Drugs Used In Psychiatry

This guide contains color reproductions of some commonly prescribed major psychotherapeutic drugs. This guide mainly illustrates tablets and capsules. A † symbol preceding the name of the drug indicates that other doses are available. Check directly with the manufacturer. (*Although the photos are intended as accurate reproductions of the drug, this guide should be used only as a quick identification aid.*)

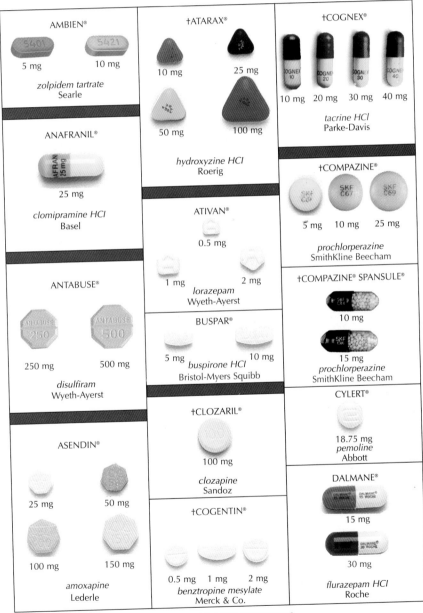

AMBIEN®
5 mg   10 mg
zolpidem tartrate
Searle

ANAFRANIL®
25 mg
clomipramine HCl
Basel

ANTABUSE®
250 mg   500 mg
disulfiram
Wyeth-Ayerst

ASENDIN®
25 mg   50 mg
100 mg   150 mg
amoxapine
Lederle

†ATARAX®
10 mg   25 mg
50 mg   100 mg
hydroxyzine HCl
Roerig

ATIVAN®
0.5 mg
1 mg   2 mg
lorazepam
Wyeth-Ayerst

BUSPAR®
5 mg   10 mg
buspirone HCl
Bristol-Myers Squibb

†CLOZARIL®
100 mg
clozapine
Sandoz

†COGENTIN®
0.5 mg   1 mg   2 mg
benztropine mesylate
Merck & Co.

†COGNEX®
10 mg   20 mg   30 mg   40 mg
tacrine HCl
Parke-Davis

†COMPAZINE®
5 mg   10 mg   25 mg
prochlorperazine
SmithKline Beecham

†COMPAZINE® SPANSULE®
10 mg
15 mg
prochlorperazine
SmithKline Beecham

CYLERT®
18.75 mg
pemoline
Abbott

DALMANE®
15 mg
30 mg
flurazepam HCl
Roche

WILLIAMS AND WILKINS©

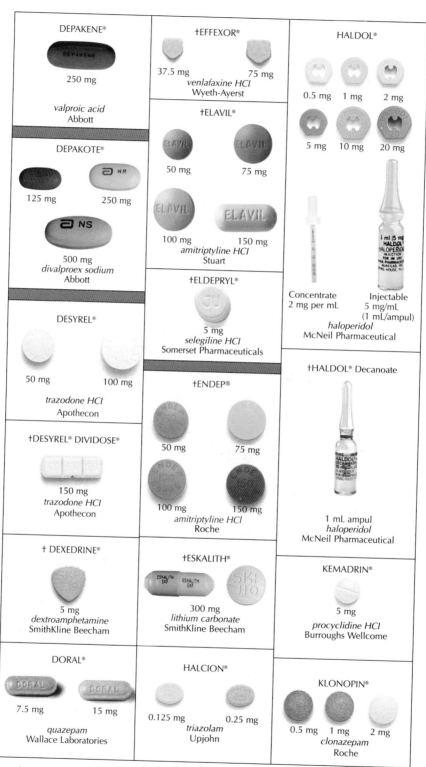

DEPAKENE®

250 mg

valproic acid
Abbott

DEPAKOTE®

125 mg   250 mg

500 mg
divalproex sodium
Abbott

DESYREL®

50 mg   100 mg

trazodone HCl
Apothecon

†DESYREL® DIVIDOSE®

150 mg
trazodone HCl
Apothecon

† DEXEDRINE®

5 mg
dextroamphetamine
SmithKline Beecham

DORAL®

7.5 mg   15 mg

quazepam
Wallace Laboratories

†EFFEXOR®

37.5 mg   75 mg
venlafaxine HCl
Wyeth-Ayerst

†ELAVIL®

50 mg   75 mg

100 mg   150 mg
amitriptyline HCl
Stuart

†ELDEPRYL®

5 mg
selegiline HCl
Somerset Pharmaceuticals

†ENDEP®

50 mg   75 mg

100 mg   150 mg
amitriptyline HCl
Roche

†ESKALITH®

300 mg
lithium carbonate
SmithKline Beecham

HALCION®

0.125 mg   0.25 mg
triazolam
Upjohn

HALDOL®

0.5 mg   1 mg   2 mg

5 mg   10 mg   20 mg

Concentrate   Injectable
2 mg per mL   5 mg/mL
                     (1 mL/ampul)
haloperidol
McNeil Pharmaceutical

†HALDOL® Decanoate

1 mL ampul
haloperidol
McNeil Pharmaceutical

KEMADRIN®

5 mg
procyclidine HCl
Burroughs Wellcome

KLONOPIN®

0.5 mg   1 mg   2 mg
clonazepam
Roche

WILLIAMS AND WILKINS©

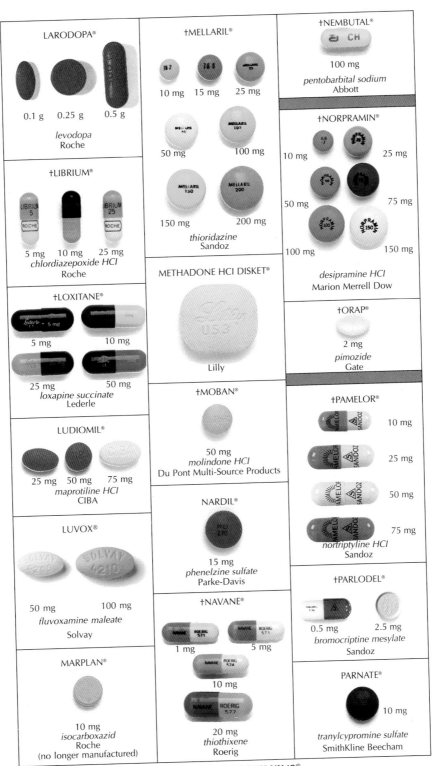

LARODOPA®

0.1 g   0.25 g   0.5 g

levodopa
Roche

†LIBRIUM®

5 mg   10 mg   25 mg
chlordiazepoxide HCl
Roche

†LOXITANE®

5 mg   10 mg

25 mg   50 mg
loxapine succinate
Lederle

LUDIOMIL®

25 mg   50 mg   75 mg
maprotiline HCl
CIBA

LUVOX®

50 mg   100 mg
fluvoxamine maleate
Solvay

MARPLAN®

10 mg
isocarboxazid
Roche
(no longer manufactured)

†MELLARIL®

10 mg   15 mg   25 mg

50 mg   100 mg

150 mg   200 mg

thioridazine
Sandoz

METHADONE HCl DISKET®

Lilly

†MOBAN®

50 mg
molindone HCl
Du Pont Multi-Source Products

NARDIL®

15 mg
phenelzine sulfate
Parke-Davis

†NAVANE®

1 mg   5 mg

10 mg

20 mg
thiothixene
Roerig

†NEMBUTAL®

100 mg
pentobarbital sodium
Abbott

†NORPRAMIN®

10 mg   25 mg

50 mg   75 mg

100 mg   150 mg

desipramine HCl
Marion Merrell Dow

†ORAP®

2 mg
pimozide
Gate

†PAMELOR®

10 mg

25 mg

50 mg

75 mg
nortriptyline HCl
Sandoz

†PARLODEL®

0.5 mg   2.5 mg
bromocriptine mesylate
Sandoz

PARNATE®

10 mg

tranylcypromine sulfate
SmithKline Beecham

WILLIAMS AND WILKINS©

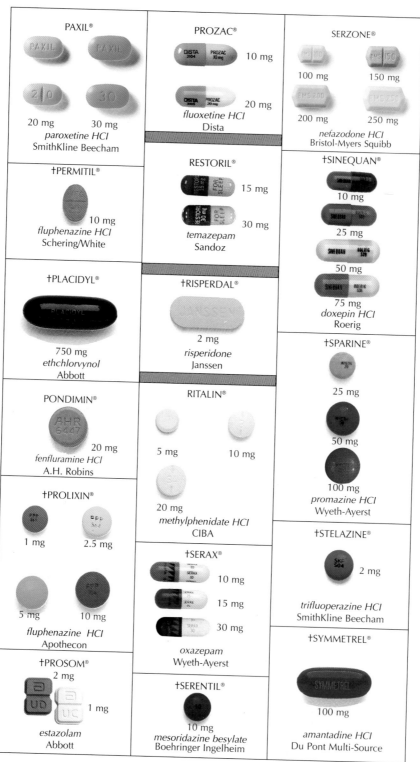

PAXIL®

20 mg   30 mg

paroxetine HCl
SmithKline Beecham

†PERMITIL®

10 mg

fluphenazine HCl
Schering/White

†PLACIDYL®

750 mg
ethchlorvynol
Abbott

PONDIMIN®

20 mg

fenfluramine HCl
A.H. Robins

†PROLIXIN®

1 mg   2.5 mg

5 mg   10 mg

fluphenazine HCl
Apothecon

†PROSOM®
2 mg

1 mg

estazolam
Abbott

PROZAC®

10 mg

20 mg

fluoxetine HCl
Dista

RESTORIL®

15 mg

30 mg

temazepam
Sandoz

†RISPERDAL®

2 mg

risperidone
Janssen

RITALIN®

5 mg   10 mg

20 mg

methylphenidate HCl
CIBA

†SERAX®

10 mg

15 mg

30 mg

oxazepam
Wyeth-Ayerst

†SERENTIL®

10 mg

mesoridazine besylate
Boehringer Ingelheim

SERZONE®

100 mg   150 mg

200 mg   250 mg

nefazodone HCl
Bristol-Myers Squibb

†SINEQUAN®

10 mg

25 mg

50 mg

75 mg
doxepin HCl
Roerig

†SPARINE®

25 mg

50 mg

100 mg
promazine HCl
Wyeth-Ayerst

†STELAZINE®

2 mg

trifluoperazine HCl
SmithKline Beecham

†SYMMETREL®

100 mg

amantadine HCl
Du Pont Multi-Source

WILLIAMS AND WILKINS©

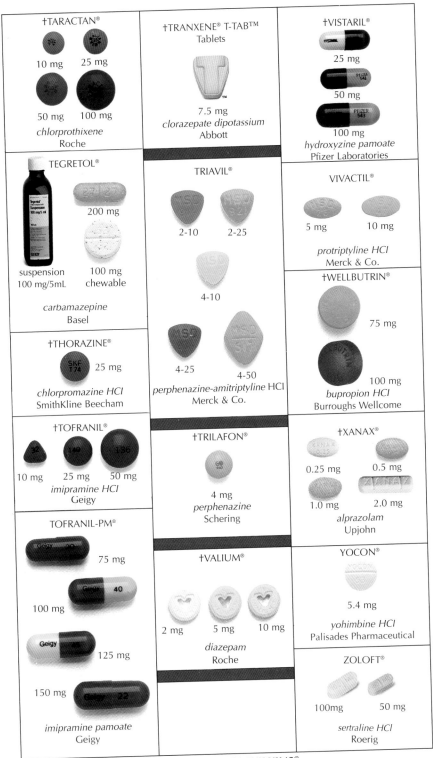

†TARACTAN®
10 mg   25 mg
50 mg   100 mg
chlorprothixene
Roche

†TRANXENE® T-TAB™
Tablets
7.5 mg
clorazepate dipotassium
Abbott

†VISTARIL®
25 mg
50 mg
100 mg
hydroxyzine pamoate
Pfizer Laboratories

TEGRETOL®
200 mg
suspension
100 mg/5mL
100 mg
chewable
carbamazepine
Basel

TRIAVIL®
2-10   2-25
4-10
4-25   4-50
perphenazine-amitriptyline HCl
Merck & Co.

VIVACTIL®
5 mg   10 mg
protriptyline HCl
Merck & Co.

†WELLBUTRIN®
75 mg
100 mg
bupropion HCl
Burroughs Wellcome

†THORAZINE®
25 mg
chlorpromazine HCl
SmithKline Beecham

†TOFRANIL®
10 mg   25 mg   50 mg
imipramine HCl
Geigy

†TRILAFON®
4 mg
perphenazine
Schering

†XANAX®
0.25 mg   0.5 mg
1.0 mg   2.0 mg
alprazolam
Upjohn

TOFRANIL-PM®
75 mg
100 mg
125 mg
150 mg
imipramine pamoate
Geigy

†VALIUM®
2 mg   5 mg   10 mg
diazepam
Roche

YOCON®
5.4 mg
yohimbine HCl
Palisades Pharmaceutical

ZOLOFT®
100mg   50 mg
sertraline HCl
Roerig

WILLIAMS AND WILKINS©

CONCISE
TEXTBOOK OF
CLINICAL PSYCHIATRY

Senior Contributing Editor

ROBERT CANCRO, M.D., MED.D.SC.

Professor and Chairman, Department of Psychiatry,
New York University School of Medicine;
Director, Department of Psychiatry, Tisch Hospital,
the University Hospital of the New York University Medical Center,
New York, New York;
Director, Nathan S. Kline Institute for Psychiatric Research,
Orangeburg, New York

CONCISE
TEXTBOOK OF
CLINICAL PSYCHIATRY

HAROLD I. KAPLAN, M.D.

Professor of Psychiatry, New York University School of Medicine,
Attending Psychiatrist, Tisch Hospital, the University Hospital of the New York University
Medical Center;
Attending Psychiatrist, Bellevue Hospital Center;
Consultant Psychiatrist, Lenox Hill Hospital,
New York, New York

BENJAMIN J. SADOCK, M.D.

Professor and Vice Chairman, Department of Psychiatry, New York University School of
Medicine;
Attending Psychiatrist, Tisch Hospital, the University Hospital of the New York University
Medical Center;
Attending Psychiatrist, Bellevue Hospital Center;
Consultant Psychiatrist, Lenox Hill Hospital,
New York, New York

Williams & Wilkins
A WAVERLY COMPANY

BALTIMORE • PHILADELPHIA • LONDON • PARIS • BANGKOK
BUENOS AIRES • HONG KONG • MUNICH • SYDNEY • TOKYO • WROCLAW

Editor: Susan M. Gay
Managing Editor: Kathleen Courtney Millet
Production Coordinator: Barbara J. Felton
Copy Editors: Bonnie Montgomery, John Daniel
Designer: Wilma E. Rosenberger
Illustration Planner: Lorraine Wrzosek
Typesetter: Maryland Composition Co., Inc.
Printer/Binder: McNaughton & Gunn

Copyright © 1996 Williams & Wilkins

351 West Camden Street
Baltimore, Maryland 21201-2436 USA

Rose Tree Corporate Center
1400 North Providence Road
Building II, Suite 5025
Media, Pennsylvania 19063-2043 USA

Notice. The indications and dosages of all drugs in this book have been recommended
in the medical literature and conform to the practices of the general medical community.
The medications described do not necessarily have specific approval by the Food and
Drug Administration for use in the diseases and dosages for which they are
recommended. The package insert for each drug should be consulted for use and
dosage as approved by the FDA. Because standards for usage change, it is advisable to
keep abreast of revised recommendations, particularly those concerning new drugs.

Printed in the United States of America

Library of Congress Cataloging-in-Publication Data

Kaplan, Harold I.
    Concise textbook of clinical psychiatry / Harold I. Kaplan, Benjamin J. Sadock.
       p.   cm.
    Derived from: Kaplan and Sadock's synopsis of psychiatry / Harold I. Kaplan,
Benjamin J. Sadock, Jack A. Grebb. 7th ed. c1994.
    Includes bibliographical references and index.
    ISBN 0-683-30009-1
    1. Mental illness. 2. Psychiatry. I. Sadock, Benjamin J.
    II. Kaplan, Harold I. Kaplan and Sadock's synopsis of psychiatry. III. Title.
    [DNLM: 1. Mental Disorders.   WM 140 K17c 1996]
RC454.K349   1996
616.89'14—dc20
DNLM/DLC
for Library of Congress   96-3941
                                                           CIP

*The publishers have made every effort to trace the copyright holders for borrowed
material. If they have inadvertently overlooked any, they will be pleased to make the
necessary arrangements at the first opportunity.*

To purchase additional copies of this book, call our customer service department at **(800)
638-0672** or fax orders to **(800) 447-8438**. For other book services, including chapter
reprints and large quantity sales, ask for the Special Sales department.

Canadian customers should call **(800) 268-4178**, or fax **(905) 470-6780**. For all other
calls originating outside of the United States, please call **(410) 528-4223** or fax us at
(410) 528-8550.

Visit Williams & Wilkins on the Internet: http://www.wwilkins.com or contact our
customer service department at **custserv@wwilkins.com**. Williams & Wilkins customer
service representatives are available from 8:30 am to 6:00 pm, EST, Monday through
Friday, for telephone access.

97 98 99 00
2 3 4 5 6 7 8 9 10

To our wives,

Nancy Barrett Kaplan

and Virginia Alcott Sadock,

without whose help and sacrifice

this textbook would not have been possible

Preface

This textbook is published as the clinical psychiatry part of a larger volume, *Kaplan and Sadocks Synopsis of Psychiatry, Seventh Edition,* that covers both the basic behavioral sciences and all of the clinical psychiatric disorders. This new smaller volume covers the clinical psychiatric disorders alone with some modification. We have added fresh material in this special concise edition since the publication of the larger *Synopsis* in 1994. Updated information about clinical syndromes and new data about recently introduced pharmacological agents are included. The larger format provides the student with a book that can be used throughout the entire four years of medical school. This smaller one is of use to the student who requires a textbook covering clinical psychiatry alone. We believe such flexibility in choice will admirably meet the needs of a variety of readers from psychiatry, psychology, psychiatric social work, psychiatric nursing, occupational and recreational therapy, and other mental health professions.

DSM-IV

The mental disorders discussed in this textbook are consistent with the nosology of the fourth edition of the American Psychiatric Association's *Diagnostic and Statistical Manual of Mental Disorders* (DSM-IV). Many psychiatrists have reservations about the DSM-IV nosology; in several sections of this book, those objections are clearly stated. Such terms as "neurosis" and "psychosomatic" are used in this book, even though those terms are not a part of the official nosology.

The inclusion of the DSM-IV nosology and diagnostic criteria means that almost every section has undergone a thorough and extensive revision. For example, DSM-IV no longer uses the term "organic mental disorders." An entirely new chapter in this textbook—has been written to reflect that change: "Delirium, Dementia, and Amnestic and Other Cognitive Disorders" and "Mental Disorders Due to a General Medial Condition." Similarly, the topic of psychoactive substance-induced organic mental disorders is now covered in Chapter 6, "Substance-Related Disorders," which is the DSM-IV classification. The entire textbook has been reorganized to reflect the DSM-IV organization, and new chapters, such as "Relational Problems" and "Problems Related to Abuse or Neglect," have been added.

NEW AND REVISED AREAS

The chapters on child and adolescent psychiatry have been heavily rewritten. As in the adult areas, the new organization is based on DSM-IV. The new chapters include "Assessment, Examination, and Psychological Testing," "Mental Retardation," "Learning Disorders," "Mood Disorders and Suicide," and "Schizophrenia with Childhood Onset." Chapter 5, "Neuropsychiatric Aspects of Human Immunodeficiency Virus (HIV) Infection and Acquired Immune Deficiency Syndrome (AIDS)," has been updated, and Section 1.3, "Medical Assessment in Psychiatry," has been added. Other extensively changed areas include geriatric psychiatry and the role of laboratory tests in psychiatry.

In this special concise edition the reader will find that every section has new references that are current and up-to-date.

BIOLOGICAL THERAPIES

Drugs used in the treatment of mental disorders are classified and discussed pharmacologically, rather than as antidepressants, antipsychotics, and the like. We use that unique format to provide the student with an understanding not only of the general principles of psychopharmacology but also of the use of each psychotherapeutic drug according to its pharmacological activity as a discrete drug, rather than as one of a family of drugs. This edition adds information about the uses, cautions, interactions, and dosages of drugs and includes information on the drugs most recently introduced in the United States. Chapter 27, "Biological Therapies," also includes information about drugs not yet on the market.

TEACHING SYSTEM

This textbook forms one part of a comprehensive system we have developed to facilitate the teaching of psychiatry and the behavioral sciences. At the head of the system is *Comprehensive Textbook of Psychiatry*, which is global in depth and scope; it is designed for and used by psychiatrists, behavioral scientists, and all workers in the mental health field. *Kaplan and Sadock's Synopsis of Psychiatry* is a relatively brief, highly modified, original, and current version useful for medical students, psychiatric residents, practicing psychiatrists, and mental health professionals. Another part of the system is *Study Guide and Self-Examination Review for Kaplan and Sadock's Synopsis of Psychiatry*, which consists of multiple-choice questions and answers; it is designed for students of psychiatry in preparation for a variety of examinations. Other parts of the system are the pocket handbooks: *Pocket Handbook of Clinical Psychiatry, Pocket Handbook of Psychiatric Drug Treatment,* and *Pocket Handbook of Emergency Psychiatric Medicine*. Those books cover the diagnosis and the treatment of psychiatric disorders, psychopharmacology, and psychiatric emergencies, respectively, and are compactly designed and concisely written to be carried in the pocket by clinical clerks and practicing physicians, whatever their specialty, to provide a quick reference. Finally, *Comprehensive Glossary of Psychiatry and Psychology* provides simply written definitions for psychiatrists and other physicians, psychologists, students, other mental health professionals, and the general public. Taken together, those books create a multipronged approach to the teaching, study, and learning of psychiatry.

FUTURE OF PSYCHIATRY

The publication of this book coincides with seismic changes in the delivery of health care in this country that are likely to affect the field of psychiatry. For example, managed-care programs are attempting to limit mental health benefits in an effort to control costs. Some proposals curtail the number of outpatient visits for psychotherapy to 5 to 20 sessions a year.

Although most types of psychotherapy can be conducted within that framework, some types of psychotherapy, particularly insight-oriented psychotherapies, require frequent visits over an extended period. In addition, before a patient can be referred to a psychiatrist, many health maintenance organizations (HMOs) require that a primary care physician (the so-called gatekeeper) see the patient for several weeks before the referral; during that time, pharmacotherapy, rather than psychotherapy, is administered. Drugs, rather than psychotherapy, will become the treatment of choice, in spite of the fact that many studies have found the superior efficacy of drugs used in conjunction with psychotherapy in the treatment of most mental disorders, particularly depressive disorders. In addition, persons who are emotionally well make fewer general medical visits than do persons with emotional disorders; the result is savings in the overall cost of general medical care.

We believe that managed-care oversight of psychiatric treatment will undermine the doctor-patient relationship. It can destroy the psychotherapeutic process, which requires confidentiality, trust, independent judgement, and freedom from external bureaucratic constraints to be effective. We believe that prejudice toward psychiatry and fear of mental illness are largely responsible for those limitations. We hope that this book will contribute to reversing the antipsychiatry forces in health care delivery systems in our society.

ACKNOWLEDGEMENTS

This book is derived from the seventh edition of *Kaplan and Sadock's Synopsis of Psychiatry*. A new author, Jack Grebb, M.D., made major contributions to that book. A distinguished clinician and scholar, Dr. Grebb helped in the conceptualization, the writing, and the implementation of every aspect of that book.

We thank our contributing editors: Glen O. Gabbard, M.D., Rebecca Jones, M.D., Peter Kaplan, M.D., Caroly Pataki, M.D., and Virginia Sadock, M.D.—Each made made major contribu-

tions in the seventh edition of *Synopsis* that were of immeasurable value.

Others who helped in the preparation of that book were Norman Sussman, M.D., in the area of psychopharmacology and Richard Perry, M.D., in the are of child psychiatry. We also thank Nancy B. Kaplan, James Sadock, Victoria Sadock, M.D., and Phillip Kaplan, M.D., for their help.

Justin Hollingsworth played a key role in assisting us in all aspects of our work. His prodigious efforts were extremely important. We also want to thank Justin Hartung and Jennifer Peters for their enormous assistance. Dorice Vieira, head of Educational Services of the Frederick L. Ehrman Medical Library of the New York University School of Medicine provided valuable assistance.

We also take this opportunity to acknowledge those who have translated this and other work into foreign languages. Current translations include French, German, Greek, Italian, Japanese, Polish, Portuguese, Russian, Spanish, and Turkish, in addition to a special Asian and international student edition of *Synopsis*.

We thank Robert Cancro, M.D., Professor and Chairman of the Department of Psychiatry at New York University School of Medicine, who participated as Senior Contributing Editor of this edition. Dr. Cancro's commitment to psychiatric education and psychiatric research is recognized throughout the world. He has been a source of great inspiration and friendship to us and has contributed immeasurably to this and previous books.

Finally, we thank our publishers, Williams & Wilkins, for their cooperation in every aspect of this textbook.

Harold I. Kaplan, M.D.
Benjamin J. Sadock, M.D.
New York University Medical Center
New York, New York
October 1995

Contents

BOOKS BY HAROLD I. KAPLAN, M.D., AND BENJAMIN J. SADOCK, M.D.

Published by Williams & Wilkins

Comprehensive Textbook of Psychiatry
1st edition, 1967 (with A.M. Freedman)
2nd edition, 1975 (with A.M. Freedman)
3rd edition, 1980 (with A.M. Freedman)
4th edition, 1985
5th edition, 1989
6th edition, 1995

Synopsis of Psychiatry
1st edition, 1972 (with A.M. Freedman)
2nd edition, 1976 (with A.M. Freedman)
3rd edition, 1981
4th edition, 1985
5th edition, 1988
6th edition, 1991
7th edition, 1994 (with J.A. Grebb)

Study Guide and Self-Examination Review for Synopsis of Psychiatry
1st edition, 1983
2nd edition, 1985
3rd edition, 1989
4th edition, 1991
5th edition, 1994

Comprehensive Group Psychotherapy
1st edition, 1971
2nd edition, 1983
3rd edition, 1993

The Sexual Experience
1976 (with A.M. Freedman)

Clinical Psychiatry
1st edition, 1988
2nd edition, 1996

Pocket Handbook of Clinical Psychiatry
1st edition, 1990
2nd edition, 1996

Comprehensive Glossary of Psychiatry and Psychology
1991

Pocket Handbook of Psychiatric Drug Treatment
1st edition, 1993
2nd edition, 1996

Pocket Handbook of Emergency Psychiatric Medicine
1993

Various editions of the above books have been translated and published in French, German, Greek, Indonesian, Italian, Japanese, Polish, Portuguese, Russian, Spanish, and Turkish. In addition, an International Asian edition has been published in English.

By other publishers

Studies in Human Behavior, 1–5, 1972
(with A.M. Freedman)
Athenaeum
1. Diagnosing Mental Illness: Evaluation in Psychiatry and Psychology
2. Interpreting Personality: A Survey of Twentieth-Century Views
3. Human Behavior: Biological, Psychological, and Sociological
4. Treating Mental Illness: Aspects of Modern Therapy
5. The Child: His Psychological and Cultural Development
   Vol. 1: Normal Development and Psychological Assessment
   Vol. 2: The Major Psychological Disorders and their Treatment

Modern Group Books I–VI, 1972
E.P. Dutton
I Origins of Group Analysis
II Evolution of Group Therapy
III Groups and Drugs
IV Sensitivity Through Encounter and Motivation
V New Models for Group Therapy
VI Group Treatment of Mental Illness

The Human Animal, 1974
(with A.M. Freedman)
K.F.S. Publications
Vol. 1: Man and His Mind
Vol. 2: The Disordered Personality

ABOUT THE AUTHORS

HAROLD IRWIN HAPLAN, M.D., is currently Professor of Psychiatry at New York University (NYU) School of Medicine, an appointment dating back to 1980. Since that time he has been an Attending Psychiatrist at Tisch Hospital (the University of the NYU Medical Center) and Bellevue Hospital Center. He is Co-Director of NYU Medical Center's Continuing Medical Education Program in Psychiatry and is Consultant Psychiatrist at Lenox Hill Hospital in New York City. From 1948 to 1980, he was Professor of Psychiatry at New York Medical College and Director of Psychiatric Education, heading the undergraduate, residency, and continuing education programs in psychiatry, and he was a Visiting Psychiatrist at Metropolitan Hospital in New York City. He received his Bachelor of Arts degree from New York University. He received his M.D. from New York Medical College in 1949 at the age of 21, interned at Jewish Hospital of Brooklyn, and served his psychiatric residency training at Kingsbridge Bronx Veterans Administration Hospital, New York's Mount Sinai Hospital, and at Jewish Board of Guardians (in child psychiatry). He has received awards for academic excellence in psychiatry from the Alumni Association of New York Medical College (1983), the Distinguished Service Award in Psychiatry from the Association of Psychiatric Outpatient Centers of America and the NYU Post-Graduate Medical School (1982), and a Founders Day Award for Scholastic Achievement from NYU (1988). During his tenure at New York Medical College, he was the principal investigator of 10 educational grants in psychiatry from NIMH, several specializing in the psychiatric training of women physicians. He was a member of the Preparatory Commission on Psychiatric Education for National Institute of Mental Health (NIMH) and the American Psychiatric Association from 1973 to 1975. In 1947 he was certified in psychiatry by the American Board of Psychiatry and Neurology and has served as an Assistant and Associate Examiner of the American Board for 12 years. He received a Certificate of Commendation from the American Psychiatric Association for his work as chairman of their Committee on Education from 1973 to 1975. Professor Kaplan was certified in psychoanalysis in 1955 by New York Medical College. He has published many papers in numerous psychiatric journals and has authored and edited the books listed in this volume. He is a Life Fellow of the American Psychiatric Association, the American College of Physicians, the New York Academy of Medicine, and the American Orthopsychiatric Association. He is also a member of the Alpha Omega Alpha Honorary Medical Society and treasurer of the NYU-Bellevue Psychiatric Society. He presently makes his home in New York City, where is he is married to actress Nancy Barrett. He has three children, Jennifer, Peter Mark, and Phillip. He maintains an active general psychiatric practice in Manhattan, which includes individual and group psychotherapy, psychiatric consultation, psychoanalysis, and psychopharmacotherapy. In his leisure time he enjous reading nonfiction, travel, and fine food.

BENJAMIN JAMES SADOCK, M.D., is currently Professor and Vice chairman of the Department of Psychiatry at the New York University (NYU) School of Medicine. He gradiated from Union College in 1955 and received his M.D. from New York Medical College in 1949. After an internship at Albany Hospital, he completed his residency at Bellevue Psychiatric Hospital and then entered military service, where he served as Assistant Chief and Acting Chief of Neuropsychiatry at Sheppard Air Force Base, Texas. He held faculty and teaching appointments at Southwestern Medical School and Parkland Hospital in Dallas and at New York Medical College, St. Luke's Hospital, the New York State Psychiatric Institute, and Metropolitan Hospital in New York City. He joined the faculty of the NTU School of Medicine in 1980 and served in various positions: Director of Medical Student Education in Psychiatry, Co-director of the Residency Training Program in Psychiatry, and Director of Graduate Medical Education. Since 1980, Dr. Sadock has been director of Student Mental Health Services, psychiatric consultant to the Admissions Committee, and Co-Director of Continuing Education in Psychiatry at the NYU School of Medicine. He is on the staff of Bellevue Hospital Center and Tisch Hospital (the University Hospital of the NYU Medical Center) and is Consultant Psychiatrist at Lenox Hill Hospital. Dr. Sadock became a Diplomate of the American Board of Psychiatry and Neurology in 1966 and served as an assistant and associate examiner for the Board for over a decade. He is a Fellow of the American Psychiatric Association (APA), the American College of Physicians, and the New York Academy of Medicine. He is also a member of the Alpha Omega Alpha Honor Society. He is active in numerous psychiatric organizations and is President and founder of the NYU-Bellevue Psychiatric Society. Dr. Sadock was a member of the National Committee on Continuing Education in Psychiatry of the APA, served on the Ad Hoc Committee on Sex Therapy Clinics of the American Medical Association, was delegate to the Conference of Recertification of the American Board of Medical Specialists, and was a representative of the APA's Task Force on the National Board of Medical Examiners and the American Board of Psychiatry and Neurology. In 1985 he received the Academic Achievement Award from New York Medical College. He is author or editor of more than 100 publications, including the books listed in this volume, and is a book reviewer for psychiatry journals. He is married to Virginia Alcott Sadock, M.D., Clinical Professor of Psychiatry and Director of the Program in Human Sexuality and Sex Therapy at NYU Medical Center. They live in Manhattan and are also in private practice specializing in individual psychotherapy, group psychotherapy, sex and marital therapy, and pharmacotherapy. They have two children, Jamaes and Victoria. Dr. Sadock is an opera lover, s skier, and an avid fly fisherman.

1/ Clinical Examination of the Psychiatric Patient

1.1 PSYCHIATRIC INTERVIEW, HISTORY, AND MENTAL STATUS EXAMINATION

PSYCHIATRIC INTERVIEW

To treat a psychiatric patient effectively—whether with medications, environmental manipulations, or psychodynamic psychotherapy—the psychiatrist must make a reliable and accurate diagnosis. To formulate such a diagnosis, the psychiatrist must learn as much as possible about who the patient is in terms of genetic, temperamental, biological, developmental, social, and psychological influences. The psychiatrist must be able to convey concern, empathy, respect, and competence to the patient in order to create a rapport and trust that allow the patient to speak honestly and intimately. The psychiatrist must develop interviewing skills and techniques that most effectively allow the patient to describe the signs and the symptoms that, gathered together, constitute the various syndromes that are potentially definable and treatable. Patients range from those who are clear, articulate, and easy to engage to those who are thought-disordered, paranoid, responding to internal stimuli, and severely disorganized. The interview itself may vary, depending on the specific challenges presented by each patient.

Management of Time

The initial consultation lasts for 30 minutes to one hour, depending on the circumstances. Interviews with psychotic or medically ill patients are brief because the patient may find the interview stressful. Long interviews may be required in the emergency room. Second visits and ongoing therapeutic interviews also vary in length. The American Board of Psychiatry and Neurology in its clinical oral examination in psychiatry allows 30 minutes for a psychiatric examination.

Patients' management of appointment times reveals important aspects of personality and coping. Most often, patients arrive a few minutes before their appointments. An anxious patient may arrive as much as a half hour early. If the patient arrives very early, the clinician may want to explore the reasons. The patient who arrives significantly late for an appointment poses another set of potential questions. The first time it occurs, the clinician may listen to the explanation offered and respond sympathetically if the lateness is due to circumstances beyond the patient's control. If the patient states, ''I forgot all about the appointment,'' that is a clue that something about going to the doctor is making the patient anxious or uncomfortable, and that needs to be explored further. The psychiatrist may ask directly, ''Did you feel reluctant to come in today?'' If the answer is ''Yes,'' the psychiatrist can begin to explore the possible reasons for the patient's reluctance. If the answer is ''No,'' it is probably best to drop the direct questioning about the lateness and just listen to the patient. By listening carefully, the psychiatrist can usually detect themes that the patient may not be aware of. Those themes can then be explored by both the patient and the psychiatrist in an attempt to understand better what the patient is experiencing.

The psychiatrist's handling of time is also an important factor in the interview. Carelessness regarding time indicates a lack of concern for the patient. If the psychiatrist is unavoidably detained for an interview, it is appropriate to express regret at having kept the patient waiting.

Seating Arrangements

The way chairs are arranged in the psychiatrist's office affects the interview. Both chairs should be of approximately equal heights, so that neither person looks down on the other. Most psychiatrists think that it is desirable to place the chairs without any furniture between the clinician and the patient. If the room contains several chairs, the psychiatrist indicates his or her own chair and then allows the patient to choose the chair in which he or she will feel most comfortable.

If the patient being interviewed is one who is potentially dangerous, the door to the interview room should be left open, the psychiatrist should sit closest to the open door, with nothing obstructing the space from the clinician to the door, and, if necessary, a third person should be asked to stand outside or even inside the room, to be available if there is trouble.

Psychiatrist's Office

A psychiatrist can never remain entirely unknown to the patient. The physician's office can tell the patient a good deal about the personality of the psychiatrist. The color of the office, paintings and diplomas on the wall, furniture, plants, books, and personal photographs all describe the psychiatrist in ways that are not directly verbalized. Patients often have reactions to their doctors' offices that may or may not be distortions, and carefully listening to any comments can help the psychiatrist understand patients. Studies have shown that patients respond more positively to male physicians who wear jackets and ties than to those who do not. No studies have been done on the dress of female physicians, but, by extrapolation, a positive response would probably be elicited by professional attire.

Note Taking

For legal and medical reasons an adequate written record of each patient's treatment must be maintained. The patient's record also aids the psychiatrist's memory. Each clinician must establish a system of record keeping and decide which information to record. Many psychiatrists make complete notes during the first few sessions while eliciting historical data. After that time most psychiatrists record only new historical information, important events in the patient's life, medications prescribed, dreams, and general comments about the patient's progress. Some psychiatrists maintain detailed process notes (verbatim record of a session) on specific patients, writing out immediately after a session as much of the session as they can remember. Process notes make it much easier to determine trends in the treatment (with regard to transference and countertransference issues) and to go back over the session to pick up ideas that may have been missed. Process notes are also helpful if the psychiatrist is working with a supervisor or a consultant who needs an accurate presentation of a particular session.

Most psychiatrists do not recommend taking extensive notes during a session, as writing can cut down on the ability to listen. Some patients, however, may express resentment if the psychiatrist does not write notes during an interview; they may fear that their comments were not important enough to record or that the psychiatrist was not interested in them. Since, presumably, not taking notes during a session has no relation to the psychiatrist's listening, that type of feeling on a patient's part can be further explored in order to understand the fear of not being taken seriously.

Subsequent Interviews

Interviews subsequent to the initial one allow the patient to correct any misinformation provided in the first meeting. It is often helpful to start the second interview by asking the patient whether he or she has thought about the first interview and for any reactions to that experience. Another variation of that technique is to say: "Frequently, people think of additional things they wanted to discuss after they leave. What thoughts have you had?"

Psychiatrists often learn something of value when they ask patients if they have discussed the interview with anyone else. If the patient has done so, the details of that conversation and with whom the patient spoke are enlightening. There are no set rules concerning which topics are best deferred until the second interview. In general, as patients' comfort and familiarity with the psychiatrist increase, they become increasingly able to reveal the intimate details of their lives.

Interviewing Situations

The manner in which an interview is conducted—the specific techniques and structure—vary depending on the setting in which the interview takes place, the interview's purpose, and the particular patient's strengths, weaknesses, and diagnosis. Psychiatrists are trained to be flexible in modifying their interview style to fit the existing situation. Patients who carry varying psychiatric diagnoses differ in their capacities to participate in an interview and differ in the challenges they present to the interviewing psychiatrist. Certain consistent themes are often observed in interviews with patients who have the same diagnosis, although, even with the same diagnosis, patients may require subtly different interview strategies.

DEPRESSED AND POTENTIALLY SUICIDAL PATIENT

Depressed patients are often unable to provide spontaneously an adequate account of their illness because of such factors as psychomotor retardation and hopelessness. The psychiatrist must be prepared to ask a depressed person specifically about history and symptoms related to depression, including questions about suicidal ideation, which the patient may not initially volunteer. Another reason for being specific in questioning a depressed patient is that the patient may not realize that such symptoms as waking during the night or increased somatic complaints are related to depressive disorders.

One of the most difficult aspects of dealing with depressed patients is experiencing their hopelessness. Many severely depressed patients believe that their current feeling will continue indefinitely and that there is no hope. The psychiatrist must be careful not to reassure such patients prematurely that everything is going to be fine, as the patients most likely will experience that reassurance as an indication that the psychiatrist does not understand the degree of pain that they are feeling. A reasonable approach is for the psychiatrist to indicate that he or she is aware how bad patients are feeling, that help is certainly possible, and that it is understandable at that point for patients not to believe that they can be helped. Furthermore, the psychiatrist must make it clear that he or she is committed to helping patients feel better, that all specific and effective pharmacological and psychological tools will be used, and that patients will not be abandoned during what may be a lengthy period of recovery. Up to that point, everything patients have done to relieve their distress has not worked, and, by the time the psychiatrist interviews them, they may be desperate. It can be a relief to depressed patients when the psychiatrist truthfully tells them that their depression can be treated but that it may take a little work and time for the psychiatrist to find the method that will most effectively treat their specific depressive disorder. That message conveys not a false sense of reassurance, which could make depressed patients feel even more depressed than before, but a sense that the psychiatrist is committed to understanding who the patient is and what treatment will work most quickly and most effectively for him or her. Every depressed person hopes, consciously or unconsciously, that the psychiatrist will magically and immediately produce a cure, but most people are willing to proceed along a therapeutic path, even when a part of them believes there is no hope. The interviewing psychiatrist must be careful not to make promises about specific treatments' being the answer. If those treatments turn out not to work for the patient, the disappointment may eliminate the patient's last hope.

Suicide

Of special concern when interviewing depressed patients is the potential for suicide. Being mindful of the possibility of suicide is imperative when interviewing any depressed patient, even if there is no apparent suicidal risk. The psychiatrist must inquire in some detail about the presence of suicidal thoughts. The psychiatrist should ask specifically, "Are you suicidal now, or do you have plans to take your own life?" A suicide note, a family history of suicide, or previous suicidal behavior on the part of the patient increases the risk for suicide. Evidence of impulsivity or of pervasive pessimism about the future also places patients at risk. If the psychiatrist decides that the patient is at imminent risk for suicidal behavior, the patient must be hospitalized or otherwise protected. A difficult situation arises when there does not seem to be an immediate risk but the potential for suicide is present as long as the patient remains depressed. If the decision is made not to hospitalize the patient immediately, the psychiatrist should insist that the patient promise to call at any time suicidal pressure mounts. In such situations the patient commonly has a crisis after midnight and calls the psychiatrist, who should assure the patient that he or she is reachable at all times. Having determined that the psychiatrist is, in fact, available, the patient is often reassured and can control the impulses and use regularly scheduled sessions for exploration of the suicidal feelings.

VIOLENT PATIENT

Potentially violent patients should be approached with some of the same attitudes and techniques used with suicidal patients. For example, indicating that one is capable of dealing with the patient's capacity for violence is important. It conveys that one is accustomed to the unpleasant, as well as the pleasant, in life and that part of one's job is to help the patient stay in control and to make sure that neither the patient nor anyone else is going to get hurt.

Frequently, the psychiatrist encounters a violent patient in the hospital setting. For example, when the police bring a patient into the emergency room, the patient is often in some type of physical restraint (for example, handcuffs). The psychiatrist must establish whether effective verbal contact can be made with the patient or whether the patient's sense of reality is so impaired that effective interviewing is impossible. If impaired reality testing is an issue, the psychiatrist may have to medicate the patient before any attempts at interviewing can begin. If reality testing is not severely impaired, however, one of the first questions to be addressed is whether it is safe to remove the physical restraints from the patient. That question can be addressed in a straightforward manner, expressing concern for the safety of the patient and other persons in the surrounding area. Many psychiatrists opt to leave restraints on the patient until at least some history has been obtained and some rapport established. Should a decision be made to undo the restraints, the psychiatrist must carefully monitor what is happening to the patient as the restraints are loosened. If the patient remains calm and seems to be relieved, the process of removing the restraints can continue. If the patient does or says anything that indicates that the removal of the restraints is leading to increased agitation, the decision to remove them should be reassessed immediately.

With or without restraints, a violent patient should not be interviewed alone; at least one other person should always be present, and in some situations that other person should be a security guard or a police officer. Other precautions include leaving the interview room's door open and sitting between the patient and the door, so that the interviewer has unrestricted access to an exit should it become necessary. The psychiatrist must make it clear, in a firm but nonangry manner, that the patient may say or feel anything but is not free to act in a violent way. That statement must be backed up by a unified, calm, consistent staff presence that the patient understands is there to lend support in efforts to maintain control, including the ability to subdue the patient physically if necessary.

Confrontation with a violent patient is to be assiduously avoided, as in any behavior that could be construed as demeaning to or disrespectful of the patient. Within the limits of safety, the interviewer should respect as must as possible the patient's need for space.

Specific questions that need to be asked of violent patients include those pertaining to their previous acts of violence and to violence experienced as a child. The psychiatrist should determine under what specific conditions the patient resorts to violence, and corroboration as to critical aspects of the patient's history must be obtained from friends and family members.

DELUSIONAL PATIENT

A patient's delusion should never be directly challenged. Delusions may be thought of as a patient's defensive and self-protective, albeit maladaptive, strategy against overwhelming anxiety, lowered self-esteem, and confusion. Challenging a delusion by insisting that it is not true or possible only increases the patient's anxiety and often leads the threatened patient to defend the belief ever more desperately. It is inadvisable, however, to pretend that one believes the patient's delusion. Often, the helpful approach is to indicate that one understands that the patient believes the delusion to be true but that one does not hold the same belief. It is probably most productive to focus on the feelings, fears, and hopes that underlie the delusional belief to understand what particular function the delusion holds for the patient. The more that patients feel that the psychiatrist respects, understands, and listens to them, the more likely they are to talk about themselves, not about the delusion.

Delusions may be excessively fixed, immutable, and chronic, or they may be subject to question and doubt by the patient and may last only a relatively brief time. The patient may or may not be influenced by the delusional beliefs and may be able to recognize their effects.

Delusions, as with most psychiatric symptoms, occur on a spectrum from severe to mild and must be evaluated for the degree of severity, fixedness, elaborateness, power to influence the patient's actions, and deviation from normal beliefs.

INTERVIEWING RELATIVES

Interviews with family members of a patient can be both valuable and fraught with difficulties. For example, a spouse may be so closely identified with the patient that anxiety overwhelms the spouse's ability to provide coherent information. Family members may not realize that certain kinds of information are best provided by an observer and that other kinds of information may be obtained only from the patient; for example, family members may be able to describe the patient's social activity, but only the patient can describe what he or she is thinking and feeling. The psychiatrist must be highly sensitive to discussions with family members; if those discussions are not properly handled by the psychiatrist, the relationship between the patient and the clinician may break down.

Interviews with family members can be viewed from a variety of perspectives. If one's goal is to diagnose a disorder, then the more facts at one's disposal, the easier it will be to formulate a diagnosis, prognosis, and treatment. From the dynamic or analytical viewpoint, however, if one sees patients' problems as largely influenced by interactions with the important figures in their lives, the external reality is less important than the patients' own perceptions. In general, the more serious a patient's presenting situation (for example, major depressive disorder, suicidal ideation, or psychotic disorder), the more likely and perhaps the more appropriate it is for the psychiatrist to deal with family members.

One of the most important aspects related to talking with family members has to do with confidentiality. Ultimately, the physician must learn to elicit information and to offer hope to family members without revealing information concerning the patient that the patient does not want revealed. Betraying a confidence can make treatment of the patient impossible. If the issues concern suicidal or homicidal ideation, however, the patient must understand that the information cannot remain entirely confidential, for the protection of the patient and others.

PSYCHIATRIC HISTORY

The psychiatric history is the record of the patient's life that allows the psychiatrist to understand who the patient is, where the patient has come from, and where the patient is likely to go in the future. The history is the patient's life story told to the psychiatrist in the patient's own words from his or her own point of view. Many times the history also includes information about the patient obtained from other sources, such as a parent or a spouse. Obtaining a comprehensive history from a patient and, if necessary, from informed sources is essential to making a correct diagnosis and formulating a specific and effective treatment plan. The psychiatric history differs slightly from histories taken in medicine or surgery. In addition to gathering the concrete and factual data related to the chronology of symptom formation and to psychiatric and medical history, the psychiatrist strives to derive from the history the elusive picture of patients' individual personality characteristics, including both their strengths and their weaknesses. The psychiatric history provides insight into the nature of relationships with those closest to the patients and includes all the important people in their past and present lives. A reasonably comprehensive picture of the patients' development, from the earliest formative years until the present, can usually be elicited.

The most important technique in obtaining the psychiatric history is to allow patients to tell their own stories in their own words in the order that they feel is most important. Skillful interviewers recognize the points, as patients relate their stories, at which they can introduce relevant questions concerning the areas described in the outline of the history and mental status examination.

The structure presented in this section is not intended as a rigid plan for interviewing a patient; it is intended as a guide to organizing the patient's history when it is written up. A number of acceptable and standard formats for the psychiatric history are available.

Identifying Data

The identifying data provide a succinct demographic summary of the patient by name, age, marital status, sex, occupation, language if other than English, ethnic background and religion insofar as they are pertinent, and current circumstances of living. The information can also include in what place or situation the current interview took place, the sources of the information, the reliability of the source, and whether the current disorder is the first episode of that type for the patient. The psychiatrist should indicate whether the patient came in on his or her own, was referred by someone else, or was brought in by someone else. The identifying data are meant to provide a thumbnail sketch of potentially important patient characteristics that may affect diagnosis, prognosis, treatment, and compliance.

An example of the written report of the identifying data is as follows:

John Jones is a 25-year-old white single Catholic man, currently unemployed and homeless, living in public shelters and on the street. The current interview occurred in the emergency room (ER) with the patient in four-point restraints in the presence of two clinical staff members and one police officer. It was the 10th such visit to the ER for Mr. Jones in the past year. The sources of information on Mr. Jones included the patient himself and the police officer who brought the patient to the ER. The police officer had witnessed the patient on the street and knew him from previous episodes.

Chief Complaint

The chief complaint, in the patient's own words, states why he or she has come or been brought in for help. It should be recorded even if the patient is unable to speak, and a description of the person who provided the information should be included.

The patient's explanation, regardless of how bizarre or irrelevant it is, should be recorded verbatim in the section on the chief complaint. The other persons present can then give their versions of the presenting events in the section on the history of the present illness.

History of Present Illness

This part of the psychiatric history provides a comprehensive and chronological picture of the events leading up to the current moment in the patient's life. It is the part of the history that will probably be most helpful in making a diagnosis: what was the onset of the current episode, and what were the immediate precipitating events or triggers? An understanding of the history of the present illness helps answer the question, ''Why now?'' Why did the patient come to the doctor at this time? What were the patient's life circumstances at the onset of the symptoms or behavioral changes, and how did they affect the patient so that the presenting disorder became manifest? Knowing what the personality was of the previously well patient also helps give perspective on the currently ill patient.

The evolution of the patient's symptoms should be determined and summarized in an organized and systematic way. Symptoms not present should also be delineated. The more detailed the history of the present illness, the more likely the clinician is to make an accurate diagnosis. What past precipitating events were part of the chain leading up to the immediate events? In what ways has the patient's illness affected his or her life activities (for example, work, important relationships)? What is the nature of the dysfunction (for example, details about changes in such factors as personality, memory, speech)? Are there psychophysiological symptoms? If so, they should be described in terms of location, intensity, and fluctuation. If there is a relation between physical and psychological symptoms, it should be noted. Evidence of secondary gain—the extent to which illness serves some additional purpose—should also be noted. A description of the patient's current anxieties, whether they are generalized and nonspecific (free-floating) or are specifically related to particular situations, is helpful. How does the patient handle those anxieties? Frequently, a relatively open-ended question—such as, ''How did this all begin?''—leads to an adequate unfolding of the history of the present illness. A well-organized patient is generally able to present a chronological account of the history. However, a disorganized patient is difficult to interview, as the chronology of events is confused. In that case, contacting other informants, such as family members and friends, can be a valuable aid in clarifying the patient's story.

Previous Illnesses

This section of the psychiatric history is a transition between the story of the present illness and the patient's personal history (anamnesis). Past episodes of both psychiatric and medical illnesses are described. Ideally, at this point a detailed account of the patient's preexisting and underlying psychological and biological substrates is given, and important clues and evidence of vulnerable areas in the patient's functioning are provided. The patient's symptoms, extent of incapacity, type of treatment received, names of hospitals, length of each illness, effects of prior treatments, and degree of compliance should all be explored and recorded chronologically. Particular attention should be paid to the first episode that signaled the onset of illness, as first episodes can often provide crucial data about precipitating events, diagnostic possibilities, and coping capabilities.

With regard to medical history, the psychiatrist should obtain a medical review of symptoms and note any major medical or surgical illnesses and major traumas, particularly those requiring hospitalization, experienced by the patient. Episodes of craniocerebral trauma, neurological illness, tumors, and seizure disorders are especially relevant to psychiatric histories and so is a history of having tested positive for the human immunodeficiency virus (HIV) or of having acquired immune deficiency syndrome (AIDS). Specific questions need to be asked about the presence of a seizure disorder, episodes of loss of consciousness, changes in usual headache patterns, changes in vision, and episodes of confusion and disorientation. A history of infection with syphilis is critical and relevant.

Causes, complications, and treatment of any illness and the effects of the illness on the patient should be noted. Specific questions about psychosomatic disorders should be asked and noted. Included in that category are hay fever, rheumatoid arthritis, ulcerative colitis, asthma, hyperthyroidism, gastrointestinal upsets, recurrent colds, and skin conditions. All patients must be asked about alcohol and other substance use, including details about the quantity and the frequency of use. It is often advisable to frame one's questions in the form of an assumption of use, such as, ''How much alcohol would you say you drink in a day?'' rather than ''Do you drink?'' The latter question may put the patient on the defensive, concerned about what the physician will think if the answer is yes. If the physician assumes that drinking is a fact, the patient is likely to feel comfortable admitting use.

Personal History (Anamnesis)

In addition to studying the patient's present illness and current life situation, the psychiatrist needs a thorough understanding of the patient's past life and its relationship to the present emotional problem. The anamnesis or personal history is usually divided into the major developmental periods of prenatal and perinatal, early childhood, middle childhood, late childhood, and adulthood. The predominant emotions associated with the different life periods (for example, painful, stressful, conflictual) should be noted. Depending on time and situation, the psychiatrist may go into detail with regard to each of those areas.

PRENATAL AND PERINATAL HISTORY

The psychiatrist considers the nature of the home situation into which the patient was born and whether the patient was planned and wanted. Were there any problems with the mother's pregnancy and delivery? Was there any evidence of defect or injury at birth? What was the mother's emotional and physical state at the time of the patient's birth? Were there any maternal health problems during pregnancy? Was the mother abusing alcohol or other substances during her pregnancy?

EARLY CHILDHOOD (BIRTH THROUGH AGE 3 YEARS)

The early childhood period consists of the first 3 years of the patient's life. The quality of the mother-child interaction during feeding and toilet training is important. It is frequently possible to learn whether the child presented problems in those areas. Early disturbances in sleep patterns and signs of unmet needs, such as head banging and body rocking, provide clues about possible maternal deprivation or developmental disability. In addition, the psychiatrist should obtain a history of human constancy during the first 3 years. Did the parents have any psychiatric or medical illness that may have interfered with parent-child interactions? Did persons other than the mother care for the patient? Did the patient exhibit excessive problems at an early period with stranger anxiety or separation anxiety? The patient's siblings and the details of his or her relationship to them should be explored. The emerging personality of the child is also a topic of crucial importance. Was the child shy, restless, overactive, withdrawn, studious, outgoing, timid, athletic, friendly? The clinician should seek data concerning the child's increasingly ability to concentrate, to tolerate frustration, and to postpone gratification. The child's preference for active or passive roles in physical play should also be noted. What were the child's favorite games or toys? Did the child prefer to play alone, with others, or not at all? What is the patient's earliest memory? Were there any recurrent dreams or fantasies during that period?

Important areas to be covered are (1) feeding habits (breastfed or bottle-fed, eating problems), early development (walking, talking, teething, language development, motor development, signs of unmet needs, sleep pattern, object constancy, stranger anxiety, maternal deprivation, separation anxiety, other caretakers in the home), (3) toilet training (age, attitude of parents, feelings about it), (4) symptoms of behavior problems (thumb sucking, temper tantrums, tics, head bumping, rocking, night terrors, fears, bed-wetting or bed soiling, nail biting, excessive masturbation), (5) personality as a child (shy, restless, overactive, withdrawn, persistent, outgoing, timid, athletic, friendly; patterns of play), and (6) early or recurrent dreams or fantasies.

MIDDLE CHILDHOOD (AGES 3 TO 11 YEARS)

In this section the psychiatrist can address such important subjects as gender identification, punishments used in the home, and who provided the discipline and influenced early conscience formation. The psychiatrist must inquire about the patient's early school experiences, especially how the patient first tolerated being separated from his or her mother. Data about the patient's earliest friendships and personal relationships are valuable. The psychiatrist should identify and define the number and the closeness of the patient's friends, describe whether the patient took the role of a leader or a follower, and describe the patient's social popularity and participation in group or gang activities. Was the child able to cooperate with peers, to be fair, to understand and comply with rules, and to develop an early conscience? Early patterns of assertion, impulsiveness, aggression, passivity, anxiety, or antisocial behavior emerge in the context of school relationships. A history of the patient's learning to read and the development of other intellectual and motor skills are important. A history of learning disabilities, their management, and their effects on the child are of particular significance. The presence of nightmares, phobias, bed-wetting, fire setting, cruelty to animals, and excessive masturbation should also be explored.

LATE CHILDHOOD (PUBERTY THROUGH ADOLESCENCE)

During late childhood, people begin to develop independence from their parents through relationships with peers and in group activities. The psychiatrist should attempt to define the values of the patient's social groups and determine who were the patient's idealized figures. That information provides useful clues concerning the patient's emerging idealized self-image.

Further exploration is indicated of the patient's school history, relationships with teachers, and favorite studies and interests, both in school and in the extracurricular area. The psychiatrist should ask about the patient's participation in sports and hobbies and inquire about any emotional or physical problems that may have first appeared during this phase. Examples of the types of questions that are commonly asked include the following: What was the patient's sense of personal identity? How extensive was the use of alcohol and other substances? Was the patient sexually active, and what was the quality of the sexual relationships? Was the patient interactive and involved with school and peers, or was he or she isolated, withdrawn, perceived as odd by others? Did the patient have a generally intact self-esteem, or was there evidence of excessive self-loathing? What was the patient's body image? Were there suicidal episodes? Were there problems in school, including excessive truancy? How did the patient use private time? What was the relationship with the parents? What were the feelings about the development of secondary sex characteristics? What was the response to menarche? What were the attitudes about dating, petting, crushes, parties, and sex games? One way to organize the diverse and large amount of information is to break late childhood into subsets of behavior (for example, social relationships, school history, cognitive and motor development, emotional and physical problems, and sexuality), as described below.

Social Relationships

Attitudes toward siblings and playmates, number and closeness of friends, leader or follower, social popularity, participation in group or gang activities, idealized figures, patterns of aggression, passivity, anxiety, antisocial behavior

School History

How far the patient progressed, adjustment to school, relationships with teachers—teacher's pet versus rebel—favorite studies or interests, particular abilities or assets, extracurricular activities, sports, hobbies, relations of problems or symptoms to any social period

Cognitive and Motor Development

Learning to read and other intellectual and motor skills, minimal cerebral dysfunctions, learning disabilities—their management and effects on the child

Emotional and Physical Problems

Nightmares, phobias, masturbation, bed-wetting, running away, delinquency, smoking, alcohol or other substance use, anorexia, bulimia, weight problems, feelings of inferiority, depression, suicidal ideas and acts

Sexuality
a. Early curiosity, infantile masturbation, sex play
b. Acquisition of sexual knowledge, attitude of parents toward sex, sexual abuse
c. Onset of puberty, feelings about it, kind of preparation, feelings about menstruation, development of secondary sex characteristics
d. Adolescent sexual activity: crushes, parties, dating, petting, masturbation, nocturnal emissions and attitudes toward them

e. Attitudes toward opposite sex: timid, shy, aggressive, need to impress, seductive, sexual conquests, anxiety
f. Sexual practices: sexual problems, paraphilias, promiscuity
g. Sexual orientation: homosexual experiences in both heterosexual and homosexual adolescents, gender identity issues, self-esteem

ADULTHOOD
Occupational History

The psychiatrist should describe the patient's choice of occupation, the requisite training and preparation, any work-related conflicts, and the long-term ambitions and goals. The interviewer should also explore the patient's feelings about his or her current job and relationships at work (with authorities, peers, and, if applicable, subordinates) and describe the job history (for example, number and duration of jobs, reasons for job changes, and changes in job status). What would the patient do for work if he or she could freely choose?

Marital and Relationship History

In this section the psychiatrist describes the history of each marriage, whether legal or common law. Significant relationships with persons with whom the patient has lived for a protracted period of time are also included. The story of the marriage or long-term relationship should give a description of the evolution of the relationship, including the age of the patient at the beginning of the marriage or the long-term relationship. The areas of agreement and disagreement—including the management of money, housing difficulties, the roles of the in-laws, and attitudes toward raising children—should be described. Other questions include: Is the patient currently in a long-term relationship? How long is the longest relationship that the patient has had? What is the quality of the patient's sexual relationship (for example, is the patient's sexual life experienced as satisfactory or inadequate)? What does the patient look for in a partner? Is the patient able to initiate a relationship or to approach someone he or she feels attracted to or compatible with? How does the patient describe the current relationship in terms of its positive and negative qualities? How does the patient perceive failures of past relationships in terms of understanding what went wrong and who was or was not to blame?

Military History

The psychiatrist should inquire about patient's general adjustment to the military, whether they saw combat or sustained an injury, and the nature of their discharges. Were they ever referred for psychiatric consultation, and did they suffer any disciplinary action during their periods of service?

Education History

The psychiatrist needs to have a clear picture of the patient's educational background. That information can provide clues as to the patient's social and cultural background, intelligence, motivation, and any obstacles to achievement. For instance, a patient from an economically deprived background who never had the opportunity to attend the best schools and whose parents never graduated from high school shows strength of character, intelligence, and tremendous motivation by graduating from college. A patient who dropped out of high school because of violence and substance use displays creativity and determination by going to school at night to obtain a high school diploma while working during the day as a drug counselor. How far did the patient go in school? What was the highest grade or graduate level attained? What did the patient like to study, and what was the level of academic performance? How far did the other members of the patient's family go in school, and how does that compare with the patient's progress? What is the patient's attitude toward academic achievement?

Religion

The psychiatrist should describe the religious background of both parents and the details of the patient's religious instruction. Was the family's attitude toward religion strict or permissive, and were there any conflicts between the parents over the child's religious education? The psychiatrist should trace the evolution of the patient's adolescent religious practices to present beliefs and activities. Does the patient have a strong religious affiliation, and, if so, how does that affiliation affect the patient's life? What does the patient's religion say about the treatment of psychiatric or medical illness? What is the religious attitude toward suicide?

Social Activity

The psychiatrist should describe the patient's social life and the nature of friendships, with an emphasis on the depth, the duration, and the quality of human relationships. What type of social, intellectual, and physical interests does the patient share with friends? What types of relationships does the patient have with people of the same sex and the opposite sex? Is the patient essentially isolated and asocial? Does the patient prefer isolation, or is the patient isolated because of anxieties and fears about other people? Who visits the patient in the hospital and how frequently?

Current Living Situation

The psychiatrist should ask the patient to describe where he or she lives in terms of the neighborhood and the residence. He or she should include the number of rooms, the number of family members living in the home, and the sleeping arrangements. The psychiatrist should inquire as to how issues of privacy are handled, with particular emphasis on parental and sibling nudity and bathroom arrangements. He or she should ask about the sources of family income and any financial hardships. If applicable, the psychiatrist may inquire about public assistance and the patient's feelings about it. If the patient has been hospitalized, have provisions been made so that he or she will not lose a job or an apartment? The psychiatrist should ask who is caring for the children at home, who visits the patient in the hospital, and how frequently.

Legal History

Has the patient ever been arrested and, if so, for what? How many times? Was the patient ever in jail? For how long? Is the patient on probation, or are charges pending? Is the patient mandated to be in treatment as part of a stipulation of probation? Does the patient have a history of assault or violence? Against whom? Using what? What is the patient's attitude toward the arrests or prison terms? An extensive legal history, as well as the patient's attitude toward it, may indicate an antisocial personality disorder. An extensive history of violence may alert the psychiatrist to the potential for violence in the future.

PSYCHOSEXUAL HISTORY

Much of the history of infantile sexuality is not recoverable, although many patients are able to recall curiosities and sexual games played from the ages of 3 to 6 years. The psychiatrist should ask how patients learned about sex and what they felt their parents' attitudes were toward their sexual development. The interviewer can also inquire if the patient was sexually abused in childhood. Some of the material discussed in this section may also be covered in the section on adolescent sexuality. It is not important where in the history it is covered, as long as it is included.

The onset of puberty and the patient's feelings about that milestone are important. The adolescent masturbatory history, including the nature of the patient's fantasies and feelings about them, is of significance. Attitudes toward sex should be described in detail. Is the patient shy, timid, aggressive? Or does the patient need to impress others and boast of sexual conquests? Did the patient experience anxiety in the sexual setting? Was there promiscuity? What is the patient's sexual orientation?

The sexual history should include any sexual symptoms, such as anorgasmia, vaginismus, impotence, premature or retarded ejaculation, lack of sexual desire, and paraphilias (for example, sexual sadism, fetishism, voyeurism). Attitudes toward fellatio, cunnilingus, and coital techniques may be discussed. The topic of sexual adjustment should include a description of how sexual activity is usually initiated, the frequency of sexual relations, and sexual preferences, variations, and techniques. It is usually appropriate to inquire if the patient has engaged in extramarital relationships and, if so, under what circumstances and whether the spouse knew of the affair. If the spouse did learn of the affair, the psychiatrist should ask the patient to describe what happened. The reasons underlying an extramarital affair are just as important as an understanding of its effect on the marriage. Attitudes toward contraception and family planning are important. What form of contraception does the patient use? However, the psychiatrist should not assume that the patient uses birth control. A lesbian patient asked by an interviewer to describe what type of birth control she uses (on the assumption that she is heterosexual) may surmise that the interviewer will not be understanding or accepting of her sexual orientation. A better question is "Do you need to use birth control?" or "Is contraception something that is part of your sexuality?"

The psychiatrist should ask whether the patient wants to mention other areas of sexual functioning and sexuality. Is the patient aware of the issues involved in safe sex? Does the patient have a sexually transmitted disease, such as herpes or AIDS? Does the patient worry about being HIV-positive?

FAMILY HISTORY

A brief statement about any psychiatric illnesses, hospitalizations, and treatments of the patient's immediate family members should be placed in this part of the report. Is there a family history of alcohol and other substance abuse or of antisocial behavior? In addition, the family history should provide a description of the personalities and the intelligence of the various people living in the patient's home from childhood to the present and descriptions of the various households lived in. The psychiatrist should also define the role each person has played in the patient's upbringing and the current relationship with the patient. What have been the family ethnic, national, and religious traditions? Informants other than the patient may be available to contribute to the family history, and the source should be cited in the written record. Often, various members of the family give different descriptions of the same people and events. The psychiatrist should determine the family's attitude toward and insight into the patient's illness. Does the patient feel that the family members are supportive, indifferent, or destructive? What is the role of illness in the family?

Other questions that provide useful information in this section include the following: What are the patient's attitudes toward his or her parents and siblings? The psychiatrist should ask the patient to describe each family member. Whom does the patient mention first? Whom does the patient leave out? What does each of the parents do for a living? What do the siblings do? How does that compare with what the patient is currently doing, and how does the patient feel about it? Whom does the patient feel he or she is most like in the family and why?

DREAMS, FANTASIES, AND VALUES

Sigmund Freud stated that the dream is the royal road to the unconscious. Repetitive dreams are of particular value. If the patient has nightmares, what are their repetitive themes? Some of the most common dream themes are food, examinations, sex, helplessness, and impotence. Can the patient describe a recent dream and discuss its possible meanings? Fantasies and daydreams are another valuable source of unconscious material. As with dreams, the psychiatrist can explore and record all manifest details and attendant feelings.

What are the patient's fantasies about the future? If the patient could make any change in his or her life, what would it be? What are the patient's most common or favorite current fantasies? Does the patient experience daydreams? Are the patient's fantasies grounded in reality, or is the patient unable to tell the difference between fantasy and reality?

The psychiatrist may inquire about the patient's system of values—both social and moral—including values that concern work, money, play, children, parents, friends, sex, community concerns, and cultural issues. For instance, are children seen as a burden or a joy? Is work experienced as a necessary evil, an avoidable chore, or an opportunity? What is the patient's concept of right and wrong?

MENTAL STATUS EXAMINATION

The mental status examination is the part of the clinical assessment that describes the sum total of the examiner's observations and impressions of the psychiatric patient at the time of the interview. Whereas the patient's history remains stable, the patient's mental status can change from day to day or hour to hour. The mental status examination is the description of the patient's appearance, speech, actions, and thoughts during the interview. Even when a patient is mute or incoherent or refuses to answer questions, one can obtain a wealth of information through careful observation. Although practitioners' organizational formats for writing up the mental status examination vary slightly, the format must contain certain categories of information. One such format is outlined in Table 1.1–1.

Table 1.1–1. Outline of the Mental Status Examination

I. General description
  A. Appearance
  B. Behavior and psychomotor activity
  C. Attitude toward examiner
II. Mood and affect
  A. Mood
  B. Affect
  C. Appropriateness
III. Speech
IV. Perceptual disturbances
V. Thought
  A. Process or form of thought
  B. Content of thought
VI. Sensorium and cognition
  A. Alertness and level of conciousness
  B. Orientation
  C. Memory
  D. Concentration and attention
  E. Capacity to read and write
  F. Visuospatial ability
  G. Abstract thinking
  H. Fund of information and intelligence
VII. Impulse control
VIII. Judgment and insight
IX. Reliability

General Description

APPEARANCE

This is a description of the patient's appearance and overall physical impression conveyed to the psychiatrist, as reflected by posture, poise, clothing, and grooming. If the patient appears particularly bizarre, one may ask, ''Has anyone ever commented on how you look?'' ''How would you describe how you look?'' ''Can you help me understand some of the choices you make in how you look?''

Examples of items in the appearance category include body type, posture, poise, clothes, grooming, hair, and nails. Common terms used to describe appearance are healthy, sickly, ill at ease, poised, old-looking, young-looking, disheveled, childlike, and bizarre. Signs of anxiety are noted: moist hands, perspiring forehead, tense posture, wide eyes.

BEHAVIOR AND PSYCHOMOTOR ACTIVITY

This category refers to both the quantitative and the qualitative aspects of the patient's motor behavior. Included are mannerisms, tics, gestures, twitches, stereotyped behavior, echopraxia, hyperactivity, agitation, combativeness, flexibility, rigidity, gait, and agility. Restlessness, wringing of hands, pacing, and other physical manifestations are described. Psychomotor retardation or generalized slowing down of body movements should be noted. Any aimless, purposeless activity should be described.

ATTITUDE TOWARD EXAMINER

The patient's attitude toward the examiner can be described as cooperative, friendly, attentive, interested, frank, seductive, defensive, contemptuous, perplexed, apathetic, hostile, playful, ingratiating, evasive, or guarded; any number of other adjectives can be used. The level of rapport established should be recorded.

Mood and Affect

MOOD

Mood is defined as a pervasive and sustained emotion that colors the person's perception of the world. The psychiatrist is interested in whether the patient remarks voluntarily about feelings or whether it is necessary to ask the patient how he or she feels. Statements about the patient's mood should include depth, intensity, duration, and fluctuations. Common adjectives used to describe mood include depressed, despairing, irritable, anxious, angry, expansive, euphoric, empty, guilty, awed, futile, self-contemptuous, frightened, and perplexed. Mood may be labile, meaning that it fluctuates or alternates rapidly between extremes (for example, laughing loudly and expansive one moment, tearful and despairing the next).

AFFECT

Affect may be defined as the patient's present emotional responsiveness. Affect is what the examiner infers from the patient's facial expression, including the amount and the range of expressive behavior. Affect may or may not be congruent with mood. Affect is described as being within normal range, constricted, blunted, or flat. In the normal range of affect, there is a variation in facial expression, tone of voice, use of hands, and body movements. When affect is *constricted*, there is a clear reduction in the range and the intensity of expression. Similarly, in *blunted* affect, emotional expression is further reduced. To diagnose *flat* affect, one should find virtually no signs of affective expression, the patient's voice should be monotonous, and the face should be immobile. ''Blunted,'' ''flat,'' and ''constricted'' are terms used to refer to the apparent depth of emotion; depressed, proud, angry, fearful, anxious, guilty, euphoric, and expansive are terms used to refer to particular moods. The psychiatrist should note the patient's difficulty in initiating, sustaining, or terminating an emotional response.

APPROPRIATENESS

The appropriateness of the patient's emotional responses can be considered in the context of the subject matter the patient is discussing. Delusional patients who are describing a delusion of persecution should be angry or frightened about the experiences they believe are happening to them. Anger or fear in that context is an appropriate expression. Some psychiatrists have reserved the term ''inappropriateness of affect'' for a quality of response found in some schizophrenic patients, in which the patient's affect is incongruent with what the patient is saying (for example, flattened affect when speaking about murderous impulses).

Speech

This part of the report describes the physical characteristics of speech. Speech can be described in terms of its quantity, rate of production, and quality. The patient may be described as talkative, garrulous, voluble, and taciturn, unspontaneous, or normally responsive to cues from the interviewer. Speech may be rapid or slow, pressured, hesitant, emotional, dramatic, monotonous, loud, whispered, slurred, staccato, or mumbled. Impairments of speech, such as stuttering, are included in this section. Unusual rhythms (termed dysprosody) and any accent that may be present should be noted. Is the patient's speech spontaneous or not?

Perceptual Disturbances

Perceptual disturbances, such as hallucinations and illusions, may be experienced in reference to the self or the environment. The sensory system involved (for example, auditory, visual, olfactory, or tactile) and the content of the illusion or the hallucinatory experience should be described. The circumstances of the occurrence of any hallucinatory experience are important, because of hypnagogic hallucinations (occurring as a person falls asleep) and hypnopompic hallucinations (occurring as a person awakens) are of much less serious significance than other types of hallucinations. Hallucinations may also occur in particular times of stress for individual patients. Feelings of depersonalization and derealization (extreme feelings of detachment from one's self or the environment) are other examples of perceptual disturbance. Formication, the feeling of bugs crawling on or under the skin, is seen in cocaine-related disorders.

Examples of questions used to elicit the experience of hallucinations include the following: Have you ever heard voices or other sounds that no one else could hear or when no one else was around? Have you experienced any strange sensations in your body that others do not seem to experience? Have you ever had visions or seen things that other people do not seem to see?

Thought

Thought is divided into process (or form) and content. Process refers to the way in which a person puts together ideas and associations, the form in which a person thinks. Process or form of thought may be logical and coherent or completely illogical and even incomprehensible. Content refers to what a person is actually thinking about: ideas, beliefs, preoccupations, obsessions.

THOUGHT PROCESS (FORM OF THINKING)

The patient may have either an overabundance or a poverty of ideas. There may be rapid thinking, which, if carried to the extreme, is called a *flight of ideas*. A patient may exhibit slow or hesitant thinking. Thought may be vague or empty. Do the patient's replies really answer the questions asked, and does the patient have the capacity for goal-directed thinking? Are the responses relevant or irrelevant? Is there a clear cause-and-effect relation in the patient's explanations? Does the patient have *loose associations* (for example, do the ideas expressed appear to be unrelated and idiosyncratically connected)? Disturbances of the continuity of thought include statements that are tangential, circumstantial, rambling, evasive, and perseverative.

Blocking is an interruption of the train of thought before an idea has been completed; the patient may indicate an inability to recall what was being said or intended to be said.

Circumstantiality indicates the loss of capacity for goal-directed thinking; in the process of explaining an idea, the patient brings in many irrelevant details and parenthetical comments but eventually does get back to the original point. *Tangentiality* is a disturbance in which the patient loses the thread of the conversation and pursues tangential thoughts stimulated by various external or internal irrelevant stimuli and never returns to the original point. Thought process impairments may be reflected by *word salad* (incoherent or incomprehensible connections of thoughts), *clang associations* (association by rhyming), *punning* (association by double meaning), and *neologisms* (new words created by the patient through the combination or the condensation of other words).

CONTENT OF THOUGHT

Disturbances in content of thought include delusions, preoccupations (which may involve the patient's illness), obsessions (''Are there ideas that you have that are intrusive and repetitive?''), compulsions (''Are there things you do over and over, in a repetitive manner?'' ''Are there things you must do in a particular way or order, and, if not done that way, must you repeat them?'' ''Do you know why you do things that way?''), phobias, plans, intentions, recurrent ideas about suicide or homicide, hypochondriacal symptoms, and specific antisocial urges. Does the patient have thoughts of doing harm to himself or herself? Is there a plan? A major category of disturbances of thought content involves delusions. Delusions may be *mood-congruent* (in keeping with a depressed or elated mood) or *mood-incongruent*. *Delusions* are fixed, false beliefs out of keeping with the patient's cultural background. The content of any delusional system should be described, and the psychiatrist should attempt to evaluate its organization and the patient's conviction as to its validity. The manner in which it affects the patient's life is appropriately described in the history of the present illness. Delusions may be bizarre and may involve beliefs about external control. Delusions may have themes that are persecutory or paranoid, grandiose, jealous, somatic, guilty, nihilistic, or erotic. Ideas of reference and ideas of influence should also be described. Examples of *ideas of reference* include beliefs that one's television or radio is speaking to or about one. Examples of *ideas of influence* are beliefs involving another person or force controlling some aspect of one's behavior.

Sensorium and Cognition

This portion of the mental status examination seeks to assess organic brain function and the patient's intelligence, capacity for abstract thought, and level of insight and judgment.

The Mini-Mental State Examination (MMSE) is a brief instrument designed to grossly assess cognitive functioning. It assesses orientation, memory, calculations, reading and writing capacity, visuospatial ability, and language. The patient is quantitatively measured on those functions; a perfect score is 30 points. The MMSE is widely used as a simple, quick assessment of possible cognitive deficits. See table 4.1–1 for an example of the MMSE.

ALERTNESS AND LEVEL OF CONSCIOUSNESS

Disturbances of consciousness usually indicate organic brain impairment. *Clouding of consciousness* is an overall reduced awareness of the environment. A patient may be unable to sustain attention to environmental stimuli or to sustain goal-directed thinking or behavior. Clouding or obtunding of consciousness is frequently not a fixed mental state. The typical patient manifests fluctuations in the level of awareness of the surrounding environment. The patient who has an altered state of consciousness often shows some impairment of orientation as well, although the reverse is not necessarily true. Some terms used to describe the patient's level of consciousness are clouding, somnolence, stupor, coma, lethargy, alertness, and fugue state.

ORIENTATION

Disorders of orientation are traditionally separated according to time, place, and person. Any impairment usually appears in that order (that is, sense of time is impaired before sense of place); similarly, as the patient improves, the impairment clears in the reverse order. The psychiatrist must determine whether patients can give the approximate date and time of day. In addition, if patients are in a hospital, do they know how long they have been there? Do the patients behave as though they are oriented to the present? In questions about the patient's orientation to place, it is not sufficient that they be able to *state* the name and the location of the hospital correctly; they should also *behave* as though they know where they are. In assessing orientation for person, the psychiatrist asks patients whether they know the names of the people around them and whether they understand their roles in relationship to them. Do they know who the examiner is? It is only in the most severe instances that patients do not know who they themselves are.

MEMORY

Memory functions have traditionally been divided into four areas: remote memory, recent past memory, recent memory, and immediate retention and recall. Recent memory may be checked by asking patients about their appetite and then inquir-

ing what they had for breakfast or for dinner the previous evening. Patients may be asked at that point if they recall the interviewer's name. Asking patients to repeat six digits forward and then backward is a test for immediate retention. Remote memory can be tested by asking patients for information about their childhood that can be later verified. Asking patients to recall important news events from the past few months checks recent past memory. In cognitive disorders, recent or short-term memory is often impaired first, and remote or long-term memory is impaired later. If there is impairment, what are the efforts made to cope with it or to conceal impairment? Is denial, confabulation, catastrophic reaction, or circumstantiality used to conceal a deficit? Reactions to the loss of memory can give important clues to underlying disorders and coping mechanisms. For instance, a patient who appears to have memory impairment but, in fact, is depressed is more likely to be concerned about memory loss than is someone with memory loss secondary to dementia. *Confabulation* (unconsciously making up false answers when memory is impaired) is most closely associated with cognitive disorders.

CONCENTRATION AND ATTENTION

A patient's concentration may be impaired for a variety of reasons. For instance, a cognitive disorder, anxiety, depression, and internal stimuli, such as auditory hallucinations—all may contribute to impaired concentration. Subtracting serial 7s from 100 is a simple task that requires that both concentration and cognitive capacities be intact. Was the patient able to subtract 7 from 100 and keep subtracting 7s? If the patient could not subtract 7s, could 3s be subtracted? Were easier tasks accompanied—$4 \times 9, 5 \times 4$? The examiner must always assess whether anxiety, some disturbance of mood or consciousness, or a learning deficit is responsible for the difficulty.

Attention is assessed by calculations or by asking the patient to spell the word ''world'' (or others) backward. The patient can also be asked to name five things that start with a particular letter.

CAPACITY TO READ AND WRITE

The patient should be asked to read a sentence (for example, ''Close your eyes'') and then to do what the sentence says. The patient should also be asked to write a simple but complete sentence.

VISUOSPATIAL ABILITY

The patient should be asked to copy a figure, such as a clock face or interlocking pentagons.

ABSTRACT THINKING

Abstract thinking is the ability of patients to deal with concepts. Patients present with disturbances in the manner in which they conceptualize or handle ideas. Can patients explain similarities, such as those between an apple and a pear or those between truth and beauty? Are the meanings of simple proverbs, such as ''A rolling stone gathers no moss,'' understood? Answers may be concrete (giving specific examples to illustrate the meaning) or overly abstract (giving too generalized an explanation). Appropriateness of answers and the manner in which answers are given should be noted. In a catastrophic reaction, brain-damaged patients become extremely emotional and cannot think abstractly.

FUND OF INFORMATION AND INTELLIGENCE

If a possible cognitive impairment is suspected, does the patient have trouble with mental tasks, such as counting the change from $10 after a purchase of $6.37? If that task is too difficult, are easy problems (such as how many nickels are in $1.35) solved? The patient's intelligence is related to vocabulary and general fund of knowledge (for example, the distance from New York to Paris, Presidents of the United States). The patient's education level (both formal and self-education) and socioeconomic status must be taken into account. A patient's handling of difficult or sophisticated concepts can be reflective of intelligence, even in the absence of formal education or an extensive fund of information. Ultimately, the psychiatrist estimates the patient's intellectual capability and whether the patient is capable of functioning at the level of basic endowment.

Impulse Control

Is the patient capable of controlling sexual, aggressive, and other impulses? An assessment of impulse control is critical in ascertaining the patient's awareness of socially appropriate behavior and is a measure of the patient's potential danger to self and others. Some patients may be unable to control impulses secondary to cognitive disorders, others secondary to psychotic disorders, and others as the result of chronic characterological defects, as observed in the personality disorders. Impulse control can be estimated from information in the patient's recent history and from behavior observed during the interview.

Judgment and Insight

JUDGMENT

During the course of the history taking, the psychiatrist should be able to assess many aspects of the patient's capability for social judgment. Does the patient understand the likely outcome of his or her behavior, and is he or she influenced by that understanding? Can the patient predict what he or she would do in imaginary situations? For instance, what would the patient do if he or she smelled smoke in a crowded movie theater?

INSIGHT

Insight is the patients' degree of awareness and understanding that they are ill. Patients may exhibit a complete denial of their illness or may show some awareness that they are ill but place the blame on others, on external factors, or even on organic factors. They may acknowledge that they have an illness but ascribe it to something unknown or mysterious in themselves.

Intellectual insight is present when patients can admit that they are ill and acknowledge that their failures to adapt are, in part, due to their own irrational feelings. However, the major limitation to intellectual insight is that patients are unable to apply the knowledge to alter future experiences. True emotional insight is present when patients' awareness of their own motives and deep feelings leads to a change in their personality or behavior patterns.

A summary of levels of insight follows:

1. Complete denial of illness
2. Slight awareness of being sick and needing help but denying it at the same time

3. Awareness of being sick but blaming it on others, on external factors, or on organic factors
4. Awareness that illness is due to something unknown in the patient
5. *Intellectual insight:* admission that the patient is ill and that symptoms or failures in social adjustment are due to the patient's own particular irrational feelings or disturbances without applying that knowledge to future experiences
6. *True emotional insight:* emotional awareness of the motives and feelings within the patient and the important persons in his or her life, which can lead to basic changes in behavior

Reliability

The mental status part of the report concludes with the psychiatrist's impressions of the patient's reliability and capacity to report his or her situation accurately. It includes an estimate of the psychiatrist's impression of the patient's truthfulness or veracity. For instance, if the patient is open about significant active substance abuse or about circumstances that the patient knows may reflect badly (for example, trouble with the law), the psychiatrist may estimate the patient's reliability to be good.

PSYCHIATRIC REPORT

When the psychiatrist has completed a comprehensive psychiatric history and mental status examination, the information obtained is written up and organized into the psychiatric report. The report follows the outline of the standard psychiatric history and mental status examination. In the psychiatric report the examiner (1) addresses the critical questions of further diagnostic studies that must be performed, (2) adds a summary of both positive and negative findings, (3) makes a tentative multiaxial diagnosis, (4) gives a prognosis, (5) gives a psychodynamic formulation, and (6) gives a set of management recommendations.

Further Diagnostic Studies

A. General physical examination
B. Neurological examination
C. Additional psychiatric diagnostic interviews
D. Interviews with family members, friends, or neighbors by a social worker
E. Psychological, neurological, or laboratory tests as indicated: electroencephalogram, computed tomography scan, magnetic resonance imaging, tests of other medical conditions, reading comprehension and writing tests, tests for aphasia, projective psychological tests, dexamethasone-suppression test, 24-hour urine test for heavy-metal intoxication

Summary of Positive and Negative Findings

Mental symptoms, historical data (for example, family history), medical and laboratory findings, and psychological and neurological test results, if available, are summarized.

Diagnosis

Diagnostic classification is made according to the fourth edition of the American Psychiatric Association's *Diagnostic and Statistical Manual of Mental Disorders* (DSM-IV). DSM-

IV uses a multiaxial classification scheme consisting of five axes, each of which should be covered in the diagnosis.

Axis I consists of all clinical syndromes (for example, mood disorders, schizophrenia, generalized anxiety disorder) and other conditions that may be a focus of clinical attention.

Axis II consists of personality disorders, mental retardation, and borderline intellectual functioning.

Axis III consists of any general medical conditions (for example, epilepsy, cardiovascular disease, endocrine disorders).

Axis IV refers to psychosocial and environmental problems (for example, divorce, injury, death of a loved one) relevant to the illness.

Axis V relates to the global assessment of functioning exhibited by the patient during the interview (for example, social, occupational, and psychological functioning); a rating scale with a continuum from 100 (superior functioning) to 1 (grossly impaired functioning) is used.

The DSM-IV multiaxial classification scheme is discussed in detail in Chapter 3.

Prognosis

The prognosis is an opinion about the probable immediate and future course, extent, and outcome of the disorder. The good and bad prognostic factors, as known, are listed.

Psychodynamic Formulation

The psychodynamic formulation is a summary of proposed psychological influences on or causes of the patient's disturbance; influences in the patient's life that contributed to the present disorder; environmental and personality factors relevant to determining the patient's symptoms and how those influences have interacted with the patient's genetic, temperamental, and biological makeup; and primary and secondary gains. An outline of the major defense mechanisms used by the patient should be listed.

Recommendations

In formulating the treatment plan, the clinician should note whether the patient requires psychiatric treatment at the time and, if so, at which problems and target symptoms the treatment is aimed, what kind of treatment or combination of treatments the patient should receive, and what treatment setting seems most appropriate. For instance, the examiner evaluates the role of medication, inpatient or outpatient treatment, frequency of sessions, probable duration of therapy, and type of psychotherapy (individual, group, or family therapy). Specific goals of therapy are noted. If hospitalization is recommended, the clinician should specify the reasons for hospitalization, the type of hospitalization indicated, the urgency with which the patient has to be hospitalized, and the anticipated duration of inpatient care. The clinician should also estimate the length of treatment.

If either the patient or family members are unwilling to accept the recommendations for treatment and the clinician thinks that the refusal of the recommendations may have serious consequences, the patient (or the parent or guardian) should sign a statement that the recommended treatment was refused.

References

American Psychiatric Association: *Diagnostic and Statistical Manual of Mental Disorders*, ed 4. American Psychiatric Association, Washington, 1994.

Corty E, Lehman A F, Myers C P: Influence of psychoactive substance use on the reliability of psychiatric diagnosis. J Consult Clin Psychol *61*: 165, 1993.

Kaplan H I, Sadock B J: Psychiatric Report. In *Comprehensive Textbook of Psychiatry*, ed 6, H I Kaplan, B J Sadock, editors, p 531. Williams & Wilkins, Baltimore, 1995.

Kosten T A, Rounsaville B J: Sensitivity of psychiatric diagnosis based on the best estimate procedure. Am J Psychiatry *149*: 1225, 1992.

Rogers P D, Speraw S R, Ozbek I: The assessment of the identified substance-abusing adolescent. Pediatr Clin North Am *42*: 351, 1995.

Strauss G D: The psychiatric interview, history, and mental status examination. In *Comprehensive Textbook of Psychiatry*, ed 6, H I Kaplan, B J Sadock, editors, p 521. Williams & Wilkins, Baltimore, 1995.

Zarin D A, Earls F: Diagnostic decision making in psychiatry. Am J Psychiatry *150*: 197, 1993.

1.2 LABORATORY TESTS IN PSYCHIATRY

Psychiatrists are more dependent than are other medical specialists on the clinical examination and on the patient's signs and symptoms. No laboratory tests in psychiatry can confirm or rule out such diagnoses as schizophrenia, bipolar I disorder, and major depressive disorder. However, with the continuing advances in biological psychiatry and neuropsychiatry, laboratory tests have become increasingly valuable, both to the clinical psychiatrist and to the biological researcher.

In clinical psychiatry, laboratory tests can help rule out potential underlying organic causes of psychiatric symptoms—for example, impaired copper metabolism in Wilson's disease and a positive result on an antinuclear antibody (ANA) test in systematic lupus erythematosus (SLE). Laboratory work is then used to monitor treatment, such as measuring the blood levels of antidepressant medications and assessing the effects of lithium (Eskalith) on electrolytes, thyroid metabolism, and renal function. However, laboratory data can serve only as an underlying support for the essential skill of clinical assessment.

BASIC SCREENING TESTS

Before initiating psychiatric treatment, a clinician should undertake a routine medical evaluation for the purposes of screening for concurrent disease, ruling out organicity, and establishing baseline values of functions to be monitored. Such an evaluation includes a medical history and routine medical laboratory tests, such as a complete blood count (CBC); hematocrit and hemoglobin; renal, liver, and thyroid function; electrolytes; and blood sugar.

Thyroid disease and other endocrinopathies may present as a mood disorder or a psychotic disorder; cancer or infectious disease may present as depression; infection and connective tissue diseases may present as short-term changes in mental status. In addition, a range of organic mental and neurological conditions may present initially to the psychiatrist. Those conditions include multiple sclerosis, Parkinson's disease, dementia of the Alzheimer's type, Huntington's disease, dementia due to human immunodeficiency virus (HIV) disease, and temporal lobe epilepsy. Any suspected medical or neurological condition should be thoroughly evaluated with appropriate laboratory tests and consultation.

NEUROENDOCRINE TESTS

Thyroid Function Tests

A number of thyroid function tests are available, including tests for thyroxine (T_4) by competitive protein binding (T_4D)

Table 1.2-1   Thyroid Monitoring for Patients Taking Lithium

Evaluation	Before Treatment	Repeat at 6 Months	Repeat Yearly
Medical			
1. Careful medical and family history to detect family history of thyroid disease	X		
2. Review of symptoms of hyperthyroidism and hypothyroidism	X	X	X
3. Physical examination, including palpation of thyroid	X		X
Laboratory			
T_3 resin uptake (T_3RU)	X		X
T_4RIA	X		X
FT_4I	X		X
TSH	X	X	X
Antithyroid antiboidies	X		X

Table adapted from J M Silver, S C Yudofsky: Psychopharmacology and electroconvulsive therapy. In *The American Psychiatric Press Textbook of Psychiatry*, J A Talbott, R E Hales, S C Yudofsky, editors, p 822. American Psychiatric Press, Washington, 1987. Used with permission. Table from A MacKinnon, S C Yudofsky: *Principles of the Psychiatric Evaluation*, p 104. Lippincott, Philadelphia, 1991. Used with permission.

and by radioimmunoassay (T_4RIA) involving a specific antigen-antibody reaction. More than 90 percent of T_4 is bound to serum protein and is responsible for thyroid-stimulating hormone (TSH) secretion and cellular metabolism. Other thyroid measures include the free T_4 index (FT_4I), triiodothyronine uptake, and total serum triiodothyronine measured by radioimmunoassay (T_3RIA). Those tests are used to rule out hypothyroidism, which can present with symptoms of depression. In some studies, up to 10 percent of patients complaining of depression and associated fatigue had incipient hypothyroid disease. Other associated signs and symptoms common to both depression and hypothyroidism include weakness, stiffness, poor appetite, constipation, menstrual irregularities, slowed speech, apathy, impaired memory, and even hallucinations and delusions. Lithium can cause hypothyroidism and, more rarely, hyperthyroidism. Table 1.2-1 outlines the suggested monitoring of thyroid function for patients taking lithium. Neonatal hypothyroidism results in mental retardation and is preventable if the diagnosis is made at birth.

THYROTROPIN-RELEASING HORMONE STIMULATION TEST

The thyrotropin-releasing hormone (TRH) stimulation test is indicated in patients who have marginally abnormal thyroid test results with suspected subclinical hypothyroidism, which may account for clinical depression. It is also used in patients with possible lithium-induced hypothyroidism. The procedure entails an intravenous (IV) injection of 500 μg of protirelin (Thyrel), which produces a sharp rise in serum TSH when measured at 15, 30, 60, and 90 minutes. TSH of from 5 to 25 μIU/mL above the baseline is normal. An increase of less than 7 μIU/mL is considered a blunted response, which may correlate with a diagnosis of a depressive disorder. Eight percent of all patients with depressive disorders have some thyroid illness.

Dexamethasone-Suppression Test

Dexamethasone (Decadron) is a long-acting synthetic glucocorticoid with a long half-life. About 1 mg of dexamethasone is equivalent to 25 mg of cortisol. The dexamethasone-suppression test (DST) is used to help confirm a diagnostic impression of major depressive disorder (fourth edition of *Diagnostic and Statistical Manual of Mental Disorders* [DSM-IV] classification) or endogenous depression (Research Diagnostic Criteria [RDC] classification).

PROCEDURE

The patient is given 1 mg of dexamethasone by mouth at 11 PM, and plasma cortisol is measured at 8 AM, 4 PM, and 11 PM. Plasma cortisol above 5 μg/dL (known as nonsuppression) is considered abnormal (that is, positive). Suppression of cortisol indicates that the hypothalamic-adrenal-pituitary axis is functioning properly. Since the 1930s, dysfunction of that axis has been known to be associated with stress.

The DST can be used to follow the response of a depressed person to treatment. Normalization of the DST, however, is not an indication to stop antidepressant treatment, because the DST may normalize before the depression resolves.

Some evidence indicates that patients with a positive DST result (especially 10 μg/dL) will have a good response to somatic treatment, such as electroconvulsive therapy (ECT) or cyclic antidepressant therapy. The sensitivity of the DST is considered to be 45 percent in major depressive disorder and 70 percent in major depressive episode with psychotic features. The specificity is 90 percent compared with controls and 77 percent compared with other psychiatric diagnoses.

Other Endocrine Tests

A variety of other hormones affect behavior. Exogenous hormonal administration has been shown to affect behavior, and known endocrine diseases have associated mental disorders.

In addition to thyroid hormones, those hormones include the anterior pituitary hormone prolactin, growth hormone, somatostatin, gonadotropin-releasing hormone (GnRH), and the sex steroids—luteinizing hormone (LH), follicle-stimulating hormone (FSH), testosterone, and estrogen. Melatonin from the pineal gland has been implicated in seasonal affective disorder (called mood disorder with seasonal pattern in DSM-IV).

Symptoms of anxiety or depression may be explained in some patients on the basis of unspecified changes in endocrine function or homeostasis.

Catecholamines

The serotonin metabolite 5-hydroxyindoleacetic acid (5-HIAA) is elevated in the urine of patients with carcinoid tumors and at times in patients who take phenothiazine medication and in persons who eat foods high in serotonin (for example, walnuts, bananas, avocados). The amount of 5-HIAA in cerebrospinal fluid is low in some persons who are in a suicidal depression

Table 1.2–2.   Other Laboratory Testing for Patients Taking Lithium

Test	Frequency
1. Complete blood count	Before treatment and yearly
2. Serum electrolytes	Before treatment and yearly
3. Fasting blood glucose	Before treatment and yearly
4. Electrocardiogram	Before treatment and yearly
5. Pregnancy testing for women of childbearing age*	Before treatment

* Take more frequently when compliance with treatment plan is uncertain.
Table from A MacKinnon, S C Yudofsky: *Principles of the Psychiatric Evaluation*, p 106. Lippincott, Philadelphia, 1991. Used with permission.

and in those who have committed suicide in particularly violent ways. Low cerebrospinal fluid 5-HIAA is associated with violence in general. Norepinephrine and its metabolic products—metanephrine, normetanephrine, and vanillylmandelic acid (VMA)—can be measured in the urine, the blood, and the plasma. Plasma catecholamines are markedly elevated in pheochromocytoma, which is associated with anxiety, agitation, and hypertension. Some cases of chronic anxiety may share elevated blood norepinephrine and epinephrine levels. Some depressed patients have a low urinary norepinephrine to epinephrine ratio (NE:E).

High levels of urinary norepinephrine and epinephrine have been found in some patients with posttraumatic stress disorder. The norepinephrine metabolite 3-methoxy-4-hydroxyphenylglycol (MHPG) level is decreased in patients with severe depressive disorders, especially in those patients who attempt suicide.

Renal Function Tests

Creatinine clearance detects early kidney damage and can be serially monitored to follow the course of renal disease. Blood urea nitrogen (BUN) is also elevated in renal disease and is excreted by way of the kidneys, and the serum BUN and the creatinine are monitored in patients taking lithium. If the serum BUN or the creatinine is abnormal, the patient's two-hour creatinine clearance and ultimately the 24-hour creatinine clearance are tested. Table 1.2–2 summarizes other laboratory testing for patients taking lithium.

Liver Function Tests

Total bilirubin and direct bilirubin are elevated in hepatocellular injury and intrahepatic bile stasis that can occur with phenothiazine or tricyclic medication and with alcohol and other substance abuse. Certain drugs—for example, phenobarbital (Luminal)—may decrease serum bilirubin. Liver damage or disease, which is reflected by abnormal findings in liver function tests (LFTs), may present with signs and symptoms of a cognitive disorder, including disorientation and delirium. Impaired hepatic function may increase the elimination half-lives of certain drugs, including some of the benzodiazepines, so that the drug may stay in the patient's system longer than it would under normal circumstances. LFTs need to be routinely monitored when using certain drugs, such as carbamazepine (Tegretol) and valproate (Depakene).

BLOOD TEST FOR SEXUALLY TRANSMITTED DISEASES

The Venereal Disease Research Laboratory (VDRL) test is used as a screening test for syphilis. If positive, the result is confirmed by using the specific fluorescent treponemal antibody-absorption test (FTA-ABS test), which uses the spirochete *Treponema pallidum* as the antigen. Central nervous system VDRL is measured in patients with suspected neurosyphilis. A positive HIV test result indicates that the person has been exposed to infection with the virus that causes acquired immune deficiency syndrome (AIDS).

TESTS RELATED TO PSYCHOTROPIC DRUGS

There is a trend in caring for patients receiving psychotropic medication to regularly measure their plasma levels of the prescribed drug. For some types of drugs, such as lithium, the monitoring is essential, but for other types of drugs, such as antipsychotics, it is mainly of academic or research interest. The clinician need not practice defensive medicine by insisting that all patients receiving psychotropic drugs have blood levels taken for medicolegal purposes. In the discussion that follows, the major classes of drugs and the suggested guidelines are outlined. The current status of psychopharmacological treatment is such that the psychiatrist's clinical judgment and experience, except in rare instances, is a better indication of a drug's therapeutic efficacy than is a plasma-level determination. Moreover, the reliance on plasma levels cannot replace clinical skills and the need to maintain the humanitarian aspects of patient care.

Benzodiazepines

No special tests are needed for patients taking benzodiazepines. Among those metabolized in the liver by oxidation, impaired hepatic function increases the half-life. Baseline LFTs are indicated in patients with suspected liver damage. Urine testing for benzodiazepines is used routinely in cases of substance abuse.

Antipsychotics

Antipsychotics can cause leukocytosis, leukopenia, mild anemia, and, in rare cases, agranulocytosis. A baseline may be desirable, but because bone marrow side effects can occur abruptly, even when the dosage of a drug has remained constant, a baseline normal CBC is not conclusive. Antipsychotics are metabolized in the liver, so LFTs may be useful. Antipsychotic plasma levels do not correlate with clinical response; however, there is a possible correlation between high plasma levels and toxic side effects, especially with chlorpromazine (Thorazine) and haloperidol (Haldol). There is known relation between antipsychotic levels and tardive dyskinesia. Plasma levels are currently of clinical use only to detect noncompliance and nonabsorption and, thus, may be useful in identifying the nonresponder.

CLOZAPINE

Because of the risk of agranulocytosis (1 to 2 percent), patients who are being treated with clozapine (Clozaril) must have a baseline white blood cell (WBC) and differential count before the initiation of treatment, a WBC count every week throughout treatment, and a WBC count for four weeks after the discontinuation of clozapine. Physicians and pharmacists who provide clozapine are required to be registered through the Clozaril National Registry (1-800-448-5938).

Tricyclic and Tetracyclic Drugs

An electrocardiogram (ECG) should be given before starting cyclic drugs to assess for conduction delays, which may lead to heart block at therapeutic levels. Some clinicians believe that all patients receiving prolonged cyclic drug therapy should have an annual ECG. At therapeutic levels, the drugs suppress arrhythmias through a quinidinelike effect. Trazodone (Desyrel), an antidepressant unrelated to tricyclic drugs, has been reported to cause ventricular arrhythmias and priapism, mild leukopenia, and neutropenia.

Blood levels should be tested routinely when using imipramine (Tofranil), desipramine (Norpramin), or nortriptyline (Pamelor) in the treatment of depressive disorders. Taking blood levels may also be of use in patients with a poor response at normal dosage ranges and in high-risk patients for whom there is an urgent need to know whether a therapeutic or toxic plasma level of the drug has been reached. Blood level tests should also include the measurement of active metabolites (for example, imipramine is converted to desipramine, amitriptyline [Elavil] to nortriptyline).

Procedure

The procedure for taking blood levels is as follows: The blood specimen should be drawn 10 to 14 hours after the last dose, usually in the morning after a bedtime dose. Patients must be on a stable daily dosage for at least five days for the test to be valid. Some patients are unusually poor metabolizers of cyclic drugs and may have levels as high as 2,000 ng/mL while taking normal dosages and before showing a favorable clinical response. Such patients must be monitored closely for cardiac side effects. Patients with levels greater than 1,000 ng/mL are generally at risk for cardiotoxicity.

Monoamine Oxidase Inhibitors

Patients taking monoamine oxidase inhibitors (MAOIs) are instructed to avoid tyramine-containing foods because of the danger of a potential hypertensive crisis. A baseline normal blood pressure (BP) must be recorded, and the BP must be monitored during treatment. MAOIs may also cause orthostatic hypotension as a direct drug effect unrelated to diet. Other than their potential for causing elevated BP when taken with certain foods, MAOIs are relatively free of other side effects. A test used both in research and in current clinical practice involves correlating the therapeutic response with the degree of platelet monoamine oxidase inhibition.

Lithium

Patients receiving lithium should have baseline thyroid function tests, electrolyte monitoring, a WBC count, renal function tests (specific gravity, BUN, and creatinine), and a baseline ECG. The rationale for those tests is that lithium can cause renal concentrating defects, hypothyroidism, and leukocytosis; sodium depletion can cause toxic lithium levels; and about 95 percent of lithium is excreted in the urine. Lithium has also been shown to cause ECG changes, including various conduction defects.

Lithium is most clearly indicated in the prophylactic treatment of manic episodes (its direct antimanic effect may take up to two weeks) and is commonly coupled with antipsychotics for the treatment of acute manic episodes. Lithium itself may also have antipsychotic activity. The maintenance level is 0.6 to 1.2 mEq per L, although acutely manic patients can tolerate up to 1.5 to 1.8 mEq per L. Some patients may respond at lower levels, whereas others may require higher levels. A response below 0.4 mEq per L is probably a placebo. Toxic reactions may occur with levels over 2.0 mEq per L. Regular lithium monitoring is essential, since there is a narrow therapeutic range beyond which cardiac problems and central nervous system (CNS) effects can occur.

Lithium levels are drawn 8 to 12 hours after the last dose, usually in the morning after the bedtime dose. The level should be measured at least twice a week while stabilizing the patient and may be drawn monthly thereafter.

Carbamazepine

A pretreatment CBC including platelet count should be done. Reticulocyte count and serum iron tests are also desirable. Those texts should be repeated weekly during the first three months of treatment and monthly thereafter. Carbamazepine can cause aplastic anemia, agranulocytosis, thrombocytopenia, and leukopenia. Because of the minor risk of hepatotoxicity, LFTs should be done every three to six months. The medication should be discontinued if the patient shows any signs of bone marrow suppression as measured with periodic CBCs. The therapeutic level of carbamazepine is 8 to 12 ng/mL, with toxicity most often reached at levels of 15 ng/mL. Most clinicians report that levels as high as 12 ng/mL are hard to achieve.

PROVOCATION OF PANIC ATTACKS WITH SODIUM LACTATE

Up to 72 percent of patients with panic disorder have a panic attack when administered an IV injection of sodium lactate. Therefore, lactate provocation is used to confirm a diagnosis of panic disorder. Lactate provocation has also been used to trigger flashbacks in patients with posttraumatic stress disorder. Hyperventilation, another known trigger of panic attacks in predisposed persons, is not as sensitive as lactate provocation in inducing panic attacks. Carbon dioxide (CO_2) inhalation also precipitates panic attacks in those so predisposed. Panic attacks triggered by sodium lactate are not inhibited by peripherally acting β-blockers but are inhibited by alprazolam (Xanax) and tricyclic drugs.

AMOBARBITAL INTERVIEW

Amobarbital (Amytal) interviews have both diagnostic and therapeutic indications. Diagnostically, the interviews are helpful in differentiating nonorganic and organic conditions, particularly in patients who present with symptoms of catatonia, stupor, and muteness. Organic conditions tend to worsen with infusions of amobarbital, but nonorganic or psychogenic conditions tend to get better because of disinhibition, decreased anxiety, or increased relaxation. Therapeutically, amobarbital interviews are useful in disorders of repression and dissociation—for example, in the recovery of memory in dissociative amnestic disorders and fugue, in the recovery of function in conversion disorder, and in the facilitation of emotional expression in posttraumatic stress disorder.

Table 1.2-3.   Substances of Abuse That Can Be Tested in Urine

Substance	Length of Time Detected in Urine
Alcohol	7–12 hours
Amphetamine	48 hours
Barbiturates	24 hours (short-acting)
	3 weeks (long-acting)
Benzodiazepine	3 days
Cannabis	3 days to 4 weeks (depending on use)
Cocaine	6–8 hours (metabolites 2–4 days)
Codeine	48 hours
Heroin	36–72 hours
Methadone	3 days
Methaqualone	7 days
Morphine	48–72 hours
Phencyclidine (PCP)	8 days
Propoxyphene	6–48 hours

URINE TESTING FOR SUBSTANCE ABUSE

A number of substances may be detected in a patient's urine if the urine is tested within a specific (and variable) period of time after ingestion. Knowledge of urine substance testing is becoming crucial for practicing physicians in view of the controversial issue of mandatory or random substance testing. Table 1.2–3 provides a summary of substances of abuse than can be tested in urine. Laboratory tests are also used in the detection of substances that may be contributing to cognitive disorders.

References

Rapp M S, Bibr J, Campbell K: The use of laboratory tests in a psychiatric hospital. Can J Psychiatry 37: 137, 1992.
Rosse R B, Deutsch L H, Deutsch S I: Medical assessment and laboratory testing in psychiatry. In *Comprehensive Textbook of Psychiatry*, ed 6, H I Kaplan, B J Sadock, editors, p 601. Williams & Wilkins, Baltimore, 1995.

1.3 MEDICAL ASSESSMENT IN PSYCHIATRY

The medical assessment of a psychiatric patient consists of a thorough medical history, a review of systems, general observation, physical examination, and diagnostic laboratory studies. Psychiatrists do not perform routine physical examinations of their patients. The complex interplay between somatic illness and psychiatric illness may require the psychiatrist to differentiate physical diseases that mimic psychiatric illnesses and vice versa. Also, the presenting symptoms of some physical illnesses may be psychiatric signs or symptoms. For example, a chief complaint of anxiety may be associated with mitral valve prolapse, which is revealed by cardiac auscultation. Some psychiatrists contend that a complete medical workup is essential for every patient; others maintain the opposite. In any case, the patient's medical status should always be considered at the outset; the psychiatrist is often called on to decide whether a medical evaluation is needed and, if so, what it should include.

MEDICAL HISTORY

In the course of conducting a psychiatric evaluation, information should be gathered about (1) known bodily diseases or dysfunctions, (2) hospitalizations and operative procedures, (3) medications taken recently or at present, (4) personal habits and occupational history, (5) family history of illnesses, and (6) specific physical complaints. Information about medical ill-

nesses should be gathered from both the patient and the referring physician.

Information about previous episodes of illness may provide valuable clues about the nature of the present disorder. For example, if the present disorder is distinctly delusional, the patient has a history of several similar episodes, and each responded promptly to diverse forms of treatment, the possibility of substance-induced psychotic disorder is strongly suggested. To pursue that lead, the psychiatrist should order a drug screen. The history of a surgical procedure may also be useful; for example, a thyroidectomy suggests hypothyroidism as the cause of depression.

An adverse effect of several medications prescribed for hypertension is depression. Medication taken in a therapeutic dosage occasionally reaches high blood levels. Digitalis intoxication, for example, may occur under such circumstances and result in impaired mental functioning. Proprietary drugs may cause or contribute to an anticholinergic delirium. Therefore, the psychiatrist must inquire about over-the-counter remedies, as well as prescribed medications.

An occupational history may provide essential information. Exposure to mercury may result in complaints suggesting a psychosis, and exposure to lead, as in smelting, may produce a cognitive disorder. The latter clinical picture can also result from imbibing moonshine with a high lead content.

In eliciting information concerning specific symptoms, the psychiatrist brings medical and psychological knowledge into full play. For example, the psychiatrist should elicit sufficient information from the patient complaining of headache to predict, with considerable certainty, whether the pain is or is not the result of intracranial disease. Also, the psychiatrist should be able to recognize that the pain in the right shoulder of a hypochondriacal patient with abdominal discomfort may be the classic referred pain of gallbladder disease.

REVIEW OF SYSTEMS

An inventory by systems should follow the open-ended inquiry. The review may be organized according to organ systems (for example, liver, pancreas), functional systems (for example, gastrointestinal), or a combination of the two, as in the outline below; however, the review should be comprehensive and thorough.

Head

Many patients give a history of headache; its duration, frequency, character, location, and severity should be ascertained. Headaches often result from substance abuse, including alcohol, nicotine, and caffeine. Vascular (migraine) headaches are precipitated by stress. Temporal arteritis causes unilateral throbbing headaches and may lead to blindness. Brain tumors are associated with headaches as a result of increases in intracranial pressure. A history of head injury may result in subdural hematoma and in boxers can cause progressive dementia with extrapyramidal symptoms. The headache of subarachnoid hemorrhage is sudden, severe, and associated with changes in the sensorium. Normal pressure hydrocephalus may follow a head injury or encephalitis and may be associated with dementia and a shuffling gait.

Eye, Ear, Nose, and Throat

Visual acuity, diplopia, hearing problems, tinnitus, glossitis, and bad taste are covered in this area. A patient taking antipsychotics who gives a history of twitching about the mouth or disturbing movements of the tongue may be in the early and potentially reversible stage of tardive dyskinesia. Impaired vision may occur with thioridazine (Mellaril) in high dosages. A history of glaucoma contraindicates drugs with anticholinergic side effects. Aphonia may be hysterical in nature. The late stage of cocaine abuse can result in perforations of the nasal septum and difficulty in breathing. A transitory episode of diplopia may herald multiple sclerosis. Delusional disorder is more common in hearing-impaired persons than in those with normal hearing.

Respiratory System

Cough, asthma, pleurisy, hemoptysis, dyspnea, and orthopnea are considered in this section. Hyperventilation is suggested if the patient's symptoms include all or a few of the following: onset at rest, sighing respirations, apprehension, anxiety, depersonalization, palpitations, inability to swallow, numbness of the feet and hands, and carpopedal spasm. Dyspnea and breathlessness may occur in depression. In pulmonary or obstructive airway disease the onset of symptoms is usually insidious, whereas in depression it is sudden. In depression, breathlessness is experienced at rest, shows little change with exertion, and may fluctuate within a matter of minutes; the onset of breathlessness coincides with the onset of a mood disorder and is often accompanied by attacks of dizziness, sweating, palpitations, and paresthesias. In obstructive airway disease, only the patients with the most advanced respiratory incapacity experience breathlessness at rest. Most striking and of greatest assistance in making a differential diagnosis is the emphasis placed on the difficulty in inspiration experienced by patients with depression and on the difficulty in expiration experienced by patients with pulmonary disease. Bronchial asthma has sometimes been associated with childhood histories of extreme dependence on the mother. Patients with bronchospasm should not receive propranolol (Inderal) because it may block catecholamine-induced bronchodilation; propranolol is specifically contraindicated for patients with bronchial asthma because epinephrine given to such patients in an emergency will not be effective.

Cardiovascular System

Tachycardia, palpitations, and cardiac arrhythmia are among the most common signs of anxiety about which the patient may complain. Pheochromocytoma usually produces symptoms that mimic anxiety disorders, such as rapid heart beat, tremors, and pallor. Increased urinary catecholamines are diagnostic of pheochromocytoma. Patients taking guanethidine (Ismelin) for hypertension should not receive tricyclic drugs, which reduce or eliminate the antihypertensive effect of guanethidine. A history of hypertension may preclude the use of monoamine oxidase inhibitors (MAOIs) because of the risk of a hypertensive crisis if such hypertensive patients inadvertently take foods high in tyramine. Patients with a suspected cardiac disease should have an electrocardiogram before tricyclics or lithium (Eskalith) is prescribed. A history of substernal pain should be evaluated, keeping in mind that psychological stress can precipitate anginal-type chest pain in the presence of normal coronary arteries.

Gastrointestinal System

This area covers such topics as appetite, distress before or after meals, food preferences, diarrhea, vomiting, constipation, laxative use, and abdominal pain. A history of weight loss is common in depressive disorders; but depression may accompany the weight loss caused by ulcerative colitis, regional enteritis, and cancer. Anorexia nervosa is accompanied by severe weight loss in the presence of normal appetite. Avoidance of certain foods may be a phobic phenomenon or part of an obsessive ritual. Laxative abuse and induced vomiting are common in bulimia nervosa. Constipation is caused by opioid dependence and by psychotropic drugs with anticholinergic side effects. Cocaine abuse and amphetamine abuse cause a loss of appetite and weight loss. Weight gain occurs under stress. Polyphagia, polyuria, and polydipsia are the triad of diabetes mellitus. Polyuria, polydipsia, and diarrhea are signs of lithium toxicity.

Genitourinary System

Urinary frequency, nocturia, pain or burning on urination, and changes in the size and the force of the stream are some of the signs and symptoms in this area. Anticholinergic side effects associated with antipsychotics and tricyclic drugs may cause urinary retention in men with prostate hypertrophy. Erectile difficulty and retarded ejaculation are also common side effects of those drugs, and retrograde ejaculation occurs with thioridazine. A baseline level of sexual responsivity before using pharmacological agents should be obtained. A history of venereal diseases—for example, gonorrheal discharge, chancre, herpes, and pubic lice—may indicate sexual promiscuity. In some cases the first symptom of acquired immune deficiency syndrome (AIDS) is the gradual onset of mental confusion leading to dementia. If a psychotic patient remains incontinent after treatment for several days with a psychotropic medication, some cause other than a mental disorder should be suspected.

Menstrual System

A menstrual history should include the age of the onset of menarche and menopause; the periods' interval, regularity, duration, and amount of flow; irregular bleeding; dysmenorrhea; and abortions. Amenorrhea is characteristic of anorexia nervosa and also occurs in women who are psychologically stressed. Women who are afraid of becoming pregnant or who have a wish to be pregnant may have delayed periods. Pseudocyesis is false pregnancy with complete cessation of the menses. Perimenstrual mood changes (for example, irritability, depression, and dysphoria) should be noted. Painful menstruation can result from uterine disease (for example, myomata), from psychological conflicts about the menses, or from a combination of the two. Many women report an increase in sexual desire premenstrually. The emotional distress that some women experience after an abortion is usually mild and self-limited.

GENERAL OBSERVATION

An important part of the medical examination is subsumed under the broad head of general observation—visual, auditory, and olfactory. Such nonverbal clues as posture, facial expression, and mannerisms should also be noted.

Visual Evaluation

The scrutiny of the patient begins at the first encounter. When the patient goes from the waiting room to the interview room, the psychiatrist should observe the patient's gait. Is the patient unsteady? Ataxia suggests diffuse brain disease, alcohol or other substance intoxication, chorea, spinocerebellar degeneration, weakness based on a debilitating process, and an underlying disorder, such as myotonic dystrophy. Does the patient walk without the usual associated arm movements and turn in a rigid fashion, like a toy soldier, as is seen in early Parkinson's disease? Does the patient have an asymmetry of gait, such as turning one foot outward, dragging a leg, or not swinging one arm, suggesting a focal brain lesion?

As soon as the patient is seated, the psychiatrist should direct attention to grooming. Is the patient's hair combed, are the nails clean, and are the teeth brushed? Has clothing been chosen with care, and is it appropriate? Although inattention to dress and hygiene is common in mental disorders—in particular, depressive disorders—it is also a hallmark of cognitive disorders. Lapses—such as mismatching socks, stockings, or shoes—may suggest a cognitive disorder.

The patient's posture and automatic movements or the lack of them should be noted. A stooped, flexed posture with a paucity of automatic movements may be due to Parkinson's disease, diffuse cerebral hemispheric disease, or the adverse effects of antipsychotics. An unusual tilt of the head may be adopted to avoid eye contact, but it can also result from diplopia, a visual field defect, or focal cerebellar dysfunction. Frequent quick, purposeless movements are characteristic of anxiety disorders, but they are equally characteristic of chorea and hyperthyroidism. Tremors, although commonly seen in anxiety disorders, may point to Parkinson's disease, essential tremor, or adverse effects of psychotropic medication. Patients with essential tremor sometimes seek psychiatric treatment because they believe the tremor must be due to unrecognized fear or anxiety, as others often suggest. Unilateral paucity or excess of movement suggests focal brain disease.

The patient's appearance is then scrutinized to assess general health. Does the patient appear to be robust, or is there a sense of ill health? Does looseness of clothing indicate recent weight loss? Is the patient short of breath or coughing? Does the patient's general physiognomy suggest a specific disease? Men with Klinefelter's syndrome have a feminine fat distribution and lack the development of secondary male sex characteristics. Acromegaly is usually immediately recognizable.

What is the patient's nutritional status? Recent weight loss, although often seen in depressive disorders and schizophrenia, may be due to gastrointestinal disease, diffuse carcinomatosis, Addison's disease, hyperthyroidism, and many other somatic disorders. Obesity may result from either emotional distress or organic disease. Moon facies, truncal obesity, and buffalo hump are striking findings in Cushing's syndrome. The puffy, bloated appearance seen in hypothyroidism and the massive obesity and periodic respiration seen in Pickwickian syndrome are easily recognized in patients referred for psychiatric help.

The skin frequently provides valuable information. The yellow discoloration of hepatic dysfunction and the pallor of anemia are reasonably distinctive. Intense reddening may be due to carbon monoxide poisoning or to photosensitivity resulting from porphyria or phenothiazines. Eruptions may be manifestations of such disorders as systemic lupus erythematosus, tuberous sclerosis with adenoma sebaceum, and sensitivity to drugs. A dusky purplish cast to the face, plus telangiectasia, is almost pathognomonic of alcohol abuse.

Careful observation may reveal clues that lead to the correct diagnosis in patients who create their own skin lesions. For example, the location and the shape of the lesions and the time of their appearance may be characteristic of dermatitis factitia.

The patient's face and head should be scanned for evidence of disease. Premature whitening of the hair occurs in pernicious anemia, and thinning and coarseness of the hair occurs in myxedema. Pupillary changes are produced by various drugs—constriction by opioids and dilation by anticholinergic agents and hallucinogens. The combination of dilated, fixed pupils and dry skin and mucous membranes should immediately suggest the likelihood of atropine use or atropinelike toxicity. Diffusion of the conjunctiva suggests alcohol abuse, cannabis abuse, or obstruction of the superior vena cava. Flattening of the nasolabial fold on one side or weakness of one side of the face—as manifested in speaking, smiling, and grimacing—may be the result of focal dysfunction of the contralateral cerebral hemisphere.

The patient's state of alertness and responsiveness should be carefully evaluated. Drowsiness and inattentiveness may be due to a psychological problem, but they are more likely to result from an organic brain dysfunction, whether secondary to an intrinsic brain disease or to an exogenous factor, such as substance intoxication.

Auditory Evaluation

Listening intently is just as important as looking intently for evidence of somatic disorders.

Slowed speech is characteristic not only of depression but also of diffuse brain dysfunction and subcortical dysfunction; unusually rapid speech is characteristic not only of manic episodes and anxiety disorders but also of hyperthyroidism. A weak voice and monotony of tone may be clues to Parkinson's disease in patients who complain mainly of depression. A slow, low-pitched, hoarse voice should suggest the possibility of hypothyroidism; that voice quality has been described as sounding like a bad record of a drowsy, slightly intoxicated person with a bad cold and a plum in the mouth.

Difficulty in initiating speech may be due to anxiety or stuttering, or it may be indicative of Parkinson's disease or aphasia. Easy fatigability of speech may sometimes be a manifestation of an emotional problem, but it is also characteristic of myasthenia gravis. Patients with those complaints are likely to be seen by a psychiatrist before the correct diagnosis is made.

Word production, as well as the quality of speech, is important. When words are mispronounced or incorrect words are used, the possibility of aphasia caused by a lesion of the dominant hemisphere should be entertained. The same possibility exists when the patient perseverates, has trouble finding a name or a word, or describes an object or an event in an indirect fashion (*paraphasia*). When not consonant with the patient's socioeconomic and educational level, coarseness, profanity, or inappropriate disclosures may indicate loss of inhibition caused by dementia.

Olfactory Evaluation

Much less is learned through the sense of smell than through the senses of sight and hearing, but occasionally smell provides useful information. The unpleasant odor of a patient who fails to bathe suggests an organic brain dysfunction and a depressive disorder. The odor of alcohol or of substances used to hide it is revealing in a patient who attempts to conceal a drinking problem. Occasionally, a uriniferous odor calls attention to bladder dysfunction due to a nervous system disease. Characteristic odors are also noted in patients with diabetic acidosis, uremia, and hepatic coma.

PHYSICAL EXAMINATION

Selection of Patients

The nature of the patient's complaints is critical in determining if a complete physical examination is required. Complaints fall into three categories involving (1) the body, (2) the mind, and (3) social interactions.

Bodily symptoms—such as headaches, erectile disorder, and palpitations—call for a thorough medical examination to determine what part, if any, somatic processes play in causing the distress. The same can be said for mental symptoms—such as depression, anxiety, hallucinations, and persecutory delusions—because they can be expressions of somatic processes. If the problem is clearly limited to the social sphere—as in long-standing difficulties in interactions with teachers, employers, parents, or a spouse—there may be no special indication for a physical examination.

Psychological Considerations

Even a routine physical examination may evoke adverse reactions; instruments, procedures, and the examining room may be frightening. A simple running account of what is being done can prevent much needless anxiety. Moreover, if the patient is consistently forewarned of what will be done, the dread of being suddenly and painfully surprised recedes. Comments such as, ''There's nothing to this'' and ''You don't have to be afraid because this won't hurt'' leave the patient in the dark and are much less reassuring than a few words about what actually will be done.

Although the physical examination is likely to engender or intensify a reaction of anxiety, it can also stir up sexual feelings. Some women with fantasies of being seduced may misinterpret an ordinary movement in the physical examination as a sexual advance. Similarly, a delusional man with homosexual fears may perceive a rectal examination as a sexual attack.

Lingering over the examination of a particular organ because an unusual but normal variation has aroused the physician's scientific curiosity is likely to raise concern in the patient that a serious pathological process has been discovered. Such a reaction in an anxious or hypochondriacal patient may be profound.

The physical examination occasionally serves a psychotherapeutic function. An anxious patient may be relieved to learn that, in spite of troublesome symptoms, there is no evidence of the serious illness that is feared. The young person who complains of chest pain and is certain that the pain heralds a heart attack can usually be reassured by the report of normal findings after a physical examination and electrocardiogram. However, the reassurance relieves only the worry occasioned by the immediate episode. Unless psychiatric treatment succeeds in dealing with the determinants of the reaction, recurrent episodes are likely.

Sending a patient who has a deeply rooted fear of malignancy for still another test that is intended to be reassuring is usually unrewarding.

In spite of repeated examinations, a patient (a physician) was convinced that he had carcinoma of the pharynx. A colleague, in an effort to produce positive proof, biopsied the area of complaint. When the patient was shown a microscopic section of normal tissue, he immediately declared that the normal section had been substituted for one showing malignant cells.

During the performance of the physical examination, an observant physician may note indications of emotional distress. For instance, during genital examinations, the patient's behavior may reveal information about their sexual attitudes and problems, and their reactions may be used later to open that area for exploration.

Deferring the Physical Examination

Occasionally, circumstances make it desirable or necessary to defer a complete medical assessment. For example, a delusional or manic patient may be combative or resistive or both. In that instance a medical history should be elicited from a family member if possible, but, unless there is a pressing reason to proceed with the examination, it should be deferred until the patient is tractable.

For psychological reasons it may be ill-advised to recommend a medical assessment at the time of an initial office visit. For example, with today's increased sensitivity to and openness about sexual matters and a proneness to turn quickly to psychiatric help, young men may complain about their failure in an initial attempt to consummate a sexual relationship. After taking a detailed history, the psychiatrist may conclude that the failure has been prematurely defined as a problem requiring attention. If that is the case, neither a physical examination nor psychotherapy should be recommended, because they would have the undesirable effect of reinforcing the notion of pathology.

Neurological Examination

If the psychiatrist suspects that the patient has an underlying somatic disorder, such as diabetes mellitus or Cushing's syndrome, referral is usually made to a medical physician for diagnosis and treatment. The situation is different if a cognitive disorder is suspected. The psychiatrist often chooses to assume responsibility in those cases, even though neurological evaluation may be especially difficult when the brain disease is in an early stage.

During the history-taking process in such cases, the patient's level of awareness, attentiveness to the details of the examination, understanding, facial expression, speech, posture, and gait are noted. It is also assumed that a thorough mental status examination will be performed. The neurological examination should then be performed with two objectives in mind: (1) to elicit signs pointing to focal, circumscribed cerebral dysfunction and (2) to elicit signs suggesting diffuse, bilateral cerebral disease. The first objective is met by the routine neurological examination, which is designed primarily to reveal asymmetries in the motor, perceptual, and reflex functions of the two sides of the body caused by focal hemispheric disease. The second objective is met by seeking to elicit signs that have been attributed to diffuse brain dysfunction and to frontal lobe disease. Those signs include the suckling, snout, palmomental, and grasp reflexes and the persistence of the glabella tap response. Regrettably, with the exception of the grasp reflex, such signs do not correlate strongly with the presence of underlying brain pathology.

Incidental Findings

Psychiatrists should be able to evaluate the significance of findings uncovered by consultants. With a patient who complains of a lump in the throat (globus hystericus) and who is found on examination to have hypertrophied lymphoid tissue, it is tempting to wonder about a cause-and-effect relation. How can one be sure that the finding is not incidental? Has the patient been known to have hypertrophied lymphoid tissue at a time when no complaint was made? Are there many persons with hypertrophied lymphoid tissue who never experience the sensation of a lump in the throat?

With a patient with multiple sclerosis who complains of an inability to walk but, on neurological examination, has only mild spasticity and a unilateral Babinski's sign, it is tempting to ascribe the symptom to the neurological disorder. However, in that instance the evidence of a neurological abnormality is out of keeping with manifest dysfunction. The same holds true for a patient with profound dementia in whom a small frontal meningioma is seen on a computed tomography (CT) scan. The knowledgeable psychiatrist should recognize that profound dementia may not result from such a small lesion so situated.

Often, a lesion is found that may account for a symptom, but the psychiatrist should make every effort to separate an incidental finding from a causative one, to separate a lesion merely found in the area of the symptom from a lesion producing the symptom.

PATIENT IN PSYCHIATRIC TREATMENT

While patients are being treated for psychiatric disorders, the psychiatrist should be alert to the possibility of intercurrent illnesses that call for diagnosis studies. Patients in psychotherapy, particularly those in psychoanalysis, may be all too willing to ascribe their new symptoms to emotional causes. Attention should be given to the possible use of denial, especially if the symptoms seem to be unrelated to the conflicts currently in focus.

Not only may patients in psychotherapy be prone to attribute new symptoms to emotional causes, but sometimes their therapists do so as well. There is an ever-present danger of providing psychodynamic explanations for physical symptoms.

Symptoms such as drowsiness and dizziness and signs such as a skin eruption and a gait disturbance, common side effects of psychotropic medication, call for a medical reevaluation if the patient fails to respond in a reasonable time to changes in the dosage or the kind of medication prescribed. If patients who are receiving tricyclic drugs or antipsychotic drugs complain of blurred vision, usually an anticholinergic side effect, and if the condition does not recede with a reduction in dosage or a change in medication, they should be evaluated to rule out other causes. In one case the diagnosis proved to be Toxoplasmic chorioretinitis. The absence of other anticholinergic side effects, such as a dry mouth and constipation, is an additional clue alerting the psychiatrist to the possibility of a concomitant medical illness.

Early in an illness, few, if any, positive physical or laboratory results may be found. In such instances, especially if the evidence of psychic trauma or emotional conflicts is glaring, all symptoms are likely to be regarded as psychosocial in origin and new symptoms seen in that light. Indications for repeating portions of the medical workup may be missed unless the psychiatrist is alert to clues suggesting that some symptoms do not fit the original diagnosis and point, instead, to a medical illness. Occasionally, a patient with an acute illness, such as encephalitis, is hospitalized with the diagnosis of schizophrenia; or a patient with a subacute illness, such as carcinoma of the pancreas, is treated in a private office or clinic with the diagnosis of a depressive disorder. Although it may not be possible to make the correct diagnosis at the time of the initial psychiatric evaluation, continued surveillance and attention to clinical details usually provide clues leading to the recognition of the cause.

The likelihood of intercurrent illness is greater with some psychiatric disorders than with others. Substance abusers, for example, because of their life patterns, are susceptible to infection and are likely to suffer from the adverse effects of trauma, dietary deficiencies, and poor hygiene.

When somatic and psychological dysfunctions are known to coexist, the psychiatrist should be thoroughly conversant with the patient's medical status. In cases of cardiac decompensation, peripheral neuropathy, and other disabling disorders, the nature and the degree of the impairment that can be attributed to the physical disorder should be assessed. It is important to answer the question: Does the patient exploit a disability, or is it ignored or denied with resultant overexertion? To answer that question, the psychiatrist must assess the patient's capabilities and limitations, rather than make sweeping judgments based on a diagnostic label.

Special vigilance regarding medical status is required for some patients in treatment for somatoform and eating disorders. Such is the case for patients with ulcerative colitis who are bleeding profusely and for patients with anorexia nervosa who are losing appreciable weight. Those disorders may become life-threatening.

Importance of Medical Illness

Numerous articles have called attention to the need for thorough medical screening of patients seen in psychiatric inpatient services and clinics. (A similar need has been shown to exist for the psychiatric evaluation of patients seen in medical inpatient services and clinics.)

Among identified psychiatric patients, anywhere from 24 percent to 60 percent have been shown to suffer from associated physical disorders. In a survey of 2,090 psychiatric clinic patients, 43 percent were found to have associated physical disorders; of those, almost half the physical disorders had not been diagnosed by the referring sources. (In that study, 69 patients were found to have diabetes mellitus, but only 12 of the cases of diabetes had been diagnosed before referral.)

Expecting all psychiatrists to be experts in internal medicine is unrealistic, but expecting them to recognize physical disorders when present is realistic. Moreover, they should make appropriate referrals and collaborate in treating patients who have both physical and mental disorders.

Psychiatric symptoms are nonspecific; they can herald medical illness, as well as psychiatric illness. Moreover, psychiatric symptoms often precede the appearance of definitive medical symptoms. Some psychiatric symptoms—such as visual hallucinations, distortions, and illusions—should call forth a high level of suspicion.

The medical literature abounds with case reports of patients whose disorders were initially considered emotional but ultimately proved to be organic in origin. The data in most of the reports revealed features pointing toward organicity. Diagnostic errors arose because such features were accorded too little weight.

References

Caine E D, Grossman H, Lyness J: Delirium, dementia, and amnestic and other cognitive disorders and mental disorders due to a general medical condition. In *Comprehensive Textbook of Psychiatry*, ed 6, H I Kaplan, B J Sadock, editors, p 705. Williams & Wilkins, Baltimore, 1995.

D'Ercole A, Skodol A E, Struening E, Curtis J, Millman J: Diagnosis of physical illness in psychiatric patients using Axis III and a standardized medical history. Hosp Community Psychiatry *42*: 395, 1991.

Rosse R B, Deutsch L H, Deutsch S I: Medical assessment and laboratory testing in psychiatry. In *Comprehensive Textbook of Psychiatry*, ed 6, H I Kaplan, B J Sadock, editors, p 601. Williams & Wilkins, Baltimore, 1995.

Yates W: Medical symptoms of psychiatric illness. Iowa Med *84*: 121, 1994.

2/ Typical Signs and Symptoms of Psychiatric Illness Defined

Psychiatry is concerned with phenomenology and the study of mental phenomena. Psychiatrists must learn to be masters of precise observation and evocative description, and learning those skills involves the learning of a new language. Part of the language in psychiatry involves the recognition and the definition of behavioral and emotional signs and symptoms. *Signs* are objective findings observed by the clinician (for example, constricted affect and psychomotor retardation); *symptoms* are subjective experiences described by the patient (for example, depressed mood and decreased energy). A *syndrome* is a group of signs and symptoms that occur together as a recognizable condition that may be less than specific than a clear-cut disorder or disease. Most psychiatric conditions are, in fact, syndromes. Becoming an expert in recognizing specific signs and symptoms allows the clinician to understandably communicate with other clinicians, accurately make a diagnosis, effectively manage treatment, reliably predict a prognosis, and thoroughly explore pathophysiology, causes, and psychodynamic issues.

The following outline comprehensively lists signs and symptoms, each with a precise definition or description. Most psychiatric signs and symptoms have their roots in essentially normal behavior and represent various points on the spectrum of behavior from normal to pathological.

I. CONSCIOUSNESS: state of awareness

Apperception: perception modified by one's own emotions and thoughts. Sensorium: state of cognitive functioning of the special senses (sometimes used as a synonym for consciousness). Disturbances of consciousness are most often associated with brain pathology.

A. Disturbances of consciousness

1. *Disorientation:* disturbance of orientation in time, place, or person
2. *Clouding of consciousness:* incomplete clear-mindedness with disturbances in perception and attitudes
3. *Stupor:* lack of reaction to and unawareness of surroundings
4. *Delirium:* bewildered, restless, confused, disoriented reaction associated with fear and hallucinations
5. *Coma:* profound degree of unconsciousness
6. *Coma vigil:* coma in which the patient appears to be asleep but ready to be aroused (also known as akinetic mutism)
7. *Twilight state:* disturbed consciousness with hallucinations
8. *Dreamlike state:* often used as a synonym for complex partial seizure or psychomotor epilepsy
9. *Somnolence:* abnormal drowsiness

B. Disturbances of attention attention is the amount of effort exerted in focusing on certain portions of an experience; ability to sustain a focus on one activity; ability to concentrate

1. *Distractibility:* inability to concentrate attention; attention drawn to unimportant or irrelevant external stimuli
2. *Selective inattention:* blocking out only those things that generate anxiety
3. *Hypervigilance:* excessive attention and focus on all internal and external stimuli, usually secondary to delusional or paranoid states
4. *Trance:* focused attention and altered consciousness, usually seen in hypnosis, dissociative disorders, and ecstatic religious experiences

C. Disturbances in suggestibility: compliant and uncritical response to an idea or influence

1. *Folie à deux (or folie à trois):* communicated emotional illness between two (or three) persons
2. *Hypnosis:* artificially induced modification of consciousness characterized by a heightened suggestibility

II. EMOTION: a complex feeling state with psychic, somatic, and behavioral components that is related to affect and mood

A. Affect: observed expression of emotion; may be inconsistent with patient's description of emotion

1. *Appropriate affect:* condition in which the emotional tone is in harmony with the accompanying idea, thought, or speech; also further described as broad or full affect, in which a full range of emotions is appropriately expressed
2. *Inappropriate affect:* disharmony between the emotional feeling tone and the idea, thought, or speech accompanying it
3. *Blunted affect:* a disturbance in affect manifested by a severe reduction in the intensity of externalized feeling tone
4. *Restricted or constricted affect:* reduction in intensity of feeling tone less severe than blunted affect but clearly reduced
5. *Flat affect:* absence or near absence of any signs of affective expression; voice monotonous, face immobile
6. *Labile affect:* rapid and abrupt changes in emotional feeling tone, unrelated to external stimuli

B. Mood: a pervasive and sustained emotion, subjectively experienced and reported by the patient and observed by others; examples include depression, elation, anger

1. *Dysphoric mood:* an unpleasant mood
2. *Euthymic mood:* normal range of mood, implying absence of depressed or elevated mood
3. *Expansive mood:* expression of one's feelings without restraint, frequently with an overestimation of one's significance or importance
4. *Irritable mood:* easily annoyed and provoked to anger
5. *Mood swings (labile mood):* oscillations between euphoria and depression or anxiety
6. *Elevated mood:* air of confidence and enjoyment; a mood more cheerful than usual
7. *Euphoria:* intense elation with feelings of grandeur
8. *Ecstasy:* feeling of intense rapture
9. *Depression:* psychopathological feeling of sadness
10. *Anhedonia:* loss of interest in and withdrawal from all regular and pleasurable activities, often associated with depression
11. *Grief or mourning:* sadness appropriate to a real loss
12. *Alexithymia:* inability or difficulty in describing or being aware of one's emotions or mood

C. Other emotions

1. *Anxiety:* feeling of apprehension caused by anticipation of danger, which may be internal or external
2. *Free-floating anxiety:* pervasive, unfocused fear not attached to any idea
3. *Fear:* anxiety caused by consciously recognized and realistic danger
4. *Agitation:* severe anxiety associated with motor restlessness
5. *Tension:* increased motor and psychological activity that is unpleasant

6. *Panic:* acute, episodic, intense attack of anxiety associated with overwhelming feelings of dread and autonomic discharge
7. *Apathy:* dulled emotional tone associated with detachment or indifference
8. *Ambivalence:* coexistence of two opposing impulses toward the same thing in the same person at the same time
9. *Abreaction:* emotional release or discharge after recalling a painful experience
10. *Shame:* failure to live up to self-expectations
11. *Guilt:* emotion secondary to doing what is perceived as wrong

D. **Physiological disturbances associated with mood:** signs of somatic (usually autonomic) dysfunction of the person, most often associated with depression (also called vegetative signs)

1. *Anorexia:* loss of or decrease in appetite
2. *Hyperphagia:* increase in appetite and intake of food
3. *Insomnia:* lack of or diminished ability to sleep
   a. Initial insomnia: difficulty in falling asleep
   b. Middle insomnia: difficulty in sleeping through the night without waking up and difficulty in going back to sleep
   c. Terminal insomnia: early morning awakening
4. *Hypersomnia:* excessive sleeping
5. *Diurnal variation:* mood is regularly worst in the morning, immediately after awakening, and improves as the day progresses
6. *Diminished libido:* decreased sexual interest, drive, and performance (increased libido is often associated with manic states)
7. *Constipation:* inability or difficulty in defecating

III. **MOTOR BEHAVIOR (CONATION):** the aspect of the psyche that includes impulses, motivations, wishes, drives, instincts, and cravings, as expressed by a person's behavior or motor activity.

1. *Echopraxia:* pathological imitation of movements of one person by another
2. *Catatonia:* motor anomalies in nonorganic disorders (as opposed to disturbances of consciousness and motor activity secondary to organic pathology)
   a. Catalepsy: general term for an immobile position that is constantly maintained
   b. Catatonic excitement: agitated, purposeless motor activity, uninfluenced by external stimuli
   c. Catatonic stupor: markedly slowed motor activity, often to a point of immobility and seeming unawareness of surroundings
   d. Catatonic rigidity: voluntary assumption of a rigid posture, held against all efforts to be moved
   e. Catatonic posturing: voluntary assumption of an inappropriate or bizarre posture, generally maintained for long periods of time
   f. *Cerea flexibilitas* (waxy flexibility): the person can be molded into a position that is then maintained; when the examiner moves the person's limb, the limb feels as if it were made of wax
3. *Negativism:* motiveless resistance to all attempts to be moved or to all instructions
4. *Cataplexy:* temporary loss of muscle tone and weakness precipitated by a variety of emotional states
5. *Stereotypy:* repetitive fixed pattern of physical action or speech
6. *Mannerism:* ingrained, habitual involuntary movement
7. *Automatism:* automatic performance of an act or acts generally representative of unconscious symbolic activity
8. *Command automatism:* automatic following of suggestions (also automatic obedience)
9. *Mutism:* voicelessness without structural abnormalities
10. *Overactivity*
    a. Psychomotor agitation: excessive motor and cognitive overactivity, usually nonproductive and in response to inner tension

b. Hyperactivity (hyperkinesis): restless, aggressive, destructive activity, often associated with some underlying brain pathology
c. Tic: involuntary, spasmodic motor movement
d. Sleepwalking (somnambulism): motor activity during sleep
e. Akathisia: subjective feeling of muscular tension secondary to antipsychotic or other medication, which can cause restlessness, pacing, repeated sitting and standing; can be mistaken for psychotic agitation
f. Compulsion: uncontrollable impulse to perform an act repetitively
   i. Dipsomania: compulsion to drink alcohol
   ii. Kleptomania: compulsion to steal
   iii. Nymphomania: excessive and compulsive need for coitus in a woman
   iv. Satyriasis: excessive and compulsive need for coitus in a man
   v. Trichotillomania: compulsion to pull out one's hair
   vi. Ritual: automatic activity, compulsive in nature, anxiety-reducing in origin
g. Ataxia: failure of muscle coordination; irregularity of muscle action
h. Polyphagia: pathological overeating
11. *Hypoactivity (hypokinesis):* decreased motor and cognitive activity, as in psychomotor retardation; visible slowing of thought, speech, and movements
12. *Mimicry:* simple, imitative motor activity of childhood
13. *Aggression:* forceful goal-directed action that may be verbal or physical; the motor counterpart of the affect of rage, anger, or hostility
14. *Acting out:* direct expression of an unconscious wish or impulse in action; unconscious fantasy is lived out impulsively in behavior
15. *Abulia:* reduced impulse to act and think, associated with indifference about consequences of action; association with neurological deficit

IV. **THINKING:** goal-directed flow of ideas, symbols, and associations initiated by a problem or a task and leading toward a reality-oriented conclusion; when a logical sequence occurs, thinking is normal; parapraxis (unconsciously motivated lapse from logic is also called Freudian slip) considered part of normal thinking

A. **General disturbances in form or process of thinking**

1. *Mental disorder:* clinically significant behavior or psychological syndrome, associated with distress or disability, not just an expected response to a particular event or limited to relations between the person and society
2. *Psychosis:* inability to distinguish reality from fantasy; impaired reality testing, with the creation of a new reality (as opposed to neurosis: mental disorder in which reality testing is intact, behavior may not violate gross social norms, relatively enduring or recurrent without treatment)
3. *Reality testing:* the objective evaluation and judgment of the world outside the self
4. *Formal thought disorder:* disturbance in the form of thought, instead of the content of thought; thinking characterized by loosened associations, neologisms, and illogical constructs; thought process is disordered, and the person is defined as psychotic
5. *Illogical thinking:* thinking containing erroneous conclusions or internal contradictions; it is psychopathological only when it is marked and when not caused by cultural values or intellectual deficit
6. *Dereism:* mental activity not concordant with logic or experience
7. *Autistic thinking:* preoccupation with inner, private world; term used somewhat synonymously with dereism

8. *Magical thinking:* a form of dereistic thought; thinking that is similar to that of the preoperational phase in children (Jean Piaget), in which thoughts, words, or actions assume power (for example, they can cause or prevent events)

9. *Primary process thinking:* general term for thinking that is dereistic, illogical, magical; normally found in dreams, abnormally in psychosis

B. Specific disturbances in form of thought

1. *Neologism:* new word created by the patient, often by combining syllables of other words, for idiosyncratic psychological reasons

2. *Word salad:* incoherent mixture of words and phrases

3. *Circumstantiality:* indirect speech that is delayed in reaching the point but eventually gets from original point to desired goal; characterized by an overinclusion of details and parenthetical remarks

4. *Tangentiality:* inability to have goal-directed associations of thought; patient never gets from desired point to desired goal

5. *Incoherence:* thought that, generally, is not understandable; running together of thoughts or words with no logical or grammatical connection, resulting in disorganization

6. *Perseveration:* persisting response to a prior stimulus after a new stimulus has been presented, often associated with cognitive disorders

7. *Verbigeration:* meaningless repetition of specific words or phrases

8. *Echolalia:* psychopathological repeating of words or phrases of one person by another; tends to be repetitive and persistent, may be spoken with mocking or staccato intonation

9. *Condensation:* fusion of various concepts into one

10. *Irrelevant answer:* answer that is not in harmony with question asked (patient appears to ignore or not attend to question)

11. *Loosening of associations:* flow of thought in which ideas shift from one subject to another in a completely unrelated way; when severe, speech may be incoherent

12. *Derailment:* gradual or sudden deviation in train of thought without blocking; sometimes used synonymously with loosening of associations

13. *Flight of ideas:* rapid, continuous verbalizations or plays on words produce constant shifting from one idea to another; the ideas tend to be connected, and in the less severe form a listener may be able to follow them

14. *Clang association:* association of words similar in sound but not in meaning; words have no logical connection, may include rhyming and punning

15. *Blocking:* abrupt interruption in train of thinking before a thought or idea is finished; after a brief pause, the person indicates no recall of what was being said or was going to be said (also known as thought deprivation)

16. *Glossolalia:* the expression of a revelatory message through unintelligible words (also known as speaking in tongues); not considered a disturbance in thought if associated with practices of specific Pentecostal religions

C. Specific disturbances in content of thought

1. *Poverty of content:* thought that gives little information because of vagueness, empty repetitions, or obscure phrases

2. *Overvalued idea:* unreasonable, sustained false belief maintained less firmly than a delusion

3. *Delusion:* false belief, based on incorrect inference about external reality, not consistent with patient's intelligence and cultural background, that cannot be corrected by reasoning
   a. Bizarre delusion: an absurd, totally implausible, strange false belief (for example, invaders from space have implanted electrodes in the patient's brain)
   b. Systematized delusion: false belief or beliefs united by a single event or theme (for example, patient is being persecuted by the CIA, the FBI, the Mafia, or the boss)
   c. Mood-congruent delusion: delusion with mood-appropriate content (for example, a depressed patient believes that he or she is responsible for the destruction of the world)
   d. Mood-incongruent delusion: delusion with content that has no association to mood or is mood-neutral (for example, a depressed patient has delusions of thought control or thought broadcasting)
   e. Nihilistic delusion: false feeling that self, others, or the world is nonexistent or ending
   f. Delusion of poverty: false belief that one is bereft or will be deprived of all material possessions
   g. Somatic delusion: false belief involving functioning of one's body (for example, belief that one's brain is rotting or melting)
   h. Paranoid delusions: includes persecutory delusions and delusions of reference, control, and grandeur (distinguished from paranoid ideation, which is suspiciousness of less than delusional proportions)
      i. Delusion of persecution: false belief that one is being harassed, cheated, or persecuted; often found in litigious patients who have a pathological tendency to take legal action because of imagined mistreatment
      ii. Delusion of grandeur: exaggerated conception of one's importance, power, or identity
      iii. Delusion of reference: false belief that the behavior of others refers to oneself; that events, objects, or other people have a particular and unusual significance, usually of a negative nature; derived from idea of reference, in which one falsely feels that one is being talked about by others (for example, belief that people on television or radio are talking to or about the patient)
   i. Delusion of self-accusation: false feeling of remorse and guilt
   j. Delusion of control: false feeling that one's will, thoughts, or feelings are being controlled by external forces
      i. Thought withdrawal: delusion that one's thoughts are being removed from one's mind by other people or forces
      ii. Thought insertion: delusion that thoughts are being implanted in one's mind by other people or forces
      iii. Thought broadcasting: delusion that one's thoughts can be heard by others, as though they were being broadcast into the air
      iv. Thought control: delusion that one's thoughts are being controlled by other people or forces
   k. Delusion of infidelity (delusional jealousy): false belief derived from pathological jealousy that one's lover is unfaithful
   l. Erotomania: delusional belief, more common in women than in men, that someone is deeply in love with them (also known as Clérambault-Kandinsky complex)
   m. *Pseudologia phantastica:* a type of lying, in which the person appears to believe in the reality of his or her fantasies and acts on them; associated with Munchausen syndrome, repeated feigning of illness

4. *Trend or preoccupation of thought:* centering of thought content on a particular idea, associated with a strong affective tone, such as a paranoid trend or a suicidal or homicidal preoccupation

5. *Egomania:* pathological self-preoccupation

6. *Monomania:* preoccupation with a single object

7. *Hypochondria:* exaggerated concern about one's health that is based not on real organic pathology but, rather, on unrealistic interpretations of physical signs or sensations as abnormal

8. *Obsession:* pathological persistence of an irresistible thought or feeling that cannot be eliminated from consciousness by logical effort, which is associated with anxiety (also termed rumination)

9. *Compulsion:* pathological need to act on an impulse that, if resisted, produces anxiety; repetitive behavior in response to an obsession or performed according to certain rules, with no true end in itself other than to prevent something from occurring in the future
10. *Coprolalia:* compulsive utterance of obscene words
11. *Phobia:* persistent, irrational, exaggerated, and invariably pathological dread of some specific type of stimulus or situation; results in a compelling desire to avoid the feared stimulus
    a. Specific phobia: circumscribed dread of a discrete object or situation (for example, dread of spiders or snakes)
    b. Social phobia: dread of public humiliation, as in fear of public speaking, performing, or eating in public
    c. Acrophobia: dread of high places
    d. Agoraphobia: dread of open places
    e. Algophobia: dread of pain
    f. Ailurophobia: dread of cats
    g. Erythrophobia: dread of red (refers to a fear of blushing)
    h. Panphobia: dread of everything
    i. Claustrophobia: dread of closed places
    j. Xenophobia: dread of strangers
    k. Zoophobia: dread of animals
12. *Noesis:* a revelation in which immense illumination occurs in association with a sense that one has been chosen to lead and command
13. *Unio mystica:* an oceanic feeling, one of mystic unity with an infinite power; not considered a disturbance in thought content if congruent with patient's religious or cultural milieu

V. SPEECH: ideas, thoughts, feelings as expressed through language; communication through the use of words and language

A. Disturbances in speech

1. *Pressure of speech:* rapid speech that is increased in amount and difficult to interrupt
2. *Volubility (logorrhea):* copious, coherent, logical speech
3. *Poverty of speech:* restriction in the amount of speech used; replies may be monosyllabic
4. *Nonspontaneous speech:* verbal responses given only when asked or spoken to directly; no self-initiation of speech
5. *Poverty of content of speech:* speech that is adequate in amount but conveys little information because of vagueness, emptiness, or stereotyped phrases
6. *Dysprosody:* loss of normal speech melody (called prosody)
7. *Dysarthria:* difficulty in articulation, not in word finding or in grammar
8. *Excessively loud or soft speech:* loss of modulation of normal speech volume; may reflect a variety of pathological conditions ranging from psychosis to depression to deafness
9. *Stuttering:* frequent repetition or prolongation of a sound or syllable, leading to markedly impaired speech fluency
10. *Cluttering:* erratic and dysrhythmic speech, consisting of rapid and jerky spurts

B. Aphasic disturbances: disturbances in language output

1. *Motor aphasia:* disturbance of speech caused by a cognitive disorder in which understanding remains but ability to speak is grossly impaired; speech is halting, laborious, and inaccurate (also known as Broca's, nonfluent, and expressive aphasia)
2. *Sensory aphasia:* organic loss of ability to comprehend the meaning of words; speech is fluid and spontaneous but incoherent and nonsensical (also known as Wernicke's, fluent, and receptive aphasia)
3. *Nominal aphasia:* difficulty in finding correct name for an object (also termed anomia and amnestic aphasia)
4. *Syntactical aphasia:* inability to arrange words in proper sequence

5. *Jargon aphasia:* words produced are totally neologistic; nonsense words repeated with various intonations and inflections
6. *Global aphasia:* combination of a grossly nonfluent aphasia and a severe fluent aphasia

VI. PERCEPTION: process of transferring physical stimulation into psychological information; mental process by which sensory stimuli are brought to awareness

A. Disturbances of perception

1. *Hallucination:* false sensory perception not associated with real external stimuli; there may or may not be a delusional interpretation of the hallucinatory experience
    a. Hypnagogic hallucination: false sensory perception occurring while falling asleep; generally considered nonpathological phenomenon
    b. Hypnopompic hallucination: false perception occurring while awakening from sleep; generally considered nonpathological
    c. Auditory hallucination: false perception of sound, usually voices but also other noises, such as music; most common hallucination in psychiatric disorders
    d. Visual hallucination: false perception involving sight consisting of both formed images (for example, people) and unformed images (for example, flashes of light); most common in medically determined disorders
    e. Olfactory hallucination: false perception of smell; most common in medical disorders
    f. Gustatory hallucination: false perception of taste, such as unpleasant taste caused by an uncinate seizure; most common in medical disorders
    g. Tactile (haptic) hallucination: false perception of touch or surface sensation, as from an amputated limb (phantom limb), crawling sensation on or under the skin (formication)
    h. Somatic hallucination: false sensation of things occurring in or to the body, most often visceral in origin (also known as cenesthesic hallucination)
    i. Lilliputian hallucination: false perception in which objects are seen as reduced in size (also termed micropsia)
    j. Mood-congruent hallucination: hallucination in which the content is consistent with either a depressed or a manic mood (for example, a depressed patient hears voices saying that the patient is a bad person; a manic patient hears voices saying that the patient is of inflated worth, power, and knowledge)
    k. Mood-incongruent hallucination: hallucination in which the content is not consistent with either depressed or manic mood (for example, in depression, hallucinations not involving such themes as guilt, deserved punishment, or inadequacy; in mania, hallucinations not involving such themes as inflated worth or power)
    l. Hallucinosis: hallucinations, most often auditory, that are associated with chronic alcohol abuse and that occur within a clear sensorium, as opposed to delirium tremens (DTs), hallucinations that occur in the context of a clouded sensorium
    m. Synesthesia: sensation or hallucination caused by another sensation (for example, an auditory sensation is accompanied by or triggers a visual sensation; a sound is experienced as being seen, or a visual experience is heard)
    n. Trailing phenomenon: perceptual abnormality associated with hallucinogenic drugs in which moving objects are seen as a series of discrete and discontinuous images
2. *Illusion:* misperception or misinterpretation of real external sensory stimuli

B. Disturbances associated with cognitive disorder:
agnosia—an inability to recognize and interpret the significance of sensory impressions

1. *Anosognosia (ignorance of illness):* inability to recognize a neurological deficit as occurring to oneself
2. *Somatopagnosia (ignorance of the body):* inability to recognize a body part as one's own (also called autotopagnosia)
3. *Visual agnosia:* inability to recognize objects or persons
4. *Astereognosis:* inability to recognize objects by touch
5. *Prosopagnosia:* inability to recognize faces
6. *Apraxia:* inability to carry out specific tasks
7. *Simultagnosia:* inability to comprehend more than one element of a visual scene at a time or to integrate the parts into a whole
8. *Adiadochokinesia:* inability to perform rapid alternating movements.

C. Disturbances associated with conversion and dissociative phenomena:
somatization of repressed material or the development of physical symptoms and distortions involving the voluntary muscles or special sense organs; not under voluntary control and not explained by any physical disorder

1. *Hysterical anesthesia:* loss of sensory modalities resulting from emotional conflicts
2. *Macropsia:* state in which objects seem larger than they are
3. *Micropsia:* state in which objects seem smaller than they are (both macropsia and micropsia can also be associated with clear organic conditions, such as complex partial seizures)
4. *Depersonalization:* a subjective sense of being unreal, strange, or unfamiliar to oneself
5. *Derealization:* a subjective sense that the environment is strange or unreal; a feeling of changed reality
6. *Fugue:* taking on a new identity with amnesia for the old identity; often involves travel or wandering to new environments
7. *Multiple personality:* one person who appears at different times to be two or more entirely different personalities and characters (called dissociative identity disorder in the fourth edition of *Diagnostic and Statistical Manual of Mental Disorders* (DSM-IV)

VII. MEMORY:
function by which information stored in the brain is later recalled to consciousness

A. Disturbances of memory

1. *Amnesia:* partial or total inability to recall past experiences; may be organic or emotional in origin
   a. Anterograde: amnesia for events occurring after a point in time
   b. Retrograde: amnesia prior to a point in time
2. *Paramnesia:* falsification of memory by distortion of recall
   a. *Fausse reconnaissance*: false recognition
   b. Retrospective falsification: memory becomes unintentionally (unconsciously) distorted by being filtered through patient's present emotional, cognitive, and experiential state
   c. Confabulation: unconscious filling of gaps in memory by imagined or untrue experiences that patient believes but that have no basis in fact; most often associated with organic pathology
   d. Déjà vu: illusion of visual recognition in which a new situation is incorrectly regarded as a repetition of a previous memory
   e. *Déjà entendu*: illusion of auditory recognition
   f. *Déjà pensé*: illusion that a new thought is recognized as a thought previously felt or expressed
   g. *Jamais vu*: false feeling of unfamiliarity with a real situation one has experienced

3. *Hypermnesia:* exaggerated degree of retention and recall
4. *Eidetic image:* visual memory of almost hallucinatory vividness
5. *Screen memory:* a consciously tolerable memory covering for a painful memory
6. *Repression:* a defense mechanism characterized by unconscious forgetting of unacceptable ideas or impulses
7. *Lethologica:* temporary inability to remember a name or a proper noun

B. Levels of memory

1. *Immediate:* reproduction or recall of perceived material within seconds to minutes
2. *Recent:* recall of events over past few days
3. *Recent past:* recall of events over past few months
4. *Remote:* recall of events in distant past

VIII. INTELLIGENCE:
the ability to understand, recall, mobilize, and constructively integrate previous learning in meeting new situations

A. Mental retardation:
lack of intelligence to a degree in which there is interference with social and vocational performance: mild (I.Q. of 50 or 55 to approximately 70), moderate (I.Q. of 35 or 40 to 50 or 55), severe (I.Q. of 20 or 25 to 35 or 40), or profound (I.Q. below 20 or 25); obsolete terms are idiot (mental age less than 3 years), imbecile (mental age of 3 to 7 years), and moron (mental age of about 8)

B. Dementia:
organic and global deterioration of intellectual functioning without clouding of consciousness

1. *Dyscalculia (acalculia):* loss of ability to do calculations not caused by anxiety or impairment in concentration
2. *Dysgraphia (agraphia):* loss of ability to write in cursive style; loss of word structure
3. *Alexia:* loss of a previously possessed reading facility; not explained by defective visual acuity

C. Pseudodementia:
clinical features resembling a dementia not caused by an organic condition; most often caused by depression (dementia syndrome of depression)

D. Concrete thinking:
literal thinking; limited use of metaphor without understanding of nuances of meaning; one-dimensional thought

E. Abstract thinking:
ability to appreciate nuances of meaning; multidimensional thinking with ability to use metaphors and hypotheses appropriately

IX. INSIGHT:
ability of the patient to understand the true cause and meaning of a situation (such as a set of symptoms)

A. Intellectual insight:
understanding of the objective reality of a set of circumstances without the ability to apply the understanding in any useful way to master the situation

B. True insight:
understanding of the objective reality of a situation, coupled with the motivation and the emotional impetus to master the situation

C. Impaired insight:
diminished ability to understand the objective reality of a situation

X. Judgment:
ability to assess a situation correctly and to act appropriately within that situation

A. Critical judgment:
ability to assess, discern, and choose among various options in a situation

B. Automatic judgment: reflex performance of an action

C. Impaired judgment: diminished ability to understand a situation correctly and to act appropriately

References

Campbell R J: *Psychiatric Dictionary*, ed 6. Oxford University Press, New York, 1989.

Kaplan H I, Sadock B J: Typical signs and symptoms of psychiatric illness. In *Comprehensive Textbook of Psychiatry*, ed 6, H I Kaplan, B J Sadock, editors, p 535. Williams & Wilkins, Baltimore, 1995.

Spitzer R L, Gibbon M, Skodol A E, Williams J B W, First M B, editors: *DSM-IV Case Book: A Learning Companion to the Diagnostic and Statistical Manual of Mental Disorders, Fourth Edition*. American Psychiatric Press, Washington, 1995.

Stoudemire A, editor: *Clinical Psychiatry for Medical Students*, ed 2. Lippincott, Philadelphia, 1994.

Yager J, Gitlin M J: Clinical manifestations of psychiatric disorders. In *Comprehensive Textbook of Psychiatry*, ed 6, H I Kaplan, B J Sadock, editors, p 637. Williams & Wilkins, Baltimore, 1995.

3/ Classification in Psychiatry and Psychiatric Rating Scales

INTERNATIONAL CLASSIFICATION OF DISEASES

The 10th revision of the International Classification of Diseases and Related Health Problems (ICD-10) is the official classification system used in Europe (Table 3–1). All the categories used in the fourth edition of *Diagnostic and Statistical Manual of Mental Disorders* (DSM-IV) are found in ICD-10, but not all ICD-10 categories are in DSM-IV. Because ICD-10 has yet to become official in the United States, the clinical modification of the ninth revision (ICD-9-CM) is used here. The terms and codes in DSM-IV are fully compatible with both ICD-9-CM and ICD-10.

DSM-IV

The fourth edition of *Diagnostic and Statistical Manual of Mental Disorders* (DSM-IV), published in 1994, is the latest and most up-to-date classification of mental disorders. DSM-IV is used by mental health professionals of all disciplines and is cited for insurance reimbursement, disability deliberations, and forensic matters.

Relation to ICD-10

The fourth edition of DSM correlates with the 10th revision of the World Health Organization's International Classification of Diseases and Related Health Problems (ICD-10), developed in 1992. Diagnostic systems used in the United States must be compatible with ICD to ensure uniform reporting of national and international health statistics. In addition, Medicare requires that billing codes for reimbursement follow ICD. However, the language used to describe each disorder often differs significantly in the two publications. For example, neurasthenia appears in ICD-10 but is not found in DSM-IV.

DSM-IV has been criticized for including too much detail in comparison with ICD-10 and for being oriented toward researchers, not clinicians. ICD-10 presents guidelines for making diagnoses and avoids the rigid research-oriented criteria that made previous editions of DSM difficult to use in everyday psychiatric practice. ICD-10 recognizes the skills of well-trained psychiatrist to fully utilize clinical material when arriving at a diagnosis. It is considerably more user-friendly than DSM-IV.

Although many psychiatrists have been critical of the many versions of DSM that have appeared since the first edition (DSM-I) appeared in 1952, DSM-IV is the official nomenclature. All terminology used in this textbook conforms to DSM-IV nomenclature.

History

The various classification systems used in psychiatry date back to Hippocrates, who introduced the terms ''mania'' and ''hysteria'' as forms of mental illness in the fifth century B.C. Since then, each era has introduced its own psychiatric classification. The first American classification was introduced in 1869

at the annual meeting of the American Medico-Psychological Association, which was then the name of the American Psychiatric Association.

In 1952 the American Psychiatric Association's Committee on Nomenclature and Statistics published the first edition of *Diagnostic and Statistical Manual of Mental Disorders* (DSM-I). Four editions have been published since then: DSM-II (1968); DSM-III (1980); a revised DSM-III, DSM-III-R (1987); and DSM-IV (1994).

The DSM-IV revision process consisted of three stages: (1) extensive scientific literature reviews to use as a data base, (2) data reanalysis to provide additional information, and (3) 12 field trials to compare sets of criteria. A 27-member task force—assisted by more than 1,000 psychiatrists, mental health professionals, and other health care experts—prepared the manual.

STATISTICAL MANUAL OR TEXTBOOK?

The editions of DSM are designed to provide a system whereby psychiatric illnesses can be classified into appropriate nosological categories. As knowledge has increased, the DSM nomenclature has expanded. In addition to setting forth the criteria on which a diagnosis is to be based, DSM has added other information, such as epidemiology and differential diagnosis. Because major categories that are present in textbooks are missing from DSM, it is not and has never claimed to be a textbook; nevertheless, it is used as a text by some groups, including insurance companies, which believe it to be a comprehensive source about mental illness. DSM is authorized, but in the authors' view it is not authoritative.

Basic Features

DESCRIPTIVE APPROACH

The approach to DSM-IV, as it was in DSM-III-R, is atheoretical with regard to causes. Thus, DSM-IV attempts to describe the manifestations of the mental disorders; only rarely does it attempt to account for how the disturbances come about. The definitions of the disorders usually consist of descriptions of the clinical features.

DIAGNOSTIC CRITERIA

Specified diagnostic criteria are provided for each specific mental disorder. Those criteria include a list of features that must be present for the diagnosis to be made. Such criteria increase the reliability of the diagnostic process among clinicians.

SYSTEMATIC DESCRIPTION

DSM-IV also systematically describes each disorder in terms of its associated features: specific age, cultural, and gender-related features; prevalence, incidence, and risk; course; complications; predisposing factors; familial pattern; and differential diagnosis. In some instances, when many of the specific disorders share common features, that information is included in

Table 3-1. ICD-10 Classification of Mental Disorders

F00-F09
Organic, including symptomatic, mental disorders

F00 Dementia in Alzheimer's disease
  F00.0 Dementia in Alzheimer's disease with early onset
  F00.1 Dementia in Alzheimer's disease with late onset
  F00.2 Dementia in Alzheimer's disease, atypical or mixed type
  F00.9 Dementia in Alzheimer's disease, unspecified

F01 Vascular dementia
  F01.0 Vascular dementia of acute onset
  F01.1 Multi-infarct dementia
  F01.2 Subcortical vascular dementia
  F01.3 Mixed cortical and subcortical vascular dementia
  F01.8 Other vascular dementia
  F01.9 Vascular dementia, unspecified

F02 Dementia in other diseases classified elsewhere
  F02.0 Dementia in Pick's disease
  F02.1 Dementia in Creutzfeldt-Jakob disease
  F02.2 Dementia in Huntington's disease
  F02.3 Dementia in Parkinson's disease
  F02.4 Dementia in human immunodeficiency virus (HIV) disease
  F02.8 Dementia in other specified diseases classified elsewhere

F03 Unspecified dementia

A fifth character may be added to specify dementia in F00-03, as follows:

  .x 0 Without additional symptoms
  .x 1 Other symptoms, predominantly delusional
  .x 2 Other symptoms, predominantly hallucinatory
  .x 3 Other symptoms, predominantly depressive
  .x 4 Other mixed symptoms

F04 Organic amnesic syndrome, not induced by alcohol and other psychoactive substances

F05 Delirium, not induced by alcohol and other psychoactive substances
  F05.0 Delirium, not superimposed on dementia, so described
  F05.1 Delirium, superimposed on dementia
  F05.8 Other delirium
  F05.9 Delirum, unspecified

F06 Other mental disorders due to brain damage and dysfunction and to physical disease
  F06.0 Organic hallucinosis
  F06.1 Organic catatonic disorder
  F06.2 Organic delusional (schizophrenialike) disorder
  F06.3 Organic mood (affective) disorders
      .30 Organic manic disorder
      .31 Organic bipolar disorder
      .32 Organic depressive disorder
      .33 Organic mixed affective disorder
  F06.4 Organic anxiety disorder
  F06.5 Organic dissociative disorder
  F06.6 Organic emotionally labile (asthenic) disorder
  F06.7 Mild cognitive disorder
  F06.8 Other specified mental disorders due to brain damage and dysfunction and to physical disease
  F06.9 Unspecified mental disorder due to brain damage and dysfunction and to physical disease

F07 Personality and behavioural disorders due to brain disease, damage and dysfunction
  F07.0 Organic personality disorder
  F07.1 Postencephalitic syndrome
  F07.2 Postconcussional syndrome
  F07.8 Other organic personality and behavioural disorders due to brain disease, damage and dysfunction
  F07.9 Unspecified organic personality and behavioural disorder due to brain disease, damage and dysfunction

F09 Unpecified organic or symptomatic mental disorder

F10-F19
Mental and behavioural disorders due to psychoactive substance use

F10—Mental and behavioural disorders due to use of alcohol

F11—Mental and behavioural disorders due to use of opioids

F12—Mental and behavioural disorders due to use of cannabinoids

F13—Mental and behavioural disorders due to use of sedatives or hypnotics

F14—Mental and behavioural disorders due to use of cocaine

F15—Mental and behavioural disorders due to use of caffeine

F16—Mental and behavioural disorders due to use of hallucinogens

F17—Mental and behavioural disorders due to use of tobacco

F18—Mental and behavioural disorders due to use of volatile solvents

F19—Mental and behavioural disorders due to multiple drug use and use of other psychoactive substances

Four- and five-character categories may be used to specify the clinical conditions, as follows:
  F1x.0 Acute intoxication
      .00 Uncomplicated
      .01 With trauma or other bodily injury
      .02 With other medical complications
      .03 With delirium
      .04 With perceptual distortions
      .05 With coma
      .06 With convulsions
      .07 Pathological intoxication

  F1x.1 Harmful use

  F1x.2 Dependence syndrome
      .20 Currently abstinent
      .21 Currently abstinent, but in a protected environment
      .22 Currently on a clinically supervised maintenanced or replacement regime (controlled dependence)
      .23 Currently abstinent, but receiving treatment with aversive or blocking drugs
      .24 Currently using the substance (active dependence)
      .25 Continuous use
      .26 Episodic use (dipsomania)

  F1x.3 Withdrawal state
      .30 Uncomplicated
      .31 Convulsions

  F1x.4 Withdrawal state with delirium
      .40 Without convulsions
      .41 With convulsions

  F1x.5 Psychotic disorder
      .50 Schizophrenialike
      .51 Predominantly delusional
      .52 Predominantly hallucinatory
      .53 Predominantly polymorphic
      .54 Predominantly depressive symptoms
      .55 Predominantly manic symptoms
      .56 Mixed

  F1x.6 Amnesic syndrome

  F1x.7 Residual and late-onset psychotic disorder
      .70 Flashbacks
      .71 Personality or behaviour disorder
      .72 Residual affective disorder
      .73 Dementia
      .74 Other persisting cognitive impairment
      .75 Late-onset psychotic disorder

  F1x.8 Other mental and behavioural disorders

  F1x.9 Unspecified mental and behavioural disorder

F20-F29
Schizophrenia, schizotypcal and delusional disorders

F20 Schizophrenia
  F20.0 Paranoid schizophrenia
  F20.1 Hebephrenic schizophrenia
  F20.2 Catatonic schizophrenia
  F20.3 Paranoid schizophrenia
  F20.4 Undifferentiated schizophrenia
  F20.5 Postschizophrenic depression
  F20.6 Residual schizophrenia
  F20.7 Simple schizophrenia
  F20.8 Other schizophrenia
  F20.9 Schizophrenia, unspecified

A fifth character may be used to classify course:
      .x 0 Continuous
      .x 1 Episodic with progressive deficit

Table 3-1. *(continued)*

.x 2 Episodic with stable deficit
.x 3 Episodic remittent
.x 4 Incomplete remission
.x 5 Complete remission
.x 8 Other
.x 9 Period of observation less than one year

F21 Schizotypal disorder

F22 Persistent delusional disorders
F22.0 Delusional disorder
F22.8 Other persistent delusional disorders
F22.9 Persistent delusional disorder, unspecified

F23 Acute and transient psychotic disorders
F23.0 Acute polymorphic psychotic disorder without symptoms of schizophrenia
F23.1 Acute polymorphic psychotic disorder with symptoms of schizophrenia
F23.2 Acute schizophrenialike psychotic disorder
F23.3 Other acute predominantly delusional psychotic disorders
F23.8 Other acute transient psychotic disorders
F23.9 Acute and transient psychotic disorders unspecified

A fifth character may be used to identify the presence or absence of associated acute stress:
.x 0 Without associated acute stress
.x 1 With associated acute stress

F24 Induced delusional disorder

F25 Schizoaffective disorders
F25.0 Schizoaffective disorder, manic type
F25.1 Schizoaffective disorder, depressive type
F25.2 Schizoaffective disorder, mixed type
F25.8 Other schizoaffective disorders
F25.9 Schizoaffective disorder, unspecified

F28 Other nonorganic psychotic disorders

F29 Unspecified nonorganic psychotic disorders

F30–F39
Mood (affective) disorders

F30 Manic episode
F30.0 Hypomania
F30.1 Mania without psychotic symptoms
F30.2 Mania with psychotic symptoms
F30.8 Other manic episodes
F30.9 Manic episode, unspecified

F31 Bipolar affective disorder
F31.0 Bipolar affective disorder, current episode hypomanic
F31.1 Bipolar affedtive disorder, current episode manic without psychotic symptoms
F31.2 Bipolar affective disorder, current episode manic with psychotic symptoms
F31.3 Bipolar affective disorder, current episode mild or moderate depression
.30 Without somatic symptoms
.31 With somatic symptoms
F31.4 Bipolar affective disorder, current episode severe depression without psychotic symptoms
F31.5 Bipolar affective disorder, current episode severe depression with psychotic symptoms
F31.6 Bipolar affective disorder, current episode mixed
F31.7 Bipolar affective disorder, currently in remission
F31.8 Other bipolar affective disorders
F31.9 Bipolar affective disorder, unspecified

F32 Depressive episode
F32.0 Mild depressive episode
.00 Without somatic symptoms
.01 With somatic symptoms
F32.1 Moderate depressive episode
.10 Without somatic symptoms
.11 With somatic symptoms
F32.3 Severe depressive episode with psychotic symptoms
F32.8 Other depressive episodes
F32.9 Depressive episode, unspecified

F33 Recurrent depressive disorder
F33.0 Recurrent depressive disorder, current episode mild
.10 Without somatic symptoms
.11 With somatic symptoms

F33.1 Recurrent depressive disorder, current episode moderate
.10 Without somatic symptoms
.11 With somatic symptoms
F33.2 Recurrent depressive disorder, current episode severe without psychotic symptoms
F33.3 Recurrent depressive disorder, current episode severe with psychotic symptoms
F33.4 Recurrent depressive disorder, currently in remission
F33.8 Other recurrent depressive disorders
F33.9 Recurrent depressive disorder, unspecified

F34 Persistent mood (affective) disorders
F34.0 Cyclothymia
F34.1 Dysthymia
F34.8 Other persistent mood (affective) disorders
F34.9 Persistent mood (affective) disorder, unspecified

F38 Other mood (affective) disorders
F38.0 Other single mood (affective) disorders
.00 Mixed affective episode
F38.1 Other recurrent mood (affective) disorders
.10 Recurrent brief depressive disorder
F38.8 Other specified mood (affective) disorders

F39 Unspecified mood (affective) disorder

F40–F48
Neurotic stress-related and somatoform disorders

F40 Phobic anxiety disorders
F40.0 Agoraphobia
.00 Without panic disorder
.01 With panic disorder
F40.1 Social phobias
F40.2 Specific (isolated) phobias
F40.3 Other phobic anxiety disorders
F40.9 Phobic anxiety disorder, unspecified

F41 Other anxiety disorders
F41.0 Panic disorder (episodic paroxysmal anxiety)
F41.1 Generalized anxiety disorder
F41.2 Mixed anxiety and depressive disorder
F41.3 Other mixed anxiety disorders
F41.8 Other specified anxiety disorders
F41.9 Anxiety disorder, unspecified

F42 Obsessive-compulsive disorder
F42.0 Predominantly obsessional thoughts or ruminations
F42.1 Predominantly compulsive acts (obssessional rituals)
F42.2 Mixed obsessional thoughts and acts
F42.8 Other obsessive-compulsive disorders
F42.9 Obsessive-compulsive disorder, unspecified

F43 Reactions to severe stress, and adjustment disorders
F43.0 Acute stress reaction
F43.1 Posttraumatic stress disorder
F43.2 Adjustment disorders
.20 Brief depressive reaction
.21 Prolonged depressive reaction
.22 Mixed anxiety and depressive reaction
.23 With predominant disturbance of other emotions
.24 With predominant disturbance of conduct
.25 With mixed disturbance of emotions and conduct
.28 With other specified predominant symptoms
F43.8 Other reactions to severe stress
F43.9 Reaction to severe stress, unspecified

F44 Dissociative (conversion) disorders
F44.0 Dissociative amnesia
F44.1 Dissociative fugue
F44.2 Dissociative stupor
F44.3 Trance and possession disorders
F44.4 Dissociative motor disorders
F44.5 Dissociative convulsions
F44.6 Dissociative anaesthesia and sensory loss
F44.7 Mixed dissociative (conversion) disorders
F44.8 Other dissociative (conversion) disorders
.80 Ganser's syndrome
.81 Multiple personality disorder
.82 Transient dissociative (conversion) disorders occurring in childhood and adolescence
.88 Other specified dissociative (conversion) disorders
F44.9 Dissociative (conversion) disorder, unspecified

(continued)

Table 3-1.   *(continued)*

F45 Somatoform disorders
  F45.0 Somatization disorder
  F45.1 Undifferentiated somatoform disorder
  F45.2 Hypochondriacal disorder
  F45.3 Somatoform autonomic dysfunction
      .30 Heart and cardiovascular system
      .31 Upper gastrointestinal tract
      .32 Lower gastrointestinal tract
      .33 Respiratory system
      .34 Genitourinary system
      .38 Other organ or system
  F45.4 Persistent somatoform pain disorder
  F45.8 Other somatoform disorders
  F45.9 Somatoform disorder, unspecified

F48 Other neurotic disorders
  F48.0 Neurasthenia
  F48.1 Depersonalization-derealization syndrome
  F48.8 Other specified neurotic disorders
  F48.9 Neurotic disorder, unspecified

F50-F59
Behavioural syndromes associated with physiological disturbances and physical factors

F50 Eating disorders
  F50.0 Anorexia nervosa
  F50.1 Atypical anorexia nervosa
  F50.2 Bulimia nervosa
  F50.3 Atypical bulimia nervosa
  F50.4 Overeating associated with other psychological disturbances
  F50.5 Vomiting associated with other psychological disturbances
  F50.8 Other eating disorders
  F50.9 Eating disorder, unspecified

F51 Nonorganic sleep disorders
  F51.0 Nonorganic insomnia
  F51.1 Nonorganic hypersomnia
  F51.2 Nonorganic disorder of the sleep-wake schedule
  F51.3 Sleepwalking (somnambulism)
  F51.4 Sleep terrors (night terrors)
  F51.5 Nightmares
  F51.8 Other nonorganic sleep disorders
  F51.9 Nonorganic sleep disorder, unspecified

F52 Sexual dysfunction, not caused by organic disorder or disease
  F52.0 Lack or loss of sexual desire
  F52.1 Sexual aversion and lack of sexual enjoyment
      .10 Sexual aversion
      .11 Lack of sexual enjoyment
  F52.2 Failure of genital response
  F52.3 Organic dysfunction
  F52.4 Premature ejaculation
  F52.5 Nonorganic vaginismus
  F52.6 Nonorganic dyspareunia
  F52.7 Excessive sexual drive
  F52.8 Other sexual dysfunction, not caused by organic disorders or disease
  F52.9 Unspecified sexual dysfunction, not caused by organic disorder or disease

F53 Mental and behavioural disorders associated with the puerperium, not elsewhere classified
  F53.0 Mild mental and behavioural disorders associated with the puerperium, not elsewhere classified
  F53.1 Severe mental and behavioural disorders associated with the puerperium, not elsewhere classified
  F53.8 Other mental and behavioural disorders associated with the puerperium, not elsewhere classified
  F53.9 Puerperal mental disorder, unspecified

F54 Psychological and behavioural factors associated with disorders or diseases classified elsewhere

F55 Abuse of nondependence-producing substances
  F55.0 Antidepressants
  F55.1 Laxatives
  F55.2 Analgesics
  F55.3 Antacids
  F55.4 Vitamins
  F55.5 Steroids or hormones
  F55.6 Specific herbal or folk remedies
  F55.8 Other substances that do not produce dependence
  F55.9 Unspecified

F59 Unspecified behavioural syndromes associated with physiological disturbances and physical factors

F60-F69
Disorders of adult personality and behaviour

F60 Specific personality disorders
  F60.0 Paranoid personality disorder
  F60.1 Schizoid personality disorder
  F60.2 Dissocial personality disorder
  F60.3 Emotionally unstable personality disorder
      .30 Impulsive type
      .31 Borderline type
  F60.4 Histrionic personality disorder
  F60.5 Anankastic personality disorder
  F60.6 Anxious (avoidant) personality disorder
  F60.7 Dependent personality disorder
  F60.8 Other specific personality disorders
  F60.9 Personality disorder, unspecified

F61 Mixed and other personality disorders
  F61.0 Mixed personality disorders
  F61.1 Troublesome personality disorders

F62 Enduring personality changes, not attributable to brain damage and disease
  F62.0 Enduring personality change after catastrophic experience
  F62.1 Enduring personality change after psychiatric illness
  F62.8 Other enduring personality changes
  F62.9 Enduring personality change, unspecified

F63 Habit and impulse disorders
  F63.0 Pathological gambling
  F63.1 Pathological fire-setting (pyromania)
  F63.2 Pathological stealing (kleptomania)
  F63.3 Trichotillomania
  F63.8 Other habit and impulse disorders
  F63.9 Habit and impulse disorder, unspecified

F64 Gender identity disorders
  F64.0 Transsexualism
  F64.1 Dual-role transvestism
  F64.2 Gender identity disorder of childhood
  F64.8 Other gender identity disorders
  F64.9 Gender identity disorder, unspecified

F65 Disorders of sexual preference
  F65.0 Fetishism
  F65.1 Fetishistic transvestism
  F65.2 Exhibitionism
  F65.3 Voyeurism
  F65.4 Paedophilia
  F65.5 Sadomasochism
  F65.6 Multiple disorders of sexual preference
  F65.8 Other disorders of sexual preference
  F65.9 Disorder of sexual preference, unspecified

F66 Psychological and behavioural disorders associated with sexual development and orientation
  F66.0 Sexual maturation disorder
  F66.1 Egodystonic sexual orientation
  F66.2 Sexual relationship disorder
  F66.8 Other psychosexual development disorders
  F66.9 Psychosexual development disorder, unspecified

A fifth character may be used to indicate assocaition with:
      .x 0 Heterosexuality
      .x 1 Homosexuality
      .x 2 Bisexuality
      .x 8 Other, including prepubertal

F68 Other disorders of adult personality and behaviour
  F68.0 Elaboration of physical symptoms for psychological reasons
  F68.1 Intentional production or feigning of symptoms or disabilities, either physical or psychological (factitious disorder)
  F68.8 Other specified disorders of adult personality and behaviour

F69 Unspecified disorders of adult personality and behaviour

F70-F79
Mental retardation

F70 Mild mental retardation

F71 Moderate mental retardation

Table 3-1. *(continued)*

F72 Severe mental retardation

F73 Profound mental retardation

F78 Other mental retardation

F79 Unspecified mental retardation

A fourth character may be used to specify the extent of associated behavioural impairment:
F7x.0 No, or minimal, impairment of behaviour
F7x.1 Significant impairment of behaviour requiring attention or treatment
F7.x8 Other impairments of behaviour
F7x.9 Without mention of impairment of behaviour

F80–F89
Disorders of psychological development

F80 Specific developmental disorders of speech and language
F80.0 Specific speech articulation disorder
F80.1 Expressive language disorder
F80.2 Receptive language disorder
F80.3 Acquired aphasia with epilepsy (Landau-Kleffner syndrome)
F80.8 Other developmental disorders of speech and language
F80.9 Developmental disorder of speech and language, unspecified

F81 Specific developmental disorders of scholastic skills
F81.0 Specific reading disorder
F81.1 Specific spelling disorder
F81.2 Specific orders of arithmetical skills
F81.3 Mixed disorder of scholastic skills
F81.8 Other developmental disorders of scholastic skills
F81.9 Developmental disorder of scholastic skills, unspecified

F82 Specific developmental disorder of motor function

F83 Mixed specific developmental disorders

F84 Pervasive developmental disorders
F84.0 Childhood autism
F84.1 Atypical autism
F84.2 Rett's syndrome
F84.3 Other childhood disintegrative disorder
F84.4 Overactive disorder associated with mental retardation and steretyped movements
F84.5 Asperger's syndrome
F84.8 Other pervasive developmental disorders
F84.9 Pervasive developmental disorder, unspecified

F88 Other disorders of psychological development

F89 Unspecified disorder or psychological development

F90–F98
Behavioural and emotional disorders with onset usually occurring in childhood and adolescence

F90 Hyperkinetic disorders
F90.0 Disturbance of activity and attention
F90.1 Hyperkinetic conduct disorder

F90.8 Other hyperkinetic disorders
F90.9 Hyperkinetic disorder, unspecified

F91 Conduct disorders
F91.0 Conduct disorder confined to the family context
F91.1 Unsocialized conduct disorder
F91.2 Socialized conduct disorder
F91.3 Oppositional defiant disorder
F91.8 Other conduct disorder
F91.9 Conduct disorder, unspecified

F92 Mixed disorders of conduct and emotions
F92.0 Depressive conduct disorder
F92.8 Other mixed disorders of conduct and emotions
F92.9 Mixed disorder of conduct and emotions, unspecified

F93 Emotionsl disorders with onset specific to childhood
F93.0 Separation anxiety disorder of childhood
F93.1 Phobic anxiety disorder of childhood
F93.2 Social anxiety disorder of childhood
F93.3 Sibling rivalry disorder
F93.8 Other childhood emotional disorders
F93.9 Childhood emotional disorder, unspecified

F94 Disorders of social functioning with onset specific to childhood and adolescence
F94.0 Elective mutism
F94.1 Reactive attachment disorder of childhood
F94.2 Disinhibited attachment disorder of childhood
F94.8 Other childhood disorders of social functioning
F94.9 Childhood disorders of social functioning, unspecified

F95 Tic disorders
F95.0 Transient tic disorder
F95.1 Chronic motor or vocal tic disorder
F95.2 Combined vocal and multiple motor tic disorder (de la Tourette's syndrome)
F95.8 Other tic disorders
F95.9 Tic disorder, unspecified

F98 Other behavioural and emotional disorders with onset usually occurring in childhood and adolescence
F98.0 Nonorganic enuresis
F98.1 Nonorganic encopresis
F98.2 Feeding disorder of infancy and childhood
F98.3 Pica of infancy and childhood
F98.4 Stereotyped movement disorders
F98.5 Stuttering (stammering)
F98.6 Cluttering
F98.8 Other specified behavioural and emotional disorders with onset usually occurring in childhood and adolescence
F98.9 Unspecified behavioural and emotional disorders with onset usually occurring in childhood and adolescence

F99
Unspecified mental disorder

F99 Mental disorder, not otherwise specified

Table from World Health Organization: *The ICD-10 Classification of Mental and Behavioural Disorders: Clinical Descriptions and Diagnostic Guidelines*, World Health Organization, Geneva, 1992. Used with permission.

the introduction to the entire section. Laboratory findings and associated physical examination signs and symptoms are described when relevant. DSM-IV does not purport to be a textbook. No mention is made of theories of causes, management, or treatment, nor are the controversial issues surrounding a particular diagnostic category discussed.

DIAGNOSTIC UNCERTAINTIES

DSM-IV provides explicit rules to be used when the information is insufficient (diagnosis to be deferred or provisional) or the patient's clinical presentation and history do not meet the full criteria of a prototypical category (an atypical, residual, or not otherwise specified [NOS] type within the general category).

Multiaxial Evaluation

DSM-IV is a multiaxial system that evaluates the patient along several variables and contains five axes. Axis I and Axis II comprise the entire classification of mental disorder, 17 major classifications and more than 300 specific disorders (Table 3–2). In many instances the patient has a disorder on both axes. For example, a patient may have major depressive disorder noted on Axis I and obsessive-compulsive personality disorder on Axis II.

AXIS I

Axis I consists of clinical disorders and other conditions that may be a focus of clinical attention (Table 3–3).

Table 3-2.   Classes or Groups of Conditions in DSM-IV

Disorders usually first diagnosed in infancy, childhood, or adolescence

Delirium, dementia, and amnestic and other cognitive disorders

Mental disorders due to a general medical condition not elsewhere classified

Substance-related disorders

Schizophrenia and other psychotic disorders

Mood disorders

Anxiety disorders

Somatoform disorders

Factitious disorders

Dissociative disorders

Sexual and gender identity disorders

Eating disorders

Sleep disorders

Impulse-control disorders not elsewhere classified

Adjustment disorders

Personality disorders

Other conditions that may be a focus of clinical attention

Table 3-3.   Axis I: Clinical Disorders and Other Conditions That May Be a Focus of Clinical Attention

Disorders usually first diagnosed in infancy, childhood, or adolescence (excluding mental retardation, which is diagnosed on Axis II)

Delirium, dementia, and amnestic and other cognitive disorders

Mental disorders due to a general medical condition

Substance-related disorders

Schizophrenia and other psychotic disorders

Mood disorders

Anxiety disorders

Somatoform disorders

Factitious disorders

Dissociative disorders

Sexual and gender identity disorders

Eating disorders

Sleep disorders

Impulse-control disorders not elsewhere classified

Adjustment disorders

Other conditions that may be a focus of clinical attention

Table from DSM-IV, *Diagnostic and Statistical Manual of Mental Disorders*, ed 4. Copyright American Psychiatric Association, Washington, 1994. Used with permission.

Table 3-4.   Axis II: Personality Disorders and Mental Retardation

Paranoid personality disorder

Schizoid personality disorder

Schizotypal personality disorder

Antisocial personality disorder

Borderline personality disorder

Histrionic personality disorder

Narcissistic personality disorder

Avoidant personality disorder

Dependent personality disorder

Obsessive-compulsive personality disorder

Personality disorder not otherwise specified

Mental retardation

Table from DSM-IV, *Diagnostic and Statistical Manual of Mental Disorders*, ed 4. Copyright American Psychiatric Association, Washington, 1994. Used with permission.

Table 3-5.   Axis III: ICD-9-CM General Medical Conditions

Infectious and parasitic diseases (001-139)

Neoplasms (140-239)

Endocrine, nutritional, and metabolic diseases and immunity disorders (240-279)

Diseases of the blood and blood-forming organs (280-289)

Diseases of the nervous system and sense organs (320-389)

Diseases of the circulatory system (390-459)

Diseases of the respiratory system (460-519)

Diseases of the digestive system (520-579)

Diseases of the genitourinary system (580-629)

Complications of pregnancy, childbirth, and the puerperium (630-676)

Diseases of the skin and subcutaneous tissue (680-709)

Diseases of the musculoskeletal system and connective tissue (710-739)

Congenital anomalies (740-759)

Certain conditions originating in the perinatal period (760-779)

Symptoms, signs, and ill-defined conditions (780-799)

Injury and poisoning (800-999)

Table from DSM-IV, *Diagnostic and Statistical Manual of Mental Disorders*, ed 4. Copyright American Psychiatric Association, Washington, 1994. Used with permission.

Axis II

Axis II consists of personality disorders and mental retardation (Table 3–4). Borderline intellectual functioning and the habitual use of a particular defense mechanism can be indicated on Axis II.

Axis III

Axis III lists any physical disorder or general medical condition that is present in addition to the mental disorder. The physical condition may be causative (for example, kidney failure causing delirium), the result of a mental disorder (for example,

alcohol gastritis secondary to alcohol dependence), or unrelated to the mental disorder. When a medical condition is causative or causally related to a mental disorder, a mental disorder due to a general condition is listed on Axis I and the general medical condition is listed on both Axis I and Axis III. In DSM-IV's example—a case in which hypothyroidism is a direct cause of major depressive disorder—the designation on Axis I is mood disorder due to hypothyroidism with depressive features, and hypothyroidism is listed again on Axis III (Table 3–5).

Axis IV

Axis IV is used to code the psychosocial and environmental problems that significantly contribute to the development or the exacerbation of the current disorder (Table 3–6).

The evaluation of stressors is based on the clinician's assessment of the stress that an average person with similar sociocultural values and circumstances would experience from the psychosocial stressors. That judgment considers the amount of change in the person's life caused by the stressor, the degree to which the event is desired and under the person's control, and the number of stressors. Stressors may be positive (for example, a job promotion) or negative (for example, the loss of a loved one). Information about stressors may be important in formulating a treatment plan that includes attempts to remove the psychosocial stressors or to help the patient cope with them.

Axis V

Axis V is a global assessment of functioning (GAF) scale in which the clinician judges the patient's overall level of func-

tioning during a particular time period (for example, the patient's level of functioning at the time of the evaluation or the patient's highest level of functioning for at least a few months during the past year). Functioning is conceptualized as a composite of three major areas: social functioning, occupational functioning, and psychological functioning. The GAF scale, based on a continuum of mental health and mental illness, is a 100-point scale, 100 representing the highest level of functioning in all areas (Table 3–7).

Patients who had a high level of functioning before an episode of illness generally have a better prognosis than do those who had a low level of functioning.

Multiaxial Evaluation Report Form

Table 3–8 shows the DSM-IV multiaxial evaluation report form. Examples of how to record the results of a DSM-IV multiaxial evaluation are given in Table 3–9.

Nonaxial Format

DSM-IV also allows clinicians who do not wish to use the multiaxial format to list the diagnoses serially, with the principal diagnosis listed first (Table 3–10).

Severity of Disorder

Depending on the clinical picture, the presence or the absence of signs and symptoms, and their intensity, the severity of a disorder may be mild, moderate, or severe, and the disorder

Table 3-6. Axis IV: Psychosocial and Environmental Problems

Problems with primary support group
Problems related to the social environment
Educational problems
Occupational problems
Housing problems
Economic problems
Problems with access to health care services
Problems related to interaction with the legal system/crime
Other psychosocial and environmental problems

Table from DSM-IV, *Diagnostic and Statistical Manual of Mental Disorders*, ed 4. Copyright American Psychiatric Association, Washington, 1994. Used with permission.

Table 3-7. Global Assessment of Functioning (GAF) Scale

Consider psychological, social, and occupational functioning on a hypothetical continuum of mental health-illness. Do not include impairment in functioning due to physical (or environmental) limitations.

Code	(Note: Use intermediate codes when appropriate, e.g., 45, 68, 72.)
100 91	**Superior functioning in a wide range of activities, life's problems never seem to get out of hand, is sought out by others because of his or her many positive qualities. No symptoms.**
90 | 81	**Absent or minimal symptoms** (e.g., mild anxiety before an exam), **good functioning in all areas, interested and involved in a wide range of activities, socially effective, generally satisfied with life, no more than everyday problems or concerns** (e.g., an occasional argument with family members).
80 | 71	**If symptoms are present, they are transient and expectable reactions to psychosocial stressors** (e.g., difficulty concentrating after family argument); **no more than slight impairment in social, occupational, or school functioning** (e.g., temporarily falling behind in schoolwork).
70 | 61	**Some mild symptoms** (e.g., depressed mood and mild insomnia) **OR some difficulty in social, occupational, or school functioning** (e.g., occasional truancy, or theft within the household), **but generally functioning pretty well, has some meaningful interpersonal relationships.**
60 | 51	**Moderate symptoms** (e.g., flat affect and circumstantial speech, occasional panic attacks) **OR moderate difficulty in social, occupational, or school functioning** (e.g., few friends, conflicts with peers or coworkers).
50 | 41	**Serious symptoms** (e.g., suicidal ideation, severe obsessional rituals, frequent shoplifting) **OR any serious impairment in social, occupational, or school functioning** (e.g., no friends, unable to keep a job).
40 | 31	**Some impairment in reality testing or communication** (e.g., speech is at times illogical, obscure, or irrelevant) **OR major impairment in several areas, such as work or school, family relations, judgments, thinking, or mood** (e.g., depressed man avoids friends, neglects family, and is unable to work; child frequently beats up younger children, is defiant at home, and is failing at school).
30 | 21	**Behavior is considerably influenced by delusions or hallucinations OR serious impairment in communication or judgment** (e.g., sometimes incoherent, acts grossly inappropriately, suicidal preoccupation) **OR inability to function in almost all areas** (e.g., stays in bed all day; no job, home or friends).
20 | 11	**Some danger of hurting self or others** (e.g., suicide attempts without clear expectation of death; frequently violent; manic excitement) **OR occasionally fails to maintain minimal personal hygiene** (e.g., smears feces) **OR gross impairment in communication** (e.g., largely incoherent or mute).
10 1	**Persistent danger of severely hurting self or others** (e.g., recurrent violence) **OR persistent inability to maintain minimal personal hygiene OR serious suicidal act with clear expectation of death.**
0	Inadequate information.

Table from DSM-IV, *Diagnostic and Statistical Manual of Mental Disorders*, ed 4. Copyright American Psychiatric Association, Washington, 1994. Used with permission.

Table 3-8.   Multiaxial Evaluation Report Form

The following form is offered as one possibility for reporting multiaxial evaluations. In some settings, this form may be used exactly as is; in other settings, the form may be adapted to satisfy special needs.

AXIS I: Clinical Disorders
   Other Conditions that May Be a Focus of
      Clinical Attention

Diagnostic code   DSM-IV name

___ ___ . ___ ___   _____

___ ___ . ___ ___   _____

AXIS II: Personality Disorders
   Mental Retardation

Diagnostic code   DSM-IV name

___ ___ . ___ ___   _____

___ ___ . ___ ___   _____

AXIS III: General Medical Conditions

ICD-9-CM code   ICD-9-CM name

___ ___ . ___ ___   _____

___ ___ . ___ ___   _____

AXIS IV: Psychosocial and Environmental Problems

Check:
☐ **Problems with primary support group**
      Specify:
☐ **Problems related to the social environment**
      Specify:
☐ **Educational problems** *Specify:* _____
☐ **Occupational problems** *Specify:* _____
☐ **Housing problems** *Specify:*
☐ **Economic problems** *Specify:* _____
☐ **Problems with access to health care services**
      Specify:
☐ **Problems related to interaction with the legal system/crime**
      Specify:
☐ **Other psychosocial and environmental problems**
      Specify:

AXIS V: Global Assessment of Functioning Scale
                              Score: _____
                         Time frame: _____

Table from DSM-IV, *Diagnostic and Statistical Manual of Mental Disorders*, ed 4. Copyright American Psychiatric Association, Washington, 1994. Used with permission.

may be in partial remission or in full remission. The following guidelines are used by DSM-IV.

MILD

Few, if any, symptoms in excess of those required to make the diagnosis are present, and symptoms result in no more than minor impairment in social or occupational functioning.

MODERATE

Symptoms or functional impairment between "mild" and "severe" are present.

SEVERE

Many symptoms in excess of those required to make the diagnosis, or several symptoms that are particularly severe, are present, or the symptoms result in marked impairment in social or occupational functioning.

IN PARTIAL REMISSION

The full criteria for the disorder were previously met, but currently only some of the symptoms or signs of the disorder remain.

Table 3-9.   Examples of How to Record the Results of a DSM-IV Multiaxial Evaluation

Example 1:

Axis I	296.23	Major depressive disorder, single episode, severe without psychotic features
	305.00	Alcohol abuse
Axis II	301.6	Dependent personality disorder Frequent use of denial
Axis III		None
Axis IV		Threat of job loss
Axis V	GAF = 35	(current)

Example 2:

Axis I	300.4	Dysthymic disorder
	315.00	Reading disorder
Axis II	V71.09	No diagnosis
Axis III	382.9	Otitis media, recurrent
Axis IV		Victim of child neglect
Axis V	GAF = 53	(current)

Example 3:

Axis I	293.83	Mood disorder due to hypothyroidism, with depressive features
Axis II	V71.09	No diagnosis, histrionic personality features
Axis III	244.9	Hypothyroidism
	365.23	Chronic angle-closure glaucoma
Axis IV		None
Axis V	GAF = 45	(on admission)
	GAF = 65	(at discharge)

Example 4:

Axis I	V61.1	Partner relational problem
Axis II	V71.09	No diagnosis
Axis III		None
Axis IV		Unemployment
Axis V	GAF = 83	(highest level past year)

Table from DSM-IV, *Diagnostic and Statistical Manual of Mental Disorders*, ed 4. Copyright American Psychiatric Association, Washington, 1994. Used with permission.

Table 3-10.   Nonaxial Format

Clinicians who do not wish to use the multiaxial format may simply list the appropriate diagnoses. Those choosing this option should follow the general rule of recording as many coexisting mental disorders, general medical conditions, and other factors that are relevant to the care and treatment of the individual. The principal diagnosis or the reason for visit should be listed first.

The examples below illustrate the reporting of diagnoses in a format that does not use the multiaxial system.

Example 1:

296.23	Major depressive disorder, single episode, severe without psychotic features
305.00	Alcohol abuse
301.6	Dependent personality disorder Frequent use of denial

Example 2:

300.4	Dysthymic disorder
315.00	Reading disorder
382.9	Otitis media, recurrent

Example 3:

293.83	Mood disorder due to hypothyroidism, with depressive features
244.9	Hypothyroidism
365.23	Chronic angle-closure glaucoma Histrionic personality features

Example 4:

V61.1	Partner relational problem

Table from DSM-IV, *Diagnostic and Statistical Manual of Mental Disorders*, ed 4. Copyright American Psychiatric Association, Washington, 1994. Used with permission.

In Full Remission

There are no longer any symptoms or signs of the disorder but it is still clinically relevant to note the disorder . . . The differentiation of in full remission from recovered requires consideration of many factors, including the characteristic course of the disorder, the length of time since the last period of disturbance, the total duration of the disturbance, and the need for continued evaluation or prophylactic treatment.

Multiple Diagnoses

When a patient has more than one Axis I disorder, the principal diagnosis is indicated by listing it first. According to DSM-IV:

The remaining disorders are listed in order of focus of attention and treatment. When a person has both an Axis I and an Axis II diagnosis, the principal diagnosis or the reason for visit will be assumed to be on Axis I unless the Axis II diagnosis is followed by the qualifying phrase ''(Principal diagnosis)'' or ''(Reason for visit).''

DSM-IV also states:

When more than one diagnosis for an individual is given in an inpatient setting, the *principal diagnosis* is the condition established after study to be chiefly responsible for occasioning the admission of the individual. When more than one diagnosis is given for an individual in an outpatient setting, the *reason for visit* is the condition that is chiefly responsible for the ambulatory care medical services received during the visit. In most cases, the principal diagnosis or the reason for visit is also the main focus of attention or treatment. It is often difficult (and somewhat arbitrary) to determine which diagnosis is the principal diagnosis or the *reason for visit*, especially in situations of ''dual diagnosis'' (a substance-related diagnosis like Amphetamine Dependence accompanied by a non-substance-related diagnosis like Schizophrenia). For example, it may be unclear which diagnosis should be considered ''principal'' for an individual hospitalized with both Schizophrenia and Amphetamine Intoxication, because each condition may have contributed equally to the need for admission and treatment.

Provisional Diagnosis

According to DSM-IV:

The modifier *provisional* can be used when there is a strong presumption that the full criteria will ultimately be met for a disorder, but not enough information is available to make a firm diagnosis. The clinician can indicate the diagnostic uncertainty by writing ''(Provisional)'' following the diagnosis.

DSM-IV Classification of Mental Disorders

Table 3–11 presents the DSM-IV classification of mental disorders (Axis I and Axis II).

Definition of Mental Disorder

According to DSM-IV:

Each of the mental disorders is conceptualized as a clinically significant behavioral or psychological syndrome or pattern that occurs in an individual and that is associated with present distress (e.g., a painful symptom) or disability (i.e., impairment in one or more important areas of functioning) or with a significantly increased risk of suffering death,

pain, disability, or an important loss of freedom. In addition, this syndrome or pattern must not be merely an expectable and culturally sanctioned response to a particular event, for example, the death of a loved one. Whatever its original cause, it must currently be considered a manifestation of a behavioral, psychological, or biological dysfunction in the individual. Neither deviant behavior (e.g., political, religious, or sexual), nor conflicts that are primarily between the individual and society are mental disorders unless the deviance or conflict is a symptom of a dysfunction in the individual, as described above . . .

Distinction Between Mental Disorder *and* General Medical Condition. The terms *mental disorder* and *general medical condition* are used throughout this manual. The term *mental disorder* is explained above. The term *general medical condition* is used merely as a convenient shorthand to refer to conditions and disorders that are listed outside the ''Mental and Behavioral Disorders'' chapter of ICD. It should be recognized that these are merely terms of convenience and should not be taken to imply that there is any fundamental distinction between mental disorders and general medical conditions, that mental disorders are unrelated to physical or biological factors or processes, or that general medical conditions are unrelated to behavioral or psychosocial factors or processes.

Decision Trees

Decision trees, also known as algorithms, are diagrammatic tracks that organize the clinician's thinking so that all differential diagnoses are considered and ruled in or out, resulting in a presumptive diagnosis. Beginning with specific signs or symptoms, the psychiatrist follows the positive or negative track down the tree (by answering ''yes'' or ''no'') until a point in the tree with no outgoing branches (known as a leaf) is found. That point is the final diagnosis. Figure 3–1 is an example of a decision tree for psychotic disorders. DSM-IV includes an appendix of diagnostic decision trees.

PSYCHOSIS AND NEUROSIS

Psychosis

Although the traditional meaning of the term ''psychotic'' emphasized loss of reality testing and impairment of mental functioning—manifested by delusions, hallucinations, confusion, and impaired memory—two other meanings have evolved during the past 50 years. In the most common psychiatric use of the term, ''psychotic'' became synonymous with severe impairment of social and personal functioning characterized by social withdrawal and inability to perform the usual household and occupational roles. The other use of the term specifies the degree of ego regression as the criterion for psychotic illness. As a consequence of those multiple meanings, the term has lost its precision in current clinical and research practice.

According to the glossary of the American Psychiatric Association, the term ''psychotic'' means grossly impaired in reality testing. The term may be used to describe the behavior of a person at a given time or a mental disorder in which at some time during its course all persons with the disorder have grossly impaired reality testing. With gross impairment in reality testing, persons incorrectly evaluate the accuracy of their perceptions and thoughts and make incorrect inferences about external reality, even in the face of contrary evidence. The term ''psy-

Table 3-11.   DSM-IV Classification

NOS = Not otherwise specified.

An *x* appearing in a diagnostic code indicates that a specified code number is required.

An ellipsis (. . .) is used in the names of certain disorders to indicate that the name of a specific mental disorder or general medical condition should be inserted when recording the name (e.g., 293.0 delirium due to hypothyroidism).

If criteria are currently met, one of the following severity specifiers may be noted after the diagnosis:
Mild
Moderate
Severe

If criteria are no longer met, one of the following specifiers may be noted:
In partial remission
In full remission
Prior history

Disorders Usually First Diagnosed in Infancy, Childhood, or Adolescence

MENTAL RETARDATION
Note: These are coded on Axis II.
317   Mild mental retardation
318.0   Moderate mental retardation
318.1   Severe mental retardation
318.2   Profound mental retardation
319   Mental retardation, severity unspecified

LEARNING DISORDERS
315.00   Reading disorder
315.1   Mathematics disorder
315.2   Disorder of written expression
315.9   Learning disorder NOS

MOTOR SKILLS DISORDER
315.4   Developmental coordination disorder

COMMUNICATION DISORDERS
315.31   Expressive language disorder
315.31   Mixed receptive-expressive language disorder
315.39   Phonological disorder
307.0   Stuttering
307.9   Communication disorder NOS

PERVASIVE DEVELOPMENTAL DISORDERS
299.00   Autistic disorder
299.80   Rett's disorder
299.10   Childhood disintegrative disorder
299.80   Asperger's disorder
299.80   Pervasive developmental disorder NOS

ATTENTION-DEFICIT AND DISRUPTIVE BEHAVIOR DISORDERS
314.xx   Attention-deficit/hyperactivity disorder
.01   Combined type
.00   Predominantly inattentive type
.01   Predominantly hyperactive-impulsive type
314.9   Attention-deficit/hyperactivity disorder NOS
312.8   Conduct disorder
         Specify type:
         childhood-onset type/adolescent-onset type
313.81   Oppositional defiant disorder
312.9   Disruptive behavior disorder NOS

FEEDING AND EATING DISORDERS OF INFANCY OR EARLY CHILDHOOD
307.52   Pica
307.53   Rumination disorder
307.59   Feeding disorder of infancy or early childhood

TIC DISORDERS
307.23   Tourette's disorder
307.22   Chronic motor or vocal tic disorder
307.21   Transient tic disorder
         Specify type:
         nocturnal only/diurnal only/
         nocturnal and diurnal
307.20   Tic disorder NOS

ELIMINATION DISORDERS
_____.__ Encopresis
787.6   With constipation and overflow incontinence
307.7   Without constipation and overflow incontinence
307.6   Enuresis (not due to a general medical condition)
         Specify type: nocturnal only/diurnal only/nocturnal and diurnal

OTHER DISORDERS OF INFANCY, CHILDHOOD, OR ADOLESCENCE
309.21   Separation anxiety disorder
         Specify if: early onset
313.23   Selective mutism
313.89   Reactive attachment disorder of infancy or early childhood
         Specify type: inhibited type/disinhibited type
307.3   Stereotypic movement disorder
         Specify if: with self-injurious behavior
313.9   Disorder of infancy, childhood, or adolescence NOS

Delirium, Dementia, and Amnestic and Other Cognitive Disorders

DELIRIUM
293.0   Delirium due to . . . *(indicate the general medical condition)*
_____.__ Substance intoxication delirium *(refer to substance-related disorders for substance-specific codes)*
_____.__ Substance withdrawal delirium *(refer to substance-related disorders for substance-specific codes)*
_____.__ Delirium due to multiple etiologies *(code each of the specific etiologies)*
780.09   Delirium NOS

DEMENTIA
290.xx   Dementia of the Alzheimer's type, with early onset *(also code 331.0 Alzheimer's disease on Axis III)*
.10   Uncomplicated
.11   With delirium
.12   With delusions
.13   With depressed mood
         Specify if: with behavioral disturbance
290.xx   Dementia of the Alzheimer's type, with late onset *(also code 331.0 Alzheimer's disease on Axis III)*
.0   Uncomplicated
.3   With delirium
.20   With delusions
.21   With depressed mood
         Specify if: with behavioral disturbance

290.xx   Vascular dementia
.40   Uncomplicated
.41   With delirium
.42   With delusions
.43   With depressed mood
         Specify if: with behavioral disturbance
294.9   Dementia due to HIV disease *(also code 043.1 HIV infection affecting central nervous system on Axis III)*
294.1   Dementia due to head trauma *(also code 854.00 head injury on Axis III)*
294.1   Dementia due to Parkinson's disease *(also code 332.0 Parkinson's disease on Axis III)*
294.1   Dementia due to Huntington's disease *(also code 333.4 Huntington's disease on Axis III)*
290.10   Dementia due to Pick's disease *(also code 333.1 Pick's disease on Axis III)*
290.10   Dementia due to Creutzfeldt-Jakob disease *(also code 046.1 Creutzfeldt-Jakob disease on Axis III)*
294.1   Dementia due to *(indicate the general medical condition not listed above) (also code the general medical condition on Axis III)*
_____.__ Substance induced persisting dementia *(refer to substance-related disorders for substance specific codes)*
_____.__ Dementia due to multiple etiologies *(code each of the specific etiologies)*
294.8   Dementia NOS

AMNESTIC DISORDERS
294.0   Amnestic disorder due to . . . *(indicate the general medical condition)*
         Specify if: transient/chronic
_____.__ Substance-induced persisting amnestic disorder *(refer to substance-related disorders for substance-specific codes)*
294.8   Amnestic disorder NOS

OTHER COGNITIVE DISORDERS
294.9   Cognitive disorder NOS

Mental Disorders Due to a General Medical Condition Not Elsewhere Classified

293.89   Catatonic disorder due to . . . *(indicate the general medical condition)*
310.1   Personality change due to . . . *(indicate the general medical condition)*
         Specify type: labile type/disinhibited type/aggressive type/apathetic type/paranoid type/other type/combined type/unspecified type
293.9   Mental disorder NOS due to . . . *(indicate the general medical condition)*

Substance-Related Disorders

The following specifiers may be applied to substance dependence:
With physiological dependence/without physiological dependence

Table 3-11.   *(continued)*

Early full remission/early partial remission/ sustained full remission/sustained partial remission

On agonist therapy/in a controlled environment

The following specifiers apply to substance-induced disorders as noted

With onset during intoxication/with onset during withdrawal

ALCOHOL-RELATED DISORDERS

Alcohol Use Disorders
303.90   Alcohol dependence[a]
305.00   Alcohol abuse

Alcohol-Induced Disorders
303.00   Alcohol intoxication
291.8   Alcohol withdrawal
         Specify if: with perceptual disturbances
291.0   Alcohol intoxication delirium
291.0   Alcohol withdrawal delirium
291.2   Alcohol-induced persisting dementia
291.1   Alcohol-induced persisting amnestic disorder
291.x   Alcohol-induced psychotic disorder
  .5   With delusions[I,W]
  .3   With hallucinations[I,W]
291.8   Alcohol-induced mood disorder[I,W]
291.8   Alcohol-induced anxiety disorder[I,W]
291.8   Alcohol-induced sexual dysfunction[I]
291.8   Alcohol-induced sleep disorder[I,W]
291.9   Alcohol-related disorder NOS

AMPHETAMINE (OR AMPHETAMINELIKE)- RELATED DISORDERS

Amphetamine Use Disorders
304.40   Amphetamine dependence[a]
305.70   Amphetamine abuse

Amphetamine-Induced Disorders
292.89   Amphetamine intoxication
         Specify if: with perceptual disturbances
292.0   Amphetamine withdrawal
292.81   Amphetamine intoxication delirium
292.xx   Amphetamine-induced psychotic disorder
  .11   With delusions[I]
  .12   With hallucinations[I]
292.84   Amphetamine-induced mood disorder[I,W]
292.89   Amphetamine-induced anxiety disorder[I]
292.89   Amphetamine-induced sexual dysfunction[I]
292.89   Amphetamine-induced sleep disorder[I,W]
292.9   Amphetamine-related disorder NOS

CAFFEINE-RELATED DISORDERS

Caffeine-Induced Disorders
305.90   Caffeine intoxication
292.89   Caffeine-induced anxiety disorder[I]
292.89   Caffeine-induced sleep disorder[I]
292.9   Caffeine-related disorder NOS

CANNABIS-RELATED DISORDERS

Cannabis Use Disorders
304.30   Cannabis dependence[a]
305.20   Cannabis abuse

Cannabis-Induced Disorders
292.89   Cannabis intoxication
         Specify if: with perceptual disturbances
292.81   Cannabis intoxication delirium
292.xx   Cannabis-induced psychotic disorder
  .11   With delusions[I]
  .12   With hallucinations[I]
292.89   Cannabis-induced anxiety disorder[I]
292.9   Cannabis-related disorder NOS

COCAINE-RELATED DISORDERS

Cocaine Use Disorders
304.20   Cocaine dependence[a]
305.60   Cocaine abuse

Cocaine-Induced Disorders
292.89   Cocaine intoxication
         Specify if: with perceptual disturbances
292.0   Cocaine withdrawal
292.81   Cocaine intoxication delirium
292.xx   Cocaine-induced psychotic disorder
  .11   With delusions[I]
  .12   With hallucinations[I]
292.84   Cocaine-induced mood disorder[I,W]
292.89   Cocaine-induced anxiety disorder[I]
292.89   Cocaine-induced sexual dysfunction[I]
292.89   Cocaine-induced sleep disorder[I,W]
292.9   Cocaine-related disorder NOS

HALLUCINOGEN-RELATED DISORDERS

Hallucinogen Use Disorders
304.50   Hallucinogen dependence[a]
305.30   Hallucinogen abuse

Hallucinogen-Induced Disorders
292.89   Hallucinogen intoxication
292.89   Hallucinogen persisting perception disorder (flashbacks)
292.81   Hallucinogen intoxication delirium
292.xx   Hallucinogen-induced psychotic disorder
  .11   With delusions[I]
  .12   With hallucinations[I]
292.84   Hallucinogen-induced mood disorder[I]
292.89   Hallucinogen-induced anxiety disorder[I]
292.9   Hallucinogen-related disorder NOS

INHALANT-RELATED DISORDERS

Inhalant Use Disorders
304.60   Inhalant dependence[a]
305.90   Inhalant abuse

Inhalant-Induced Disorders
292.89   Inhalant intoxication
292.81   Inhalant intoxication delirium
292.82   Inhalant-induced persisting dementia
292.xx   Inhalant-induced psychotic disorder
  .11   With delusions[I]
  .12   With hallucinations[I]
292.84   Inhalant-induced mood disorder[I]
292.89   Inhalant-induced anxiety disorder[I]
292.9   Inhalant-related disorder NOS

NICOTINE-RELATED DISORDERS

Nicotine Use Disorders
305.10   Nicotine dependence[a]

Nicotine-Induced Disorder
292.0   Nicotine withdrawal
292.9   Nicotine-related disorder NOS

OPIOID-RELATED DISORDERS

Opioid Use Disorders
304.00   Opioid dependence[a]
305.50   Opioid abuse

Opioid-Induced Disorders
292.89   Opioid intoxication
         Specify if: with perceptual disturbances
292.0   Opioid withdrawal
292.81   Opioid intoxication delirium
292.xx   Opioid-induced psychotic disorder
  .11   With delusions[I]
  .12   With hallucinations[I]
292.84   Opioid-induced mood disorder[I]
292.89   Opioid-induced sexual dysfunction[I]
292.89   Opioid-induced sleep disorder[I,W]
292.9   Opioid-related disorder NOS

PHENCYCLIDINE (OR PHENCYCLIDINELIKE)- RELATED DISORDERS

Phencyclidine Use Disorders
304.90   Phencyclidine dependence[a]
305.90   Phencyclidine abuse

Phencyclidine-Induced Disorders
292.89   Phencyclidine intoxication
         Specify if: with perceptual disturbances
292.81   Phencyclidine intoxication delirium
292.xx   Phencyclidine-induced psychotic disorder
  .11   With delusions[I]
  .12   With hallucinations[I]
292.84   Phencyclidine-induced mood disorder[I]
292.89   Phencyclidine-induced anxiety disorder[I]
292.9   Phencyclidine-related disorder NOS

SEDATIVE-, HYPNOTIC-, OR ANXIOLYTIC- RELATED DISORDERS

Sedative, Hypnotic, or Anxiolytic Use Disorders
304.10   Sedative, hypnotic, or anxiolytic dependence[a]
305.40   Sedative, hypnotic, or anxiolytic abuse

Sedative-, Hypnotic-, or Anxiolytic-Induced Disorders
292.89   Sedative, hypnotic, or anxiolytic intoxication
292.0   Sedative, hypnotic, or anxiolytic withdrawal
         Specify if: with perceptual disturbances
292.81   Sedative, hypnotic, or anxiolytic intoxication delirium
292.81   Sedative, hypnotic, or anxiolytic withdrawal delirium
292.82   Sedative-, hypnotic-, or anxiolytic-induced persisting dementia
292.83   Sedative-, hypnotic-, or anxiolytic-induced persisting amnestic disorder
292.xx   Sedative-, hypnotic-, or anxiolytic-induced psychotic disorder
  .11   With delusions[I,W]
  .12   With hallucinations[I,W]
292.84   Sedative-, hypnotic-, or anxiolytic-induced mood disorder[I,W]
292.89   Sedative-, hypnotic-, or anxiolytic-induced anxiety disorder[W]

(continued)

Table 3-11. *(Continued)*

292.89 Sedative-, hypnotic-, or anxiolytic-induced sexual dysfunction[i]
292.89 Sedative-, hypnotic-, or anxiolytic-induced sleep disorder[i,W]
292.9   Sedative-, hypnotic-, or anxiolytic-related disorder NOS

POLYSUBSTANCE-RELATED DISORDER
304.80 Polysubstance dependence[a]

OTHER (OR UNKNOWN) SUBSTANCE-RELATED DISORDERS

Other (or Unknown) Substance Use Disorders
304.90 Other (or unknown) substance dependence[a]
305.90 Other (or unknown) substance abuse

Other (or unknown) Substance-Induced Disorders
292.89 Other (or unknown) substance intoxication
        Specify if: with perceptual disturbances
292.0   Other (or unknown) substance withdrawal
        Specify if: with perceptual disturbances
292.81 Other (or unknown) substance-induced delirium
292.82 Other (or unknown) substance-induced persisting dementia
292.83 Other (or unknown) substance-induced persisting amnestic disorder
292.xx Other (or unknown) substance-induced psychotic disorder
  .11   With delusions[i,W]
  .12   With hallucinations[i,W]
292.84 Other (or unknown) substance-induced mood disorder[i,W]
292.89 Other (or unknown) substance-induced anxiety disorder[i,W]
292.89 Other (or unknown) substance-induced sexual dysfunction[i]
292.89 Other (or unknown) substance-induced sleep disorder[i,W]
292.9   Other (or unknown substance-related disorder NOS)

Schizophrenia and Other Psychotic Disorders
295.xx Schizophrenia

The following classification of longitudinal course applies to all subtypes of schizophrenia:
Episodic with interepisode residual symptoms (*specify if:* with prominent negative symptoms)/episodic with no interepisode residual symptoms/continuous (*specify if:* with prominent negative symptoms)

Single episode in partial remission (*specify if:* with prominent negative symptoms)/single episode in full remission

Other or unspecified pattern
  .30   Paranoid type
  .10   Disorganized type
  .20   Catatonic type
  .90   Undifferentiated type
  .60   Residual type
295.40 Schizophreniform disorder
        Specify if: without good prognostic features/with good prognostic features
295.70 Schizoaffective disorder
        Specify type: bipolar type/depressive type

297.1   Delusional disorder
        Specify type: erotomanic type/grandiose type/jealous type/persecutory type/somatic type/mixed type/unspecified type
298.8   Brief psychotic disorder
        Specify if: with marked stressor(s)/without marked stressor(s)/with postpartum onset
297.3   Shared psychotic disorder
293.xx Psychotic disorder due to . . . *(indicate the general medical condition)*
  .81   With delusions
  .82   With hallucinations
_____   Substance-induced psychotic disorder *(refer to substance-related disorders for substance specific codes)*
        Specify if: with onset during intoxication/with onset during withdrawal
298.9   Psychotic disorder NOS

Mood Disorders
Code current state of major depressive disorder or bipolar I disorder in fifth digit:
1 = mild
2 = moderate
3 = Severe without psychotic features
4 = Severe with psychotic features
        Specify: mood-congruent psychotic features/mood-incongruent psychotic features
5 = in partial remission
6 = in full remission
0 = unspecified

The following specifiers apply (for current or most recent episode) to mood disorders as noted:

[a]Severity/psychotic remission specifiers/[b]chronic/[c]with catatonic features/[d]with melancholic features/[e]with atypical features/[f]with postpartum onset

The following specifiers apply to mood disorders as follows:

[g]With or without full interepisode recovery/[h]with seasonal pattern/[i]with rapid cycling

DEPRESSIVE DISORDERS
296.xx Major depressive disorder
  .2x   Single episode[a,b,c,d,e,f]
  .3x   Recurrent[a,b,c,d,e,f,g,h]
300.4   Dysthymic disorder
        Specify if: early onset/late onset
        Specify: with atypical features
311   Depressive disorder NOS

BIPOLAR DISORDERS
296.xx Bipolar I disorder
  .0x   Single manic episode[a,c,f]
          Specify if: mixed
  .40   Most recent episode hypomanic[g,h,i]
  .4x   Most recent episode manic[a,c,f,g,h,i]
  .6x   Most recent episode mixed[a,c,f,g,h,i]
  .5x   Most recent episode depressed[a,b,c,d,e,f,g,h,i]
  .7   Most recent episode unspecified[g,h,i]
296.89 Bipolar II disorder[a,b,c,d,e,f,g,h,i]
        Specify (current or most recent episode): hypomanic/depressed
301.13 Cyclothymic disorder
296.80 Bipolar disorder NOS

293.83 Mood disorder due to . . . *(indicate the general medical condition)*

        Specify type: with depressive features/with major depressivelike episode/with manic features/with mixed features
_____   Substance-induced mood disorder *(refer to substance-related disorders for substance-specific codes)*
        Specify type: with depressive features/with manic features/with mixed features
        Specify if: with onset during intoxication/with onset during withdrawal
296.90 Mood disorder NOS

Anxiety Disorders

300.1   Panic disorder without agoraphobia
300.21 Panic disorder with agoraphobia
300.22 Agoraphobia without history of panic disorder
300.29 Specific phobia
        Specify type: animal type/natural environment type/blood-injection-injury type/situational type/other type
300.23 Social phobia
        Specify if: generalized
300.3   Obsessive-compulsive disorder
        Specify if: with poor insight
309.81 Posttraumatic stress disorder
        Specify if: acute/chronic
        Specify if: with delayed onset
308.3   Acute stress disorder
300.02 Generalized anxiety disorder
293.89 Anxiety disorder due to . . . *(indicate the general medical condition)*
        Specify if: with generalized anxiety/with panic attacks/with obsessive-compulsive symptoms
_____   Substance-induced anxiety disorder *(refer to substance-related disorders for substance-specific codes)*
        Specify if: with generalized anxiety/with panic attacks/with obsessive-compulsive symptoms/with phobic symptoms
        Specify if: with onset during intoxication/with onset during withdrawal
300.00 Anxiety disorder NOS

Somatoform Disorders

300.81 Somatization disorder
300.81 Undifferentiated somatoform disorder
300.11 Conversion disorder
        Specify type: with motor symptom or deficit/with sensory symptom or deficit/with seizures or convulsions/with mixed presentation
307.xx Pain disorder
  .80   Associated with psychological factors
  .89   Associated with both psychological factors and a general medical condition
        Specify if: acute/chronic
300.7   Hypochondriasis
        Specify if: with poor insight
300.7   Body dysmorphic disorder
300.81 Somatoform disorder NOS

Table 3-11.   *(continued)*

Factitious Disorders

300.xx Factitious disorder
.16   With predominantly psychological signs and symptoms
.19   With predominantly physical signs and symptoms
.19   With combined psychological and physical signs and symptoms
300.19 Factitious disorder NOS

Dissociative Disorders

301.12 Dissociative amnesia
301.13 Dissociative fugue
301.14 Dissociative identity disorder
300.6   Depersonalization disorder
300.15 Dissociative disorder NOS

Sexual and Gender Identity Disorders

SEXUAL DYSFUNCTIONS
The following specifiers apply to all primary sexual dysfunctions:
Lifelong type/acquired type
Generalized type/situational type
Due to psychological factors/due to combined factors

Sexual Desire Disorders
302.71 Hypoactive sexual desire disorder
302.79 Sexual aversion disorder

Sexual Arousal Disorders
302.72 Female sexual arousal disorder
302.72 Male erectile disorder

Orgasmic Disorders
302.73 Female orgasmic disorder
302.74 Male orgasmic disorder
302.75 Premature ejaculation

Sexual Pain Disorders
302.76 Dyspareunia (not due to a general medical condition)
306.51 Vaginismus (not due to a general medical condition)

Sexual Dysfunction Due to a General Medical Condition
625.8   Female hypoactive sexual desire disorder due to . . . *(indicate the general medical condition)*
608.89 Male hypoactive sexual desire disorder due to . . . *(indicate the general medical condition)*
607.84 Male erectile disorder due to . . . *(indicate the general medical condition)*
625.0   Female dyspareunia due to . . . *(indicate the general medical condition)*
608.89 Male dyspareunia due to . . . *(indicate the general medical condition)*
625.8   Other female sexual dysfunction due to . . . *(indicate the general medical condition)*
608.89 Other male sexual dysfunction due to . . . *(indicate te general medical condition)*
_____ Substance-induced sexual dysfunction *(refer to substance-related disorders for substance-specific codes)*

Specify if: with impaired desire/with impaired arousal/with impaired orgasm/with sexual pain
Specify if: with onset during intoxication
302.70 Sexual dysfunction NOS

PARAPHILIAS
302.4   Exhibitionism
302.81 Fetishism
302.89 Frotteurism
302.2   Pedophilia
Specify if: Sexually attracted to males/sexually attracted to females/sexually attracted to both
Specify if: limited to incest
Specify type: exclusive type/nonexclusive type
302.83 Sexual masochism
302.84 Sexual sadism
302.3   Transvestic fetishism
Specify if: with gender dysphoria
302.82 Voyeurism
302.9   Paraphilia NOS

GENDER IDENTITY DISORDERS
302.xx Gender identity disorder
.6   in children
.85   in adolescents or adults
Specify if: sexually attracted to males/sexually attracted to females/sexually attracted to both/sexually attracted to neither
302.6   Gender identity disorder NOS

302.9   Sexual disorder NOS

Eating Disorders

307.1   Anorexia nervosa
Specify type: restricting type; binge-eating/purging type
307.51 Bulimia nervosa
Specify type: purging type/nonpurging type
307.50 Eating disorder NOS

Sleep Disorders

PRIMARY SLEEP DISORDERS

Dyssomnias
307.42 Primary insomnia
307.44 Primary hypersomnia
Specify if: recurrent
347   Narcolepsy
780.59 Breathing-related sleep disorder
307.45 Circadian rhythm sleep disorder
Specify type: delayed sleep phase type/jet lag type/shift work type/unspecified type
307.47 Dyssomnia NOS

Parasomnias
307.47 Nightmare disorder
307.46 Sleep terror disorder
307.46 Sleepwalking disorder
307.47 Parasomnia NOS

SLEEP DISORDERS RELATED TO ANOTHER MENTAL DISORDER
307.42 Insomnia related to . . . *(indicated the Axis I or Axis II disorder)*
307.44 Hypersomnia related to . . . *(indicate the Axis I or Axis II disorder)*

OTHER SLEEP DISORDERS
780.xx Sleep disorder due to . . . *(indicate the general medical condition)*
.52   Insomnia type
.54   Hypersomnia type
.59   Parasomnia type
.59   Mixed type
_____ Substance-induced sleep disorder *(refer to substance-related disorders for substance-specific codes)*
Specify type: insomnia type/hypersomnia type/parasomnia type/mixed type
Specify if: with onset during intoxication/with onset during withdrawal

Impulse-Control Disorders Not Elsewhere Classified

312.34 Intermittent explosive disorder
312.32 Kleptomania
312.33 Pyromania
312.31 Pathological gambling
312.39 Trichotillomania
312.30 Impulse-control disorder NOS

Adjustment Disorders

309.xx Adjustment disorder
.0   With depressed mood
.24   With anxiety
.28   With mixed anxiety and depressed mood
.3   With disturbance of conduct
.4   With mixed disturbance of emotions and conduct
.9   Unspecified
Specify if: acute/chronic

Personality Disorders

Note: These are coded on Axis II.
301.0   Paranoid personality disorder
301.20 Schizoid personality disorder
301.22 Schizotypal personality disorder
301.7   Antisocial personality disorder
301.83 Borderline personality disorder
301.50 Histrionic personality disorder
301.81 Narcissistic personality disorder
301.82 Avoidant personality disorder
301.6   Dependent personality disorder
301.4   Obsessive-compulsive personality disorder
301.9   Personality disorder NOS

Other Conditions That May Be a Focus of Clinical Attention

PSYCHOLOGICAL FACTORS AFFECTING MEDICAL CONDITION
316   . . . *(Specified psychological factor)* Affecting . . . *(indicate the general medical condition)*
Choose name based on nature of factors:
Mental disorder affecting medical condition
Psychological symptoms affecting medical condition
Personality traits or coping style affecting medical condition

(continued)

Table 3-11. *(continued)*

Maladaptive health behaviors affecting medical condition	V61.20 Parent-child relational problem	V62.3 Academic problem
Stress-related physiological response affecting medical condition	V61.1 Partner relational problem	V62.2 Occupational problem
	V61.8 Sibling relational problem	313.82 Identity problem
	V62.81 Relational problem NOS	V62.89 Religious or spiritual problem
Other or unspecified psychological factors affecting medical condition	**PROBLEMS RELATED TO ABUSE OR NEGLECT**	V62.4 Acculturation problem
	V61.21 Physical abuse of child *(code 995.5 if focus of attention is on victim)*	V62.89 Phase of life problem

MEDICATION-INDUCED MOVEMENT DISORDERS

332.1 Neuroleptic-induced parkinsonism	V61.21 Sexual abuse of child *(code 995.5 if focus of attention is on victim)*	**Additional Codes**
333.92 Neuroleptic malignant syndrome	V61.21 Neglect of child *(code 995.5 if focus of attention is on victim)*	
333.7 Neuroleptic-induced acute dystonia	V61.1 Physical abuse of adult *(code 995.81 if focus of attention is on victim)*	300.9 Unspecified mental disorder (nonpsychotic)
333.99 Neuroleptic-induced acute akathisia		V71.09 No diagnosis or condition on Axis I
333.82 Neuroleptic-induced tardive dyskinesia	V61.1 Sexual abuse of adult *(code 995.81 if focus of attention is on victim)*	799.9 Diagnosis or condition deferred on Axis I
333.1 Medication-induced postural tremor		V71.09 No diagnosis on Axis II
333.9 Medication-induced movement disorder NOS	**ADDITIONAL CONDITIONS THAT MAY BE A FOCUS OF CLINICAL ATTENTION**	799.9 Diagnosis deferred on Axis II
	V15.81 Noncompliance with treatment	
OTHER MEDICATION-INDUCED DISORDER	V65.2 Malingering	**Multiaxial System**
995.2 Adverse effects of medication NOS	V71.01 Adult antisocial behavior	
	V71.02 Child or adolescent antisocial behavior	Axis I Clinical disorders
RELATIONAL PROBLEMS	V62.89 Borderline intellectual functioning **Note:** *This is coded on Axis II.*	Other conditions that may be a focus of clinical attention
V61.9 Relational problem related to a mental disorder or general medical condition	780.9 Age-related cognitive decline	Axis II Personality disorders Mental retardation
	V62.82 Bereavement	Axis III General medical conditions
		Axis IV Psychosocial and environmental problems
		Axis V Global assessment of functioning

Table from DSM-IV, *Diagnostic and Statistical Manual of Mental Disorders,* ed 4. Copyright American Psychiatric Association, Washington, 1994. Used with permission.

chotic'' does not apply to minor distortions of reality that involve matters of relative judgment. For example, depressed persons who underestimate their achievements are not described as psychotic, whereas those who believe that they have caused natural catastrophes are so described.

Direct evidence of psychotic behavior is the presence of either delusions or hallucinations without insight into their pathological nature. The term ''psychotic'' is sometimes appropriate when behavior is so grossly disorganized that a reasonable inference can be made that reality testing is disturbed. Examples include markedly incoherent speech without apparent awareness by the person that the speech is not understandable and the agitated, inattentive, and disoriented behavior seen in alcohol intoxication delirium. A person with a nonpsychotic mental disorder may exhibit psychotic behavior, although rarely. For example, a person with obsessive-compulsive disorder may at times come to believe in the reality of the danger of being contaminated by shaking hands with strangers. In DSM-IV the psychotic disorders include schizophrenia, schizophreniform disorder, schizoaffective disorder, delusional disorder, brief psychotic disorder, shared psychotic disorder, psychotic disorder due to a general medical condition, substance-induced psychotic disorder, and psychotic disorder not otherwise specified. In addition, some severe mood disorders have psychotic features.

Neurosis

A neurosis is a chronic or recurrent nonpsychotic disorder characterized mainly by anxiety, which is experienced or expressed directly or is altered through defense mechanisms; it appears as a symptom, such as an obsession, a compulsion, a phobia, or a sexual dysfunction. Although not used in DSM-IV, the term ''neurosis'' is still found in the literature and in ICD-10. In the third edition of DSM (DSM-III), a neurotic disorder was defined as follows:

A mental disorder in which the predominant disturbance is a symptom or group of symptoms that is distressing to the individual and is recognized by him or her as unacceptable and alien (ego-dystonic); reality testing is grossly intact. Behavior does not actively violate gross social norms (though it may be quite disabling). The disturbance is relatively enduring or recurrent without treatment, and is not limited to a transitory reaction to stressors. There is no demonstrable organic etiology or factor.

DSM-IV contains no overall diagnostic class called ''neuroses''; however, many clinicians consider the following diagnostic categories neuroses: anxiety disorders, somatoform disorders, dissociative disorders, sexual disorders, and dysthymic disorder. The term ''neuroses'' encompasses a broad range of disorders of various signs and symptoms. As such, it has lost any degree of precision except to signify that the person's gross reality testing and personality organization are intact. However, a neurosis can be and usually is sufficient to impair the person's functioning in a number of areas. The authors believe that the term is useful in contemporary psychiatry and should be retained.

ICD-10

In ICD-10 a class called neurotic, stress-related, and somatoform disorders encompasses the following: phobic anxiety disorders, other anxiety disorders (including panic disorder, generalized anxiety disorder, and mixed anxiety and depressive disorder), obsessive-compulsive disorder, adjustment disorders, dissociative (conversion) disorders, and somatoform disorders. In addition, ICD-10 includes neurasthenia as a neurotic disorder characterized by mental and physical fatigability, a sense of

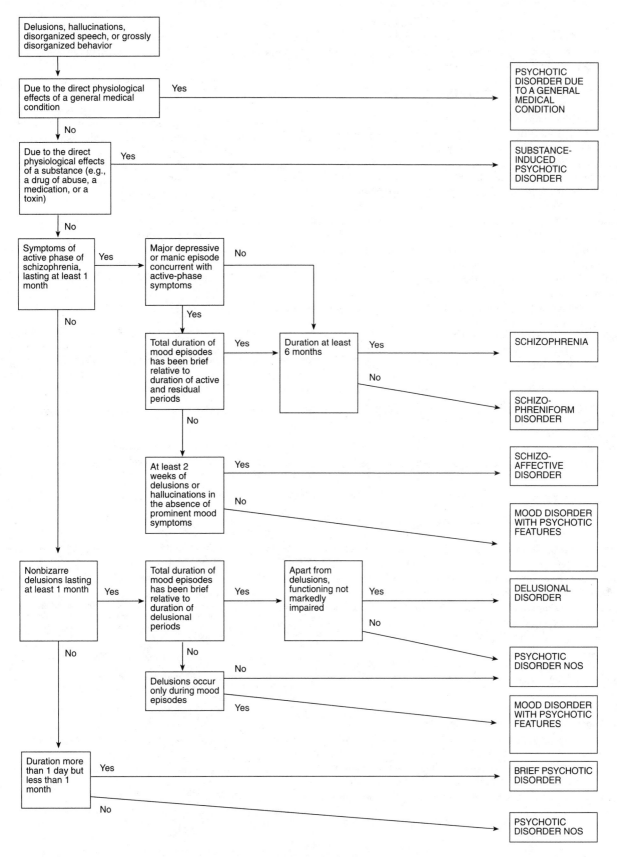

Figure 3-1. Differential diagnosis of psychotic disorders. (Figure from DSM-IV, *Diagnostic and Statistical Manual of Mental Disorders,* ed 4. Copyright American Psychiatric Association, Washington, 1994. Used with permission.)

general instability, irritability, anhedonia, and sleep disturbances. Many of the cases so diagnosed outside the United
States fit the descriptions of anxiety disorders and depressive
disorders and are diagnosed as such by American psychiatrists.

PSYCHIATRIC RATING SCALES

Psychiatric rating scales, also called rating instruments, provide a way to quantify aspects of a patient's psyche, behavior,
and relationships with individuals and society. The measurement of pathology in those areas of a person's life may initially
seem to be much less straightforward than the measurement of
pathology—hypertension, for example—seen by other medical
specialists. Nevertheless, many psychiatric rating scales can
measure carefully chosen features of well-formulated concepts.
Moreover, psychiatrists who do not use those rating scales are
left with only their clinical impressions, which are difficult to
record in a manner that allows for reliable comparison and communication in the future. Without psychiatric rating scales,
quantitative data in psychiatry are crude (for example, length
of hospitalization or other treatment, discharge and readmission
to hospital, length to relationships or employment, and the presence of legal troubles).

Characteristics of Rating Scales

Rating scales can be specific or comprehensive, and they
can measure both internally experienced variables (for example,
mood) and externally observable variables (for example, behavior). Specific scales measure discrete thoughts, moods, or behaviors, such as obsessive thoughts and temper tantrums; comprehensive scales measure broad abstractions, such as
depression and anxiety.

SIGNS AND SYMPTOMS

Classic items from the mental status examination are the
most frequently assessed items on rating scales. Those items
include thought disorders, mood disturbances, and gross behaviors. Another type of information covered by rating scales is
the assessment of adverse effects from psychotherapeutic drugs.
Social adjustments (for example, occupational success and quality of relationships) and psychoanalytic concepts (for example,
ego strength and defense mechanisms) are also measured by
some rating scales, although the reliability and the validity of
such scales are lowered by the absence of agreed-on norms, the
high level of inference required on some items, and the lack of
independence between measures.

OTHER CHARACTERISTICS

Other characteristics of rating scales include the time period
covered, the level of judgment required, and the method of
recording the answers. The time period covered by a rating scale
must be specified, and the rater must adhere to that time period.
For example, a particular rating scale may rate a five-minute
observation period, a week-long period of time, or the entire
life of the patient.

The most reliable rating scales require a limited amount of
judgment or inference on the part of the rater. Whatever the
level of judgment required, clear definitions of the answer scale,
preferably with clinical examples, should be provided by the
developer of the scale and should be read by the rater.

The actual answer given may be recorded as either a dichotomous variable (for example, true or false, present or absent) or
a continuous variable. Continuous items may ask the rater to
choose a term to describe severity (absent, slight, mild, moderate, severe, or extreme) or frequency (never, rarely, occasionally, often, very often, or always). Although many psychiatric
symptoms are thought of as existing in dichotomous states—for
example, the presence or the absence of delusions—most experienced clinicians know that the world is not that simple.

Rating Scales Used in DSM-IV

Rating scales form an integral part of DSM-IV. The rating
scales used are broad and measure the overall severity of the
patient's illness.

GAF SCALE

Axis V in DSM-IV uses the Global Assessment of Functioning (GAF) Scale (see Table 3–7). That axis is used for reporting
the clinician's judgment of the patient's overall level of functioning. The information is used to decide on a treatment plan
and later to measure the plan's effect.

SOCIAL AND OCCUPATIONAL FUNCTIONING ASSESSMENT SCALE

This scale can be used to track the patient's progress in social
and occupational areas. It is independent of the psychiatric diagnosis and of the severity of the patient's psychological symptoms.

OTHER SCALES

Two other scales in DSM-IV that may be useful are the
Global Assessment of Relational Functioning (GARF) Scale
and the Defensive Functioning Scale.

References

American Psychiatric Association: *Diagnostic and Statistical Manual of Mental Disorders*, ed 4. American Psychiatric Association, Washington, 1994.

Mezzich J E: International perspectives on psychiatric diagnosis. In *Comprehensive Textbook of Psychiatry*, ed 6, H I Kaplan, B J Sadock, editors, p 692. Williams & Wilkins, Baltimore, 1995.

Ormel J, Oldehinkel A J, Goldberg D P, Hodiamont P P, Wilmink F W, Bridges K: The structure of common psychiatric symptoms: How many dimensions of neurosis? Psychol Med *25*: 521, 1995.

Sadock B J, Kaplan H I: Classification of mental disorders. In *Comprehensive Textbook of Psychiatry*, ed 6, H I Kaplan, B J Sadock, editors, p 671. Williams & Wilkins, Baltimore, 1995.

Wilson M: DSM-III and the transformation of American psychiatry: A history. Am J Psychiatry *150*: 399, 1993.

World Health Organization: *The ICD-10 Classification of Mental and Behavioral Disorders: Clinical Descriptions and Diagnostic Guidelines*. World Health Organization, Geneva, 1992.

World Health Organization: *The ICD-10 Classification of Mental and Behavioral Disorders: Diagnostic Criteria for Research*. World Health Organization, Geneva, 1993.

Zarin D A, Earls F: Diagnostic decision making in psychiatry. Am J Psychiatry *150*: 197, 1993.

Zimmerman M: Is DSM-IV needed at all? Am J Psychiatry *147*: 974, 1990.

4/ Delirium, Dementia, and Amnestic and Other Cognitive Disorders and Mental Disorders Due to a General Medical Condition

4.1 OVERVIEW

ORGANIC VERSUS FUNCTIONAL DISORDERS

Traditionally, *organic brain disorders* have been defined as disorders for which there is an identifiable cause (for example, brain tumor, cerebrovascular disease, drug intoxication). Those brain disorders for which there is no generally accepted organic basis (for example, schizophrenia, depression) have been called *functional disorders*. Historically, the field of neurology has been associated with the treatment of the so-called organic disorders, and psychiatry has been associated with the treatment of the so-called functional disorders.

The authors of the fourth edition of the *Diagnostic and Statistical Manual of Mental Disorders* (DSM-IV) have decided that the century-old distinction between organic disorders and functional disorders is outdated enough to be dropped from the nomenclature. The medical, neurological, and psychiatric journals, as well as this and other textbooks, are filled with reports and data about the organic basis of the major psychiatric disorders. Any unbiased evaluation of the available data would conclude that every psychiatric disorder has an organic (that is, biological) component. Because of that assessment of the data, the concept of functional disorders has been determined to be misleading, and both the term "functional" and its historical opposite, "organic," are dropped from DSM-IV.

STRUCTURAL VERSUS FUNCTIONAL DISORDERS

The other context in which the term "functional" is used is in basic science, in which functional abnormalities are contrasted with structural abnormalities. That distinction is also antiquated, since basic neuroscience can now identify structural correlates of functional abnormalities at the level of genes and other molecules. The division between structural and functional rests solely on which biological level is arbitrarily chosen as the cutoff point. An accurate approach is to accept the idea that each biological disorder, including mental illness, has a structural pathology at some level or assortment of levels and that the structural abnormality is reflected as a disorder of function or regulation.

COGNITIVE DISORDERS

DSM-IV classifies three groups of disorders—delirium, dementia, and the amnestic disorders—into a broad category that acknowledges the primary symptoms common to all the disorders—that is, an impairment in cognition (for example, memory, language, or attention). Although DSM-IV acknowledges that other psychiatric disorders can include a degree of cognitive impairment as a symptom, cognitive impairment is the cardinal symptom in delirium, dementia, and the amnestic disorders. Within each of those diagnostic categories, DSM-IV delimits specific types.

For each of the three major categories (delirium, dementia, and amnestic disorders), there are subcategories for disorders caused by (1) general medical conditions, (2) substance use, and (3) causes not otherwise specified (NOS). For delirium and dementia, DSM-IV includes a diagnostic category for multiple causes, which is a commonly encountered clinical situation. For dementia, DSM-IV includes seven general medical conditions as diagnostic possibilities.

Evaluation of Cognitive Impairment

Although formal evaluation of cognitive impairment requires time-consuming consultation with an expert in psychological testing, one practical and clinically useful test for the practitioner is the Mini-Mental State Examination (MMSE) (Table 4.1–1). The MMSE is a screening test that can be used during the clinical examination of a patient. It is also a practical test to track how a patient's cognitive state changes with time. Out of a possible 30 points, a score of less than 25 suggests impairment, and a score of less than 20 indicates definite impairment.

Cognitive Disorder Not Otherwise Specified

DSM-IV allows for the diagnosis of cognitive disorders that do not fit into the other categories available. Those disorders fit into the not otherwise specified (NOS) category (Table 4.1–2). Patients with syndromes of cognitive impairment that do not meet the criteria for delirium, dementia, or amnestic disorders are classified with the NOS category. The causes of those syndromes are presumed to involve a specific general medical condition, a pharmacologically active agent, or possibly both.

MENTAL DISORDERS DUE TO A GENERAL MEDICAL CONDITION

DSM-IV introduces two major changes to the nomenclature. First, DSM-IV drops the term "organic" and substitutes the phrase "due to a general medical condition." Second, the psychiatric disorders due to general medical condition are now included within the DSM-IV diagnostic categories that contain other disorders with the same primary symptom. For example anxiety disorder due to a general medical condition is now included within the anxiety disorders section of DSM-IV. The inclusion of the secondary psychiatric disorder within the general anxiety disorders section is meant to facilitate a clinician's formulation regarding the differential diagnosis of patients who present with a particular system. Delirium, dementia, or amnesia due to a general medical condition is contained in the diagnostic section on delirium, dementia, and amnestic and other cognitive disorders.

The use of the phrase "due to a general medical condition" requires some clarification. The term is meant to convey the clinician's opinion that a particular psychiatric symptom (for example, depression) is probably primarily related to a specific

Table 4.1–1. Mini-Mental State Examination (MMSE) Questionnaire

Orientation (score 1 if correct)

Name this hospital or building. _____

What city are you in now? _____

What year is it? _____

What month is it? _____

What is the date today? _____

What state are you in? _____

What county is this? _____

What floor of the building are you on? _____

What day of the week is it? _____

What season of the year is it? _____

Registration

Name three objects and have the patient repeat them. Score number repeated by the patient. Name the three objects several more times if needed for the patient to repeat correctly (record trials ___) _____

Attention and calculation

Subtract 7 from 100 in serial fashion to 65. Maximum score = 5 _____

Recall

Do you recall the three objects named before? _____

Language tests

Confrontation naming: watch, pen = 2 _____

Repetition: ``No ifs, ands, or buts'' = 1 _____

Comprehension: Pick up the paper in your right hand, fold it in half, and set it on the floor = 3 _____

Read and perform the command ``close your eyes'' = 1 _____

Write any sentence (subject, verb, object) = 1 _____

Construction

Copy the design below = 1 _____

Total MMSE questionnaire score (maximum) = 30 _____

Table adapted from M F Folstein, S Folstein, P R McHugh: Mini-mental state: A practical method for grading the cognitive state of patients for the clinician. J. Psychiatr Res *12*: 189, 1975. Used with permission.

---

nonpsychiatric disorder (for example, pancreatic cancer), and the DSM-IV-defined disorder (for example, mood disorder due to pancreatic cancer with depressive features) is a distinct diagnosis that requires its own treatment plan. The phrase ``due to a general medical condition'' does not imply a specific temporal relation to the associated nonpsychiatric condition. In the above example, depression associated with pancreatic cancer may be the presenting complaint and, thus, may be identified before the pancreatic cancer is diagnosed. The use of the phrase ``due to a general medical condition'' can perhaps be criticized as being overly simplistic, since it disregards the other variables that may affect the appearance of a psychiatric symptom in association with a general medical condition. Such other variables may include other biological factors (for example, a genetic diathesis to depression), psychosocial problems, prescribed or illicit drug use, and psychological stressors. Realistically, any diagnostic nosological system must reduce the available information somewhat, and the intent of DSM-IV is to highlight the principal causative factor involved.

Table 4.1–2. Diagnostic Criteria for Cognitive Disorder Not Otherwise Specified

This category is for disorders that are characterized by cognitive dysfunction presumed to be due to the direct physiological effect of a general medical condition that do not meet criteria for any of the specific deliriums, dementias, or amnestic disorders listed in this section and that are not better classified as delirium not otherwise specified, dementia not otherwise specified, or amnestic disorder not otherwise specified. For cognitive dysfunction due to a specific or unknown substance, the specific substance-related disorder not otherwise specified category should be used.

Examples include

1. Mild neurocognitive disorder: impairment in cognitive functioning as evidenced by neuropsychological testing or quantified clinical assessment, accompanied by objective evidence of a systemic general medical condition or central nervous system dysfunction
2. Postconcussional disorder: following a head trauma, impairment in memory or attention with associated symptoms

Table from DSM-IV, *Diagnostic and Statistical Manual of Mental Disorders*, ed 4. Copyright American Psychiatric Association, Washington, 1994. Used with permission.

Within DSM-IV, most mental disorders due to a general medical condition are listed with other diagnoses for the major symptom, including psychotic disorder due to a general medical condition, mood disorder due to a general medical condition, anxiety disorder due to a general medical condition, sexual dysfunction due to a general medical condition, and sleep disorder due to a general medical condition. The three disorders listed in the DSM-IV section called mental disorders due to a general medical condition not elsewhere classified are catatonic disorder due to a general medical condition, personality change due to a general medical condition, and mental disorder not otherwise specified due to a general medical condition.

References

Caine E D: Should age-associated cognitive decline be included in DSM-IV? J Neuropsychiatry Clin Neurosci *5*: 1, 1993.

Caine E D: Delirium, dementia, and amnestic and other cognitive disorders and mental disorders due to a general medical condition. In *Comprehensive Textbook of Psychiatry*, ed 6, H I Kaplan, B J Sadock, editors, p 705. Williams & Wilkins, Baltimore, 1995.

Lipowski Z J: Is ``organic'' obsolete? Psychosomatics *31*: 342, 1990.

Spitzer R L, First M B, Williams J B W, Kendler K, Pincus H A, Tucker G: Now is the time to retire the term ``organic mental disorders.'' Am J Psychiatry *149*: 240, 1992.

Spitzer R L, Williams J B W, First M B, Kendler K S: A proposal for DSM-IV: Solving the ``organic/nonorganic problem.'' J Neuropsychiatry *147*: 947, 1990.

Sullivan M D: Organic or functional? Why psychiatry needs a philosophy of mind. Psychiatr Ann *20*: 271, 1990.

4.2 DELIRIUM

The hallmark symptom of delirium is an impairment of consciousness, usually seen in association with global impairments of cognitive functions. Abnormalities of mood, perception, and behavior are common psychiatric symptoms; tremor, asterixis, nystagmus, incoordination, and urinary incontinence are common neurological symptoms. Classically, delirium has a sudden onset (hours or days), a brief and fluctuating course, and a rapid improvement when the causative factor is identified and eliminated. However, each of those characteristic features can vary in individual patients.

Delirium is a syndrome, not a disease. Delirium is acknowledged to have many causes, all of which result in a similar pattern of symptoms relating to the patient's level of consciousness and cognitive impairment. Most of the causes of delirium lie outside the central nervous system—for example, renal or hepatic failure.

Delirium remains an underrecognized and underdiagnosed clinical disorder. Part of the problem is that the syndrome is called a wide variety of other names—for example, acute confusional state, acute brain syndrome, metabolic encephalopathy, toxic psychosis, and acute brain failure. The intent of *Diagnostic and Statistical Manual of Mental Disorders* in its third edition (DSM-III), revised third edition (DSM-III-R), and fourth edition (DSM-IV) has been to help consolidate the myriad terms into a single diagnostic label.

The importance of recognizing delirium involves (1) the clinical need to identify and treat the underlying cause and (2) the need to avert the development of delirium-related complications. Such complications include accidental injury because of the patient's clouded consciousness or impaired coordination or the unnecessary use of restraints. The disruption of ward routine is an especially troubling problem on nonpsychiatric units, such as intensive care units and general medical and surgical wards.

EPIDEMIOLOGY

Delirium is a common disorder. About 10 to 15 percent of patients on general surgical wards and 15 to 25 percent of patients on general medical wards experience delirium during their hospital stays. About 30 percent of patients in surgical intensive care units and cardiac intensive care units and 40 to 50 percent of patients who are recovering from surgery for hip fractures have an episode of delirium. An estimated 20 percent of patients with severe burns and 30 percent of patients with acquired immune deficiency syndrome (AIDS) have episodes of delirium while hospitalized. The causes of *postoperative delirium* include the stress of surgery, postoperative pain, insomnia, pain medication, electrolyte imbalances, infection, fever, and blood loss.

Advanced age is a major risk factor for the development of delirium. About 30 to 40 percent of hospitalized patients more than 65 years old have an episode of delirium. Other predisposing factors for the development of delirium are young age (that is, children), preexisting brain damage (for example, dementia, cerebrovascular disease, tumor), a history of delirium, alcohol dependence, diabetes, cancer, sensory impairment (for example, blindness), and malnutrition.

The presence of delirium is a bad prognostic sign. The three-month mortality rate of patients who have an episode of delirium is estimated to be 23 to 33 percent. The one-year mortality rate for patients who have an episode of delirium may be as high as 50 percent.

ETIOLOGY

The major causes of delirium are central nervous system disease (for example, epilepsy), systemic disease (for example, cardiac failure), and either intoxication or withdrawal from pharmacological or toxic agents. When evaluating a delirious patient, the clinician should assume that any drug the patient has taken may be causatively relevant to the delirium.

The major neurotransmitter hypothesized to be involved in delirium is acetylcholine, and the major neuroanatomical area is the reticular formation. Several types of studies have reported that a variety of delirium-inducing factors result in decreased acetylcholine activity in the brain. Also, one of the most common causes of delirium is toxicity from too many prescribed medications that have anticholinergic activity. In addition to the anticholinergic drugs themselves, amitriptyline (Elavil), doxepin (Sinequan), nortriptyline (Aventyl), imipramine (Tofranil), thioridazine (Mellaril), and chlorpromazine (Thorazine) are among the most anticholinergic drugs used in psychiatry. The reticular formation of the brainstem is the principal area regulating attention and arousal, and the major pathway implicated in delirium is the dorsal tegmental pathway, which projects from the mesencephalic reticular formation to the tectum and the thalamus.

Other pathophysiological mechanisms have been suggested for delirium. In particular, the delirium associated with alcohol withdrawal has been associated with hyperactivity of the locus ceruleus and its noradrenergic neurons. Other neurotransmitters that have been implicated are serotonin and glutamate.

Lithium-Induced Delirium

Patients with lithium serum concentrations greater than 1.5 mEq per L are at risk for delirium. The onset of delirium in those patients may be heralded by general lethargy, stammering, stuttering, and muscle fasciculations that develop over the course of several days to a week. Lithium-induced delirium may take up to two weeks to resolve even after lithium administration has been stopped. The appearance of seizures and episodes of stupor during recovery is common. The primary treatments, in addition to stopping lithium administration, are supportive treatment, maintenance of the patient's electrolyte balance, and facilitation of lithium excretion. Proximal segment-acting drugs (for example, aminophylline, acetazolamide [Diamox]) are more effective than distal tubule-acting drugs. The most effective way to eliminate lithium from the patient's body is hemodialysis, especially if the hemodialysis is done early in the course of disorder.

DIAGNOSIS

DSM-IV strives to group all the causes of delirium under one section. Thus, delirium due to a general medical condition (Table 4.2–1), substance intoxication delirium (Table 4.2–2),

---

Table 4.2-1.   Diagnostic Criteria for Delirium Due to a General Medical Condition

A. Disturbance of consciousness (i.e., reduced clarity of awareness of the environment) with reduced ability to focus, sustain, or shift attention.

B. A change in cognition (such as memory deficit, disorientation, language disturbance) or the development of a perceptual disturbance that is not better accounted for by a preexisting, established, or evolving dementia.

C. The disturbance develops over a short period of time (usually hours to days) and tends to fluctuate during the course of the day.

D. There is evidence from the history, physical examination, or laboratory findings that the disturbance is caused by the direct physiological consequences of a general medical condition.

Table from DSM-IV, *Diagnostic and Statistical Manual of Mental Disorders*, ed 4. Copyright American Psychiatric Association, Washington, 1994. Used with permission.

Table 4.2–2.   Diagnostic Criteria for Substance Intoxication Delirium

A. Disturbance of consciousness (i.e., reduced clarity of awareness of the environment) with reduced ability to focus, sustain, or shift attention.

B. A change in cognition (such as memory deficit, disorientation, language disturbance) or the development of a perceptual disturbance that is not better accounted for by a preexisting, established, or evolving dementia.

C. The disturbance develops over a short period of time (usually hours to days) and tends to fluctuate during the course of the day.

D. There is evidence from the history, physical examination, or laboratory findings of either (1) or (2):

   (1) the symptoms in criteria A and B developed during substance intoxication
   (2) medication use is etiologically related to the disturbance

Table from DSM-IV, *Diagnostic and Statistical Manual of Mental Disorders*, ed 4. Copyright American Psychiatric Association, Washington, 1994. Used with permission.

Table 4.2–3.   Diagnostic Criteria for Substance Withdrawal Delirium

A. Disturbance of consciousness (i.e., reduced clarity of awareness of the environment) with reduced ability to focus, sustain, or shift attention.

B. A change in cognition (such as memory deficit, disorientation, language disturbance) or the development of a perceptual disturbance that is not better accounted for by a preexisting, established, or evolving dementia.

C. The disturbance develops over a short period of time (usually hours to days) and tends to fluctuate during the course of the day.

D. There is evidence from the history, physical examination, or laboratory findings that the symptoms in criteria A and B developed during, or shortly after, a withdrawal syndrome.

Table from DSM-IV, *Diagnostic and Statistical Manual of Mental Disorders*, ed 4. Copyright American Psychiatric Association, Washington, 1994. Used with permission.

Table 4.2–4.   Diagnostic Criteria for Delirium Due to Multiple Etiologies

A. Disturbance of consciousness (i.e., reduced clarity of awareness of the environment) with reduced ability to focus, sustain, or shift attention.

B. A change in cognition (such as memory deficit, disorientation, language disturbance) or the development of a perceptual disturbance that is not better accounted for by a preexisting, established, or evolving dementia.

C. The disturbance develops over a short period of time (usually hours to days) and tends to fluctuate during the course of the day.

D. There is evidence from the history, physical examination, or laboratory findings that the delirium has more than one etiology (e.g., more than one etiological general medical condition, a general medical condition plus substance intoxication or medication side effect).

Table from DSM-IV, *Diagnostic and Statistical Manual of Mental Disorders*, ed 4. Copyright American Psychiatric Association, Washington, 1994. Used with permission.

substance withdrawal delirium (Table 4.2–3), and delirium due to multiple etiologies (Table 4.2–4) are included in the section on delirium. A diagnostic category of delirium not otherwise specified (NOS) is included for states of delirium due to causes not included in the other categories. DSM-IV gives delirium related to sensory deprivation as an example of such a situation.

Physical and Laboratory Examination

Delirium is usually diagnosed at the bedside and is characterized by the sudden onset of symptoms. The use of a bedside mental status examination—such as the Mini-Mental State Examination (MMSE), the Mental Status Examination, or the Face-Hand Test can be useful in documenting the cognitive impairment and providing a baseline from which to measure the patient's clinical course. The physical examination often reveals clues to the cause of the delirium. The presence of a known physical illness or a history of head trauma or alcohol or other substance dependence increases the likelihood of the diagnosis.

The laboratory workup of a patient with delirium should include standard tests and additional studies indicated by the clinical situation. The electroencephalogram (EEG) in delirium characteristically shows a generalized slowing of activity and may be useful in differentiating delirium from depression or psychosis. The EEG of a delirious patient sometimes shows focal areas of hyperactivity. In rare cases, it may be difficult to differentiate delirium related to epilepsy from delirium related to other causes.

CLINICAL FEATURES

The key feature of delirium is an impairment of consciousness, which DSM-IV describes as being a ''reduced clarity of awareness of the environment,'' with reduced ability to focus, sustain, or shift attention. Indeed, some investigators have suggested that the inability of delirious patients to maintain attention is the central feature of delirium. Most commonly, the impairment of consciousness and the inability to attend fluctuate over the course of a day, such that relatively lucid periods alternate with symptomatic periods. The delirious state may be preceded over a few days by the development of anxiety, drowsiness, insomnia, transient hallucinations, nightmares, and restlessness. The appearance of those symptoms in a patient who is at risk for delirium should prompt the clinician to monitor the patient carefully. Moreover, patients who have had a prior episode of delirium are likely to have a recurrent episode under the same conditions.

Arousal

Two general patterns of abnormal arousal have been noted in patients with delirium. One pattern is characterized by hyperactivity associated with increased alertness. The other pattern is characterized by hypoactivity associated with decreased alertness. Patients with delirium related to substance withdrawal often have the hyperactive delirium, which can also be associated with autonomic signs, such as a flushing, pallor, sweating, tachycardia, dilated pupils, nausea, vomiting, and hyperthermia. Patients with the hypoactive symptoms are occasionally classified as being depressed, catatonic, or demented. Patients with a mixed symptom pattern of hypoactivity and hyperactivity are also seen in clinical settings.

Orientation

Orientation to time, place, and person should be tested in a patient with delirium. Orientation to time is commonly lost, even in mild cases of delirium. Orientation to place and the ability to recognize other persons (for example, the doctor, family members) may also be impaired in severe cases. A delirious patient rarely loses orientation to self.

Language and Cognition

Patients with delirium often have abnormalities in language. The abnormalities may include rambling, irrelevant, or incoherent speech, and an impaired ability to comprehend speech. However, DSM-IV no longer requires the presence of an abnormality of language for diagnosis, since such an abnormality may be impossible to diagnosis in a mute patient.

Other cognitive functions that may be impaired in a delirious patient include memory and generalized cognitive functions. The ability to register, retain, and recall memories may be impaired, although the recall of remote memories may be preserved. In addition to decreased attention, patients may have a dramatically decreased cognitive output as a characteristic of the hypoactive symptoms of delirium. Delirious patients also have impaired problem-solving abilities and may also have unsystematized, often paranoid, delusions.

Perception

Patients with delirium often have a generalized inability to discriminate sensory stimuli and to integrate present perceptions with their past experiences. Therefore, patients are often distracted by irrelevant stimuli or become agitated when presented with new information. Hallucinations are also relatively common in delirious patients. The hallucinations are most often visual or auditory, although they can also be tactile or olfactory. The visual hallucinations can range from simple geometric figures or colored patterns to fully formed people and scenes. Visual and auditory illusions are often common in delirium.

Mood

Patients with delirium often have abnormalities in the regulation of mood. The most common symptoms are anger, rage, and unwarranted fear. Other abnormalities of mood seen in patients are apathy, depression, and euphoria. Some patients rapidly alternate among those emotions within the course of a day.

Associated Symptoms

SLEEP-WAKE DISTURBANCES

The sleep of delirious patients is characteristically disturbed. Patients are often drowsy during the day and can be found napping in their beds or in the dayrooms. The sleep of delirious patients, however, is almost always short and fragmented. Sometimes the entire sleep-wake cycle of patients with delirium is simply reversed. Patients sometimes have an exacerbation of delirious symptoms just about bedtime, a clinical situation widely known as *sundowning*. Occasionally, the nightmares and the disturbing dreams of delirious patients continue into wakefulness as hallucinatory experiences.

NEUROLOGICAL SYMPTOMS

Patients with delirium commonly have associated neurological symptoms, including dysphasia, tremor, asterixis, incoordination, and urinary incontinence. Focal neurological signs an

also be seen as part of the symptom pattern of patients with delirium.

DIFFERENTIAL DIAGNOSIS

Delirium versus Dementia

It is necessary to distinguish delirium from dementia, and a number of clinical features help in the differentiation. In contrast to the sudden onset of delirium, the onset of dementia is usually insidious. Although both conditions include cognitive impairment, the changes in dementia are more stable over time and do not fluctuate over the course of a day, for example. A patient with dementia is usually alert; a patient with delirium has episodes of decreased consciousness. Occasionally, delirium occurs in a patient suffering from dementia, a condition known as *beclouded dementia*. A diagnosis of delirium can be made when there is a definite history of preexisting dementia.

Delirium versus Psychosis or Depression

Delirium must also be differentiated from schizophrenia and depressive disorder. Patients with factitious disorders may attempt to simulate the symptoms of delirium; however, they usually reveal the factitious nature of their symptoms by inconsistencies on their mental status examinations, and an EEG can easily separate the two diagnoses. Some patients with psychotic disorders, usually schizophrenia, or manic episodes may have episodes of extremely disorganized behavior that may be difficult to distinguish from delirium. In general, however, the hallucinations and the delusions of schizophrenic patients are more constant and better organized than are those of delirious patient. Also, schizophrenic patients usually experience no change in their level of consciousness or orientation. Patients with hypoactive symptoms of delirium may appear somewhat similar to severely depressed patients but can be distinguished on the basis of an EEG. Other psychiatric diagnoses to consider in the differential diagnosis of delirium are brief psychotic disorder, schizophreniform disorder, and dissociative disorders.

COURSE AND PROGNOSIS

Although the onset of delirium is usually sudden, prodromal symptoms (for example, restlessness and fearfulness) may occur in the days preceding the onset of florid symptoms. The symptoms of delirium usually last as long as the causally relevant factors are present, although delirium generally lasts less than a week. After the identification and the removal of the causative factors, the symptoms of delirium usually recede over a three- to seven-day period, although some symptoms may take up to two weeks to resolve completely. The older a patient is and the longer the patient has been delirious, the longer it takes for the delirium to resolve. Recall of what transpired during a delirium, once it is over, is characteristically spotty, and the patient may refer to it as a bad dream or a nightmare that is remembered only vaguely. As mentioned in the discussion on epidemiology, the occurrence of delirium is associated with a high mortality rate in the next year, primarily because of the serious nature of the associated medical conditions that lead to delirium.

Whether delirium progresses to dementia has not been demonstrated in carefully controlled studies, although many clinicians believe they have seen such a progression. A clinical observation that has been validated by some studies, however, is that periods of delirium are sometimes followed by depression or posttraumatic stress disorder.

TREATMENT

The primary goal is to treat the underlying condition that is causing the delirium. When the condition is anticholinergic toxicity, the use of physostigmine salicylate (Antilirium) 1 to 2 mg intravenously (IV) or intramuscularly (IM), with repeated doses in 15 to 30 minutes, may be indicated. The other important goal of treatment is the provision of physical, sensory, and environmental support. Physical support is necessary so that delirious patients do not get into situations in which they may have accidents. Patients with delirium should be neither sensory-deprived nor overly stimulated by the environment. Usually, delirious patients are helped by having a friend or a relative in the room or by the presence of a regular sitter. Familiar pictures and decorations, the presence of a clock or a calendar, and regular orientations to person, place, and time help delirious patients be comfortable. Delirium can sometimes occur in elderly patients with eye patches after cataract surgery (blackpatch-delirium). Such patients can be helped by placing pin holes in the patches to let in some stimuli or by occasionally removing one patch at a time during recovery.

Pharmacological Treatment

The two major symptoms of delirium that may require pharmacological treatment are psychosis and insomnia. The drug of choice for psychosis is haloperidol (Haldol), a butyrophenone antipsychotic drug. Depending on the patient's age, weight, and physical condition, the initial dose may range from 2 to 10 mg IM, repeated in an hour if the patient remains agitated. As soon as the patient is calm, oral medication in liquid concentrate or tablet form should begin. Two daily oral doses should suffice, with two thirds of the dose being given at bedtime. To achieve the same therapeutic effect, the oral dose should be about 1.5 times higher than the parenteral dose. The effective total daily dosage of haloperidol may range from 5 to 50 mg for the majority of delirious patients.

Droperidol (Inapsine) is a butyrophenone that is available as an alternative IV formulation, although careful monitoring of the electrocardiogram may be prudent with that treatment. Phenothiazines should be avoided in delirious patients, because those drugs are associated with significant anticholinergic activity.

Insomnia is best treated with either benzodiazepines with short half-lives or with hydroxyzine (Vistaril), 25 to 100 mg. Benzodiazepines with long half-lives and barbiturates should be avoided unless they are being used as part of the treatment for the underlying disorder (for example, alcohol withdrawal).

References

Caine E D: Delirium, dementia, and amnestic and other cognitive disorders and mental disorders due to a general medical condition. In *Comprehensive Textbook of Psychiatry*, ed 6, H I Kaplan, B J Sadock, editors, p 705. Williams & Wilkins, Baltimore, 1995.

Lipowski Z J: Update on delirium. Psychiatr Clin North Am *15*: 335, 1992.

Parikh S S, Chung F: Postoperative delirium in the elderly. Anesth Analg *80*: 1223, 1995.

Rummans T A, Evans J M, Krahn L E, Fleming K C, Delirium in elderly patients: Evaluation and management. Mayo Clin Proc *70*: 989, 1995.

Shapira J, Roper J, Schulzinger J: Managing delirious patients. Nursing *23*: 78, 1993.

Taylor D, Lewis S: Delirium. J Neurol Neurosurg Psychiatry *56*: 742, 1993.

4.3 DEMENTIA

Dementia is a syndrome characterized by multiple impairments in cognitive functions without impairment in consciousness. The cognitive functions that can be affected in dementia include general intelligence, learning and memory, language, problem solving, orientation, perception, attention and concentration, judgment, and social abilities. The patient's personality is also affected. If the patient has an impairment of consciousness, then the patient probably fits the diagnostic criteria for delirium. In addition, a diagnosis of dementia, according to the fourth edition of *Diagnostic and Statistical Manual of Mental Disorders* (DSM-IV), requires that the symptoms result in a significant impairment in social or occupational functioning and represent a significant decline from a previous level of functioning.

The critical clinical points of dementia are the identification of the syndrome and the clinical workup of its cause. The disorder may be progressive or static, permanent or reversible. An underlying cause is always assumed, although in rare cases it is impossible to determine a specific cause. The potential reversibility of dementia is related to the underlying pathology and to the availability and the application of effective treatment. An estimated 15 percent of persons with dementia have illnesses that are reversible if the physician initiates timely treatment, before irreversible damage has taken place.

EPIDEMIOLOGY

Dementia is essentially a disease of the aged. Of Americans over the age of 65, about 5 percent have severe dementia, and 15 percent have mild dementia. Of Americans over the age of 80, about 20 percent have severe dementia. Of all patients with dementia, 50 to 60 percent have dementia of the Alzheimer's type, the most common type of dementia. About 5 percent of all persons who reach age 65 have dementia of the Alzheimer's type, compared with 15 to 25 percent of all persons age 85 or older. Patients with dementia of the Alzheimer's type occupy more than 50 percent of nursing home beds. The risk factors for the development of dementia of the Alzheimer's type include being female, having a first-degree relative with the disorder, and having a history of head injury. Down's syndrome is also characteristically associated with the development of dementia of the Alzheimer's type.

The second most common type of dementia is vascular dementia—that is, dementia causally related to cerebrovascular diseases. Vascular dementias account for 15 to 30 percent of all dementia cases. Vascular dementia is most common in persons between the ages of 60 and 70 and is more common in men than in women. Hypertension predisposes a person to the disease. About 10 to 15 percent of patients have coexisting vascular dementia and dementia of the Alzheimer's type.

Other common causes of dementia, each representing 1 to 5 percent of all cases, include head trauma, alcohol-related dementias, and various movement disorder–related dementias—for example, Huntington's disease and Parkinson's disease. Because dementia is a fairly general syndrome, it has many causes, and clinicians must embark on a careful clinical workup of a demented patient to establish the cause of the dementia in that particular patient.

The cost of dementia to society is staggering. By the year 2030 an estimated 20 percent of the population will be more than 65 years old. Thus, the current annual cost of $15 billion for caring for dementia patients is likely to increase even further.

ETIOLOGY

Dementia has many causes; however, dementia of the Alzheimer's type and vascular dementia together represent as much as 75 percent of all cases. Other causes of dementia that are specified in DSM-IV are Pick's disease, Creutzfeldt-Jakob disease, Huntington's disease, Parkinson's disease, human immunodeficiency virus (HIV), and head trauma.

Dementia of the Alzheimer's Type

Alois Alzheimer first described the condition that later assumed his name: in 1906 he described a 51-year-old woman with a $4\frac{1}{2}$-year course of progressive dementia. The final diagnosis of Alzheimer's disease is based on a neuropathological examination of the brain; nevertheless, dementia of the Alzheimer's type is commonly diagnosed in the clinical setting after other causes of dementia have been excluded from diagnostic consideration.

Although the cause of dementia of the Alzheimer's type remains unknown, progress has been made in understanding the molecular basis of the amyloid deposits that are a hallmark of the disorder's neuropathology. Some studies have indicated that as many as 40 percent of patients have a family history of dementia of the Alzheimer's type; thus, genetic factors are presumed to play a part in the disorder's development in at least some cases. Additional support for a genetic influence is that the concordance rate for monozygotic twins is higher than the rate for dizygotic twins. Furthermore, in several well-documented cases the disorder has been transmitted in families through an autosomal dominant gene, although such transmission in rare.

NEUROPATHOLOGY

The classic gross neuroanatomical observation of a brain from a patient with Alzheimer's disease is diffuse atrophy with flattened cortical sulci and enlarged cerebral ventricles. The classic and pathognomonic microscopic findings are senile plaques, neurofibrillary tangles, neuronal loss (particularly in the cortex and the hippocampus), synaptic loss (perhaps as much as 50 percent in the cortex), and granulovascular degeneration of the neurons. Neurofibrillary tangles are composed of cytoskeletal elements, primarily phosphorylated tau protein, although other cytoskeletal proteins are also present. Neurofibrillary tangles are not unique to Alzheimer's disease, since they are also found in Down's syndrome, dementia pugilistica (punch-drunk syndrome), Parkinson-dementia complex of Guam, Hallervorden-Spatz disease, and the brains of normal aging persons. Neurofibrillary tangles are commonly found in the cortex, the hippocampus, the substantia nigra, and the locus ceruleus.

Senile plaques, also referred to as amyloid plaques, are much more indicative of Alzheimer's disease, although they are also present in Down's syndrome and, to some extent, in normal aging. Senile plaques are composed of a particular protein, β/A4, and astrocytes, dystrophic neuronal processes, and microglia. The number and the density of senile plaques present in postmortem brains have been correlated with severity of the disease.

AMYLOID PRECURSOR PROTEIN

The gene for amyloid precursor protein is on the long arm of chromosome 21. Through the process of differential splicing, there are actually four forms of amyloid precursor protein. The β/A4 protein, which is the major constituent of senile plaques, is a 42-amino-acid peptide that is a breakdown product of amyloid precursor protein. In Down's syndrome (trisomy 21), there are three copies of the amyloid precursor protein gene, and in a disease in which there is a mutation at codon 717 in the amyloid precursor protein gene, a pathological process results in the excessive deposition of β/A4 protein. The question of whether abnormal amyloid precursor protein processing is of primary causative significance in Alzheimer's disease remains unanswered; however, many research groups are actively studying both the normal metabolic processing of amyloid precursor protein and its processing in patients with dementia of the Alzheimer's type in an attempt to answer that question.

NEUROTRANSMITTER ABNORMALITIES

The neurotransmitters that are most implicated in the pathophysiology are acetylcholine and norepinephrine, both of which are hypothesized to be hypoactive in Alzheimer's disease. Several studies have reported data consistent with the hypothesis that a specific degeneration of cholinergic neurons is present in the nucleus basalis of Meynert in patients with Alzheimer's disease. Other data in support of a cholinergic deficit in Alzheimer's disease are decreases in acetylcholine and choline acetyltransferase concentrations in the brains. Choline acetyltransferase is the key enzyme for the synthesis of acetylcholine, and a reduction in choline acetyltransferase concentrations suggests a decrease in the number of cholinergic neurons. Additional support for the cholinergic deficit hypothesis comes from the observation that cholinergic antagonists, such as scopolamine and atropine, impair cognitive abilities, whereas cholinergic agonists, such as physostigmine and arecoline, have been reported to enhance cognitive abilities. The decrease in norepinephrine activity in Alzheimer's disease is suggested by the decrease in norepinephrine-containing neurons in the locus ceruleus that has been found in some pathological examinations of brains from patients with Alzheimer's disease. Two other neurotransmitters that have been implicated in the pathophysiology of Alzheimer's disease are two neuroactive peptides, somatostatin and corticotropin, both of which have been reported to be decreased in Alzheimer's disease.

OTHER POTENTIAL CAUSES

Other causative theories have been proposed to explain the development of Alzheimer's disease. One theory is that an abnormality in the regulation of membrane phospholipid metabolism results in membranes that are less fluid—that is, more rigid—than normal. Several investigators are using molecular resonance spectroscopic (MRS) imaging to assess that hypothesis directly in patients with dementia of the Alzheimer's type. Aluminum toxicity has also been hypothesized to be a causative factor, since high levels of aluminum have been found in the brains of some patients with Alzheimer's disease.

A gene (E4) has been implicated in the etiology of Alzheimer's disease. Persons with one copy of the gene had Alzheimer's disease three times more frequently than those with no E4 gene. Persons with two E4 genes had the disease eight times more frequently than persons with no E4 gene.

Vascular Dementia

The primary cause of vascular dementia is presumed to be multiple cerebral vascular disease, resulting in a symptom pattern of dementia. Vascular dementia is most common in men, especially those with preexisting hypertension or other cardiovascular risk factors. The disorder primarily affects small and medium-size cerebral vessels, which undergo infarction and produce multiple parenchymal lesions spread over wide areas of the brain. The cause of the infarctions may include occlusion of the vessels by arteriosclerotic plaque or thromboemboli from distant origins (for example, heart valves). An examination of the patient may reveal carotid bruits, funduscopic abnormalities, or enlarged cardiac chambers.

BINSWANGER'S DISEASE

Binswanger's disease is also known as subcortical arteriosclerotic encephalopathy. It is characterized by the presence of many small infarctions of the white matter, thus sparing the cortical regions. Although Binswanger's disease was previously considered a rare condition, the advent of sophisticated and powerful imaging techniques, such as magnetic resonance imaging (MRI), has revealed that the condition is more common than was previously thought.

Pick's Disease

In contrast to the parietal-temporal distribution of pathology in Alzheimer's disease, Pick's disease is characterized by a preponderance of atrophy in the frontotemporal regions. Those regions also have neuronal loss, gliosis, and the presence of neuronal Pick's bodies, which are masses of cytoskeletal elements. Pick's bodies are seen in some postmortem specimens but are not necessary for the diagnosis. The cause of Pick's disease is not known. Pick's disease constitutes about 5 percent of all irreversible dementias. It is most common in men, especially those who have a first-degree relative with the condition. Pick's disease is difficult to distinguish from dementia of the Alzheimer's type, although the early stages of Pick's disease are more often characterized by personality and behavioral changes, with a relative preservation of other cognitive functions. Features of Klüver-Bucy syndrome (for example, hypersexuality, placidity, and hyperorality) are much more common in Pick's disease than in Alzheimer's disease.

Creutzfeldt-Jakob Disease

Creutzfeldt-Jakob disease is a rare degenerative brain disease caused by a slowly progressive, transmissible (that is, infective) agent, most probably a prion, which is a proteinaceous agent that does not contain DNA or RNA. Other prion-related diseases are scrapie (a disease of sheep), kuru (a fatal central nervous system degenerative disorder of New Guinea highland tribes in which the prion is transmitted through ritualistic cannibalism), and Gerstmann-Sträussler syndrome (a rare, familial progressive dementia). All of the prion-related disorders result in a spongiform degeneration of the brain, characterized by the absence of an inflammatory immune response.

Evidence exists that in humans Creutzfeldt-Jakob disease can be transmitted iatrogenically, through infected, transplanted corneas or surgical instruments. Most cases of the disease, however, appear to be sporadic, affecting persons in their 50s. There is evidence that the incubation period may be relatively short (one to two years) or relatively long (8 to 16 years). The onset of the illness is characterized by the development of tremor, ataxia of gait, myoclonus, and dementia. The disease is usually rapidly progressive, leading to severe dementia and death in 6 to 12 months. Examination of the cerebrospinal fluid usually reveals no abnormalities, and the computed tomographic (CT) or MRI scan may be normal until late in the course of the disorder. The disease is characterized by the presence of an unusual pattern on the electroencephalogram (EEG), consisting of bursts of high-voltage slow waves.

Huntington's Disease

Huntington's disease is classically associated with the development of dementia. The dementia seen in Huntington's disease is the *subcortical type of dementia*, which is characterized by more motor abnormalities and fewer language abnormalities than the cortical type of dementia. The dementia of Huntington's disease is characterized by psychomotor slowing and difficulty with complex tasks, but memory, language, and insight remain relatively intact in the early and middle stages of the illness. As the disease progresses, however, the dementia becomes complete, and the features distinguishing it from dementia of the Alzheimer's type are the high incidence of depression and psychosis, in addition to the classic choreoathetoid movement disorder.

Parkinson's Disease

Like Huntington's disease, parkinsonism is a disease of the basal ganglia that is commonly associated with dementia and depression. An estimated 20 to 30 percent of patients with Parkinson's disease have dementia, and an additional 30 to 40 percent have a measurable impairment in cognitive abilities. The slow movements of a patient with Parkinson's disease are paralleled in the slow thinking of some affected patients, a feature that some clinicians refer to as *bradyphrenia*.

HIV-Related Dementia

Infection with HIV commonly leads to dementia and other psychiatric symptoms. Patients infected with HIV experience dementia at an annual rate of about 14 percent. An estimated 75 percent of patients with acquired immune deficiency syndrome (AIDS) have involvement of the central nervous system (CNS) at the time of autopsy. The development of dementia in HIV-infected patients is often paralleled by the appearance of parenchymal abnormalities in MRI scans.

Head Trauma–Related Dementia

Dementia can be a sequela of head trauma, as can a wide range of neuropsychiatric syndromes.

Table 4.3-1. Diagnostic Criteria for Dementia of the Alzheimer's Type

A. The development of multiple cognitive deficits manifested by both

   (1) memory impairment (impaired ability to learn new information or to recall previously learned information)
   (2) one (or more) of the following cognitive disturbances:

      (a) aphasia (language disturbance)
      (b) apraxia (impaired ability to carry out motor activities despite intact motor function)
      (c) agnosia (failure to recognize or identify objects despite intact sensory function)
      (d) disturbance in executive functioning (i.e., planning, organizing, sequencing, abstracting)

B. The cognitive deficits in criteria A1 and A2 each cause significant impairment in social or occupational functioning and represent a significant decline from a previous level of functioning.

C. The course is characterized by gradual onset and continuing cognitive decline.

D. The cognitive deficits in criteria A1 and A2 are not due to any of the following:

   (1) other central nervous system conditions that cause progressive deficits in memory and cognition (e.g.,cerebrovascular disease, Parkinson's disease, Huntington's disease, subdural hematoma, normal-pressure hydrocephalus, brain tumor)
   (2) systemic conditions that are known to cause dementia (e.g., hypothyroidism, vitamin B_{12} or folic acid deficiency, niacin deficiency, hypercalcemia, neurosyphilis, HIV infection)
   (3) substance-induced conditions

E. The deficits do not occur exclusively during the course of a delirium.

F. The disturbance is not better accounted for by another Axis I disorder (e.g., major depressive disorder, schizophrenia).

Table from DSM-IV, *Diagnostic and Statistical Manual of Mental Disorders*, ed 4. Copyright American Psychiatric Association, Washington, 1994. Used with permission.

Table 4.3-2. Diagnostic Criteria for Vascular Dementia

A. The development of multiple cognitive deficits manifested by both

   (1) memory impairment (impaired ability to learn new information or to recall previously learned information)
   (2) one (or more) of the following cognitive disturbances:

      (a) aphasia (language disturbance)
      (b) apraxia (impaired ability to carry out motor activities despite intact motor function)
      (c) agnosia (failure to recognize or identify objects despite intact sensory function)
      (d) disturbance in executive functioning (i.e., planning, organizing, sequencing, abstracting)

B. The cognitive deficits in criteria A1 and A2 each cause significant impairment in social or occupational functioning and represent a significant decline from a previous level of functioning.

C. Focal neurological signs and symptoms (e.g., exaggeration of deep tendon reflexes, extensor plantar response, pseudobulbar palsy, gait abnormalities, weakness of an extremity) or laboratory evidence indicative of cerebrovascular disease (e.g., multiple infarctions involving cortex and underlying white matter) that are judged to be etiologically related to the disturbance.

D. The deficits do not occur exclusively during the course of a delirium.

Table from DSM-IV, *Diagnostic and Statistical Manual of Mental Disorders*, ed 4. Copyright American Psychiatric Association, Washington, 1994. Used with permission.

Table 4.3-3. Diagnostic Criteria for Dementia Due to Other General Medical Conditions

A. The development of multiple cognitive deficits manifested by both

   (1) memory impairment (impaired ability to learn new information or to recall previously learned information)
   (2) one (or more) of the following cognitive disturbances:

      (a) aphasia (language disturbance)
      (b) apraxia (impaired ability to carry out motor activities despite intact motor function)
      (c) agnosia (failure to recognize or identify objects despite intact sensory function)
      (d) disturbance in executive functioning (i.e., planning, organizing, sequencing, abstracting)

B. The cognitive deficits in criteria A1 and A2 each cause significant impairment in social or occupational functioning and represent a significant decline from a previous level of functioning.

C. There is evidence from the history, physical examination, or laboratory findings that the disturbance is the direct physiological consequence of one of the general medical conditions listed below.

D. The deficits do not occur exclusively during the course of a delirium.

Table from DSM-IV, *Diagnostic and Statistical Manual of Mental Disorders*, ed 4. Copyright American Psychiatric Association, Washington, 1994. Used with permission.

DIAGNOSIS

DSM-IV

The dementia diagnoses in DSM-IV are dementia of the Alzheimer's type (DAT) (Table 4.3–1), vascular dementia (Table 4.3–2), dementia due to other general medical conditions (Table 4.3–3), substance-induced persisting dementia (Table 4.3–4), dementia due to multiple etiologies (Table 4.3–5), and dementia not otherwise specified (NOS).

DEMENTIA OF THE ALZHEIMER'S TYPE

The DSM-IV diagnostic criteria for dementia of the Alzheimer's type emphasize the presence of memory impairment and the associated presence of at least one other symptom of cognitive decline (aphasia, apraxia, agnosia, or abnormal executive functioning). The diagnostic criteria also require a continuing and gradual decline in functioning, impairment in social or occupational functioning, and the exclusion of other causes of dementia. DSM-IV suggests that the age of onset be characterized as early (at age 65 or below) or late (after age 65) and that a predominant behavioral symptom be coded with the diagnosis, if appropriate.

VASCULAR DEMENTIA

The general symptoms of vascular dementia are the same as those for dementia of the Alzheimer's type, but the diagnosis of vascular dementia requires the presence of either clinical or laboratory evidence supportive of a vascular cause of the dementia.

DEMENTIA DUE TO OTHER GENERAL MEDICAL CONDITIONS

DSM-IV lists six specific causes of dementia that can be coded directly: HIV disease, head trauma, Parkinson's disease, Huntington's disease, Pick's disease, and Creutzfeldt-Jakob disease. A seventh category allows the clinician to specify other nonpsychiatric medical conditions associated with dementia.

Table 4.3–4.   Diagnostic Criteria for Substance-Induced Persisting Dementia

A. The development of multiple cognitive deficits manifested by both

　(1) memory impairment (impaired ability to learn new information or to recall previously learned information)
　(2) one (or more) of the following cognitive disturbances:

　　(a) aphasia (language disturbance)
　　(b) apraxia (impaired ability to carry out motor activities despite intact motor function)
　　(c) agnosia (failure to recognize or identify objects despite intact sensory function)
　　(d) disturbance in executive functioning (i.e., planning, organizing sequencing, abstracting)

B. The cognitive deficits in criteria A1 and A2 each cause significant impairment in social or occupational functioning and represent a significant decline from a previous level of functioning.

C. The deficits do not occur exclusively during the course of a delirium and persist beyond the usual duration of substance intoxication or withdrawal.

D. There is evidence from the history, physical examination, or laboratory findings that the deficits are etiologically related to the persisting effects of substance use (e.g., a drug of abuse, a medication).

Table from DSM-IV, *Diagnostic and Statistical Manual of Mental Disorders*, ed 4. Copyright American Psychiatric Association, Washington, 1994. Used with permission.

Table 4.3–5.   Diagnostic Criteria for Dementia Due to Multiple Etiologies

A. The development of multiple cognitive deficits manifested by both

　(1) memory impairment (impaired ability to learn new information or to recall previously learned information)
　(2) one (or more) of the following cognitive disturbances:

　　(a) aphasia (language disturbance)
　　(b) apraxia (impaired ability to carry out motor activites despite intact motor function)
　　(c) agnosia (failure to recognize or identify objects despite intact sensory function)
　　(d) disturbance in executive functioning (i.e, planning, organizing, sequencing, abstracting)

B. The cognitive deficits in criteria A1 and A2 each cause significant impairment in social or occupational functioning and represent a significant decline from a previous level of functioning.

C. There is evidence from the history, physical examination, or laboratory findings that the disturbance has more than one etiology (e.g., head trauma plus chronic alcohol use, dementia of the Alzheimer's type with the subsequent development of vascular dementia).

D. The deficits do not occur exclusively during the course of a delirium.

Table from DSM-IV, *Diagnostic and Statistical Manual of Mental Disorders*, ed 4. Copyright American Psychiatric Association, Washington, 1994. Used with permission.

SUBSTANCE-INDUCED PERSISTING DEMENTIA

The primary reason that this DSM-IV category is listed with both the dementias and the substance-related disorders is to facilitate the clinician's thinking regarding differential diagnosis. The specific substances that DSM-IV cross-references are alcohol; inhalant; sedative, hypnotic, or anxiolytic; and other or unknown substances.

Clinical Diagnosis

The diagnosis of dementia is based on a clinical examination of the patient, including a mental status examination, and on information from the patient's family, friends, and employers. Complaints of a personality change in a patient more than 40 years old suggest that a diagnosis of dementia should be carefully considered.

Complaints by the patient about intellectual impairment and forgetfulness should be noted, as should any evidence of evasion, denial, or rationalization aimed at concealing cognitive deficits. Excessive orderliness, social withdrawal, or a tendency to relate events in minute detail can be characteristic. Sudden outbursts of anger or sarcasm may occur. The patient's appearance and behavior should be noted. Lability of emotions, sloppy grooming, uninhibited remarks, silly jokes, or a dull, apathetic, or vacuous facial expression and manner suggest the presence of dementia, especially when coupled with memory impairment.

CLINICAL FEATURES

At the initial stages of dementia, the patient shows difficulty in sustaining mental performance, fatigue, and a tendency to fail when a task is novel or complex or requires a shift in problem-solving strategy. The inability to perform tasks becomes increasingly severe and spreads to everyday tasks, such as grocery shopping, as the dementia progresses. Eventually, the demented patient may require constant supervision and help in order to perform even the most basic tasks of daily living. The major defects in dementia involve orientation, memory, perception, intellectual functioning, and reasoning. All those functions become progressively affected as the disease process advances. Affective and behavioral changes, such as defective control of impulses and lability of mood, are frequent, as are accentuations and alterations of premorbid personality traits.

Memory Impairment

Memory impairment is typically an early and prominent feature in dementia, especially in dementias involving the cortex, such as dementia of the Alzheimer's type. Early in the course of dementia, memory impairment is mild and is usually most marked for recent events, such as forgetting telephone numbers, conversations, and events of the day. As the course of dementia progresses, memory impairment becomes severe, and only the most highly learned information (for example, place of birth) is retained.

Orientation

Inasmuch as memory is important for orientation to person, place, and time, orientation can be progressively affected during the course of a dementing illness. For example, patients with dementia may forget how to get back to their rooms after going to the bathroom. No matter how severe the disorientation seems, however, the patient shows no impairment in the level of consciousness.

Language Impairment

Dementing processes that affect the cortex, primarily dementia of the Alzheimer's type and vascular dementia, can affect the patient's language abilities. In fact, DSM-IV includes aphasia as one of the diagnostic criteria. The language difficulty may be characterized by a vague, stereotyped, imprecise, or circumstantial locution. The patient may also have difficulty in naming objects.

Personality Changes

Changes in a demented person's personality are among the most disturbing features for the families of affected patients. Preexisting personality traits may be accentuated during the development of a dementia. Patients with dementia may also become introverted and may seem to be less concerned about the effects of their behavior on others. Demented patients who have paranoid delusions are generally hostile to family members and caretakers. Patients with frontal and temporal involvement are likely to have marked personality changes and may be irritable and explosive.

Psychosis

An estimated 20 to 30 percent of demented patients, primarily patients with dementia of the Alzheimer's type, have hallucinations, and 30 to 40 percent have delusions, primarily of a paranoid or persecutory and unsystematized nature, although complex, sustained, and well-systematized delusions are also reported by demented patients. Physical aggression and other forms of violence are common in demented patients who also have psychotic symptoms.

Other Impairments

PSYCHIATRIC

In addition to psychosis and personality changes, depression and anxiety are major symptoms in an estimated 40 to 50 percent of demented patients, although the full syndrome of depressive disorder may be present in only 10 to 20 percent of demented patients. Patients with dementia may also exhibit pathological laughter or crying—that is, extremes of emotions with no apparent provocation.

NEUROLOGICAL

In addition to the aphasias in demented patients, apraxias and agnosias are common, and their presence is included as potential diagnostic criteria in DSM-IV. Other neurological signs that can be associated with dementia are seizures, seen in about 10 percent of patients with dementia of the Alzheimer's type and 20 percent of patients with vascular dementia, and atypical neurological presentations, such as nondominant parietal lobe syndromes. Primitive reflexes—such as the grasp, snout, suck, tonic-foot, and palmomental reflexes—may be present on neurological examination, and myoclonic jerks are present in 5 to 10 percent of patients.

Patients with vascular dementia may have additional neurological symptoms—such as headaches, dizziness, faintness, weakness, focal neurological signs, and sleep disturbances—that may be attributable to the location of the cerebrovascular disease. Pseudobulbar palsy, dysarthria, and dysphagia are also more common in vascular dementia than in other dementing conditions.

CATASTROPHIC REACTION

The dementia patient also exhibits a reduced ability to apply what Kurt Goldstein called the abstract attitude. The patient has difficulty in generalizing from a single instance, in forming concepts, and in grasping similarities and differences among concepts. Further, the ability to solve problems, to reason logically, and to make sound judgments is compromised. Goldstein also described a *catastrophic reaction*, which is marked by agitation secondary to the subjective awareness of one's intellectual deficits under stressful circumstances. Patients usually attempt to compensate for defects by using strategies to avoid demonstrating failures in intellectual performance, such as changing the subject, making jokes, or otherwise diverting the interviewer. Lack of judgment and poor impulse control are commonly found, particularly in dementias that primarily affect the frontal lobes. Examples of those impairments include coarse language, inappropriate jokes, the neglect of personal appearance and hygiene, and a general disregard for the conventional rules of social conduct.

SUNDOWNER SYNDROME

Sundowner syndrome is characterized by drowsiness, confusion, ataxia, and accidental falls. It occurs in the elderly who are overly sedated and in demented patients who react adversely to even a small dose of a psychoactive drug. The syndrome also occurs in demented patients when external stimuli, such as light and interpersonal orienting cues, are diminished.

DIFFERENTIAL DIAGNOSIS

A comprehensive laboratory workup must be performed when evaluating a patient with dementia. The purposes of the workup are to detect reversible causes of dementia and to provide the patient and the family with a definitive diagnosis.

Continued improvements in brain imaging techniques, particularly MRI, have made the differentiation between dementia of the Alzheimer's type and vascular dementia somewhat more straightforward than in the past in some cases. An active area of research is the use of single photon emission computed tomography (SPECT) to detect patterns of brain metabolism in various types of dementia; within the near future, the use of SPECT images may help in the clinical differential diagnosis of dementing illnesses.

Dementia of the Alzheimer's Type versus Vascular Dementia

Classically, vascular dementia has been distinguished from dementia of the Alzheimer's type by the decremental deterioration that may accompany cerebrovascular disease over a period of time. Although the discrete, stepwise deterioration may not be apparent in all cases, focal neurological symptoms are more common in vascular dementia than in dementia of the Alzheimer's type, as are the standard risk factors for cerebrovascular disease.

Vascular Dementia versus Transient Ischemic Attacks

Transient ischemic attacks are brief episodes of focal neurological dysfunction lasting less than 24 hours (usually 5 to 15 minutes). Although a variety of mechanisms may be responsible, the episodes are frequently the result of microembolization from a proximal intracranial arterial lesion that produces transient brain ischemia, and the episodes usually resolve without significant pathological alteration of the parenchymal tissue. About a third of untreated patients with transient ischemic attacks later experience a brain infarction; therefore, recognition of transient ischemic attacks is an important clinical strategy to prevent brain infarction.

The clinician should distinguish episodes involving the vertebrobasilar system from those involving the carotid arterial system. In general, symptoms of vertebrobasilar disease reflect a transient functional disturbance in either the brainstem or the occipital lobe; carotid distribution symptoms reflect unilateral retinal or hemispheric abnormality. Anticoagulant therapy, antiplatelet agglutinating drugs such as acetylsalicylic acid (aspirin), and extracranial and intracranial reconstructive vascular surgery have been reported to be effective in reducing the risk of infarction in patients with transient ischemic attacks.

Delirium

The differentiation between delirium and dementia can be more difficult than the DSM-IV classification indicates. In general, however, delirium is distinguished by rapid onset, brief duration, fluctuation of cognitive impairment during the course of the day, nocturnal exacerbation of symptoms, marked disturbance of the sleep-wake cycle, and prominent disturbances in attention and perception.

Depression

Some patients with depression have symptoms of cognitive impairment that can be difficult to distinguish from symptoms of dementia. The clinical picture is sometimes referred to as *pseudodementia*, although the term *depression-related cognitive dysfunction* is a preferable and more descriptive term. In general, patients with depression-related cognitive dysfunction have prominent depressive symptoms, have more insight into their symptoms than do demented patients, and often have a past history of depressive episodes.

Factitious Disorder

Persons who attempt to simulate memory loss, as in factitious disorder, do so in an erratic and inconsistent manner. In true dementia, memory for time and place is lost before memory for person, and recent memory is lost before remote memory.

Schizophrenia

Although schizophrenia may be associated with some degree of acquired intellectual impairment, its symptoms are much less severe than are the related symptoms of psychosis and thought disorder seen in dementia.

Normal Aging

Aging is not necessarily associated with any significant cognitive decline, but a minor degree of memory problems can occur as a normal part of aging. Those normal occurrences are sometimes referred to as *benign senescent forgetfulness* or *age-associated memory impairment*. They are distinguished from dementia by their minor severity and by the fact that they do not significantly interfere with the patient's social or occupational life.

COURSE AND PROGNOSIS

The classic course of dementia is an onset in the patient's 50s or 60s, with gradual deterioration over 5 to 10 years, leading eventually to death. The age of onset and the rapidity of deterioration vary among different types of dementia and within individual diagnostic categories. For example, the mean survival for patients with dementia of the Alzheimer's type is about 8 years, with a range of 1 to 20 years. Data suggest that patients with an early onset of dementia or with a family history of dementia are likely to have a rapid course. Once dementia is diagnosed, the patient must undergo a complete medical and neurological workup, since 10 to 15 percent of all patients with dementia have a potentially reversible condition if treatment is initiated before permanent brain damage occurs.

The most common course of dementia begins with a number of subtle signs that may, at first, be ignored by both the patient and the people closest to the patient. A gradual onset of symptoms is most commonly associated with dementia of the Alzheimer's type, vascular dementia, endocrinopathies, brain tumors, and metabolic disorders. Conversely, the onset of dementia resulting from head trauma, cardiac arrest with cerebral hypoxia, or encephalitis may be sudden. Although the symptoms of the early phase of dementia are subtle, the symptoms become conspicuous as the dementia progresses, and family members may then bring the patient to a physician's attention. Demented patients may be sensitive to the use of benzodiazepines or alcohol, which may precipitate agitated, aggressive, or psychotic behavior. In the terminal stages of dementia, patients become empty shells of their former selves—profoundly disoriented, incoherent, amnestic, and incontinent of urine and feces.

With psychosocial and pharmacological treatment and possibly because of self-healing properties of the brain, the symptoms of dementia may progress only slowly for a time or even recede a bit. That regression of symptoms is certainly a possibility of reversible dementias (for example, dementias caused by hypothyroidism, normal pressure hydrocephalus, and brain tumors) once treatment is initiated. The course of the dementia varies from a steady progression (commonly seen with dementia of the Alzheimer's type) to an incrementally worsening dementia (commonly seen with vascular dementia) to a stable dementia (as may be seen in dementia related to head trauma).

Psychosocial Factors

The severity and the course of dementia can be affected by psychosocial factors. For example, the greater the patient's premorbid intelligence and education, the better is the patient's ability to compensate for intellectual deficits. Patients who have a rapid onset of dementia use fewer defenses than do patients who experience an insidious onset. Anxiety and depression may intensify and aggravate the symptoms.

Pseudodementia occurs in depressed patients who complain of impaired memory but are, in fact, suffering from a depressive disorder. When the depression is treated, the cognitive defects disappear.

Dementia of the Alzheimer's Type

Dementia of the Alzheimer's type may begin at any age. DSM-IV suggests that the age of onset be specified and classified as early onset (at age 65 or below) or as late onset (after age 65). About half of all patients with dementia of the Alzheimer's type experience their first symptoms between the ages of 65 and 70. The course of the disorder is characteristically one of gradual decline over 8 to 10 years, although the course may be much more rapid or much more gradual that that. Once the symptoms of dementia have become severe, death often follows in a short time.

Vascular Dementia

In contrast to the onset of dementia of the Alzheimer's type, the onset of vascular dementia is likely to be sudden. Also in contrast to dementia of the Alzheimer's type, there is a greater preservation of personality in patients with vascular dementia. The course of vascular dementia has been described as stepwise and patchy; however, refinements in brain imaging techniques have revealed that the clinical course of vascular dementia can be as gradual and smooth as the clinical course characteristic of dementia of the Alzheimer's type.

TREATMENT

Some cases of dementia are regarded as treatable because the dysfunctional brain tissue may retain the capacity for recovery if treatment is timely. A complete medical history, physical examination, and laboratory tests, including appropriate brain imaging, should be undertaken as soon as the diagnosis is suspected. If the patient is suffering from a treatable cause of dementia, therapy is directed toward treating the underlying disorder.

The general treatment approach to demented patients is to provide supportive medical care, emotional support for the patients and their families, and pharmacological treatment for specific symptoms, including disruptive behavior. The maintenance of the patient's physical health, a supportive environment, and symptomatic psychopharmacological treatment are indicated in the treatment of most types of dementia. Symptomatic treatment includes the maintenance of a nutritious diet, proper exercise, recreational and activity therapies, attention to visual and auditory problems, and the treatment of associated medical problems, such as urinary tract infections, decubitus ulcers, and cardiopulmonary dysfunction. Particular attention must be provided to caretakers and family members who deal with frustration, grief, and psychological burnout as they care for the patient over a long period.

When the diagnosis of vascular dementia is made, risk factors contributing to cerebrovascular disease should be identified and therapeutically addressed. Those factors include hypertension, hyperlipidemia, obesity, cardiac disease, diabetes, and alcohol dependence. Patients who smoke should be encouraged to stop, since smoking cessation is associated with improved cerebral perfusion and cognitive functioning.

Pharmacological Treatments

CURRENTLY AVAILABLE TREATMENTS

The clinician may prescribe benzodiazepines for insomnia and anxiety, antidepressants for depression, and antipsychotic drugs for delusions and hallucinations; however, the clinician should be aware of possible idiosyncratic drug effects in the elderly (such as paradoxical excitement, confusion, and in-

creased sedation). In general, drugs with high anticholinergic activity should be avoided, although some data indicate that thioridazine (Mellaril), which does have high anticholinergic activity, may be an especially effective drug in controlling behavior in demented patients when given in low dosages. Short-acting benzodiazepines in small dosages are the preferred anxiolytic and sedative medication for demented patients. Zolpidem (Ambien) may also be used for sedation.

Tacrine (Cognex) has been approved by the Food and Drug Administration (FDA) as a treatment for Alzheimer's disease. The drug is a moderately long-acting inhibitor of cholinesterase activity, and well-controlled trials have shown a clinically significant improvement in 20 to 25 percent of patients who take it. Because of the cholinomimetic activity of the drug, some patients are not able to tolerate it because of side effects. Some patients also have to discontinue the drug because of elevations in liver enzymes.

Psychodynamic Factors

The deterioration of mental faculties has significant psychological meaning for patients with dementia. The experience of oneself as having continuity over time depends on memory. Since recent memory is lost before remote memory in most cases of dementia, many patients are highly distressed because they can clearly recall how they used to function while observing their obvious deterioration. At the most fundamental level, the self is a product of brain functioning. Hence, the patients' identities fade as the illness progresses, and patients can recall less and less of their past. Emotional reactions ranging from depression to severe anxiety to catastrophic terror can stem from the realization that the sense of self is disappearing before one's eyes.

From a psychodynamic standpoint, there is no such thing as an untreatable dementia. Patients often benefit from a supportive and educational psychotherapy in which the nature and the course of their illness are clearly explained to them. They may also benefit from assistance in grieving and accepting the extent of their disability. At the same time, they can benefit from attention to self-esteem issues. Any areas of intact functioning should be maximized by helping the patient identify activities in which successful functioning is possible. A psychodynamic assessment of defective ego functions and cognitive limitations can also be useful. The clinician can assist patients in finding ways to deal with the defective ego functions, such as keeping calendars for orientation problems, making schedules to help structure activities, and taking notes for memory problems.

Psychodynamic interventions with family members of dementia patients may be of enormous assistance. Loved ones who take care of the patient struggle with feelings of guilt, grief, anger, and exhaustion as they watch the family member gradually deteriorate. A common problem that develops among caregivers is that they sacrifice themselves in the service of caring for the patient. The gradually developing resentment from that self-sacrifice is often suppressed because of the guilt feelings it produces. Clinicians can help caretakers understand the complex mixture of feelings associated with seeing a loved one decline and can provide understanding and permission to express those feelings. Attention must also be given to tendencies to blame oneself or others for the patient's illness and for an appreciation of the role that the dementia patient plays in the lives of family members.

References

Caine E D: Delirium, dementia, and amnestic and other cognitive disorders and mental disorders due to a general medical condition. In *Comprehensive Textbook of Psychiatry*, ed 6, H I Kaplan, B J Sadock, editors, p 705. Williams & Wilkins, Baltimore, 1995.

Corder E H, Saunders A M, Strittmatter W J, Schmechel D E, Gaskell P C, Small G W, Roses A D, Haines J L, Pericak-Vance M A: Gene dose of apolipoprotein E type 4 allele and the risk of Alzheimer's disease in late onset families. Science *261*: 921, 1993.

Davis R E, Emmerling M R, Jaen J C, Moos W H, Spiegel K: Therapeutic intervention in dementia. Crit Rev Neurobiol 7: 41, 1993.

Greenamyre J T, Maragos W F: Neurotransmitter receptors in Alzheimer disease. Cerebrovasc Brain Metab Rev 5: 61, 1993.

Simonian N A, Hyman B T: Functional alterations in neural circuits in Alzheimer's disease. Neurobiol Aging *16*: 305, 1995.

Yesauage J: Differential diagnosis between depression and dementia. Am J Med *94* (Suppl, 5): 235, 1993.

4.4 AMNESTIC DISORDERS

The amnestic disorders are characterized primarily by the single symptom of a memory disorder that causes significant impairment in social or occupational functioning. The diagnosis of amnestic disorder cannot be made when the patient has other signs of cognitive impairment, such as those seen in dementia, or when the patient has impaired attention or consciousness, such as that seen in delirium. The amnestic disorders are differentiated from the dissociative disorders (for example, dissociative amnesia, dissociative fugue, dissociative identity disorder) by the identified or presumed presence of a causally related general medical condition (for example, a history of head trauma, carbon monoxide poisoning).

EPIDEMIOLOGY

No adequate studies have been reported on the incidence or the prevalence of the amnestic disorders. However, some studies report the incidence or the prevalence of memory impairments in specific disorders (for example, multiple sclerosis). Amnesia is most commonly found in alcohol use disorders and head injury. In general practice and hospital settings, the frequency of amnesia related to chronic alcohol abuse has decreased, and the frequency of amnesia related to head trauma has increased.

ETIOLOGY

The major neuroanatomical structures involved in memory and the development of an amnestic disorder are particular diencephalic structures (for example, dorsomedial and midline nuclei of the thalamus) and midtemporal lobe structures (for example, the hippocampus, the mammillary bodies, the amygdala). Although amnesia is usually the result of bilateral damage to those structures, some cases of unilateral damage result in an amnestic disorder, and evidence indicates that the left hemisphere may be more critical than the right hemisphere in the development of memory disorders. Many studies of memory and amnesia in animals have suggested that other brain areas may also be involved in the symptoms that accompany amnesia. For example, frontal lobe involvement may result in such symptoms as confabulation and apathy, which can be seen in patients with amnestic disorders.

Amnestic disorders have many potential causes. Thiamine

deficiency, hypoglycemia, hypoxia (including carbon monoxide poisoning), and herpes simplex encephalitis all have a predilection to damage the temporal lobes, particularly the hippocampi. Thus, those conditions can be associated with the development of amnestic disorders. Similarly, when tumors, cerebrovascular diseases, surgical procedures, or multiple sclerosis plaques involve the diencephalic or temporal regions of the brain, the symptoms of an amnestic disorder may develop in a patient. General insults to the brain—for example, seizures, electroconvulsive therapy (ECT), and head trauma—may also result in memory impairments. Transient global amnesia is presumed to be a cerebrovascular disorder involving transient impairment in blood flow through the vertebrobasilar arteries.

Many drugs have been associated with the development of amnesia, and a review of all drugs that a patient has taken, including nonprescription drugs, should be considered in the diagnostic workup of an amnestic patient. The benzodiazepines are the most commonly used prescription drugs associated with amnesia. One benzodiazepine in particular, the short-acting hypnotic triazolam (Halcion), has been inaccurately singled out by the popular press as being associated with anterograde amnesia. A review of the scientific data has concluded that all benzodiazepines can be associated with amnesia and that the association is related to dosage. When triazolam is used in doses (generally less than or equal to 0.25 mg) equivalent to standard doses of other benzodiazepines, amnesia is no more often associated with triazolam than with other benzodiazepines.

DIAGNOSIS

For the diagnosis of amnestic disorder, the fourth edition of *Diagnostic and Statistical Manual of Mental Disorders* (DSM-IV) requires the "development of memory impairment as manifested by impairment in the ability to learn new information or the inability to recall previously learned information" and that the "memory disturbance causes significant impairment in social or occupational functioning." A diagnosis of amnestic disorder due to a general medical condition (Table 4.4–1) is made when there is evidence of a causatively relevant specific medical condition (including physical trauma). DSM-IV further categorizes the diagnosis as being transient or chronic. A diagnosis of substance-induced persisting amnestic disorder is made when there is evidence that the symptoms are due to the persisting

---

Table 4.4–1. Diagnostic Criteria for Amnestic Disorder Due to a General Medical Condition

A. The development of memory impairment as manifested by impairment in the ability to learn new information or the inability to recall previously learned information.

B. The memory disturbance causes significant impairment in social or occupational functioning and represents a significant decline from a previous level of functioning.

C. The memory disturbance does not occur exclusively during the course of a delirium or a dementia.

D. There is evidence from the history, physical examination, or laboratory findings that the disturbance is the direct physiological consequence of a general medical condition (including physical trauma).

Table from DSM-IV, *Diagnostic and Statistical Manual of Mental Disorders*, ed 4. Copyright American Psychiatric Association, Washington, 1994. Used with permission.

Table 4.4-2. Diagnostic Criteria for Substance-Induced Persisting Amnestic Disorder

A. The development of memory impairment as manifested by impairment in the ability to learn new information or the inability to recall previously learned information.

B. The memory disturbance causes significant impairment in social or occupational functioning and represents a significant decline from a previous level of functioning.

C. The memory disturbance does not occur exclusively during the course of a delirium or a dementia and persists beyond the usual duration of substance intoxication or withdrawal.

D. There is evidence from the history, physical examination, or laboratory findings that the memory disturbance is etiologically related to the persisting effects of substance use (e.g., drug of abuse, a medication).

Table from DSM-IV, *Diagnostic and Statistical Manual of Mental Disorders*, ed 4. Copyright American Psychiatric Association, Washington, 1994. Used with permission.

effects related to the use of a substance (Table 4.4–2). DSM-IV refers the clinician to specific diagnoses within substance-related disorders: alcohol-induced persisting amnestic disorder; sedative-, hypnotic-, or anxiolytic-induced persisting amnestic disorder; and other (or unknown) substance-induced persisting amnestic disorder. DSM-IV also provides for the diagnosis of amnestic disorder not otherwise specified (NOS).

CLINICAL FEATURES AND ASSOCIATED CONDITIONS

The central symptom of amnestic disorders is the development of a memory disorder characterized by impairment in the ability to learn new information (*anterograde amnesia*) and the inability to recall previously remembered knowledge (*retrograde amnesia*). The symptom must result in significant problems for patients in their social or occupational functioning. The period of time for which a patient is amnestic may begin directly at the point of trauma or may include a period before the trauma. Memory for the time during the physical insult (for example, during a cerebrovascular event) may also be lost.

Short-term memory and recent memory are usually impaired. Patients cannot remember what they had for breakfast or lunch, the name of the hospital, or their doctor. In some patients the amnesia is so profound that the patients cannot orient themselves to city and time, although orientation to person is seldom lost in amnestic disorders. Memory for over-learned information or events from the remote past, such as childhood experiences, is intact; but memory for events from the less remote past (over the past decade) is impaired. Immediate memory (tested, for example, by asking the patient to repeat six numbers) remains intact. With improvement, the patient may experience a gradual shrinking of the time period for which memory has been lost, although some patients experience a gradual improvement in their memory for the entire period.

The onset of symptoms may be sudden—as in trauma, cerebrovascular events, and neurotoxic chemical assaults—or gradual, as in nutritional deficiency and cerebral tumors. The amnesia can be of short duration (specified as transient by DSM-IV if lasting a month or less) or of long duration (specified as chronic by DSM-IV if lasting more than one month).

A variety of other symptoms can be associated with amnestic disorders. However, if the patient has other cognitive impairments, a diagnosis of dementia or delirium is more appropriate than a diagnosis of an amnestic disorder. Both subtle and gross changes in personality can accompany the symptoms of memory impairment in amnestic disorders. Patients with amnestic disorders may be apathetic, lack initiative, have unprovoked episodes of agitation, or appear to be overly friendly or agreeable. Patients with amnestic disorders may also appear bewildered and confused and may attempt to cover their confusion with confabulatory answers to questions. Characteristically, patients with amnestic disorders do not have good insight about their neuropsychiatric conditions.

Cerebrovascular Diseases

Cerebrovascular diseases affecting the hippocampus involve the posterior cerebral and basilar arteries and their branches. Infarctions are rarely limited to the hippocampus; they often involve the occipital or parietal lobes. Thus, common accompanying symptoms of cerebrovascular diseases in that region are focal neurological signs involving vision or sensory modalities. Cerebrovascular diseases affecting the bilateral medial thalamus, particularly the anterior portions, are often associated with symptoms of amnestic disorders. A few case studies report amnestic disorders from ruptures of an aneurysm of the anterior communicating artery, resulting in an infarction of the basal forebrain region.

Multiple Sclerosis

The pathophysiological process of multiple sclerosis involves the seemingly random formation of plaques within the brain parenchyma. When the plaques occur in the temporal lobe and the diencephalic regions, symptoms of memory impairment can occur. In fact, the most common cognitive complaints in patients with multiple sclerosis involve impaired memory, which occurs in 40 to 60 percent of patients. Characteristically, digit span memory is normal, but immediate recall and delayed recall of information are impaired. The memory impairment can affect both verbal and nonverbal material.

Korsakoff's Syndrome

Korsakoff's syndrome is the amnestic syndrome caused by thiamine deficiency, which is most commonly associated with the poor nutritional habits of persons with chronic alcohol abuse. Other causes of poor nutrition (for example, starvation), gastric carcinoma, hemodialysis, hyperemesis gravidarum, prolonged intravenous hyperalimentation, and gastric plication may also result in thiamine deficiency. Korsakoff's syndrome is often associated with *Wernicke's encephalopathy*, which is the associated syndrome of confusion, ataxia, and ophthalmoplegia. In patients with those thiamine deficiency-related symptoms, the neuropathological findings include hyperplasia of the small blood vessels with occasional hemorrhages, hypertrophy of astrocytes, and subtle changes in neuronal axons. Although the delirium clears up within a month or so, the amnestic syndrome either accompanies or follows untreated Wernicke's encephalopathy in about 85 percent of all cases.

The onset of Korsakoff's syndrome may be gradual. Recent memory tends to be affected more than remote memory; however, that feature is variable. Confabulation, apathy, and passivity are often prominent symptoms in the syndrome. With treatment, patients may remain amnestic for up to three months and then gradually improve over the next year. The administration of thiamine may prevent the development of additional amnestic symptoms, but rarely is the treatment able to reverse severe amnestic symptoms, once they are present. About a third to a quarter of all patients recover completely, and about a quarter of all patients have no improvement of their symptoms.

Electroconvulsive Therapy

Electroconvulsive therapy (ECT) treatments are usually associated with a retrograde amnesia for a period of several minutes before the treatment and an anterograde amnesia after the treatment, although the anterograde amnesia usually resolves within five hours of the treatment. Mild memory deficits may remain for one to two months after a course of ECT treatments, but the symptoms are completely resolved six to nine months after treatment.

Head Injury

Head injuries (both closed and penetrating) can result in a wide range of neuropsychiatric symptoms, including dementia, depression, personality changes, and amnestic disorders. Amnestic disorders caused by head injuries are commonly associated with a period of retrograde amnesia leading up to the traumatic incident and amnesia for the traumatic incident itself. The severity of the brain injury is somewhat correlated with the duration and the severity of the amnestic syndrome, but the best correlate of eventual improvement is the degree of clinical improvement of the amnesia during the first week after the patient has regained consciousness.

Transient Global Amnesia

Transient global amnesia is characterized by the abrupt loss of the ability to recall recent events or to remember new information. The syndrome is often characterized by a lack of insight regarding the problem, a clear sensorium, some mild degree of confusion, and, occasionally, the ability to perform some well-learned complex tasks. Episodes last from 6 to 24 hours. Studies suggest that transient global amnesia occurs in 5 to 10 cases per 100,000 people per year, although, for patients more than 50 years old, the rate may be as high as 30 cases per 100,000 people per year. The pathophysiology is unknown, but it is likely to involve ischemia of the temporal lobe and the diencephalic brain regions. Several studies of patients with single photon emission computed tomography (SPECT) have found decreased blood flow in the temporal and parietal-temporal regions, particularly in the left hemisphere. Patients with transient global amnesia almost universally experience complete improvement, although one study found that about 20 percent of patients may have a recurrence of the episode, and another study found that about 7 percent of patients may have epilepsy. Patients with transient global amnesia have been differentiated from patients with transient ischemic attacks as having less diabetes, hypercholesterolemia, and hypertriglyceridemia but more hypertension and migrainous episodes.

DIFFERENTIAL DIAGNOSIS

To make the diagnosis of an amnestic disorder, the clinician must obtain the patient's history, conduct a complete physical examination, and order all appropriate laboratory tests. However, other diagnoses can be confused with the amnestic disorders.

Dementia and Delirium

The clinician must differentiate amnestic disorders from dementia and delirium. Memory impairment is commonly present in dementia but is accompanied by other cognitive deficits. Memory impairment is also commonly present in delirium but occurs in the setting of an impairment in attention and consciousness.

Alcoholic Blackouts

An acute impairment in memory may be associated with alcohol intoxication. In some persons with severe alcohol abuse, the syndrome commonly referred to as an alcoholic blackout may occur. Characteristically, the alcoholic person awakens in the morning with a conscious awareness of being unable to remember a period of time the night before, while intoxicated. Sometimes specific behaviors (hiding money in a secret place and provoking fights) are associated with a person's blackouts.

Normal Aging

Some minor impairment in memory may accompany normal aging; however, the DSM-IV requirement that the memory impairment cause significant impairment in social or occupational functioning should exclude normal aging patients from the diagnosis.

Dissociative Disorders

The dissociative disorders can sometimes be difficult to differentiate from the amnestic disorders. However, patients with dissociative disorders are more likely to have lost their orientation to self and may have more selective memory deficits than do patients with amnestic disorders. For example, patients with dissociative disorders may not know their names or home addresses but may still be able to learn new information and to remember selected past memories. Dissociative disorders are also often associated with emotionally stressful life events involving money, the legal system, or troubled relationships.

Factitious Disorders

Patients with factitious disorders who are mimicking an amnestic disorder often have inconsistent results on memory tests and have no evidence of an identifiable cause. Those findings, coupled with evidence of primary or secondary gain by the patient, should suggest a factitious disorder.

COURSE AND PROGNOSIS

The specific cause of the amnestic disorder determines its course and the prognosis for a patient. The onset may be sudden or gradual; the symptoms may be transient or chronic; and the outcome can range from no improvement to complete recovery. Transient amnestic disorder with full recovery is common in temporal lobe epilepsy, ECT, the intake of such drugs as benzodiazepines and barbiturates, and resuscitation from cardiac arrest. Permanent amnestic syndromes may follow a head trauma, carbon monoxide poisoning, a cerebral infarction, subarachnoid hemorrhage, and herpes simplex encephalitis.

TREATMENT

The primary approach is to treat the underlying cause of the amnestic disorder. While the patient is amnestic, supportive prompts regarding the date, the time, and the patient's location can be helpful and can reduce the patient's anxiety. After the resolution of the amnestic episode, psychotherapy of some type (for example, cognitive, psychodynamic, or supportive) may help patients incorporate the amnestic experience into their lives.

Psychodynamic Factors

Psychodynamic interventions may be of considerable value for patients suffering from amnestic disorders that result from insults to the brain. Understanding the course of recovery in such patients helps the clinician be sensitive to the narcissistic injury inherent in damage to the central nervous system.

The first phase of recovery, in which the patient is incapable of processing what happened because the ego defenses are overwhelmed, requires that the clinician serve as a supportive auxiliary ego who explains to the patient what is happening and provides missing ego functions. In the second phase of recovery, as the realization of the injury sets in, the patient may become angry and feel victimized by the malevolent hand of fate. The patient may view others, including the clinician, as bad or destructive, and the clinician must contain those projections without becoming punitive or retaliatory. The clinician can build a therapeutic alliance with the patient by explaining slowly and clearly what happened and by offering an explanation for the patient's internal experience. The third phase of recovery is an integrative one. As the patient accepts what happened, the clinician can help the patient form a new identity by connecting current experiences of the self with past experiences of the self. Grieving over one's lost faculties may be an important feature of the third phase.

Most patients who are amnestic from a brain injury engage in denial. The clinician must respect and empathize with the patients' need to deny the reality of what has happened. Insensitive and blunt confrontations will destroy any developing therapeutic alliance and may cause patients to feel attacked. A sensitive approach is to help the patients accept their cognitive limitations by exposing them to those deficits bit by bit over time. When the patients fully accept what has happened, they may need assistance in forgiving themselves and any others involved, so that they can get on with their lives. Clinicians must also be wary of being seduced into thinking that all the patient's symptoms are directly related to the brain insult. An evaluation of preexisting personality disorders—such as borderline, antisocial, and narcissistic personality disorders—must be part of the overall assessment, because many patients with personality disorders place themselves in situations that predispose them to injuries. Those personality features may become a crucial part of the psychodynamic psychotherapy.

References

Caine E D: Delirium, dementia, and amnestic and other cognitive disorders and mental disorders due to a general medical condition. In *Comprehensive Textbook of Psychiatry*, ed 6, H I Kaplan, B J Sadock, editors, p 705. Williams & Wilkins, Baltimore, 1995.

Caine E D: Amnesic disorders. J Neuropsychiatry Clin Neurosci 5: 6, 1993.
Gabbard G O: *Psychodynamic Psychiatry in Clinical Practice: The DSM-IV Edition*. American Psychiatric Press, Washington, 1994.
Hodges J R, McCarthy R A: Loss of remote memory: A cognitive neuropsychological perspective. Curr Opin Neurobiol 5: 178, 1995.
Jonides J, Smith E E, Koeppe R A, Awh E, Minoshima S, Mintun M A: Spatial working memory in humans as revealed by PET. Nature 363: 623, 1993.
Krupa D J, Thompson J K, Thompson R F: Localization of a memory trace in the mammalian brain. Science 260: 989, 1993.

4.5 MENTAL DISORDERS DUE TO A GENERAL MEDICAL CONDITION

An assessment that a mental disorder is due to a general medical condition indicates that the clinician, on the weight of the available data, thinks that the psychiatric symptoms are part of a syndrome caused by a nonpsychiatric medical condition. An example is the depression associated with Cushing's disease. The diagnosis of a mental disorder due to a general medical condition also implies that the clinician thinks that the psychiatric symptom is severe enough to warrant treatment as an identified problem.

The fourth edition of *Diagnostic and Statistical Manual of Mental Disorders* (DSM-IV) has three additional diagnostic categories for clinical presentations of mental disorders due to a general medical condition that do not meet the diagnostic criteria for specific diagnoses. The first of the diagnoses is catatonic disorder due to a general medical condition (Table 4.5–1). The second diagnosis is personality change due to a general medical condition (Table 4.5–2). The third diagnosis is mental disorder not otherwise specified (NOS) due to a general medical condition.

In addition to the mental disorders due to a general medical condition within the DSM-IV symptom categories, diagnoses for substance-induced psychiatric disorders appear. Specifically, DSM-IV allows for the diagnosis of intoxication-related or withdrawal-related substance-induced disorders with features of psychotic, mood, anxiety, and sleep disorders.

As a general rule, the differential diagnosis for a mental syndrome in a patient should always include consideration of any general medical disease or disorder a patient may have and consideration of any prescription, nonprescription, or illegal substances a patient may be taking. Although some general medical conditions have classically been associated with mental

Table 4.5–1. Diagnostic Criteria for Catatonic Disorder Due to a General Medical Condition

A. The presence of catatonia as manifested by motoric immobility, excessive motor activity (that is apparently purposeless and not influenced by external stimuli), extreme negativism or mutism, peculiarities of voluntary movement, or echolalia or echopraxia.

B. There is evidence from the history, physical examination, or laboratory findings that the disturbance is the direct physiological consequence of a general medical condition.

C. The disturbance is not better accounted for by another mental disorder (e.g., manic episode)

D. The disturbance does not occur exclusively during the course of a delirium.

Table 4.5–2.   Diagnostic Criteria for Personality Change Due to a General Medical Condition

A. A persistent personality disturbance that represents a change from the individual's previous characteristic personality pattern. (In children, the disturbance involves a marked deviation from normal development or a significant change in the child's usual behavior patterns lasting at least 1 year).

B. There is evidence from the history, physical examination, or laboratory findings that the disturbance is the direct physiological consequence of a general medical condition.

C. The disturbance is not better accounted for by another mental disorder (including other mental disorders due to a general medical condition).

D. The disturbance does not occur exclusively during the course of a delirium and does not meet criteria for a dementia.

E. The disturbance causes clinically significant distress or impairment in social, occupational, or other important areas of functioning.

Table from DSM-IV, *Diagnostic and Statistical Manual of Mental Disorders,* ed 4. Copyright American Psychiatric Association, Washington, 1994. Used with permission.

syndromes, a much larger number of general medical conditions have been associated with mental syndromes in case reports and small studies.

DEGENERATIVE DISORDERS

Degenerative disorders affecting the basal ganglia are commonly associated not only with movement disorders but also with depression, dementia, and psychosis. The most widely known examples of the degenerative disorders are Parkinson's disease, Huntington's disease, Wilson's disease, and Fahr's disease. Parkinson's disease involves a degeneration primarily of the substantia nigra, and it usually has an unknown cause. Huntington's disease involves a degeneration primarily of the caudate nucleus, and it is an autosomal dominant disease. Wilson's disease is an autosomal recessive disease that results in the destructive deposition of copper in the lenticular nuclei. Fahr's disease is a rare hereditary disorder that involves the calcification and destruction of the basal ganglia.

EPILEPSY

Epilepsy is the most common chronic neurological disease in the general population, affecting about 1 percent of the population in the United States. For psychiatrists the major concerns regarding epilepsy are consideration of an epileptic diagnosis in psychiatric patients, the psychosocial ramifications of a diagnosis of epilepsy for a patient, and the psychological and cognitive effects of commonly used antiepileptic drugs. With regard to the first of those concerns, 30 to 50 percent of all epileptic persons have psychiatric difficulties sometime during the course of their illness. The most common behavioral symptom of epilepsy is a change in personality; psychosis, violence, and depression are much less common symptoms of an epileptic disorder.

Definitions

A *seizure* is a transient paroxysmal pathophysiological disturbance of cerebral function that is caused by a spontaneous, excessive discharge of neurons. Patients are said to have *epilepsy* if they have a chronic condition characterized by recurrent

seizure. The *ictus* or *ictal event* of a seizure is the seizure itself. The nonictal time periods can be categorized as preictal, postictal, and interictal. The symptoms present during the ictal event are primarily determined by the site of origin in the brain for the seizure and by the pattern of the spread of the seizure activity through the brain. Interictal symptoms are influenced by the ictal event and other neuropsychiatric and psychosocial factors, such as coexisting psychiatric or neurological disorders, the presence of psychosocial stressors, and premorbid personality traits.

Classification

The two major categories of seizures are partial and generalized. *Partial seizures* involve epileptiform activity in localized brain regions; *generalized seizures* involve the entire brain.

GENERALIZED SEIZURES

Generalized tonic-clonic seizures have the classic symptoms of loss of consciousness, generalized tonic-clonic movements of the limbs, tongue biting, and incontinence. Although the diagnosis of the ictal events of the seizure is relatively straightforward, the postictal state—which is characterized by a slow, gradual recovery of consciousness and cognition—occasionally presents a diagnostic dilemma for a psychiatrist in an emergency room. The period of recovery from a generalized tonic-clonic seizure ranges from a few minutes to many hours. The clinical picture is that of a gradually clearing delirium. The most common psychiatric problems associated with generalized seizures involve helping the patient adjust to a chronic neurological disorder and assessing the cognitive or behavioral effects of antiepileptic drugs.

Absences (Petit Mal)

A difficult type of generalized seizure for a psychiatrist to diagnose is an absence or petit mal seizure. The epileptic nature of the episodes may go unrecognized, because the characteristic motor or sensory manifestations of epilepsy may be absent or so slight that they do not arouse the physician's suspicion. Petit mal epilepsy usually begins in childhood between the ages of 5 and 7 years and ceases by puberty. Brief disruptions of consciousness, during which the patient suddenly loses contact with the environment, are characteristic of petit mal epilepsy; however, the patient has no true loss of consciousness or convulsive movements during the episodes. The electroencephalogram (EEG) produces a characteristic pattern of three-per-second spike-and-wave activity. In rare instances, petit mal epilepsy has its onset during adulthood. Adult-onset petit mal epilepsy can be characterized by sudden, recurrent psychotic episodes or deliriums that appear and disappear abruptly. The symptoms may be accompanied by a history of falling or fainting spells.

PARTIAL SEIZURES

Partial seizures are classified as either simple (without alterations in consciousness) or complex (with an alteration in consciousness). Somewhat more than half of all patients with partial seizures have complex partial seizures. Other terms used for complex partial seizures are temporal lobe epilepsy, psychomotor seizures, and limbic epilepsy; however, those terms are not accurate descriptions of the clinical situation. Complex partial epilepsy is the most common form of epilepsy in adults, affecting about 3 in 1,000 persons.

Symptoms

PREICTAL SYMPTOMS

Preictal events (auras) in complex partial epilepsy include autonomic sensations (for example, fullness in the stomach, blushing, and changes in respiration), cognitive sensations (for example, déjà vu, *jamais vu*, forced thinking, and dreamy states), affective states (for example, fear, panic, depression, and elation), and, classically, automatisms (for example, lip smacking, rubbing, and chewing).

ICTAL SYMPTOMS

Brief, disorganized, and uninhibited behavior characterizes the ictal event. Although some defense attorneys may claim otherwise, rarely does a person exhibit organized, directed violent behavior during an epileptic episode. The cognitive symptoms include amnesia for the time during the seizure and a period of resolving delirium after the seizure. In patients with complex partial epilepsy, a seizure focus can be found on an EEG in 25 to 50 percent of all patients. The use of sphenoidal or anterior temporal electrodes and of sleep-deprived EEGs may increase the likelihood of finding an EEG abnormality. Multiple normal EEGs are often obtained for a patient with complex partial epilepsy; therefore, normal EEGs cannot be used to exclude a diagnosis of complex partial epilepsy. The use of long-term EEG recordings (usually 24 to 72 hours) can help the clinician detect a seizure focus in some patients. Most studies show that the use of nasopharyngeal leads does not add much to the sensitivity of an EEG, but they certainly add to the discomfort of the procedure for the patient.

INTERICTAL SYMPTOMS

Personality Disturbances

The most frequent psychiatric abnormalities reported in epileptic patients are personality disorders, and they are especially likely to occur in patients with epilepsy of temporal lobe origin. The most common features are changes in sexual behavior, a quality usually called viscosity of personality, religiosity, and a heightened experience of emotions. The syndrome in its complete form is relatively rare, even in those with complex partial seizures of temporal lobe origin. Many patients are not affected by personality disturbances; others suffer from a variety of disturbances that differ strikingly from the classic syndrome.

Changes in sexual behavior may be manifested by hypersexuality; deviations in sexual interest, such as fetishism and transvestism; and, most commonly, hyposexuality. The hyposexuality is characterized both by a lack of interest in sexual matters and by reduced sexual arousal. Some patients with the onset of complex partial epilepsy before puberty may fail to reach a normal level of sexual interest after puberty, although that characteristic may not disturb the patient. For patients with the onset of complex partial epilepsy after puberty, the change in sexual interest may be bothersome and worrisome.

The symptom of viscosity of personality is usually most noticeable in a patient's conversation, which is likely to be slow, serious, ponderous, pedantic, overly replete with nonessential details, and often circumstantial. The listener may grow bored but be unable to find a courteous and successful way to disengage from the conversation. The speech tendencies are often mirrored in the patient's writing, resulting in a symptom known as hypergraphia, which some clinicians consider virtually pathognomonic for complex partial epilepsy.

Religiosity may be striking and may be manifested not only by increased participation in overtly religious activities but also by unusual concern for moral and ethical issues, preoccupation with right and wrong, and heightened interest in global and philosophical concerns.

The hyperreligious features can sometimes seem like the prodromal symptoms of schizophrenia and can result in a diagnostic problem in an adolescent or a young adult.

Psychotic Symptoms

Interictal psychotic states are more common than ictal psychoses. Schizophrenialike interictal episodes can occur in patients with epilepsy, particularly those with temporal lobe origins. An estimated 10 to 30 percent of all patients with complex partial epilepsy have psychotic symptoms. Risk factors for the symptoms include female gender, left-handedness, the onset of seizures during puberty, and a left-sided lesion.

The onset of psychotic symptoms in epilepsy varies. Classically, psychotic symptoms appear in patients who have had epilepsy for a long time, and the onset of psychotic symptoms is preceded by the development of personality changes related to the epileptic brain activity.

The most characteristic symptoms of the psychoses are hallucinations and paranoid delusions. Usually, patients remain warm and appropriate in affect, in contrast to the abnormalities of affect that are commonly seen in schizophrenic patients. The thought disorder symptoms in psychotic epilepsy patients are most commonly those involving conceptualization and circumstantiality, rather than the classic schizophrenic symptoms of blocking and looseness.

Violence

Episodic violence has been a problem in some patients with epilepsy, especially epilepsy of temporal and frontal lobe origin. Whether the violence is a manifestation of the seizure itself or is of interictal psychopathology is uncertain. To date, most of the evidence points to the extreme rarity of violence as an ictal phenomenon. Only in rare cases should an epileptic patient's violence be attributed to the seizure itself.

Mood Symptoms

Mood disorder symptoms, such as depression and mania, are seen less often in epilepsy than are schizophrenialike symptoms. The mood disorder symptoms that do occur tend to be episodic and to occur most often when the epileptic foci affect the temporal lobe of the nondominant cerebral hemisphere. The importance of the mood disorder symptoms in epilepsy may be attested to by the increased incidence of attempted suicide in persons with epilepsy.

Diagnosis

A correct diagnosis of epilepsy can be particularly difficult when the ictal and interictal symptoms of epilepsy are severe manifestations of psychiatric symptoms in the absence of significant changes in consciousness and cognitive abilities. Therefore, psychiatrists must maintain a high level of suspicion during the evaluation of a new patient and must consider the possibility of an epileptic disorder, even in the absence of the classic signs and symptoms. Another differential diagnosis to consider is that of *pseudoseizure*, in which a patient has some conscious control over mimicking the symptoms of a seizure.

In patients who have previously received a diagnosis of epilepsy, the appearance of new psychiatric symptoms should be considered as possibly representing an evolution in their epileptic symptoms. The appearance of psychotic symptoms, mood disorder symptoms, personality changes, or symptoms of anxiety (for example, panic attacks) should cause the clinician to evaluate the control of the patient's epilepsy and to assess the patient for the presence of an independent mental disorder. In such circumstances the clinician should evaluate the patient's compliance with the antiepileptic drug regimen and should consider whether the psychiatric symptoms could be toxic effects from the antiepileptic drugs themselves. When psychiatric symptoms appear in a patient in whom epilepsy has been diagnosed or in whom such a diagnosis has been considered in the past, the clinician should obtain one or more EEG examinations.

In patients who have not previously received a diagnosis of epilepsy, four characteristics should cause the clinician to be suspicious of the possibility: the abrupt onset of psychosis in a person previously regarded as psychologically healthy, the abrupt onset of delirium without a recognized cause, a history of similar episodes with abrupt onset and spontaneous recovery, and a history of previous unexplained falling or fainting spells.

Treatment

Carbamazepine (Tegretol) and valproic acid (Depakene) may be helpful in controlling the symptoms of irritability and outbursts of aggression, as are the typical antipsychotic drugs. Psychotherapy, family counseling, and group therapy may be useful in addressing the psychosocial issues that may be associated with epilepsy. In addition, the clinician should be aware that many antiepileptic drugs have a mild to moderate degree of cognitive impairment, and an adjustment of the dosage or a change in medications should be considered if symptoms of cognitive impairment are a problem in a particular patient.

BRAIN TUMORS

Brain tumors and cerebrovascular diseases can cause virtually any psychiatric symptom or syndrome. However, cerebrovascular diseases, by the nature of their onset and symptom pattern, are rarely misdiagnosed as mental disorders. In general, tumors are associated with much less psychopathology than are cerebrovascular diseases affecting a similar volume of brain tissue. The two key approaches to the diagnosis of either condition are a comprehensive clinical history and a complete neurological examination. The choice of the appropriate brain imaging technology is usually the final diagnostic procedure; the imaging should usually confirm the clinical diagnosis, rather than discover an unsuspected cause.

Clinical Features, Course, and Prognosis

At some time during the course of their illnesses, about 50 percent of patients with brain tumors experience mental symptoms. About 80 percent of brain tumor patients with mental symptoms have their tumors in frontal or limbic brain regions, rather than in parietal or temporal regions. Another general guideline is that meningiomas are likely to cause focal symptoms, since they compress a limited region of the cortex, whereas gliomas are likely to cause diffuse symptoms. Delirium is most often a component of rapidly growing, large, or metastatic tumors. If the patient's history and a physical examination reveal bowel or bladder incontinence, a frontal lobe tumor should be suspected; if the history and the examination reveal abnormalities in memory and speech, a temporal lobe tumor should be suspected.

COGNITION

Impaired intellectual functioning often accompanies the presence of a brain tumor, regardless of its type or location.

LANGUAGE SKILLS

Disorders of language function may be severe, particularly if the tumor growth is rapid. In fact, defects of language function often obscure all other mental symptoms.

MEMORY

Loss of memory is a frequent symptom of brain tumors. Patients with brain tumors may present with Korsakoff's syndrome, retaining no memory of events that occurred since the illness began. Events of the immediate past, even painful ones, are lost. Old memories, however, are retained, and patients are unaware of their loss of recent memory.

PERCEPTION

Prominent perceptual defects are often associated with behavioral disorders, especially when the patient needs to integrate tactile, auditory, and visual perceptions.

AWARENESS

Alterations of consciousness are common late symptoms of increased intracranial pressure caused by a brain tumor. Tumors arising in the upper part of the brainstem may produce a unique symptom called akinetic mutism or vigilant coma. The patient is immobile and mute, yet alert.

Colloid Cysts

Although not, strictly speaking, brain tumors, colloid cysts located in the third ventricle can exert physical pressure on structures within the diencephalon, resulting in such mental symptoms as depression, emotional lability, psychotic symptoms, and personality changes. The classic associated neurological symptoms are position-dependent intermittent headaches.

HEAD TRAUMA

Head trauma can result in an array of mental symptoms. Head trauma can lead to a diagnosis of dementia due to head trauma or mental disorder not otherwise specified due to a general medical condition (for example, postconcussional disorder). The postconcussive syndrome remains controversial, since it focuses on the wide range of psychiatric symptoms, some quite serious, that can follow what seem to be minor head traumas. DSM-IV includes a set of research criteria for postconcussional disorder in an appendix (Table 4.5–3).

Pathophysiology

Head trauma is a common clinical situation; an estimated 2 million incidents involve head trauma each year. Head trauma most commonly occurs in persons 15 to 25 years of age, and it has a male-to-female predominance of about 3 to 1. Gross estimates based on the severity of the head trauma suggest that virtually all patients with serious head trauma, more than half of all patients with moderate head trauma, and about 10 percent of all patients with mild head trauma have ongoing neuropsychiatric sequelae resulting from the head trauma.

Head trauma can be grossly divided into penetrating head trauma (for example, a bullet) and blunt trauma, in which there is no physical penetration of the skull. Blunt trauma is far more common than penetrating head trauma, and motor vehicle accidents account for more than half of all the incidents of blunt

Table 4.5-3. Research Criteria for Postconcussional Disorder

A. A history of head trauma that has caused signficant cerebral concussion.

   Note: The manifestations of concussion include loss of consciousness, posttraumatic amnesia, and, less commonly, posttraumatic onset of seizures. The specific method of defining this criterion needs to be established by further research.

B. Evidence from neuropsychological testing or quantified cognitive assessment of difficulty in attention (concentrating, shifting focus of attention, performing simultaneous cognitive tasks) or memory (learning or recalling information).

C. Three (or more) of the following occur shortly after the trauma and last at least 3 months:

   (1) becoming fatigued easily
   (2) disordered sleep
   (3) headache
   (4) vertigo or dizziness
   (5) irritability or aggression on little or no provocation
   (6) anxiety, depression, or affective lability
   (7) changes in personality (e.g., social or sexual inappropriateness)
   (8) apathy or lack of spontaneity

D. The symptoms in criteria B and C have their onset following head trauma or else represent a substantial worsening of preexisting symptoms.

E. The disturbance causes significant impairment in social or occupational functioning and represents a significant decline from a previous level of functioning. In school-age children, the impairment may be manifested by a significant worsening in school or academic performance dating from the trauma.

F. The symptoms do not meet criteria for dementia due to head trauma and are not better accounted for by another mental disorder (e.g., amnestic disorder due to head trauma, personality change due to head trauma).

Table from DSM-IV, *Diagnostic and Statistical Manual of Mental Disorders*, ed 4. Copyright American Psychiatric Association, Washington, 1994. Used with permission.

central nervous system (CNS) trauma. Falls, violence, and sports-related head trauma account for most of the remaining cases of blunt head trauma.

Whereas brain injury from penetrating wounds is usually localized to the areas directly affected by the missile, brain injury from blunt trauma involves several mechanisms. During the actual head trauma, the head usually moves back and forth violently, thus causing the brain to crash repeatedly against the skull as it and the skull are mismatched in their rapid deceleration and acceleration. That crashing results in focal contusions. The stretching of the brain parenchyma results in diffuse axonal injury. Later-developing processes, such as edema and hemorrhaging, may result in further damage to the brain.

Symptoms

The two major clusters of symptoms related to head trauma are those of cognitive impairment and those of behavioral sequelae. After a period of posttraumatic amnesia, there is usually a 6- to 12-month period of recovery, after which the remaining symptoms are likely to be permanent. The most common cognitive problems are decreased speed in information processing, decreased attention, increased distractibility, deficits in problem solving and in the ability to sustain effort, and problems with memory and learning new information. A variety of language disabilities may also be present.

Behaviorally, the major symptoms involve changes in personality, depression, increased impulsivity, and increased aggression. Those symptoms may be further exacerbated by the use of alcohol, which was often involved in the head trauma event itself. A debate has ensued about how preexisting character and personality traits affect the development of behavioral symptoms after a head trauma. The critical studies needed to answer the question definitively have not been done yet, but the weight of opinion is leaning toward a biologically and neuroanatomically based association between the head trauma and the behavioral sequelae.

Treatment

The treatment of the cognitive and behavioral disorders in head trauma patients is basically similar to the treatment approaches used in other patients with those symptoms. One difference is that head trauma patients may be particularly susceptible to the side effects associated with psychotropic drugs; therefore, those agents should be initiated in lower dosages than usual and should be titrated upward more slowly than usual. Standard antidepressants can be used to treat depression, and either anticonvulsants or antipsychotics can be used to treat aggression and impulsivity. Other approaches to the symptoms include lithium (Eskalith), calcium channel inhibitors, and β-adrenergic receptor antagonists.

The clinician must support the patient through individual and group psychotherapy and should support the major caretakers through couples and family therapy. Especially with minor and moderate head traumas, the patients will rejoin their families and restart their jobs, so all involved parties need help to adjust to any changes in the affected patient's personality and mental abilities.

DEMYELINATING DISORDERS

The major demyelinating disorder is multiple sclerosis (MS). Other demyelinating disorders include amyotrophic lateral sclerosis, metachromatic leukodystrophy, adrenoleukodystrophy, gangliosidoses, subacute sclerosing panencephalitis, and Kufs disease. All those disorders can be associated with neurological, cognitive, and behavioral symptoms.

Multiple Sclerosis

MS is characterized by multiple episodes of symptoms, pathophysiologically related to multifocal lesions in the white matter of the CNS. The cause remains unknown, but studies have focused on slow viral infections and disturbances in the immune system.

The estimated prevalence of MS in the Western hemisphere is 50 patients per 100,000 people. The disease is much more frequent in cold and temperate climates than in the tropics and subtropics. It is more common in women than in men and is predominantly a disease of young adults. The onset in the vast majority of patients is between the ages of 20 and 40 years.

The neuropsychiatric symptoms of MS can be divided into the cognitive symptoms and the behavioral symptoms. Research reports have found that 30 to 50 percent of patients with MS have some cognitive impairment and that 20 to 30 percent of MS patients have serious cognitive impairments. Although evidence indicates that MS patients experience a decline in their general intelligence, memory is the most commonly affected cognitive function. The severity of the memory impairment does not seem to be correlated with the severity of the neurological symptoms or the duration of the illness. Other cognitive impairments can be seen in MS, as is expected for a disease in which any part of the brain can be affected by the white matter lesions.

The behavioral symptoms associated with MS are euphoria, depression, and personality changes. Psychosis is a rare complication of MS. About 25 percent of patients with MS have a euphoric mood that is not hypomanic in severity but, rather, somewhat more cheerful than their situation warrants and not necessarily in character with their disposition before the onset of MS. Only 10 percent of MS patients have a sustained and elevated mood, although it is still not truly hypomanic in severity. Depression, however, is common, affecting 25 to 50 percent of patients with MS and resulting in a higher rate of suicide than is seen in the general population. Risk factors for suicide in MS patients are male sex, the onset of MS before age 30, and a relatively recent diagnosis of the disorder. Personality changes are also common in MS patients, affecting 20 to 40 percent of patients and often characterized by increased irritability or apathy.

Amyotrophic Lateral Sclerosis

Amyotrophic lateral sclerosis (ALS) is a progressive, non-inherited disease of asymmetrical muscle atrophy. It begins in adult life and progresses over months or years to involve all the striated muscles except the cardiac and ocular muscles. In addition to muscle atrophy, patients have signs of pyramidal tract involvement. The illness is rare, occurring in about 16 persons per 1,000,000 a year. A few of the patients have concomitant dementia. The disease progresses rapidly, and death generally occurs within four years of onset.

INFECTIOUS DISEASES

Herpes Simplex Encephalitis

Herpes simplex encephalitis is the most common type of focal encephalitis; it most commonly affects the frontal and temporal lobes. The symptoms often involve anosmia, olfactory and gustatory hallucinations, and personality changes and can also involve bizarre or psychotic behaviors. Complex partial epilepsy may also develop in patients with herpes simplex encephalitis. Although the mortality for the infection has decreased, a high morbidity involves personality changes, symptoms of memory loss, and psychotic symptoms.

Rabies Encephalitis

The inoculation period for rabies ranges from 10 days to one year, after which symptoms of restlessness, overactivity, and agitation can develop. *Hydrophobia*, present in up to 50 percent of patients, is characterized by an intense fear of drinking water. The fear develops from the severe laryngeal and diaphragmatic spasms that the patients experience from drinking water. Once rabies encephalitis develops, the disease is fatal within days or weeks.

Neurosyphilis

Neurosyphilis (also known as general paresis) appears 10 to 15 years after the primary *Treponema* infection. Since the ad-

vent of penicillin, neurosyphilis has become a rare disorder, although acquired immune deficiency syndrome (AIDS) has reintroduced neurosyphilis into medical practice in some urban settings. Neurosyphilis generally affects the frontal lobes, resulting in personality changes, the development of poor judgment, irritability, and decreased care for self. Delusions of grandeur develop in 10 to 20 percent of affected patients. The disease progresses with the development of dementia and tremor, resulting eventually in bedridden patients with paretic neurosyphilis. The neurological symptoms include Argyll-Robertson pupils, which are small, irregular, and unequal and have light-near reflex dissociation; tremor; dysarthria; and hyperreflexia. A cerebrospinal fluid (CSF) examination of the patients shows a lymphocytosis, increased protein, and a positive result on a Venereal Disease Research Laboratory (VDRL) test.

Chronic Meningitis

Chronic meningitis is also seen more often today than in the recent past because of the immunocompromised condition of AIDS patients. The most usual causative agents are *Mycobacterium tuberculosis, Cryptococcus,* and *Coccidioides.* The usual symptoms are headache, memory impairment, confusion, and fever.

Subacute Sclerosing Panencephalitis

Subacute sclerosing panencephalitis is a disease of childhood and early adolescence, with a male-to-female ratio of 3 to 1. The onset usually follows either an infection with measles or a vaccination for measles. The initial symptoms may be a change in behavior, temper tantrums, sleepiness, and hallucinations, but the classic symptoms of myoclonus, ataxia, seizures, and intellectual deterioration eventually develop. The disease relentlessly progresses to coma and death in one to two years.

Creutzfeldt-Jakob Disease

Creutzfeldt-Jakob disease is a rare degenerative brain disease caused by a slow virus infection. A progressive dementia occurs, accompanied by ataxia, extrapyramidal signs, choreoathetosis, and dysarthria. The disease is most common in adults in their 50s, and death occurs usually within one year of the diagnosis. Men and women are affected equally. No treatment is known. Computed tomography (CT) scans show cerebellar and cortical atrophy, and specific EEG changes occur in the late stages.

Kuru

Kuru is a progressive dementia accompanied by extrapyramidal signs. It is found among the natives of New Guinea who practice cannibalistic rites. By eating the brains of infected persons, the natives take in the slow virus that produces the fatal disease.

IMMUNE DISORDERS

The major immune disorder affecting contemporary society is AIDS. However, other immune disorders can also present diagnostic and treatment challenges to mental health clinicians.

Systemic Lupus Erythematosus

Systemic lupus erythematosus (SLE) is an autoimmune disease that involves a sterile inflammation of multiple organ systems. The officially accepted diagnosis of SLE requires that the patient have 4 of 11 criteria that have been defined by the American Rheumatism Association. Between 5 and 50 percent of SLE patients have mental symptoms at the initial presentation, and about 50 percent of patients eventually show neuropsychiatric manifestations. The major symptoms are depression, insomnia, emotional lability, nervousness, and confusion. Treatment with steroids commonly induces further psychiatric complications, including mania and psychosis.

ENDOCRINE DISORDERS

Thyroid Disorders

Hyperthyroidism is characterized by confusion, anxiety, and an agitated depressive syndrome. Patients may also complain of easy fatigability and generalized weakness. Insomnia, weight loss in spite of increased appetite, tremulousness, palpitations, and increased perspiration are also common symptoms. Serious psychiatric symptoms include impairments in memory, orientation, and judgment; manic excitement; delusions; and hallucinations.

Hypothyroidism was called "myxedema madness" in 1949 by Irvin Asher. In its most severe form, it is characterized by paranoia, depression, hypomania, and hallucinations. Slowed thinking and delirium can also be part of the symptom picture. The physical symptoms include weight gain, a deep voice, thin and dry hair, loss of the lateral eyebrow, facial puffiness, cold intolerance, and impaired hearing. About 10 percent of all patients have residual neuropsychiatric symptoms after hormone replacement therapy.

Parathyroid Disorders

Dysfunction of the parathyroid gland results in the abnormal regulation of calcium metabolism. Excessive secretion of the parathyroid hormone causes hypercalcemia, which can result in delirium, personality changes, and apathy in 50 to 60 percent of patients and in cognitive impairments in about 25 percent of patients. Neuromuscular excitability, which depends on proper calcium ion concentration, is reduced, and muscle weakness may appear.

Hypocalcemia can occur with hypoparathyroid disorders and can result in neuropsychiatric symptoms of delirium and personality changes. If the calcium level drops gradually, the clinician may see the psychiatric symptoms without the characteristic tetany seen with hypocalcemia. Other symptoms of hypocalcemia are cataract formation, seizures, extrapyramidal symptoms, and increased intracranial pressure.

Adrenal Disorders

Adrenal disorders cause changes in the normal secretion of hormones from the adrenal cortex and produce significant neurological and psychological changes. Patients with chronic adrenocortical insufficiency (Addison's disease), which is most frequently the result of adrenocortical atrophy or granulomatous invasion caused by tuberculous or fungal infection, exhibit mild

mental symptoms, such as apathy, easy fatigability, irritability, and depression. Occasionally, psychotic reactions or confusion develop. Cortisone or one of its synthetic derivatives is effective in correcting such abnormalities.

Excessive quantities of cortisol produced endogenously by an adrenocortical tumor or hyperplasia (Cushing's syndrome) lead to a secondary mood disorder, a syndrome of agitated depression, and, often, suicide. Decreased concentration and memory deficits may also be present. Psychotic reactions, with schizophrenialike symptoms, are seen in a small number of patients. The administration of high dosages of exogenous corticosteroids typically leads to a secondary mood disorder similar to mania. Severe depression may follow the termination of steroid therapy.

Pituitary Disorders

Total pituitary failure can present with psychiatric symptoms, particularly in a postpartum woman who has hemorrhaged into her pituitary, a condition known as *Sheehan's syndrome*. Patients have a combination of symptoms, especially of thyroid and adrenal disorders, and can present with virtually any psychiatric symptom.

METABOLIC DISORDERS

Metabolic encephalopathy is a common cause of organic brain dysfunction and can produce alterations in mental processes, behavior, and neurological functions. The diagnosis should be considered whenever recent and rapid changes in behavior, thinking, and consciousness have occurred. The earliest signals are likely to be an impairment of memory, particularly recent memory, and an impairment of orientation. Some patients become agitated, anxious, and hyperactive; others become quiet, withdrawn, and inactive. As metabolic encephalopathies progress, confusion or delirium gives way to decreased responsiveness, to stupor, and, eventually, to death.

Hepatic Encephalopathy

Severe hepatic failure can result in hepatic encephalopathy, characterized by alterations in consciousness, asterixis, hyperventilation, and EEG abnormalities. The alterations in consciousness can range from apathy to drowsiness to coma. Associated psychiatric symptoms are changes in memory, in general intellectual skills, and in personality.

Uremic Encephalopathy

Renal failure is associated with alterations in memory, orientation, and consciousness. Restlessness, crawling sensations on the limbs, muscle twitching, and persistent hiccups are also associated symptoms. In young people with brief episodes of uremia, the neuropsychiatric symptoms tend to be reversible; in elderly people with long episodes of uremia, the neuropsychiatric symptoms can be irreversible.

Hypoglycemic Encephalopathy

Hypoglycemic encephalopathy can be caused either by the excessive endogenous production of insulin or by excessive exogenous insulin administration. The premonitory symptoms, which do not occur in every patient, include nausea, sweating, tachycardia, and feelings of hunger, apprehension, and restlessness. With the progression of the disorder, disorientation, confusion, and hallucinations can develop, as well as other neurological and medical symptoms. Stupor and coma can develop, and a residual and persistent dementia can sometimes be a serious neuropsychiatric sequela of the disorder.

Diabetic Ketoacidosis

Diabetic ketoacidosis begins with feelings of weakness, easy fatigability, and listlessness and with increasing polyuria and polydipsia. Headache and sometimes nausea and vomiting appear. Patients with diabetes mellitus have an increased likelihood of a chronic dementia with general arteriosclerosis.

Acute Intermittent Porphyria

The porphyrias are disorders of heme biosynthesis, resulting in the excessive accumulation of porphyrins. The triad of symptoms are (1) acute, colicky abdominal pain, (2) motor polyneuropathy, and (3) psychosis. Acute intermittent porphyria is an autosomal dominant disorder that affects more women than men and that has its onset between ages 20 and 50. The psychiatric symptoms include anxiety, insomnia, lability of mood, depression, and psychosis. Some studies have found that between 0.2 and 0.5 percent of chronic psychiatric patients may have undiagnosed porphyrias. Barbiturates precipitate or aggravate the attacks of acute porphyria. The use of barbiturates for any reason is absolutely contraindicated in a person with acute intermittent porphyria and in anyone who has a relative with the disease.

NUTRITIONAL DISORDERS

Niacin Deficiency

Dietary insufficiency of niacin (nicotinic acid) and its precursor, tryptophan, is associated with *pellagra*, a nutritional deficiency disease of global importance. Pellagra is seen in association with alcohol abuse, vegetarian diets, and extreme poverty and starvation. The neuropsychiatric symptoms include apathy, irritability, insomnia, depression, and delirium. The medical symptoms include dermatitis, peripheral neuropathies, and diarrhea. Traditionally, pellagra was described with five Ds: dermatitis, diarrhea, delirium, dementia, and death. The response to treatment with nicotinic acid is rapid; however, dementia from prolonged illness may improve only slowly and incompletely.

Thiamine Deficiency

Thiamine (vitamin B_1) deficiency leads to *beriberi*, characterized chiefly by cardiovascular and neurological changes, and to Wernicke-Korsakoff syndrome, which is most often associated with chronic alcohol abuse. Beriberi occurs primarily in Asia and in areas of famine and poverty. The psychiatric symptoms include apathy, depression, irritability, nervousness, and poor concentration; severe memory disorders can develop with severe and prolonged deficiencies.

Cobalamin Deficiency

Deficiencies in cobalamin (vitamin B_{12}) arise because of the failure of the gastric mucosal cells to secrete a specific substance, intrinsic factor, which is required for the normal absorption of vitamin B_{12} from the ileum. The deficiency state is characterized by the development of a chronic macrocytic megaloblastic anemia (pernicious anemia) and by neurological manifestations resulting from degenerative changes in the peripheral nerves, the spinal cord, and the brain. Neurological changes are seen in about 80 percent of all patients. Those changes are commonly associated with megaloblastic anemia, but they occasionally precede the onset of hematological abnormalities.

Mental changes such as apathy, depression, irritability, and moodiness are common. In a few patients, encephalopathy and its associated delirium, delusions, hallucinations, dementia, and sometimes paranoid features are prominent and are sometimes called megaloblastic madness. The neurological manifestations of vitamin B_{12} deficiency can be completely and rapidly arrested by the early and continued administration of parenteral vitamin therapy.

TOXINS

Environmental toxins are becoming an increasingly serious threat to physical and mental health in contemporary society. Although the delirium and the dementia associated with arsenic is of historical interest, mercury poisoning is an increasingly important differential diagnosis.

Mercury

Both inorganic mercury and organic mercury can cause mercury poisoning. Inorganic mercury poisoning results in the Mad Hatter syndrome (mercury is used in the hat industry), with depression, irritability, and psychosis. Associated neurological symptoms are headache, tremor, and weakness. Organic mercury poisoning can come from contaminated fish or grain and can result in depression, irritability, and cognitive impairments. Associated symptoms are sensory neuropathies, cerebellar ataxia, dysarthria, paresthesias, and visual field defects.

References

Biller J, Kathol R H: The interface of psychiatry and neurology. Psychiatr Clin North Am *15* (2): 283, 1992.

Caine E D: Delirium, dementia, and amnestic and other cognitive disorders and mental disorders due to a general medical condition. In *Comprehensive Textbook of Psychiatry*, ed 6, H I Kaplan, B J Sadock, editors, p 705. Williams & Wilkins, Baltimore, 1995.

Chiu H F: Psychiatric aspects of progressive supranuclear palsy. Gen Hosp Psychiatry *17*: 135, 1995.

Currier M B, Murray G B, Elch C C: Electroconvulsive therapy for poststroke depressed geriatric patients. J Neuropsychiatry Clin Neurosci *4*: 140, 1992.

Fornazzari L, Farcnik K, Smith I, Heasman G A, Ichise M: Violent visual hallucinations and aggression in frontal lobe dysfunction: Clinical manifestations of deep orbitofrontal foci. J Neuropsychiatry Clin Neurosci *4*: 42, 1992.

Iverson G L: Psychopathology associated with systemic lupus erythematosus: A methodological review. Semin Arthritis Rheum *22*: 242, 1993.

Jorge R E, Robinson R G, Starkstein S E, Arndt S V: Depression and anxiety following traumatic brain injury. J Neuropsychiatry *5*: 369, 1993.

5/ Neuropsychiatric Aspects of Human Immunodeficiency Virus (HIV) Infection and Acquired Immune Deficiency Syndrome (AIDS)

Acquired immune deficiency syndrome (AIDS) results from infection by the human immunodeficiency virus (HIV), which is causally related to a broad array of other medical conditions and neuropsychiatric syndromes. HIV is a ribonucleic acid (RNA)-containing retrovirus that was isolated and identified in 1983. HIV infects cells of the immune system and the nervous system. Infection of T4 (helper) lymphocytes eventually results in impaired cell-mediated immunity, dramatically limiting the ability of the body to protect itself from other infectious agents and to prevent the development of specific neoplastic disorders. Infection of cells (primarily astrocytes) within the central nervous system (CNS) results directly in the development of neuropsychiatric syndromes, which are commonly further complicated in patients with AIDS by the neuropsychiatric effects of opportunistic CNS infections, CNS neoplasms, antiviral treatment-related adverse effects, independent psychiatric syndromes, and myriad psychosocial stresses related to having an HIV-related disorder.

HIV-related disorders (including AIDS) have profoundly changed the face of health care worldwide. Mental health clinicians have had a major role in the health care system in the efforts to cope with HIV-related disorders. Mental health clinicians are involved in three major areas of care for HIV-infected patients: First, pathological involvement of the brain has been reported to be present in 75 to 90 percent of autopsies performed on persons who had had AIDS. Clinically, neuropsychiatric complications (for example, HIV encephalopathy) occur in at least 50 percent of HIV-infected patients and may be the first signs of the disease in about 10 percent of patients. Mental health clinicians are, therefore, involved in the assessment and the treatment of those neuropsychiatric syndromes. Second, classic psychiatric syndromes (for example, anxiety disorders, depressive disorders, and psychotic disorders) are commonly associated with HIV-related disorders. Mental health clinicians are essential to the assessment and the treatment of those syndromes with both pharmacological and psychotherapeutic modalities. Third, the entire field of mental health has been involved in helping society cope with the effects of this modern plague. Mental health professionals and mental health organizations (for example, the National Institute of Mental Health) have used their influence to educate people about the societal effects of HIV-related disorders and about the need for change in behaviors that are generally held to be private, such as sexual and substance-using behaviors.

HIV AND ITS TRANSMISSION

At least two types of HIV have been identified, HIV-1 and HIV-2. HIV-1 is the causative agent for the vast majority of HIV-related diseases; however, infection by HIV-2 seems to be increasing in Africa. HIV is a retrovirus related to the human T-cell leukemia viruses (HTLVs) and to a variety of retroviruses that infect animals, including nonhuman primates.

HIV is present in the blood, the semen, cervical and vaginal secretions, and, to a smaller extent, the saliva, tears, breast milk, and cerebrospinal fluid of infected persons. HIV is usually transmitted through sexual intercourse or the transfer of contaminated blood between persons. Unprotected anal, vaginal, and oral sex are the sexual activities most likely to transmit the virus. Health providers should be aware of the guidelines for safe sexual practices and should advise their patients to practice safe sex.

Although male-to-male transmission has been the most common route of sexual transmission, male-to-female transmission and female-to-male transmission have been documented and represent an increasingly large percentage of the transmission routes. Some studies have found that about 50 percent of the regular sex partners of HIV-infected persons have become infected themselves, suggesting that some persons have an as yet not understood immunity or resistance to HIV infection.

Transmission by contaminated blood most often occurs when intravenous (IV) substance-dependent persons share hypodermic needles without proper sterilization techniques. Transmission of HIV through blood transfusions, organ transplantation, and artificial insemination is no longer a problem because of the testing of donors for HIV infection. Tragically, the transfusions of blood products did infect many hemophiliacs before HIV was identified as the causative agent.

Children can be infected in utero or through breast feeding when their mothers are infected with HIV.

Health workers are theoretically at risk because of potential contact with bodily fluids from HIV-infected patients. In practice, however, the incidence of such transmission is very low, and almost all reported cases have been traced back to accidental needle punctures with contaminated hypodermic needles.

No evidence has been found that HIV can be contracted through casual contact, such as sharing a living space or a classroom with an HIV-infected person, although direct and indirect contact with an infected person's body fluids (for example, blood and semen) should be avoided.

The estimated length of time to the development of AIDS after infection with HIV is 8 to 11 years, although that time is gradually increasing because of early implementation of treatment. Once a person is infected by HIV, the virus primarily targets the T4 (helper) lymphocyte, also called the CD4 + lymphocyte, to which the virus binds because a glycoprotein (gp-120) on the viral surface has a high and selective affinity for the CD4 receptor on T4 lymphocytes. After binding, the virus is able to inject its RNA into the infected lymphocyte; there the RNA is transcribed into deoxyribonucleic acid (DNA) by the action of reverse transcriptase. The resultant DNA can then be incorporated into the host's cell genome and translated and eventually transcribed, once the lymphocyte is stimulated to divide. When the viral proteins have been produced by lymphocytes, the various components of the virus can assemble, and new, mature viruses can then bud off from the host cell. Although the process of budding may cause lysis of the lymphocyte, a variety of other pathophysiological mechanisms by HIV can gradually disable a patient's entire complement of T4 lymphocytes.

AIDS

The definition of AIDS has changed over time as researchers have learned more about the disease. The Centers for Disease Control and Prevention (CDC) originally described AIDS as the presence of a ''a disease, at least moderately predictive of a defect in cell-mediated immunity, occurring in a person with no known cause for diminished resistance to that disease. Such diseases include Kaposi's sarcoma (KS), *Pneumocystis carinii* pneumonia (PCP), and other serious opportunistic infections.'' Other conditions considered indicative of AIDS are HIV encephalopathy, HIV wasting syndrome, recurrent salmonella septicemia, lymphoid interstitial pneumonia, extrapulmonary tuberculosis, and multiple and recurrent pyogenic infections in children.

The 1987 CDC AIDS criteria, which are still commonly used, classified AIDS into four groups: group I, acute infection, often with seroconversion illness; group II, asymptomatic infection; group III, asymptomatic infection, with the exception of the presence of persistent, generalized lymphadenopathy; and group IV, the presence of AIDS-defining diseases, such as constitutional and neurological syndromes, and secondary infections and cancers. That 1987 classification system is being replaced by a two-dimensional classification system for persons who are known to be infected by HIV. One dimension is the degree of immunosuppression, as indicated by the T4 cell count; the second dimension records the presence of complications (for example, infections, cancers, and encephalopathies).

Epidemiology

The first patient with AIDS was reported in 1981; however, analysis of specimens retained from people who had died previously has shown that cases of HIV infection were present as early as 1959, suggesting that, in the 1960s and the 1970s, HIV-related disorders and AIDS were increasingly common but unrecognized, particularly in Africa and North America. At the end of 1995, more than 510,000 cases of AIDS were reported (including more than 320,000 deaths), and an estimated 1 million persons were infected in the United States. The ratio of men to women who are infected is estimated to be 6 to 1, but the number of infected women is growing four times faster than the number of infected men. At the end of 1993, the World Health Organization (WHO) estimated that, worldwide, 2.5 million adults and 1 million children had AIDS, and about 18 million persons were infected with HIV. Although estimates of future cases have varied widely, it appears likely that by the turn of the century, 30 to 40 million persons worldwide will be infected with HIV.

In the United States the major groups at risk have been homosexual and bisexual men and IV substance abusers; they account for about 60 percent and 20 percent, respectively, of the first 100,000 cases of AIDS. Because of changes in sexual behaviors by homosexual and bisexual men and because of the continued spread of the virus through heterosexual sex, the percentage of total cases for homosexual and bisexual men has gradually declined, but the percentage of total cases for other groups has

increased—specifically, IV substance abusers, women, heterosexual men, children, and minority groups (particularly blacks and Hispanics). More women are now being infected through heterosexual intercourse than through IV substance use. Some reports have linked the use of crack cocaine with HIV infection in women. Although the geographical distribution is heavily skewed toward large urban centers—with the cities of New York, Los Angeles, San Francisco, and Miami accounting for more than 50 percent of all cases—cases of AIDS have been reported in every state.

Diagnosis

SERUM TESTING

Two assay techniques are now widely available to detect the presence of anti-HIV antibodies in human serum. Both health care workers and their patients must understand that the presence of HIV antibodies indicates infection, not immunity to infection. Persons with a positive finding on an HIV test have been exposed to the virus, have the virus within their bodies, have the potential to transmit the virus to another person, and will almost certainly have AIDS eventually. Persons with a negative HIV test result either have not been exposed to the HIV virus and are not infected or were exposed to the HIV virus but do not yet have antibodies, a possibility if the exposure occurred less than a year before the testing.

The two assay techniques are the enzyme-linked immunosorbent assay (ELISA) and the Western blot assay. The ELISA is used as an initial screening test because it is less expensive than the Western blot assay and more easily used to screen a large number of samples. The ELISA is sensitive and reasonably specific; although it is unlikely to report a false-negative result, it may indicate a false-positive result. For that reason, positive results from an ELISA are confirmed by using the more expensive and cumbersome Western blot assay, which is sensitive and specific.

Seroconversion is the change, after infection with HIV, from a negative HIV antibody test result to a positive HIV antibody test result. Seroconversion most commonly occurs between 6 and 12 weeks after infection, although in rare cases seroconversion can take 6 to 12 months.

COUNSELING

The major issues regarding the counseling of persons about HIV serum testing are (1) who, in general, should be tested, (2) why a particular person should be (or should not be) tested, (3) what the test results signify, and (4) what the implications are. Although it is increasingly an arguable point to have the entire world population tested for HIV, specific groups of people are at high risk for contracting HIV and should probably be tested. In addition, any person who wants to be tested should probably be tested, although the reasons for requesting a test should be ascertained to detect unspoken concerns and motivations that may merit psychotherapeutic intervention. Counseling both before and after testing should be done in person, not over the telephone, and should cover both the significance of the test results and their implications for behavioral changes. It is good practice to repeat the meaning of the test results and their implications several times at both pretest and posttest interviews because many people are so anxious at those sessions that they may miss anything that is said only once.

Pretest counseling should review past practices that may have put the testee at risk for HIV infection and should include education about safe sexual practices. During posttest counseling a negative test finding should suggest to the person that safe sexual behavior and the avoidance of shared hypodermic needles are recommended to remain free of HIV infection. A positive test result indicates that the person is infected with HIV and is capable of spreading the disease. Persons with positive results must receive counseling regarding safe practices and potential treatment options. They may need additional psychotherapeutic interventions if anxiety or depressive disorders develop after they discover that they are infected. Common issues and concerns are fear of disclosure, relationships with friends and family, employment and financial security, their medical condition, and such psychological issues as self-esteem and self-blame. A person may react to a positive HIV test finding with a syndrome similar to that of posttraumatic stress disorder. Concern about minor physical symptoms, insomnia, and dependence on health care workers are commonly seen. Adjustment disorder with anxiety or depressed mood may develop in as many as 25 percent of persons informed of a positive HIV test result. The clinical interactions with the patient should emphasize the meaning of a positive test result and should encourage the reestablishment of emotional and functional stability.

Couples who are considering taking the HIV antibody test need to decide who will be tested and whether to go alone or together. The therapist should ask why they are considering taking the test, because often the partners first discuss issues of commitment, honesty, and trust, such as sexual contacts outside the relationship. They need to be prepared for the possibility that one or both are infected and what effect it will have on their relationship.

CONFIDENTIALITY

Confidentiality is a key issue in serum testing. No person should be given HIV tests without their prior knowledge and consent, although various jurisdictions and organizations (for example, the military) now require HIV testing for all its inhabitants or members. The results of an HIV test can be shared with other members of a medical team, although that information should be provided to no one else except in the special circumstances discussed below. The patient should be advised against too readily disclosing the results of HIV testing to employers, friends, and family members, since the information may result in discrimination in employment, housing, and insurance.

The major exception to an approach of restricted disclosure is the need to notify potential and past sexual or IV substance partners. The majority of HIV-positive patients act responsibility. If, however, the treating physician knows that an HIV-infected patient is putting another person at risk of becoming infected, the physician may try either to hospitalize the infected person involuntarily to prevent danger to others or to notify the potential victim. The clinician should be aware of the laws concerning such issues, which vary among the states. The guidelines also apply to inpatient psychiatric wards when an HIV-infected patient is believed to be sexually active with other patients.

CLINICAL FEATURES
Nonneurological

About 30 percent of HIV-infected persons experience a flu-like syndrome three to six weeks after becoming infected; the majority of persons never notice any symptoms immediately or shortly after their infection. When symptoms do appear, the flulike syndrome includes fever, myalgia, headaches, fatigue, gastrointestinal symptoms, and sometimes a rash. The syndrome may be accompanied by splenomegaly and lymphadenopathy. Rarely, an acute aseptic meningitis develops shortly after infection, as does an encephalopathy or Guillain-Barré syndrome.

In the United States the median duration of the asymptomatic stages is 10 years, although nonspecific symptoms—such as lymphadenopathy, chronic diarrhea, weight loss, malaise, fatigue, fevers, and night sweats—may make variable appearances. During the asymptomatic period, however, the T4 cell count almost always declines from normal values ($>1,000/mm^3$) to grossly abnormal values ($<200/mm^3$).

The most common infection affecting HIV-infected persons who have AIDS is *Pneumocystis carinii* pneumonia, which is characterized by a chronic, nonproductive cough and dyspnea that are sometimes severe enough to result in hypoxemia and resultant cognitive effects. Diagnosis is made with fiberoptic bronchoscopy and alveolar lavage. The pneumonia is usually treatable with co-trimoxazole (Bactrim, Septra), a combination of trimethoprim and sulfamethoxazole, or pentamidine isethionate (Pentam), which can also be used for prophylaxis against the pneumonia. The other disease that was initially associated with the development of AIDS is Kaposi's sarcoma, a previously rare, blue-purple-tinted skin lesion. For unknown reasons, Kaposi's sarcoma is less commonly associated with AIDS recently diagnosed.

Although *Pneumocystis carinii* pneumonia and Kaposi's sarcoma are the two classic AIDS-related infectious and neoplastic disorders, the severely disabled cellular immune system of HIV-infected patients permits the development of a staggering array of infections and neoplasms. The most common infections are from protozoa (for example, *Toxoplasma gondii*), fungi (for example, *Cryptococcus neoformans* and *Candida albicans*), bacteria (for example, *Mycobacterium avium-intracellulare*), and viruses (for example, cytomegalovirus and herpes simplex virus).

For the psychiatrist, the importance of those nonneurological, nonpsychiatric complications lies in their biological effects on the patient's brain function (for example, hypoxia with *Pneumocystis carinii* pneumonia) and their psychological effects on the patient's mood and state of anxiety. In addition, since each of the conditions is usually treated by an additional drug, the psychiatrist needs to be aware of the adverse CNS effects of the large armamentarium of drugs.

Neurological

An extensive array of disease processes can affect the brain of an HIV-infected patient. The most important disease for mental health workers is HIV encephalopathy, which is associated with the development of a subcortical type of dementia and which may affect 50 percent of HIV-infected patients to some degree. The other diseases and complications of treatment must also be considered in the differential diagnosis of an HIV-infected patient with neuropsychiatric symptoms. Symptoms such as photophobia, headache, stiff neck, motor weakness, sensory loss, and changes in level of consciousness should alert a mental health worker that the patient should be examined for the possible development of a CNS opportunistic infection or a CNS neoplasm. HIV infection can also result in a variety of peripheral neuropathies that should prompt the mental health clinician to reconsider the extent of CNS involvement.

HIV ENCEPHALOPATHY

Although the means by which HIV enters the CNS remains controversial, it is known that HIV does enter the CNS, where it infects primarily glial cells, particularly astrocytes. The virus is also harbored within immune cells in the CNS. The neuropathological picture includes multinucleated giant cells, microglial nodules, diffuse astrocytosis, perivascular lymphocyte cuffing, cortical atrophy, and white matter vacuolation and demyelination. HIV encephalopathy was previously referred to as "AIDS dementia complex"; however, the fact that HIV-related encephalopathy and dementia can develop in a patient who does not meet the diagnostic criteria for AIDS makes "HIV encephalopathy" a preferable term.

Clinical Symptoms

HIV encephalopathy is a subacute encephalitis that results in a progressive subcortical dementia without focal neurological signs. The major differentiating feature between the two types of dementia is the absence of classic cortical symptoms (for example, aphasia) until late in the illness. Patients with HIV encephalitis or their friends usually notice subtle mood and personality changes, problems with memory and concentration, and some psychomotor slowing. Additional symptoms include apathy, distractibility, confusion, malaise, anhedonia, and social withdrawal. Some of those symptoms are virtually indistinguishable from those of depressive disorders, although careful cognitive testing may help suggest the correct diagnosis. In addition to an overlap with the symptoms of depressive disorders, HIV encephalopathy can result in a delirium that may present symptoms suggesting manic episodes or schizophrenia. The presence of motor symptoms may also suggest a diagnosis of HIV encephalopathy. Motor symptoms associated with subcortical dementia include hyperreflexia, spastic or ataxic gait, paraparesis, and increased muscle tone.

Children infected in utero with HIV have a variety of symptoms, including microcephaly, severe cognitive defects, weakness, failure to reach developmental milestone, pseudobulbar palsy, extrapyramidal rigidity, and seizures.

Differential Diagnosis

The differential diagnosis for HIV encephalopathy includes aseptic meningitis and other CNS-related conditions. Aseptic meningitis occurs shortly after HIV infection and is characterized by a flulike illness in the presence of fluctuating levels of consciousness, meningeal signs, and facial palsies. Diagnostic testing should include detailed psychometric testing, cerebrospinal fluid (CSF) examination, and brain imaging studies. The CSF examination may show slight elevations in protein concentrations and, in about one quarter of all HIV-infected patients, a mononuclear pleocytosis. Magnetic resonance imaging (MRI) and computed tomography (CT) studies of HIV-infected patients often show cortical atrophy, ventricular enlargement, and areas of demyelination within the white matter. Positron emission tomography (PET) and single photon emission computed tomography (SPECT) studies have reported hypermetabolism of the basal ganglia early in the course of HIV encephalopathy, progressing to subcortical and cortical hypometabolism later in the course of the illness. Electroencephalographic (EEG) studies usually show generalized slowing, and evoked potential (EP) studies may show a delay in the P300 wave.

Psychiatric Syndromes

DEMENTIA

The fourth edition of *Diagnostic and Statistical Manual of Mental Disorders* (DSM-IV) allows for the diagnosis of dementia due to HIV disease (Section 4.3). Although HIV encephalopathy is found in a large proportion of HIV-infected patients, other causes of dementia in HIV-infected patients need to be considered. Those causes include CNS infections, CNS neoplasms, CNS abnormalities caused by systemic disorders and endocrinopathies, and adverse CNS responses to drugs. The development of dementia is generally a poor prognostic sign; 50 to 75 percent of patients with dementia die within six months.

DELIRIUM

Delirium can result from the same variety of causes that lead to dementia in HIV-infected patients. Delirious states characterized by both increased activity and decreased activity have been described. Delirium in HIV-infected patients is probably underdiagnosed; however, delirium should always precipitate a medical workup of an HIV-infected patient to determine whether a new CNS-related process has begun.

ANXIETY DISORDERS

Patients with HIV infection may have any of the anxiety disorders, but generalized anxiety disorder, posttraumatic stress disorder, and obsessive-compulsive disorder are particularly common.

ADJUSTMENT DISORDER

Adjustment disorder with anxiety or depressed mood has been reported to occur in 5 to 20 percent of HIV-infected patients. The incidence of adjustment disorder is higher than usual in some special populations, such as military recruits and prison inmates.

DEPRESSIVE DISORDERS

A range of 4 to 40 percent of HIV-infected patients have been reported to meet the diagnostic criteria for depressive disorders. The pre-HIV infection prevalence of depressive disorders may be higher than usual in some groups who are at risk for contracting HIV. Another reason for the variation in prevalence rates is the variable application of the diagnostic criteria, since some of the criteria for depressive disorders (poor sleep and weight loss) can also be caused by the HIV infection itself.

SUBSTANCE ABUSE

Substance abuse is a problem not only for IV substance abusers who contract HIV-related diseases but also for all other HIV patients, who may have used illegal substances only occasionally in the past but who may be tempted to use them regularly in an attempt to deal with depression or anxiety.

SUICIDE

Suicidal ideation and suicide attempts may be increased in patients with HIV infection and AIDS. The risk factors for suicide in the HIV-infected population are having friends who died from AIDS, recent notification of HIV seropositivity, relapses, difficult social issues relating to homosexuality, inadequate social and financial support, and the presence of dementia or delirium.

WORRIED WELL

The worried well are persons in high-risk groups who, although they are seronegative and disease-free, are anxious or have an obsession about contracting the virus. Some of those persons are reassured by repeated negative serum test results. Others, however, obsess about the possible long incubation period and cannot be reassured. Their symptoms can include generalized anxiety, panic attacks, obsessive-compulsive disorder, and hypochondriasis.

TREATMENT

The primary approach to HIV infection should be prevention. All persons at any risk for HIV infection should be informed about safe-sex practices and the need to avoid sharing contaminated hypodermic needles. Preventive strategies are complicated by the complex societal values surrounding sexual acts, sexual orientation, birth control, and substance abuse. Many public health officials have advocated condom distribution in schools and the distribution of clean needles to drug addicts, but those issues remain controversial. Condoms have been shown to be a fairly (although not completely) safe and effective preventive strategy against HIV infection. Some conservative and religious persons argue that sexual abstinence should be the educational message. Many university laboratories and pharmaceutical companies are attempting to develop a vaccine that will protect people from infection by HIV. However, the development of such a vaccine is probably at least a decade away.

Medical Treatment

Primary prevention involves protecting people from getting the disease; secondary prevention involves modification of the course of the disease. Zidovudine (Retrovir) is an inhibitor of reverse transcriptase and has been shown to slow the course of the disease in many patients and to prolong the survival of some patients. The use of zidovudine is often limited by associated severe adverse effects, although other antiretroviral drugs are being used clinically—for example, dideoxyinosine (Didanosine)—and other pharmacological approaches are also in development. The prophylactic use of aerosolized pentamidine and of trimethoprim and sulfamethoxazole against the development of *Pneumocystis carinii* pneumonia is also in common practice now. In addition, most physicians advise patients to get adequate nutrition, rest, and exercise and to minimize their use of alcohol and other psychoactive substances.

A number of studies have reported that treatment with antiretroviral agents, such as zidovudine, prevents or reverses the neuropsychiatric symptoms associated with HIV encephalopathy. Although dopamine antagonists, such as haloperidol (Haldol), may be required for the control of agitation, they should be used in as low a dosage as possible because of the patients' increased sensitivity for extrapyramidal effects and the development of neuroleptic malignant syndrome.

Because of HIV-infected patients' susceptibility to delirium, the use of psychoactive medications with significant anticholinergic activity should be avoided.

An attempt to treat some aspects of anxiety disorders in HIV-infected patients with an appropriate psychotherapeutic technique can be made; however, the use of anxiolytic drugs—benzodiazepine or nonbenzodiazepine (for example, buspirone [BuSpar]) sedatives—or the use of antidepressant drugs may become necessary. When using a benzodiazepine, most clini-

cians prefer to use one with either a short or a medium half-life.

Many clinicians believe that depressive disorders in HIV-infected patients should be aggressively treated with antidepressant medications. The starting dose of antidepressants should be about one quarter of that normally used in adults, and the dosage should be raised in small increments every two to three days until a therapeutic effect is reached. Tricyclic drugs and serotonin-specific reuptake inhibitors have both been used effectively by HIV-infected patients. The use of sympathomimetic drugs (for example, amphetamine) is also a reasonable treatment approach, as is electroconvulsive therapy (ECT) if a neurological examination confirms the absence of increased intracranial pressure or space-occupying CNS lesions.

Manic and psychotic symptoms may require the use of typical antipsychotic drugs to control grossly disorganized behavior or to reduce delusions or hallucinations. HIV-infected patients are sensitive to the adverse effects of those drugs; therefore, both initial and maintenance dosages should be lower than usual. HIV-infected patients who had previously been treated with lithium for the control of bipolar I disorder can continue to take lithium; however, the lithium concentrations must be monitored closely, especially if the patient has significant gastrointestinal disturbances (for example, vomiting and diarrhea) that may affect lithium absorption and excretion. The use of anticonvulsants—for example, carbamazepine (Tegretol) and valproic acid (Depakene)—may also be effective for treating episodic disturbances of impulse control.

Psychotherapy

Major psychodynamic themes for HIV-infected patients involve self-blame, self-esteem, and issues regarding death. The psychiatrist can help patients deal with feelings of guilt regarding behaviors that contributed to the development of AIDS. Some AIDS patients feel that they are being punished for a deviant life-style. Difficult health care decisions, such as whether to participate in an experimental drug trial, and terminal care and life-support systems should be explored. Major practical themes for the patients involve employment, medical benefits, life insurance, career plans, and relationships with families and friends. The entire range of psychotherapeutic approaches may be appropriate for patients with HIV-related disorders. Both individual therapy and group therapy can be effective. Individual therapy may be either short-term or long-term and may be supportive, cognitive, behavioral, or psychodynamic. Group therapy techniques can range from psychodynamic to completely supportive in nature.

The homosexual community has provided a significant support system for HIV-infected people, particularly homosexual and bisexual persons. Public education campaigns within that community have resulted in significant (more than 50 percent) reductions in the highest-risk sexual practices, although some homosexual men still practice high-risk sex. Homosexual men are likely to practice safe sex if they know the safe-sex guidelines, have access to a support group, are in a steady relationship, and have a close relationship with a person with AIDS. Unfortunately, IV substance abusers with AIDS have received little support, partly because of the many biases about them. It is particularly unfortunate that there has been little progress in educating IV substance abusers, since they are a major reservoir from which the virus is spreading to women, heterosexual men, and children.

The assessment of HIV-infected patients should include a complete sexual and substance-abuse history, a psychiatric history, and an evaluation of the support systems available to the patient. The clinician must understand the patient's history with regard to sexual orientation and substance abuse, and the patient must feel that the therapist is not judging past or present behaviors. A sense of trust and empathy can often be encouraged by the therapist's asking specific, well-informed, and straightforward questions about the homosexual or substance-using culture. The therapist must also determine the patient's level of knowledge about HIV and AIDS.

Countertransference issues and the burnout of therapists who treat many HIV-infected patients are two key issues to evaluate regularly. Therapists must acknowledge to themselves their predetermined attitudes toward sexual orientation and substance abuse so that those attitudes do not interfere with the treatment of the patients. Issues regarding the therapist's own sexual identity, past behaviors, and eventual death may also give rise to countertransference issues. For some psychotherapists who have practices with many HIV-infected patients, professional burnout can begin to affect their effectiveness. Some studies have found that seeing many HIV-infected patients in a short period of time seems to be more stressful to therapists than seeing a smaller number of HIV-infected patients over a long period of time.

The treatment approach to adjustment disorder in HIV-infected patients usually involves either individual or group psychotherapy, sometimes supplemented with short-term (two to three weeks) use of anxiolytic drugs.

Direct counseling regarding substance abuse and its potential adverse effects on the HIV-infected patient's health is indicated. Specific treatments for particular substance abuse disorders should be initiated if necessary for the total well-being of the patient.

Some concern among healthy members of high-risk groups is warranted, but when the concern evolves into psychological symptoms that impair functioning, psychiatric attention is warranted. Supportive or insight-oriented psychotherapy is indicated in those cases.

Afflicted children may require special schooling. Children with AIDS who come from single-parent homes or who have parents who are unable to provide care may require foster care placement. HIV-infected children who are not severely neurologically impaired can attend regular schools without putting fellow classmates at risk for infection as long as reasonable guidelines are followed.

INVOLVEMENT OF SIGNIFICANT OTHERS

The patient's family, lover, and close friends are often important allies in treatment. The patient's spouse or lover may have guilt feelings about possibly having infected the patient or may experience anger at the patient for possibly infecting him or her. The involvement of members of the patient's support group can help the therapist assess the patient's cognitive function and can also aid in planning financial and living arrangements. The patient's significant others may themselves benefit from the attention of the therapist in helping them cope with the illness and the impending loss of a friend or family member.

LEGAL ISSUES

Mental health care workers are often enlisted to help the patient deal with legal matters, such as making a will and taking care of hospital and other medical expenses. The resolution of such matters is of such practical importance that is often well worth the time of the mental health workers to make sure that those matters are addressed satisfactorily.

References

Empfield M, Cournos F, Meyer I, McKinnon K, Horwarth E, Silver M, Schrage H, Herman R: HIV seroprevalence among homeless patients admitted to a psychiatric inpatient unit. Am J Psychiatry *150*: 47, 1993.

Graham N M H, Zeger S L, Park L P, Vermund S H, Detels R, Rinaldo C R, Phair J P: The effects on survival of early treatment of human immunodeficiency virus infection. N Engl J Med *326*: 1037, 1992.

Grant I, Atkinson H Jr: Psychiatric aspects of acquired immune deficiency syndrome. In *Comprehensive Textbook of Psychiatry*, ed 6, H I Kaplan, B J Sadock, editors, p 1644. Williams & Wilkins, Baltimore, 1995.

Hirsch M S, D'Aquilla R T: Therapy for human immunodeficiency virus infection. N Engl J Med *328*: 1686, 1993.

Lyketsos C G, Fishman M, Treisman G: Psychiatric issues and emergencies in HIV infection. Emerg Med Clin North Am *13*: 163, 1995.

Mapou R L, Law W A, Martin A, Kampen D, Salazar A M, Rundell JR: Neuropsychological performance, mood, and complaints of cognitive and motor difficulties in individuals infected with the human immunodeficiency virus. J Neuropsychiatry Clin Neurosci *5*: 86, 1993.

Silverman D C: Psychosocial impact of HIV-related caregiving on health providers: A review and recommendations for the role of psychiatry. Am J Psychiatry *150*: 705, 1993.

6/ Substance-Related Disorders

6.1 OVERVIEW

The phenomenon of substance abuse has many implications for brain research, clinical psychiatry, and society in general. Simply stated, some substances can affect both internally perceived mental states (for example, mood) and externally observable activities (that is, behavior). The ramifications of that simple statement, however, are staggering. One of the ramifications is that the substances can cause neuropsychiatric symptoms that are indistinguishable from those of common psychiatric disorders with no known causes (for example, schizophrenia and mood disorders). That observation can then be taken to suggest that psychiatric disorders and disorders involving the use of brain-altering substances are related. If the depressive symptoms seen in some persons who have not taken a brain-altering substance are indistinguishable from the depressive symptoms in a person who has taken a brain-altering substance, there may be some brain-based commonality between substance-taking behavior and depression. The fact that brain-altering substances exist is a fundamental clue as to how the brain works in both normal and abnormal states.

TERMINOLOGY

The complexity engendered by illicit substance use is reflected in its associated terminology. The word ''substance'' is generally preferable to the word ''drug,'' since ''drug'' implies a manufactured chemical, whereas many of the substances associated with abuse patterns are naturally occurring (for example, opium) or not meant for human consumption (for example, airplane glue). Thus, in the fourth edition of *Diagnostic and Statistical Manual of Mental Disorders* (DSM-IV) the topic is best described by the general heading of substance-related disorders.

Although all substances (except nicotine) considered by DSM-IV in the substance-related disorders category are associated with a pathological intoxication state, the substances vary as to whether or not a pathological state is associated with withdrawal or persists after the elimination of the substance from the body. Within the DSM-IV system, patients who are experiencing substance intoxication or withdrawal accompanied by psychiatric symptoms but who do not meet the criteria for a specific syndromal pattern of symptoms (for example, depression) receive the diagnosis of substance intoxication (Table 6.1–1) or substance withdrawal (Table 6.1–2), possibly along with dependence or abuse.

Substance Dependence and Abuse

In 1964 the World Health Organization concluded that the term ''addiction'' is no longer a scientific term and recommended substituting the term ''drug dependence.'' The concept of substance dependence has had many officially recognized meanings and many commonly used meanings over the decades. Basically, two concepts have been invoked regarding the definition of dependence—behavioral dependence and physical dependence. *Behavioral dependence* has emphasized the substance-seeking activities and related evidence of pathological use patterns, and *physical dependence* has emphasized the physical (that is, physiological) effects of multiple episodes of substance use. Definitions of dependence that have emphasized physical dependence have used the presence of tolerance or withdrawal in their classification criteria. DSM-IV allows the clinician to specify whether or not symptoms of physiological dependence are present (Table 6.1–3).

Psychological dependence, also referred to as habituation, is characterized by a continuous or intermittent craving for the substance in order to avoid a dysphoric state.

DSM-IV defines substance abuse as being characterized by the presence of at least one specific symptom that indicates that substance use has interfered with the person's life (Table 6.1–4). Persons cannot meet the criteria for substance abuse for a particular substance if they have ever met the criteria for dependence on the same substance.

EPIDEMIOLOGY

One large recent survey found that the lifetime prevalence of a diagnosis of substance abuse or dependence among the United States population over the age of 18 was 16.7 percent. The lifetime prevalence for alcohol abuse or dependence was 13.8 percent, and for nonalcoholic substances it was 6.2 percent. Alcohol and nicotine (cigarettes) are the most commonly used substances, but marijuana, hashish, and cocaine are also commonly used. In general, however, for all four of those substances—alcohol, marijuana, cigarettes, and cocaine—there has been a gradual but consistent decrease in use. However, some evidence indicates that substance abuse is again increasing among children and adolescents under age 18.

Abuse and dependence on substances is more common in men than in women, with the difference more marked for nonalcoholic substances than for alcohol. Substance abuse is also higher among the unemployed and among some minority groups than among working people and majority groups. Substance use is not limited to adults. As shown by a recent survey of high school seniors, about 30 percent of them had tried a nonalcoholic substance at least once, and about 16 percent of them had tried a nonalcoholic, nonmarijuana substance (for example, amphetamine, inhalant, hallucinogen, sedative, or cocaine) at least once.

Substance use is more common among medical professionals than among nonmedical professionals of equal levels of training (for example, lawyers). One possible explanation for the difference is simply the relative ease of access that medical professionals have to some classes of substances (for example, sedatives and stimulants).

COMORBIDITY

Comorbidity (also known as dual diagnosis) is the diagnosis of two or more psychiatric disorders in a single patient. A recent large community survey found that 76 percent of men and 65 percent of women with a diagnosis of substance abuse or depen-

Table 6.1-1.   Criteria for Substance Intoxication

A. The development of a reversible substance-specific syndrome due to recent ingestion of (or exposure to) a substance. **Note:** Different substances may produce similar or identical syndromes.

B. Clinically significant maladaptive behavioral or psychological changes that are due to the effect of the substance on the central nervous system (e.g., belligerence, mood lability, cognitive impairment, impaired judgment, impaired social or occupational functioning) and develop during or shortly after use of the substance.

C. The symptoms are not due to a general medical condition and are not better accounted for by another mental disorder.

Table from DSM-IV, *Diagnostic and Statistical Manual of Mental Disorders*, ed 4. Copyright American Psychiatric Association, Washington, 1994. Used with permission.

Table 6.1-2.   Criteria for Substance Withdrawal

A. The development of substance-specific syndrome due to the cessation of (or reduction in) substance use that has been heavy and prolonged.

B. The substance-specific syndrome causes clinically significant distress or impairment in social, occupational, or other important areas of functioning.

C. The symptoms are not due to a general medical condition and are not better accounted for by another mental disorder.

Table from DSM-IV, *Diagnostic and Statistical Manual of Mental Disorders*, ed 4. Copyright American Psychiatric Association, Washington, 1994. Used with permission.

dence had an additional psychiatric diagnosis. The most common comorbidity involves two substances of abuse, usually alcohol and some other substance. Other psychiatric diagnoses that are commonly associated with substance abuse are antisocial personality disorder, anxiety disorders, major depressive disorder, and dysthymic disorder. In general, the most potent and dangerous substances have the highest comorbidity rates. For example, comorbidity of psychiatric disorders is more common for opioid and cocaine use than for marijuana use.

ETIOLOGY

Psychosocial and Psychodynamic Theories

The range of psychodynamic theories regarding substance abuse reflects the various psychodynamic theories that have had their periods of popularity during the past 100 years. Classic theories suggest that substance abuse is a masturbatory equivalent, a defense against homosexual impulses, or a manifestation of oral regression. Recent psychodynamic formulations involve a relation between substance use and depression or involve substance use as a reflection of disturbed ego functions.

Psychodynamic approaches to persons with substance abuse are more widely valued and accepted than they are in the treatment of alcoholic patients. In contrast to alcoholic patients, those with polysubstance abuse are more likely to have had unstable childhoods, more likely to self-medicate with substances, and more likely to benefit from psychotherapy. Considerable research links personality disorders with the development of substance dependence.

COADDICTION

The concept of coaddiction or codependence has become popularized in recent years, although some experts in the addic-

Table 6.1-3.   Criteria for Substance Dependence

A maladaptive pattern of substance use, leading to clinically significant impairment or distress, as manifested by three (or more) of the following, occurring at any time in the same 12-month period:

(1) tolerance, as defined by either of the following:
  (a) a need for markedly increased amounts of the substance to achieve intoxication or desired effect
  (b) markedly diminished effect with continued use of the same amount of the substance

(2) withdrawal, as manifested by either of the following:
  (a) the characteristic withdrawal syndrome for the substance (refer to criteria A and B of the criteria sets for withdrawal from the specific substances)
  (b) the same (or a closely related) substance is taken to relieve or avoid withdrawal symptoms

(3) the substance is often taken in larger amounts or over a longer period than was intended

(4) there is a persistent desire or unsuccessful efforts to cut down or control substance use

(5) a great deal of time is spent in activities necessary to obtain the substance (e.g., visiting multiple doctors or driving long distances), use the substance (e.g., chain-smoking), or recover from its effects

(6) important social, occupational, or recreational activities are given up or reduced because of substance use

(7) the substance use is continued despite knowledge of having a persistent or recurrent physical or psychological problem that is likely to have been caused or exacerbated by the substance (e.g., current cocaine use despite recognition of cocaine-induced depression, or continued drinking despite recognition that an ulcer was made worse by alcohol consumption)

Table from DSM-IV, *Diagnostic and Statistical Manual of Mental Disorders*, ed 4. Copyright American Psychiatric Association, Washington, 1994. Used with permission.

Table 6.1-4.   Criteria for Substance Abuse

A. A maladaptive pattern of substance use leading to clinically significant impairment or distress, as manifested by one (or more) of the following, occurring within a 12-month period:

  (1) recurrent substance use resulting in a failure to fulfill major role obligations at work, school, or home (e.g., repeated absences or poor work performance related to substance use; substance-related absences, suspensions, or expulsions from school; neglect of children or household)
  (2) recurrent substance use in situations in which it is physically hazardous (e.g., driving an automobile or operating a machine when impaired by substance use)
  (3) recurrent substance-related legal problems (e.g., arrests for substance-related disorderly conduct)
  (4) continued substance use despite having persistent or recurrent social or interpersonal problems caused or exacerbated by the effects of the substance (e.g., arguments with spouse about consequences of intoxication, physical fights)

B. The symptoms have never met the criteria for substance dependence for this class of substance.

Table from DSM-IV, *Diagnostic and Statistical Manual of Mental Disorders*, ed 4. Copyright American Psychiatric Association, Washington, 1994. Used with permission.

tion field reject the concept of coaddiction as invalid. Coaddiction occurs when persons, usually a couple, have a relationship that is primarily responsible for the maintenance of addictive behavior in at least one of the persons. Each person may have enabling behaviors that help perpetuate the situation, and denial of the situation is a prerequisite for such a dyadic relationship to develop. The treatment of such a coaddictive situation involves directly addressing the elements of the enabling behavior and the denial.

BEHAVIORAL THEORIES

Some behavioral models of substance abuse have focused on substance-seeking behavior, rather than the symptoms of physical dependence. For a behavioral model to have relevance to all substances, the model must not depend on the presence of withdrawal symptoms or tolerance, since many substances of abuse are not associated with the development of physiological dependence. Some researchers hypothesize that four major behavioral principles are at work in inducing substance-seeking behavior. The first and second principles are the positive reinforcing qualities and the adverse effects of some substances. Most substances of abuse are associated with a positive experience after taking them the first time; thus, the substance acts as a positive reinforcer for substance-seeking behavior. Many substances are also associated with adverse effects, which act to reduce substance-seeking behavior. Third, the person must be able to discriminate the substance of abuse from other substances. Fourth, almost all substance-seeking behavior is associated with other cues that become associated with the substance-taking experience.

Genetic Theories

Strong evidence from studies of twins, adoptees, and siblings raised apart indicates that the cause of alcohol abuse has a genetic component. Many less conclusive data suggest that other types of substance abuse or substance dependence have a genetic pattern in their development. Some studies, however, have found a genetic basis for nonalcoholic substance dependence and abuse. Recently, researchers have used the technology of restriction fragment length polymorphism (RFLP) in the study of substance abuse and substance dependence, and a few reports of RFLP associations have been published.

Neurochemical Theories

For most substances of abuse, with the exception of alcohol, researchers have identified particular neurotransmitters or neurotransmitter receptors on which the substances have their effects. For example, the opioids act on the opioid receptors. Thus, a person who has too little endogenous opioid activity (for example, low concentrations of endorphins) or who has too much activity of an endogenous opioid antagonist may be at risk for the development of opioid dependence. Even in a person with completely normal endogenous receptor function and neurotransmitter concentration, the long-term use of a particular substance of abuse may eventually modulate those receptor systems in the brain, so that the brain requires the presence of the exogenous substance to maintain homeostasis. Such a receptor-level process may be the mechanism for the development of tolerance within the central nervous system (CNS). In fact, however, modulation of neurotransmitter release and neurotransmitter receptor function has proved to be difficult to demonstrate, and recent research focuses on the effects of substances on the second-messenger system and on gene regulation.

PATHWAYS AND NEUROTRANSMITTERS

The major neurotransmitters that may be involved in the development of substance abuse and substance dependence are the opioid, catecholamine (particularly dopamine), and γ-aminobutyric acid (GABA) systems. Of particular importance are the dopaminergic neurons in the ventral tegmental area that project to the cortical and limbic regions, especially the nucleus accumbens. That particular pathway is thought to be involved in the sensation of reward and is thought to be the major mediator of the effects of such substances as amphetamine and cocaine. The locus ceruleus, the largest group of adrenergic neurons, is thought to be involved in the mediation of the effects of the opioids.

TREATMENT

Treatment approaches for substance abuse vary according to the substance, the pattern of abuse, the availability of psychosocial support systems, and the individual features of the patient. In general, substance abuse involves two major goals of treatment. The first goal is abstinence from the substance. Although some persons have been able to change from an abusive pattern of use to a moderate pattern of use, they are exceptions to the majority of abusers, in whom complete abstinence is the only way to control the problem. The second goal is the physical, psychiatric, and psychosocial well-being of the patient. Significant damage has often been done to the patient's support systems during a prolonged period of substance abuse. If a patient is going to stop a pattern of substance abuse successfully, then adequate psychosocial supports must be in place to foster that difficult change in behavior.

Initial treatment approaches to substance abuse may be conducted in either an inpatient setting or an outpatient setting. Although an outpatient setting is more naturalistic than an inpatient setting, the temptations available to an outpatient may present too high a hurdle for the initiation of treatment. Inpatient treatment is also indicated in the presence of severe medical or psychiatric symptoms, a history of failed outpatient treatments, a lack of psychosocial supports, or a particularly severe or long-term history of substance abuse. After an initial period of detoxification, the patient needs a sustained period of rehabilitation. Throughout the treatment period, individual, family, and group therapies can be effective. Education about substance abuse and support for the patient's efforts are essential factors in treatment. In some cases the use of a psychotherapeutic drug—for example, disulfiram (Antabuse)—may be indicated to discourage the patient from using the abused substance, to reduce the effects of withdrawal (for example, methadone [Dolophine]), or to treat a presumptive underlying psychiatric disorder (for example, antidepressants).

Psychotherapy

The role of psychotherapy in alcohol dependence is highly controversial, but some patients who cannot or will not make use of Alcoholics Anonymous (AA) may require psychotherapeutic intervention. Alcohol dependence is a highly heterogeneous disorder, and individual personalities must always be taken into account in treatment planning. Although no specific personality traits are connected with alcohol dependence, clinicians have observed that alcohol may serve the function of replacing missing psychological structures and, therefore, serve to restore a sense of self-esteem in the patient. For some patients, psychotherapy and AA work synergistically—AA helps them achieve abstinence, and psychotherapy deals with psychological and interpersonal factors that caused distress in their lives.

The early psychoanalytic interpretation of substance abuse as a regression to the oral stage of psychosexual development has recently been replaced by a view of most substance abuse as adaptive and defensive, rather than regressive. Regressive states may actually be reversed by using substances because the substance reinforces weakened defenses against intense affects, such as shame and rage. Moreover, those with substance dependence tend to have significant deficits in self-care, resulting from early developmental disturbances that contribute to the impaired internalization of parents. As a consequence, those with substance dependence find it difficult to soothe themselves and to regulate impulse control and self-esteem.

Methodologically rigorous research has shown that the addition of psychotherapy to the overall treatment plan of those with opioid dependence produces far greater benefit than do treatment plans without psychotherapy. Those patients with significant psychiatric symptoms make little or no progress with counseling alone but are the best candidates for psychotherapy and benefit the most from it. However, abstinence from the abused substance is a requirement for psychotherapy to be effective in dealing with the underlying psychiatric disturbances.

RESIDUAL DIAGNOSTIC CATEGORIES

Other Substance Use Disorders

DSM-IV includes a diagnostic category for substances that are not listed in the specific sections. DSM-IV also allows for a complete range of substance-induced syndromes caused by other or unknown substances. And DSM-IV allows for the diagnosis of other (or unknown) substance use disorder not otherwise specified to cover any syndrome that is assessed to be causally related to any substance.

ANABOLIC (ANDROGENIC) STEROIDS

The naturally occurring anabolic-androgenic steroid in men is testosterone; many synthetic anabolic steroids are now available—for example, Dianabol, Anavar, and Winstrol-V. Those preparations are available in both oral and intramuscular formulations. Anabolic steroids are schedule III drugs and, therefore, are subject to the same regulatory requirements for dispensing as are narcotics. Although anabolic steroids have legitimate medical uses, they are illegally used primarily by men to enhance their physical performance and appearance as measured by muscle bulk, muscle definition, and athletic prowess. An estimated $400 million a year is spent in illegal sales of anabolic steroids in the United States, although many young athletes, some as young as 10 years of age, spend a lot of money on blanks—that is, useless and sometimes harmful nonsteroid formulations. Although virtually every athletic regulatory agency has officially forbidden the use of anabolic steroids, sophisticated athletes and less-than-honest trainers have developed the use of the steroids to a fine art and are able to adjust the amount and the timing of doses to remain undetected by currently used screening tests.

An estimated 1 million people in the United States have used illegal steroids at least once. Male users of anabolic steroids greatly outnumber female users, approximately 50 to 1. About half of the users start before the age of 16. The users are primarily middle-class and white. Although the steroids are used to enhance muscle mass and athletic performance, perhaps one third to one half of all users are not currently engaged in serious competitive sports activities. Many young users report that they have been influenced by muscle magazines and by reports of steroid use by successful sports stars. The users tend to use the steroids in cycles of 6 to 12 months. The users also tend to stack their use—that is, they take small amounts of two or more types of anabolic steroids at the same time, believing that doing so maximizes the desired effects while minimizing the risks.

Anabolic steroid use has obvious physical effects. The most obvious effect is that their use causes rapid development and enhancement of muscle bulk, definition, and power. Males who abuse steroids also have acne, premature balding, yellowing of the skin and the eyes, gynecomastia, and decreased size of the testicles and the prostate. Young boys abusing anabolic steroids can have a painful enlargement of the genitalia. The use of anabolic steroids in young adolescents can also lead to stunted growth, because the use causes premature closure of the bone plates. In females who abuse anabolic steroids, the voice may deepen, the breasts may shrink, the clitoris may enlarge, and the menstrual cycle may become irregular.

Laboratory values may also be changed, including elevated liver function, decreased high-density lipoproteins, and increased low-density lipoproteins. Decreased spermatogenesis has been reported, as has an association between anabolic steroid abuse and myocardial infarction and cerebrovascular diseases.

Anabolic steroids have come to the attention of psychiatrists because of the steroid's psychiatric effects. Initially, anabolic steroids may induce euphoria and hyperactivity, but after relatively short periods their use can become associated with increased anger, arousal, irritability, hostility, anxiety, somatization, and depression (especially during periods off the steroids). A number of studies have found that from 2 to 15 percent of anabolic steroid abusers experience hypomanic or manic episodes, and a smaller percentage may have clear psychotic symptoms. Also disturbing is an association between abuse of the steroids and violence, termed ''roid rage'' in the parlance of users. A number of murders and other violent crimes have been reported in steroid abusers who had no prior record of sociopathy or violence.

The steroids are apparently addictive substances. When abusers stop taking the steroids, they can become depressed, anxious, and concerned about the physical state of their bodies. Some similarities are noted between those athlete's views of their muscles and the views of patients with anorexia nervosa regarding their own bodies. Both groups seem to distort the realistic assessment of their bodies. Treatment for anabolic steroid abuse involves the same basic principles as for any other substance abuse problem—abstinence in an environment that provides the necessary psychosocial support.

NITRITE INHALANTS

The nitrite inhalants include amyl, butyl, and isobutyl nitrites, all of which are referred to as ''poppers'' in popular jargon. Nitrite inhalant use is specifically excluded from the inhalant use disorders, as is anesthetic gas use, because the intoxication syndromes seen with nitrites can be markedly different from the syndromes seen with the standard inhalant substances (for example, lighter fluid and airplane glue). Nitrite inhalants are used by persons who seek the associated mild euphoria, altered sense of time, feeling of fullness in the head, and possibly increased sexual feelings. The nitrite compounds are used by some homosexual men to reduce sexual inhibitions, to delay orgasm, and to relax the anal sphincter for penile penetration. Under such circumstances a person may inhale the substance from a small bottle from a few times to dozens of times within several hours. Adverse reactions include a toxic syndrome characterized by nausea, vomiting, headache, hypotension, drowsiness, and irritation of the respiratory tract. Some evidence indicates that nitrite inhalants may adversely affect the immune function.

NITROUS OXIDE

Nitrous oxide is a widely available anesthetic agent that is commonly known as laughing gas. It is subject to abuse because its use is associated with a feeling of light-headedness and of floating, which some persons can experience as pleasurable. With long-term abuse patterns, nitrous oxide use has been associated with delirium and paranoia. Female dental assistants who have been exposed to high levels of nitrous oxide have been reported to have reduced fertility.

OTHER SUBSTANCES

Nutmeg, the spice, can be ingested in a number of preparations; if taken in high-enough doses, it can induce some depersonalization, derealization, and a feeling of heaviness in the limbs. Morning glory seeds, in high-enough doses, can produce a syndrome similar to that seen with lysergic acid diethylamide (LSD), characterized by altered sensory perceptions and mild visual hallucinations. Catnip can produce a marijuanalike intoxication in low doses and LSD-like intoxication in high doses. The betel nut, when chewed, can produce a mild euphoria and a feeling of floating in space. Kava, which is derived from a pepper plant in the South Pacific, can produce sedation and incoordination and is associated with hepatitis, lung abnormalities, and weight loss. DSM-IV also notes that over-the-counter and prescription medications—such as cortisol, antiparkinsonian agents, and antihistamines—can be subject to abuse by some persons.

Polysubstance-Related Disorder

Substance users often abuse more than one substance. DSM-IV allows for a diagnosis of polysubstance dependence if, for a period of at least 12 months, the person has repeatedly used substances from at least three categories of substances (not including nicotine and caffeine), even if the diagnostic criteria for a substance-related disorder are not met for any single substance, as long as, during that period, the criteria for substance dependence have been met for the substances considered as a group.

References

DuRant R H, Rickert V I, Ashworth C S, Newman C, Slavens G: Use of multiple drugs among adolescents who use anabolic steroids. N Engl J Med *328*: 922, 1993.
Jaffe J H: Introduction and overview. In *Comprehensive Textbook of Psychiatry*, ed 6, H I Kaplan, B J Sadock, editors, p 755. Williams & Wilkins, Baltimore, 1995.
Nestler E J: Molecular mechanisms of drug addiction. J Neurosci *12*: 2439, 1992.
Satel S L, Kosten T R, Schuckit M A, Fischman M W: Should protracted withdrawal from drugs be introduced in DSM-IV? Am J Psychiatry *150*: 695, 1993.
Stolerman I: Drugs of abuse: Behavioral principles, methods and terms. Trends Pharmacol Sci *13*: 170, 1992.

Warner L A, Kessler R C, Hughes M, Anthony J C, Nelson C B: Prevalence and correlates of drug use and dependence in the United States. Results from the National Comorbidity Survey. Arch General Psychiatry *52*: 219, 1995.

6.2 ALCOHOL-RELATED DISORDERS

Alcohol abuse and dependence are, by far, the most common substance-related disorders. The direct and indirect cost to society in the United States for alcohol-related disorders is estimated to be more than $150 billion, about $600 per capita. Alcohol abuse and dependence are commonly referred to as alcoholism; however, because the term ''alcoholism'' lacks a precise definition, it is not used in the fourth edition of *Diagnostic and Statistical Manual of Mental Disorders* (DSM-IV) or in most other officially recognized diagnostic systems.

EPIDEMIOLOGY

About 85 percent of all United States residents have had an alcohol-containing drink at least once in their lives, and about 51 percent of all United States adults are current users of alcohol. Those figures merely support the observation that the drinking of alcohol-containing beverages is generally considered an acceptable and common habit. After heart disease and cancer, alcohol-related disorders constitute the third largest health problem in the United States today. In the United States, beer accounts for about half of all alcohol consumption, liquor for about a third, and wine for about a sixth. About 30 to 45 percent of all adults in the United States have had at least one transient episode of alcohol-related problems, usually involving an alcohol-induced amnestic episode (for example, a blackout), driving a motor vehicle while intoxicated, or having missed school or work because of excessive drinking. About 10 percent of women and 20 percent of men have met the diagnostic criteria for alcohol abuse during their life-times, and 3 to 5 percent of women and 10 percent of men have met the diagnostic criteria for the more serious diagnosis of alcohol dependence during their lifetimes. About 200,000 deaths each year are directly related to alcohol abuse. The common causes of death among persons with alcohol-related disorders are suicide, cancer, heart disease, and hepatic disease. Although not always involving persons who meet the diagnostic criteria for an alcohol-related disorder, about half of all automotive fatalities involve a drunken driver, and that percentage increases to about 75 percent if only accidents occurring in the late evening are considered. Alcohol use and alcohol-related disorders are also associated with about 50 percent of all homicides and 25 percent of all suicides. Alcohol abuse reduces life expectancy by about 10 years. Alcohol leads all other substance in substance-related deaths.

Age and Sex

The age group with the highest percentage of active alcohol users, which is also the age group that consumes the most alcohol, is the group in the ages from 20 to 35. That fact, however, risks overshadowing the fact that about 50 percent of adolescents aged 12 to 17 have tried alcohol-containing beverages at least once, and about 25 percent of that age group describe themselves as current users of alcohol. Most persons who drink had their first drinks during their early to middle teens. Although the peak ages of alcohol use extends to age 35, persons in their subsequent decades—their 40s, 50s, 60s, and 70s—have a gradually declining pattern of alcohol use. Among persons 65 years and older, abstainers exceed drinkers in both sexes, and only 7 percent of men and 2 percent of women in that age group are considered heavy drinkers (defined as those who drink almost every day and become intoxicated several times a month).

More men than women use alcohol, and the ratio of men to women for alcohol-related disorder diagnoses is about 2 to 1 or 3 to 1. The course of alcohol abuse also differs between the sexes. Although the symptoms of an alcohol-related disorder may be present in a man while he is in his 20s, the presence of the condition is often not recognized until the man is in his 30s, perhaps because of the relative lack of obligations a man in his 20s has compared with a man in his 30s, who may by then have a family and a responsible job. It is rare for the symptoms of an alcohol-related disorder to appear in a man after age 45, and the appearance of such symptoms should prompt the physician to evaluate the patient for the presence of a mood disorder or secondary psychiatric syndrome. In contrast to the predictable course of alcohol-related disorders among men, the course of the disorders among women varies. The onset of alcohol abuse is generally later in women than in men.

Race and Locale

Although the rate of alcohol-related disorders has traditionally been highest among young white men, evidence now indicates that young black men and young Hispanic men may have surpassed young white men in their rates of alcohol-related disorders. Native American and Inuit (Eskimo) men and women also have a high prevalence of alcohol-related disorders. Asian-Americans have a low prevalence of alcohol-related disorders, although some data suggest that the prevalence is rising among young Asian-Americans.

The consumption of alcohol varies markedly in geographic areas. Drinking is more common in urban areas than in rural areas. In the United States, alcohol consumption is greatest in the Northeast and lowest in the South. Expectancy rates for alcohol-related disorders are about the same in the United States as in Germany, Sweden, Denmark, and England. Expectancy rates are higher in Portugal, Spain, Italy, France, and the former Soviet Union than in the United States.

Psychosocial Factors

Alcohol-related disorders are present in persons from all socioeconomic classes. In fact, stereotyped skid-row alcoholic persons constitute less than 5 percent of persons with alcohol-related disorders in the United States. Moreover, alcohol-related disorders are particularly high in persons who have attained advanced degrees and are in high socioeconomic classes.

In high school, alcohol-related problems are correlated with a history of school difficulties. High school dropouts and persons with a record of frequent truancy and delinquency appear to be at a particularly high risk for alcohol abuse. Those epidemiological data are consistent with the high comorbidity seen between alcohol-related disorders and antisocial personality disorder.

Comorbidity

The most common associated psychiatric diagnoses with the alcohol-related disorders are other substance-related disorders, antisocial personality disorder, mood disorders, and anxiety disorders. Although the data are somewhat controversial, most data suggest that persons with alcohol-related disorders have a markedly higher suicide rate than do the general population.

ANTISOCIAL PERSONALITY DISORDER

A relation between antisocial personality disorder and alcohol-related disorders has frequently been reported. Some studies have suggested that antisocial personality disorder is particularly common in men with an alcohol-related disorder and can precede the development of the alcohol-related disorder. Other studies have suggested that antisocial personality disorder and alcohol-related disorders are completely distinct entities that are not causally related.

MOOD DISORDERS

About 30 to 40 percent of persons with an alcohol-related disorder meet the diagnostic criteria for major depressive disorder sometime during their lifetimes. Depression is more common in alcoholic women than in alcoholic men. Several studies found that depression is likely to occur in alcohol-related disorder patients who have a high daily consumption of alcohol and who have a family history of alcohol abuse. Persons with an alcohol-related disorder and major depressive disorder are at great risk for attempting suicide and are likely to have other substance-related disorder diagnoses. According to some clinicians, depressive symptoms that remain after two to three weeks of sobriety should be treated with antidepressant drugs. Bipolar I disorder patients are thought to be at risk for the development of an alcohol-related disorder because they may use alcohol to self-medicate their manic episodes. Some studies have shown that persons with both alcohol-related disorder and depressive disorder diagnoses have low cerebrospinal fluid (CSF) concentrations of dopamine metabolites (homovanillic acid) and γ-aminobutyric acid (GABA).

ANXIETY DISORDERS

Alcohol is effective in alleviating anxiety, and many persons use alcohol for that reason. Although the comorbidity between alcohol-related disorders and mood disorders is fairly widely recognized, it is less well known that perhaps 25 to 50 percent of all persons with alcohol-related disorders also meet the diagnostic criteria for an anxiety disorder. Phobias and panic disorder are particularly frequent comorbid diagnoses in those patients. Some data indicate that alcohol may be used in an attempt to self-medicate symptoms of agoraphobia or social phobia, but an alcohol-related disorder is likely to precede the development of panic disorder or generalized anxiety disorder.

SUICIDE

Most estimates of the prevalence of suicide among alcohol-related disorder patients range from 10 to 15 percent, although alcohol use itself may be involved in a much higher percentage of suicides. Some investigators have questioned whether the suicide rate among persons with alcohol-related disorder is as high as those numbers suggest. Factors that have been associated with suicide among persons with alcohol-related disorder include the presence of a major depressive episode, weak psychosocial support systems, a serious coexisting medical condition, unemployment, and living alone.

ETIOLOGY

Alcohol-related disorders, like virtually all other psychiatric conditions, probably represent a heterogeneous group of disease processes. In any individual case, psychosocial, genetic, or behavioral factors may be more important than other factors. Within any single set of factors—biological factors, for example—one element (such as a neurotransmitter receptor gene) may be more critically involved than another element (such as a neurotransmitter uptake pump). Except for research purposes, it is not necessary to identify the single causative factor, since the treatment approach to the alcohol-related disorder should be to do whatever is effective, regardless of theory.

Childhood History

Several factors have been identified in the childhood histories of persons who later have an alcohol-related disorder and in the children who are at high risk for having an alcohol-related disorder because one or both of their parents are affected. Children at high risk for alcohol-related disorder have been found in experimental studies to have, on average, a range of deficits on neurocognitive testing, a decreased amplitude of the P300 wave on evoked potential testing, and a variety of abnormalities on electroencephalogram (EEG) recordings. Studies of high-risk offspring in their 20s have also shown a generally blunted effect of alcohol compared with the effect seen in persons who do not have parents with alcohol-related disorder diagnoses. Those findings suggest that some biological heritable brain function may predispose a person to an alcohol-related disorder.

A childhood history of attention-deficit/hyperactivity disorder, conduct disorder, or both increases a child's risk for an alcohol-related disorder as an adult. Personality disorders, especially antisocial personality disorder, as noted above, also predispose a person to an alcohol-related disorder.

Psychoanalytic Factors

Psychoanalytic theories regarding alcohol-related disorders have centered on hypotheses regarding overly punitive superegos and fixation at the oral stage of psychosexual development. According to psychoanalytic theory, persons with harsh superegos who are self-punitive turn to alcohol as a way of diminishing their unconscious stress. Anxiety in persons fixated at the oral stage may be reduced by taking substances, such as alcohol, by mouth. Some psychodynamic psychiatrists describe the general personality of a person with an alcohol-related disorder as shy, isolated, impatient, irritable, anxious, hypersensitive, and sexually repressed. A common psychoanalytic aphorism is that the superego is soluble in alcohol. On a less theoretical level, alcohol may be abused by some persons as a way of reducing tension, anxiety, and various types of psychic pain. Alcohol consumption in some persons also leads to a sense of power and increased self-worth.

Social and Cultural Factors

Some social settings commonly lead to excessive drinking. College dormitories and military bases are two examples of settings where excessive drinking and frequent drinking are often seen as completely normal and socially expected behaviors. Recently, colleges and universities have tried to educate students about the health risks of drinking large quantities of alcohol. Some cultural and ethnic groups are more restrained than others about alcohol consumption. For example, Asian and conservative Protestant persons use alcohol less frequently than do liberal Protestant and Catholic persons.

Behavioral and Learning Factors

Just as cultural factors can affect drinking habits, so can the habits within the family itself, specifically the parental drinking habits. However, some evidence indicates that, although familial drinking habits do affect the children's drinking habits, familial drinking habits are less directly linked to the development of alcohol-related disorders than was previously thought. From a behavioral point of view, the emphasis is on the positive reinforcing aspects of alcohol, which can induce feelings of well-being and euphoria in a person. Furthermore, alcohol consumption can reduce fear and anxiety, which may further encourage drinking.

Genetic and Other Biological Factors

The data strongly indicate a genetic component in at least some forms of alcohol-related disorders. The data for the heritability of alcohol-related disorders in males are stronger than the data for the heritability of alcohol-related disorders in females. Both the design of the studies and the interpretation of their results are complicated, however, by the likely heterogeneity of the disorders and by the likely polygenic causes. Many studies have shown that persons with first-degree relatives affected with an alcohol-related disorder are three to four times more likely to have an alcohol-related disorder than are persons without affected first-degree relatives. And alcohol-related disorder patients with family histories of alcohol abuse are more likely to have severe forms of the disorder and to have higher rates of alcohol intake and more alcohol-related problems than are patients without such family histories. That finding is supported by studies of monozygotic and dizygotic twins, which consistently show a much higher concordance rate among monozygotic twins than among dizygotic twins, who are no more likely to be concordant for alcohol-related disorder than are siblings who are not twins.

The effects of shared environmental factors have been approached through adoptee studies. Those studies show that the children of parents with alcohol-related disorders are still at risk for an alcohol-related disorder, even if the children are raised by families in which the parental figures do not have an alcohol-related disorder. Moreover, children whose biological parents do not have an alcohol-related disorder are not put at increased risk for the disorder if they are raised in households in which the paternal figures do have an alcohol-related disorder.

A single drink is usually considered to contain about 12 grams of ethanol, which is the content of 12 ounces of beer (7.2-proof, 3.6 percent ethanol in the United States), one 4-ounce glass of nonfortified wine, or 1 ounce to 1.5 ounces of an 80-proof (40 percent ethanol) liquor (for example, whiskey or gin). In calculating a patient's intake of alcohol, however, the clinician should be aware that beers vary in their content of alcohol, that beers come in small and large cans and mugs, that glasses of wine range from two to six ounces, and that mixed drinks at some bars and in most homes contain two to three ounces of liquor. Nonetheless, using the moderate sizes of drinks, a clinician can estimate that a single drink increases the blood alcohol level of a 150-pound man 15 to 20 mg/dL, which is about the concentration of alcohol that an average person can metabolize in one hour.

ABSORPTION

About 10 percent of consumed alcohol is absorbed from the stomach, with the remainder absorbed from the small intestine. Peak blood concentration of alcohol is reached in 30 to 90 minutes, usually in 45 to 60 minutes, depending on whether the alcohol was taken on an empty stomach, which enhances absorption, or with food, which delays absorption. The time to peak blood concentration is also a factor of the time during which the alcohol was consumed; a short time reduces the time to peak concentration, and a long time increases the time to peak concentration. Absorption is most rapid with 15 to 30 percent (30- to 60-proof) alcohol-containing beverages. There is some dispute about whether carbonation (for example, in champagne and mixed drinks with seltzer) enhances the absorption of alcohol.

The body has protective devices against inundation by alcohol. For example, if the concentration of alcohol becomes too high in the stomach, mucus is secreted, and the pyloric valve closes. Those actions slow the absorption and keep the alcohol from passing into the small intestine, where no significant restraints to absorption exist. Thus, a large amount of alcohol can remain unabsorbed in the stomach for hours. Furthermore, the pylorospasm often results in nausea and vomiting.

Once alcohol is absorbed into the bloodstream, it is distributed to all the tissues of the body. Because alcohol is uniformly dissolved in the water of the body, tissues containing a high proportion of water receive a high concentration of alcohol. The intoxicating effects are greater when the blood alcohol concentration is rising than when it is falling (the *Mellanby effects*). For that reason the rate of absorption has a direct bearing on the intoxication response.

Metabolism

About 90 percent of absorbed alcohol is metabolized through oxidation in the liver; the remaining 10 percent is excreted unchanged by the kidneys and the lungs. The rate of oxidation by the liver is constant and is independent of the body's energy requirements. The body can metabolize about 15 mg/dL an hour, with a range of 10 to 34 mg/dL an hour. Stated another way, the average person oxidizes three fourths of an ounce of 40 percent (80 proof) alcohol in an hour. In persons who have a history of alcohol consumption, there is an up-regulation of the necessary enzymes, resulting in fast metabolism of the alcohol.

Alcohol is metabolized by two enzymes: alcohol dehydrogenase (ADH) and aldehyde dehydrogenase. ADH catalyzes the conversion of alcohol into acetaldehyde, which is a toxic compound. Aldehyde dehydrogenase catalyzes the conversion of acetaldehyde into acetic acid. Aldehyde dehydrogenase is inhibited by disulfiram (Antabuse), which is often used in the treatment of alcohol-related disorders. Some studies have shown that women have a lower ADH content than do men, which may account for women's tendency to become more intoxicated than men after drinking the same amount of alcohol. The decreased function of alcohol-metabolizing enzymes in some Asian persons can also lead to easy intoxication and toxic symptoms.

Effects on the Brain

BIOCHEMISTRY

In contrast to most other substances of abuse that have identified receptor targets—for example, the N-methyl-D-aspartate (NMDA) receptor of phencyclidine—no single molecular target has been identified as the mediator for the effects of alcohol. The long-standing theory regarding the biochemical effects of alcohol involves its effects on the membranes of neurons. Data support the hypothesis that alcohol has its effects by intercalating itself into membranes, resulting in increased fluidity of the membranes with short-term use. With long-term use, however, the theory hypothesizes that the membranes become rigid or stiff. The fluidity of the membranes is critical to the normal functioning of receptors, ion channels, and other membrane-bound functional proteins. Recent studies attempt to identify specific molecular targets for the effects of alcohol. Most of the attention has been focused on the effects of alcohol at ion channels. Specifically, studies have found that alcohol ion channel activities associated with the nicotinic acetylcholine, serotonin (5-hydroxytryptamine) type 3 (5-HT$_3$), and GABA type A (GABA$_A$) receptors are enhanced by alcohol, whereas ion channel activities associated with glutamate receptors and voltage-gated calcium channels are inhibited.

BEHAVIORAL EFFECTS

The net result of the molecular activities is that alcohol functions as a depressant, much like the barbiturates and the benzodiazepines, with which there is some degree of cross-tolerance and cross-dependence. At a level of 0.05 percent alcohol in the blood, thought, judgment, and restraint are loosened and sometimes disrupted. At a concentration of 0.1 percent, voluntary motor actions usually become perceptibly clumsy. In most states, legal intoxication ranges from 0.1 to 0.15 percent blood alcohol level. At 0.2 percent the function of the entire motor area of the brain is measurably depressed; the parts of the brain that control emotional behavior are also affected. At 0.3 percent a person is commonly confused or may become stuporous. At 0.4 to 0.5 percent a person is in a coma. At higher levels the primitive centers of the brain, which control breathing and heart rate, are affected, and death ensues. Death is secondary to direct respiratory depression or to the aspiration of vomitus. Persons with long-term histories of alcohol abuse, however, are able to tolerate much higher concentrations of alcohol than can alcohol-naive persons and may falsely appear to be less intoxicated than they really are because of their tolerance.

SLEEP EFFECTS

Although alcohol intake in the evening usually results in an increased ease of falling asleep (that is, decreased sleep latency), alcohol also has adverse effects on sleep architecture. Specifically, alcohol use is associated with decreased rapid eye movement sleep (REM or dream sleep), decreased deep sleep (stage 4), and increased sleep fragmentation, including more and longer episodes of awakening. Therefore, it is a myth that drinking alcohol aids sleeping.

Other Physiological Effects

LIVER

The major adverse effects associated with alcohol use are related to liver damage. Alcohol use, even short (week-long) episodes of increased drinking, can result in an accumulation of fats and proteins, resulting in the appearance of a fatty liver, which is sometimes found on physical examination as an enlarged liver. The association between fatty infiltration of the liver and serious liver damage remains unclear. However, alcohol use is associated with the development of alcoholic hepatitis and hepatic cirrhosis.

GASTROINTESTINAL SYSTEM

Long-term heavy drinking is associated with the development of esophagitis, gastritis, achlorhydria, and gastric ulcers. The development of esophageal varices can accompany particularly heavy alcohol abuse, and the rupture of the varices is a medical emergency that often results in death due to exsanguination. Occasionally, disorders of the small intestine also occur. Pancreatitis, pancreatic insufficiency, and pancreatic cancer are also associated with heavy alcohol use. Heavy alcohol intake may interfere with the normal processes of food digestion and absorption. As a result, the food that is consumed is inadequately digested. Alcohol abuse also appears to inhibit the capacity of the intestine to absorb various nutrients, including vitamins and amino acids. That effect, coupled with the often poor dietary habits of persons with alcohol-related disorders, can result in serious vitamin deficiencies, particularly of the B vitamins.

OTHER BODILY SYSTEMS

A significant intake of alcohol has been associated with increased blood pressure, dysregulation of lipoproteins and triglycerides, and increased risk for myocardial infarctions and cerebrovascular diseases. Alcohol has been shown to affect the hearts of even nonalcoholic persons, increasing the resting cardiac output, heart rate, and myocardial oxygen consumption. Evidence indicates that alcohol intake can adversely affect the hematopoietic system and can increase the incidence of cancer, particularly head, neck, esophageal, stomach, hepatic, colonic, and lung cancer. Acute intoxication may also be associated with hypoglycemia, which, when unrecognized, may be responsible for some of the sudden deaths of intoxicated people. Muscle weakness is a side effect of alcoholism.

LABORATORY TESTS

The adverse effects of alcohol are reflected in common laboratory tests, which can be useful diagnostic aids in identifying persons with alcohol-related disorders. The γ-glutamyltranspeptidase levels are elevated in about 80 percent of all persons with alcohol-related disorders, and the mean corpuscular volume (MCV) is elevated in about 60 percent, more so in women than in men. Other laboratory test results that may be elevated in association with alcohol abuse are uric acid, triglycerides, serum glutamic-oxaloacetic transaminase (SGOT), also called aspartate aminotransferase (AST), and serum glutamic-pyruvic transaminase (SGPT), also called alanine aminotransferase (ALT).

Drug Interactions

The interaction between alcohol and other substances can be dangerous, even fatal. Certain substances, such as alcohol and phenobarbital (Luminal) are metabolized by the liver; their prolonged use may lead to an acceleration of their metabolism. When alcoholic persons are sober, that accelerated metabolism makes them unusually tolerant to many drugs, such as sedatives and hypnotics; but, when alcoholic persons are intoxicated, those drugs compete with the alcohol for the same detoxification mechanisms, and potentially toxic blood levels of all involved substances can accumulate.

The effects of alcohol and other central nervous system (CNS) depressants are usually synergistic. Sedatives, hypnotics, and drugs that relieve pain, motion sickness, head colds, and allergy symptoms must be used with caution by alcoholic persons. Narcotics depress the sensory areas of the cerebral cortex, resulting in pain relief, sedation, apathy, drowsiness, and sleep. High doses can result in respiratory failure and death. Increasing the dosages of sedative-hypnotic drugs, such as chloral hydrate (Noctec) and benzodiazepines, especially when they are combined with alcohol, produces a range of effects from sedation to motor and intellectual impairment and progressing to stupor, coma, and death. Since sedatives and other psychotropics can potentiate the effects of alcohol, patients should be instructed about the dangers of combining CNS depressants and alcohol, particularly when they are driving or operating machinery.

DISORDERS

Alcohol Dependence and Alcohol Abuse

DIAGNOSIS AND CLINICAL FEATURES

In DSM-IV all substance-related disorders have the same criteria for dependence and abuse (see Tables 6.1–3 and 6.1–4). With regard to alcohol dependence and alcohol abuse, the need for the daily use of large amounts of alcohol for adequate functioning, a regular pattern of heavy drinking limited to weekends, and long periods of sobriety interspersed with binges of heavy alcohol intake lasting for weeks or months are strongly suggestive of those alcohol use disorders. The patterns are often associated with such behaviors a (1) the inability to cut down or stop drinking, (2) repeated efforts to control or reduce excessive drinking by going on the wagon (periods of temporary abstinence) or restricting drinking to certain times of the day, (3) binges (remaining intoxicated throughout the day for at least two days), (4) the occasional consumption of a fifth of spirits (or its equivalent in wine or beer), (5) amnestic periods for events occurring while intoxicated (blackouts), (6) the continuation of drinking despite a serious physical disorder that the person knows is exacerbated by alcohol use, and (7) the drinking of nonbeverage alcohol, such as fuel and commercial products containing alcohol. In addition, people with alcohol dependence and alcohol abuse show impaired social or occupational functioning because of alcohol use, such as violence while intoxicated, absence from work, loss of job, legal difficulties (for example, arrest for intoxicated behavior and traffic accidents while intoxicated), and arguments or difficulties with family members or friends because of excessive alcohol use.

Table 6.2–1. Diagnostic Criteria for Alcohol Intoxication

A. Recent ingestion of alcohol.

B. Clinically significant maladaptive behavioral or psychological changes (e.g., inappropriate sexual or aggressive behavior, mood lability, impaired judgment, impaired social or occupational functioning) that developed during, or shortly after, alcohol ingestion.

C. One (or more) of the following signs, developing during, or shortly after, alcohol use:

(1) slurred speech
(2) incoordination
(3) unsteady gait
(4) nystagmus
(5) impairment in attention or memory
(6) stupor or coma

D. The symptoms are not due to a general medical condition and are not better accounted for by another mental disorder.

Table from DSM-IV, *Diagnostic and Statistical Manual of Mental Disorders*, ed 4. Copyright American Psychiatric Association, Washington, 1994. Used with permission.

Table 6.2–2. Diagnostic Criteria for Alcohol Withdrawal

A. Cessation of (or reduction in) alcohol use that has been heavy and prolonged.

B. Two (or more) of the following, developing within several hours to a few days after criterion A:

(1) automatic hyperactivity (e.g., sweating or pulse rate greater than 100)
(2) increased hand tremor
(3) insomnia
(4) nausea or vomiting
(5) transient visual, tactile, or auditory hallucinations or illusions
(6) psychomotor agitation
(7) anxiety
(8) grand mal seizures

C. The symptoms in criterion B cause clinically significant distress or impairment in social, occupational, or other important areas of functioning.

D. The symptoms are not due to a general medical condition and are not better accounted for by another mental disorder.

Table from DSM-IV, *Diagnostic and Statistical Manual of Mental Disorders*, ed 4. Copyright American Psychiatric Association, Washington, 1994. Used with permission.

Alcohol Intoxication

DIAGNOSIS AND CLINICAL FEATURES

DSM-IV has formal criteria regarding the diagnosis of alcohol intoxication (Table 6.2–1). The criteria emphasize a sufficient amount of alcohol consumption, specific maladaptive behavioral changes, signs of neurological impairment, and the absence of other confounding diagnoses or conditions. Alcohol intoxication is not a trivial condition. Extreme alcohol intoxication can lead to coma, respiratory depression, and death, either because of respiratory arrest or because of the aspiration of vomitus. Treatment for severe alcohol intoxication involves mechanical ventilatory support in an intensive care unit, with attention to the patient's acid-base balance, electrolytes, and temperature. Some studies of cerebral blood flow (CBF) during alcohol intoxication have found a modest increase in CBF after the ingestion of small amounts of alcohol, but CBF decreases with continued drinking.

The severity of the symptoms of alcohol intoxication correlates roughly with the blood concentration of alcohol, which reflects the alcohol concentration in the brain. At the onset of intoxication, some persons become talkative and gregarious; some become withdrawn and sullen; others become belligerent. Some patients show a liability of mood, with intermittent episodes of laughing and crying. A short-term tolerance to alcohol may occur, such that the person seems to be less intoxicated after many hours of drinking than after only a few hours.

The medical complications of intoxication include those that result from falls, such as subdural hematomas and fractures. Telltale signs of frequent bouts of intoxication are facial hematomas, particularly about the eyes, which are the result of falls or fights while drunk. In cold climates, hypothermia and death may occur because the intoxicated person is exposed to the elements. A person with alcohol intoxication may also be predisposed to infections, secondary to a suppression of the immune system.

Alcohol Withdrawal

DIAGNOSIS AND CLINICAL FEATURES

Conditions that may predispose to or aggravate withdrawal symptoms include fatigue, malnutrition, physical illness, and depression. The DSM-IV criteria for alcohol withdrawal (Table 6.2–2) require the cessation or reduction of alcohol use that was heavy and prolonged, as well as the presence of specific physical or neuropsychiatric symptoms. The DSM-IV diagnosis also allows for the specification of "with perceptual disturbances." One recent positron emission tomographic (PET) study of blood flow during alcohol withdrawal in otherwise healthy persons with alcohol dependence found a globally low rate of metabolic activity, although, with further inspection of the data, the authors concluded that activity was especially decreased in the left parietal and right frontal areas.

The classic sign of alcohol withdrawal is tremulousness, although the spectrum of symptoms can expand to include psychotic and perceptual symptoms (for example, delusions and hallucinations), seizures, and the symptoms of delirium tremens (DTs), called alcohol withdrawal delirium in DSM-IV. Tremulousness (commonly called the shakes or jitters) develops six to eight hours after the cessation of drinking, the psychotic and perceptual symptoms start in 8 to 12 hours, seizures in 12 to 24 hours, and DTs within 72 hours, although physicians should watch for the development of DTs for the first week of withdrawal. The syndrome of withdrawal sometimes skips the usual progression and, for example, goes directly to DTs.

The tremor of alcohol withdrawal can be similar either to physiological tremor, with a continuous tremor of great amplitude and of more than 8 Hz, or to familial tremor, with bursts of tremor activity slower than 8 Hz. Other symptoms of withdrawal include general irritability, gastrointestinal symptoms (for example, nausea and vomiting), and sympathetic autonomic hyperactivity, including anxiety, arousal, sweating, facial flushing, mydriasis, tachycardia, and mild hypertension. Patients experiencing alcohol withdrawal are generally alert but may startle easily.

SEIZURES

Seizures associated with alcohol withdrawal are stereotyped, generalized, and tonic-clonic in character. Patients often have more than one seizure in the three to six hours after the first seizure. Status epilepticus is relatively rare in alcohol withdrawal patients, occurring in less than 3 percent of all patients.

Although anticonvulsant medications are not required in the management of alcohol withdrawal seizures, the cause of the seizures is difficult to establish when a patient is first assessed in the emergency room; thus, many patients with withdrawal seizures receive anticonvulsant medications, which are then discontinued once the cause of the seizures is recognized. Seizure activity in patients with known alcohol abuse histories should still prompt the clinician to consider other possible causative factors, including head injuries, CNS infections, CNS neoplasms, and other cerebrovascular diseases; long-term severe alcohol abuse can result in hypoglycemia, hyponatremia, and hypomagnesemia—all of which can also be associated with seizures.

TREATMENT

The primary medications for the control of alcohol withdrawal symptoms are the benzodiazepines. Many studies have found that benzodiazepines help control seizure activity, delirium, anxiety, tachycardia, hypertension, diaphoresis, and tremor associated with alcohol withdrawal. Benzodiazepines can be given either orally or parenterally; however, neither diazepam (Valium) nor chlordiazepoxide (Librium) should be given intramuscularly (IM) because of their erratic absorption by that route. The clinician must titrate the dosage of the benzodiazepine, starting with a high dosage and lowering the dosage as the patient recovers. Sufficient benzodiazepines should be used to keep patients calm and sedated but not so sedated that they cannot be aroused for the clinician to perform appropriate procedures, including neurological examinations.

Although benzodiazepines are the standard treatment for alcohol withdrawal, a number of studies have shown that carbamazepine (Tegretol) in dosages of 800 mg a day is as effective as benzodiazepines and has the added benefit of minimal abuse liability. That use of carbamazepine is gradually becoming common in the United States and Europe. The β-adrenergic receptor antagonists and clonidine (Catapres) have also been used to block the symptoms of sympathetic hyperactivity; however, neither of those drugs is an effective treatment for seizures or delirium.

Alcohol Delirium

DIAGNOSIS AND CLINICAL FEATURES

DSM-IV contains the diagnostic criteria for alcohol intoxication delirium in the category of substance intoxication delirium and the diagnostic criteria for alcohol withdrawal delirium in the category of substance withdrawal delirium (Section 4.2). Patients with recognized alcohol withdrawal symptoms should be carefully monitored to prevent progression to alcohol withdrawal delirium, also known as the DTs. Alcohol withdrawal delirium is a medical emergency that can result in significant morbidity and mortality. Delirious patients are a danger to themselves and to others because of the unpredictability of their behavior. The patients may be assaultive or suicidal or may be acting on hallucinations or delusional thoughts as if they were genuine dangers. Untreated, DTs has a mortality rate of 20 percent, usually as a result of an intercurrent medical illness, such as pneumonia, renal disease, hepatic insufficiency, or heart failure. Although withdrawal seizures commonly precede the development of alcohol withdrawal delirium, the delirium can also appear unheralded. The essential feature of the syndrome is

delirium that occurs within one week after the person stops drinking or reduces his or her intake of alcohol. In addition to the symptoms of delirium, the features include (1) autonomic hyperactivity, such as tachycardia, diaphoresis, fever, anxiety, insomnia, and hypertension; (2) perceptual distortions, which are most frequently visual or tactile hallucinations; and (3) fluctuating levels of psychomotor activity, ranging from hyperexcitability to lethargy.

About 5 percent of all alcoholic persons who are hospitalized have DTs. Since the syndrome usually develops on the third hospital day, a patient admitted for an unrelated condition may unexpectedly go into an episode of delirium, which is the first sign of a previously undiagnosed alcohol-related disorder. Episodes of DTs usually begin in the patient's 30s or 40s after 5 to 15 years of heavy drinking, typically of the binge type. Physical illness (for example, hepatitis or pancreatitis) predisposes to the syndrome; a person in good physical health rarely has DTs during alcohol withdrawal.

TREATMENT

The best treatment for DTs is its prevention. Patients who are withdrawing from alcohol who exhibit any withdrawal phenomena should receive a benzodiazepine, such as 25 to 50 mg of chlordiazepoxide every two to four hours until they seem to be out of danger. Once the delirium appears, however, 50 to 100 mg of chlordiazepoxide should be given every four hours orally, or intravenous (IV) lorazepam (Ativan) should be used if oral medication is not possible. A high-calorie, high-carbohydrate diet supplemented by multivitamins is also important. Physically restraining patients with the DTs is risky, since they may fight against the restraints to a dangerous level of exhaustion. When patients are disorderly and uncontrollable, a seclusion room can be used. Dehydration, often contributed to by diaphoresis and fever, can be corrected with fluids by mouth or intravenously. Anorexia, vomiting, and diarrhea often occur during withdrawal. Antipsychotic medications should be avoided because they may reduce the seizure threshold in the patient.

The need for warm, supportive psychotherapy in the treatment of DTs is essential. Patients are often bewildered, frightened, and anxious because of their tumultuous symptoms. Skillful verbal support is imperative.

The emergence of focal neurological symptoms, lateralizing seizures, increased intracranial pressure, evidence of skull fractures, or other indications of CNS pathology should prompt the clinician to examine the patient for additional neurological diseases. Nonbenzodiazepine anticonvulsant medication is not useful in preventing or treating alcohol withdrawal convulsions, although benzodiazepines are generally effective.

Alcohol-Induced Persisting Dementia

The legitimacy of the concept of alcohol-induced persisting dementia remains controversial, inasmuch as some clinicians and researchers believe that it is difficult to separate the toxic effects of alcohol abuse from the CNS damage done by poor nutrition, multiple trauma, and the CNS damage that follows the malfunctioning of other bodily organs (for example, the liver, the pancreas, and the kidneys). Although several studies have found enlarged ventricles and cortical atrophy in persons with dementia and a history of alcohol dependence, the studies do not help clarify the cause of the dementia. Nonetheless, the diagnosis of alcohol-induced persisting dementia is contained in DSM-IV (Section 4.3). The controversy regarding the diagnosis should encourage the clinician to complete a diagnostic assessment of the dementia before concluding that the dementia was caused by alcohol.

Alcohol-Induced Persisting Amnestic Disorder

DIAGNOSIS AND CLINICAL FEATURES

The diagnostic criteria of alcohol-induced persisting amnestic disorder are contained in the DSM-IV category of substance-induced persisting amnestic disorder (Section 4.4). The essential feature of alcohol-induced persisting amnestic disorder is a disturbance in short-term memory caused by the prolonged heavy use of alcohol. Since the disorder usually occurs in persons who have been drinking heavily for many years, the disorder is rare in persons under the age of 35.

WERNICKE-KORSAKOFF SYNDROME

The classic names for alcohol-induced persisting amnestic disorder are Wernicke's encephalopathy (a set of acute symptoms) and Korsakoff's syndrome (a chronic condition). Whereas Wernicke's syndrome is completely reversible with treatment, only about 20 percent of Korsakoff's syndrome patients recover. The pathophysiological connection between the two syndromes is thiamine deficiency, caused either by poor nutritional habits or by malabsorption problems. Thiamine is a cofactor for several important enzymes, and it may also be involved in the conduction of the axon potential along the axon and in synaptic transmission. The neuropathological lesions are symmetrical and paraventricular, involving the mammillary bodies, the thalamus, the hypothalamus, the midbrain, the pons, the medulla, the fornix, and the cerebellum.

Wernicke's encephalopathy is an acute neurological disorder characterized by ataxia (affecting primarily the gait), vestibular dysfunction, confusion, and a variety of ocular motility abnormalities, including horizontal nystagmus, lateral rectal palsy, and gaze palsy. Usually, those eye signs are bilateral, although not necessarily symmetrical. Other eye signs may include a sluggish reaction to light and anisocoria. Wernicke's encephalopathy may clear spontaneously in a few days or weeks, or it may progress into Korsakoff's syndrome.

TREATMENT

The early stages of Wernicke's encephalopathy respond rapidly to large doses of parenteral thiamine, which is believed to be effective in preventing the progression into Korsakoff's syndrome. The dosage of thiamine is usually initiated at 100 mg by mouth two to three times daily and is continued for one to two weeks. In patients with alcohol-related disorders who are being given IV administrations of glucose solution, it is good practice to include 100 mg of thiamine in each liter of the glucose solution.

Korsakoff's syndrome is the chronic amnestic syndrome that can follow Wernicke's syndrome, and the two syndromes are believed to be pathophysiologically related. The cardinal features of Korsakoff's syndrome are impaired mental syndrome (especially recent memory) and anterograde amnesia in an alert and responsive patient. The patient may or may not have the symptom of confabulation. Treatment of Korsakoff's syndrome

is also 100 mg thiamine given by mouth two to three times daily; the treatment should be continued for 3 to 12 months. Few patients who progress to Korsakoff's syndrome ever fully recover, although a substantial proportion have some improvement in their cognitive abilities with thiamine and nutritional support.

BLACKOUTS

Alcohol-related blackouts are not included in DSM-IV's diagnostic classification, although the symptom of alcohol intoxication does exist and is common. Blackouts are similar to episodes of transient global amnesia (Section 4.4) in that they are discrete episodes of anterograde amnesia, although blackouts occur in association with alcohol intoxication. The periods of amnesia can be particularly distressing because people may fear that they have unknowingly harmed someone or behaved imprudently while intoxicated.

Alcohol-Induced Psychotic Disorder

DIAGNOSIS AND CLINICAL FEATURES

The diagnostic criteria for alcohol-induced psychotic disorder (for example, delusions, hallucinations) are found in the DSM-IV category of substance-induced psychotic disorder (Section 8.1). DSM-IV further allows the specification of onset (during intoxication or withdrawal) and whether hallucinations or delusions are present. The most common hallucinations are auditory, usually voices, but they are often unstructured. The voices are characteristically maligning, reproachful, or threatening, although some patients report that the voices are pleasant and nondisruptive. The hallucinations usually last less than a week, although during that week impaired reality testing is common. After the episode, most patients realize the hallucinatory nature of the symptoms.

Hallucinations after alcohol withdrawal are considered rare symptoms, and the syndrome is distinct from that of alcohol withdrawal delirium. The hallucinations can occur at any age, but they are usually associated with persons who have been abusing alcohol for a long time. Although the hallucinations usually resolve within a week, some may linger; in those cases, the clinician must begin to consider other psychotic disorders in the differential diagnosis. Alcohol withdrawal–related hallucinations are differentiated from the hallucinations of schizophrenia by the temporal association with alcohol withdrawal, the absence of a classic history of schizophrenia, and the usually short-lived duration of the hallucinations. Alcohol withdrawal–related hallucinations are differentiated from the DTs by the presence of a clear sensorium in the patients.

TREATMENT

The treatment of alcohol withdrawal–related hallucinations is much like the treatment of DTs—benzodiazepines, adequate nutrition, and fluids if necessary. If that regimen fails and in long-term cases, antipsychotics may be used.

Other Alcohol-Related Disorders

ALCOHOL-INDUCED MOOD DISORDER

DSM-IV allows for the diagnosis of alcohol-induced mood disorder with manic, depressive, or mixed features (Section 9.3) and for the specification of onset during either intoxication or withdrawal. As with all the secondary and substance-induced disorders, the clinician must consider whether the abused substance and the symptoms have a causal relation.

ALCOHOL-INDUCED ANXIETY DISORDER

DSM-IV allows for the diagnosis of alcohol-induced anxiety disorder (Section 10.1). DSM-IV further suggests that the diagnosis specify whether the symptoms are those of generalized anxiety, panic attacks, obsessive-compulsive symptoms, or phobic symptoms and whether the onset was during intoxication or during withdrawal. The association between alcohol use and anxiety symptoms has been discussed above; deciding whether the anxiety symptoms are primary or secondary can be difficult.

ALCOHOL-INDUCED SEXUAL DYSFUNCTION

DSM-IV allows for the diagnosis of symptoms of sexual dysfunction associated with alcohol intoxication. The formal diagnosis is alcohol-induced sexual dysfunction (Section 14.2).

ALCOHOL-INDUCED SLEEP DISORDER

DSM-IV allows for the diagnosis of sleep disorders that have their onset during either alcohol intoxication or alcohol withdrawal. The diagnostic criteria for alcohol-induced sleep disorder are found in the sleep disorders section (Section 17.2).

ALCOHOL-RELATED USE DISORDER NOT OTHERWISE SPECIFIED

DSM-IV allows for the diagnosis of alcohol-related disorder not otherwise specified (NOS) for alcohol-related disorders that do not meet the diagnostic criteria for any of the other diagnoses.

Idiosyncratic Alcohol Intoxication

A significant debate concerns whether the diagnostic entity of idiosyncratic alcohol intoxication really exists; it is not recognized as an official diagnosis in DSM-IV. Several well-controlled studies of persons who supposedly have the disorder have raised questions regarding its validity. The condition has been variously called pathological, complicated, atypical, and paranoid alcohol intoxication; all those terms indicate that a severe behavioral syndrome develops rapidly after the person consumes a small amount of alcohol that, in most people, has minimal behavioral effects. The importance of the diagnosis lies in the forensic arena. Alcohol intoxication is generally not accepted as grounds for not being held responsible for one's activities. Idiosyncratic alcohol intoxication, however, can be used in a person's defense if a defense lawyer can successfully argue that the defendant has an unexpected, idiosyncratic, and pathological reaction to a minimal amount of alcohol.

The treatment of idiosyncratic alcohol intoxication involves protecting patients from harming themselves and others. Physical restraint may be necessary but is difficult because of the abrupt onset of the condition. Once the patient has been restrained, an injection of an antipsychotic drug, such as haloperidol (Haldol), is useful for controlling assaultiveness.

The condition must be differentiated from other causes of abrupt behavioral change, such as complex partial epilepsy. Several persons with the disorder have been reported to show temporal lobe spiking on an electroencephalogram (EEG) after ingesting small amounts of alcohol.

Other Alcohol-Related Neurological Disorders

ALCOHOLIC PELLAGRA ENCEPHALOPATHY

One diagnosis is of potential interest to psychiatrists who may be presented with a patient who appears to be afflicted with Wernicke's syndrome or Korsakoff's syndrome but who has no response to thiamine treatment. The symptoms of alcoholic pellagra encephalopathy include confusion, clouding of consciousness, myoclonus, oppositional hypertonias, fatigue, apathy, irritability, anorexia, insomnia, and sometimes delirium. The patients suffer from a deficiency of niacin (nicotinic acid), and the specific treatment is 50 mg of niacin by mouth four times daily or 25 mg parenterally two to three times daily.

Fetal Alcohol Syndrome

The data clearly indicate that women who are pregnant or who are breast-feeding should not drink alcohol. Fetal alcohol syndrome is the result of exposing fetuses to alcohol in utero when their mothers drink alcohol. Fetal alcohol syndrome is the leading cause of mental retardation in the United States. The presence of the alcohol inhibits intrauterine growth and postnatal development. Microcephaly, craniofacial malformations, and limb and heart defects are common in affected infants. Short stature as adults and the development of a range of adult maladaptive behaviors have also been associated with fetal alcohol syndrome.

The risk of an alcoholic woman's having a defective child is as high as 35 percent. Although the precise mechanism of the damage to the fetus is unknown, the damage seems to be the result of exposure in utero to ethanol or its metabolites. Alcohol may also cause hormone imbalances that increase the risk of abnormalities.

TREATMENT

Although some clinicians and groups are proponents of the concept of controlled drinking, most clinicians and the majority of well-controlled research studies indicate that complete abstinence from alcohol has to be the centerpiece of a successful treatment strategy for alcohol abuse. Most people with alcohol-related disorders come to treatment as a result of pressure from a spouse or an employer or fear that continued drinking will have a fatal outcome. The patients who are persuaded, encouraged, or even coerced into treatment by persons who are meaningful to them are more apt to remain in treatment and have a better prognosis than are those who are not so pressured. The best prognosis, however, is for the affected persons who come to a mental health worker voluntarily because they conclude that they are alcoholics and that they need help.

Psychotherapy

When psychotherapy focuses on the reasons that the person drinks, it is more successful than when it focuses on vague psychodynamic issues. The specific focus is on the situations in which the patient drinks, the motivating forces behind the drinking, the expected results from drinking, and alternative ways of dealing with those situations. Involving an interested and cooperative spouse in conjoint therapy for at least some of the sessions is highly effective.

The initial contact with a person with an alcohol-related disorder is crucial to successful treatment. In the early encounter the therapist needs to be active and supportive, because patients with alcohol problems often anticipate rejection and may misinterpret a passive therapeutic role as rejecting. The patients often have an ambivalent relation to therapy, and they may miss appointments or have relapses with regard to drinking. Many therapists attempt to view alcohol abuse less in terms of an individual patient and more in terms of how that patient interacts with family members, work or school colleagues, and society in general.

The therapist must also deal with alcohol as a psychological defense; the removal of the emotional and intellectual barriers between the patient and the therapist should be an early goal. The therapist must be prepared to have the therapeutic bond tested again and again and cannot hide behind the screen of the patient's lack of motivation when relapses become threatening to the therapist. Depressions can be countered by the active, supportive role of the therapist and at times by the addition of antidepressant drug medication.

Medication

DISULFIRAM

Disulfiram (Antabuse) competitively inhibits the enzyme aldehyde dehydrogenase, so that even a single drink usually causes a toxic reaction because of acetaldehyde accumulation in the blood. Administration of the drug should not begin until 24 hours have elapsed since the patient's last drink. The patient must be in good health, highly motivated, and cooperative. The physician must warn the patient about the consequences of ingesting alcohol while taking the drug and for as long as two weeks thereafter. Those who drink while taking the 250-mg daily dose of disulfiram experience flushing and feelings of heat in the face, the sclera, the upper limbs, and the chest. They may become pale, hypotensive, and nauseated and experience serious malaise. They may also experience dizziness, blurred vision, palpitations, air hunger, and numbness of the extremities. The most serious potential consequence is severe hypotension. Patients may also have a response to alcohol ingested in such substances as sauces and vinegars and even to inhaled alcohol vapors from after-shave lotions. The syndrome, once elicited, typically lasts some 30 to 60 minutes but can persist longer. With dosages of more than 250 mg, toxic psychoses can occur, with memory impairment and confusion. The drug can also exacerbate psychotic symptoms in some schizophrenic patients in the absence of alcohol intake.

PSYCHOTROPICS

Naltrexone (ReVia) decreases alcohol craving, probably by blocking the release of endogenous opioids. Both antianxiety agents and antidepressants may be useful in the treatment of anxiety and depressive symptoms in patients with alcohol-related disorders. However, increasing attention is being given to the possibility of using psychoactive drugs in the control of the sensation of craving for alcohol. Several trials of lithium (Eskalith) in patients who have both an alcohol-related disorder and a mood disorder of any type have shown a reduction in both the desire to drink and the mood cycles. Other studies with lithium have not consistently confirmed those results. There is also increasing interest in the use of serotonergic drugs in the control of drinking and alcohol craving. Some evidence indicates that the serotonin-specific reuptake inhibitors or trazodone (Desyrel) may be effective. Recent research focuses on specific serotonin receptor agonists and serotonin type 3 (5-HT$_3$) receptor antagonists. Some data indicate that dopaminergic agonists, such as low dosages of apomorphine or bromocriptine (Parlo-

del), may also be effective in reducing the patient's craving. For the most part, however, the treatment strategies directed at reducing the craving are still in early stages of research and require further validation.

Behavior Therapy

Behavior therapy teaches the person with an alcohol-related disorder other ways to reduce anxiety. Relaxation training, assertiveness training, self-control skills, and new strategies to master the environment are emphasized. A number of operant conditioning programs condition people with alcohol-related disorders to modify their drinking behavior or to stop drinking. The reinforcements have included monetary rewards, an opportunity to live in an enriched inpatient environment, and access to pleasurable social interactions.

Alcoholics Anonymous

Alcoholics Anonymous (AA) is a voluntary supportive fellowship of hundreds of thousands of persons with alcohol-related disorders that was founded in 1935 by two alcohol-dependent men, a stockbroker and a surgeon. Physicians should refer alcoholic patients to AA as part of a multiple-treatment approach. Frequently, patients who object when AA is initially suggested later derive much benefit from the organization and become enthusiastic participants. Its members make a public admission of their alcohol-related disorder, and abstinence is the rule.

AL-ANON

Al-Anon is an organization for the spouses of persons with alcohol-related disorders; it is structured along the same lines as AA. The aims of Al-Anon are, through group support, to assist the efforts of the spouses to regain self-esteem, to refrain from feeling responsible for the spouse's drinking, and to develop a rewarding life for themselves and their families. Alateen is directed toward the children of alcohol-dependent persons to help them understand their parents' alcohol dependence.

Halfway Houses

The discharge of an alcoholic patient from a hospital often poses serious placement problems. Home or other familiar environments may be counterproductive, unsupportive, or too unstructured. A halfway house is an important treatment resource that provides emotional support, counseling, and progressive entry back into society.

References

Babor T F, Hofman M, DelBoca F K, Hesselbrock V, Meyer R E, Dolinsky Z S, Rounsaville B: Types of alcoholics: I. Evidence for an empirically derived typology based on indicators of vulnerability and severity. Arch Gen Psychiatry 49: 599, 1992.

Noble E P: The D$_2$ dopamine receptor gene: A review of association studies in alcoholism. Behav Genet 23: 119, 1993.

O'Malley S S: Integration of opioid antagonists and psychosocial therapy in the treatment of narcotic and alcohol dependence. J Clin Psychiatry 56: 30, 1995.

Rubino F A: Neurologic complications of alcoholism. Psychiatr Clin North Am 15: 359, 1992.

Schuckit M A: Alcohol-related disorders. In Comprehensive Textbook of Psychiatry, ed 6, H I Kaplan, B J Sadock, editors, p 775. Williams & Wilkins, Baltimore, 1995.

Schuckit M A, Smith T L, Anthenelli R, Irwin M: Clinical course of alcoholism in 636 male inpatients. Am J Psychiatry 150; 786, 1993.

6.3 AMPHETAMINE (OR AMPHETAMINELIKE)-RELATED DISORDERS

The racemate amphetamine (Benzedrine) was first synthesized in 1887 and was introduced to clinical practice in 1932 as an over-the-counter inhaler for the treatment of nasal congestion and asthma. In 1937 amphetamine tablets were introduced for the treatment of narcolepsy, postencephalitic parkinsonism, depression, and lethargy. The production, the legal use, and the illicit use of amphetamines increased until the 1970s, when a variety of social and regulatory factors began to curb their widespread use. The currently approved indications for amphetamine are limited to attention-deficit/hyperactivity disorder, narcolepsy, and depressive disorders. Amphetamines are also used in the treatment of obesity, although their efficacy and safety for that indication are controversial.

FORMS

Currently, the major amphetamines available in the United States are dextroamphetamine (Dexedrine), methamphetamine (Desoxyn), and methylphenidate (Ritalin). Those drugs go by such street names as crack, crystal, crystal meth, and speed. As a general class, the amphetamines are also referred to as sympathomimetics, stimulants, and psychostimulants.

The typical amphetamines are used to increase performance and to induce a euphoric feeling. Students studying for examinations, long-distance truck drivers on long hauls, business people with important deadlines, and athletes in competition are some examples of the people and situations for which amphetamines are used. Amphetamines are addictive drugs, although not as addictive as cocaine.

Other amphetamine-related substance are ephedrine and propranolamine, which are available over the counter in the United States as nasal decongestants. Phenylpropanolamine (PPA) is also available as an appetite suppressant. Although less potent than the classic amphetamines, ephedrine and propranolamine are subject to abuse, partly because of their easy availability and low price. Both drugs, propranolamine in particular, can dangerously exacerbate hypertension, precipitate a toxic psychosis, or result in death. The safety margin for propranolamine is particularly narrow, and three to four times the normal dose can result in life-threatening hypertension.

Ice

Ice is a pure form of methamphetamine that can be inhaled, smoked, or injected intravenously by abusers of the substance. Ice has been used most heavily on the West Coast of the United States and in Hawaii. The psychological effects of ice last for hours and are described as being particularly powerful. Unlike crack cocaine, which has to be imported, ice is a synthetic drug that can be manufactured in domestic illicit laboratories. Some law enforcement agencies and urban emergency room physicians think that ice may become a widespread drug of abuse over the next five years.

Amphetamine-Related Substances

The classic amphetamine drugs (dextroamphetamine, methamphetamine, and methylphenidate) have their major effects through the dopaminergic system. A number of so-called designer amphetamines have been synthesized and have neurochemical effects on both the serotonergic and the dopaminergic systems and behavioral effects that reflect a combination of amphetaminelike and hallucinogenlike activities. Some psychopharmacologists classify the designer amphetamines as hallucinogens; however, this textbook classifies them with the amphetamines because they are closely related structurally. Examples of the designer amphetamines include 3,4-methylenedioxyamphetamine (MDMA), also referred to as ecstasy, X, and Adam; N-ethyl-3,4-methylenedioxyamphetamine (MDEA), also referred to as Eve; 5-methoxy-3,4-methylenedioxyamphetamine (MMDA); and 2,5-dimethoxy-4-methylamphetamine (DOM), also referred to as STP. Of those drugs, MDMA has been studied most closely and is perhaps the most widely available.

EPIDEMIOLOGY

In 1991 about 7 percent of the United States population had used stimulants at least once, although fewer than 1 percent were current users. The 18- to 25-year-old age group had the highest level of use, with 9 percent reporting use at least once and 1 percent describing themselves as current users. Use among the 12-to 17-year-old age group is alarmingly high, with 3 percent reporting use at least once and 1 percent reporting current use. Amphetamine use is present in all socioeconomic groups, and the general trend is for amphetamine use to be high among white professionals. Since amphetamines are available by prescription for specific indications, the prescribing physician must be aware of the risk of abuse of the amphetamine by others, including friends and family members of the patient receiving the amphetamine. No reliable data are available on the epidemiology of designer amphetamine use.

NEUROPHARMACOLOGY

All the amphetamines are rapidly absorbed orally and are associated with a rapid onset of action, usually within one hour when taken orally. The classic amphetamines are also taken intravenously; by that route they have an almost immediate effect. Nonprescribed amphetamines and designer amphetamines are also ingested by inhaling (snorting). Tolerance does develop with both the classic amphetamines and the designer amphetamines, although amphetamine users often overcome the tolerance by taking more of the drug. Amphetamine is less addictive than cocaine, as evidenced by the animal experiments in which not all the rats spontaneously self-administered low doses of amphetamine. The further study of such animal models may help clinicians understand the susceptibility of some patients to amphetamine dependence.

The classic amphetamines (dextroamphetamine, methamphetamine, and methylphenidate) have their primary effects by causing the release of catecholamines, particularly dopamine, from presynaptic terminals. The effects are particularly potent for the dopaminergic neurons that project from the ventral tegmental area to the cerebral cortex and the limbic areas. That pathway has been termed the reward pathway, and its activation is probably the major addicting mechanism for the amphetamines.

The designer amphetamines (for example, MDMA, MDEA, MMDA, and DOM) cause the release of catecholamines (that

Table 6.3-1. Diagnostic Criteria for Amphetamine Intoxication

A. Recent use of amphetamine or a related substance (e.g., methylphenidate).

B. Clincally significant maladaptive behavioral or psychological changes (e.g., euphoria or affective blunting; changes in sociability; hypervigilance; interpersonal sensitivity; anxiety, tension, or anger; stereotyped behaviors; impaired judgment; or impaired social or occupational functioning) that developed during, or shortly after, use of amphetamine or a related substance.

C. Two (or more) of the following, developing during, or shortly after, use of amphetamine or a related substance:

(1) tachycardia or bradycardia
(2) pupillary dilation
(3) elevated or lowered blood pressure
(4) perspiration or chills
(5) nausea or vomiting
(6) evidence of weight loss
(7) psychomotor agitation or retardation
(8) muscular weakness, respiratory depression, chest pain, or cardiac arrhythmias
(9) confusion, seizures, dyskinesias, dystonias, or coma

D. The symptoms are not due to a general medical condition and are not better accounted for by another mental disorder.

Table from DSM-IV, *Diagnostic and Statistical Manual of Mental Disorders*, ed 4. Copyright American Psychiatric Association, Washington, 1994. Used with permission.

Table 6.3-2. Diagnostic Criteria for Amphetamine Withdrawal

A. Cesstion of (or reduction in) amphetamine (or a related substance) use that has been heavy and prolonged.

B. Dysphoric mood and two (or more) of the following physiological changes, developing within a few hours to several days after criterion A:

(1) fatigue
(2) vivid, unpleasant dreams
(3) insomnia or hypersomnia
(4) increased appetite
(5) psychomotor retardation or agitation

C. The symptoms in criterion B cause clinically significant distress or impairment in social, occupational, or other important areas of functioning.

D. The symptoms are not due to a general medical condition and are not better accounted for by another mental disorder.

Table from DSM-IV, *Diagnostic and Statistical Manual of Mental Disorders*, ed 4. Copyright American Psychiatric Association, Washington, 1994. Used with permission.

is, dopamine and norepinephrine) and the release of serotonin. Serotonin is the neurotransmitter that is implicated as the major neurochemical pathway involved in the effects of the hallucinogens. Therefore, the clinical effects of the designer amphetamines is a cross between the effects of the classic amphetamines and the effects of the hallucinogens. The pharmacology of MDMA is the best understood of the group. MDMA is taken up in serotonergic neurons by the serotonin transporter responsible for serotonin reuptake. Once in the neuron, MDMA causes a rapid release of a bolus of serotonin and inhibits the activity of the serotonin-producing enzymes. As a result, patients who are taking a serotonin-specific reuptake inhibitor—for example, fluoxetine (Prozac)—cannot get high when they take MDMA because the serotonin-specific reuptake inhibitor prevents the MDMA from being taken up into the serotonergic neurons.

DIAGNOSIS

The fourth edition of *Diagnostic and Statistical Manual of Mental Disorders* (DSM-IV) lists many amphetamine (or amphetaminelike)-related disorders but specifies the diagnostic criteria only for amphetamine intoxication (Table 6.3–1), amphetamine withdrawal (Table 6.3–2), and amphetamine-related disorder not otherwise specified in the section on amphetamine (or amphetaminelike)-related disorders. The diagnostic criteria for the other amphetamine (or amphetaminelike)-related disorders are contained in the DSM-IV sections that deal with the primary phenomenological symptom (for example, psychosis).

Dependence and Abuse

The DSM-IV criteria for dependence and abuse are applied to amphetamine and its related substances (see Tables 6.1–3 and 6.1–4). Amphetamine dependence can result in a rapid down-spiral of a person's abilities to cope with work-related and family-related obligations and stresses. An amphetamine-

abusing person requires increasingly high doses of amphetamine to obtain the usual high, and physical signs of amphetamine abuse (for example, decreased weight and paranoid ideas) almost always develop with continued abuse.

Intoxication

The intoxication syndromes that result from cocaine (which blocks dopamine reuptake) and amphetamines (which cause the release of dopamine) are similar. Because more rigorous and in-depth research has been done on cocaine abuse and intoxication than on amphetamines, the clinical literature on amphetamines has been strongly influenced by the clinical findings of cocaine abuse. In DSM-IV, the diagnostic criteria for amphetamine intoxication (see Table 6.3–1) and cocaine intoxication (see Table 6.6–1) are separated but are virtually the same. DSM-IV allows for the specification of the presence of perceptual disturbances. If reality testing is not intact, a diagnosis of amphetamine-induced psychotic disorder with onset during intoxication is indicated. The symptoms of amphetamine intoxication are mostly resolved after 24 hours and are generally completely resolved after 48 hours.

Withdrawal

The crash after amphetamine intoxication can be associated with anxiety, tremulousness, dysphoric mood, lethargy, fatigue, nightmares (accompanied by rebound rapid eye movement [REM] sleep), headache, profuse sweating, muscle cramps, stomach cramps, and insatiable hunger. The withdrawal symptoms generally peak in two to four days and are resolved in a week. The most serious withdrawal symptom is depression, which can be particularly severe after the sustained use of high doses of amphetamine and which can be associated with suicidal ideation or behavior. The DSM-IV diagnostic criteria for amphetamine withdrawal (Table 6.3–2) specify that a dysphoric mood and a number of physiological changes are necessary for the diagnosis.

Delirium

Amphetamine intoxication delirium is a DSM-IV diagnosis (Section 4.2). Delirium associated with amphetamine is usually the result of high doses of amphetamine or the sustained use of amphetamine, such that sleep deprivation affects the clinical presentation. The combination of amphetamines with other substances and the use of amphetamines by a person with preexisting brain damage can also result in the development of delirium.

Psychotic Disorder

Amphetamine-induced psychosis has been extensively studied in psychiatry because of its close resemblance to paranoid schizophrenia. The clinical similarity has prompted researchers to attempt to understand the pathophysiology of paranoid schizophrenia by studying the neurochemistry of amphetamine-induced psychosis. The hallmark of amphetamine-induced psychotic disorder is the presence of paranoia. Paranoid schizophrenia can be distinguished from amphetamine-induced psychotic disorder by a number of differentiating characteristics associated with amphetamine-induced psychotic disorder, including a predominance of visual hallucinations, generally appropriate affects, hyperactivity, hypersexuality, confusion and incoherence, and little evidence of disordered thinking (for example, looseness of associations). Several studies have also found that, although the positive symptoms of schizophrenia and amphetamine-induced psychotic disorder are similar, the effective flattening and alogia of schizophrenia are generally absent in amphetamine-induced psychotic disorder. Clinically, however, acute amphetamine-induced psychotic disorder can be completely indistinguishable from schizophrenia, and only the resolution of the symptoms in a few days or a positive finding in a urine drug screen test eventually reveals the correct diagnosis. Some evidence indicates that the long-term use of amphetamines is associated with an increased vulnerability to the development of psychosis under a number of circumstances, including alcohol intoxication and stress. The treatment of choice for amphetamine-induced psychotic disorder is the short-term use of dopamine receptor antagonists—for example, haloperidol (Haldol). DSM-IV lists the diagnostic criteria for amphetamine-induced psychotic disorder with the other psychotic disorders (Section 8.1). DSM-IV allows the clinician to specify whether delusions or hallucinations are the predominant symptoms.

Mood Disorder

DSM-IV allows the clinician to diagnose amphetamine-induced mood disorder with onset during intoxication or withdrawal (Section 9.3). In general, intoxication is associated with manic or mixed mood features, whereas withdrawal is associated with depressive mood features.

Anxiety Disorder

DSM-IV allows for the possibility of amphetamine-induced anxiety disorder with onset during intoxication or withdrawal (Section 10.1). Amphetamine, like cocaine, can induce symptoms similar to those seen in obsessive-compulsive disorder, panic disorder, and phobic disorders, in particular.

Sexual Dysfunction

Although amphetamine is often used to enhance sexual experiences, high doses and long-term use are associated with impo-

tence and other sexual dysfunction. Those sexual dysfunctions are classified in DSM-IV as amphetamine-induced sexual dysfunction with onset during intoxication (Section 14.2).

Sleep Disorder

The diagnostic criteria for amphetamine-induced sleep disorder with onset during intoxication or withdrawal are found in the DSM-IV section on sleep disorders (Section 17.2). Amphetamine intoxication is associated with insomnia and sleep deprivation, whereas amphetamine withdrawal can be associated with hypersomnolence and nightmares.

Disorder Not Otherwise Specified

If an amphetamine (or amphetaminelike)-related disorder does not meet the criteria of one or more of the above categories, it can be diagnosed as an amphetamine-related disorder not otherwise specified (NOS). With the increasing illicit use of the designer amphetamines, syndromes may arise that do not meet the criteria outlined in DSM-IV, necessitating the frequent use of the NOS category for those designer amphetamines.

CLINICAL FEATURES

Classic Amphetamines

In persons who have not previously used amphetamines, a single 5-mg dose increases their sense of well-being and induces elation, euphoria, and friendliness. Small doses generally improve their attention and increase their performance on written, oral, and performance tasks. There is also an associated decrease in fatigue, an induction of anorexia, and a heightening of the pain threshold. Undesirable effects accompany the use of high doses for long periods of time.

Designer Amphetamines

Because of their effects on the dopaminergic system, the designer amphetamines are activating and energizing. Their effects on the serotonergic system, however, color the experience of those drugs with a hallucinogenic character. The designer amphetamines are associated with much less disorientation and perceptual distortion than are the classic hallucinogens—for example, lysergic acid diethylamide (LSD). A sense of closeness with other people and of comfort with oneself and an increased luminescence of objects are commonly reported effects of MDMA. Some psychotherapists have used and advocated further research into the use of designer amphetamines as adjuvants to psychotherapy. That suggestion is controversial; other clinicians emphasize the potential dangers of the use of such drugs.

Adverse Effects

PHYSICAL

Cerebrovascular, cardiac, and gastrointestinal effects are among the most serious adverse effects associated with amphetamine abuse. The specific life-threatening conditions include myocardial infarction, severe hypertension, cerebrovascular disease, and ischemic colitis. A continuum of neurological symptoms, from twitching to tetany to seizures to coma and death, is associated with increasingly high amphetamine doses. The intravenous use of amphetamines is associated with the transmission of human immunodeficiency virus (HIV) and hepatitis and with the development of lung abscesses, endocarditis, and necrotizing angiitis. Several studies have found that information about safe-sex practices and the use of condoms is not well-known by abusers of amphetamines. The less than life-threatening adverse effects include flushing, pallor, cyanosis, fever, headache, tachycardia, palpitations, nausea, vomiting, bruxism, shortness of breath, tremor, and ataxia. The use of amphetamines by pregnant women has been associated with low birth weight, small head circumference, early gestational age, and growth retardation.

PSYCHOLOGICAL

The adverse psychological effects associated with amphetamine use include restlessness, dysphoria, insomnia, irritability, hostility, and confusion. Symptoms of anxiety disorders, such as generalized anxiety disorder and panic disorder, can be induced by amphetamine use. Ideas of reference, paranoid delusions, and hallucinations can be caused by amphetamine use.

TREATMENT

The treatment of amphetamine-related disorders is like that of the cocaine-related disorders in that it is difficult to help the patient remain abstinent from the drug, which has powerfully reinforcing qualities and which induces craving. An inpatient setting and the use of multiple therapeutic modalities (individual, family, and group psychotherapy) are usually necessary to achieve a lasting abstinence from the substance. The treatment of specific amphetamine-induced disorders (for example, amphetamine-induced psychotic disorder and amphetamine-induced anxiety disorder) with specific drugs (for example, antipsychotics and anxiolytics) may be necessary on a short-term basis. Antipsychotics, either a phenothiazine or haloperidol, may be prescribed for the first few days. In the absence of psychosis, diazepam (Valium) is useful to treat the patient's agitation and hyperactivity.

The physician should establish a therapeutic alliance with the patient to deal with the underlying depression or personality disorder or both; however, because many patients are heavily dependent on the drug, psychotherapy may be especially difficult.

References

Cox D E: ''Rave'' to the grave. Forensic Sci Int 60: 5, 1993.
Green A R, Cross A J, Goodwin G M: Review of the pharmacology and clinical pharmacology of 3,4-methylenedioxymethamphetamine (MDMA or ''Ecstasy''). Psychopharmacology 119: 247, 1995.
Hall W, Darke S, Ross M, Wodak A: Patterns of drug use and risk-taking among injecting amphetamine and opioid drug users in Sydney, Australia. Addiction 88: 509, 1993.
Jaffe, J H: Amphetamine (or amphetaminelike)-related disorder. In Comprehensive Textbook of Psychiatry, ed 6, H I Kaplan, B J Sadock, editors, p 791. Williams & Wilkins, Baltimore, 1995.
Koelega H S: Stimulant drugs and vigilance performance: A review. Psychopharmacology 111: 1, 1993.
Ragland A S Ismail Y, Arsura E L: Myocardial infarction after amphetamine use. Am Heart J 125: 247, 1993.

6.4 CAFFEINE-RELATED DISORDERS

Caffeine, most often in the form of coffee or tea, is the most widely used psychoactive substance in Western countries.

About 80 percent of North American adults regularly drink caffeine-containing beverages. The fourth edition of *Diagnostic and Statistical Manual of Mental Disorders* (DSM-IV) has provisions for the diagnosis of caffeine intoxication, caffeine-induced anxiety disorder, and caffeine-induced sleep disorder. DSM-IV does not have diagnostic categories for caffeine dependence and caffeine withdrawal, in spite of the fact that a number of studies have reported data consistent with the presence of caffeine-related physical dependence and withdrawal phenomena. However, research criteria for caffeine withdrawal are included in an appendix.

EPIDEMIOLOGY

Caffeine is contained in a variety of drinks, foods, prescription medicines, and over-the-counter medicines. The average adult in the United States consumes about 200 mg of caffeine a day, although 20 to 30 percent of all adults consume more than 500 mg a day. The per capita use of coffee in the United States is 10.2 pounds a year. A cup of coffee generally contains 100 to 150 mg of caffeine; tea contains about one third as much. Many over-the-counter medications contain one third to one half as much caffeine as that in a cup of coffee, although some migraine medications and over-the-counter stimulants contain more caffeine than does a cup of coffee. Significant amounts of caffeine are contained in cocoa, chocolate, and soft drinks. The amount of caffeine contained in those products can be enough to cause some symptoms of caffeine intoxication in small children when they ingest a candy bar and a 12-ounce cola drink.

NEUROPHARMACOLOGY

Caffeine, a methylxanthine, is more potent than another commonly used methylxanthine, theophylline (Primatene). The half-life of caffeine in the human body is 3 to 10 hours, and the time of peak concentration is 30 to 60 minutes. Caffeine readily crosses the blood-brain barrier. The primary mechanism of action for caffeine is as an antagonist of the adenosine receptors. Activation of adenosine receptors activates an inhibitory G protein (G_i), thus inhibiting the formation of the second-messenger cyclic adenosine monophosphate (cAMP). Caffeine intake, therefore, results in an increase in intraneuronal cAMP concentrations in neurons that have adenosine receptors. It has been estimated that three cups of coffee results in so much caffeine in the brain that about 50 percent of the adenosine receptors are occupied by caffeine. Several experiments indicate that caffeine, especially at high doses or concentrations, can affect dopamine and noradrenergic neurons. Specifically, dopamine activity may be enhanced by caffeine, which may explain clinical reports associating caffeine intake with an exacerbation of psychotic symptoms in patients with schizophrenia. Activation of noradrenergic neurons has been hypothesized to be involved in the mediation of some of the symptoms associated with caffeine withdrawal.

Caffeine as a Substance of Abuse

Caffeine evidences all the traits that are associated with commonly accepted substances of abuse. First, caffeine can act as a positive reinforcer, particularly at low doses. Caffeine doses of about 100 mg induce a mild euphoria in humans and behavioral effects in other animals that are associated with repeated substance-seeking behavior. Caffeine doses of 300 mg, however, are associated with increased anxiety and mild dysphoria in humans and do not act as positive reinforcers. Second, studies in animals and humans have found that caffeine can be discriminated from a placebo in blinded experimental conditions. Third, both animal and human studies have found that physical tolerance to some effects of caffeine does develop and that withdrawal symptoms do occur.

Effects on Cerebral Blood Flow

Most studies have found that caffeine results in global cerebral vasoconstriction, with a resultant decrease in cerebral blood flow (CBF), although that effect may not occur in persons more than 65 years of age. One recent study found that tolerance does not develop to those vasoconstrictive effects and that the CBF shows a rebound increase after withdrawal from caffeine.

DIAGNOSIS

The diagnosis of caffeine intoxication or other caffeine-related disorders depends primarily on the clinician's taking a comprehensive history of the patient's intake of caffeine-containing products. The history should cover whether or not the patient has experienced any symptoms of caffeine withdrawal during periods when caffeine consumption was either stopped or severely reduced. The differential diagnosis for caffeine-related disorders should include the following psychiatric diagnoses: generalized anxiety disorder, panic disorder with or without agoraphobia, bipolar II disorder, attention-deficit/hyperactivity disorder, and sleep disorders. The differential diagnosis should also include the abuse of caffeine-containing over-the-counter medications, anabolic steroids, and other stimulants, such as amphetamines and cocaine. A urine sample may be needed to screen for those substances. The differential diagnosis should also include hyperthyroidism and pheochromocytoma.

DSM-IV provides diagnostic criteria for caffeine intoxication (Table 6.4–1) but does not formally recognize a diagnosis

of caffeine withdrawal, which is classified as a caffeine-related disorder not otherwise specified (NOS). The diagnostic criteria for the other two caffeine-related disorders are contained in those sections specific for the principal symptom (for example, as a substance-induced anxiety disorder for caffeine-induced anxiety disorder).

Caffeine Intoxication

DSM-IV specifies the diagnostic criteria for caffeine intoxication (Table 6.4–1), which include the recent consumption of caffeine, usually in excess of 250 mg. The annual incidence of caffeine intoxication is an estimated 10 percent, although some clinicians and investigators suspect that the actual incidence is much higher than that figure. The common symptoms associated with caffeine intoxication include anxiety, psychomotor agitation, restlessness, irritability, and psychophysiological complaints, such as muscle twitching, flushed face, nausea, diuresis, gastrointestinal distress, excessive perspiration, tingling in the fingers and toes, and insomnia. The consumption of more than 1 gram of caffeine can be associated with rambling speech, confused thinking, cardiac arrhythmias, inexhaustibility, marked agitation, tinnitus, and mild visual hallucinations (light flashes). The consumption of more than 10 grams of caffeine can cause generalized tonic-clonic seizures, respiratory failure, and death.

Caffeine Withdrawal

In spite of the fact that DSM-IV does not include a diagnosis of caffeine withdrawal, a number of well-controlled studies indicate that caffeine withdrawal does exist, and DSM-IV does give research criteria for caffeine withdrawal (Table 6.4–2). The appearance of withdrawal symptoms is a reflection of the tolerance and the physiological dependence that develops with continued caffeine use. Several epidemiological studies have reported symptoms of caffeine withdrawal in 50 to 75 percent of all caffeine users studied. The most common symptoms of caffeine withdrawal are headache and fatigue; other symptoms include anxiety, irritability, mild depressive symptoms, impaired psychomotor performance, nausea, vomiting, craving for caffeine, and muscle pain and stiffness. The number and the severity of the withdrawal symptoms is correlated with the amount of caffeine that had been taken and the abruptness of

---

Table 6.4–1.   Diagnostic Criteria for Caffeine Intoxication

A. Recent consumption of caffeine, usually in excess of 250 mg (e.g., more than 2–3 cups of brewed coffee).

B. Five (or more) of the following signs, developing during, or shortly after, caffeine use:

    (1) restlessness
    (2) nervousness
    (3) excitement
    (4) insomnia
    (5) flushed face
    (6) diuresis
    (7) gastrointestinal disturbance
    (8) muscle twitching
    (9) rambling flow of thought and speech
    (10) tachycardia or cardiac arrhythmia
    (11) periods of inexhaustibility
    (12) psychomotor agitation

C. The symptoms in criterion B cause clinically significant distress or impairment in social, occupational, or other important areas of functioning.

D. The symptoms are not due to a general medical condition and are not better accounted for by another mental disorder (e.g., an Anxiety Disorder).

Table 6.4–2.   Research Criteria for Caffeine Withdrawal

A. Prolonged daily use of caffeine.

B. Abrupt cessation of caffeine use, or reduction in the amount of caffeine used, closely followed by headache and one (or more) of the following symptoms:

    (1) marked fatigue or drowsiness
    (2) marked anxiety or depression
    (3) nausea or vomiting

C. The symptoms in criterion B cause clinically significant distress or impairment in social, occupational, or other important areas of functioning.

D. The symptoms are not due to the direct physiological effects of a general medical condition (e.g., migraine, viral illness) and are not better accounted for by another mental disorder.

the withdrawal. Caffeine withdrawal symptoms have their onset 12 to 24 hours after the last dose; the symptoms peak in 24 to 48 hours and resolve within one week.

The induction of caffeine withdrawal can sometimes be iatrogenic. Physicians often ask their patients to discontinue caffeine intake before certain medical procedures, such as endoscopy, colonoscopy, and cardiac catheterization. Physicians also often recommend stopping caffeine intake by patients who have anxiety symptoms, cardiac arrhythmias esophagitis, hiatal hernias, fibrocystic disease of the breast, and insomnia. Some persons simply decide that it would be good for them to stop using caffeine-containing products. In all those situations the caffeine user should taper the use of caffeine-containing products over a 7-to 14-day period, rather than stop abruptly.

Caffeine-Induced Anxiety Disorder

Caffeine-induced anxiety disorder, which can occur during caffeine intoxication, is a DSM-IV diagnosis (Section 10.1). The anxiety related to caffeine use can appear to be similar to the anxiety symptoms associated with generalized anxiety disorder. Patients with the disorder may be perceived as wired, overly talkative, and irritable, and they may complain of not sleeping well and of having energy to burn. Although caffeine induces and exacerbates panic attacks in persons with a panic disorder, a causative association between caffeine and a panic disorder has not yet been demonstrated.

Caffeine-Induced Sleep Disorder

Caffeine-induced sleep disorder, which can occur during caffeine intoxication, is a DSM-IV diagnosis (Section 17.2). Caffeine is associated with a delay in falling asleep, an inability to remain asleep, and early morning awakening.

Caffeine-Related Disorder Not Otherwise Specified

DSM-IV contains a residual category for caffeine-related disorders, caffeine-related disorder not otherwise specified. The category is for caffeine-related diagnoses that do not meet the criteria for caffeine intoxication, caffeine-induced anxiety disorder, or caffeine-induced sleep disorder.

Other Substance-Related Disorders

Persons with caffeine-related disorders are more likely to have additional substance-related disorders than are persons without diagnoses of caffeine-related disorders. About two thirds of the persons who consume large amounts of caffeine every day also use sedative and hypnotic drugs.

CLINICAL FEATURES

After the ingestion of 50 to 100 mg of caffeine, common symptoms include increased alertness, a mild sense of well-being, and a sense of improved verbal and motor performance. Caffeine ingestion is also associated with diureses, cardiac muscle stimulation, increased intestinal peristalsis, increased gastric acid secretion, and a usually mild increase in blood pressure.

Adverse Effects

Although caffeine is not associated with cardiac-related risks in healthy persons, those with preexisting cardiac disease are often advised to limit their caffeine intake because of a possible association between cardiac arrhythmias and caffeine. Caffeine is clearly associated with increased gastric acid secretion, so clinicians usually advise patients with gastric ulcers not to ingest any caffeine-containing products. Limited data suggest that caffeine is associated with fibrocystic disease of the breasts in women. Although the question of whether caffeine is associated with birth defects remains controversial, women who are pregnant or breast-feeding should probably avoid caffeine-containing products. No solid data link caffeine intake with cancer.

TREATMENT

The primary treatment of caffeine-related disorders is either the elimination or the severe reduction of caffeine-containing products from the person's diet or habits. Education of patients regarding the wide range of products that contain caffeine is essential for therapeutic success. Clinicians can advise patients to substitute other beverages—for example, water and decaffeinated soft drinks and coffee—to help deal with the habit of frequent drinks during the day. Spouses or significant others can often help the patients stop their caffeine use. Usually, the spouses or significant others agree to eliminate caffeine from their own diets.

Analgesics, such as aspirin, are almost always sufficient for the control of the headaches and muscle aches that may accompany caffeine withdrawal. Rarely do patients require benzodiazepines for the relief of the withdrawal symptoms. If benzodiazepines are used for that indication, they should be used in small dosages for a brief period of time, about 7 to 10 days at the longest.

References

Battig K: Acute and chronic cardiovascular and behavioural effects of caffeine, aspirin and ephedrine. Int J Obes *17* (2, Suppl): 61, 1993.

Greden J F, Pomerleau O: Caffeine-related disorders and nicotine-related disorders. In *Comprehensive Textbook of Psychiatry*, ed 6, H I Kaplan, B J Sadock, editors, p 799. Williams & Wilkins, Baltimore, 1995.

Hughes J R, Oliveto A H, Bickel W K, Higgins S T, Badger G J: Caffeine self-administration and withdrawal: Incidence, individual differences and interrelationships. Drug Alcohol Depend *32*: 239, 1993.

Kozlowski L T, Henningfield J E, Keenan R M, Lei H, Leight G, Jelinek L C, Pope M A, Haertzen C A: Patterns of alcohol, cigarette, and caffeine and other drug use in two drug abusing populations. J Subst Abuse Treat *10*: 171, 1993.

Rogers P J, Richardson N J, Dernoncourt C: Caffeine use: is there a net benefit for mood and psychomotor performance? Neuropsychobiology *31*: 195, 1995.

Silverman K, Evans S M, Strain E C, Griffiths R R: Withdrawal syndrome after the double-blind cessation of caffeine consumption. N Engl J Med *327*: 1109, 1992.

6.5 CANNABIS-RELATED DISORDERS

Cannabis is the abbreviated name for the hemp plant *Cannabis sativa*. All parts of the plant contain psychoactive cannabinoids, of which $(-)\Delta^9$-tetrahydrocannabinol (Δ^9-THC) is most abundant. The cannabis plant is usually cut, dried, chopped, and then rolled into cigarettes (commonly called joints), which are then smoked. The common names for cannabis are marijuana, grass, pot, weed, tea, and Mary Jane. Other names for cannabis, which describe cannabis types of various strengths, are hemp, chasra, bhang, ganja, dagga, and sinsemilla. The most potent forms of cannabis come from the flowering tops of the plants or from the dried, black-brown, resinous exudate from the leaves, which is referred to as hashish or hash.

The euphoriant effects of cannabis have been known for thousands of years. The potential medicinal effects of cannabis as an analgesic, anticonvulsant, and hypnotic were recognized in the 19th and early 20th centuries. Recently, cannabis and its primary active component, Δ^9-THC, have been used successfully to treat nausea secondary to cancer treatment drugs and to stimulate appetite in patients with acquired immune deficiency syndrome (AIDS). Some less convincing reports concern the use of Δ^9-THC in the treatment of glaucoma.

EPIDEMIOLOGY

Cannabis is the most commonly used illicit substance in the United States. In 1991 about one third of the total population had used cannabis at least once, and about 5 percent were current users. Within the 18- to 25-year-old age group, about 50 percent had used cannabis at least once, and 13 percent were current users. Within the 12-to 17-year-old age group, about 13 percent had used cannabis at least once, and 4 percent were current users. In general, however, cannabis use has decreased from its high levels in the late 1970s.

NEUROPHARMACOLOGY

As previously stated, the principal component of cannabis is Δ^9-THC; however, the cannabis plant contains more than 400 chemicals, of which about 60 are chemically related to Δ^9-THC. In the human, Δ^9-THC is rapidly converted into 11-hydroxy-Δ^9-THC, the metabolite that is active in the central nervous system (CNS).

A specific receptor for the cannabinols has been identified, cloned, and characterized. The receptor is a member of the G protein-linked family of receptors. The cannabinoid receptor is linked to the inhibitory G protein (G_i), which is linked to adenylyl cyclase in an inhibitory fashion. The cannabinoid receptor is found in highest concentrations in the basal ganglia, the hippocampus, and the cerebellum, with lower concentrations in the cerebral cortex. The receptor is not found in the brainstem, a fact that is consistent with the minimal effects cannabis has on respiratory and cardiac functions. Studies in animals have found that the cannabinoids affect the monoamine and γ-aminobutyric acid (GABA) neurons.

Most studies have shown that animals do not self-administer cannabinoids, as they do most other substances of abuse. Moreover, some debate concerns whether the cannabinoids stimulate the so-called reward centers of the brain, such as the dopaminergic neurons of the ventral tegmental area. However, tolerance to cannabis does develop, and psychological dependence has been found, but the evidence for physiological dependence is not strong. Withdrawal symptoms in humans are limited to modest increases in irritability, restlessness, insomnia, anorexia, and mild nausea; all those symptoms are seen only when a person abruptly stops taking high doses of cannabis.

When cannabis is smoked, the euphoric effects appear within minutes, peak in about 30 minutes, and last two to four hours. Some of the motor and cognitive effects last 5 to 12 hours. Cannabis can also be taken orally when it is prepared in food, such as brownies and cakes. About two to three times as much cannabis must be taken orally to be as potent as cannabis taken by the inhalation of its smoke. Many variables affect the psychoactive properties of cannabis, including the potency of the cannabis used, the route of administration, the smoking technique, the effects of pyrolysis on the cannabinoid content, the dose, the setting, the user's past experience, the user's expectations, and the user's unique biological vulnerability to the effects of cannabinoids.

DIAGNOSIS AND CLINICAL FEATURES

The most common physical effects of cannabis are dilation of the conjunctival blood vessels (that is, red eye) and a mild tachycardia. At high doses, orthostatic hypotension may appear. Increased appetite—often referred to as the munchies—and dry mouth are other common effects of cannabis intoxication. There has never been a clearly documented case of death caused by cannabis intoxication alone, which reflects the substance's lack of effect on the respiratory rate. The most serious potential adverse effects of cannabis use come from the inhalation of the same carcinogenic hydrocarbons that are present in conventional tobacco, and some data indicate that heavy cannabis users are at risk for chronic respiratory disease and lung cancer. The practice of smoking cannabis-containing cigarettes to their very ends, so-called roaches, further increases the intake of tar (that is, particulate matter). Many reports indicate that long-term cannabis use is associated with cerebral atrophy, seizure susceptibility, chromosomal damage, birth defects, impaired immune reactivity, alterations in testosterone concentrations, and dysregulation of menstrual cycles; however, those reports have not been conclusively replicated, and the association between those effects and cannabis use is uncertain.

The fourth edition of *Diagnostic and Statistical Manual of Mental Disorders* (DSM-IV) lists the cannabis-related disorders but has specific criteria within the cannabis-related disorders section only for cannabis intoxication (Table 6.5–1). The diagnostic criteria for the other cannabis-related disorders are contained in those DSM-IV sections that focus on the major phenomenological symptom—for example, cannabis-induced psychotic disorder, with delusions, in the DSM-IV section on substance-induced psychotic disorder (Section 8.1).

Cannabis Dependence and Cannabis Abuse

DSM-IV includes the diagnoses of cannabis dependence and cannabis abuse (see Tables 6.1–3 and 6.1–4). The experimental

---

Table 6.5–1. Diagnostic Criteria for Cannabis Intoxication

A. Recent use of cannabis.

B. Clinically significant maladaptive behavioral or psychological changes (e.g., impaired motor coordination, euphoria, anxiety, sensation of slowed time, impaired judgment, social withdrawal) that developed during, or shortly after, cannabis use.

C. Two (or more) of the following signs, developing within 2 hours of cannabis use:

    (1) conjunctival injection
    (2) increased appetite
    (3) dry mouth
    (4) tachycardia

D. The symptoms are not due to a general medical condition and are not better accounted for by another mental disorder.

Table from DSM-IV, *Diagnostic and Statistical Manual of Mental Disorders*, ed 4. Copyright American Psychiatric Association, Washington, 1994. Used with permission.

data clearly show tolerance to many of the effects of cannabis; however, the data are less supportive of the presence of physical dependence. Psychological dependence on cannabis use does develop in long-term users.

Cannabis Intoxication

DSM-IV formalizes the diagnostic criteria for cannabis intoxication (see Table 6.5–1). The diagnostic criteria specify that the diagnosis can be augmented with the phrase "with perceptual disturbances." If reality testing is not intact, the diagnosis is cannabis-induced psychotic disorder.

Cannabis intoxication commonly heightens the user's sensitivity to external stimuli, reveals new details, makes colors seem brighter and richer than usual, and subjectively slows down the appreciation of time. In high doses, the user may also experience depersonalization and derealization.

Motor skills are impaired by cannabis use, and the impairment in motor skills remains after the subjective, euphoriant effects have resolved. For 8 to 12 hours after using cannabis, the user has an impairment of motor skills that interferes with the operation of motor vehicles and other heavy machinery. Moreover, those effects are additive to those of alcohol, which is commonly used in combination with cannabis.

Cannabis Intoxication Delirium

Cannabis intoxication delirium is a DSM-IV diagnosis (Section 4.2). The delirium associated with cannabis intoxication is characterized by marked impairment on cognition and performance tasks. Even modest doses of cannabis result in impairment in memory, reaction time, perception, motor coordination, and attention. High doses that also impair the user's level of consciousness have marked effects on those cognitive measures.

Cannabis-Induced Psychotic Disorder

Cannabis-induced psychotic disorder (Section 8.1) is diagnosed in the presence of a cannabis-induced psychosis. Cannabis-induced psychotic disorder is rare, but transient paranoid ideation is more common. Florid psychosis is somewhat common in countries in which some persons have long-term access to cannabis of a particularly high potency. The psychotic episodes are sometimes referred to as hemp insanity. Cannabis use is rarely associated with a bad-trip experience, which is often associated with hallucinogen intoxication. When cannabis-induced psychotic disorder does occur, it may be associated with a preexisting personality disorder in the affected person.

Cannabis-Induced Anxiety Disorder

Cannabis-induced anxiety disorder (Section 10.1) is a common diagnosis for acute cannabis intoxication, which in many persons induces short-lived anxiety states that are often provoked by paranoid thoughts. In such circumstances, panic attacks may be induced, based on ill-defined and disorganized fears. The appearance of anxiety symptoms is correlated with the dose and is the most frequent adverse reaction to the moderate use of smoked cannabis. Inexperienced users are much more likely to experience anxiety symptoms than are experienced users.

Cannabis-Related Disorder Not Otherwise Specified

DSM-IV does not formally recognize cannabis-induced mood disorders; therefore, such disorders are classified as cannabis-related disorders not otherwise specified (NOS). Cannabis intoxication can be associated with depressive symptoms, although such symptoms may suggest long-term cannabis use. Hypomania, however, is a common symptom in cannabis intoxication.

DSM-IV also does not formally recognize cannabis-induced sleep disorders or cannabis-induced sexual dysfunction; therefore, both are classified as cannabis-related disorders NOS. When either sleep disorder symptoms or sexual dysfunction symptoms are present and related to cannabis use, they almost always resolve within days or a week after the cessation of cannabis use.

FLASHBACKS

Persisting perceptual abnormalities after cannabis use are not formally classified in DSM-IV, although there are case reports of persons who have experienced sensations related to cannabis intoxication—at times significantly—after the short-term effects of the substance have disappeared. Debate continues as to whether flashbacks are related to cannabis use alone or whether they are related to the concomitant use of hallucinogens or of cannabis tainted with phencyclidine (PCP).

AMOTIVATIONAL SYNDROME

Another controversial cannabis-related syndrome is amotivational syndrome. The debate involves whether the syndrome is related to cannabis use or whether it reflects characterological traits in a subgroup of persons, regardless of cannabis use. Traditionally, the amotivational syndrome has been associated with long-term heavy use and has been characterized by a person's unwillingness to persist in a task—be it at school, at work, or in any setting that requires prolonged attention or tenacity. The person is described as becoming apathetic and anergic, usually gaining weight, and appearing slothful.

TREATMENT

Treatment of cannabis use rests on the same principles as does treatment of other substances of abuse—abstinence and support. Abstinence can be achieved through direct interventions, such as hospitalization, or through careful outpatient monitoring by the use of urine tests, which can detect cannabis for a period of three days to four weeks after use. Support can be achieved through the use of individual, family, and group psychotherapies. Education should be a cornerstone for both abstinence and support programs, since a patient who does not understand the intellectual reasons for addressing the substance-abuse problem shows little motivation to stop. For some patients an antianxiety drug may be useful for the short-term relief of withdrawal symptoms. For other patients the cannabis use may be related to an underlying depressive disorder that may respond to specific antidepressant treatment.

References

Abood M E, Martin B R: Neurobiology of marijuana abuse. Trends Pharmacol Sci *13*: 201, 1992.

Chait L D, Zacny J P: Reinforcing and subjective effects of oral delta 9-THC and smoked marijuana in humans. Psychopharmacology *107*: 255, 1992.

Friedman H, Klein T W, Newton C, Daaka Y: Marijuana, receptors and immuno-modulation. Adv Exp Med Biol *373*: 103, 1995.

Munro S, Thomas K L, Abu-Shaar M: Molecular characterization of a peripheral receptor for cannabinoids. Nature *365*: 61, 1993.

Nahas G, Latour C: The human toxicity of marijuana. Med J Aust *156*: 495, 1992.

Woody G E, MacFadden W: Cannabis-related disorders. In *Comprehensive Textbook of Psychiatry*, ed 6, H I Kaplan, B J Sadock, editors, p 810. Williams & Wilkins, Baltimore, 1995.

6.6 COCAINE-RELATED DISORDERS

Cocaine is one of the most addictive, commonly abused substances and one of the most dangerous. Cocaine—variously referred to as snow, coke, girl, and lady—is also abused in its most potent forms, freebase and crack (crack cocaine). Cocaine is an alkaloid that is derived from the shrub *Erythroxylon coca*, which is indigenous to South America, where the leaves of the shrub are chewed by the local inhabitants to obtain the stimulating effects. The cocaine alkaloid was first isolated in 1860 and was first used as a local anesthetic in 1880. Cocaine is still used as a local anesthetic, especially for eye, nose, and throat surgery, for which its vasoconstrictive effects are also helpful. In 1884 Sigmund Freud made a study of its general pharmacological effects. In the 1880s and 1890s, cocaine was widely touted as a cure for many ills. In 1914, however, cocaine was classified as a narcotic, along with morphine and heroin, because its addictive and adverse effects had by then been recognized.

EPIDEMIOLOGY

About 1.9 million Americans, including 1.9 percent of high school seniors, have used cocaine within the past month; however, cocaine use is on the decline. The decrease in the use of cocaine in the United States is primarily due to increased awareness of the risks involved with cocaine use; that awareness has likely been affected by a comprehensive public campaign about cocaine and its effects. The societal effects of the decrease in the use of cocaine, however, have been somewhat offset by the emergence over the past decade of the frequent use of crack, a highly potent form of cocaine. Crack use is most common in persons aged 18 to 25, who are particularly susceptible to the low street price of a single 50- to 100-mg dose of crack, usually around $10. Cocaine usually sells for around $100 to $150 for each one-gram vial.

In 1991 about 12 percent of the United States population had used cocaine at least once, and 1.9 percent had used crack at least once. The highest use was in the 18- to 25-year-old age group; 18 percent of them had used cocaine at least once, and 2 percent were current users. In that age group, 3.8 percent had used crack at least once. Although cocaine use is highest among the unemployed, cocaine is also used by highly educated persons in high socioeconomic groups. Cocaine use among males is twice as frequent as cocaine use among females. Although cocaine use among blacks and whites had declined since the mid-1980s, its use among Hispanics has increased. Cocaine is a dangerous drug, associated not only with gross behavioral disorders but also with medical morbidity. There were about 80,000 cocaine-related emergency room visits in the United States in 1990.

NEUROPHARMACOLOGY

The primary pharmacodynamic effect of cocaine that is related to its behavioral effects is competitive blockade of dopamine reuptake by the dopamine transporter. Blockade of that reuptake mechanism increases the concentration of dopamine in the synaptic cleft and results in increased activation of both dopamine type 1 (D_1) and dopamine type 2 (D_2) receptors. The effects of cocaine on the activity mediated by D_3, D_4, and D_5 receptors is not well understood at this time, but at least one preclinical study has implicated the D_3 receptor. Although the behavioral effects are thought to be mediated primarily by the blockade of dopamine reuptake, cocaine also blocks the reuptake of the other major catecholamine, norepinephrine, and the reuptake of serotonin. The behavioral effects related to those activities are receiving increased attention in the scientific literature. The effects of cocaine on cerebral blood flow and cerebral glucose use have also been studied. In general, most studies have found that cocaine is associated with decreased cerebral blood flow and possibly with the development of patchy areas of decreased glucose use.

The behavioral effects of cocaine are felt almost immediately and last for a relatively brief time (30 to 60 minutes), thus necessitating repeated administration to maintain the effects of intoxication. Although the behavioral effects are short-lived, metabolites of cocaine may be present in the blood and the urine for up to 10 days.

Cocaine has potent addictive qualities. A psychological dependence on cocaine can develop after a single use because of its potency as a positive reinforcer of behavior. With repeated administration, both tolerance and sensitivity to various effects of cocaine can develop, although the development of tolerance or sensitivity is apparently due to many factors and is not easily predicted. Physiological dependence on cocaine does develop, although cocaine withdrawal is mild compared with the effects of withdrawal from opiates and opioids.

METHODS OF USE

The cocaine that is available on the street varies greatly in purity, since drug dealers often dilute the cocaine powder with sugar or procaine. Cocaine is sometimes cut with amphetamine. The most common method of using cocaine is by inhaling the finely chopped powder into the nose, a practice referred to as snorting or tooting. Other methods of ingesting cocaine are subcutaneous or intravenous (IV) injection and smoking (free-basing). Free-basing involves mixing street cocaine with chemically extracted pure cocaine alkaloid (the freebase) to get an increased effect. Smoking is also the method used for ingesting crack cocaine. Inhaling is the least dangerous method of cocaine use; IV injection and smoking are the most dangerous methods. The most direct methods of ingestion are often associated with cerebrovascular diseases, cardiac abnormalities, and death. Although cocaine can be taken orally, that route is rarely used because it is the least effective route.

Crack

Crack is an extremely potent, freebase form of cocaine. Crack is sold in small, ready-to-smoke amounts, often called rocks. Crack cocaine is highly addictive; even one or two experiences with the drug can cause intense craving for more. Users have been known to resort to extremes of behavior to obtain the money to buy more crack. Anecdotal reports from urban emergency rooms have also associated extremes of violence with crack abuse.

Table 6.6–1.   Diagnostic Criteria for Cocaine Intoxication

A. Recent use of cocaine.

B. Clincally significant maladaptive behavioral or psychological changes (e.g., euphoria or affective blunting, changes in sociability; hypervigilance; interpersonal sensitivity; anxiety, tension, or anger; stereotyped behaviors; impaired judgment; or impaired social or occupational functioning) that developed during, or shortly after, use of cocaine.

C. Two (or more) of the following, developing during, or shortly after, cocaine use:

    (1) tachycardia or bradycardia
    (2) pupillary dilation
    (3) elevated or lowered blood pressure
    (4) perspiration or chills
    (5) nausea or vomiting
    (6) evidence of weight loss
    (7) psychomotor agitation or retardation
    (8) muscular weakness, respiratory depression, chest pain, or cardiac arrhythmias
    (9) confusion, seizures, dyskinesias, dystonias, or coma

D. The symptoms are not due to a general medical condition and are not better accounted for by another mental disorder.

Table from DSM-IV, *Diagnostic and Statistical Manual of Mental Disorders*, ed 4. Copyright American Psychiatric Association, Washington, 1994. Used with permission.

Table 6.6–2.   Diagnostic Criteria for Cocaine Withdrawal

A. Cessation of (or reduction in) cocaine use that has been heavy and prolonged.

B. Dysphoric mood and two (or more) of the following physiological changes, developing within a few hours to several days after criterion A:

    (1) fatigue
    (2) vivid, unpleasant dreams
    (3) insomnia or hypersomnia
    (4) increased appetite
    (5) psychomotor retardation or agitation

C. The symptoms in criterion B cause clinically significant distress or impairment in social, occupational, or other important areas of functioning.

D. The symptoms are not due to a general medical condition and are not better accounted for by another mental disorder.

Table from DSM-IV, *Diagnostic and Statistical Manual of Mental Disorders*, ed 4. Copyright American Psychiatric Association, Washington, 1994. Used with permission.

DIAGNOSIS AND CLINICAL FEATURES

The fourth edition of *Diagnostic and Statistical Manual of Mental Disorders* (DSM-IV) lists many cocaine use disorders but specifies the diagnostic criteria for only cocaine intoxication (Table 6.6–1) and cocaine withdrawal (Table 6.6–2) within the cocaine-related disorders section. The diagnostic criteria for the other cocaine-related disorders are in the DSM-IV sections that focus on the principal symptom—for example, cocaine-induced mood disorder in the mood disorders section (Section 9.3).

DSM-IV uses the general guidelines for substance dependence and substance abuse to diagnose cocaine dependence and cocaine abuse (see Tables 6.1–3 and 6.1–4). Clinically and practically, cocaine dependence or cocaine abuse can be suspected in patients who evidence unexplained changes in their personalities. Common changes associated with cocaine use are irritability, impaired ability to concentrate, compulsive behavior, severe insomnia, and weight loss. Colleagues at work and

family members may notice a general and increasing inability to perform the expected tasks associated with work and family life. The patient may show new evidence of increased debt or inability to pay bills on time because of the large sums used to buy cocaine. Cocaine abusers often excuse themselves from work or social situations every 30 to 60 minutes to find a secluded place in which they can inhale some more cocaine. Because of the vasoconstricting effects of cocaine, its users almost always develop nasal congestion, which they may attempt to self-medicate with decongestant sprays.

Comorbidity (Dual Diagnosis)

As with other substance-related disorders, cocaine-related disorders are often accompanied by other psychiatric disorders. In general, the development of mood disorders and alcohol-related disorders follows the onset of cocaine-related disorders, whereas anxiety disorders, antisocial personality disorder, and attention-deficit/hyperactivity disorder are thought to precede the development of cocaine-related disorders. Most studies of comorbidity in patients with cocaine-related disorders have shown that major depressive disorder, bipolar II disorder, cyclothymic disorder, anxiety disorders, and antisocial personality disorder are the most commonly associated psychiatric diagnoses.

Adverse Effects

A common adverse effect associated with cocaine use is nasal congestion, although serious inflammation, swelling, bleeding, and ulceration of the nasal mucosa can also occur. Long-term use of cocaine can also lead to the perforation of the nasal septa. Free-basing and smoking crack can cause damage to the bronchial passages and the lungs. The IV use of cocaine is associated with infection, embolisms, and the transmission of the human immunodeficiency virus (HIV). Minor neurological complications with cocaine use include the development of acute dystonia, tics, and migrainelike headaches. The major complications of cocaine use, however, are its cerebrovascular, epileptic, and cardiac effects. About two thirds of those acute toxic effects occur within one hour of intoxication; about one fifth occur in one to three hours; the remainder occur up to several days later.

CEREBROVASCULAR EFFECTS

The most common cerebrovascular diseases associated with cocaine use are nonhemorrhagic cerebral infarctions. When hemorrhagic infarctions do occur, they can include subarachnoid hemorrhages, intraparenchymal hemorrhages, and interventricular hemorrhages. Transient ischemic attacks have also been associated with cocaine use. Although those vascular disorders usually affect the brain, spinal cord hemorrhages have also been reported. The obvious pathophysiological mechanism for those vascular disorders is through vasoconstriction, but other pathophysiological mechanisms have also been proposed.

SEIZURES

Seizures have been reported to account for 3 to 8 percent of cocaine-related emergency room visits. Cocaine is the substance of abuse that is most commonly associated with seizures; the second most common substance is amphetamine. Usually, cocaine-induced seizures are single events, although multiple seizures and status epilepticus are also possible. A rare and easy-to-misdiagnose complication of cocaine use is partial complex status epilepticus, which should be considered in a patient who seems to have cocaine-induced psychotic disorder with an unusually fluctuating course. The risk of having cocaine-induced seizures is highest in patients who have a history of epilepsy, who use high doses of cocaine, and who use crack.

CARDIAC EFFECTS

Myocardial infarctions and arrhythmias are perhaps the most common cocaine-induced cardiac abnormalities. Cardiomyopathies can develop with the long-term use of cocaine. Cardioembolic cerebral infarctions can be a further complication arising from cocaine-induced myocardial dysfunction.

DEATH

High doses of cocaine are associated with seizures, respiratory depression, cerebrovascular diseases, and myocardial infarctions—all of which can lead to death in cocaine users. The users may experience warning signs of syncope or chest pain but may ignore those signs because of the irrepressible desire to take more cocaine. Deaths have also been reported with the ingestion of speedballs, which are combinations of opioids and cocaine.

Cocaine Intoxication

DSM-IV specifies the diagnostic criteria for cocaine intoxication (Table 6.6–1), emphasizing the behavioral and physical signs and symptoms of cocaine use. The DSM-IV diagnostic criteria allow for the specification of the presence of perceptual disturbances. If hallucinations are present in the absence of intact reality testing, the appropriate diagnosis is cocaine-induced psychotic disorder, with hallucinations.

Cocaine is used because it characteristically causes elation, euphoria, heightened self-esteem, and perceived improvement on mental and physical tasks. Actually, some studies have indicated that low doses of cocaine can be associated with improved performance on some cognitive tasks. With high doses of cocaine, however, the symptoms of intoxication include agitation, irritability, impaired judgment, impulsive and potentially dangerous sexual behavior, aggression, a generalized increase in psychomotor activity, and, potentially, symptoms of mania. The major associated physical symptoms are tachycardia, hypertension, and mydriasis.

Cocaine Withdrawal

After the cessation of cocaine use or after acute intoxication, a postintoxication depression (crash) is characterized by dysphoria, anhedonia, anxiety, irritability, fatigue, hypersomnolence, and sometimes agitation. With mild to moderate cocaine use, those withdrawal symptoms are over within 18 hours. With heavy use, such as that seen with cocaine dependence, the withdrawal symptoms can last up to a week, usually peaking in two to four days. Some patients and anecdotal reports have described cocaine withdrawal syndromes that have lasted for weeks or months. The withdrawal symptoms can also be associated with suicidal ideation in the affected person. In the state of withdrawal, the craving for cocaine can be powerful and intense,

since the person knows that taking cocaine can eliminate the uncomfortable symptoms of cocaine withdrawal. Persons experiencing cocaine withdrawal often attempt to self-medicate the symptoms with alcohol, sedatives, hypnotics, or antianxiety agents, such as diazepam (Valium). DSM-IV has formalized the diagnostic criteria for cocaine withdrawal (Table 6.6–2).

Cocaine Intoxication Delirium

DSM-IV has specified a diagnosis for cocaine intoxication delirium (Section 4.2). Cocaine intoxication delirium is most common when high doses of cocaine are used; when the cocaine has been used over a short period of time, thereby resulting in a rapid increase in cocaine blood concentrations; or when the cocaine is mixed with other psychoactive substances (for example, amphetamine, opiates, opioids, and alcohol). Persons with preexisting brain damage (often resulting from previous episodes of cocaine intoxication) are also at increased risk for cocaine intoxication delirium.

Cocaine-Induced Psychotic Disorders

Paranoid delusions and hallucinations may occur in as many as 50 percent of all cocaine users. The occurrence of those psychotic symptoms depends on the dose, the duration of use, and the user's individual sensitivity to the substance. Cocaine-induced psychotic disorders are most common with IV users and crack users. Males are much more likely to have psychotic symptoms than are females. Of the psychotic symptoms, paranoid delusions are the most frequent, although auditory hallucinations are also common. Visual and tactile hallucinations may be less common than paranoid delusions. The sensation of bugs crawling just beneath the skin (formication) has been reported to be associated with cocaine use. The development of psychotic disorders can be associated with grossly inappropriate sexual behavior, generally bizarre behavior, and homicidal or other violent behavior related to the content of the paranoid delusions or hallucinations. The DSM-IV diagnostic criteria of cocaine-induced psychotic disorders are listed in Section 8.1. The clinician can further specify whether delusions or hallucinations are the predominant symptoms.

Cocaine-Induced Mood Disorder

DSM-IV allows for the diagnosis of cocaine-induced mood disorder (Section 9.3), which can begin during either intoxication or withdrawal. Classically, the mood disorder symptoms associated with intoxication are hypomanic or manic in character. The mood disorder symptoms associated with withdrawal are characteristic of depression.

Cocaine-Induced Anxiety Disorder

DSM-IV also allows for the diagnosis of cocaine-induced anxiety disorder (Section 10.1). Common anxiety disorder symptoms associated with cocaine intoxication or cocaine withdrawal are those of obsessive-compulsive disorder, panic disorders, and phobias.

Cocaine-Induced Sexual Dysfunction

DSM-IV allows for the diagnosis of cocaine-induced sexual dysfunction (Section 14.2), which can begin when a person is intoxicated with cocaine. Although cocaine is used as an aphrodisiac and as a way to delay orgasm, its repeated use can result in impotence.

Cocaine-Induced Sleep Disorder

Cocaine-induced sleep disorder, which can begin during either intoxication or withdrawal, is described under the heading of substance-induced sleep disorder (Section 17.2). Cocaine intoxication is associated with the inability to sleep; cocaine withdrawal is associated with disrupted sleep or hypersomnolence.

Cocaine-Related Disorder Not Otherwise Specified

DSM-IV provides a diagnosis of cocaine-related disorder not otherwise specified (NOS) for cocaine-related disorders that cannot be classified into one of the other diagnoses.

TREATMENT

Many cocaine users do not come to treatment voluntarily. Their experience with the substance is too positive and the negative effects are perceived as too minimal to warrant seeking treatment. One study of cocaine users who sought treatment compared with those who did not seek treatment found that those who did not seek treatment more often had a polysubstance-related disorder, fewer negative consequences associated with cocaine use, fewer work-related or family-related obligations, and increased contact with the legal system and with illegal activities. The major hurdle to overcome in the treatment of cocaine-related disorders is the intense craving that the cocaine user has for the drug. Although animal studies have shown that cocaine is a powerful inducer of cocaine self-administration, those studies have also shown that animals limit their use of cocaine if negative reinforcers are experimentally linked to the cocaine intake. In humans, negative reinforcers may take the form of work-related and family-related problems that are brought on by cocaine use. Therefore, the clinician must take a broad treatment approach and include social, psychological, and perhaps biological strategies in the treatment program.

To attain abstinence from cocaine, the clinician may have to institute complete or partial hospitalization to remove patients from the usual social settings in which they had obtained or used cocaine. Frequent and unscheduled urine testing is almost always necessary to monitor patients' continued abstinence, especially in the first weeks and months of treatment.

Psychological intervention usually involves individual, group, and family modalities. Individual therapy is most effectively focused on the dynamics that led to the cocaine use, the perceived positive effects of the cocaine, and how those aims may be met in a different manner. Group therapy and support groups (such as Narcotics Anonymous) often involve discussions with other cocaine abusers and the sharing of past experiences and effective coping methods. Family therapy is often an essential component of the treatment strategy. Common issues in family therapy are discussing how past behavior has harmed the family and allowing other family members to voice their responses to those behaviors. However, the therapy should maintain a focus on the future and on how changes in the family's activities may help the cocaine abuser stay off the drug and direct energies in different directions.

A variety of pharmacological strategies have been used to help cocaine abusers resist the urge to take cocaine. The two most successful classes of drugs are the dopaminergic agonists and some of the tricyclic drugs. The two most commonly used dopaminergic agonists are amantadine (Symadine), 100 mg twice daily, and bromocriptine (Parlodel), 2.5 mg twice daily; both have been reported to reduce the patient's craving, increase energy, and normalize sleep. Carbamazepine (Tegretol) has also been used as a pharmacological approach to cocaine detoxification. Carbamazepine has been found to be effective in reducing craving, except in patients with coexisting antisocial personality disorder.

References

Caine S B, Koob G F: Modulation of cocaine self-administration in the rat through D-3 dopamine receptors. Science *260*: 1814, 1993.
Gallanter M, Egelko S, De Leon G, Rohrs C, Franco H: Crack-cocaine abusers in the general hospital: Assessment and initiation of care. Am J Psychiatry *149*: 810, 1992.
Higgins S T, Budney A J, Bickel W K, Hughes J R, Foerg F, Badger G: Achieving cocaine abstinence with a behavioral approach. Am J Psychiatry *150*: 763, 1993.
Jaffe J H: Cocaine-related disorders. In *Comprehensive Textbook of Psychiatry*, ed 6, H I Kaplan, B J Sadock, editors, p 817. Williams & Wilkins, Baltimore, 1995.
Withers N W, Pulvirenti L, Koob G F, Gillin J C: Cocaine abuse and dependence. J Clin Psychopharmacology *15*: 63, 1995.
Woolverton W L, Johnson K M: Neurobiology of cocaine abuse. Trends Pharmacol Sci *13*: 193, 1992.

6.7 HALLUCINOGEN-RELATED DISORDERS

The hallucinogens are variously called psychedelics or psychotomimetics because, besides inducing hallucinations, they cause loss of contact with reality and an expanding and heightening of consciousness. The hallucinogens are classified as schedule I drugs; the Food and Drug Administration (FDA) has decreed that they have no medical use and a high abuse potential. More than 100 natural and synthetic hallucinogens are used by humans. The classic naturally occurring hallucinogens are psilocybin (from some mushrooms) and mescaline (from peyote cactus). Other naturally occurring hallucinogens are harmine, harmaline, ibogaine, and dimethyltryptamine (DMT). The classic synthetic hallucinogen is lysergic acid diethylamide (LSD), which was synthesized in 1938 by Albert Hoffman, who later accidentally ingested some of the drug and experienced the first LSD-induced hallucinogenic episode.

EPIDEMIOLOGY

In the United States an estimated 8.1 percent of the inhabitants have used a hallucinogen at least once, 1.2 percent have used a hallucinogen in the preceding year, and 0.3 percent have used a hallucinogen in the preceding month. Hallucinogen use is most common among young (15 to 35 years of age) white males. The ratio of whites to blacks who have used a hallucinogen is 2 to 1, and the white-to-Hispanic ratio is around 1.5 to 1. Males represent 62 percent of those who have ever used a hallucinogen and 75 percent of those who have used a hallucinogen in the preceding month, thus reflecting a pattern of more frequent use than by females. Those 26 to 34 years of age have the highest use of hallucinogens, with 15.5 percent having used a hallucinogen at least once. Those 18 to 25 years of age have the highest recent use of a hallucinogen—1.2 percent of the

Table 6.7-1.   Diagnostic Criteria for Hallucinogen Intoxication

A. Recent use of a hallucinogen.

B. Clinically significant maladaptive behavioral or psychological changes (e.g., marked anxiety or depression, ideas of reference, fear of losing one's mind, paranoid ideation, impaired judgment, or impaired social or occupational functioning) that developed during, or shortly after, hallucinogen use.

C. Perceptual changes occurring in a state of full wakefulness and alertness (e.g., subjective intensification of perceptions, depersonalization, derealization, illusions, hallucinations, synesthesias) that developed during, or shortly after, hallucinogen use.

D. Two (or more) of the following signs, developing during, or shortly after, hallucinogen use:

(1) pupillary dilation
(2) tachycardia
(3) sweating
(4) palpitations
(5) blurring of vision
(6) tremors
(7) incoordination

E. The symptoms are not due to a general medical condition and are not better accounted for by another mental disorder.

Table from DSM-IV, *Diagnostic and Statistical Manual of Mental Disorders*, ed 4. Copyright American Psychiatric Association, Washington, 1994. Used with permission.

Table 6.7-2.   Diagnostic Criteria for Hallucinogen Persisting Perception Disorder (Flashbacks)

A. The reexperiencing, following cessation of use of a hallucinogen, of one or more of the perceptual symptoms that were experienced while intoxicated with the hallucinogen (e.g., geometric hallucinations, false perceptions of movement in the peripheral visual fields, flashes of color, intensified colors, trails of images of moving objects, positive after-images, halos around objects, macropsia, and micropsia).

B. The symptoms in criterion A cause clinically significant distress or impairment in social, occupational, or other important areas of functioning.

C. The symptoms are not due to a general medical condition (e.g., anatomical lesions and infections of the brain, visual epilepsies) and are not better accounted for by another mental disorder (e.g., delirium, dementia, schizophrenia) or hypnopompic hallucinations.

Table from DSM-IV, *Diagnostic and Statistical Manual of Mental Disorders*, ed 4. Copyright American Psychiatric Association, Washington, 1994. Used with permission.

age group. Cultural factors influence the use of hallucinogens; their use in the western United States is significantly higher than in the southern United States. Hallucinogen use is associated with less morbidity and less mortality than are some other substances. For example, one study found that only 1 percent of substance-related emergency room visits were related to hallucinogens, in comparison with 40 percent for cocaine-related problems. However, of those visiting the emergency room, more than 50 percent were under 20 years of age. There is a reported resurgence in the popularity of hallucinogens.

NEUROPHARMACOLOGY

Although the myriad hallucinogenic substances vary in their pharmacological effects, LSD can be discussed as a general prototype of a hallucinogen. The fundamental pharmacodynamic effect of LSD remains controversial, although it is generally well accepted that the principal effects are on the serotonergic system. The controversy regards whether LSD acts as an antagonist or as an agonist; the data at this time suggest that LSD acts as a partial agonist at postsynaptic serotonin receptors.

Most hallucinogens are well absorbed after oral ingestion, although some types of hallucinogens are ingested by inhalation, smoking, or intravenous injection. Tolerance for LSD and other hallucinogens develops rapidly and is virtually complete after three or four days of continuous use. Tolerance also reverses quickly, usually in four to seven days. There is no physical dependence on hallucinogens, and there are no withdrawal symptoms. However, a psychological dependence can develop to the insight-inducing experiences that a user may associate with episodes of hallucinogen use.

DIAGNOSIS

The fourth edition of *Diagnostic and Statistical Manual of Mental Disorders* (DSM-IV) lists a number of hallucinogen-related disorders but contains specific diagnostic criteria only for hallucinogen intoxication (Table 6.7–1) and hallucinogen persisting perception disorder (flashbacks) (Table 6.7–2). The diagnostic criteria for the other hallucinogen use disorders are contained in the DSM-IV sections that are specific to each symptom—for example, hallucinogen-induced mood disorder (Section 9.3).

Hallucinogen Dependence and Hallucinogen Abuse

Long-term hallucinogen use is not common. There is no physical addiction; although psychological dependence occurs, it is rare, partly because each LSD experience is different and partly because there is no reliable euphoria. Nonetheless, hallucinogen dependence and hallucinogen abuse do exist, and both syndromes are defined by DSM-IV criteria (see Tables 6.1–3 and 6.1–4).

Hallucinogen Intoxication

Intoxication with hallucinogens is defined in DSM-IV as being characterized by maladaptive behavioral and perceptual changes and by certain physiological signs (Table 6.7–1). The differential diagnosis for hallucinogen intoxication includes anticholinergic and amphetamine intoxication and alcohol withdrawal. The preferred treatment for hallucinogen intoxication is *talking down* the patient; during that process, guides can reassure patients that the symptoms are drug-induced, that the patients are not going crazy, and that the symptoms will resolve shortly. In the most severe cases, dopaminergic antagonists—for example, haloperidol (Haldol)—or benzodiazepines—for example, diazepam (Valium)—can be used for a limited time. In general, no withdrawal syndrome is associated with hallucinogen intoxication.

Hallucinogen Persisting Perception Disorder

At times distant to the ingestion of a hallucinogen, a person can experience a flashback involving hallucinogenic symptoms. The syndrome is diagnosed as hallucinogen persisting perception disorder (Table 6.7–2) in DSM-IV. Various studies have reported that from 15 to 80 percent of hallucinogen users report having experienced flashbacks. The differential diagnosis for flashbacks includes migraine, seizures, visual system abnormalities, and posttraumatic stress disorder. A flashback experience can be triggered by emotional stress, sensory deprivation (for example, monotonous driving), or the use of another psychoactive substance (for example, alcohol or marijuana).

The flashback is a spontaneous, transitory recurrence of the substance-induced experience. Most flashbacks are episodes of visual distortion, geometric hallucinations, hallucinations of sounds or voices, false perceptions of movement in peripheral fields, flashes of color, trails of images from moving objects, positive afterimages and halos, macropsia, micropsia, time expansion, physical symptoms, or relived intense emotion. The episodes usually last a few seconds to a few minutes, but sometimes they last longer than that.

Most often, even in the presence of distinct perceptual disturbances, the person has insight into the pathological nature of the disturbance. Suicidal behavior, major depressive disorder, and panic disorders are potential complications.

Hallucinogen Intoxication Delirium

DSM-IV allows for the diagnosis of hallucinogen delirium (Section 4.2). The disorder is thought to be relatively rare. It begins during intoxication in persons who have ingested pure hallucinogens. However, hallucinogens are often mixed with other substances, and the other components or their interactions with the hallucinogens can result in a clinical delirium.

Hallucinogen-Induced Psychotic Disorders

If psychotic symptoms are present in the absence of retained reality testing, a diagnosis of hallucinogen-induced psychotic disorder may be warranted (Section 8.1). DSM-IV also allows the clinician to specify whether hallucinations or delusions are the prominent symptoms. The most common adverse effect of LSD and related substances is a bad trip, which resembles the acute panic reaction to cannabis but which can be more severe; a bad trip occasionally produces true psychotic symptoms. The bad trip generally ends when the immediate effects of the hallucinogen wear off. However, the course of a bad trip is variable, and occasionally a protracted psychotic episode is difficult to distinguish from a nonorganic psychotic disorder. Whether a chronic psychosis after a drug ingestion is the result of the drug ingestion or is unrelated to the drug ingestion or is a combination of both the drug ingestion and predisposing factors is currently an unanswerable question.

Occasionally, the psychotic disorder is prolonged; prolonged reactions are thought to be most common is persons with preexisting schizoid personality disorder and prepsychotic personalities, an unstable ego balance, or a great deal of anxiety. Such persons cannot cope with the perceptual changes, body-image distortions, and symbolic unconscious material stimulated by the hallucinogen. The rate of previous mental instability in persons hospitalized for LSD reactions is high. In the late 1960s a number of adverse reactions occurred because LSD was being promoted as a self-prescribed psychotherapy for emotional crises in the lives of seriously disturbed people. Because that is happening less today, prolonged adverse reactions are much less commonly seen now than in the past.

Hallucinogen-Induced Mood Disorder

DSM-IV provides a diagnostic category for hallucinogen-induced mood disorder (Section 9.3). Unlike cocaine-induced mood disorder and amphetamine-induced mood disorder, in which the symptoms are somewhat predictable, mood disorder symptoms accompanying hallucinogen abuse can vary. Abusers may experience maniclike symptoms involving grandiose delusions or depressionlike feelings and ideas or mixed symptoms. As with the hallucinogen-induced psychotic disorder symptoms, the symptoms of hallucinogen-induced mood disorder almost invariably resolve once the drug has been eliminated from the patient's body.

Hallucinogen-Induced Anxiety Disorder

Hallucinogen-induced anxiety disorder (Section 10.1) also varies in its symptom pattern, and few data regarding symptom patterns are available. Anecdotally, physicians who treat patients who come into emergency rooms with hallucinogen-related disorders have frequently reported panic disorder with agoraphobia.

Hallucinogen-Related Disorder Not Otherwise Specified

If a patient with a hallucinogen-related disorder does not meet the diagnostic criteria for any of the standard hallucinogen-related disorders, the patient may be classified as having hallucinogen-related disorder not otherwise specified (NOS). DSM-IV does not have a diagnostic category of hallucinogen withdrawal, but some clinicians anecdotally report a syndrome with depression and anxiety that follows the cessation of frequent hallucinogen use. Such a syndrome may best fit the diagnosis of hallucinogen-related disorder NOS.

CLINICAL FEATURES

The onset of action of LSD occurs within one hour, peaks in two to four hours, and lasts 8 to 12 hours. The sympathomimetic effects of LSD include tremors, tachycardia, hypertension, hyperthermia, sweating, blurring of vision, and mydriasis. Death can be caused by hallucinogenic use. The cause of death can be related to cardiac or cerebrovascular pathology related to hypertension or hyperthermia. A syndrome similar to neuroleptic malignant syndrome has been reported to be associated with LSD use. The cause of death can also be related to a physical injury after the use of impaired judgment—for example, regarding traffic or the person's ability to fly. The psychological effects are usually well tolerated; however, if persons are unable to recall experiences or unable to appreciate that the experiences are substance-induced, they may fear the onset of insanity.

With hallucinogen use, perceptions become unusually brilliant and intense. Colors and textures seem to be richer than usual, contours sharpened, music more emotionally profound, and smells and tastes heightened. Synesthesia is common; colors may be heard or sounds seen. Changes in body image and alterations of time and space perception also occur. Hallucinations are usually visual, often of geometric forms and figures, but auditory and tactile hallucinations are sometimes experienced. Emotions become unusually intense and may change abruptly and often; two seemingly incompatible feelings may be experienced at the same time. Suggestibility is greatly heightened, and sensitivity or detachment from other people may arise. Other features that often appear are a seeming awareness of internal organs, the recovery of lost early memories, the release of unconscious material in symbolic form, and regression and the apparent reliving of past events, including birth. Introspective reflection and feelings of religious and philosophical insight are common. The sense of self is greatly changed, sometimes to the point of depersonalization, merging with the external world, separation of self from body, or total dissolution of the ego in mystical ecstasy.

There is no clear evidence of drastic personality change or chronic psychosis produced by long-term LSD use in moderate users not otherwise predisposed to those conditions. However, some heavy users of hallucinogens may suffer from chronic anxiety or depression and may benefit from a psychological or pharmacological approach that addresses the underlying problem.

Many persons maintain that a single experience with LSD has given them increased creative capacity, new psychological insight, relief from neurotic or psychosomatic symptoms, or a desirable change in personality. Psychiatrists in the 1950s and 1960s showed great interest in LSD and related substances, both as a potential model for functional psychosis and as possible pharmacotherapeutic agents. The availability of those compounds to researchers in the basic neurosciences has led to many scientific advances.

TREATMENT

The treatment of choice for acute psychiatric symptoms associated with hallucinogen intoxication is supportive counseling (talking down). The best treatment for a person who is having a severely unpleasant experience under the influence of LSD is protection, companionship, and reassurance. Occasionally, a short course of psychotherapeutic drugs may be necessary, usually with dopamine receptor antagonists for psychotic symptoms or with benzodiazepines for anxiety symptoms. When a hallucinogen-induced drug experience is temporally related to the onset of a persisting psychiatric condition (for example, a depressive disorder, manic episodes, or schizophrenia), the treatment of the persisting psychiatric condition should generally follow the usual guidelines for that diagnosis.

References

Behan W M, Bakheit A M, Behan P O, More I A: The muscle findings in the neuroleptic malignant syndrome associated with lysergic acid diethylamide. J Neurol Neurosurg Psychiatry 54: 741, 1991.
Cousineau D, Savard M, Allard D: Illicit drug use among adolescent students. A peer phenomenon? Can Fam Physician Med Fam Can 39: 523, 1993.
Crowley T J: Hallucinogen-related disorders. In Comprehensive Textbook of Psychiatry, ed 6, H I Kaplan, B J Sadock, editors, p 831. Williams & Wilkins, Baltimore, 1995.
Dinges M M, Oetting E R: Similarity in drug use patterns between adolescents and their friends. Adolescence 28: 253, 1993.
Johnston L D, O'Malley P M, Bachman J G: Drug abuse among American high school seniors, college students, and young adults, 1975–1990. Department of Health and Human Services, Washington, 1991.
Schwartz R H: LSD: Its rise, fall, and renewed popularity among high school students. Pediatr Clin North Am 42: 403, 1995.

6.8 INHALANT-RELATED DISORDERS

In the fourth edition of *Diagnostic and Statistical Manual of Mental Disorders* (DSM-IV), the category of inhalant-related disorders includes the psychiatric syndromes resulting from the use of solvents, glues, adhesives, aerosol propellants, paint thinners, and fuels. Specific examples of those substances include gasoline, varnish remover, lighter fluid, airplane glue, rubber cement, cleaning fluid, spray paint, shoe conditioner, and typewriter correction fluid. A resurgence of inhalants' popularity among the young has been reported. The active compounds in those inhalants include toluene, acetone, benzene, trichloroethane, perchloroethylene, trichloroethylene, 1,2-dichloropropane, and halogenated hydrocarbons. DSM-IV specifically excludes anesthetic gases (for example, nitrous oxide and ether) and short-acting vasodilators (for example, amylnitrite) from the inhalant-related disorders; DSM-IV classifies those as other (or unknown) substance-related disorders.

EPIDEMIOLOGY

Inhalant substances are available legally, inexpensively, and easily. Those three factors contribute to the high use of inhalants among the poor and the young. In 1991 about 5 percent of the total United States population had used inhalants at least once, and about 1 percent were current users. Among young adults 18 to 25 years old, 11 percent had used inhalants at least once, and 2 percent were current users. Among youths 12 to 17 years old, 7 percent had used inhalants at least once, and 2 percent were current users. In one study of high school seniors, 18 percent reported having used inhalants at least once, and 2.7 percent reported having used inhalants within the preceding month. White users of inhalants are more common than either black or Hispanic users. Some data suggest that, in the United States, inhalant use may be more common in suburban communities than in urban communities.

Inhalant use accounts for 1 percent of all substance-related deaths and fewer than 0.5 percent of all substance-related emergency room visits. About 20 percent of the emergency room visits for inhalant use involve persons less than 18 years old. Inhalant use among adolescents may be most common in those who have parents or older siblings who use illegal substances. Inhalant use among adolescents is also associated with an increased likelihood of being classified as having conduct disorder or antisocial personality disorder.

NEUROPHARMACOLOGY

The inhalants are usually delivered to the lungs by using a tube, a can, a plastic bag, or an inhalant-soaked rag, through or from which the user can sniff the inhalant through the nose or huff the inhalant through the mouth. The general action of inhalants is as a central nervous system (CNS) depressant. Tolerance for inhalants does develop, although the withdrawal symptoms are usually fairly mild and are not classified in DSM-IV as a disorder.

The inhalants are rapidly absorbed through the lungs and are rapidly delivered to the brain. The effects appear within five minutes and may last for 30 minutes to several hours, depending on the inhalant substance and the dose. For example, 15 to 20 breaths of a 1-percent solution of gasoline may result in a high that lasts several hours. The blood concentrations of many inhalant substances are increased when used in combination with alcohol, perhaps because of competition for hepatic enzymes. Although about one fifth of an inhalant substance is excreted unchanged by the lungs, the remainder is metabolized by the liver. Inhalants are detectable in the blood for 4 to 10 hours after use, and blood samples should be taken in the emergency room if inhalant use is suspected.

Much like alcohol, inhalants have specific pharmacodynamic effects that are not well understood. Because their effects are generally similar to and additive to the effects of other CNS depressants (for example, ethanol, barbiturates, and benzodiazepines), some investigators have suggested that the inhalants operate through an enhancement of the γ-aminobutyric acid (GABA) system. Other investigators have suggested that inhalants have their effects through membrane fluidization, which has also been hypothesized to be a pharmacodynamic effect of ethanol.

DIAGNOSIS

DSM-IV lists a number of inhalant-related disorders but contains specific diagnostic criteria only for inhalant intoxication (Table 6.8–1) within the inhalant-related disorders section. Diagnostic criteria for the other inhalant-related disorders are specified in the DSM-IV sections that specifically address the major symptoms—for example, inhalant-induced psychotic disorders (Section 8.1).

Inhalant Dependence and Inhalant Abuse

Most persons probably use inhalants for a short time and do not develop a pattern of long-term use that results in dependence and abuse. Nonetheless, dependence and abuse of inhalants do occur and are diagnosed according to the standard DSM-IV criteria for those syndromes (see Tables 6.1–3 and 6.1–4).

Inhalant Intoxication

The DSM-IV diagnostic criteria for inhalant intoxication (Table 6.8–1) specify the presence of maladaptive behavioral changes and at least two physical symptoms. The intoxicated state is often characterized by apathy, diminished social and occupational functioning, impaired judgment, and impulsive or

Table 6.8–1.   Diagnostic Criteria for Inhalant Intoxication

A. Recent intentional use or short-term, high-dose exposure to volatile inhalants (excluding anesthetic gases and short-acting vasodilators).

B. Clinically significant maladaptive behavioral or psychological changes (e.g., belligerence, assaultiveness, apathy, impaired judgment, impaired social or occupational functioning) that developed during, or shortly after, use of or exposure to volatile inhalants.

C. Two (or more) of the following signs, developing during, or shortly after, inhalant use or exposure:

    (1) dizziness
    (2) nystagmus
    (3) incoordination
    (4) slurred speech
    (5) unsteady gait
    (6) lethargy
    (7) depressed reflexes
    (8) psychomotor retardation
    (9) tremor
    (10) generalized muscle weakness
    (11) blurred vision or diplopia
    (12) stupor or coma
    (13) euphoria

D. The symptoms are not due to a general medical condition and are not better accounted for by another mental disorder.

Table from DSM-IV, *Diagnostic and Statistical Manual of Mental Disorders*, ed 4. Copyright American Psychiatric Association, Washington, 1994. Used with permission.

aggressive behavior. The person may later be amnestic for the period of intoxication. Intoxication is often accompanied by nausea, anorexia, nystagmus, depressed reflexes, and diplopia. The user's neurological status can progress to stupor and unconsciousness with high doses and long exposures. Clinicians can sometimes identify a recent user of inhalants by rashes around the patient's nose and mouth; unusual breath odors; the residue of the inhalant substances on the patient's face, hands, or clothing; and irritation of the patient's eyes, throat, lungs, and nose.

Inhalant Intoxication Delirium

DSM-IV provides a diagnostic category for inhalant intoxication delirium (Section 4.2). Delirium can be induced by the effects of the inhalants themselves, by pharmacodynamic interactions with other substances, and by the hypoxia that may be associated with either the inhalant or its method of inhalation. If the delirium results in severe behavioral disturbances, short-term treatment with a dopamine receptor antagonist—for example, haloperidol (Haldol)—may be necessary. Benzodiazepines should be avoided because of the possibility of adding to the patient's respiratory depression.

Inhalant-Induced Persisting Dementia

Inhalant-induced persisting dementia (Section 4.3), like delirium, may be due to the neurotoxic effects of the inhalants themselves, the neurotoxic effects of the metals commonly used in inhalants (for example, lead), or the effects of frequent and prolonged periods of hypoxia. The dementia caused by inhalants is likely to be irreversible in all but the mildest cases.

Inhalant-Induced Psychotic Disorder

Inhalant-induced psychotic disorder is a DSM-IV diagnosis (Section 8.1). The clinician can specify whether hallucinations or delusions are the predominant symptoms. Paranoid states are probably the most common psychotic syndromes during inhalant intoxication.

Inhalant-Induced Mood Disorder and Inhalant-Induced Anxiety Disorder

Inhalant-induced mood disorder (Section 9.3) and inhalant-induced anxiety disorder (Section 10.1) are DSM-IV diagnoses that allow the classification of inhalant-related disorders that are characterized by prominent mood and anxiety symptoms. Depressive disorders are the most common mood disorders associated with inhalant use, and panic disorders and generalized anxiety disorder are the most common anxiety disorders.

Inhalant-Related Disorder Not Otherwise Specified

The diagnosis of inhalant-related disorder not otherwise specified (NOS) is the recommended DSM-IV diagnosis for inhalant-related disorders that do not fit into one of the above diagnostic categories.

CLINICAL FEATURES

In small initial doses the inhalants may be disinhibiting and may result in feelings of euphoria, excitement, and pleasant floating sensations; the drugs are presumably used for those effects. Other psychological symptoms of high doses of the substance can include fearfulness, sensory illusions, auditory and visual hallucinations, and distortions of body size. The neurological symptoms can include slurred speech, decreased speed of talking, and ataxia. Use over a long period can be associated with irritability, emotional lability, and impaired memory.

Tolerance for inhalants does develop; although not recognized by DSM-IV, a withdrawal syndrome can accompany the cessation of inhalant use. The withdrawal syndrome does not occur frequently; when it does, it can be characterized by sleep disturbances, irritability, jitteriness, sweating, nausea, vomiting, tachycardia, and sometimes delusions and hallucinations.

Adverse Effects

The inhalants are associated with many potentially serious adverse effects. The most serious adverse effect is death, which can result from respiratory depression, cardiac arrhythmias, asphyxiation, the aspiration of vomitus, or accident or injury (for example, by driving while intoxicated with inhalants). Other serious adverse effects associated with long-term inhalant use include irreversible hepatic or renal damage and permanent muscle damage associated with rhabdomyolysis. The combination of organic solvents and high concentrations of copper, zinc, and heavy metals has been associated with the development of brain atrophy, temporal lobe epilepsy, decreased intelligence quotient (I.Q.), and a variety of electroencephalographic (EEG) changes. Several studies of house painters and factory workers who have been exposed to solvents for long periods have found evidence of brain atrophy on computed tomography (CT) scans and decreases in cerebral blood flow. Additional adverse effects include cardiovascular and pulmonary symptoms (for example, chest pain and bronchospasm), gastrointestinal symptoms (for example, pain, nausea, vomiting, and hematemesis), and other neurological signs and symptoms (for example, peripheral neuritis, headache, paresthesia, cerebellar signs, and lead encephalopathy). There are reports of brain atrophy, renal tubular acidosis, and long-term motor impairment in toluene users. A number of reports concern serious adverse effects on fetal development when the pregnant mother uses or is exposed to inhalant substances.

TREATMENT

Usually, the use of inhalants is a relatively short-lived period in a person's life. The person either ceases substance-taking activity or moves on to other substances of abuse. The identification of inhalant use in an adolescent is an indication that the teenager should receive counseling and education about the general topic of substance use. The presence of an associated diagnosis of conduct disorder or antisocial personality disorder should prompt the clinician to address the situation in depth because of the increased likelihood that the adolescent will become further involved in substance use. For the most part, however, persons with inhalant abuse or inhalant dependence are older, debilitated persons who need substantial social interventions as part of the treatment approach.

References

Crowley T J: Inhalant-related disorders. In *Comprehensive Textbook of Psychiatry*, ed 6, H I Kaplan, B J Sadock, editors, p 838. Williams & Wilkins, Baltimore, 1995.

Dinwiddie, S H: Abuse of inhalants: A review. Addiction *89*: 925, 1994.
Espeland K: Inhalant abuse: Assessment guidelines. J Psychosoc Nurs Ment Health Serv *31*: 11, 1993.
Farrow J A, Schwartz R H: Adolescent drug and alcohol usage: A comparison of urban and suburban pediatric practices. J Natl Med Assoc *84*: 409, 1992.
Tenenbein M, Pillay N: Sensory evoked potentials in inhalant (volatile solvent) abuse. J Paediatr Child Health *29*: 206, 1993.
Wheeler M G, Rozycki A A, Smith R P: Recreational propane inhalation in an adolescent male. J Toxicol Clin Toxicol *30*: 135, 1992.

6.9 NICOTINE-RELATED DISORDERS

In 1988 *The Surgeon General's Report on the Health Consequences of Smoking: Nicotine Addiction* was published. It clearly stated that nicotine is an addicting drug, just as cocaine and heroin are addicting drugs. As a result of that report and other public health information campaigns, the percentage of persons who smoke in the United States has decreased from 44 percent in 1964 to approximately 27 percent in 1992. The fact that 27 percent of all persons in the United States continue to smoke in spite of the mountain of data showing how dangerous the habit is to their health is testament to the powerfully addictive properties of nicotine. The ill effects of cigarette smoking are reflected in the estimate that 60 percent of the direct health care costs in the United States go to treat tobacco-related illnesses and come to an estimated $1 billion a day.

In 1995 President William Clinton announced proposed rules that will allow the Food and Drug Administration (FDA) to govern the sale and distribution of nicotine-containing cigarettes and smokeless tobacco products to children and adolescents by reducing easy access and decreasing the appeal of these products. The proposed rule would not restrict the use of tobacco products by adults.

EPIDEMIOLOGY

The number of Americans who smoke is decreasing, but it still estimated that 22 percent of all Americans will still be smoking in the year 2000. The rate of quitting smoking has been fastest among well-educated, white men and slower among women, blacks, teenagers, and persons with low levels of education.

The most common form of nicotine is tobacco, which is smoked in cigarettes, cigars, and pipes. Tobacco can also be used as snuff and chewing tobacco (also called smokeless tobacco); both forms are increasingly popular in the United States. About 3 percent of all persons in the United States are current users of snuff or chewing tobacco; however, about 6 percent of young adults aged 18 to 25 use those forms of tobacco.

Children

Children are becoming addicted to nicotine. The average teenage smoker starts at $14\frac{1}{2}$ years old and becomes a daily smoker before age 18. More than 80 percent of all adult smokers had tried smoking by their 18th birthday, and more than half of them had already become regular smokers by that age. Studies show that if people do not begin to smoke as teenagers or children, it is unlikely they will ever do so.

Each and every day, another 3,000 young people become regular smokers, and nearly 1,000 of them will eventually die as a result of their smoking. Currently, more than 3 million children and adolescents smoke cigarettes, and 1 million adolescent boys currently use smokeless tobacco. Smoking by young people is rising sharply. Between 1991 and 1994, the percentage of eighth graders who smoke increased 30 percent, and the percentage of tenth graders who smoke increased 22 percent.

COMORBIDITY

America's youth are engaged in risky health behaviors, and those who smoke cigarettes are the most likely to have many poor health habits. In a National Center for Health Statistics (NCHS) survey of the unhealthy behaviors of youth aged 12 to 21 years, the data showed that over one quarter of adolescents and young adults were smokers. Current smokers were 3 to 17 times more likely to have recently used other substances than adolescents who had never smoked. Smokers were more likely to have engaged in binge drinking and to have been involved in physical fighting and in carrying weapons, including guns and knives.

Adverse Effects

The primary adverse effect of cigarette smoking is death. Tobacco use is associated with approximately 400,000 premature deaths each year in the United States, representing 25 percent of all deaths. The causes of death include chronic bronchitis and emphysema (51,000 deaths), bronchogenic cancer (106,000 deaths), 35 percent of fatal myocardial infarctions (115,000 deaths), cerebrovascular disease, cardiovascular disease, and almost all cases of chronic obstructive pulmonary disease and lung cancer. Lung cancer is now the leading cause of cancer-related deaths in women, having recently surpassed breast cancer. The increased use of chewing tobacco and snuff has been associated with the development of oropharyngeal cancer.

NEUROPHARMACOLOGY

The psychoactive component of tobacco is nicotine, which affects the central nervous system (CNS) by acting as an agonist at the nicotinic subtype of acetylcholine receptors. About 25 percent of the nicotine inhaled when smoking a cigarette reaches the blood, through which the nicotine reaches the brain within 15 seconds. The half-life of nicotine is about two hours. Nicotine is believed to have its positive reinforcing and addictive properties because it activates the dopaminergic pathway projecting from the ventral tegmental area to the cerebral cortex and the limbic system. In addition to activating that reward dopamine system, nicotine causes an increase in the concentrations of circulating norepinephrine and epinephrine and an increase in the release of vasopressin, β-endorphin, adrenocorticotropic hormone (ACTH), and cortisol. Those hormones are thought to contribute to the basic stimulatory effects of nicotine on the CNS.

DIAGNOSIS

The fourth edition of *Diagnosis and Statistical Manual of Mental Disorders* (DSM-IV) lists three nicotine-related disorders but contains specific diagnostic criteria for only nicotine

Table 6.9-1.   Diagnostic Criteria for Nicotine Withdrawal

A. Daily use of nicotine for at least several weeks.

B. Abrupt cessation of nicotine use, or reduction in the amount of nicotine used, followed within 24 hours by four (or more) of the following signs:

    (1) dysphoric or depressed mood
    (2) insomnia
    (3) irritability, frustration, or anger
    (4) anxiety
    (5) difficulty concentrating
    (6) restlessness
    (7) decreased heart rate
    (8) increased appetite or weight gain

C. The symptoms in criterion B cause clinically significant distress or impairment in social, occupational, or other important areas of functioning.

D. The symptoms are not due to a general medical condition and are not better accounted for by another mental disorder.

Table from DSM-IV, *Diagnostic and Statistical Manual of Mental Disorders*, ed 4. Copyright American Psychiatric Association, Washington, 1994. Used with permission.

withdrawal (Table 6.9–1) in the nicotine-related disorders section. The other nicotine-related disorders recognized by DSM-IV are nicotine dependence and nicotine-related disorder not otherwise specified.

Nicotine Dependence

DSM-IV allows for the diagnosis of nicotine dependence (see Table 6.1–3) but not nicotine abuse. Dependence on nicotine develops quickly, probably because of the activation by nicotine of the ventral tegmental area dopaminergic system, the same system affected by cocaine and amphetamine. The development of dependence is enhanced by strong social factors that encourage smoking in some settings and by the powerful effects of tobacco company advertising. Persons are likely to smoke if they have parents or siblings who smoke and who serve as role models. Several recent studies have also suggested a genetic diathesis toward nicotine dependence. Most persons who smoke want to quit and have tried many times to quit but have been unsuccessful in their efforts.

Nicotine Withdrawal

DSM-IV does not have a diagnostic category for nicotine intoxication; however, DSM-IV does have a diagnostic category for nicotine withdrawal (see Table 6.9–1). Withdrawal symptoms from nicotine can develop within two hours of smoking the last cigarette, generally peak in the first 24 to 48 hours, and can last for weeks or months. The common symptoms include an intense craving for nicotine, tension, irritability, difficulty in concentrating, drowsiness and paradoxical trouble in sleeping, decreased heart rate and blood pressure, increased appetite and weight gain, decreased motor performance, and increased muscle tension. A mild syndrome of nicotine withdrawal can appear when a smoker switches from regular cigarettes to low-nicotine cigarettes.

Nicotine-Related Disorder Not Otherwise Specified

Nicotine-related disorder not otherwise specified (NOS) is a diagnostic category for nicotine-related disorders that do not fit into one of the categories discussed above. Such diagnoses may include nicotine intoxication, nicotine abuse, and mood disorders and anxiety disorders associated with nicotine use.

CLINICAL FEATURES

Behaviorally, the stimulatory effects of nicotine result in improved attention, learning, reaction time, and problem-solving ability. Users of tobacco also report that cigarette smoking lifts their mood, decreases tension, and lessens depressive feelings. The effects of nicotine on the cerebral blood flow (CBF) have been studied, and the results suggest that short-term nicotine exposure increases the CBF without changing cerebral oxygen metabolism but that long-term nicotine exposure is associated with decreases in the CBF. In contrast to its stimulatory CNS effects, nicotine acts as a skeletal muscle relaxant.

Adverse Effects

Nicotine is a highly toxic chemical. Doses of 60 mg in an adult are fatal secondary to respiratory paralysis; doses of 0.5 mg are delivered by smoking the average cigarette. In low doses the signs and symptoms of nicotine toxicity include nausea, vomiting, salivation, pallor (caused by peripheral vasoconstriction), weakness, abdominal pain (caused by increased peristalsis), diarrhea, dizziness, headache, increased blood pressure, tachycardia, tremor, and cold sweats. Toxicity is also associated with an inability to concentrate, confusion, and sensory disturbances. Nicotine is further associated with a decrease in the user's amount of rapid eye movement (REM) sleep. Tobacco use during pregnancy has been associated with an increased incidence of low-birth-weight babies.

Health Benefits of Smoking Cessation

In a report by the Surgeon General in 1990 on the health benefits to smoking cessation, the following five major conclusions were reached: (1) Smoking cessation has major and immediate health benefits for persons of all ages and provides benefits for persons with and without smoking-related diseases. (2) Former smokers live longer than do those who continue to smoke. (3) Smoking cessation decreases the risk for lung cancer and other cancers, myocardial infarction, cerebrovascular diseases, and chronic lung diseases. (4) Women who stop smoking before pregnancy during the first three to four months of pregnancy reduce their risk for having low-birth-weight infants to that of women who never smoked. (5) The health benefits of smoking cessation substantially exceed any risks from the average five-pound (2.3-kilogram) weight gain or any adverse psychological effects after quitting.

TREATMENT

The combined use of transdermal nicotine administration (nicotine patches) and behavioral counseling has resulted in sustained abstinence rates of 60 percent in well-controlled clinical trials. That figure is significantly greater than the estimated 10 percent success rate for persons who quit cigarette smoking without specific support treatment. The most effective behavioral support programs address such issues as how to perform common daily activities (for example, eating, driving, and socializing) without smoking and how to cope with the dysphoric mood and the weight gain that can accompany smoking cessation. A further advantage of transdermal nicotine use is that doses of the nicotine can be individually titrated to patients' needs and their experiences of nicotine withdrawal symptoms. A variety of other psychopharmacological agents have also been used with some success in maintaining abstinence from nicotine. Those other preparations and drugs include nicotine-containing chewing gum, lobeline (a congener of nicotine), clonidine (Catapres), antidepressants—particularly fluoxetine (Prozac)—and buspirone (BuSpar). In addition, people who successfully discontinue smoking are likely to have been encouraged by someone close to them (such as a spouse or children), to have been fearful of the ill effects of smoking, and to have joined a support group of some type for ex-smokers. Encouragement from a nonsmoking physician is also highly correlated with abstinence.

References

Brautbar N: Direct effects of nicotine on the brain: Evidence for chemical addiction. Arch Environ Health *50*: 263, 1995.
DeGrandpre R J, Bickel W K Rizvi S A, Hughes J R: Effects of income on drug choice in humans. J Exp Anal Behav *59*: 483, 1993.
Greden J F, Pomerleau O F: Caffeine-related disorders and nicotine-related disorders. In *Comprehensive Textbook of Psychiatry*, ed 6, H I Kaplan, B J Sadock, editors, p 799. Williams & Wilkins, Baltimore, 1995.
Perkins K A, Grobe J E, Epstein L H, Caggiula A, Stiller R L, Jacob R G: Chronic and acute tolerance to subjective effects of nicotine. Pharmacol Biochem Behav *45*: 375, 1993.
Russell M A, Stapleton J A, Feyerabend C, Wiseman S M, Gustavsson G, Sawe U, Connor P: Targeting heavy smokers in general practice: Randomised controlled trial of transdermal nicotine patches. Br Med J *306*: 1308, 1993.
Schwartz J L: Methods of smoking cessation. Med Clin North Am 76: 451, 1992.

6.10 OPIOID-RELATED DISORDERS

The words "opiate" and "opioid" come from the word "opium," the juice of the opium poppy, *Papaver somniferum*, which contains approximately 20 opium alkaloids, including morphine. (The fourth edition of *Diagnostic and Statistical Manual of Mental Disorders* [DSM-IV] uses the word "opioid" to encompass "opiate," any preparation or derivative of opium, as well as "opioid," a synthetic narcotic that resembles an opiate in action but that is not derived from opium.) The naturally occurring opiates are smuggled into the United States from the Middle East and the Far East, where the opium poppy is a major revenue-producing crop. Other naturally occurring opiates or opioids that are synthesized from naturally occurring opiates are heroin (diacetylmorphine), codeine (3-methoxymorphine), and hydromorphone (Dilaudid). Heroin is about twice as potent as morphine and is the most commonly used opiate in persons with opioid-related disorders.

Heroin, which is pharmacologically similar to morphine, induces analgesia, drowsiness, and changes in mood. Although the manufacture, the sale, and the possession of heroin are illegal in the United States, attempts have been made to make heroin available to pain-ridden terminal cancer patients because of its excellent analgesic and euphoric effects. Many people, including some legislators, favor a change in the law, but such legislation has been repeatedly voted down by the United States Congress.

A large number of synthetic opioids have been manufactured, including meperidine (Demerol), methadone (Dolophine), pentazocine (Talwin), and propoxyphene (Darvon). Methadone is the current gold standard in the treatment of opioid dependence. Opioid antagonists have been synthesized to treat opioid overdose and opioid dependence, and that class of drugs includes naloxone (Narcan), naltrexone (ReVia), nalorphine, levallorphan, and apomorphine. A number of compounds with mixed agonist and antagonist activity at opioid receptors have been synthesized, and they include pentazocine, butorphanol (Stadol), and buprenorphine (Buprenex). A number of studies have found buprenorphine to be an effective treatment for opioid dependence.

EPIDEMIOLOGY

Heroin is the most widely used opiate in persons with opioid dependence. In 1991 an estimated 1.3 percent of the United States population had used heroin at least once. About 500,000 persons with opioid dependence are in the United States, about half of them in New York City. The male-to-female ratio of persons with opioid dependence is about 3 to 1. Typically, users of opiates and opioids started to use substances in their teens and early 20s; currently, most persons with opioid dependence are in their 30s and 40s. In the United States, persons tend to experience their first opioid-induced experience in their early teens or even as young as 10 years old. Such early induction into the drug culture is likely to happen in communities in which substance abuse is rampant and in families in which the parents are substance abusers. Heroin habits can cost a person hundreds of dollars a day; thus, the person with opioid dependence needs to obtain money through criminal activities and prostitution. The involvement of persons with opioid dependence in prostitution accounts for much of the spread of HIV.

NEUROPHARMACOLOGY

The primary effects of the opiates and the opioids are mediated through the opiate receptors, which were discovered in the second half of the 1970s. The μ-opioid receptors are involved in the regulation and the mediation of analgesia, respiratory depression, constipation, and dependence; the κ-opioid receptors with analgesia, diuresis, and sedation; and the Δ-opioid receptors possibly with analgesia.

In 1974 enkephalin, an endogenous pentapeptide with opiatelike actions, was identified. That discovery led to the identification of three classes of endogenous opioids within the brain, including the endorphins and the enkephalins. Endorphins are involved in neural transmission and serve to suppress pain. They are released naturally in the body when a person is physically hurt and account in part for the absence of pain during acute injuries.

The opioids also have significant effects on the dopaminergic and noradrenergic neurotransmitter systems. Several types of data indicate that the addictive rewarding properties of opiates and opioids are mediated through the activation of the ventral tegmental area dopaminergic neurons that project to the cerebral cortex and the limbic system.

Heroin is the most commonly abused opiate and is more potent and lipid-soluble than morphine. Because of those properties, heroin crosses the blood-brain barrier in less time and has a more rapid onset than does morphine. Heroin was first introduced as a treatment of morphine addiction, but it is, in fact, more dependence-producing than is morphine. Codeine, which occurs naturally as about 0.5 percent of the opioid alkaloids in opium, is absorbed easily through the gastrointestinal

tract and is subsequently transformed into morphine in the body. At least one positron emission tomographic (PET) study has suggested that one effect of all opiates and opioids is a decrease in cerebral blood flow in selected brain regions in persons with opioid dependence.

Tolerance and Dependence

Tolerance to opiates and opioids develops rapidly and can, for example, be so profound that terminally ill cancer patients may need 200 to 300 mg a day of morphine, whereas a dose of 60 mg can easily be fatal to an opioid-naive person. The symptoms of opioid withdrawal, however, do not occur unless a person has been using opioids for a long time or when the cessation is particularly abrupt, as functionally occurs when an opiate antagonist is given. The long-term use of opiates or opioids results in changes in the number and the sensitivity of opioid receptors, which are mediators for at least some of the effect of tolerance and withdrawal. Although long-term use is associated with increased sensitivity of the dopaminergic, cholinergic, and serotonergic neurons, the effect of opiates and opioids on the noradrenergic neurons is probably the primary mediator of the symptoms of opioid withdrawal. Short-term use of opioids decreases the activity of the noradrenergic neurons in the locus ceruleus; long-term use activates a compensatory homeostatic mechanism within the neurons; and opioids withdrawal results in a rebound hyperactivity. That hypothesis also provides a basis for why clonidine (Catapres), an α_2-adrenergic receptor agonist that decreases the release of norepinephrine, is useful in the treatment of opioid withdrawal symptoms.

ETIOLOGY

Societal and Cultural Factors

Opioid dependence is not limited to the low socioeconomic classes, although the incidence of opioid dependence is higher in those groups than in higher socioeconomic classes. A variety of social factors associated with urban poverty probably contribute to opioid dependence. About 50 percent of urban heroin users are children of single parents or divorced parents and are from families in which at least one other member has a substance-related disorder. Children from such settings are at high risk for opioid dependence, especially if they also evidence behavioral problems in school or other signs of conduct disorder.

Some consistent behavior patterns seem to be especially pronounced in adolescents with opioid dependence. Those patterns have been called the *heroin behavior syndrome*: underlying depression, often of an agitated type and frequently accompanied by anxiety symptoms; impulsiveness expressed by a passive-aggressive orientation; fear of failure; use of heroin as an antianxiety agent to mask feelings of low self-esteem, hopelessness, and aggression; limited coping strategies and low frustration tolerance, accompanied by the need for immediate gratification; sensitivity to drug contingencies, with a keen awareness of the relation between good feelings and the act of drug taking; feelings of behavioral impotence counteracted by momentary control over the life situation by means of substances; and disturbances in social and interpersonal relationships with peers maintained by mutual substance experiences.

Table 6.10-1.   Diagnostic Criteria for Opioid Intoxication

A. Recent use of an opioid.

B. Clinically significant maladaptive behavioral or psychological changes (e.g., initial euphoria followed by apathy, dysphoria, psychomotor agitation or retardation, impaired judgment, or impaired social or occupational functioning) that developed during, or shortly after, opioid use.

C. Pupillary constriction (or pupillary dilation due to anoxia from severe overdose) and one (or more) of the following signs, developing during, or shortly after, opioid use:

   (1) drowsiness or coma
   (2) slurred speech
   (3) impairment in attention or memory

D. The symptoms are not due to a general medical condition and are not better accounted for by another mental disorder.

Table from DSM-IV, *Diagnostic and Statistical Manual of Mental Disorders*, ed 4. Copyright American Psychiatric Association, Washington, 1994. Used with permission.

Comorbidity

About 90 percent of persons with opioid dependence have an additional psychiatric diagnosis. The most common comorbid psychiatric diagnoses are major depressive disorder, alcohol-related disorders, antisocial personality disorder, and anxiety disorders. About 15 percent of persons with opioid dependence attempt to commit suicide at least once. The high prevalence of comorbidity with other psychiatric diagnoses highlights the need to develop a broad-based treatment program that also addresses the associated psychiatric disorders in the patient.

Biological and Genetic Factors

A person with an opioid-related disorder may have had a genetically determined hypoactivity of the opiate system. Such hypoactivity may be caused by opiate receptors that were too few or were less sensitive than possible, by having too little release of endogenous opiates, or by having too high concentrations of a hypothesized endogenous opiate antagonist. A number of researchers are investigating those possibilities. A biological predisposition to an opioid-related disorder may also be associated with abnormal functioning in either the dopaminergic neurotransmitter system or the noradrenergic neurotransmitter system. Because of the difficulties inherent in the study of substance-related disorders, the data are still limited; however, some data do support the idea that there are genetic determinants for the development of opioid-related disorders.

Psychoanalytic Theory

In the psychoanalytic literature the behavior of narcotic addicts was described in terms of libidinal fixation, with regression to pregenital, oral, or even more archaic levels of psychosexual development. The need to explain the relation of drug abuse, defense mechanisms, impulse control, affective disturbances, and adaptive mechanisms led to the shift from psychosexual formulations to formulations emphasizing ego psychology. Serious ego pathology is often thought to be associated with substance abuse and is considered to be indicative of profound developmental disturbances. Problems of the relation between the ego and affects emerge as a key area of difficulty.

DIAGNOSIS

DSM-IV lists a number of opioid-related disorders but contains specific diagnostic criteria only for opioid intoxication (Table 6.10–1) and opioid withdrawal (Table 6.10–2) within

Table 6.10-2.   Diagnostic Criteria for Opioid Withdrawal

A. Either of the following:

   (1) cessation of (or reduction in) opioid use that has been heavy and prolonged (several weeks or longer)
   (2) administration of an opioid antagonist after a period of opioid use

B. Three (or more) of the following, developing within minutes to several days after criterion A:

   (1) dysphoric mood
   (2) nausea or vomiting
   (3) muscle aches
   (4) lacrimation or rhinorrhea
   (5) pupillary dilation, piloerection, or sweating
   (6) diarrhea
   (7) yawning
   (8) fever
   (9) insomnia

C. The symptoms in criterion B cause clinically significant distress or impairment in social, occupational, or other important areas of functioning.

D. The symptoms are not due to a general medical condition and are not better accounted for by another mental disorder.

Table from DSM-IV, *Diagnostic and Statistical Manual of Mental Disorders*, ed 4. Copyright American Psychiatric Association, Washington, 1994. Used with permission.

the section on opioid-related disorders. The diagnostic criteria for the other opioid-related disorders are contained within the DSM-IV sections that deal specifically with the predominant symptom—for example, opioid-induced mood disorder (Section 9.3).

Opioid Dependence and Opioid Abuse

Opioid dependence and opioid abuse are defined in DSM-IV according to the general criteria for those disorders (see Tables 6.1–3 and 6.1–4).

Opioid Intoxication

DSM-IV defines opioid intoxication as including maladaptive behavioral changes and some specific physical symptoms of opioid use (Table 6.10–1). In general, the presence of an altered mood, psychomotor retardation, drowsiness, slurred speech, and impaired memory and attention in the presence of other indicators of recent opioid use strongly suggests a diagnosis of opioid intoxication. DSM-IV allows for the specification of ''with perceptual disturbances.''

Opioid Withdrawal

The general rule regarding the onset and the duration of withdrawal symptoms is that substances with short durations of action tend to produce short, intense withdrawal syndromes, and that substances with long durations of action produce prolonged but mild withdrawal syndromes. An exception to the rule is that narcotic antagonist-precipitated withdrawal after long-acting opioid dependence can be severe.

An abstinence syndrome can be precipitated by the administration of an opiate antagonist. The symptoms may begin within seconds of such an intravenous injection and may peak in about one hour. Opioid craving rarely occurs in the context of analgesic administration for pain from physical disorders or surgery. The full withdrawal syndrome, including intense craving for opiates or opioids, usually occurs only secondary to an abrupt cessation of use in persons with opioid dependence.

MORPHINE AND HEROIN

The morphine and heroin withdrawal syndrome begins in six to eight hours after the last dose, usually after a one- to two-week period of continuous use or the administration of a narcotic antagonist. The withdrawal syndrome reaches its peak intensity during the second or third day and subsides during the next 7 to 10 days. However, some symptoms may persist for six months or longer.

MEPERIDINE

The withdrawal syndrome from meperidine begins quickly, reaches a peak in 8 to 12 hours, and is complete in four to five days.

METHADONE

Methadone withdrawal usually begins one to three days after the last dose and is complete in 10 to 14 days.

SYMPTOMS

Opioid withdrawal is officially defined in DSM-IV (Table 6.10–2). The disorder consists of severe muscle cramps and bone aches, profuse diarrhea, abdominal cramps, rhinorrhea, lacrimation, piloerection or gooseflesh (from which comes the term "cold turkey" for the abstinence syndrome), yawning, fever, pupillary dilation, hypertension, tachycardia, and temperature dysregulation, including hypothermia and hyperthermia. A person with opioid dependence seldom dies from opioid withdrawal, unless the person has a severe preexisting physical illness, such as cardiac disease. Residual symptoms—such as insomnia, bradycardia, temperature dysregulation, and a craving for opiates or opioids—may persist for months after withdrawal. At any time during the abstinence syndrome, a single injection of morphine or heroin eliminates all the symptoms. Associated features of opioid withdrawal include restlessness, irritability, depression, tremor, weakness, nausea, and vomiting.

Opioid Intoxication Delirium

Opioid intoxication delirium is a diagnostic category within DSM-IV (Section 4.2). Opioid intoxication delirium is most likely when opiates or opioids are used in high doses, are mixed with other psychoactive compounds, or are used by a person with preexisting brain damage or a central nervous system (CNS) disorder (for example, epilepsy).

Opioid-Induced Psychotic Disorder

Opioid-induced psychotic disorder can begin during opioid intoxication. The DSM-IV diagnostic criteria are contained in the section on schizophrenia and other psychotic disorders (Section 8.1). The clinician can specify whether the predominant symptoms are hallucinations or delusions.

Opioid-Induced Mood Disorder

Opioid-induced mood disorder, which can begin during opioid intoxication, is a diagnostic category in DSM-IV (Section 9.3). Opioid-induced mood disorder symptoms may be of a manic, depressed, or mixed nature, depending on the person's response to the opiates or opioids. A person coming to psychiatric attention with opioid-induced mood disorder usually has mixed symptoms, combining irritability, expansiveness, and depression.

Opioid-Induced Sleep Disorder and Opioid-Induced Sexual Dysfunction

Opioid-induced sleep disorder (Section 17.2) and opioid-induced sexual dysfunction (Section 14.2) are diagnostic categories in DSM-IV. Hypersomnia is likely to be a more common sleep disorder with opiates or opioids than is insomnia. The most common sexual dysfunction is likely to be impotence.

Opioid-Related Disorder Not Otherwise Specified

DSM-IV includes diagnoses for opioid-related disorders with symptoms of delirium, abnormal mood, psychosis, abnormal sleep, and sexual dysfunction. Clinical situations that do not fit into those categories are examples of appropriate cases for the use of the DSM-IV diagnosis of opioid-related disorder not otherwise specified (NOS).

CLINICAL FEATURES

Opiates and opioids can be taken orally, snorted intranasally, injected intravenously, or injected subcutaneously. Opiates and opioids are subjectively addictive because of the euphoric high (the rush) experienced by opioid users, especially those who take the substances intravenously. The associated symptoms include a feeling of warmth, heaviness of the extremities, dry mouth, itchy face (especially the nose), and facial flushing. The initial euphoria is followed by a period of sedation, known in street parlance as *nodding off*. For opioid-naive persons, the use of opiates or opioids can induce dysphoria, nausea, and vomiting.

The physical effects of opiates and opioids include respiratory depression, pupillary constriction, smooth-muscle contraction (including the ureters and the bile ducts), constipation, and changes in blood pressure, heart rate, and body temperature. The respiratory depressant effects are mediated at the level of the brainstem and are additive to the effects of the phenothiazines and the monoamine oxidase inhibitors.

Adverse Effects

The most common and most serious adverse effect associated with the opioid-related disorders is the potential transmission of hepatitis and HIV through the use of contaminated needles by more than one person. Another serious adverse effect is an idiosyncratic drug interaction between meperidine and monoamine oxidase inhibitors (MAOIs) that can result in gross autonomic instability, severe behavioral agitation, coma, seizures, and death. Idiosyncratic allergic reactions to opiates and opioids can also occur, resulting in anaphylactic shock, pulmonary edema, and death if the person does not receive prompt and adequate treatment.

Opioid Overdose

Death from an overdose of an opiate or an opioid is almost always due to respiratory arrest from the respiratory depressant effect of the drug. The symptoms of overdose include marked unresponsiveness, coma, slow respiration, hypothermia, hypotension, and bradycardia. When presented with the clinical triad of coma, pinpoint pupils, and respiratory depression, the clinician should consider opiate or opioid overdose as a primary diagnosis. The clinician can also inspect the patient's body for needle tracks in the arms, legs, ankles, groin, and even the dorsal vein of the penis.

OVERDOSE TREATMENT

Opioid overdose is a medical emergency. The patient's respiration is severely depressed, and the patient may be semicomatose, comatose, or in shock. The first task is to make sure that the patient has an open airway and that vital signs are maintained. Naloxone, an opioid antagonist, can be administered, 0.4 mg intravenously; that dose can be repeated four to five times within the first 30 to 45 minutes. The patient generally becomes responsive, but, because naloxone has a short duration of action, the patient may relapse into a semicomatose state in four or five hours; therefore, careful observation is imperative. Grand mal seizures occur with meperidine overdose and can be prevented by naloxone. Antagonists must be used carefully because they can precipitate a severe withdrawal reaction. Other narcotic antagonists useful in the treatment of overdose include nalorphine and levallorphan.

MPTP-Induced Parkinsonism

In 1976, after ingesting an opioid contaminated with N-methyl-4-phenyl-1,2,3,6 tetrahydropyridine (MPTP), a number of persons had a syndrome of irreversible parkinsonism. The mechanism for the neurotoxic effect is as follows: MPTP is converted into 1-methyl-4-phenylpyridinium (MPP^+) by the enzyme monoamine oxidase and is then taken up by dopaminergic neurons. Because MPP^+ binds to melanin in substantia nigra neurons, MPP^+ is concentrated in those neurons and eventually kills the cells. Positron emission tomographic (PET) studies of persons who ingested MPTP but who remained asymptomatic have shown a decrease in the number of dopamine-binding sites in the substantia nigra, thus reflecting a loss in the number of dopaminergic neurons in that region.

TREATMENT

Education and Needle Exchange

Although the core treatment of opioid use disorders is the encouragement of abstinence from opiates and opioids, education about the transmission of HIV must receive equal priority. Persons with opioid dependence who use intravenous or subcutaneous routes of administration must be educated about safe-sex practices available to them. Although subject to intense political and societal pressures, free needle-exchange programs, where allowed, should be made available to persons with opioid dependence. Several studies have indicated that unsafe needle sharing is common when it is difficult to obtain a sufficient supply of clean needles and is common in persons with legal difficulties, severe substance problems, and psychiatric symptoms. Those are just the persons who may be most likely to be involved in the continued transmission of HIV.

Methadone

Methadone is a synthetic opioid that substitutes for heroin and can be taken orally. It is given to addicts in place of their usual substance of abuse, and it suppresses withdrawal symptoms. The action of methadone is such that 20 to 80 mg a day is sufficient to stabilize a patient, although dosages of up to 120 mg a day have been used. Methadone has a duration of action exceeding 24 hours; thus once-daily dosing is adequate. Methadone maintenance is continued until the patient can be withdrawn from methadone, which itself causes dependence. Patients are detoxified from methadone more easily than from heroin, although a similar abstinence syndrome occurs with methadone withdrawal. Usually, clonidine (Catapres) (0.1 to 0.3 mg three to four times a day) is given during the detoxification period.

Methadone maintenance has several advantages. First, it frees the person with opioid dependence from dependence on injectable heroin, thus reducing the chance of spreading HIV through the use of contaminated needles. Second, methadone causes minimal euphoria and rarely causes drowsiness or depression when taken for a long time. Third, methadone allows the patient to engage in gainful employment, instead of criminal activity. The major disadvantage is that the patient remains dependent on a narcotic.

Other Opioid Substitutes

Levomethadyl acetate (ORLAMM), a longer-acting opioid than methadone, is also used for the treatment of persons with opioid dependence. In contrast to the daily methadone treatment, levomethadyl acetate can be administered in dosages of 30 to 80 mg three times a week. Buprenorphine is a mixed agonist-antagonist at the opiate receptor, and a number of studies have reported promising data regarding its use as an opioid substitute in treatment strategies.

Opioid Antagonists

Opioid antagonists block or antagonize the effects of opiates and opioids. Unlike methadone, they do not in themselves exert narcotic effects and do not cause dependence. The antagonists include the following drugs: naloxone, which is used in the treatment of opiate and opioid overdose because it reverses the effects of narcotics, and naltrexone, which is the longest-acting (72 hours) antagonist. The theory behind the use of an antagonist for opioid-related disorders is that the blocking of opioid agonist effects, particularly euphoria, discourages persons with opioid dependence from substance-seeking behavior and thus deconditions their substance-seeking behaviors. The major weakness of the antagonist treatment model is the lack of any mechanism that compels the person to continue to take the antagonist.

Pregnant Women with Opioid Dependence

Neonatal addiction is a significant problem; about three fourths of all infants born to addicted mothers experience the withdrawal syndrome.

Although opioid withdrawal is almost never fatal for the otherwise healthy adult, opioid withdrawal is hazardous to the fetus and can lead to miscarriage or fetal death. Maintaining the pregnant woman with opioid dependence on a low dosage of methadone (10 to 40 mg a day) may be the least hazardous course to follow. At that dosage, neonatal withdrawal is usually mild and can be managed with low doses of paregoric. If the pregnancy begins while the woman is taking high doses of methadone, the dosage should be reduced slowly (for example, 1 mg every three days), and fetal movements should be monitored. If withdrawal is necessary or desired, it is accomplished with least hazard during the second trimester.

FETAL AIDS TRANSMISSION

The other major risk for the fetus of a woman with opioid dependence is AIDS. Pregnant women can pass HIV, the causative agent of AIDS, to the fetus through the placental circulation. The HIV-infected mother can also pass HIV to the infant through breast feeding.

Psychotherapies

The entire range of psychotherapeutic modalities is appropriate for the treatment of opioid-related disorders in individual cases. Individual psychotherapy, behavioral therapy, cognitive-behavioral therapy, family therapy, support groups (such as Narcotics Anonymous), and social skills training may all prove to be effective treatments for specific patients. Social skills training should be particularly emphasized for patients who have few social skills with which to operate in the community. Family therapy is almost always indicated when family members are still living with the patient.

Therapeutic Communities

The therapeutic community is a residence composed of members who all have the same problem of substance abuse. Abstinence is the rule; in order to be admitted to such a community, the person must show a high level of motivation. The goals are to effect a complete change of life-style, including abstinence from substances; the development of personal honesty, responsibility, and useful social skills; and the elimination of antisocial attitudes and criminal behavior.

The staff members of most therapeutic communities are former substance-dependent persons, who often put the prospective candidate through a rigorous screening process to test the person's motivation. Self-help through the use of confrontational groups of isolation from the outside world and from friends associated with the drug life are emphasized. The prototypical community for substance-dependent persons is Phoenix House, where the residents live for long periods (usually 12 to 18 months) while receiving treatment. They are allowed to return to their old environments only when they have demonstrated their ability to handle increased responsibility within the therapeutic community. Therapeutic communities are effective, but they require large staffs and extensive facilities. Moreover, dropout rates are high; as many as 75 percent of those who enter therapeutic communities leave within the first month.

References

Di Chiara G, North R A: Neurobiology of opiate abuse. Trends Pharmacol Sci *13*: 185, 1992.

Jaffe J H: Opioid-related disorders. In *Comprehensive Textbook of Psychiatry*, ed 6, H I Kaplan, B J Sadock, editors, p 842. Williams & Wilkins, Baltimore, 1995.

Gintzler A R: Relevance of opioid bimodality to tolerance/dependence formation: From transmitter release to second messenger formation. Adv Exp Med Biol *373*: 73, 1995.

Koob G F, Maldonado R, Stinus L: Neural substrates of opiate withdrawal. Trends Neurosci *15*: 186, 1992.

Kosten T A, Bianchi M S, Kosten T R: The predictive validity of the dependence syndrome in opiate abusers. Am J Drug Alcohol Abuse *18*: 145, 1992.

Kreek M J: Rationale for maintenance pharmacotherapy of opiate dependence. Res Publ Assoc Res Nerv Ment Dis *70*: 2, 1992.

6.11 PHENCYCLIDINE (OR PHENCYCLIDINELIKE)-RELATED DISORDERS

Phencyclidine [1-(1-phenylcyclohexy-1)piperidine] is the most commonly abused arylcyclohexylamine. Phencyclidine is most commonly known as PCP, but it is also referred to as angel dust, crystal, peace pill, supergrass (when sprinkled on a cannabis cigarette), hog, rocket fuel, and horse tranqs. PCP was developed and is classified as a dissociative anesthetic; however, its use as an anesthetic in humans was associated with disorientation, agitation, delirium, and unpleasant hallucinations on awakening. For those reasons, PCP is no longer used as an anesthetic in humans, although it is used in some countries in veterinary medicine as an anesthetic. A related compound, ketamine, is still used as a human anesthetic in the United States; it has not been associated with the same adverse effects, although ketamine is also subject to abuse by humans.

PCP was first used illicitly in San Francisco in the late 1960s. Since then, about 30 chemical analogues have been produced and are intermittently available on the streets of major United States cities.

The effects of PCP are similar to those of such hallucinogens as lysergic acid diethylamide (LSD); however, because of differing pharmacology and some difference in clinical effects, DSM-IV classifies the arylcyclohexylamines as a separate category. PCP has also been of interest to schizophrenia researchers, who have used PCP-induced chemical and behavioral changes in animals as a possible model of schizophrenia.

EPIDEMIOLOGY

PCP and some of the related substances are relatively easy to synthesize in illegal laboratories and are relatively inexpensive to buy on the streets. The variable quality of the laboratories, however, results in a range of potency and purity. PCP use varies most markedly as a factor of geography. Some areas of some cities have a 10-fold higher usage rate of PCP than do other areas. The highest PCP use in the United States is in the District of Columbia, where PCP accounts for 18 percent of all substance-related deaths. In Los Angeles, Chicago, and Baltimore the comparable figure is 6 percent. The national average is 3 percent. In general, PCP is used by men, aged 20 to 40, who are members of a minority group. Most users of PCP also use other substances, particularly alcohol but also opiates, opioids, marijuana, amphetamines, and cocaine.

NEUROPHARMACOLOGY

PCP and its related compounds are variously sold as a crystalline powder, paste, liquid, or drug-soaked paper (blotter). PCP is most commonly used as an additive to a cannabis- or parsley-containing cigarette. Experienced users report that the effects of 2 to 3 mg of smoked PCP occur in about five minutes and plateau in 30 minutes. PCP has a bioavailability of about 75 percent when taken intravenously and a bioavailability of about 30 percent when smoked. The half-life of PCP in humans is about 20 hours.

The primary pharmacodynamic effect of PCP is as an antagonist at the N-methyl-D-aspartate (NMDA) subtype of glutamate receptors. PCP binds to a site within the NMDA-associated calcium channel and prevents the influx of calcium ions. Another effect of PCP is the activation of the dopaminergic neurons of the ventral tegmental area, which project to the cerebral cortex and the limbic system. The activation of those neurons is usually involved in mediating the reinforcing qualities of PCP.

Tolerance for the effects of PCP does occur in humans, although physical dependence generally does not occur. However, in animals that are administered more PCP per pound for longer periods of time than in virtually any humans, PCP does induce physical dependence, such that marked withdrawal symptoms consisting of lethargy, depression, and craving do occur. Physical symptoms of withdrawal in humans are rare, probably as a function of dose and duration of use. Although physical dependence is rare in humans, psychological dependence is common, as some users become psychologically dependent on the PCP-induced psychological state.

The fact that PCP is made in illicit laboratories contributes to the increased likelihood of impurities in the final product. One such contaminant is 1-piperidenocyclohexane carbonitrite, which releases hydrogen cyanide in small quantities when ingested. Another contaminant is piperidine, which can be recognized by its strong fishy odor.

DIAGNOSIS

The fourth edition of *Diagnostic and Statistical Manual of Mental Disorders* (DSM-IV) lists a number of phencyclidine (or phencyclidinelike)-related disorders but outlines the specific diagnostic criteria for only phencyclidine intoxication (Table 6.11–1) within the phencyclidine (or phencyclidinelike)-related disorders section. The diagnostic criteria of other phencyclidine (or phencyclidinelike)-related disorders are listed in the sections that deal with specific symptoms—for example, phencyclidine-induced anxiety disorder in the anxiety disorders section of DSM-IV (Section 10.1).

Dependence and Abuse

DSM-IV uses the general criteria for phencyclidine dependence and phencyclidine abuse (see Tables 6.1–3 and 6.1–4).

Table 6.11–1.   Diagnostic Criteria for Phencyclidine Intoxication

A. Recent use of phencyclidine (or a related substance).

B. Clinically significant maladaptive behavioral changes (e.g., belligerence, assaultiveness, impulsiveness, unpredictability, psychomotor agitation, impaired judgment, or impaired social or occupational functioning) that developed during, or shortly after, phencyclidine use.

C. Within an hour (less when smoked, ''snorted,'' or used intravenously), two (or more) of the following signs:

  (1) vertical or horizontal nystagmus
  (2) hypertension or tachycardia
  (3) numbness or diminished responsiveness to pain
  (4) ataxia
  (5) dysarthria
  (6) muscle rigidity
  (7) seizures or coma
  (8) hyperacusis

D. The symptoms are not due to a general medical condition and are not better accounted for by another mental disorder.

Some long-term users of PCP are said to be crystallized, a syndrome characterized by dulled thinking, decreased reflexes, loss of memory, loss of impulse control, depression, lethargy, and impaired concentration.

Intoxication

Short-term phencyclidine intoxication can have potentially severe complications and often must be considered a psychiatric emergency. Phencyclidine intoxication is defined by specific criteria in DSM-IV (Table 6.11–1). The clinician can specify the presence of perceptual disturbances.

Some patients may be brought to psychiatric attention within hours of ingesting PCP, but often two to three days elapse before psychiatric help is sought. The long interval between drug ingestion and the appearance of the patient in a clinic usually reflects the attempts of friends to deal with the psychosis by talking down; persons who lose consciousness are brought for help earlier than are those who remain conscious. Most patients recover completely within a day or two, but some remain psychotic for as long as two weeks. Patients who are first seen in a coma often manifest disorientation, hallucinations, confusion, and difficulty in communication on regaining consciousness. Those symptoms may also be seen in noncomatose patients, but their symptoms appear to be less severe than the comatose patients' symptoms. Sometimes the behavioral disturbances are severe; they may include public masturbation, stripping off clothes, violence, urinary incontinence, crying, and inappropriate laughing. Frequently, the patient has amnesia for the entire period of the psychosis.

Intoxication Delirium

Phencyclidine intoxication delirium is included as a diagnostic category in DSM-IV (Section 4.2). An estimated 25 percent of all PCP-related emergency room patients may meet the criteria for the disorder, which can be characterized by agitated, violent, and bizarre behavior.

Psychotic Disorder

Phencyclidine-induced psychotic disorder is included as a diagnostic category in DSM-IV (Section 8.3). The clinician can further specify whether delusions or hallucinations are the predominant symptoms. An estimated 6 percent of PCP-related emergency room patients may meet the criteria for the disorder. About 40 percent of those patients have physical signs of hypertension and nystagmus, and 10 percent have been injured accidentally during the psychosis. The psychosis can last from 1 to 30 days, with an average of four to five days.

Mood Disorder

Phencyclidine-induced mood disorder is included as a diagnostic category in DSM-IV (Section 9.3). An estimated 3 percent of PCP-related emergency room patients meet the criteria for the disorder, with most fitting the criteria for a maniclike episode. About 40 to 50 percent of those persons have been accidentally injured during the course of their manic symptoms.

Anxiety Disorder

Phencyclidine-induced anxiety disorder is included as a diagnostic category in DSM-IV (Section 10.1). Anxiety is probably the most common symptom that brings a PCP-intoxicated person to the emergency room seeking help.

Phencyclidine-Related Disorder Not Otherwise Specified

The diagnosis of phencyclidine-related disorder not otherwise specified (NOS) is the appropriate diagnosis for a patient who does not fit into any of the above diagnoses.

CLINICAL FEATURES

The amount of PCP varies greatly among PCP-laced cigarettes; 1 gram may be used to make as few as four or as many as several dozen cigarettes. Less than 5 mg of PCP is considered a low dose, and doses above 10 mg are considered high. The variability of dose makes it difficult to predict the effect, although smoking PCP is the easiest and most reliable way users can titrate the dose.

People who have just taken PCP are frequently uncommunicative, appear to be oblivious, and report active fantasy production. They experience speedy feelings, euphoria, bodily warmth, tingling, peaceful floating sensations, and occasionally feelings of depersonalization, isolation, and estrangement. Sometimes they have auditory and visual hallucinations. They often have striking alterations of body image, distortions of space and time perception, and delusions. They may experience an intensification of dependence feelings, confusion, and disorganization of thought. Users may be sympathetic, sociable, and talkative at one moment but hostile and negative at another. Anxiety is sometimes reported; it is often the most prominent presenting symptom during an adverse reaction. Nystagmus, hypertension, and hyperthermia are common effects of PCP. Head-rolling movements, stroking, grimacing, muscle rigidity on stimulation, repeated episodes of vomiting, and repetitive chanting speech are sometimes observed.

The short-term effects last three to six hours and sometimes give way to a mild depression in which the user becomes irritable, somewhat paranoid, and occasionally belligerent, irrationally assaultive, suicidal, or homicidal. The effects can last for several days. Users sometimes find that it takes one to two days to recover completely; laboratory tests show that PCP may remain in the patient's blood and urine for more than a week.

Adverse Effects

As with the other effects of PCP, neurological and physiological symptoms are dose-related. PCP doses of more than 20 mg are likely to cause convulsions, coma, and death. Death can also be caused by hyperthermia and autonomic instability, for which benzodiazepine treatment may be useful. Another serious adverse effect associated with PCP use is rhabdomyolysis with associated renal failure, which may occur in 2 percent of all PCP users. A mild increase in muscle-derived creatinine phosphokinase occurs in about 70 percent of all PCP users. Among the common symptoms seen in emergency rooms are hypertension, increased pulse rate, and nystagmus (horizontal or vertical or both). At low doses, the patient may experience dysarthria, gross ataxia, and muscle rigidity, particularly of the face and the neck. Increased deep tendon reflexes and diminished response to pain are commonly observed. High doses may lead to massive heat production and fatal hyperthermia, agitated and repetitive

movements, athetosis or clonic jerking of the extremities, and occasionally opisthotonic posturing. With even higher doses, patients may be drowsy, stuporous with their eyes open, comatose, and, in some instances, responsive only to noxious stimuli. Clonic movements and muscle rigidity may sometimes precede generalized seizure activity, and status epilepticus has been reported. Cheyne-Stokes breathing has also been observed; respiratory arrest can occur and be fatal. Vomiting, probably of central origin, may occur; hypersalivation and diaphoresis are occasional symptoms, and ptosis, usually bilateral, has been observed.

DIFFERENTIAL DIAGNOSIS

Depending on the patient's status at the time of admission, the differential diagnosis may include sedative or narcotic overdose, psychotic disorder as a consequence of the use of psychedelic drugs, and brief psychotic disorder. Laboratory analysis may be helpful in establishing the diagnosis, particularly in the many cases in which the substance history is unreliable or unattainable.

TREATMENT

The treatment for each of the phencyclidine (or phencyclidinelike)-related disorders is symptomatic. Talking down, which may work after hallucinogen use, is generally not useful for phencyclidine intoxication. Benzodiazepines and dopamine receptor antagonists are the drugs of choice for controlling behavior pharmacologically. The physician must monitor the patient's level of consciousness, blood pressure, temperature, and muscle activity and must be ready to treat severe medical abnormalities as necessary.

The clinician must carefully monitor unconscious patients, particularly those who have toxic reactions to PCP, because excessive secretions may interfere with already-compromised respiration. In an alert patient who has recently taken PCP, gastric lavage presents a risk of inducing laryngeal spasm and aspiration of emesis. Muscle spasms and seizures are best treated with diazepam (Valium). The environment should afford minimal sensory stimulation. Ideally, one person stays with the patient in a quiet, dark room. Four-point restraint is dangerous, because it may lead to rhabdomyolysis; total body immobilization may occasionally be necessary. A benzodiazepine is often effective in reducing agitation, but a patient with severe behavioral disturbances may require short-term treatment with a dopamine receptor antagonist—for example, haloperidol (Haldol). For patients with severe hypertension, a hypotensive-inducing drug such as phentolamine (Regitine) may be needed. Ammonium chloride in the early stage and ascorbic acid or cranberry juice later on are used to acidify the patient's urine and promote the elimination of the substance, although the efficacy of the procedure is controversial.

If the symptoms are not severe and if one can be certain that enough time has elapsed so that all the PCP has been absorbed, the patient may be monitored in the outpatient department and, if the symptoms improve, released to family or friends. Even at low doses, however, symptoms may worsen, requiring that the person be hospitalized to prevent violence and suicide.

References

Baldridge E B, Bessen H A: Phencyclidine. Emerg Med Clin North Am 8: 541, 1990.

Crowley T J: Phencyclidine (or phencyclidinelike)-related disorders. In *Comprehensive Textbook of Psychiatry*, ed 6, H I Kaplan, B J Sadock, editors, p 864. Williams & Wilkins, Baltimore, 1995.

Javitt D C, Zukin S R: Recent advances in the phencyclidine model of schizophrenia. Am J Psychiatry *148*: 1301, 1991.

National Institute on Drug Abuse: National Household Survey on Drug Abuse: Highlights, 1991. U S Government Printing Office, Washington, 1991.

Polkis A, Graham M, Maginn D, Branch C A, Gantner G E: Phencyclidine and violent deaths in St. Louis, Missouri: A survey of medical examiners' cases from 1977 through 1986. Am J Drug Alcohol Abuse *16*: 265, 1990.

Rahbar F, Fomufod A, White D, Westney L S: Impact of intrauterine exposure to phencyclidine (PCP) and cocaine on neonates. J Natl Med Assoc *85*: 349, 1993.

6.12 SEDATIVE-, HYPNOTIC-, OR ANXIOLYTIC-RELATED DISORDERS

Sedatives are drugs that reduce subjective tension and induce mental calmness. The term "sedative" is virtually synonymous with the term "*anxiolytic*," which is a drug that reduces anxiety. *Hypnotics* are drugs that are used to induce sleep. The differentiation between anxiolytics and sedatives as daytime drugs and hypnotics as nighttime drugs is not accurate. When sedatives and anxiolytics are given in high doses, they can induce sleep, just as the hypnotics do. Conversely, when hypnotics are given in low doses, they can induce daytime sedation, just as the sedatives and anxiolytics do. In some literature, especially old literature, the sedatives, anxiolytics, and hypnotics are grouped together as the *minor tranquilizers*. That term is poorly defined and subject to ambiguous meanings and, therefore, is best avoided.

The drugs contained within this class of substance-related disorders are the benzodiazepines (for example, flunitrazepam (Rohypnol), diazepam [Valium]), barbiturates (for example, secobarbital [Seconal]), and the barbituratelike substances, which include methaqualone, meprobamate (Miltown, Equanil), and glutethimide. The major nonpsychiatric indications for those drugs are as antiepileptics, muscle relaxants, anesthetics, and anesthetic adjuvants. All drugs of this class and alcohol are cross-tolerant, and their effects are additive. Physiological and psychological dependence develop to all the drugs, and all are associated with withdrawal symptoms.

SUBSTANCES

Benzodiazepines

A wide variety of benzodiazepines, differing primarily in their half-lives, are available in the United States. Examples of benzodiazepines are diazepam, flurazepam (Dalmane), oxazepam (Serax), and chlordiazepoxide (Librium). Benzodiazepines are used primarily as anxiolytics, hypnotics, antiepileptics, and anesthetics and for alcohol withdrawal. After their introduction in the United States in the 1960s, the benzodiazepines rapidly became the most prescribed drugs; about 15 percent of all persons in this country have had a benzodiazepine prescribed by a physician. However, increasing awareness of the risks for dependence on benzodiazepines and increased regulatory requirements have caused a decrease in the number of benzodiazepine prescriptions. All benzodiazepines are classified as schedule IV controlled substances by the Drug Enforcement Agency (DEA).

Barbiturates

Before the introduction of the benzodiazepines, the barbiturates were frequently prescribed; however, because of their high abuse potential, they are rarely used. Secobarbital (popularly known as reds, red devils, seggies, and downers), pentobarbital (Nembutal) (known as yellow jackets, yellows, and nembies), and a combination of secobarbital and amobarbital (Amytal) (known as reds and blues, rainbows, double-trouble, and tooies) are easily available on the street from drug dealers. Pentobarbital, secobarbital, and amobarbital are now under the same federal legal controls as morphine.

The first barbiturate, barbital (Veronal), was introduced in the United States in 1903. Barbital and phenobarbital (Luminal), which was introduced shortly thereafter, are long-acting drugs with half-lives of 12 to 24 hours. Amobarbital is an intermediate-acting barbiturate with a half-life of 6 to 12 hours. Pentobarbital and secobarbital are short-acting barbiturates with half-lives of three to six hours.

Barbituratelike Substances

The most commonly abused barbituratelike substance is methaqualone, which is no longer manufactured in the United States. Methaqualone is often used by young people who believe that the substance heightens the pleasure of sexual activity. Abusers of methaqualone commonly take one or two standard tablets (usually 300 mg a tablet) to obtain the desired effects. The street names for methaqualone include mandrakes (from the United Kingdom preparation Mandrax) and soapers (from the brand name Sopor). Luding out (from the brand name Quaalude) means getting high on methaqualone, which is often combined with excessive alcohol intake.

EPIDEMIOLOGY

About one quarter to one third of all substance-related emergency room visits involve substances from this class. The patients have a female-to-male ratio of 3 to 1 and a white-to-black ratio of 2 to 1. Benzodiazepines are abused alone, but cocaine abusers often use them to reduce withdrawal symptoms, and opiate and opioid abusers use them to enhance the euphoric effects of opiates and opioids. Benzodiazepines, because they are easily obtained, are also used by abusers of stimulants, hallucinogens, and phencyclidine (PCP) to help reduce the anxiety effects that can be caused by those substances.

Whereas barbiturate abuse is common among mature adults who have long histories of abuse of those substances, benzodiazepines are abused by a younger age group, usually under 40 years of age. That group of benzodiazepine abusers may have a slight male predominance, and a white-to-black ratio of about 2 to 1. Benzodiazepines are probably not abused as frequently as are other substances for the purpose of getting high, in the sense of inducing a euphoric feeling.

NEUROPHARMACOLOGY

The benzodiazepines, barbiturates, and barbituratelike substances all have their primary effects on the γ-aminobutyric acid (GABA) type A (GABA$_A$) receptor complex, which contains a chloride ion channel, a binding site for GABA, and a well-defined binding site for benzodiazepines. The barbiturates and

Table 6.12–1.   Diagnostic Criteria for Sedative, Hypnotic, or Anxiolytic Intoxication

A. Recent use of a sedative, hypnotic, or anxiolytic.

B. Clinically significant maladaptive behavioral or psychological changes (e.g., inappropriate sexual or aggressive behavior, mood lability, impaired judgment, impaired social or occupational functioning) that developed during, or shortly after, sedative, hypnotic, or anxiolytic use.

C. One (or more) of the following signs, developing during, or shortly after, sedative, hypnotic, or anxiolytic use:

(1) slurred speech
(2) incoordination
(3) unsteady gait
(4) nystagmus
(5) impairment in attention or memory
(6) stupor or coma

D. The symptoms are not due to a general medical condition and are not better accounted for by another mental disorder.

Table from DSM-IV, *Diagnostic and Statistical Manual of Mental Disorders*, ed 4. Copyright American Psychiatric Association, Washington, 1994. Used with permission.

Table 6.12–2.   Diagnostic Criteria for Sedative, Hypnotic, or Anxiolytic Withdrawal

A. Cessation of (or reduction in) sedative, hypnotic, or anxiolytic use that has been heavy and prolonged.

B. Two (or more) of the following, developing within several hours to a few days after criterion A:

(1) autonomic hyperactivity (e.g., sweating or pulse rate greater than 100)
(2) increased hand tremor
(3) insomnia
(4) nausea or vomiting
(5) transient visual, tactile, or auditory hallucinations or illusions
(6) psychomotor agitation
(7) anxiety
(8) grand mal seizures

C. The symptoms in criterion B cause clinically significant distress or impairment in social, occupational, or other important areas of functioning.

D. The symptoms are not due to a general medical condition and are not better accounted for by another mental disorder.

Table from DSM-IV, *Diagnostic and Statistical Manual of Mental Disorders*, ed 4. Copyright American Psychiatric Association, Washington, 1994. Used with permission.

barbituratelike substances are also believed to bind somewhere on the GABA$_A$ receptor complex. When a benzodiazepine, barbiturate, or barbituratelike substance does bind to the complex, the effect is to increase the affinity of the receptor for its endogenous neurotransmitter, GABA, and to increase the flow of chloride ions through the channel into the neuron. The effect of the influx of negatively charged chloride ions into the neuron is inhibitory, since it hyperpolarizes the neuron relative to the extracellular space.

Although all the substances in this class induce tolerance and physical dependence, the mechanisms behind those effects are best understood for the benzodiazepines. After long-term benzodiazepine use there is an attenuation of the receptor effects caused by the agonist. Specifically, after the long-term use of benzodiazepines, GABA stimulation of the GABA$_A$ receptors results in less influx of chloride than was caused by GABA stimulation before the benzodiazepine administration. That down-regulation of receptor response is not due to a decrease in receptor number or to a decrease in the affinity of the receptor for GABA. The basis for the down-regulation seems to be in the coupling between the GABA binding site and the activation of the chloride ion channel. That decreased efficiency in coupling may be regulated within the GABA$_A$ receptor complex itself or by other neuronal mechanisms.

DIAGNOSIS

The fourth edition of *Diagnostic and Statistical Manual of mental Disorders* (DSM-IV) lists a number of sedative-, hypnotic-, or anxiolytic-related disorders but contains specific diagnostic criteria only for sedative, hypnotic, or anxiolytic intoxication (Table 6.12–1) and sedative, hypnotic, or anxiolytic withdrawal (Table 6.12–2). The diagnostic criteria for other sedative-, hypnotic-, or anxiolytic-related disorders are outlined in those DSM-IV sections that are specific for the major symptom—for example, sedative-, hypnotic-, or anxiolytic-induced psychotic disorder (Section 8.1).

Dependence and Abuse

Sedative, hypnotic, or anxiolytic dependence and sedative, hypnotic, or anxiolytic abuse are diagnosed according to the general criteria in DSM-IV for substance dependence and substance abuse (see Tables 6.1–3 and 6.1–4).

Intoxication

DSM-IV contains single set of diagnostic criteria for intoxication by any sedative, hypnotic, or anxiolytic substance (Table 6.12–2). Although the intoxication syndromes induced by all those drugs are similar, subtle clinical differences are observable, especially with intoxications that involve low doses. The diagnosis of intoxication by one of this class of substances is best confirmed by obtaining a blood sample for substance screening.

BENZODIAZEPINES

Benzodiazepine intoxication can be associated with behavioral disinhibition, potentially resulting in hostile or aggressive behavior in some persons. The effect is perhaps most common when benzodiazepines are taken in combination with alcohol. Benzodiazepine intoxication is associated with less euphoria than is intoxication by other drugs in this class. That characteristic is the basis for the lower abuse and dependence potential of benzodiazepines when compared with the barbiturates.

BARBITURATES AND BARBITURATELIKE SUBSTANCES

When barbiturates and barbituratelike substances are taken in relatively low doses, the clinical syndrome of intoxication is indistinguishable from that associated with alcohol intoxication. The symptoms include sluggishness, incoordination, difficulty in thinking, poor memory, slowness of speech and comprehension, faulty judgment, disinhibition of sexual aggressive impulses, a narrowed range of attention, emotional lability, and an exaggeration of basic personality traits. The sluggishness usually resolves after a few hours, but the impaired judgment, distorted mood, and impaired motor skills may remain for 12 to 24 hours, depending primarily on the half-life of the abused substance. Other potential symptoms are hostility, argumentativeness, moroseness, and, occasionally, paranoid and suicidal ideation. The neurological effects include nystagmus, diplopia, strabismus, ataxic gait, positive Romberg's sign, hypotonia, and decreased superficial reflexes.

Withdrawal

DSM-IV contains a single set of diagnostic criteria for withdrawal from any sedative, hypnotic, or anxiolytic substance (see Table 6.12–2). The clinician can specify ''with perceptual disturbances'' if illusions, altered perceptions, or hallucinations are present but are accompanied by intact reality testing. Two important issues to remember about withdrawal are that benzodiazepines are associated with a withdrawal syndrome and that withdrawal from barbiturates can be life-threatening. Withdrawal from benzodiazepines can also result in serious medical complications, such as seizures.

BENZODIAZEPINES

The severity of the withdrawal syndrome associated with the benzodiazepines varies significantly according to the average dose and the duration of use. However, a mild withdrawal syndrome can follow even short-term use of relatively low doses of benzodiazepines. A significant withdrawal syndrome is likely to occur at the cessation of dosages in the 40-mg-a-day range for diazepam, for example, although 10 to 20 mg a day, taken for a month, can also result in a withdrawal syndrome when the drug is stopped. The onset of withdrawal symptoms usually occurs two to three days after the cessation of use, but with long-acting drugs, such as diazepam, the latency before onset may be five or six days. The symptoms include anxiety, dysphoria, intolerance for bright lights and loud noises, nausea, sweating, muscle twitching, and sometimes seizures (generally at dosages of 50 mg a day or more of diazepam).

BARBITURATES AND BARBITURATELIKE SUBSTANCES

The barbiturate and barbituratelike substances withdrawal syndrome ranges from mild symptoms (for example, anxiety, weakness, sweating, and insomnia) to severe symptoms (for example, seizures, delirium, cardiovascular collapse, and death). Persons who have been abusing pentobarbital in the range of 400 mg a day may experience mild withdrawal symptoms; persons who have been abusing the substance in the range of 800 mg a day experience orthostatic hypotension, weakness, tremor, and severe anxiety. About 75 percent of those persons have withdrawal-related seizures. Users of dosages even higher than 800 mg a day may experience anorexia, delirium, hallucinations, and repeated seizures.

Most of the symptoms appear in the first three days of abstinence, and seizures generally occur on the second or third day, when the symptoms are worst. If seizures do occur, they always precede the development of delirium. The symptoms rarely occurs more than a week after stopping the substance. A psychotic disorder, if it develops, starts on the third to eighth day. The various symptoms generally run their course within two to three days but may last as long as two weeks. The first episode of the syndrome usually occurs after 5 to 15 years of heavy substance use.

Delirium

DSM-IV allows for the diagnosis of sedative, hypnotic, or anxiolytic intoxication delirium and sedative, hypnotic, or anxiolytic withdrawal delirium (Section 4.2). Delirium that is indistinguishable from delirium tremens associated with alcohol withdrawal is more commonly seen with barbiturate withdrawal than with benzodiazepine withdrawal. Delirium associated with intoxication can be seen with either barbiturates or benzodiazepines if the dosages are high enough.

Persisting Dementia

DSM-IV allows for the diagnosis of sedative-, hypnotic-, or anxiolytic-induced persisting dementia (Section 4.3). The existence of the disorder is controversial, inasmuch as there is uncertainty whether a persisting dementia is due to the substance use itself or to associated features of the substance use. It will be necessary to evaluate the diagnosis further, using DSM-IV criteria to ascertain its validity.

Persisting Amnestic Disorder

DSM-IV allows for the diagnostic of sedative-, hypnotic-, or anxiolytic-induced persisting amnestic disorder (Section 4.4). Amnestic disorders associated with sedatives, hypnotics, and anxiolytics may have been underdiagnosed. One exception has been the increased number of reports of amnestic episodes associated with the short-term use of benzodiazepines with short half-lives (such as triazolam [Halcion]).

Psychotic Disorders

The psychotic symptoms of barbiturate withdrawal can be indistinguishable from those of alcohol-associated delirium tremens. Agitation, delusions, and hallucinations are usually visual, but sometimes tactile or auditory features develop after about one week of abstinence. Psychotic symptoms associated with intoxication or withdrawal are much more common with barbiturates than with benzodiazepines and are diagnosed as sedative-, hypnotic-, or anxiolytic-induced psychotic disorders (Section 10.1). The clinician can further specify whether delusions or hallucinations are the predominant symptoms.

Other Disorders

Sedative, hypnotic, and anxiolytic use has also been associated with mood disorders (Section 9.3), anxiety disorders (Section 12.1), sleep disorders (Section 17.2), and sexual dysfunctions (Section 14.2). When none of the above diagnostic categories is appropriate for a person with a sedative, hypnotic, or anxiolytic use disorder, the appropriate diagnosis is sedative-, hypnotic-, or anxiolytic-related disorder not otherwise specified (NOS).

CLINICAL FEATURES

Patterns of Abuse

ORAL USE

The sedatives, hypnotics, and anxiolytics can all be taken orally, either occasionally to achieve a time-limited specific effect or regularly to obtain a constant, usually mild, intoxication state. The occasional-use pattern is associated with young persons who take the substance to achieve specific effects—relaxation for an evening, intensification of sexual activities, and a short-lived period of mild euphoria. The user's personality and expectations about the substance's effects and the setting in which the substance is taken also affect the substance-induced experience. The regular-use pattern is associated with middle-aged, middle-class people who usually obtain the substance from the family physician as a prescription for insomnia or anxiety. Abusers of that type may have prescriptions from several physicians, and the pattern of abuse may go undetected until obvious signs of abuse or dependence are noticed by the person's family, coworkers, or physicians.

INTRAVENOUS USE

A severe form of abuse involves the intravenous use of this class of substances. The users are mainly young adults intimately involved with illegal substances. Intravenous barbiturate use is associated with a pleasant, warm, drowsy feeling, and users may be inclined to use barbiturates more than opiates or opioids because of the low cost of barbiturates. The physical dangers of injection include the transmission of the human immunodeficiency virus (HIV), cellulitis, vascular complications from accidental injection into an artery, infections, and allergic reactions to contaminants. Intravenous use is associated with a rapid and profound degree of tolerance and dependence and with a severe withdrawal syndrome.

Overdose

BENZODIAZEPINES

The benzodiazepines, in contrast to the barbiturates and the barbituratelike substances, have a large margin of safety when taken in overdoses, a feature that contributed significantly to their rapid acceptance. The ratio of lethal-to-effective dose is about 200 to 1 or higher because of the minimal degree of respiratory depression associated with the benzodiazepines. Even when grossly excessive amounts (more than 2 grams) are taken in suicide attempts, the symptoms include only drowsiness, lethargy, ataxia, some confusion, and mild depression of the user's vital signs. A much more serious condition prevails when benzodiazepines are taken in overdose in combination with other sedative-hypnotic substances, such as alcohol. In such cases, small does of benzodiazepines can cause death. The availability of flumazenil (Romazicon), a specific benzodiazepine antagonist, has reduced the lethality of the benzodiazepines, since flumazenil can be used in emergency rooms to reverse the effects of the benzodiazepines.

BARBITURATES

Barbiturates are lethal when taken in overdose because of their induction of respiratory depression. In addition to intentional suicide attempts, accidental or unintentional overdoses are common. Barbiturates in home medicine cabinets are a common cause of fatal drug overdoses in children. As with benzodiazepines, the lethal effects of the barbiturates are additive to those of other sedative-hypnotics, including alcohol and benzodiazepines. Barbiturate overdose is characterized by the induction of coma, respiratory arrest, cardiovascular failure, and death.

The lethal dose varies with the route of administration and the degree of tolerance for the substance after a history of long-term abuse. For the most commonly abused barbiturates, the ratio of lethal-to-effective dose ranges between 3 to 1 and 30 to 1. Dependent users often take an average daily dose of 1.5 grams of a short-acting barbiturate, and some have been reported to take as much as 2.5 grams a day for months. The lethal dose is not much greater for the long-term abuser than it is for the neophyte. Tolerance develops quickly to the point at which withdrawal in a hospital becomes necessary to prevent accidental death from overdose.

BARBITURATELIKE SUBSTANCES

The barbiturate substances vary in their lethality and are usually intermediate between the relative safety of the benzodiazepines and the high lethality of the barbiturates. An overdose of methaqualone, for example, may result in restlessness, delirium, hypertonia, muscle spasms, convulsions, and, in very high doses, death. Unlike barbiturates, methaqualone rarely causes severe cardiovascular or respiratory depression, and most fatalities result from combining methaqualone with alcohol.

TREATMENT

Withdrawal

BENZODIAZEPINES

Because some benzodiazepines are eliminated from the body slowly, the symptoms of withdrawal may continue to develop for several weeks. To prevent seizures and other withdrawal symptoms, the clinician should reduce the dosage gradually. Several reports indicate that carbamazepine (Tegretol) may be useful in the treatment of benzodiazepine withdrawal.

BARBITURATES

To avoid sudden death during barbiturate withdrawal, the clinician must follow conservative clinical guidelines. The clinical should not give barbiturates to a patient who is comatose or grossly intoxicated. The clinician should attempt to determine the patient's usual daily dose of barbiturates and then verify that dosage clinically. For example, the clinician can give a test dose of 200 mg of pentobarbital every hour until a mild intoxication is present but withdrawal symptoms are absent. The clinician can then taper the total daily dose at a rate of about 10 percent of the total daily dose. Once the correct dosage is determined, a long-acting barbiturate can be used for the detoxification period. During that process the patient may begin to experience withdrawal symptoms, in which case, the clinician should halve the daily decrement.

Phenobarbital may be substituted in the withdrawal procedure for the more commonly abused short-acting barbiturates. The effects of phenobarbital last longer, and, because there is less fluctuation of barbiturate blood levels, phenobarbital does not produce observable toxic signs or a serious overdose. An adequate dose is 30 mg of phenobarbital for every 100 mg of the short-acting substance. The user should be maintained for at least two days at that level before the dosage is reduced further. The regimen is analogous to the substitution of methadone for heroin.

After withdrawal is complete, the patient must overcome the desire to start taking the substance again. Although it has been suggested that nonbarbiturate sedative-hypnotics be substituted for barbiturates as a preventive therapeutic measure, doing so often results in replacing one substance dependence with another. If a user is to remain substance-free, follow-up treatment, usually with psychiatric help and community support, is vital. Otherwise, the patient will almost certainly return to barbiturates or to substances with similar hazards.

Overdose

The treatment of overdose of this general class of substances involves gastric lavage, activated charcoal, and careful monitoring of vital signs and central nervous system (CNS) activity. Overdose patients who come to medical attention while awake should be kept from slipping into unconsciousness. Vomiting should be induced, and activated charcoal should be administered to delay gastric absorption. If the patient is comatose, the clinician must establish an intravenous fluid line, monitor the patient's vital signs, insert an endotracheal tube to maintain a patent airway, and provide mechanical ventilation, if necessary. Hospitalization of a comatose patient in an intensive care unit is usually required during the early stages of recovery from such overdoses.

LEGAL ISSUES

State and federal agencies have attempted to restrict the distribution of benzodiazepines by requiring special reporting forms. For example, through the use of New York State triplicate prescription forms, the names of doctors and patients are kept on file in a data bank. Such measures have been taken to stem the tide of abuse. But most abuse is the result of the illicit manufacture, sale, and diversion of substances, particularly to cocaine and opioid addicts, and not from physicians' prescriptions or legitimate pharmaceutical companies. To attempt to curtail the use of substances that have unquestionable and invaluable therapeutic benefits, is an example of increasing governmental interference in the practice of medicine and in the confidential relationship between doctor and patient. Such restrictions will do little to curb cocaine, opioid, or benzodiazepine abuse.

The number of benzodiazepine prescriptions has decreased in New York State, but whether that decrease is due to improved medical prescribing standards of practice or to the intimidation of physicians is open to question.

New York is now among 10 states that regulate level II controlled substances with multiple-copy prescriptions (triplicates). California has the oldest triplicate program (established in 1939), but in 1989 New York, with its reported high prescription abuse rate, became the first state to extend triplicate regulation to benzodiazepines, against the recommendation of most physicians in New York. In 1991, a symposium sponsored by the Medical Society of the State of New York concluded that triplicate prescriptions jeopardize patient care.

References

Ciraulo D A, Greenblatt D J: Sedative-, hypnotic-, or anxiolytic-related disorders. In *Comprehensive Textbook of Psychiatry*, ed 6, H I Kaplan, B J Sadock, editors, p 872. Williams & Wilkins, Baltimore, 1995.
Juergens S M: Benzodiazepines and addiction. Psychiatr Clin North Am *16*: 75, 1993.
Lader M, Farr I, Morton S: A comparison of alpidem and placebo in relieving benzodiazepine withdrawal symptoms. Int Clin Psychopharmacol *8*: 31, 1993.
Rickels K, Warren G C, Schweizer E, Garcia-España F, Fridman R: Long-term benzodiazepine users 3 years after participation in a discontinuation program. Am J Psychiatry *148*: 757, 1991.
Schweizer E, Rickels K, Case W G, Greenblatt D J: Carbamazepine treatment in patients discontinuing long-term benzodiazepine therapy: Effects on withdrawal severity and outcome. Arch Gen Psychiatry *48*: 448, 1991.
Seiverwright N, Dougal W: Withdrawal symptoms from high dose benzodiazepines in poly drug users. Drug Alcohol Depend *32*: 15, 1993.

7/ Schizophrenia

The 1990s have brought major advances in the understanding of schizophrenia in three major areas. First, advances in brain imaging techniques, especially magnetic resonance imaging (MRI), and refinements in neuropathological techniques have focused much interest on the limbic system as central to the pathophysiology of schizophrenia. The particular brain areas of interest are the amygdala, the hippocampus, and the parahippocampal gyrus. The focus on those brain regions does not negate interest in other brain areas but does increasingly generate hypotheses that can be tested as the knowledge base regarding schizophrenia expands. Second, after the introduction of clozapine (Clozaril), an atypical antipsychotic with minimal neurological side effects, there has been a significant amount of research regarding other atypical antipsychotic drugs, particularly risperidone (Risperdal). Risperidone and other atypical drugs that will be introduced in the second half of the 1990s could be more effective in reducing the negative symptoms of schizophrenia and could be associated with a low incidence of neurological adverse effects. Third, as drug treatments improve and as a solid biological basis for schizophrenia is broadly recognized, there is an increase in interest in the psychosocial factors affecting schizophrenia, including those that may affect onset, relapse, and treatment outcome.

HISTORY

The history of psychiatrists and neurologists who have written and theorized about schizophrenia parallels the history of psychiatry itself. The magnitude of the clinical problem has consistently attracted the attention of major figures throughout the history of the discipline. Emil Kraepelin (1856–1926) and Eugen Bleuler (1857–1939) are the two key figures in the history of schizophrenia. Benedict A. Morel (1809–1873), a French psychiatrist, used the term *démense précoce* for deteriorated patients whose illness had begun in adolescence; Karl Ludwig Kahlbaum (1828–1899) described the symptoms of catatonia; and Ewold Hecker (1843–1909) wrote about the bizarre behavior of hebephrenia.

Emil Kraepelin

Emil Kraepelin latinized Morel's term to *dementia precox*, a term that emphasized a distinct cognitive process (dementia) and the early onset (precox) that is characteristic of the disorder. Kraepelin further distinguished patients with dementia precox from those he classified as being afflicted with manic-depressive psychosis or paranoia. Patients with dementia precox were characterized as having a long-term deteriorating course and common clinical symptoms of hallucinations and delusions. Kraepelin's views regarding the course of schizophrenia are sometimes misrepresented in terms of the certainty of a deteriorating course, since he did acknowledge that about 4 percent of his patients had complete recoveries and 13 percent had significant remissions. Patients with manic-depressive psychosis were differentiated from patients with dementia precox by the presence of distinct episodes of illness that were separated by periods of normal functioning. Patients with paranoia had persistent persecutory delusions as their major symptom but did not have the deteriorating course of dementia precox or the intermittent symptoms of manic-depressive psychosis.

Eugen Bleuler

Eugen Bleuler coined the term "schizophrenia," and the term replaced "dementia precox" in the literature. Bleuler conceptualized the term to signify the presence of a schism between thought, emotion, and behavior in affected patients. However, the term is widely misunderstood, especially by the lay public, as signifying a split personality. Split personality (now called dissociative identity disorder) is an entirely different disorder that is categorized in the fourth edition of *Diagnostic and Statistical Manual of Mental Disorders* (DSM-IV) with the other dissociative disorders. A major distinction that Bleuler drew between his concept of schizophrenia and Kraepelin's concept of dementia precox was that a deteriorating course is not necessary in the concept of schizophrenia, as it was in dementia precox. One effect of Bleuler's conceptualization was to increase the number of patients who meet the conceptual criteria for a diagnosis of schizophrenia. That widening of the diagnosis may have led to as much as a twofold difference in the incidence of schizophrenia before the introduction of the third edition of DSM (DSM-III) when comparing European countries (which tended to follow Kraepelin's principles) with the United States (which tended to follow Bleuler's principles). Since the introduction of DSM-III, the United States diagnostic system has clearly moved toward Kraepelin's ideas, although Bleuler's term, "schizophrenia," has become the internationally accepted label for the disorder.

THE FOUR AS

To explain further his theory regarding the internal mental schisms of affected patients, Bleuler described specific *fundamental (or primary) symptoms* of schizophrenia, including a thought disorder characterized by associational disturbances, particularly looseness. Other fundamental symptoms were affective disturbances, autism, and ambivalence. Thus, Bleuler's four As consist of associations, affect, autism, and ambivalence. Bleuler also described *accessory (secondary) symptoms*, which included hallucinations and delusions, symptoms that had been a prominent part of Kraepelin's conceptualization of the disorder.

Other Theorists

Adolf Meyer, Harry Stack Sullivan, Gabriel Langfeldt, and Kurt Schneider also made major contributions to the understanding of the many facets of schizophrenia. Meyer, the founder of psychobiology, believed that schizophrenia and other mental disorders are reactions to a variety of life stresses, so he called the syndrome a schizophrenic reaction. Sullivan, the founder of the interpersonal psychoanalytic school, emphasized social isolation as both a cause and a symptom of schizophrenia.

Ernst Kretschmer's data supported the idea that schizophrenia is more common in patients with asthenic, athletic, and dysplastic body types than in patients with pyknic body types, who are more likely to have bipolar disorders. Although that observation seems unusual, it is not inconsistent with a superficial impression regarding the body types of many homeless persons.

GABRIEL LANGFELDT

Langfeldt divided the patients with major psychotic symptoms into two groups, those with true schizophrenia and those with schizophreniform psychosis. Langfeldt emphasized the importance of depersonalization, autism, emotional blunting, an insidious onset, and feelings of derealization in his description of *true schizophrenia*. True schizophrenia also came to be known as nuclear schizophrenia, process schizophrenia, and nonremitting schizophrenia in the literature that followed Langfeldt's papers.

KURT SCHNEIDER

Kurt Schneider described a number of first-rank symptoms that he considered in no way specific for schizophrenia but of pragmatic value in making a diagnosis. Schizophrenia, Schneider pointed out, can also be diagnosed exclusively on the basis of second-rank symptoms and an otherwise typical clinical appearance. Schneider did not mean those symptoms to be applied rigidly. He warned the clinician that the diagnosis of schizophrenia should be made in certain patients who failed to show first-rank symptoms. Unfortunately, that warning is frequently ignored, and the absence of such symptoms in a single interview is sometimes taken as evidence that the person does not have schizophrenia.

KARL JASPERS

Karl Jaspers was a psychiatrist and a philosopher, and he was a major contributor to existential psychoanalysis. Jaspers approached psychopathology with the idea that there are no firm conceptual frameworks or fundamental principles. In his theories regarding schizophrenia, therefore, Jaspers attempted to remain unencumbered by traditional concepts, such as subject and object, cause and effect, and reality and fantasy. One specific development of that philosophy was his interest in the content of psychiatric patients' delusions.

EPIDEMIOLOGY

In the United States the lifetime prevalence of schizophrenia has been variously reported as ranging from 1 to 1.5 percent; consistent with that range, the National Institute of Mental Health (NIMH)-sponsored Epidemiologic Catchment Area (ECA) study reported a lifetime prevalence of 1.3 percent. About 0.025 to 0.05 percent of the total population are treated for schizophrenia in any one year. Although two thirds of those treated patients require hospitalization, only about half of all schizophrenic patients obtain treatment, in spite of the severity of the disorder.

Age and Sex

Schizophrenia is equally prevalent in men and women. However, the two sexes show several differences in the onset and the course of illness. Men have an earlier onset of schizophrenia than do women. More than half of all male schizophrenic patients but only a third of all female schizophrenic patients have their first psychiatric hospital admission before age 25. The

peak ages of onset for men are 15 to 25; for women the peak ages are 25 to 35. The onset of schizophrenia before age 10 or after age 50 is extremely rare. About 90 percent of the patients in treatment of schizophrenia are between 15 and 55 years old. Some studies have indicated that men are more likely than are women to be impaired by negative symptoms and that women are more likely to have better social functioning than men. In general, the outcome for female schizophrenic patients is better than the outcome for male schizophrenic patients.

Seasonality of Birth

A robust finding in schizophrenia research is that persons who later have schizophrenia are more likely to have been born in the winter and early spring and less likely to have been born in late spring and summer. Specifically, in the northern hemisphere, including the United States, schizophrenic persons were more often born in the months from January to April. In the southern hemisphere, schizophrenic persons were more often born in the months from July to September. Various hypotheses to explain that observation have been put forward. They include the hypothesis that some season-specific risk factor is operative, such as a virus or a seasonal change in diet. Another hypothesis is that persons who have the genetic predisposition for schizophrenia have an increased biological advantage to survive season-specific insults.

Geographical Distribution

Schizophrenia is not evenly distributed geographically throughout the United States or throughout the world. Historically, the prevalence of schizophrenia in the Northeast and the West in the United States was higher than in other areas, although that unequal distribution has eroded. However, some geographical regions in the world have an unusually high prevalence of schizophrenia. Some have interpreted those geographical pockets of schizophrenia as evidence of an infective (for example, viral) cause of schizophrenia.

Reproduction Rates

The use of psychotherapeutic drugs, the open-door policies in hospitals, the deinstitutionalization in state hospitals, the emphasis on rehabilitation, and the community-based care for patients with schizophrenia have all led to a general increase in the marriage and fertility rates among schizophrenic persons. Because of those factors, the number of children born to schizophrenic parents doubled from 1935 to 1955. The fertility rate for schizophrenic persons is now close to the rate of the general population.

Medical Illness

Schizophrenic persons have a higher mortality rate from accidents and natural causes than do the general population. That increase in mortality is not explained by institution-related or treatment-related variables. The higher rate may be related to the fact that the diagnosis and the treatment of medical and surgical conditions in schizophrenic patients can be a clinical challenge. Several studies have found that up to 80 percent of all schizophrenic patients have significant concurrent medical illnesses and that up to 50 percent of those conditions may be undiagnosed.

Suicide

Suicide is a common cause of death among schizophrenic patients, partly because clinicians still tend to associate suicide more with mood disorders than with the psychotic disorders. About 50 percent of all patients with schizophrenia attempt suicide at least once in their lifetimes, and 10 to 15 percent of schizophrenic patients die by suicide. Male and female schizophrenic patients are equally likely to commit suicide. The major risk factors for suicide among schizophrenic persons include the presence of depressive symptoms, young age, and high levels of premorbid functioning (especially a college education). That group may realize the devastating significance of their illness more than do other groups of schizophrenic patients and may see suicide as a reasonable alternative. Treatment approaches to such patients may include pharmacological treatment of the depression, addressing issues of loss in psychotherapy, and the use of support groups to help direct the patient's ambitions toward some obtainable goal.

Associated Substance Use and Abuse

CIGARETTE SMOKING

Most surveys have reported that more than three fourths of all schizophrenic patients smoke cigarettes, compared with less than half of psychiatric patients as a whole. In addition to the well-known health risks associated with smoking, cigarette smoking affects other aspects of a schizophrenic patient's care. Several studies have reported that cigarette smoking is associated with the use of high dosages of antipsychotic drugs, possibly because cigarette smoking increases the metabolism rate of those drugs. However, cigarette smoking is associated with a decrease in antipsychotic drug-related parkinsonism, possibly because of nicotine-dependent activation of dopamine neurons.

SUBSTANCE ABUSE

Comorbidity of schizophrenia and substance-related disorders is common, although the implications of substance abuse in schizophrenic patients are unclear. About 30 to 50 percent of schizophrenic patients may meet the diagnostic criteria for alcohol abuse or alcohol dependence; and the other two most commonly used substances are cannabis (about 15 to 25 percent) and cocaine (about 5 to 10 percent). Patients tend to report that they use those substances to obtain pleasure and to reduce their depression and anxiety. In general, most studies have associated the comorbidity of substance-related disorders with schizophrenia as an indicator of poor prognosis.

Cultural and Socioeconomic Considerations

Schizophrenia has been described in all cultures and socioeconomic status groups. In industrialized nations a disproportionate number of schizophrenic patients are in the low socioeconomic groups. That observation has been explained by the *downward drift hypothesis*, which suggests that affected persons either move into a lower socioeconomic group or fail to rise out of a low socioeconomic group because of the illness. An alternative explanation is the *social causation hypothesis*, which proposes that stresses experienced by members of low socioeconomic groups contribute to the development of schizophrenia.

In addition to hypothesizing that the stress of industrialization causes schizophrenia, some investigators have presented data indicating that the stress of immigration can lead to a schizophrenialike condition. Some studies report a high prevalence of schizophrenia among recent immigrants, and that finding has implicated abrupt cultural change as a stressor involved in the cause of schizophrenia. Perhaps consistent with both hypotheses is the observation that the prevalence of schizophrenia appears to rise among third-world populations as contact with technologically advanced cultures increases.

Advocates of a social cause for schizophrenia argue that cultures may be more or less schizophrenogenic, depending on how mental illness is perceived in the culture, the nature of the patient role, the available system of social and family supports, and the complexity of social communication. Schizophrenia has been reported to be prognostically more benign in less developed nations where patients are reintegrated into their communities and families more completely than they are in highly civilized Western societies.

HOMELESSNESS

The problem of the homeless in large cities may be related to the deinstitutionalization of schizophrenic patients who were not adequately followed up. Although the exact percentage of homeless persons who are schizophrenic is difficult to obtain, an estimated one third to two thirds of the homeless are probably afflicted with schizophrenia.

FINANCIAL COST TO SOCIETY

The estimation of an illness's cost to society is a complex task; nevertheless, the financial cost of schizophrenia to the United States is widely acknowledged to be enormous. About 1 percent of the United States national income goes toward the treatment of mental illness (excluding substance-related disorders); that percentage came to about $40 billion in 1985. When the indirect costs to society (for example, lost production and mortality) are added, the figure tops $100 billion annually. The majority of that amount is related to covering the direct and indirect costs of schizophrenia.

Mental Hospital Beds

Both the development of effective antipsychotic drugs and changes in political and popular attitudes toward the treatment and the rights of mentally ill people have resulted in a dramatic change in the patterns of hospitalization for schizophrenic patients over the past four decades. The probability of readmission within two years after discharge from the first hospitalization is about 40 to 60 percent. Schizophrenic patients occupy about 50 percent of all mental hospital beds and account for about 16 percent of all psychiatric patients who receive any type of treatment.

ETIOLOGY

Although schizophrenia is discussed as if it were a single disease, the diagnostic category can include a variety of disorders that present with somewhat similar behavioral symptoms. Schizophrenia probably comprises a group of disorders with heterogeneous causes and definitely includes patients with various clinical presentations, treatment responses, and courses of illness.

Stress-Diathesis Model

One model for the integration of biological factors and psychosocial and environmental factors is the stress-diathesis model. That model postulates that a person may have a specific vulnerability (diathesis) that, when acted on by some stressful environment influence, allows the symptoms of schizophrenia to develop. In the most general stress-diathesis model diathesis or the stress can be biological, environmental, or both. The environmental component can be either biological (for example, an infection) or psychological (for example, a stressful family situation or the death of a close relative). The biological basis of a diathesis can be further shaped by epigenetic influences, such as substance abuse, psychosocial stress, and trauma.

Biological Factors

The cause of schizophrenia is not known. In the past decade, however, an increasing amount of research has implicated a pathophysiological role for certain areas of the brain, including the limbic system, the frontal cortex, and the basal ganglia. Those three areas are, of course, interconnected, so that dysfunction in one area may involve primary pathology in another area. Two types of research have implicated the limbic system as a potential site for the primary pathology in at least some proportion, perhaps even the majority, of schizophrenic patients. Those two types of research are brain imaging of living persons and neuropathological examination of postmortem brain tissue.

The time a neuropathological lesion appears in the brain and the interaction of the lesion with environmental and social stressors remain areas of active research. The basis for the appearance of the abnormality may lie in abnormal development (for example, abnormal migration of neurons along the radial glial cells during development) or in degeneration of neurons after development (for example, abnormally early preprogrammed cell death, as appears to occur in Huntington's disease). However, theorists are still left with the fact that monozygotic twins have a 50 percent discordance rate, thus implying that there is some poorly understood interaction between the environment and the development of schizophrenia. An alternative explanation is that, although monozygotic twins have the same genetic information, the regulation of gene expression as they go through their separate lives may be different. The factors regulating gene expression are just beginning to be understood; possibly through differential gene regulation, one monozygotic twin has schizophrenia, whereas the other does not.

INTEGRATION OF BIOLOGICAL THEORIES

The major brain areas implicated in schizophrenia are the limbic structures, the frontal lobes, and the basal ganglia. The thalamus and the brainstem have also been implicated because of the role of the thalamus as an integrating mechanism and the fact that the brainstem and the midbrain are the primary locations for the ascending aminergic neurons. However, the limbic system is increasingly the focus of much of the theory-building exercises. For example, one study of twins who were discordant for schizophrenia used both MRI and the measurement of re-

gional cerebral blood flow. The investigators had previously determined that the hippocampal area of almost every affected twin was smaller than that of the unaffected twin and that the affected twin also had a smaller increase in blood flow to the dorsolateral prefrontal cortex while performing a psychological-activation procedure. The study found a correlation between those two abnormalities, suggesting that the two findings were related, although some third factor may have affected both variables.

DOPAMINE HYPOTHESIS

The simplest formulation of the *dopamine hypothesis of schizophrenia* posits that schizophrenia results from too much dopaminergic activity. The theory evolved out of two observations. First, except for clozapine, the efficacy and the potency of antipsychotics is correlated with their abilities to act as antagonists of the dopamine type 2 (D_2) receptor. Second, drugs that increase dopaminergic activity, most notably amphetamine, are psychotomimetic. The basic theory does not elaborate on whether the dopaminergic hyperactivity is due to too much release of dopamine, too many dopamine receptors, hypersensitivity of the dopamine receptors to dopamine, or some combination of those mechanisms. Nor does the basic theory specify which dopamine tracts in the brain may be involved, although the mesocortical and mesolimbic tracts are most often implicated. The dopaminergic neurons in those tracts project from their cell bodies in the midbrain to dopaminoceptive neurons in the limbic system and the cerebral cortex.

The dopamine hypothesis of schizophrenia continues to be refined and expanded. One area of speculation is that the dopamine type 1 (D_1) receptor may play a role in negative symptoms, and some researchers are interested in using D_1 agonists as a treatment approach for those symptoms. The recently discovered dopamine type 5 (D_5) receptor is related to the D_1 receptor and may merit research. In a parallel fashion the dopamine type 3 (D_3) and dopamine type 4 (D_4) receptors are related to the D_2 receptor and will be the subject of increasing research as specific agonists and antagonists are developed for those receptors. At least one study has reported an increase in D_4 receptors in postmortem brain samples from schizophrenic patients.

Although the dopamine hypothesis of schizophrenia has stimulated schizophrenia research for more than two decades and remains the leading neurochemical hypothesis, the hypothesis has two major problems. First, dopamine antagonists are effective in treating virtually all psychotic and severely agitated patients, regardless of diagnosis. It is not possible, therefore, to conclude that dopaminergic hyperactivity is unique to schizophrenia. For example, dopamine antagonists are also used in the treatment of acute mania. Second, some electrophysiological data suggest that dopaminergic neurons may increase their firing rate in response to long-term exposure to antipsychotic drugs. The data imply that the initial abnormality in schizophrenia may involve a hypodopaminergic state.

A significant role for dopamine in the pathophysiology of schizophrenia is consistent with studies that have measured plasma concentrations of the major dopamine metabolite, homovanillic acid. Several preliminary studies have indicated that, under carefully controlled experimental conditions, plasma homovanillic acid concentrations can reflect central nervous system (CNS) concentrations of homovanillic acid. Those studies have reported a positive correlation between high pretreatment concentrations of homovanillic acid and two factors: the severity of the psychotic symptoms and the treatment response to antipsychotic drugs. Studies of plasma homovanillic acid have also reported that, after a transient increase in plasma homovanillic acid concentrations, the concentrations decline steadily. That decline is correlated with symptom improvement in at least some patients.

Other Neurotransmitters

Although dopamine is the neurotransmitter that has received the most attention in schizophrenia research, increasing attention is being paid to other neurotransmitters. The consideration of other neurotransmitters is warranted for at least two reasons. First, since schizophrenia is likely to be a heterogeneous disorder, it is possible that abnormalities in different neurotransmitters lead to the same behavioral syndrome. For instance, hallucinogenic substances that affect serotonin—for example, lysergic acid diethylamide (LSD)—and high doses of substances that affect dopamine—for example, amphetamine—can cause psychotic symptoms that are difficult to distinguish from intoxication. Second, basic neuroscience research has clearly shown that a single neuron may contain more than one neurotransmitter and may have neurotransmitter receptors for a half dozen more neurotransmitters. Thus, the various neurotransmitters in the brain are involved in complex interactional relations, and abnormal functioning may result from changes in any single neurotransmitter substance.

Serotonin

Serotonin has become a subject of much interest in schizophrenia research since the observation that many of the so-called atypical antipsychotics have potent serotonin-related activities (for example, clozapine, risperidone, ritanserin). Specifically, antagonism at the serotonin (5-hydroxytryptamine) type 2 (5-HT$_2$) receptor has been emphasized as important in reducing psychotic symptoms and in mitigating against the development of D$_2$-antagonism-related movement disorders. As has also been suggested in the research on mood disorders, serotonin activity has been implicated in suicidal and impulsive behavior that can also be seen in schizophrenic patients.

Norepinephrine

Several investigators have reported that long-term antipsychotic administration decreases the activity of noradrenergic neurons in the locus ceruleus and that the therapeutic effects of some antipsychotics may involve their activities at α_1-adrenergic and α_2-adrenergic receptors. Although the relation between dopaminergic and noradrenergic activity remains unclear, an increasing body of data suggests that the noradrenergic system modulates the dopaminergic system in such a way that abnormalities of the noradrenergic system predispose a patient to frequent relapse.

Amino Acids

The inhibitory amino acid neurotransmitter (γ-aminobutyric acid (GABA) has also been implicated in the pathophysiology of schizophrenia. The available data are consistent with the hypothesis that some patients with schizophrenia have a loss of GABA-ergic neurons in the hippocampus. The loss of inhibitory GABA-ergic neurons could theoretically lead to the hyperactivity of dopaminergic and noradrenergic neurons.

The excitatory amino acid neurotransmitter glutamate has also been reported to be involved in the biological basis of schizophrenia. A range of hypotheses have been put forth regarding glutamate, including hyperactivity, hypoactivity, and glutamate-induced neurotoxicity hypotheses.

Neuropathology

Although the failure of neuropathologists in the 19th century to find a neuropathological basis for schizophrenia led to the classification of schizophrenia as a functional disorder, the past decade of neuropathological research has made significant strides in revealing a potential neuropathological basis for schizophrenia. The two brain areas that have received the most attention are the limbic system and the basal ganglia, although several controversial reports concern neuropathological or neurochemical abnormalities in the cerebral cortex, the thalamus, and the brainstem.

Limbic System

The limbic system, because of its role in the control emotions, has been hypothesized to be involved in the pathophysiological basis of schizophrenia. In fact, the limbic system has proved to be the most fertile area for neuropathological studies of schizophrenia. More than a half-dozen well-controlled studies of postmortem schizophrenic brain samples have found a decrease in the size of the region including the amygdala, the hippocampus, and the parahippocampal gyrus. That neuropathological finding supports a similar observation made by using MRI of living schizophrenic patients. A disorganization of the neurons within the hippocampus of schizophrenic patients has also been reported.

Basal Ganglia

The basal ganglia have been of theoretical interest in schizophrenia for at least two reasons. First, many schizophrenic patients have odd movements, even in the absence of medication-induced movement disorders (for example, tardive dyskinesia). The odd movements can include an awkward gait, facial grimacing, and stereotypies. Inasmuch as the basal ganglia are involved in the control of movement, pathology in the basal ganglia is thereby implicated in the pathophysiology of schizophrenia. Second, of all the neurological disorders in which psychosis can be an associated symptom, the movement disorders involving the basal ganglia (for example, Huntington's disease) are the ones most commonly associated with psychosis in affected patients. Another factor implicating the basal ganglia in the pathophysiology of schizophrenia is the fact that the basal ganglia are reciprocally connected to the frontal lobes, thus raising the possibility that the abnormalities in frontal lobe function seen in some brain imaging studies may be due to pathology within the basal ganglia, rather than in the frontal lobes themselves.

Neuropathological studies of the basal ganglia have produced variable and inconclusive reports concerning cell loss or the reduction of volume of the globus pallidus and the substantia nigra. In contrast, many studies have shown an increase in the number of D$_2$ receptors in the caudate, the putamen, and the nucleus accumbens; however, the question remains whether the increase is secondary to the patients' having received antipsychotic medications. Some investigators have begun to study the serotonergic system in the basal ganglia, since a role for serotonin in psychotic disorders is suggested by the clinical usefulness of antipsychotic drugs with serotonergic activity (for example, clozapine, risperidone).

Brain Imaging

Before the advent of brain imaging technologies, the study of schizophrenia depended on the distant measurement of brain activity—for example, the measurement of neurotransmitters in cerebrospinal fluid (CSF), plasma, or urine—in living patients or the direct measurement of the brain in deceased persons. Brain imaging techniques now allow researchers to make specific measurements of neurochemicals or brain function in living patients. However, the technology of those methods can be seductive. The reader of the research literature must be aware that many assumptions are used to develop models regarding the calculation of the data derived from the brain imaging machines. Differences in those mathematical models between two research groups can lead to different conclusions from the same data. To protect against that possibility, researchers in those fields are constantly exchanging their ideas regarding the appropriate mathematical models to use.

Computed Tomography

The initial studies using computed tomography (CT) in schizophrenic populations may have produced the earliest and most convincing data that schizophrenia is a bona fide brain disease. Those studies have consistently shown that the brains of schizophrenic patients have lateral and third-ventricular enlargement and some degree of reduction in cortical volume. Those findings can be interpreted as consistent with the presence of less than usual brain tissue in affected patients; whether that decrease in the amount of brain tissue is due to abnormal development or to degeneration remains unresolved.

Other CT studies have reported abnormal cerebral asymmetry, reduced cerebellar volume, and brain density changes in schizophrenic patients. Many of the CT studies have correlated the presence of CT scan abnormalities with the presence of negative or deficit symptoms, neuropsychiatric impairment, increased neurological signs, frequent extrapyramidal symptoms from antipsychotics, and poor premorbid adjustment. Although not all CT studies have confirmed those associations, it makes intuitive sense that the more evidence of neuropathology present, the more serious the symptoms are. However, the abnormalities reported in CT studies of schizophrenic patients have also been reported in other neuropsychiatric conditions, including mood disorders, alcohol-related disorders, and dementias. Thus, those changes are not likely to be specific for the pathophysiological processes underlying schizophrenia.

A number of studies have attempted to determine whether the abnormalities detected by CT are progressive or static. Some of the studies have concluded that the lesions observed on CT are present at the onset of the illness and do not progress. Other studies, however, have concluded that the pathology visualized on CT continues to progress during the illness. Thus, whether an active pathological process is continuing to evolve in schizophrenic patients is still uncertain.

Although the enlarged ventricles in schizophrenic patients can be shown when groups of patients and controls are used, the difference between affected and unaffected persons is variable and usually small. Therefore, the use of CT in the diagnosis of schizophrenia is limited. However, some data indicate that ventricles are more enlarged in patients with tardive dyskinesia than in patients who do not have tardive dyskinesia. Also, some data indicate that the enlargement of ventricles is seen more often in male patients than in female patients.

Magnetic Resonance Imaging

Magnetic resonance imaging (MRI) was initially used to verify the findings of the CT studies but has subsequently been used to expand the knowledge about the pathophysiology of schizophrenia. One of the most important MRI studies examined monozygotic twins who were discordant for schizophrenia. The study found that virtually all the affected twins had larger cerebral ventricles than did the nonaffected twins, although the cerebral ventricles of most of the affected twins were within a normal range.

Investigators using MRI in schizophrenia research have used its properties of superior resolution, compared with CT, and the qualitative information obtainable by using various signal sequences to get T_1- or T_2-weighted images, for example. MRI's superior resolution has resulted in several reports that the volumes of the hippocampal-amygdala complex and the parahippocampal gyrus are reduced in schizophrenic patients. One recent study found a specific reduction of those brain areas in the left hemisphere and not in the right, although other studies have found bilateral reductions in volume. Some of the studies have correlated the reduction in limbic system volume with the degree of

psychopathology or other measures of severity of illness. There have also been reports of differential T_1 and T_2 relaxation times in schizophrenic patients, particularly as measured in the frontal and temporal regions.

Magnetic Resonance Spectroscopy

Magnetic resonance spectroscopy (MRS) is a technique that allows the measurement of the concentrations of specific molecules—for example, adenosine triphosphate (ATP)—in the brain. Although the technique is still early in its development, several preliminary reports of using MRS to study schizophrenia have appeared in the literature. One study that used MRS imaging of the dorsolateral prefrontal cortex found that, compared with a control group, schizophrenic patients had lower levels of phosphomonoesters and inorganic phosphate and higher levels of phosphodiesters and adenosine triphosphate. Those data concerning the metabolism of phosphate-containing compounds were consistent with hypoactivity of that brain region, thus supporting the findings of other brain imaging studies—for example, positron emission tomography (PET).

Positron Emission Tomography

Although many studies using positron emission tomography (PET) to study schizophrenia have been reported, few clear conclusions can be drawn at this time. Most PET studies have measured either glucose utilization or cerebral blood flow, and the positive findings have included hypoactivity of the frontal lobes, impaired activation of certain brain areas after psychological test stimulation, and hyperactivity of the basal ganglia relative to the cerebral cortex. A number of studies, however, have failed to replicate those findings, although the abnormal-activation results seem to be a robust finding. In those studies the person's blood flow is assayed by using PET, single photon emission computed tomography (SPECT), or regional cerebral blood flow (rCBF) brain imaging systems. While the cerebral blood flow is being measured, the person is asked to perform a psychological task that presumably activates a particular part of the cerebral cortex in normal control subjects. One of the best-controlled studies of that design found that schizophrenic patients, in contrast to the control group, failed to increase the blood flow to the dorsolateral prefrontal cortex while performing the Wisconsin Card-Sorting Test.

A second type of PET study has used radioactive ligands to estimate the quantity of D_2 receptors present. The two most discussed studies disagree; one group reported an increased number of D_2 receptors in the basal ganglia, and the other group reported no change in the number of D_2 receptors in the basal ganglia. The difference between the two studies may involve the use of different ligands, different types of schizophrenic patients, or other differences in method or data analysis. The controversy remains unresolved at this time. However, the technique will continue to be used in the study of schizophrenia, and subsequent research reports will use ligands for other neurotransmitter systems, such as the noradrenergic and glutamate systems.

ELECTROPHYSIOLOGY

Electroencephalographic (EEG) studies of schizophrenic patients indicate that a high number of patients have abnormal records, increased sensitivity to activation procedures (for example, frequent spike activity after sleep deprivation), decreased alpha activity, increased theta and delta activity, possibly higher than usual epileptiform activity, and possibly more than usual left-sided abnormalities.

Complex Partial Epilepsy

Schizophrenialike psychoses have been reported to occur more frequently than expected in patients with complex partial seizures, especially seizures involving the temporal lobes. Factors associated with the development of psychosis in those patients include a left-sided seizure focus, medial temporal location of the lesion, and early onset of seizures. The first-rank symptoms described by Schneider may be similar to symptoms seen in patients with complex partial epilepsy and may reflect the presence of temporal lobe pathology when seen in patients with schizophrenia.

Evoked Potentials

A large number of abnormalities in evoked potentials in schizophrenic patients have been described in the research literature. The P300 wave has been most studied and is defined as a large, positive evoked-potential wave that occurs about 300 milliseconds after a sensory stimulus is detected. The major source of the P300 wave may be located in the limbic system structures of the medical temporal lobes. In schizophrenic patients the P300 wave has been reported to be statistically smaller and later than in comparison groups. Abnormalities in the P300 wave have also been reported to be more common in children who are at high risk for schizophrenia because of having affected parents. Whether the characteristics of the P300 wave represent a state phenomenon or a trait phenomenon remains controversial. Other evoked potentials that have been reported to be abnormal in schizophrenic patients are the N100 wave and the contingent negative variation. The N100 is a negative wave that occurs about 100 milliseconds after the stimulus, and the contingent negative variation is a slowly developing, negative-voltage shift that follows the presentation of a sensory stimulus that is a warning for an upcoming stimulus. The evoked-potential data have been interpreted as indicating that although schizophrenic patients are unusually sensitive to sensory stimulus (larger early evoked potentials), they compensate for the increased sensitivity by blunting the processing of information at higher cortical levels (indicated by smaller late evoked potentials).

EYE MOVEMENT DYSFUNCTION

The inability of a person to accurately follow a moving visual target is the defining basis for the disorders of smooth visual pursuit and the disinhibition of saccadic eye movements seen in schizophrenic patients. Eye movement dysfunction may be a trait marker for schizophrenia, since it is independent of drug treatment and clinical state, and it is also seen in first-degree relatives of schizophrenic probands. Various studies have reported abnormal eye movements in 50 to 85 percent of schizophrenic patients, in comparison with about 25 percent in nonschizophrenic psychiatric patients and less than 10 percent in nonpsychiatrically ill control subjects. Since eye movement is partly controlled by centers in the frontal lobes, a disorder in eye movement is consistent with theories that implicate frontal lobe pathology in schizophrenia.

PSYCHONEUROIMMUNOLOGY

A number of immunological abnormalities have been associated with schizophrenic patients. The abnormalities include decreased T cell interleukin-2 production, reduced number and responsiveness of peripheral lymphocytes, abnormal cellular and humoral reactivity to neurons, and the presence of brain-directed (antibrain) antibodies. The data can be interpreted variously as representing the effects of a neurotoxic virus or of an endogenous autoimmune disorder. Most carefully conducted investigations that have searched for evidence of neurotoxic viral infections in schizophrenia have had negative results, although epidemiological data show a high incidence of schizophrenia after prenatal exposure to influenza during several epidemics of the disease. Other data that support a viral hypothesis are an increased number of physical anomalies at birth, an increased rate of pregnancy and birth complications, seasonality

of birth consistent with viral infection, geographical clusters of adult cases, and seasonality of hospitalizations. Nonetheless, the inability to detect genetic evidence of viral infection reduces the significance of all circumstantial data. The possibility of autoimmune brain antibodies has some data to support it; however, the pathophysiological process, if it exists, probably explains only a subset of the schizophrenic populations.

PSYCHONEUROENDOCRINOLOGY

Many reports describe neuroendocrine differences between groups of schizophrenic patients and groups of normal control subjects. For example, the dexamethasone-suppression test has been reported to be abnormal in various subgroups of schizophrenic patients, although the practical or predictive value of the test in schizophrenia has been questioned. However, one carefully done report has correlated persistent nonsuppression on the dexamethasone-suppression test in schizophrenia with a poor long-term outcome.

Some data suggest decreased concentrations of luteinizing hormone/follicle stimulating hormone (LH/FSH), perhaps correlated with age of onset and length of illness. Two additional reported abnormalities are a blunted release of prolactin and growth hormone to gonadotropin-releasing hormone (GnRH) or thyrotropin-releasing hormone (TRH) stimulation and a blunted release of growth hormone to apomorphine stimulation that may be correlated with the presence of negative symptoms.

Genetics

A wide range of genetic studies strongly suggested a genetic component to the inheritance of schizophrenia. The early, classic studies of the genetics of schizophrenia, done in the 1930s, found that a person is likely to have schizophrenia if other members of the family also have schizophrenia and that the likelihood of the person's having schizophrenia is correlated with the closeness of the relationship (for example, first-degree or second-degree relative) (Table 7–1). Monozygotic twins have the highest concordance rate. The studies of adopted monozygotic twins show that twins who are reared by adoptive parents have schizophrenia at the same rate as their twin siblings raised by their biological parents. That finding suggests that the genetic influence outweighs the environmental influence. In further support of the genetic basis is the observation that the more severe the schizophrenia, the more likely the twins are to be concordant for the disorder. One study that supports the stress-diathesis model showed that adopted monozygotic twins who later had schizophrenia were likely to have been adopted by psychologically disordered families.

Table 7–1. Prevalence of Schizophrenia in Specific Populations

Population	Prevalence (%)
General population	1
Nontwin sibling of a schizophrenic patient	8
Child with one schizophrenic parent	12
Dizygotic twin of a schizophrenic patient	12
Child of two schizophrenic parents	40
Monozygotic twin of a schizophrenic patient	47

CHROMOSOMAL MARKERS

Current approaches in genetics are directed toward identifying large pedigrees of affected persons and investigating the families for restriction fragment length polymorphisms (RFLPs) that segregate with disease phenotype. Many associations between particular chromosomal sites and schizophrenia have been reported in the literature since the widespread application of the techniques of molecular biology. More than half of the chromosomes have been associated with schizophrenia in those various reports, but the most commonly reported have been the long arms of chromosomes 5, 11, and 18; the short arm of chromosome 19; and the X chromosome. At this time, the literature is best summarized as indicating a potentially heterogeneous genetic basis for schizophrenia.

Psychosocial Factors

The rapidly evolving understanding regarding the biology of schizophrenia and the introduction of effective and safe pharmacological treatments have further emphasized the important need for an understanding of individual, family, and social issues that affect the patient with schizophrenia. If schizophrenia is a disease of the brain, it is likely to parallel diseases of other organs (for example, myocardial infarctions and diabetes) whose courses are affected by psychosocial stress. Schizophrenia also parallels other chronic diseases (for example, chronic congestive pulmonary disease) in that drug therapy alone is rarely sufficient to obtain maximal clinical improvement. Thus, the clinician should consider the psychosocial factors that affect schizophrenia. Although, historically, it has been argued that some of the psychosocial factors are directly and causally linked to the development of schizophrenia, that prior view should not prevent the contemporary clinician from using the relevant theories and guidelines from those past observations and hypotheses.

THEORIES REGARDING THE INDIVIDUAL PATIENT

Regardless of the controversies regarding the cause or causes of schizophrenia, it remains irrefutable that schizophrenia affects individual patients, each of whom has a unique psychological makeup. Although many psychodynamic theories regarding the pathogenesis of schizophrenia seem out of date to contemporary readers, their perceptive clinical observations can help the contemporary clinician understand how the disease may affect the patient's psyche.

Psychoanalytic Theories

Sigmund Freud postulated that schizophrenia results from fixations in development that occurred earlier than those that result in the development of neuroses. Freud also postulated the presence of an ego defect that also contributes to the symptoms of schizophrenia. Ego disintegration is a return to the time when the ego was not yet established or had just begun to be established. Thus, intrapsychic conflict resulting from the early fixations and the ego defect, which may have resulted from poor early object relations, fuel the psychotic symptoms. Central to Freud's theories regarding schizophrenia were a decathexis of objects and a regression in response to frustration and conflict with others. Many of Freud's ideas regarding schizophrenia were colored by his lack of intensive involvement with schizophrenic patients. In contrast, Harry Stack Sullivan engaged schizophrenic patients in intensive psychoanalysis and concluded that the illness results from early interpersonal difficulties, particularly those related to what he considered faulty, overly anxious mothering.

The general psychoanalytic view of schizophrenia hypothesizes that the ego defect affects the interpretation of reality and the control of inner drives, such as sex and aggression. The disturbances occur as a consequence of distortions in the reciprocal relationship between the infant and the mother. As described by Margaret Mahler, the child is unable to separate and progress beyond the closeness and complete dependence that characterizes the mother-child relationship in the oral phase of development. The schizophrenic person never achieves object constancy, which is characterized by a sense of secure identity and which results from a close attachment to the mother during infancy. Paul Federn concluded that the fundamental disturbance in schizophrenia is the patient's early inability to achieve self-object differentiation. Some psychoanalysts hypothesize that the defect in rudimentary ego functions permits intense hostility and aggression to distort the mother-infant relationship, leading to a personality organization that is vulnerable to stress. The onset of symptoms during adolescence occurs at a time when the person requires a strong ego to deal with the need to function independently, to separate from the parents, to identify tasks, to control increased internal drives, and to cope with intense external stimulation.

Psychoanalytic theory also postulates that the various symptoms of schizophrenia have symbolic meaning for the individual patient. For example, fantasies of the world coming to an end may indicate a perception that the person's internal world has broken down. Feelings of grandeur may reflect reactivated narcissism, in which persons believe that they are omnipotent. Hallucinations may be substitutes for the patients' inability to deal with objective reality and may represent their inner wishes or fears. Delusions, similar to hallucinations, are regressive, restitutive attempts to create a new reality or to express hidden fears or impulses.

Psychodynamic Theories

Genetic studies clearly suggest that schizophrenia is an illness with a biological substrate. Nevertheless, studies of monozygotic twins repeatedly show that environmental and psychological factors have some importance in the development of schizophrenia, since many twins are discordant for the illness. Freud regarded schizophrenia as a regressive response to overwhelming frustration and conflict with persons in the environment. That regression involves a withdrawal of emotional investment or *cathexis* from both internal object representations and actual persons in the environment, leading to a return to an autoerotic stage of development. The patient's cathexis is reinvested in the self, thus giving the appearance of autistic withdrawal. Freud later added that, although neurosis involves a conflict between the ego and the id, psychosis can be viewed as a conflict between the ego and the external world in which reality is disavowed and subsequently remodeled.

Later psychodynamic views of schizophrenia have differed from Freud's complex model. They tend to regard the constitutionally based hypersensitivity to perceptual stimuli as deficit. Indeed, a good deal of research suggests that patients with schizophrenia find it difficult to screen out various stimuli and to focus on one piece of data at a time. That defective stimulus barrier creates difficulty throughout every phase of development during childhood and places particular stress on interpersonal relatedness. Psychodynamic views of schizophrenia are often mistakenly regarded as parent-blaming, when actually they focus on psychological and neurophysiological difficulties that create problems for most people in close relationships with the schizophrenic patient.

Regardless of which theoretical model is preferred, all psychodynamic approaches operate from the premise that psychotic symptoms have meaning in schizophrenia. For example, patients may become grandiose after an injury to their self-esteem. Similarly, all theories recognize that human relatedness may be terrifying for persons suffering from schizophrenia. Although the research on the efficacy of psychotherapy with schizophrenia shows mixed results, concerned persons who offer human compassion and a sanctuary from a confusing world must be a cornerstone of any overall treatment plan. Long-term follow-up studies find that some patients who seal over psychotic episodes probably do not benefit from exploratory psychotherapy, but those who are able to integrate the psychotic experience into their lives may benefit from some insight-oriented approaches.

Learning Theories

According to learning theorists, children who later have schizophrenia learn irrational reactions and ways of thinking by imitating parents who may have their own significant emotional problems. The poor interpersonal relationships of schizophrenic persons, according to learning theory, also develop because of poor models from which to learn during childhood.

THEORIES REGARDING THE FAMILY

No well-controlled evidence indicates that any specific family pattern plays a causative role in the development of schizophrenia. That is an important point for clinicians to understand, since many parents of schizophrenic children still harbor anger against the psychiatric community, which for a long time was fairly outspoken regarding a correlation between dysfunctional families and the development of schizophrenia. Some schizophrenic patients do come from dysfunctional families, just as many nonpsychiatrically ill persons come from dysfunctional families. It is clinically relevant, however, to recognize pathological family behavior, since such behavior can significantly increase the emotional stress that a vulnerable schizophrenic patient must cope with.

Double Bind

The double bind concept was formulated by Gregory Bateson to describe a hypothetical family in which children receive conflicting parental messages regarding their behavior, attitudes, and feelings. Within that hypothesis, children withdraw into their own psychotic state to escape the unsolvable confusion of the double bind. Unfortunately, the family studies that were conducted to prove the theory were seriously flawed methodologically and cannot be taken to validate the theory.

Schisms and Skewed Families

Theodore Lidz described two abnormal patterns of family behavior. In one type of family, there is a prominent schism between the parents, and one parent gets overly close to child of the opposite sex. In the other type of family, a skewed relationship with one parent involves a power struggle between the parents and the resulting dominance of one parent.

Pseudomutual and Pseudohostile Families

Lyman Wynne described families in which emotional expression is suppressed by the consistent use of a pseudomutual or pseudohostile verbal communication. That suppression results in the development of a verbal communication that is unique to that family and not necessarily comprehensible to anyone outside the family; problems arise when the child leaves home and has to relate to other people.

Expressed Emotion

Expressed emotion (EE) is usually defined as including the criticism, hostility, and overinvolvement that can characterize the behavior of parents or other caretakers toward a schizophrenic person. Many studies have indicated that, in families with high levels of EE, the relapse rate for schizophrenia is high. The assessment of EE involves analyzing both what is said and the manner in which it is said.

SOCIAL THEORIES

Some theories have suggested that industrialization and urbanization are involved in the causes of schizophrenia. Although some data support such theories the stresses are now thought to have their major effects on the timing of the onset and the severity of the illness.

DIAGNOSIS

The DSM-IV diagnostic criteria are largely unchanged from those in the revised third edition of DSM (DSM-III-R), although the DSM-IV course specifiers offer more options to the clinician and more description of actual clinical situations (Table 7–2). Neither hallucinations nor delusions are required for the diagnosis of schizophrenia, since patients can meet the diagnosis if they have two of the symptoms listed as symptoms 3 to 5 in criterion A.

DSM-IV Subtypes

DSM-IV uses five subtypes of schizophrenia: paranoid, disorganized, catatonic, undifferentiated, and residual types (Table

Table 7–2. Diagnostic Criteria for Schizophrenia

A. *Characteristic symptoms:* Two (or more) of the following, each present for a significant portion of time during a 1-month period (or less if successfully treated):
   (1) delusions
   (2) hallucinations
   (3) disorganized speech (e.g., frequent derailment or incoherence)
   (4) grossly disorganized or catatonic behavior
   (5) negative symptoms, i.e., affective flattening, alogia, or avolition

   Note: Only one criterion A symptom is required if delusions are bizarre or hallucinations consist of a voice keeping up a running commentary on the person's behavior or thoughts, or two or more voices conversing with each other.

B. *Social/occupational dysfunction:* For a significant portion of the time since the onset of the disturbance, one or more major areas of functioning such as work, interpersonal relations, or self-care are markedly below the level achieved prior to the onset (or when the onset is in childhood or adolescence, failure to achieve expected level of interpersonal academic, or occupational achievement).

C. *Duration:* Continuous signs of the disturbance persist for at least 6 months. This 6-month period must include at least 1 month of symptoms (or less if successfully treated) that meet criterion A (i.e., active-phase symptoms) and may include periods of prodromal or residual symptoms. During these prodromal or residual periods, the signs of the disturbance may be manifested by only negative symptoms or two or more symptoms listed in criterion A present in an attenuated form (e.g., odd beliefs, unusual perceptual experiences).

D. *Schizoaffective and mood disorder exclusion:* Schizoaffective disorder and mood disorder with psychotic features have been ruled out because either (1) no major depressive, manic, or mixed episodes have occurred concurrently with the active-phase symptoms; or (2) if mood episodes have occurred during active-phase symptoms, their total duration has been brief relative to the duration of the active and residual periods.

E. *Substance/general medical condition exclusion:* The disturbance is not due to the direct physiological effects of a substance (e.g., a drug of abuse, a medication) or general medical condition.

F. *Relationship to a pervasive developmental disorder:* If there is a history of autistic disorder or another pervasive developmental disorder, the additional diagnosis of schizophrenia is made only if prominent delusions or hallucinations are also present for at least a month (or less if successfully treated).

Table from DSM-IV, *Diagnostic and Statistical Manual of Mental Disorders*, ed 4. Copyright American Psychiatric Association, Washington, 1994. Used with permission.

Table 7-3. Diagnostic Criteria for Schizophrenia Subtypes

Paranoid Type
A type of schizophrenia in which the following criteria are met:

A. Preoccupation with one or more delusions or frequent auditory hallucinations.

B. None of the following is prominent: disorganized speech, disorganized or catatonic behavior, or flat or inappropiate affect.

Disorganized Type
A type of schizophrenia in which the following criteria are met:

A. All of the following are prominent:

  (1) disorganized speech
  (2) disorganized behavior
  (3) flat or inappropriate affect

B. The criteria are not met for catatonic type.

Catatonic Type
A type of schizophrenia in which the clinical picture is dominated by at least two of the following:

  (1) motoric immobility as evidenced by catalepsy (including waxy flexibility) or stupor
  (2) excessive motor activity (that is apparently purposeless and not influenced by external stimuli)
  (3) extreme negativism (an apparently motiveless resistance to all instructions or maintenance of a rigid posture against attempts to be moved) or mutism
  (4) peculiarities of voluntary movement as evidenced by posturing (voluntary assumption of inappropriate or bizarre postures), stereotyped movements, prominent mannerisms, or prominent grimacing
  (5) echolalia or echopraxia

Undifferentiated Type
A type of schizophrenia in which symptoms that meet criterion A are present, but the criteria are not met for the paranoid, disorganized, or catatonic type.

Residual Type
A type of schizophrenia in which the following criteria are met:

A. Absence of prominent delusions, hallucinations, disorganized speech, and grossly disorganized or catatonic behavior.

B. There is continuing evidence of the disturbance, as indicated by the presence of negative symptoms or two or more symptoms listed in criterion A for schizophrenia, present in an attenuated form (e.g., odd beliefs, unusual perceptual experiences).

Table from DSM-IV, Diagnostic and Statistical Manual of Mental Disorders, ed 4. Copyright American Psychiatric Association, Washington, 1994. Used with permission.

Table 7-4. Features Weighting toward Good to Poor Prognosis in Schizophrenia

Good Prognosis	Poor Prognosis
Late onset	Young onset
Obvious precipitating factors	No precipitating factors
Acute onset	Insidious onset
Good premorbid social, sexual, and work histories	Poor premorbid social, sexual, and work histories
Mood disorder symptoms (especially depressive disorders)	Withdrawn, autistic behavior
Married	Single, divorced, or widowed
Familiy history of mood disorders	Family history of schizophrenia
Good support systems	Poor support systems
Positive symptoms	Negative symptoms
	Neurological signs and symptoms
	History of perinatal trauma
	No remissions in three years
	Many relapses
	History of assaultiveness

of their mental faculties, emotional response, and behavior than do the other types of schizophrenic patients.

Typical paranoid schizophrenic patients are tense, suspicious, guarded, and reserved. They can also be hostile or aggressive. Paranoid schizophrenic patients occasionally conduct themselves adequately in social situations. Their intelligence in areas not invaded by their psychosis tends to remain intact.

DISORGANIZED TYPE

The disorganized (formerly called hebephrenic) type is characterized by a marked regression to primitive, disinhibited, and unorganized behavior and by the absence of symptoms that meet the criteria for the catatonic type. The onset is usually early, before age 25. Disorganized patients are usually active but in an aimless, nonconstructive manner. Their thought disorder is pronounced, and their contact with reality is poor. Their personal appearance and their social behavior are dilapidated. Their emotional responses are inappropriate, and they often burst out laughing without any apparent reason. Incongruous grinning and grimacing are common in this type of patient, whose behavior is best described as silly or fatuous.

CATATONIC TYPE

Although the catatonic type was common several decades ago, it is now rare in Europe and North America. The classic feature of the catatonic type is a marked disturbance in motor function, which may involve stupor, negativism, rigidity, excitement, or posturing. Sometimes the patient shows a rapid alteration between extremes of excitement and stupor. Associated features include stereotypies, mannerisms, and waxy flexibility. Mutism is particularly common. During catatonic stupor or excitement, schizophrenic patients need careful supervision to avoid hurting themselves or others. Medical care may be needed because of malnutrition, exhaustion, hyperpyrexia, or self-inflicted injury.

UNDIFFERENTIATED TYPE

Frequently, patients who are clearly schizophrenic cannot be easily fitted into one of the other types. DSM-IV classifies those patients as the undifferentiated type.

RESIDUAL TYPE

According to DSM-IV, the residual type is characterized by the presence of continuing evidence of the schizophrenic

7-3). The DSM-IV subtyping scheme is based predominantly on clinical presentation. The DSM-IV subtypes are not closely correlated with differentiations of prognosis; such differentiation can best be done by looking at specific predictors of prognosis (Table 7-4).

PARANOID TYPE

DSM-IV specifies that the paranoid type is characterized by preoccupation with one or more delusions or frequent auditory hallucinations and that other specific behaviors suggestive of the disorganized or catatonic type are absent. Classically, the paranoid type of schizophrenia is characterized mainly by the presence of delusions of persecution or grandeur. Paranoid schizophrenic patients are usually older than catatonic or disorganized schizophrenic patients when they have the first episode of illness. Patients who have been well up to their late 20s or 30s have usually established a social life that may help them through their illness. Also, the ego resources of paranoid patients tend to be greater than those of catatonic and disorganized patients. Paranoid schizophrenic patients show less regression disturbance, in the absence of a complete set of active symptoms or sufficient symptoms to meet another type of schizophrenia (Table 7–3). Emotional blunting, social withdrawal, eccentric behavior, illogical thinking, and mild loosening of associations are common in the residual type. If delusions or hallucinations are present, they are not prominent and are not accompanied by strong affect.

Type I and Type II

While DSM-IV was being written, a major discussion in the literature concerned whether to use a subtyping scheme based on the presence or the absence of positive (or productive) and negative (or deficit) symptoms. In 1980 T. J. Crow proposed a classification of schizophrenic patients into type I and type II. Although that system was not accepted as part of the DSM-IV classification, the clinical distinction of those two types has significantly influenced psychiatric research. The *negative symptoms* include affective flattening or blunting, poverty of speech or speech content, blocking, poor grooming, lack of motivation, anhedonia, social withdrawal, cognitive defects, and attention deficits. The *positive symptoms* include loose associations, hallucinations, bizarre behavior, and increased speech. Type I patients tend to have mostly positive symptoms, normal brain structures on CT scans, and relatively good responses to treatment; type II patients tend to have mostly negative symptoms, structural brain abnormalities on CT scans, and poor responses to treatment.

OTHER SUBTYPES

The subtyping of schizophrenia has had a long history, and other subtyping schemes can be found in the literature, especially from countries other than the United States.

The names of some of those subtypes are self-explanatory—for example, late-onset, childhood, and process. *Late-onset schizophrenia* is usually defined as schizophrenia that has an onset after age 45. *Schizophrenia with a childhood onset* is simply called schizophrenia in DSM-IV, although even the literature in the United States tends to refer to childhood schizophrenia. *Process schizophrenia* means schizophrenia with a particularly debilitating and deteriorating course.

BOUFFÉE DÉLIRANTE (ACUTE DELUSIONAL PSYCHOSIS)

This French diagnostic concept is differentiated from schizophrenia primarily on the basis of a symptom duration of less than three months. The diagnosis is similar to the DSM-IV diagnosis of schizophreniform disorder. French clinicians report that about 40 percent of patients with a diagnosis of *bouffée délirante* progress in their illness and are eventually classified as having schizophrenia.

LATENT

The concept of latent schizophrenia developed during a time when there was a broad diagnostic conceptualization of schizophrenia. Currently, patients must be very mentally ill to warrant a diagnosis of schizophrenia; however, with a broad diagnostic conceptualization of schizophrenia, patients who would not today be seen as severely ill can receive a diagnosis of schizophrenia. Latent schizophrenia, for example, was often the diagnosis used for patients with what now may be called schizoid and schizotypal personality disorders. Those patients may occa-

sionally present peculiar behaviors or thought disorders but do not consistently manifest psychotic symptoms. The syndrome was also termed borderline schizophrenia in the past.

ONEIROID

The oneiroid state is a dreamlike state in which the patient may be deeply perplexed and not fully oriented in time and place. The term ''oneiroid schizophrenic'' has been used for schizophrenic patients who are particularly engaged in their hallucinatory experiences to the exclusion of involvement in the real world. When an oneiroid state is present, the clinician should be particularly careful to examine the patient for a medical or neurological cause of the symptoms.

PARAPHRENIA

This term is sometimes used as a synonym for ''paranoid schizophrenia.'' In other usages the term is used for either a progressively deteriorating course of illness or the presence of a well-systematized delusional system. The multiple meanings of the term render it not very useful in communicating information.

PSEUDONEUROTIC

Occasionally, patients who initially present such symptoms as anxiety, phobias, obsessions, and compulsions later reveal symptoms of thought disorder and psychosis. Those patients are characterized by symptoms of pananxiety, panphobia, panambivalence, and sometimes a chaotic sexuality. Unlike patients suffering from anxiety disorders, they have anxiety that is free-floating and that hardly ever subsides. In clinical descriptions of the patients, they rarely become overtly and severely psychotic.

SIMPLE SCHIZOPHRENIA

As with ''latent schizophrenia,'' the term ''simple schizophrenia'' was used during a period when schizophrenia had a broad diagnostic conceptualization. Simple schizophrenia was characterized by a gradual, insidious loss of drive and ambition. Patients with the disorder were usually not overtly psychotic and did not experience persistent hallucinations or delusions. The primary symptom is the withdrawal of the patient from social and work-related situations. The syndrome may reflect depression, a phobia, a dementia, or an exacerbation of personality traits. The clinician should be sure that the patient truly meets the diagnostic criteria for schizophrenia before making that diagnosis. In spite of those reservations, simple deteriorative disorder (simple schizophrenia) appears as a diagnostic category in an appendix of DSM-IV.

CLINICAL FEATURES

The clinical signs and symptoms of schizophrenia raise three key issues. First, no clinical sign or symptom is pathognomonic for schizophrenia; every sign or symptom seen in schizophrenia can be seen in other psychiatric and neurological disorders. That observation is contrary to the often-heard clinical opinion that certain signs and symptoms are diagnostic of schizophrenia. Therefore, a clinician cannot diagnose schizophrenia simply by a mental status examination. The patient's history is essential for the diagnosis of schizophrenia. Second, a patient's symptoms change with time. For example, a patient may have intermittent hallucinations and a varying ability to perform adequately in social situations. Or, for another example, significant symptoms of a mood disorder may also come and go during the course of schizophrenia. Third, the clinician must take into account the patient's educational level, intellectual ability, and cultural and subcultural membership. An impaired ability to understand abstract concepts, for example, may reflect the patient's education or intelligence. Various religious organizations and cults may have customs that seem strange to those outside that organization but that are considered perfectly normal to those within the cultural setting.

Premorbid Signs and Symptoms

In theoretical formulations of the course of schizophrenia, premorbid signs and symptoms appear before the prodromal phase of the illness. That differentiation implies that premorbid signs and symptoms exist before the disease process evidences itself and that the prodromal signs and symptoms are parts of the evolving disorder. The typical but not invariable premorbid history of schizophrenic patients is one of schizoid or schizotypal personality. Such a personality may be characterized as quiet, passive, and introverted; as a result, the child had few friends. A preschizophrenic adolescent may have had no close friends and no dates and may have avoided team sports. Such an adolescent may enjoy watching movies and television or listening to music to the exclusion of social activities.

The prodromal signs and symptoms are almost invariably recognized retrospectively after the diagnosis of schizophrenia has been made. Therefore, their validity is uncertain; once schizophrenia is diagnosed, the retrospective remembrance of early signs and symptoms is affected. Nevertheless, although the first hospitalization is often considered the beginning of the disorder, signs and symptoms have often been present for months or even years. They may have started with complaints about somatic symptoms, such as headache, back and muscle pain, weakness, and digestive problems. The initial diagnosis may be malingering or somatization disorder. Family and friends may eventually notice that the person has changed and is no longer functioning well in occupational, social, and personal activities. During that stage the patient may begin to develop a new interest in abstract ideas, philosophy, the occult, or religious matters. Additional prodromal signs and symptoms may include markedly peculiar behavior, abnormal affects, unusual speech, bizarre ideas, and strange perceptual experiences.

Mental Status Examination

GENERAL DESCRIPTION

The general appearance of a schizophrenic patient can cover a broad range—from that of a completely disheveled, screaming, agitated person to an obsessively groomed, completely silent, and immobile person. Between those two poles, the patient may be talkative and may exhibit bizarre postures. The behavior may become agitated or violent, apparently unprovoked but usually in response to hallucinations. That behavior contrasts dramatically with catatonic stupor (often referred to merely as catatonia), in which the patient seems completely lifeless and may exhibit such signs as muteness, negativism, and automatic obedience. Waxy flexibility used to be a common sign in catatonia, but it is now rare. A less extreme presentation of that type may

include marked social withdrawal and egocentricity, lack of spontaneous speech or movement, and an absence of goal-directed behavior. Catatonic patients may sit immobile and speechless in their chairs, respond only with short answers to questions, and move only when directed to. Other obvious behavior may include an odd clumsiness or stiffness in body movements, signs that are now seen as possibly indicating pathology in the basal ganglia. Schizophrenic patients often have poor grooming, fail to bathe, and dress much too warmly for the prevailing temperatures. Other odd behaviors include tics, stereotypies, mannerisms, and, occasionally, *echopraxia*, in which the patient imitates the posture or the behaviors of the examiner.

Precox Feeling

Some clinicians report a precox feeling, an intuitive experience of their inability to establish an emotional rapport with the patient. Although the experience is common, no data indicate that it is a valid or reliable criterion in the diagnosis of schizophrenia.

MOOD, FEELINGS, AND AFFECT

Depression can be a feature of acute psychosis and an aftermath of a psychotic episode. The depressive symptoms are sometimes referred to as secondary depression in schizophrenia or as postpsychotic depressive disorder of schizophrenia. Some studies indicate that about 25 percent of all schizophrenic patients meet carefully defined criteria for postpsychotic depressive disorder of schizophrenia. Some data indicate that depression correlates with the presence of antipsychotic-induced extrapyramidal symptoms. Those data could suggest that schizophrenic patients with depressive features are sensitive to the extrapyramidal side effects of antipsychotics. Other feeling tones include perplexity, terror, a sense of isolation, and overwhelming ambivalence. Postpsychotic depressive disorder of schizophrenia is further discussed in Section 8.1.

Other Affective Symptoms

Two other common affective symptoms in schizophrenia are reduced emotional responsiveness, which is sometimes severe enough to warrant the label of anhedonia, and overly active and inappropriate emotions, such as extremes of rage, happiness, and anxiety. A flat or blunted affect can be a symptom of the illness itself, the parkinsonian effects of antipsychotic medications, or a symptom of depression. The differentiation of those symptoms can be a clinical challenge. Overly emotional patients may describe exultant feelings of omnipotence, religious ecstasy, terror at the disintegration of their souls, or paralyzing anxiety about the destruction of the universe.

PERCEPTUAL DISTURBANCES

Any of the five senses may be affected by hallucinatory experiences in schizophrenic patients. However, the most common hallucinations are auditory. The voices are often threatening, obscene, accusatory, or insulting. Two or more voices may converse among themselves, or a voice may comment on the patient's life or behavior. Visual hallucinations are common, but tactile, olfactory, and gustatory hallucinations are unusual; their presence should prompt the clinician to consider the possibility of an underlying medical or neurological disorder that is causing the entire syndrome.

Cenesthetic Hallucinations

Cenesthetic hallucinations are unfounded sensations of altered states in bodily organs. Example of cenesthetic hallucinations include a burning sensation in the brain, a pushing sensation in the blood vessels, and a cutting sensation in the bone marrow.

Illusions

Illusions, as differentiated from hallucinations, are distortions of real images or sensations, whereas *hallucinations* are not based on real images or sensations. Illusions can occur in schizophrenic patients during active phases of the disorder, but they also occur during the prodromal phases of the disorder and during periods of remission. Whenever illusions or hallucinations occur, the clinician should still consider the possibility of a substance-related cause for the symptoms, even in a patient who has already received a diagnosis of schizophrenia.

THOUGHT

Disorders of thought are the most difficult symptoms to understand for many clinicians and students. Disorders of thought may, in fact, be the core symptoms of schizophrenia. One way to clarify the disorders of thought is to divide them into disorders of thought content, form of thought, and thought process.

Thought Content

Disorders of thought content reflect the patient's ideas, beliefs, and interpretations of stimuli. Delusions are the most obvious example of a disorder of thought content. Delusions can be varied in schizophrenia—persecutory, grandiose, religious, or somatic. Patients may believe that some outside entity is controlling their thoughts or behavior or, conversely, that they are controlling outside events in some extraordinary fashion (for example, causing the sun to rise and set and preventing earthquakes). Patients may have an intense and consuming preoccupation with esoteric, abstract, symbolic, psychological, or philosophical ideas. Patients may also be concerned about allegedly life-threatening but completely bizarre and implausible somatic conditions—for example, the presence of aliens inside the patient's testicles and affecting his ability to have children.

The phrase "loss of ego boundaries" describes the lack of a clear sense of where the patient's own body, mind, and influence end and where those of other animate and inanimate objects begin. For example, patients may think that other people, the television, or the newspapers are making reference to them (*ideas of reference*). Other symptoms of the loss of ego boundaries include the sense that the patient has physically fused with an outside object (for example, a tree or another person) or that the patient has disintegrated and fused with the entire universe. Given that state of mind, some schizophrenic patients have doubts as to what sex they are or what their sexual orientation is. Those symptoms should not be confused with transvestism, transsexuality, or homosexuality.

Form of Thought

Disorders of the form of thought are objectively observable in patients' spoken and written language. The disorders include looseness of associations, derailment, incoherence, tangentiality, circumstantiality, neologisms, echolalia, verbigeration, word salad, and mutism. Although looseness of associations was once described as pathognomonic for schizophrenia, the symptom is frequently seen in mania. Distinguishing between looseness of associations and tangentiality can be difficult for even the most experienced clinician.

Thought Process

Disorders in thought process concern the way ideas and language are formulated. The examiner infers a disorder from what and how the patient speaks, writes, or draws. The examiner may also assess the patient's thought process by observing the patient's behavior, especially in carrying out discrete tasks in occupational therapy, for example. Disorders of thought process include flight of ideas, thought blocking, impaired attention, poverty of thought content, poor abstraction abilities, perseveration, idiosyncratic associations (for example, identical predicates and clang associations), overinclusion, and circumstantiality.

IMPULSIVENESS, SUICIDE, AND HOMICIDE

Patients with schizophrenia may be agitated and have little impulse control when ill. They may also have decreased social sensitivity, appearing to be impulsive when, for example, they grab another patient's cigarettes, change television channels abruptly, or throw food on the floor. Some apparently impulsive behavior, including suicide and homicide attempts, may be in response to hallucinations commanding the patient to act.

Suicide

Perhaps the most underappreciated factor involved in the suicide of schizophrenic patients is depression that has been misdiagnosed as flat affect or a medication-induced side effect. Other precipitants of suicide include feelings of absolute emptiness, a need to escape from the mental torture, or auditory hallucinations that command patients to kill themselves. The risk factors for suicide are the patient's awareness of the illness, being male, a college education, young age, a change in the course of the disease, an improvement after a relapse, dependence on the hospital, overly high ambitions, prior suicide attempts early in the course of the illness, and living alone.

Homicide

In spite of the sensational attention that the news media provide when a patient with schizophrenia murders someone, the available data indicate that a schizophrenic patient is no more likely to commit homicide than is a member of the general population. When a schizophrenic patient does commit homicide, it may be for unpredictable or bizarre reasons based on hallucinations or delusions. Possible predictors of homicidal activity are a history of prior violence, dangerous behavior while hospitalized, and hallucinations or delusions involving such violence.

SENSORIUM AND COGNITION

Orientation

Schizophrenic patients are usually oriented to person, time, and place. The lack of such orientation should prompt the clinician to investigate the possibility of a medical or neurological brain disorder. Some schizophrenic patients may give incorrect or bizarre answers to questions regarding orientation—for example, "I am Christ; this is heaven; and it is 35 A.D."

Memory

Memory, as tested in the mental status examination, is usually intact. It may be impossible, however, to get a patient to attend closely enough to the memory tests to permit adequate assessment.

JUDGMENT AND INSIGHT

Classically, schizophrenic patients are described as having poor insight into the nature and the severity of their disorder. The so-called lack of insight is associated with poor compliance with treatment. When examining a schizophrenic patient, the clinician should carefully define various aspects of insight, such as awareness of symptoms, trouble in getting along with people, and the reasons for those problems. Such information can be clinically useful in tailoring a treatment strategy and theoretically useful in postulating what areas of the brain contribute to the observed lack of insight (for example, the parietal lobes).

RELIABILITY

A schizophrenic patient is no less reliable than is any other psychiatric or nonpsychiatric patient. However, the nature of the disorder requires that the examiner verify important information through additional sources.

Neurological Findings

Localizing and nonlocalizing neurological signs (also known as hard and soft signs, respectively) have been reported to be present more commonly in patients with schizophrenia than in other psychiatric patients. Nonlocalizing signs include dysdiadochokinesia, astereognosis, mirror sign, primitive reflexes, and diminished dexterity. The presence of neurological signs and symptoms correlates with increased severity of illness, affective blunting, and a poor prognosis. Other abnormal neurological signs include tics, stereotypies, grimacing, impaired fine motor skills, abnormal motor tone, and abnormal movements. One study has found that only about 25 percent of schizophrenic patients are aware of their own abnormal involuntary movements and that the lack of awareness is correlated with lack of insight regarding the primary psychiatric disorder and the duration of illness.

Eye Examination

In addition to the disorder of smooth ocular pursuit, schizophrenic patients have an elevated blink rate. The elevated blink rate is thought to reflect hyperdopaminergic activity. In primates, blinking can be increased by dopamine agonists and reduced by dopamine antagonists.

Speech

Although the disorders of speech in schizophrenia (for example, looseness of associations) are classically thought of as indicating a thought disorder, the disorders of speech may also indicate a *forme fruste* of an aphasia, perhaps implicating the dominant parietal lobe. The inability of schizophrenic patients to perceive the prosody of speech or to inflect their own speech can be seen as a neurological symptom of a disorder in the nondominant parietal lobe. Other parietal lobelike symptoms in schizophrenia include the inability to carry out tasks (that is, *apraxia*), right-left disorientation, and lack of concern about the disorder.

Other Physical Findings

An increased incidence of minor physical anomalies is associated with the diagnosis of schizophrenia. Such anomalies are most likely associated with early stages of embryonic and fetal growth, usually during the first trimester. Such physical anomalies have been reported to be present in 30 to 75 percent of schizophrenic patients, compared with 0 to 13 percent of normal persons. Some studies now suggest that such anomalies are more common in males than in females and are probably associated with genetic factors, although obstetric complication cannot be ruled out as a causative factor.

Psychological Tests

Neuropsychological Testing

Formal neuropsychological assessment of cognitive functions in schizophrenic patients often provides data that may be used clinically. Objective measures of neuropsychological performance, such as the Halstead-Reitan Neuropsychological Battery and the Luria-Nebraska Neuropsychological Battery, often give abnormal findings, but the results may suggest practical approaches to take with patients that account for their cognitive weaknesses. In general, the test results are consistent with bilateral frontal and temporal lobe dysfunction, including impairments in attention, retention time, and problem-solving ability.

Intelligence Tests

When groups of schizophrenic patients are compared with groups of nonschizophrenic psychiatric patients or with the general population, the schizophrenic patients tend to have lower scores on intelligence tests. Statistically, the evidence suggests that low intelligence is often present at the onset, and intelligence may continue to deteriorate with the progression of the disorder.

Projective and Personality Tests

Projective tests—for example, the Rorschach test and the Thematic Apperception Test (TAT)—may indicate bizarre ideation. Personality inventories—for example, the Minnesota Multiphasic Personality Inventory (MMPI)—often give abnormal results in schizophrenia, but the contribution to diagnosis and treatment planning is minimal.

DIFFERENTIAL DIAGNOSIS

Secondary Psychotic Disorders

Symptoms of psychosis and catatonia can be caused by a wide range of nonpsychiatric medical conditions and can be induced by a wide range of substances. When psychosis or catatonia is caused by a nonpsychiatric medical condition or induced by a substance, the most appropriate diagnosis is *psychotic disorder due to a general medical condition*, *catatonic disorder due to a general medical condition*, or *substance-induced psychotic disorder*. The psychiatric manifestations of many of the nonpsychiatric medical conditions can come early in the course of the illness, often before the development of other symptoms. Therefore, the clinician must consider a wide range of nonpsychiatric medical conditions in the differential diagnosis of psychosis, even in the absence of obvious physical symptoms. Generally, patients with neurological disorders have more insight into their illnesses and more distress from their psychiatric symptoms than do schizophrenic patients, a fact that can help the clinician differentiate the two groups of patients.

When evaluating a psychotic patient, the clinician should follow the general guidelines regarding the assessment of nonpsychiatric conditions. First, the clinician should be especially aggressive in pursuing an undiagnosed nonpsychiatric medical condition if the patient exhibits any unusual or rare symptoms or any variation in the level of consciousness. Second, the clinician should attempt to obtain a complete family history, including a history of medical, neurological, and psychiatric disorders. Third, the clinician should consider the possibility of a nonpsychiatric medical condition, even in patients with previous diagnoses of schizophrenia. A schizophrenia patient is just as likely to have a brain tumor resulting in psychotic symptoms as is a nonschizophrenic patient.

Malingering and Factitious Disorders

Either malingering or a factitious disorder may be an appropriate diagnosis in a patient who is imitating the symptoms of schizophrenia but does not actually have schizophrenia. People have faked schizophrenic symptoms and been admitted into and treated at psychiatric hospitals. Patients who are completely in control of their symptom production may qualify for a diagnosis of malingering; such patients usually have some obvious financial or legal reason to be considered insane. Patients who are less in control of their falsification of psychotic symptoms may qualify for a diagnosis of a factitious disorder. However, some patients with schizophrenia sometimes falsely complain of an exacerbation of psychotic symptoms to obtain increased assistance benefits or to gain admission to a hospital.

Other Psychotic Disorders

The psychotic symptoms seen in schizophrenia can be identical to those seen in schizophreniform disorder, brief psychotic disorder, and schizoaffective disorder. *Schizophreniform disorder* differs from schizophrenia in having a duration of symptoms that is at least one month but less than six months. Brief psychotic disorder is the appropriate diagnosis if the symptoms have lasted at least one day but less than one month and if the patient has not returned to the premorbid level of functioning. *Schizoaffective disorder* is the appropriate diagnosis when a manic or depressive syndrome develops concurrently with the major symptoms of schizophrenia.

A diagnosis of *delusional disorder* is warranted if nonbizarre delusions have been present for at least one month in the absence of the other symptoms of schizophrenia or a mood disorder.

Mood Disorders

The differential diagnosis of schizophrenia and mood disorders can be difficult, but it is important because of the availability of specific and effective treatments for mania and depression. Affective or mood symptoms in schizophrenia should be brief relative to the duration of the primary symptoms. In the absence of information other than a single mental status examination, the clinician should delay a final diagnosis or should assume the presence of mood disorder, rather than make a diagnosis of schizophrenia prematurely.

Personality Disorders

A variety of personality disorders may present with some features of schizophrenia; schizotypal, schizoid, and borderline personality disorders are the personality disorders with the most similar symptoms. Personality disorders, unlike schizophrenia, have mild symptoms, a history of being present throughout the patient's life, and the absence of an identifiable date of onset.

COURSE AND PROGNOSIS

Course

A premorbid pattern of symptoms may be the first evidence of illness, although the import of the symptoms is usually recognized only retrospectively. Characteristically, the symptoms begin in adolescence, followed by the development of prodromal symptoms in days to a few months. The onset of the disturbing symptoms may seem to have been precipitated by a social or environmental change, such as moving away to college, an experience with substances, or the death of a relative. The prodromal syndrome may last a year or more before the onset of overt psychotic symptoms.

After the first psychotic episode, the patient has a gradual period of recovery, which can be followed by a lengthy period of relatively normal functioning. However, a relapse usually occurs, and the general pattern of illness that is evidenced in the first five years after the diagnosis is usually predictive of the course that the patient follows. Each relapse of the psychosis is followed by a further deterioration in the patient's baseline functioning. The classic course of schizophrenia is one of exacerbations and remissions. The major distinction between schizophrenia and the mood disorders is the schizophrenic patient's failure to return to baseline functioning after each relapse. Sometimes a clinically observable postpsychotic depression follows a psychotic episode, and the schizophrenic patient's vulnerability to stress is usually lifelong. Positive symptoms tend to become less severe with time, but the socially debilitating negative or deficit symptoms may increase in severity. Although about one third of all schizophrenic patients have some marginal or integrated social existence, the majority have lives characterized by aimlessness, inactivity, frequent hospitalizations, and, in urban settings, homelessness and poverty.

Prognosis

Several studies have found that over the 5- to 10-year period after the first psychiatric hospitalization for schizophrenia, only about 10 to 20 percent of the patients can be described as having a good outcome. More than 50 percent of the patients can be described as having a poor outcome, with repeated hospitalizations, exacerbations of symptoms, episodes of major mood disorders, and suicide attempts. In spite of those glum figures, schizophrenia does not always run a deteriorating course, and a number of factors have been associated with a good prognosis.

The range of recovery rates reported in the literature is from 10 to 60 percent, and a reasonable estimate is that 20 to 30 percent of all schizophrenic patients are able to lead somewhat normal lives. About 20 to 30 percent of patients continue to experience moderate symptoms, and 40 to 60 percent of patients remain significantly impaired by their disorder for their entire lives. Schizophrenic patients do much less well than do patients with mood disorders, although 20 to 25 percent of mood disorder patients are also severely disturbed at long-term follow-up.

TREATMENT

Three fundamental observations about schizophrenia warrant attention when considering the treatment of the disorder. First, regardless of cause, schizophrenia occurs in a person who has a unique individual, familial, and social psychological profile. The treatment approach must be tailored to how the particular patient has been affected by the disorder and how the particular patient will be helped by the treatment. Second, the fact that the concordance rate for schizophrenia among monozygotic twins is 50 percent has been taken by many investigators to suggest that unknown but probably specific environmental and psychological factors have contributed to the development of the disorder. Thus, just as pharmacological agents are used to address presumed chemical imbalances, nonpharmacological strategies must address nonbiological issues. Third, schizophrenia is a complex disorder, and any single therapeutic approach is rarely sufficient to address the multifaceted disorder satisfactorily.

Although antipsychotic medications are the mainstay of the treatment of schizophrenia, research has found that psychosocial interventions can augment the clinical improvement. Psychosocial modalities should be carefully integrated into the drug treatment regimen and should support it. Most schizophrenic patients benefit from the combined use of antipsychotics and psychosocial treatment.

Hospitalization

The primary indications for hospitalization are for diagnostic purposes, stabilization on medications, patient safety because of suicidal or homicidal ideation, and grossly disorganized or inappropriate behavior, including the inability to take care of basic needs, such as food, clothing, and shelter. A primary goal of hospitalization should be to establish an effective link between the patient and community support systems.

Introduced in the early 1950s, antipsychotic medications have revolutionized the treatment of schizophrenia. About two to four times as many patients relapse when treated with a placebo than when treated with antipsychotics. However, antipsychotics treat the symptoms of the disorder and are not a cure for schizophrenia.

Other aspects of clinical management flow logically from a medical model of the disorder. Rehabilitation and adjustment imply that the patient's specific handicaps are taken into account when treatment strategies are planned. The physician must also educate the patient and the patient's caretakers and family about schizophrenia.

Hospitalization decreases stress on patients and helps them structure their daily activities. The length of hospitalization depends on the severity of the patient's illness and the availability of outpatient treatment facilities. Research has shown that short hospitalizations (four to six weeks) are just as effective as long-term hospitalizations and that hospitals with active behavioral approaches are more effective than custodial institutions and insight-oriented therapeutic communities.

The hospital treatment plan should have a practical orientation toward issues of living, self-care, quality of life, employment, and social relationships. Hospitalization should be directed toward aligning patients with aftercare facilities, including their family homes, foster families, board-and-care homes, and halfway houses. Day care and home visits can sometimes help patients remain out of the hospital for long periods and can improve the quality of the patients' daily lives.

Somatic Treatments

ANTIPSYCHOTICS

The antipsychotic drugs are sometimes referred to as "neuroleptics," which is an acceptable term. The term "major tranquilizers," however, should be avoided, since it has been used to indicate various types of drugs and inaccurately implies that the antipsychotics have a sedative or tranquilizing effect as a major mode of action. The antipsychotics include dopamine receptor antagonists, risperidone, and clozapine.

Choice of Drug

The dopamine receptor antagonists are the classic antipsychotic drugs and are effective in the treatment of schizophrenia. The drugs have two major shortcomings. First, only a small percentage of patients (perhaps 25 percent) are helped sufficiently to recover a reasonable amount of normal mental functioning. As noted above, even with treatment, about 50 percent of schizophrenic patients lead severely debilitated lives. Second, the dopamine receptor antagonists are associated with both annoying and serious adverse effects. The most common annoying effects are akathisia and parkinsonianlike symptoms of rigidity and tremor. The potential serious effects include tardive dyskinesia and neuroleptic malignant syndrome.

Risperidone is a serotonin-dopamine antagonist (SDA), an antipsychotic drug with significant antagonist activity at the 5-HT$_2$ receptor and at the D$_2$ receptor. Research data indicate that it may be more effective than currently available dopamine receptor antagonists at treating both the positive symptoms and the negative symptoms of schizophrenia. The available research data also indicate that risperidone is associated with significantly fewer and less severe neurological adverse effects than are typical dopaminergic antagonist drugs.

Clozapine is an effective antipsychotic drug. Its mechanism of action is not well understood, although it is known that clozapine is weak antagonist of the D$_2$ receptor but appears to be a potent antagonist of the D$_4$ receptor and has antagonistic activity at the serotonergic receptors. Clozapine, unfortunately, is associated with a 1 to 2 percent incidence of agranulocytosis, an adverse effect that necessitates the weekly monitoring of the blood indexes. Clozapine is indicated in patients with tardive dyskinesia because the available data indicate that clozapine is not associated with the development or the exacerbation of that disorder.

Therapeutic Principles

The use of antipsychotic medications in schizophrenia should follow five major principles. (1) The clinician should carefully define the target symptoms to be treated. (2) An antipsychotic that has worked well in the past for the patient should be used again. In the absence of such information, the choice of an antipsychotic is usually based on the side-effect profile. Currently available data indicate that risperidone and similar drugs that may be introduced in the next few years may offer a superior side-effect profile and the possibility of superior efficacy. Within the standard dopaminergic antagonists, all members of that class are equally efficacious. (3) The minimum length of an antipsychotic trial is four to six weeks at adequate dosages. If the trial is unsuccessful, a different antipsychotic, usually from a different class, can be tried. However, an unpleasant experience by the patient to the first dose of an antipsychotic drug correlates highly with future poor response and noncompliance. Negative experiences can include a peculiar subjective negative feeling, oversedation, or an acute dystonic reaction. If a severe and negative initial reaction is observed, the clinician may consider switching to a different antipsychotic drug in less than four weeks. (4) In general, the use of more than one antipsychotic medication at a time is rarely, if ever, indicated, although some psychiatrists use thioridazine (Mellaril) for treating insomnia in a patient who is receiving another antipsychotic for the treatment of schizophrenic symptoms. In particularly treatment-resistant patients, combinations of antipsychotics with other drugs—for example, carbamazepine (Tegretol)—may be indicated. (5) Patients should be maintained on the lowest possible effective dosage of medication. The dosage is often lower than the dosage that was needed to achieve symptom control during the psychotic episode.

OTHER DRUGS

If adequate trials with at least one dopaminergic receptor antagonist have all been unsuccessful, combination therapy with one of those drugs and an adjuvant medication may be indicated. The adjuvant medications with the most supportive data are lithium, two anticonvulsants (carbamazepine and valproate [Depakene]), and the benzodiazepines.

Lithium

Lithium may be effective in further reducing psychotic symptoms in up to 50 percent of patients with schizophrenia. Lithium may also be a reasonable drug to try in patients who are unable to take any of the antipsychotic medications.

Anticonvulsants

Carbamazepine or valproate may be used alone or in combination with lithium or an antipsychotic. Although neither of the anticonvulsants has been shown to be effective in reducing psychotic symptoms in schizophrenia when used alone, data suggest that the anticonvulsants may be effective in reducing episodes of violence in some schizophrenic patients.

Benzodiazepines

Data support the practice of coadministering alprazolam (Xanax) with antipsychotics to patients who have not responded to antipsychotic administration alone. There are also reports of schizophrenic patients responding to high dosages of diazepam (Valium) alone. However, the severity of the psychosis may be exacerbated after the withdrawal of a benzodiazepine.

OTHER SOMATIC TREATMENTS

Although much less effective than antipsychotics, electroconvulsive therapy (ECT) may be indicated for catatonic patients and for patients who for some reason cannot take antipsychotics. Patients who have been ill for less than one year are most likely to respond.

In the past, schizophrenia was treated with insulin-induced coma and barbiturate-induced coma. Those treatments are no longer used because of the associated hazards. Psychosurgery, particularly frontal lobotomies, was used from 1935 to 1955 for the treatment of schizophrenia. Although sophisticated approaches to psychosurgery for schizophrenia may eventually be developed, psychosurgery is no longer considered an appropriate treatment of schizophrenia, but it is being used on a limited experimental basis.

Psychosocial Treatments

BEHAVIOR THERAPY

Treatment planning for schizophrenia should address both the abilities and the deficits of the patient. Behavioral techniques use token economies and social skills training to increase social abilities, self-sufficiency, practical skills, and interpersonal communication. Adaptive behaviors are reinforced by praise or tokens that can be redeemed for desired items, such as hospital privileges and passes. Consequently, the frequency of maladaptive or deviant behavior—such as talking loudly, talking to oneself in public, and bizarre posturing—can be reduced.

Behavioral Skills Training

Behavioral skills training is sometimes referred to as social skills therapy; regardless of the name, the therapy can be directly supportive and useful to the patient and is naturally additive to pharmacological therapy. In addition to the personal symptoms of schizophrenia, some of the most noticeable symptoms of schizophrenia involve the patient's relationships with others, including poor eye contact, unusual delays in response, odd facial expressions, lack of spontaneity in social situations, and inaccurate perceptions or lack or perception of emotions in other people. Those behaviors are specifically addressed in behavioral skills training. Behavioral skills training involves the use of videotapes of

others and of the patient, role playing in therapy, and homework assignments regarding the specific skills being practiced.

FAMILY-ORIENTED THERAPIES

A variety of family-oriented therapies are useful in the treatment of schizophrenia. Because schizophrenic patients are often discharged in an only partially remitted state, a family to which a schizophrenic patient is returning can often benefit from a brief but intensive (as often as daily) course of family therapy. The focus of the therapy should be on the immediate situation and should include identifying and avoiding potentially troublesome situations. When problems do emerge with the patient in the family, the focus of the therapy should be on the rapid resolution of the problem.

Subsequent to the immediate postdischarge period, an important topic to cover in family therapy is the recovery process, particularly its length and its rate. Too often, family members, in a well-meaning fashion, encourage a schizophrenic relative to resume regular activities too quickly. That overly optimistic plan stems both from ignorance about the nature of schizophrenia and from denial regarding its severity. The therapist must help the family and the patient understand schizophrenia without being overly discouraging. The therapist may discuss the psychotic episode itself and the events leading up to it. The common practice of ignoring the psychotic episode often adds to the shame associated with the event and does not take advantage of the recency of the event as a source of discussion, education, and understanding. Family members are often frightened by the psychotic symptoms, and open discussion with the psychiatrist and the schizophrenic relative can often be helpful for all parties. Subsequent family therapy can be directed toward the long-range implementation of stress-reducing and coping strategies and toward gradual reinvolvement of the patient in activities.

In any family session with schizophrenic patients, the therapist must control the emotional intensity of the session. The excessive expression of emotion during a session can be damaging to the recovery process of a schizophrenic patient and can undermine the potential success of subsequent family therapy sessions. A number of studies have found family therapy to be especially effective in reducing relapse. However, each of those studies used a different type of family therapy, and the commonality among the therapies remains unclear. In controlled studies the reduction in relapse rate was dramatic—25 to 50 percent annual relapse rate without family therapy and 5 to 10 percent with family therapy.

NAMI

The National Alliance for the Mentally Ill (NAMI) and similar groups are support groups for the family members and the friends of mentally ill patients and for the patients themselves. Such organizations give emotional and practical advice about obtaining care in a sometimes overly complex health care delivery system. NAMI is often a supportive group to which family members can be referred. NAMI has also waged a campaign to destigmatize mental illness and to increase awareness in government regarding the needs and the rights of the mentally ill and their families.

GROUP THERAPY

Group therapy for schizophrenia generally focuses on real-life plans, problems, and relationships. Groups may be behaviorally oriented, psychodynamically or insight-oriented, or supportive. Some doubt exists about whether dynamic interpretation and insight therapy are valuable for the typical schizophrenic patient. However, group therapy is effective in reducing social isolation, increasing the sense of cohesiveness, and improving reality testing for patients with schizophrenia. Groups led in a supportive manner, rather than in an interpretative way, appear to be most helpful for schizophrenic patients.

INDIVIDUAL PSYCHOTHERAPY

The best-conducted studies of the effects of individual psychotherapy in the treatment of schizophrenia have provided data that the therapy is helpful and is additive to the effects of pharmacological treatment. The types of therapies studied include supportive psychotherapy and insight-oriented psychotherapy. A critical concept in the psychotherapy for a schizophrenic patient is the development of a therapeutic relationship that the patient experiences as safe. That experience is affected by the reliability of the therapist, the emotional distance between the therapist and the patient, and the genuineness of the therapist as interpreted by the patient. Inexperienced psychotherapists often provide interpretations too quickly to schizophrenic patients. The psychotherapy for a schizophrenic patient should be conceptualized in terms of decades, rather than sessions, months, or even years. That reality makes it unfortunate that residency training programs permit only a few years, at most, for residents to spend with schizophrenic patients.

Some clinicians and researchers have emphasized that the ability of a schizophrenic patient to form a therapeutic alliance with a therapist can predict the outcome. At least one study found that schizophrenic patients who were able to form a good therapeutic alliance were likely to remain in psychotherapy, to remain compliant with their medications, and to have good outcomes at a two-year follow-up evaluation.

The relationship between the clinician and the patient is different from that encountered in the treatment of nonpsychotic patients. Establishing a relationship is often difficult; the schizophrenic patient is desperately lonely yet defends against closeness and trust and is likely to become suspicious, anxious, hostile, or regressed when someone attempts to draw close. The scrupulous observance of distance and privacy, simple directness, patience, sincerity, and sensitivity to social conventions are preferable to premature informality and the condescending use of first names. Exaggerated warmth or professions of friendship are out of place and are likely to be perceived as attempts at bribery, manipulation, or exploitation.

However, in the context of a professional relationship, flexibility may be essential in establishing a working alliance with the patient. The therapist may have meals with the patient, sit on the floor, go for a walk, eat at a restaurant, accept and give gifts, play table tennis, remember the patient's birthday, or just sit silently with the patient. The major aim is to convey the idea that the therapist can be trusted, wants to understand the patient and will try to do so, and has faith in the patient's potential as a human being, no matter how disturbed, hostile, or bizarre the patient may be at the moment. Mandred Bleuler stated that the correct therapeutic attitude toward schizophrenic patients is to accept them, rather than watch them as persons who have become unintelligible and different from the therapist.

References

Abi-Dargham A, Laruelle M, Lipska B, Jaskiw G E, Wong D T, Robertson D W, Weinberger D R, Kleinman J E: Serotonin 5-HT₃ receptors in schizophrenia: A postmortem study in the amygdala. Brain Res 616: 53, 1993.

Andreasen N C, Flaum M: Schizophrenia: The characteristic symptoms. Schizophr Bull 17: 27, 1991.

Basset A S: Chromosomal aberrations and schizophrenia: Autosomes. Br J Psychiatry 61: 323, 1992.

Bogerst B, Lieberman J A, Ashtari M, Bilder R M, Degreef G, Lerner G, Johns C, Masiar S: Hippocampus-amygdala volumes and psychopathology in chronic schizophrenia. Biol Psychiatry 33: 236, 1993.

Gabbard G O: Psychodynamic Psychiatry in Clinical Practice: The DSM-IV Edition. American Psychiatric Press, Washington, 1994.

Goldberg T E, Gold J M, Greenberg R, Griffin S, Schulz S C, Pickar D, Kleinman J E, Weinberger D R: Contrasts between patients with affective disorders and patients with schizophrenia on a neuropsychological test battery. Am J Psychiatry 150: 1355, 1993.

Gur R E, Pearlson G D: Neuroimaging in schizophrenia research. Schizophr Bull 19: 337, 1993.

Harrison P J: On the neuropathology of schizophrenia and its dementia: neurodevelopmental, neurodegenerative, or both?. Neurodegeneration 4: 1, 1995.

Heinrichs R W, Awad A G: Neurocognitive subtypes of chronic schizophrenia. Schizophr Res 9: 49, 1993.

Kaplan H I, Sadock B J, editors: Schizophrenia. In Comprehensive Textbook of Psychiatry, ed 6, H I Kaplan, B J Sadock, editors, p 889. Williams & Wilkins, Baltimore, 1995.

Kendler K S, Diehl S R: The genetics of schizophrenia: A current, genetic-epidemiologic perspective. Schizophr Bull 19: 261, 1993.

Lieberman J A, Koreen A R: Neurochemistry and neuroendocrinology of schizophrenia: A selective review. Schizophr Bull 19: 371, 1993.

Maas J W, Contreras S A, Miller A L, Berman N, Bowden C L, Javors M A, Seleshi E, Weintraub S: Studies of catecholamine metabolism in schizophrenia/psychosis: I. Neuropsychopharmacology 8: 97, 1993.

Moller H J: Neuroleptic treatment of negative symptoms in schizophrenic patients: Efficacy problems and methodological difficulties. Eur Neuropsychopharmacol 3: 1, 1993.

Nordstrom A-L, Farde L, Wiesel F-A, Forslund K, Pauline S, Halldin C, Uppfeldt G: Central D2-dopamine receptor occupancy in relation to antipsychotic drug effects: A double-blind PET study of schizophrenic patients. Biol Psychiatry 33: 227, 1993.

Shalev A, Hermesh H, Rothberg J, Munitz H: Poor neuroleptic response in acutely exacerbated schizophrenic patients. Acta Psychiatr Scand 87: 86, 1993.

Sharma R P, Javaid J I, Pandey G N, Janicak P G, Davis J M: Behavioral and biochemical effects of methylphenidate in schizophrenic and non-schizophrenic patients. Biol Psychiatry 30: 459, 1991.

Siegel B V, Buchsbaum M S, Bunney W E, Gottschalk L A, Haier R J, Lohr J B, Lottenberg S, Najafi A, Nuechterlein K H, Potkin S G, Wu J C: Cortical-striatal-thalamic circuits and brain glucose metabolic activity in 70 unmedicated male schizophrenic patients. Am J Psychiatry 150: 1325, 1993.

Stoll A L, Tohen M, Baldessarini R J, Goodwin D C, Stein S, Katz S, Geenens D, Swinson R P, Goethe J W, McGlashan T: Shifts in diagnostic frequencies of schizophrenia and major affective disorders at six North American psychiatric hospitals, 1972–1988. Am J Psychiatry 150: 1668, 1993.

8/ Other Psychotic Disorders

8.1 OVERVIEW

Schizophrenia is both the classic and the most common psychotic disorder. There are, however, many other psychotic syndromes that do not meet the diagnostic criteria for schizophrenia. The other major psychotic syndromes are schizophreniform disorder, schizoaffective disorder, delusional disorder, and brief psychotic disorder. Briefly, the symptoms of *schizophreniform disorder* are identical to those of schizophrenia except that the symptoms have been present for at least one month but less than six months. *Schizoaffective disorder* is characterized by the presence of a complete syndrome of symptoms for both schizophrenia and a mood disorder. *Delusional disorder*, like schizophrenia, is a chronic disorder but is characterized by the presence of delusions as the predominant symptom. And *brief psychotic disorder* is characterized primarily by the brief duration (at least one day but less than one month) of schizophrenic symptoms.

In the evaluation of any psychotic patient, the possibility that the psychosis is caused by a general medical condition or is induced by a substance must be considered. Those two situations are classified in the fourth edition of *Diagnostic and Statistical Manual of Mental Disorders* (DSM-IV) as *psychotic disorder due to a general medical condition* and *substance-induced psychotic disorder*, respectively. DSM-IV also includes a diagnosis of *catatonic disorder due to a general medical condition* to emphasize the special considerations regarding the differential diagnosis of catatonic symptoms (see Section 4.5).

DSM-IV introduces into an appendix two new psychotic disorder diagnoses. *Postpsychotic depressive disorder of schizophrenia* is characterized by the presence of all the symptoms of a major depressive episode during the residual phase of schizophrenia. *Simple deteriorative disorder (simple schizophrenia)*, a still controversial diagnostic category, is characterized as the progressive development of symptoms of social withdrawal and other symptoms similar to the deficit symptoms of schizophrenia.

Beyond the common psychotic disorders and the newly introduced DSM-IV diagnoses, a variety of rare or atypical psychotic disorders have been either officially or clinically recognized. DSM-IV includes diagnostic criteria for *shared psychotic disorder*, which is the classification for persons with psychotic symptoms that develop because of their association with another psychotic person. *Postpartum psychosis* occurs in some women after the delivery of a child. In addition to those and other atypical psychoses, there are a variety of culture-bound psychotic syndromes, such as amok and koro.

SECONDARY DISORDERS

The evaluation of a psychotic patient requires the consideration of the possibility that the psychotic symptoms are the result of a general medical condition (for example, a brain tumor) or the ingestion of a substance (for example, phencyclidine [PCP]).

Epidemiology

Relevant epidemiological data about psychotic disorder due to a general medical condition and substance-induced psychotic disorder are lacking. The disorders are most often encountered in patients who abuse alcohol or other substances on a long-term basis. The delusional syndrome that may accompany complex partial seizures is more common in women than in men.

Etiology

Physical conditions—such as cerebral neoplasms, particularly of the occipital or temporal areas—can cause hallucinations. Sensory deprivation, as occurs in blind and deaf persons, can also result in hallucinatory or delusional experiences. Lesions involving the temporal lobe and other cerebral regions, especially the right hemisphere and the parietal lobe, are associated with delusions.

Psychoactive substances are common causes of psychotic syndromes. The most commonly involved substances are alcohol, indole hallucinogens—for example, lysergic acid diethylamide (LSD)—amphetamine, cocaine, mescaline, PCP, and ketamine (Ketalar). Many other substances, including steroids and levothyroxine (Levoxyl, Levothroid, Synthroid), can be associated with substance-induced hallucinations.

Diagnosis

PSYCHOTIC DISORDER DUE TO A GENERAL MEDICAL CONDITION

The DSM-IV diagnosis of psychotic disorder due to a general medical condition (Table 8.1–1) combines into one diagnosis the two similar diagnostic categories in the revised third edition of DSM (DSM-III-R), organic delusional disorder and organic hallucinosis. The phenomena of the psychotic disorder are defined in DSM-IV by further specifying the predominant symptoms. With this diagnosis, the medical condition, along with the predominant symptoms pattern, should be included in the diagnosis—for example, psychotic disorder due to a brain tumor, with delusions. The DSM-IV criteria further specify that the disorder does not occur exclusively while the patient is delirious or demented and that the symptoms are not better accounted for by another mental disorder.

SUBSTANCE-INDUCED PSYCHOTIC DISORDER

The diagnosis of substance-induced psychotic disorder (Table 8.1–2) is reserved for persons who have substance-induced psychotic symptoms and impaired reality testing. Persons who have substance-induced psychotic symptoms (for example, hallucinations) but who have retained reality testing should be classified as having another substance-related disorder—for example, phencyclidine intoxication with perceptual disturbances. The intent of including the diagnosis of substance-induced psychotic disorder with the other psychotic disorder diagnoses is to prompt the clinician to consider the possibility that a substance is causally involved in the production of the psychotic symptoms. The full diagnosis of substance-induced psychotic disorder should include the type of substance involved, the stage

Table 8.1-1.   Diagnostic Criteria for Psychotic Disorder Due to a General Medical Condition

A. Prominent hallucinations or delusions.

B. There is evidence from the history, physical examination, or laboratory findings that the disturbance is the direct physiological consequence of a general medical condition.

C. The disturbance is not better accounted for by another mental disorder.

D. The disturbance does not occur exclusively during the course of a delirium.

Table from DSM-IV, *Diagnostic and Statistical Manual of Mental Disorders*, ed 4. Copyright American Psychiatric Association, Washington, 1994. Used with permission.

Table 8.1-2.   Diagnostic Criteria for Substance-Induced Psychotic Disorder

A. Prominent hallucinations or delusions. **Note:** Do not include hallucinations if the person has insight that they are substance-induced.

B. There is evidence from the history, physical examination, or laboratory findings of either (1) or (2):

   (1) the symptoms in criterion A developed during, or within a month of, substance intoxication or withdrawal
   (2) medication use is etiologically related to the disturbance

C. The disturbance is not better accounted for by a psychotic disorder that is not substance induced. Evidence that the symptoms are better accounted for by a psychotic disorder that is not substance induced might include the following: the symptoms precede the onset of the use (or medication use); the symptoms persist for a substantial period of time (e.g., about a month) after the cessation of acute withdrawal or severe intoxication, or are substantially in excess of what would be expected given the type or amount of the substance used or the duration of use; or there is other evidence that suggests the existence of an independent non-substance-induced psychotic disorder (e.g., history of recurrent non-substance-related episodes).

D. The disturbance does not occur exclusively during the course of a delirium.

Table from DSM-IV, *Diagnostic and Statistical Manual of Mental Disorders*, ed 4. Copyright American Psychiatric Association, Washington, 1994. Used with permission.

of substance use when the disorder began (for example, during intoxication or withdrawal), and the clinical phenomena (for example, hallucinations or delusions).

Clinical Features

HALLUCINATIONS

Hallucinations may occur in one or more sensory modalities. Tactile hallucinations (such as the sensation of bugs crawling on the skin) are characteristic of cocaine use. Auditory hallucinations are usually associated with psychoactive substance abuse; auditory hallucinations may also occur in deaf people. Olfactory hallucinations can occur in temporal lobe epilepsy. Visual hallucinations may occur in people who are blind from cataracts. Hallucinations are either recurrent or persistent. They are experienced in a state of full wakefulness and alertness, and the patient shows no significant changes in cognitive functions. Visual hallucinations often take the form of scenes involving diminutive (lilliputian) human figures or various small animals. Rare musical hallucinations typically feature religious songs. Patients with psychotic disorder due to a general medical condi-

tion and substance-induced psychotic disorder may act on their hallucinations. In alcohol-related hallucinations, threatening, critical, or insulting voices speak about the patients in the third person. They may tell the patients to harm either themselves or others; such patients are dangerous and are at significant risk for suicide or homicide. The patient may or may not believe that the hallucinations are real.

DELUSIONS

Secondary and substance-induced delusions are usually present in a state of full wakefulness. The patient experiences no change in the level of consciousness, although mild cognitive impairment may be observed. The delusions may be systematized or fragmentary, and their content may vary. Persecutory delusions are the most common. The person may appear confused, disheveled, or eccentric. Speech may be tangential or even incoherent. Hyperactivity and apathy may be observed. An associated dysphoric mood is thought to be common.

Differential Diagnosis

Psychotic disorder due to a general medical condition and substance-induced psychotic disorder need to be distinguished from delirium, in which the patient has a clouded sensorium; from dementia, in which the patient has major intellectual deficits; and from schizophrenia, in which the patient has other symptoms of thought disorder and impaired functioning. Psychotic disorder due to a general medical condition and substance-induced psychotic disorder must also be differentiated from psychotic mood disorders, in which other affective symptoms are pronounced.

Treatment

Treatment involves the identification of the general medical condition or the particular substance involved. At that point, treatment is directed toward the underlying condition and the immediate behavioral control of the patient. Hospitalization may be necessary to evaluate the patient completely and to ensure the patient's safety. Antipsychotic agents may be necessary for the immediate and short-term control of psychotic or aggressive behavior, although benzodiazepines may also be useful for the control of agitation and anxiety.

PSYCHOTIC DISORDERS IN DSM-IV APPENDIX

Postpsychotic Depressive Disorder of Schizophrenia

Depressive symptoms after a psychotic episode in a schizophrenic patient were categorized as an example of depressive disorder not otherwise specified in DSM-III-R. In DSM-IV the syndrome has been given its own diagnostic classification in an appendix.

EPIDEMIOLOGY

Without specific diagnostic criteria, the reported incidence of postpsychotic depression of schizophrenia varied widely from less than 10 to more than 70 percent. A reasonable estimate from the large studies is about 25 percent, although a definitive incidence figure must wait for controlled studies using the DSM-IV criteria.

PROGNOSTIC SIGNIFICANCE

The prognostic significance of the DSM-IV diagnosis is uncertain at this point, since studies using the official diagnostic category have not yet been conducted. Nonetheless, data from other studies show that patients with postpsychotic depressive disorder of schizophrenia are likely to have had poor premorbid adjustment, marked schizoid personality disorder traits, and an insidious onset of their psychotic symptoms. Patients with postpsychotic depressive disorder of schizophrenia are also likely to have first-degree relatives with mood disorders. Postpsychotic depressive disorder of schizophrenia has been inconsistently associated in the literature with a less favorable prognosis, a higher likelihood of relapse, and an increased incidence of suicide than is seen in schizophrenic patients without postpsychotic depressive disorder. Although some data indicate that schizophrenic patients with and without postpsychotic depressive disorder may differ in several biological variables—for example, in dexamethasone-suppression test (DST) and thyrotropin-releasing hormone (TRH) test results and in monoamine oxidase (MAO) activity—the validity and the usefulness of those tests in the diagnosis are still uncertain.

DIAGNOSIS AND DIFFERENTIAL DIAGNOSIS

The clinical boundaries of the diagnosis are hard to define operationally. The symptoms of postpsychotic depressive disorder of schizophrenia can closely resemble the symptoms of the residual phase of schizophrenia and the side effects of commonly used antipsychotic medications. It can also be difficult to distinguish the diagnosis from schizoaffective disorder, depressive type. The DSM-IV criteria specify that the criteria for a major depressive episode be met and that the symptoms occur only during the residual phase of schizophrenia. The symptoms cannot be substance-induced or part of a mood disorder due to a general medical condition.

A major criticism of the disorder is that it may be almost entirely due to the effects of antipsychotic medications. But several types of data indicate that antipsychotic medications cannot explain the entire extent of the symptoms. First, depressive symptoms are often present during the psychotic episode itself and, generally, decrease in severity, along with the psychotic symptoms, with successful antipsychotic treatment. Second, the severity of depressive symptoms in postpsychotic schizophrenic patients has not been correlated with the dosage of antipsychotic medication. Third, depressive symptoms have been frequently reported in nonmedicated schizophrenic patients who are recovering from psychotic episodes. Nonetheless, the clinician should not confuse the antipsychotic-induced side effects of akathisia and akinesia as symptoms of postpsychotic depressive disorder of schizophrenia.

TREATMENT

The use of antidepressants in the treatment of postpsychotic depressive disorder of schizophrenia has been reported in a number of studies. About half of the studies have reported positive effects, and the other half have reported no effects in the relief of the depressive symptoms. Antidepressant medications probably relieve depressive symptoms in some patients, but the mixed result of the studies reflect the current inability to distinguish those patients who will respond from those who will not.

Simple Deteriorative Disorder

Simple deteriorative disorder (simple schizophrenia) is a controversial diagnostic category. The use of the DSM-IV research criteria in subsequent studies will help either refute or support the reliability and the validity of the diagnostic category. The research criteria outline the gradual and progressive onset of symptoms that are similar to the deficit symptoms and the cognitive decline that can be seen in schizophrenia. Hallucinations and delusions are not part of the proposed symptom pattern.

Although few clinicians would say that they have not seen patients who meet the research criteria of simple schizophrenia, many researchers and clinicians have raised serious concerns about the diagnosis: (1) The term ''simple schizophrenia'' may incorrectly imply a close relation to schizophrenia and may unfairly stigmatize patients given the diagnosis. (2) The criteria may define an overinclusive group of patients, who may be better classified as having major depressive disorder, dysthymic disorder, substance abuse, or personality disorder. In fact, the overlap with those other diagnostic categories is obviously present and demands the use of variable and unpredictable clinical judgment in deciding among the diagnostic alternatives. (3) The lack of a scientific literature regarding the criteria limits their usefulness in terms of predicting prognosis or suggesting treatment.

The diagnostic category may eventually be shown to have prognostic and treatment implications. While clinicians are waiting for the appropriate studies to be completed, they should use the diagnosis with caution and forethought.

ATYPICAL PSYCHOTIC DISORDERS

Shared Psychotic Disorder

Shared psychotic disorder is a rare disorder and is perhaps better known as *folie à deux*. A patient is classified as having shared psychotic disorder when the symptoms developed during a long-term relationship with another person who had a similar psychotic syndrome before the onset of symptoms in the patient with shared psychotic disorder. The disorder most commonly involves two people—a dominant person (the inducer, the principal, or the primary patient) and a submissive person, who is the patient with shared psychotic disorder. Occasionally, cases involving more than two persons have been reported and have been called *folie à trois*, *folie à quatre*, *folie à cinq*, and so on. One case involving an entire family (*folie à famille*) involved 12 persons (*folie à douze*). Jules Baillarger first described the syndrome, calling it *folie à communiquée*, in 1860; however, the first description is commonly attributed to Ernest Charles Lasègue and Jules Falret, who described the condition in 1877 and gave it the name *folie à deux*. The syndrome has also been called communicated insanity, contagious insanity, infectious insanity, psychosis of association, and double insanity. Marandon de Montyel divided *folie à deux* into three groups (*folie imposée*, *folie simultanée*, and *folie communiquée*) and Heinz Lehmann added a fourth group, *folie induite*. *Folie imposée* is the most common and classic form of the disorder; the dominant person develops a delusional system and then progressively imposes that delusional system onto the usually younger and more passive person. In *folie simultanée* similar delusional systems develop independently in two persons who are closely associated. In contrast to *folie imposée*, in which separation often causes an improvement of the symptoms in the submissive person, separation of the two persons in *folie simultanée* does not lead to improvement in either person. In *folie communiquée* the dominant person is involved in the induction of a similar delusional system in the submissive person, but the submissive person develops his or her own delusional system, which does not remit after the separation of the two parties. In *folie induite* one delusional person has his or her delusions extended by taking on the delusions of a second person. The various types of *folie* are difficult to differentiate in practice and are of historical interest more than clinical interest.

EPIDEMIOLOGY

More than 95 percent of all cases of shared psychotic disorder involve two members of the same family. About a third of the cases involve two sisters; another third involve a husband and a wife or a mother and her child. Two brothers, a brother and a sister, and a father and his child have been reported less frequently. The dominant person is usually affected by schizophrenia or a similar psychotic disorder. In about 25 percent of all cases, the submissive person is affected with physical disabilities, including deafness, cerebrovascular diseases, or other disabilities that increase the submissive person's dependence on the dominant person. Shared psychotic disorder may be more common in low socioeconomic groups than in high socioeconomic groups. Shared psychotic disorder is more common in women than in men.

ETIOLOGY

The disorder has a psychosocial basis. Although the primary theory regarding the disorder is psychosocial, the fact that the affected persons are in the same family more than 95 percent of the time has also been interpreted to suggest a significant genetic component to the disorder. A modest amount of data indicates that affected persons often have a family history of schizophrenia.

The dominant member of the dyad has a preexisting psychotic disorder, almost always schizophrenia or a related psychotic disorder and rarely an affective or dementia-related psychosis. The dominant person is usually older, more intelligent, and better educated and possesses stronger personality traits than the submissive person, who is usually dependent on the dominant person. The two (or more) persons inevitably live together or have an extremely close personal relationship. The closeness is associated with a background of shared life experiences, common needs and hopes, and, often, a deep emotional rapport with each other. The relationship between the involved persons is usually somewhat or completely isolated from external societal and cultural influences.

The submissive person may be predisposed to a mental disorder and may have a history of a personality disorder with dependent or suggestible qualities. The submissive person may also have a history of depression, suspiciousness, and social isolation. The relationship between the two persons, although one of dependence, may also be characterized by ambivalence, with deeply held feelings of both love and hate. The dominant person may be moved to induce the delusional system in the submissive person as a mechanism for maintaining contact with another person in spite of the dominant person's psychosis. The dominant person's psychotic symptoms may develop in the submis-

Table 8.1–3.   Diagnostic Criteria for Shared Psychotic Disorder

A. A delusion develops in an individual in the context of a close relationship with another person(s), who has an already-established delusion.

B. The delusion is similar in content to that of the person who already has the established delusion.

C. The disturbance is not better accounted for by another psychotic disorder (e.g., schizophrenia) or a mood disorder with psychotic features and is not due to the direct physiological effects of a substance (e.g., a drug of abuse, a medication) or a general medical condition.

Table from DSM-IV, *Diagnostic and Statistical Manual of Mental Disorders*, ed 4. Copyright American Psychiatric Association, Washington, 1994. Used with permission.

sive person through the process of identification. By adopting the psychotic symptoms of the dominant person, the submissive person gains the acceptance of the dominant person. However, the admiration the submissive person has for the dominant person may evolve into hatred, which the submissive person considers unacceptable, and so that hatred is directed inward, often resulting in depression and sometimes suicide.

DIAGNOSIS

The DSM-IV criteria for shared psychotic disorder (Table 8.1–3) include the development of delusions in a person who has a close relationship with a person who already has a similar delusional system. The person with shared psychotic disorder does not have a preexisting psychotic disorder.

CLINICAL FEATURES

The key symptom is the unquestioning acceptance of the delusions of another person. The delusions themselves are often in the realm of possibility and usually not as bizarre as those seen in many patients with schizophrenia. The content of the delusions is often persecutory or hypochondriacal. Symptoms of a coexisting personality disorder may be present, but signs and symptoms that meet the diagnostic criteria for schizophrenia, mood disorders, and delusional disorder are absent. The patient may have ideation about suicide or pacts regarding homicide; that information must be elicited during the clinical interview.

DIFFERENTIAL DIAGNOSIS

Malingering, factitious disorder with predominantly psychological signs and symptoms, psychotic disorder due to a general medical condition, and substance-induced psychotic disorder need to be considered in the differential diagnosis of the condition. The boundary between shared psychotic disorder and generic group madness, such as the Jonestown massacre in Guyana, is unclear.

COURSE AND PROGNOSIS

The nature of the disorder suggests that separation of the submissive person, the person who has shared psychotic disorder, from the dominant person should result in the resolution and the disappearance of the submissive person's psychotic symptoms. In fact, this happens in perhaps only 10 percent and probably no more than 40 percent of all cases. Often, the submissive person requires treatment with antipsychotic drugs, just as the dominant person needs antipsychotic drugs for his or her psychotic disorder. Because the persons almost always come from the same family, they usually move back together after release from a hospital.

TREATMENT

The first step in treatment is the separation of the affected person from the source of the delusions, the dominant partner. The patient may need significant support to compensate for that loss. The patient with shared psychotic disorder should be observed for the remission of the delusional symptoms. Antipsychotic drugs can be used if the delusional symptoms have not abated in one or two weeks.

Psychotherapy with nondelusional members of the patient's family should be undertaken, and psychotherapy with both the patient with shared psychotic disorder and the dominant partner may be indicated later in the course of treatment. In addition, the mental disorder of the dominant partner should be treated.

To prevent the recurrence of the syndrome, the clinician must use family therapy and social support to modify the family dynamics and to prevent the redevelopment of the syndrome. It is often useful to make sure that the family unit is exposed to input from outside sources to decrease the family's isolation.

Other Atypical Psychotic Disorders

AUTOSCOPIC PSYCHOSIS

The characteristic symptom of autoscopic psychosis is a visual hallucination of all or part of the person's own body. The hallucinatory perception, which is called a phantom, is usually colorless and transparent and is perceived as though appearing in a mirror, since the phantom imitates the person's movements. The phantom tends to appear suddenly and without warning.

Epidemiology

Autoscopy is a rate phenomenon. Some persons have an autoscopic experience only once or a few times; other persons have the experience more often. Although the data are limited, sex, age, heredity, and intelligence do not appear related to the occurrence of the syndrome.

Etiology

The cause of the autoscopic phenomenon is unknown. A biological hypothesis is that abnormal, episodic activity in areas of the temporoparietal lobes is involved with one's sense of self, perhaps combined with abnormal activity in parts of the visual cortex. Psychological theories have associated the syndrome with personalities characterized by imagination, visual sensitivity, and, possibly, narcissistic personality disorder traits. Such persons may be likely to experience autoscopic phenomena during periods of stress.

Course and Prognosis

The classic descriptions of the phenomenon indicate that usually the syndrome is neither progressive nor incapacitating. The affected persons usually maintain some emotional distance from the phenomenon, possibly suggesting a specific neuroanatomical lesion. Rarely do the symptoms reflect the onset of schizophrenia or other psychotic disorders.

CAPGRAS'S SYNDROME

The characteristic symptom of Capgras's syndrome is the delusion that other persons, usually persons closely related to the affected person, have been replaced by exact doubles, who are imposters. Those imposters assume the roles of the persons

they impersonate and behave identically. The syndrome was originally described in 1923 by the French psychiatrist Jean Marie Joseph Capgras, who called it *l'illusion des sosies*, which means the illusion of doubles.

Epidemiology

This rare syndrome is more frequently occurring in women than in men. The condition is sometimes classified as a delusional disorder, although it may also be a symptom of schizophrenia in some patients.

Etiology

Capgras explained the nature of the delusion as a result of feelings of strangeness, combined with a paranoid tendency to distrust. A biological hypothesis is that it is a neurobiological dysfunction in the brain areas that usually relate perceptions to the recognition of persons. A psychoanalytic hypothesis posits that what the patients feel about the persons with whom they are confronted (for example, anger or fear) is displaced to the doubles, who are imposters and, therefore, may be safely and righteously rejected.

Prognosis and Treatment

The symptoms of Capgras's syndrome respond to antipsychotic treatment. However, when patients have Capgras's syndrome as the sole symptom of their psychotic disorder, the clinician should do an extensive neuropsychological workup to identify any organic lesions that may be causing the syndrome.

COTARD'S SYNDROME

In the 19th century the French psychiatrist Jules Cotard described several patients who suffered from a syndrome referred to as *délire de négation*. The syndrome is sometimes called nihilistic delusional disorder. Patients with the syndrome complain of having lost not only possessions, status, and strength but also their heart, blood, and intestines. The world beyond them is reduced to nothingness.

Epidemiology

The syndrome is usually seen as a precursor to a schizophrenic or depressive episode. It is relatively rare; with the common use today of antipsychotic drugs, the syndrome is seen even less frequently than in the past.

Etiology

In its pure form the syndrome is seen in patients suffering from depression, schizophrenia, and psychotic disorder due to a general medical condition, often associated with dementia.

Prognosis and Treatment

The syndrome usually lasts only a few days or weeks and responds to treatment directed at the underlying disorder. Long-term forms of the syndrome are usually associated with dementing syndromes, such as dementia of the Alzheimer's type.

ATYPICAL SCHIZOPHRENIA

A particular form of schizophrenia was described by R. Gjessing and called periodic catatonia. Patients affected with the disorder have periodic bouts of stuporous or excited catatonia, which Gjessing believed were related to metabolic shifts in nitrogen balance. The syndrome is rarely seen, responds well to standard antipsychotic agents, and is prevented by maintenance medication.

CULTURE-BOUND PSYCHOTIC SYNDROMES

The literature describes a variety of culture-bound psychotic syndromes. In general, the culture-bound psychotic syndromes can be fit into one or another DSM-IV diagnosis, including psychotic disorder not otherwise specified. However, the existence of the syndromes raises two possibilities. First, if the syndromes are unique and limited to specific cultures, they raise the possibility that specific cultural or biological factors are contributing to the psychosis. Second, if the syndromes are forms of standard diagnoses—schizophrenia, for example—their existence suggests that the content of their delusions and hallucinations can be strongly influenced by the society and the culture.

Amok

The Malayan word ''amok'' means to engage furiously in battle. The amok syndrome consists of a sudden, unprovoked outburst of wild rage that causes affected persons to run about madly, indiscriminately attacking and maiming any persons and animals in their way. The savage homicidal attack is generally preceded by a period of preoccupation, brooding, and mild depression. After the attack, the person feels exhausted, has no memory of the attack, and often commits suicide. The Malayan natives also refer to the attack as *mata elap* (darkened eye). Examples of persons with a syndrome similar to amok in the United States are commonly reported in the newspapers. Often, those persons are suffering from schizophrenia, a bipolar disorder, or a depressive disorder. In other cases, the cause may be a general medical condition, such as epilepsy or another brain lesion. A cultural explanation of the syndrome is this: in a culture that imposes strict restrictions on adolescents and adults but allows children free rein to express their aggression, some persons may be especially prone to psychopathological reactions of the amok type. The belief in magical possession by demons and evil spirits, as is the case in some primitive cultures, may be another cultural factor that contributes to the development of the amok syndrome.

The only immediate treatment consists of overpowering amok persons and gaining complete physical control over them. The attack is usually over within a few hours. Afterward, the patient may require treatment for a chronic psychotic disorder, which may have been the underlying cause.

Koro

Koro is characterized by the patient's delusion that his penis is shrinking and may disappear into his abdomen and that he may die. The koro syndrome occurs among the people of Southeast Asia and in some areas of China, where it is known as *suk-yeong*. A corresponding disorder in women involves complaints of the shrinkage of the vulva, the labia, and the breasts. Occasional cases of koro syndrome among people belonging to a Western culture have been reported. Koro has usually been thought of as a psychogenic disorder resulting from the interaction of cultural, social, and psychodynamic factors in especially predisposed persons. Culturally elaborated fears about nocturnal emission, masturbation, and sexual overindulgence seem to give rise to the condition. Alternatively, the disorder may be seen as a delusional disorder or as a symptom of another psychotic disorder.

Patients have been treated with psychotherapy, antipsychotic drugs, and, in a few cases, electroconvulsive therapy. As with other psychiatric disorders, the prognosis is related to the patient's premorbid personality adjustment and to any associated pathology. Some cultures prescribe fellatio as a cure.

Pibloktoq

Occurring among Eskimos and sometimes called Arctic hysteria, pibloktoq is characterized by attacks lasting from one to two hours, during which patients (usually women) begin to scream and to tear off and destroy their clothing. While imitating the cry of some animal or bird, the patients may throw themselves on the snow or run wildly about on the ice, although the temperature may be well below zero. After the attack, the persons appear normal and usually have no memory of the episode. The Eskimos are reluctant to touch afflicted persons during the attacks because they believe that the attacks involve evil spirits. Pibloktoq is almost certainly a hysterical state of a dissociative disorder. It has become much less frequent than it used to be among Eskimos.

Wihtigo

Wihtigo or windigo psychosis is a psychiatric disorder confined to the Cree, Ojibwa, and Salteaux Indians of North America. Affected persons believe that they may be transformed into a *wihtigo*, a giant monster that eats human flesh. During times of starvation, affected persons may have the delusion that they have been transformed into a *wihtigo*, and they may feel and express a craving for human flesh. Because of the patient's belief in witchcraft and in the possibility of such a transformation, symptoms concerning the alimentary tract, such as loss of appetite and nausea from trivial causes, may sometimes cause the patient to become greatly excited for fear of being transformed into a *wihtigo*.

PSYCHOTIC DISORDER NOT OTHERWISE SPECIFIED

This DSM-IV category is used for patients who have psychotic symptoms (for example, delusions, hallucinations, and disorganized speech and behavior) but who do not meet the diagnostic criteria for other specifically defined psychotic disorders. In some cases the diagnosis of psychotic disorder not otherwise specified may be used when not enough information is available to make a specific diagnosis. DSM-IV has listed some examples of the diagnosis to help guide clinicians (Table 8.1–4).

Postpartum Psychosis

Postpartum psychosis, an example of psychotic disorder not otherwise specified, is a syndrome most often characterized by depression, delusions, and thoughts by the mother of harming either the infant or herself. Such ideation of suicide or infanticide must be carefully monitored, since some mothers have acted on those ideas. Most of the available data suggest a close relation between postpartum psychosis and the mood disorders, particularly bipolar disorders and major depressive disorder.

EPIDEMIOLOGY

The incidence of postpartum psychosis is about 1 per 1,000 childbirths, although some reports have suggested that the incidence may be

Table 8.1–4. Diagnostic Criteria for Psychotic Disorder Not Otherwise Specified

This category includes psychotic symptomatology (i.e., delusions, hallucinations, disorganized speech, grossly disorganized or catatonic behavior) about which there is inadequate information to make a specific diagnosis or about which there is contradictory information, or disorders with psychotic symptoms that do not meet the criteria for any specific psychotic disorder.

Examples include:

1. Postpartum psychosis that does not meet criteria for mood disorder with psychotic features, brief psychotic disorder, psychotic disorder due to a general medical condition, or substance-induced psychotic disorder
2. Psychotic symptoms that have lasted for less than 1 month but that have not yet remitted, so that the criteria for brief psychotic disorder are not met
3. Persistent auditory hallucinations in the absence of any other features
4. Persistent nonbizarre delusions with periods of overlapping mood episodes that have been present for a substantial portion of the delusional disturbance
5. Situations in which the clinician has concluded that a psychotic disorder is present, but is unable to determine whether it is primary, due to a general medical condition, or substance induced

Table from DSM-IV, *Diagnostic and Statistical Manual of Mental Disorders*, ed 4. Copyright American Psychiatric Association, Washington, 1994. Used with permission.

---

as high as 2 per 1,000 childbirths. About 50 to 60 percent of the affected women have just had their first child, and about 50 percent of the cases involved deliveries associated with nonpsychiatric perinatal complications. About 50 percent of the affected women have a family history of mood disorders. Although postpartum psychosis is fundamentally a disorder of women, some rare cases affect fathers. In those rare instances the husband may feel displaced by the child and may be competitive for the mother's love and attention. However, the father probably has a coexisting major mental disorder that has been exacerbated by the stress of fatherhood.

ETIOLOGY

The most robust data indicate that an episode of postpartum psychosis is essentially an episode of a mood disorder, usually a bipolar disorder but possibly a depressive disorder. Relatives of persons with postpartum psychosis have an incidence of mood disorders that is similar to the incidence in relatives of persons with mood disorders. Schizoaffective disorder and delusional disorder are rarely appropriate diagnoses. The validity of those diagnoses is usually verified in the year after the birth, when as many as two thirds of the patients may have a second episode of the underlying disorder. The delivery process may best be seen as a nonspecific stress, perhaps through a major hormonal mechanism, that causes the development of an episode of a major mood disorder.

A few instances of postpartum psychosis result from a general medical condition associated with perinatal events, such as infection, drug intoxication—for example, scopolamine and meperidine (Demerol)—toxemia, and blood loss. The sudden fall in estrogen and progesterone concentrations immediately after delivery may also contribute to the disorder. However, treatment with those hormones has not been effective.

Some investigators have written that a purely psychosocial causal mechanism is suggested by the preponderance of primiparous mothers and an association between postpartum psychosis and recent stressful events. Psychodynamic studies of postpartum mental illness have suggested the presence of conflicted feelings in the mother about her mothering experience. Some women may not have wanted to become pregnant; others may feel trapped in unhappy marriages by motherhood. Marital discord during pregnancy has been associated with an increased incidence of illness, although the discord may be related to the slow development of mood disorder symptoms in the mother.

DIAGNOSIS

Specific diagnostic criteria are not included in DSM-IV. The diagnosis can be made when psychosis occurs in close temporal association with childbirth, although a DSM-IV diagnosis of a mood disorder should be considered in the differential diagnosis. Characteristic symptoms include delusions, cognitive deficits, motility disturbances, mood abnormalities, and occasionally hallucinations. The content of the psychotic material revolves around mothering and pregnancy. DSM-IV also allows for the diagnosis of brief psychotic disorder with postpartum onset (see Section 8.5).

CLINICAL FEATURES

The symptoms of postpartum psychosis can often begin within days of the delivery, although the mean time to onset is two to three weeks and almost always within eight weeks of delivery. Characteristically, the patient begins to complain of fatigue, insomnia, and restlessness and may have episodes of tearfulness and emotional lability. Later, suspiciousness, confusion, incoherence, irrational statements, and obsessive concerns about the baby's health and welfare may be present. Delusions may be present in 50 percent of all patients and hallucinations in about 25 percent. Complaints regarding the inability to move, stand, or walk are also common.

The patient may have feelings of not wanting to care for the baby, of not loving the baby, and, in some cases, of wanting to do harm to the baby, to self, or to both. Delusional material may involve the idea that the baby is dead or defective. The patient may deny the birth and may express thoughts of being unmarried, virginal, persecuted, influenced, or perverse. Hallucinations may occur with similar content and may involve voices telling the patient to kill the baby.

DIFFERENTIAL DIAGNOSIS

As with any psychotic disorder, the clinician should consider the possibility of either a psychotic disorder due to a general medical condition or a substance-induced psychotic disorder. Potential general medical conditions include hypothyroidism and Cushing's syndrome. Substance-induced psychotic disorder may be associated with the use of pain medications—for example, pentazocine (Talwin)—or antihypertensive drugs during the pregnancy. Other potential medical causes include infections, toxemia, and neoplasms. Women with a history of a mood disorder should be classified as having recurrences of that disorder. Postpartum psychosis should not be confused with the so-called postpartum blues, a normal condition that occurs in up to 50 percent of women after childbirth. Postpartum blues is self-limited, lasts only a few days, and is characterized by tearfulness, fatigue, anxiety, and irritability that begin shortly after childbirth and lessen in severity over the course of a week.

COURSE AND PROGNOSIS

The onset of florid psychotic symptoms is usually preceded by prodromal signs, such as insomnia, restlessness, agitation, lability of mood, and mild cognitive deficits. Once the psychosis occurs, the patient may be a danger to herself or to her newborn, depending on the content of her delusional system and her degree of agitation. In one study, 5 percent of the patients committed suicide, and 4 percent committed infanticide. A favorable outcome is associated with a good premorbid adjustment and a supportive family network.

Since an episode of postpartum psychosis is most likely an episode of a mood disorder, the course of the syndrome is similar to that seen in patients with mood disorders. Specifically, mood disorders are usually episodic disorders and patients with postpartum psychosis often experience another episode of symptoms within a year or two of the birth. Subsequent pregnancies are associated with an increased risk of having another episode.

TREATMENT

Postpartum psychosis is a psychiatric emergency. Antidepressants and lithium (Eskalith), sometimes in combination, are the treatments of choice. No pharmacological agents should be prescribed to a woman who is breast-feeding. Suicidal patients may require transfer to a psychiatric unit to help prevent a suicide attempt.

It is usually advantageous for the mother to have contact with her baby if she so desires. But the visits must be closely supervised, especially if the mother is preoccupied with doing harm to the infant. Psychotherapy is indicated after the period of acute psychosis is past. Therapy is usually directed at the conflictual areas that have become evident during the evaluation. Therapy may involve helping the patient accept and be comfortable with the mothering role. Changes in environmental factors may also be indicated. Increased support from the husband and other persons in the environment may help reduce the woman's stress. Most studies report high rates of recovery from the acute illness.

References

Gaines A D: Culture-specific delusions: Sense and nonsense in cultural context. Psychiatr Clin North Am *18* : 281, 1995.

Manshreck T C: Delusional disorder and shared psychotic disorder. In *Comprehensive Textbook of Psychiatry*, ed 6, H I Kaplan, B J Sadock, editors, p 1031. Williams & Wilkins, Baltimore, 1995.

Mezzich J E, Keh-Ming L: Acute and Transient Psychotic Disorders and Culture-Bound Syndromes. In *Comprehensive Textbook of Psychiatry*, ed 6, H I Kaplan, B J Sadock, editors, p 1049. Williams & Wilkins, Baltimore, 1995.

Parry B L: Postpartum Psychiatric Syndromes. In *Comprehensive Textbook of Psychiatry*, ed 6, H I Kaplan, B J Sadock, editors, p 1059. Williams & Wilkins, Baltimore, 1995.

Popkin M K, Tucker G J: "Secondary" and drug-induced mood, anxiety psychotic, catatonic, and personality disorders: A review of the literature. J Neuropsychiatry Clin Neurosci *4* : 369, 1992.

Tsuang D, Coryell W: An 8-year follow-up of patients with DSM-III-R psychotic depression, schizoaffective disorder, and schizophrenia. Am J Psychiatry *150* : 1182, 1993.

8.2 SCHIZOPHRENIFORM DISORDER

Schizophreniform disorder is identical in every respect to schizophrenia except that its symptoms last at least one month but less than six months. Patients with schizophreniform disorder return to their baseline level of functioning once the schizophreniform disorder has resolved. In contrast, for a patient to meet the diagnostic criteria for schizophrenia, the symptoms must have been present for at least six months.

EPIDEMIOLOGY

The incidence, the prevalence, and the sex ratio of schizophreniform disorder have not yet been reported in the literature. Some clinicians have the impression that the disorder is most common in adolescents and young adults, and most investigators believe that the disorder is less than half as common as schizophrenia.

Family History

Several studies have shown that the relatives of patients with schizophreniform disorder are at high risk of having psychiatric disorders; however, the distribution of the disorders differs from the distribution seen in the relatives of patients with schizophrenia and bipolar disorders. Specifically, the relatives of patients with schizophreniform disorders are more likely to have mood disorders than are the relatives of patients with schizophrenia. In addition, the relatives of patients with schizophreniform disorder are more likely to have a diagnosis of a psychotic mood disorder than are the relatives of patients with bipolar disorders.

ETIOLOGY

As in all the classic psychotic disorders, the cause of schizophreniform disorder is not known. As Gabriel Langfeldt noted in 1939, patients with the diagnostic label are likely to be heterogeneous. In general, some patients have a disorder similar to schizophrenia, whereas others have a disorder similar to a mood disorder. Because of their generally good outcome, the disorder probably has similarities to the episodic nature of mood disorders. However, some data suggest a close relation to schizophrenia.

In support of the relation to mood disorders, several studies have shown that schizophreniform disorder patients, as a group, have more affective symptoms (especially mania) and a better outcome than do schizophrenic patients. Also, the increased presence of mood disorders in the relatives of patients with schizophreniform disorder indicates a relation to mood disorders. Thus, the biological and epidemiological data are most consistent with the hypothesis that the current diagnostic category defines a group of patients, some of whom have a disorder similar to schizophrenia and others of whom have a disorder similar to a mood disorder.

Brain Imaging

As for schizophrenia, a relative activation deficit in the inferior prefrontal region of the brain while the patient is performing a region-specific psychological task (the Wisconsin Card-Sorting Test) has been reported in schizophreniform disorder patients. In one study the deficit was limited to the left hemisphere. That study also found impaired striatal activity suppression, also limited to the left hemisphere, during the activation procedure. The data can be interpreted to suggest a physiological similarity between the psychosis of schizophrenia and the psychosis of schizophreniform disorder. Additional central nervous system (CNS) factors, as yet unidentified, may lead to either the long-term course of schizophrenia or the foreshortened course of schizophreniform disorder.

Some data suggest that patients with schizophreniform disorder may have enlarged cerebral ventricles, as determined by computed tomography (CT) and magnetic resonance imaging (MRI). However, other data indicate that, unlike the enlargement seen in schizophrenia, the ventricular enlargement in schizophreniform disorder is not correlated with outcome measures or other biological measures.

Other Biological Measures

Although brain imaging studies point to a similarity between schizophreniform disorder and schizophrenia, at least one study of electrodermal activity has suggested a difference. Schizophrenic patients born during the winter and spring months (a period of high risk for the birth of schizophrenic patients) had hyporesponsive skin conductances, but that association was absent in patients with schizophreniform disorder. The significance and the meaning of that single study are difficult to interpret; however, the results do suggest caution in assuming similarity between schizophrenic patients and schizophreniform disorder patients. Data from at least one study of eye tracking

Table 8.2–1. Diagnostic Criteria for Schizophreniform Disorder

A. Criteria A, D, and E of schizophrenia are met.

B. An episode of the disorder (including prodromal, active, and residual phases) lasts at least one month but less than six months. (When the diagnosis must be made without waiting for recovery, it should be qualified as ''provisional.'')

Specify if:
Without good prognostic features
With good prognostic features as evidenced by two (or more)/ of the following:

(1) onset of prominent psychotic symptoms within four weeks of the first noticeable change in usual behavior or functioning
(2) confusion or perplexity at the height of the psychotic episode
(3) good premorbid social and occupational functioning
(4) absence of blunted or flat affect

Table from DSM-IV, *Diagnostic and Statistical Manual of Mental Disorders*, ed 4. Copyright American Psychiatric Association, Washington, 1994. Used with permission.

in schizophreniform disorder patients and schizophrenic patients also indicate that the two groups may differ in some biological measures.

DIAGNOSIS

The diagnostic criteria for schizophreniform disorder in the fourth edition of *Diagnostic and Statistical Manual of Mental Disorders* (DSM-IV) (Table 8.2–1) include three criteria identical to those for schizophrenia. The first criterion is the presence of active symptoms (for example, delusions, hallucinations, and flat affects) for one month. The next two criteria are exclusion criteria for schizoaffective disorder, mood disorder with psychotic features, substance-related disorders, and mental disorders due to a general medical condition. The other criteria for schizophreniform disorder specify that the entire episode, including the prodromal and residual phases, last at least one month but less than six months.

The diagnosis of provisional schizophreniform disorder is made while waiting to see if the symptoms resolve. A diagnosis of schizophreniform disorder is more accurate than a diagnosis of schizophrenia when the clinician is unable to obtain a reliable history from psychotic patients regarding the duration of their symptoms. However, a patient's personal history of prodromal symptoms may mislead the physician away from a correct diagnosis of schizophrenia; a patient's personal history of affective symptoms may cause the physician to miss a diagnosis of a mood disorder or schizoaffective disorder.

Prognostic Subtypes

DSM-IV allows for the specification of the presence or the absence of good prognostic features (see Table 8.2–1). The good prognostic features include a rapid onset, a degree of cognitive impairment, good premorbid adjustment, and the absence of deficit affective symptoms. One study found that schizophreniform disorder patients with poor prognoses exhibit affective flattening, alogia (inability to speak), and poor eye contact with examiners.

CLINICAL FEATURES

The clinical signs and symptoms and the mental status examination for a patient with schizophreniform disorders are identical to those for a patient with schizophrenia. However, the presence of affective symptoms may predict a favorable course. Alternatively, a flat or blunted affect may predict an unfavorable course.

DIFFERENTIAL DIAGNOSIS

The differential diagnosis for schizophreniform disorder is identical to that for schizophrenia. Factitious disorder with predominantly psychological signs and symptoms, psychotic disorder due to a general medical condition, and substance-induced psychotic disorder must be ruled out. A general medical condition that should be considered is infection with human immunodeficiency virus (HIV). Temporal lobe epilepsy, CNS tumors, and cerebrovascular diseases can also be associated with relatively short-lived psychotic episodes. There has also been an increasing frequency of reports of psychosis associated with the use of anabolic steroids by young men who are attempting to build up their musculature to perform better in athletic endeavors.

COURSE AND PROGNOSIS

The prognosis of schizophreniform disorder varies, a fact addressed in DSM-IV by distinguishing patients with and without good prognostic features. The good prognostic features noted in DSM-IV were gathered from the literature. However, the validity of those features has been questioned. Confusion or perplexity at the height of the psychotic episode is the feature best correlated with a good outcome. The validity of the other features remains uncertain.

Beyond the predictors of a good prognosis in DSM-IV, the shorter the period of illness, the better the prognosis is likely to be. There is a significant risk of suicide in patients with schizophreniform disorder. They are likely to have a period of depression after the psychotic period, and psychotherapy addressed to helping the patient understand the psychotic episode is likely to improve the prognosis and speed the patient's recovery.

By definition, schizophreniform disorder resolves within six months with a return to baseline mental functioning. Studies have suggested that the requirement for at least six months of symptoms in schizophrenia weighs heavily toward a poor prognosis; therefore, schizophreniform disorder patients have a better prognosis than do most schizophrenic patients.

TREATMENT

Hospitalization is often necessary in the treatment of patients with schizophreniform disorder. Hospitalization allows for an effective assessment, treatment, and supervision of the patient's behavior. The psychotic symptoms can usually be treated by a three- to six-month course of antipsychotic drugs. Several studies have shown that patients with schizophreniform disorder respond much more rapidly to antipsychotic treatment than do patients with schizophrenia. One study found that about three fourths of the schizophreniform disorder patients, in comparison with only one fifth of the schizophrenic patients, responded to antipsychotic medications within eight days. Electroconvulsive therapy (ECT) may be indicated for some patients, especially those with marked catatonic or depressed features. A trial of lithium, carbamazepine (Tegretol), or valproate (Depakene) may be warranted for treatment and prophylaxis if a patient has a recurrent episode. Psychotherapy is usually necessary to help patients integrate the psychotic experience into their understanding of their minds, brains, and lives.

References

Cuesta M J, Peralta V: Does formal thought disorder differ among patients with schizophrenic, schizophreniform and manic schizoaffective disorders? Schizophr Res 10: 151, 1993.

Rao M L, Gross G, Halaris A, Huber G, Marler M, Strebel B, Braunig P: Hyperdopaminergia in schizophreniform psychosis: A chronobiological study. Psychiatry Res 47: 187, 1993.

Rubin P, Holm S, Friberg L, Videbech P, Andersen H S, Bendsen B B, Strømsøn N, Larsen J K, Lassen N A, Hemmingsen R: Altered modulation of prefrontal and subcortical brain activity in newly diagnosed schizophrenia and schizophreniform disorder: A regional cerebral blood flow study. Arch Gen Psychiatry 48: 987, 1991.

Sautter F, McDermott B, Garver D: The course of DSM-III-R schizophreniform disorder. J Clin Psychol 49: 339, 1993.

Siris S G, Lavin, M R: Schizoaffective disorder, schizophreniform disorder, and brief psychotic disorder. In Comprehensive Textbook of Psychiatry, ed 6, H I Kaplan, B J Sadock, editors, p 1019. Williams & Wilkins, Baltimore, 1995.

8.3 SCHIZOAFFECTIVE DISORDER

As the term implies, schizoaffective disorder has features of both schizophrenia and affective disorders (now called mood disorders). The diagnostic criteria for schizoaffective disorder have changed over time, mostly as a reflection of changes in the diagnostic criteria for schizophrenia and the mood disorders. Whatever the mutable nature of the diagnosis, it remains the best diagnosis for patients whose clinical syndrome would be distorted if it were considered as only schizophrenia or only a mood disorder.

EPIDEMIOLOGY

The lifetime prevalence of schizoaffective disorder is less than 1 percent, possibly in the range of 0.5 to 0.8 percent. However, those figures are estimates, since the various studies of schizoaffective disorder have used varying diagnostic criteria. In clinical practice a preliminary diagnosis of schizoaffective disorder is frequently used when the clinician is uncertain of the diagnosis.

Gender Differences

The literature describing gender differences among patients with schizoaffective disorder is limited. However, some preliminary observations may eventually be replicated in subsequent studies. The prevalence of the disorder has been reported to be lower in men than in women, particularly married women; the age of onset for women is later than the age for men, as in schizophrenia. Men with schizoaffective disorder are likely to exhibit antisocial behavior and to have marked flatness or inappropriateness of affect.

ETIOLOGY

The cause of schizoaffective disorder is unknown, but four conceptual models have been advanced. (1) Schizoaffective disorder may be either a type of schizophrenia or a type of mood disorder. (2) Schizoaffective disorder may be the simultaneous expression on schizophrenia and a mood disorder. (3) Schizoaffective disorder may be a distinct third type of psychosis, one that is not related to either schizophrenia or a mood disorder. (4) The most likely possibility is that schizoaffective disorder is a heterogenous group of disorders encompassing all the first three possibilities.

Studies designed to explore those possibilities have examined family histories, biological markers, short-term treatment responses, and long-term outcomes. Most of the studies have considered patients with schizoaffective disorder as a homogeneous group. Recent studies have examined the bipolar and depressive types of schizoaffective disorder separately.

Although much of the family and genetic work done to study schizoaffective disorder is based on the premise that schizophrenia and the mood disorders are completely separate entities, some data suggest that schizophrenia and the mood disorders may be related genetically. Some confusion that arises in the family studies of schizoaffective disorder patients may reflect the nonabsolute distinction between the two primary disorders. Not surprisingly, therefore, studies of the relatives of patients with schizoaffective disorder have reported inconsistent results. An increased prevalence of schizophrenia is not found among the relatives of probands with schizoaffective disorder, bipolar type; however, the relatives of patients with schizoaffective disorder, depressive type, may be at higher risk for schizophrenia than for a mood disorder.

Depending on the type of schizoaffective disorder studied, an increased prevalence of schizophrenia or mood disorders may be found in the relatives of schizoaffective disorder probands. The possibility that schizoaffective disorder is distinct from schizophrenia and mood disorders is not supported by the observation that only a small percentage of the relatives of schizoaffective disorder probands have schizoaffective disorder.

As a group, schizoaffective disorder patients have a better prognosis than do patients with schizophrenia and a worse prognosis than do patients with mood disorders. As a group, schizoaffective disorder patients respond to lithium (Eskalith) and tend to have a nondeteriorating course.

Consolidation of Data

One reasonable conclusion from the available data is that patients with schizoaffective disorder are a heterogenous group: some have schizophrenia with prominent affective symptoms, others have a mood disorder with prominent schizophrenic symptoms, and a third group have a distinct clinical syndrome. The hypothesis that schizoaffective disorder patients have both schizophrenia and a mood disorder is untenable, because the calculated co-occurrence of the two disorders is much lower than the incidence of schizoaffective disorder.

CLINICAL FEATURES

The clinical signs and symptoms of schizoaffective disorder include all the signs and symptoms of schizophrenia, manic episodes, and depressive disorders. The schizophrenic and mood disorder symptoms can present together or in an alternating fashion. The course can vary from one of exacerbations and remissions to one of a long-term deteriorating course.

Many researchers and clinicians have speculated about the mood-incongruent psychotic features; the psychotic content (that is, hallucinations or delusions) is not consistent with the

Table 8.3–1. Diagnostic Criteria for Schizoaffective Disorder

A. An uninterrupted period of illness during which, at some time, there is either a major depressive episode, a manic episode, or a mixed episode concurrent with symptoms that meet criterion A for schizophrenia.

   Note: The major depressive episode must include criterion A1: depressed mood.

B. During the same period of illness, there have been delusions or hallucinations for at least 2 weeks in the absence of prominent mood symptoms.

C. Symptoms that meet criteria for a mood episode are present for a substantial portion of the total duration of the active and residual periods of the illness.

D. The disturbance is not due to the direct physiological effects of a substance (e.g., drug of abuse, a medication) or a general medical condition.

Specify type:
   Bipolar type: if the disturbance includes a manic or a mixed episode (or a manic or a mixed episode and major depressive episodes)
   Depressive type: if the disturbance only includes major depressive episodes

Table from DSM-IV, *Diagnostic and Statistical Manual of Mental Disorders*, ed 4. Copyright American Psychiatric Association, Washington, 1994. Used with permission.

prevailing mood. In general, the presence of mood-incongruent psychotic features in a mood disorder is likely to be an indicator of a poor prognosis. That association is likely to be true for schizoaffective disorder as well, although the data are limited.

DIAGNOSIS

The primary diagnostic criteria for schizoaffective disorder (Table 8.3–1) are that the patient has met the diagnostic criteria for a major depressive episode or a manic episode concurrently with meeting the diagnostic criteria for the active phase of schizophrenia. In addition, the patient must have had delusions or hallucinations for at least two weeks in the absence of prominent mood disorder symptoms. The mood disorder symptoms must also be present for a substantial part of the active and residual psychotic periods. Essentially, the criteria are written to help the clinician avoid diagnosing a mood disorder with psychotic features as schizoaffective disorder.

The fourth edition of *Diagnostic and Statistical Manual of Mental Disorders* (DSM-IV) also allows the clinician to specify whether the patient has schizoaffective disorder, bipolar type, or schizoaffective disorder, depressive type. A patient is classified as having the bipolar type if the present episode is of the manic type or a mixed episode or a manic or a mixed episode and major depressive episodes. Otherwise, the patient is classified as having the depressive type.

DIFFERENTIAL DIAGNOSIS

All the conditions listed in the differential diagnoses of schizophrenia and mood disorders need to be considered in the differential diagnosis of schizoaffective disorder. Patients treated with steroids, abusers of amphetamine and phencyclidine (PCP), and some patients with temporal lobe epilepsy are particularly likely to present with concurrent schizophrenic and affective symptoms.

The psychiatric differential diagnosis also includes all the

possibilities usually considered for schizophrenia and mood disorders. In clinical practice, psychosis at the time of the presentation may hinder the detection of current or past mood disorder symptoms. Therefore, the clinician may delay making a final psychiatric diagnosis until the most acute symptoms of psychosis have been controlled.

COURSE AND PROGNOSIS

As a group, patients with schizoaffective disorder have prognoses intermediate between prognoses of patients with schizophrenia and the prognoses of patients with mood disorders. As a group, patients with schizoaffective disorder have much worse prognoses than do patients with depressive disorders, have worse prognoses than do patients with bipolar disorders, and better prognoses than do patients with schizophrenia. Those generalities have been supported by several studies that followed patients for two to five years after the index episode and that assessed social and occupational functioning, as well as the course of the disorder itself.

Data suggest that patients with schizoaffective disorder, bipolar type, have prognoses similar to those for patients with bipolar I disorder and that patients with schizoaffective disorder, depressive type, have prognoses similar to those for patients with schizophrenia. No matter the type, the following variables weigh toward a poor prognosis: a poor premorbid history; an insidious onset; no precipitating factor; a predominance of psychotic symptoms, especially deficit or negative symptoms; an early onset; an unremitting course; and a family history of schizophrenia. The opposite of each of those characteristics weighs toward a good outcome. The presence or the absence of Schneiderian first-rank symptoms does not seem to predict the course.

Although there do not appear to be gender-related differences in outcome for schizoaffective disorder, some data suggest that suicidal behavior may be more common in women with schizoaffective disorder than in men with the disorder. The incidence of suicide among patients with schizoaffective disorder is thought to be at least 10 percent.

TREATMENT

The major treatment modalities for schizoaffective disorder are hospitalization, medication, and psychosocial interventions. The basic principles underlying pharmacotherapy for schizoaffective disorder are that antidepressant and antimanic protocols be followed if at all indicated and that antipsychotics be used only as needed for short-term control. If thymoleptic protocols are not effective in controlling the symptoms on an ongoing basis, antipsychotic medications may be indicated. Patients with schizoaffective disorder, bipolar type, should receive trials of lithium, carbamazepine (Tegretol), valproate (Depakene), or some combination of those drugs if one drug alone is not effective. Patients with schizoaffective disorder, depressive type, should be given trials of antidepressants and electroconvulsive therapy (ECT) before they are found unresponsive to antidepressant treatment.

References

Beatty W W, Jocic Z, Monson N, Staton R D: Memory and frontal lobe dysfunction in schizophrenia and schizoaffective disorder. J Nerv Ment Dis *181*: 448, 1993.
del Rio Vega J M, Ayuso-Gutierrez J L: Course of schizoaffective psychosis: Further data from a retrospective study. Acta Psychiatr Scand *85*: 328, 1992.

Grossman L S, Harrow M, Goldberg J F, Fichtner C G: Outcome of schizoaffective disorder at two long-term follow-ups: Comparisons with outcome of schizophrenia and affective disorders. Am J Psychiatry *148:* 1359, 1991.

Keck P E Jr, Wilson D R, Strakowski S M, McElroy S L, Kizer D L, Balistreri
T M, Holtman H M, DePriest M: Clinical predictors of acute risperidone response in schizophrenia, schizoaffective disorder, and psychotic mood disorders. J Clin Psychiatry *56:* 466, 1995.

Siris S G, Lavin, M R: Schizoaffective disorder, schizophreniform disorder, and
brief psychotic disorder. In *Comprehensive Textbook of Psychiatry,* ed 6, H I
Kaplan, B J Sadock, editors, p 1019. Williams & Wilkins, Baltimore, 1995.

Smith T E, Deutsch A, Schwartz F, Terkelsen K G: The role of personality in
the treatment of schizophrenic and schizoaffective disorder inpatients: A pilot
study. Bull Menninger Clin *57:* 88, 1993.

Tsuang D, Coryell W: An 8-year follow-up of patients with DSM-III-R psychotic
depression, schizoaffective disorder, and schizophrenia. Am J Psychiatry *150:*
1182, 1993.

8.4 DELUSIONAL DISORDER

Delusional disorder is defined as a psychiatric disorder in which the predominant symptoms are delusions. Delusional disorder was formerly called paranoia or paranoid disorder. Those terms, however, incorrectly imply that the delusions are always persecutory in content, and that is not so. The delusions in delusional disorder can also be grandiose, erotic, jealous, somatic, and mixed in primary content.

Delusional disorder must be differentiated from both mood disorders and schizophrenia. Although patients with delusional disorder may have a mood that is consistent with the content of their delusions, they do not evidence the pervasiveness of the affective symptoms seen in the mood disorders. Similarly, patients with delusional disorder differ from schizophrenic patients in the nonbizarre nature of their delusions (for example, ''being followed by the FBI,'' which is unlikely but possible, versus ''being controlled by Martians,'' which is not possible). Patients with delusional disorder also lack other symptoms seen in schizophrenia, such as prominent hallucinations, affective flattening, and additional symptoms of thought disorder.

EPIDEMIOLOGY

An accurate assessment of the epidemiology of delusional disorder is hampered by the relative uncommonness of the disorder, as well as by the changing definitions of the disorder over recent history. Moreover, delusional disorder may be underreported because delusional patients rarely seek psychiatric help unless forced to do so by their families or by the courts. Even in the face of those limitations, however, the literature does support the contention that delusional disorder, although an uncommon disorder, has been present in the population at a relatively steady rate.

The prevalence of delusional disorder in the United States is currently estimated to be 0.025 to 0.03 percent. Thus, delusional disorder is much rarer than schizophrenia, which has a prevalence of about 1 percent, and the mood disorders, which have a prevalence of about 5 percent. The annual incidence of delusional disorder is one to three new cases per 100,000 population, about 4 percent of all first admissions to psychiatric hospitals for psychoses not due to a general medical condition or a substance.

The mean age of onset is about 40 years, but the range for the age of onset runs from 18 to the 90s. There is a slight preponderance of female patients. Many patients are married and employed, but there may be some association with recent immigration and low socioeconomic status.

ETIOLOGY

As with all the major psychiatric disorders, the cause of delusional disorder is not known. Moreover, the patients currently classified as having delusional disorder probably have a heterogeneous group of conditions with delusions as the predominant symptom. The central concept regarding the cause of delusional disorder is its distinctness from schizophrenia and the mood disorders. Delusional disorder is much rarer than either schizophrenia or mood disorders, thus suggesting that is a separate disorder. In addition, delusional disorder has a later onset than does schizophrenia and has a much less pronounced female predominance than that seen in the mood disorders. The most convincing data come from family studies that report an increased prevalence of delusional disorder and related personality traits (for example, suspiciousness, jealousy, and secretiveness) in the relatives of delusional disorder probands. Family studies have reported neither an increased incidence of schizophrenia and mood disorders in the families of delusional disorder probands nor an increased incidence of delusional disorder in the families of schizophrenic probands. Long-term followup of delusional disorder patients suggests that the diagnosis of delusional disorder be relatively stable: less than one quarter of the patients are eventually reclassified as having schizophrenia and less than 10 percent are eventually reclassified as having a mood disorder. Those data indicate that delusional disorder is not simply an early stage in the development of one or both of those two more common disorders.

Biological Factors

A wide range of nonpsychiatric medical conditions and substances can cause delusions, thus suggesting that clear-cut biological factors can cause delusions. However, not everyone with a brain tumor, for example, has delusions. Unique and as yet not understood factors in a patient's brain and personality are likely to be relevant to the specific pathophysiology of delusional disorder.

The neurological conditions most commonly associated with delusions are conditions that affect the limbic system and the basal ganglia. Patients who have delusions caused by neurological diseases in the absence of intellectual impairment tend to have complex delusions that are similar to those seen in patients with delusional disorder. Conversely, neurological disorder patients with intellectual impairments often have simple delusions that are unlike those seen in patients with delusional disorder. Thus, delusional disorder may involve pathology of the limbic system or basal ganglia in patients who have intact cerebral cortical functioning.

Delusional disorder may arise as a normal response to abnormal experiences in the environment, the peripheral nervous system, or the central nervous system. Thus, if patients have erroneous sensory experiences of being followed (for example, people staring, hearing footsteps), they may come to believe that they are actually being followed. That hypothesis hinges on the presence of hallucinatorylike experiences that need to be explained. The presence of such hallucinatory experiences in delusional disorder has not been proved.

Psychodynamic Factors

Practitioners have a strong clinical impression that many patients with delusional disorder are socially isolated and have attained less than expected levels of achievement. Specific psychodynamic theories regarding the cause and the evolution of delusional symptoms involve suppositions regarding hypersensitive persons and specific ego mechanisms: reaction formation, projection, and denial.

FREUD'S CONTRIBUTIONS

Sigmund Freud believed that delusions, rather than being symptoms of the disorder, are part of a healing process. In 1896 he described projection as the main defense mechanism in paranoia. Later, Freud read *Memories of My Nervous Illness*, an autobiographical account by Daniel Paul Schreber. Although he never personally met Schreber, Freud theorized from his review of the autobiography that unconscious homosexual tendencies are defended against by denial and projection. According to classic psychodynamic theory, the dynamics underlying the formation of delusions for a female patient are the same as for a male patient.

Freud theorized that, because homosexuality is consciously inadmissible to some paranoid patients, male patients' feeling of "I love him" is denied and changed by reaction formation into "I do not love him; I hate him." That feeling is further transformed through projection into "It is not I who hate him; it is he who hates me." In a full-blown paranoid state the feeling is elaborated into "I am persecuted by him." Patients are then able to rationalize their anger by consciously hating those they perceive to hate them. Instead of being aware of the passive homosexual impulses, the patients reject the love of anyone except themselves. In erotomanic delusions the male patient changes "I love him" to "I love her," and that feeling, through projection, becomes "She loves me." In delusional grandiosity "I do not love him" becomes "I love myself."

Freud also believed that unconscious homosexuality is the cause of delusions of jealousy. In an attempt to ward off threatening impulses, the patient becomes preoccupied by jealous thoughts; thus, the male patient asserts, "I do not love him; she [a wife, for example] loves him." Freud believed that the man the paranoid patient suspects his wife of loving is a man to whom the patient feels sexually attracted.

Clinical evidence has not supported Freud's thesis. A significant number of delusional patients do not have demonstrable homosexual inclinations, and the majority of homosexual men do not have symptoms of paranoia or delusions.

PARANOID PSEUDOCOMMUNITY

Norman Cameron described seven situations that favor the development of delusional disorders: (1) an increased expectation of receiving sadistic treatment, (2) situations that increase distrust and suspicion, (3) social isolation, (4) situations that increase envy and jealousy, (5) situations that lower self-esteem, (6) situations that cause persons to see their own defects in others, and (7) situations that increase the potential for rumination over probable meanings and motivations. When frustration from any combination of those conditions exceeds the limit that the persons can tolerate, they become withdrawn and anxious; they realize that something is wrong and seek an explanation for the problem. The crystallization of a delusional system offers a solution. Elaboration of the delusion to include imagined persons and the attribution of malevolent motivations to both real and imagined people results in the organization of the *pseudocommunity*—that is, a perceived community of plotters. That

delusional entity hypothetically binds together projected fears and wishes to justify the patient's aggression and to provide a tangible target for the patient's hostilities.

OTHER FACTORS

Clinical observations suggest that some paranoid patients experience a lack of trust in relationships. That distrust has been hypothesized to be related to a consistently hostile family environment, often with an overcontrolling mother and a distant or sadistic father.

Patients with delusional disorder primarily use the defense mechanisms of reaction formation, denial, and projection. *Reaction formation* is used as a defense against aggression, dependence needs, and feelings of affection. The need for dependence is transformed into staunch independence. *Denial* is used to avoid awareness of painful reality. Consumed with anger and hostility and unable to face responsibility for the rage, the patients project their resentment and anger onto others. *Projection* is used to protect patients from recognizing unacceptable impulses in themselves.

Hypersensitivity and feelings of inferiority have been hypothesized to lead, through reaction formation and projection, to delusions of superiority and grandiosity. Delusions of erotic ideas have been suggested as replacements for feelings of rejection. Some clinicians have noted that children who are expected to perform impeccably and are undeservedly punished when they fail to do so may develop elaborate fantasies as a way of enhancing their injured self-esteem. Their secret thoughts may eventually evolve into delusions. Critical and frightening delusions are often described as projections of superego criticism.

The delusions of female paranoid patients often involve accusations of prostitution. As a child, the female paranoiac turned to her father for the material love that she was unable to receive from her mother. Incestuous desires developed. Later heterosexual encounters are an unconscious reminder of the incestuous desires of childhood; those desires are defended against by superego projections accusing the female paranoiac of prostitution.

Somatic delusions can be psychodynamically explained as a regression to the infantile narcissistic state, in which patients withdraw emotional involvement from other people and fixate on their physical selves. In erotic delusions the love can be understood as projected narcissistic love used as a defense against low self-esteem and severe narcissistic injury. Delusions of grandeur may be a regression to the omnipotent feelings of childhood, in which feelings of undenied and undiminished powers predominated.

DIAGNOSIS

The fourth edition of *Diagnostic and Statistical Manual of Mental Disorders* (DSM-IV) has two criteria for describing the clinical symptoms of delusional disorder (Table 8.4–1). Criterion A requires the presence of delusions for at least one month and describes the delusions as nonbizarre in an attempt to assist the clinician in discriminating those delusions from the bizarre delusions seen in schizophrenic patients. Criterion B requires the absence of other symptoms of schizophrenia at any time during the course of the disorder. One exception to that exclusion is the presence of tactile or olfactory hallucinations if they are consistent with the delusional system. DSM-IV also speci-

Table from DSM-IV, *Diagnostic and Statistical Manual of Mental Disorders*, ed 4. Copyright American Psychiatric Association, Washington, 1994. Used with permission.

Table 8.4–1.   Diagnostic Criteria for Delusional Disorder

A. Nonbizarre delusions (i.e., involving situations that occur in real life, such as being followed, poisoned, infected, loved at a distance, or deceived by spouse or lover, or having a disease) of at least 1 month's duration.

B. Criterion A for schizophrenia has never been met. **Note:** Tactile and olfactory hallucinations may be present in delusional disorder if they are related to the delusional theme.

C. Apart from the impact of the delusion(s) or its ramifications, functioning is not markedly impaired and behavior is not obviously odd or bizarre.

D. If mood episodes have occurred concurrently with delusions, their total duration has been brief relative to the duration of the delusional periods.

E. The disturbance is not due to the direct physiological effects of a substance (e.g., a drug of abuse, a medication) or a general medical condition.

Specify type (the following types are assigned based on the predominant delusional theme):

Erotomanic type: delusions that another person, usually of higher status, is in love with the individual
Grandiose type: delusions of inflated worth, power, knowledge, identity, or special relationship to a deity or famous person
Jealous type: delusions that the individual's sexual partner is unfaithful
Persecutory type: delusions that the person (or someone to whom the person is close) is being malevolently treated in some way
Somatic type: delusions that the person has some physical defect or general medical condition
Mixed type: delusions characteristic of more than one of the above types but no one theme predominates
Unspecified type

fies that the effects of the disorder on the patient's functioning are limited to the effects that the delusions themselves have on the patient's life. That criterion is meant to exclude patients who have functional impairment because of characteristic schizophrenic symptoms, such as ambivalence.

Types

DSM-IV allows the clinician to specify one of seven types of delusional disorder, based on the predominant content of the delusions (see Table 8.4–1). The types include erotomanic type, grandiose type, jealous type, persecutory type, and somatic type. Two additional types are mixed type, for patients with delusions containing more than one theme, and unspecified type, for patients with delusions that do not fit into any of the above categories. Persecutory and jealous types are the most common; grandiose type is not as common; erotomanic and somatic types are the most unusual.

Other Delusions

Other delusions have been given specific names in the literature. Lacking an organic explanation, patients with those delusions may be classified according to DSM-IV either as having delusional disorder (unspecified type) or as having a psychotic disorder not otherwise specified. *Capgras's syndrome* is the delusion that familiar people have been replaced by identical impostors. *Fregoli's phenomenon* is the delusion that a persecutor is taking on a variety of faces, like an actor. *Lycanthropy*

is the delusion of being a werewolf, and *heutoscopy* is the false belief that one has a double. *Cotard's syndrome* was originally called *délire de négation*; persons with the syndrome may believe that they have lost everything—possessions, strength, and even bodily organs, such as the heart.

CLINICAL FEATURES

Mental Status

GENERAL DESCRIPTION

The patient is usually well groomed and well dressed, without evidence of gross disintegration of personality or daily activities. However, the patient may seem eccentric, odd, suspicious, or hostile. The patient is sometimes litigious and may make that inclination clear to the examiner. If the patient attempts to engage the clinician as an ally in a delusion, the clinician should not pretend to accept the delusion, since doing so further confounds reality and sets the stage for eventual distrust between the patient and the therapist. What is usually most remarkable about patients with delusional disorder is that the mental status examination shows them to be remarkably normal except for the presence of a markedly abnormal delusional system.

MOOD, FEELINGS, AND AFFECT

The patient's mood is consistent with the content of the delusion. A patient with grandiose delusions is euphoric; a patient with persecutory delusions is suspicious. Whatever the nature of the delusional system, the examiner may sense some mild depressive qualities.

PERCEPTUAL DISTURBANCES

By definition, patients with delusional disorder do not have prominent or sustained hallucinations. According to DSM-IV, tactile of olfactory delusions may be present if they are consistent with the delusion (for example, somatic delusion of body odor). A few delusional patients have other hallucinatory experiences—virtually always auditory, rather than visual.

THOUGHT

Disorder of thought content, in the form of delusions, is the key symptom of the disorder. The delusions are usually systematized and are characterized as being possible—for example, delusions of being persecuted, having an unfaithful spouse, being infected with a virus, and being loved by a famous person. Those examples of delusional content are contrasted with the bizarre and impossible delusional content seen in some schizophrenic patients. The delusional system itself may be complex or simple. The patient lacks other signs of thought disorder, although some patients may be verbose, circumstantial, or idiosyncratic in their speech when they talk about their delusions. The clinician should not assume that all unlikely scenarios are delusional. The veracity of an identified patient's beliefs should be checked before automatically considering their content to be delusional.

SENSORIUM AND COGNITION

Orientation

Patients with delusional disorder usually have no abnormality in orientation unless they have a specific delusion concerning person, place, or time.

Memory

Memory and other cognitive processes are intact in patients with delusional disorder.

IMPULSE CONTROL

The clinician must evaluate patients with delusional disorder for ideation or plans to act on their delusional material by suicide, homicide, or other violence. The incidence of those behaviors in delusional disorder patients is not known. The therapist should not hesitate to ask patients about their suicidal, homicidal, or sexual plans. Destructive aggression is most common in patients with a history of violence. If aggressive feelings existed in the past, the therapist should ask patients how they managed those feelings. If the patients are unable to control their impulses, hospitalization is probably necessary. The therapist can sometimes help foster a therapeutic alliance by openly discussing how hospitalization can help patients gain additional control of their impulses.

JUDGMENT AND INSIGHT

Patients with delusional disorder have virtually no insight into their condition and are almost always brought to the hospital by the police, family members, or employers. Judgment can best be assessed by evaluating the patient's past, present, and planned behavior.

RELIABILITY

Patients with delusional disorder are usually reliable in their information, unless it impinges on their delusional system.

Types

EROTOMANIC TYPE

In the erotomanic type the central delusion is that the affected patient is loved intensely by another person—usually a famous person, such as a movie star, or a superior at work. Patients with erotic delusions are significant sources of harassment to public figures. The erotomanic type of delusional disorder has also been called erotomania, *psychose passionelle*, and de Clerambault syndrome. The onset of the symptom can be sudden and often becomes the central focus of the affected person's life. Efforts to contact the object of the delusion—through telephone calls, letters, gifts, visits, and even surveillance and stalking—are common, although occasionally the person attempts to keep the delusion secret. The symptom of paradoxical conduct consists of interpreting all verbal and physical denials of love as cryptic proof of love.

Whereas in clinical samples most patients with the erotomanic type are women, in forensic samples most are men. Some people with the disorder, particularly men, come into the conflict with the law in their efforts to pursue the objects of their delusions or in misguided efforts to rescue them from some imagined dangers. For example, a man with delusional disorder may attempt to murder the husband of a woman whom he believes is really in love with him.

Affected persons are often found to have lived isolated and withdrawn lives. They are usually single and have had limited sexual contacts. Affected persons are often employed in modest occupations.

GRANDIOSE TYPE

The grandiose type of delusion disorder has also been called megalomania. The most common form of grandiose delusion is the belief that one has some great but unrecognized talent or insight or has made some important discovery. The patient may take this discovery to various governmental agencies, such as the Federal Bureau of Investigation (FBI) and the United States Patent Office. Less common is the delusion that one has a special relationship with a prominent person, such as the President of the United States. Grandiose delusions may have a religious content, and persons with the delusions can become leaders of religious cults.

JEALOUS TYPE

The jealous type of delusional disorder is also known, when the delusion concerns the fidelity of the spouse, as conjugal paranoia and Othello syndrome. Men are more commonly affected than women. The disorder is rare, affecting probably less than 0.2 percent of all psychiatric patients. The onset is often sudden, and the symptoms may resolve only after separation or the death of the spouse. The jealous delusion can lead to significant verbal and physical abuse against the spouse and can even result in the spouse's murder. In 1891 Richard von Krafft-Ebing emphasized the frequent association between alcoholism and jealous delusions.

When a person is affected with the jealous type of delusional disorder, bits of "evidence," such as disarrayed clothing and spots on the sheets, may be collected and used to justify the delusion. Almost invariably, persons with the delusion confront their spouses or lovers and may take extraordinary steps to intervene in the imagined infidelity. Those attempts may include restricting autonomy by insisting that the spouse or lover never leave the house unaccompanied, secretly following the spouse or lover, and investigating the other "lover."

PERSECUTORY TYPE

This is the most common type of delusional disorder. The persecutory delusion may be simple or elaborate. It usually involves a single theme or a series of connected themes, such as being conspired against, cheated, spied on, followed, poisoned or drugged, maliciously maligned, harassed, or obstructed in the pursuit of long-term goals. Small slights may be exaggerated and become the focus of a delusional system. In certain cases the focus of the delusion is some injustice that must be remedied by legal action (*querulous paranoia*), and the affected person often engages in repeated attempts to obtain satisfaction by appeals to the courts and other government agencies. Persons with persecutory delusions are often resentful and angry, and they may resort to violence against those they believe to be hurting them.

SOMATIC TYPE

The somatic type of delusional disorder is also known as monosymptomatic hypochondriacal psychosis. The differentiation between hypochondriasis and the somatic type of delusional disorder rests on the degree of conviction that patients with delusional disorder have about their presumed illness. The most common delusional afflictions are infection (for example, bacteria, viruses, parasites); infestation of insects on or in the skin; dysmorphophobia (for example, misshapen nose or breasts); delusions regarding body odors coming from the skin, mouth, or vagina; and delusions that certain parts of the body, such as the large intestine, are not functioning. The somatic type affects both sexes equally and is thought to be rare, although most patients probably go to nonpsychiatric physicians. Histories of substance abuse or head injury may be common in patients with the disorder. The frustration caused by the symptom may lead some patients to suicide.

DIFFERENTIAL DIAGNOSIS

Many medical and neurological illnesses can present with delusions. The most common sites for lesions are the basal ganglia and the limbic system. The medical evaluation should include toxicology screening and routine admission laboratory work. Neuropsychological testing (such as the Bender Gestalt test and the Wechsler memory scale) and an electroencephalogram (EEG) or a computed tomography (CT) scan may be indicated at the time of the initial presentation, especially if other signs or symptoms suggest cognitive impairment or electrophysiological or structural lesions.

Delirium, Dementia, and Substance-Related Disorders

Delirium and dementia need to be considered in the differential diagnosis of a patient with delusions. Delirium can be differentiated by the presence of a fluctuating level of consciousness or impaired cognitive abilities. Delusions early in the course of a dementing illness, as in dementia of the Alzheimer's type, may give the appearance of a delusional disorder; however, neuropsychological testing usually detects cognitive impairment. Although alcohol abuse is an associated feature for patients with delusional disorder, delusional disorder should be distinguished from alcohol-induced psychotic disorder with hallucinations. Intoxication with sympathomimetics (including amphetamines), marijuana, or levodopa (Larodopa) is likely to result in delusional symptoms.

Other Disorders

The psychiatric differential diagnosis for delusional disorder includes malingering and factitious disorder with predominantly psychological signs and symptoms. The nonfactitious disorders in the differential diagnosis are schizophrenia, mood disorders, obsessive-compulsive disorder, somatoform disorders, and paranoid personality disorder. Delusional disorder is distinguished from schizophrenia by the absence of other schizophrenic symptoms and by the nonbizarre quality of the delusions. Also, patients with delusional disorder lack the impairment of functioning seen in schizophrenia. The somatic type of delusional disorder may resemble a depressive disorder or a somatoform disorder. The somatic type of delusional disorder is differential from depressive disorders by the absence of other signs of depression and by the lack of a pervasive quality to the depression. Delusional disorder can be differentiated from somatoform disorders by the degree to which the somatic belief is held by the patient. Patients with somatoform disorders allow for the possibility that their disorder does not exist, whereas patients with delusional disorder have no doubt. Separating paranoid personality disorder from delusional disorder requires the sometimes difficult clinical distinction between extreme suspiciousness and a frank delusion. In general, if the clinician

doubts that the symptom is a delusion, the diagnosis of delusional disorder should not be made.

COURSE AND PROGNOSIS

Some clinicians and some research data indicate that an identifiable psychosocial stressor is often present at the onset of the disorder. The nature of the stressor may be such that some degree of suspicion or concern by the patient is warranted. Examples of such stressors are recent immigration, social conflict with family members or friends, and social isolation. In general, a sudden onset is thought to be more common than an insidious onset. Some clinicians believe that the premorbid personality of a patient with delusional disorder is likely to be extroverted, dominant, and hypersensitive. Some clinicians also believe that a patient with delusional disorder is likely to be below average in intelligence. The patient's initial suspicions or concerns gradually become elaborate, consuming much of the patient's attention, and finally become delusional. Patients may begin quarreling with coworkers, may seek protection from the FBI or the police, or may begin visiting many medical or surgical doctors to seek consultations. Thus, the initial contact with the patient may be not with a psychiatrist but, rather, with lawyers regarding suits, primary care physicians regarding medical complaints, or the police regarding delusional suspicions.

Delusional disorder is thought to be a fairly stable diagnosis. Less than 25 percent of all patients with delusional disorder go on to schizophrenia; less than 10 percent of patients with delusional disorder go on to a mood disorder. About 50 percent of patients are recovered at long-term follow-up; another 20 percent have a decrease in their symptoms; and 30 percent have no change in their symptoms. The following factors correlate with a good prognosis: high levels of occupational, social, and functional adjustments; female sex; onset before age 30; sudden onset; short duration of illness; and the presence of precipitating factors. Although reliable data are limited, patients with persecutory, somatic, and erotic delusions are thought to have a better prognosis than do patients with grandiose and jealous delusions.

TREATMENT

Hospitalization

In general, patients with delusional disorder can be treated on an outpatient basis. However, a clinician should consider hospitalization for a few specific reasons. First, a complete medical and neurological evaluation of the patient may be needed to find whether a nonpsychiatric medical condition is causing the delusional symptoms. Second, patients need to be assessed regarding their ability to control violent impulses, such as suicide and homicide, that may be related to the delusional material. Third, patients' behavior regarding the delusions may have significantly affected their ability to function within their families or occupational settings, thereby requiring professional intervention to stabilize the social or occupational relationships.

If the physician is convinced that the patient would be best treated in a hospital, an attempt should be made to persuade the patient to accept hospitalization; failing that, legal commitment may be indicated. Often, if the physician convinces the patient that hospitalization is inevitable, the patient voluntarily enters a hospital to avoid legal commitment.

Pharmacotherapy

In an emergency, severely agitated patients should be given an antipsychotic drug intramuscularly. Although adequately conducted clinical trials with large numbers of patients have not been conducted, most clinicians think that antipsychotic drugs are the treatment of choice for delusional disorder. Delusional disorder patients are likely to refuse medication because they can easily incorporate the administration of drugs into their delusional system. The physician should not insist on medication immediately after hospitalization but, rather, should spend a few days establishing rapport with the patient. The physician should explain potential side effects to the patient, so that the patient does not later suspect that the physician lied.

The patient's history of medication response is the best guide in choosing a drug. Often, the physician should start with low doses—for example, 2 mg of haloperidol (Haldol)—and increase the dosage slowly. If a patient fails to respond to the drug at a reasonable dosage in a six-week trial, antipsychotics from other classes should be given clinical trials. Some investigators have suggested that pimozide (Orap) may be particularly effective in delusional disorder, especially in patients with somatic delusions. A common cause of drug failure is noncompliance, and that possibility should be evaluated.

If the patient receives no benefit from antipsychotic medication, the drug should be discontinued. In patients who do respond to antipsychotics, some data suggest that maintenance dosages can be low. Although essentially no data evaluate the use of antidepressants, lithium (Eskalith), or anticonvulsants—for example, carbamazepine (Tegretol) and valproate (Depakene)—in the treatment of delusional disorder, trials with those drugs may be warranted in patients who are unresponsive to antipsychotic drugs. Trials of those drugs should be considered when a patient has either the features of a mood disorder or a family history of mood disorders.

Psychotherapy

The essential element in effective psychotherapy is establishing a relationship in which the patient begins to trust the therapist. Individual therapy appears more effective than group therapy. Insight-oriented supportive, cognitive, and behavioral therapies are often effective. Initially, the therapist should neither agree with nor challenge the patient's delusions. Although the therapist must ask about the delusion to establish its extent, persistent questioning about the delusion should probably be avoided. The physician may stimulate the motivation to receive help by emphasizing a willingness to help patients with their anxiety or irritability, without suggesting that the delusions be treated. However, the therapist should not actively support the notion that the delusions represent reality.

The therapist's unwavering reliability is essential. The therapist should be on time and make appointments as regularly as possible, the goal being to develop a solid and trusting relationship with the patient. Overgratification may actually increase the patient's hostility and suspiciousness because of the core realization that not all demands can be met. The therapist can avoid overgratification by not extending the designated appointment period, by not giving extra appointments unless absolutely necessary, and by not being lenient about the fee.

Therapists should not make disparaging remarks about patients' delusions or ideas but can sympathetically suggest to patients that their preoccupation with their delusions both distresses themselves and interferes with a constructive life. When patients begin to waver in their delusional beliefs, therapists may increase reality testing by asking patients to clarify their concerns.

Psychodynamic Factors

The internal experience of delusional patients is that they are victims of a world that persecutes them. Projection is the principal defense mechanism, and all malevolence is projected into persons or institutions in the environment. By substituting an external threat for an internal one, delusional patients feel a sense of control. The need to control everyone around them reflects the low self-esteem at the core of paranoia. Paranoid patients compensate for feelings of weakness and inferiority by assuming that they are so special that governmental agencies, famous people, and a host of other significant persons are all deeply concerned about them and trying to persecute them.

Clinicians who attempt to treat patients with delusional disorder must respect the patient's need for the defense of projection. Psychotherapists must be willing to serve as a container for all the negative feelings projected by the patient; any efforts to turn such feelings prematurely will result in the patient's feeling attacked and blamed. One corollary of that principle is that delusions should not be challenged when working psychotherapeutically with delusional patients. Instead, the therapist should simply ask for further elaborations of the patient's perceptions and feelings.

Another approach that is useful in building a therapeutic alliance is to empathize with the patient's internal experience of being overwhelmed by persecution. It may be helpful to make such comments as, "You must be exhausted, considering what you've been through." Without agreeing with every delusional misperception, the therapist can acknowledge that, from the patient's perspective, such perceptions create a good deal of distress. The ultimate goal is to help the patient entertain the possibility of a doubt about the perceptions. As the patient becomes less rigid, feelings of weakness and inferiority associated with some depression may surface. When the patient allows feelings of vulnerability to enter into the therapy, a positive therapeutic alliance has been established, and constructive therapeutic work becomes a possibility.

Family Therapy

When family members are available, the clinician may decide to involve them in the treatment plan. Without being delusionally seen as siding with the enemy, the clinician should attempt to enlist the family as allies in the treatment process. Consequently, both the patient and the family members need to understand that physician-patient confidentiality will be maintained by the therapist and that communications from relatives will be discussed at some point the patient. The family may benefit from the support of the therapist and may thus be supportive of the patient.

A good therapeutic outcome depends on the psychiatrist's ability to respond to the patient's mistrust of others and the resulting interpersonal conflicts, frustrations, and failures. The mark of successful treatment may be a satisfactory social adjustment, rather than an abatement of the patient's delusions.

References

Alford B A, Beck A T: Cognitive therapy of delusional beliefs. Behav Res Ther *32*: 369, 1994.

Fink M: Convulsive therapy in delusional disorders. Psychiatr Clin North Am *18*: 393, 1995.

Gabbard G O: *Psychodynamic Psychiatry in General Practice: The DSM-IV Edition.* American Psychiatric Press, Washington, 1994.

Gambini O, Colombo C, Cavallaro R, Scarone S: Smooth pursuit eye movements and saccadic eye movements in patients with delusional disorder. Am J Psychiatry *150*: 1411, 1993.

Manschreck T C: Delusional disorder and shared psychotic disorder. In *Comprehensive Textbook of Psychiatry*, ed 6, H I Kaplan, B J Sadock, editors, p 1031. Williams & Wilkins, Baltimore, 1995.

Marino C, Nobile M, Bellodi L, Smeraldi E: Delusional disorder and mood disorder: Can they coexist? Psychopathology *26*: 53, 1993.

Munro A: The classification of delusional disorders. Psychiatr Clin North Am *18*: 199, 1995.

Opjordsmoen S, Retterstol N: Outcome in delusional disorder in different periods of time: Possible implications for treatment with neuroleptics. Psychopathology *26*: 90, 1993.

8.5 BRIEF PSYCHOTIC DISORDER

The fourth edition of *Diagnostic and Statistical Manual of Mental Disorders* (DSM-IV) combines two diagnostic concepts into the diagnosis of brief psychotic disorder. First, the disorder has lasted a short time, defined in DSM-IV as less than one month but at least one day; the symptoms may or may not meet the diagnostic criteria for schizophrenia. Second, the disorder may have developed in response to a severe psychosocial stressor or group of stressors. The grouping of those in DSM-IV as brief psychotic disorder acknowledges the practical difficulty of differentiating those concepts in routine clinical practice.

EPIDEMIOLOGY

Few studies were conducted on the epidemiology of the revised third edition of DSM (DSM-III-R) diagnosis of brief reactive psychosis, and none have been conducted using the DSM-IV criteria. Therefore, reliable estimates of the incidence, the prevalence, the sex ratio, and the average age of onset for the disorder are not available. In general, the disorder is considered uncommon, as indicated by one study of military recruits in which the incidence of DSM-III-R brief reactive psychosis was estimated to be 1.4 per 100,000 recruits. With the inclusion of brief psychotic episodes not associated with a precipitating factor in DSM-IV, the incidence for the DSM-IV diagnosis may be higher than that figure. Another widely held clinical impression is that the disorder is more common among young patients than among older patients, although some case reports present case histories that do involve older people.

Some clinicians suggest that the disorder may be seen most frequently in patients from low socioeconomic classes and in patients with preexisting personality disorders (most commonly, historic, narcissistic, paranoid, schizotypal, and borderline personality disorders). Persons who have experienced disasters or who have gone through major cultural changes (for example, immigrants) may also be at risk for the disorder after subsequent psychosocial stressors. Those clinical impressions, however, have not been shown to be true in well-controlled clinical studies.

ETIOLOGY

Patients with brief psychotic disorder who have had a personality disorder may have biological or psychological vulnerability toward the development of psychotic symptoms. Although patients with brief psychotic disorder as a group may not have an increased incidence of schizophrenia in their families, some data suggest an increased incidence of mood disorders. Psychodynamic formulations have emphasized the presence of inadequate coping mechanisms and the possibility of secondary gain for those patients with psychotic symptoms. As with the biological theories for the disorder, the psychological theories have not been validated by carefully controlled clinical studies. Additional psychodynamic theories suggest that the psychotic symptoms are a defense against a prohibited fantasy, the fulfillment of an unattained wish, or an escape from a specific psychosocial situation.

DIAGNOSIS

DSM-IV has a continuum of diagnoses for psychotic disorders, based primarily on the duration of the symptoms. For psychotic symptoms that last at least one day but less than one month and that are not associated with a mood disorder, a substance-related disorder, or a psychotic disorder due to a general medical condition, a diagnosis of brief psychotic disorder is likely to be the appropriate diagnosis. For psychotic symptoms that last more than one month, the appropriate diagnoses to consider are delusional disorder (if delusions are the primary psychotic symptoms), schizophreniform disorder (if the symptoms have lasted less than six months), and schizophrenia (if the symptoms have lasted more than six months).

Thus, brief psychotic disorder is classified in DSM-IV as a psychotic disorder of short duration (Table 8.5–1). The diagnostic criteria specify the presence of at least one clearly psychotic symptom lasting from one day to one month. DSM-IV further allows the specification of two features: (1) the presence or the absence of one or more marked stressors and (2) a postpartum onset.

As with any acutely ill psychiatric patient, the history necessary to make the diagnosis may not be obtainable solely from

---

Table 8.5–1.   Diagnostic Criteria for Brief Psychotic Disorder

A. Presence of one (or more) of the following symptoms:
   (1) delusions
   (2) hallucinations
   (3) disorganized speech (e.g., frequent derailment or incoherence)
   (4) grossly disorganized or catatonic behavior

   Note: Do not include a symptom if it is a culturally sanctioned response pattern.

B. Duration of an episode of the disturbance is at least 1 day but less than 1 month, with eventual full return to premorbid level of functioning.

C. The disturbance is not better accounted for by a mood disorder with psychotic features, schizoaffective disorder, or schizophrenia and is not due to the direct physiological effects of a substance (e.g., a drug of abuse, a medication) or a general medical condition.

Table from DSM-IV, *Diagnostic and Statistical Manual of Mental Disorders*, ed 4. Copyright American Psychiatric Association, Washington, 1994. Used with permission.

the patient. Although the presence of psychotic symptoms may be obvious, information about prodromal symptoms, previous episodes of a mood disorder, and the recent history of the ingestion of a psychotomimetic substance may not be available from the clinical interview alone. In addition, the clinician may not be able to obtain accurate information regarding the presence or the absence of precipitating stressors. Such information is usually best and most accurately obtained from a relative or a friend.

CLINICAL FEATURES

The symptoms of brief psychotic disorder always include at least one major symptom of psychosis, usually with an abrupt onset, but do not always include the entire symptom pattern seen in schizophrenia. Some clinicians have observed that affective symptoms, confusion, and impaired attention may be more common in brief psychotic disorder than in the chronic psychotic disorders. Characteristic symptoms in brief psychotic disorder include emotional volatility, outlandish dress or behavior, screaming or muteness, and impaired memory for recent events. Some symptoms seen in the disorder suggest a diagnosis of delirium and certainly warrant a complete organic workup, although the results may be negative.

The Scandinavian and other European literature differentiate several characteristic symptom patterns seen in brief psychotic disorder, although the symptom patterns may not hold exactly for this side of the Atlantic Ocean. The symptom patterns include acute paranoid reactions, reactive confusions, reactive excitations, and reactive depressions. Some data suggest that, in the United States, paranoia is often the predominant symptom in the disorder. In French psychiatry, *bouffée délirante* is similar to brief psychotic disorder.

Precipitating Stressors

The clearest examples of precipitating stressors are major life events that would cause any person significant emotional upset. Such events include the loss of a close family member and a severe auto accident. Some clinicians argue that the severity of the event must be considered in relation to the patient's life. Although that view is reasonable, it may broaden the definition of precipitating stressor to include events that were not related to the psychotic episode. Others have argued that the stressor may be a series of modestly stressful events, rather than a single markedly stressful event. But the summation of the degree of stress caused by a sequence of events calls for an almost impossible degree of clinical judgment.

DIFFERENTIAL DIAGNOSIS

The clinician must not assume that the correct diagnosis for a briefly psychotic patient is brief psychotic disorder, even when a clear precipitating psychosocial factor is identified. Such a factor may be merely coincidental. Other diagnoses to consider in the differential diagnosis include factitious disorder with predominantly psychological signs and symptoms, malingering, psychotic disorder due to a general medical condition, and substance-induced psychotic disorder. A patient may be unwilling to admit the use of illicit substances, thereby making the assessment of substance intoxication or substance withdrawal difficult without the use of laboratory testing. Patients with epilepsy or delirium can also present with psychotic symptoms that resemble those seen in brief psychotic disorder. Additional psychiatric disorders to be considered in the differential diagnosis include dissociative identity disorder and psychotic episodes associated with borderline and schizotypal personality disorders.

COURSE AND PROGNOSIS

By definition, the course of brief psychotic disorder is less than one month. Nonetheless, the development of such a significant psychiatric disorder may signify a mental vulnerability in the patient. An unknown percentage of patients who are first classified as having brief psychotic disorder later display chronic psychiatric syndromes, such as schizophrenia and mood disorders. In general, however, patients with brief psychotic disorder have good prognoses, and European studies have suggested that 50 to 80 percent of all patients have no further major psychiatric problems.

The length of the acute and residual symptoms is often just a few days. Occasionally, depressive symptoms follow the resolution of the psychotic symptoms. Suicide is a concern during both the psychotic phase and the postpsychotic depressive phase. Several indicators—for example, good premorbid adjustment, few premorbid schizoid traits, severe precipitating stressor, sudden onset of symptoms, affective symptoms—have been associated with a good prognosis. Patients with those features are not likely to have subsequent episodes and are not likely to later have schizophrenia or a mood disorder.

TREATMENT

Hospitalization

When a patient is acutely psychotic, a brief hospitalization may be necessary for both the evaluation and the protection of the patient. The evaluation of the patient requires close monitoring of the symptoms and an assessment of the patient's level of danger to self and others. In addition, the quiet and structured setting of a hospital may help patients regain their sense of reality. While the clinician is waiting for the setting or drugs to have their effects, seclusion, physical restraints, or one-to-one monitoring of the patient may be necessary.

Pharmacotherapy

The two major classes of drugs to be considered in the treatment of brief psychotic disorder are the dopamine receptor antagonist antipsychotic drugs and the benzodiazepines. When an antipsychotic is chosen, a high-potency antipsychotic—for example, haloperidol (Haldol)—is usually used. Especially in patients who are at high risk for the development of extrapyramidal side effects (for example, young men), an anticholinergic drug should probably be coadministered with the antipsychotic as prophylaxis against medication-induced movement disorder symptoms. Alternatively, benzodiazepines can be used in the short-term treatment of psychosis. Although benzodiazepines have limited or no usefulness in the long-term treatment of psychotic disorders, they can be effective for a short time and are associated with fewer side effects than are the antipsychotics. In rare cases the benzodiazepines are associated with increased agitation and, more rarely still, withdrawal seizures, which usually occur only with the sustained use of high dosages. The use of other drugs in the treatment of brief psychotic disorder, although reported in case reports, has not been supported in any large-scale studies. However, hypnotic medications are often useful during the first two to three weeks after the resolution of the psychotic episode. The long-term use of any medication should be avoided in the treatment of the disorder. If maintenance medication is necessary, the clinician may have to reconsider the diagnosis.

Psychotherapy

Although hospitalization and pharmacotherapy are likely to control short-term situations, the difficult part of treatment is psychological integration of the experience (and possibly the precipitating trauma, if one was present) into the lives of patients and their families. Individual, family, and group psychotherapies may be indicated. The stressors, the psychotic episode, and the development of coping strategies are the major topics for discussion in such therapies. Associated issues include helping the patient cope with the loss of self-esteem and confidence.

References

Beighley P S, Brown G R, Thompson J W: DSM-III-R brief reactive psychosis among Air Force recruits. J Clin Psychiatry 53: 283, 1992.
Siris S G, Lavin, M R: Schizoaffective disorder, schizophreniform disorder, and brief psychotic disorder. In *Comprehensive Textbook of Psychiatry*, ed 6, H I Kaplan, B J Sadock, editors, p 1019. Williams & Wilkins, Baltimore, 1995.
Vanderhart O, Witztum E, Friedman B: From hysterical psychosis to reactive dissociative psychosis. J Traumatic Stress 6: 43, 1993.

9/ Mood Disorders

9.1 MAJOR DEPRESSIVE DISORDER AND BIPOLAR I DISORDER

As clinical and biological researchers have studied the mood disorders, previously recognized clinical distinctions among patients have become appreciated and are now officially recognized by the fourth edition of *Diagnostic and Statistical Manual of Mental Disorders* (DSM-IV). The two major mood disorders are major depressive disorder and bipolar I disorder. Major depressive disorder and bipolar I disorder are often referred to as affective disorders; however, the critical pathology in those disorders is one of *mood*, the sustained internal emotional state of a person, and not one of *affect*, the external expression of present emotional content. Patients who are afflicted with only depressive episodes are said to have major depressive disorder, sometimes called unipolar depression (not a DSM-IV term). Patients with both manic and depressive episodes and patients with manic episodes alone are said to have bipolar I disorder. The terms ''unipolar mania'' and ''pure mania'' (not DSM-IV terms) are sometimes used for bipolar I disorder patients who do not have depressive episodes.

Two additional mood disorders, dysthymic disorder and cyclothymic disorder, have also been appreciated clinically for some time. Dysthymic disorder and cyclothymic disorder are characterized by the presence of symptoms that are less severe than the symptoms of major depressive disorder and of bipolar I disorder, respectively. DSM-IV has codified additional mood disorders, both in the main body of the text and in the appendixes. Those disorders include syndromes related to depression (minor depressive disorder, recurrent brief depressive disorder, and premenstrual dysphoric disorder) and disorders related to bipolar I disorder (bipolar II disorder). In minor depressive disorder the symptom severity does not reach the severity necessary for a diagnosis of major depressive disorder; in recurrent brief depressive disorder the depressive episodes do reach the severity of symptoms required for a diagnosis of major depressive disorder but do so for only a brief period, insufficient in length to meet the diagnostic criteria for major depressive disorder. Bipolar II disorder is characterized by the presence of major depressive episodes alternating with episodes of hypomania—that is, episodes of manic symptoms that do not meet the full criteria for the manic episodes seen in bipolar I disorder. Additional mood disorder diagnoses include mood disorder due to a general medical condition, substance-induced mood disorder, and mood disorder not otherwise specified (NOS).

At least three major theories consider the relation between major depressive disorder and bipolar I disorder. The most accepted hypothesis, which is supported by several types of genetic and biochemical studies, is that major depressive disorder and bipolar I disorder are two different disorders. Recently, some investigators have suggested that bipolar I disorder is a more severe expression of the same pathophysiological process seen in major depressive disorder. The third hypothesis is that depression and mania are two extremes of a continuum of emotional experience; that idea is not supported by the common clinical observation that many patients have mixed states with both depressed and manic features.

EPIDEMIOLOGY

Major depressive disorder is a common disorder, with a lifetime prevalence of about 15 percent, perhaps as high as 25 percent for women. The incidence of major depressive disorder is also higher than usual in primary care patients, in whom it approaches 10 percent, and in medical inpatients, in whom it approaches 15 percent. Bipolar I disorder is less common than major depressive disorder, with a lifetime prevalence of about 1 percent, similar to the figure for schizophrenia. Since it is increasingly appreciated that the course of bipolar I disorder is not as favorable as the course for major depressive disorder, the cost of bipolar I disorder to patients, their families, and society is significant. Another difference between bipolar I disorder and major depressive disorder is that, whereas most persons with bipolar I disorder eventually come to the attention of a physician and receive treatment, only about half of all persons with major depressive disorder ever receive specific treatment. Although the National Institute of Mental Health (NIMH) has begun a program to increase the awareness of depression in the general population and among physicians, the symptoms of depression are often inappropriately dismissed as understandable reactions to stress, evidence of a weakness of will, or simply a conscious attempt to achieve some secondary gain.

Sex

An almost universal observation, independent of country or culture, is the twofold greater prevalence of major depressive disorder in women than in men. Although the reasons for the difference are unknown, research has clearly shown that the difference in Western countries is not solely because of socially biased diagnostic practices. The reasons for the difference have been hypothesized to involve hormonal differences, the effects of childbirth, differing psychosocial stressors for women and for men, and behavioral models of learned helplessness. In contrast to major depressive disorder, bipolar I disorder has a prevalence that is equal for men and women.

Age

In general, the onset of bipolar I disorder is earlier than that for major depressive disorder. The age of onset for bipolar I disorder ranges from childhood (as early as age 5 or 6) to 50 years or even older in rare cases, with a mean age of 30. The mean age of onset for major depressive disorder is about 40 years; 50 percent of all patients have an onset between the ages of 20 and 50. Major depressive disorder can also have its onset in childhood or in old age, although that is uncommon. Some recent epidemiological data suggest that the incidence of major depressive disorder may be increasing among persons less than 20 years old. If that observation is true, it may be related to the increased use of alcohol and other substances in that age group.

Race

The prevalence of mood disorders does not differ from race to race. However, clinicians tend to underdiagnose mood disorders and to overdiagnose schizophrenia in patients who have racial or cultural backgrounds different from their own. White psychiatrists, for example, tend to underdiagnose mood disorders in blacks and Hispanics.

Marital Status

In general, major depressive disorder occurs most often in persons who have no close interpersonal relationships or who are divorced or separated. Bipolar I disorder may be more common in divorced and single persons than among married persons, but that difference may reflect the early onset and the resulting marital discord that are characteristic of the disorder.

Socioeconomic and Cultural Considerations

No correlation has been found between socioeconomic status and major depressive disorder; a higher than average incidence of bipolar I disorder does appear among the upper socioeconomic groups, possibly because of biased diagnostic practices. Depression may be more common in rural areas than in urban areas. Bipolar I disorder is more common in persons who did not graduate from college than in college graduates, probably reflecting the relatively early age of onset for the disorder.

ETIOLOGY

The causal basis for mood disorders is not known. The many attempts to identify a biological or psychosocial cause of mood disorders may have been hampered by the heterogeneity of the patient population defined by any of the available, clinically based diagnostic systems, including DSM-IV. The causative factors can artificially be divided into biological factors, genetic factors, and psychosocial factors. That division is artificial because of the likelihood that the three realms interact among themselves. For example, psychosocial factors and genetic factors can affect biological factors (for example, concentrations of a certain neurotransmitter). Biological and psychosocial factors can also affect gene expression. And biological and genetic factors can affect the response of a person to psychosocial factors.

Biological Factors

Many studies have reported various abnormalities in biogenic amine metabolites—such as 5-hydroxyindoleacetic acid (5-HIAA), homovanillic acid (HVA), and 3-methoxy-4-hydroxyphenylglycol (MHPG)—in blood, urine, and cerebrospinal fluid (CSF) from patients with mood disorders. The data reported are most consistent with the hypothesis that mood disorders are associated with heterogeneous dysregulations of the biogenic amines.

BIOGENIC AMINES

Of the biogenic amines, norepinephrine and serotonin are the two neurotransmitters most implicated in the pathophysiology of mood disorders.

Norepinephrine

The correlation suggested by basic science studies between the down-regulation of β-adrenergic receptors and clinical antidepressant responses is probably the single most compelling piece of data suggesting a direct role for the noradrenergic system in depression. Other types of evidence have also implicated the presynaptic α_2-adrenergic receptors in depression, since activation of those receptors results in a decrease in the amount of norepinephrine released. Presynaptic α_2-adrenergic receptors are also located on serotonergic neurons and regulate the amount of serotonin released. The existence of almost purely noradrenergic, clinically effective antidepressant drugs—for example, desipramine (Norpramin)—is further support of a role for norepinephrine in the pathophysiology of at least the symptoms of depression.

Serotonin

With the huge effect that the serotonin-specific reuptake inhibitors (SSRIs)—for example, fluoxetine (Prozac)—have made on the treatment of depression, serotonin has become the biogenic amine neurotransmitter that is most commonly associated with depression. The identification of multiple serotonin receptor subtypes has also increased the excitement within the research community regarding the development of even more specific treatments for depression. Besides the fact that SSRIs and other serotonergic antidepressants are effective in the treatment of depression, other types of data indicate that serotonin is involved in the pathophysiology of depression. Depletion of serotonin may precipitate depression, and some suicidal patients have low CSF concentrations of serotonin metabolites and low concentrations of serotonin uptake sites on platelets, as measured by imipramine (Tofranil) binding to platelets. Some depressed patients also have abnormal neuroendocrine responses—for example, growth hormone, prolactin, and adrenocorticotropic hormone (ACTH)—to challenges with serotonergic agents. Although current serotonin-active antidepressants act primarily through the blockade of serotonin reuptake, future generations of antidepressants may have other effects on the serotonin system, including antagonism of the serotonin type 2 (5-HT$_2$) receptor (for example, nefazodone [Serzone]) and agonism of the serotonin type 1$_A$ (5-HT$_{1A}$) receptor (for example, ipsapirone).

Dopamine

Although norepinephrine and serotonin are the biogenic amines most often associated with the pathophysiology of depression, dopamine has also been theorized to play a role in depression. The data suggest that dopamine activity may be reduced in depression and increased in mania. The discovery of new subtypes of the dopamine receptors and increasing understanding of the presynaptic and postsynaptic regulation of dopamine function have further enriched the research into the relation between dopamine and mood disorders. Drugs that reduce dopamine concentrations—for example, reserpine—and diseases that reduce dopamine concentrations (for example, Parkinson's disease) are associated with depressive symptoms. Also, drugs that increase dopamine concentrations—for example, tyrosine, amphetamine, and bupropion (Wellbutrin)—reduce the symptoms of depression. Two recent theories regarding dopamine and depression are that the mesolimbic dopamine pathway may be dysfunctional in depression and that the dopamine type 1 (D$_1$) receptor may be hypoactive in depression.

OTHER NEUROCHEMICAL FACTORS

Although the data are not conclusive at this time, amino acid neurotransmitters—particularly γ-aminobutyric acid (GABA)—and neuroactive peptides (particularly vasopressin and the endogenous opiates) have been implicated in the pathophysiology of mood disorders. Some investigators have suggested that second-messenger systems—such as adenylate cyclase, phosphatidylinositol, and calcium regulation—may also be of causal relevance.

NEUROENDOCRINE REGULATION

The hypothalamus is central to the regulation of the neuroendocrine axes and itself receives many neuronal inputs that use biogenic amine neurotransmitters. A variety of neuroendocrine dysregulations have been reported in patients with mood disorders. Therefore, the abnormal regulation of neuroendocrine axes may be a result of abnormal functioning of biogenic amine-containing neurons. Although it is theoretically possible for a particular dysregulation of a neuroendocrine axis (for example, thyroid axis, adrenal axis) to be involved in the cause of a mood disorder, the dysregulations are more likely reflections of a fundamental underlying brain disorder. The major neuroendocrine axes of interest in mood disorders are the adrenal, thyroid, and growth hormone axes. Other neuroendocrine abnormalities described in patients with mood disorders include decreased nocturnal secretion of melatonin, decreased prolactin release to tryptophan administration, decreased basal levels of follicle-stimulating hormone (FSH) and luteinizing hormone (LH), and decreased testosterone levels in men.

Thyroid Axis

Thyroid disorders are often associated with affective symptoms, and researchers have described abnormal regulation of the thyroid axis in patients with mood disorders. One direct clinical implication of the association is the critical importance of testing all affectively ill patients to determine their thyroid status. A consistent finding in studies has been that about one third of all patients with major depressive disorder who have an otherwise normal thyroid axis have a blunted release of thyrotropin—that is, thyroid-stimulating hormone (TSH)—to an infusion of a synthetic thyrotropin-releasing hormone (TRH), protirelin (Thyrel); however, that same abnormality has been reported in a wide range of other psychiatric diagnoses, thus limiting the diagnostic usefulness of the test. Moreover, attempts to subtype depressed patients on the basis of their TRH test results have been contradictory.

Growth Hormone

Several studies have found a statistical difference between depressed patients and normal persons in the regulation of growth hormone release. Depressed patients have a blunted sleep-induced stimulation of growth hormone release. Because sleep abnormalities are common symptoms of depression, a neuroendocrine marker related to sleep is an avenue for research. Studies have also found that depressed patients have a blunted response to clonidine (Catapres) when used to induce increases in growth hormone secretion.

SLEEP ABNORMALITIES

Problems with sleeping—initial and terminal insomnia, multiple awakenings, hypersomnia—are common and classic symptoms of depression, and perceived decreased need for sleep is a classic symptom of mania. Researchers have long recognized that the sleep electroencephalograms (EEGs) of many depressed persons show abnormalities. Common abnormalities are delayed sleep onset, shortened rapid eye movement (REM) latency (the time between falling asleep and the first REM period), an increased length of the first REM period, and abnormal delta sleep. Some investigators have attempted to use the sleep EEG in the diagnostic assessment of patients with mood disorders.

KINDLING

Kindling is the electrophysiological process in which repeated subthreshold stimulation of a neuron eventually generates an action potential. At the organ level, repeated subthreshold stimulation of an area of the brain results in a seizure. The clinical observation that anticonvulsants—for example, carbamazepine (Tegretol) and valproate (Depakene)—are useful in the treatment of mood disorders, particularly bipolar I disorder, has given rise to the theory that the pathophysiology of mood disorders may involve kindling in the temporal lobes.

CIRCADIAN RHYTHMS

The abnormalities of sleep architecture in depression and the transient clinical improvement in depression associated with sleep deprivation have led to theories that depression reflects an abnormal regulation of circadian rhythms. Some experimental studies with animals indicate that many standard antidepressant treatments are effective in changing the setting of internal biological clocks (that is, endogenous *zeitgebers*.)

NEUROIMMUNE REGULATION

Researchers have reported immunological abnormalities in depressed persons and in persons who are grieving the loss of a relative, spouse, or close friend. The dysregulation of the cortisol axis may affect the immune status; there may be abnormal hypothalamic regulation of the immune system. A less likely possibility is that in some patients a primary pathophysiological process involving the immune system leads to the psychiatric symptoms of mood disorders.

BRAIN IMAGING

Brain imaging studies of patients with mood disorders have provided some inconclusive clues regarding abnormal brain function in those disorders. Although studies have not reported consistent findings, the data do suggest the following: (1) a significant set of bipolar I disorder patients, predominantly male patients, have enlarged cerebral ventricles; (2) ventricular enlargement is much less common in patients with major depressive disorder than in patients with bipolar I disorder.

Many reports in the literature concern cerebral blood flow in mood disorders, usually measured by using single photon emission computed tomography (SPECT) or positron emission tomography (PET). A slight majority of the studies have reported decreased blood flow affecting the cerebral cortex in general and the frontal cortical areas in particular. In contrast, one study found increases in cerebral blood flow in patients with major depressive disorder. That study found state-dependent increases in the cortex, the basal ganglia, and the medial thalamus, with the suggestion of a trait-dependent increase in the amygdala.

NEUROANATOMICAL CONSIDERATIONS

Both the symptoms of mood disorders and biological research findings support the hypothesis that mood disorders involve pathology of the limbic system, the basal ganglia, and the hypothalamus. Neurological disorders of the basal ganglia and the limbic system (especially excitatory lesions of the nondominant hemisphere) are likely to present with depressive symptoms. The limbic system and the basal ganglia are intimately connected, and a major role in the production of emotions is hypothesized for the limbic system. Dysfunction of the hypothalamus is suggested by the depressed patient's alterations in sleep, appetite, and sexual behavior and by the biological changes in endocrine, immunological, and chronobiological measures. The depressed patient's stooped posture, motor slowness, and minor cognitive impairment are similar to the signs seen in disorders of the basal ganglia, such as Parkinson's disease and other subcortical dementias.

Genetic Factors

The genetic data strongly indicate that a significant factor in the development of a mood disorder is genetics. However, the pattern of genetic inheritance is clearly through complex mechanisms; not only is it impossible to exclude psychosocial effect, but nongenetic factors probably play causative roles in the development of mood disorders in at least some people. In addition, there is a stronger genetic component for the transmission of bipolar I disorder than for the transmission of major depressive disorder.

FAMILY STUDIES

Family studies have repeatedly found that the first-degree relatives of bipolar I disorder probands are 8 to 18 times more likely than are the first-degree relatives of control subjects to have bipolar I disorder and 2 to 10 times more likely to have major depressive disorder. Family studies have also found that the first-degree relatives of major depressive disorder probands are 1.5 to 2.5 times more likely to have bipolar I disorder than are the first-degree relatives of normal control subjects and two to three times more likely to have major depressive disorder. Family studies have found that the likelihood of having a mood disorder decreases as the degree of relationship widens. For example, a second-degree relative (for example, a cousin) is less likely to be affected than is a first-degree relative (for example, a brother). The inheritability of bipolar I disorder is also shown by the fact that about 50 percent of all bipolar I disorder patients have at least one parent with a mood disorder, most often major depressive disorder. If one percent has bipolar I disorder, there is a 25 percent chance that any child has a mood disorder; if both parents have bipolar I disorder, there is a 50 to 75 percent chance that a child has a mood disorder.

ADOPTION STUDIES

Adoption studies have also produced data that support the genetic basis for the inheritance of mood disorders. Two of three adoption studies have found a strong genetic component for the inheritance of major depressive disorder; the only adoption study for bipolar I disorder also suggested a genetic basis. Essentially, those adoption studies have found that the biological children of affected parents remain at increased risk of a mood disorder, even if they are reared in nonaffected, adoptive families. Adoption studies have also shown that the biological parents of adopted mood-disordered children have a prevalence of mood disorder similar to that of the parents of nonadopted mood-disordered children. The prevalence of mood disorders in the adoptive parents is similar to the baseline prevalence in the general population.

TWIN STUDIES

Twin studies have shown that the concordance rate for bipolar I disorder in monozygotic twins is 33 to 90 percent, depending on the particular study; for major depressive disorder the concordance rate in monozygotic twins is about 50 percent. By contrast, the concordance rates in dizygotic twins are about 5 to 25 percent for bipolar I disorder and 10 to 25 percent for major depressive disorder.

LINKAGE STUDIES

The availability of modern techniques of molecular biology, including restriction fragment length polymorphisms (RFLPs), has led to many studies that have reported, replicated, or failed to replicate various associations between specific genes or gene markers and one of the mood disorders. At this time, no genetic association has been consistently replicated. The most reasonable interpretation of the studies is that the particular genes identified in the positive studies may be involved with the genetic inheritance of the mood disorder in the family studies but may not be involved in the genetic inheritance of the mood disorder in other families. Associations between the mood disorders, particularly bipolar I disorder, and genetic markers have been reported for chromosomes 5, 11, and X. The D_1 receptor gene is located on chromosome 5. The gene for tyrosine hydroxylase, the rate-limiting enzyme for catecholamine synthesis, is located on chromosome 11.

Chromosome 11 and Bipolar I Disorder

A study reported in 1987 an association between bipolar I disorder among members of an Old Order Amish family and genetic markers on the short arm of chromosome 11. With subsequent extension of that pedigree and the development of bipolar I disorder in previously unaffected family members, the statistical association ceased to apply. That turn of events effectively suggested the degree of caution that must be used in carrying out and interpreting genetic linkage studies in mental disorders.

X Chromosome and Bipolar I Disorder

Linkage has long been suggested between bipolar I disorder and a region on the X chromosome that contains genes for color blindness and glucose-6-phosphate dehydrogenase deficiency. As with most linkage studies in psychiatry, the application of molecular genetic techniques has produced contradictory results; some studies find a linkage and others do not. The most conservative interpretation remains the possibility that an X-linked gene is a factor in the development of bipolar I disorder in some patients and families.

Psychosocial Factors

LIFE EVENTS AND ENVIRONMENTAL STRESS

One long-standing clinical observation that has been replicated is that stressful life events more often precede the first episodes of mood disorders than subsequent episodes. That association has been reported for both major depressive disorder and bipolar I disorder patients. One theory proposed to explain the observation is that the stress that accompanies the first episode results in long-lasting changes in the biology of the brain. Those long-lasting changes may result in changes in the functional states of various neurotransmitter and intraneuronal signaling systems. The changes may even include the loss of neurons and an excessive reduction in synaptic contacts. The net result of the changes is to cause the person to be at a higher risk of suffering from subsequent episodes of a mood disorder, even without an external stressor.

Some clinicians strongly believe that life events play the primary or principal role in depression; other clinicians suggest that life events have only a limited role in the onset and the timing of depression. The most compelling data indicate that the life event most associated with the later development of depression is the loss of the parent before age 11. The environmental stressor most associated with the onset of an episode of depression is the loss of a spouse.

Family

Several theoretical articles and many anecdotal reports concern the relation between family functioning and the onset the course of mood disorders, particularly major depressive disorder. Several reports have indicated that the psychopathology observed in the family during the time the identified patient is being treated tends to remain, even after the patient has recovered. Moreover, the degree of psychopathology in the family may affect the rate of recovery, the return of symptoms, and the patient's postrecovery adjustment. The clinical and anecdotal data support the clinical importance of evaluating the family life of a patient and of addressing any identified family-related stresses.

PREMORBID PERSONALITY FACTORS

No single personality trait or type uniquely predisposes one to depression. All humans, of whatever personality pattern, can and do become depressed under appropriate circumstances; however, certain personality types—oral-dependent, obsessive-compulsive, hysterical—may be at greater risk for depression than are antisocial, paranoid, and other personality types who use projection and other externalizing defense mechanisms. No evidence shows that any particular personality disorder is associated with the later development of bipolar I disorder. However, dysthymic disorder and cyclothymic disorder are associated with the later development of bipolar I disorder.

PSYCHOANALYTIC AND PSYCHODYNAMIC FACTORS

In attempting to understand depression, Sigmund Freud postulated a relation between object loss and melancholia. He suggested that the depressed patient's rage is internally directed because of identification with the lost object. Freud believed that introjection may be the only way for the ego to relinquish an object. He differentiated melancholia or depression from grief on the basis that the depressed patient feels profound self-depreciation in association with guilt and self-reproach, while the mourner does not.

Melanie Klein later linked depression to the depressive position. She understood manic-depressive cycles as a reflection of a failure in childhood to establish loving introjects. In her view, depressed patients suffer from the concern that they may have destroyed loving objects through their own destructiveness and greed. Because of that fantasied destruction, they experience persecution by the remaining hated objects. The worthless feeling that is characteristic of depressed patients grows out of a sense that their good internal parents have been transformed into persecutors because of the patients' destructive fantasies and impulses. Klein regarded mania as a set of defensive operations designed to idealize others, deny any aggression or destructiveness toward others, and restore the lost love objects.

E. Bibring regarded depression as a primary affective state that has little to do with aggression turned inward. Instead, he regarded depression as an affect arising from tension within the ego between one's aspirations and one's reality. When depressed patients realize that they have not lived up to their ideals, they feel helpless and powerless as a result. In essence, depression can be summarized as a partial or complete collapse of the self-esteem within the ego.

Recently, Heinz Kohut redefined depression in terms of self psychology. When self-object needs for mirroring, twinship, or idealization are not forthcoming from significant people, the depressed person feels a sense of incompleteness and despair at not receiving the longed-for response. Within that idea, certain responses in the environment are necessary to sustain self-esteem and a feeling of wholeness.

LEARNED HELPLESSNESS

In experiments in which animals were repeatedly exposed to electric shocks from which they could not escape, the animals eventually gave up and made no attempt to escape future shocks. They learned that they were helpless. In humans who are depressed, one can find a similar state of helplessness. According to learned-helplessness theory, depression can improve if the clinician instills in the depressed patient a sense of control and mastery of the environment. The clinician uses behavioral techniques of reward and positive reinforcement in such efforts.

COGNITIVE THEORY

According to cognitive theory, common cognitive misinterpretations involve negative distortions of life experience, negative self-evaluation, pessimism, and hopelessness. Those learned negative views then lead to the feeling of depression. A cognitive therapist attempts to identify negative cognitions by using behavioral tasks, such as recording and consciously modifying the patient' thoughts.

DIAGNOSIS

Major Depressive Disorder

DSM-IV lists the criteria for a major depressive episode separately from the diagnostic criteria for depression-related diagnoses (Table 9.1–1). DSM-IV requires that the disorder has caused social or occupational impairment or has caused marked distress to the patient.

WITH PSYCHOTIC FEATURES

The presence of psychotic features in major depressive disorder reflects severe disease and is a poor prognostic indicator. Clinicians and researchers have dichotomized depressive illness along a psychotic-neurotic continuum. A review of the literature comparing psychotic with nonpsychotic major depressive disorder indicates that the two conditions may be distinct in their pathogenesis. One difference is that bipolar I disorder is more common in the families of probands with psychotic depression than in the families of probands with nonpsychotic depression.

The psychotic symptoms themselves are often categorized as either *mood-congruent*—that is, in harmony with the mood disorder ("I deserve to be punished because I am so bad")—or *mood-incongruent*—that is, not in harmony with the mood disorder. Although mood disorder patients with mood-congruent psychoses have a psychotic type of mood disorder, mood disorder patients with mood-incongruent psychotic symptoms have been variously typed as having schizoaffective disorder or a subtype of schizophrenia or some completely distinct diagnostic entity. Although the classification of those mood-incongruent patients remains controversial, the weight of the research data and the guidelines in DSM-IV suggest that one should classify such patients as having a psychotic mood disorder.

Psychotic features are generally a sign of a poor prognosis

Table 9.1-1.   Criteria for Major Depressive Episode

A. Five (or more) of the following symptoms have been present during the same 2-week period and represent a change from previous functioning; at least one of the symptoms is either (1) depressed mood or (2) loss of interest or pleasure.

   (1) depressed mood most of the day, nearly every day, as indicated by either subjective report (e.g., feels sad or empty) or observation made by others (e.g., appears tearful). **Note:** In children and adolescents, can be irritable mood.
   (2) markedly diminished interest or pleasure in all, or almost all, activities most of the day, nearly every day (as indicated by either subjective account or observation made by others)
   (3) significant weight loss when not dieting or weight gain (e.g., a change of more than 5% of body weight in a month), or decrease or increase in appetite nearly every day. **Note:** In children, consider failure to make expected weight gains.
   (4) insomnia or hypersomnia nearly every day
   (5) psychomotor agitation or retardation nearly every day (observable by others, not merely subjective feelings of restlessness or being slowed down)
   (6) fatigue or loss of energy nearly every day
   (7) feelings of worthlessness or excessive or inappropriate guilt (which may be delusional) nearly every day (not merely self-reproach or guilt about being sick)
   (8) diminished ability to think or concentrate, or indecisiveness, nearly every day (either by subjective account or as observed by others)
   (9) recurrent thoughts of death (not just fear of dying), recurrent suicidal ideation without a specific plan, or a suicide attempt or a specific plan for committing suicide.

B. The symptoms do not meet criteria for a mixed episode.

C. The symptoms cause clinically significant distress or impairment in social, occupational, or other important areas of functioning.

D. The symptoms are not due to the direct physiological effects of a substance (e.g., a drug of abuse, a medication) or a general medical condition (e.g., hypothyroidism).

E. The symptoms are not better accounted for by bereavement, i.e., after the loss of a loved one, the symptoms persist for longer than 2 months or are characterized by marked functional impairment, morbid preoccupation with worthlessness, suicidal ideation, psychotic symptoms, or psychomotor retardation.

Table from DSM-IV, *Diagnostic and Statistical Manual of Mental Disorders*, ed 4. Copyright American Psychiatric Association, Washington, 1994. Used with permission.

for patients with mood disorders. The following factors have been associated with a poor prognosis: long duration of episodes, temporal dissociation between the mood disorder and the psychotic symptoms, and a poor premorbid history of social adjustment. The presence of psychotic features also has significant treatment implications; patients with psychotic features almost invariably require antipsychotic drugs in addition to antidepressants or may require electroconvulsive therapy (ECT) to obtain clinical improvement.

Major Depressive Disorder, Single Episode

DSM-IV specifies the diagnostic criteria for the first episode of major depressive disorder. The differentiation between patients who have a single episode of major depressive disorder and patients who have two or more episodes of major depressive disorder is justified because of the uncertain course of the patients who have just one episode.

Major Depressive Disorder, Recurrent

Patients who are experiencing at least their second episode of depression are classified in DSM-IV as having major depressive

disorder, recurrent. The major problem with diagnosing recurrent episode of major depressive disorder is deciding what criteria to use to designate the resolution of each period. The two variables are the degree of resolution of the symptoms and the length of the resolution. DSM-IV requires that distinct episodes of depression be separated by at least a two-month period, during which the patient has no significant symptoms of depression.

Bipolar I Disorder

The designation bipolar I disorder is synonymous with what was known as bipolar disorder—that is, a syndrome with a complete set of symptoms for mania during the course of the disorder (Table 9.1–2). DSM-IV has now formalized the diagnostic criteria for a disorder known as bipolar II disorder; it is characterized by the presence during the course of the disorder of depressive episodes and hypomanic episodes—that is, episodes of manic symptoms that do not quite meet the diagnostic criteria for a full manic syndrome (Table 9.1–3). Bipolar II disorder is discussed in Section 9.3.

DSM-IV specifically states (see Table 9.1–2) that manic episodes that are clearly precipitated by antidepressant treatment (for example, pharmacotherapy, electroconvulsive therapy [ECT]) are not indicative of bipolar I disorder.

Bipolar I Disorder, Single Manic Episode

According to DSM-IV, patients must be experiencing their first manic episode to meet the diagnostic criteria for bipolar I disorder, single manic episode. The logic rests on the fact that patients who are having their first episode of bipolar I disorder depression cannot be distinguished from patients with major depressive disorder.

Table 9.1-2.   Criteria for Manic Episode

A. A distinct period of abnormally and persistently elevated, expansive, or irritable mood, lasting at least 1 week (or any duration if hospitalization is necessary).

B. During the period of mood disturbance, three (or more) of the following symptoms have persisted (four if the mood is only irritable) and have been present to a significant degree:

   (1) inflated self-esteem or grandiosity
   (2) decreased need for sleep (e.g., feels rested after only 3 hours of sleep)
   (3) more talkative than usual or pressure to keep talking
   (4) flight of ideas or subjective experience that thoughts are racing
   (5) distractibility (i.e., attention too easily drawn to unimportant or irrelevant external stimuli)
   (6) increase in goal-directed activity (either socially, at work or school, or sexually) or psychomotor agitation
   (7) excessive involvement in pleasurable activities that have a high potential for painful consequences (e.g., engaging in unrestrained buying sprees, sexual indiscretions, or foolish business investments)

C. The symptoms do not meet criteria for a mixed episode.

D. The mood disturbance is sufficiently severe to cause marked impairment in occupational functioning or in usual social activities or relationships with others, or to necessitate hospitalization to prevent harm to self or others, or there are psychotic features.

E. The symptoms are not due to the direct physiological effects of a substance (e.g., a drug of abuse, a medication, or other treatment) or a general medical condition (e.g., hyperthyroidism).

Table from DSM-IV, *Diagnostic and Statistical Manual of Mental Disorders*, ed 4. Copyright American Psychiatric Association, Washington, 1994. Used with permission.

Table 9.1–3.   Criteria for Hypomanic Episode

A. A distinct period of persistently elevated, expansive, or irritable mood, lasting throughout at least 4 days, that is clearly different from the usual nondepressed mood.

B. During the period of mood disturbance, three (or more) of the following symptoms have persisted (four if the mood is only irritable) and have been present to a significant degree:

   (1) inflated self-esteem or grandiosity
   (2) decreased need for sleep (e.g., feels rested after only 3 hours of sleep)
   (3) more talkative than usual or pressure to keep talking
   (4) flight of ideas or subjective experience that thoughts are racing
   (5) distractibility (i.e., attention too easily drawn to unimportant or irrelevant external stimuli)
   (6) increase in goal-directed activity (either socially, at work or school, or sexually) or psychomotor agitation
   (7) excessive involvement in pleasurable activities that have a high potential for painful consequences (e.g., the person engages in unrestrained buying sprees, sexual indiscretions, or foolish business investments)

C. The episode is associated with an unequivocal change in functioning that is uncharacteristic of the person when not symptomatic.

D. The disturbance in mood and the change in functioning are observable by others.

E. The episode is not severe enough to cause marked impairment in social or occupational functioning, or to necessitate hospitalization, and there are no psychotic features.

F. The symptoms are not due to the direct physiological effects of a substance (e.g., drug of abuse, a medication, or other treatment) or a general medical condition (e.g., hyperthyroidism).

Table from DSM-IV, *Diagnostic and Statistical Manual of Mental Disorders*, ed 4. Copyright American Psychiatric Association, Washington, 1994. Used with permission.

BIPOLAR I DISORDER, RECURRENT

The issues regarding the definition of the end of an episode of depression also apply to the definition of the end on an episode of mania. In DSM-IV, episodes are considered distinct if they are separated by at least two months without significant symptoms of mania or hypomania.

Cross-Sectional Symptom Features

DSM-IV defines three additional symptom features that can be used to describe patients with various mood disorders. Two of the cross-sectional symptom features (melancholic features and atypical features) are limited to the description of depressive episodes. The third cross-sectional symptom feature (catatonic features) can be applied to the description of either depressive or manic episodes.

WITH MELANCHOLIC FEATURES

In the literature on the melancholic features of depression, about 10 systems have been suggested, with almost three times as many specific criteria for symptoms and course specifiers. In view of the absence of sufficient data on any one of those systems and the absence of adequate comparative studies of those systems, any decision regarding the specific criteria is essentially arbitrary. Moreover, the arbitrary nature of the decisions has not succeeded in discouraging frequent changes in the officially accepted definition of melancholia. The potential importance of identifying the melancholic features of major

depressive episodes is to identify a group of patients whom some data indicate are more responsive to pharmacotherapeutic treatment than are nonmelancholic depressed patients.

The DSM-IV melancholic features can be applied to major depressive episodes in major depressive disorder, bipolar I disorder, or bipolar II disorder (Table 9.1–4).

WITH ATYPICAL FEATURES

The introduction of a formally defined type of depression with atypical features is in response to research and clinical data suggesting that patients with atypical features have specific, predictable characteristics. The classic atypical features are overeating and oversleeping. Those symptoms have sometimes been called reversed vegetative symptoms, and the symptom pattern has sometimes been called hysteroid dysphoria. When major depressive disorder patients with the features are compared with major depressive disorder patients without the features, the patients with the atypical features are found to have a younger age of onset, a more severe degree of psychomotor slowing, and more frequent coexisting diagnoses of panic disorder, substance abuse or dependence, and somatization disorder. The high incidence and the severity of anxiety symptoms in patients with atypical features have been correlated in some research with the likelihood of their being misclassified as having an anxiety disorder, rather than a mood disorder. Patients with atypical features may also be likely to have a long-term course, a diagnosis of bipolar I disorder, or a seasonal pattern to their disorder. The major treatment implication of atypical features is that the patients are more likely to respond to monoamine oxidase inhibitors (MAOIs) than to tricyclic drugs. However, the significance of atypical features remains controversial, as does the preferential treatment response to MAOIs. Moreover, the absence of specific diagnostic criteria has limited the ability to assess their validity and prevalence and to ascertain the existence of any other biological or psychological factors that may differentiate it from other symptom patterns.

Table 9.1–4.   Criteria for Melancholic Features Specifier

Specify if:
With melancholic features (can be applied to the current or most recent major depressive episode in major depressive disorder and to a major depressive episode in bipolar I or bipolar II disorder only if it is the most recent type of mood episode)

A. Either of the following, occuring during the most severe period of the current episode.

   (1) loss of pleasure in all, or almost all, activities
   (2) lack of reactivity to usually pleasurable stimuli (does not feel much better, even temporarily, when something good happens)

B. Three (or more) of the following:

   (1) distinct quality of depressed moods (i.e., the depressed mood is experienced as distinctly different from the kind of feeling experienced after the death of a loved one)
   (2) depression regularly worse in the morning
   (3) early morning awakening (at least 2 hours before usual time of awakening)
   (4) marked psychomotor retardation or agitation
   (5) significant anorexia or weight loss
   (6) excessive or inappropriate guilt

Table from DSM-IV, *Diagnostic and Statistical Manual of Mental Disorders*, ed 4. Copyright American Psychiatric Association, Washington, 1994. Used with permission.

WITH CATATONIC FEATURES

The decision to include a specific classification for catatonic features in the mood disorders category was motivated by two factors. First, since one intent of DSM-IV is to be helpful in the differential diagnosis of mental disorders, the inclusion of a specific catatonic type of mood disorder helps balance the presence of a catatonic type of schizophrenia. Catatonia is a symptom that can be present in some mental disorders, most commonly schizophrenia and the mood disorders. Second, although as yet incompletely studied, the presence of catatonic features in patients with mood disorders will probably be shown to have prognostic and treatment significance.

The hallmark symptoms of catatonia—stupor, blunted affect, extreme withdrawal, negativism, and marked psychomotor retardation—can be seen in both catatonic and noncatatonic schizophrenia, major depressive disorder (often with psychotic features), and medical and neurological disorders. However, catatonic symptoms are probably most commonly associated with bipolar I disorder. That association is often not made in the clinician's mind, because of the marked contrast between the symptoms of stuporous catatonia and the classic symptoms of mania. The most important clinical point is that catatonic symptoms are a behavioral syndrome that can be seen in a number of medical and psychiatric conditions; catatonic symptoms do not imply a single diagnosis.

In DSM-IV catatonic features can be applied to the most recent manic episode or major depressive episode in major depressive disorder, bipolar I disorder, or bipolar II disorder.

NON-DSM-IV TYPES

Other systems also identify types of patients with mood disorders; those systems usually separate patients with good and poor prognoses or patients who may respond to a particular treatment. The differentiations include endogenous-reactive and primary-secondary schemes.

The endogenous-reactive continuum is a controversial division because it implies that endogenous depressions are biological and that reactive depressions are psychological; the division is based primarily on the presence or the absence of an identifiable precipitating stress. Other symptoms of endogenous depression have been described as diurnal variation, delusions, psychomotor retardation, early morning awakening, and feelings of guilt; thus, endogenous depression is similar to the DSM-IV diagnosis of major depressive disorder with psychotic features or melancholic features or both. Symptoms of reactive depression have been described as including initial insomnia, anxiety, emotional lability, and multiple somatic complaints.

Primary depressions are what DSM-IV refers to as mood disorders except for the diagnoses of mood disorder due to a general medical condition and substance-induced mood disorder, which are considered secondary depressions. *Double depression* is the condition in which major depressive disorder is superimposed on dysthymic disorder. A *depressive equivalent* is a symptom or syndrome that may be a *forme fruste* of a depressive episode. For example, a triad of truancy, alcohol abuse, and sexual promiscuity in a formerly well-behaved adolescent may constitute a depressive equivalent.

Course Specifiers

DSM-IV includes criteria for three distinct course specifiers for mood disorders. One of the course specifiers, with rapid cycling, is restricted to bipolar I disorder and bipolar II disorder. Another course specifier, with seasonal pattern, can be applied to bipolar I disorder, bipolar II disorder, and major depressive disorder, recurrent. The third course specifier, with postpartum onset, can be applied to major depressive or manic episodes in bipolar I disorder, bipolar II disorder, major depressive disorder, and brief psychotic disorder.

RAPID CYCLING

Rapid cycling bipolar I disorder patients are likely to be female and to have had depressive and hypomanic episodes. No data shows that rapid cycling has a familial pattern of inheritance; this suggests that some external factor (for example, stress or drug treatment) is involved in the pathogenesis of rapid cycling. The DSM-IV criteria specify that the patient must have at least four episodes within a 12-month period.

SEASONAL PATTERN

Patients with a seasonal pattern to their mood disorders tend to experience depressive episodes during a particular time of the year, most commonly winter. The pattern has become known as seasonal affective disorder (SAD), although that term is not used in DSM-IV. Two types of evidence suggest that the seasonal pattern may represent a separate diagnostic entity. First, the patients are likely to respond to treatment with light therapy, although adequate studies to evaluate light therapy in nonseasonally depressed patients have not been conducted. Second, at least one PET study has found that the patients have decreased metabolic activity in the orbital frontal cortex and in the left inferior parietal lobule. Although that study has yet to be replicated, future studies will probably attempt to differentiate depressed persons with seasonal pattern from other depressed persons.

POSTPARTUM ONSET

DSM-IV allows for the specification of a postpartum mood disturbance if the onset of symptoms is within four weeks postpartum. Postpartum mental disorders commonly include psychotic symptoms. Postpartum psychotic disorders are discussed in Section 8.1.

LONGITUDINAL COURSE SPECIFIERS

DSM-IV includes specific descriptions of longitudinal courses for both major depressive disorder and bipolar I disorder. The purpose of the inclusion of the longitudinal course specifiers in DSM-IV is to allow clinicians and researchers to use the criteria to identify prospectively any treatment or prognostic significance in various longitudinal courses. Although preliminary studies of the DSM-IV longitudinal course specifiers indicate that clinicians can assess the longitudinal course, more and larger studies are needed to develop a solid appreciation of the assessment and the implications of variations in the longitudinal course. The cyclothymic and dysthymic features in the longitudinal course specifiers are described in Section 9.2.

CLINICAL FEATURES

There are two basic symptom patterns in mood disorders, one for depression and one for mania. Depressive episodes can occur in both major depressive disorder and bipolar I disorder.

Many studies have attempted with great difficulty to find reliable differences between bipolar I disorder depressive episodes and episodes of major depressive disorder. In the clinical situation, only the patient's history, family history, and future course can help differentiate the two conditions. Some patients with bipolar I disorder have mixed states with both manic and depressive features. Also, some bipolar I disorder patients seem to experience brief—minutes to a few hours—episodes of depression during manic episodes.

Depressive Episodes

A depressed mood and a loss of interest or pleasure are the key symptoms of depression. Patients may say that they feel blue, hopeless, in the dumps, or worthless. For the patient the depressed mood often has a distinct quality that differentiates it from the normal emotion of sadness or grief. Patients often describe the symptom of depression as one of agonizing emotional pain. Depressed patients sometimes complain about being unable to cry, a symptom that resolves as they improve.

About two thirds of all depressed patients contemplate suicide, and 10 to 15 percent commit suicide. However, depressed patients sometimes seem unaware of their depression and do not complain of a mood disturbance, though they exhibit withdrawal from family, friends, and activities that previously interested them.

Almost all depressed patients (97 percent) complain about reduced energy that results in difficulty in finishing tasks, school and work impairment, and decreased motivation to undertake new projects. About 80 percent of patients complain of trouble in sleeping, especially early morning awakening (that is, terminal insomnia) and multiple awakenings at night, during which they ruminate about their problems.

Many patients have decreased appetite and weight loss. Some patients, however, have increased appetite, weight gain, and increased sleep. Those patients are classified in DSM-IV as having atypical features and are also known as having hysteroid dysphoria. Anxiety, in fact, is a common symptom of depression, affecting as many as 90 percent of all depressed patients. The various changes in food intake and rest can aggravate coexisting medical illnesses, such as diabetes, hypertension, chronic obstructive lung disease, and heart disease. Other vegetative symptoms include abnormal menses and decreased interest and performance in sexual activities. Sexual problems can sometimes lead to inappropriate referrals, such as to marital counseling and sex therapy, or the clinician fails to recognize the underlying depressive disorder.

Anxiety (including panic attacks), alcohol abuse, and somatic complaints (such as constipation and headaches) often complicate the treatment of depression. About 50 percent of all patients describe a diurnal variation in their symptoms, with an increased severity in the morning and a lessening of symptoms by evening. Cognitive symptoms include subjective reports of an inability to concentrate (84 percent of patients in one study) and impairments in thinking (67 percent of patients in another study).

DEPRESSION IN CHILDREN AND ADOLESCENTS

School phobia and excessive clinging to parents may be symptoms of depression in children. Poor academic performance, substance abuse, antisocial behavior, sexual promiscu-

ity, truancy, and running away may be symptoms of depression in adolescents. Chapter 46 discusses this area further.

DEPRESSION IN THE ELDERLY

Depression is more common in the elderly than it is in the general population. Various studies have reported prevalence rates ranging from 25 to almost 50 percent, although what percentage of those cases are major depressive disorder is uncertain. A number of studies have reported data suggesting that depression in the elderly may be correlated with low socioeconomic status, the loss of a spouse, a concurrent physical illness, and social isolation. Several studies have indicated that depression in the elderly is underdiagnosed and undertreated, perhaps particularly by general practitioners. The underrecognition of depression in the elderly may be due to the observation that depression is more often present with somatic complaints in the elderly than in younger age groups. Also, more than an element of ageism may be found in physicians, who may unconsciously accept more depressive symptoms in elderly patients than in younger patients.

Manic Episodes

An elevated, expansive, or irritable mood is the hallmark of a manic episode. The elevated mood is euphoric and often infectious, sometimes causing a countertransferential denial of illness by an inexperienced clinician. Although uninvolved people may not recognize the unusual nature of the patient's mood, those who know the patient recognize it as abnormal. Alternatively, the mood may be irritable, especially when the patient's overtly ambitious plans are thwarted. Often, a patient exhibits a change of predominant mood from euphoria early in the course of the illness to irritability later in the disorder.

The treatment of manic patients on an inpatient ward can be complicated by their testing of the limits of ward rules, a tendency to shift responsibility for their acts onto others, exploitation of the weaknesses of others, and a tendency to divide staffs. Outside the hospital, manic patients often drink alcohol excessively, perhaps in an attempt to self-medicate. Their disinhibited nature is reflected in their excessive use of the telephone, especially the making of long-distance calls during the early hours of the morning. Pathological gambling, a tendency to disrobe in public places, clothing and jewelry of bright colors in unusual combinations, and an inattention to small details (such as forgetting to hang up the telephone) are also symptomatic of the disorder. The impulsive nature of many of the patients' acts is coupled with a sense of conviction and purpose. Patients are often preoccupied by religious, political, financial, sexual, or persecutory ideas that can evolve into complex delusional systems. Occasionally, manic patients become regressed and play with their urine and feces.

MANIA IN ADOLESCENTS

Mania in adolescents is often misdiagnosed as antisocial personality disorder or schizophrenia. Symptoms of mania in adolescents may include psychosis, alcohol or other substance abuse, suicide attempts, academic problems, philosophical brooding, obsessive-compulsive disorder symptoms, multiple somatic complaints, marked irritability resulting in fights, and other antisocial behaviors. Although many of those symptoms are seen in normal adolescence, severe or persistent symptoms should cause the clinician to consider bipolar I disorder in the differential diagnosis.

Coexisting Disorders

ANXIETY

In the anxiety disorders, DSM-IV notes the existence of mixed anxiety-depressive disorder. Significant symptoms of anxiety can and often do coexist with significant symptoms of depression. Whether patients who exhibit significant symptoms of both anxiety and depression are affected by two distinct disease processes or by a single disease process that produces both sets of symptoms is not yet resolved. Patients of both types may constitute the group of patients with mixed anxiety-depressive disorder.

ALCOHOL DEPENDENCE

Alcohol dependence frequently coexists with mood disorders. Both major depressive disorder patients and bipolar I disorder patients are likely to meet the diagnostic criteria for an alcohol use disorder. The available data indicate that alcohol dependence in women is more strongly associated with a coexisting diagnosis of depression than is alcohol dependence in men. In contrast, the genetic and family data regarding men who have both a mood disorder and alcohol dependence suggest that they are likely to be suffering from two genetically distinct disease processes.

OTHER SUBSTANCE-RELATED DISORDERS

Substance-related disorders other than alcohol dependence are also commonly associated with mood disorders. In any individual patient the abuse of substances may be involved in the precipitation of an episode of illness, or, conversely, the abuse of substances may be patients' attempts to treat their own illnesses. Although manic patients seldom use sedatives to dampen their euphoria, depressed patients often use stimulants, such as cocaine and amphetamines, to relieve their depression.

MEDICAL CONDITIONS

Depression commonly coexists with medical conditions, especially in the elderly. When depression and medical conditions coexist, the clinician must try to determine whether the underlying medical condition is pathophysiologically related to the depression or whether any drugs that the patient is taking for the medical condition are causing the depression. Many studies suggest that treatment of a coexisting major depressive disorder can improve the course of the underlying medical disorder, including cancer.

MENTAL STATUS EXAMINATION

Depressive Episodes

GENERAL DESCRIPTION

Generalized psychomotor retardation is the most common symptom, although psychomotor agitation is also seen, especially in elderly patients. Hand wringing and hair pulling are the most common symptoms of agitation. Classically, a depressed patient has a stooped posture, no spontaneous movements, and a downcast, averted gaze. On clinical examination, depressed patients exhibiting gross symptoms of psychomotor retardation

may appear identical to patients with catatonic schizophrenia. That fact is recognized in DSM-IV by the inclusion of the symptom qualifier "with catatonic features" for some mood disorders.

MOOD, AFFECT, AND FEELINGS

Depression is the key symptom, although about half of the patients deny depressive feelings and do not appear particularly depressed. Those patients are often brought in by family members or employers because of social withdrawal and generally decreased activity.

SPEECH

Many depressed patients evidence a decreased rate and volume of speech, responding to questions with single words and exhibiting delayed responses to questions. The examiner may literally have to wait two or three minutes for a response to a question.

PERCEPTUAL DISTURBANCES

Depressed patients with delusions or hallucinations are said to have a major depressive episode with psychotic features. Some clinicians also use the term "psychotic depression" for grossly regressed depressed patients—mute, not bathing, soiling—even without delusions or hallucinations. Such patients are probably better described as having catatonic features.

Delusions and hallucinations that are consistent with a depressed mood are said to be mood-congruent. Mood-congruent delusions in a depressed person include those of guilt, sinfulness, worthlessness, poverty, failure, persecution, and terminal somatic illnesses (for example, cancer and "rotting" brain). The content of the mood-incongruent delusions or hallucinations is not consistent with the depressed mood. Mood-incongruent delusions in a depressed person involve grandiose themes of exaggerated power, knowledge, and worth—for example, the belief that one is being persecuted because one is the Messiah. Hallucinations also occur in major depressive episodes with psychotic features but are relatively rare.

THOUGHT

Depressed patients customarily have a negative view of the world and of themselves. Their thought content often involves nondelusional ruminations about loss, guilt, suicide, and death. About 10 percent of all depressed patients have marked symptoms of a thought disorder, usually thought blocking and profound poverty of content.

SENSORIUM AND COGNITION

ORIENTATION

Most depressed patients are oriented to person, place, and time, although some may not have enough energy or interest to answer questions about those subjects during an interview.

Memory

About 50 to 75 percent of all depressed patients have a cognitive impairment sometimes called depressive pseudodementia. Such patients commonly complain of impaired concentration and forgetfulness.

IMPULSE CONTROL

About 10 to 15 percent of all depressed patients complete suicide, and about two thirds have suicidal ideation. Depressed patients with psychotic features occasionally consider killing a person involved with their delusional systems. However, the most severely depressed patients often lack the motivation or the energy to act in an impulsive or violent way. Patients with depressive disorders are at increased risk of suicide as they begin to improve and to regain the energy needed to plan and carry out a suicide (paradoxical suicide). It is usually not clinically wise to give a depressed patient a large prescription for antidepressants, especially tricyclic drugs, on discharge from the hospital.

JUDGMENT AND INSIGHT

Patients' judgment is best assessed by reviewing their actions in the recent past and their behavior during the interview. Depressed patients' insight into their disorder is often excessive; they over-emphasize their symptoms, their disorder, and their life problems. It is difficult to convince such patients that improvement is possible.

RELIABILITY

All information obtained from a depressed patient overemphasizes the bad and minimizes the good. A common clinical mistake is to unquestioningly believe a depressed patient who says that a previous trial of antidepressant medications did not work. Such statements may be false, and they require confirmation from another source. The psychiatrist should not view the patients' misinformation as an intentional fabrication, since the admission of any hopeful information may be impossible for a person in a depressed state of mind.

OBJECTIVE RATING SCALES FOR DEPRESSION

Objective rating scales for depression can be useful in clinical practice for the documentation of the depressed patient's clinical state.

Manic Episodes

GENERAL DESCRIPTION

Manic patients are excited, talkative, sometimes amusing, and frequently hyperactive. At times they are grossly psychotic and disorganized, requiring physical restraints and the intramuscular injection of sedating drugs.

MOOD, AFFECT, AND FEELINGS

Manic patients are classically euphoric but can also be irritable, especially when the mania has been present for some time. They also have a low frustration tolerance, which may lead to feelings of anger and hostility. Manic patients may be emotionally labile, switching from laughter to irritability to depression in minutes or hours.

SPEECH

Manic patients cannot be interrupted while they are speaking, and they are often intrusive nuisances to those around them. Speech is often disturbed. As the mania gets more intense, speech becomes louder, more rapid, and difficult to interpret. As the activated state increases, speech becomes full of puns, jokes, rhymes, plays on words, and irrelevancies. As the activity level increases still more, associations become loosened. The ability to concentrate fades, leading to flight of ideas, word salad, and neologisms. In acute manic excitement, speech may be totally incoherent and indistinguishable from that of a schizophrenic person.

PERCEPTUAL DISTURBANCES

Delusions are present in 75 percent of all manic patients. Mood-congruent manic delusions often involve great wealth, abilities, or power. Delusions and hallucinations that are bizarre and mood-incongruent are also seen in mania.

THOUGHT

Manic patients' thought content includes themes of self-confidence and self-aggrandizement. Manic patients are often easily distracted. The cognitive functioning of the manic state is characterized by an unrestrained and accelerated flow of ideas.

SENSORIUM AND COGNITION

Although much has been written about the cognitive deficits seen in schizophrenic patients, much less has been written about similar deficits in bipolar I disorder patients, who may have similar minor cognitive deficits. The cognitive deficits reported can be interpreted as reflecting diffuse cortical dysfunction, although subsequent work may be able to localize the abnormal areas. Grossly, orientation and memory are intact, although some manic patients may be so euphoric that they answer incorrectly. The symptom was called ''delirious mania'' by Emil Kraepelin.

IMPULSE CONTROL

About 75 percent of all manic patients are assaultive or threatening. Manic patients do attempt suicide and homicide, but the incidence of those behaviors is not known. Patients who threaten particularly important people (such as the President of the United States) more often have bipolar I disorder than schizophrenia.

JUDGMENT AND INSIGHT

Impaired judgment is a hallmark of manic patients. They may break laws regarding credit cards, sexual activities, and finances, sometimes involving their families in financial ruin. Manic patients also have little insight into their disorder.

RELIABILITY

Manic patients are notoriously unreliable in their information. Lying and deceit are common in mania, often causing inexperienced clinicians to treat manic patients with inappropriate disdain.

DIFFERENTIAL DIAGNOSIS

Major Depressive Disorder

MEDICAL DISORDERS

When a nonpsychiatric medical condition causes a mood disorder, the DSM-IV diagnosis is mood disorder due to a general medical condition. When a substance causes a mood disorder, the DSM-IV diagnosis is substance-induced mood disorder. Both of those diagnostic categories are discussed in Section 9.3.

Failure to obtain a good clinical history or to consider the context of the patient's current life situation may lead to diagnostic errors. Depressed adolescents should be tested for mononucleosis. Patients who are markedly overweight or underweight should be tested for adrenal and thyroid dysfunctions. Homosexual and bisexual men and intravenous substance abusers should be tested for the human immunodeficiency virus (HIV). Elderly patients should be evaluated for viral pneumonia and other medical conditions.

Many neurological and medical disorders and pharmacological agents can produce symptoms of depression. Many patients with depressive disorders first go to their general practitioners with somatic complaints. Most organic causes of depressive disorders can be detected with a comprehensive medical history, a complete physical and neurological examination, and routine blood and urine tests. The workup should include tests for thyroid and adrenal functions, because disorders of both of those endocrine systems can present as depressive disorders. In substance-induced mood disorder, a reasonable rule of thumb is that any drug a depressed patient is taking should be considered a potential factor in the mood disorder. Cardiac drugs, antihypertensives, sedatives, hypnotics, antipsychotics, antiepileptics, antiparkinsonian drugs, analgesics, antibacterials, and antineoplastics are all commonly associated with depressive symptoms.

Neurological Conditions

The most common neurological problems that manifest depressive symptoms are Parkinson's disease, dementing illnesses (including dementia of the Alzheimer's type), epilepsy, cerebrovascular diseases, and tumors. About 50 to 75 percent of all patients with Parkinson's disease have marked symptoms of depressive disorder that are not correlated with the patient's degree of physical disability, age, or duration of illness but are correlated with the presence of abnormalities found on neuropsychological tests. The symptoms of depressive disorder may be masked by the almost identical motor symptoms of Parkinson's disease. Depressive symptoms often respond to antidepressant drugs or ECT.

The interictal changes associated with temporal lobe epilepsy can mimic a depressive disorder, especially if the epileptic focus is on the right side. Depression is a common complicating feature of cerebrovascular diseases, particularly in the two years after the episode. Depression is more common after anterior events than after posterior events. The depression often responds to antidepressant medications. Tumors of the diencephalic and temporal regions are particularly likely to be associated with depressive disorder symptoms.

Pseudodementia

The clinician can usually differentiate the pseudodementia of major depressive disorder from the dementia of a disease, such as Alzheimer's disease, on clinical grounds. The cognitive symptoms in major depressive disorder have a sudden onset, and other symptoms of major depressive disorder, such as self-reproach, are present. A diurnal variation to the cognitive problems that is not seen in primary dementias may be present. Depressed patients with cognitive difficulties often do not try to answer questions (''I don't know''), whereas demented patients may confabulate. In depressed patients, recent memory is more affected than is remote memory. Also, depressed patients can sometimes be coached and encouraged during an interview into remembering, an ability that demented patients lack.

MENTAL DISORDERS

Depression can be a feature of virtually any mental disorder listed in DSM-IV, but the mental disorders listed in Table 9.1–5 should be particularly considered in the differential diagnosis.

Other Mood Disorders

First, the clinician must rule out mood disorder due to a general medical condition and substance-induced mood disorder. Next, the clinician must determine whether the patient has had episodes of maniclike

Table 9.1–5. Mental Disorders That Commonly Have Depressive Features

Adjustment disorder with depressed mood

Alcohol use disorders

Anxiety disorders
   Generalized anxiety disorder
   Mixed anxiety-depressive disorder
   Panic disorder
   Posttraumatic stress disorder
   Obsessive-compulsive disorder

Eating disorders
   Anorexia nervosa
   Bulimia nervosa

Mood disorders
   Bipolar I disorder
   Bipolar II disorder
   Cyclothymic disorder
   Dysthymic disorder
   Major depressive disorder
   Minor depressive disorder
   Mood disorder due to a general medical condition
   Recurrent brief depressive disorder
   Substance-induced mood disorder

Schizophrenia

Schizophreniform disorder

Somatoform disorders (especially somatization disorder)

symptoms, indicating bipolar I disorder (complete manic and depressive syndromes), bipolar II disorder (recurrent major depressive episodes with hypomania), or cyclothymic disorder (incomplete depressive and manic syndromes). If the patient's symptoms are limited to those of depression, the clinician must assess the severity and the duration of the symptoms to differentiate among major depressive disorder (complete depressive syndrome for two weeks), minor depressive disorder (incomplete but episodic depressive syndrome), recurrent brief depressive disorder (complete depressive syndrome but for less than two weeks per episode), and dysthymic disorder (incomplete depressive syndrome without clear episodes).

Other Mental Disorders

Substance-related disorders, psychotic disorders, eating disorders, adjustment disorders, somatoform disorders, and anxiety disorders are all commonly associated with depressive symptoms and must be considered in the differential diagnosis of a patient with depressive symptoms. Perhaps the most difficult differential is between anxiety disorders with depression and depressive disorders with marked anxiety. The difficulty of making the differentiation is reflected in the inclusion of the diagnosis of mixed anxiety-depressive disorder in DSM-IV. An abnormal result on the dexamethasone-suppression test (DST), the presence of shortened REM latency on a sleep EEG, and a negative lactate infusion test result support a diagnosis of major depressive disorder in particularly troublesome cases.

Uncomplicated Bereavement

Uncomplicated bereavement is not considered a mental disorder, although about one third of all bereaved spouses meet the diagnostic criteria for major depressive disorder for a time. Some patients with uncomplicated bereavement do go on to major depressive disorder. However, the diagnosis is not made unless a resolution of the grief does not occur; the differentiation is based on the symptoms' severity and length. The symptoms commonly seen in major depressive disorder that evolve from unresolved bereavement are a morbid preoccupation with worthlessness, suicidal ideation, feelings that one has committed an act (not just an omission) that caused the death, mummification (keeping the deceased's belongings exactly as they were), and a particularly severe anniversary reaction, which sometimes includes a suicide attempt.

Table 9.1–6.   Drugs Associated with Manic Symptoms

Amphetamines
Baclofen
Bromide
Bromocriptine
Captopril
Cimetidine
Cocaine
Corticosteroids (including ACTH)
Cyclosporine
Disulfiram
Hallucinogens (intoxication and flashbacks)
Hydralazine
Isoniazid
Levodopa
Methylphenidate
Metrizamide (following myelography)
Opiates and opioids
Procarbazine
Procyclidine

Bipolar I Disorder

MEDICAL DISORDERS

In contrast to depressive symptoms, which are present in almost all psychiatric disorders, manic symptoms are more distinctive, although they can be caused by a wide range of medical and neurological conditions and substances (Table 9.1–6). Antidepressant treatment can also be associated with the precipitation of mania in some patients.

MENTAL DISORDERS

When a bipolar I disorder patient presents with a depressive episode, the differential diagnosis is the same as that for a patient who is being considered for a diagnosis of major depressive disorder. When a patient is manic, however, the differential diagnosis includes bipolar I disorder, bipolar II disorder, cyclothymic disorder, mood disorder due to a general medical condition, and substance-induced mood disorder. Of special consideration with manic symptoms are borderline, narcissistic, histrionic, and antisocial personality disorders.

Schizophrenia

A great deal has been published about the clinical difficulty of separating a manic episode from schizophrenia. Although difficult, a differential diagnosis is possible with a few clinical guidelines. Merriment, elation, and infectiousness of mood are much more common in manic episodes than in schizophrenia. The combination of a manic mood, rapid or pressured speech, and hyperactivity weights heavily toward a diagnosis of manic episode. The onset in a manic episode is often rapid and is perceived as a marked change from the patient's previous behavior. Half of all bipolar I disorder patients have a family history of a mood disorder. Catatonic features may be a depressive phase in bipolar I disorder. When evaluating catatonic patients, the clinician should carefully look for a history of manic or depressive episodes and for a family history of mood disorders. Manic symptoms in minorities (particularly blacks and Hispanics) are often misdiagnosed as schizophrenic symptoms.

COURSE AND PROGNOSIS

Major Depressive Disorder

COURSE

Onset

About 50 percent of patients in the first episode of major depressive disorder had significant depressive symptoms before the first identified episode. One implication of that observation is that early identification and treatment of early symptoms may prevent the development of a full depressive episode. Although symptoms may have been present, patients with major depressive disorder usually have not had a premorbid personality disorder. The first depressive episode occurs before age 40 in about 50 percent of patients. A later onset is associated with the absence of a family history of mood disorders, antisocial personality disorder, and alcohol abuse.

Duration

An untreated depressive episode lasts 6 to 13 months; most treated episodes last about three months. The withdrawal of antidepressants before three months has elapsed almost always results in the return of the symptoms. As the course of the disorder progresses, patients tend to have more frequent episodes that last longer. Over a 20-year period the mean number of episodes is five or six.

Development of Manic Episodes

About 5 to 10 percent of patients with an initial diagnosis of major depressive disorder have a manic episode 6 to 10 years after the first depressive episode. The mean age for that switch is 32 years, and it often occurs after two to four depressive episodes. Although the data are inconsistent and controversial, some clinicians report that the depression of patients who are later classified as bipolar I disorder patients is often characterized by hypersomnia, psychomotor retardation, psychotic symptoms, a history of postpartum episodes, a family history of bipolar I disorder, and a history of antidepressant-induced hypomania.

PROGNOSIS

Major depressive disorder is not a benign disorder. It tends to be chronic, and patients tend to relapse. Patients who have been hospitalized for a first episode of major depressive disorder have about a 50 percent chance of recovering in the first year. The percentage of patients recovering after hospitalization decreases with passing time, and after five years posthospitalization, 10 to 15 percent of patients have not recovered. Many unrecovered patients remain affected with dysthymic disorder. Recurrences of major depressive episodes are also common. About 25 percent of patients experience a recurrence in the first six months after release from a hospital, about 30 to 50 percent in the first two years, and about 50 to 75 percent in five years. The incidence of relapse is much lower than those figures in patients who continue prophylactic psychopharmacological treatment and in patients who have had only one or two depressive episodes. Generally, as a patient experiences more and more depressive episodes, the time between the episodes decreases, and the severity of each episode increases.

Prognostic Indicators

Many studies have attempted to identify both good and bad prognostic indicators in the course of major depressive disorder. Mild episodes, the absence of psychotic symptoms, and a short hospital stay are good prognostic indicators. Psychosocial indicators of a good course include a history of solid friendships during adolescence, stable family functioning, and a generally solid social functioning for the five years preceding the illness. Additional good prognostic signs are the absence of a comorbid psychiatric disorder, the absence of a personality disorder, no more than one previous hospitalization for major depressive disorder, and an advanced age of onset. The possibility of a poor prognosis is increased by coexisting dysthymic disorder, abuse of alcohol and other substances, anxiety disorder symptoms, and a history of more than one previous depressive episode. Men are more likely than women to experience a chronically impaired course.

Bipolar I Disorder

COURSE

The natural history of bipolar I disorder is such that is often useful to make a graph of the patient's disorder and to keep the graph up-to-date as treatment progresses. Although cyclothymic disorder is sometimes diagnosed retrospectively in bipolar I disorder patients, no identified personality traits are specifically associated with bipolar I disorder. Bipolar I disorder most often starts with depression (75 percent of the time in women, 67 percent in men) and is a recurring disorder. Most patients experience both depressive and manic episodes, although 10 to 20 percent experience only manic episodes. The manic episodes typically have a rapid onset (hours or days), but they may evolve over a few weeks. An untreated manic episode lasts about three months; therefore, the clinician should not discontinue drugs before that time. As the disorder progresses, the time between episodes often decreases. After about five episodes, however, the interepisode interval often stabilizes at six to nine months. Some bipolar I disorder patients have rapidly cycling episodes.

Bipolar I Disorder in Children and the Elderly

Bipolar I disorder can affect both the very young and the elderly. The incidence of bipolar I disorder in children and adolescents is about 1 percent, and the onset can be as early as age 8. Common misdiagnoses are schizophrenia and oppositional defiant disorder. Bipolar I disorder with such an early onset is associated with a poor prognosis. Manic symptoms are common in the elderly, although the range of causes is broad, including nonpsychiatric medical conditions, dementia, delirium, and bipolar I disorder. Currently available data suggest that the onset of true bipolar I disorder in the elderly is relatively uncommon.

PROGNOSIS

Patients with bipolar I disorder have a poorer prognosis than do patients with major depressive disorder. About 40 to 50 percent of bipolar I disorder patients may have a second manic episode within two years of the first episode. Although lithium (Eskalith) prophylaxis improves the course and the prognosis of bipolar I disorder, probably only 50 to 60 percent of patients achieve significant control of their symptoms with lithium. One four-year follow-up study of patients with bipolar I disorder found that a premorbid poor occupational status, alcohol dependence, psychotic features, depressive features, interepisode depressive features, and male gender were all factors that weighted toward a poor prognosis. Short duration of manic episodes, advanced age of onset, few suicidal thoughts, and few coexisting psychiatric or medical problems weight toward a good prognosis.

About 7 percent of all bipolar I disorder patients do not have a recurrence of symptoms, 45 percent have more than one episode, and 40 percent have a chronic disorder. Patients may have from 2 to 30 manic episodes, although the mean number is about nine. About 40 percent of all patients have more than

10 episodes. On long-term follow-up, 15 percent of all bipolar I disorder patients are well, 45 percent are well but have multiple relapses, 30 percent are in partial remission, and 10 percent are chronically ill. One third of all bipolar I disorder patients have chronic symptoms and evidence of significant social decline.

TREATMENT

The treatment of patients with mood disorders must be directed toward several goals. First, the safety of the patient must be guaranteed. Second, a complete diagnostic evaluation of the patient must be carried out. Third, a treatment plan must be initiated that addresses not only the immediate symptoms but also the patient's prospective well-being. Although the current emphasis is on pharmacotherapy and psychotherapy addressed to the individual patient, stressful life events are also associated with increases in relapse rates among patients with mood disorders. Thus, treatment must reduce the number and the severity of the stressors in patients' lives.

Overall, the treatment of mood disorders is rewarding for the psychiatrist. Specific treatments are now available for both manic and depressive episodes, and the data indicate that prophylactic treatment is also effective. Because the prognosis for each episode is good, optimism is always warranted and welcomed by both the patient and the patient's family, even if initial treatment results are not promising. However, mood disorders are chronic, and the patient and the family must be advised about future treatment strategies.

Hospitalization

The first and most critical decision the physician must make is whether to hospitalize the patient or to attempt outpatient treatment. Clear indications for hospitalization are the need for diagnostic procedures, the risk of suicide or homicide, and the patient's grossly reduced ability to get food and shelter. A history of rapidly progressing symptoms and the rupture of the patient's usual support systems are also indications for hospitalization.

Mild depression or hypomania may be safely treated in the office if the physician evaluates the patient frequently. Clinical signs of impaired judgment, weight loss, or insomnia should be minimal. The patient's support system should be strong, neither overinvolved nor withdrawing from the patient. Any adverse changes in the patient's symptoms or behavior or the attitude of the patient's support system may be sufficient to warrant hospitalization.

Patients with mood disorders are often unwilling to enter a hospital voluntarily, so they may have to be involuntarily committed. Patients with major depressive disorder are often incapable of making decisions because of their slowed thinking, negative *Weltanschauung* (world view), and hopelessness. Manic patients often have such a complete lack of insight into their disorder that hospitalization seems absolutely absurd to them.

Psychosocial Therapies

Although most studies indicate—and most clinicians and researchers believe—that combined psychotherapy and pharmacotherapy is the most effective treatment for major depressive disorder, some data suggest a different view. Specifically, some data indicate that either pharmacotherapy or psychotherapy alone is effective, at least in patients with mild major depressive episodes, and that the regular use of combined therapy adds to the cost of treatment and exposes patients to unnecessary side effects.

Three types of short-term psychotherapies—cognitive therapy, interpersonal therapy, and behavior therapy—have been studied regarding their efficacy in the treatment of major depressive disorder. Psychoanalytically oriented psychotherapy, although not as well researched regarding its efficacy in major depressive disorder, has long been used for depressive disorders, and many clinicians use the technique as their primary method. What differentiates the three short-term psychotherapy modalities from the psychoanalytically oriented approach are the active and directive roles of the therapist, the directly recognizable goals, and the endpoints for short-term therapy.

COGNITIVE THERAPY

Cognitive therapy, developed originally by Aaron Beck, focuses on the cognitive distortions postulated to be present in major depressive disorder. Such distortions include selective attention to the negative aspects of circumstances and unrealistically morbid inferences about consequences. For example, apathy and low energy are results of the patient's expectation of failure in all areas. The goal of cognitive therapy is to alleviate depressive episodes and to prevent their recurrence by helping patients identify and test negative cognitions; develop alternative, flexible, and positive ways of thinking; and rehearse new cognitive and behavioral responses.

About a dozen studies have found that cognitive therapy is effective in the treatment of major depressive disorder; most of the studies found that cognitive therapy is equal in efficacy to pharmacotherapy, associated with fewer side effects than is pharmacotherapy, and associated with better follow-up than is pharmacotherapy. However, most of the studies can be criticized for using antidepressant dosages that were too low and for using the antidepressant medications for too short a period. Some of the best controlled studies have shown that the combination of cognitive therapy and pharmacotherapy is more efficacious than either therapy alone, although other studies have not found that additive effect. At least one study, the NIMH Treatment of Depression Collaborative Research Program, found that pharmacotherapy, either alone or with psychotherapy, may be the treatment of choice for patients with severe major depressive episodes.

INTERPERSONAL THERAPY

Interpersonal therapy, developed by Gerald Klerman, focuses on one or two of the patient's current interpersonal problems, using two assumptions: First, current interpersonal problems are likely to have their roots in early dysfunctional relationships. Second, current interpersonal problems are likely to be involved in precipitating or perpetuating the current depressive symptoms. Several controlled trials have compared interpersonal therapy, cognitive therapy, pharmacotherapy, and the combination of pharmacotherapy with psychotherapy. Those trials suggested that interpersonal therapy is effective in the treatment of major depressive disorder and may, not surprisingly, be specifically helpful in addressing interpersonal problems. The data are less solid regarding the efficacy of interpersonal therapy in the treatment of severe major depressive episodes, although some data indicate that interpersonal therapy may be the most effective modality for severe major depressive episodes when the treatment choice is psychotherapy alone.

The interpersonal therapy program usually consists of 12 to 16 weekly sessions. The therapy is characterized by an active, therapeutic approach. Intrapsychic phenomena, such as defense mechanisms and internal conflicts, are not addressed in the therapy. Discrete behaviors—such as lack of assertiveness, impaired social skills, and distorted thinking—may be addressed but only in the context of their meaning or their effect on interpersonal relationships.

BEHAVIOR THERAPY

Behavior therapy is based on the hypothesis that maladaptive behavioral patterns result in a person's receiving little positive feedback from society and perhaps outright rejection. By addressing maladaptive behaviors in therapy, patients learn to function in the world in such a way that they receive positive reinforcement. Behavior therapy for major depressive disorder has not been the subject of many controlled studies yet, although individual and group therapies have been studied. The data to date indicate that behavior therapy is an effective treatment modality for major depressive disorder.

PSYCHOANALYTICALLY ORIENTED THERAPY

The psychoanalytic approach to mood disorders is based on the psychoanalytic theories about depression and mania. In general, the goal of psychoanalytic psychotherapy is to effect a change in the patient's personality structure or character, not simply to alleviate symptoms. Improvements in interpersonal trust, intimacy, coping mechanisms, the capacity to grieve, and the ability to experience a wide range of emotions are some of the aims of psychoanalytic therapy. Treatment often requires the patient to experience heightened anxiety and distress during the course of therapy, which may continue for several years.

FAMILY THERAPY

Family therapy is not generally viewed as a primary therapy for the treatment of major depressive disorder, but increasing evidence shows that helping a patient with a mood disorder reduce stress and cope with stress can reduce the chance of a relapse. Family therapy is indicated if the disorder jeopardizes the patient's marriage or family functioning or if the mood disorder is promoted or maintained by the family situation. Family therapy examines the role of the mood-disordered member in the overall psychological well-being of the whole family; it also examines the role of the entire family in the maintenance of the patient's symptoms. Patients with mood disorders have a high rate of divorce, and about 50 percent of all spouses report that they would not have married the patient or had children if they had known that the patient was going to have a mood disorder.

Pharmacotherapy

Although the specific, short-term psychotherapies (for example, interpersonal therapy and cognitive therapy) have influenced the treatment approaches to major depressive disorder, the pharmacotherapeutic approach to mood disorders has revolutionized their treatment and has dramatically affected the courses of mood disorders and reduced their inherent costs to society.

The physician must integrate pharmacotherapy with psychotherapeutic interventions. If physicians view mood disorders as fundamentally evolving from psychodynamic issues, their ambivalence about the use of drugs may result in a poor response, noncompliance, and probably inadequate dosages for too short a treatment period. Alternatively, if physicians ignore the psychosocial needs of the patient, the outcome of pharmacotherapy may be compromised.

MAJOR DEPRESSIVE DISORDER

Effective and specific treatments (for example, tricyclic drugs) have been available for the treatment of major depressive disorder for 40 years. The use of specific pharmacotherapy approximately doubles the chance that a depressed patient will recover in one month. Several problems remain in the treatment of major depressive disorder: some patients do not respond to the first treatment; all currently available antidepressants take three to four weeks to exert significant therapeutic effects, although they may begin to show their effects earlier; and, until relatively recently, all available antidepressants have been toxic in overdoses and have had adverse effects. Now, however, the introduction of bupropion and the SSRIs—fluoxetine, fluvoxamine (Luvox), paroxetine (Paxil), and sertraline (Zoloft)—gives clinicians drugs that are much safer and much better tolerated than previous drugs but that are equally effective. Recent indications (for example, eating disorders and anxiety disorders) for antidepressant medications make the grouping of those drugs under the single label of antidepressants somewhat confusing.

The principal indication for antidepressants is a major depressive episode. The first symptoms to improve are often poor sleep and appetite patterns, although that may be less true when SSRIs are used than when tricyclic drugs are used. Agitation, anxiety, depressive episodes, and hopelessness are the next symptoms to improve. Other target symptoms include low energy, poor concentration, helplessness, and decreased libido.

The physician must always consider the risk of suicide in mood disorder patients. Most antidepressants are lethal if taken in large amounts. It is unwise to give most mood disorder patients large prescriptions when they are discharged from the hospital unless another person will monitor the drug's administration.

Alternatives to Drug Treatment

Two organic therapies that are alternatives to pharmacotherapy are ECT and phototherapy. ECT is generally used when (1) the patient is unresponsive to pharmacotherapy, (2) the patient cannot tolerate pharmacotherapy, or (3) the clinical situation is so severe that the rapid improvement seen with ECT is needed. Although the use of ECT is often limited to those three situations, it is an effective antidepressant treatment and can be reasonably considered as the treatment of choice in some patients, such as elderly depressed persons. Phototherapy is a novel treatment used with patients with a seasonal pattern to their mood disorder. Phototherapy can be used alone for patients with mild cases of mood disorder with a seasonal pattern, and it can be used in combination with pharmacotherapy for severely affected patients, although studies of the efficacy of that combination have not yet produced definitive results.

Available Drugs

Drugs available for antidepressant therapy are listed in Table 9.1–7.

Choice of Drug

Because of the many antidepressant drugs now available on the commercial market, the physician faces many clinical considerations in the choice of a first-line drug. In the treatment of all mental disorders, the best reason for choosing a particular drug is a history of a good response to that agent by the patient or a family member. If such information is not available, the choice of a drug is based principally on the adverse effects of the drug (Table 9.1–8). The clinician must consider both the severity and the frequency of potential adverse effects when using side effects as the basis for choosing among available antidepressants. Most clinicians choose either one of the tricyclic or tetracyclic drugs or one of the SSRIs as the first-line drug in the treatment of major depressive disorder. Tricyclic and tetracyclic drugs are often chosen because of the level of the clinician's comfort with these old drugs. They are also less expensive than the new drugs, because most of the tricyclic and tetracyclic drugs are available in generic formulations. SSRIs are frequently chosen by clinicians whose experience supports the research data that SSRIs are as efficacious as the tricyclic and tetracyclic drugs and are much better tolerated. The tricyclic and tetracyclic drugs also differ in their side-effect profiles, with nortriptyline (Pamelor), desipramine, and protriptyline (Vivactil)—that is, the secondary amine tricyclic and tetracyclic drugs—generally having a more benign side-effect profile than the tertiary tricyclic and tetracyclic drugs (for example, imipramine).

As first-line drugs, the MAOIs, the sympathomimetics, and other atypical drugs (for example, alprazolam [Xanax], trazodone [Desyrel], and bupropion) are chosen less often than the tricyclic and tetracyclic drugs and the SSRIs. The MAOIs are usually not chosen as first-line drugs because of their association with tyramine-induced hypertensive crises, which are caused when a patient taking conventional MAOIs ingests certain drugs or foods with a high tyramine content. Although that adverse interaction can be avoided if the patient follows simple dietary guidelines, the potentially life-threatening nature of a hypertensive crisis and the need for dietary restrictions limit the acceptability of MAOIs. The sympathomimetics are rarely used as first-line drugs because of their high potential for abuse. Alprazolam, a benzodiazepine, is not a common first-line drug because of its potential for sedation, motor impairment, and abuse. Trazodone as a first-line drug is limited by its significant sedative properties and its association with priapism in men. Although bupropion is basically a safe and effective antidepressant drug, its association with seizures when used incorrectly may have inappropriately limited its choice as a first-line drug.

General Clinical Guidelines

The most common clinical mistake leading to an unsuccessful trial of an antidepressant drug is the use of too low a dosage for too short a time. Unless adverse events prevent it, the dosage of an antidepressant should be raised to the maximum recommended level and maintained at that level for at least four weeks before a drug trial can be considered unsuccessful. Alternatively, if a patient is improving clinically on a low dosage of the drug, that dosage should not be raised unless clinical improvement stops before the maximal benefit is obtained. If a patient does not begin to respond to appropriate dosages of a drug after two or three weeks, the clinician may decide to obtain a plasma concentration of the drug if a test is available. The test may indicate either noncompliance or particularly unusual pharmacokinetic disposition of the drug, thereby suggesting an alternative dosage.

Duration and Prophylaxis

Antidepressant treatment should be maintained for at least six months or the length of a previous episode, whichever is greater. Several studies show that prophylactic treatment with antidepressants is effective in reducing the number and the severity of recurrences. One study concluded that, if episodes are less than $2\frac{1}{2}$ years apart, prophylactic treatment for five years is probably indicated. Another factor suggesting prophylactic treatment is the seriousness of previous depressive episodes. Episodes that have involved significant suicidal ideation or impairment of psychosocial functioning may indicate that the clinician should consider prophylactic treatment. When antidepressants are

Table 9.1–7. Considerations When Selecting an Antidepressant: Comparison of Classes

Consideration	Tricyclic and Tetracyclic Drugs (e.g., nortriptyline)	SSRIs (e.g., sertraline)	Triazolopyridines (i.e., trazodone)	Aminoketones (i.e, bupropion)	MAOIs (e.g., tranylcypromine)
Likelihood of response	High	Equivalent to tricyclic in outpatients	Possibly less than tricyclics	Less than tricyclics	Less then tricyclics
Unique spectrum of activity	Can work when SSRI fail	Can work in tricyclic failures	None shown	Can work in tricyclic failures	Can work in tricyclic failures
Maintenance of response	Evidence of controlled studies	Evidence of controlled studies	None shown	None shown	None shown
Safety	Serious systemic toxicity can result from overdose (either heavy ingestion or gradual accumulation because of slow clearance)	No serious systemic toxicity shown	Minimal serious systemic toxicity because of acute overdose	Seizures as primary acute systemic toxicity because of acute overdose; easily managed in medical setting	Serious systemic toxicity can result from heavy ingestion
Tolerability	Generally good with secondary amine tricyclics, much superior to tertiary amine tricyclics	Generally good, especially if dosage is kept to effective minimum dosage	Sedation and cognitive slowing are frequently problems, even at effective minimum dosage	Generally good, especially if dosage is kept to effective minimum dosage	Generally good except for the occurrence of hypotension and the need for dietary restrictions
Pharmacokinetic interactions	Can be affected by other drugs (e.g., SSRIs) to a clinically significant extent but do not affect other drugs	Can inhibit oxidative metabolism of a variety of drugs but considerable differences among class in terms of magnitude and duration of effect; no known clinically significant effect of other drugs on SSRIs	Neither affected by other drugs nor affect other drugs in a clinically significant way	Can be affected by some SSRIs (e.g., fluoxetine) and possibly others in a clinically significant way; no known effect on the metabolism of other drugs	Neither affected by other drugs nor affect other drugs in a clinically significant way
Pharmacodynamic interactions	Multiple because of large number of effects of tricyclics; can be agonistic (additive or potentiating) or antagonistic; such interactions are more likely and more significant with tertiary as opposed to secondary amines	See MAOI interaction; may occur with other serotonin agonists; fluoxetine can have agonistic interaction with dopamine agonists in terms of extrapyramidal effects; minimal experience with sertraline in this regard	Can have interactions with other agents that decrease arousal or impair cognitive performance; can interact with adrenergic agents affecting blood pressure regulation; complex interactions with other serotonin-active agents	Can have interactions with dopamine agonists and antoganists	Clinically significant interactions with: Tyramine and sympathomimetic agents on blood pressure Serotonin-active agents inducing the central serotonin syndrome
Physician confidence	Excellent because of extensive data base in terms of human exposure (e.g., patient-years of exposure, total number of patients exposed, variety of patients exposed)	Excellent primarily because of efficacy and safety profile; less extensive data base in terms of human exposure compared with tricyclics but rapidly expanding	Satisfactory because of substantial data base in terms of human exposure; concerns are with spectrum of activity and tolerability	Reserved because of less extensive data base concerning human exposure coupled with concerns about safety caused by seizure risk	Caution because of safety concerns primarily about patient compliance with dietary restrictions
Ease of administration	Excellent, generally can be administered once a day	Excellent for sertraline because of once-a-day administration; good for fluoxetine, typically administered once a day, but long half-life of parent compound and active metabolite makes dosage difficult and has a long carryover effect	Satisfactory but require multiple dosing for antidepressant effect	Satisfactory but require multiple dosing for antidepressant effect	Satisfactory but clinical practice generally is to give in divided doses.

Table from S H Preskorn, M Burke: Somatic therapy for major depressive disorder: Selection of an antidepressant. J Clin Psychiatry 53: (9, Suppl): 8, 1992. Used with permission.

Table 9.1–8.   Adverse Drug Reaction Profiles

Drug and Risk	Severity		
	Nuisance	Moderate Discomfort	Intolerable or Unacceptable
Fluoxetine			
Frequent	Nausea	Anxiety	
		Insomnia	
Occasional		Sedation	
		Decreased libido	
		Headaches	
Rare	Anorexia	Rash	Vomiting
		Flatulence	
		Anorgasmia	
		Weight gain	
		Impotence	
Bupropion			
Frequent	Nausea	Anxiety	
Occasional	Jitteriness		
	Insomnia		
Rare		Sexual dysfunction	Seizure
		Cognitive difficulties	
Tertiary Amines: Imipramine, Amitriptyline, Doxepine, and Trimipramine			
Frequent	Sedation	Constipation	
	Dry mouth		
Occasional	Light-headedness	Severe constipation	Fainting, falling
	Dizziness	Sweating	
	Urinary hesitancy	Weight gain of 10 lbs	
		Tachycardia	
		Urinary hesitancy	
		Skin rash	
		Blurry vision	
Rare		Pain on ejaculation	Seizues
		Memory problems	Urinary blockage
		Severe blurry vision	Paralytic ilcus
		Tremor	Delirium
		Agitation, akithisia	Mania
Secondary Amines: Nortriptyline, Desipramine, and Protriptyline			
Frequent	Mild dry mouth	Tremor	
		Tachycardia	
Occasional	Dry mouth	Jitteriness	
	Dizziness	Anxiety	
		Constipation	
		Sweating	
Rare		Sedation	Seizures
		Rash	Memory problems
		Urinary hesitancy	Mania
Monamine Oxidase Inhibitors: Phenelzine, Tranylcypromine, and Isocarboxazid			
Frequent	Insomnia	Weight gain	
Occasional	Daytime sedation	Light-headedness	Hypertension episode
		Anorgasmia	
		Decreased blood pressure	
Rare		Profuse sweating	Fainting
		Dry mouth	Liver toxicity
		Urinary hesitancy	Hypertensive crisis
			Cerebrovascular disease
			Mania
Trazodone			
Frequent		Sedation	
Occasional	Dry mouth	Nausea	Vomiting
	Constipation	Headache	
	Light-headedness	Flulike malaise	
Rare		Weight gain	Fainting
			Priapism
			Mania

Table from A A Nierenberg, J O Cole: Antidepressant adverse drug reactions. J Clin Psychiatry *52*: 45, 1991. Used with permission.

stopped, they should be tapered gradually over one to two weeks, depending on the half-life of the particular compound.

Failure of Drug Trial

If the first antidepressant drug has been used for an adequate trial and, if appropriate, the clinician is sure that adequate plasma concentrations were obtained, two options face the clinician—augmenting the drug with lithium, liothyronine (L-triiodothyronine) (Cytomel), or L-tryptophan or switching to an alternative primary agent. A now rarely used strategy is the combination of a tricyclic or tetracyclic drug with an MAOI. When switching agents, the clinician should switch a patient who has been taking a tricyclic or tetracyclic drug to an SSRI (or possibly an MAOI). A patient who has been taking an SSRI should be switched to a tricyclic or tetracyclic drug (or possibly an MAOI). At least two weeks should elapse between the use of an SSRI and the use of an MAOI, and the two drugs should never be used concurrently. The clinician can also consider switching a first-line drug nonresponder to trazodone or bupropion.

BIPOLAR I DISORDER

Whereas the treatment of major depressive disorder has been changed by the introduction of the SSRIs, the treatment of bipolar I disorder has been changed by the many studies that have demonstrated the efficacy of two anticonvulsants—carbamazepine and valproate—in the treatment of manic episodes and probably in the prophylaxis of manic and depressive episodes in bipolar I disorder. Although the data in support of the efficacy of lithium (Eskalith) are many, sufficient data have accumulated to warrant consideration of the two anticonvulsants as first-line treatments of bipolar I disorder. Such a decision should be based primarily on the compatibility between the patient and the relevant side effects of the drugs. The long-term treatment of bipolar I disorder is an indication for those anticonvulsants, but the initial stages of manic episodes often require the addition of drugs with potent sedative effects. Drugs commonly used at the initiation of therapy for bipolar I disorder include clonazepam (Klonopin) (1 mg every four to six hours), lorazepam (Ativan) (2 mg every four to six hours), and haloperidol (Haldol) (5 mg every two to four hours). The physician should taper those medications and discontinue them as soon as the initial phase of the manic episode has subsided and the effects of the lithium, carbamazepine, or valproate are beginning to be seen clinically.

Whereas lithium, valproate, and possibly carbamazepine are the first-line drugs for the treatment of bipolar I disorder, the second-line drugs now include another anticonvulsant (clonazepam), a calcium channel inhibitor (verapamil [Calan]), an α_2-adrenergic receptor agonist (clonidine), and antipsychotics (especially clozapine [Clozaril]); ECT is another second-line treatment.

Lithium

Lithium is still the standard treatment of bipolar I disorder. The adverse effects that may limit the use of lithium and cause the clinician to consider using either carbamazepine or valproate include renal effects (thirst, polyuria), nervous system effects (tremor, memory loss), metabolic effects (weight gain), gastrointestinal effects (diarrhea), dermatological effects (acne, psoriasis), and thyroid effects (goiter, myxedema). Of potentially serious concern with lithium treatment is its effects on the kidneys, which can include moderate and occasionally severe impairment of tubular function; uncommon, moderate, and unspecific morphological changes; and rarely, a nephrotic syndrome. Those many adverse effects require careful monitoring of the patient's renal and thyroid status.

Compliance with lithium treatment is increased with the early initiation of treatment, adequate treatment of concomitant illness, treatment of coexisting substance abuse, the early detection and prevention of side effects, and the inclusion of the patient in individual and group psychotherapy. Responsiveness to lithium treatment is improved when adequate lithium levels are maintained, adjunctive medication is used as indicated, and laboratory and clinical monitoring is carried out. Nonresponsiveness to lithium treatment is most likely with severe illness, the presence of schizoaffective disorder symptoms, mixed manic and depressive symptoms, somatic symptoms, alcohol abuse and other substance abuse, rapid cycling, and the absence of a family history of bipolar I disorder.

Anticonvulsants

As stated above, the efficacy data for valproate and carbamazepine are now sufficient to warrant their consideration as first-line drugs. It also warrants their use either as adjuvants to lithium or as alternatives to lithium for patients who are not responsive to lithium alone or who are intolerant of lithium-induced adverse effects. The decision to use carbamazepine or valproate is based on the presence of adverse effects and possibly the price of prescriptions. Carbamazepine is associated with sedation, nausea, blurred vision, rash, blood dyscrasias, and hyponatremia. Valproate has a relatively benign safety profile but is associated with gastrointestinal symptoms, tremor, hair loss, weight gain, and blood dyscrasias. Both valproate and carbamazepine require routine blood monitoring for hepatic and hematological indexes of function.

Maintenance

The decision to maintain a patient on lithium (or other drug) prophylaxis is based on the severity of the patient's disorder, the risk of adverse effects from the particular drug, and the quality of the patient's support systems. In general, maintenance treatment is indicated for the prophylaxis of bipolar I disorder in any patient who has had more than one episode. The rationale for that practice is the relative safety of the available drugs, their demonstrated efficacy, and the significant potential for psychosocial problems if another bipolar I disorder episode occurs.

References

Bauer M S, Whybrow P C: Validity of rapid cycling as a modifier for bipolar disorder in DSM-IV. Depression *1*: 11, 1993.

Coffey C E, Wilkinson W E, Weiner R D, Parashos I A, Djang W T, Webb W C, Figiel G S, Spritzer C F: Quantitative cerebral anatomy in depression: A controlled magnetic resonance imaging study. Arch Gen Psychiatry *50*: 7, 1993.

Dantzler A, Salzman C: Treatment of bipolar depression. Psychiatr Serv *46*: 229, 1995.

Jorge R E, Robinson R G, Starkstein S E, Arndt S V, Forrester A W, Geisler F M: Secondary mania following traumatic brain injury. Am J Psychiatry *150*: 916, 1993.

Kaplan H I, Sadock B J, editors.: Mood Disorders. In *Comprehensive Textbook of Psychiatry*, ed 6, p 1067. Williams & Wilkins, Baltimore, 1995.

Solomon D A, Keitner G I, Miller I W, Shea M T, Keller M: Course of illness and maintenance treatments for patients with bipolar disorder. J Clin Psychiatry *56*: 5, 1995.

Workman E A, Short D D: Atypical antidepressants versus imipramine in the treatment of major depression: A meta-analysis. J Clin Psychiatry *54*: 5, 1993.

9.2 DYSTHYMIC DISORDER AND CYCLOTHYMIC DISORDER

Dysthymic disorder and cyclothymic disorder are sometimes known in unofficial parlance as subaffective disorders. That term suggests that dysthymic disorder and cyclothymic disorder are mild forms of major depressive disorder and bipolar I disorder, respectively. However, some research data suggest that, although the disorders may be related, they probably have fundamental biological and psychosocial differences. One major difference is that, whereas major depressive disorder is characterized by discrete episodes of symptoms, dysthymic disorder is characterized by chronic, nonepisodic symptoms.

The inclusion of the so-called subaffective disorders, such as dysthymic disorder and cyclothymic disorder, with the mood disorders is controversial in the field of psychiatry. Their inclusion with the major mood disorders implies similarities in cause, genetic bases, prognoses, and treatment responses. In disagreement with that view, some psychodynamically oriented psychiatrists believe that dysthymic disorder and cyclothymic disorder are understood as primarily the results of incompletely resolved issues in a person's psychodynamic development.

DYSTHYMIC DISORDER

Dysthymic disorder is a chronic disorder characterized by the presence of a depressed (or irritable in children and adolescents) mood that lasts most of the day and is present on most days. The term ''dysthymia,'' which means ill-humored, was introduced in 1980 and changed to ''dysthymic disorder'' in the fourth edition of *Diagnostic Statistical Manual of Mental Disorders* (DSM-IV). Before 1980, most patients now classified as having dysthymic disorder were classified as having depressive neurosis (also called neurotic depression), although some patients were classified as having cyclothymic personality. The diagnosis of depressive neurosis was the most common psychiatric diagnosis in the 1970s. In fact, its patently obvious heterogeneity and the lack of clinical agreement about the diagnosis may have helped increase the appreciation of the need for a diagnostic manual such as the third edition of DSM (DSM-III).

Epidemiology

Dysthymic disorder is a common disorder among the general population, affecting 3 to 5 percent of all persons, and it is common among patients in general psychiatric clinics, affecting between one half and one third of all clinic patients. At least one study reported prevalences of dysthymic disorder among young adolescents of about 8 percent in boys and 5 percent in girls. Dysthymic disorder is more common in women less than 64 years old than in men of any age. Dysthymic disorder is also more common among unmarried and young persons and in persons with low incomes. Moreover, dysthymic disorder frequently co-exists with other mental disorders, especially major depressive disorder, anxiety disorders (especially panic disorder), substance abuse, and, probably, borderline personality disorder. Such patients with dysthymic disorder are likely to be taking a wide range of psychiatric medications, including antidepressants, antimanic agents—for example, lithium (Eskalith) and carbamazepine (Tegretol)—and sedative-hypnotics.

Etiology

BIOLOGICAL FACTORS

Some studies of biological measures in dysthymic disorder support the classification of dysthymic disorder with the mood disorders; other studies question that association. One hypothesis drawn from the data is that the biological bases for the symptoms of dysthymic disorder and major depressive disorder are similar; however, the biological bases for the underlying pathophysiology in the two disorders are different.

Sleep Studies

Decreased rapid eye movement (REM) latency and increased REM density are two state markers of depression in major depressive disorder that are also found in a significant proportion of patients with dysthymic disorder. Some investigators have reported preliminary data suggesting that the presence of those sleep abnormalities in patients with dysthymic disorder predicts a response to antidepressant drugs.

Neuroendocrine Studies

The two most studied neuroendocrine axes in major depressive disorder and dysthymic disorder are the adrenal axis and the thyroid axis, which have been tested by using the dexamethasone-suppression test (DST) and the thyrotropin-releasing hormone (TRH) stimulation test, respectively. Although the studies are not absolutely consistent, most of the studies indicate that patients with dysthymic disorder are much less likely to have abnormal results on a DST than are patients with major depressive disorder. The studies of the TRH-stimulation test have been fewer but have produced preliminary data suggesting that abnormalities in the thyroid axis may be a trait variable associated with chronic illness. That hypothesis is supported by a generally increased percentage of patients with dysthymic disorder who have thyroid axis abnormalities when compared with normal controls.

PSYCHOSOCIAL FACTORS

Psychodynamic theories regarding the development of dysthymic disorder posit that the disorder results from personality and ego development, culminating in difficulty in adapting to adolescence and young adulthood. Karl Abraham, for example, thought that the conflicts of depression center on oral and anal-sadistic traits. Anal traits include excessive orderliness, guilt, and concern for others; anal traits are postulated to be a defense against preoccupation with anal matter and with disorganization, hostility, and self-preoccupation. A major defense mechanism used is reaction formation. Low self-esteem, anhedonia, and introversion are often associated with the depressive character.

Freud

In ''Mourning and Melancholia'' Sigmund Freud asserted that a vulnerability to depression can be caused by an interpersonal disappointment early in life that leads to ambivalent love relationships as an adult; real or threatened losses in adult life that trigger depression. Persons prone to depression are orally dependent and require constant narcissistic gratification. If deprived of love, affection, and care, they become clinically depressed. When those persons experience a real loss, they internalize or introject the loss object and turn their anger on it and, thus, on themselves.

Cognitive Theory

The cognitive theory of depression also applies to dysthymic disorder; it holds that a disparity between actual and fantasized situations leads to diminished self-esteem and a sense of helplessness. The success of cognitive therapy in the treatment of some patients with dysthymic disorder may provide some support for the theoretical model.

Diagnosis

The DSM-IV diagnostic criteria for dysthymic disorder require the presence of a depressed mood most of the time for at least two years (or one year for children and adolescents) (Table

Table 9.2-1. Diagnostic Criteria for Dysthymic Disorder

A. Depressed mood for most of the day, for more days than not, as indicated either by subjective account or observation by others, for at least 2 years. Note: In children and adolescents, mood can be irritable and duration must be at least 1 year.

B. Presence, while depressed, of two (or more) of the following:

    (1) poor appetite or overeating
    (2) insomnia or hypersomnia
    (3) low energy or fatigue
    (4) low self-esteem
    (5) poor concentration or difficulty making decisions
    (6) feelings of hopelessness

C. During the 2-year period (1 year for children or adolescents) of the disturbance, the person has never been without the symptoms in criteria A and B for more than 2 months at a time.

D. No major depressive episode has been present during the first 2 years of the disturbance (1 year for children and adolescents); i.e., the disturbance is not better accounted for by chronic major depressive disorder, or major depressive disorder, in partial remission.

E. There has never been a manic episode, a mixed episode, or a hypomanic episode, and criteria have never been met for cyclothymic disorder.

F. The disturbance does not occur exclusively during the course of a chronic psychotic disorder, such as schizophrenia or delusional disorder.

G. The symptoms are not due to the direct physiological effects of a substance (e.g., a drug of abuse, a medication) or a general medical condition (e.g., hypothyroidism).

H. The symptoms cause clinically significant distress or impairment in social, occupational, or other important areas of functioning.

Table from DSM-IV, *Diagnostic and Statistical Manual of Mental Disorders*, ed 4. Copyright American Psychiatric Association, Washington, 1994. Used with permission.

9.2–1). To meet the diagnostic criteria, the patient should not have symptoms that are better accounted for as major depressive disorder. The patient should never have had a manic or hypomanic episode. DSM-IV allows the clinician to specify whether the onset was early (before age 21) or late (age 21 or older). DSM-IV also allows for the specification of atypical features in dysthymic disorder.

Clinical Features

Dysthymic disorder is a chronic disorder characterized not by episodes of illness but, rather, by the steady presence of symptoms. Nevertheless, dysthymic disorder patients can have some temporal variation in the severity of their symptoms. The symptoms themselves are similar to those for major depressive disorder, and the presence of a depressed mood—characterized by feeling sad, blue, down in the dumps, or low and by a lack of interest in the patient's usual activities—is central to the disorder. The severity of the depressive symptoms in dysthymic disorder is generally less than in major depressive disorder, but it is the lack of discrete episodes that most weights toward the diagnosis of dysthymic disorder.

Patients with dysthymic disorder can often be sarcastic, nihilistic, brooding, demanding, and complaining. They can be tense and rigid and resistant to therapeutic interventions, although they come regularly to appointments. As a result, the clinician may feel angry toward the patient and may even disregard the patient's complaints. By definition, dysthymic disorder patient do not have any psychotic symptoms.

ASSOCIATED SYMPTOMS

Associated symptoms include changes in appetite and sleep patterns, low self-esteem, loss of energy, psychomotor retardation, decreased sexual drive, and obsessive preoccupation with health matters. Pessimism, hopelessness, and helplessness may cause dysthymic disorder patients to be seen as masochistic. However, if the pessimism is directed outward, the patients may rant against the world and complain that they have been poorly treated by relatives, children, parents, colleagues, and the system.

SOCIAL IMPAIRMENT

Impairment in social functioning is sometimes the reason patients with dysthymic disorder seek treatment. In fact, divorce, unemployment, and social problems are common problems for those patients. They may complain that they have difficulty in concentrating and may report that their school or work performance is suffering. Because of complaints of physical illness, patients may miss workdays and social occasions. Dysthymic disorder patients may have marital problems resulting from sexual dysfunction (for example, impotence) or from an inability to sustain emotional intimacy.

COEXISTING DIAGNOSES

As mentioned previously, the diagnosis of dysthymic disorder is frequently made for persons who are also suffering from other mental disorders. Data indicate that the comorbidity of dysthymic disorder with other mental disorders is a significant negative predictor of a good prognosis. That is, the presence of a chronic, untreated depressive disorder appears to limit the rate and the extent of improvement a patient can obtain in other mental disorders. Frequently found comorbid disorders are major depressive disorder and substance-related disorders.

Double Depression

An estimated 40 percent of patients with major depressive disorder also meet the criteria for dysthymic disorder. That combination of disorders is often called double depression. Available data support the conclusion that patients with double depression have a poorer prognosis than do patients with only major depressive disorder. The treatment of patients with double depression should be directed toward both disorders, since the resolution of the symptoms of major depressive episode in those patients still leaves them with significant psychiatric impairment.

Alcohol and Other Substance Abuse

Patients with dysthymic disorder commonly meet the diagnostic criteria for a substance-related disorder. That comorbidity may be seen as logical, given the propensity of dysthymic disorder patients to develop coping methods for their chronically depressed state. Therefore, patients with dysthymic disorder are likely to use alcohol, stimulants (for example, cocaine), or marijuana, the choice perhaps depending primarily on the patient's social context. The presence of a comorbid diagnosis of substance abuse presents a diagnostic dilemma for the clinician, since the long-term use of many substances can result in a symptom picture indistinguishable from that of dysthymic disorder.

Differential Diagnosis

The differential diagnosis for dysthymic disorder is essentially identical to that for major depressive disorder. Many substances and medical illnesses can cause chronic depressive symptoms. Two disorders are particularly important to consider in the differential diagnosis of dysthymic disorder—minor depressive disorder and recurrent brief depressive disorder.

MINOR DEPRESSIVE DISORDER

Minor depressive disorder, discussed in Section 9.3, is characterized by episodes of depressive symptoms that are less severe than those seen in major depressive disorder. The difference between dysthymic disorder and minor depressive disorder is primarily the episodic nature of the symptoms in minor depressive disorder. Between episodes, patients with minor depressive disorder have a euthymic mood, whereas patients with dysthymic disorder have virtually no euthymic periods.

RECURRENT BRIEF DEPRESSIVE DISORDER

Recurrent brief depressive disorder, discussed in Section 9.3, is characterized by brief periods (less than two weeks) during which depressive episodes are present. Patients with the disorder would meet the diagnostic criteria for major depressive disorder if their episodes lasted longer. Patients with recurrent brief depressive disorder differ from dysthymic disorder patients on two counts: first, they have an episodic disorder, and, second, the severity of their symptoms is greater.

Course and Prognosis

About 50 percent of dysthymic disorder patients experience an insidious onset of the symptoms before age 25. Despite the early onset, patients often suffer with the symptoms for a decade before seeking psychiatric help. Those affected may consider early-onset dysthymic disorder simply as part of life. Patients who have an early onset of symptoms are at risk for either major depressive disorder or bipolar I disorder in the course of their disorder. Studies of patients with the diagnosis of depressive neurosis indicated that about 20 percent of them progressed to major depressive disorder, 15 percent to bipolar II disorder, and less than 5 percent to bipolar I disorder.

The prognosis for patients with dysthymic disorder is variable. Future studies may show that the use of new antidepressive agents—for example, fluoxetine (Prozac) and bupropion (Wellbutrin)—or specific types of psychotherapy (for example, cognitive and behavior therapies) have positive effects on the course and the prognosis of dysthymic disorder. The available data regarding previously available treatments indicate that only 10 to 15 percent of dysthymic disorder patients are in remission one year after the initial diagnosis. About 25 percent of all dysthymic disorder patients never attain a complete recovery.

Treatment

Historically, patients with dysthymic disorder received no treatment or were seen as candidates for long-term, insight-oriented psychotherapy. Contemporary data offer objective support for only cognitive therapy, behavior therapy, and pharmacotherapy. The combination of pharmacotherapy and either cognitive or behavior therapy may be the most effective treatment for the disorder. Other therapies may be beneficial; however, the benefit has yet to be proved in well-controlled studies.

COGNITIVE THERAPY

Cognitive therapy is a technique in which patients are taught new ways of thinking and behaving to replace faulty negative attitudes about themselves, the world, and the future. It is a short-term therapy program oriented toward current problems and their resolution.

BEHAVIOR THERAPY

Behavior therapy for depressive disorders is based on the theory that depression is caused by a loss of positive reinforcement because of separation, death, or sudden environmental change. The various treatment methods focus on specific goals to increase activity, to provide pleasant experiences, and to teach patients how to relax. Altering personal behavior in depressed patients is believed to be the most effective way to change the associated depressed thoughts and feelings. Behavior therapy is often used to treat the learned helplessness of some patients who seem to meet every life challenge with a sense of impotence.

INSIGHT-ORIENTED (PSYCHOANALYTIC) PSYCHOTHERAPY

Individual insight-oriented psychotherapy is the most common treatment modality for dysthymic disorder, and many clinicians believe it to be the treatment of choice. The psychotherapeutic approach attempts to relate the development and the maintenance of depressive symptoms and maladaptive personality features to unresolved conflicts from early childhood. Insight into depressive equivalents (such as substance abuse) or into childhood disappointments as antecedents to adult depression can be gained through treatment. Ambivalent current relationships with parents, friends, and others in the patient's current life are examined. Patients' understanding of how they try to gratify an excessive need for outside approval to counter low self-esteem and a harsh superego is an important goal in the therapy.

Dysthymic disorder involves a chronic state of depression that becomes a way of life for certain persons. They consciously experience themselves to be at the mercy of a tormenting internal object that is unrelenting in its persecution of them. Usually understood as a harsh superego, the internal agency criticizes them, punishes them for not measuring up to expectations, and generally contributes to their feelings of misery and unhappiness. The pattern may be associated with self-defeating tendencies, because they do not feel that they deserve to be successful. They may also have a long-standing sense of despair about ever getting their emotional needs met by important people in their lives. The patients' bleak outlook on life and their pessimism about relationships result in a self-fulfilling prophecy: many people avoid them because their company is unpleasant.

INTERPERSONAL THERAPY

In interpersonal therapy for depressive disorders, the patient's current interpersonal experiences and ways of copying with stress are examined to reduce depressive symptoms and improve self-esteem. Interpersonal therapy consists of about 12 to 16 weekly sessions and can be combined with antidepressant medication.

FAMILY AND GROUP THERAPIES

Family therapy may help both the patient and the patient's family deal with the symptoms of the disorder, especially when a biologically based subaffective syndrome may be present. Group therapy may help withdrawn patients learn new ways to overcome their interpersonal problems in social situations.

PHARMACOTHERAPY

Because of long-standing and commonly held theoretical beliefs that dysthymic disorder is primarily a psychologically determined disorder, many clinicians avoid the use of antidepressants in patients with the disorder. Many studies have had therapeutic success with antidepressants in the disorder. In general, however, the data suggest that monoamine oxidase inhibitors (MAOIs) may be more beneficial than tricyclic drugs. The relatively recent introduction of the well-tolerated serotonin-specific reuptake inhibitors (SSRIs) has led to their frequent use by patients with dysthymic disorder; preliminary reports indicate that the SSRIs may be the drugs of choice for the disorder. Similarly, initial reports suggest that bupropion may be an effective treatment for patients with dysthymic disorder. Sympathomimetics, such as amphetamine, have also been of use in selected patients.

Failure of Therapeutic Trial

A therapeutic trial of an antidepressant in the treatment of dysthymic disorder should use maximal tolerated dosages for a minimum of eight weeks before the clinician concludes that the trial was not effective. If a drug trial is unsuccessful, the clinician should reconsider the diagnosis, especially regarding the possibility of an underlying medical disorder (especially a thyroid disorder) or adult attention-deficit disorder. If a reconsideration of the differential diagnosis still leaves dysthymic disorder as the most likely diagnosis, the clinician may follow the same therapeutic strategy one would follow in major depressive disorder. Specifically, the clinician may attempt to augment the first antidepressant by adding lithium or liothyronine (Cytomel), although augmentation strategies have not been studied for dysthymic disorder. Or the clinician may decide to switch to an antidepressant from a completely different class of drugs. For example, if a trial with an SSRI is unsuccessful, the clinician may switch to bupropion or an MAOI.

HOSPITALIZATION

Hospitalization is usually not indicated for dysthymic disorder patients; however, the presence of particularly severe symptoms, marked social or professional incapacitation, the need for extensive diagnostic procedures, and suicidal ideation are all indications for hospitalization.

CYCLOTHYMIC DISORDER

Cyclothymic disorder is symptomatically a mild form of bipolar II disorder; it is characterized by episodes of hypomania and episodes of mild depression. In DSM-IV, cyclothymic disorder is differentiated from bipolar II disorder, which is characterized by the presence of major depressive episodes and hypomanic episodes. As with dysthymic disorder, the categorization of cyclothymic disorder with the mood disorders implies a relation, probably biological, to bipolar I disorder. However, some psychiatrists understand cyclothymic disorder as distinct from bipolar I disorder and as resulting from chaotic object relations early in life.

The history of cyclothymic disorder is based to some extent on the observations of Emil Kraepelin and Kurt Schneider that one third to two thirds of patients with mood disorders exhibit personality disorders. Kraepelin described four types of personality disorders: depressive (gloomy), manic (cheerful and uninhibited), irritable (labile and explosive), and cyclothymic. Kraepelin described the irritable personality as the simultaneous presence of the depressive and manic personalities, and he described the cyclothymic personality as the alternation of the depressive and manic personalities.

Epidemiology

Patients with cyclothymic disorder may constitute from 3 to 10 percent of all psychiatric outpatients, perhaps particularly those with significant complaints regarding marital and interpersonal difficulties. In the general population the lifetime prevalence of cyclothymic disorder is estimated to be about 1 percent. That figure is probably lower than the actual prevalence, since, as with bipolar I disorder patients, the patients may not be aware that they have a psychiatric problem. Cyclothymic disorder, like dysthymic disorder, frequently coexists with borderline personality disorder. An estimated 10 percent of outpatients and 20 percent of inpatients with borderline personality disorder have a coexisting diagnosis of cyclothymic disorder. The female-to-male ratio in cyclothymic disorder is about 3 to 2, and 50 to 75 percent of all patients have an onset between ages 15 and 25.

Etiology

As with dysthymic disorder, controversy concerns whether cyclothymic disorder is related to the mood disorders, either biologically or psychologically. Some researchers have postulated that cyclothymic disorder has a closer relation to borderline personality disorder than to the mood disorders. In spite of those controversies, the preponderance of the biological and genetic data favors the conceptualization of cyclothymic disorder as a bona fide mood disorder.

BIOLOGICAL FACTORS

The genetic data are the strongest supports for the hypothesis that cyclothymic disorder is a mood disorder. About 30 percent of all cyclothymic disorder patients have positive family histories for bipolar I disorder; that rate is similar to the rate for patients with bipolar I disorder. Moreover, the pedigrees of families with bipolar I disorder often contain generations of bipolar I disorder patients linked by a generation with cyclothymic disorder. Conversely, the prevalence of cyclothymic disorder in the relatives of bipolar I disorder patients is much higher than is the prevalence of cyclothymic disorder either in the relatives of patients with other mental disorders or in mentally healthy persons. The observations that about one third of patients with cyclothymic disorder subsequently have major mood disorders, that they are particularly sensitive to antidepressant-induced hypomania, and that about 60 percent respond to lithium add further support to the conceptualization of cyclothymic disorder as a mild or attenuated form of bipolar I disorder.

PSYCHOSOCIAL FACTORS

Most psychodynamic theories postulate that the development of cyclothymic disorder lies in traumas and fixations during the oral stage of infant development. Freud hypothesized that the cyclothymic state is the ego's attempt to overcome a harsh and punitive superego. Hypomania is explained psychodynamically as occurring when a depressed person throws off the burden of an overly harsh superego, resulting in a lack of self-criticism and an absence of inhibitions. The major defense mechanism in hypomania is denial, by which the patient avoids external problems and internal feelings of depression.

Patients with cyclothymic disorder are characterized by periods of depression alternating with periods of hypomania. Psychoanalytic exploration of such patients reveals that underlying depressive themes are defended against by euphoric or hypomanic periods. Hypomania is frequently triggered by a profound interpersonal loss. The false euphoria generated in such instances is a way the patient denies dependence on love objects while simultaneously disavowing any aggression or destructiveness that may have contributed to the loss of the loved person. Hypomania may also be associated with an unconscious fantasy that the lost object has been restored. That denial is generally short-lived, and the patient soon resumes the preoccupation with suffering and misery characteristic of dysthymic disorder.

Diagnosis

Although many patients seek psychiatric help for depression, their problems are often related to the chaos that their manic episodes have caused. The clinician must consider a diagnosis of cyclothymic disorder when a patient presents with what may seem to be sociopathic behavioral problems. Marital difficulties and instability in relationships are common complaints because cyclothymic disorder patients are often promiscuous and irritable while in manic and mixed states. Although there are anecdotal reports of increased productivity and creativity while patients are hypomanic, most clinicians report that their patients become disorganized and ineffective in work and school during those periods.

The DSM-IV diagnostic criteria for cyclothymic disorder (Table 9.2–2) require that the patient has never met the criteria for a major depressive episode and did not meet the criteria for a manic episode during the first two years of the disturbance. The criteria also require the more or less constant presence of symptoms for two years (or one year for children and adolescents).

Clinical Features

The symptoms of cyclothymic disorder are identical to the symptoms seen in bipolar I disorder, except that they are generally less severe. On occasion, however, the symptoms may be equal in severity but be of shorter duration than those seen in bipolar I disorder. About half of all cyclothymic disorder patients have depression as their major symptom, and those patients are most likely to seek psychiatric help while depressed. Some cyclothymic disorder patients have primarily hypomanic symptoms and are less likely to consult a psychiatrist than are primarily depressed patients. Almost all cyclothymic disorder patients have periods of mixed symptoms with marked irritability.

Most cyclothymic disorder patients seen by psychiatrists have not succeeded in their professional and social lives because of their disorder. However, a few cyclothymic disorder patients have become high achievers who have worked especially long hours and have required little sleep. The ability of some persons to successfully control the symptoms of the disorder depends on multiple individual, social, and cultural attributes.

The lives of most cyclothymic disorder patients are difficult. The cycles of cyclothymic disorder tend to be much shorter than those in bipolar I disorder. In cyclothymic disorder the changes in mood are irregular and abrupt, sometimes occurring within hours. Occasional periods of normal mood and the unpredictable nature of the mood changes cause the patients a great deal of stress. Patients often feel that their moods are out of control. In irritable, mixed periods the patients may become involved in unprovoked disagreements with friends, family, and coworkers.

SUBSTANCES ABUSE

Alcohol abuse and other substance abuse are common in cyclothymic disorder patients; they may use substances either to self-medicate (with alcohol, benzodiazepines, and marijuana) or to achieve even further stimulation (with cocaine, amphetamines, and hallucinogens) when they are manic. About 5 to 10 percent of all cyclothymic disorder patients have substance dependence. Cyclothymic disorder persons often have a history of multiple geographical moves, involvements in religious cults, and dilettantism.

Differential Diagnosis

When a diagnosis of cyclothymic disorder is under consideration, all the possible medical and substance-related causes of depression and mania must be considered. Seizures and particular substances (cocaine, amphetamine, and steroids) need to be considered in the differential diagnosis. Borderline, antisocial, histrionic, and narcissistic personality disorders should also be considered in the differential diagnosis. Attention-deficit/hyperactivity disorder can be difficult to differentiate from cyclothymic disorder in children and adolescents. A trial of stimulants helps most patients with attention-deficit/hyperactivity disorder and exacerbates the symptoms of most patients with cyclothymic disorder. Bipolar II disorder, discussed in Section 9.3, is characterized by the combination of major depressive episodes and hypomanic episodes.

Course and Prognosis

Some patients with cyclothymic disorder are characterized as having been sensitive, hyperactive, or moody as young children. The onset of frank symptoms of cyclothymic disorder

Table 9.2–2.   Diagnostic Criteria for Cyclothymic Disorder

A. For at least 2 years, the presence of numerous periods with hypomanic symptoms and numerous periods with depressive symptoms that do not meet criteria for a major depressive episode. **Note:** In children and adolescents, the duration must be at least 1 year.

B. During the above 2-year period (1 year in children and adolescents), the person has not been without the symptoms in criterion A for more than 2 months at a time.

C. No major depressive episode, manic episode, or mixed episode has been present during the first 2 years of the disturbance.

D. The symptoms in criterion A are not better accounted for by schizoaffective disorder and are not superimposed on schizophrenia, schizophreniform disorder, delusional disorder, or psychotic disorder not otherwise specified.

E. The symptoms are not due to the direct physiological effects of a substance (e.g., a drug of abuse, a medication) or a general medical condition (e.g., hyperthyroidism).

F. The symptoms cause clinically significant distress or impairment in social, occupational, or other important areas of functioning.

Table from DSM-IV, *Diagnostic and Statistical Manual of Mental Disorders*, ed 4. Copyright American Psychiatric Association, Washington, 1994. Used with permission.

often occurs insidiously in the person's teens and early 20s. The emergence of symptoms at that time can hinder the person's performance in school and ability to establish friendships with peers. The reactions of patients to such a disorder vary; patients with adaptive coping strategies or ego defenses have better outcomes than do patients with poor coping strategies. About one third of all cyclothymic disorder patients go on to have a major mood disorder, most often bipolar II disorder.

Treatment

BIOLOGICAL TREATMENT

The antimanic drugs are the first line of treatment of patients with cyclothymic disorder. Although the experimental data are limited to studies with lithium, other antimanic agents—for example, carbamazepine and valproate (Depakene)—are also effective, and such results have been reported. Dosages and plasma concentrations of those agents should be the same as in bipolar I disorder. The treatment of depressed cyclothymic disorder patients with antidepressants should be done with caution, because of their increased susceptibility to antidepressant-induced hypomanic or manic episodes. About 40 to 50 percent of all cyclothymic disorder patients treated with antidepressants experience such episodes.

PSYCHOSOCIAL TREATMENT

The psychotherapy for cyclothymic disorder patients is best directed toward increasing the patients' awareness of their condition and helping them develop coping mechanisms for their mood swings. Therapists usually need to help patients repair any damage done during episodes of hypomania. Such damage may include both work-related and family-related problems.

Because of the long-term nature of cyclothymic disorder, patients often require lifelong treatment. Family and group therapies may be supportive, educational, and therapeutic for the patients and those involved in their lives.

References

Akiskal H S: Dysthymic and cyclothymic depressions: Therapeutic considerations. J Clin Psychiatry 55: 46, 1994.
Hellerstein D J, Yanowitch P, Rosenthal J, Samstag L W, Maurer M, Kasch K, Burrows L, Poster M, Cantillon M, Winston A: A randomized double-blind study of fluoxetine versus placebo in the treatment of dysthymic. Am J Psychiatry 150: 1169, 1993.
Howland R H, Thase M E: A comprehensive review of cyclothymic disorder. J Nerv Ment Dis 181: 485, 1993.
Kaplan H I, Sadock B J, editors: Mood Disorders. In Comprehensive Textbook of Psychiatry, ed 6, p 1067. Williams & Wilkins, Baltimore, 1995.
Osser D N: A systematic approach to the classification and pharmacotherapy of nonpsychotic major depression and dysthymia. J Clin Psychopharmacol 13: 133, 1993.
Zisook S: Treatment of dysthymia and atypical depression. J Clin Psychiatry Monogr 10: 15, 1992.

9.3 OTHER MOOD DISORDERS

DEPRESSIVE DISORDERS

The diagnostic criteria for major depressive disorder specify a certain level of severity and a certain duration of symptoms as minimum requirements to meet the diagnosis. Although the criteria reflect a great deal of research and discussion, they are, by necessity, arbitrary. Many clinicians, especially primary care physicians, report that they have seen many patients who have depressive symptoms and suffer psychosocial impairment from them but who do not meet the diagnostic criteria for major depressive disorder. Usually, such patients fall short of the criteria either because their symptoms are not severe enough or because their symptoms have not lasted long enough. The fourth edition of Diagnostic and Statistical Manual of Mental Disorders (DSM-IV) addresses the diagnostic problem posed by those patients by including two additional diagnostic categories.

The research criteria for minor depressive disorder apply to patients who have depressive symptoms that fail to meet the criteria for major depressive disorder in terms of severity but that do meet the criteria for duration. The diagnostic criteria for recurrent brief depressive disorder are derived from the 10th revision of the International Classification of Diseases (ICD-10). The criteria apply to patients who have depressive symptoms that fail to meet the criteria for major depressive disorder in terms of duration but that do meet the criteria for severity.

Minor depressive disorder and recurrent brief depressive disorder differ from dysthymic disorder, discussed in Section 9.2. Dysthymic disorder is a chronic depressive disorder that is not characterized by discrete episodes. In contrast, both minor depressive disorder and recurrent brief depressive disorder are characterized by discrete episodes.

Depressive Disorder Not Otherwise Specified

If a patient exhibits depressive symptoms as the major feature and does not meet the diagnostic criteria for any other mood disorder or other DSM-IV mental disorder, the most appropriate diagnosis is depressive disorder not otherwise specified (NOS). Listed as examples here and also discussed in the appendixes are minor depressive disorder, recurrent brief depressive disorder, and premenstrual dysphoric disorder.

MINOR DEPRESSIVE DISORDER

The literature in the United States on minor depressive disorder is limited, partly by the fact that the term ''minor depression'' is used to describe a wide range of disorders, including what is called dysthymic disorder in DSM-IV. The European literature on minor depressive disorder, although limited, is more extensive than the United States literature. The information about minor depressive disorder is helped considerably by the introduction in the appendix of DSM-IV of specific diagnostic guidelines that allow researchers to use a single definition of the disorder.

Epidemiology

The epidemiology of minor depressive disorder is not known, but preliminary data show that it may be as common as major depressive disorder—that is, about 5 percent prevalence in the general population. Preliminary data also indicate that the disorder is more common in women than in men. Minor depressive disorder probably affects persons of virtually any age, from childhood to old age.

Etiology

The cause of minor depressive disorder is not known. The same causative considerations given major depressive disorder should be considered. Specifically, the biological theories involve the activities of noradrenergic and serotonergic biogenic amine systems and the thyroid and adrenal neuroendocrine axes. The psychological theories center on issues of loss, guilt, and punitive superegos.

Diagnosis

The DSM-IV research criteria for minor depressive disorder list symptoms equal in duration to those of major depressive disorder but of less severity. The availability of the diagnostic category allows for the specific diagnosis of patients whose lives are affected by depressive symptoms but whose symptoms do not meet the severity required for a diagnosis of major depressive disorder.

Clinical Features

The clinical features of minor depressive disorder are virtually identical to the clinical features of major depressive disorder, except that they are of less severity. The central symptom of both disorders is the same—that is, a depressed mood.

Differential Diagnosis

The differential diagnosis for minor depressive disorder is the same as that for major depressive disorder. Of special importance for the differential diagnosis of minor depressive disorder are dysthymic disorder and recurrent brief depressive disorder. Dysthymic disorder is characterized by the presence of chronic depressive symptoms, whereas recurrent brief depressive disorder is characterized by multiple brief episodes of severe depressive symptoms.

Course And Prognosis

No definitive data on the course and the prognosis of minor depressive disorder are available. However, minor depressive disorder is probably similar to major depressive disorder: a long-term course that may require long-term treatment. A significant proportion of patients with minor depressive disorder are probably at risk for other mood disorders, including dysthymic disorder, bipolar I disorder, bipolar II disorder, and major depressive disorder.

Treatment

The treatment of minor depressive disorder can include psychotherapy or pharmacotherapy or both. Some psychotherapists advocate the use of multiple psychotherapeutic approaches, but using the psychotherapy data for major depressive disorder is a more conservative approach. Insight-oriented psychotherapy, cognitive therapy, interpersonal therapy, and behavior therapy are the psychotherapeutic treatments for major depressive disorder and, by implication, for minor depressive disorder. Although the experimental data are limited, patients with minor depressive disorder are probably responsive to pharmacotherapy, particularly serotonin-specific reuptake inhibitors (SSRIs) and bupropion (Wellbutrin).

RECURRENT BRIEF DEPRESSIVE DISORDER

Recurrent brief depressive disorder is characterized by multiple, relatively brief episodes (less than two weeks) of depressive symptoms that, except for their brief duration, meet the diagnostic criteria for major depressive disorder. Recurrent brief depressive disorder has been written about mostly in the European literature; however, with its introduction as a diagnostic category in the appendix of DSM-IV, the disorder is likely to gain rapid acceptance in the United States. Its acceptance in the United States will likely be further facilitated by clinicians' increasing awareness that recurrent brief depressive disorder is a relatively common disorder associated with significant morbidity.

Epidemiology

Extensive studies on the epidemiology of recurrent brief depressive disorder have not been conducted in the United States. Available data indicate that the 10-year prevalence rate for the disorder is estimated to be 10 percent for persons in their 20s; the one-year prevalence rate for the general population is estimated to be 5 percent. Those figures indicate that recurrent brief depressive disorder is most common among young adults, but many more studies must be conducted to refine the data.

Etiology

One study found that patients with recurrent brief depressive disorder share several biological abnormalities with patients with major de-

pressive disorder when compared with mentally healthy control subjects. The variables include nonsuppression on the dexamethasone-suppression test (DST), a blunted response to thyrotropin-releasing hormone (TRH) (that is, protirelin [Thyrel]), and a shortening of REM sleep latency. The data are consistent with the idea that recurrent brief depressive disorder is closely related to major depressive disorder in its cause and pathophysiology. The available data also indicate that family histories of mood disorders are similar for recurrent brief depressive disorder and major depressive disorder, suggesting a close relation between the two disorders.

Diagnosis

The DSM-IV research criteria for recurrent brief depressive disorder specify that the symptom duration for each episode is less than two weeks. Otherwise, the diagnostic criteria for recurrent brief depressive disorder and major depressive disorder are essentially identical.

Clinical Features

The clinical features of recurrent brief depressive disorder are almost identical to those of major depressive disorder. One subtle difference is that the lives of patients with recurrent brief depressive disorder may seem more disrupted or chaotic because of the frequent changes in their moods when compared with the lives of patients with major depressive disorder, whose depressive episodes occur at a measured pace. One study calculated the mean length of time between depressive episodes in recurrent brief depressive disorder to be 18 days. Another study reported that episodes of sleep disturbance closely coincide with the episodes of depression, thus helping the clinician establish the periodicity of the depressive episodes.

Differential Diagnosis

The differential diagnosis for recurrent brief depressive disorder is the same as that for major depressive disorder. The clinician should consider bipolar disorders and major depressive disorder with seasonal pattern in the differential diagnosis. Research into recurrent brief depressive disorder may find an association with the rapid cycling type of bipolar disorders. The clinician should also assess whether there is a seasonal pattern to the recurrence of depressive episodes in a patient being evaluated for a diagnosis of recurrent brief depressive disorder. At least one researcher has proposed that patients with recurrent brief depressive disorder be subtyped according to the relative frequencies of their depressive episodes. That differentiation is not included in DSM-IV, although the differentiation may yet prove to have prognostic or treatment implications.

Course and Prognosis

The course and the prognosis for patients with recurrent brief depressive disorder are not well known. Based on the available data, their course, including age of onset, and their prognosis are similar to those of patients with major depressive disorder.

Treatment

The treatment of patients with recurrent brief depressive disorder should be similar to the treatment of patients with major depressive disorder. The main treatments should be psychotherapy (insight-oriented psychotherapy, cognitive therapy, interpersonal therapy, or behavioral therapy) and pharmacotherapy with the standard antidepressant drugs. Some treatments for bipolar I disorder—lithium (Eskalith) and anticonvulsants—may be of therapeutic value, but those agents have not yet been studied in patients with recurrent brief depressive disorder.

PREMENSTRUAL DYSPHORIC DISORDER

DSM-IV includes suggested diagnostic criteria for premenstrual dysphoric disorder in its appendixes to help researchers and clinicians in the evaluation of the validity of the diagnosis. Premenstrual dysphoric disorder has also been called late luteal phase dysphoric disorder, and premenstrual syndrome (PMS). Whether the syndrome warrants an official diagnosis remains controversial. Nevertheless, the generally recognized syndrome is one involving mood symptoms (for example, lability), behavior symptoms (for example, changes in eating patterns), and physical symptoms (for example, breast tenderness, edema, and headaches). That pattern of symptoms occurs at a specific time during the menstrual cycle, and the symptoms resolve for some time between menstrual cycles.

Epidemiology

Because of the absence of generally agreed on diagnostic criteria, the epidemiology of premenstrual dysphoric disorder is not known with certainty. One study reported that about 40 percent of women have at least mild symptoms of the disorder and that from 2 to 10 percent meet the full diagnostic criteria for the disorder.

Etiology

On the one hand, the cause of premenstrual dysphoric disorder is not known. On the other hand, because of the timing of the symptoms with the menstrual cycle, the hormonal changes occurring during the menstrual cycle are probably involved in the production of symptoms. Among the theories that have been put forth for the disorder, one of the most commonly stated is that the disorder is characterized by an abnormally high estrogen-to-progesterone ratio in affected women. Other hypotheses are that affected women have biogenic amine neurons that are abnormally affected by changes in the hormones, that the disorder is an example of a chronobiological phase disorder, and that the disorder is the result of abnormal prostaglandin activity. In addition to the biological theories, societal and personal issues regarding menstruation and womanhood may affect the symptoms of individual patients.

Diagnosis

An appendix of DSM-IV contains suggested research criteria for premenstrual dysphoric disorder. The criteria include symptoms regarding abnormal mood, abnormal behavior, and somatic complaints.

Clinical Features

The most common mood and cognitive symptoms are lability of mood, irritability, anxiety, decreased interest in activities, increased fatigability, and difficulty in concentrating. Behavioral symptoms often include changes in appetite and sleep patterns. The most common somatic complaints are headache, breast tenderness, and edema. In affected women the symptoms appear during most (if not all) menstrual cycles, although the symptoms usually remit before the end of the blood flow. Affected women are symptom-free for at least a week during each menstrual cycle.

Differential Diagnosis

If symptoms are present throughout the menstrual cycle, with no intercycle symptom relief, the clinician should consider one of the nonmenstrual-cycle-related mood disorders and anxiety disorders. Even if the symptoms have a cyclical nature, the presence of especially severe symptoms should prompt the clinician to consider other mood disorders and anxiety disorders.

Course and Prognosis

The course and the prognosis of premenstrual dysphoric disorder have not been adequately studied to reach any reasonable conclusions. Anecdotally, the symptoms tend to be chronic unless effective treatment is initiated.

Treatment

Treatment of premenstrual dysphoric disorder includes support for the patient regarding the presence and the recognition of the symptoms.

In preliminary studies, progesterone supplementation, fluoxetine (Prozac), and alprazolam (Xanax) have all been reported to be effective, although no treatment has been conclusively shown to be effective in multiple well-controlled trials.

BIPOLAR DISORDERS

Clinicians have long reported that in some patients the primary symptom seems to be depressive episodes, but the course of the disorder is interspersed with episodes of mild manic symptoms (that is, hypomanic episodes). Such disorders have been called bipolar II disorder (by those researchers who think that the disorder belongs in the bipolar disorders spectrum) and major depressive disorder with hypomanic episodes (by those researchers who think that the disorder belongs in the depressive disorders spectrum). The distinction between bipolar II disorder and recurrent major depressive episodes with hypomania has important implications for prognostic and treatment assessments and decisions.

Bipolar II Disorder

Bipolar II disorder, alternatively called recurrent major depressive episodes with hypomania, is a new diagnostic category in DSM-IV. Patients with the disorder were formerly classified as having bipolar disorder not otherwise specified (NOS).

EPIDEMIOLOGY

The epidemiology of bipolar II disorder is not known accurately at this time because of the relatively recent recognition of the disorder.

ETIOLOGY

Although the classification of bipolar II disorder with the mood disorders implies a close association with the mood disorders, some investigators have hypothesized that bipolar II disorder is related to borderline personality disorder. However, some data indicate that bipolar II disorder tends to be inherited as bipolar II disorder, thus suggesting that it has its own unique genetic predisposition.

DIAGNOSIS

The diagnostic criteria for bipolar II disorder specify a particular severity, frequency, and duration of the hypomanic symptoms. The diagnostic criteria for a hypomanic episode (see Table 9.1–3) are listed separately from the criteria for bipolar II disorder (Table 9.3–1). The criteria have been established to decrease the overdiagnosis of hypomanic episodes and the incorrect classification of patients with major depressive disorder as patients

Table 9.3-1. Diagnostic Criteria for Bipolar II Disorder

A. Presence (or history) of one or more major depressive episodes.

B. Presence (or history) of at least one hypomanic episode.

C. There has never been a manic episode or a mixed episode.

D. The mood symptoms in criteria A and B are not better accounted for by schizoaffective disorder and are not superimposed on schizophrenia, schizophreniform disorder, delusional disorder, or psychotic disorder not otherwise specified.

E. The symptoms cause clinically significant distress or impairment in social, occupational, or other important areas of functioning.

Table from DSM-IV, *Diagnostic and Statistical Manual of Mental Disorders*, ed 4. Copyright American Psychiatric Association, Washington, 1994. Used with permission.

with bipolar II disorder. Clinically, the psychiatrist may find it difficult to distinguish euthymia from hypomania in a patient who has been chronically depressed for many months or years. As with bipolar I disorder, antidepressant-induced hypomanic episodes are not diagnostic of bipolar II disorder.

Specifiers

DSM-IV allows the qualification of the diagnosis of bipolar II disorder with specific terms, including the specification of the symptom picture as being with melancholic (see Table 9.1–4), atypical, or catatonic features. DSM-IV also allows the following course specifiers: with rapid cycling, with seasonal pattern, and with postpartum onset.

CLINICAL FEATURES

The clinical features of bipolar II disorder are those of major depressive disorder combined with those of hypomanic episode. Although the data are limited, a few studies indicate that bipolar II disorder is associated with more marital disruption and onset at an earlier age than is bipolar I disorder. Evidence also indicates that bipolar II disorder patients are at greater risk of both attempting and completing suicide than are bipolar I disorder and major depressive disorder patients.

DIFFERENTIAL DIAGNOSIS

The differential diagnosis of patients being evaluated for a diagnosis of bipolar II disorder should include bipolar I disorder, major depressive disorder, and borderline personality disorder. The differentiation between bipolar II disorder on the one hand and major depressive disorder and bipolar I disorder on the other hand rests on the clinical evaluation of the maniclike episodes. The clinician should not mistake euthymia in a chronically depressed patient as a hypomanic or manic episode. Patients with borderline personality disorder often have the same type of severely disrupted life that patients with bipolar II disorder have, because of the multiple episodes of significant mood disorder symptoms.

COURSE AND PROGNOSIS

The course and the prognosis of bipolar II disorder have just begun to be studied; however, preliminary data indicate that it is a stable diagnosis, as shown by the high likelihood that patients with bipolar II disorder will have the same diagnosis up to five years later. The data indicate that bipolar II disorder is a chronic disease that warrants long-term treatment strategies.

TREATMENT

The treatment of bipolar II disorder must be approached cautiously, since the treatment of depressive episodes with antidepressants can frequently precipitate a manic episode. Whether typical bipolar I disorder medication strategies (for example, lithium and anticonvulsants) are effective in the treatment of bipolar II disorder patients is still under investigation. A trial of such agents seems warranted, especially when treatment with antidepressants alone has not been successful.

Bipolar Disorder Not Otherwise Specified

If patients exhibit depressive and manic symptoms as the major features of their disorder and do not meet the diagnostic criteria for any other mood disorder or other DSM-IV mental disorder, the most appropriate diagnosis is bipolar disorder not otherwise specified. DSM-IV allows for the further specification of with rapid cycling, with seasonal pattern, or with postpartum onset.

ATYPICAL CYCLOID PSYCHOSES

This group of disorders shows some features of bipolar I disorder but generally do not meet the complete diagnostic criteria for that category. Some patients with atypical cycloid psychoses may be classified as having bipolar disorder not otherwise specified.

Motility Psychosis

The two forms of motility psychosis are akinetic and hyperkinetic. The akinetic form of motility psychosis has a clinical presentation similar to that of catatonic stupor. In contrast to the catatonic type of schizophrenia, however, akinetic motility psychosis has a rapidly resolving and favorable course that does not lead to personality deterioration. In its hyperkinetic form, motility psychosis may resemble manic or catatonic excitement. As with the akinetic form, the hyperkinetic form has a rapidly resolving and favorable course.

Confusional Psychosis

Excited confusional psychosis, as originally described, was differentiated from mania by several characteristics: in excited confusional psychosis, more anxiety, less distractibility, and a degree of speech incoherence out of proportion to the severity of the flight of ideas. Confusional psychosis is probably a clinical variation of the mania seen in bipolar I disorder.

Anxiety-Blissfulness Psychosis

Anxiety-blissfulness psychosis may resemble agitated depression, but it may also be characterized by so much inhibition that the patient can hardly move. Periodic states of overwhelming anxiety and paranoid ideas of reference are characteristic of the condition, but self-accusation, hypochondriacal preoccupation, other depressive symptoms, and hallucinations may also accompany it. The blissful phase manifests itself most frequently in expansive behavior and grandiose ideas, which are concerned less with self-aggrandizement than with the mission of making others happy and saving the world.

OTHER MOOD DISORDERS

Two mood disorder diagnoses to be considered in the differential diagnosis of any patient with mood disorder symptoms are mood disorder due to a general medical condition and substance-induced mood disorder. DSM-IV includes those diagnostic categories within the mood disorders to encourage and facilitate the process of differential diagnosis.

It can be difficult to determine whether mood disorder symptoms in a patient with a general medical condition are (1) secondary to the effects on the brain of the general medical condition (classified as a mood disorder due to a general medical condition), (2) secondary to the effects on the brain of drugs used to treat the general medical condition (classified as a substance-induced mood disorder), (3) reflecting an adjustment disorder caused by the general medical condition (classified as an adjustment disorder), or (4) reflecting a primary mood disorder (for example, major depressive disorder). The difficulty of the clinical differentiation is recognized in DSM-IV by the grouping of the disorders (except for adjustment disorder) in the mood disorders section.

Mood Disorder Due to a General Medical Condition

When depressive or manic symptoms are present in a patient with a general medical condition, attributing the depressive symptoms to either the general medical condition or a mood disorder can be difficult. Many general medical conditions present depressive symptoms, such as poor sleep, decreased appetite, and fatigue.

EPIDEMIOLOGY

The epidemiology of mood disorder due to a general medical condition is not known. However, the disorder is probably common and often undiagnosed.

ETIOLOGY

Many somatic disorders have been implicated as causes of mood disorder symptoms, including endocrine disorders, especially Cushing's syndrome, and neurological disorders, such as brain tumors, encephalitis, and epilepsy. Structural damage to the brain, similar to what occurs in hemispheric cerebrovascular diseases, is a common cause of mood disorder due to a general medical condition.

DIAGNOSIS

The DSM-IV diagnostic criteria for mood disorder due to a general medical condition (Table 9.3–2) allow the clinician to specify whether the symptoms are manic (full or partial symptoms), depressive (full or partial symptoms), or mixed.

CLINICAL FEATURES

Disturbances of mood resembling those observed in depressive and manic states are the predominant and essential clinical features. To make the diagnosis, the physician must find a general medical condition that antedates the onset of the mood disorder symptoms. The disorder varies in severity from mild to severe or psychotic and may be indistinguishable from the symptoms seen in major depressive disorder and bipolar I disor-

Table 9.3–2.   Diagnostic Criteria for Mood Disorder Due to a General Medical Condition

A. A prominent and persistent disturbance in mood predominates in the clinical picture and is characterized by either (or both) of the following:
    (1) depressed mood or markedly diminished interest or pleasure in all, or almost all, activities
    (2) elevated, expansive, or irritable mood

B. There is evidence from the history, physical examination, or laboratory findings that the disturbance is the direct physiological consequence of a general medical condition.

C. The disturbance is not better accounted for by another mental disorder (e.g., adjustment disorder with depressed mood in response to the stress of having a general medical condition).

D. The disturbance does not occur exclusively during the course of a delirium.

E. The symptoms cause clinically significant distress or impairment in social, occupational, or other important areas of functioning.

Specify type:
    With depressive features: if the predominant mood is depressed but the full criteria are not met for a major depressive episode
    With major depressivelike episode: if the full criteria are met (except criterion D) for a major depressive episode
    With manic features: if the predominant mood is elevated, euphoric, or irritable
    With mixed features: if the symptoms of both mania and depression are present but neither predominates

der. Delusions and hallucinations may be present, as well as mild to moderate cognitive impairment.

DIFFERENTIAL DIAGNOSIS

The differential diagnosis should include substance-induced mood disorder (involving substances used to treat the medical condition), the primary mood disorders, and adjustment disorders. In some health delivery systems, malingering must also be considered in the differential diagnosis.

COURSE AND PROGNOSIS

The onset of the symptoms may be sudden or insidious, and the course varies, depending on the underlying cause. The removal of the cause does not necessarily result in the patient's prompt recovery from the mood disorder. The disorder may persist for weeks or months after the successful treatment of the underlying physical condition. As with the other mood disorders, suicide is a risk for patients with mood disorder due to a general medical condition.

TREATMENT

Management of the disorder involves determining the cause and treating the underlying disorder. Psychopharmacological treatment may be indicated and should follow the guidelines applicable to the treatment of depression or mania, with due regard for the coexisting physical condition. Psychotherapy may be useful as an adjunct to other treatments.

Substance-Induced Mood Disorder

Substance-induced mood disorder must always be considered in the differential diagnosis of mood disorder symptoms. In general, the clinician should consider three possibilities: First, the patient may be taking drugs for the treatment of nonpsychiatric medical problems. Second, the patient may have been accidentally and perhaps unknowingly exposed to neurotoxic chemicals. Third, the patient may have taken a substance for recreational purposes or may be dependent on such a substance.

EPIDEMIOLOGY

The epidemiology of substance-induced mood disorder is not known. However, the prevalence is probably high, given the number of prescription drugs that can cause depression and mania, the number of toxic chemicals in the environment and the workplace, and the widespread use of so-called recreational drugs.

ETIOLOGY

Medications, especially antihypertensives, are probably the most frequent cause of substance-induced mood disorder, although a wide range of drugs can cause depression and mania. Drugs such as reserpine (Serpasil) and methyldopa (Aldomet), both antihypertensive agents, can precipitate a depressive disorder, presumably by depleting serotonin, as happens in more than 10 percent of all persons who take the drugs.

DIAGNOSIS

The DSM-IV diagnostic criteria for substance-induced mood disorder allow the specification of (1) the substance involved, (2) whether the onset was during intoxication or withdrawal, and (3) the nature of the symptoms (for example, manic or

Table 9.3–3. Diagnostic Criteria for Substance-Induced Mood Disorder

A. A prominent and persistent disturbance in mood predominates in the clinical picture and is characterized by either (or both) of the following:

  (1) depressed mood or markedly diminished interest or pleasure in all, or almost all, activities
  (2) elevated, expansive, or irritable mood

B. There is evidence from the history, physical examination, or laboratory findings of either (1) or (2):

  (1) the symptoms in criterion A developed during, or within a month of, substance intoxication or withdrawal
  (2) medication use is etiologically related to the disturbance

C. The disturbance is not better accounted for by a mood disorder that is not substance induced. Evidence that the symptoms are better accounted for by a mood disorder that is not substance induced might include the following: the symptoms precede the onset of the substance use (or medication use); the symptoms persist for a substantial period of time (e.g., about a month) after the cessation of acute withdrawal or severe intoxication or are substantially in excess of what would be expected given the type or amount of the substance used or the duration of use; or there is other evidence that suggests the existence of an independent non-substance-induced mood disorder (e.g., a history of recurrent major depressive episodes).

D. The disturbance does not occur exclusively during the course of a delirium.

E. The symptoms cause clinically significant distress or impairment in social, occupational, or other important areas of functioning.

Table from DSM-IV, *Diagnostic and Statistical Manual of Mental Disorders*, ed 4. Copyright American Psychiatric Association, Washington, 1994. Used with permission.

depressed) (Table 9.3–3). A maximum of a month between the use of the substance and the appearance of the symptoms is allowed in DSM-IV, although the usual period is probably shorter than a month. However, the diagnosis may sometimes be warranted after more than a month.

CLINICAL FEATURES

The substance-induced manic and depressive features can be identical to those of bipolar I disorder and major depressive disorder. However, substance-induced mood disorder may present more waxing and waning of the symptoms and a fluctuation in the patient's level of consciousness.

DIFFERENTIAL DIAGNOSIS

The presence of a history of mood disorders in the patient or the patient's family weights toward the diagnosis of a primary mood disorder, although such a history does not rule out the possibility of substance-induced mood disorder. Substances may also trigger an underlying mood disorder in a patient who is biologically vulnerable to mood disorders.

COURSE AND PROGNOSIS

The course and the prognosis of substance-induced mood disorder are variable; in general, shortly after the substance has been cleared from the body, a normal mood returns. Sometimes, however, the substance exposure seems to precipitate a long-lasting mood disorder that may take weeks or months to resolve completely.

TREATMENT

The primary treatment of substance-induced mood disorder is the identification of the causally involved substance. Usually, stopping the intake of the substance is sufficient to cause the mood disorder symptoms to abate. If the symptoms linger, treatment with appropriate psychiatric drugs may be necessary.

Mood Disorder Not Otherwise Specified

If patients exhibit depressive or manic symptoms or both as the major features of their disorder and do not meet the diagnostic criteria for any other mood disorder or other DSM-IV mental disorder, including depressive disorder not otherwise specified and bipolar disorder not otherwise specified, the most appropriate diagnosis is mood disorder not otherwise specified (NOS).

References

Akiskal H S: Mood disorders: Clinical features. In *Comprehensive Textbook of Psychiatry*, ed 6, H I Kaplan, B J Sadock, editors, p 1123. Williams & Wilkins, Baltimore, 1995.

Christensen A P, Oei T P: The efficacy of cognitive behaviour therapy in treating premenstrual dysphoric changes. J Affect Disord *33*: 57, 1995.

Evans D L, Byerly M J, Greer R A: Secondary mania: Diagnosis and treatment. J Clin Psychiatry *56* (Suppl 3): 31, 1995.

Heun R, Maier W: The distinction of bipolar II disorder from bipolar I and recurrent unipolar depression: results of a controlled family study. Acta Psychiatr Scand *87*: 279, 1993.

Lazarus A A: The multimodal approach to the treatment of minor depression. Am J Psychother *46*: 50, 1992.

Moline M L: Pharmacologic strategies for managing premenstrual syndrome. Clin Pharm *12*: 181, 1993.

Paykel E, moderator: Workshop IV: Depression in medical illness. Int Clin Psychopharmacol *7*: 205, 1993.

Simpson S G, Folstein S E, Meyers D A, McMahon F J, Brusco D M, DePaulo J R Jr: Bipolar II: the most common bipolar phenotype? Am J Psychiatry *150*: 901, 1993.

Stuart J W, Quitkin F M, Klein D F: The pharmacotherapy of minor depression. Am J Psychother *46*: 23, 1992.

Sunblad C, Hedberg M A, Eriksson E: Clomipramine administered during the luteal-phase reduces the symptoms of premenstrual-syndrome—A placebo-controlled trial. Neuropsychopharmacology *9*: 133, 1993.

Tannock C, Katona C: Minor depression in the aged. Concepts, prevalence and optimal management. Drugs Aging *6*: 278, 1995.

Weiss M K, Tohen M, Zarate C Jr, Iversen A: Diagnosis and management of bipolar II disorder. Compr Ther *20*: 121, 1994.

10/ Anxiety Disorders

10.1 ANXIETY DISORDERS: OVERVIEW

When evaluating a patient with anxiety, the clinician must still distinguish between normal and pathological types of anxiety. On a practical level, pathological anxiety is differentiated from normal anxiety by the assessments made by patients, their families, their friends, and the clinician that pathological anxiety is, in fact, present. Such assessments are based on the patients' reported internal states, their behaviors, and their abilities to function. A patient with pathological anxiety requires a complete neuropsychiatric evaluation and an individually tailored treatment plan. The clinician must be aware that anxiety can be a component of many medical conditions and other mental disorders, especially depressive disorders.

Because it is clearly to one's advantage to respond with anxiety in certain threatening situations, one can speak of normal anxiety in contrast to abnormal or pathological anxiety. For example, anxiety is normal for the infant who is threatened by separation from parents or by loss of love, for children on their first day in school, for adolescents on their first date, for adults when they contemplate old age and death, and for anyone who is faced with illness. Anxiety is a normal accompaniment of growth, of change, of experiencing something new and untried, and of finding one's own identity and meaning in life. Pathological anxiety, by contrast, is an inappropriate response to given stimulus by virtue of either its intensity or its duration.

NORMAL ANXIETY

The sensation of anxiety is commonly experienced by virtually all humans. The feeling is characterized by a diffuse, unpleasant, vague sense of apprehension, often accompanied by autonomic symptoms, such as headache, perspiration, palpitations, tightness in the chest, and mild stomach discomfort. An anxious person may also feel restless, as indicated by an inability to sit or stand still for long. The particular constellation of symptoms present during anxiety tends to vary among people.

Fear and Anxiety

Anxiety is an alerting signal; it warns of impending danger and enables the person to take measures to deal with a threat. Fear, a similar alerting signal, should be differentiated from anxiety. Fear is a response to a threat that is known, external, definite, or nonconflictual in origin; anxiety is a response to a threat that is unknown, internal, vague, or conflictual in origin.

The distinction between fear and anxiety arose by accident. Freud's early translator mistranslated ''angst,'' the German word for fear, as anxiety. Freud himself generally ignored the distinction that associates anxiety with a repressed, unconscious object and fear with a known, external object. The distinction may be difficult to make because fear may also be due to an unconscious, repressed, internal object displaced to another object in the external world. For example, a boy may be afraid of barking dogs because he is actually afraid of his father and unconsciously associates his father with barking dogs.

According to post-Freudian psychoanalytic formulations, the separation of fear and anxiety is psychologically justifiable. The emotion caused by a rapidly approaching car as one crosses the street differs from the vague discomfort one may experience when one meets new people in a strange setting. The main psychological difference between the two emotional responses is the acuteness of fear and the chronicity of anxiety.

Adaptive Functions of Anxiety

When considered simply as an alerting signal, anxiety can be considered basically the same emotion as fear. Anxiety warns of an external or internal threat; it has lifesaving qualities. At a lower level, anxiety warns of threats of bodily damage, pain, helplessness, possible punishment, or the frustration of social or bodily needs; of separation from loved ones; of a menace to one's success or status; and ultimately of threats to one's unity or wholeness. It prompts the person to take the necessary steps to prevent the threat or to lessen its consequences. Examples of warding off threats in daily life include getting down to the hard work of preparing for an examination, dodging a ball thrown at one's head, sneaking into the dormitory after curfew to prevent punishment, and running to catch the last commuter train. Thus, anxiety prevents damage by alerting the person to carry out certain acts that forestall the danger.

Stress, Conflict, and Anxiety

Whether an event is perceived as stressful depends on the nature of the event and on the person's resources, psychological defenses, and coping mechanisms. All involve the ego, a collective abstraction for the process by which a person perceives, thinks, and acts on external events or internal drives. A person whose ego is functioning properly is in adaptive balance with both external and internal worlds; if the ego is not functioning properly and the resulting imbalance continues long enough, the person experiences chronic anxiety.

Whether the imbalance is external, between the pressures of the outside world and the person's ego, or internal, between the patient's impulses (for example, aggressive, sexual, and dependent impulses) and conscience, the imbalance produces a conflict. Conflicts caused by external events are usually interpersonal, whereas those caused by internal events are intrapsychic or intrapersonal. A combination of the two is possible, as in the case of employees who have an excessively demanding or critical boss and who must control their impulses to hit the boss for fear of losing their jobs. Interpersonal and intrapsychic conflicts are, in fact, usually combined, because human beings are social and their main conflicts are usually with other people.

Psychological and Cognitive Symptoms

The experience of anxiety has two components: (1) the awareness of the physiological sensations (such as palpitations and sweating) and (2) the awareness of being nervous or frightened. The anxiety may be increased by a feeling of shame—''Others will recognize that I am frightened.'' Many persons are astonished to find out that others are not cognizant of their anxiety or, if others are cognizant, do not appreciate the intensity of the anxiety.

In addition to its motor and visceral effects, anxiety affects thinking, perception, and learning. Anxiety tends to produce confusion and distortions of perception, not only of time and space but of people and the meaning of events. Those distortions can interfere with learning by lowering concentrations, reducing recall, and impairing the ability to relate one item to another—that is, to make associations.

PATHOLOGICAL ANXIETY

Psychological Theories

Three major schools of psychological theory—psychoanalytic, behavioral, and existential—have contributed theories regarding the causes of anxiety. Each of those theories has both conceptual and practical usefulness in the treatment of patients with anxiety disorders.

PSYCHOANALYTIC THEORIES

Within psychoanalytic theory, anxiety is seen as falling into four major categories, depending on the nature of the feared consequences: id or impulse anxiety, separation anxiety, castration anxiety, and superego anxiety. Those varieties of anxiety are hypothesized to develop at various stages of growth and development. Id or impulse anxiety is related to the primitive, diffuse discomforts of infants when they feel overwhelmed with needs and stimuli over which their helpless state provides no control. Separation anxiety occurs in somewhat older but still preoedipal children, who fear the loss of love or even abandonment by their parents if they fail to control and direct their impulses in conformity with their parents' standards and demands. The fantasies of castration that characterize the oedipal child, particularly in relation to the child's developing sexual impulses, are reflected in the castration anxiety of the adult. Superego anxiety is the direct result of the final development of the superego that marks the passing of the Oedipus complex and the advent of the prepubertal period of latency.

Psychoanalysts differ about the sources and the nature of anxiety. Otto Rank, for example, traced the genesis of all anxiety back to the trauma of birth. Harry Stack Sullivan emphasized the early relationship between the mother and the child and the transmission of the mother's anxiety to her infant. Regardless of the school of psychoanalysis, however, treatment of anxiety disorders usually involves long-term, insight-oriented psychotherapy or psychoanalysis directed toward the formation of a transference, which allows the reworking of the development problem and the resolution of the neurotic symptoms.

BEHAVIORAL THEORIES

The behavioral or learning theories of anxiety have spawned some of the most effective treatments for anxiety disorders. Behavioral theories state that anxiety is a conditioned response to specific environmental stimuli. In a model of classical conditioning, a person who does not have any food allergies may become sick after eating contaminated shellfish in a restaurant. Subsequent exposures to shellfish may cause that person to feel sick. Through generalization, such a person may come to distrust all food prepared by others. As an alternative causal possibility, persons may learn to have an internal response of anxiety by imitating the anxiety responses of their parents (social learning theory). In either case, treatment is usually with some form of desensitization by repeated exposure to the anxiogenic stimulus, coupled with cognitive psychotherapeutic approaches.

In recent years, proponents of behavioral theories have shown increasing interest in cognitive approaches to conceptualizing and treating anxiety disorders, and cognitive theorists have proposed alternatives to traditional learning theory causal models of anxiety. Cognitive conceptualization of nonphobic anxiety states state that faulty, distorted, or counterproductive thinking patterns accompany or precede maladaptive behaviors and emotional disorders. According to one model, patients suffering from anxiety disorders tend to overestimate the degree of danger and the probability of harm in a given situation and tend to underestimate their abilities to cope with perceived threats to their physical or psychological well-being. That model asserts that patients with panic disorder often have thoughts of loss of control and fears of dying that follow inexplicable physiological sensations (such as palpitations, tachycardia, and light-headedness) but precede and then accompany panic attacks.

EXISTENTIAL THEORIES

Existenial theories of anxiety provide models for generalized anxiety disorder, in which there is no specifically identifiable stimulus for a chronically anxious feeling. The central concept of existential theory is that persons become aware of a profound nothingness in their lives, feelings that may be even more profoundly discomforting than an acceptance of their inevitable death. Anxiety is the person's response to that vast void of existence and meaning. Existential concerns may have increased since the development of nuclear weapons.

Biological Theories

Biological theories regarding anxiety have developed out of preclinical studies with animal models of anxiety, the study of patients in whom biological factors were ascertained, the growing knowledge regarding basic neuroscience, and the actions of psychotherapeutic drugs. One pole of thought posits that measurable biological changes in patients with anxiety disorders reflect the results of psychological conflicts; the opposite pole posits that the biological events precede the psychological conflicts. Both situations may exist in specific persons, and a range of biologically based sensitivities may exist among persons with the symptoms of anxiety disorders.

AUTONOMIC NERVOUS SYSTEM

Stimulation of the autonomic nervous system causes certain symptoms—cardiovascular (for example, tachycardia), muscular (for example, headache), gastrointestinal (for example, diarrhea), and respiratory (for example, tachypnea). Those peripheral manifestations of anxiety are neither peculiar to anxiety disorders nor necessarily correlated with the subjective experience of anxiety. In the first third of the 20th century, Walter Cannon demonstrated that cats exposed to barking dogs exhibit behavioral and physiological signs of fear that are associated with the adrenal release of epinephrine. The James-Lange theory states that subjective anxiety is a response to peripheral phenomena. It is now generally thought that central nervous system (CNS) anxiety precedes the peripheral manifestations of anxiety, except when a specific peripheral cause is present, such as when a patient has a pheochromocytoma. Some anxiety disorder patients, especially those with panic disorder, have autonomic nervous systems that exhibit increased sympathetic tone, adapt slowly to repeated stimuli, and respond excessively to moderate stimuli.

NEUROTRANSMITTERS

The three major neurotransmitters associated with anxiety on the basis of animal studies and responses to drug treatment are norepinephrine, serotonin, and γ-aminobutyric acid (GABA). Much of the basic neuroscience information about anxiety comes from animal experiments involving behavioral paradigms and psychoactive agents. One such animal model of anxiety is the conflict test, in which the animal is simultaneously presented with stimuli that are positive (for example, food) and negative (for example, electric shock). Anxiolytic drugs (for example, benzodiazepines) tend to facilitate the adaptation of the animal to that situation, whereas other drugs (for example, amphetamines) further disrupt the behavioral responses of the animal.

Norepinephrine

The general theory regarding the role of norepinephrine in anxiety disorders is that affected patients may have a poorly regulated noradrenergic system that has occasional bursts of activity. The cell bodies of the noradrenergic system are primarily localized to the locus ceruleus in the rostral pons, and they project their axons to the cerebral cortex, the limbic system, the brainstem, and the spinal cord. Experiments in primates have demonstrated that stimulation of the locus ceruleus produces a fear response in the animals and that ablation of the same area inhibits or completely blocks the ability of the animals to form a fear response.

Human studies have found that in patients with panic disorder, β-adrenergic agonists—for example, isoproterenol (Isuprel)—and α_2-adrenergic antagonists—for example, yohimbine (Yocon)—can provoke frequent and severe panic attacks. Conversely, clonidine (Catapres), an α_2-adrenergic agonist, reduces anxiety symptoms in some experimental and therapeutic situations. A less consistent finding is that patients with anxiety disorders, particularly panic disorder, have elevated cerebrospinal fluid (CSF) or urinary levels of the noradrenergic metabolite 3-methoxy-4-hydroxyphenylglycol (MHPG).

Serotonin

The identification of many serotonin receptor types has stimulated the search for a role for serotonin in the pathogenesis of anxiety disorders. The interest in that relation was initially motivated by the observation that serotonergic antidepressants have therapeutic effects in some anxiety disorders—for example, clomipramine (Anafranil) in obsessive-compulsive disorder. The effectiveness of buspirone (BuSpar), a serotonergic type 1A ($5-HT_{1A}$) receptor agonist, in the treatment of anxiety disorders also suggests the possibility of an association between serotonin and anxiety. The cell bodies of most of the serotonergic neurons are located in the raphe nuclei in the rostral brainstem and project to the cerebral cortex, the limbic system (especially the amygdala and the hippocampus), and the hypothalamus. Although the administration of serotonergic agents to animals results in behavior suggestive of anxiety, the data on similar effects in humans are less robust. Several reports indicate that m-chlorophenylpiperazine (mCPP), a drug with multiple serotonergic and nonserotonergic effects, and fenfluramine (Pondimin), which causes the release of serotonin, do cause increased anxiety in patients with anxiety disorders; and many anecdotal reports indicate that serotonergic hallucinogens and stimulants—for example, lysergic acid diethylamide (LSD) and 3,4-methylenedioxymethamphetamine (MDMA)—are associated with the development of both acute and chronic anxiety disorders in persons who use those drugs.

GABA

A role of GABA in anxiety disorders is most strongly supported by the undisputed efficacy of benzodiazepines, which enhance the activity of GABA at the $GABA_A$ receptor, in the treatment of some types of anxiety disorders. Although low-potency benzodiazepines are most effective for the symptoms of generalized anxiety disorder, high-potency benzodiazepines, such as alprazolam (Xanax), are effective in the treatment of panic disorder. Studies in primates have found that autonomic nervous system symptoms of anxiety disorders are induced when a benzodiazepine inverse agonist, β-carboline-3-carboxylic acid (BCCE), is administered. BCCE also causes anxiety in normal control volunteers. A benzodiazepine antagonist, flumazenil (Romazicon), causes frequent severe panic attacks in patients with panic disorder. Those data have led researchers to hypothesize that some patients with anxiety disorders have abnormal functioning of their $GABA_A$ receptors, although that connection has not been proved directly.

Aplysia

A neurotransmitter model for anxiety disorders is based on the study of *Aplysia california*, a sea snail that reacts to danger by moving away, withdrawing into its shell, and decreasing its feeding behavior. Those behaviors can be classically conditioned, so that the snail responds to a neutral stimulus as if it were a dangerous stimulus. The snail can also be sensitized by random shocks, so that it exhibits a flight response in the absence of real danger. Parallels have previously been drawn between classical conditioning and human phobic anxiety. The classically conditioned aplysia shows measurable changes in presynaptic facilitation, resulting in the release of increased amounts of neurotransmitter. Although the sea snail is a simple animal, that work shows an experimental approach to complex neurochemical processes potentially involved in anxiety disorders in humans.

BRAIN-IMAGING STUDIES

A range of brain-imaging studies, almost always conducted with a specific anxiety disorder, have found several possible leads in the understanding of anxiety disorders. Structural studies—for example, computed tomography (CT) and magnetic resonance imaging (MRI)—have occasionally found some increase in the size of cerebral ventricles. In one study the increase was correlated with the length of time patients had been taking benzodiazepines. In one MRI study a specific defect in the right temporal lobe was noted in patients with panic disorder. Several other brain-imaging studies have reported abnormal findings in the right hemisphere but not the left hemisphere, suggesting that some types of cerebral asymmetry may be important in the development of anxiety disorder symptoms in specific patients. Functional brain-imaging studies—for example, positron emission tomography (PET), single photon emission tomography (SPECT), and electroencephalography (EEG)—of anxiety disorder patients have variously reported abnormalities in the frontal cortex, the occipital and temporal areas, and, in one study, the parahippocampal gyrus in a study of panic disorder. A conservative interpretation of those data is that some patients with anxiety disorders have demonstrable functional cerebral pathology and that the pathology may be causally relevant to their anxiety disorder symptoms.

GENETIC STUDIES

Genetic studies have produced solid data that at least some genetic component contributes to the development of anxiety disorders. Almost half of all patients with panic disorder have at least one affected relative. The figures for other anxiety disorders, although not as high, also indicate a higher frequency of the illness in first-degree relatives of affected patients than in the relatives of nonaffected persons. Although adoption studies with anxiety disorders have not been reported, data from twin registers also support the hypothesis that anxiety disorders are at least partially genetically determined.

NEUROANATOMICAL CONSIDERATIONS

The locus ceruleus and the raphe nuclei project primarily to the limbic system and the cerebral cortex. In combination with the data from brain-imaging studies, those areas have become the focus of much hypothesis-building regarding the neuroanatomical substrates of anxiety disorders.

Limbic System

In addition to receiving noradrenergic and serotonergic innervation, the limbic system also contains a high concentration of $GABA_A$ receptors. Ablation and stimulation studies in nonhuman primates have also implicated the limbic system in the generation of anxiety and fear responses. Two areas of the limbic system have received special attention in the literature: increased activity in the septohippocampal pathway may lead to anxiety, and the cingulate gyrus has been implicated, particularly in the pathophysiology of obsessive-compulsive disorder.

Cerebral Cortex

The frontal cerebral cortex is connected with the parahippocampal region, the cingulate gyrus, and the hypothalamus; therefore, it may be involved in the production of anxiety disorders. The temporal cortex has also been implicated as a pathophysiological site in anxiety disorders. That association is based in part on the similarity in clinical presentation and electrophysiology between some patients with temporal lobe epilepsy and patients with obsessive-compulsive disorder.

DSM-IV ANXIETY DISORDERS

The fourth edition of *Diagnostic and Statistical Manual of Mental Disorders* (DSM-IV) lists the following anxiety disorders: panic disorder with agoraphobia, panic disorder without agoraphobia, agoraphobia without a history of panic disorder, specific phobia, social phobia, obsessive-compulsive disorder, posttraumatic stress disorder, acute stress disorder, generalized anxiety disorder (all discussed in other sections in this chapter), anxiety disorder due to a general medical condition, substance-induced anxiety disorder, and anxiety disorder not otherwise specified, including mixed anxiety-depressive disorder (all discussed below) (Table 10.1–1).

Anxiety Disorder Due to a General Medical Condition

As with other major syndromes (for example, psychosis and mood disorder symptoms), anxiety disorder due to a general

medical condition has been included within the relevant section to encourage the formulation and the consideration of a complete differential diagnosis.

EPIDEMIOLOGY

The occurrence of anxiety symptoms related to general medical conditions is common, although the incidence of the disorder varies for each specific general medical condition.

ETIOLOGY

A wide range of medical conditions can cause symptoms similar to those seen in anxiety disorders. Hyperthyroidism, hypothyroidism, hypoparathyroidism, and vitamin B_{12} deficiency are frequently associated with anxiety symptoms. A pheochromocytoma produces epinephrine, which can cause paroxysmal episodes of anxiety symptoms. Certain lesions of the brain and postencephalitic states reportedly produce symptoms identical to those seen in obsessive-compulsive disorder. Some other medical conditions, such as cardiac arrhythmia, can produce physiological symptoms of panic disorder. Hypoglycemia can also mimic the symptoms of an anxiety disorder. The diverse list of medical conditions that can cause symptoms of anxiety disorder may do so through a common mechanism, the noradrenergic system, although the effects on the serotonergic system are also being studied.

DIAGNOSIS

The DSM-IV diagnosis of anxiety disorder due to a general medical condition (Table 10.1–2) requires the presence of symptoms of an anxiety disorder. DSM-IV allows clinicians to specify if the disorder is characterized by symptoms of generalized anxiety, panic attacks, or obsessive-compulsive symptoms.

The clinician should have an increased level of suspicion for the diagnosis when chronic or paroxysmal anxiety is associated with a physical disease that is known to cause such symptoms in some patients. Paroxysmal bouts of hypertension in an anxious patient may indicate that a workup for a pheochromocytoma is appropriate. A general medical workup may reveal diabetes, an adrenal tumor, thyroid disease, or a neurological condition. For example, extreme episodes of anxiety or fear are the only manifestation of the epileptic activity in some patients with complex partial epilepsy.

Table 10.1–1. Psychoanalytic Neuroses and Disorders in DSM-IV

Classic Neuroses	DSM-IV Classification
Anxiety	Generalized anxiety disorder
Phobic	Agoraphobia, specific and social phobias
Obsessive-compulsive	Obsessive-compulsive disorder
Depressive	Dysthymic disorder
Hysterical (conversion)	Conversion disorder
Hysterical (dissociative)	Depersonalization disorder
Hypochondriacal	Hypochondriasis
Paraphilic	Sexual disorders

Table 10.1–2. Diagnostic Criteria for Anxiety Disorder Due to a General Medical Condition

A. Prominent anxiety, panic attacks, or obsessions or compulsions predominate in the clinical picture.

B. There is evidence from the history, physical examination, or laboratory findings that the disturbance is the direct physiological consequence of a general medical condition.

C. The disturbance is not better accounted for by another mental disorder (e.g., adjustment disorder with anxiety in which the stressor is a serious general medical condition.)

D. The disturbance does not occur exclusively during the course of a delirium.

E. The disturbance causes clinically significant distress or impairment in social, occupational, or other important areas of functioning.

Table from DSM-IV, *Diagnostic and Statistical Manual of Mental Disorders*, ed 4. Copyright American Psychiatric Association, Washington, 1994. Used with permission.

CLINICAL FEATURES

The symptoms of anxiety disorder due to a general medical condition can be identical to those of the primary anxiety disorders. A syndrome similar to panic disorder is the most common clinical picture, and a syndrome similar to a phobia is the least common.

Panic Attacks

Patients who have cardiomyopathy may have the highest incidence of panic disorder secondary to a general medical condition. One study reported that 83 percent of cardiomyopathy patients awaiting cardiac transplantation had panic disorder symptoms. Increased noradrenergic tone in those patients may be the provoking stimulus for the panic attacks. In some studies, about 25 percent of patients with Parkinson's disease and chronic obstructive pulmonary disease have symptoms of panic disorder. Other medical disorders associated with panic disorder include chronic pain, primary biliary cirrhosis, and epilepsy, particularly when the focus is in the right parahippocampal gyrus.

Generalized Anxiety

A high prevalence of generalized anxiety disorder symptoms in patients with Sjögren's syndrome has been reported, and that may be related to the effects of Sjögren's syndrome on cortical and subcortical functions and on thyroid function. The highest prevalence of generalized anxiety disorder symptoms in a medical disorder seems to be Graves' disease, in which as many as two thirds of all patients meet the criteria for generalized anxiety disorder.

Obsessive-Compulsive Symptoms

Reports in the literature have associated the development of obsessive-compulsive disorder symptoms with Sydenham's chorea and multiple sclerosis.

DIFFERENTIAL DIAGNOSIS

Anxiety is a symptom can be associated with many psychiatric disorders, in addition to the anxiety disorders themselves. A mental status examination is necessary to determine the presence of mood symptoms or psychotic symptoms that may suggest another psychiatric diagnosis. For the clinician to conclude that a patient has an anxiety disorder due to a general medical condition, the patient should clearly have anxiety as the predominant symptom and should have a specific causative nonpsychiatric medical disorder. To ascertain the degree to which a general medical condition is causing the anxiety, the clinician should know how closely related the medical condition and the anxiety symptoms have been related in the literature, the age of onset (primary anxiety disorders usually have their onset before age 35), and the patient's family history of both anxiety disorders and relevant general medical conditions (for example, hyperthyroidism). A diagnosis of adjustment disorder with anxiety must also be considered in the differential diagnosis.

COURSE AND PROGNOSIS

The unremitting experience of anxiety can be disabling, interfering with every aspect of life, including social, occupational, and psychological functioning. A sudden change in level of anxiety may prompt the affected person to seek medical or psychiatric help more quickly than when the onset is insidious. The treatment or the removal of the primary medical cause of the anxiety usually initiates a clear course of improvement in the anxiety disorder symptoms. In some cases, however, the anxiety disorder symptoms continue even after the primary

medical condition is treated—for example, in continuing anxiety after an episode of encephalitis. Also, some symptoms, particularly obsessive-compulsive disorder symptoms, linger for a longer time than do other anxiety disorder symptoms. When anxiety disorder symptoms are present for a significant period after the medical disorder has been treated, the remaining symptoms should probably be treated as if they were primary—that is, with psychotherapy or pharmacotherapy or both.

TREATMENT

The primary treatment for anxiety disorder due to a general medical condition is the treatment of the underlying medical condition. If the patient also has an alcohol or other substance use disorder, that disorder must also be therapeutically addressed to gain control of the anxiety disorder symptoms. If the removal of the primary medical condition does not reverse the anxiety disorder symptoms, treatment of those symptoms should follow the treatment guidelines for the specific mental disorder. In general, behavioral modification techniques, anxiolytic agents, and serotonergic antidepressants have been the most effective treatment modalities.

Substance-Induced Anxiety Disorder

DSM-IV includes the substance-induced mental disorders in the categories for the relevant mental disorder syndromes. Substance-induced anxiety disorder, therefore, is contained in the category of anxiety disorders.

EPIDEMIOLOGY

Substance-induced anxiety disorder is common, both as the result of the ingestion of so-called recreational drugs and as the result of prescription drug use.

ETIOLOGY

A wide range of substances can cause symptoms of anxiety that can mimic any of the DSM-IV anxiety disorders. Although sympathomimetics (for example, amphetamine, cocaine, and caffeine) have been most associated with the production of anxiety disorder symptoms, many serotonergic drugs (for example, LSD and MDMA) can also cause both acute and chronic anxiety syndromes in users of those drugs. A wide range of prescription medications are also associated with the production of anxiety disorder symptoms in susceptible persons.

DIAGNOSIS

The DSM-IV diagnostic criteria for substance-induced anxiety disorder require the presence of prominent anxiety, panic attacks, obsessions, or compulsions (Table 10.1–3). The DSM-IV guidelines state that the symptoms should have developed while the substance was being used or within a month of the cessation of substance use. However, DSM-IV encourages the clinician to use appropriate clinical judgment to assess the relation between substance exposure and anxiety symptoms. The structure of the diagnosis includes specification of the substance (for example, cocaine), specification of the appropriate state during the onset (for example, intoxication), and mention of the specific symptom pattern (for example, panic attacks).

CLINICAL FEATURES

The associated clinical features vary with the particular substance involved. Even infrequent use of psychostimulants can

Table 10.1–3.   Diagnostic Criteria for Substance-Induced Anxiety Disorder

A. Prominent anxiety, panic attacks, or obsessions or compulsions predominate in the clinical picture.

B. There is evidence from the history, physical examination, or laboratory findings of either (1) or (2):

   (1) the symptoms in criterion A developed during, or within 1 month of, substance Intoxication or withdrawal
   (2) medication use is etiologically related to the disturbance

C. The disturbance is not better accounted for by an anxiety disorder that is not substance induced. Evidence that the symptoms are better accounted for by an anxiety disorder that is not substance induced might include the following: the symptoms precede the onset of the substance use (or medication use); the symptoms persist for a substantial period of time (e.g., about a month) after the cessation of acute withdrawal or severe intoxication or are substantially in excess of what would be expected given the type or amount of the substance used or the duration of use; or there is other evidence suggesting the existence of an independent non-substance-induced anxiety disorder (e.g., a history of recurrent non-substance-related episodes).

D. The disturbance does not occur exclusively during the course of a delirium.

E. The disturbances causes clinically significant distress or impairment in social, occupational, or other important areas of functioning.

Table from DSM-IV, *Diagnostic and Statistical Manual of Mental Disorders*, ed 4. Copyright American Psychiatric Association, Washington, 1994. Used with permission.

result in anxiety disorder symptoms in some persons. Associated with the anxiety disorder symptoms may also be cognitive impairments in comprehension, calculation, and memory. Those cognitive deficits are usually reversible if the substance use is stopped.

DIFFERENTIAL DIAGNOSIS

The differential diagnosis includes the primary anxiety disorders, anxiety disorder due to a general medical condition (for which the patient may be receiving an implicated drug), and mood disorders, which are frequently accompanied by symptoms of anxiety disorders. Personality disorders and malingering must be considered in the differential diagnosis, particularly in some urban emergency rooms.

COURSE AND PROGNOSIS

The course and the prognosis generally depend on the removal of the causally involved substance and the long-term ability of the affected patient to limit the use of the substance. The anxiogenic effects of most drugs are reversible. When the anxiety does not reverse with the cessation of the drug, the clinician should reconsider the diagnosis of substance-induced anxiety disorder or consider the possibility that the substance causes irreversible brain damage.

TREATMENT

The primary treatment for substance-induced anxiety disorder is the removal of the causally involved substance. Treatment then must focus on finding an alternative treatment if the substance was a medically indicated drug, on limiting the patient's exposure if the substance was introduced through environmental exposure, or on treating the underlying substance-related disorder. If anxiety disorder symptoms continue even though the substance use has stopped, treatment of the anxiety disorder symptoms with appropriate psychotherapeutic or pharmacotherapeutic modalities may be appropriate.

Anxiety Disorder Not Otherwise Specified

Some patients have symptoms of anxiety disorders that do not meet the criteria for any specific DSM-IV anxiety disorder or adjustment disorder with anxiety or mixed anxiety and depressed mood. One example is mixed anxiety-depressive disorder. Such patients are most appropriately classified as having anxiety disorder not otherwise specified (NOS).

References

Fick S N, Roy-Byrne P P, Cowley D S, Shores M M, Dunner D L: DSM-III-R personality disorders in a mood and anxiety disorders clinic: Prevalence, comorbidity, and clinical correlates. J Aff Disorders 27: 71–79, 1993.
Gorman J M, Papp L A, editors: Anxiety disorders. In *Review of Psychiatry*, vol 11, A Tasman, M B Riba, editors, p 243. American Psychiatric Press, Washington, 1992.
Johnson E O, Kamilaris T C, Chrousos G P, Gold P W: Mechanisms of stress: A dynamic overview of hormonal and behavioral homeostases. Neurosci Biobehav Rev 16: 115, 1992.
Journal of Clinical Psychiatry: Mixed anxiety and depression: A nosologic reality? J Clin Psychiatry 54 (1, Suppl): 2, 1993.
McNally R J: Automaticity and the anxiety disorders. Behav Res Ther 33: 747, 1995.
Papp, L A, Gorman, J M: Generalized anxiety disorder. In *Comprehensive Textbook of Psychiatry*, ed 6, H I Kaplan, B J Sadock, editors, p 1236. Williams & Wilkins, Baltimore, 1995.

10.2 PANIC DISORDER AND AGORAPHOBIA

Panic disorder is characterized by the spontaneous, unexpected occurrence of panic attacks. *Panic attacks* are relatively short-lived (usually less than one hour) periods of intense anxiety or fear, which are accompanied by such somatic symptoms as palpitations and tachypnea. Because patients with panic attacks often present to medical clinics, the symptoms may be misdiagnosed as either a serious medical condition (for example, myocardial infarction) or a so-called hysterical symptom. The frequency with which patients with panic disorder experience panic attacks varies from multiple attacks during a single day to only a few attacks during the course of a year. Panic disorder is often accompanied by *agoraphobia*, the fear of being alone in public places (for example, supermarkets), especially places from which a rapid exit would be difficult if the person experienced a panic attack. Agoraphobia can be the most disabling of the phobias, since its presence may significantly interfere with a person's ability to function in social and work situations outside the home.

EPIDEMIOLOGY

Epidemiological studies have reported lifetime prevalence rates of 1.5 to 3 percent for panic disorder and 3 to 4 percent for panic attacks. One recent study of more than 1,600 randomly selected adults in Texas found a lifetime prevalence rate of 3.8 percent for panic disorder, 5.6 percent for panic attacks, and 2.2 percent for panic attacks with limited symptoms that did not meet the full diagnostic criteria.

The lifetime prevalence of agoraphobia has been reported as ranging from as low as 0.6 percent to as high as 6 percent. The major factor leading to that wide range of estimates is the use of varying diagnostic criteria and assessment methods.

Although studies of agoraphobia in psychiatric settings have reported that at least three fourths of the affected patients have panic disorder as well, studies of agoraphobia in community samples have found that as many as half of the patients have agoraphobia without panic disorder. The reasons for those divergent findings are not known but probably involve differences in ascertainment techniques. In many cases the onset of agoraphobia follows a traumatic event.

ETIOLOGY

Biological Factors

Research regarding the biological basis of panic disorder has produced a range of findings; one interpretation is that the symptoms of panic disorder can result in a range of biological abnormalities in brain structure and brain function. The greatest amount of work has been done in the area of using biological stimulants to induce panic attacks in patients with panic disorder. Those and other studies have resulted in hypotheses implicating both peripheral and central nervous system dysregulation in the pathophysiology of panic disorder. The autonomic nervous systems of some panic disorder patients have been reported to exhibit increased sympathetic tone, to adapt slowly to repeated stimuli, and to respond excessively to moderate stimuli. Studies of the neuroendocrine status of panic disorder patients have reported several abnormalities, although the studies have been inconsistent in their findings.

The major neurotransmitter systems that have been implicated are those for norepinephrine, serotonin, and γ-aminobutyric acid (GABA). The totality of the biological data has led to a focus on the brainstem (particularly the noradrenergic neurons of the locus ceruleus and the serotonergic neurons of the median raphe nucleus), the limbic system (possibly responsible for the generation of anticipatory anxiety), and the prefrontal cortex (possibly responsible for the generation of phobic avoidance).

PANIC-INDUCING SUBSTANCES

Panic-inducing substances (sometimes called panicogens) are substances that induce panic attacks in a majority of patients with panic disorder and in a much smaller proportion of persons without panic disorder or a history of panic attacks. The use of panic-inducing substances is strictly limited to the research setting; there are no clinically indicated reasons to stimulate panic attacks in patients. So-called respiratory panic-inducing substances cause respiratory stimulation and a shift in the acid-base balance. Those substances include carbon dioxide (5 to 35 percent mixtures), sodium lactate, and bicarbonate. Neurochemical panic-inducing substances, which act through specific neurotransmitter systems, include yohimbine (Yocon), an α_2-adrenergic receptor antagonist; fenfluramine (Pondimin), a serotonin-releasing agent; m-chlorophenylpiperazine (mCPP), an agent with multiple serotonergic effects; β-carboline drugs; $GABA_B$ receptor inverse agonists; flumazenil, a $GABA_B$ receptor antagonist; cholecystokinin; and caffeine. Isoproterenol (Isuprel) is also a panic-inducing substance, although its mechanism of action in inducing panic attacks is poorly understood. The respiratory panic-inducing substances may act initially at the peripheral cardiovascular baroreceptors and relay their signal by vagal afferents to the nucleus tractus solitarii and then on to the nucleus

paragigantocellularis of the medulla. The neurochemical panic-inducing substances are presumed to have their primary effects directly on the noradrenergic, serotonergic, and GABA receptors of the central nervous system.

BRAIN IMAGING

Structural brain-imaging studies—for example, magnetic resonance imaging (MRI)—in panic disorder patients have implicated pathology in the temporal lobes, particularly the hippocampus. For example, one MRI study reported abnormalities, particularly cortical atrophy, in the right temporal lobe of panic disorder patients. Functional brain-imaging studies—for example, positron emission tomography (PET)—have implicated a dysregulation of cerebral blood flow. Specifically, anxiety disorders and panic attacks are associated with cerebral vasoconstriction, which may result in central nervous system symptoms, such as dizziness, and in peripheral nervous system symptoms that may be induced by hyperventilation and hypocapnia. Most functional brain-imaging studies have used a specific panic-inducing substance (for example, lactate, caffeine, or yohimbine) in combination with PET or single photon emission tomography (SPECT) to assess the effects of the panic-inducing substance and the induced panic attack on cerebral blood flow.

Genetic Factors

Although the number of well-controlled studies of the genetic basis of panic disorder and agoraphobia is small, the data to date support the conclusion that the disorders have a distinct genetic component. In addition, some data indicate that panic disorder with agoraphobia is a severe form of panic disorder without agoraphobia and is thus more likely to be inherited. Various studies have found a fourfold to eightfold increase in the risk for panic disorder among the first-degree relatives of panic disorder patients compared with first-degree relatives of other psychiatric patients. The twin studies conducted to date have generally reported that monozygotic twins are more likely to be concordant for panic disorder than are dizygotic twins.

Psychosocial Factors

Both cognitive-behavioral and psychoanalytic theories have been developed to explain the pathogenesis of panic disorder and agoraphobia. The success of cognitive-behavioral approaches to the treatment of those disorders may add credence to the cognitive-behavioral theories.

COGNITIVE BEHAVIORAL THEORIES

Behavioral theories posit that anxiety is a learned response either from modeling parental behavior or through the process of classical conditioning. In a classical conditioning approach to panic disorder and agoraphobia, a noxious stimulus (for example, a panic attack) that occurs with a neutral stimulus (for example, a bus ride) can result in the avoidance of the neutral stimulus. Other behavioral theories posit a linkage between the sensation of minor somatic symptoms (for example, palpitations) and the generation of a complete panic attack. Although cognitive-behavioral theories can help explain the development of agoraphobia or an increase in the number or the severity of panic attacks, they do not explain the occurrence of the first unprovoked and unexpected panic attack that an affected patient experiences.

Psychoanalytic Theories

Psychoanalytic theories conceptualize panic attacks as resulting from an unsuccessful defense against anxiety-provoking impulses. What was previously a mild signal anxiety becomes an overwhelming feeling of apprehension, complete with somatic symptoms. In agoraphobia, psychoanalytic theories emphasize the loss of a parent in childhood and a history of separation anxiety. Being alone in public places revives the childhood anxiety about being abandoned. The defense mechanisms used include repression, displacement, avoidance, and symbolization. Traumatic separations during childhood may affect the child's developing nervous system in such a manner that the child becomes susceptible to anxieties in adulthood.

Many patients describe panic attacks as coming out of the blue, as though no psychological factors were involved, but psychodynamic exploration frequently reveals a clear psychological trigger for the panic attack. Although panic attacks are correlated neurophysiologically with the locus ceruleus, the onset of panic is generally related to environmental or psychological factors. Patients with panic disorder have a higher incidence of stressful life events, particularly loss, compared with controls in the months before the onset of panic disorder. Moreover, the patients typically experience greater distress about life events than do controls.

The research indicates that the cause of panic attacks is likely to involve the unconscious meaning of stressful events and that the pathogenesis of the panic attacks may be related to neurophysiological factors triggered by the psychological reactions. Psychodynamic clinicians should always thoroughly investigate possible triggers whenever a diagnostic assessment is being performed on a patient with panic disorder.

DIAGNOSIS

Panic Attacks

In DSM-IV the diagnostic criteria for a panic attack are listed as a separate set of criteria (Table 10.2–1). The major reason to have a separate set of diagnostic criteria for a panic attack is that panic attacks can occur in mental disorders other than panic disorder, particularly in specific phobia, social phobia, and posttraumatic stress disorder. Furthermore, the inclusion of

Table 10.2–1.   Criteria for Panic Attack

A discrete period of intense fear or discomfort, in which four (or more) of the following symptoms developed abruptly and reached a peak within 10 minutes:

(1) palpitations, pounding heart, or accelerated heart rate
(2) sweating
(3) trembling
(4) sensations of shortness of breath or smothering
(5) feeling of choking
(6) chest pain or discomfort
(7) nausea or abdominal distress
(8) feeling dizzy, unsteady, lightheaded, or faint
(9) derealization (feelings of unreality) or depersonalization (being detached from oneself)
(10) fear of losing control or going crazy
(11) fear of dying
(12) paresthesias (numbness or tingling sensations)
(13) chills or hot flashes

Table from DSM-IV, *Diagnostic and Statistical Manual of Mental Disorders*, ed. 4. Copyright American Psychiatric Association, Washington, 1994. Used with permission.

the criteria for a panic attack within the diagnostic criteria for panic disorder implied that panic attacks had to be unexpected or uncued to meet the diagnostic criteria. Unexpected panic attacks occur out of the blue and are not associated with any identifiable situational stimulus. However, panic attacks do not need to be unexpected, since panic attacks in patients with social and specific phobias are usually expected or cued to a recognized or specific stimulus. Some panic attacks do not fit easily into the distinction between unexpected and expected, and those attacks are referred to as situationally predisposed panic attacks; they may or may not occur when a patient is exposed to a specific trigger, or they may occur either immediately after exposure or after a considerable delay.

Panic Disorder

DSM-IV contains two diagnostic criteria for panic disorder, one without agoraphobia (Table 10.2–3) and the other with agoraphobia (Table 10.2–4), but both require the presence of panic attacks as described in Table 10.2–1. Some community surveys have indicated that panic attacks are common, and a major issue in the development of the diagnostic criteria for panic disorder was the determination of a threshold number or frequency of panic attacks required to meet the diagnosis. Setting the threshold too low results in the diagnosis of panic disorder in patients who do not have an impairment from an occasional panic attack; setting the threshold too high results in a situation in which patients who are impaired by their panic attacks do not meet the diagnostic criteria. The vagaries of setting the threshold are evidenced by the range of thresholds set in various diagnostic criteria. The Research Diagnostic Criteria (RDC) requires six panic attacks during a six-week period. The 10th revision of the International Classification of Diseases (ICD-10) requires three attacks in three weeks (for moderate disease) or four attacks in four weeks (for severe disease). DSM-IV does not specify a minimum number of panic attacks or a time frame but does require that at least one attack be followed by at least a month-long period of concern about having another panic attack or about the implications of the attack or a signifi-

Table 10.2–2.   Criteria for Agoraphobia

A. Anxiety about being in places or situations from which escape might be difficult (or embarrassing) or in which help may not be available in the event of having an unexpected or situationally predisposed panic attack or paniclike symptoms. Agoraphobic fears typically involve characteristic clusters of situations that include being outside the home alone; being in a crowd or standing in a line; being on a bridge; and traveling in a bus, train, or automobile.

B. The situations are avoided (e.g., travel is restricted) or else are endured with marked distress or with anxiety about having a panic attack or paniclike symptoms, or require the presence of a companion.

C. The anxiety or phobic avoidance is not better accounted for by another mental disorder, such as social phobia (e.g., avoidance limited to social situations because of fear of embarrassment), specific phobia (e.g., avoidance limited to a single situation like elevators), obsessive-compulsive disorder (e.g., avoidance of dirt in someone with an obsession about contamination), posttraumatic stress disorder (e.g., avoidance of stimuli associated with a severe stressor), or separation anxiety disorder (e.g., avoidance of leaving home or relatives).

Table from DSM-IV, *Diagnostic and Statistical Manual of Mental Disorders*, ed 4. Copyright American Psychiatric Association, Washington, 1994. Used with permission.

Table 10.2–3. Diagnostic Criteria for Panic Disorder Without Agoraphobia

A. Both (1) and (2):

  (1) recurrent unexpected panic attacks
  (2) at least one of the attacks has been followed by 1 month (or more) of one (or more) of the following:

    (a) persistent concern about having additional attacks
    (b) worry about the implications of the attack or its consequences (e.g., losing control, having a heart attack, ''going crazy'')
    (c) a significant change in behavior related to the attacks

B. Absence of Agoraphobia

C. The panic attacks are not due to the direct physiological effects of a substance (e.g., a drug of abuse, a medication) or a general medical condition (e.g., hyperthyroidism).

D. The panic attacks are not better accounted for by another mental disorder, such as social phobia (e.g., occurring on exposure to feared social situations), specific phobia (e.g., on exposure to a specific phobic situation), obsessive-compulsive disorder (e.g., on exposure to dirt in someone with an obsession about contamination), posttraumatic stress disorder (e.g., in response to stimuli associated with a severe stressor), or separation anxiety disorder (e.g., in response to being away from home or close relatives).

Table from DSM-IV, *Diagnostic and Statistical Manual of Mental Disorders*, ed 4. Copyright American Psychiatric Association, Washington, 1994. Used with permission.

Table10.2–4. Diagnostic Criteria for Panic Disorder With Agoraphobia

A. Both (1) and (2):

  (1) recurrent unexpected panic attacks
  (2) at least one of the attacks has been followed by 1 month (or more) of one (or more) of the following:

    (a) persistent concern about having additional attacks
    (b) worry about the implications of the attack or its consequences (e.g., losing control, having a heart attack, ''going crazy'')
    (c) a significant change in behavior related to the attacks

B. The presence of agoraphobia.

C. The panic attacks are not due to the direct physiological effects of a substance (e.g., a drug of abuse, a medication) or a general medical condition (e.g., hyperthyroidism).

D. The panic attacks are not better accounted for by another mental disorder, such as social phobia (e.g., occurring on exposure to feared social situations), specific phobia (e.g., on exposure to a specific phobic situation), obsessive-compulsive disorder (e.g., on exposure to dirt in someone with an obsession about contamination), posttraumatic stress disorder (e.g., in response to stimuli associated with a severe stressor), or separation anxiety disorder (e.g., in response to being away from home or close relatives).

Table from DSM-IV, *Diagnostic and Statistical Manual of Mental Disorders*, ed 4. Copyright American Psychiatric Association, Washington, 1994. Used with permission.

cant change in behavior. DSM-IV also requires that the panic attacks generally be unexpected but allows expected or situationally predisposed attacks. Table 10.2–2 lists criteria for agoraphobia.

Agoraphobia Without History of Panic Disorder

The DSM-IV diagnostic criteria for agoraphobia without history of panic disorder (Table 10.2–5) includes criteria based on the fear of a sudden incapacitating or embarrassing symptom. In contrast, the ICD-10 criteria require the presence of interre-

Table 10.2–5. Diagnostic Criteria for Agoraphobia Without History of Panic Disorder

A. The presence of agoraphobia related to fear of developing paniclike symptoms (e.g., dizziness or diarrhea).

B. Criteria have never been met for panic disorder.

C. The disturbance is not due to the direct physiological effects of a substance (e.g., a drug of abuse, a medication) or a general medical condition.

D. If an associated general medical condition is present, the fear described in criterion A is clearly in excess of that usually associated with the condition.

Table from DSM-IV, *Diagnostic and Statistical Manual of Mental Disorders*, ed 4. Copyright American Psychiatric Association, Washington, 1994. Used with permission.

lated or overlapping phobias but do not require that fear of incapacitating or embarrassing symptoms be present.

The DSM-IV criteria also address the avoidance of situations that are based on a concern related to a medical disorder (for example, fear of a myocardial infarction in a patient with severe heart disease).

CLINICAL FEATURES

Panic Disorder

The first panic attack is often completely spontaneous, although panic attacks occasionally follow excitement, physical exertion, sexual activity, or moderate emotional trauma. DSM-IV emphasizes that at least the first attacks must be unexpected (uncued) to meet the diagnostic criteria for panic disorder. The clinician should attempt to ascertain any habit or situation that commonly precedes a patient's panic attacks. Such activities may include the use of caffeine, alcohol, nicotine, or other substances; unusual patterns of sleeping or eating; and specific environmental settings, such as harsh lighting at work.

The attack often begins with a 10-minute period of rapidly increasing symptoms. The major mental symptoms are extreme fear and a sense of impending death and doom. Patients are usually not able to name the source of their fear. The patients may feel confused and have trouble in concentrating. The physical signs often include tachycardia, palpitations, dyspnea, and sweating. Patients often try to leave whatever situation they are in to seek help. The attack generally lasts 20 to 30 minutes and rarely more than an hour. A formal mental status examination during a panic attack may reveal rumination, difficulty in speaking (for example, stammering), and an impaired memory. Patients may experience depression or depersonalization during an attack. The symptoms may disappear quickly or gradually. Between attacks, patients may have anticipatory anxiety about having another attack. The differentiation between anticipatory anxiety and generalized anxiety disorder can be difficult, although pain disorder patients with anticipatory anxiety are able to name the focus of their anxiety.

Somatic concerns of death from a cardiac or respiratory problem may be the major focus of patients' attention during panic attacks. Patients may believe that the palpitations and the pain in the chest indicate that they are about to die. As many as 20 percent of such patients actually have syncopal episodes during a panic attack. The patients may present to emergency rooms as young (20s), physically healthy persons who nevertheless insist that are about to die from a heart attack. Rather than immediately diagnosing hypochondriasis, the emergency room physician should consider a diagnosis of panic disorder. Hyperventilation may produce respiratory alkalosis and other symptoms. The age-old treatment of breathing into a paper bag sometimes helps.

Agoraphobia

Agoraphobic patients rigidly avoid situations in which it would be difficult to obtain help. They prefer to be accompanied by a friend or a family member in such places as busy streets, crowded stores, closed-in spaces (such as tunnels, bridges, and elevators), and closed-in vehicles (such as subways, buses, and airplanes). The patients may insist that they be accompanied every time they leave the house. The behavior may result in marital discord, which may be misdiagnosed as the primary problem. Severely affected patients may simply refuse to leave the house. Particularly before a correct diagnosis is made, patients may be terrified that they are going crazy.

Associated Symptoms

Depressive symptoms are often present in panic disorder and agoraphobia, and in some patients a depressive disorder coexists with the panic disorder. Studies have found that the lifetime risk of suicide in persons with panic disorder is higher than it is in persons with no mental disorder. The clinician should be alert to the risk of suicide. In addition to agoraphobia, other phobias and obsessive-compulsive disorder can coexist with panic disorder. The psychosocial consequences of panic disorder and agoraphobia, in addition to marital discord, can include time lost from work, financial difficulties related to the loss of work, and alcohol and other substance abuse.

DIFFERENTIAL DIAGNOSIS

Panic Disorder

The differential diagnosis for a patient with panic disorder includes a large number of medical disorders, as well as many mental disorders.

MEDICAL DISORDERS

Whenever a patient, regardless of age or risk factors, reports to an emergency room with symptoms of a potentially fatal condition (for example, myocardial infarction), a complete medical history must be obtained and a physical examination performed. Standard laboratory procedures include a complete blood count; studies of electrolytes, fasting glucose, calcium concentrations, liver function, urea, creatinine, and thyroid; a urinalysis; a drug screen; and an electrocardiogram (ECG). Once the presence of an immediately life-threatening condition has been ruled out, the clinical suspicion is that the patient has panic disorder. The possibility that additional medical diagnostic procedures will reveal a medical condition must be weighed against the procedures' potentially adverse effects on helping the patient accept a diagnosis of panic disorder. Nevertheless, the presence of atypical symptoms (for example, vertigo, loss of bladder control, and unconsciousness) or the late onset of the first panic attack (above age 45) should cause the clinician to reconsider the presence of an underlying nonpsychiatric medical condition.

MENTAL DISORDERS

The psychiatric differential diagnosis for panic disorder includes malingering, factitious disorders, hypochondriasis, depersonalization disorder, social and specific phobias, posttraumatic stress disorder, depressive disorders, and schizophrenia. In the differential diagnosis, the clinician must determine whether the panic attack was unexpected, situationally bound, or situationally predisposed. Unexpected panic attacks are the hallmark of panic disorder; situationally bound panic attacks generally indicate a different condition, such as social phobia or specific phobia (when exposed to the phobic situation), obsessive-compulsive disorder (when trying to resist a compulsion), or a depressive disorder (when overwhelmed with anxiety). The focus of the anxiety or the fear is also important. Was there no focus (as in panic disorder), or was there a specific focus (for example, fear of becoming tongue-tied in a person with social phobia)? Somatoform disorders should also be considered in the differential diagnosis, although a patient may meet the criteria for both somatoform disorder and panic disorder.

Specific And Social Phobias

DSM-IV addresses the sometimes difficult diagnostic task of distinguishing between panic disorder with agoraphobia, on the one hand, and specific and social phobias, on the other hand. Some patients who experience a single panic attack in a specific setting (for example, an elevator) may go on to have a long-lasting avoidance of the specific setting, regardless of whether they ever have another panic attack. Those patients meet the diagnostic criteria for a specific phobia, and clinicians must use their judgment about what is the most appropriate diagnosis. In another example, a person who experiences one or more panic attacks may go on to a fear of public speaking for fear of having a panic attack in such a situation. Although the clinical picture is almost identical to the clinical picture in social phobia, a diagnosis of social phobia is excluded because the avoidance of the public situation is based on fear of having a panic attack, rather than fear of the public speaking itself. Because empirical data on the distinctions are limited, DSM-IV advises clinicians to use their clinical judgment to make the diagnosis in difficult cases.

Agoraphobia Without History of Panic Disorder

The differential diagnosis for agoraphobia without a history of panic disorder includes all the medical disorders that may cause anxiety or depression. The psychiatric differential diagnosis includes major depressive disorder, schizophrenia, paranoid personality disorder, avoidance personality disorder, and dependent personality disorder.

COURSE AND PROGNOSIS

Panic Disorder

Panic disorder usually has its onset during late adolescence or early adulthood, although onset during childhood, early adolescence, and midlife does occur. Some data implicate increased psychosocial stressors with the onset of panic disorder, although no psychosocial stressor can be definitely identified in most cases.

Panic disorder, in general, is a chronic disorder, although its course varies both among patients and within a single patient. The available long-term follow-up studies of panic disorder are difficult to interpret because they have not controlled for the effects of treatment. Nevertheless, about 30 to 40 percent of patients seem to be symptom-free at long-term follow-up; about 50 percent have symptoms that are mild enough not to affect their lives significantly; and about 10 to 20 percent continue to have significant symptoms.

After the first one to two panic attacks, patients may be relatively unconcerned about their condition; however, with repeated attacks, the symptoms may become a major concern. Patients may attempt to keep the panic attacks secret, thereby causing their families and friends concern about unexplained changes in behavior. The frequency and the severity of the panic attacks may fluctuate. Panic attacks may occur several times in a day or less than once a month. The excessive intake of caffeine or nicotine may exacerbate the symptoms.

Depression may complicate the symptom picture in anywhere from 40 to 80 percent of all patients, as estimated by various studies. Although the patients do not tend to talk about suicidal ideation, they are at increased risk for committing suicide. Alcohol and other substance dependence occurs in about 20 to 40 percent of all patients, and obsessive-compulsive disorder may also develop. Performance in school and at work and family interactions commonly suffer. Patients with good premorbid functioning and a brief duration of symptoms tend to have good prognoses.

Agoraphobia

Most cases of agoraphobia are thought to be due to panic disorder. If the panic disorder is treated, the agoraphobia often improves with time. For a rapid and complete reduction of agoraphobia, behavior therapy is sometimes indicated. Agoraphobia without a history of panic disorder is often incapacitating and chronic. Depressive disorders and alcohol dependence often complicate the course of agoraphobia.

TREATMENT

With treatment, most patients have a dramatic improvement in the symptoms of panic disorder and agoraphobia. The two most effective treatments are pharmacotherapy and cognitive-behavioral therapy. Family and group therapy may help affected patients and their families adjust to the fact that the patients have the disorder and to the psychosocial difficulties the disorder may have precipitated.

Pharmacotherapy

Tricyclic and tetracyclic drugs, monoamine oxidase inhibitors (MAOIs), serotonin-specific reuptake inhibitors (SSRIs), and the benzodiazepines are effective in the treatment of panic disorder. However, β-adrenergic receptor antagonists—for example, propranolol (Inderal)—are not effective for the treatment of panic disorder, and the currently available azaspirodecanediones—for example, buspirone (BuSpar)—are probably not effective, although definitive trials have not been conducted. A conservative approach based on currently available data is to use a tricyclic drug—for example, clomipramine (Anafranil) or imipramine (Tofranil)—as the first-line drug, followed by trials of an MAOI, an SSRI, or a benzodiazepine if the tricyclic drug is not effective or is not tolerated. Alternatively, some clinicians choose to use an MAOI, an SSRI, or a benzodiazepine as the first-line drug.

TRICYCLIC AND TETRACYCLIC DRUGS

Among tricyclic drugs, the most robust data show that clomipramine and imipramine are effective in the treatment of panic disorder. However, clinical experience indicates that clomipramine and imipramine should be initiated at low dosages, 10 mg a day, and titrated slowly at first in intervals of 10 mg a day every two to three days, then more rapidly, in intervals of 25 mg a day every two to three days, if the low dosages are well-tolerated. The most common adverse effect that causes noncompliance in panic disorder patients treated with clomipramine and imipramine is overstimulation during the initiation of treatment. The overstimulation is usually avoided by using the slow dosage titration schedule. Although early studies indicated that panic disorder patients respond more quickly and to lower dosages than do depressive disorder patients, later studies showed that that is not the case. Panic disorder patients need full dosages of clomipramine and imipramine and generally require a long time to respond, usually 8 to 12 weeks, rather than the 6 to 8 weeks for depression.

Some data support the efficacy of desipramine (Norpramin) in the treatment of panic disorder; other data indicate that maprotiline (Ludiomil) and trazodone (Desyrel) are less effective than desipramine. Anecdotal reports and case reports indicate that other tricyclic drugs are effective, including nortriptyline (Aventyl), amitriptyline (Limbitrol), and doxepin (Adapin). Clinical trials with nortriptyline may be indicated because that tricyclic drug is generally associated with fewer adverse effects, especially orthostatic hypotension, than are other tricyclic drugs.

MONOAMINE OXIDASE INHIBITORS

Monoamine oxidase inhibitors (MAOIs) are also effective in the treatment of panic disorder. Most studies have used phenelzine (Nardil), although some have used tranylcypromine (Parnate). Some studies have indicated that MAOIs are more effective than tricyclic drugs, and anecdotal reports indicate that patients who do not respond to tricyclic drugs may be likely to respond to MAOIs. When they are treated with MAOIs, panic disorder patients do not seem to have the initial side effect of overstimulation that can occur with tricyclic drugs. The dosages of MAOIs must reach those used for the treatment of depression, and a therapeutic trial should last 8 to 12 weeks.

SEROTONIN-SPECIFIC REUPTAKE INHIBITORS

Four SSRIs are available in the United States: fluoxetine (Prozac), sertraline (Zoloft), paroxetine (Paxil), and fluvoxamine (Luvox). The data from well-controlled studies of the efficacy of SSRIs in panic disorder are limited, but the efficacy of clomipramine in panic disorder patients suggests that the SSRIs should also be effective. A well-controlled study of fluvoxamine indicated that the drug is effective in the treatment of panic disorder. Anecdotal reports, however, indicate that panic disorder patients are particularly sensitive to overstimulation caused by SSRIs and that the clinician must titrate the dosages of the drugs slowly. Slow titration for fluoxetine is possible by dissolving a capsule in water or fruit juice or by using the fluoxetine elixir that is now available. Starting dosages can be as low as 2 or 4 mg a day and should be raised in intervals of 2 to 4 mg a day every two to four days. The goal should be to reach a full therapeutic dosage of at least 20 mg a day.

BENZODIAZEPINES

The use of benzodiazepines in the treatment of panic disorder has been limited because of concerns about dependence, cognitive impairment, and abuse. However, benzodiazepines are effective in the treatment of panic disorder and may have a more rapid onset (onset at one to two weeks, peaking after four to eight weeks) than do other pharmacotherapies. With some patients the clinician may initiate treatment with a benzodiazepine, titrate in another drug (for example, clomipramine), and then taper off (over 4 to 10 weeks) the benzodiazepine after 8 to 12 weeks. The best data are available for the use of alprazolam (Xanax) in the treatment of panic disorder, although case reports indicate that clonazepam (Klonopin), which is about twice as potent as alprazolam, and lorazepam (Ativan), which is about half as potent as alprazolam, are also effective treatments. Alprazolam treatment can be initiated at 0.5 mg four times daily. Although the Food and Drug Administration (FDA) approves dosages up to 10 mg a day for the treatment of panic disorder, the most commonly effective dosages are between 4 and 6 mg a day. The major risks in benzodiazepine treatment are dependence and abuse. Dependence may develop in patients who are treated for several months, thus requiring a gradual tapering of the benzodiazepine, especially alprazolam, when the decision is made to stop the medication. However, solid data indicate that patients do not become tolerant to the antipanic effects of the benzodiazepines, as indicated by the lack of a need to increase the dosage of the benzodiazepine when treatment is long-term.

TREATMENT FAILURES

If a drug from one class (for example, a tricyclic drug) is not effective, a drug from a different class (for example, an MAOI) should be tried. If treatment with a single agent is not effective, combinations can be tried (a benzodiazepine and a tricyclic drug, an SSRI and a tricyclic drug, lithium [Eskalith] and a tricyclic drug). Some reports indicate that anticonvulsants—for example, carbamazepine (Tegretol) and valproate (Depakene)—have been effective, and other reports indicate that calcium channel inhibitors—for example, verapamil (Calan)—have been effective in the treatment of panic disorder. When faces with treatment failure, clinicians should reconsider the diagnosis, assess the patient's compliance with the treatment regimen (possibly with plasma concentrations of the drug), and consider potentially complicating factors (comorbid psychiatric diagnoses—for example, depression—and alcohol, marijuana, and other substance use).

DURATION OF PHARMACOTHERAPY

Once effective, pharmacological treatment should generally continue for 8 to 12 months. The available data indicate that panic disorder is a chronic, perhaps lifelong, condition that will recur when treatment is discontinued. Studies have reported that from 30 to 90 percent of successfully treated panic disorder patients relapse when their medication is discontinued. Patients may be likely to relapse if they are treated with benzodiazepines and the benzodiazepine therapy is terminated in such a way as to cause withdrawal symptoms.

Cognitive and Behavior Therapies

Cognitive and behavior therapies are effective treatments for panic disorder. Various reports have concluded that cognitive and behavior therapies are superior to pharmacotherapy alone; other reports have concluded the opposite. Several studies and reports have found that the combination of cognitive or behavior therapy with pharmacotherapy is more effective than either therapeutic approach alone. Several studies have included long-term follow-up of patients treated with cognitive or behavior therapy and have found that the therapies are effective in producing the long-lasting remission of symptoms.

COGNITIVE THERAPY

The two major foci of cognitive therapy for panic disorder are instruction regarding the patient's false beliefs and information regarding panic attacks. The instruction regarding false beliefs centers on the patient's tendency to misinterpret mild bodily sensations as indicative of impending panic attacks, doom, or death. The information about panic attacks includes explanations that panic attacks, when they occur, are time-limited and not life-threatening.

APPLIED RELAXATION

The goal of applied relaxation (for example, Herbert Benson's relaxation training) is to instill a sense of control in patients regarding their levels of anxiety and relaxation. Through the use of standardized techniques for muscle relaxation and the imagining of relaxing situations, patients learn techniques that may help them through a panic attack.

RESPIRATORY TRAINING

Since the hyperventilation associated with panic attacks is probably related to some symptoms, such as dizziness and faintness, one direct approach to control panic attacks is to train patients how to control the urge to hyperventilate. After that training, patients can use the technique to help control hyperventilation during a panic attack.

IN VIVO EXPOSURE

In vivo exposure used to be the primary behavior treatment for panic disorder. The technique involves sequentially greater exposure of the patient to the feared stimulus; over time, the patient becomes desensitized to the experience. Previously, the focus was on external stimuli; recently, the technique has included exposure of the patient to internal feared sensations (for example, tachypnea and fear of having a panic attack).

Combined Psychotherapy and Pharmacotherapy

Even when pharmacotherapy is effective in eliminating the primary symptoms of panic disorder, psychotherapy may be needed to treat secondary symptoms. Glen O. Gabbard wrote:

Panic-disordered patients frequently require a combination of drug therapy and psychotherapy . . . Even when patients with panic attacks and agoraphobia have their symptoms pharmacologically controlled, they are often reluctant to venture out into the world again and may require psychotherapeutic interventions to help overcome this fear . . . Some patients will adamantly refuse any medication because they believe that it stigmatizes them as being mentally ill, so psychotherapeutic intervention is required to help them understand and eliminate their resistance to pharmacotherapy . . . For a comprehensive and effective treatment plan, these patients require psychotherapeutic approaches in addition to appropriate medications. In all patients with symptoms of panic disorder or agoraphobia, a careful psychodynamic evaluation will help weigh the contributions of biological and dynamic factors.

References

Black D W, Wesner R, Bowers W, Gabel J: A comparison of fluvoxamine, cognitive therapy, and placebo in the treatment of panic disorder. Arch Gen Psychiatry *50*: 44, 1993.

Fyer A J, Mannuzza S, Coplan J D: Panic disorders and agoraphobia. In *Comprehensive Textbook of Psychiatry*, ed 6, H I Kaplan, B J Sadock, editors, p 1191. Williams & Wilkins, Baltimore, 1995.

Johnson M R, Lydiard R B, Ballenger JC: Panic disorder. Pathophysiology and drug treatment. Drugs *49*: 328, 1995.

Katerndahl D A, Realini J P: Lifetime prevalence of panic states. Am J Psychiatry *150*: 246, 1993.

Keller M B, Hanks D L: Course and outcome in panic disorder. Prog Neuro Psychopharmacol Biol Psychiatry *17*: 551, 1993.

Shear M K, Cooper A M, Klerman G L, Busch F N, Shapiro T: A psychodynamic model of panic disorder. Am J Psychiatry *150*: 859, 1993.

10.3 SPECIFIC PHOBIA AND SOCIAL PHOBIA

Recent epidemiological studies have found that phobias are the most common mental disorders in the United States. An estimated 5 to 10 percent of the population are afflicted with those troubling and sometimes disabling disorders. Less conservative estimates have ranged up to 25 percent of the population. The distress associated with phobias, especially when they are not recognized or acknowledged as mental disorders, can lead to further psychiatric complications, including other anxiety disorders, major depressive disorder, and substance-related disorders, especially alcohol use disorders. The underrecognition of phobias is particularly unfortunate, since recent research studies have found that phobias often respond to treatment with cognitive and behavioral psychotherapies and to treatment with specific pharmacotherapies, including tricyclic drugs, monoamine oxidase inhibitors, and β-adrenergic receptor antagonists.

A *phobia* is an irrational fear resulting in a conscious avoidance of the feared object, activity, or situation. Either the presence or the anticipation of the phobic entity elicits severe distress in the affected person, who recognizes that the reaction is excessive. Nevertheless, the phobic reaction results in a disruption of the person's ability to function in life.

EPIDEMIOLOGY

As mentioned above, phobias are common mental disorders, although a large percentage of phobic persons either do not come to the attention of clinicians for their phobias or are misdiagnosed when they do come to psychiatric or medical attention.

Specific Phobia

Specific phobia is more common than social phobia. Specific phobia is the most common mental disorder among women and the second most common among men, second only to substance-related disorders. The six-month prevalence of specific phobia is about 5 to 10 per 100 persons. The female-to-male ratio is about 2 to 1, although the ratio is closer to 1 to 1 for the blood-injection-injury type. The peak age of onset for the natural environment type and the blood-injection-injury type is in the range of 5 to 9 years, although onset also occurs at older ages. In contrast, the peak age of onset for the situational type (except fear of heights) is higher, in the mid-20s, which is closer to the age of onset for agoraphobia. The feared objects and situations in specific phobia (listed in descending frequency of appearance) are animals, storms, heights, illness, injury, and death.

Social Phobia

Social phobia, also called social anxiety disorder, is characterized by an excessive fear of humiliation or embarrassment in various social settings, such as public speaking, urinating in a public rest room (also called shy bladder), and speaking to a date. The six-month prevalence for social phobia is about 2 to 3 per 100 persons. In epidemiological studies, females are affected more often than males, but in clinical samples the reverse is often true. The reasons for those varying observations are not known. The peak age of onset for social phobia is in the person's teens, although onset is common in persons as young as 5 years of age and as old as 35.

ETIOLOGY

Both specific phobia and social phobia have types, and the precise causes of those types are likely to differ. Even within the types, as in all mental disorders, causative heterogeneity is found. The pathogenesis of the phobias, once it is understood, may prove to be a clear model for interactions between biological and genetic factors on the one hand, and environmental events on the other hand. In the blood-injection-injury type of specific phobia, affected persons may have inherited a particularly strong vasovagal reflex, which becomes associated with phobic emotions.

General Principles

BEHAVIORAL FACTORS

In 1920 John B. Watson wrote an article called "Conditioned Emotional Reactions," in which he recounted his experiences with Little Albert, an infant with a fear of rats and rabbits. Unlike Sigmund Freud's Little Hans, who had phobic symptoms in the natural course of his maturation, Little Albert's difficulties were the direct result of the scientific experiments of two psychologists who used techniques that had successfully induced conditioned responses in laboratory animals.

Watson's formulation invoked the traditional Pavlovian stimulus-response model of the conditioned reflex to account for the creation of the phobia. That is, anxiety is aroused by a naturally frightening stimulus that occurs in contiguity with a second inherently neutral stimulus. As a result of the contiguity, especially when the two stimuli are paired on several successive occasions, the originally neutral stimulus takes on the capacity to arouse anxiety by itself. The neutral stimulus, therefore, becomes a conditioned stimulus for anxiety production.

In the classic stimulus-response theory the conditioned stimulus gradually loses its potency to arouse a response if it is not reinforced by a periodic repetition of the unconditioned stimulus. In the phobic symptom, the attenuation of the response to the phobic—that is, conditioned—stimulus does not occur; the symptom may last for years without any apparent external reinforcement. Operant conditioning theory provides a model to explain that phenomenon. In operant conditioning theory, anxiety is a drive that motivates the organism to do what it can to obviate the painful affect. In the course of its random behavior, the organism learns that certain actions enable it to avoid the anxiety-provoking stimulus. Those avoidance patterns remain stable for long periods of time as a result of the reinforcement they receive from their capacity to diminish activity. That model is readily applicable to phobias in that avoidance of the anxiety-provoking object or situation plays a central part. Such avoidance behavior becomes fixed as a stable symptom because of its effectiveness in protecting the person from the phobic anxiety.

Learning theory has a particularly relevance to phobias and provides simple and intelligible explanations for many aspects of phobic symptoms. Critics contend, however, that it deals mostly with surface mechanisms of symptom formation and is less useful than psychoanalytic theories in providing an understanding of some of the complex underlying psychic processes involved.

PSYCHOANALYTIC FACTORS

Sigmund Freud presented a formulation of phobic neurosis that has remained the analytic explanation of specific phobia and social phobia. Freud hypothesized that the major function of anxiety is to signal the ego that a forbidden unconscious drive is pushing for conscious expression, thus altering the ego to strengthen and marshall its defenses against the threatening instinctual force. Freud viewed the phobia—anxiety hysteria, as he continued to call it—as a result of conflicts centered on an unresolved childhood oedipal situation. Because the sex drive continues to have a strong incestuous coloring in the adult, sexual arousal tends to kindle an anxiety that is characteristically a fear of castration. When repression fails to be entirely successful, the ego must call on auxiliary defenses. In phobic patients the defense involves primarily the use or displacement; that is, the sexual conflict is displaced from the person who evokes the conflict to a seemingly unimportant, irrelevant object or situation, which then has the power to arouse the constellation of affects, including signal anxiety. The phobic object or situation may have a direct associative connection with the primary source of the conflict and, thus, symbolizes it (the defense mechanism of symbolization). Furthermore, the situation or the object is usually one that the person is able to keep away from; by that additional defense mechanism of avoidance, the person can escape suffering serious anxiety. Freud first discussed the theoretical formulation of phobia formation in his famous case history of Little Hans, a 5-year-old boy who had a fear of horses.

Although theorists originally thought that phobias resulted from castration anxiety, recent psychoanalytic theorists have suggested that other types of anxiety may be involved. In agoraphobia, for example, separation anxiety clearly plays a leading role, and in erythrophobia (a fear of red that can be manifested as a fear of blushing), the element of shame implies the involvement of superego anxiety. Clinical observations lead to the view that anxiety associated with phobias has a variety of sources and colorings.

Phobias illustrate the interaction between a genetic constitutional diathesis and environmental stressors. Longitudinal studies suggest that certain children are constitutionally predisposed to phobias because they are born with a specific temperament known as behavioral inhibition to the unfamiliar. However, some type of chronic environmental stress must act on that temperamental disposition to create a full-blown phobia. Such stressors as the death of a parent, separation from a parent, criticism or humiliation by an older sibling, and violence in the household may activate the latent diathesis within the child, so that the child becomes symptomatic.

Counterphobic Attitude

Otto Fenichel called attention to the fact that phobic anxiety can be hidden attitudes and behavior patterns that represent a denial, either that the dreaded object or situation is dangerous or that one is afraid of it. Basic to the phenomenon is a reversal of the situation in which one is the passive victim of external circumstances to a position of actively attempting to confront and master what one fears. The counterphobic person seeks out situations of danger and rushes enthusiastically toward them. The devotee of potentially dangerous sports, such as parachute jumping and rock climbing, may be exhibiting counterphobic behavior. Such patterns may be secondary to phobic anxiety or may be used as normal means of dealing with a realistically dangerous situation. The play of children may contain counterphobic elements, as when children play doctor and give the doll the shot they received earlier in the day in the pediatrician's office. That pattern of behavior may involve the related defense mechanism of identification with the aggressor.

Specific Phobia

The development of specific phobia may result from the pairing of a specific object or situation with the emotions of fear and panic. Various mechanisms for the pairing have been postulated. In general, a nonspecific tendency to experience fear or anxiety forms the backgroup; when a specific event (for example, driving) is paired with an emotional experience (for example, an accident), the person is susceptible to a permanent emotional association between driving or cars and fear or anxiety. The emotional experience itself can be either responsive to an external incident, as in a traffic accident, or an internal incident, most commonly a panic attack. Although a person may never experience a panic attack again and may not meet the diagnostic criteria for panic disorder, such a person may have a generalized fear of driving and not an expressed fear of having a panic attack while driving. Other mechanisms of association between the phobic object and the phobic emotions include modeling, in which a person observes the reaction in another (for example, a parent), and information transfer, in which a person is taught or warned about the dangers of specific objects (for example, venomous snakes).

GENETIC FACTORS

Specific phobia tends to run in families. The blood, injection, injury type has a particularly high familial tendency. Studies have reported that two thirds to three fourths of affected probands have at least one first-degree relative with specific phobia of the same type. However, the necessary twin and adoption studies have not been conducted to rule out a significant contribution by nongenetic transmission of specific phobia.

Social Phobia

Several studies have reported the possible presence of a trait in some children that is characterized by a consistent pattern of behavioral inhibition. That trait may be particularly common in the children of parents who are affected with panic disorder and may develop into severe shyness as the children grow older. At least some persons with social phobia may have exhibited behavioral inhibition during childhood. Perhaps associated with that trait, which is thought to be biologically based, are the psychologically based data indicating that the parents of persons with social phobia were, as a group, less caring, more rejecting, and more overprotective of their children than were other parents. Some social phobia research has referred to the spectrum from dominance to submission that is observed in the animal kingdom. For example, dominant humans may tend to walk with their chins in the air and to make eye contact, whereas submissive humans may tend to walk with their chins down and to avoid eye contact.

NEUROCHEMICAL FACTORS

The success of pharmacotherapies in treating social phobia has generated two specific neurochemical hypotheses regarding two types of social phobia. Specifically, the use of β-adrenergic antagonists—for example, propranolol (Inderal)—for performance phobias (for example, public speaking) has led to the development of an adrenergic theory for those phobias. Patients with performance phobias may release more norepinephrine or epinephrine, both centrally and peripherally, than do nonphobic persons, or such patients may be sensitive to a normal level of adrenergic stimulation. The observation that monoamine oxidase inhibitors (MAOIs) may be more effective than tricyclic drugs in the treatment of generalized social phobia, in combination with preclinical data, has led some investigators to hypothesize that dopaminergic activity is related to the pathogenesis of the disorder.

GENETIC FACTORS

First-degree relatives of persons with social phobia are about three times more likely to be affected with social phobia than are first-degree relatives of persons without mental disorders. And some preliminary data indicate that monozygotic twins are more often concordant than are dizygotic twins, although in social phobia it is particularly important to study twins reared apart to help control for environmental factors.

DIAGNOSIS

Specific Phobia

Because a review of the literature indicated that specific phobia is associated with varying ages of onset, sex ratios, family histories, and physiological responses, the fourth edition of *Diagnostic and Statistical Manual of Mental Disorders* (DSM-IV) includes distinctive types of specific phobia: animal type; natural environment type (for example, storms); blood-injection-injury type; situational type (for example, cars); and other type (for specific phobias that do not fit into the previous four types) (Table 10.3–1). Preliminary data indicate that the natural environment type is most common in children under 10 years old and the situational type is most common in persons in their early 20s. The blood-injection-injury type is differentiated from the others in that bradycardia and hypotension often follow the initial tachycardia that is common in all phobias. The blood-injection-injury type of specific phobia is particularly likely to affect many members and generations of a family. One type of specific phobia that has been reported recently is space phobia, in which patients are afraid of falling when there is no nearby support, such as a wall or a chair. Some data indicate that af-

Table 10.3–1.   Diagnostic Criteria for Specific Phobia

A. Marked and persistent fear that is excessive or unreasonable, cued by the presence or anticipation of a specific object or situation (e.g., flying, heights, animals, receiving an injection, seeing blood).

B. Exposure to the phobic stimulus almost invariably provokes an immediate anxiety response, which may take the form of a situationally bound or situationally predisposed panic attack. **Note:** In children, the anxiety may be expressed by crying, tantrums, freezing, or clinging.

C. The person recognizes that the fear is excessive or unreasonable. **Note:** In children, this feature may be absent.

D. The phobic situation(s) is avoided or else is endured with intense anxiety or distress.

E. The avoidance, anxious anticipation, or distress in the feared situation(s) interferes significantly with the person's normal routine, occupational (or academic) functioning, or social activities or relationships, or there is marked distress about having the phobia.

F. In individuals under age 18 years, the duration is at least 6 months.

G. The anxiety, panic attacks, or phobic avoidance associated with the specific object or situation are not better accounted for by another mental disorder, such as obsessive-compulsive disorder (e.g., fear of dirt in someone with an obsession about contamination), posttraumatic stress disorder (e.g., avoidance of stimuli associated with a severe stressor), separation anxiety disorder (e.g., avoidance of school), social phobia (e.g., avoidance of social situations because of fear of embarrassment), panic disorder with agoraphobia, or agoraphobia without history of panic disorder.

Table from DSM-IV, *Diagnostic and Statistical Manual of Mental Disorders*, ed 4. Copyright American Psychiatric Association, Washington, 1994. Used with permission.

fected patients may have abnormal function in the right hemisphere, possibly resulting in a visual-spatial impairment.

Social Phobia

The DSM-IV diagnostic criteria for social phobia (Table 10.3–2) encourages the use of clinical judgment in making the final diagnosis. DSM-IV adds a type of social phobia, generalized type, which may be of use in the prediction of course, prognosis, and treatment response. DSM-IV excludes a diagnosis of social phobia when the symptoms are a result of social avoidance stemming from embarrassment about another psychiatric or nonpsychiatric medical condition.

CLINICAL FEATURES

Phobias are characterized by the arousal of severe anxiety when the patient is exposed to a specific situation or object or when the patient even anticipates exposure to the situation or object. DSM-IV emphasizes the possibility that panic attacks can and frequently do occur in patients with specific and social phobias, but the panic attacks, except perhaps for the first few, are expected. Exposure to the phobic stimulus or anticipation of it almost invariably results in a panic attack in a panic attack-prone person.

Patients with phobias, by definition, try to avoid the phobic stimulus. Some patients go to great trouble to avoid anxiety-provoking situations. For example, a phobic patient may take a bus across the United States, rather than fly, to avoid contact with the object of the patient's phobia, an airplane. Perhaps as another way to avoid the stress of the phobic stimulus, many

Table 10.3-2.   Diagnostic Criteria for Social Phobia

A. A marked and persistent fear of one or more social or performance situations in which the person is exposed to unfamiliar people or to possible scrutiny by others. The individual fears that he or she will act in a way (or show anxiety symptoms) that will be humiliating or embarrassing. **Note:** In children, there must be evidence of the capacity for age-appropriate social relationships with familiar people and the anxiety must occur in peer settings, not just in interactions with adults.

B. Exposure to the feared social situation almost invariably provokes anxiety, which may take the form of a situationally bound or situationally predisposed panic attack. **Note:** In children, the anxiety may be expressed by crying, tantrums, freezing, or shrinking from social situations with unfamiliar people.

C. The person recognizes that the fear is excessive or unreasonable. **Note:** In children, this feature may be absent.

D. The feared or social or performance situations are avoided or else are endured with intense anxiety or distress.

E. The avoidance, anxious anticipation, or distress in the feared social or performance situation(s) interferes significantly with the person's normal routine, occupational (academic) functioning, or social activities or relationships or there is marked distress about having the phobia.

F. In individuals under age 18 years, the duration is at least 6 months.

G. The fear or avoidance is not due to the direct physiological effects of a substance (e.g., a drug of abuse, a medication) or a general medical condition and is not better accounted for by another mental disorder (e.g., panic disorder with or without agoraphobia, separation anxiety disorder, body dysmorphic disorder, a pervasive developmental disorder, or schizoid personality disorder.

H. If a general medical condition or another mental disorder is present, the fear in criterion A is unrelated to it, e.g., the fear is not of stuttering, trembling in Parkinson's disease, or exhibiting abnormal eating behavior in anorexia nervosa or bulimia nervosa.

Table from DSM-IV, *Diagnostic and Statistical Manual of Mental Disorders*, ed 4. Copyright American Psychiatric Association, Washington, 1994. Used with permission.

phobic patients have substance-related disorders, particularly alcohol use disorders. Moreover, an estimated one third of patients with social phobia have major depressive disorder.

The major finding on the mental status examination is the presence of an irrational and ego-dystonic fear of a specific situation, activity, or object; patients are able to describe how they avoid contact with the phobic situation. Depression is commonly found on the mental status examination and may be present in as many as one third of all phobic patients.

DIFFERENTIAL DIAGNOSIS

Specific phobia and social phobia need to be differentiated from appropriate fear and normal shyness, respectively. DSM-IV aids in the differentiation by requiring that the symptoms impair the patient's ability to function appropriately. Nonpsychiatric medical conditions that can result in the development of a phobia include the use of substances (particularly hallucinogens and sympathomimetics), central nervous system tumors, and cerebrovascular diseases. Phobic symptoms in those instances are unlikely in the absence of additional suggestive findings on physical, neurological, and mental status examinations. Schizophrenia is also in the differential diagnosis of both specific phobia and social phobia, since schizophrenic patients can have phobic symptoms as part of their psychoses. However,

unlike schizophrenic patients, phobic patients have insight into the irrationality of their fears and lack the bizarre quality and other psychotic symptoms that accompany schizophrenia.

In the differential diagnosis of both specific phobia and social phobia, the clinician must consider panic disorder, agoraphobia, and avoidant personality disorder. DSM-IV acknowledges that the differentiation among panic disorder, agoraphobia, social phobia, and specific phobia can be difficult in individual cases, and the clinician is advised to use clinical judgment. In general, however, patients with specific phobia or nongeneralized social phobia tend to experience anxiety immediately when presented with the phobic stimulus. Furthermore, their anxiety or panic is limited to the identified situation, and, in general, the patients are not abnormally anxious when they are neither confronted with the phobic stimulus nor caused to anticipate the stimulus.

An agoraphobic patient is often comforted by the presence of another person in an anxiety-provoking situation, whereas the patient with social phobia is made more anxious than before by the presence of other people. Whereas breathlessness, dizziness, a sense of suffocation, and a fear of dying are common in panic disorder and agoraphobia, the symptoms associated with social phobia usually involve blushing, muscle twitching, and anxiety about scrutiny. The differentiation between social phobia and avoidant personality disorder can be difficult and can require extensive interviews and psychiatric histories.

Specific Phobia

Other diagnoses to consider in the differential diagnosis of specific phobia are hypochondriasis, obsessive-compulsive disorder, and paranoid personality disorder. Hypochondriasis is the fear of having a disease, whereas specific phobia of the illness type is the fear of contracting the disease. Some patients with obsessive-compulsive disorder manifest behavior that is indistinguishable from that of a patient with specific phobia. For example, patients with obsessive-compulsive disorder may avoid knives because they have a compulsive thought about killing their children, whereas patients with specific phobia involving knives may avoid knives for fear of cutting themselves. Paranoid personality disorder can be distinguished from specific phobia by the generalized fear in patients with paranoid personality disorder.

Social Phobia

Two additional differential diagnostic considerations for social phobia are major depressive disorder and schizoid personality disorder. The avoidance of social situations can often be a symptom in depression; however, a psychiatric interview with the patient is likely to elicit a broad constellation of depressive symptoms. In patients with schizoid personality disorder, the lack of interest in socializing, not fear of socializing, leads to the avoidant social behavior.

COURSE AND PROGNOSIS

Not a great deal is known about the course and the prognosis of specific phobia and social phobia because of their relatively recent recognition as important mental disorders. The introduction of specific psychotherapies and pharmacotherapies to treat the phobias will also affect the interpretation of data on course and prognosis unless the studies control for the treatment strategies.

Phobic disorders may be associated with more morbidity than was previously recognized. Depending on the degree to which the phobic behavior interferes with the person's ability to function, the affected patient may depend financially on others as adults and have varying degrees of impairment in their social lives, occupational successes, and, in the case of young people, school performance. The development of associated substance-related disorders can also adversely affect the course and the prognosis of the disorders.

TREATMENT

Insight-Oriented Psychotherapy

Early in the development of psychoanalysis and the dynamically oriented psychotherapies, theorists believed that those methods were the treatments of choice for phobic neurosis, which was then thought to stem from oedipal-genital conflicts. Soon, however, therapists recognized that, in spite of progress in uncovering and analyzing unconscious conflicts, patients frequently failed to lose their phobic symptoms. Moreover, by continuing to avoid the phobic situation, patients excluded a significant degree of anxiety and its related associations from the analytic process. Both Freud and his pupil Sandor Ferenczi recognized that, if progress in analyzing those symptoms was to be made, therapists had to go beyond their analytic roles and actively urge phobic patients to seek out the phobic situation and experience the anxiety and resultant insight. Since then, psychiatrists have generally agreed that a measure of activity on the part of the therapist is often required to treat phobic anxiety successfully. The decision to apply the techniques of psychodynamic insight-oriented therapy should be based not on the presence of the phobic symptom alone but on positive indications from the patient's ego structure and life patterns for the use of that method of treatment. Insight-oriented therapy enables the patient to understand the origin of the phobia, the phenomenon of secondary gain, and the role of resistance and enables the patient to seek healthy ways of dealing with anxiety-provoking stimuli.

Other Therapies

Hypnosis, supportive therapy, and family therapy may be useful in the treatment of phobias. Hypnosis is used to enhance the therapist's suggestions that the phobic object is not dangerous, and self-hypnosis can be taught to the patient as a method of relaxation when confronted with the phobic object. Supportive psychotherapy and family therapy are often useful in helping the patient actively confront the phobic object during treatment. Not only can family therapy enlist the aid of the family in treating the patient, but it may help the family understand the nature of the patient's problem. An additional therapeutic and supportive activity for patients may be involvement in the Anxiety Disorders Association of America (ADAA).

Specific Phobia

The most commonly used treatment for specific phobia is exposure therapy, a type of behavior therapy originally pioneered by Joseph Wolpe. The therapist desensitizes the patient, using a series of gradual, self-paced exposures to the phobic stimulus. The therapist teaches the patient various techniques to deal with the anxiety, including relaxation, breathing control, and cognitive approaches to the situation. The cognitive approaches include reinforcing the realization that the situation is, in fact, safe. The key aspects of successful behavior therapy are (1) the patient's commitment to treatment, (2) clearly identified problems and objectives, and (3) available alternative strategies for coping with the patient's feelings. In the special situation of blood, injection, injury phobia, some therapists recommend that patients tense their bodies during the exposure and remain seated during the exposure to help avoid the possibility of fainting from a vasovagal reaction to the phobic stimulation. Some preliminary reports indicate that β-adrenergic receptor antagonists can be useful in the treatment of specific phobia. When specific phobia is associated with panic attacks, pharmacotherapy or psychotherapy directed to the panic attacks may also be of benefit.

Social Phobia

The treatment of social phobia uses both psychotherapy and pharmacotherapy, and varying approaches are indicated for the generalized type and performance situations. Some studies indicate that the use of both pharmacotherapy and psychotherapy produces better results than either therapy alone, although the finding may not be applicable to all situations and patients.

Several well-controlled studies have found that monoamine oxidase inhibitors, especially phenelzine (Nardil), are effective in the treatment of the generalized type of social phobia. Other drugs that have been reported to be effective, although not in as many well-controlled trials, include alprazolam (Xanax), clonazepam (Klonopin), and possibly the serotonin-specific reuptake inhibitors. Dosages for those drugs parallel those for their use in depressive disorders, and the response can take the usual four to six weeks. Some data indicate that tricyclic drugs and buspirone (BuSpar) may not be effective in social phobia, although the data are limited and not definite.

The psychotherapy for the generalized type of social phobia usually involves a combination of behavioral and cognitive methods, including cognitive retraining, desensitization, rehearsal during sessions, and a range of homework assignments.

The treatment of social phobia associated with performance situations frequently involves the use of β-adrenergic receptor antagonists shortly before exposure to the phobic stimulus. The two compounds most widely used are atenolol (Tenormin), 50 to 100 mg every morning or one hour before the performance, and propranolol (20 to 40 mg). Cognitive, behavioral, and exposure techniques can also be useful in performance situations.

References

Barlow D H, Liebowitz M R: Specific phobia and social phobia. In *Comprehensive Textbook of Psychiatry*, ed 6, H I Kaplan, B J Sadock, editors, p 1204. Williams & Wilkins, Baltimore, 1995.
Chapman T F, Fyer A J, Mannuzza S, Klein D F: A comparison of treated and untreated simple phobia. Am J Psychiatry *150*: 816, 1993.
Greist J H: The diagnosis of social phobia. J Clin Psychiatry *56*: 5, 1995.
Potts N L S, Davidson J R T: Social phobia: Biological aspects and pharmacotherapy. Prog Neuropsychopharmacol Biol Psychiatry *16*: 635, 1992.
Van Ameringen M, Mancini C, Streiner D L: Fluoxetine efficacy in social phobia. J Clin Psychiatry *54*: 27, 1993.

10.4 OBSESSIVE-COMPULSIVE DISORDER

Obsessive-compulsive disorder is an example of the positive effects that modern research can have on a disorder in a short time. As recently as the 1980s, obsessive-compulsive disorder was considered an uncommon disorder and poorly responsive to treatment. It is now recognized that obsessive-compulsive disorder is common and very responsive to treatment.

An *obsession* is a recurrent and intrusive thought, feeling, idea, or sensation. A *compulsion* is a conscious, standardized, recurrent thought or behavior, such as counting, checking, or avoiding. Obsessions increase a person's anxiety, whereas carrying out compulsions reduces a person's anxiety. However, when a person resists carrying out a compulsion, anxiety is increased. A person with obsessive-compulsive disorder generally realizes the irrationality of the obsessions and experiences both the obsession and the compulsion as ego-dystonic. Obsessive-compulsive disorder can be a disabling disorder, because the obsessions can be time-consuming and can interfere significantly with the person's normal routine, occupational functioning, usual social activities, or relationships with friends and family members.

EPIDEMIOLOGY

The lifetime prevalence of obsessive-compulsive disorder in the general population is an estimated 2 to 3 percent. Some researchers have estimated that obsessive-compulsive disorder is found in as many as 10 percent of the outpatients in psychiatric clinics. Those figures make obsessive-compulsive disorder the fourth most common psychiatric diagnosis after phobias, substance-related disorders, and major depressive disorder. Epidemiological studies in Europe, Asia, and Africa have confirmed those rates across cultural boundaries.

ETIOLOGY

Biological Factors

NEUROTRANSMITTERS

The many clinical trials that have been conducted with various drugs support the hypothesis that a dysregulation of serotonin is involved in the symptom formation of obsessions and compulsions in the disorder. Data show that serotonergic drugs are more effective than drugs that affect other neurotransmitter systems. However, whether serotonin is involved in the cause of obsessive-compulsive disorder is not clear at this time. Clinical studies have assayed cerebrospinal fluid (CSF) concentrations of serotonin metabolites—for example, 5-hydroxyindoleacetic acid (5-HIAA)—and affinities and numbers of platelet binding sites of tritiated imipramine (which binds to serotonin reuptake sites) and have reported variable findings of those measures in obsessive-compulsive disorder patients. Some researchers have said that the cholinergic and dopaminergic neurotransmitter systems in obsessive-compulsive disorder patients are two areas for future research studies.

BRAIN-IMAGING STUDIES

A variety of functional brain-imaging studies—for example, positron emission tomography (PET)—have found increased activity (for example, metabolism and blood flow) in the frontal lobes, the basal ganglia (especially the caudate), and the cingulum of patients with obsessive-compulsive disorder. Pharmacological and behavioral treatments reportedly reverse those abnormalities. The data from the functional brain-imaging studies are consistent with the data from structural brain-imaging studies. Both computed tomographic (CT) and magnetic resonance imaging (MRI) studies have found decreased sizes of caudates bilaterally in patients with obsessive-compulsive disorder. Both functional and structural brain-imaging studies are also consistent with the observation that neurological procedures involving the cingulum are sometimes effective in the treatment of obsessive-compulsive disorder patients. One recent MRI study reported increased T_1 relaxation times in the frontal cortex, a finding that is consistent with the location of abnormalities found in PET studies.

GENETICS

Available genetic data on obsessive-compulsive disorder are consistent with the hypothesis that the inheritance of obsessive-compulsive disorder has a significant genetic component. The data, however, do not yet distinguish the influence of cultural and behavioral effects on the transmission of the disorder. The studies of concordance in twins for obsessive-compulsive disorder have consistently found a significantly higher concordance rate for monozygotic twins than for dizygotic twins. Family studies of obsessive-compulsive disorder patients have found that 35 percent of the first-degree relatives of obsessive-compulsive disorder patients are also afflicted with the disorder.

OTHER BIOLOGICAL DATA

Electrophysiological studies, sleep electroencephalogram (EEG) studies, and neuroendocrine studies have contributed data that indicate some commonalties between depressive disorders and obsessive-compulsive disorder. A higher than usual incidence of nonspecific EEG abnormalities are found in obsessive-compulsive disorder patients. Sleep EEG studies have found abnormalities similar to those seen in depressive disorders, such as decreased rapid eye movement (REM) latency. Neuroendocrine studies have also found some similarities to depressive disorders, such as nonsuppression on the dexamethasone-suppression test in about one third of the patients and decreased growth hormone secretion with clonidine (Catapres) infusions.

Behavioral Factors

According to learning theorists, obsessions are conditioned stimuli. A relatively neutral stimulus becomes associated with fear or anxiety through a process of respondent conditioning by being paired with events that are by nature noxious or anxiety-producing. Thus, previously neutral objects and thoughts become conditioned stimuli capable of provoking anxiety or discomfort.

Compulsions are established in a different way. A person discovers that a certain action reduces the anxiety attached to an obsessional thought. Thus, active avoidance strategies in the form of compulsions or ritualistic behaviors are developed to control anxiety. Gradually, because of their efficacy in reducing a painful secondary drive (the anxiety), the avoidance strategies become fixed as learned patterns of compulsive behaviors. Learning theory provides useful concepts for explaining certain aspects of the obsessive-compulsive phenomena—for example, the anxiety-provoking capacity of ideas that are not necessarily frightening in themselves and the establishment of compulsive patterns of behavior.

Psychosocial Factors

PERSONALITY FACTORS

Obsessive-compulsive disorder is different from obsessive-compulsive personality disorder. The majority of obsessive-compulsive disorder patients do not have premorbid compulsive symptoms; therefore, such personality traits are neither necessary nor sufficient for the development of obsessive-compulsive disorder. Only about 15 to 35 percent of obsessive-compulsive disorder patients have had premorbid obsessional traits.

PSYCHODYNAMIC FACTORS

Sigmund Freud described three major psychological defense mechanisms that determine the form and the quality of obsessive-compulsive symptoms and character traits: isolation, undoing, and reaction formation.

Isolation

Isolation is a defense mechanism that protects a person from anxiety-provoking affects and impulses. Under ordinary circumstances a person experiences in consciousness both the affect and the imagery of an emotion-laden idea, whether it be a fantasy or the memory of an event. When isolation occurs, the affect and the impulse of which it is a derivative are separated from the ideational component and are pushed out of consciousness. If isolation is completely successful, the impulse and its associated affect are totally repressed, and the patient is consciously aware only of the affectless idea that is related to it.

Undoing

Because of the constant threat that the impulse may escape the primary defense of isolation and break free, secondary defensive operations are required to combat the impulse and to quiet the anxiety that its imminent eruption into consciousness arouses. The compulsive act constitutes the surface manifestation of a defensive operation aimed at reducing anxiety and at controlling the underlying impulse that has not been sufficiently contained by isolation. A particularly important secondary defensive operation is the mechanism of undoing. As the word suggests, undoing is a compulsive act that is performed in an attempt to prevent or undo the consequences that the patient irrationally anticipates from a frightening obsessional thought or impulse.

Reaction Formation

Both isolation and undoing are defensive maneuvers that are intimately involved in the production of clinical symptoms. Reaction formation results in the formation of character traits, rather than symptoms. As the term implies, reaction formation involves manifest patterns of behavior and consciously experienced attitudes that are exactly the opposite of the underlying impulses. Often, the patterns seem to an observer to be highly exaggerated and inappropriate.

Other Psychodynamic Factors

In classic psychoanalytic theory, obsessive-compulsive disorder was termed obsessive-compulsive neurosis and was a regression from the oedipal phase to the anal psychosexual phase of development. When patients with obsessive-compulsive disorder feel threatened by anxiety about retaliation or the loss of a significant object's love, they retreat from the oedipal position and regress to an intensely ambivalent emotional stage associated with the anal phase. The ambivalence is connected to the unraveling of the smooth fusion between sexual and aggressive drives characteristic of the oedipal phase. The coexistence of hatred and love toward the same person leaves the patient paralyzed with doubt and indecision.

One of the striking features of patients with obsessive-compulsive disorder is the degree to which they are preoccupied with aggression or cleanliness, either overtly in the content of their symptoms or in the associations that lie behind them. Therefore, the psychogenesis of obsessive-compulsive disorder may lie in disturbances in normal growth and development related to the anal-sadistic phase of development.

Ambivalence.   Ambivalence is the direct result of a change in the characteristics of the impulse life. It is an important feature of the normal child during the anal-sadistic developmental phase; that is, the child feels both love and murderous hate toward the same object, sometimes simultaneously. The obsessive-compulsive disorder patient often consciously experiences both love and hate toward an object. That conflict of opposing emotions may be seen in the patient's doing-undoing patterns of behavior and paralyzing doubt in the face of choices.

Magical thinking.   In magical thinking the regression uncovers early modes of thought, rather than impulses; that is, ego functions, as well as id functions, are affected by regression. Inherent in magical thinking is omnipotence of thought. Persons feel that, merely by thinking about an event in the external world, they can cause that event to occur without intermediate physical actions. That feeling makes having an aggressive thought frightening to obsessive-compulsive disorder patients.

DIAGNOSIS

The fourth edition of *Diagnostic and Statistical Manual of Mental Disorders* (DSM-IV) introduces the clinical observation that thoughts (that is, mental acts) can be either obsessions or compulsions, depending on whether they increase anxiety (obsessions) or reduce anxiety (compulsions) (Table 10.4–1). DSM-IV allows the clinician to specify that patients have the poor insight type of obsessive-compulsive disorder if they generally do not recognize the excessiveness of their obsessions and compulsions.

CLINICAL FEATURES

Patients with obsessive-compulsive disorder often go to physicians other than psychiatrists. Patients with both obsessions and compulsions constitute at least 75 percent of the affected patients. Some researchers and clinicians believe that the number may be much closer to 100 percent if patients are carefully assessed for the presence of mental compulsions in addition to behavioral compulsions. For example, an obsession about hurting a child may be followed by a mental compulsion to repeat a specific prayer a specific number of times. However, some researchers and clinicians believe that some patients do have only obsessive thoughts and do not have compulsions. Such patients are likely to have repetitious thoughts of some sexual or aggressive act that is reprehensible to the patient.

Obsessions and compulsions have certain features in common: (1) An idea or an impulse intrudes itself insistently and persistently into the person's conscious awareness. (2) A feeling of anxious dread accompanies the central manifestation and frequently leads the person to take countermeasures against the initial idea or impulse. (3) The obsession or the compulsion is ego-alien; that is, it is experienced as being foreign to the person's experience of himself or herself as a psychological being. (4) No matter how vivid and compelling the obsession or the compulsion is, the person usually recognizes it as absurd and irrational. (5) The person suffering from obsessions and compulsions usually feels a strong desire to resist them. However, about half of all patients offer little resistance to the compulsion. About 80 percent of all patients believe that the compulsion is irrational. Sometimes obsessions and compulsions become overvalued to the patients—for example, patients may insist that compulsive cleanliness is morally correct, even though they lost their jobs because of time spent cleaning.

Table 10.4-1. Diagnostic Criteria for Obsessive-Compulsive Disorder

A. Either obsessions or compulsions:

Obsessions as defined by (1), (2), (3), and (4):
(1) recurrent and persistent thoughts, impulses, or images that are experienced, at some time during the disturbance, as intrusive and inappropriate and that cause marked anxiety or distress
(2) the thoughts, impulses, or images are not simply excessive worries about real-life problems
(3) the person attempts to ignore or suppress such thoughts, impulses, or images, or to neutralize them with some other thought or action
(4) the person recognizes that the obsessional thoughts, impulses, or images, are a product of his or her own mind (not imposed from without as in thought insertion)

Compulsions as defined by (1) and (2):
(1) repetitive behaviors (e.g., hand washing, ordering, checking) or mental acts (e.g., praying, counting, repeating words silently) that the person feels driven to perform in response to an obsession, or according to rules that must be applied rigidly
(2) the behaviors or mental acts are aimed at preventing or reducing distress or preventing some dreaded event or situation; however, these behaviors or mental acts either are not connected in a realistic way with what they are designed to neutralize or prevent or are clearly excessive

B. At some point during the course of the disorder, the person has recognized that the obsessions or compulsions are excessive or unreasonable. **Note:** This does not apply to children.

C. The obsessions or compulsions cause marked distress, are time consuming (take more than 1 hour a day), or significantly interfere with the person's normal routine, occupational (or academic) functioning, or usual social activities or relationships.

D. If another Axis I disorder is present, the content of the obsessions or compulsions is not restricted to it (e.g., preoccupation with food in the presence of an eating disorder; hair pulling in the presence of trichotillomania; concern with appearance in the presence of body dysmorphic disorder; preoccupation with drugs in the presence of substance use disorder; preoccupation with having a serious illness in the presence of hypochondriasis; preoccupation with sexual urges or fantasies in the presence of a paraphilia; or guilty ruminations in the presence of major depressive disorder).

E. The disturbance is not due to the direct physiological effects of a substance (e.g., a drug of abuse, a medication) or a general medical condition.

Table from DSM-IV, *Diagnostic and Statistical Manual of Mental Disorders*, ed 4. Copyright American Psychiatric Association, Washington, 1994. Used with permission.

The presentation of obsessions and compulsions is heterogeneous in adults and in children and adolescents. The symptoms of an individual patient may overlap and change with time, but obsessive-compulsive disorder has four major symptom patterns. The most common pattern is an obsession of contamination, followed by washing or accompanied by compulsive avoidance of the presumably contaminated object. The feared object is often hard to avoid (for example, feces, urine, dust, or germs). Patients may literally rub the skin off their hands by excessive hand washing or may be unable to leave their homes because of fear of germs. Although anxiety is the most common emotional response to the feared object, obsessive shame and disgust are also common. Patients with contamination obsessions usually believe that the contamination is spread from object to object or person to person by the slightest contact.

The second most common pattern is an obsession of doubt, followed by a compulsion of checking. The obsession often implies some danger of violence (such as forgetting to turn off the stove or not locking a door). The checking may involve multiple trips back into the house to check the stove, for example. The patients have an obsessional self-doubt, as they always feel guilty for having forgotten or committed something.

The third most common pattern is one with merely intrusive obsessional thoughts without a compulsion. Such obsessions are usually repetitive thoughts of some sexual or aggressive act that is reprehensible to the patient.

The fourth most common pattern is the need for symmetry or precision, which can lead to a compulsion of slowness. Patients can literally take hours to eat a meal or shave their faces. Religious obsessions and compulsive hoarding are common in obsessive-compulsive patients. *Trichotillomania* (compulsive hair pulling) and nail biting may be compulsions related to obsessive-compulsive disorder.

Mental Status Examination

On the mental status examination, obsessive-compulsive disorder patients show symptoms of depressive disorders. Such symptoms are present in about 50 percent of all patients. Some obsessive-compulsive disorder patients have character traits suggestive of obsessive-compulsive personality disorder, but most do not. Obsessive-compulsive disorder patients, especially men, have a higher than average celibacy rate. A greater than usual amount of marital discord is found in these patients.

DIFFERENTIAL DIAGNOSIS

Medical and Neurological Conditions

The DSM-IV diagnostic requirement of personal distress and functional impairment differentiates obsessive-compulsive disorder from ordinary or mildly excessive thoughts and habits. The major neurological disorders to consider in the differential diagnosis are Tourette's disorder, other tic disorders, temporal lobe epilepsy, and, occasionally, trauma and postencephalitic complications.

TOURETTE'S DISORDER

The characteristic symptoms of Tourette's disorder are motor and vocal tics that occur frequently and virtually every day. Tourette's disorder and obsessive-compulsive disorder have a similar age of onset and similar symptoms. About 90 percent of Tourette's disorder patients have compulsive symptoms, and as many as two thirds meet the diagnostic criteria for obsessive-compulsive disorder.

Psychiatric Conditions

The major psychiatric considerations in the differential diagnosis of obsessive-compulsive disorder are schizophrenia, obsessive-compulsive personality disorder, phobias, and depressive disorders. Obsessive-compulsive disorder can usually be distinguished from schizophrenia by the absence of other schizophrenic symptoms, by the less bizarre nature of the symptoms, and by patients' insight into their disorder. Obsessive-compulsive personality disorder does not have the degree of functional impairment associated with obsessive-compulsive disorder. Phobias are distinguished by the absence of a relation between the obsessive thoughts and the compulsions. Major depressive disorder can sometimes be associated with obsessive ideas, but patients with just obsessive-compulsive disorder fail to meet the diagnostic criteria for major depressive disorder.

Other psychiatric conditions that may be closely related to obsessive-compulsive disorder are hypochondriasis, body dysmorphic disorder, and possibly other impulse disorders, such as kleptomania and pathological gambling. In all those disorders the patient has either a repetitive thought (for example, concern about one's body) or a repetitive behavior (for example, stealing). Several research groups are investigating those disorders, their relations to obsessive-compulsive disorder, and their responses to various treatments.

COURSE AND PROGNOSIS

More than half of patients with obsessive-compulsive disorder have a sudden onset of symptoms. About 50 to 70 percent of the patients have the onset of symptoms after a stressful event, such as a pregnancy, a sexual problem, or the death of a relative. Because many patients manage to keep their symptoms secret, there is often a delay of 5 to 10 years before they come to psychiatric attention, although the delay is probably shortening with increased awareness of the disorder among lay and professional people. The course is usually long but variable; some patients experience a fluctuating course, and others experience a constant course.

Symptoms improve significantly in about 20 to 30 percent of patients and improve moderately in 40 to 50 percent. The remaining 20 to 40 percent of patients either remain ill or their symptoms worsen.

About one third of patients with obsessive-compulsive disorder have major depressive disorder, and suicide is a risk for all patients with obsessive-compulsive disorder. A poor prognosis is indicated by yielding to (rather than resisting) compulsions, childhood onset, bizarre compulsions, the need for hospitalization, a coexisting major depressive disorder, delusional beliefs, the presence of overvalued ideas (that is, some acceptance of obsessions and compulsions), and the presence of a personality disorder (especially schizotypal personality disorder). A good prognosis is indicated by a good social and occupational adjustment, the presence of a precipitating event, and episodic symptoms. The obsessional content does not seem to be related to the prognosis.

TREATMENT

With mounting evidence that obsessive-compulsive disorder is largely determined by biological factors, the classic psychoanalytic theory has fallen out of favor. Moreover, because obsessive-compulsive disorder symptoms appear to be largely refractory to psychodynamic psychotherapy and psychoanalysis, pharmacological and behavioral treatments have become common. However, psychodynamic factors may be of considerable benefit in understanding what precipitates exacerbations of the disorder and in treating various forms of resistance to treatment, such as noncompliance with medication.

Many obsessive-compulsive disorder patients tenaciously resist treatment efforts. They may refuse to take medication and may resist carrying out homework assignments and other prescribed activities given by behavior therapists. The obsessive-compulsive symptoms themselves, no matter how biologically based, may have important psychological meanings that make patients reluctant to give them up. A psychodynamic exploration of the patient's resistance to treatment may result in improved compliance.

Well-controlled studies have found that pharmacotherapy or behavior therapy or the combination significantly reduces the symptoms of obsessive-compulsive disorder patients. The decision regarding which therapy to use is based on the clinician's judgment and experience and on the patient's acceptance of the various modalities.

Pharmacotherapy

The efficacy of pharmacotherapy in obsessive-compulsive disorder has been proved in many clinical trials. The efficacy is enhanced by the observation that studies find a placebo response rate of about 5 percent. That percentage is low compared with the 30 to 40 percent placebo response rate often seen in studies of antidepressants and anxiolytic drugs.

The available data indicate that the drugs, all of which are used to treat depressive disorders or other mental disorders, can be used in their usual dosage ranges. Initial effects are generally seen after four to six weeks of treatment, although 8 to 16 weeks are usually needed to obtain the maximum therapeutic benefit. Although treatment with antidepressant drugs is still controversial, a significant proportion of patients with obsessive-compulsive disorder who respond to treatment with antidepressant drugs seem to relapse if the drug therapy is discontinued.

The standard approach is to start with a serotonergic drug—for example, clomipramine (Anafranil) or a serotonin-specific reuptake inhibitor (SSRI), such as fluvoxamine (Luvox), or fluoxetine (Prozac)—and then to move to other pharmacological strategies if the serotonin-specific drugs are not effective.

CLOMIPRAMINE

The standard drug for the treatment of obsessive-compulsive disorder is clomipramine, a serotonin-specific tricyclic drug that is also used for the treatment of depressive disorders. The efficacy of clomipramine in obsessive-compulsive disorder is supported by many clinical trials. Clomipramine is usually initiated at dosages of 25 to 50 mg at bedtime and can be increased by increments of 25 mg a day every two to three days, up to a maximum dosage of 250 mg a day or the appearance of dose-limiting side effects. Because clomipramine is a tricyclic drug, it is associated with the usual side effects of those drugs, including sedation, hypotension, sexual dysfunction, and anticholinergic side effects (for example, dry mouth).

SEROTONIN-SPECIFIC REUPTAKE INHIBITORS

The SSRIs available in the United States include fluoxetine, sertraline (Zoloft), paroxetine (Paxil), and fluvoxamine. Several clinical trials have shown the efficacy of fluvoxamine, fluoxetine, and sertraline in obsessive-compulsive disorder, and paroxetine may also be effective. Studies of fluoxetine in obsessive-compulsive disorder have used dosages up to 80 mg a day to achieve therapeutic benefits. Although SSRIs are associated with overstimulation, restlessness, headaches, insomnia, nausea, and gastrointestinal adverse effects, the SSRIs as a group are better tolerated than are the tricyclic drugs and, therefore, are sometimes used as the first-line drugs in the treatment of obsessive-compulsive disorder.

OTHER DRUGS

If treatment with clomipramine or an SSRI is unsuccessful, many therapists augment the first drug by the addition of lithium (Eskalith). Other drugs that can be tried in the treatment of obsessive-compulsive disorder are the monoamine oxidase inhibitors (MAOIs), especially phenelzine (Nardil). Less well studied pharmacological agents for the treatment of unresponsive patients include buspirone (BuSpar), fenfluramine (Pondimin), L-tryptophan, and clonazepam (Klonopin).

Behavior Therapy

Although few head-to-head comparisons have been made, behavior therapy is as effective as pharmacotherapies in obsessive-compulsive disorder, and some data indicate that the beneficial effects are longer-lasting with behavior therapy. Therefore, many clinicians consider behavior therapy to be the treatment of choice for obsessive-compulsive disorder. Behavior therapy can be conducted in both outpatient and inpatient settings. The principal behavioral approaches in obsessive-compulsive disorder are exposure and response prevention. Desensitization, thought stopping, flooding, implosion therapy, and aversive conditioning have also been used in obsessive-compulsive disorder patients. In behavior therapy the patient must be truly committed to improvement.

Psychotherapy

In the absence of adequate studies of insight-oriented psychotherapy for obsessive-compulsive disorder, any valid generalizations about its effectiveness are hard to make, although there are anecdotal reports of successes. Individual analysts have seen striking and lasting changes for the better in patients with obsessive-compulsive personality disorder, especially when they are able to come to terms with the aggressive impulses lying behind the patient's character traits. Likewise, analysts and dynamically oriented psychiatrists have observed marked symptomatic improvement in patients with obsessive-compulsive disorder in the course of analysis or prolonged insight psychotherapy.

Supportive psychotherapy undoubtedly has its place, especially for those obsessive-compulsive disorder patients who, despite symptoms of varying degrees of severity, are able to work and make social adjustments. With continuous and regular contact with an interested, sympathetic, and encouraging professional person, patients may be able to function by virtue of that help, without which their symptoms would incapacitate them. Occasionally, when obsessional rituals and anxiety reach an intolerable intensity, it is necessary to hospitalize the patient until the shelter of an institution and the removal from external environmental stresses bring the symptoms down to a tolerable level.

The patient's family members are often driven to the verge of despair by the patient's behavior. Any psychotherapeutic endeavors must include attention to the family members through the provision of emotional support, reassurance, explanation, and advice on how to manage and respond to the patient.

Other Therapies

Family therapy is often useful in supporting the family, helping reduce marital discord resulting from the disorder, and building a treatment alliance with the family members for the good of the patient.

Group therapy is useful as a support system for some patients.

For severely treatment-resistant patients, electroconvulsive therapy (ECT) and psychosurgery should be considered. ECT is not as effective as psychosurgery but should probably be tried before surgery is tried. The most common psychosurgical procedure for obsessive-compulsive disorder is cingulotomy, which is successful in treating 25 to 30 percent of otherwise treatment-unresponsive patients. The most common complication of psychosurgery is the development of seizures, which are almost always controlled by treatment with phenytoin (Dilantin). Some patients who do not respond to psychosurgery alone and who did not respond to pharmacotherapy or behavior therapy before the operation do respond to pharmacotherapy or behavior therapy after psychosurgery.

References

Baxter L R, Schwartz J M, Bergman K S, Szuba M P, Guze B H, Mazziotta J C, Alazraki A, Selin C E, Ferng H-K, Munford P, Phelps M E: Caudate glucose metabolic rate changes with both drug and behavior therapy for obsessive-compulsive disorder. Arch Gen Psychiatry 49: 681, 1992.

Gabbard G O: *Psychodynamic Psychiatry in Clinical Practice: The DSM-IV Edition.* American Psychiatric Press, Washington, 1994.

Jenike M A: Obsessive-compulsive disorder. In *Comprehensive Textbook of Psychiatry,* ed 6, H I Kaplan, B J Sadock, editors, p 1218. Williams & Wilkins, Baltimore, 1995.

Jenike M A, editor: Obsessional disorders. Psychiatr Clin North Am *15*: 743, 1992.

McDougle C J, Gordman W K, Price L H: The pharmacotherapy of obsessive-compulsive disorder. Pharmacopsychiatry *26* (Suppl): 24, 1993.

Wong C M: Obsessive-compulsive spectrum disorders. J Clin Psychiatry *56*: 3, 1995.

10.5 POSTTRAUMATIC STRESS DISORDER AND ACUTE STRESS DISORDER

For patients to be classified as having posttraumatic stress disorder, they must have experienced an emotional stress that was of a magnitude that would be traumatic for almost anyone. Such traumas include combat experience, natural catastrophes, assault, rape, and serious accidents (for example, automobile accidents and building fires). Posttraumatic stress disorder consists of (1) the reexperiencing of the trauma through dreams and waking thoughts, (2) persistent avoidance of reminders of the trauma and numbing of responsiveness to such reminders, and (3) persistent hyperarousal. Common associated symptoms of posttraumatic stress disorder are depression, anxiety, and cognitive difficulties (for example, poor concentration). In the fourth edition of *Diagnostic and Statistical Manual of Mental Disorders* (DSM-IV), the minimum duration of symptoms of posttraumatic stress disorder is one month.

DSM-IV introduces a new diagnosis, acute stress disorder, for patients in whom the symptoms occur within four weeks of the traumatic event and in whom the symptoms last for two days to four weeks.

EPIDEMIOLOGY

The lifetime prevalence of posttraumatic stress disorder is estimated to be from 1 to 3 percent of the general population, although an additional 5 to 15 percent may experience subclinical forms of the disorder. Among high-risk groups whose members experienced traumatic events, the lifetime prevalence rates range from 5 to 75 percent. About 30 percent of Vietnam veterans experienced posttraumatic stress disorder, and an additional 25 percent experienced subclinical forms of the disorder.

Although posttraumatic stress disorder can appear at any age, it is most prevalent in young adults, because of the nature of the precipitating situations. However, children can have posttraumatic stress disorder. The trauma for men is usually combat experience, and the trauma for women is most commonly assault or rape. The disorder is most likely to occur in those who are single, divorced, widowed, economically handicapped, or socially withdrawn.

ETIOLOGY

Stressor

By definition, the stressor is the prime causative factor in the development of posttraumatic stress disorder. But not everyone experiences posttraumatic stress disorder after a traumatic event; although the stressor is necessary, it is not sufficient to cause the disorder. The clinician must also consider individual preexisting biological factors, preexisting psychosocial factors, and events that happened after the trauma. For example, being part of a group who live through a disaster sometimes enables a person to deal with the trauma because others shared the experience. However, survivor guilt sometimes complicates the management of posttraumatic stress disorder.

Recent research on posttraumatic stress disorder has placed greater emphasis on a person's subjective response to trauma than on the severity of the stressor itself. Although posttraumatic stress disorder symptoms were once thought to be directly proportional to the severity of the stressor, empirical studies have proved otherwise. As a result, the growing consensus is that the disorder has a great deal to do with the stressor's subjective meaning to the patient

Even when faced with overwhelming trauma, the majority of people do not experience posttraumatic stress disorder symptoms. Similarly, events that may appear mundane or less than catastrophic to most people may produce posttraumatic stress disorder in some persons because of the subjective meaning of the event. The predisposing vulnerability factors that appear to play primary roles in determining whether the disorder develops include (1) the presence of childhood trauma, (2) borderline, paranoid, dependent, or antisocial personality disorder traits, (3) an inadequate support system, (4) genetic-constitutional vulnerability to psychiatric illness, (5) recent stressful life changes, (6) perception of an external locus of control, rather than an internal one, and (7) recent excessive alcohol intake.

Psychodynamic studies of persons who have survived severe psychic traumas have identified *alexithymia*—the inability to identify or verbalize feeling states—as a common feature. If psychic trauma occurs in childhood, an arrest of emotional development frequently results. If the trauma occurs in adulthood, an emotional regression often occurs. In either case, survivors of trauma usually cannot use internal emotional states as signals and may experience psychosomatic symptoms. They are also incapable of soothing themselves when under stress.

Psychodynamic Factors

The cognitive model of posttraumatic stress disorder posits that affected persons are unable to process or rationalize the trauma that precipitated the disorder. They continue to experience the stress and attempt to avoid the reexperiencing of the stress by avoidance techniques. Consistent with their partial ability to cope cognitively with the event, the patients experience alternating periods of acknowledging the event and blocking it.

The behavioral model of posttraumatic stress disorder indicates that the disorder has two phases in its development. First, the trauma (the unconditioned stimulus) is paired, through classical conditioning, with a conditioned stimulus (physical or mental reminders of the trauma). Second, through instrumental learning, the patient develops a pattern of avoidance of both the conditioned stimulus and the unconditioned stimulus.

The psychoanalytic model of the disorder hypothesizes that the trauma has reactivated a previously quiescent, yet unresolved psychological conflict. The revival of the childhood trauma results in regression and the use of the defense mechanisms of repression, denial, and undoing. The ego relives and thereby tries to master and reduce the anxiety. The patient also receives secondary gains from the external world, the common gains being monetary compensation, increased attention or sympathy, and the satisfaction of dependence needs. Those gains reinforce the disorder and its persistence. A cognitive view of posttraumatic stress disorder is that the brain is trying to process the massive amount of information that the trauma provoked by alternating periods of acknowledging and blocking the event.

Biological Factors

The biological theories regarding posttraumatic stress disorder have developed from both preclinical studies of animal models of stress and from measures of biological variables of clinical populations with posttraumatic stress disorder. Many neurotransmitter systems have been implicated by both sets of data. Preclinical models of learned helplessness, kindling, and sensitization in animals have led to theories regarding norepinephrine, dopamine, endogenous opiate, and benzodiazepine receptors and the hypothalamic-pituitary-adrenal axis. In clinical populations, data have supported hypotheses that the noradrenergic and endogenous opiate systems, as well as the hypothalamic-pituitary-adrenal-axis, are hyperactive in at least some patients with posttraumatic stress disorder.

The other major biological findings are increased activity and responsiveness of the autonomic nervous system, as evidenced by elevated heart rates and blood pressure readings, and abnormal sleep architecture (for example, sleep fragmentation and increased sleep latency). Some researchers have suggested a similarity between posttraumatic stress disorder and two other psychiatric disorders, major depressive disorder and panic disorder.

DIAGNOSIS

The DSM-IV diagnostic criteria for posttraumatic stress disorder allow the clinician to specify whether the disorder is acute

Table 10.5.-1   Diagnostic Criteria for Posttraumatic Stress Disorder

A. The person has been exposed to a traumatic event in which both of the following were present:

  (1) the person experienced, witnessed, or was confronted with an event or events that involved actual or threatened death or serious injury, or a threat to the physical integrity of self or others

  (2) the person's response involved intense fear, helplessness, or horror. **Note:** In children, this may be expressed instead by disorganized or agitated behavior.

B. The traumatic event is persistently reexperienced in one (or more) of the following ways:

  (1) recurrent and intrusive distressing recollections of the event, including images, thoughts, or perceptions. **Note:** In young children, repetitive play may occur in which themes or aspects of the trauma are expressed.

  (2) recurrent distressing dreams of the event. **Note:** In children, there may be frightening dreams without recognizable content.

  (3) acting or feeling as if the traumatic event were recurring (includes a sense of reliving the experience, illusions, hallucinations, and dissociative flashback episodes, including those that occur on awakening or when intoxicated). **Note:** In young children, trauma-specific reenactment may occur.

  (4) intense psychological distress at exposure to internal or external cues that symbolize or resemble an aspect of the traumatic event

  (5) physiological reactivity on exposure to internal or external cues that symbolize or resemble an aspect of the traumatic event

C. Persistent avoidance of stimuli associated with the trauma and numbing of general responsiveness (not present before the trauma), as indicated by three (or more) of the following:

  (1) efforts to avoid thoughts, feelings, or conversations associated with the trauma

  (2) efforts to avoid activities, places, or people that arouse recollections of the trauma

  (3) inability to recall an important aspect of the trauma

  (4) markedly diminished interest or participation in significant activities

  (5) feeling of detachment or estrangement from others

  (6) restricted range of affect (e.g., unable to have loving feelings)

  (7) sense of a foreshortened future (e.g., does not expect to have a career, marriage, children, or a normal life span)

D. Persistent symptoms of increased arousal (not present before the trauma), as indicated by two (or more) of the following:

  (1) difficulty falling or staying asleep

  (2) irritability or outbursts of anger

  (3) difficulty concentrating

  (4) hypervigilance

  (5) exaggerated startle response

E. Duration of the disturbance (symptoms in criteria B, C, and D) is more than 1 month.

F. The disturbance causes clinically significant distress or impairment in social, occupational, or other important areas of functioning.

Table from DSM-IV, *Diagnostic and Statistical Manual of Mental Disorders*, ed 4. Copyright American Psychiatric Association, Washington, 1994. Used with permission.

Table 10.5-2.   Diagnostic Criteria for Acute Stress Disorder

A. The person has been exposed to a traumatic event in which both of the following were present:

  (1) the person experienced, witnessed, or was confronted with an event or events that involved actual or threatened death or serious injury, or a threat to the physical integrity of self or others

  (2) the person's response involved intense fear, helplessness, or horror

B. Either while experiencing or after experiencing the distressing event, the individual has three (or more) of the following dissociative symptoms:

  (1) a subjective sense of numbing, detachment, or absence of emotional responsiveness

  (2) a reduction in awareness of his or her surroundings (e.g., "being in a daze")

  (3) derealization

  (4) depersonalization

  (5) dissociative amnesia (i.e., inability to recall an important aspect of the trauma)

C. The traumatic event is persistently reexperienced in at least one of the following ways: recurrent images, thoughts, dreams, illusions, flashback episodes, or a sense of reliving the experience; or distress on exposure to reminders of the traumatic event.

D. Marked avoidance of stimuli that arouse recollections of the trauma (e.g., thoughts, feelings, conversations, activities, places, people).

E. Marked symptoms of anxiety or increased arousal (e.g., difficulty sleeping, irritability, poor concentration, hypervigilance, exaggerated startle response, motor restlessness).

F. The disturbance causes clinically significant distress or impairment in social, occupational, or other important areas of functioning or impairs the individual's ability to pursue some necessary task, such as obtaining necessary assistance or mobilizing personal resources by telling family members about the traumatic experience.

G. The disturbance lasts for a minimum of 2 days and a maximum of 4 weeks and occurs within 4 weeks of the traumatic event.

H. The disturbance is not due to the direct physiological effects of a substance (e.g., a drug of abuse, a medication) or a general medical condition, is not better accounted for by brief psychotic disorder, and is not merely an exacerbation of a preexisting Axis I or Axis II disorder.

Table from DSM-IV, *Diagnostic and Statistical Manual of Mental Disorders*, ed 4. Copyright American Psychiatric Association, Washington, 1994. Used with permission.

CLINICAL FEATURES

The principal clinical features of posttraumatic stress disorder are the painful reexperiencing of the event, a pattern of avoidance and emotional numbing, and fairly constant hyperarousal. The disorder may not develop until months or even years after the event. The mental status examination often reveals feelings of guilt, rejection, and humiliation. The patient may also describe dissociative states and panic attacks. Illusions and hallucinations may be present. Cognitive testing may reveal that the patient has impairments of memory and attention.

Associated symptoms can include aggression, violence, poor impulse control, depression, and substance-related disorders. The patients have elevated Sc, D, F, and Ps scores on the Minnesota Multiphasic Personality Inventory (MMPI), and the Rorschach test findings often include aggressive and violent material.

DIFFERENTIAL DIAGNOSIS

A major consideration in the diagnosis of posttraumatic stress disorder is the possibility that the patient also incurred a

(if the symptoms have lasted less than three months) or chronic (if the symptoms have lasted three months or more) (Table 10.5–1). DSM-IV also allows the clinician to specify that the disorder was with delayed onset if the onset of the symptoms was six months or more after the stressful event. DSM-IV specifies that the symptoms of reexperiencing, avoidance, and hyperarousal have lasted more than one month. For patients in whom symptoms have been present less than one month, the appropriate diagnosis may be acute stress disorder (Table 10.5–2).

head injury during the trauma. Other organic considerations that can both cause and exacerbate the symptoms are epilepsy, alcohol use disorders, and other substance-related disorders. Acute intoxication or withdrawal from some substances may also present a clinical picture that is difficult to distinguish from posttraumatic stress disorder until the effects of the substance have worn off.

Posttraumatic stress disorder is commonly misdiagnosed as some other mental disorder, resulting in inappropriate treatment of the condition. The clinician must consider posttraumatic stress disorder in patients who have pain disorder, substance abuse, other anxiety disorders, and mood disorders. In general, posttraumatic stress disorder can be distinguished from other mental disorders by interviewing the patient regarding previous traumatic experiences and by the nature of the current symptoms. Borderline personality disorder, dissociative disorders, factitious disorders, and malingering should also be considered. Borderline personality disorder can be difficult to distinguish from posttraumatic stress disorder. The two disorders may coexist or even may be causally related. Patients with dissociative disorders do not usually have the degree of avoidance behavior, the autonomic hyperarousal, or the history of trauma that patients with posttraumatic stress disorder report. Partly because of the publicity that posttraumatic stress disorder has received in the popular press, clinicians should also consider the possibility of a factitious disorder and malingering.

COURSE AND PROGNOSIS

Posttraumatic stress disorder usually develops some time after the trauma. The delay can be as short as one week or as long as 30 years. Symptoms can fluctuate over time and may be most intense during periods of stress. About 30 percent of patients recover completely, 40 percent continue to have mild symptoms, 20 percent continue to have moderate symptoms, and 10 percent remain unchanged or become worse. A good prognosis is predicted by a rapid onset of the symptoms, the short duration of the symptoms (less than six months), good premorbid functioning, strong social supports, and the absence of other psychiatric, medical, or substance-related disorders.

In general, the very young and the very old have more difficulty with traumatic events than do those in midlife. For example, about 80 percent of young children who sustain a burn injury show symptoms of posttraumatic stress disorder one or two years after the initial injury; only 30 percent of adults who suffer such an injury have a posttraumatic stress disorder after one year. Presumably, young children do not yet have adequate coping mechanisms to deal with the physical and emotional insults of the trauma. Likewise, elderly people, when compared with younger adults, are likely to have more rigid coping mechanisms and to be less able to muster a flexible approach to dealing with the effects of the trauma. Furthermore, the effects of the trauma may be exacerbated by physical disabilities characteristics of late life, particularly disabilities of the nervous system and the cardiovascular system such as reduced cerebral blood flow, failing vision, palpitations, and arrhythmias. Preexisting psychiatric disability, whether a personality disorder or a more serious condition, also increases the effects of particular stressors. The availability of social supports may also influence the development, the severity, and the duration of posttraumatic stress disorder. In general, patients who have a good network of social support are not likely to have the disorder or to experience it in its severe forms.

TREATMENT

When a clinician is faced with a patient who has experienced a significant trauma, the major approaches are support, encouragement to discuss the event, and education regarding a variety of coping mechanisms (for example, relaxation). The use of sedatives and hypnotics can also be helpful. When a clinician is faced with a patient who experienced a traumatic event in the past and now has posttraumatic stress disorder, the emphasis should be on education regarding the disorder and its treatment, both pharmacological and psychotherapeutic. Additional support for the patient and the family can be obtained through local and national support groups for patients with posttraumatic stress disorder.

Pharmacotherapy

The efficacy of imipramine (Tofranil) and amitriptyline (Elavil), two tricyclic drugs, in the treatment of posttraumatic stress disorder are supported by a number of well-controlled clinical trials. Although some trials of the two drugs have had negative findings, most of those trials had serious design flaws, including too short a duration. Dosages of imipramine and amitriptyline should be the same as those used to treat depressive disorders, and the minimum length of an adequate trial should be eight weeks. Patients who respond well should probably continue the pharmacotherapy for at least one year before an attempt is made to withdraw the drug. Some studies indicate that pharmacotherapy is more effective in treating the depression, anxiety, and hyperarousal than in treating the avoidance, denial, and emotional numbing.

Other drugs that may be useful in the treatment of posttraumatic stress disorder include the serotonin-specific reuptake inhibitors (SSRIs), the monoamine oxidase inhibitors (MAOIs), and the anticonvulsants (for example, carbamazepine [Tegretol], valproate [Depakene]). Clonidine (Catapres) and propranolol (Inderal) are suggested by the theories regarding noradrenergic hyperactivity in the disorder. Although some anecdotal reports point to the effectiveness of alprazolam (Xanax) in posttraumatic stress disorder, the use of that drug is complicated by the high association of substance-related disorders in patients with the disorder and by the emergence of withdrawal symptoms on discontinuation of the drug. Almost no positive data concern the use of antipsychotic drugs in the disorder, so the use of those drugs—for example, haloperidol (Haldol)—should be avoided except perhaps for the short-term control of severe aggression and agitation.

Psychotherapy

Psychodynamic psychotherapy may be useful in the treatment of many patients with posttraumatic stress disorder. In some cases, reconstruction of the traumatic events with associated abreaction and catharsis may be therapeutic. However, psychotherapy must be individualized, because some patients are overwhelmed by reexperiencing the traumas.

Psychotherapeutic interventions for posttraumatic stress disorder include behavior therapy, cognitive therapy, and hypnosis. Many clinicians advocate time-limited psychotherapy for the victims of trauma. Such therapy usually takes a cognitive approach and also provides support and security. The short-term nature of the psychotherapy minimizes the risk of dependence and chronicity. Issues of suspicion, paranoia, and trust often adversely affect compliance. The therapist should overcome patients' denial of the traumatic event, encourage them to relax, and remove them from the source of the stress. The patient should be encouraged to sleep, using medication if necessary. Support from the environment (such as friends and relatives) should be provided. The patient should be encouraged to review and abreact emotional feelings associated with the traumatic event and plan for future recovery.

Psychotherapy after a traumatic event should follow a model of crisis intervention with support, education, and the development of coping mechanisms and acceptance of the event. When posttraumatic stress disorder has developed, two major psychotherapeutic approaches can be taken. The first is exposure to the traumatic event through imaginal techniques or in vivo exposure. The exposures can be intense, as in implosive therapy, or graded, as in systematic desensitization. The second approach is to teach the patient methods of stress management, including relaxation techniques and cognitive approaches to coping with stress. Some preliminary data indicate that, although stress management techniques are effective more rapidly than are exposure techniques, the results of exposure techniques are more longlasting.

In addition to individual therapy techniques, group therapy and family therapy have been reported to be effective in cases of posttraumatic stress disorder. The advantages of group therapy include the sharing of multiple traumatic experiences and support from other group members. Group therapy has been particularly successful with Vietnam veterans. Family therapy often helps sustain a marriage through periods of exacerbated symptoms. Hospitalization may be necessary when symptoms are particularly severe or when there is a risk of suicide or other violence.

References

Boudewyns P A: Posttraumatic stress disorder: Conceptualization and treatment. Prog Behav Modif 30: 165, 1996.
Bremmer J D, Scott T M, Delaney R C, Southwick S M, Mason J W, Johnson D R, Innis R B, McCarthy G, Charney D S: Deficits in short-term memory in posttraumatic stress disorder. Am J Psychiatry 150: 1015, 1993.
Bremmer J D, Steinberg M, Southwick S M, Johnson D R, Charney D S: Use the structured clinical interview for DSM-IV dissociative disorders for systematic assessment of dissociative symptoms in posttraumatic stress disorder. Am J Psychiatry 150: 1011, 1993.
Davidson J R T: Posttraumatic stress disorder and acute stress disorder. In Comprehensive Textbook of Psychiatry, ed 6, H I Kaplan, B J Sadock, editors, p 1227. Williams & Wilkins, Baltimore, 1995.
Davidson J R T, Kudler H S, Saunders W B, Erickson L, Smith R D, Stein R M, Lipper S, Hammett E B, Mahorney S L, Cavenar J O Jr: Predicting response to amitriptyline in posttraumatic stress disorder. Am J Psychiatry 150: 1024, 1993.
Gabbard G O: Psychodynamic Psychiatry in Clinical Practice: The DSM-IV Edition. American Psychiatric Press, Washington, 1994.

10.6 GENERALIZED ANXIETY DISORDER

Generalized anxiety disorder is defined in the *Diagnostic and Statistical Manual of Mental Disorders* (DSM-IV) as excessive and pervasive worry, accompanied by a variety of somatic symptoms, that causes significant impairment in social or occupational functioning or marked distress in the patient.

EPIDEMIOLOGY

Generalized anxiety disorder is a common condition. Reasonable estimates for the one-year prevalence of generalized anxiety range from 3 to 8 percent. Generalized anxiety disorder is probably the disorder most often found with the coexisting mental disorder, usually another anxiety disorder or a mood disorder. Perhaps 50 percent of patients with generalized anxiety disorder have another mental disorder.

The ratio of women to men is about 2 to 1, but the ratio of women to men who are receiving inpatient treatment for the disorder is about 1 to 1. The age of onset is difficult to specify, since most patients with the disorder report that they have been anxious for as long as they can remember. Patients usually come to a clinician's attention in their 20s, although the first contact with a clinician can occur at virtually any age. Only a third of patients who have generalized anxiety disorder seek psychiatric treatment. Many patients go to general practitioners, internists, cardiologists, pulmonary specialists, or gastroenterologists, seeking treatment for the somatic component of the disorder.

ETIOLOGY

As with most mental disorders, the cause of generalized anxiety disorder is not known. As currently defined, generalized anxiety disorder probably affects a heterogeneous group of patients. Perhaps because a certain degree of anxiety is normal and adaptive, differentiating normal anxiety from pathological anxiety and differentiating biological causative factors from psychosocial factors are difficult. Biological and psychological factors probably work together.

Biological Factors

The therapeutic efficacies of benzodiazepines and the azaspirodecanediones—for example, buspirone (BuSpar)—have focused biological research efforts on the γ-aminobutyric acid (GABA) and serotonin (5-hydroxytryptamine [5-HT]) neurotransmitter systems. Benzodiazepines (which are benzodiazepine receptor agonists) are known to reduce anxiety, whereas flumazenil (Romazicon) (a benzodiazepine receptor antagonist) and the β-carbolines (benzodiazepine receptor reverse agonists) are known to induce anxiety. Although no convincing data indicate that the benzodiazepine receptors are abnormal in patients with generalized anxiety disorder, some researchers have focused on the occipital lobe, which has the highest concentrations of benzodiazepine receptors in the brain. Other brain areas that have been hypothesized to be involved in generalized anxiety disorder are the basal ganglia, the limbic system, and the frontal cortex. Because buspirone is an agonist at the 5-HT_{1A} receptor, several research groups are focusing on the hypothesis that the regulation of the serotonergic system in generalized anxiety disorder is abnormal. Other neurotransmitter systems that have been the subject of research in generalized anxiety disorder include the norepinephrine, glutamate, and cholecystokinin neurotransmitter systems. Some evidence indicates that the patients with generalized anxiety disorder may have a subsensitivity of their α_2-adrenergic receptors, as indicated by a blunted release of growth hormone after clonidine (Catapres) infusion.

Only a limited number of brain-imaging studies of patients with generalized anxiety disorder have been conducted. One positron emission tomography (PET) study reported a lower metabolic rate in basal ganglia and white matter in generalized anxiety disorder patients than in normal controls. A few genetic studies have also been conducted in the field. One study found that a genetic relation may exist between generalized anxiety disorder and major depressive disorder in women. Another study found a distinct but difficult-to-quantitate genetic component in generalized anxiety disorder. About 25 percent of first-degree relatives of patients with generalized anxiety disorder are also affected. Male relatives are likely to have an alcohol use disorder. Some twin studies report a concordance rate of 50 percent in monozygotic twins and 15 percent in dizygotic twins.

A variety of electroencephalogram (EEG) abnormalities have been noted in alpha rhythm and evoked potentials. Sleep EEG studies have reported increased sleep discontinuity, decreased delta sleep, decreased stage 1 sleep, and reduced rapid eye movement (REM) sleep. Those changes in sleep architecture are different from the changes seen in depressive disorders.

Psychosocial Factors

The two major schools of thought regarding the psychosocial factors leading to the development of generalized anxiety disorder are the cognitive-behavioral school and the psychoanalytic school. The cognitive-behavioral school hypothesizes that patients with generalized anxiety disorder are responding to incorrectly and inaccurately perceived dangers. The inaccuracy is generated by selective attention to negative details in the environment, by distortions in information processing, and by an overly negative view of one's own ability to cope. The psychoanalytic school hypothesizes that anxiety is a symptom of unresolved unconscious conflicts. That psychological theory of anxiety was first presented by Sigmund Freud in 1909 with his description of Little Hans; before then, Freud had conceptualized anxiety as having a physiological basis.

A hierarchy of anxieties are related to various developmental levels. At the most primitive level, anxiety may relate to the fear of annihilation or of fusion with another person. At a more mature level of development, anxiety is related to separation from a love object. At a still more mature level, the anxiety is connected to the loss of love from an important object. Castration anxiety is related to the oedipal phase of development and is considered one of the highest levels of anxiety. Superego anxiety, the fear of disappointing one's own ideals and values (derived from internalized parents), is the most mature form of anxiety.

DIAGNOSIS

The DSM-IV diagnostic criteria (Table 10.6–1) includes some modifications to make them easier to use and to help the clinician differentiate among generalized anxiety disorder, normal anxiety, and other mental disorders. The distinction between generalized anxiety disorder and normal anxiety is emphasized by the use of the words "excessive" and "difficult to control" in the criteria and by the specification that the symptoms cause significant impairment or distress. The distinction between generalized anxiety disorder and other mental disorders is aided in DSM-IV by examples of distinguishing features in criterion D.

Table 10.6–1. Diagnostic Criteria for Generalized Anxiety Disorder

A. Excessive anxiety and worry (apprehensive expectation), occurring more days than not for at least 6 months, about a number of events or activities (such as work or school performance).

B. The person finds it difficult to control the worry.

C. The anxiety and worry are associated with three (or more) of the following six symptoms (with at least some symptoms present for more days than not for the past 6 months). **Note:** Only one item is required in children.

   (1) restlessness or feeling keyed up or on edge
   (2) being easily fatigued
   (3) difficulty concentrating or mind going blank
   (4) irritability
   (5) muscle tension
   (6) sleep disturbance (difficulty falling or staying asleep, or restless unsatisfying sleep)

D. The focus of the anxiety and worry is not confined to features of an Axis I disorder, e.g., the anxiety or worry is not about having a panic attack (as in panic disorder), being embarrassed in public (as in social phobia), being contaminated (as in obsessive-compulsive disorder), being away from home or close relatives (as in separation anxiety disorder), gaining weight (as in anorexia nervosa), having multiple physical complaints (as in somatization disorder), or having a serious illness (as in hypochondriasis), and the anxiety and worry do not occur exclusively during posttraumatic stress disorder.

E. The anxiety, worry, or physical symptoms cause clinically significant distress or impairment in social, occupational, or other important areas of functioning.

F. The disturbance is not due to the direct physiological effects of a substance (e.g., a drug of abuse, a medication) or a general medical condition (e.g., hyperthyroidism) and does not occur exclusively during a mood disorder, a psychotic disorder, or a pervasive developmental disorder.

Table from DSM-IV, *Diagnostic and Statistical Manual of Mental Disorders*, ed 4. Copyright American Psychiatric Association, Washington, 1994. Used with permission.

CLINICAL FEATURES

The primary symptoms of generalized anxiety disorder are anxiety, motor tension, autonomic hyperactivity, and cognitive vigilance. The anxiety is excessive and interferes with other aspects of the patient's life. The motor tension is most commonly manifested as shakiness, restlessness, and headaches. The autonomic hyperactivity is commonly manifested by shortness of breath, excessive sweating, palpitations, and various gastrointestinal symptoms. The cognitive vigilance is evidenced by the patient's irritability and the ease with which the patient is startled.

Most commonly, patients with generalized anxiety disorder seek out a general practitioner or internist for help with some somatic symptom. Alternatively, the patients go to a specialist for a specific symptom—for example, chronic diarrhea. A specific nonpsychiatric medical disorder is rarely found, and patients vary in their doctor-seeking behavior. Some patients accept a diagnosis of generalized anxiety disorder and the appropriate treatment; others seek additional medical consultations for their problems.

DIFFERENTIAL DIAGNOSIS

The differential diagnosis of generalized anxiety disorder includes all the medical disorders that may cause anxiety (see

Table 10.1–2). The medical workup should include the standard blood chemistry tests, an electrocardiogram, and thyroid function tests. The clinician must rule out caffeine intoxication, stimulant abuse, alcohol withdrawal, and sedative, hypnotic, or anxiolytic withdrawal. The mental status examination and the history should explore the diagnostic possibilities of panic disorder, phobias, and obsessive-compulsive disorder. In general, patients with panic disorder seek treatment earlier, are more disabled by their disorder, have had a sudden onset of symptoms, and are less troubled by their somatic symptoms than are patients with generalized anxiety disorder. Distinguishing generalized anxiety disorder from major depressive disorder and dysthymic disorder can be difficult; in fact, the disorders frequently coexist. Other diagnostic possibilities are adjustment disorder with anxiety, hypochondriasis, adult attention-deficit/hyperactivity disorder, somatization disorder, and personality disorders.

COURSE AND PROGNOSIS

Because of the high incidence of comorbid mental disorders in patients with generalized anxiety disorder, the clinical course and the prognosis of the disorder is difficult to predict. Nonetheless, some data indicate that life events are associated with the onset of generalized anxiety disorder: the occurrence of several negative life events greatly increases the likelihood that the disorder will develop. By definition, generalized anxiety disorder is a chronic condition that may well be lifelong. As many as 25 percent of the patients eventually experience panic disorder. An additional high percentage of patients are likely to have major depressive disorder.

TREATMENT

The most effective treatment of patients with generalized anxiety disorder is probably one that combines psychotherapeutic, pharmacotherapeutic, and supportive approaches. The treatment may take a significant amount of time for the involved clinician, regardless of whether the clinician is a psychiatrist, a family practitioner, or another specialist.

Psychotherapy

The major psychotherapeutic approaches to generalized anxiety disorder are cognitive-behavioral, supportive, and insight-oriented. Data are still limited on the relative merits of those approaches, although the most sophisticated studies have been with the cognitive-behavioral techniques, which seem to have both short-term and long-term efficacy. Cognitive approaches directly address the patient's hypothesized cognitive distortions, and behavioral approaches address the somatic symptoms directly. The major techniques used in the behavioral approaches are relaxation and biofeedback. Some preliminary data indicate that the combination of cognitive and behavioral approaches is more effective than either technique used alone. Supportive therapy offers patients reassurance and comfort, although its long-term efficacy is doubtful. Insight-oriented psychotherapy focuses on uncovering unconscious conflicts and identifying ego strengths. The efficacy of insight-oriented psychotherapy for generalized anxiety disorder is reported in many anecdotal case reports, but large controlled studies are lacking.

Most patients experience a marked lessening of anxiety when given the opportunity to discuss their difficulties with a concerned and sympathetic physician. If the clinician discovers external situations that are anxiety-provoking, the clinician may be able—alone with the help of the patients or their families—to change the environment and thus reduce the stressful pressures. A reduction in symptoms often allows the patients to function effectively in their daily work and relationships, which provides new rewards and gratification that are in themselves therapeutic.

The psychoanalytic perspective is that in certain cases anxiety is a signal of unconscious turmoil that deserves investigation. The anxiety can be normal, adaptive, maladaptive, too intense, or too mild, depending on the circumstances. Anxiety appears in numerous situations over the course of the life cycle; in many cases, symptom relief is not the most appropriate course of action.

For patients who are psychologically minded and motivated to understand the sources of their anxiety, psychotherapy may be the treatment of choice. Psychodynamic therapy proceeds with the assumption that anxiety may increase with effective treatment. The goal of the dynamic approach may be to increase the patient's *anxiety tolerance* (defined as a capacity to experience anxiety without having to discharge it), rather than to eliminate anxiety. Empirical research indicates that many patients for whom psychotherapeutic treatment is successful may continue to experience anxiety after termination of the psychotherapy. However, their increased ego mastery allows them to use the anxiety symptoms as a signal to reflect on internal struggles and to expand their insight and understanding. A psychodynamic approach to the patient with generalized anxiety disorder involves a search for the patient's underlying fear.

Pharmacotherapy

The decision to prescribe an anxiolytic to patients with generalized anxiety disorder should rarely be made on the first visit. Because of the long-term nature of the disorder, a treatment plan must be carefully thought out. The two major drugs to be considered for the treatment of generalized anxiety disorder are buspirone and the benzodiazepines. Other drugs that may be useful are the tricyclic drugs—for example, imipramine (Tofranil)—antihistamines, and the β-adrenergic receptor antagonists—for example, propranolol (Inderal).

Although drug treatment of generalized anxiety disorder is sometimes seen as a 6- to 12-month treatment, some evidence indicates that treatment should be long-term, perhaps lifelong. About 25 percent of patients relapse in the first month after the discontinuation of therapy, and 60 to 80 percent relapse over the course of the next year. Although some patients become dependent on the benzodiazepines, no tolerance develops to the therapeutic effects of either the benzodiazepines or buspirone.

BENZODIAZEPINES

Benzodiazepines have been the drugs of choice for generalized anxiety disorder. Benzodiazepines can be prescribed on an as-needed basis, so that patients take a rapidly acting benzodiazepine when they feel particularly anxious. The alternative approach is to prescribe benzodiazepines for a limited period, during which psychosocial therapeutic approaches are implemented.

Several problems are associated with the use of benzodiazepines in generalized anxiety disorder. About 25 to 30 percent of all patients fail to respond, and tolerance and dependence may occur. Some patients also experience impaired alertness while taking the drugs and are, therefore, at risk for accidents involving automobiles and machinery.

The clinical decision to initiate treatment with a benzodiazepine should be a considered and specific one. The patient's diagnosis, the specific target symptoms, and the duration of treatment—all should be defined, and the information should be shared with the patient. Treatment for most anxiety conditions lasts for two to six weeks, followed by one or two weeks of tapering the drug before it is discontinued. The most common clinical mistake with benzodiazepine treatment is to decide passively to continue treatment indefinitely.

For the treatment of anxiety, it is usual to begin a drug at the low end of its therapeutic range and to increase the dosage to achieve a therapeutic response. The use of a benzodiazepine with an intermediate half-life (8 to 15 hours) is likely to avoid some of the adverse effects associated with the use of benzodiazepines with long half-lives. The use of divided doses prevents the development of adverse effects associated with high peak plasma levels. The improvement produced by benzodiazepines may go beyond a simple antianxiety effect. For example, the drugs may cause the patient to regard various occurrences in a positive light. The drugs may also have a mild disinhibiting action, similar to that observed after modest amounts of alcohol.

BUSPIRONE

Buspirone is most likely effective in 60 to 80 percent of patients with generalized anxiety disorder. Data indicate that buspirone is more effective in reducing the cognitive symptoms of generalized anxiety disorder than in reducing the somatic symptoms. Evidence also indicates that patients who have previously been treated with benzodiazepines are not likely to respond to treatment with buspirone. The lack of response may be due to the absence, with buspirone treatment, of some of the nonanxiolytic effects of benzodiazepines (such as muscle relaxation and the additional sense of well-being). Nonetheless,

the improved benefit-risk ratio, the lack of cognitive and psychomotor effects, and the absence of withdrawal symptoms may make buspirone the first-line drug in the treatment of generalized anxiety disorder. The major disadvantage of buspirone is that its effects take two to three weeks to become evident, in contrast to the almost immediate anxiolytic effects of the benzodiazepines. Buspirone is not an effective treatment for benzodiazepine withdrawal.

OTHER DRUGS

If treatment with buspirone or a benzodiazepine is not effective or not completely effective, treatment with a tricyclic drug or a β-adrenergic antagonist can be considered. The tricyclic drugs have been proved to be effective in the treatment of anxiety. The β-adrenergic drugs are limited in their effectiveness to the treatment of the peripheral symptoms of anxiety (for example, palpitations and tremor). Another alternative is to use combinations of drugs, such as benzodiazepines and buspirone or one of those drugs with a tricyclic drug or a β-adrenergic receptor antagonist.

References

Borkovec T D, Roemer L: Perceived functions of worry among generalized anxiety disorder subjects: distraction from more emotionally distressing topics? J Behav Ther Exp Psychiatry 26: 25, 1995.

Butler G: Predicting outcome after treatment for generalized anxiety disorder. Behav Res Ther 31: 211, 1993.

Gabbard G O: Psychodynamic psychiatry in the "decade of the brain." Am J Psychiatry 149: 991, 1992.

Massion A O, Warshaw M G, Keller M B: Quality of life and psychiatric morbidity in panic disorder and generalized anxiety disorder. Am J Psychiatry 150: 600, 1993.

Mathews A, Mogg K, Kentish J, Eysenck M: Effect of psychological treatment on cognitive bias in generalized anxiety disorder. Behav Res Ther 33: 293, 1995.

Noyes R Jr, Woodman C, Garvey M J, Cook B L, Suelzer M, Clancy J, Anderson D J: Generalized anxiety disorder vs panic disorder: Distinguishing characteristics and patterns of comorbidity. J Nerv Ment Dis 180: 369, 1992.

Papp L A, Gorman J M: Generalized anxiety disorder. In Comprehensive Textbook of Psychiatry, ed 6, H I Kaplan, B J Sadock, editors, p 1236. Williams & Wilkins, Baltimore, 1995.

Rickels K, Schweizer E: The treatment of generalized anxiety disorder in patients with depression symptomatology. J Clin Psychiatry 54 (1, Suppl): 20, 1993.

11/ Somatoform Disorders

The somatoform disorders are a group of disorders that include physical symptoms (for example, pain, nausea, and dizziness) for which an adequate explanation cannot be found. The somatic symptoms and complaints are serious enough to cause the patient significant emotional distress or impairment in the patient's ability to function in social and occupational roles. A diagnosis of a somatoform disorder reflects the clinician's assessment that psychological factors are a large contributor to the symptoms' onset, severity, and duration. Somatoform disorders are not the result of conscious malingering or factitious disorders.

SOMATIZATION DISORDER

Somatization disorder is characterized by many somatic symptoms that cannot be explained adequately on the basis of physical and laboratory examinations. Somatization disorder is distinguished from other somatoform disorders because of the multiplicity of the complaints and the multiple organ systems (for example, gastrointestinal and neurological) that are affected. The disorder is chronic (with symptoms present for several years and beginning before age 30) and is associated with significant psychological distress, impairment in social and occupational functioning, and excessive medical help-seeking behavior.

Epidemiology

The lifetime prevalence of somatization disorder in the general population is estimated to be 0.1 or 0.2 percent, although several research groups believe that the actual figure may be closer to 0.5 percent. Women with somatization disorder outnumber men by 5 to 20 times, although the highest estimates may be due to the early tendency not to diagnose somatization disorder in male patients. Nevertheless, with a 5-to-1 female-to-male ratio, the lifetime prevalence of somatization disorder among women in the general population may be 1 or 2 percent; it is not an uncommon disorder. Among patients in the offices of general practitioners and family practitioners, as many as 5 to 10 percent of patients may meet the diagnostic criteria for somatization disorder. The disorder is inversely related to social position, occurring most often among little-educated and poor patients. Somatization disorder is defined as beginning before age 30; it most often begins during a person's teens.

Etiology

PSYCHOSOCIAL FACTORS

The cause of somatization disorder is unknown. Psychosocial formulations of the cause involve interpretations of the symptoms as a type of social communication, the result of which is to avoid obligations (for example, going to a job one does not like), to express emotions (for example, anger at one's spouse), or to symbolize a feeling or a belief (for example, a pain in one's guts). Strict psychoanalytic interpretations of symptoms rest on the hypothesis that the symptoms are substitutions for repressed instinctual impulses.

A behavioral perspective on somatization disorder emphasizes that parental teaching, parental example, and ethnic mores may teach some children to somatize more than do others. In addition, some patients with somatization disorder come from unstable homes and have been physically abused. Social, cultural, and ethnic factors may also be involved in the development of symptoms in somatization disorder.

BIOLOGICAL FACTORS

Some studies point to a neuropsychological basis for somatization disorder. Those studies propose that the patients have characteristic attention and cognitive impairments that result in the faulty perception and assessment of somatosensory inputs. The reported impairments include excessive distractibility, inability to habituate to repetitive stimuli, the grouping of cognitive constructs on an impressionistic basis, partial and circumstantial associations, and lack of selectivity, as indicated in some studies of evoked potentials. A limited number of brain-imaging studies have reported decreased metabolism in the frontal lobes and in the nondominant hemisphere.

One new area of basic neuroscience research that may be relevant to somatization disorder and other somatoform disorders concerns the cytokines. Cytokines are messenger molecules that the immune system uses to communicate within itself and to communicate with the nervous system, including the brain. Examples of cytokines are interleukins, tumor necrosis factor, and interferons. Some preliminary experiments indicate that the cytokines may help cause some of the nonspecific symptoms of disease, especially infections, such as hypersomnia, anorexia, fatigue, and depression. Although no data yet support the hypothesis, abnormal regulation of the cytokine system may result in some of the symptoms seen in somatoform disorders.

Diagnosis

For the diagnosis of somatoform disorder, the fourth edition of *Diagnostic and Statistical Manual of Mental Disorders* (DSM-IV) requires the onset of the symptoms before age 30 (Table 11–1). During the course of the disorder, the patient must have complained of at least four pain symptoms, two gastrointestinal symptoms, one sexual symptom, and one pseudoneurological symptom, none of which is completely explained by physical or laboratory examinations.

Clinical Features

Patients with somatization disorder have many somatic complaints and long, complicated medical histories. Nausea and vomiting (other than during pregnancy), difficulty in swallowing, pain in the arms and the legs, shortness of breath unrelated to exertion, amnesia, and complications of pregnancy and menstruation are among the most common symptoms. The belief that one has been sickly most of one's life is also common.

Psychological distress and interpersonal problems are prominent; anxiety and depression are the most prevalent psychiatric conditions. Suicide threats are common, but actual suicide is rare. If suicide does occur, it is often associated with substance

Table 11-1.   Diagnostic Criteria for Somatization Disorder

A. A history of many physical complaints beginning before age 30 years that occur over a period of several years and result in treatment being sought or significant impairment in social, occupational, or other important areas of functioning.

B. Each of the following criteria must have been met, with individual symptoms occuring at any time during the course of the disturbance:

   (1) *four pain symptoms:* a history of pain related to at least four differenct sites or functions (e.g., head, abdomen, back, joints, extremities, chest, rectum, during menstruation, during sexual intercourse, or during urination)

   (2) *two gastrointestinal symptoms:* a history of at least two gastrointestinal symptoms other than pain (e.g., nausea, bloating, vomiting other than during pregnancy, diarrhea, or intolerance of several different foods)

   (3) *one sexual symptom:* a history of at least one sexual or reproductive symptom other than pain (e.g., sexual indifference, erectile or ejaculatory dysfunction, irregular menses, excessive menstrual bleeding, vomiting throughout pregnancy)

   (4) *One pseudoneurological symptom:* a history of at least one symptom or deficit suggesting a neurological condition not limited to pain (conversion symptoms such as impaired coordination or balance, paralysis or localized weakness, difficulty swallowing or lump in throat, aphonia, urinary retention, hallucinations, loss of touch or pain sensation, double vision, blindness, deafness, seizures; dissociative symptoms such as amnesia; or loss of consciousness other than fainting)

C. Either (1) or (2):

   (1) after appropriate investigation, each of the symptoms in criterion B cannot be fully explained by a known general medical condition or the direct effects of a substance (e.g., a drug of abuse, a medication)

   (2) when there is a related general medical condition, the physical complaints or resulting social or occupational impairment are in excess of what would be expected from the history, physical examination, or laboratory findings

D. The symptoms are not intentionally produced or feigned (as in factitious disorder or malingering).

Table from DSM-IV, *Diagnostic and Statistical Manual of Mental Disorders*, ed 4. Copyright American Psychiatric Association, Washington, 1994. Used with permission.

abuse. The patients' medical histories are often circumstantial, vague, imprecise, inconsistent, and disorganized. The patients classically but not always describe their complaints in a dramatic, emotional, and exaggerated fashion, with vivid and colorful language. Such patients may confuse temporal sequences and cannot clearly distinguish current symptoms from past symptoms. Female patients with somatization disorder may dress in an exhibitionistic manner. The patients may be perceived as dependent, self-centered, hungry for admiration or praise, and manipulative.

Somatization disorder is commonly associated with other mental disorders, including major depressive disorder, personality disorders, substance-related disorders, generalized anxiety disorder, and phobias. The combination of those disorders and the chronic symptoms result in an increased incidence of martial, occupational, and social problems.

Differential Diagnosis

The clinician must always rule out nonpsychiatric medical conditions that may explain the patient's symptoms. A number of medical disorders often present with nonspecific, transient abnormalities in the same age group. Those medical disorders include multiple sclerosis, myasthenia gravis, systemic lupus erythematosus, acquired immune deficiency syndrome (AIDS), acute intermittent porphyria, hyperparathyroidism, hyperthyroidism, and chronic systemic infections. The onset of multiple somatic symptoms in patients over 40 should be presumed to be caused by a nonpsychiatric medical condition until an exhaustive medical workup has been completed.

Many mental disorders are considered in the differential diagnosis, which is made complicated by the observation that at least 50 percent of patients with somatization disorder have a coexisting mental disorder. Major depressive disorder, generalized anxiety disorder, and schizophrenia may all present with an initial complaint that focuses on somatic symptoms. In all those disorders, however, the symptoms of depression, anxiety, or psychosis eventually predominate over the somatic complaints. Although patients with panic disorder may complain of many somatic symptoms related to their panic attacks, those patients are not bothered by somatic symptoms in between panic attacks.

Course and Prognosis

Somatization disorder is a chronic and often debilitating disorder. By definition, the symptoms should have begun before age 30 and been present for several years. Episodes of increased symptom severity and the development of new symptoms are thought to last six to nine months and may be separated by less symptomatic periods lasting 9 to 12 months. Rarely, however, does a patient with somatization disorder go for more than a year without seeking some medical attention. There is often an association between periods of increased or new stress and the exacerbation of somatic symptoms.

Treatment

Somatization disorder patients are best treated when they have a single identified physician as the primary caretaker. When more than one clinician is involved, the patient has increased opportunities to express somatic complaints. The primary physician should see the patient during regularly scheduled visits, usually at monthly intervals. The visits should be relatively brief; although a partial physical examination should be conducted to respond to each new somatic complaint, additional laboratory and diagnostic procedures should generally be avoided. Once somatization disorder has been diagnosed, the treating physician should listen to the somatic complaints as emotional expressions, rather than as medical complaints. However, patients with somatization disorder can also have bona fide physical illnesses; therefore, physicians must always use their judgment about what symptoms to work up and to what extent. A reasonable long-range strategy for a primary care physician who is treating a patient with somatization disorder is to increase the patient's awareness of the possibility that psychological factors are involved in the symptoms until the patient is willing to see a mental health clinician, probably a psychiatrist, on a regular basis.

Psychotherapy, both individual and group, decreases somatization disorder patients' personal health care expenditures by 50 percent, largely by decreasing their rates of hospitalization. In psychotherapy settings, patients are helped to cope with their symptoms, to express underlying emotions, and to develop alternative strategies for expressing their feelings.

Giving psychotropic medications whenever somatization disorder coexists with a mood or anxiety disorder is always a risk, but psychopharmacological treatment, as well as psychotherapeutic treatment, of the coexisting disorder is indicated. Medication must be monitored, because somatization disorder patients tend to use drugs erratically and unreliably. In patients without coexisting mental disorders, few available data indicate that pharmacological treatment is effective.

UNDIFFERENTIATED SOMATOFORM DISORDER

The diagnosis of *undifferentiated somatoform disorder* (Table 11–2) is appropriate for patients who present with one or more physical complaints that cannot be explained by a known medical condition or that grossly exceed the expected complaints in a medical condition but who do not meet the diagnostic criteria for somatoform disorder (Table 11–1). The symptoms must have been present at least six months and must cause the patient significant emotional distress or impair the patient's social or occupational functioning.

Two types of symptom patterns may be seen in patients with undifferentiated somatoform disorder: those involving the autonomic nervous system and those involving sensations of fatigue or weakness. In what is sometimes referred to as autonomic arousal disorder, some patients are affected with somatoform disorder symptoms that are limited to bodily functions innervated by the autonomic nervous system. Such patients have complaints involving the cardiovascular, respiratory, gastrointestinal, urogenital, and dermatological systems. Other patients have complaints of mental and physical fatigue, physical weakness and exhaustion, and inability to perform many everyday activities because of their symptoms. That syndrome is often referred to as neurasthenia by clinicians and in other diagnostic systems. The syndrome may overlap chronic fatigue syndrome, which various research reports have hypothesized to involved psychiatric, virological, and immunological factors.

Table 11–2. Diagnostic Criteria for Undifferentiated Somatoform Disorder

A. One or more physical complaints (e.g., fatigue, loss of appetite, gastrointestinal or urinary complaints).

B. Either (1) or (2):

   (1) after appropiate investigation, the symptoms cannot be fully explained by a known general medical condition or the direct effects of a substance (e.g., a drug of abuse, a medication)

   (2) when there is a related general medical condition, the physical complaints or resulting social or occupational impairment is in excess of what would be expected from the hisory, physical examination, or laboratory findings

C. The symptoms cause clinically significant distress or impairment in social, occupational, or other important areas of functioning.

D. The duration of the disturbance is at least 6 months.

E. The disturbance is not better accounted for by another mental disorder (e.g., another somatoform disorder, sexual dysfunction, mood disorder, anxiety disorder, sleep disorder, or psychotic disorder).

F. The symptom is not intentionally produced or feigned (as in factitious disorder or malingering).

Table from DSM-IV, *Diagnostic and Statistical Manual of Mental Disorders*, ed 4. Copyright American Psychiatric Association, Washington, 1994. Used with permission.

CONVERSION DISORDER

DSM-IV defines *conversion disorder* as a disorder characterized by the presence of one or more neurological symptoms (for example, paralysis, blindness, and paresthesias) that cannot be explained by a known neurological or medical disorder. In addition, the diagnosis requires that psychological factors be associated with the initiation or the exacerbation of the symptoms.

Epidemiology

The prevalence of some symptoms of conversion disorder that are not severe enough to warrant the diagnosis may occur in as many as one-third the general population sometime during their lives. One community survey reported that the annual incidence of conversion disorder was 22 per 100,000. Among specific populations, the occurrence of conversion disorder may be higher than that, perhaps making conversion disorder the most common somatoform disorder in some populations. Several studies have reported that 5 to 15 percent of psychiatric consultations in a general hospital and 25 to 30 percent of admissions to a Veterans Affairs hospital involve patients with conversion disorder diagnoses.

The ratio of women to men among adult patients is at least 2 to 1 and as much as 5 to 1; children have an even higher predominance of girls. Men with conversion disorder have often been involved in occupational or military accidents. Conversion disorder can have its onset at any age, from childhood to old age, but it is most common in adolescents and young adults. Data indicate that conversion disorder is most common among rural populations, little-educated persons, those with low intelligence quotients, persons in low socioeconomic groups, and military personnel who have been exposed to combat situations. Conversion disorder is commonly associated with comorbid diagnoses of major depressive disorder, anxiety disorders, and schizophrenia.

Etiology

PSYCHOANALYTIC FACTORS

According to psychoanalytic theory, conversion disorder is caused by the repression of unconscious intrapsychic conflict and the conversion of anxiety into a physical symptom. The conflict is between an instinctual impulse (for example, aggressive or sexual) and the prohibitions against its expression. The symptoms allow the partial expression of the forbidden wish or urge but disguise it, so that the patients need not consciously confront their unacceptable impulses; that is, the conversion disorder symptom has a symbolic relation to the unconscious conflict. The conversion disorder symptoms also enable the patients to communicate that they need a special consideration and special treatment. Such symptoms may function as a nonverbal means of controlling or manipulating others.

BIOLOGICAL FACTORS

Increasing data implicate biological and neuropsychological factors in the development of conversion disorder symptoms. Preliminary brain-imaging studies have found hypometabolism of the dominant hemisphere and hypermetabolism of the nondominant hemisphere and have implicated impaired hemispheric communication in the cause of conversion disorder. The symptoms may be caused by an excessive cortical arousal that sets off negative feedback loops between the cerebral cortex and the brainstem reticular formation. Elevated levels of cortico-fugal output, in turn, inhibit the patient's awareness of bodily sensation, which in some conversion disorder patients may explain the observed sensory deficits. In some conversion disorder patients, neuropsychological tests reveal subtle cerebral impairments in verbal communication, memory, vigilance, affective incongruity, and attention.

Diagnosis

The diagnosis of conversion disorder requires that the clinician find a necessary and critical association between the cause of the neurological symptom and psychological factors, although the symptom cannot be the result of malingering or factitious disorder. The diagnosis of conversion disorder also excludes symptoms of pain and sexual dysfunction and symptoms that occur only in somatization disorder. DSM-IV allows the specification of the type of symptom or deficit seen in conversion disorder (Table 11–3).

Clinical Features

Paralysis, blindness, and mutism are the most common conversion disorder symptoms. Conversion disorder may be most commonly associated with passive-aggressive, dependent, antisocial, and histrionic personality disorders. Depressive and anxiety disorder symptoms can often accompany the symptoms of conversion disorder, and affected patients are at risk for suicide.

SENSORY SYMPTOMS

In conversion disorder, anesthesia and paresthesia are common, especially of the extremities. All sensory modalities can be involved, and the distribution of the disturbance is usually inconsistent with that of either central or peripheral neurological disease. Thus, one may see the characteristic stocking-and-glove anesthesia of the hands or the feet or the hemianesthesia of the body beginning precisely along the midline.

Conversion disorder symptoms may involve the organs of special sense, producing deafness, blindness, and tunnel vision. Those symptoms may be unilateral or bilateral. However, neurological evaluation reveals intact sensory pathways. In conversion disorder blindness, for example, patients walk around without collisions or self-injury, their pupils react to light, and their cortical evoked potentials are normal.

MOTOR SYMPTOMS

The motor symptoms include abnormal movements, gait, disturbance, weakness, and paralysis. Gross rhythmical tremors, choreiform movements, tics, and jerks may be present. The movements generally worsen when attention is called to them. One gait disturbance seen in conversion disorder is astasia-abasia, which is a wildly ataxic, staggering gait accompanied by gross, irregular, jerky truncal movements and thrashing and waving arm movements. Patients with the symptoms rarely fall; if they do, they are generally not injured.

Other common motor disturbances are paralysis and paresis involving one, two, or all four limbs, although the distribution of the involved muscles does not conform to the neural pathways. Reflexes remain normal; the patient has no fasciculations or muscle atrophy (except after long-standing conversion paralysis); electromyography findings are normal.

SEIZURE SYMPTOMS

Pseudoseizures are another symptom in conversion disorder. The clinician may find it difficult by clinical observation alone to differentiate a pseudoseizure from an actual seizure. Moreover, about a third of the patients who have pseudoseizures also have a coexisting epileptic disorder. Tongue biting, urinary incontinence, and injuries after falling can occur in pseudoseizures, although those symptoms are generally not present. Pupillary and gag reflexes are retained after pseudoseizure, and the patient has no postseizure increase in prolactin concentrations.

OTHER ASSOCIATED FEATURES

Several psychological symptoms have also been associated with conversion disorder.

Primary Gain

Patients achieve primary gain by keeping internal conflicts outside their awareness. The symptom has symbolic value in that it represents the unconscious psychological conflict.

Secondary Gain

Patients accrue tangible advantages and benefits as a result of their being sick, such as being excused from obligations and difficult life situations, receiving support and assistance that might not otherwise be forthcoming, and controlling other people's behavior.

La Belle Indifférence

La belle indifférence is the patient's inappropriately cavalier attitude toward a serious symptom; that is, the patient seems to be unconcerned about what appears to be a major impairment. That bland indifference may be lacking in some conversion disorder patients; it is also seen in some seriously ill medical patients who develop a stoic attitude. The

---

Table 11–3.   Diagnostic Criteria for Conversion Disorder

A. One or more symptoms or deficits affecting voluntary motor or sensory function that suggest a neurological or other general medical condition.

B. Psychological factors are judged to be associated with the symptom or deficit because the initiation or exacerbation of the symptom or deficit is preceded by conflicts or other stressors.

C. The symptom or deficit is not intentionally produced or feigned (as in factitious disorder or malingering).

D. The symptom or deficit cannot, after appropriate investigation, be fully explained by a general medical condition, or by the direct effects of a substance, or as a culturally sanctioned behavior or experience.

E. The symptom or deficit causes clinically significant distress or impairment in social, occupational, or other important areas of functioning or warrants medical evaluation.

F. The symptom or deficit is not limited to pain or sexual dysfunction, does not occur exclusively during the course of somatization disorder and is not better accounted for by another mental disorder.

Specify type of symptom or deficit:
With motor symptom or deficit
With sensory symptom or deficit
With seizures or convulsions
With mixed presentation

Table from DSM-IV, *Diagnostic and Statistical Manual of Mental Disorders,* ed 4. Copyright American Psychiatric Association, Washington, 1994. Used with permission.

presence or the absence of *la belle indifférence* is an inaccurate measure of whether a patient has conversion disorder.

Identification

Conversion disorder patients may unconsciously model their symptoms on those of someone important to them. For example, a parent or a person who has recently died may serve as a model for conversion disorder. It is common during pathological grief reaction for the bereaved person to have symptoms of the deceased.

Differential Diagnosis

One of the major problems in diagnosing conversion disorder is the difficulty in definitively ruling out a medical disorder. Concomitant nonpsychiatric medical disorders are common in hospitalized patients with conversion disorder, and evidence of a current or prior neurological disorder or of a systematic disease affecting the brain has been reported in 18 to 64 percent of such patients. An estimated 25 to 50 percent of patients classified as having conversion disorder eventually are diagnosed with neurological or nonpsychiatric medical disorders that could have caused their earlier symptoms. Therefore, a thorough medical and neurological workup is essential in all cases. If the symptoms can be resolved by suggestion, hypnosis, or parenteral amobarbital (Amytal) or lorazepam (Ativan), they are probably the result of conversion disorder.

Neurological disorders (such as dementia and other degenerative diseases), brain tumors, and basal ganglia disease must be considered in the differential diagnosis. For example, weakness may be confused with myasthenia gravis, polymyositis, acquired myopathies, or multiple sclerosis. Optic neuritis may be misdiagnosed as conversion disorder blindness. Other diseases that may cause confusing symptoms are Guillain-Barré syndrome, Creutzfeldt-Jakob disease, periodic paralysis, and early neurological manifestations of acquired immune deficiency syndrome (AIDS). Conversion disorder symptoms occur in schizophrenia, depressive disorders, and anxiety disorders; however, those other disorders are associated with their own distinct symptoms that eventually make differential diagnosis possible.

Sensorimotor symptoms also occur in somatization disorder. But somatization disorder is a chronic illness that begins early in life and includes symptoms in many other organ systems. In hypochondriasis the patient has no actual loss or distortion of function; the somatic complaints are chronic and are not limited to neurological symptoms, and the characteristic hypochondriacal attitudes and beliefs are present. If the patient's symptoms are limited to pain, pain disorder can be diagnosed. The patient whose complaints are limited to sexual function is classified as having a sexual dysfunction, rather than conversion disorder.

In both malingering and factitious disorder, the symptoms are under conscious, voluntary control. The malingerer's history is usually more inconsistent and contradictory than is the conversion disorder patient's history, and the malingerers fraudulent behavior is clearly goal-directed.

Course and Prognosis

In the vast majority of patients with conversion disorder—perhaps 90 to 100 percent—the initial symptoms resolve in a few days or less than a month. A reported 75 percent of patients may not experience another episode, but 25 percent of patients may have additional episodes during periods of stress.

Associated with a good prognosis are a sudden onset, an easily identifiable stressor, good premorbid adjustment, no comorbid psychiatric or medical disorders, and no ongoing litigation. The longer the conversion disorder symptoms are present, the worse the prognosis is. As mentioned above, 25 to 50 percent of patients may later have neurological disorders or nonpsychiatric medical conditions affecting the nervous system. Therefore, patients with conversion disorder must have complete medical and neurological evaluations at the time of the diagnosis.

Treatment

Resolution of the conversion disorder symptom is usually spontaneous, although resolution is probably facilitated by insight-oriented supportive or behavior therapy; the most important feature of the therapy is a caring and authoritative therapeutic relationship. With patients who are resistant to the idea of psychotherapy, the physician can suggest that the psychotherapy will focus on issues of stress and coping. Telling such patients that their symptoms are imaginary often makes the symptoms worse, rather than better. Hypnosis, anxiolytics, and behavioral relaxation exercises are effective in some cases. Parenteral amobarbital or lorazepam may be helpful in obtaining additional historical information, especially if a traumatic event was recently experienced. Psychodynamic approaches include psychoanalysis and insight-oriented psychotherapy, in which patients explore intrapsychic conflicts and the symbolism of the conversion disorder symptom. Brief and direct forms of short-term psychotherapy have also been used to treat conversion disorder. The longer that conversion disorder patients have been in the sick role and the more they have regressed, the more difficult the treatment is.

HYPOCHONDRIASIS

The term ''hypochondriasis'' is derived from the old medical term ''hypochondrium,'' which means below the ribs, and reflects the common abdominal complaints that many patients with the disorder have. Hypochondriasis results from patient's unrealistic or inaccurate interpretations of physical symptoms or sensations, leading to preoccupations and fear that they have serious diseases, even though no known medical causes can be found. The patient's preoccupations result in significant distress to the patients and impair their ability to function in their personal, social, and occupational roles.

Epidemiology

One recent study reported a six-month prevalence of 4 to 6 percent in a general medical clinic population. Men and women are equally affected by hypochondriasis. Although the onset of symptoms can occur at any age, the onset is most common between 20 and 30 years of age. Some evidence indicates that the diagnosis is more common among blacks than among whites, but social position, education level, and marital status do not appear to affect the diagnosis.

Etiology

The diagnostic criteria for hypochondriasis note that the symptoms reflect a misinterpretation of bodily symptoms. A reasonable body of data indicates that hypochondriacal persons augment and amplify their somatic sensations; they have lower than usual thresholds for and a lower tolerance of physical discomfort. For example, what a person normally perceives as abdominal pressure, the hypochondriacal person experiences as abdominal pain. The hypochondriacal person may focus on bodily sensations, misinterpret them, and become alarmed by them because of a faulty cognitive scheme.

A second theory is that hypochondriasis is understandable on the basis of a social learning model. The symptoms of hypochondriasis are viewed as a request for admission to the sick role made by a person who is facing seemingly insurmountable and insolvable problems. The sick role offers a way out, because the sick patient is allowed to avoid noxious obligations and to postpone unwelcome challenges and is excused from usually expected duties.

A third theory regarding the cause of hypochondriasis is that it is a variant form of other mental disorders. The disorders most frequently hypothesized to be related to hypochondriasis are depressive disorders and anxiety disorders. An estimated 80 percent of patients with hypochondriasis may have coexisting depressive disorders or anxiety disorders.

A fourth school of thought regarding hypochondriasis is the psychodynamic school, which posits that aggressive and hostile wishes toward others are transferred (through repression and displacement) into physical complaints. The anger of hypochondriacal patients originates in past disappointments, rejections, and losses, but the patients express their anger in the present by soliciting the help and concern of other people and then rejecting them as ineffective. Hypochondriasis is also viewed as a defense against guilt, a sense of innate badness, an expression of low self-esteem, and a sign of excessive self-concern. Pain and somatic suffering thus becomes a means of atonement and expiation (undoing) and can be experienced as deserved punishment for past wrongdoing (either real or imaginary) and the sense that one is wicked and sinful.

Diagnosis

The DSM-IV diagnostic criteria for hypochondriasis require that the patient be preoccupied with the false belief that he or she has a serious disease and that the false belief be based on a misinterpretation of physical signs or sensations (Table 11–4). The criteria require that the belief last at least six months despite the absence of pathological findings on medical and neurological examinations. The diagnostic criteria also require that the belief not have the intensity of a delusion (more appropriately diagnosed as delusional disorder) and that it not be restricted to distress about appearance (more appropriately diagnosed as body dysmorphic disorder). However, the symptoms of hypochondriasis are required to be intense enough to cause emotional distress or impairment in the patient's ability to function in important areas of life. The clinician may specify the presence of poor insight if the patient does not consistently recognize that the concerns about disease are excessive.

Clinical Features

Hypochondriacal patients believe that they have a serious disease that has not yet been detected, and they cannot be persuaded to the contrary. Hypochondriacal patients may maintain a belief that they have one particular disease, or as time pro-

Table 11–4. Diagnostic Criteria for Hypochondriasis

A. Preoccupation with fears of having, or the idea that one has a serious disease based on the person's misinterpretation of bodily symptoms.

B. The preoccupation persists despite appropriate medical evaluation and reassurance.

C. The belief in criterion A is not of delusional intensity (as in delusional disorder somatic type) and is not restricted to a circumscribed concern about appearance (as in body dysmorphic disorder).

D. The preoccupation causes clinically significant distress or impairment in social, occupational, or other important areas of functioning.

E. The duration of the disturbance is at least 6 months.

F. The preoccupation is not better accounted for by generalized anxiety disorder, obsessive-compulsive disorder, panic disorder, a major depressive episode, separation anxiety, or another somatoform disorder.

Specify if:
With poor insight: if, for most of the time during the current episode, the person does not recognize that the concern about having a serious illness is excessive or unreasonable

Table from DSM-IV, *Diagnostic and Statistical Manual of Mental Disorders*, ed 4. Copyright American Psychiatric Association, Washington, 1994. Used with permission.

gresses, they may change their belief about the specific disease. The conviction persists despite negative laboratory results, the benign course of the alleged disease over time, and appropriate reassurances from physicians. But the belief is not so fixed that it is a delusion. Hypochondriasis is often accompanied by symptoms of depression and anxiety, and it commonly coexists with a depressive or anxiety disorder.

Although DSM-IV specifies that the symptoms must be present for at least six months, transient hypochondriacal states can occur after major stresses, most commonly the death or serious illness of someone important to the patient or a serious (perhaps life-threatening) illness that has been resolved but that leaves the patient temporarily hypochondriacal in its wake. Such hypochondriacal states that last fewer than six months should be diagnosed as somatoform disorder not otherwise specified. Transient hypochondriacal responses to external stress generally remit when the stress is resolved, but they can become chronic if reinforced by people in the patient's social system or by health professionals.

Differential Diagnosis

Hypochondriasis must be differentiated from nonpsychiatric medical conditions, especially disorders that can present with symptoms that are not necessarily easily diagnosed. Such diseases include AIDS, endocrinopathies, myasthenia gravis, multiple sclerosis, degenerative diseases of the nervous system, systemic lupus erythematosus, and occult neoplastic disorders.

Hypochondriasis is differentiated from somatization disorder by the emphasis in hypochondriasis on fear of having a disease and emphasis in somatization disorder on concern about many symptoms. A subtle distinction is that patients with hypochondriasis usually complain about fewer symptoms than do patients with somatization disorder. Somatization disorder usually has an onset before age 30, whereas hypochondriasis has a less specific age of onset. The somatization disorder patient is more likely to be a woman than is the patient with hypochondriasis, which has an equal distribution of men to women.

Hypochondriasis must also be differentiated from the other somatoform disorders. Conversion disorder is acute and generally transient and usually involves a symptom rather than a particular disease. The presence or the absence of *la belle indifférence* is an unreliable feature with which to differentiate the two conditions. Pain disorder is chronic, as is hypochondriasis, but the symptoms are limited to complaints of pain. Body dysmorphic disorder patients wish to appear normal but believe that others notice that they are not, whereas hypochondriacal patients seek out attention for their presumed diseases.

Hypochondriacal symptoms can also occur in depressive disorders and anxiety disorders. If a patient meets the full diagnostic criteria for both hypochondriasis and another major mental disorder, such as major depressive disorder or generalized anxiety disorder, the patient should receive both diagnoses, unless the hypochondriacal symptoms occur only during episodes of the other mental disorder. Patients with panic disorder may initially complain that they are affected by some disease (for example, heart trouble), but careful questioning during the medical history usually uncovers the classic symptoms of a panic attack. Delusional hypochondriacal beliefs occur in schizophrenia and other psychotic disorders but can be differentiated from hypochondriasis by their delusional intensity and by the presence of other psychotic symptoms. In addition, schizophrenic patients' somatic delusions tend to be bizarre, idiosyncratic, and out of keeping with their cultural milieus.

Hypochondriasis is distinguished from factitious disorder with predominantly physical signs and symptoms and from malingering in that hypochondriacal patients actually experience and do not simulate the symptoms they report.

Course and Prognosis

The course of hypochondriasis is usually episodic; the episodes last from months to years and are separated by equally long quiescent periods. There may be an obvious association between exacerbations of hypochondriacal symptoms and psychosocial stressors. Although well-conducted large outcome studies have not yet been reported, an estimated one third to one half of all hypochondriasis patients eventually improve significantly. A good prognosis is associated with a high socioeconomic status, treatment-responsive anxiety or depression, the sudden onset of symptoms, the absence of a personality disorder, and the absence of a related nonpsychiatric medical condition. Most hypochondriacal children recover by late adolescence or early adulthood.

Treatment

Hypochondriacal patients are usually resistant to psychiatric treatment. Some hypochondriacal patients accept psychiatric treatment if it takes place in a medical setting and focuses on stress reduction and education in coping with chronic illness. Among such patients, group psychotherapy is the modality of choice, in part because it provides the social support and social interaction that seem to reduce their anxiety. Individual insight-oriented psychotherapy may be useful, but it is generally not successful.

Frequent, regularly scheduled physical examinations are useful to reassure the patients that they are not being abandoned by their doctors and that their complaints are being taken seriously. However, invasive diagnostic and therapeutic procedures should be undertaken only when objective evidence calls for them. When possible, the clinician should refrain from treating equivocal or incidental physical examination findings.

Pharmacotherapy alleviates hypochondriacal symptoms only when the patient has an underlying drug-responsive condition, such as an anxiety disorder or major depressive disorder. When hypochondriasis is secondary to some other primary mental disorder, that disorder must be treated in its own right. When hypochondriasis is a transient situational reaction, the clinician must help patients cope with the stress without reinforcing their illness behavior and their use of the sick role as a solution to the problem.

BODY DYSMORPHIC DISORDER

Body dysmorphic disorder is a preoccupation with an imagined bodily defect (for example, a misshapen nose) or an exaggerated distortion of a minimal or minor defect. For such a concern to be considered a mental disorder, the concern must cause the patient significant distress or be associated with impairment in the patient's personal, social, or occupational life.

Epidemiology

Body dysmorphic disorder is a poorly studied condition, partly because the patients are more likely to go to dermatologists, internists, or plastic surgeons than to psychiatrists. One study of patients attending a plastic surgery clinic found that only 2 percent of those patients met the diagnostic criteria, thus indicating that patients with the complete diagnostic criteria may be rare.

Available data indicate that the most common age of onset is between 15 and 20 years and that women are somewhat more often affected than are men. Affected patients are also likely to be unmarried. Body dysmorphic disorder commonly coexists with other mental disorders. One study found that more than 90 percent of the body dysmorphic disorder patients had experienced a major depressive episode in their lifetimes, about 70 percent had had an anxiety disorder, and about 30 percent had had a psychotic disorder.

Etiology

The cause of body dysmorphic disorder is unknown. The high comorbidity with depressive disorders, a higher-than-expected family history of mood disorders and obsessive-compulsive disorder, and the reported responsiveness of the condition to serotonin-specific drugs indicate that, in at least some patients, the pathophysiology of the disorder may involve serotonin and may be related to other mental disorders. There may be significant cultural or social effects on body dysmorphic disorder patients because of the emphasis on stereotyped concepts of beauty that may be emphasized in certain families and within the culture at large. In psychodynamic models, body dysmorphic disorder is seen as reflecting the displacement of a sexual or emotional conflict onto a nonrelated body part. Such an association occurs through the defense mechanisms of repression, dissociation, distortion, symbolization, and projection.

Table 11-5.   Diagnostic Criteria for Body Dysmorphic Disorder

A. Preoccupation with an imagined defect in appearance. If a slight physical anomaly is present, the person's concern is markedly excessive.

B. The preoccupation causes clinically significant distress or impairment in social, occupational, or other important areas of functioning.

C. The preoccupation is not better accounted for by another mental disorder (e.g., dissatisfaction with body shape and size in anorexia nervosa).

Table from DSM-IV, *Diagnostic and Statistical Manual of Mental Disorders*, ed 4. Copyright American Psychiatric Association, Washington, 1994. Used with permission.

Diagnosis

The DSM-IV diagnostic criteria for body dysmorphic disorder require a preoccupation with an imagined defect in appearance or an overemphasis on a slight defect (Table 11–5). The preoccupation causes the patient significant emotional distress or markedly impairs the patient's ability to function in important areas.

Clinical Features

The most common concerns involve facial flaws, particularly those involving specific parts (for example, the nose). Sometimes the concern is vague and difficult to understand, such as extreme concern over a "scrunchy" chin. One study found that, on average, patients had concerns about four body regions during the course of the disorder. The body part of specific concern may change during the time the patient is affected with the disorder. Common associated symptoms include ideas or frank delusions of reference (usually regarding people's noticing the alleged body flaw), either excessive mirror checking or avoidance of reflective surfaces, and attempts to hide the presumed deformity (with makeup or clothing). The effects on a person's life can be significant; almost all affected patients avoid social and occupational exposure. As many as a third of the patients may be housebound by their concern about being ridiculed for their alleged deformities, and as many as a fifth of the affected patients attempt suicide. As previously mentioned, comorbid diagnoses of depressive disorders and anxiety disorders are common, and the patients may also have traits of obsessive-compulsive, schizoid, and narcissistic personality disorders.

Differential Diagnosis

Distortions of body image occur in anorexia nervosa, gender identity disorders, and some specific types of brain damage (for example, neglect syndromes); body dysmorphic disorder should not be diagnosed in those situations. Body dysmorphic disorder also needs to be distinguished from normal concern about one's appearance. The differentiating feature is that in body dysmorphic disorder the person experiences significant emotional distress and functional impairment as a result of the concern. Although making the distinction between a strongly held idea and a delusion is difficult, if the perceived body defect is, in fact, of delusional intensity, the appropriate diagnosis is delusional disorder, somatic type. Other diagnostic considerations are narcissistic personality disorder, depressive disorders, obsessive-compulsive disorder, and schizophrenia.

Course and Prognosis

The onset of body dysmorphic disorder is usually gradual. An affected person may experience increasing concern over a particular body part until the person notices that functioning is being affected by the concern. At that point the person may seek medical or surgical help to address the presumed problem. The level of concern about the problem may wax and wane over time, although body dysmorphic disorder is generally a chronic disorder if left untreated.

Treatment

Treatment of patients with body dysmorphic disorder with surgical, dermatological, dental, and other medical procedures to address the alleged defects is almost invariably unsuccessful. Although tricyclic drugs, monoamine oxidase inhibitors, and pimozide (Orap) have been reported to be useful in individual cases, a larger body of data indicate that serotonin-specific drugs—for example, clomipramine (Anafranil) and fluoxetine (Prozac)—are effective in reducing symptoms in at least 50 percent of patients. In any patient with a coexisting mental disorder, such as a depressive disorder or an anxiety disorder, the coexisting disorder should be treated with the appropriate pharmacotherapy and psychotherapy. How long treatment should be continued when the symptoms of body dysmorphic disorder have remitted is unknown.

PAIN DISORDER

The primary symptom of *pain disorder* is the presence of pain in one or more sites that is not fully accounted for by a nonpsychiatric medical or neurological condition. The symptoms of pain are associated with emotional distress and functional impairment, and the disorder has a plausible causal relation with psychological factors. The disorder has been called somatoform pain disorder, psychogenic pain disorder, idiopathic pain disorder, and the euphemistic atypical pain disorder.

Epidemiology

Pain is perhaps the most frequent complaint in medical practice. Intractable pain syndromes are also common. Low back pain has disabled an estimated 7 million Americans and accounts for more than 8 million physician office visits annually. Pain disorder is diagnosed twice as frequently in women as in men. The peak ages of onset are in the fourth and fifth decades of life, perhaps because the tolerance for pain declines with age. Pain disorder is most common in persons with blue-collar occupations, perhaps because of increased likelihood of job-related injuries. First-degree relatives of pain disorder patients have an increased likelihood for the same disorder, thus indicating the possibility of a genetic inheritance or behavioral mechanisms in the transmission of the disorder. Depressive disorders, anxiety disorders, and substance abuse are also more common in the families of pain disorder patients than in the general population.

Etiology

PSYCHODYNAMIC FACTORS

Patients who experience aches and pains in their bodies without identifiable adequate physical causes may be symbolically expressing an intrapsychic conflict through the body. Some patients suffer from alexithymia, in which they are unable to articulate their internal feeling states in words, so the body expresses the feelings for them. Other patients may unconsciously regard emotional pain as weak and somehow lacking in legitimacy. By displacing the problem to the body, they may feel that they have a legitimate claim to the fulfillment of their dependence needs. The symbolic meaning of body disturbances may also relate to atonement for perceived sin, expiation of guilt, or suppressed aggression. Many patients have pain that is intractable and unresponsive because they are convinced that they deserve to suffer.

Pain can function as a method of obtaining love, a punishment for wrongdoing, and a way of expiating guilt and of atoning for an innate sense of badness. Among the defense mechanisms used by patients with pain disorder are displacement, substitution, and repression. Identification plays a role when the patient takes on the role of an ambivalent love object who also has pain, such as a parent.

BEHAVIORAL FACTORS

Pain behaviors are reinforced when rewarded and are inhibited when ignored or punished. For example, moderate pain symptoms may become intense when followed by the solicitous and attentive behavior of others, by monetary gain, or by the successful avoidance of distasteful activities.

INTERPERSONAL FACTORS

Intractable pain has been conceptualized as a means for manipulation and gaining advantage in interpersonal relationships—for example, to ensure the devotion of a family member or to stabilize a fragile marriage. Such secondary gain is most important to patients with pain disorder.

BIOLOGICAL FACTORS

The cerebral cortex can inhibit the firing of afferent pain fibers. Serotonin is probably the main neurotransmitter in the descending inhibitory pathways, and endorphins also play a role in the central nervous system's modulation of pain. Endorphin deficiency seems to correlate with the augmentation of incoming sensory stimuli. Some patients may have pain disorder, rather than another mental disorder, because of sensory and limbic structural or chemical abnormalities that predispose them to experience pain.

Diagnosis

The DSM-IV diagnostic criteria for pain disorder require the presence of clinically significant complaints of pain (Table 11–6). The complaints of pain must be judged to be significantly affected by psychological factors, and the symptoms must result in significant emotional distress or functional impairment (for example, social or occupational) to the patient. DSM-IV requires that the pain disorder be further defined as being associated primarily with psychological factors or as being associated

Table 11–6. Diagnostic Criteria for Pain Disorder

A. Pain in one or more anatomical sites is the predominant focus of the clinical presentation and is of sufficient severity to warrant clinical attention.

B. The pain causes clinically significant distress or impairment in social, occupational, or other important areas of functioning.

C. Psychological factors are judged to have an important role in the onset, severity, exacerbation, or maintenance of the pain.

D. The symptom or deficit is not intentionally produced or feigned (as in factitious disorder or malingering).

E. The pain is not better accounted for by a mood, anxiety, or psychotic disorder and does not meet criteria for dyspareunia.

Table from DSM-IV, *Diagnostic and Statistical Manual of Mental Disorders*, ed 4. Copyright American Psychiatric Association, Washington, 1994. Used with permission.

with both psychological factors and a general medical condition. DSM-IV further specifies that pain disorder associated solely with a general medical condition be diagnosed as an Axis III condition. DSM-IV also allows the clinician to specify whether the pain disorder is acute or chronic, depending on whether the symptoms have lasted six months or longer.

Clinical Features

Pain disorder patients do not constitute a uniform group but, instead, are a collection of heterogeneous patients with various pains, such as low back pain, headache, atypical facial pain, and chronic pelvic pain. The patient's pain may be posttraumatic, neuropathic, neurological, iatrogenic, or musculoskeletal; however, to meet a diagnosis of pain disorder, the disorder must have a psychological factor that is judged to be significantly involved in the pain symptoms and their ramifications.

Pain disorder patients often have long histories of medical and surgical care, visiting many doctors and requesting many medications. They may be especially insistent in their desire for surgery. Indeed, they can be completely preoccupied with their pain, citing it as the source of all their misery. Such patients often deny any other sources of emotional dysphoria and maintain that their lives are blissful except for the pain. Pain disorder patients may have the clinical picture complicated by substance-related disorders, because they attempt to reduce the pain through the use of alcohol and other substances.

At least one study has correlated the number of pain symptoms to the likelihood and the severity of symptoms of somatization disorder, depressive disorders, and anxiety disorders. Major depressive disorder is present in about 25 to 50 percent of all pain disorder patients, and dysthymic disorder or depressive disorder symptoms are reported in 60 to 100 percent of the patients. Some investigators believe that chronic pain is almost always a variant of a depressive disorder, suggesting that it is a masked or somatized form of depression. The most prominent depressive symptoms in pain disorder patients are anergia, anhedonia, decreased libido, insomnia, and irritability; diurnal variation, weight loss, and psychomotor retardation appear to be less common than those symptoms.

Differential Diagnosis

Purely physical pain can be difficult to distinguish from purely psychogenic pain, especially because they are not mutually exclusive. Physical pain fluctuates in intensity and is highly sensitive to emotional, cognitive, attentional, and situational influences. Pain that does not vary and is insensitive to any of those factors is likely to be psychogenic. If the pain does not wax and wane and is not even temporarily relieved by distraction or analgesics, the clinician can suspect an important psychogenic component.

Pain disorder must be distinguished from other somatoform disorders, although some somatoform disorders can coexist. Hypochondriacal patients may complain of pain, and aspects of the clinical presentation of hypochondriasis, such as bodily preoccupation and disease conviction, can also be present in pain disorder patients. However, hypochondriacal patients tend to have many more symptoms than do pain disorder patients, and their symptoms tend to fluctuate more than do the symptoms of pain disorder patients. Conversion disorder is generally short-lived, whereas pain disorder is chronic. In additional, pain is, by definition, not a symptom in conversion disorder. Malingering patients consciously provide false reports, and their complaints are usually connected to clearly recognizable goals.

The differential diagnosis can be difficult because pain disorder patients often receive disability compensation or a litigation award. They are not, however, pretending to be in pain. For example, muscle contraction (tension) headaches have a pathophysiological mechanism to account for the pain and so are not diagnosed as pain disorder.

Course and Prognosis

The pain in pain disorder generally begins abruptly and increases in severity over the next few weeks or months. The prognosis for pain disorder patients varies, although pain disorder can often be chronic, distressful, and completely disabling. When psychological factors predominate in pain disorder, the pain may subside with treatment or after the elimination of external reinforcement. The patients with the poorest prognoses, with or without treatment, have preexisting characterological problems, especially pronounced passivity; are involved in litigation or receive financial compensation; use addictive substances; and have long histories of pain.

Treatment

Since it may not be possible to reduce the pain, the treatment approach must address rehabilitation. The clinician should discuss the issue of psychological factors early in treatment, telling patients frankly that such factors are important in the cause and the consequences of both physical and psychogenic pain. The therapist should also explain how various brain circuits that are involved with emotions (such as the limbic system) may also influence the sensory pain pathways. For example, hitting one's head while happy at a party can seem to hurt less than hitting one's head while angry and at work. However, the therapist must fully understand that the patient's experience of pain is real.

PHARMACOTHERAPY

Analgesic medications are not generally helpful for most pain disorder patients. In addition, substance abuse and dependence are often major problems for pain disorder patients who receive long-term analgesic treatment. In addition, sedatives and antianxiety agents are not especially beneficial and often be-

come problems in themselves because of their frequent abuse, misuse, and side effects.

Antidepressants—such as amitriptyline (Elavil), imipramine (Tofranil), and doxepin (Sinequan)—are useful. Whether antidepressants reduce pain through their antidepressant action or exert an independent, direct analgesic effect (possibly by stimulating efferent inhibitory pain pathways) remains controversial. Preliminary data indicate that the serotonergic antidepressants (for example, clomipramine and fluoxetine) also reduce pain in pain disorder patients. The success of those agents supports the hypothesis that serotonin is important in the pathophysiology of the disorder.

BEHAVIORAL TREATMENT

Biofeedback can be helpful in the treatment of pain disorder, particularly with migraine pain, myofacial pain, and muscle tension states, such as tension headaches. Hypnosis, transcutaneous nerve stimulation, and dorsal column stimulation also have been used. Nerve blocks and surgical ablative procedures are ineffective for most pain disorder patients; the pain returns after 6 to 18 months.

PSYCHOTHERAPY

Some outcome data indicate that psychodynamic psychotherapy is helpful to patients with pain disorder. The first step in psychotherapy is to develop a solid therapeutic alliance by empathizing with the patient's suffering. Clinicians should not confront somatoform disorder patients with comments such as, "This is all in your head." For the patient, the pain is real, and clinicians must acknowledge the reality of the pain, even though they suspect that it is largely intrapsychic in origin. A useful entry point into the emotional aspects of the pain is to examine the interpersonal ramifications of the pain in the patient's life. By exploring marital problems, for example, the psychotherapist may soon get to the source of the patient's psychological pain and the function of the physical complaints in significant relationships.

PAIN CONTROL PROGRAMS

It may sometimes be necessary to remove the patients from their usual settings and place them in a comprehensive inpatient pain control program. Multidisciplinary pain units use many modalities, such as cognitive, behavior, and group therapies. They provide extensive physical conditioning through physical therapy and exercise and offer vocational evaluation and rehabilitation. Concurrent mental disorders are diagnosed and treated, and patients dependent on analgesics and hypnotics are detoxified. Inpatient treatment programs generally report encouraging results.

SOMATOFORM DISORDER NOT OTHERWISE SPECIFIED

The DSM-IV diagnostic category of somatoform disorder not otherwise specified (NOS) is a residual category for patients who have symptoms suggestive of a somatoform disorder but who do not meet the specific diagnostic criteria for other somatoform disorders. Such patients may have a symptom not covered in the other somatoform disorders (for example, pseudocyesis) or may not have met the six-month criterion of the other somatoform disorders.

References

Barsky A J, Cleary P D, Sarnie M K, Klerman G L: The course of transient hypochondriasis. Psychiatry *150*: 484, 1993.

Barsky A J, Coeytaux R R, Sarnie M K, Cleary P D: Hypochondriacal patients' beliefs about good health. Am J Psychiatry *150*: 1085, 1993.

Bass C, Benjamin S: The management of chronic somatisation. Br J Psychiatry *162*: 472, 1993.

Creed F, Guthrie E: Techniques for interviewing the somatising patient. Br J Psychiatry *162*: 467, 1993.

Ford C V: Dimensions of somatization and hypochondriasis. Neurol Clin *13*: 241, 1995.

Guggenheim F G, Smith G R: Somatoform disorders. In *Comprehensive Textbook of Psychiatry*, ed 6, H I Kaplan, B J Sadock, editors, p 1251. Williams & Wilkins, Baltimore, 1995.

Kirmayer L J, Robbins J M, Dworkind M, Yaffe M J: Somatization and the recognition of depression and anxiety in primary care. Am J Psychiatry *150*: 734, 1993.

Mayou R: Somatization. Psychother Psychosom *59*: 69, 1993.

Phillips K A, McElroy S L, Keck P E Jr, Pope H G, Judson J I: Body dysmorphic disorder: 30 cases of imagined ugliness. Am J Psychiatry *150*: 302, 1993.

12/ Factitious Disorders

Patients with factitious disorders intentionally produce signs of medical or mental disorders and misrepresent their histories and symptoms. The only apparent objective of the behavior is to assume the role of a patient. For many persons, hospitalization itself is a primary objective and often a way of life. The disorders have a compulsive quality, but the behaviors are considered voluntary in that they are deliberate and purposeful, even if they cannot be controlled.

EPIDEMIOLOGY

The prevalence of factitious disorders is unknown, although some clinicians believe that they are more common than is acknowledged. They appear to occur most frequently in men and among hospital and health care workers. One study reported a 9-percent rate of factitious disorders among all patients admitted to a hospital; another study found factitious fever in 3 percent of all patients. A data bank of persons who feign illness has been established to alert hospitals about such patients, many of whom travel from place to place, seeking admission under different names or simulating different illnesses.

ETIOLOGY

The psychodynamic underpinnings of factitious disorders are poorly understood because the patients are difficult to engage in an exploratory psychotherapy process. They may insist that their symptoms are physical and, therefore, that psychologically oriented treatment is useless. Anecdotal case reports indicate that many of the patients suffered childhood abuse or deprivation, resulting in frequent hospitalizations during early development. In such circumstances an inpatient stay may have been regarded as an escape from a traumatic home situation, and the patient may have found a series of caregivers (such as doctors, nurses, and hospital workers) loving and caring. In contrast, the patients' families of origin usually contained a rejecting mother or an absent father. The usual history reveals that the patient perceives one or both parents as rejecting figures who are unable to form close relationships. The facsimile of genuine illness, therefore, is used to re-create the desired positive parent-child bond. The disorders are a form of repetition compulsion—repeating the basic conflict of needing and seeking acceptance and love while expecting that they will not be forthcoming. Hence, the patient transforms the physicians and staff members into rejecting parents.

Patients who seek out painful procedures, such as surgical operations and invasive diagnostic tests, may have a masochistic personality makeup in which pain serves as punishment for past sins, imagined or real. Some patients may attempt to master the past and early trauma of serious medical illness or hospitalization by assuming the role of the patient and reliving the painful and frightening experience over and over again through multiple hospitalizations.

Patients who feign psychiatric illness may have had a relative who was hospitalized with the illness they are simulating. Through identification, the patients hope to reunite with the relative in a magical way.

Many of the patients have the poor identity formation and disturbed self-image that is characteristic of someone with borderline personality disorder. Some patients are as-if personalities who have assumed the identities of those around them. If those patients are health professionals, they are often unable to differentiate themselves from the patients with whom they come in contact.

The cooperation or the encouragement of other persons in simulating a factitious illness occurs in a rare variant of the disorder, suggesting another possible causative factor. Although the majority of the patients act alone, friends or relatives participate in fabricating the illness in some instances.

Significant defense mechanisms are repression, identification, identification with the aggressor, regression, and symbolization.

DIAGNOSIS AND CLINICAL FEATURES

The diagnostic criteria for factitious disorder in the fourth edition of *Diagnostic and Statistical Manual of Mental Disorders* (DSM-IV) are given in Table 12–1.

The psychiatric examination should emphasize securing information from any available friend, relative, or other informant, because interviews with reliable outside sources often reveal the false nature of the patient's illness. Although time-consuming and tedious, verifying all the facts presented by the patient concerning prior hospitalizations and medical care is essential.

Psychiatric evaluation is requested on a consultation basis in about 50 percent of the cases, usually after the presence of a simulated illness is suspected. The psychiatrist is often asked to confirm the diagnosis of factitious disorder. Under those circumstances it is necessary to avoid pointed or accusatory questioning that may provoke truculence, evasion, or flight from the hospital. There may be a danger of provoking frank psychosis if vigorous confrontation is used, because in some instances the feigned illness serves an adaptive function and is a desperate attempt to ward off further disintegration.

Psychological testing may reveal specific underlying pathology in individual patients. Features that are overrepresented in factitious disorder patients include normal or above-average intelligence quotient (I.Q.); absence of a formal thought disorder; poor sense of identity, including confusion over sexual identity; poor sexual adjustment; poor frustration tolerance; strong dependence needs; and narcissism.

Factitious Disorder with Predominantly Psychological Signs and Symptoms

Some patients present with psychiatric symptoms that are judged to be feigned. That determination can be difficult and is often made only after a prolonged investigation. The feigned symptoms often include depression, hallucinations, dissociative and conversion symptoms, and bizarre behavior. Because the patient does not improve after routine therapeutic measures are administered, the patient may receive large doses of psychoactive drugs and may undergo electroconvulsive therapy.

Factitious psychological symptoms resemble the phenome-

Table 12-1. Diagnostic Criteria for Factitious Disorder

A. Intentional production or feigning of physical or psychological signs or symptoms.

B. The motivation for the behavior is to assume the sick role.

C. External incentives for the behavior (such as economic gain, avoiding legal responsibility, or improving physical well-being, as malingering) are absent.

Table from DSM-IV, *Diagnostic and Statistical Manual of Mental Disorders*, ed 4. Copyright American Psychiatric Association, Washington, 1994. Used with permission.

non of *pseudomalingering*, defined as satisfying the need to maintain an intact self-image, which would be marred by admitting psychological problems that are beyond the person's capacity to master through conscious effort. In that case, deception is a transient ego-supporting device.

Recent findings indicate that factitious psychotic symptoms are more common than was previously suspected. The presence of simulated psychosis as a feature of other disorders, such as mood disorders, indicates a poor overall prognosis.

Psychotic inpatients found to have factitious disorder with predominantly psychological signs and symptoms—that is, exclusively simulated psychotic symptoms—generally have a concurrent diagnosis of borderline personality disorder. In those cases, the outcome appears to be worse than that of bipolar I disorder or schizoaffective disorder.

Patients may present as depressed, offering as the reason a false history of the recent death of a significant friend or relative. Elements of the history that may suggest factitious bereavement include a violent or bloody death, a death under dramatic circumstances, and the dead person's being a child or a young adult. Other patients may present with both recent and remote memory loss or with both auditory and visual hallucinations.

Other symptoms, which also appear in the psychological type of factitious disorder, include pseudologia phantastica and impostorship. In pseudologia phantastica, limited factual material is mixed with extensive and colorful fantasies. The listener's interest pleases the patient and, thus, reinforces the symptom. However, the distortion of truth is not limited to the history or an illness's symptoms; the patients often give false and conflicting accounts about other areas of their lives (such as claiming the death of a parent, so as to play on the sympathy of others). Impostorship is commonly related to lying in those cases. Many patients assume the identity of a prestigious person. Men, for example, report being war heroes, attributing their surgical scars to wounds received during battle or other dramatic and dangerous exploits. Similarly, they may say that they have ties to accomplished or renowned figures.

Factitious Disorder with Predominantly Physical Signs and Symptoms

Factitious disorder with predominantly physical signs and symptoms has been designated by a variety of labels, the best known being Munchausen syndrome, named after the German Baron von Münchausen, who lived in the 18th century and wrote many travel and adventure stories. The disorder has also been called hospital addiction, polysurgical addiction, and professional patient syndrome, among other names.

The essential feature of patients with the disorder is their ability to present physical symptoms so well that they are able to gain admission to and stay in a hospital. To support their history, the patients may feign symptoms suggestive of a disorder that may involve any organ system. They are familiar with the diagnoses of most disorders that usually require hospital admission or medication and can give excellent histories capable of deceiving even the most experienced clinician. Clinical presentations are myriad and include hematoma, hemoptysis, abdominal pain, fever, hypoglycemia, lupuslike syndromes, nausea, vomiting, dizziness, and seizures. Urine is contaminated with blood or feces; anticoagulants are taken to simulate bleeding disorders; insulin is used to produce hypoglycemia; and so on. Such patients often insist on surgery, claiming adhesions from previous surgical procedures. The patients may acquire a gridiron abdomen from multiple procedures. Complaints of pain, especially that simulating renal colic, are common, with the patients wanting narcotics. In about half the reported cases, the patients demand treatment with specific medications, usually analgesics. Once in the hospital, they continue to be demanding and difficult. As each test is returned with a negative result, they may accuse the doctor of incompetence, threaten litigation, and become generally abusive. Some may sign out abruptly shortly before they believe they are going to be confronted with their factitious behavior. They then go to another hospital in the same or another city and begin the cycle again. Specific predisposing factors are true physical disorders during childhood leading to extensive medical treatment, a grudge against the medical profession, employment as a medical paraprofessional, and an important relationship with a physician in the past.

Factitious Disorder with Combined Psychological and Physical Signs and Symptoms

In combined forms of factitious disorder, both psychological and physical signs and symptoms are present. If neither type predominates in the clinical presentation, a diagnosis of factitious disorder with combined psychological and physical signs and symptoms should be made.

Factitious Disorder Not Otherwise Specified

Some patients with factitious signs and symptoms do not meet the DSM-IV criteria for a specific factitious disorder and should be classified as having factitious disorder not otherwise specified. The most notable example of the diagnosis is factitious disorder by proxy, which is also included in a DSM-IV appendix. In factitious disorder by proxy, someone intentionally produces physical signs or symptoms in another person who is under the first person's care. The only apparent purpose of the behavior is for the caretaker to indirectly assume the sick role. The most common case of factitious disorder by proxy involves a mother who deceives medical personnel into believing that her child is ill. The deception may involve a false medical history, the contamination of laboratory samples, the alteration of records, or the induction of injury and illness in the child.

DIFFERENTIAL DIAGNOSIS

Any disorder in which physical signs and symptoms are prominent should be considered in the differential diagnosis, and the possibility of authentic or concomitant physical illness must always be explored.

Somatoform Disorders

A factitious disorder is differentiated from somatization disorder (Briquet's syndrome) by the voluntary production of factitious symptoms, the extreme course of multiple hospitalizations, and the patient's seeming willingness to undergo an extraordinary number of mutilating procedures. Patients with conversion disorder are not usually conversant with medical terminology and hospital routines, and their symptoms have a direct temporal relation or symbolic reference to specific emotional conflicts.

Hypochondriasis differs from factitious disorder in that the hypochondriacal patient does not voluntarily initiate the production of symptoms, and hypochondriasis typically has a later age of onset. As is the case with somatization disorder, patients with hypochondriasis do not usually submit to potentially mutilating procedures.

Personality Disorders

Because of their pathological lying, lack of close relationships with others, hostile and manipulative manner, and associated substance and criminal history, factitious disorder patients are often classified as having antisocial personality disorder; however, antisocial persons do not usually volunteer for invasive procedures or resort to a way of life marked by repeated or long-term hospitalization.

Because of attention-seeking and an occasional flair for the dramatic, factitious disorder patients may be classified as having histrionic personality disorder. But not all factitious disorder patients have a dramatic flair; many are withdrawn and bland.

Consideration of the patient's chaotic lifestyle, past history of disturbed interpersonal relationships, identity crisis, substance abuse, self-damaging acts, and manipulative tactics may lead to the diagnosis of borderline personality disorder.

Factitious disorder persons usually do not have the eccentricities of dress, thought, or communication that characterize schizotypal personality disorder patients.

Schizophrenia

The diagnosis of schizophrenia is often based on patients' admittedly bizarre lifestyles, but factitious disorder patients do not usually meet the diagnostic criteria for schizophrenia unless they have the fixed delusion that they are actually ill and act on that belief by seeking hospitalization. Such a practice seems to be the exception, for few patients with factitious disorder show evidence of a severe thought disorder or bizarre delusions.

Malingering

Factitious disorders must be distinguished from malingering. Malingerers have an obvious, recognizable environmental goal in producing signs and symptoms. They may seek hospitalization to secure financial compensation, evade the police, avoid work, or merely obtain free bed and board for the night; but they always have some apparent end for their behavior. Moreover, they can usually stop producing their signs and symptoms when they are no longer considered profitable or when the stakes rise too high and the patients risk life and limb.

Substance Use Disorders

Although patients with factitious disorders may have a complicating history of substance abuse, they should be considered not merely as substance abusers but as having coexisting diagnoses.

Ganser's Syndrome

Ganser's syndrome, a controversial condition most typically associated with prison inmates, is characterized by the use of approximate answers. Persons with the syndrome respond to simple questions with astonishingly incorrect answers. For example, when asked about the color of a blue car, the person answers ''red.'' Ganser's syndrome may be a variant of malingering, in that the patients avoid punishment or responsibility for their actions. Ganser's syndrome is classified in DSM-IV as a dissociative disorder not otherwise specified when it is not associated with dissociative amnesia or dissociative fugue.

COURSE AND PROGNOSIS

Factitious disorders typically begin in early adult life, although they may appear during childhood or adolescence. The onset of the disorder or of discrete episodes of treatment-seeking may follow a real illness, loss, rejection, or abandonment. Usually, the patient or a close relative was hospitalized in childhood or early adolescence for a genuine physical illness. Thereafter, a long pattern of successive hospitalizations unfolds, beginning insidiously. If that is the case, the onset was earlier than generally reported. As the disorder progresses, the patient becomes knowledgeable about medicine and hospitals.

Factitious disorders are incapacitating to the patient, often producing severe traumas or untoward reactions related to treatment. As may seem obvious, a course of repeated or long-term hospitalization is incompatible with meaningful vocational work and sustained interpersonal relationships. The prognosis in most cases is poor. A few patients occasionally spend time in jail, usually for minor crimes, such as burglary, vagrancy, and disorderly conduct. The patient may also have a history of intermittent psychiatric hospitalization.

Although no adequate data are available about the ultimate outcome for the patients, a few of them probably die as a result of needless medication, instrumentation, or surgery. In view of the patients' often expert simulation and the risks that they take, some may die without the disorder being suspected. Possible features that indicate a favorable prognosis are (1) the presence of a depressive-masochistic personality, (2) functioning at a borderline, not a continuously psychotic, level, and (3) the presence of minimal psychopathic antisocial personality disorder attributes.

TREATMENT

No specific psychiatric therapy has been effective in treating factitious disorders. It is a clinical paradox that patients with the disorders simulate serious illness, seeking and submitting to unnecessary treatment, while denying to themselves and others their true illness. Ultimately, the patients elude meaningful therapy by abruptly leaving the hospital or failing to keep follow-up appointments.

Treatment, thus, is best focused on management, rather than on cure. Perhaps the single most important factor in successful management is a physician's early recognition of the disorder. The physician can then forestall the patient's undergoing a multitude of painful and potentially dangerous diagnostic procedures. Good liaison between psychiatrists and the medical or surgical staff is strongly advised.

Legal intervention has been obtained in several instances, particularly with children. An obstacle to successful court action is the senselessness of the disorder and the denial of false action by parents, thereby often making conclusive proof unobtainable. In such cases the child welfare services should be notified and arrangements made for the ongoing monitoring of the children's health.

The personal reactions of physicians and staff members are of great significance in treating and establishing a working alliance with the patients, who invariably evoke feelings of futility, bewilderment, betrayal, hostility, and even contempt. In essence, staff members are forced to abandon a basis element of their relationship with patients: acceptance of the truthfulness of the patient's statements. One appropriate psychiatric intervention is to suggest to the staff ways of maintaining an awareness that, even though the patient's illness is factitious, the patient is ill.

Physicians should try not to feel resentment when patients dispute their diagnostic ability, and they should avoid any unmasking ceremony that sets up the patients as adversaries and precipitates their flight from the hospital. Staff anger may also be manifested by performing unnecessary procedures or by discharging patients abruptly.

Clinicians who find themselves involved with patients suffering from factitious disorders often become enraged at the patient for lying and deceiving them. Hence, therapists must be mindful of countertransference whenever they suspect factitious disorder. Often, the diagnosis is unclear because a definitive physical cause cannot be entirely ruled out. Although the use of confrontation is controversial, at some point in the treatment, the patient must be made to face reality. The majority of patients simply leave treatment when their method of gaining attention is identified and brought out into the open. In some cases the clinician should reframe the factitious disorder as a cry for help, so that the patient does not view the clinician's response as a punitive one. A major role for psychiatrists in working with factitious disorder patients is to help other staff members in the hospital deal with their own sense of outrage at having been duped. Education about the disorder and some attempt to understand the patient's motivations may help the staff members maintain their professional conduct in the face of extreme frustration.

Although a few cases of individual psychotherapy have been reported in the literature, no consensus exists regarding the best approach. In general, working in concert with the patient's primary care physician is more effective than working with the patient in isolation.

References

Folks D G: Munchausen's syndrome and other factitious disorders. Special Issue: Malingering and conversion reactions. Neurol Clin *13*: 267, 1995.

French J: Pseudoseizures in the era of video-electroencephalogram monitoring. Curr Opin Neurol 8: 117, 1995.

Heron E A, Kritchevsky M, Delis D C: Neuropsychological presentation of Ganser symptoms. J Clin Exp Neuropsychol *13*: 552, 1991.

Houck C A: Medicolegal aspects of factitious disorder. Psychiatr Med *10*: 105, 1992.

Jones R M: Factitious disorders. In *Comprehensive Textbook of Psychiatry*, ed 6, H I Kaplan, B J Sadock, editors, p 1271. Williams & Wilkins, Baltimore, 1995.

Jureidini J: Obstetric factitious disorder and Munchausen syndrome by proxy. J Nerv Ment Dis *181*: 135, 1993.

Schmaling K B, Rosenberg S J, Oppenheimer J, Moran M G: Factitious disorder with respiratory symptoms. Psychosomatics *32*: 457, 1991.

Schreier H A: The perversion of mothering: Munchausen syndrome by proxy. Bull Menninger Clin *56*: 421, 1992.

Songer D A: Factitious AIDS. A case reported and literature review. Psychosomatics *36*: 406, 1995.

13/ Dissociative Disorders

In a state of mental health, a person has a unitary sense of self as a single human being with a single basic personality. The key dysfunction in the dissociative disorders is a loss of that unitary state of consciousness; the person feels the lack of such an identity or confusion regarding his or her identity or has multiple identities. The unifying experience of self usually consists of an integration of a person's thoughts, feelings, and actions into a unique personality. Although that unifying experience of personality is abnormal in the dissociative disorders, patients with the disorders exhibit a range of dissociative experiences from normal to pathological.

Dissociation arises as a self-defense against trauma. Dissociative defenses perform the dual function of helping victims remove themselves from trauma at the time it occurs while also delaying the necessary working through that places the trauma in perspective with the rest of their lives. In the case of repression, a horizontal split is created by the repression barrier, and the material is transferred to the dynamic unconscious. Dissociation differs by creating a vertical split, so that the mental contents exist in a series of parallel consciousnesses.

In the majority of dissociative states, contradictory representations of the self are maintained in separate mental compartments, because they are in conflict with one another. In the extreme form of dissociative identity disorder (multiple personality), those separate representations of the self take on the metaphoric existence of separate personalities known as alters.

DISSOCIATIVE AMNESIA

The symptom of amnesia is common to dissociative amnesia, dissociative fugue, and dissociative identity disorder. Dissociative amnesia is the appropriate diagnosis when the dissociative phenomena are limited to amnesia. The key symptom of dissociative amnesia is the inability to recall information already stored in the patient's memory. The forgotten information is usually about a stressful or traumatic event in the person's life. The inability to remember the information cannot be explained by ordinary forgetfulness, and there is no evidence of an underlying brain disorder. The capacity to learn new information is retained.

A common form of dissociative amnesia involves amnesia for one's personal identity but intact memory of general information. That clinical picture is exactly the reverse of the clinical picture seen in dementia, in which patients may remember their names but forget general information, such as what they had for lunch. Except for their amnesia, patients with dissociative amnesia appear completely intact and function coherently. By contrast, in most amnesias due to a general medical condition (such as postictal and toxic amnesia), the patients may be confused and have disorganized behavior. Other types of amnesias (for example, transient global amnesia and postconcussion amnesia) are associated with an ongoing anterograde amnesia, which does not occur in dissociative amnesia patients.

Epidemiology

Amnesia is the most common dissociative symptom, since it occurs in almost all the dissociative disorders. Dissociative amnesia is thought to be the most common of the dissociative disorders, although epidemiological data on all the dissociative disorders are limited and uncertain. Nevertheless, dissociative amnesia is thought to occur more often in women than in men and more often in young adults than in older adults. Inasmuch as the disorder is usually associated with stressful and traumatic events, its incidence probably increases during times of war and natural disasters. Cases of dissociative amnesia that are related to domestic settings—for example, spouse abuse and child abuse—are probably constant in number.

Etiology

The neuroanatomical, neurophysiological, and neurochemical processes of memory storage and retrieval are much better understood today than they were a decade ago. The differentiation between short-term memory and long-term memory, the central role of the hippocampus, and the involvement of neurotransmitter systems have been clarified. The newly appreciated complexity of the formation and the retrieval of memories may make dissociative amnesia intuitively understandable because of the many potential areas for dysfunction. However, the vast majority of patients with dissociative amnesia are unable to retrieve painful memories of stressful and traumatic events. Thus, the emotional content of the memory is clearly related to the pathophysiology and the cause of the disorder.

One particularly relevant observation about normal people is that learning is often state-dependent—that is, dependent on the context in which the learning occurs. Information that is learned or experienced during a particular behavior (for example, while driving a car), a pharmacological state (for example, while drinking alcohol), or a neurochemical state (for example, possibly associated with an emotion such as happiness) or in a particular physical setting (for example, seeing a certain flower) is often recalled only while reexperiencing the original state or is most easily recalled while reexperiencing the original state. Thus, people can remember where the light switch is in their cars more easily while they are driving than when they are watching television. The theory of state-dependent learning applies to dissociative amnesia in that the memory of a traumatic event is laid down during the event, and the emotional state may be so out of the ordinary for the affected person that it is hard for the person to remember information learned during that state.

The psychoanalytic approach to dissociative amnesia is to consider the amnesia primarily as a defense mechanism, in which the person alters consciousness as a way of dealing with an emotional conflict or an external stressor. Secondary defenses involved in dissociative amnesia include repression (disturbing impulses are blocked from consciousness) and denial (some aspect of external reality is ignored by the conscious mind).

Diagnosis

The diagnostic criteria for dissociative amnesia in the fourth edition of *Diagnostic and Statistical Manual of Mental Disor-*

Table 13-1. Diagnostic Criteria for Dissociative Amnesia

A. The predominant disturbance is one or more episodes of inability to recall important personal information, usually of a traumatic or stressful nature, that is too extensive to be explained by ordinary forgetfulness.

B. The disturbance does not occur exclusively during the course of dissociative identity disorder, dissociative fugue, posttraumatic stress disorder, acute stress disorder, or somatization disorder and is not due to the direct physiological effects of a substance (e.g., a drug of abuse, a medication) or a neurological or other general medical condition (e.g., amnestic disorder due to head trauma).

C. The symptoms cause clinically significant distress or impairment in social, occupational, or other important areas of functioning.

Table from DSM-IV, *Diagnostic and Statistical Manual of Mental Disorders*, ed 4. Copyright American Psychiatric Association, Washington, 1994. Used with permission.

ders (DSM-IV) (Table 13–1) emphasize that the forgotten information is usually of a traumatic or stressful nature. Dissociative amnesia can be diagnosed only if the symptoms are not limited to amnesia that occurs in the course of dissociative identity disorder and are not the result of a general medical condition (for example, head trauma) or the ingestion of a substance.

Although rare episodes of dissociative amnesia occur spontaneously, the history usually reveals some precipitating emotional trauma charged with painful emotions and psychological conflict—for example, a natural disaster in which patients witnessed severe injuries or feared for their lives. A fantasized or actual expression of an impulse (sexual or aggressive) with which the patient is unable to deal may also act as the precipitant. Amnesia may follow an extramarital affair that the patient finds morally reprehensible.

Although not necessary for diagnosis, the onset is often abrupt, and the patients are usually aware that they have lost their memories. Some patients are upset about the memory loss, but others appear to be unconcerned or indifferent. With patients who are not aware of their memory loss but whom the clinician suspects of having dissociative amnesia, it is often useful to ask specific questions that may reveal the symptoms. Amnestic patients are usually alert before and after the amnesia occurs. A few patients, however, report a slight clouding of consciousness during the period immediately surrounding the amnestic period. Depression and anxiety are common predisposing factors and are frequently present on the mental status examination of the patient.

The amnesia of dissociative amnesia may take one of several forms: (1) *localized amnesia*, the most common type, is the loss of memory for the events of a short period of time (a few hours to a few days); (2) *generalized amnesia* is the loss of memory for a whole lifetime of experience; (3) *selective* (also known as *systematized*) *amnesia* is the failure to recall some but not all events during a short period of time.

Amnesia may have a primary gain or a secondary gain. The woman who is amnestic for the birth of a dead baby achieves a primary gain by protecting herself from painful emotions. An example of secondary gain is a soldier who has sudden amnesia and is removed from combat as a result.

Differential Diagnosis

The differential diagnosis of dissociative amnesia involves a consideration of both general medical conditions and other

mental disorders. A medical history, a physical examination, a laboratory workup, a psychiatric history, and a mental status examination should be conducted.

Amnesia associated with dementia and delirium is usually associated with many other easily recognized cognitive symptoms. When the patient has amnesia for personal information in those conditions, the dementia or the delirium is usually advanced and easily differentiated from dissociative amnesia. Especially in a case of delirium, the patient may evidence confabulation during the interview. In general, a prompt return of memory usually indicates dissociative amnesia, rather than amnestic disorder due to a general medical condition.

In postconcussion amnesia the memory disturbance follows a head trauma, is often retrograde (as opposed to the anterograde disturbance of dissociative amnesia), and usually does not extend beyond one week. The clinical evaluation of a patient with postconcussion amnesia may reveal a history of unconsciousness, external evidence of trauma, or other evidence of a brain injury. Some researchers have hypothesized that a history of head trauma may predispose a person to a dissociative disorder. Epilepsy can lead to sudden memory impairment associated with motor and electroencephalogram (EEG) abnormalities. Patients with epilepsy are prone to seizures during periods of stress, and some researchers have hypothesized that an epilepticlike pathology may be involved in the dissociative disorders. A history of an aura, head trauma, or incontinence can help the clinician recognize amnesia related to epilepsy.

TRANSIENT GLOBAL AMNESIA

Transient global amnesia is an acute and transient retrograde amnesia that affects recent memories more than remote memories. Although patients are usually aware of the amnesia, they may still perform highly complex mental and physical acts during the 6 to 24 hours that transient global amnesia episodes usually last. Recovery from the disorder is usually complete. Transient global amnesia is most often caused by transient ischemic attacks (TIAs) that affect limbic midline brain structures. Transient global amnesia can also be associated with migraine headaches, seizures, and intoxication with sedative-hypnotic drugs.

Transient global amnesia can be differentiated from dissociative amnesia in several ways. Transient global amnesia is associated with an anterograde amnesia during the episode; dissociative amnesia is not. Patients with transient global amnesia tend to be more upset and concerned about the symptoms than are patients with dissociative amnesia. The personal identity of the patient with dissociative amnesia is lost; that of the patient with transient global amnesia is retained. The memory loss of a patient with dissociative amnesia may be selective for certain areas and usually does not show a temporal gradient; the memory loss of a patient with transient global amnesia is generalized, and remote events are remembered better than recent events. Because of the association of transient global amnesia with vascular problems, the disorder is most common in patients in their 60s and 70s, whereas dissociative amnesia is most common in patients in their 20s to 40s, a period associated with the common types of psychological stressors seen in those patients.

OTHER MENTAL DISORDERS

Two other dissociative disorders, dissociative fugue and dissociative identity disorder, should be considered in the differential diagnosis. Those disorders are distinguished on the basis of their additional symptoms.

In DSM-IV sleepwalking disorder is classified as a parasomnia, a type of sleep disorder. Patients suffering from sleepwalking disorder behave in a strange manner that resembles the behavior of someone in a dissociative state. In sleepwalking disorder, patients exhibit an altered state of conscious awareness of their surroundings; they often have vivid hallucinatory recollections of an emotionally traumatic event in the past of which there is no memory during the usual waking state. Such patients are out of contact with the environment, appear preoccupied with a private world, and stare into space if their eyes are open. They may appear emotionally upset, speak excitedly in words and sentences that are frequently hard to understand, or engage in a pattern of seemingly meaningful activities that is repeated every time an episode occurs. The patient has amnesia for the sleepwalking episode once it has ended.

Although amnesia for a period of immediate past experience is found in patients with sleepwalking disorder and with localized and general amnesia, the state of consciousness during the period for which they are amnestic differs in character. Patients with sleepwalking disorder seem out of touch with the environment and appear to be dreaming. Amnestic patients, by contrast, usually give no indication to observers that anything is amiss and seem entirely alert both before and after the amnesia occurs.

Posttraumatic stress disorder, acute stress disorder, and the somatoform disorders (especially somatization disorder and conversion disorder) should be considered in the differential diagnosis and may coexist with dissociative amnesia. The somatoform disorders may be associated with the same type of traumatic events that are usually seen in dissociative amnesia. Malingering, in this case a deliberate attempt to mimic amnesia, may be difficult to confirm. Any possible secondary gain, especially in regard to escaping punishment for criminal activity, should increase the clinician's suspicion, although such secondary gain does not rule out the diagnosis of dissociative amnesia.

Course and Prognosis

The symptoms of dissociative amnesia usually terminate abruptly, and recovery is generally complete with few recurrences. In some cases, especially if there is secondary gain, the condition may last a long time. The clinician should try to restore the patient's lost memories to consciousness as soon as possible; otherwise, the repressed memory may form a nucleus in the unconscious mind around which future amnestic episodes may develop.

Treatment

Interviewing may give the clinician clues to the psychologically traumatic precipitant. Intermediate and short-acting barbiturates, such as thiopental (Pentothal) and amobarbital (Amytal) given intravenously, and benzodiazepines may be used to help patients recover their forgotten memories. Hypnosis can be used primarily as a means of relaxing the patient enough to recall what has been forgotten. The patient is placed in a somnolent state, at which point mental inhibitions are diminished, and the amnestic material emerges into consciousness and is then recalled. Once the lost memories have been retrieved, psychotherapy is generally recommended to help patients incorporate the memories into their conscious states.

DISSOCIATIVE FUGUE

The behavior of patients with dissociative fugue is more purposefully integrated with their amnesia than is that of patients with dissociative amnesia. Patients with dissociative fugue have physically traveled away from their customary homes or work situations and fail to remember important aspects of their previous identities (name, family, occupation). Such a patient often, but not necessarily, takes on an entirely new identity and occupation, although the new identity is usually less complete than are the alternate personalities seen in dissociative identity disorder. Also, in dissociative fugue the old and the new identities do not alternate, as they do in dissociative identity disorder.

Epidemiology

Dissociative fugue is rare and, like dissociative amnesia, occurs most often during wartime, after natural disasters, and as a result of personal crises with intense internal conflicts (for example, extramarital affairs).

Etiology

Although heavy alcohol abuse may predispose a person to dissociative fugue, the cause of the disorder is thought to be basically psychological. The essential motivating factor appears to be a desire to withdraw from emotionally painful experiences. Patients with mood disorders and certain personality disorders (for example, borderline, histrionic, and schizoid personality disorders) are predisposed to the development of dissociative fugue.

A variety of stressors and personal factors predispose a person to the development of dissociative fugue. The psychosocial factors include marital, financial, occupational, and war-related stressors. Other associated predisposing features include depression, suicide attempts, organic disorders (especially epilepsy), and a history of substance abuse. A history of head trauma also predisposes a person to dissociative fugue.

Diagnosis

The diagnosis of dissociative fugue requires that the onset of the symptoms be sudden (Table 13–2). DSM-IV requires that a person either be confused about his or her identity or assume a new identity. The diagnosis is excluded if the symp-

---

Table 13-2.   Diagnostic Criteria for Dissociative Fugue

A. The predominant disturbance is sudden, unexpected travel away from home or one's customary place of work, with inability to recall one's past.

B. Confusion about personal identity or assumption of a new identity (partial or complete).

C. The disturbance does not occur exclusively during the course of dissociative identity disorder and is not due to the direct physiological effects of a substance (e.g., a drug of abuse, a medication) or a general medical condition (e.g., temporal lobe epilepsy).

D. The symptoms cause clinically significant distress or impairment in social, occupational, or other important areas of functioning.

Table from DSM-IV, *Diagnostic and Statistical Manual of Mental Disorders*, ed 4. Copyright American Psychiatric Association, Washington, 1994. Used with permission.

toms occur only during the course of dissociative identity disorder or are the result of substance ingestion or a general medical condition (for example, temporal lobe epilepsy).

Clinical Features

Dissociative fugue has several typical features. Patients wander in a purposeful way, usually far from home and often for days at a time. During that period they have complete amnesia for their past lives and associations, but, unlike patients with dissociative amnesia, they are generally unaware that they have forgotten anything. Only when they suddenly return to their former selves do they recall the time antedating the onset of fugue, but then they remain amnestic for the period of the fugue itself. Patients with dissociative fugue do not seem to others to be behaving in extraordinary ways, nor do they give evidence of acting out any specific memory of a traumatic event. On the contrary, dissociative fugue patients lead quiet, prosaic, reclusive existences; work at simple occupations; live modestly; and, in general, do nothing to draw attention to themselves.

Differential Diagnosis

The differential diagnosis for dissociative fugue is similar to that for dissociative amnesia. The wandering that is seen in dementia or delirium is usually distinguished from the traveling of a dissociative fugue patient by the aimlessness and the absence of complex and socially adaptive behaviors in the former. Complex partial epilepsy may be associated with episodes of travel, but the patient does not usually assume a new identity, and the episodes are generally not precipitated by psychological stress. Dissociative amnesia presents with a loss of memory as the result of psychological stress, but there are no episodes of purposeful travel or of a new identity. Malingering may be difficult to distinguish from dissociative fugue. Any evidence of a clear secondary gain should raise the clinician's suspicions. Hypnosis and amobarbital interviews may be useful in clarifying the clinical diagnosis.

Course and Prognosis

The fugue is usually brief—hours to days. Less commonly, a fugue lasts many months and involves extensive travel covering thousands of miles. Generally, recovery is spontaneous and rapid, and recurrences are rare.

Treatment

Treatment of dissociative fugue is similar to the treatment of dissociative amnesia. Psychiatric interviewing, drug-assisted interviewing, and hypnosis may help reveal to the therapist and to the patient the psychological stressors that precipitated the fugue episode. Psychotherapy is generally indicated to help patients incorporate the precipitating stressors into their psyches in a healthy and integrated manner. The treatment of choice for dissociative fugue is expressive-supportive psychodynamic psychotherapy. The most widely accepted technique requires a mixture of abreaction of the past trauma and integration of the trauma into a cohesive self that no longer requires fragmentation to deal with the trauma.

DISSOCIATIVE IDENTITY DISORDER

Dissociative identity disorder is the DSM-IV name for what has been commonly known as multiple personality disorder. Dissociative identity disorder is a chronic dissociative disorder, and its cause almost invariably involves a traumatic event, usually childhood physical or sexual abuse. The concept of personality conveys the sense of an integration of the way person thinks, feels, and behaves and the appreciation of himself or herself as a unitary being. Persons with dissociative identity disorder have two or more distinct personalities, each of which determines behavior and attitudes during any period when it is the dominant personality. Dissociative identity disorder is usually considered the most serious of the dissociative disorders, although some clinicians who are diagnosing a wide range of patients with the disorder have suggested that there may be a wider range of severity than was previously appreciated.

Epidemiology

Anecdotal and research reports about dissociative identity disorder have varied in their estimates of the prevalence of the disorder. On one extreme, some investigators believe that dissociative identity disorder is extremely rare; on the other extreme, some investigators believe that dissociative identity disorder is vastly under-recognized. Well-controlled studies have reported that from 0.5 to 2 percent of general psychiatric hospital admissions meet the diagnostic criteria for dissociative identity disorder, as do perhaps as many as 5 percent of all psychiatric patients. Patients who are diagnosed with dissociative identity disorder are overwhelmingly women—90 to 100 percent of most samples reported. However, many clinicians and researchers believe that men are underreported in clinical samples because, they believe, most men with the disorder enter the criminal justice system, rather than the mental health system.

The disorder is most common in late adolescence and young adult life, with a mean age of diagnosis of 30 years, although patients have usually had symptoms for 5 to 10 years before the diagnosis. Several studies have found that the disorder is more common in the first-degree biological relatives of people with the disorder than in the general population.

Dissociative identity disorder frequently coexists with other mental disorders, including anxiety disorders, mood disorders, somatoform disorders, sexual dysfunctions, substance-related disorders, eating disorders, sleeping disorders, and posttraumatic stress disorder. The symptoms of dissociative identity disorder are similar to those seen in borderline personality disorder, and the differentiation between the two disorders can be difficult. Suicide attempts are common in patients with dissociative identity disorder, and some studies have reported that as many as two thirds of all patients with dissociative identity disorder do attempt suicide during the course of their illness.

Etiology

The cause of dissociative identity disorder is unknown, although the histories of the patients almost invariably (approaching 100 percent) involve a traumatic event, most often in childhood. In general, four types of causative factors have been identified: (1) a traumatic life event, (2) a tendency for the disorder to develop, (3) formative environmental factors, and (4) the absence of external support.

The traumatic event is usually childhood physical or sexual abuse, commonly incestuous. Other traumatic events may include the death of a close relative or friend during childhood and witnessing a trauma or a death.

The tendency for the disorder to develop may be biologically or psychologically based. The variable ability of persons to be hypnotized may be one example of a risk factor for the development of dissociative identity disorder. Epilepsy has been hypothesized to be involved in the cause of dissociative identity disorder, and a high percentage of abnormal EEG activity has been reported in some studies of affected patients. One study of regional cerebral blood flow revealed temporal hyperperfusion in one of the subpersonalities but not in the main personality. Although several studies have found differences in pain sensitivity and other physiological measures among the personalities, the use of those data as proof of the existence of dissociative identity disorder should be approached with great caution.

The formulative environmental factors involved in the pathogenesis of dissociative identity disorder are nonspecific and are likely to involve such factors as role models and the availability of other mechanisms with which to deal with stress.

In many cases of dissociative identity disorder, a factor in the development of the disorder seems to have been the absence of support from significant others—for example, parents, siblings, other relatives, and nonrelated people, such as teachers.

Diagnosis

In the diagnostic criteria (Table 13–3), DSM-IV requires an amnestic component, which research has found to be an essential component of the complete clinical picture. The diagnosis of dissociative identity disorder requires the presence of at least two distinct personality states. The diagnosis of dissociative personality disorder is excluded if the symptoms are the result of a substance (for example, alcohol) or a general medical condition (for example, complex partial seizures).

Clinical Features

Patients with dissociative identity disorder are often thought to have a personality disorder (commonly borderline personality disorder), schizophrenia, or a rapid-cycling bipolar disorder. Clinicians must be aware of the diagnostic category and must listen for specific suggestive features of dissociative identity

Table 13-3. Diagnostic Criteria for Dissociative Identity Disorder

A. The presence of two or more distinct identities or personality states (each with its own relatively enduring pattern of perceiving, relating to, and thinking about the environment and self).

B. At least two of these identities or personality states recurrently take control of the person's behavior.

C. Inability to recall important personal information that is too extensive to be explained by ordinary forgetfulness.

D. The disturbance is not due to the direct physiological effects of a substance (e.g., blackouts or chaotic behavior during alcohol intoxication) or a general medical condition (e.g., complex partial seizures). **Note:** In children, the symptoms are not attributable to imaginary playmates or other fantasy play.

disorder in the clinical interview. In spite of stories in the popular press about patients with more than 20 personalities, the median number of personalities in dissociative identity disorder is in the range of 5 to 10. Often, only two or three of the personalities are evident at diagnosis; the others are recognized during the course of treatment.

The transition from one personality to another is often sudden and dramatic. The patient generally has amnesia during each personality state for the existence of the others and for the events that took place when another personality was dominant. Sometimes, however, one personality state is not bound by such amnesia and retains complete awareness of the existence, qualities, and activities of the other personalities. At other times, the personalities are aware of all or some of the others to varying degrees and may experience the others as friends, companions, or adversaries. In classic cases, each personality has a fully integrated, highly complex set of associated memories and characteristic attitudes, personal relationships, and behavior patterns. Most often, the personalities have proper names; occasionally, one or more is given the name of its function—for example, the protector. Although some clinicians have emphasized that one of the personalities tends to be the dominant personality, that is not always the case. In fact, sometimes one personality masquerades as one of the others. However, usually a host personality is the one who presents for treatment and carries the patient's legal name. That host personality is likely to be depressed or anxious, may have masochistic personality traits, and may seem overly moral.

The first appearance of the secondary personality or personalities may be spontaneous or may emerge in relation to what seems to be a precipitant (including hypnosis or a drug-assisted interview). The personalities may be of both sexes, of various races and ages, and from families different from the patient's family of origin. The most common subordinate personality is childlike. Often, the personalities are disparate and may even be opposites. In the same person, one of the personalities may be extroverted, even sexually promiscuous, and others may be introverted, withdrawn, and sexually inhibited.

On examination, patients often show nothing unusual in their mental status, other than a possible amnesia for periods of varying durations. Often, only with prolonged interviews or many contacts with a patient with dissociative identity disorder is a clinician able to detect the presence of multiple personalities. Sometimes, by asking a patient to keep a diary, the clinician finds the multiple personalities revealed in the diary entries. An estimated 60 percent of patients switch into alternate personalities only occasionally; another 20 percent of patients not only have rare episodes but also are adept at covering the switches.

Differential Diagnosis

The differential diagnosis includes two other dissociative disorders, dissociative amnesia and dissociative fugue. However, both of those disorders lack the shifts in identity and the awareness of the original identity that are seen in dissociative identity disorder. Psychotic disorders, notably schizophrenia, may be confused with dissociative identity disorder only because schizophrenic persons may be delusional and believe that they have separate identities or report hearing other personalities' voices. In schizophrenia, a formal thought disorder, chronic social deterioration and other distinguishing signs are present.

Recently, clinicians have increasingly appreciated rapid-cycling bipolar disorders. The symptoms of rapid-cycling bipolar disorders appear to be similar to those of dissociative identity disorder; however, interviewing reveals the presence of discrete personalities in dissociative identity disorder patients. Borderline personality disorder may coexist with dissociative identity disorder, but the alteration of personalities in dissociative identity disorder may be mistakenly interpreted as nothing more than the irritability of mood and self-image problems that are characteristic of borderline personality disorder patients. Malingering presents a difficult diagnostic problem. Clear secondary gain raises suspicion, and drug-assisted interviews may be helpful in making the diagnosis. Among the neurological disorders to consider, complex partial epilepsy is the most likely to imitate the symptoms of dissociative identity disorder.

Course and Prognosis

Dissociative identity disorder can develop in children as young as 3 years of age. In children the symptoms may appear trancelike and may be accompanied by changes in abilities, depressive disorder symptoms, amnestic periods, hallucinatory voices, disavowal of behaviors, and suicidal or self-injurious behaviors. In spite of the female predominance in the disorder, affected children are more likely to be boys than girls. In adolescence the female predominance develops. Two symptom patterns in affected female adolescents have been observed: One symptom pattern is of a chaotic life with promiscuity, drug use, somatic symptoms, and suicide attempts. Such patients may be classified as having an impulse control disorder, schizophrenia, rapid-cycling bipolar I disorder, or histrionic or borderline personality disorder. A second pattern is characterized by withdrawal and childlike behaviors. Sometimes those patients are misclassified as having a mood disorder, a somatoform disorder, or generalized anxiety disorder. In male adolescents with dissociative identity disorder, the symptoms may get them into trouble with the law or school officials, and they may eventually end up in prison.

The earlier the onset of dissociative identity disorder, the worse the prognosis. One or more of the personalities may function relatively well, while others function marginally. The level of impairment ranges from moderate to severe, the determining variables being the number, the type, and the chronicity of the various personalities. The disorder is considered the most severe and chronic of the dissociative disorders, and recovery is generally incomplete. In addition, individual personalities may have their own separate mental disorders; mood disorders, personality disorders, and other dissociative disorders are the most common.

Treatment

The most efficacious approaches to dissociative identity involve insight-oriented psychotherapy, often in association with hypnotherapy or drug-assisted interviewing techniques. Hypnotherapy or drug-assisted interviewing can be useful in obtaining additional history, identifying previously unrecognized personalities, and fostering abreaction. A psychotherapeutic treatment plan should begin by confirming the diagnosis and by identifying and characterizing the various personalities. If any of the personalities are inclined toward self-destructive or otherwise violent behavior, the therapist should engage the patient and the appropriate personalities in treatment contracts regarding those dangerous behaviors. Hospitalization may be necessary in some cases.

The use of antipsychotic medications in the patients is almost never indicated. Some data indicate that antidepressants and antianxiety medications may be useful as adjuvants to psychotherapy. A few uncontrolled studies report that anticonvulsant medications—for example, carbamazepine (Tegretol)—help selected patients.

DEPERSONALIZATION DISORDER

DSM-IV characterizes depersonalization disorder as a persistent or recurrent alteration in the perception of the self to the extent that the sense of one's own reality is temporarily lost. Patients with depersonalization disorder may feel that they are mechanical, in a dream, or detached from their bodies. The episodes are ego-dystonic, and the patients realize the unreality of the symptoms.

Some clinicians distinguish between depersonalization and derealization. *Depersonalization* is the feeling that one's body or one's personal self is strange and unreal; *derealization* is the perception of objects in the external world as being strange and unreal. The distinction provides a more accurate description of each phenomenon than is achieved by grouping them together under the rubric of depersonalization.

Epidemiology

As an occasional isolated experience in the lives of many persons, depersonalization is a common phenomenon and is not necessarily pathological. Studies indicate that transient depersonalization may occur in as much as 70 percent of a given population, with no significant difference between men and women. Depersonalization is a frequent event in children as they develop the capacity for self-awareness, and adults often undergo a temporary sense of unreality when they travel to new and strange places.

Information about the epidemiology of pathological depersonalization is scanty. In a few recent studies, depersonalization was found to occur in women at least twice as frequently as in men; it is rarely found in persons over 40 years of age.

Etiology

Depersonalization disorder may be caused by psychological, neurological, or systemic disease. Experiences of depersonalization have been associated with epilepsy, brain tumors, sensory deprivation, and emotional trauma. Depersonalization disorder is associated with an array of substances, including alcohol, barbiturates, benzodiazepines, scopolamine (Donnagel), clioquinol (Vioform), β-adrenergic antagonists, marijuana, and virtually any phencyclidinelike or hallucinogenic substance. Depersonalization phenomena have been caused by electrical stimulation of the cortex of the temporal lobes during neurosurgery. Systemic causes include endocrine disorders of the thyroid and the pancreas. Anxiety and depression are predisposing factors, as is severe stress, such as what one experiences in combat or in an automobile accident. Depersonalization is a symptom frequently associated with anxiety disorders, depressive disorders, and schizophrenia.

Table 13-4.   Diagnostic Criteria for Depersonalization Disorder

A. Persistent or recurrent experiences of feeling detached from, and as if one is an outside observer of, one's mental processes or body (e.g., feeling like one is in a dream).

B. During the depersonalization experience, reality testing remains intact.

C. The depersonalization causes clinically significant distress or impairment in social, occupational, or other important areas of functioning.

D. The depersonalization experience does not occur exclusively during the course of another mental disorder, such as schizophrenia, panic disorder, acute stress disorder, or another dissociative disorder, and is not due to the direct physiological effects of a substance (e.g., a drug of abuse, a medication) or a general medical condition (e.g., temporal lobe epilepsy).

Table from DSM-IV, *Diagnostic and Statistical Manual of Mental Disorders*, ed 4. Copyright American Psychiatric Association, Washington, 1994. Used with permission.

Diagnosis

The DSM-IV diagnostic criteria for depersonalization disorder (Table 13–4) require persistent or recurrent episodes of depersonalization that result in significant distress to patients or an impairment in their ability to function in social, occupational, or interpersonal relationships. The disorder is largely differentiated from psychotic disorders by the diagnostic requirement that reality testing remains intact in depersonalization disorder. The disorder cannot be diagnosed if the symptoms are better accounted for by another mental disorder, substance ingestion, or a general medical condition.

Clinical Features

The central characteristic of depersonalization is the quality of unreality and estrangement. Inner mental processes and external events seem to go on exactly as before, but they feel different and no longer seem to have any relation or significance to the person. Parts of the body or the entire physical being may seem foreign, as may mental operations and accustomed behavior. Particularly common is the sensation of a change in the patient's body; for instance, patients may feel that their extremities are bigger or smaller than usual. Hemidepersonalization, the patient's feeling that half of the body is unreal or does not exist, may be related to contralateral parietal lobe disease. Anxiety often accompanies the disorder, and many patients complain of distortions in their senses of time and space.

An occasional phenomenon is doubling; patients feel that the point of conscious I-ness is outside their bodies, often a few feet overhead; from there they observe themselves, as if they were totally separate persons. Sometimes patients believe that they are in two places at the same time, a condition known as reduplicative paramnesia or double orientation. Most patients are aware of the disturbances in their sense of reality; that awareness is considered one of the salient characteristics of the disorder.

Differential Diagnosis

Depersonalization may occur as a symptom in numerous other disorders. The common occurrence of depersonalization in patients with depressive disorders and schizophrenia should alert the clinician to the possibility that the patient who initially complains of feelings of unreality and estrangement is suffering from one of those more common disorders. A history and the mental status examination usually disclose the characteristic features of depressive disorders and schizophrenia. Because psychotomimetic drugs often induce long-lasting changes in the experience of the reality of the self and the environment, the clinician must inquire about the use of those substances. The presence of other clinical phenomena in patients complaining of a sense of unreality should usually take precedence in determining the diagnosis. In general, the diagnosis of depersonalization disorder is reserved for those conditions in which depersonalization constitutes the predominating symptom.

The fact that depersonalization phenomena may result from gross disturbances in brain function underlies the necessity for a neurological evaluation, especially when the depersonalization is not accompanied by common and obvious psychiatric symptoms. In particular, the possibility of a brain tumor or epilepsy should be considered. The experience of depersonalization may be the earliest presenting symptom of a neurological disorder.

Course and Prognosis

In the large majority of patients, the symptoms of depersonalization disorder first appear suddenly; only a few patients report a gradual onset. The disorder starts most often between the ages of 15 and 30 years, but it has been seen in patients as young as 10 years of age; it occurs less frequently after age 30 and almost never in the late decades of life. A few follow-up studies indicate that, in more than half of the cases, depersonalization tends to be a long-lasting condition. In many patients the symptoms run a steady course without any significant fluctuation of intensity, but the symptoms may occur episodically, interspersed with symptom-free intervals. Little is known about precipitating factors, although the disorder has been observed to begin during a period of relaxation after a person has experienced fatiguing psychological stress. The disorder is sometimes ushered in by an attack of acute anxiety that is frequently accompanied by hyperventilation.

Treatment

Little attention has been given to the treatment of patients with depersonalization disorder. Data on which a specific pharmacological treatment can be based currently are insufficient. However, the anxiety usually responds to antianxiety agents. An underlying disorder (for example, schizophrenia) can also be treated pharmacologically. Psychotherapeutic approaches are equally untested. As with all patients with neurotic symptoms, the decision to use psychoanalysis or insight-oriented psychotherapy is determined not by the presence of the symptom itself but by a variety of positive indications derived from an assessment of the patient's personality, human relationships, and life situation.

DISSOCIATIVE DISORDER NOT OTHERWISE SPECIFIED

The diagnosis of dissociative disorder not otherwise specified (NOS) is meant for disorders with dissociative features that do not meet the diagnostic criteria for dissociative amnesia, dissociative fugue, dissociative identity disorder, or depersonalization disorder.

Dissociative Trance Disorder

DSM-IV includes, as an example of dissociative disorder NOS, patients with single or episodic alterations in consciousness that are limited to particular locations or cultures. The example states that the "dissociative or trance disorder is not a normal part of a broadly accepted collective cultural or religious practice." DSM-IV includes in its appendixes a suggested set of diagnostic criteria for dissociative trance disorder. The disorder is similar to the diagnosis of trance and possession disorder in ICD-10. The DSM-IV diagnostic criteria require that the symptoms cause the patient significant distress or an impairment in the ability to function.

Trance states are altered states of consciousness, and patients exhibit diminished responsibility to environmental stimuli. Children may have repeated amnestic periods or trancelike states after physical abuse or trauma. Possession and trance states are curious and imperfectly understood forms of dissociation. A common example of a trance state is the medium who presides over a spiritual seance. Typically, mediums enter a dissociative state, during which a person from the so-called spirit world takes over much of the mediums' conscious awareness and influences their thoughts and speech.

Automatic writing and crystal-gazing are less common manifestations of possession or trance states. In automatic writing the dissociation affects only the arm and the hand that write the message, which often discloses mental contents of which the writer was unaware. Crystal-gazing results in a trance state in which visual hallucinations are prominent.

Phenomena related to trance states include highway hypnosis and the similar mental states experienced by airplane pilots. The monotony of moving at high speeds through environments that provide little in the way of distractions to the operator of the vehicle leads to a fixation on a single object—for example, a dial on the instrument panel or the never-ending horizon of a road running straight ahead for miles. A trancelike state of consciousness results in which visual hallucinations may occur and in which the danger of a serious accident is always present. Possibly in the same order of phenomena are the hallucinations and dissociated mental states in patients who have been confined to respirators for long periods without adequate environmental distractions.

The religions of many cultures recognize that the practice of concentration may lead to a variety of dissociative phenomena, such as hallucinations, paralyses, and other sensory disturbances. Hypnosis occasionally precipitates a self-limited but sometimes prolonged trance state.

Ganser's Syndrome

Ganser's syndrome is the voluntary production of severe psychiatric symptoms, sometimes described as the giving of approximate answers or talking past the point (for example, when asked to multiply 4 times 5, the patient answers "21"). The syndrome may occur in persons with other mental disorders, such as schizophrenia, depressive disorders, toxic states, paresis, alcohol use disorders, and factitious disorder. The psychological symptoms generally represent the patient's sense of mental illness, rather than any recognized diagnostic category. The syndrome is commonly associated with such dissociative phenomena as amnesia, fugue, perceptual disturbances, and conversion symptoms. Ganser's syndrome is apparently most common in men and in prisoners, although prevalence data and familial patterns are not established. A major predisposing factor is the existence of a severe personality disorder. The differential diagnosis may be extremely difficult. Unless the patient is able to admit the factitious nature of the presenting symptoms or unless conclusive evidence from objective psychological tests indicates that the symptoms are false, the clinician may not be able to determine whether the patient has a true disorder. The syndrome may be recognized by its pansymptomatic nature or by the fact that the symptoms are often worse when patients believe they are being watched. Recovery from the syndrome is sudden; patients claim amnesia for the events. Ganser's syndrome was previously classified as a factitious disorder.

Dissociated States

Certain degrees of dissociation may occur in persons who have been subjected to periods of prolonged and intensive coercive persuasion (such as brainwashing, thought reform, and indoctrination while being held captive by terrorists or cultists). Whether the states are truly dissociative disorders is open to question, since some evidence, especially in victims of Nazi concentration camps, indicates that the persons are often alexithymic, which results from massive regression rather than from dissociation.

References

Fleisher W P, Anderson G: Dissociative disorders in adolescence. Adolesc Psychiatry *20*: 203, 1995.

Gabbard G O: *Psychodynamic Psychiatry in Clinical Practice: The DSM-IV Edition*. American Psychiatric Press, Washington, 1994.

Nemiah J C: Dissociative disorders. In *Comprehensive Textbook of Psychiatry*, ed 6, H I Kaplan, B J Sadock, editors, p 1281. Williams & Wilkins, Baltimore, 1995.

Putnam F W, Loewenstein R J: Treatment of multiple personality disorder: A survey of current practices. Am J Psychiatry *150*: 1048, 1993.

Saxe G N, van der Kolk B A, Berkowitz R, Chinman G, Hall K, Lieberg G, Schwartz J: Dissociative disorders in psychiatric inpatients. Am J Psychiatry *150*: 1037, 1993.

Simeon D, Hollander E: Depersonalization disorder. Psychiatr Ann *23*: 382, 1993.

Steinberg M: *Handbook for the Assessment of Dissociation: A Clinical Guide*. American Psychiatric Press, Washington, 1995.

14/ Human Sexuality

14.1 NORMAL SEXUALITY

Sexual behavior is diverse and determined by a complex interaction of factors. It is affected by one's relationships with others, by one's life circumstances, and by the culture in which one lives. A person's sexuality is enmeshed with other personality factors, with biological makeup, and with a general sense of self. It includes the perception of being male or female, and it reflects developmental experiences with sex throughout the life cycle. A rigid definition of normal sexuality is difficult to draw and is clinically impractical. It is easier to define abnormal sexuality—that is, sexual behavior that is destructive to oneself or others, that cannot be directed toward a partner, that excludes stimulation of the primary sex organs, that is inappropriately associated with guilt and anxiety, or that is compulsive. Sex outside of marriage, masturbation, and various forms of sexual stimulation involving other than the primary sexual organs may still fall within normal limits, depending on the total context.

PSYCHOSEXUALITY

A person's sexuality and total personality are so entwined that it is virtually impossible to speak of sexuality as a separate entity. The term ''psychosexual'' is, therefore, used to imply personality development and functioning as those are affected by one's sexuality. ''Psychosexual'' is clearly not limited to sexual feelings and behavior, nor is it synonymous with libido in the broad Freudian sense.

In Sigmund Freud's view, all pleasurable impulses and activities are ultimately sexual and should be so designated from the start. That generalization has led to endless misinterpretations of Freudian sexual concepts by the laity and to confusion of one motivation with another by psychiatrists. For example, some oral activities are directed toward obtaining food, whereas others are directed toward achieving sexual gratification. Just because both are pleasure-seeking behaviors and both use the same organs, they are not, as Freud contended, necessarily sexual. Labeling all pleasure-seeking behaviors ''sexual'' precludes the clarification of motivation. A person may also use sexual activities for gratification of nonsexual needs, such as dependent, aggressive, and status needs. Although sexual and nonsexual impulses may motivate behavior jointly, the analysis of behavior depends on understanding the underlying individual motivations and their interactions.

SEXUAL LEARNING IN CHILDHOOD

Not until Freud described the effects of children's experiences on their characters as adults did the world recognize the universality of sexual activity and sexual learning in children. Most sexual learning experiences in childhood occur without the parent's awareness, but consciousness of the child's sex does influence parental behavior. Male infants, for instance, tend to be handled more vigorously, and female infants tend to be cuddled more. Fathers spend more time with their infant sons than with their daughters, and fathers also tend to be more aware of their sons' adolescent concerns than of their daughters'

anxieties. Boys are more likely than are girls to be physically disciplined. The child's sex affects parental tolerance for aggression and the reinforcement or the extinction of activity or passivity and of intellectual, aesthetic, and athletic interests.

Direct observation of children in various situations reveals that genital play in infants is part of the normal pattern of development. According to Harry Harlow, interaction with mothers and peers is necessary for the development of effective adult sexual behavior in monkeys, a finding that has relevance to the normal socialization of children. There is a critical period in development beyond which infants may be immune or resistant to certain types of stimulation but during which they are particularly susceptible to such stimuli. The detailed relation of critical periods to psychosexual development has yet to be established; presumably, Freud's stages of psychosexual development—oral, anal, phallic, latent, and genital—provide a broad framework of development.

PSYCHOSEXUAL FACTORS

A person's sexuality depends on four interrelated factors: sexual identity, gender identity, sexual orientation, and sexual behavior. Those factors affect personality growth, development, and functioning, and their totality is called psychosexual factors. Sexuality is something more than physical sex, coital or noncoital, and something less than every aspect of behavior directed toward attaining pleasure.

Sexual Identity and Gender Identity

Sexual identity is a person's biological sexual characteristics: chromosomes, external genitalia, internal genitalia, hormonal composition, gonads, and secondary sex characteristics. In normal development, they form a cohesive pattern, so that a person has no doubt about his or her sex.

Gender identity is a person's sense of maleness or femaleness.

SEXUAL IDENTITY

Modern embryological studies have shown that all mammalian embryos—the genetically male and the genetically female—are anatomically female during the early stages of fetal life. Differentiation of the male from the female results from the action of fetal androgen; the action begins about the sixth week of embryonic life and is completed by the end of the third month. Recent studies have explained the effects of fetal hormones on the masculinization or the feminization of the brain. In animals, prenatal hormonal stimulation of the brain is necessary for male and female reproductive and copulatory behavior. The fetus is also vulnerable to exogenously administered androgen during that period. For instance, if the pregnant mother receives sufficient exogenous androgen, a female fetus processing ovaries can develop external genitalia resembling those of a male.

GENDER IDENTITY

By the age of 2 to 3 years, almost everyone has a firm conviction that ''I am male'' or ''I am female.'' Yet even if maleness and femaleness develop normally, the person still has the adaptive task of developing a sense of masculinity or femininity.

Gender identity, according to Robert Stoller, "connotes psychological aspects of behavior related to masculinity and femininity." He considers gender social and sex biological: "Most often the two are relatively congruent, that is, males tend to be manly and females womanly." But sex and gender may develop in conflicting or even opposite ways. Gender identity results from an almost infinite series of cues derived from experiences with family members, teachers, friends, and coworkers and from cultural phenomena. Physical characteristics derived from one's biological sex—such as general physique, body shape, and physical dimensions—interrelate with an intricate system of stimuli, including rewards and punishment and parental gender labels, to establish gender identity.

The formation of gender identity is based on parental and cultural attitudes, the infant's external genitalia, and a genetic influence, which is physiologically active by the sixth week of fetal life. Even though family, cultural, and biological influences may complicate the establishment of a sense of masculinity or femininity, the standard and healthy outcome is a relatively secure sense of identification with one's biological sex—a stable gender identity.

Gender Role

Related to and in part derived from gender identity is gender role behavior. John Money described gender role behavior as all those things that a person says or does to disclose himself or herself as having the status of boy or man, girl or woman, respectively. A gender role is not established at birth but is built up cumulatively through experiences encountered and transacted through casual and unplanned learning, through explicit instruction and inculcation, and through spontaneously putting two and two together to make sometimes four and sometimes, erroneously, five.

The standard and healthy outcome is a congruence of gender identity and gender role. Although biological attributes are significant, the major factor in attaining the role appropriate to one's sex is learning.

Research on sex differences in behavior in children reveals more psychological similarities than differences. However, girls are found to be less prone to tantrums after the age of 18 months than are boys, and boys generally are more aggressive than girls—both physically and verbally—from age 2 onward. Little girls and little boys are similarly active, but the boys are more easily stimulated to sudden bursts of activity when they are in groups. Some researchers speculate that, although aggression is a learned behavior, male hormones may have sensitized boys' neural organizations to absorb those lessons better than girls do.

Gender role can appear to be in opposition to gender identity. Persons may identify with their own sex and yet adopt the dress, hairstyle, or other characteristics of the opposite sex. Or they may identify with the opposite sex yet for expediency adopt much of the behavior characteristics of their own sex.

A further discussion of gender issues (including gender identity disorder) appears in Chapter 15.

Sexual Orientation

Sexual orientation describes the object of a person's sexual impulses: heterosexual (opposite sex), homosexual (same sex), or bisexual (both sexes).

Sexual Behavior

PHYSIOLOGICAL RESPONSES

Sexual response is a true psychophysiological experience. Arousal is triggered by both psychological and physical stimuli,

levels of tension are experienced both physiologically and emotionally, and, with orgasm, there is normally a subjective perception of a peak of physical reaction and release. Psychosexual development, psychological attitudes toward sexuality, and attitudes toward one's sexual partner are directly involved with and affect the physiology of human sexual response.

Normal men and women experience a sequence of physiological responses to sexual stimulation. In the first detailed description of those responses, William Masters and Virginia Johnson observed that the physiological process involves increasing levels of vasocongestion and myotonia (tumescence) and the subsequent release of the vascular activity and muscle tone as a result of orgasm (detumescence). Tables 14.1–1 and 14.1–2 describe the male and female sexual response cycles. The fourth edition of *Diagnostic and Statistical Manual of Mental Disorders* (DSM-IV) defines a four-phase response cycle: phase 1, desire; phase 2, excitement; phase 3, orgasm; phase 4, resolution.

Phase 1: Desire

The desire (or appetitive) phase is distinct from any phase identified solely through physiology, and it reflects the psychiatrist's fundamental concern with motivations, drives, and personality. The phase is characterized by sexual fantasies and the desire to have sexual activity.

Phase 2: Excitement

The excitement phase is brought on by psychological stimulation (fantasy or the presence of a love object) or physiological stimulation (stroking or kissing) or a combination of the two. It consists of a subjective sense of pleasure. The excitement phase is characterized by penile tumescence leading to erection in the man and by vaginal lubrication in the woman. The nipples of both sexes become erect, although nipple erection is more common in women than in men. The woman's clitoris becomes hard and turgid, and her labia minora become thicker as a result of venous engorgement. Initial excitement may last several minutes to several hours. With continued stimulation, the man's testes increase in size 50 percent and elevate. The woman's vaginal barrel shows a characteristic constriction along the outer third, known as the orgasmic platform. The clitoris elevates and retracts behind the symphysis pubis. As a result, the clitoris is not easily accessible. As the area is stimulated, however, traction on the labia minora and the prepuce occurs, and there is intrapreputial movement of the clitoral shaft. Breast size in the woman increases 25 percent. Continued engorgement of the penis and the vagina produces specific color changes, particularly in the labia minora, which become bright or deep red. Voluntary contractions of large muscle groups occur, the rates of heartbeat and respiration increase, and blood pressure rises. Heightened excitement lasts 30 seconds to several minutes.

Phase 3: Orgasm

The orgasm phase consists of a peaking of sexual pleasure, with the release of sexual tension and the rhythmic contraction of the perineal muscles and the pelvic reproductive organs. A subjective sense of ejaculatory inevitability triggers the man's orgasm. The forceful emission of semen follows. The male orgasm is also associated with four to five rhythmic spasms of the prostate, seminal vesicles, vas, and urethra. In the woman, orgasm is characterized by 3 to 15 involuntary contractions of the lower third of the vagina and by strong sustained contractions of the uterus, flowing from the fundus downward to the cervix. Both men and women have involuntary contractions of the internal and external sphincters. Those and the other contractions during orgasm occur at intervals of 0.8 second. Other manifestations include voluntary and involuntary movements of the large muscle groups, including facial grimacing and carpopedal spasm. Blood pressure rises 20 to 40 mm (both

Table 14.1–1.   Male Sexual Response Cycle*

Organ	Excitement Phase	Orgasmic Phase	Resolution Phase
	Lasts several minutes to several hours; heightened excitement before orgasm, 30 seconds to 3 minutes	3 to 15 seconds	10 to 15 minutes; if no orgasm, $\frac{1}{2}$ to 1 day
Skin	Just before orgasm: sexual flush inconsistently appears; maculopapular rash originates on abdomen and spreads to anterior chest wall, face, and neck and can include shoulders and forearms	Well-developed flush	Flush disappears in reverse order of appearance; inconsistently appearing film of perspiration on soles of feet and palms of hands
Penis	Erection in 10 to 30 seconds caused by vasocongestion of erectile bodies of corpus cavernosa of shaft; loss of erection may occur with introduction of asexual stimulus, loud noise; with heightened excitement, size of glans and diameter of penile shaft increase further	Ejaculation; emission phase marked by three to four contractions of 0.8 second of vas, seminal vesicles, prostate; ejaculation proper marked by contractions of 0.8 second of urethra and ejaculatory spurt of 12 to 20 inches at age 18, decreasing with age to seepage at 70	Erection: partial involution in 5 to 10 seconds with variable refractory period; full detumescence in 5 to 30 minutes
Scrotum and testes	Tightening and lifting of scrotal sac and elevation of testes; with heightened excitement, 50% increase in size of testes over unstimulated state and flattening against perineum, signaling impending ejaculation	No change	Decrease to baseline size because of loss of vasocongestion; testicular and scrotal descent within 5 to 30 minutes after orgasm; involution may take several hours if no orgasmic release takes place
Cowper's glands	2 to 3 drops of mucoid fluid that contain viable sperm are secreted during heightened excitement	No change	No change
Other	Breasts: inconsistent nipple erection with heightened excitement before orgasm Myotonia: semispastic contractions of facial, abdominal, and intercostal muscles Tachycardia: up to 175 a minute Blood pressure: rise in systolic 20 to 80 mm; in diastolic 10 to 40 mm Respiration: increased	Loss of voluntary muscular control Rectum: rhythmical contractions of sphincter Heart rate: up to 180 beats a minute Blood pressure: up to 40 to 100 mm systolic; 20 to 50 mm diastolic Respiration: up to 40 respirations a minute	Return to baseline state in 5 to 10 minutes

* A desire phase consisting of sex fantasies and desire to have sex precedes excitement phase. Table by Virginia Sadock, MD.

systolic and diastolic), and the heart rate increases up to 160 beats a minute. Orgasm lasts from 3 to 25 seconds and is associated with a slight clouding of consciousness.

Phase 4: Resolution

Resolution consists of the disgorgement of blood from the genitalia (detumescence), and that detumescence brings the body back to its resting state. If orgasm occurs, resolution is rapid; if it does not occur, resolution may take two to six hours and may be associated with irritability and discomfort. Resolution through orgasm is characterized by a subjective sense of well-being, general relaxation, and muscular relaxation.

After orgasm, men have a refractory period that may last from several minutes to many hours; in that period they cannot be stimulated to further orgasm. The refractory period does not exist in women, who are capable of multiple and successive orgasms.

DIFFERENCES IN EROTIC STIMULI

Explicit sexual fantasies are common to men and women. The external stimuli for the fantasies frequently differ for the sexes. Men respond to visual stimuli of nude or barely dressed women, who are depicted as lust-driven and interested in only physical satisfaction. Women respond to romantic stories with tender, demonstrative heroes whose passion for the heroine impels him toward a lifetime commitment to her.

MASTURBATION

Masturbation is usually a normal precursor of object-related sexual behavior. It has been said that no other form of sexual activity has been more frequently discussed, more roundly condemned, and more universally practiced than masturbation. Research by Alfred C. Kinsey into the prevalence of masturbation indicated that nearly all men and three fourths of all women masturbate sometime during their lives.

Longitudinal studies of development show that sexual self-stimulation is common in infancy and childhood. Just as infants learn to explore the functions of their fingers and mouths, they do the same with their genitalia. At about 15 to 19 months

Table 14.1–2. Female Sexual Response Cycle*

Organ	Excitement Phase	Orgasmic Phase	Resolution Phase
	Lasts several minutes to several hours; heightened excitement before orgasm, 30 seconds to 3 minutes	3 to 15 seconds	10 to 15 minutes; if no orgasm, ½ to 1 day
Skin	Just before orgasm: sexual flush inconsistently appears; maculopapular rash originates on abdomen and spreads to anterior chest wall, face, and neck; can include shoulders and forearms	Well-developed flush	Flush disappears in reverse order of appearance; inconsistently appearing film of perspiration on soles of feet and palms of hands
Breasts	Nipple erection in two thirds of women, venous congestion and areolar enlargement; size increases to one fourth over normal	Breasts may become tremulous	Return to normal in about ½ hour
Clitoris	Enlargement in diameter of glans and shaft; just before orgasm, shaft retracts into pupuce	No change	Shaft returns to normal position in 5 to 10 seconds; detumescence in 5 to 30 minutes; if no orgasm, detumescence takes several hours
Labia majora	Nullipara: elevate and flatten against perineum Multipara: congestion and edema	No change	Nullipara: increase to normal size in 1 to 2 minutes Multipara: decrease to normal size in 10 to 15 minutes
Labia minora	Size increase two to three times over normal; change to pink, red, deep red before orgasm	Contractions of proximal labia minora	Return to normal within 5 minutes
Vagina	Color change to dark purple; vaginal transudate appears 10 to 30 seconds after arousal; elongation and ballooning of vagina; lower third of vagina constricts before orgasm	3 to 15 contractions of lower third of vagina at intervals of 0.8 second	Ejaculate forms seminal pool in upper two thirds of vagina; congestion disappears in seconds or, if no orgasm, in 20 to 30 minutes
Uterus	Ascends into false pelvis; laborlike contractions begin in heightened excitement just before orgasm	Contractions throughout orgasm	Contractions cease, and uterus descends to normal position
Other	Myotonia A few drops of mucoid secretion from Bartholin's glands during heightened excitement Cervix swells slightly and is passively elevated with uterus	Loss of voluntary muscular control Rectum: rhythmical contractions of sphincter Hyperventilation and tachycardia	Return to baseline status in seconds to minutes Cervix color and size return to normal, and cervix descends into seminal pool

* A desire phase consisting of sex fantasies and desire to have sex precedes excitement phase. Table by Virginia Sadock, MD.

of age, both sexes begin genital self-stimulation. Pleasurable sensations result from any gentle touch to the genital region. Those sensations, coupled with the ordinary desire for exploration of one's body, produce a normal interest in masturbatory pleasure at that time. Children also develop an increased interest in the genitalia of others—parents, children, and even animals. As youngsters acquire playmates, the curiosity about their own and others' genitalia motivates episodes of exhibitionism or genital exploration. Such experiences, unless blocked by guilty fear, contribute to continued pleasure from sexual stimulation.

With the approach of puberty, the upsurge of sex hormones, and the development of secondary sex characteristics, sexual curiosity is intensified, and masturbation increases. Adolescents are physically capable of coitus and orgasm but are usually inhibited by social restraints. They are under the dual and often conflicting pressures of establishing their sexual identities and controlling their sexual impulses. The result is a great deal of physiological sexual tension that demands release, and mastur-

bation is a normal way of reducing sexual tensions. An important emotional difference between the pubescent child and the youngster of earlier years is the presence of coital fantasies during masturbation in the adolescent. Those fantasies are an important adjunct to the development of sexual identity; in the comparative safety of the imagination, the adolescent learns to perform the adult sex role. That autoerotic activity is usually maintained into the young adult years, when it is normally replaced by coitus.

Couples in a sexual relationship do not abandon masturbation entirely. When coitus is unsatisfactory or is unavailable because of illness or the absence of the partner, self-stimulation often serves an adaptive purpose, combining sensual pleasure and tension release.

Kinsey found that, when women masturbate, most prefer clitoral stimulation to any other. Masters and Johnson reported that women prefer the shaft of the clitoris to the glans because the glans is hypersensitive to intense stimulation.

Moral taboos against masturbation have generated myths that masturbation causes mental illness or a decrease in sexual potency. No scientific evidence supports such claims. Masturbation is a psychopathological symptom only when it becomes a compulsion beyond the willful control of the person. It is then a symptom of emotional disturbance—not because it is sexual but because it is compulsive. Masturbation is almost a universal and inevitable aspect of psychosexual development, and in most cases it is adaptive.

HOMOSEXUALITY

In 1973 homosexuality was eliminated as a diagnostic category by the American Psychiatric Association and was removed from DSM-IV. Doing so was the result of the view that homosexuality was not a pathological disorder, and that it occurs with some regularity as a variant of human sexuality. As David Hawkins wrote, "The presence of homosexuality does not appear to be a matter of choice; the expression of it is a matter of choice."

Definitions

The term "homosexual" is used most often to describe a person's overt behavior, sexual orientation, and sense of personal or social identity. Hawkins wrote that the terms "gay" and "lesbian" refer to a combination of self-perceived identity and social identity; the terms reflect the fact that the person has some sense of being part of the social group that is similarly labeled.

Homophobia is a negative attitude toward or fear of homosexuality or homosexuals. *Heterosexism* is the belief that a heterosexual relationship is preferable to all others; it implies discrimination against and persecution of those practicing other forms of sexuality.

Prevalence

The first major study of the incidence of homosexuality was conducted by Kinsey in 1948; he found that 10 percent of men are homosexual. For women the figure was 5 percent. Kinsey also found that 37 percent of all persons reported a homosexual experience at some time in their lives, including adolescent sexual activities.

Since 1948, numerous surveys have revised those figures in a downward direction. A 1988 survey by the United States Bureau of the Census concluded that the male prevalence rate for homosexuality is 2 to 3 percent. A 1989 University of Chicago study found that less than 1 percent of both sexes are exclusively homosexual. In 1993 the Alan Guttmacher Institute found that the percentage of men reporting exclusively homosexual activity in the previous year was 1 percent and that 2 percent reported a lifetime history of having homosexual experiences.

Since sex surveys are unreliable, no accurate data are available, but government agencies such as the Centers for Disease Control and Prevention no longer use Kinsey's figures for national projections of homosexual behavior.

Some homosexuals, particularly males, report being aware of same-sex romantic attractions before puberty. According to Kinsey's data, about half of all prepubertal boys have some genital experience with a same-sex partner. However, that experience is often exploratory—particularly if shared with a peer,

not an adult—and typically lacks a strong affective component. Most male homosexuals recall the onset of romantic and erotic attractions to same-sex partners during early adolescence. For females the onset of romantic feelings toward same-sex partners may also be in preadolescence. However, the clear recognition of a same-sex partner preference typically occurs in middle to late adolescence or not until young adulthood. More homosexual women that homosexual men appear to have heterosexual experiences during their primary homosexual careers. In one study 56 percent of a lesbian sample had heterosexual intercourse before their first genital homosexual experience, compared with 19 percent of a male homosexual sample who had heterosexual intercourse first. Nearly 40 percent of the lesbians had had heterosexual intercourse during the year preceding the survey.

Theoretical Issues

PSYCHOLOGICAL FACTORS

The determinants of homosexual behavior are enigmatic. Freud viewed homosexuality as an arrest of psychosexual development. Castration fears for the male and fears of maternal engulfment in the preoedipal phase of psychosexual development are mentioned. According to psychodynamic theory, early-life situations that can result in male homosexual behavior include a strong fixation on the mother, lack of effective fathering, inhibition of masculine development by the parents, fixation or regression at the narcissistic stage of development, and losing competition with brothers and sisters. Freud's views on the causes of female homosexuality included a lack of resolution of penis envy in association with unresolved oedipal conflicts.

Freud did not consider homosexuality to be a mental illness. In *Three Essays on the Theory of Sexuality*, he wrote that homosexuality "is found in people who exhibit no other serious deviations from normal . . . whose efficiency is unimpaired and who are indeed distinguished by specially high intellectual development and ethical culture." In "Letter to an American Mother," Freud wrote, "homosexuality is assuredly no advantage, but it is nothing to be ashamed of, no vice, no degradation, it cannot be classified as an illness; we consider it to be a variation of the sexual functions produced by a certain arrest of sexual development."

NEW PSYCHOANALYTIC FACTORS

Some psychoanalysts have advanced new psychodynamic formulations, in contrast to classic psychoanalytic theory. Richard Isay described same-sex fantasies in children aged 3 to 5 years that can be recovered from homosexuals and that occur at about the same ages when heterosexuals have opposite-sex fantasies.

Isay wrote that, in homosexual men, same-sex erotic fantasies center on the father or the father surrogate:

The child's perception of and exposure to these erotic feelings may account for such "atypical" behavior as greater secretiveness than other boys, self-isolation, and excessive emotionality. Some "feminine" traits may also be caused by identification with the mother or a mother surrogate. Such characteristics usually develop as a way of attracting the father's love and attention in a manner similar to the way the heterosexual boy may pattern himself after his father to gain his mother's attention.

The psychodynamics of homosexuality in women may be similar. The little girl does not give up her original fixation on the mother as a love object and continues to seek it in adulthood.

BIOLOGICAL FACTORS

Recent studies indicate that genetic and biological components may contribute to homosexual orientation. Homosexual men reportedly exhibit lower levels of circulatory androgen than do heterosexual men. There have also been reports of atypical estrogen feedback patterns among homosexual males. Such males show abnormal rebound increases in luteinizing hormone (LH) levels after estrogen injections. But neither of those results has been replicated in similar studies. Prenatal hormones appear to play a role in the organization of the central nervous system. The effective presence of androgens in prenatal life is purported to contribute to a sexual orientation toward females, and a deficiency of prenatal androgens (or a tissue insensitivity to them) may lead to a sexual orientation toward males. Preadolescent girls exposed to large amounts of androgens before birth are unusually aggressive and unfeminine, and boys exposed to excessive female hormones in utero are less athletic, less assertive, and less aggressive than other boys. Women with hyperadrenocorticalism become bisexual or homosexual in greater proportion than is expected in the general population.

Genetic studies have found a higher incidence of homosexual concordance among monozygotic twins than among dizygotic twins, which suggests a genetic predisposition, but chromosome studies have been unable to differentiate homosexuals from heterosexuals. Male homosexuals also show a familial distribution; homosexual men have more brothers who are homosexual than do heterosexual men. One study found that 33 of 40 pairs of homosexual brothers shared a genetic marker on the bottom half of the X chromosome. Another study found a group of cells in the hypothalamus that were smaller in women and in homosexual men than in heterosexual men. Those studies require replication.

SEXUAL BEHAVIOR PATTERNS

The behavioral features of male and female homosexuals are as varied as those of male and female heterosexuals. Sexual practices engaged in by homosexuals are the same as for heterosexuals, with the obvious differences imposed by anatomy.

A variety of ongoing relationship patterns exist among homosexuals, as they do among heterosexuals. Some homosexual dyads live in a common household in either a monogamous or a primary relationship for decades, and other homosexual persons typically have only fleeting sexual contacts. Although more stable male-male relationships exist than were previously thought, male-male relationships appear to be less stable and more fleeting than are female-female relationships. The amount of male homosexual promiscuity is reported to have diminished since the onset of acquired immune deficiency syndrome (AIDS) and its rapid spread in the homosexual community through sexual contact.

Homosexual male couples are subjected to civil and social discrimination and do not have the legal social support system of marriage or the biological capacity for childbearing that bonds some otherwise incompatible heterosexual couples together. Female-female couples experience less social stigmatization and appear to have more enduring monogamous or primary relationships.

PSYCHOPATHOLOGY

The range of psychopathology that may be found among distressed homosexuals parallels that found among heterosexuals. Distress resulting only from conflict between the homosexual and the societal value structure is not classifiable as a disorder. If the distress is sufficiently severe to warrant a diagnosis, adjustment disorder to a depressive disorder is to be considered. Some homosexuals suffering from major depressive disorder may experience guilt and self-hatred that becomes directed toward their sexual orientation; then the desire for sexual reorientation is only a symptom of the depressive disorder.

COMING OUT

According to Richelle Klinger and Robert Cabaj, *coming out* is a "process by which an individual acknowledges his or her sexual orientation in the face of societal stigma and with successful resolution accepts himself or herself." They wrote:

> Successful coming out involves the individual accepting his or her sexual orientation and integrating it into all spheres (e.g., social, vocational, and familial). Another milestone that individuals and couples must eventually confront is the degree of disclosure of sexual orientation to the external world. Some degree of disclosure is probably necessary for successful coming out . . .
>
> Difficulty in negotiating coming out and disclosure is a common cause of relationship difficulties. For each individual, problems in resolving the coming out process may contribute to poor self-esteem caused by internalized homophobia and lead to deleterious effects on the individual's ability to function in the relationship. Conflict can also arise within a relationship when there is disagreement on the degree of disclosure between partners.

LOVE AND INTIMACY

There are many kinds of love: sexual, parental, filial, fraternal, anaclitic, and narcissistic love, as well as love for group, school, and country. A desire to maintain closeness to the love object typifies being in love. The development of sexuality and the development of the ability to love have reciprocal effects.

A person able to give and receive love with a minimum of fear and conflict has the capacity to develop genuinely intimate relationships with others. When involved in an intimate relationship, the person actively strives for the growth and the happiness of the loved person. Mature heterosexual love is marked by the intimacy that is a special attribute of the relationship between a man and a woman. The quality of intimacy in a mature sexual relationship is what Rollo May called "active receiving," in which a person, while loving, permits himself or herself to be loved. That capability indicates a profound awareness of love for another and for oneself. In such a loving relationship, sex acts as a catalyst. May described the values of sexual love as an expansion of one's self-awareness, the experience of tenderness, an increase of self-affirmation and pride, and sometimes, at the moment of orgasm, even loss of feelings of separateness. In that setting, sex and love are reciprocally enhancing and healthily fused.

A person is attracted to a potential mate for various reasons. One reason may be a purely physical attraction, which ordinarily establishes a transient relationship. Another reason may be a magical desire to find the perfect lover, whose qualities will be reminiscent of the idealized qualities of one's parents or other past sources of love and affection. Expectations of a partner may or may not be realistic. One neurotic motivation for marrying is an inability to separate on one's own from one's parents. Another neurotic motivation is selecting a partner to compensate for unmet childhood needs. Expectations and neurotic themes such as those probably exist in all personalities and in all matings. When they predominate and the couple act mainly to exchange patterns of exploitation or when interlocking complementary needs fail to bring sufficient security or happiness, discomfort and anxiety occur, and a breakdown in the relationship is possible.

References

Farber M: *Human Sexuality*. Macmillan, New York, 1985.
Hawkins D M: Group psychotherapy with gay men and lesbians. In *Comprehensive Group Psychotherapy*, ed 3, H I Kaplan, B J Sadock, editors, p 506. Williams & Wilkins, Baltimore, 1993.
Money J, Ehrhardt A A: *Man and Woman/Boy and Girl*. Johns Hopkins University Press, Baltimore, 1972.
Sadock V A: Normal human sexuality. In *Comprehensive Textbook of Psychiatry*, ed 6, H I Kaplan, B J Sadock, editors, p 1295. Williams & Wilkins, Baltimore, 1995.
Schiavi R C, Segraves R T: The biology of sexual function. Psychiatr Clin North Am *18*: 7, 1995.
Sherfey M J: *The Nature and Evolution of Female Sexuality*. Random House, New York, 1972.

14.2 Sexual Dysfunctions

Seven major categories of sexual dysfunction are listed in the fourth edition of *Diagnostic and Statistical Manual of Mental Disorders* (DSM-IV): (1) sexual desire disorders, (2) sexual arousal disorders, (3) orgasm disorders, (4) sexual pain disorders, (5) sexual dysfunction due to a general medical condition, (6) substance-induced sexual dysfunction, and (7) sexual dysfunction not otherwise specified.

It is useful to think of the sexual dysfunctions as disorders related to a particular phase of the sexual response cycle. Thus, sexual desire disorders are associated with the first phase of the response cycle, known as the desire phase. Table 14.2–1 lists each of the DSM-IV phases of the sexual response cycle and the sexual dysfunctions usually associated with it.

Sexual dysfunctions can be symptomatic of biological problems (biogenic) or intrapsychic or interpersonal conflicts (psychogenic) or a combination of those factors. Sexual function can be adversely affected by stress of any kind, by emotional disorders, or by ignorance of sexual function and physiology. The dysfunction may be lifelong or acquired—that is, develop after a period of normal functioning. The dysfunction may be generalized or situation—that is, limited to a specific partner or a certain situation—and it is coded that way in DSM-IV (Table 14.2–2).

In considering each of the disorders, the clinician needs to rule out an acquired medical condition and the use of a pharmacological substance that could account for or contribute to the dysfunction. It the disorder is biogenic, it is coded on Axis III, unless there is substantial evidence of dysfunctional episodes apart from the onset of physiological or pharmacological influences. In some cases a patient suffers from more than one dysfunction—for example, premature ejaculation and male erectile disorder.

SEXUAL DESIRE DISORDERS

Sexual desire disorders are divided into two classes: hypoactive sexual desire disorder, characterized by a deficiency or the absence of sexual fantasies and desire for sexual activity (Table 14.2–3), and sexual aversion disorder, characterized by an aversion to and avoidance of genital sexual contact with a sexual partner (Table 14.2–4). The former condition is more common than the latter. An estimated 20 percent of the total population have hypoactive sexual desire disorder. The complaint is more common among women than among men.

A variety of causative factors are associated with sexual desire disorders. Patients with desire problems often use inhibition of desire in a defensive way to protect against unconscious fears about sex. Unacceptable homosexual impulses can also suppress libido or cause an aversion to heterosexual contact.

Table 14.2–1.   DSM-IV Phases of the Sexual Response Cycle and Associated Sexual Dysfunctions*

Phases	Characteristics	Dysfunction
1. Desire	This phase is distinct from any identified solely through physiology and reflects the patient's motivations, drives, and personality. The phase is characterized by sexual fantasies and the desire to have sex.	Hypoactive sexual desire disorder; sexual aversion disorder; hypoactive sexual desire disorder due to a general medical condition (male or female); substance-induced sexual dysfunction with impaired desire
2. Excitement	This phase consists of a subjective sense of sexual pleasure and accompanying physiological changes. All the physiological responses noted in Masters and Johnson's excitement and plateau phases are combined and occur in this phase.	Female sexual arousal disorder; male erectile disorder (may also occur in stage 3 and in stage 4); male erectile disorder due to a general medical condition; dyspareunia due to a general medical condition (male or female); substance-induced sexual dysfunction with impaired arousal
3. Orgasm	This phase consists of a peaking of sexual pleasure, with release of sexual tension and rhythmic contraction of the perineal muscles and pelvic reproductive organs.	Female orgasmic disorder; male orgasmic disorder; premature ejaculation; other sexual dysfunction due to a general medical condition (male or female); substance-induced sexual dysfunction with impaired orgasm
4. Resolution	This phase entails a sense of general relaxation, well-being, and muscle relaxation. During this phase men are refractory to orgasm for a period of time that increases with age, whereas women are capable of having multiple orgasms without a refractory period.	Postcoital dysphoria; postcoital headache

* DSM-IV consolidates the Masters and Johnson excitement and plateau phases into a single excitement phase, which is preceded by the desire (appetitive) phase. The orgasm and resolution phases remain the same as originally described by Masters and Johnson.

Table 14.2-2. Subtypes of Sexual Dysfunctions

Subtypes are provided to indicate the onset, context, and etiological factors associated with the sexual dysfunctions. If multiple sexual dysfunctions are present, the appropriate subtypes for each may be noted. These subtypes do not apply to a diagnosis of sexual dysfunction due to a general medical condition or substance-induced sexual dysfunction.

One of the following subtypes may be used to indicate the nature of the onset of the sexual dysfunction:

Lifelong type. This subtype applies if the sexual dysfunction has been present since the onset of sexual functioning.

Acquired type. This subtype applies if the sexual dysfunction develops only after a period of normal functioning.

One of the following subtypes may be used to indicate the context in which the sexual dysfunction occurs:

Generalized type. This subtype applies if the sexual dysfunction is not limited to certain types of stimulation, situations, or partners.

Situational type. This subtype applies if the sexual dysfunction is limited to certain types of stimulation, situations, or partners. Although in most instances the dysfunctions occur during sexual activity with a partner, in some cases it may be appropriate to identify dysfunctions that occur during masturbation.

One of the following subtypes may be used to indicate etiological factors associated with the sexual dysfunction:

Due to Psychological Factors. This subtype applies when psychological factors are judged to have the major role in the onset, severity, exacerbation, or maintenance of the sexual dysfunction, and general medical conditions and substances play no role in the etiology of the sexual dysfunction.

Due to Combined Factors. This subtype applies when 1) psychological factors are judged to have a role in the onset, severity, exacerbation, or maintenance of the sexual dysfunction; and 2) a general medical condition or substance use is also judged to be contributory but is not sufficient to account for the sexual dysfunction. If a general medical condition or substance use (including medication side effects) is sufficient to account for the sexual dysfunction, sexual dysfunction due to a general medical condition and/or substance-induced sexual dysfunction is diagnosed.

Table from DSM-IV, *Diagnostic and Statistical Manual of Mental Disorders*, ed 4. Copyright American Psychiatric Association, Washington, 1994. Used with permission.

Table 14.2-3. Diagnostic Criteria for Hypoactive Sexual Desire Disorder

A. Persistently or recurrently deficient (or absent) sexual fantasies and desire for sexual activity. The judgment of deficiency or absence is made by the clinician, taking into account factors that affect sexual functioning, such as age and the context of the person's life.

B. The disturbance causes marked distress or interpersonal difficulty.

C. The sexual dysfunction is not better accounted for by another Axis I disorder (except another sexual dysfunction), and is not due exclusively to the direct physiological effects of a substance (e.g., a drug of abuse, a medication) or a general medical condition.

Table from DSM-IV, *Diagnostic and Statistical Manual of Mental Disorders*, ed 4. Copyright American Psychiatric Association, Washington, 1994. Used with permission.

Sigmund Freud conceptualized low sexual desire as the result of inhibition during the phallic psychosexual phase and unresolved oedipal conflicts. Some men, fixated at the phallic state of development, are fearful of the vagina, believing that they will be castrated if they approach it, a concept Freud called *vagina dentata*, because they believe unconsciously that the vagina has

Table 14.2-4. Diagnostic Criteria for Sexual Aversion Disorder

A. Persistent or recurrent extreme aversion to, and avoidance of, all (or almost all) genital sexual contact with a sexual partner.

B. The disturbance causes marked distress or interpersonal difficulty.

C. The sexual dysfunction is not better accounted for by another Axis I disorder (except another sexual dysfunction).

Table from DSM-IV, *Diagnostic and Statistical Manual of Mental Disorders*, ed 4. Copyright American Psychiatric Association, Washington, 1994. Used with permission.

teeth. Hence, they avoid contact with the female genitalia entirely. Lack of desire can also be the result of chronic stress, anxiety, or depression.

Abstinence from sex for a prolonged period sometimes results in suppression of the sexual impulse. Loss of desire may also be an expression of hostility or the sign of a deteriorating relationship.

In one study of young married couples who ceased having sexual relations for a period of two months, marital discord was the reason most frequently given for the cessation or the inhibition of sexual activity.

The presence of desire depends on several factors: biological drive, adequate self-esteem, previous good experiences with sex, the availability of an appropriate partner, and a good relationship in nonsexual areas with one's partner. Damage to any of those factors may result in diminished desire.

In making the diagnosis, the clinician must evaluate the patient's age, general health, and life stresses. The clinician should attempt to establish a baseline of sexual interest before the disorder began. The need for sexual contact and satisfaction varies among persons and over time in any given person. In a group of 100 couples with stable marriages, 8 percent reported having intercourse less than once a month. In another group of couples, one third reported episodic lack of sexual relations for periods averaging eight weeks. The diagnosis should not be made unless the lack of desire is a source of distress to the patient.

SEXUAL AROUSAL DISORDERS

The sexual arousal disorders are divided by DSM-IV into (1) female sexual arousal disorder, characterized by the persistent or recurrent partial or complete failure to attain or maintain the lubrication-swelling response of sexual excitement until the completion of the sexual act, and (2) male erectile disorder, characterized by the recurrent and persistent partial or complete failure to attain or maintain an erection until the completion of the sex act. The diagnosis takes into account the focus, the intensity, and the duration of the sexual activity in which the patient engages (Tables 14.2–5 and 14.2–6). If sexual stimulation is inadequate in focus, intensity, or duration, the diagnosis should not be made.

Female Sexual Arousal Disorder

The prevalence of female sexual arousal disorder is generally underestimated. Women who have excitement-phase dysfunction often have orgasm problems as well. In one study of relatively happy married couples, 33 percent of the women described difficulty in maintaining sexual excitement.

Table 14.2-5. Diagnostic Criteria for Female Sexual Arousal Disorder

A. Persistent or recurrent inability to attain, or to maintain until completion of the sexual activity, an adequate lubrication-swelling response of sexual excitement.

B. The disturbance causes marked distress or interpersonal difficulty.

C. The sexual dysfunction is not better accounted for by another Axis I disorder (except another sexual dysfunction) and is not due exclusively to the direct physiological effects of a substance (e.g., a drug of abuse, a medication) or a general medical condition.

Table from DSM-IV, *Diagnostic and Statistical Manual of Mental Disorders,* ed 4. Copyright American Psychiatric Association, Washington, 1994. used with permission.

Table 14.2-6. Diagnostic Criteria for Male Erectile Disorder

A. Persistent or recurrent inability to attain, or to maintain until completion of the sexual activity, an adequate erection.

B. The disturbance causes marked distress or interpersonal difficulty.

C. The erectile dysfunction is not better accounted for by another Axis I disorder (other than a sexual dysfunction) and is not due exclusively to the direct physiological effects of a substance (e.g., a drug of abuse, a medication) or a general medical condition.

Table from DSM-IV. *Diagnostic and Statistical Manual of Mental Disorders,* ed 4. Copyright American Psychiatric Association, Washington, 1994. Used with permission.

Many psychological factors (for example, anxiety, guilt, and fear) are associated with female sexual arousal disorder. In some women, excitement-phase disorders are associated with dyspareunia and with lack of desire.

Physiological studies of sexual dysfunctions indicate that a hormonal pattern may contribute to responsiveness in women who have excitement-phase dysfunction. William Masters and Virginia Johnson found women to be particularly desirous of sex before the onset of the menses. However, some women report that they feel the greatest sexual excitement immediately after the menses or at the time of ovulation. Alterations in testosterone, estrogen, prolactin, and thyroxin levels have been implicated in female sexual arousal disorder. Also, medications with antihistaminic or anticholinergic properties cause a decrease in vaginal lubrication. Some evidence indicates that dysfunctional women are less aware of the physiological responses of their bodies, such as vasocongestion, during arousal than are other women.

Male Erectile Disorder

Male erectile disorder is also called erectile dysfunction and impotence. A man with lifelong male erectile disorder has never been able to obtain an erection sufficient for vaginal insertion. In acquired male erectile disorder the man has successfully achieved vaginal penetration at some time in his sexual life but is later unable to do so. In situational male erectile disorder the man is able to have coitus in certain circumstances but not in others; for example, a man may function effectively with a prostitute but be impotent with his wife.

Acquired male erectile disorder has been reported in 10 to 20

percent of all men. Freud declared it to be a common complaint among his patients. Among all men treated for sexual disorders, more than 50 percent have impotence as the chief complaint. Lifelong male erectile disorder is a rare disorder, occurring in about 1 percent of men under age 35. The incidence of impotence increases with age. Among young adults it has been reported in about 8 percent of the population. Alfred Kinsey reported that 75 percent of all men were impotent at age 80. Masters and Johnson reported a fear of impotence in all men over 40, which the researchers believe reflects the masculine fear of loss of virility with advancing age. However, male erectile disorder is not universal in aging men; having an available sex partner is closely related to continuing potency, as is a history of consistent sexual activity.

The causes of male erectile disorder may be organic or psychological or a combination of both, but most are psychological. A good history is of primary importance in determining the cause of the dysfunction. If a man reports having spontaneous erections at times when he does not plan to have intercourse, having morning erections, or having good erections with masturbation or with partners other than his usual one, the organic causes of his impotence can be considered negligible, and costly diagnostic procedures can be avoided. Male erectile disorder caused by a general medical condition or a pharmacological substance is discussed below.

Freud described one type of impotence as caused by an inability to reconcile feelings of affection toward a woman with feelings of desire for her. Men with such conflicting feelings can function only with women whom they see as degraded. Other factors that have been cited as contributing to impotence include a punitive superego, an inability to trust, and feelings of inadequacy or a sense of being undesirable as a partner. The man may be unable to express the sexual impulse because of fear, anxiety, anger, or moral prohibition. In an ongoing relationship, impotence may reflect difficulties between the partners, particularly if the man cannot communicate his needs or his anger in a direct and constructive way. In addition, episodes of impotence are reinforcing, with the man becoming increasingly anxious before each sexual encounter.

ORGASM DISORDERS

Female Orgasmic Disorder

Female orgasmic disorder, also called inhibited female orgasm and anorgasmia, is defined as the recurrent or persistent inhibition of the female orgasm, as manifested by the recurrent delay in orgasm or the absence of orgasm after a normal sexual excitement phase that the clinician judges to be adequate in focus, intensity, and duration. It is the inability of the woman to achieve orgasm by masturbation or coitus. Women who can achieve orgasm with one of those methods are not necessarily categorized as anorgasmic, although some degree of sexual inhibition may be postulated (Table 14.2–7).

Research on the physiology of the female sexual response has shown that orgasms caused by clitoral stimulation and those caused by vaginal stimulation are physiologically identical. Freud's theory that women must give up clitoral sensitivity for vaginal sensitivity to achieve sexual maturity is now considered misleading; however, some women say that they gain a special sense of satisfaction from an orgasm precipitated by coitus. Some

Table 14.2–7. Diagnostic Criteria for Female Orgasmic Disorder

A. Persistent or recurrent delay in, or absence of, orgasm following a normal sexual excitement phase. Women exhibit wide variability in the type or intensity of stimulation that triggers orgasm. The diagnosis of female orgasmic disorder should be based on the clinician's judgment that the woman's orgasmic capacity is less than would be reasonable for her age, sexual experience, and the adequacy of sexual stimulation she receives.

B. The disturbance causes marked distress or interpersonal difficulty.

C. The orgasmic dysfunction is not better accounted for by another Axis I disorder (except another sexual dysfunction) and is not due exclusively to the direct physiological effects of a substance (e.g., a drug of abuse, a medication) or a general medical condition.

Table from DSM-IV, *Diagnostic and Statistical Manual of Mental Disorders*, ed 4. Copyright American Psychiatric Association, Washington, 1994. Used with permission.

Table 14.2–8. Diagnostic Criteria for Male Orgasmic Disorder

A. Persistent or recurrent delay in, or absence of, orgasm following a normal sexual excitement phase during sexual activity that the clinician, taking into account the person's age, judges to be adequate in focus, intensity, and duration.

B. The disturbance causes marked distress or interpersonal difficulty.

C. The orgasmic dysfunction is not better accounted for by another Axis I disorder (except another sexual dysfunction) and is not due exclusively to the direct physiological effects of a substance (e.g., a drug of abuse, a medication) or a general medical condition

Table from DSM-IV, *Diagnostic and Statistical Manual of Mental Disorders*, ed 4. Copyright American Psychiatric Association, Washington, 1994. Used with permission.

workers attribute that satisfaction to the psychological feeling of closeness engendered by the act of coitus, but others maintain that the coital orgasm is a physiologically different experience. Many women achieve orgasm during coitus by a combination of manual clitoral stimulation and penile vaginal stimulation.

Lifelong female orgasmic disorder exists when the woman has never experienced orgasm by any kind of stimulation. Acquired orgasmic disorder exists if the woman has previously experienced at least one orgasm, regardless of the circumstances or means of stimulation, whether by masturbation or during sleep while dreaming. Kinsey found that the proportion of married women over 35 years of age who had never achieved orgasm by any means was only 5 percent. The incidence of orgasm increases with age. According to Kinsey, the first orgasm occurs during adolescence in about 50 percent of women; the rest usually experience orgasm as they get older. Lifelong female orgasmic disorder is more common among unmarried women than among married women. Increased orgasmic potential in women over 35 has been explained on the basis of less psychological inhibition or greater sexual experience or both.

Acquired female orgasmic disorder is a common complaint in clinical populations. One clinical treatment facility reported having about four times as many nonorgasmic women in its practice as patients with all other sexual disorders. In another study 46 percent of the women complained of difficulty in reaching orgasm. The true prevalence of problems in maintaining excitement is not known, but inhibition of excitement and orgasmic problems often occur together. The overall prevalence of female orgasmic disorder from all causes is estimated to be 30 percent.

Numerous psychological factors are associated with female orgasmic disorder. They include fears of impregnation, rejection by the sex partner, or damage to the vagina; hostility toward men; and feelings of guilt regarding sexual impulses. For some women, orgasm is equated with loss of control or with aggressive, destructive, or violent behavior; their fear of those impulses may be expressed through inhibition of excitement or orgasm. Cultural expectations and social restrictions on women are also relevant. Nonorgasmic women may be otherwise symptom-free or may experience frustration in a variety of ways, including such pelvic complaints as lower abdominal pain, itching, and vaginal discharge, as well as increased tension, irritability, and fatigue.

Male Orgasmic Disorder

In male orgasmic disorder, the man achieves ejaculation during coitus with great difficulty, if at all. A man suffers from lifelong orgasmic disorder if he has never been able to ejaculate during coitus. The disorder is diagnosed as acquired if it develops after previous normal functioning (Table 14.2–8).

Some workers think that a differentiation should be made between orgasm and ejaculation. Some men ejaculate but complain of a decreased or absent subjective sense of pleasure during the orgasmic experience (orgasmic anhedonia).

The incidence of male orgasmic disorder is much lower than the incidence of premature ejaculation or impotence. Masters and Johnson reported an incidence of male orgasmic disorder in only 3.8 percent in one group of 447 sexual dysfunction cases. A general prevalence of 5 percent has been reported.

Lifelong male orgasmic disorder is indicative of severe psychopathology. The man often comes from a rigid, puritanical background; he may perceive sex as sinful and the genitals as dirty; and he may have conscious or unconscious incest wishes and guilt. He usually has difficulties with closeness that extend beyond the area of sexual relations.

In an ongoing relationship, acquired male orgasmic disorder frequently reflects interpersonal difficulties. The disorder may be the man's way of coping with real or fantasized changes in the relationship. Those changes may include plans for pregnancy about which the man is ambivalent, the loss of sexual attraction to the partner, or demands by the partner for greater commitment as expressed by sexual performance. In some men the inability to ejaculate reflects unexpressed hostility toward the woman. That problem is more common among men with obsessive-compulsive disorder than among others.

Premature Ejaculation

In premature ejaculation the man persistently or recurrently achieves orgasm and ejaculation before he wishes to. There is no definite time frame within which to define the dysfunction. The diagnosis is made when the man regularly ejaculates before or immediately after entering the vagina. The clinician needs to consider factors that affect the duration of the excitement phase, such as age, the novelty of the sex partner, and the frequency and the duration of coitus (Table 14.2–9). Masters and Johnson conceptualized the disorder in terms of the couple and considered a man a premature ejaculator if he cannot control ejaculation for a sufficient length of time during intravaginal

Table 14.2-9.   Diagnostic Criteria for Premature Ejaculation

A. Persistent or recurrent ejaculation with minimal sexual stimulation before, on, or shortly after penetration and before the person wishes it. The clinician must take into account factors that affect duration of the excitement phase, such as age, novelty of the sexual partner or situation, and recent frequency of sexual activity.

B. The disturbance causes marked distress or interpersonal difficulty.

C. The premature ejaculation is not due exclusively to the direct effects of a substance (e.g., withdrawal from opioids).

Table from DSM-IV, *Diagnostic and Statistical Manual of Mental Disorders*, ed 4. Copyright American Psychiatric Association, Washington, 1994. Used with permission.

Table 14.2-10.   Diagnostic Criteria for Dyspareunia

A. Recurrent or persistent genital pain associated with sexual intercourse in either a male or a female.

B. The disturbance causes marked distress or interpersonal difficulty.

C. The disturbance is not caused exclusively by vaginismus or lack of lubrication, is not better accounted for by another Axis I disorder (except another sexual dysfunction), and is not due exclusively to the direct physiological effects of a substance (e.g., a drug of abuse, a medication) or a general medical condition.

Table from DSM-IV, *Diagnostic and Statistical Manual of Mental Disorders*, ed 4. Copyright American Psychiatric Association, Washington, 1994. Used with permission.

Table 14.2-11.   Diagnostic Criteria for Vaginismus

A. Recurrent or persistent involuntary spasm of the musculature of the outer third of the vagina that interferes with sexual intercourse.

B. The disturbance causes marked distress or interpersonal difficulty.

C. The disturbance is not better accounted for by another Axis I disorder (e.g., somatization disorder) and is not due exclusively to the direct physiological effects of a general medical condition.

Table from DSM-IV, *Diagnostic and Statistical Manual of Mental Disorders*, ed 4. Copyright American Psychiatric Association, Washington, 1994. Used with permission.

containment to satisfy his partner in at least half of their episodes of coitus. That definition assumes that the female partner is capable of an orgasmic response. Like the other dysfunctions, premature ejaculation is not caused exclusively by organic factors and is not symptomatic of any other clinical psychiatric syndrome.

Premature ejaculation is more common today among college-educated men than among men with less education. The disorder is thought to be related to their concern for partner satisfaction; however, the true incidence of the disorder has not been determined. About 35 to 40 percent of men treated for sexual disorders have premature ejaculation as the chief complaint. Difficulty in ejaculatory control may be associated with anxiety regarding the sex act or with unconscious fears about the vagina. It may also result from negative cultural conditioning. The man who has most of his early sexual contacts with prostitutes who demand that the sex act proceed quickly or in situations in which discovery would be embarrassing (such as in the back seat of a car or in the parental home) may become conditioned to achieve orgasm rapidly. In ongoing relationships the partner has a great influence on the premature ejaculator. A stressful marriage exacerbates the disorder. The development background and the psychodynamics found in premature ejaculation and in impotence are similar.

Other Orgasm Disorders

Data on female premature orgasm are lacking; no separate category of premature orgasm for women is included in DSM-IV. A case of multiple spontaneous orgasms has been seen in a woman without sexual stimulation that was caused by an epileptogenic focus in the temporal lobe.

SEXUAL PAIN DISORDERS

Dyspareunia

Dyspareunia is recurrent or persistent genital pain occurring before, during, or after intercourse in either the man or the woman. Much more common in women than in men, dyspareunia is related to and often coincides with vaginismus. Repeated episodes of vaginismus may lead to dyspareunia and vice versa; in either case, somatic causes must be ruled out. Dyspareunia should not be diagnosed when an organic basis for the pain is found or when, in a woman, it is cause exclusively by vaginismus or by a lack of lubrication (Table 14.2–10). The incidence of dyspareunia is unknown.

In the majority of cases, dynamic factors are considered causative. Chronic pelvic pain is a common complaint in women with a history of rape or childhood sexual abuse. Painful coitus may result from tension and anxiety about the sex act that cause the woman to involuntarily contract her vaginal muscles. The pain is real and makes intercourse unpleasant or unbearable. The anticipation of further pain may cause the woman to avoid coitus altogether. If the partner proceeds with intercourse regardless of the woman's state of readiness, the condition is aggravated.

Vaginismus

Vaginismus is an involuntary muscle constriction of the outer third of the vagina that interferes with penile insertion and intercourse. That response may occur during a gynecological examination when involuntary vaginal constriction prevents the introduction of the speculum into the vagina. The diagnosis is not made if the dysfunction is caused exclusively by organic factors or if it is symptomatic of another Axis I mental disorder (Table 14.2–11).

Vaginismus is less prevalent than female orgasmic disorder. It most often afflicts highly educated women and those in the high socioeconomic groups. The woman suffering from vaginismus may consciously wish to have coitus but unconsciously wish to keep the penis from entering her body. A sexual trauma such as rape may result in vaginismus. Women with psychosexual conflicts may perceive the penis as a weapon. In some women, pain or the anticipation of pain at the first coital experience causes vaginismus. A strict religious upbringing that associates sex with sin is frequently noted in those cases. Other women have problems in the dyadic relationship; if the woman feels emotionally abused by her partner, she may protest in that nonverbal fashion.

SEXUAL DYSFUNCTION DUE TO A GENERAL MEDICAL CONDITION

This category covers sexual dysfunction that results in marked distress and interpersonal difficulty when there is evidence from the history, the physical examination, or the labora-

Table 14.2–12. Diagnostic Criteria for Sexual Dysfunction Due to a General Medical Condition

A. Clinically significant sexual dysfunction that results in marked distress or interpersonal difficulty predominates in the clinical picture.

B. There is evidence from the history, physical examination, or laboratory findings that the sexual dysfunction is fully explained by the direct physiological effects of a general medical condition.

C. The disturbance is not better accounted for by another mental disorder (e.g., major depressive disorder)

Table from DSM-IV, *Diagnostic and Statistical Manual of Mental Disorders*, ed 4. Copyright American Psychiatric Association, Washington, 1994. Used with permission.

tory findings of a general medical condition judged to be causally related to the sexual dysfunction (Table 14.2–12).

Male Erectile Disorder Due to a General Medical Condition

The incidence of psychological as opposed to organic male erectile disorder has been the focus of many studies. Statistics indicate that 20 to 50 percent of men with erectile disorder have an organic basis for the disorder. The organic causes of male erectile disorder are listed in Table 14.2–13. Side effects of medication may impair male sexual functioning in a variety of ways (Table 14.2–14). Castration (removal of the testes) does not always lead to sexual dysfunction, depending on the person. Erection may still occur after castration. A reflex arc, fired when the inner thigh is stimulated, passes through the sacral cord erectile center to account for the phenomenon.

A number of procedures, benign and invasive, are used to help differentiate organically caused impotence from functional impotence. The procedures include monitoring nocturnal penile

Table 14.2–13. Diseases and Other Medical Conditions Implicated in Male Erectile Disorder

Infectious and parasitic diseases
  Elephantiasis
  Mumps
Cardiovascular disease*
  Atherosclerotic disease
  Aortic aneurysm
  Leriche's syndrome
  Cardiac failure
Renal and urological disorders
  Peyronie's disease
  Chronic renal failure
  Hydrocele and varicocele
Hepatic disorders
  Cirrhosis (usually associated with alcohol dependence)
Pulmonary disorders
  Respiratory failure
Genetics
  Klinefelter's syndrome
  Congenital penile vascular and structural abnormalities
Nutritional disorders
  Malnutrition
  Vitamin deficiencies
Endocrine disorders *
  Diabetes mellitus
  Dysfunction of the pituitary-adrenal-testis axis
  Acromegaly
  Addison's disease
  Chromophobe adenoma
  Adrenal neoplasia
  Myxedema
  Hyperthyroidism

Neurological disorders
  Multiple sclerosis
  Transverse myelitis
  Parkinson's disease
  Temporal lobe epilepsy
  Traumatic and neoplastic spinal cord diseases*
  Central nervous system tumor
  Amyotrophic lateral sclerosis
  Peripheral neuropathy
  General paresis
  Tabes deorsalis
Pharmacological contributants
  Alcohol and other dependence-inducing substances (heroin, methadone, morphine, cocaine, amphetamines, and barbiturates)
  Prescribed drugs (psychotropic drugs, antihypertensive drugs, estrogens, and antiandrogens)
Poisoning
  Lead (plumbism)
  Herbicides
Surgical procedures*
  Perineal prostatectomy
  Abdominal-perineal colon resection
  Sympathectomy (frequently interferes with ejaculation)
  Aortoiliac surgery
  Radical cystectomy
  Retroperitoneal lymphadenectomy
Miscellaneous
  Radiation therapy
  Pelvic fracture
  Any severe systemic disease or debilitating condition

* In the United States an estimated 2 million men are impotent because they suffer from diabetes mellitus; an additional 300,000 are impotent because of other endocrine diseases; 1.5 million are impotent as a result of vascular disease; 180,000 because of multiple sclerosis; 400,000 because of trauma and fractures leading to pelvic fractures or spinal cord injuries; and another 650,000 are important as a result of radical surgery, including prostatectomies, Table by Virginia A. Sadock, MD.

Table 14.2–14.   Pharmacological Agents Implicated in Male Sexual Dysfunctions

Drug	Impairs Erection	Impairs Ejaculation
Psychiatric drugs		
Cyclic drugs*	+	
Imipramine (Tofranil)		+
Protriptyline (Vivactil)	+	+
Desipramine (Pertofrane)	+	+
Clomipramine (Anafranil)	+	+
Amitriptyline (Elavil)	+	+
Trazodone (Desyrel)†	–	–
Monoamine oxidase inhibitors		
Tranylcypromine (Parnate)	+	
Phenelzine (Nardil)	+	+
Phargyline (Eutonyl)	–	+
Isocarboxazid (Marplan)	–	+
Other mood-active drugs		
Lithium (Eskalith)	+	
Amphetamines	+	+
Fluoxetine (Prozac)	–	+
Antipsychotics‡		
Fluphenazine (Prolixin)	+	
Thioridazine (Mellaril)	+	+
Chlorprothiexene (Taractan)	–	+
Mesoridazine (Serentil)	–	+
Perphenazine (Trilafon)	–	+
Trifluoperazine (Stelazine)	–	+
Reserpine (Serpasil)	+	+
Haloperidol (Haldol)	–	+
Antianxiety agent§		
Chlordiazepoxide (Librium)	–	+
Antihypertensive drugs		
Clinidine (Catapres)	+	
Methyldopa (Aldomet)	+	+
Spironolactone (Aldactone)	+	–
Hydrochlorothiazide	+	–
Guanethidine (Ismelin)	+	+
Commonly abused substances		
Alcohol	+	+
Barbiturates	+	+
Cannabis	+	–
Cocaine	+	+
Heroin	+	+
Methadone	+	–
Morphine	+	+
Miscellaneous drugs		
Antiparkinsonian agents	+	+
Clofibrate (Atromid-S)	+	–
Digoxin (Lanoxin)	+	
Glutehimide (Doriden)	+	+
Indomethacin (Indocin)	+	–
Phentolamine (Regitine)	–	+
Propranolol (Inderal)	+	–

* The incidence of male erectile disorder associated with the use of tricyclic drugs is low.
† Trazodone has been causative in some cases of priapism.
‡ Impairment of sexual function is not a common complication of the use of antipsychotics. Priapism has occasionally occurred in association with the use of antipsychotics.
§ Benzodiazepines have been reported to decrease libido, but in some patients the diminution of anxiety caused by those drugs enhances sexual function.
Table by Virginia A. Sadock, MD.

tumescence (erections that occur during sleep), normally associated with rapid eye movement; monitoring tumescence with a strain gauge; measuring blood pressure in the penis with a penile plethysmograph or an ultrasound (Doppler) flow meter, both of which assess blood flow in the internal pudendal artery; and measuring pudendal nerve latency time. Other diagnostic tests that delineate organic bases for impotence include glucose tolerance tests, plasma hormone assays, liver and thyroid function tests, prolactin and follicle-stimulating hormone (FSH) determi-

nations, and cystometric examinations. Invasive diagnostic studies include penile arteriography, infusion cavernosography, and radioactive xenon penography. Invasive procedures require expert interpretation and are used only for patients who are candidates for vascular reconstructive procedures.

Dyspareunia Due to a General Medical Condition

An estimated 30 percent of all surgical procedures on the female genital area result in temporary dyspareunia. In addition, of women with the complaint who are seen in sex therapy clinics, 30 to 40 percent have pelvic pathology.

Organic abnormalities leading to dyspareunia and vaginismus include irritated or infected hymenal remnants, episiotomy scars, Bartholin's gland infection, various forms of vaginitis and cervicitis, and endometriosis. Postcoital pain has been reported by women with myomata and endometriosis and is attributed to the uterine contractions during orgasm. Postmenopausal women may have dyspareunia resulting from thinning of the vaginal mucosa and reduced lubrication.

Dyspareunia can also occur in men, but it is uncommon and is usually associated with an organic condition, such as Peyronie's disease, which consists of sclerotic plaques on the penis that cause penile curvature.

Hypoactive Sexual Desire Disorder Due to a General Medical Condition

Desire commonly decreases after major illness or surgery, particularly when the body image is affected after such procedures as mastectomy, ileostomy, hysterectomy, and prostatectomy. Illnesses that deplete a person's energy, chronic conditions that require physical and psychological adaptation, and serious illnesses that may cause the person to become depressed can all result in a marked lessening of sexual desire in both men and women.

In some cases, biochemical correlates are associated with hypoactive sexual desire disorder (Table 14.2–15). A recent study found markedly decreased levels of serum testosterone in men complaining of low desire when they were compared with normal controls in a sleep-laboratory situation. Drugs that depress the central nervous system (CNS) or decrease testosterone production can decrease desire.

Other Male Sexual Dysfunction Due to a General Medical Condition

This category is used when some other dysfunctional feature is predominant (for example, orgasmic disorder) or no feature predominates.

Male orgasmic disorder may have physiological causes and can occur after surgery on the genitourinary tract, such as prostatectomy. It may also be associated with Parkinson's disease and other neurological disorders involving the lumbar or sacral sections of the spinal cord. The antihypertensive drug guanethidine monosulfate (Ismelin), methyldopa (Aldomet), the phenothiazines, the tricyclic drugs, and fluoxetine (Prozac), among others, have been implicated in retarded ejaculation. Male orgasmic disorder must also be differentiated from retrograde ejaculation, in which ejaculation occurs but the seminal fluid

Table 14.2–15. Psychiatric Drugs Implicated in Female Orgasmic Disorder*

Amoxapine (Asendin)†

Clomipramine (Anafranil)‡

Fluoxetine (Prozac)§

Imipramine (Tofranil)

Isocarboxazid (Marplan)¶

Nortriptyline (Aventyl)§

Phenelzine (Nardil)¶

Thioridazine (Mellaril)

Tranylcypromine (Parnate)¶

Trifluoperazine (Stelazine)

---

* The interrelation between female sexual dysfunctions and pharmacological agents has been less extensively evaluated than have male reactions. Oral contraceptives are reported to decrease libido in some women, and some drugs with anticholinergic side effects may impair arousal and orgasm. Benzodiazepines have been reported to decrease libido, but in some patients the diminution of anxiety caused by those drugs enhances sexual function.

Both increases and decreases in libido have been reported with psychoactive agents. It is difficult to separate those effects from the underlying condition or from improvement of the condition. Sexual dysfunction associated with the use of a drug disappears when the drug is discontinued.
ᵈ Bethanechol (Urecholine) can reverse the effects of amoxapine-induced anorgasmia.
‡ Clomipramine is also reported to increase arousal and orgasmic potential.
§ Cyproheptadine (Periactin) reverses fluoxetine- and nortriptyline-induced anorgasmia.
¶ MAOI-induced anorgasmia may be a temporary reaction to the medication that disappears even though administration of the drug is continued.
Table by Virginia A. Sadock, MD

passes backward into the bladder. Retrograde ejaculation always has an organic cause. It can develop after genitourinary surgery and is also associated with medications that have anticholinergic side effects, such as the phenothiazines.

Other Female Sexual Dysfunction Due to a General Medical Condition

This category is used when some other feature (for example, orgasmic disorder) is predominant or when no feature predominates.

Some medical conditions—specifically, such endocrine diseases as hypothyroidism, diabetes mellitus, and primary hyperprolactinemia—can affect a woman's ability to have orgasms. Also, a number of drugs affect some women's capacity to have orgasms (Table 14.2–16). Antihypertensive medications, CNS stimulants, tricyclic drugs, fluoxetine, and, frequently, monoamine oxidase (MAO) inhibitors have interfered with female orgasmic capacity. However, one study of women taking MAO inhibitors found that, after 16 to 18 weeks of pharmacotherapy, that side effect of the medication disappeared, and the women were able to reexperience orgasms, although they continued taking an undiminished dosage of the drug.

SUBSTANCE-INDUCED SEXUAL DYSFUNCTION

This diagnosis is used when there is evidence from the history, the physical examination, or the laboratory findings of substance intoxication or withdrawal. Distressing sexual dysfunction occurs within a month of significant substance intoxication or withdrawal. Specified substances include alcohol; amphetamines or related substances; cocaine; opioids; sedatives, hypnotics, or anxiolytics; and other or unknown substances.

Table 14.2–16. Diagnostic Criteria for Substance-Induced Sexual Dysfunction

A. Clinically significant sexual dysfunction that results in marked distress or interpersonal difficulty predominates in the clinical picture.

B. There is evidence from the history, physical examination, or laboratory findings that the sexual dysfunction is fully explained by substance use as manifested by either (1) or (2):

  (1) the symptoms in criterion A developed during, or within a month of, substance intoxication

  (2) medication use is etiologically related to the disturbance

C. The disturbance is not better accounted for by a sexual dysfunction that is not substance induced. Evidence that the symptoms are better accounted for by a sexual dysfunction that is not substance induced might include the following: the symptoms precede the onset of the substance use or dependence (or medication use); the symptoms persist for a substantial period of time (e.g., about a month) after the cessation of intoxication, or are substantially in excess of what would be expected given the type or amount of the substance used or the duration of use; or there is other evidence that suggests the existence of an independent non-substance-induced sexual dysfunction (e.g., a history of recurrent non-substance-related episodes).

Table from DSMI-IV, *Diagnostic and Statistical Manual of Mental Disorders*, ed 4. Copyright American Psychiatric Association, Washington, 1994. Used with permission.

Abused recreational substances affect sexual function in various ways. In small doses, many of the substances enhance sexual performance by decreasing inhibition or anxiety or by causing a temporary elation of mood. However, with continued use, erectile, orgasmic, and ejaculatory capacities become impaired. The abuse of sedatives, anxiolytics, hypnotics, and particularly opiates and opioids nearly always depresses desire. Alcohol may foster the initiation of sexual activity by removing inhibition, but it impairs performance. Cocaine and amphetamines produce similar effects. Although no direct evidence indicates that sexual drive is enhanced, the user initially has a feeling of increased energy and may become sexually active. Ultimately, dysfunction occurs. Men usually go through two stages: the man experiences prolonged erection without ejaculation and then undergoes a gradual loss of erectile capability.

Recovering substance-dependent patients may need therapy to regain sexual function. In part, that is one piece of psychological readjustment to a nondependent state. Many substance abusers have always had difficulty with intimate interactions. Others have missed the experiences that would have enabled them to learn social and sexual skills because they spent their crucial developmental years under the influence of some substance.

SEXUAL DYSFUNCTION NOT OTHERWISE SPECIFIED

This category is for sexual dysfunctions that cannot be classified under the categories described above. Examples include persons who experience the physiological components of sexual excitement and orgasm but report no erotic sensation or even anesthesia (orgasmic anhedonia). Women with conditions analogous to premature ejaculation in men are classified here. Orgasmic women who desire but have not experienced multiple orgasms can be classified under this heading as well. Also, disorders of excessive rather than inhibited dysfunction, such as compulsive masturbation or coitus (sex addiction), may be classified here, as in genital pain occurring during masturbation. Other unspecified disorders are found in persons who have one or more sexual fantasies about which they feel guilty or otherwise dysphoric. However, the range of common sexual fantasies is broad.

Postcoital Headache

Postcoital headache is characterized by headache immediately after coitus and may last for several hours. It is usually described as throbbing, and it is localized in the occipital or frontal area. The cause is unknown. There may be vascular, muscle contraction (tension), or psychogenic causes. Coitus may precipitate migraine or cluster headaches in predisposed persons.

Orgasmic Anhedonia

Orgasmic anhedonia is a condition in which the person has no physical sensation of orgasms, even though the physiological component (for example, ejaculation) remains intact. Organic causes, such as sacral and cephalic lesions that interfere with afferent pathways from the genitalia to the cortex, must be ruled out. Psychic causes usually relate to extreme guilt about experiencing sexual pleasure. Those feelings produce a type of dissociative response that isolates the affective component of the orgasmic experience from consciousness.

Masturbatory Pain

In some cases, persons may experience pain during masturbation. Organic causes should always be ruled out. A small vaginal tear or early Peyronie's disease may produce a painful sensation. The condition should be differentiated from compulsive masturbation. People may masturbate to the extent that they do physical damage to their genitals and eventually experience pain during subsequent masturbatory acts. Such cases constitute a separate sexual disorder and should be so classified.

Certain masturbatory practices have resulted in what has been called autoerotic asphyxiation. The practices may involve masturbating while hanging oneself by the neck to heighten erotic sensations and the intensity of the orgasm through the mechanism of mild hypoxia. Although the persons intend to release themselves from the noose after orgasm, an estimated 500 to 1,000 persons a year accidentally kill themselves by hanging. Most who indulge in the practice are male; transvestism is often associated with the habit, and the majority of deaths occur among adolescents. Such masochistic practices are usually associated with severe mental disorders, such as schizophrenia and major mood disorders.

TREATMENT

Before 1970 the most common treatment of sexual dysfunctions was individual psychotherapy. Classic psychodynamic theory holds that sexual inadequacy has its roots in early development conflicts, and the sexual disorder is treated as part of a pervasive emotional disturbance. Treatment focuses on the exploration of unconscious conflicts, motivation, fantasy, and various interpersonal difficulties. One of the assumptions of therapy is that the removal of the conflicts will allow the sexual impulse to become structurally acceptable to the patient's ego and thereby find appropriate means of satisfaction in the environment. Unfortunately, the symptoms of sexual dysfunctions frequently become secondarily autonomous and continue to persist, even when other problems evolving from the patient's pathology have been resolved. The addition of behavioral techniques is often necessary to cure the sexual problem.

Dual-Sex Therapy

The theoretical basis of the dual-sex therapy approach is the concept of the marital unit or dyad as the object of therapy; the approach represents the major advance in the diagnosis and treatment of sexual disorders in this century. The methodology was originated and developed by William Masters and Virginia Johnson. In dual-sex therapy, there is no acceptance of the idea of a sick half of a patient couple. Both are involved in a sexually distressing relationship, and both must, therefore, participate in the therapy program.

The sexual problem often reflects other areas of disharmony or misunderstanding in the marriage. The marital relationship as a whole is treated, with emphasis on sexual functioning as a part of that relationship. The psychological and physiological aspects of sexual functioning are discussed, and an educative attitude is used. Suggestions are made for specific sexual activities, and those suggestions are followed in the privacy of the couple's home. The keystone of the program is the roundtable session in which a male and female therapy team clarifies, discusses, and works through the problems with the couple. The four-way sessions require active participation on the part of the patients. The aim of the therapy is establish or reestablish communication within the marital unit. Sex is emphasized as a natural function that flourishes in the appropriate domestic climate, and improved communication is encouraged toward that end.

Treatment is short-term and is behaviorally oriented. The therapists attempt to reflect the situation as they see it, rather than interpret underlying dynamics. An undistorted picture of the relationship presented by the therapists often corrects the myopic, narrow view held by each marriage partner. The new perspective can interrupt the couple's vicious circle of relating, and improved, more effective communication can be encouraged.

Specific exercises are prescribed for the couple to help them with their particular problem. Sexual inadequacy often involves lack of information, misinformation, and performance fear. Therefore, the couple are specifically prohibited from any sexual play other than that prescribed by the therapists. Beginning exercises usually focus on heightening sensory awareness to touch, sight, sound, and smell. Initially, intercourse is interdicted, and the couple learn to give and receive bodily pleasure without the pressure of performance. At the same time, they learn how to communicate nonverbally in a mutually satisfactory way and learn that sexual foreplay is as important as intercourse and orgasm.

During the sensate focus exercises, the couple receive much reinforcement to reduce their anxiety. They are urged to use fantasies to distract them from obsessive concerns about performance (spectatoring). The needs of both the dysfunctional partner and the nondysfunctional partner are considered. If either partner becomes sexually excited by the exercises, the other is encouraged to bring him or her to orgasm by manual or oral means. Open communication between the partners is urged, and the expression of mutual needs is encouraged. Resistances, such as claims of fatigue or not enough time to complete the exercises, are common and must be dealt with by the therapists. Genital stimulation is eventually added to general body stimulation. The couple are instructed sequentially to try various positions for intercourse, without necessarily completing the act, and to use varieties of stimulating techniques before they are instructed to proceed with intercourse.

Psychotherapy sessions follow each new exercise period, and problems and satisfactions, both sexual and in other areas of the couple's lives, are discussed. Specific instructions and the introduction of new exercises geared to the individual couple's progress are reviewed in each session. Gradually, the couple gain confidence and learn to communicate, verbally and sexually. Dual-sex therapy is most effective when the sexual dysfunction exists apart from other psychopathology.

SPECIFIC TECHNIQUES AND EXERCISES

Various techniques are used to treat the various dysfunctions. In cases of vaginismus, the woman is advised to dilate her vaginal opening with her fingers or with other dilators.

In cases of premature ejaculation, an exercise known as the squeeze technique is used to raise the threshold of penile excitability. In that exercise the man or the woman stimulates the erect penis until the earliest sensations of impending ejaculation are felt. At that point, the woman forcefully squeezes the coronal ridge of the glans, the erection is diminished, and ejaculation is inhibited. The exercise program eventually raises the threshold of the sensation of ejaculatory inevitability and allows the man to become aware of his sexual sensations and confident about his sexual performance. A variant of the exercise is the stop-start technique developed by James H. Semans, in which the woman stops all stimulation of the penis when the man first senses an impending ejaculation. No squeeze is used. Research has shown that the presence or the absence of circumcision has no bearing on a man's ejaculatory control; the glans is equally sensitive in the two states. Sex therapy has been most successful in the treatment of premature ejaculation.

A man with a sexual desire disorder or male erectile disorder is sometimes told to masturbate to prove that full erection and ejaculation are possible. In cases of lifelong female orgasmic disorder, the woman is directed to masturbate, sometimes using a vibrator. The shaft of the clitoris is the masturbatory site most preferred by women, and orgasm depends on adequate clitoral stimulation. An area on the anterior wall of the vagina has been identified in some women as a site of sexual excitation known as the G-spot; however, reports of an ejaculatory phenomenon at orgasm in women have not been satisfactorily verified. Men masturbate by stroking the shaft and the glans of the penis.

Male orgasmic disorder is managed by extravaginal ejaculation initially and gradual vaginal entry after stimulation to the point near ejaculation.

Hypnotherapy

Hypnotherapists focus specifically on the anxiety-producing symptom—that is, the particular sexual dysfunction. The successful use of hypnosis enables the patient to gain control over the symptom that has been lowering self-esteem and disrupting psychological homeostasis. The cooperation of the patient is first obtained and encouraged during a series of nonhypnotic sessions with the therapist. Those discussions permit the development of a secure doctor-patient relationship, a sense of physical and psychological comfort on the part of the patient, and the establishment of mutually desired treatment goals. During that time the therapist assesses the patient's capacity for the trance experience. The nonhypnotic

sessions also permit the clinician to take a psychiatric history and perform a mental status examination before beginning hypnotherapy. The focus of treatment is on symptom removal and attitude alteration. The patient is instructed in developing alternative means of dealing with the anxiety-provoking situation, the sexual encounter.

Patients are also taught relaxation techniques to use on themselves before sexual relations. With those methods to alleviate anxiety, the physiological responses to sexual stimulation can readily result in pleasurable excitation and discharge. Psychological impediments to vaginal lubrication, erection, and orgasms are removed, and normal sexual functioning ensues. Hypnosis may be added to a basic individual psychotherapy program to accelerate the effects of psychotherapeutic intervention.

Behavior Therapy

Behavior therapists assume that sexual dysfunction is learned maladaptive behavior. Behavioral approaches were initially designed for the treatment of phobias. In cases of sexual dysfunction, the therapist sees the patient as being fearful of sexual interaction. Using traditional techniques, the therapist sets up a hierarchy of anxiety-provoking situations for the patient, ranging from at least threatening to the most threatening situation. Mild anxiety may be experienced at the thought of kissing, and massive anxiety may be felt when imagining penile penetration. The behavior therapist enables the patient to master the anxiety through a standard program of systematic desensitization. The program is designed to inhibit the learned anxious response by encouraging behaviors antithetical to anxiety. The patient first deals with the least anxiety-producing situation in fantasy and progresses by steps to the most anxiety-producing situation. Medication, hypnosis, or special training in deep muscle relaxation is sometimes used to help with the initial mastery of anxiety.

Assertiveness training is helpful in teaching the patient to express sexual needs openly and without fear. Exercises in assertiveness are given in conjunction with sex therapy; the patient is encouraged to make sexual requests and to refuse to comply with requests perceived as unreasonable. Sexual exercises may be prescribed for the patient to perform at home, and a hierarchy may be established, starting with those activities that have proved most pleasurable and successful in the past.

One treatment variation involves the participation of the patient's sexual partner in the desensitization program. The partner, rather than the therapist, presents items of increasing stimulation value to the patient. In such situations a cooperative partner is necessary to help the patient carry gains made during treatment sessions to sexual activity at home.

Group Therapy

Group therapy has been used to examine both intrapsychic and interpersonal problems in patients with sexual disorders. The therapy group provides a strong support system for a patient who feels ashamed, anxious, or guilty about a particular sexual problem. It is a useful forum in which to counteract sexual myths, correct misconceptions, and provide accurate information regarding sexual anatomy, physiology, and varieties of behavior.

Groups for the treatment of sexual disorders can be organized in several ways. Members may all share the same problem, such as premature ejaculation; members may all be of the same sex with different sexual problems; or groups may be composed of both men and women who are experiencing a variety of sexual problems. Group therapy may be an adjacent to other forms of therapy or the prime mode of treatment. Groups organized to treat a particular dysfunction are usually behavioral in approach.

Groups composed of sexually dysfunctional married couples have also been effective. The group provides the opportunity to gather accurate information, provides consensual validation of individual preferences, and enhances self-esteem and self-acceptance. Techniques such as role playing and psychodrama may be used in treatment. Such groups are not indicated for couples when one partner is uncooperative, when a patient is suffering from a severe depressive disorder or psychosis, when a patient has a strong repugnance for explicit sexual audiovisual material, or when the patient has a strong fear of groups.

Analytically Oriented Sex Therapy

One of the most effective treatment modalities is the use of sex therapy integrated with psychodynamic and psychoanalytically oriented psychotherapy. The sex therapy is conducted over a longer than usual time period, and the extended schedule of treatment allows for the learning or the relearning of sexual satisfaction under the realities of the patients' day-to-day lives. The addition of psychodynamic conceptualizations to the behavioral techniques used to treat sexual dysfunctions allows for the treatment of patients with sex disorders associated with other psychopathology.

The themes and the dynamics that emerge in patients in analytically oriented sex therapy are the same as those seen in psychoanalytic therapy, such as relevant dreams, fear of punishment, aggressive feelings, difficulty with trusting the partner, fear of intimacy, oedipal feelings, and fear of genital mutilation.

The combined approach of analytically oriented sex therapy is used by the general psychiatrist, who carefully judges the optimal timing of sex therapy and the ability of patients to tolerate the directive approach that focuses on their sexual difficulties.

Biological Treatments

Biological forms of treatment have limited application, but more attention than in the past is being given to the approach. Intravenous methohexital sodium (Brevital) has been used in desensitization therapy. Antianxiety agents may have application in tense patients, although the drugs can also interfere with sexual response. Sometimes the side effects of such drugs as thioridazine (Mellaril) and the tricyclic drugs are used to prolong the sexual response in such conditions as premature ejaculation. The use of tricyclics has also been advocated in the treatment of patients who are phobic about sex.

Pharmacological approaches also involve treating any underlying mental disorder that may be contributing to the sexual dysfunction. For example, patients whose sexual functioning is impaired as a result of depression usually show improved performance as their depression responds to antidepressant medication.

Specific medications to deal with the sexual dysfunctions are not generally successful. Testosterone, which affects libido, is beneficial to those patients who have a demonstrated low testosterone level. In women, however, testosterone leads to masculinization—such as deep voice, enlarged clitoris, and hirsutism—which may not be reversible on discontinuing the medication. Testosterone is contraindicated when fertility needs to be maintained. Case reports indicate that cyproheptadine (Periactin) can reverse drug-induced female orgasmic disorder and male orgasmic disorder in men taking fluoxetine. Clomipramine (Anafranil) has been reported to both induce spontaneous orgasms and inhibit orgasms in women. There are no known aphrodisiacs. Although recent studies report improvement in erectile responses in men ingesting yohimbine (Yocon), those findings remain controversial. Also controversial is the use of gonadotropin-releasing hormone as an inhalant. Such substances as powdered rhinoceros horn, used in Asia for their alleged stimulant effects, are of benefit only through the power of suggestion in a particular culture.

Surgical treatment is rarely advocated, but improved penile prosthetic devices are available for men with inadequate erectile responses who are resistant to other treatment methods or who have deficiencies of organic origin. The placement of a penile prosthesis in a man who has lost the ability to ejaculate or have an orgasm because of organic causes will not enable him to recover those functions. Men with prosthetic devices have generally reported satisfaction with their subsequent sexual functioning. Their wives, however, report much less satisfaction than do the men. Presurgical counseling is strongly recommended so that the couple have a realistic expectation of what the prosthesis can do for their sex lives. Some physicians are attempting revascularization of the penis as a direct approach to treating erectile dysfunction caused by vascular disorders. In patients with corporal shunts that allow normally entrapped blood to leak from the corporal spaces, leading to inadequate erections (steal phenomenon), such surgical procedures are indicated. There are limited reports of prolonged success with the technique. Endarterectomy can be of benefit if aortoiliac occlusive disease is responsible for erectile dysfunction.

Surgical approaches to female sexual dysfunctions include hymenectomy in the case of dyspareunia in an unconsummated marriage, vaginoplasty in multiparous women who complain of reduced vaginal sensations, and the release of clitoral adhesions in women with sexual arousal disorder. Such surgical treatments have not been carefully studied and should be considered with great caution.

Injections of vasoactive materials into the corporal bodies of the penis produce erections for several hours; usually, a mixture of papaverine (Cerespan), prostaglandin E, and phentolamine (Regitine) is used. Usually, a urologist teaches the patient to inject himself in a series of training sessions. However, fibrosis and prolonged erections (lasting many hours) are occasional side effects of the approach. In addition, some patients become resistant to treating themselves. Vacuum pumps can also be used by patients without vascular disease to obtain erections but they are not very satisfactory.

References

Hawton K, Catalan J, Fagg J: Sex therapy for erectile dysfunction: Characteristics of couples, treatment outcome, and prognostic factors. Arch Sex Behav *21*: 161, 1992.

Rowland D L, Slob A K: Understanding and diagnosing sexual dysfunction:

Recent progress through psychophysiological and psychophysical methods. Neurosci Biobehav Rev *19*: 201, 1995.

Sadock V A: Normal human sexuality and sexual dysfunction. In *Comprehensive Textbook of Psychiatry*, ed 6, H I Kaplan, B J Sadock, editors, p 1295. Williams & Wilkins, Baltimore, 1995.

Schiavi R C, Karstaedt A, Schreiner-Engel P, Mandeli J: Psychometric characteristics of individuals with sexual dysfunction and their partners. J Sex Marital Ther *18*: 219, 1992.

Segraves R T: Effects of psychotropic drugs on human erections and ejaculation. Arch Gen Psychiatry *46*: 782, 1989.

Zorgniotto A W, Leflueck R S: Autoinjection of corpus cavernosum with vasoactive drug combination with vasculogenic impotence. J Urol *133*: 39, 1985.

14.3 PARAPHILIAS AND SEXUAL DISORDER NOS

PARAPHILIAS

Paraphilias are sexual disorders characterized by specialized sexual fantasies and intense sexual urges and practices that are usually repetitive and distressing to the person. The special fantasy, with its unconscious and conscious components, is the pathognomonic element, sexual arousal and orgasm being associated phenomena. The influence of the fantasy and its behavioral manifestations extend beyond the sexual sphere to pervade the person's life. The major functions of sexual behavior for human beings are to assist in bonding, to express and enhance love between two persons, and to procreate. Paraphilias are divergent behaviors in that they are concealed by their participants, appear to exclude or harm others, and disrupt the potential for bonding between persons. Paraphiliac arousal may be transient in some persons who act out their impulses only during periods of stress or conflict.

Classification

The major categories of paraphilias in the fourth edition of *Diagnostic and Statistical Manual of Mental Disorders* (DSM-IV) are exhibitionism, fetishism, frotteurism, pedophilia, sexual masochism, sexual sadism, voyeurism, transvestic fetishism, and a separate category for other paraphilias not otherwise specified (NOS)—for example, zoophilia. A given person may have multiple paraphiliac disorders.

Epidemiology

Paraphilias are practiced by a small percentage of the population. However, the insistent, repetitive nature of the disorders results in the high frequency of the commission of paraphiliac acts; thus, a large proportion of the population have been victimized by persons with paraphilias.

Among legally identified cases of paraphilias, pedophilia is far more common than the others. Ten to 20 percent of all children have been molested by age 18. Because a child is the object, the act is taken more seriously, and greater effort is spent tracking down the culprit than in other paraphilias. Persons with exhibitionism, who publicly display themselves to young children, are also commonly apprehended. Those with voyeurism may be apprehended, but their risk is not great. Twenty percent of adult females have been the targets of persons with exhibitionism and voyeurism. Sexual masochism and sexual sadism are underrepresented in any prevalence estimates. Sexual sadism usually comes to attention only in sensational cases of rape,

brutality, and lust murder. The excretory paraphilias are scarcely reported, since any activity usually takes place between consenting adults or between prostitute and client. Persons with fetishism ordinarily do not become entangled in the legal system. Those with transvestic fetishism may be arrested occasionally on disturbing-the-peace or other misdemeanor charges if they are obviously men dressed in women's clothes, but arrest is more common among those with the gender identity disorders. Zoophilia as a true paraphilia is rare.

As usually defined, the paraphilias seem to be largely male conditions. Fetishism almost always occurs in men.

More than 50 percent of all paraphilias have their onset before age 18. Paraphilia patients frequently have three to five paraphilias, either concurrently or at different times in their lives. That is especially the case with exhibitionism, fetishism, sexual masochism, sexual sadism, transvestic fetishism, voyeurism, and zoophilia.

The occurrence of paraphiliac behavior peaks between ages 15 and 25 and gradually declines; in men of 50 paraphiliac acts are rare, except for those that occur in isolation or with a cooperative partner.

Etiology

PSYCHOSOCIAL FACTORS

In the classic psychoanalytic model, a person with a paraphilia is someone who has failed to complete the normal developmental process toward heterosexual adjustment; however, the model has been modified by new psychoanalytic approaches. What distinguished one paraphilia from another is the method chosen by the person (usually male) to cope with the anxiety caused by the threat of (1) castration by the father and (2) separation from the mother. However bizarre its manifestation, the resulting behavior provides an outlet for the sexual and aggressive drives that would otherwise have been channeled into proper sexual behavior.

Failure to resolve the oedipal crisis by identifying with the father-aggressor (for boys) or mother-aggressor (for girls) results either in improper identification with the opposite-sex parent or in an improper choice of object for libido cathexis. Regardless of the DSM-IV classifications, classic psychoanalytic theory holds that transsexualism and transvestic fetishism are both disorders because each involves identification with the opposite-sex parent, instead of the same-sex parent. For instance, a man dressing in women's clothes is believed to identify with his mother. Exhibitionism and voyeurism are also seen as expressions of feminine identification, since persons with the paraphilias must constantly examine their own or others' genitals to calm their anxiety about castration. Fetishism is an attempt to avoid anxiety by displacing libidinal impulses to inappropriate objects. The person with a shoe fetish unconsciously denies that women have lost their penises through castration by attaching libido to a phallic object, the shoe, that symbolizes the female penis. Persons with pedophilia and sexual sadism have a need to dominate and control their victims, as though to compensate for their feelings of powerlessness during the oedipal crisis. Some theorists believe that the choice of a child as a love object is a narcissistic choice. Persons with sexual masochism overcome their fear of injury and their sense of powerlessness by showing that they are impervious to harm. Although recent developments in psychoanalysis place more emphasis on treating defense mechanisms than an oedipal trauma, the course of psychoanalytic therapy for the patient with a paraphilia remains consistent with Sigmund Freud's theory.

Other theories attribute the development of a paraphilia to early experiences that condition or socialize the child into committing a paraphiliac act. The first shared sexual experience can be important in that regard. Molestation as a child can predispose the person toward being the recipient of continued abuse as an adult or, conversely, toward becoming an abuser of others. The onset of paraphiliac acts can result from modeling one's behavior on the behavior of others who have carried out paraphiliac acts, mimicking sexual behavior depicted in the media, or recalling emotionally laden events from one's past, such as one's own molestation. Learning theory indicates that, because the fantasizing of paraphiliac interests begins at an early age and because personal fantasies and thoughts are not shared with others (who could block or discourage such ideas), the use and the misuse of paraphiliac fantasies and urges continue uninhibited until late in life. Only then does the person begin to realize that such paraphiliac interests and urges are inconsistent with societal norms. Unfortunately, by that time the repetitive use of such fantasies has become ingrained; the person's sexual thoughts and behaviors have become associated with or conditioned to paraphiliac fantasies.

ORGANIC FACTORS

A number of studies have identified abnormal organic findings in persons with paraphilias. None has used random samples of such persons; the studies are, instead, extensive investigations of paraphilia patients who have been referred to large medical centers. Of those persons evaluated at referral centers who had positive organic findings, 74 percent had abnormal hormone levels, 27 percent had hard or soft neurological signs, 24 percent had chromosomal abnormalities, 9 percent had seizures, 9 percent had dyslexia, 4 percent had abnormal electroencephalograms (EEGs) without seizures, 4 percent had major mental disorders, and 4 percent were mentally retarded. The remaining question is whether those abnormalities are causatively related to paraphiliac interests or are incidental findings that bear no relevance to the development of paraphiliac interests.

Psychophysiological tests have been developed to measure penile volumetric size in response to paraphiliac and nonparaphiliac stimuli. The procedures may be of use in diagnosis and treatment but are of questionable diagnostic validity because some men are able to suppress their erectile responses.

Diagnosis and Clinical Features

In DSM-IV the diagnosis criteria for paraphilias include the presence of a pathognomonic fantasy and an intense urge to act out the fantasy, which may distress the patient, or its behavior elaboration. The fantasy contains unusual sexual material that is relatively fixed and shows only minor variations. Arousal and orgasm depend on the mental elaboration or the behavioral playing out of the fantasy. Sexual activity is ritualized or stereotyped and makes use of degraded, reduced, or dehumanized objects.

EXHIBITIONISM

Exhibitionism is the recurrent urge to expose one's genitals to a stranger or an unsuspecting person (Table 14.3–1). Sexual excitement occurs in anticipation of the exposure, and orgasm

Table 14.3-1.   Diagnostic Criteria for Exhibitionism

A. Over a period of at least 6 months, recurrent, intense sexually arousing fantasies, sexual urges, or behaviors involving the exposure of one's genitals to an unsuspecting stranger.

B. The fantasies, sexual urges, or behaviors cause clinically significant distress or impairment in social, occupational, or other important areas of functioning.

Table from DSM-IV, *Diagnostic and Statistical Manual of Mental Disorders,* ed 4. Copyright American Psychiatric Association, Washington, 1994. Used with permission.

Table 14.3-2.   Diagnostic Criteria for Fetishism

A. Over a period of at least 6 months, recurrent, intense sexually arousing fantasies, sexual urges, or behaviors involving the use of nonliving objects (e.g., female undergarments).

B. The fantasies, sexual urges, or behaviors cause clinically significant distress or impairment in social, occupational, or other important areas of functioning.

C. The fetish objects are not articles of female clothing used in cross-dressing (as in transvestic fetishism) or devices designed for the purpose of tactile genital stimulation (e.g., a vibrator).

Table from DSM-IV, *Diagnostic and Statistical Manual of Mental Disorders,* ed 4. Copyright American Psychiatric Association, Washington, 1994. Used with permission.

is brought about by masturbation during or after the event. In almost 100 percent of the cases, those with exhibitionism are males exposing themselves to females.

The dynamic of the man with exhibitionism is to assert his masculinity by showing his penis and by watching the reaction of the victim—fright, surprise, disgust. Unconsciously, the man feels castrated and impotent. Wives of men with exhibitionism often substitute for the mother to whom the men were excessively attached during childhood.

In other related paraphilias the central themes involve derivatives of looking or showing.

FETISHISM

In fetishism the sexual focus is on objects (such as shoes, gloves, pantyhose, and stockings) that are intimately associated with the human body (Table 14.3–2). The particular fetish is linked to someone closely involved with the patient during childhood and has some quality associated with that loved, needed, or even traumatizing person. Usually, the disorder begins by adolescence, although the fetish may have been established in childhood. Once established, the disorder tends to be chronic.

Sexual activity may be directed toward the fetish itself (for example, masturbation with or into a shoe), or the fetish may be incorporated into sexual intercourse (for example, the demand that high-heeled shoes be worn). The disorder is almost exclusively found in males. According to Freud, the fetish serves as a symbol of the phallus because the person has unconscious castration fears. Learning theorists believe that the object was associated with sexual stimulation at an early age.

FROTTEURISM

Frotteurism is usually characterized by the male's rubbing his penis against the buttocks or other body part of a fully

Table 14.3-3.   Diagnostic Criteria for Frotteurism

A. Over a period of at least 6 months, recurrent, intense sexually arousing fantasies, sexual urges, or behaviors involving touching and rubbing against a nonconsenting person.

B. The fantasies, sexual urges, or behaviors cause clinically significant distress or impairment in social, occupational, or other important areas of functioning.

Table from DSM-IV. *Diagnostic and Statistical Manual of Mental Disorders*, ed 4. Copyright American Psychiatric Association, Washington, 1994. Used with permission.

Table 14.3-4.   Diagnostic Criteria for Pedophilia

A. Over a period of at least 6 months, recurrent, intense sexually arousing fantasies, sexual urges, or behaviors involving sexual activity with a prepubescent child or children (generally age 13 years or younger).

B. The fantasies, sexual urges, or behaviors cause clinically significant distress or impairment in social, occupational, or other important areas of functioning.

C. The person is at least 16 years and at least 5 years older than the child or children in criterion A.

Note: Do not include an individual in late adolescence involved in an ongoing sexual relationship with a 12- or 13-year-old

Table from DSM-IV. *Diagnostic and Statistical Manual of Mental Disorders*, ed 4. Copyright American Psychiatric Association, Washington, 1994. Used with permission.

Table 14.3-5.   Diagnostic Criteria for Sexual Masochism

A. Over a period of at least 6 months, recurrent, intense sexually arousing fantasies, sexual urges, or behaviors involving the act (real, not simulated) of being humiliated, beaten, bound, or otherwise made to suffer.

B. The fantasies, sexual urges, or behaviors cause clinically significant distress or impairment in social, occupational, or other important areas of functioning.

Table from DSM-IV. *Diagnostic and Statistical Manual of Mental Disorders*, ed 4. Copyright American Psychiatric Association, Washington, 1994. Used with permission.

Table 14.3-6.   Diagnostic Criteria for Sexual Sadism

A. Over a period of at least 6 months, recurrent, intense sexually arousing fantasies, sexual urges, or behaviors involving acts (real, not simulated) in which the psychological or physical suffering (including humiliation) of the victim is sexually exciting to the person.

B. The fantasies, sexual urges, or behaviors cause clinically significant distress or impairment in social, occupational, or other important areas of functioning.

Table from DSM-IV. *Diagnostic and Statistical Manual of Mental Disorders*, ed 4. Copyright American Psychiatric Association, Washington, 1994. Used with permission.

clothed woman to achieve orgasm (Table 14.3–3). At other times, he may use his hands to rub an unsuspecting victim. The acts usually occur in crowded places, particularly subways and buses. The person with frotteurism is extremely passive and isolated, and frottage is often his only source of sexual gratification.

PEDOPHILIA

Pedophilia involves, over a period of at least six months, recurrent intense sexual urges toward or arousal by children 13 years of age or younger. The person with pedophilia is at least 16 years of age and at least five years older than the victim (Table 14.3–4). When the perpetrator is a late adolescent involved in an ongoing sexual relationship with a 12- or 13-year-old, the diagnosis is not warranted.

The vast majority of child molestations involve genital fondling or oral sex. Vaginal or anal penetration of the child is an infrequent occurrence except in cases of incest. Although the majority of child victims coming to public attention are girls, that finding appears to be a product of the referral process. Offenders report that, when they touch the child, the majority (60 percent) of the victims are boys. That figure is in sharp contrast to that for non-touching victimization of children, such as window peeping and exhibitionism, which is 99 percent of all cases is perpetrated against girls. Moreover, 95 percent of those with pedophilia are heterosexual, and 50 percent have consumed alcohol to excess at the time of the incident. In addition to their pedophilia, a significant number of the perpetrators are concomitantly or have previously been involved in exhibitionism, voyeurism, or rape.

Incest is related to pedophilia by the frequent selection of an immature child as a sex object, the subtle or overt element of coercion, and, occasionally, the preferential nature of the adult-child liaison.

SEXUAL MASOCHISM

Masochism takes its name from the activities of Leopold von Sacher-Masoch, a 19th-century Austrian novelist whose characters derived sexual pleasure from being abused and dominated by women. According to DSM-IV, persons with sexual masochism have a recurrent preoccupation with sexual urges and fantasies involving the act of being humiliated, beaten, bound, or otherwise made to suffer (Table 14.3–5). Sexual masochistic practices are more common among men than among women. Freud believed masochism to result from destructive fantasies turned against the self. In some cases, persons can allow themselves to experience sexual feelings only if punishment for them follows. Persons with sexual masochism may have had childhood experiences that convinced them that pain is a prerequisite for sexual pleasure. About 30 percent of those with sexual masochism also have sadistic fantasies. Moral masochism involves a need to suffer but is not accompanied by sexual fantasies.

SEXUAL SADISM

The DSM-IV diagnostic criteria for sexual sadism are presented in Table 14.3–6. The onset is usually before the age of 18 years, and most persons with sexual sadism are male. According to psychoanalytic theory, sadism is a defense against fears of castration—the persons with sexual sadism do to others what they fear will happen to them. Pleasure is derived from expressing the aggressive instinct. The disorder was named after the Marquis de Sade, an 18th-century French author, who was repeatedly imprisoned for his violent sexual acts against women. Sexual sadism is related to rape, although rape is more aptly considered a form of aggression. Some sadistic rapists, however, kill their victims after having sex (so-called lust murders). In many cases, those persons have underlying schizophrenia. John Money believes that lust murderers have the dissociative disorder of dissociative identity disorder and may have had a history of head trauma. He lists five contributory causes of sexual sad-

Table 14.3-7. Diagnostic Criteria for Voyeurism

A. Over a period of at least 6 months, recurrent, intense sexually arousing fantasies, sexual urges, or behaviors involving the act of observing an unsuspecting person who is naked, in the process of disrobing, or engaging in sexual activity.

B. The fantasies, sexual urges, or behaviors cause clinically significant distress or impairment in social, occupational, or other important areas of functioning.

Table from DSM-IV. *Diagnostic and Statistical Manual of Mental Disorders*, ed 4. Copyright American Psychiatric Association, Washington, 1994. Used with permission.

Table 14.3-8. Diagnostic Criteria for Transvestic Fetishism

A. Over a period of at least 6 months, in a heterosexual male, recurrent, intense sexually arousing fantasies, sexual urges, or behaviors involving cross-dressing.

B. The fantasies, sexual urges, or behaviors cause clinically significant distress or impairment in social, occupational, or other important areas of functioning.

Specify if:
With gender dysphoria: if the person has persistent discomfort with gender role or identity.

Table from DSM-IV. *Diagnostic and Statistical Manual of Mental Disorders*, ed 4. Copyright American Psychiatric Association, Washington, 1994. Used with permission.

ism: hereditary predisposition, hormonal malfunctioning, pathological relationships, a history of sexual abuse, and the presence of other mental disorders.

VOYEURISM

Voyeurism is the recurrent preoccupation with fantasies and acts that involve observing people who are naked or are engaged in grooming or in sexual activity (Table 14.3–7). It is also known as scopophilia. Masturbation to orgasm usually occurs during or after the event. The first voyeuristic act usually occurs during childhood and is most common in males. When persons with voyeurism are apprehended, it is usually for loitering.

TRANSVESTIC FETISHISM

Transvestic fetishism is marked by fantasies and sexual urges by heterosexual men to dress in female clothes for purposes of arousal and as an adjunct to masturbation or coitus (Table 14.3–8). Transvestic fetishism typically begins in childhood or early adolescence. As years pass, some men with transvestic fetishism want to dress and live permanently as women. Such persons are classified in DSM-IV as persons with transvestic fetishism with gender dysphoria. Usually, more than one article of clothing is involved; frequently, an entire wardrobe is involved. When a person with transvestic fetishism is cross-dressed, the appearance of femininity may be striking, although usually not to the degree found in transsexualism. When not dressed in women's clothes, men with transvestic fetishism may be hypermasculine in appearance and occupation. Cross-dressing exists on a gradient from solitary, depressed, guilt-ridden dressing to ego-syntonic, social membership in a transvestite subculture.

The overt clinical syndrome of transvestic fetishism may begin in latency, but it is more often seen around pubescence or in adolescence. Frank dressing in women's clothes usually does not begin until mobility and relative independence from parents are well-established.

PARAPHILIA NOT OTHERWISE SPECIFIED

The classification of paraphilia not otherwise specified (NOS) includes varied paraphilias that do not meet the criteria for any of the aforementioned categories.

Telephone Scatologia

In telephone scatologia, characterized by obscene phone calling, tension and arousal begin in anticipation of phoning, an unsuspecting partner is involved, the recipient of the call listens while the telephoner (usually male) verbally exposes his preoccupations or induces her to talk about her sexual activity, and the conversation is accompanied by masturbation, which is often completed after the contact is interrupted.

People also use computer interactive networks to transmit obscene messages by electronic mail. In addition, people use computer networks to transmit sexually explicit messages and video images. Some persons compulsively use those services.

Necrophilia

Necrophilia is obsession with obtaining sexual gratification from cadavers. Most persons with necrophilia find corpses for their exploitation from morgues. Some have been known to rob graves. At times, persons murder to satisfy their sexual urges. In the few cases studied, the persons with necrophilia believed that they were inflicting the greatest conceivable humiliation on their lifeless victims. According to Richard Krafft-Ebing, the diagnosis of psychosis is, under all circumstances, justified.

Partialism

In partialism the person focuses on one part of the body to the exclusion of all other parts. Mouth-genital contact—such as cunnilingus (oral contact with the external female genitals), fellatio (oral contact with the penis), and anilingus (oral contact with the anus)—is an activity normally associated with foreplay. Freud recognized the mucosal surfaces of the body as being erotogenic and capable of producing pleasurable sensation. But when a person uses those activities as the sole source of sexual gratification and cannot have coitus or refuses to have coitus, a paraphilia exists. It is also known as oralism.

Zoophilia

In zoophilia, animals—which may be trained to participate—are preferentially incorporated into arousal fantasies or sexual activities, including intercourse, masturbation, and oral-genital contact. Zoophilia as an organized paraphilia is rare. For a number of people, animals are the major source of relatedness, so it is not surprising that a broad variety of domestic animals are sensually or sexually used. Sexual relations with animals may occasionally be an out-growth of availability or convenience, especially in parts of the world where rigid convention precludes premarital sexuality and in situations of enforced isolation. However, because masturbation is also available in such situations, some predilection for animal contact is probably present in opportunistic zoophilia.

Coprophilia And Klismaphilia

Coprophilia is attraction to sexual pleasure associated with the desire to defecate on a partner, to be defecated on, or to eat feces (coprophagia). A variant is the compulsive utterance of obscene words (coprolalia). Those paraphilias are associated with fixation at the anal stage of psychosexual development. Similarly, the use of enemas as part of sexual stimulation, klismaphilia, is related to anal fixation.

Urophilia

Urophilia is interest in sexual pleasure associated with the desire to urinate on a partner or to be urinated on; it is a form of urethral eroticism. It may be associated with masturbatory techniques involving the insertion of foreign objects into the urethra for sexual stimulation in both men and women.

Masturbation

Masturbation is a normal activity that is common in all stages of life from infancy to old age. It was not always thought to be so. Freud believed neurasthenia to be caused by excessive masturbation. In the early 1900s, masturbatory insanity was a common diagnosis in hospitals for the criminally insane in the United States. Masturbation can be defined as the achieving of sexual pleasure—usually resulting in orgasm—by oneself (autoeroticism). Alfred Kinsey found it to be more prevalent in males than in females, but that difference may no longer exist. The frequency of masturbation varies from three to four times a week in adolescence to one to two times a week in adulthood. It is common among married people; Kinsey reported that it occurred on the average of once a month among married couples.

The techniques of masturbation vary in both sexes and among persons. The most common technique is direct stimulation of the clitoris or the penis with the hand or the fingers. Indirect stimulation may also be used, such as rubbing against a pillow or squeezing the thighs. Kinsey found that 2 percent of women are capable of achieving orgasm through fantasy alone. Men and women have been known to insert objects into the urethra to achieve orgasm. The hand vibrator is now used as a masturbatory device by both sexes.

Masturbation is abnormal when it is the only type of sexual activity performed, when it is done with such frequency as to indicate a compulsion or sexual dysfunction, or when it is consistently preferred to sex with a partner.

Hypoxyphilia

Hypoxyphilia is the desire to achieve an altered state of consciousness secondary to hypoxia while experiencing orgasm. In the disorder the persons may use a drug (such as a volatile nitrite or nitrous oxide) that produces hypoxia. Autoerotic asphyxiation is also associated with hypoxic states but should be classified as a form of sexual masochism. A discussion of autoerotic asphyxiation appears in Section 14.2.

Differential Diagnosis

The clinician needs to differentiate a paraphilia from experimentation in which the act is done for its novel effect and not recurrently or compulsively. Paraphiliac activity is most likely to occur during adolescence. Some paraphilias (especially the bizarre types) are part of another mental disorder, such as schizophrenia. Brain diseases may release perverse impulses.

Course and Prognosis

A poor prognosis for paraphilias is associated with an early age of onset, a high frequency of the acts, no guilt or shame about the act, and substance abuse. The course and the prognosis are good when the patient has a history of coitus in addition to the paraphilia, when the patient has a high motivation for change, and when the patient is self-referred, rather than referred by a legal agency.

Treatment

Insight-oriented psychotherapy is the most common approach to treating the paraphilias. Patients have the opportunity to understand their dynamics and the events that caused the paraphilia to develop. In particular, they become aware of the daily events that cause them to act on their impulses (for example, a real or fantasized rejection). Psychotherapy also allows the patients to regain self-esteem and to improve their interpersonal skills and find acceptable methods for sexual gratification. Group therapy is also useful.

Sex therapy is an appropriate adjunct to the treatment of patients who suffer from specific sexual dysfunctions when they attempt nondeviant sexual activities with partners.

Behavior therapy is used to disrupt the learned paraphiliac pattern. Noxious stimuli, such as electric shocks and bad odors, have been paired with the impulse, which then diminishes. The stimuli can be self-administered and used by patients whenever they feel that they will act on the impulse.

Drug therapy, including antipsychotic or antidepressant medication, is indicated for the treatment of schizophrenia or depressive disorders if the paraphilia is associated with those disorders. Antiandrogens, such as cyproterone acetate in Europe and medroxyprogesterone acetate (Depo-Provera) in the United States, have been used experimentally in hypersexual paraphilias. Some cases have reported decreases in the hypersexual behavior. Medroxyprogesterone acetate seems to benefit those patients whose driven hypersexuality (for example, virtually constant masturbation, sexual contact at every opportunity, compulsively assaultive sexuality) is out of control or dangerous. Serotonergic agents such as fluoxetine (Prozac) have been used in some paraphiliac cases with limited success.

SEXUAL DISORDER NOT OTHERWISE SPECIFIED

Many sexual disorders are not classifiable as sexual dysfunctions or paraphilias. Those unclassified disorders are rare, poorly documented, not easily classified, or not specifically described in DSM-IV.

Postcoital Dysphoria

Postcoital dysphoria is not listed in DSM-IV. It occurs during the resolution phase of sexual activity, when the person normally experiences a sense of general well-being and muscular and psychological relaxation. Some persons, however, experience postcoital dysphoria. After an otherwise satisfactory sexual experience, they become depressed, tense, anxious, and irritable and show psychomotor agitation. They often want to get away from the partner and may become verbally or even physically abusive. The incidence of the disorder is unknown, but it is more common in men than in women. The causes are several and relate to the attitude of the person toward sex in general and toward the partner in particular. It may occur in adulterous sex and with prostitutes. The fear of acquired immune deficiency syndrome (AIDS) causes some persons to experience postcoital dysphoria. Treatment requires insight-oriented psychotherapy to help patients understand the unconscious antecedents to their behavior and attitudes.

Couple Problems

At times, a complaint must be viewed in terms of the spousal unit or the couple, rather than as an individual dysfunction. An example is a couple in which one prefers morning sex while the other functions more readily at night; another example is a couple with unequal frequencies of desire.

Unconsummated Marriage

A couple involved in an unconsummated marriage have never had coitus and are typically uninformed and inhibited about sexuality. Their feelings of guilt, shame, or inadequacy are increased by their problem, and they experience conflict between their need to seek help and their need to conceal their difficulty. Couples present with the problem after having been married several months or several years. William Masters and Virginia Johnson reported an unconsummated marriage of 17 years' duration.

Frequently, the couple do not seek help directly, but the woman may reveal the problem to her gynecologist on a visit ostensibly concerned with vague vaginal or other somatic complaints. On examining her, the gynecologist may find an intact hymen. In some cases, though, the wife may have undergone a hymenectomy to resolve the problem. That surgical procedure is another stress and often increases the feelings of inadequacy in the couple. The wife may feel put on, abused, or mutilated, and the husband's concern about his manliness may increase. The hymenectomy usually aggravates the situation without solving the basic problem. The inquiry of a physician who is comfortable in dealing with sexual problems may be the first opening to a frank discussion of the couple's distress. Often, the pretext of the medical visit is a discussion of contraceptive methods or—even more ironically—a request for an infertility workup. Once presented, the complaint can often be successfully treated. The duration of the problem does not significantly affect the prognosis or the outcome of the case.

The causes of unconsummated marriage are varied: lack of sex education, sexual prohibitions overly stressed by parents or society, problems of an oedipal nature, immaturity in both partners, overdependence on primary families, and problems in sexual identification. Religious orthodoxy, with severe control of sexual and social development or the equation of sexuality with sin or uncleanliness, has also been cited as a dominant cause. Many women involved in an unconsummated marriage have distorted concepts about their vaginas. They may fear that it is too small or too soft, or they may confuse the vagina with the rectum, leading to feelings of being unclean. The man may share in those distortions about the vagina and, in addition, perceive it as dangerous to himself. Similarly, both partners may have distortions about the man's penis, perceiving it as a weapon, as too large, or as too small. Many patients can be helped by simple education about genital anatomy and physiology, by suggestions for self-exploration, and by correct information from a physician. The problem of the unconsummated marriage is best treated by seeing both members of the couple. Dual-sex therapy involving a male-female cotherapist team has been markedly effective. However, other forms of conjoint therapy, marital counseling, traditional psychotherapy on a one-to-one basis, and counseling from a sensitive family physician, gynecologist, or urologist are all helpful.

Body Image Problems

Some persons are ashamed of their bodies and experience feelings of inadequacy related to self-imposed standards of masculinity or femininity. They may insist on sex only during total darkness, not allow certain body parts to be seen or touched, or seek unnecessary operative procedures to deal with their imagined inadequacies. Body dysmorphic disorder should be ruled out.

Don Juanism

Some men who appear to be hypersexual, as manifested by their need to have many sexual encounters or conquests, use their sexual activities to mask deep feelings of inferiority. Some have unconscious homosexual impulses, which they deny by compulsive sexual contacts with women. After having sex, most Don Juans are no longer interested in the woman. The condition is sometimes referred to as satyriasis or sex addiction.

Nymphomania

Nymphomania signifies excessive or pathological desire for coitus in a woman. There have been few scientific studies of the condition. Those patients who have been studied usually have had one or more sexual disorders, usually including female orgasmic disorder. The woman often has an intense fear of her loss of love. The woman attempts to satisfy her dependence needs, rather than to gratify her sexual impulses, through her actions. This is a form of sex addiction.

Persistent and Marked Distress about Sexual Orientation

Distress about one's sexual orientation is characterized by a dissatisfaction with homosexual arousal patterns, a desire to increase heterosexual arousal, and strong negative feelings about being homosexual. Occasional statements to the effect that life would be easier if the person were not homosexual do not constitute persistent and marked distress about sexual orientation.

Treatment of sexual orientation distress is controversial. One study reported that, with a minimum of 350 hours of psychoanalytic therapy, about a third of about 100 bisexual and homosexual men achieved a heterosexual reorientation at a five-year follow-up, but that study has been challenged. Behavior therapy and avoidance conditioning techniques have also been used, but a basic problem with behavioral techniques is that the behavior may be changed in the laboratory setting but not outside the laboratory. Prognostic factors weighing in favor of heterosexual reorientation for men include being under 35 years of age, some experience of heterosexual arousal, and a high motivation for reorientation.

Another style of intervention is directed at enabling the person with persistent and marked distress about sexual orientation to live comfortably as a homosexual without shame, guilt, anxiety, or depression. Gay counseling centers are engaged with patients in such treatment programs. At present, outcome studies of such centers have not been reported in detail.

As for the treatment of women with persistent and marked distress about sexual orientation, few data are available, and those are primarily single-case studies with variable outcomes. Section 14.1 presents a further discussion on sexual orientation, homosexuality, and coming out.

References

Abel G G, Osborn C: The paraphilias: The extent and nature of sexually deviant and criminal behavior. Psychiatr Clin North Am *15*: 675, 1992.
Langevin R: Biological factors contributing to paraphilic behavior. Psychiatr Ann *22*: 307, 1992.
Levine S M, Stava L: Personality characteristics of sex offenders: A review. Arch Sex Behav *16*: 57, 1987.
Meyer J K: Paraphilias. In *Comprehensive Textbook of Psychiatry*, ed 6, H I Kaplan, B J Sadock, editors, p 1334. Williams & Wilkins, Baltimore, 1995.
Money J: Forensic sexology: Paraphilic serial rape (biastophilia) and lust murder (erotophonophilia). Am J Psychother *44*: 26, 1990.
Stein D J, Hollander E, Anthony D T, Schneier F R: Serotonergic medications for sexual obsessions, sexual addictions, and paraphilias. J Clin Psychiatry *53*: 267, 1992.

15/ Gender Identity Disorders

Gender identity disorders are characterized by persistent feelings of discomfort with one's biological sex or the gender role of one's sex. An understanding of the disorder requires that the complex and varied terminology used in discussing this condition be described clearly to avoid confusion.

Gender identity is a psychological state that reflects the inner sense of oneself as being male or female. Gender identity is based on culturally determined sets of attitudes, behavior patterns, and other attributes usually associated with masculinity or femininity. The person with a healthy gender identity is able to say with certainty, ''I am male'' or ''I am female.'' *Gender role* is the external behavioral pattern that reflects the person's inner sense of gender identity. It is a public declaration of gender; the image of maleness versus femaleness is communicated to others.

Under ideal circumstances, gender identity and gender role are congruent; that is, a woman who has a sense of herself as a woman conveys that to the outside world by acting as a woman; similarly, a man who views himself as a man acts as a man. Gender role is everything that one says or does to indicate to others or to oneself the degree to which one is male or female. Gender identity and gender role must be distinguished from *sex* (also known as biological sex), which is strictly limited to the anatomical and physiological characteristics that indicate whether one is male or female (for example, a penis or a vagina).

All those terms must be distinguished from *sexual orientation*, the person's erotic-response tendency (for example, homosexual or heterosexual). Sexual orientation takes into account one's object choice (man or woman) and one's fantasy life—for example, erotic fantasies about men, women, or both.

EPIDEMIOLOGY

Almost no information is available about the prevalence of gender identity disorders among children, teenagers, and adults. Most estimates of prevalence are based on the number of people seeking sex-reassignment surgery, a number that indicates a male preponderance. The ratios of boys to girls reported in three child gender identity clinics were 30 to 1, 17 to 1, and 6 to 1, indicating little experience with girls. That disparity may indicate a greater male vulnerability to gender identity disorders or a greater sensitivity to and worry about cross-gender-identified boys than cross-gender-identified girls in our culture.

ETIOLOGY

Biological Factors

For mammals, the resting state of tissue is initially female; as the fetus develops, a male is produced only if androgen (set off by the Y chromosome, which is responsible for testicular development) is added. Without testes and androgen, female external genitalia develop. Thus, maleness and masculinity depend on fetal and perinatal androgens. Lower animals' sexual behavior is governed by sex steroids; as one ascends the evolutionary scale, that effect diminishes. Sex steroids influence the expression of sexual behavior in the mature man or woman;

that is, testosterone can increase libido and aggressiveness in women, and estrogen can decrease libido and aggressiveness in men. But masculinity, femininity, and gender identity are products more of postnatal life events than of prenatal hormonal organization.

Psychosocial Factors

Children develop a gender identity consonant with their sex of rearing (also known as assigned sex). The formation of gender identify is influenced by the interaction of the child's temperament and the parents' qualities and attitudes.

The quality of the mother-child relationship in the first years of life is paramount in establishing gender identity. During that period, mothers normally facilitate their children's awareness of and pride in their gender. The child is valued as a little boy or girl. At the same time, the separation-individuation process is unfolding. Devaluing, hostile mothering can result in gender problems. When those problems become associated with separation-individuation problems, the result can be the use of sexuality to remain in relationships characterized by shifts between a desperate infantile closeness and a hostile, devaluing distance.

Some children are given the message that they would be more valued if they adopted the gender identity of the opposite sex. Rejected or abused children may act on the belief that they would be better treated if they were the other sex. Gender identity problems can also triggered by the mother's death, extended absence, or depression, to which a young boy may react by totally identifying with her—that is, becoming a mother to replace her.

The role of the father is also important in those early years. His presence normally helps the separation-individuation process. The absence of a father figure risks the mother and child's remaining in an overly close bond. For a girl, the father is normally the prototype of future love objects; for a boy, the father is a model for male identification.

DIAGNOSIS AND CLINICAL FEATURES

According to the fourth edition of *Diagnostic and Statistical Manual of Mental Disorders* (DSM-IV), the essential feature of gender identity disorders is a persistent and intense distress about one's assigned sex and the desire to be or an insistence that one is of the other sex. In children, both girls and boys show an aversion to normative stereotypical feminine or masculine clothing and repudiate their respective anatomical characteristics. Table 15–1 lists the DSM-IV diagnostic criteria for the disorder.

At the extreme of gender identity disorder in children are those boys who, by the standards of their cultures, are as feminine as are the most feminine of girls and those girls who are as masculine as are the most masculine of boys. No sharp line can be drawn on the continuum of gender identity disorder between children who should receive a formal diagnosis and those who should not. Girls with the disorder regularly have male companions and an avid interest in sports and rough-and-tumble play; they show no interest in dolls or playing house (unless

Table 15-1. Diagnostic Criteria for Gender Identity Disorder

A. A strong and persistent cross-gender identification (not merely a desire for any perceived cultural advantages of being the other sex).

   In children, the disturbance is manifested by four (or more) of the following:

   (1) repeatedly stated desire to be, or insistence that he or she is, the other sex
   (2) in boys, preference for cross-dressing or simulating female attire; in girls, insistence on wearing only stereotypical masculine clothing
   (3) strong and persistent preferences for cross-sex roles in make-believe play or persistent fantasies of being the other sex
   (4) intense desire to participate in the stereotypical games and pastimes of the other sex
   (5) strong preference for playmates of the other sex

   In adolescents and adults, the disturbance is manifested by symptoms such as a stated desire to be the other sex, frequent passing as the other sex, desire to live or be treated as the other sex, or the conviction that he or she has the typical feelings and reactions of the other sex.

B. Persistent discomfort with his or her sex or sense of inappropriateness in the gender role of that sex.

   In children, the disturbance is manifested by any of the following: in boys, assertion that his penis or testes are disgusting or will disappear or assertion that it would be better not to have a penis, or aversion toward rough-and-tumble play and rejection of male stereotypical toys, games, and activities; in girls, rejection of urinating in a sitting position, assertion that she has or will grow a penis, or assertion that she does not want to grow breasts or menstruate, or marked aversion toward normative feminine clothing.

   In adolescents and adults, the disturbance is manifested by symptoms such as preoccupation with getting rid of primary and secondary sex characteristics (e.g., request for hormones, surgery, or other procedures to physically alter sexual characteristics to simulate the other sex) or belief that he or she was born the wrong sex.

C. The disturbance is not concurrent with a physical intersex condition.

D. The disturbance causes clinically significant distress or impairment in social, occupational, or other important areas of functioning.

Table from DSM-IV, *Diagnostic and Statistical Manual of Mental Disorders*, ed 4. Copyright American Psychiatric Association, Washington, 1994. Used with permission.

they play the father or another male role). A girl with the disorder may refuse to urinate in a sitting position, claim that she has or will grow a penis, not want to grow breasts or to menstruate, and assert that she will grow up to become a man (not merely in role). A boy with the disorder is usually preoccupied with female stereotypical activities. He may have a preference for dressing in girls' or women's clothes or may improvise such items from available material when the genuine articles are not available. (The cross-dressing typically does not cause sexual excitement, as in transvestic fetishism.) He often has a compelling desire to participate in the games and pastimes of girls. Female dolls are often his favorite toys, and girls are regularly his preferred playmates. When playing house, he takes the role of a female. His gestures and actions are often judged to be feminine, and he is usually subjected to male peer group teasing and rejection, whereas that rarely occurs in a girl until adolescence. A boy with the disorder may assert that he will grow up to become a woman (not merely in role). A boy with the disorder may claim that his penis or testes are disgusting or will disappear or that it would be better not to have a penis or testes.

In adolescents and adults, the signs and symptoms are similar. Adolescents and adults with the disorder manifest a stated desire to be the other sex; they frequently try to pass as a member of the other sex; and they desire to live or to be treated as the other sex. In addition, they desire to acquire the sex characteristics of the opposite sex. They may believe that they were born the wrong sex and may make such characteristic statements as, "I feel that I'm a woman trapped in a male body" or vice versa.

Adolescents and adults frequently make requests for medical or surgical procedures to alter their physical appearance. In DSM-IV those persons are categorized simply as having a gender identity disorder. However, many clinicians find the term "transsexual" useful and will probably continue to use it. In addition, transsexualism is included in the 10th revision of the International Classification of Diseases and Related Health Problems (ICD-10). Also, persons refer to themselves as transsexuals. The transsexual person has a persistent preoccupation with getting rid of his or her primary and secondary sex characteristics and with acquiring the sex characteristics of the other sex. The wish to dress and live as a member of the other sex is always present.

Most retrospective studies of transsexuals report gender identity problems during childhood; however, prospective studies of children with gender identity disorders indicate that few become transsexuals—that is, want to change their sex. The disorder is much more common in men (1 per 30,000 men) than in women (1 per 100,000 women).

Adult transsexuals usually complain that they are uncomfortable wearing the clothes of their assigned sex; therefore, they dress in clothes of the other sex. They engage in activities associated with the other sex. They find their genitals repugnant, a feeling that may lead to persistent requests for surgery. That desire may override all other wishes.

Men take estrogen to create breasts and other feminine contours, have electrolysis to remove their male hair, and have surgery to remove the testes and the penis and to create an artificial vagina. Women bind their breasts or have a double mastectomy, a hysterectomy, and an oophorectomy; take testosterone to build up their muscle mass and deepen the voice; and have surgery in which an artificial phallus is created. Those procedures may make the person indistinguishable from members of the other sex. Some investigators describe behavior in sex-reassigned persons that is almost a caricature of male and female roles.

Sexual Object Choice

Persons with gender identity disorder may be (1) sexually attracted to males, (2) sexually attracted to females, (3) sexually attracted to both, or (4) sexually attracted to neither males nor females. In almost all cases, such persons do not consider themselves to be homosexual, even if they have undergone a male-to-female change and are attracted to men. Similarly, persons with a female-to-male change who are attracted to women may not consider themselves to be homosexual. Because they believe themselves to be members of the opposite sex, they believe themselves to be heterosexual.

According to DSM-IV, once a diagnosis of gender identity disorder is made, the object of sexual attraction should be specified (for example, male, female, both, or neither).

Gender Identity Disorder Not Otherwise Specified

This diagnosis is reserved for persons who cannot be classified as having a gender identity disorder with the characteristics described above. Three examples are listed in DSM-IV: (1) persons with intersex conditions and gender dysphoria, (2) adults with transient, stress-related cross-dressing behavior, and (3) persons who have a persistent preoccupation with castration or penectomy without a desire to acquire the sex characteristics of the other sex.

INTERSEX CONDITIONS

Intersex conditions include a variety of syndromes that produce persons with gross anatomical or physiological aspects of the opposite sex.

Turner's Syndrome

In Turner's syndrome, one sex chromosome is missing (XO). The result is an absence (agenesis) or minimal development (dysgenesis) of the gonads; no significant sex hormones, male or female, are produced in fetal life or postnatally. The sexual tissues remain in a female resting state. Because the second X chromosome, which seems responsible for full femaleness, is missing, the girls have an incomplete sexual anatomy and, lacking adequate estrogens, develop no secondary sex characteristic without treatment. They often suffer other stigmata, such as web neck, low posterior hairline margin, short stature, and cubitus valgus. The infant is born with normal-appearing female external genitals and so is unequivocally assigned to the female sex and is so reared. All the children develop as unremarkably feminine, heterosexually oriented girls; however, later medical management is necessary to assist them with their infertility and absence of secondary sex characteristics.

Klinefelter's Syndrome

A person (usually XXY) with Klinefelter's syndrome has a male habitus, under the influence of the Y chromosome, but the effect is weakened by the presence of the second X chromosome. Although the patient is born with a penis and testes, the testes are small and infertile, and the penis may also be small. Beginning in adolescence, some patients develop gynecomastia and other feminine-appearing contours. Their sexual desire is usually weak. Sex assignment and rearing should lead to a clear sense of maleness, but the patients often have gender disturbances, ranging from a complete reversal, as in transsexualism, to an intermittent desire to put on women's clothes. As a result of lessened androgen production, the fetal hypogonadal state in some patients seems to have interfered with the completion of the central nervous system organization that should underlie masculine behavior. In fact, many patients have a wide variability of psychopathology, ranging from emotional instability to mental retardation.

Congenital Virilizing Adrenal Hyperplasia (Adrenogenital Syndrome)

Congenital virilizing adrenal hyperplasia results from an excess of androgen acting on the fetus. When the condition occurs in females, excessive fetal androgens from the adrenal gland cause androgenization of the external genitals, ranging from mild clitoral enlargement to external genitals that look like a normal scrotal sac, testes, and a penis; however, hidden behind those external genitals are a vagina and a uterus. The patients are otherwise normally female. At birth, if the genitals look male, the child is assigned to the male sex and is so reared. The result is a clear sense of maleness and unremarkable masculinity; however, if the child is assigned to the female sex and is so reared, a sense of femaleness and femininity results. If the parents are uncertain to which sex their child belongs, a hermaphroditic identity results. The resultant gender identity reflects the rearing

practices, but androgens may help determine behavior; children raised unequivocally as girls have a tomboy quality more intense than that found in a control group. The girls nonetheless do have a heterosexual orientation.

Pseudohermaphroditism

Infants may be born with ambiguous genitals, which is an obstetrical emergency, because the sex assignment determines gender identity. Male pseudohermaphroditism is incomplete differentiation of the external genitalia, even though a Y chromosome is present. Testes are present but rudimentary. Female pseudohermaphroditism is the presence of virilized genitals in a person who is XX, the most common cause being the adrenogenital syndrome described above.

The genitals' appearance at birth determines the sex assignment, and the core gender identity is male, female, or hermaphroditic, depending on the family's conviction as to the child's sex. Usually, a panel of experts determine the sex of rearing, basing their decision on buccal smears, chromosome studies, and parental wishes. Assignment should usually be made within 24 hours, so that the parents can adapt accordingly. If surgery is necessary to correct the genital deformity, it is generally done before the age of 3 years.

True hermaphroditism is characterized by the presence of both testes and ovaries in the same person; it is a rare condition.

Androgen Insensitivity Syndrome

Androgen insensitivity syndrome, a congenital X-linked recessive trait disorder—also known as testicular feminization syndrome—results from an inability of target tissues to respond to androgens. Unable to respond, the fetal tissues remain in their female resting state, and the central nervous system is not organized as masculine. The infant at birth appears to be an unremarkable female, although she is later found to have cryptorchid testes, which produce the testosterone to which the tissues do not respond, and minimal or absent internal sexual organs. Secondary sex characteristics at puberty are female because of the small but sufficient amounts of estrogens typically produced by the testes. The patients invariably sense themselves as females and are feminine.

CROSS-DRESSING

DSM-IV lists cross-dressing—that is, dressing in clothes of the opposite sex—as a gender identity disorder if it is transient and related to stress. If the disorder is not stress-related, persons who cross-dress are classified as having transvestic fetishism, which is classified as a paraphilia in DSM-IV. An essential feature of transvestic fetishism is that it produces sexual excitement. Stress-related cross-dressing sometimes produces sexual excitement, but it reduces tension and anxiety in the patient. The patient may harbor fantasies of cross-dressing but act them out only under stress. Most male adult cross-dressers have the fantasy that they are female, in whole or in part.

Cross-dressing is commonly known as transvestism and the cross-dresser as a transvestite. Although those terms are no longer used in DSM-IV, they remain in common parlance.

Cross-dressing phenomena range from the occasional solitary wearing of female clothes to extensive feminine identification in men and masculine identification in women and involvement in a transvestic subculture. More than one article of clothing of the other sex is involved, and the person may dress entirely as a member of the opposite sex. The degree to which the cross-dressed person appears as a member of the other sex varies, depending on mannerisms, body habitus, and cross-dressing skill. When not cross-dressed, the persons usually appear as unremarkable members of their assigned sex. Cross-dressing may coexist with paraphilias, such as sexual sadism, sexual masochism, and pedophilia.

Cross-dressing differs from transsexualism in that the patients have no persistent preoccupation with getting rid of their primary and secondary sex characteristics and acquiring the sex characteristics of the other sex.

Some people with the disorder once had transvestic fetishism but no longer become sexually aroused by cross-dressing. Other people with the disorder are homosexuals who cross-dress. The disorder is common among female impersonators.

COURSE AND PROGNOSIS

The prognosis for gender identity disorder depends on the age of onset and the intensity of the symptoms. Boys begin to have the disorder before the age of 4 years, and peer conflict develops during the early school years, at about the age of 7 or 8 years. Grossly feminine mannerisms may lessen as the boy grows older, especially if attempts are made to discourage such behavior. Cross-dressing may be part of the disorder, and 75 percent of boys who cross-dress begin to do so before age 4. The age of onset is also early for girls, but most give up masculine behavior by adolescence.

In both sexes, homosexuality is likely to develop in one third to two thirds of all cases, although fewer girls than boys have a homosexual orientation, for reasons that are not clear. Steven Levine reported that follow-up studies of gender-disturbed boys consistently indicated that homosexual orientation was the usual adolescent outcome. Transsexualism—that is, the desire for sex-reassignment surgery—occurs in less than 10 percent of cases. Retrospective data on homosexual men indicate a high frequency of cross-gender identifications and feminine gender role behavior during childhood.

Impaired social and occupational functioning as a result of the person's wanting to participate in the desired (and opposite) gender role is common. Depression is also a common problem, especially if the person feels hopeless about obtaining a sex change with surgery or hormones. Men have been known to castrate themselves, not as a suicide attempt but as a way of forcing a surgeon to deal with their problem.

TREATMENT

Treatment of gender identity disorders is a complex problem and rarely successful if the goal is to reverse the disorder. Most persons with gender identity disorders have fixed ideas and values and are unwilling to change. If and when they enter psychotherapy, it is most often because of depression or anxiety that they attribute to their condition. Countertransference problems must be addressed assiduously by therapists, many of whom are uncomfortable with gender identity disorder patients.

Children with cross-gender behavior patterns are generally brought to a psychiatrist by the parents. Richard Green developed a treatment program designed to inculcate culturally acceptable behavior patterns in boys. Green uses a one-to-one play relationship with the child in which adults or peers role-model masculine behavior. Parental counseling in conjunction with group meetings of parents and their children with the same problem is also used. Parents' encouragement of the child's atypical behavior (such as dressing a boy in girl's clothing or not giving him haircuts) is examined when parents are unaware of how they are fostering cross-gender behavior.

Adolescent patients are difficult to treat because of the coexistence of normal identity crises and gender identity confusion. Acting out is common, and the adolescents rarely have a strong motivation to alter their stereotypical cross-gender roles.

Adult patients generally enter psychotherapy to learn how to deal with their disorder, not to alter it. The therapist generally sets the goal with the patients of helping them become comfortable with the gender identity they desire; the goal is not to create a person with a conventional sexual identity. Therapy also explores sex-reassignment surgery and the indications and contraindications for such procedures, which are often impulsively decided on by severely distressed and anxious patients.

Sex-Reassignment Surgery

Surgical treatment is definitive, and because there is no turning back, careful standards preceding the surgery have been developed, which include the following: (1) The patients must go through a trial of cross-gender living for at least three months and sometimes up to one year. For some transsexuals the real-life test may make them change their minds, because they find it uncomfortable to relate to friends, coworkers, and lovers in that role. (2) The patients must receive hormone treatments, with estradiol and progesterone in male-to-female changes and testosterone in female-to-male changes. Many transsexuals like the changes in their bodies that occur as a result of that treatment, and some stop at that point. About 50 percent of transsexuals who meet the above criteria go on to sex-reassignment surgery. Outcome studies are highly variable in terms of how success is defined and measured (for example, successful intercourse and body-image satisfaction).

About 70 percent of male-to-female and 80 percent of female-to-male sex-reassignment surgery patients report satisfactory results. Unsatisfactory results correlate with a preexisting mental disorder. Suicide in postoperative sex-reassignment surgery patients has been reported in up to 2 percent of all cases. Sex-reassignment surgery is a highly controversial measure that is undergoing much scrutiny.

Hormonal Treatment

Both sexes may be treated with hormones in lieu of surgery. Biological males take estrogen, and biological females take testosterone. Patients who take estrogen usually report immediate psychological satisfaction, based on a sense of tranquility, less frequent erections, and fewer sexual drive manifestations than before the hormone treatment. Their new sterility is not of concern to them. After several months, bodily contours become rounded, a limited but pleasing breast enlargement develops, and testicular volume decreases. The quality of the voice does not change. Patients need to be watched for hypertension, hyperglycemia, hepatic dysfunction, and thromboembolic phenomena.

Women who take androgens quickly notice an increased sexual drive, clitoral tingling and enlargement, and, after several months, amenorrhea and hoarseness. If weight lifting is undertaken, a pronounced increase in muscle mass may occur. Depending on the hair distribution already present, the patients may have a moderate increase in the amount and the coarseness of facial and body hair; some develop frontal balding. Thromboembolic phenomena, hepatic dysfunction, and elevations of cholesterol and triglycerides are possible.

Treatment of Intersex Conditions

Since intersex conditions are present at birth, treatment must be timely, and some physicians believe the conditions to be true medical emergencies. Since the appearance of the genitalia in diverse conditions is often ambiguous, a decision must be made about the assigned sex (boy or girl) and how the child should be reared.

Assignment should be agreed on as early as possible, so that the entire family can regard the patient in a consistent, relaxed manner. When surgery is necessary to normalize genital appearance, it is generally undertaken well before the age of 3 years. It is easier to assign a child to be female than to assign a child to be male, because male-to-female genital surgical procedures are far more advanced than female-to-male surgical procedures.

Intersex patients may have gender identity problems because of complicated biological influences and familial confusion about their actual sex. When intersex conditions are discovered, a panel of pediatric experts usually determines the sex of rearing on the basis of clinical examination, urological studies, buccal smears, chromosomal analyses, and assessment of the parental wishes.

Treatment of Cross-Dressing

A combined approach, using psychotherapy and pharmacotherapy, is often useful in the treatment of cross-dressing. The stress factors that precipitate the behavior are identified in therapy. The goal is to help the patient cope with the stressors appropriately and, if possible, eliminate them. Intrapsychic dynamics about attitudes toward the same sex and the opposite sex are examined, and unconscious conflicts are identified. Medication is used to treat the symptoms—for example, antianxiety and antidepressant agents. Because cross-dressing may occur impulsively, medications that reinforce impulse control may be helpful—for example, thioridazine (Mellaril) and fluoxetine (Prozac). Behavior therapy, aversive conditioning, and hypnosis are alternative methods that may be of use in selected cases.

References

Green R, Blanchard R: Gender identity disorders. In *Comprehensive Textbook of Psychiatry*, ed 6, H I Kaplan, B J Sadock, editors, p 1347. Williams & Wilkins, Baltimore, 1995.

Levine S B: Gender-disturbed males. J Sex Marital Ther *19*: 131, 1993.

Meyer-Bahlburg FL: Intersexuality and the diagnosis of gender identity disorder. Arch Sex Behav *23:* 21, 1994.

Sugar M: A clinical approach to childhood gender identity disorder. Am J Psychother *49*: 260, 1995.

Zucker K J, Wild J, Bradley S J, Lowry C B: Physical attractiveness of boys with gender identity disorder. Arch Sex Behav *22*: 23, 1993.

16/ Eating Disorders

16.1 Anorexia Nervosa

Anorexia nervosa is characterized by a profound disturbance of body image and the relentless pursuit of thinness, often to the point of starvation. The disorder has been recognized for many decades and has been described in various persons with remarkable uniformity. The disorder is much more prevalent in females than in males and usually has its onset in adolescence. Hypotheses of an underlying psychological disturbance in young women with the disorder include conflicts surrounding the transition from girlhood to womanhood. Psychological issues related to feelings of helplessness and to difficulty in establishing autonomy have also been suggested as contributing to the development of the disorder.

In the fourth edition of *Diagnostic and Statistical Manual of Mental Disorders* (DSM-IV), the diagnostic criteria for anorexia nervosa consist of a persistent refusal to maintain body weight at or above a minimum expected weight or a failure to gain the expected weight during a period of growth. In either case, body weight less than 85 percent of the expected weight is cause for concern. To meet the diagnostic criteria for anorexia nervosa, postmenarchal females must have an absence of at least three consecutive menstrual cycles. DSM-IV has added two types of anorexia nervosa. In the restricting type, the person restricts intake during the episode of anorexia nervosa but does not regularly engage in binge eating or purging by vomiting or using laxatives or diuretics. In the binge eating/purging type, during the episode of anorexia nervosa, the person regularly engages in binge eating or purging through self-induced vomiting or the use of laxatives or diuretics.

EPIDEMIOLOGY

Eating disorders of various kinds have been reported in up to 4 percent of adolescent and young adult students. Anorexia nervosa has been reported more frequently over the past several decades than in the past, with increasing reports of the disorder in prepubertal girls and in males. Most commonly, the onset of anorexia nervosa comes during the mid-teenage years, but up to 5 percent of anorectic patients experience onset of the disorder in their early 20s. Anorexia nervosa is estimated to occur in about 0.5 to 1 percent of adolescent girls. It occurs 10 to 20 times more often in females than in males. The prevalence of young women with some symptoms of anorexia nervosa but who do not meet the diagnostic criteria is estimated to be close to 5 percent. Although the disorder was initially reported most often among the upper classes, recent epidemiological surveys do not show that distribution. It is most frequent in developed countries, and it may be seen with greatest frequency among young women in professions that require thinness, such as modeling and ballet.

ETIOLOGY

Biological, social, and psychological factors are implicated in the causes of anorexia nervosa. Some evidence points to higher concordance rates in monozygotic twins than in dizygotic twins. Sisters of anorexia nervosa patients are likely to be afflicted, but that association may reflect social influences more than genetic factors. Major mood disorders are more common in family members than in the general population. Neurochemically, diminished norepinephrine turnover and activity are suggested by reduced 3-methoxy-4-hydroxyphenylglycol (MHPG) in the urine and the cerebrospinal fluid (CSF) of some anorexia nervosa patients. An inverse relation is seen between MHPG and depression in patients with anorexia nervosa: an increase in MHPG is associated with a decrease in depression.

DIAGNOSIS AND CLINICAL FEATURES

The onset of anorexia nervosa usually occurs between the ages of 10 and 30 years. Patients outside that range are not typical, and so their diagnoses should be questioned. After the age of 13, the frequency of onset increases rapidly; maximum frequency is 17 to 18 years of age. About 85 percent of all anorexia nervosa patients experience onset of the illness between the ages of 13 to 20 years. Some anorexia nervosa patients, before age 10, were picky eaters or had frequent digestive problems. The DSM-IV diagnostic criteria for anorexia nervosa are given in Table 16.1–1.

Most of the aberrant behavior directed toward losing weight occurs in secret. Anorexia nervosa patients usually refuse to eat with their families or in public places. They lose weight by a drastic reduction in their total food intake, with a disproportionate decrease in high-carbohydrate and fatty foods.

Unfortunately, the term "anorexia," meaning loss of appetite, is a misnomer, because the loss of appetite is usually rare until late in the disorder. Evidence that the patients are constantly thinking about food is their passion for collecting recipes and preparing elaborate meals for others. Some patients cannot continuously control their voluntary restriction of food intake, and so they have eating binges. Those binges usually occur secretly and often at night. Self-induced vomiting frequently follows the eating binge. Patients abuse laxatives and even diuretics to lose weight. Ritualistic exercising, extensive cycling, walking, jogging, and running are common activities.

Patients with the disorder exhibit peculiar behavior regarding food. They hide food all over the house and frequently carry large quantities of candies in their pockets and purses. While eating meals, they try to dispose of food in their napkins or hide it in their pockets. They cut their meat into very small pieces and spend a great deal of time rearranging the food pieces on their plates. If the patients are confronted about their peculiar behavior, they often deny that their behavior is unusual or flatly refuse to discuss it.

An intense fear of gaining weight and becoming obese is present in all patients with the disorder and undoubtedly contributes to their lack of interest in therapy and even resistance to it.

Obsessive-compulsive behavior, depression, and anxiety are the other psychiatric symptoms in anorexia nervosa most frequently noted in the literature. Patients tend to be rigid and perfectionistic. Somatic complaints, especially epigastric discomfort, are usual. Compulsive stealing, usually of candies and

Table 16.1-1. Diagnostic Criteria for Anorexia Nervosa

A. Refusal to maintain body weight at or above a minimally normal weight for age and height (e.g., weight loss leading to maintenance of body weight less than 85% of that expected; or failure to make expected weight gain during period of growth, leading to body weight less than 85% of that expected).

B. Intense fear of gaining weight or becoming fat, even though underweight.

C. Disturbance in the way in which one's body weight or shape is experienced; undue influence of body weight or shape on self-evaluation, or denial of the seriousness of the current low body weight.

D. In postmenarchal females, amenorrhea, i.e., the absence of at least three consecutive menstrual cycles. (A woman is considered to have amenorrhea if her periods occur only following hormone, e.g., estrogen, administration.)

Table from DSM-IV, *Diagnostic and Statistical Manual of Mental Disorders*, ed 4. Copyright American Psychiatric Association, Washington, 1994. Used with permission.

laxatives but occasionally of clothes and other items, is common.

Poor sexual adjustment is frequently described in patients with the disorder. Many adolescent anorexia nervosa patients have delayed psychosocial sexual development, and adults often have a markedly decreased interest in sex accompanying the onset of the disorder. An unusual minority of anorexia nervosa patients have a premorbid history of promiscuity or substance abuse or both, and during the disorder they do not show a decreased interest in sex.

Patients usually come to medical attention when their weight loss becomes apparent. As the weight loss becomes profound, physical signs such as hypothermia (as low as 358C), dependent edema, bradycardia, hypotension, and lanugo (the appearance of neonatallike hair) appear, and the patient presents a variety of metabolic changes. Some female anorexia nervosa patients come to medical attention because of amenorrhea, which often appears before their weight loss is noticeable.

Some anorexia nervosa patients induce vomiting or abuse purgatives and diuretics, causing concern about hypokalemic alkalosis. Impaired water diuresis may be noted.

Electrocardiographic (ECG) changes—such as flattening or inversion of the T waves, ST segment depression, and lengthening of the QT interval—have been noted in the emaciated stage of anorexia nervosa. ECG changes may also occur from potassium loss, which may lead to death. Gastric dilation is a rare complication of anorexia nervosa. In some patients, aortography has shown a superior mesenteric artery syndrome.

DSM-IV identifies two types of anorexia nervosa—the restricting type and the binge eating/purging type. Binge eating/purging is common, developing in up to 50 percent of anorexia nervosa patients. Each type appears to have distinct historic and clinical features. Binge eating/purging anorectic persons share many features with persons who have bulimia nervosa but not anorexia nervosa. Binge eating/purging persons tend to have families in which some members are obese, and they themselves have histories of heavier premorbid body weights than do restricting persons. Binge eating/purging persons are likely to be associated with substance abuse, impulse-control disorders, and personality disorders. Restricting anorexia nervosa persons limit their food selection, take in as few calories as possible, and often have obsessive-compulsive traits concerning food and

other matters. Both types are preoccupied with weight and body image, and both may exercise for hours every day and exhibit bizarre eating behaviors. Social isolation, depressive disorder symptoms, and diminished sexual interest may be found in either type. Some anorexia nervosa persons purge but do not binge.

DIFFERENTIAL DIAGNOSIS

The differential diagnosis of anorexia nervosa is complicated by the patient's denial of the symptoms, the secrecy surrounding the patient's bizarre eating rituals, and the patient's resistance to seeking treatment. Thus, identifying the mechanism of weight loss and the patient's associated ruminative thoughts regarding distortions of body image may be difficult.

The clinician must ascertain that the patient does not have a medical illness that can account for the weight loss (for example, a brain tumor or cancer). Weight loss, peculiar eating behaviors, and vomiting can occur in several mental disorders. Depressive disorders and anorexia nervosa have several features in common (for example, depressed feeling, crying spells, sleep disturbance, obsessive ruminations, and occasional suicidal thoughts); however, the two disorders have several distinguishing features. Generally, a patient with a depressive disorder has a decreased appetite, whereas an anorexia nervosa patient claims to have a normal appetite and to feel hungry. Only in the severe stages of anorexia nervosa does the patient have an actual decrease in appetite. In contrast to depressive agitation, the hyperactivity seen in anorexia nervosa is planned and ritualistic. The preoccupation with the caloric content of food, recipes, and the preparation of gourmet feasts is typical of the anorexia nervosa patient and is not present in the patient with a depressive disorder; in depressive disorders the patient has no intense fear of obesity or disturbance of body image as the anorexia nervosa patient has.

Weight fluctuations, vomiting, and peculiar food handling may occur in somatization disorder. On rare occasions a patient fulfills the diagnostic criteria for both somatization disorder and anorexia nervosa; in such a case a dual diagnosis should be made. Generally, the weight loss in somatization disorder is not as severe as that in anorexia nervosa, nor does the patient with somatization disorder express a morbid fear of becoming overweight as is common in the anorexia nervosa patient. Amenorrhea for three months or longer is unusual in somatization disorder.

Delusions about food in schizophrenia are seldom concerned with the caloric content of food. A patient with schizophrenia is rarely preoccupied with a fear of becoming obese and does not have the hyperactivity seen in the anorexia nervosa patient. Schizophrenic patients may have bizarre eating habits but not the entire syndrome of anorexia nervosa.

Anorexia nervosa must be differentiated from bulimia nervosa, a disorder in which episodic binge eating (followed by depressive moods, self-deprecating thoughts, and often self-induced vomiting) occurs while patients maintain their weight within a normal range. In bulimia nervosa the patient seldom has as much as a 15 percent weight loss; however, the two conditions frequently coexist.

COURSE AND PROGNOSIS

The course of anorexia nervosa varies greatly—spontaneous recovery without treatment, recovery after a variety of treatments, a fluctuating course of weight gains followed by relapses, a gradually deteriorating course resulting in death caused by complications of starvation. Usually, the prognosis is not good. In those who have regained sufficient weight, preoccupation with food and body weight often continues, social relationships are often poor, and many patients are depressed. The short-term response of patients to most hospital treatment programs is good. Studies have shown a range of mortality rates from 5 to 18 percent.

Indicators of a favorable outcome are the admission of hunger, less denial, less immaturity, and improved self-esteem. Such factors as childhood neuroticism, parental conflict, bulimia nervosa, vomiting, laxative abuse, and various behavioral manifestations (obsessive-compulsive, hysterical, depressive, psychosomatic, neurotic, and denial symptoms) have been related to poor outcome in some studies but have not been significant in others.

From 30 to 50 percent of anorexia nervosa patients have the symptoms of bulimia nervosa, and usually the bulimic symptoms occur within $1\frac{1}{2}$ years after the beginning of anorexia nervosa. Sometimes, the bulimic symptoms precede the onset of anorexia nervosa.

TREATMENT

Given the complicated psychological and medical implications of anorexia nervosa, a comprehensive treatment plan, including hospitalization when necessary and both individual and family therapy, is recommended. Behavioral, interpersonal, and cognitive approaches and occasionally medication should be considered.

Hospitalization

The first consideration in the treatment of anorexia nervosa is to restore the patient's nutritional state, since dehydration, starvation, and electrolyte imbalances can lead to serious health compromises and, sometimes, death. The decision to hospitalize the patient is based on the patient's medical condition and the structure needed to ensure patient cooperation. Usually, anorexia nervosa patients who are 20 percent below the expected weight for their height are recommended for inpatient programs; patients who are 30 percent below their expected weight require psychiatric hospitalization for 2 to 6 months.

Inpatient psychiatric programs for anorexia nervosa patients generally use a combination of behavioral management, individual psychotherapy, family education and therapy, and, sometimes, psychotropic medications. Successful treatment is promoted by the ability of staff members to maintain a firm yet supportive approach to the patient, often through a combination of positive reinforcers (praise) and negative reinforcers (restriction of exercise and purging behavior). However, some flexibility in the program is needed to tailor the treatment to meet the patient's needs and cognitive abilities. Ultimately, the patient must become a willing participant in the treatment for it to succeed.

Most patients are uninterested in psychiatric treatment and even resistant to it; they are brought to a doctor's office unwillingly by agonizing relatives or friends. The patients rarely accept the recommendation of hospitalization without arguing and criticizing the program being offered. Emphasizing the benefits,

such as the relief of insomnia and the patient's depressive signs and symptoms, may help persuade the patients to admit themselves willingly to the hospital. The relatives' support and confidence in the physician and the treatment team are essential when firm recommendations must be carried out. The patients' families should be warned that the patients will resist admission and, for the several weeks of treatment, will make many dramatic pleas for the family's support to obtain release from the hospital program. Only when the risk of death from the complications of malnutrition is likely should compulsory admission or commitment be obtained. On rare occasions, patients prove that the doctor's statements about the probable failure of outpatient treatment are wrong. Those patients may gain a specified amount of weight by the time of each outpatient visit; however, that behavior is uncommon, and usually a period of inpatient care is necessary.

The general management of anorexia nervosa patients during a hospitalized treatment program should include certain procedures. Each patient should be weighed daily early in the morning after emptying the bladder. The daily fluid intake and urine output should be recorded. If vomiting is occurring, the hospital staff members must obtain serum electrolytes regularly and watch for the development of hypokalemia. Because food is often regurgitated after meals, the staff can probably control the vomiting by making the bathroom inaccessible for at least two hours after meals or by having an attendant in the bathroom to prevent vomiting. Constipation in anorexia nervosa patients is relieved when they begin to eat normally. Occasionally, stool softeners are given but never laxatives. If diarrhea occurs, it usually means that the patient is surreptitiously taking laxatives. Because of the rare complication of stomach dilation and possible circulatory overload, if the patient immediately starts eating an enormous number of calories, the hospital staff should start to give patients about 500 calories over the amount required to maintain their present weight (usually 1,500 to 2,000 calories a day). Giving those calories in six equal feedings throughout the day is wise, so that the patients do not have to eat a large amount of food in one sitting. Starting to give patients a liquid food supplement, such as Sustagen, may be advisable, because they may be less apprehensive about gaining weight slowly with the formula than by eating food.

After patients are discharged from the hospital, the clinician usually finds it necessary to continue some type of outpatient supervision of whatever problems are identified in the patients and their families.

Psychotherapy

Dynamic expressive-supportive psychotherapy is sometimes used in the treatment of anorexia nervosa patients. Patients' resistances, however, may make the process difficult and painstaking. Because the patients view their symptoms as forming the core of their specialness, therapists must avoid excessive investment in trying to change their eating behaviors. The opening phase of the psychotherapy process must be geared to building a therapeutic alliance. Patients may experience early interpretations as though someone else were telling them what they really feel while their own experiences are minimized and invalidated. However, therapists who empathize with patients' points of view and take an active interest in their thoughts and feelings convey to patients that their autonomy is respected. Above all, psychotherapists must be flexible, persistent, and durable in the face of patients' tendencies to defeat any efforts to help them.

Many clinicians prefer cognitive-behavioral approaches to monitor weight gain and maintenance and to address eating behaviors. Cognitive or interpersonal strategies have also been recommended to explore other issues related to the disorder. Family therapy has been used to examine interactions among family members and the disorder's possible secondary gain for the patient.

Biological Treatment

Pharmacological studies have not yet identified any medication resulting in definitive improvement of the core symptoms of anorexia nervosa. Some reports support the use of cyproheptadine (Periactin), a drug with antihistaminic and antiserotonergic properties, in the restricting type of anorexia nervosa. Amitriptyline (Elavil) has been reported to have some benefit in patients with anorexia nervosa. Other medications tried by anorexia nervosa patients—including clomipramine (Anafranil), pimozide (Orap), and chlorpromazine (Thorazine)—have not yielded positive responses. Uncontrolled trials of fluoxetine (Prozac) have resulted in some reports of weight gain. In anorexia nervosa patients with coexisting depressive disorders, other antidepressants have been tried with little benefit. Concern exists regarding the use of tricyclic drugs in low-weight, depressed anorexia nervosa patients, since they may be vulnerable to hypotension, cardiac arrhythmia, and dehydration. Once an adequate nutritional status has been attained, the risks of serious side effects from the tricyclics may decrease. However, sometimes the depression improves with weight gain and normalized nutritional status.

Some evidence suggests that electroconvulsive therapy (ECT) is beneficial in certain cases of anorexia nervosa and major depressive disorder.

References

American Psychiatric Association: Practice guidelines for eating disorders. Am J Psychiatry *150*: 212, 1993.
Brewerton T D, Lydiard R B, Ballenger J C, Herzog D B: Eating disorders and social phobia. Arch Gen Psychiatry *50*: 70, 1993.
Gabbard G O: *Psychodynamic Psychiatry in Clinical Practice: The DSM-IV Edition*. American Psychiatric Press, Washington, 1994.
Garfinkel P E: Eating disorders. In *Comprehensive Textbook of Psychiatry*, ed 6, H I Kaplan, B J Sadock, editors, p 1361. Williams & Wilkins, Baltimore, 1995.
Herzog D B, Sacks N R, Keller M B, Lavori P W, von Ranson K B, Gray H M: Patterns and predictors of recovery in anorexia nervosa and bulimia nervosa. J Am Acad Child Adolesc Psychiatry *32*: 835, 1993.
Ponton L E: A review of eating disorders in adolescents. Adolesc Psychiatry *20*: 267, 1995.
Wilson G T, Fairburn C G: Cognitive treatments for eating disorders. J Consult Clin Psychol *61*: 261, 1993.

16.2 BULIMIA NERVOSA AND EATING DISORDER NOS

BULIMIA NERVOSA

Bulimia nervosa, which is more common than anorexia nervosa, consists of recurrent episodes of eating large amounts of food accompanied by a feeling of being out of control. Social interruption or the physical discomfort of abdominal pain or nausea terminates the binge eating, which is often followed by feelings of guilt, depression, or self-disgust. The person also has recurrent compensatory behaviors—such as purging (self-induced vomiting, repeated laxative use, or diuretic use), fasting, or excessive exercise—to prevent weight gain. Unlike anorexia nervosa patients, those with bulimia nervosa may maintain a normal body weight.

Epidemiology

Bulimia nervosa is more prevalent than is anorexia nervosa. Estimates of bulimia nervosa range from 1 to 3 percent of young women. Like anorexia nervosa, bulimia nervosa is much more common in females than in males, but its onset is often later in adolescence than the onset of anorexia nervosa or in early adulthood. Occasional symptoms of bulimia nervosa, such as isolated episodes of binge eating and purging, have been reported in up to 40 percent of college women. Although bulimia nervosa is often present in normal-weight young women, they sometimes have a history of obesity.

Etiology

BIOLOGICAL FACTORS

Some investigators have attempted to associate cycles of binging and purging with various neurotransmitters. Because antidepressants often benefit patients with bulimia nervosa, serotonin and norepinephrine have been implicated.

Plasma endorphin levels are raised in some of those bulimia nervosa patients who vomit, leading to the possibility that the feelings of well-being experienced by some patients after vomiting may be medicated by raised endorphin levels.

SOCIAL FACTORS

Patients with bulimia nervosa, like those with anorexia nervosa, tend to be high achievers and to respond to societal pressures to be thin. As with anorexia nervosa patients, many bulimia nervosa patients are depressed and have increased familial depression. However, the families of such patients are generally different from those of anorexia nervosa patients. Families of bulimia nervosa patients are less close and more conflictual than the families of anorexia nervosa patients. Bulimia nervosa patients describe their parents as neglectful and rejecting.

PSYCHOLOGICAL FACTORS

Patients with bulimia nervosa, like those with anorexia nervosa, have difficulties with adolescent demands, but bulimia nervosa patients are more outgoing, angry, and impulsive than are anorexia nervosa patients. Alcohol dependence, shoplifting, and emotional lability (including suicide attempts) are associated with bulimia nervosa. Bulimia nervosa patients generally experience their uncontrolled eating as more ego-dystonic than do anorexia nervosa patients, so bulimia nervosa patients more readily seek help.

Diagnosis and Clinical Features

According to the fourth edition of *Diagnostic and Statistical Manual of Mental Disorders* (DSM-IV), the essential features of bulimia nervosa are recurrent episodes of binge eating; a sense of lack of control over eating during the eating binges; self-induced vomiting, the misuse of laxatives or diuretics, fasting, or excessive exercise to prevent weight gain; and persistent self-evaluation unduly influenced by body shape and weight

Table 16.2–1.   Diagnostic Criteria for Bulimia Nervosa

A. Recurrent episodes of binge eating. An episode of binge eating is characterized by both of the following:

    (1) eating, in a discrete period of time (e.g., within any 2 hour period), an amount of food that is definitely larger than most people would eat during a similar period of time and under similar circumstances

    (2) a sense of lack of control over eating during the episode (e.g., a feeling that one cannot stop eating or control what or how much one is eating)

B. Recurrent inappropriate compensatory behavior in order to prevent weight gain, such as self-induced vomiting; misuse of laxatives, diuretics, enemas, or other medications; fasting; or excessive exercise.

C. The binge eating and inappropriate compensatory behaviors both occur, on average, at least twice a week for 3 months.

D. Self-evaluation is unduly influenced by body shape and weight.

E. The disturbance does not occur exclusively during episodes of anorexia nervosa.

Table from DSM-IV, *Diagnostic and Statistical Manual of Mental Disorders,* ed 4. Copyright American Psychiatric Association, Washington, 1994. Used with permission.

(Table 16.2–1). Binging usually precedes vomiting by about one year.

Vomiting is common and is usually induced by sticking a finger down the throat, although some patients can vomit at will. Vomiting decreases the abdominal pain and the feeling of being bloated and allows the patients to continue eating without fear of gaining weight. Depression often follows the episode and has been called postbinge anguish. During their binges patients eat food that is sweet, high in calories, and generally smooth or soft, such as cakes and pastry. The food is eaten secretly and rapidly and is sometimes not even chewed.

Most bulimia nervosa patients are within their normal weight range, but some may be either underweight or overweight. Bulimia nervosa patients are concerned about their body image and their appearance, worry about how others see them, and are concerned about their sexual attractiveness. Most bulimia nervosa patients are sexually active, compared with anorexia nervosa patients, who are not interested in sex. Pica and struggles during meals are sometimes revealed in the histories of bulimia nervosa patients.

Patients with the purging type of bulimia nervosa may be at risk for certain medical complications, such as hypokalemia from vomiting or laxative abuse, and hypochloremic alkalosis. Those who vomit repeatedly are at risk for gastric and esophageal tears, although those complications are rare. Bulimia nervosa patients who purge may have a course different from that of patients who binge and then diet or exercise.

Bulimia nervosa occurs in persons with high rates of mood disorders and impulse control disorders. Bulimia nervosa is also reported to occur in those at risk for substance-related disorders and a variety of personality disorders. Bulimia nervosa patients also have increased rates of anxiety disorders, bipolar I disorder, and dissociative disorders, and histories of sexual abuse.

Differential Diagnosis

The diagnosis of bulimia nervosa cannot be made if the binge eating and purging behaviors occur exclusively during episodes of anorexia nervosa. In such cases the diagnosis is anorexia nervosa, binge eating/purging type.

The clinician must ascertain that the patient has no neurological disease, such as epileptic-equivalent seizures, central nervous system tumors, Klüver-Bucy syndrome, or Kleine-Levin syndrome. The pathological features manifested by Klüver-Bucy syndrome are visual agnosia, compulsive licking and biting, the examination of objects by the mouth, inability to ignore any stimulus, placidity, altered sexual behavior (hypersexuality), and altered dietary habits, especially hyperphagia. The syndrome is exceedingly rare and is unlikely to cause a problem in differential diagnosis. Kleine-Levin syndrome consists of periodic hypersomnia lasting for two to three weeks and hyperphagia. As in bulimia nervosa, the onset is usually during adolescence; the syndrome is more common in men than in women. Borderline personality disorder patients sometimes binge eat, but the eating is associated with the other signs of the disorder.

Course and Prognosis

Little is known about the long-term course of bulimia nervosa, and the short-term outcome is variable. Overall, bulimia nervosa seems to have a better prognosis than does anorexia nervosa. In the short run, bulimia nervosa patients who can engage in treatment have reported more than 50 percent improvement in binge eating and purging; among outpatients, improvement seems to last more than five years. However, the patients are not symptom-free during periods of improvement; bulimia nervosa is a chronic disorder with a waxing and waning course. Some patients with mild courses have long-term remissions. Other patients are disabled by the disorder and have been hospitalized; less than one third are doing well on a three-year follow-up, more than one third have some improvement in their symptoms, and about one third have a poor outcome, with chronic symptoms, within three years.

The prognosis depends on the severity of the purging sequelae; that is, whether the patient has electrolyte imbalances and to what degree the frequent vomiting results in esophagitis, amylasemia, salivary gland enlargement, and dental caries.

In some cases of untreated bulimia nervosa, spontaneous remission occurs in one to two years.

Treatment

Most patients with uncomplicated bulimia nervosa do not require hospitalization. Overall, patients with bulimia nervosa are not as secretive about their symptoms as are patients with anorexia nervosa; therefore, outpatient treatment is usually not difficult. However, psychotherapy is frequently stormy and may be prolonged. Some obese bulimia nervosa patients who have had prolonged psychotherapy do surprisingly well. In some cases—when eating binges are out of control, outpatient treatment does not work, or the patient exhibits such additional psychiatric symptoms as suicidality and substance abuse—hospitalization may become necessary. In addition, in cases of severe purging, resulting electrolyte and metabolic disturbances may require hospitalization.

PSYCHOTHERAPY

Some reports encourage the use of cognitive-behavioral psychotherapy to address the specific behaviors surrounding and leading up to episodes of eating binges. Some helpful programs include a behavioral contract and desensitization to the thoughts and feelings that bulimia nervosa patients have just before binge eating. However, many bulimia nervosa patients have psychopathology that exceeds the binging behaviors; therefore, additional psychotherapeutic approaches, such as psychodynamic, interpersonal, and family therapies, can be useful.

PHARMACOTHERAPY

Antidepressant medications can reduce binge eating and purging independent of the presence of a mood disorder. Thus, for particularly difficult binge-purge cycles that are not responsive to psychotherapy alone, antidepressants have been successfully used. Imipramine (Tofranil), desipramine (Norpramin), trazodone (Desyrel), and monoamine oxidase inhibitors have been helpful. Fluoxetine (Prozac) is also promising as an effective treatment. In general, most of the antidepressants have been effective at dosages usually given in the treatment of depressive disorders. However, dosages of fluoxetine that are effective in decreasing binge eating may be higher (60 mg a day) than those used for depressive disorders. In cases of comorbid depressive disorders and bulimia nervosa, medication is helpful. Carbamazepine (Tegretol) and lithium (Eskalith) have not shown impressive results as treatments for binge eating, but they have been used in the treatment of bulimia nervosa patients with comorbid mood disorders, such as bipolar I disorder.

EATING DISORDER NOT OTHERWISE SPECIFIED

The DSM-IV diagnostic classification of eating disorder not otherwise specified (NOS) is a residual category used for eating disorders that do not meet the criteria for a specific eating disorder (Table 16.2–2). Binge eating disorder—that is, recurrent episodes of binge eating without the inappropriate compensatory behaviors characteristic of bulimia nervosa—falls into the category. Such patients are not fixated on body shape and weight.

References

Advokat C, Kutlesic V: Pharmacotherapy of the eating disorders: A commentary. Neurosci Biobehav Rev *19*: 59, 1995.

Table 16.2–2.   Diagnostic Criteria for Eating Disorder Not Otherwise Specified

The eating disorder not otherwise specified category is for disorders of eating that do not meet the criteria for any specific eating disorder. Examples include

1. For females, all of the criteria for anorexia nervosa are met except that the individual has regular menses.
2. All of the criteria for anorexia nervosa are met except that, despite significant weight loss, the individual's current weight is in the normal range.
3. All of the criteria for bulimia nervosa are met except that the binge eating and inappropriate compensatory mechanisms occur at a frequency of less than twice a week or for a duration of less than 3 months.
4. The regular use of inappropriate compensatory behavior by an individual of normal body weight after eating small amounts of food (e.g., self-induced vomiting after the consumption of two cookies).
5. Repeatedly chewing and spitting out, but not swallowing, large amounts of food.
6. Binge-eating disorder: recurrent episodes of binge eating in the absence of the regular use of inappropriate compensatory behaviors characteristic of bulimia nervosa.

Table from DSM-IV, *Diagnostic and Statistical Manual of Mental Disorders*, ed 4. Copyright American Psychiatric Association, Washington, 1994. Used with permission.

Childress A C, Brewerton T D, Hodges E L, Jarrell M P: The Kids' Eating Disorders Survey (KEDS): A study of middle school students. J Am Acad Child Adolesc Psychiatry *32*: 843, 1993.

Cohen P: Seasonal patterns of bulimia nervosa. Am J Psychiatry *150*: 357, 1993.

Gabbard G O: *Psychodynamic Psychiatry in Clinical Practice: The DSM-IV Edition*. American Psychiatric Press, Washington, 1994.

Garfinkel P E: Eating disorders. In *Comprehensive Textbook of Psychiatry*, ed 6, H I Kaplan, B J Sadock, editors, p 1361. Williams & Wilkins, Baltimore, 1995.

Garner D M, Rockert W, Davis R, Garner M V: Comparison of cognitive-behavioral and supportive-expressive therapy for bulimia nervosa. Am J Psychiatry *150*: 37, 1993.

Striegel-Moore R H, Silberstein L R, Rodin J: The social self in bulimia nervosa: Public self-consciousness, social anxiety, and perceived fraudulence. J Abnorm Psychol *102*: 297, 1993.

Woodside D B: A review of anorexia nervosa and bulimia nervosa. Curr Probl Pediatr *25*: 67, 1995.

17/ Normal Sleep and Sleep Disorders

17.1 NORMAL SLEEP

Sleep is a regular, recurrent, easily reversible physiological state characterized by relative quiescence and by a great increase in the threshold of response to external stimuli compared with the waking state. Close monitoring of sleep is an important part of clinical practice, since sleep disturbance is often an early symptom of impending mental illness. Some mental disorders are associated with characteristic changes in sleep physiology.

As persons fall asleep, their brain waves go through certain characteristic changes. The waking electroencephalogram (EEG) is characterized by alpha waves of 8 to 12 cycles a second, a low-voltage activity of mixed frequency. As the person falls asleep, alpha activity begins to disappear. Stage 1, considered the lightest stage of sleep, is characterized by low-voltage, regular activity at 3 to 7 cycles a second. After a few seconds or minutes, that stage gives way to stage 2, a pattern showing frequent spindle-shaped tracings at 12 to 14 cycle a second (sleep spindles) and slow, triphasic waves known as K complexes. Soon after that, in stage 3, delta waves, high-voltage activity at 0.5 to 2.5 cycles a second, make their appearance and occupy less than 50 percent of the tracing. Eventually, in stage 4, delta waves occupy more than 50 percent of the record. It is common practice to describe stages 3 and 4 as delta sleep or slow-wave sleep (SWS) because of their characteristic appearance on the EEG record.

POLYSOMNOGRAM REM FINDINGS

Sleep is made up of two physiological states: nonrapid eye movement (NREM) sleep and rapid eye movement (REM) sleep. NREM sleep is composed of stages 1 through 4. As compared with wakefulness, most physiological functions are markedly reduced during NREM sleep. REM sleep is a quantitatively different kind of sleep characterized by a highly active brain and physiological activity levels similar to those in wakefulness. About 90 minutes after sleep onset, NREM yields to the first REM episode of the night. That REM latency of 90 minutes is a consistent finding in normal adults. A shortening of REM latency frequently occurs with such disorders as depressive disorders and narcolepsy. The EEG records the rapid conjugate eye movements that are the identifying feature of the sleep state. (There are no or few rapid eye movements in NREM sleep.) The EEG pattern consists of low-voltage, random fast activity with sawtooth waves; the electromyograph (EMG) shows a marked reduction in muscle tone.

In normal persons NREM sleep is a peaceful state compared with waking. The pulse rate is typically slowed 5 to 10 beats a minute below the level of restful waking and is very regular. Respiration behaves in the same way. Blood pressure also tends to be low, with few minute-to-minute variations. The resting muscle potential of the body musculature is lower in REM sleep than in a waking state. Episodic, involuntary body movements are present in NREM sleep. There are few rapid eye movements, if any, and seldom any penile erections. The blood flow through most tissues, including cerebral blood flow, is slightly reduced.

The deepest portions of NREM sleep—stages 3 and 4—are sometimes associated with unusual arousal characteristics. When persons are aroused a half hour to one hour after sleep onset—usually in slow-wave sleep—they are disoriented, and their thinking is disorganized. Brief arousals from slow-wave sleep are also associated with amnesia for events that occur during the arousal. The disorganization during arousal from stage 3 or stage 4 may result in specific problems, including enuresis, somnambulism, and stage 4 nightmares or night terrors.

Polygraphic measures during REM sleep show irregular patterns, sometimes close to aroused waking patterns. Indeed, if a clinician were not aware of the person's behavioral stage and happened to be recording several physiological measures (but not muscle tone) during REM periods, that clinician would undoubtedly conclude that the person was in an active waking state. Because of that observation, REM sleep has also been called paradoxical sleep. Pulse, respiration, and blood pressure in humans are all high during REM sleep—much higher than during NREM sleep and often higher than during waking. Even more striking than the level or the rate is the variability from minute to minute. Brain oxygen use increases during REM sleep. The ventilatory response to increased levels of carbon dioxide (CO_2) is depressed during REM sleep, so that there is no increase in tidal volume as partial pressure of carbon dioxide (pCO_2) increases. Thermoregulation is altered during REM sleep. In contrast to the homeothermic condition of temperature regulation present during wakefulness or NREM sleep, a poikilothermic condition (a state in which animal temperature varies with temperature changes of the surrounding medium) is present during REM sleep. Poikilothermia, which is characteristic of reptiles, results in a failure to respond to changes in ambient temperature with shivering or sweating, whichever is appropriate to maintaining body temperature. Almost every REM period is accompanied by a partial or full penile erection. That finding is of significant clinical value in evaluating the cause of impotence. The nocturnal penile tumescence study is one of the most commonly requested sleep laboratory tests. Another psychological change that occurs during REM sleep is the near total paralysis of the skeletal (postural) muscles. Because of that motor inhibition, body movement is absent during REM sleep. Probably the most distinctive feature of REM sleep is dreaming. Persons awakened during REM sleep frequently (60 to 90 percent of the time) report that they had been dreaming. Dreams during REM sleep are typically abstract and surreal. Dreaming does occur during NREM sleep, but it is typically lucid and purposeful.

The cyclical nature of sleep is regular and reliable; a REM period occurs about every 90 to 100 minutes during the night (Figure 17.1-1). The first REM period tends to be the shortest, usually lasting less than 10 minutes; the later REM periods may last 15 to 40 minutes each. Most REM periods occur in the last third of the night, whereas most stage 4 sleep occurs in the first third of the night.

Sleep patterns change over the life span. In the neonatal period, REM sleep represents more than 50 percent of total sleep time. Newborns sleep about 16 hours a day, with brief

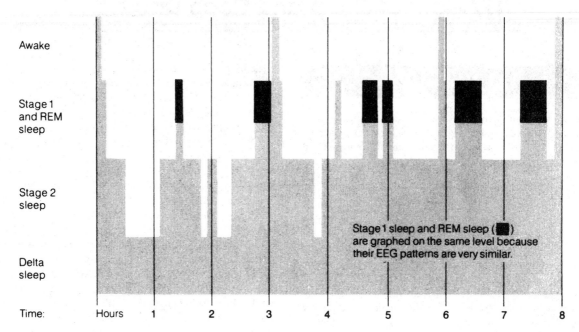

Figure 17.1–1. Typical sleep pattern of a young human adult. (Figure from P Hauri: *The Sleep Disorders, Current Concepts,* p 8. Upjohn, Kalamazoo, MI, 1982. Used with permission.)

periods of wakefulness. In the neonatal period, the EEG pattern goes from the alert state directly to the REM state without going through stages 1 through 4. By 4 months of age, the pattern shifts, so that the total percentage of REM sleep drops to less than 40 percent, and entry into sleep occurs with an initial period of NREM sleep. By young adulthood, the distribution of sleep stages is as follows:

NREM (75 percent)
  Stage 1: 5 percent
  Stage 2: 45 percent
  Stage 3: 12 percent
  Stage 4: 13 percent
REM (25 percent)

That distribution remains relatively constant into old age, although a reduction occurs in both slow-wave sleep and REM sleep in the elderly.

SLEEP REGULATION

The prevailing view is that there is not a simple sleep control center but a few interconnecting systems or centers that are chiefly located in the brainstem and that mutually activate and inhibit one another. Many studies support the role of serotonin in sleep regulation. Prevention of serotonin synthesis or destruction of the dorsal raphe nucleus of the brainstem, which contains nearly all the brain's serotonergic cell bodies, reduces sleep for a considerable time. Synthesis and release of serotonin by serotonergic neurons are influenced by the availability of amino acid precursors of that neurotransmitter, such as ryptophan. Ingestion of large amounts of L-tryptophan (1 to 15 g) reduces sleep latency and nocturnal awakenings. Conversely, tryptophan deficiency is associated with less time spent in REM sleep.

Norepinephrine-containing neurons with cell bodies in the locus ceruleus play an important role in controlling normal sleep patterns. Drugs and manipulations that increase the firing of those noradrenergic neurons produce a marked reduction in REM sleep (REM-off neurons) and an increase in wakefulness. Electrical stimulation of the locus ceruleus in humans with implanted electrodes (for the control of spasticity) profoundly disrupts all sleep parameters.

Brain acetylcholine is also involved in sleep, particularly in the production of REM sleep. In animal studies the injection of cholinergic-muscarinic agonists into pontine reticular formation neurons (REM-on neurons) results in a shift from wakefulness to REM sleep. Disturbances in central cholinergic activity are associated with the sleep changes observed in major depressive disorder. As compared with healthy persons and nondepressed psychiatric controls, depressed patients have marked disruptions of REM sleep patterns. Those disruptions include shortened REM latency (60 minutes or less), an increased percentage of REM sleep, and a shift in REM distribution from the last half to the first half of the night. The administration of a muscarinic agonist, such as arecoline, to depressed patients during the first or second NREM period results in a rapid onset of REM sleep. Depression may be associated with an underlying supersensitivity to acetylcholine.

Drugs that reduce REM sleep, such as antidepressants, produce beneficial effects in depression. Indeed, about half the patients with major depressive disorder experience temporary improvement when they are deprived of sleep or when sleep is restricted. Conversely, reserpine (Serpasil), which is one of the few drugs that increase REM sleep, also produces depression.

Patients with dementia of the Alzheimer's type have sleep disturbances characterized by reduced REM and slow-wave sleep. The loss of cholinergic neurons in the basal forebrain has been implicated as the cause of those changes. Melatonin secretion from the pineal gland is inhibited by bright light, so the lowest serum melatonin concentrations occur during the day.

The suprachiasmatic nucleus of the hypothalamus may act as the anatomical site of a circadian pacemaker that regulates melatonin secretion and the entrainment of the brain to a 24-hour sleep-wake cycle.

Evidence shows that dopamine has an alerting effect. Drugs that increase brain dopamine tend to produce arousal and wakefulness. In contrast, dopamine blockers, such as pimozide (Orap) and the phenothiazines, tend to increase sleep time.

A hypothesized homeostatic drive to sleep, perhaps in the form of an endogenous substance (process S) may accumulate during wakefulness and act to induce sleep. Another compound (process C) may act as a regulator of body temperature and sleep duration.

FUNCTIONS OF SLEEP

The functions of sleep have been examined in a variety of ways: most investigators conclude that sleep serves a restorative homeostatic function and appears to be crucial for normal thermoregulation and energy conservation.

Sleep Deprivation

Prolonged periods of sleep deprivation sometimes lead to ego disorganization, hallucinations, and delusions. Depriving persons of REM sleep by awakening them at the beginning of REM cycles produces an increase in the number of REM periods and in the amount of REM sleep (rebound increase) when they are allowed to sleep without interruption. REM-deprived patients may exhibit irritability and lethargy.

Sleep Requirements

Some persons are normally short sleepers who require fewer than six hours of sleep each night to function adequately. Long sleepers are those who need to sleep more than nine hours each night to function adequately. Long sleepers have more REM periods and more rapid eye movements within each period (known as REM density) than do short sleepers. Those movements are sometimes considered a measure of the intensity of REM sleep and are related to the vividness of dreaming. Short sleepers are generally efficient, ambitious, socially adept, and content. Long sleepers tend to be mildly depressed, anxious, and socially withdrawn. Increased sleep needs occur with physical work, exercise, illness, pregnancy, general mental stress, and increased mental activity. REM periods increase after strong psychological stimuli, such as difficult learning situations and stress, and after the use of chemicals or drugs that decrease brain catecholamines.

SLEEP-WAKE RHYTHM

Without external clues, the natural body clock follows a 25-hour cycle. The influence of external factors—such as the light-dark cycle, daily routines, meal periods, and other external synchronizers—entrains persons to the 24-hour clock.

Sleep is also influenced by biological rhythms. Within a 24-hour period, adults sleep once, sometimes twice. That rhythm is not present at birth but develops over the first two years of life. Naps taken at different times of the day differ greatly in their content of REM and NREM sleep. In a normal nighttime sleeper, a nap taken in the morning or at noon contains a great deal of REM sleep, whereas a nap taken in the afternoon or the early evening contains much less REM sleep. Apparently, a circadian cycle affects the tendency to have REM sleep.

Sleep patterns are not physiologically the same when one sleeps in the daytime or during the time one's body is accustomed to being awake; the psychological and behavioral effects of sleep differ as well. In a world of industry and communications that often functions 24 hours a day, those interactions are becoming increasingly significant.

Even in persons who work at night, interference with the various rhythms can produce problems. The best-known example is jet lag, in which, after flying east to west, one tries to convince one's body to go to sleep at a time that is out of phase with some body cycles. Most bodies adapt within a few days, but some require more time. Conditions in those bodies apparently involve long-term cycle disruption and interference.

References

Akerstedt T: Sleepiness as a consequence of shift work. Sleep *11*: 17, 1988.
Hobson A J: Sleep and dreaming. J Neurosci *10*: 371, 1990.
O'Hara B F, Young K A, Watson F L, Heller H C Kilduff T: Immediate early gene expression in brain during sleep deprivation. Sleep *16*: 1, 1993.
Shapiro C M, Flanigan M J: Function of sleep. Br Med J *306*: 383, 1993.
Waterhouse J: Circadian rhythms. Br Med J *306*: 448, 1993.
Williams, R L, Karacan I, Moore C A, Hirshkowitz M: Sleep disorders. In *Comprehensive Textbook of Psychiatry*, ed 6, H I Kaplan, B J Sadock, editors, p 1373. Williams & Wilkins, Baltimore, 1995.

17.2 SLEEP DISORDERS

MAJOR SYMPTOMS

Four major symptoms characterize most sleep disorders: insomnia, hypersomnia, parasomnia, and sleep-wake schedule disturbance. The symptoms often overlap.

Insomnia

Insomnia is difficulty in initiating or maintaining sleep. It is the most common sleep complaint. Insomnia may be transient or persistent. Common causes of insomnia are given in Table 17.2–1.

A brief period of insomnia is most often associated with anxiety, either as a sequela to an anxious experience or in anticipation of an anxiety-provoking experience (for example, an examination or an impending job interview). In some persons, transient insomnia of that kind may be related to grief, loss, or almost any life change. The condition is not likely to be serious, although a psychotic episode or a severe depression sometimes begins with an acute insomnia. Specific treatment for the condition is usually not required. When treatment with hypnotic medication is indicated, the physician and the patient should both be clear that the treatment is of short duration and that some symptoms, including a brief recurrence of the insomnia, may be expected when the medication is discontinued.

Persistent insomnia is a fairly common type. It consists of a group of conditions in which the problem is most often difficulty in falling asleep, rather than in remaining asleep, and involves two sometimes separable but often intertwined problems: (1) somatized tension and anxiety and (2) a conditioned associative response. The patients often have no clear complaint other than insomnia. They may not experience anxiety per se but discharge the anxiety through physiological channels. They may

Table 17.2-1.   Common Causes of Insomnia

Symptom	Insomnias Secondary to Medical Conditions	Insomnias Secondary to Psychiatric or Environmental Conditions
Difficulty in falling asleep	Any painful or uncomfortable condition CNS lesions Conditions listed below, at times	Anxiety Tension anxiety, muscular Environmental changes Circadian rhythm sleep disorder
Difficulty in remaining asleep	Sleep apnea syndromes Nocturnal myoclonus and restless legs syndrome Dietary factors (probably) Episodic events (parasomnias) Direct substance effects (including alcohol) Substance withdrawal effects (including alcohol) Substance interactions Endocrine or metabolic diseases Infectious, neoplastic, or other diseases Painful or uncomfortable conditions Brainstem or hypothalamic lesions or diseases Aging	Depression, especially primary depression Environmental changes Circadian rhythm sleep disorder Posttraumatic stress disorder Schizophrenia

Table by Ernest L. Hartmann, MD.

Table 17.2-2.   Common Causes of Hypersomnia

Symptom	Chiefly Medical	Chiefly Psychiatric or Environmental
Excessive sleep (hypersomnia)	Kleine-Levin syndrome Menstrual-associated somnolence Metabolic or toxic conditions Encephalitic conditions Alcohol and depressant medications Withdrawal from stimulants	Depression (some) Avoidance reactions
Excessive daytime sleepiness	Narcolepsy and narcolepsylike syndromes Sleep apneas Hypoventilation syndrome Hyperthyroidism and other metabolic and toxic conditions Alcohol and depressant medications Withdrawal from stimulants Sleep deprivation or insufficient sleep Any condition producing serious insomnia	Depression (some) Avoidance reactions Circadian rhythm sleep disorder

Table by Ernest Hartmann, MD.

complain chiefly of apprehensive feelings or ruminative thoughts that appear to keep them from falling asleep. Sometimes but not always, a patient describes how the condition is exacerbated at times of stress at work or at home and remits during vacations.

Hypersomnia

Hypersomnia manifests as excessive sleep and excessive daytime sleepiness (somnolence). In some situations both symptoms are present. The term "somnolence" should be reserved for patients who complain of sleepiness and have a clearly demonstrable tendency to fall asleep suddenly in the waking state, who have sleep attacks, and who cannot remain awake; it should not be used for persons who are simply physically tired or weary. The distinction, however, is not always clear. The complaints of hypersomnia are much less frequent than are the complaints of insomnia, but they are by no means rare if the clinician is alert to them. More than 100,000 narcoleptics are estimated to live in the United States. Narcolepsy is just one well-known condition clearly producing hypersomnia. If one includes substance-related conditions, hypersomnia is a common symptom.

Table 17.2–2 lists some common causes of hypersomnia.

As with insomnia, hypersomnia is associated with borderline conditions, situations that are hard to classify, and idiopathic cases.

According to a recent survey, the most common conditions responsible for hypersomnia severe enough to be evaluated by all-night recordings at a sleep disorders center were sleep apnea and narcolepsy. Individual sleep requirements vary. Many people are long sleepers and require 9 to 10 hours of sleep a night but, like short sleepers, they do not have a sleep problem.

Transient and situational hypersomnia is a disruption of the normal sleep-wake pattern. It is marked by excessive difficulty in remaining awake and a tendency to remain in bed for unusually long periods or to return to bed frequently during the day to nap. The pattern is experienced suddenly in response to an identifiable recent life change, conflict, or loss. It is much less common than insomnia. It is seldom marked by definite sleep attacks or unavoidable sleep but, instead, is marked by tiredness or falling asleep sooner than usual and by difficulty in arising in the morning.

Parasomnia

Parasomnia is an unusual or undesirable phenomenon that appears suddenly during sleep or that occurs at the threshold between waking and sleeping. Parasomnia usually occurs in stages 3 and is 4 and thus associated with poor recall of the disturbance.

Sleep-Wake Schedule Disturbance

Sleep-wake schedule disturbance involves the displacement of sleep from its desired circadian period. The common symptom is that patients cannot sleep when they wish to sleep, although they can sleep at other times. Correspondingly, they cannot be fully awake when they want to be fully awake, but they can be awake at other times. The disturbance does not produce precisely insomnia or somnolence. In practice the initial complaint is often either insomnia or somnolence. The above inabilities are elicited only on careful questioning.

CLASSIFICATION

The fourth edition of *Diagnostic and Statistical Manual of Mental Disorders* (DSM-IV) classifies sleep disorders based on clinical diagnostic criteria and presumed etiology. The three major categories of sleep disorders in DSM-IV are primary sleep disorders, sleep disorders related to another mental disorder, and other sleep disorders, most notably those due to a general medical condition or substance-induced. The disorders described in DSM-IV are only a fraction of the known sleep disorders; they provide a framework for a clinical assessment.

PRIMARY SLEEP DISORDERS

Dyssomnias

PRIMARY INSOMNIA

Primary insomnia is diagnosed when the chief complaint is difficulty in initiating or maintaining sleep or is nonrestorative sleep, and the complaint continues for at least a month (Table 17.2–3). The term ''primary'' indicates that the insomnia occurs independently of any known physical mental condition. Primary insomnia is often characterized by both difficulty falling asleep and repeated awakenings. Increased nighttime physiological or psychological arousal and negative conditioning for sleep are frequently evident. Usually, patients with primary insomnia are preoccupied with getting enough sleep. The more the individual

Table 17.2–3.   Diagnostic Criteria for Primary Insomnia

A. The predominant complaint is difficulty initiating or maintaining sleep, or nonrestorative sleep, for at least one month.

B. The sleep disturbance (or associated daytime fatigue) causes clinically significant distress or impairment in social, occupational, or other important areas of functioning.

C. The sleep disturbance does not occur exclusively during the course of narcolepsy, breathing-related sleep disorder, a circadian rhythm sleep disorder, or a parasomnia.

D. The disturbance does not occur exclusively during the course of another mental disorder (e.g., major depressive disorder, generalized anxiety disorder, a delirium).

E. The disturbance is not due to the direct physiological effects of a substance (e.g., a drug of abuse, a medication) or a general medical condition.

Table from DSM-IV, *Diagnostic and Statistical Manual of Mental Disorders*, ed 4. Copyright American Psychiatric Association, Washington, 1994. Used with permission.

Table 17.2–4.   Nonspecific Measures to Induce Sleep (Sleep Hygiene)

1. Arise at the same time daily.
2. Limit daily in-bed time to the usual amount present before the sleep disturbance.
3. Discontinue CNS-acting drugs (caffeine, nicotine, alcohol, stimulants).
4. Avoid daytime naps (except when sleep chart shows they induce better night sleep).
5. Establish physical fitness by means of a graded program of vigorous exercise early in the day.
6. Avoid evening stimulation; substitute radio or relaxed reading for television.
7. Try very hot, 20-minute, body temperature-raising bath soaks near bedtime.
8. Eat at regular times daily; avoid large meals near bedtime.
9. Practice evening relaxation routines, such as progressive muscle relaxation or meditation.
10. Maintain comfortable sleeping conditions.

Table from Q R Regestein: Sleep disorders. In *Clinical Psychiatry for Medical Students*, A Stoudemire, editor, p 578. Lippincott, Philadelphia, 1990. Used with permission.

tries to sleep, the greater the sense of frustration and distress and the more difficult it becomes to sleep.

Treatment of primary insomnia is difficult. When the conditioned component is prominent, a deconditioning technique may be useful. The patients are asked to use the bed for sleeping and for nothing else; if they are not asleep after five minutes in bed, they are instructed to simply get up and do something else. Sometimes, changing to another bed or to another room is useful. When somatized tension or muscle tension is prominent, relaxation tapes, transcendental meditation, and practicing the relaxation response and biofeedback are occasionally helpful. Psychotherapy has not been very useful in the treatment of primary insomnia.

Primary insomnia is commonly treated with benzodiazepine hypnotics, chloral hydrate (Noctec), and other sedatives. Hypnotic drugs should be used with care. Various nonspecific measures—so-called sleep hygiene—can be helpful in improving sleep (Table 17.2–4). Light therapy is also used.

Repeated Rapid Eye Movement (REM) Sleep Interruptions

Repeated REM sleep interruptions are rare but are examples of a primary insomnia. Their cause is unknown. They have been related to psychological difficulties and periods of nightmares or other disturbing dreams. In those cases they may be a conditioned avoidance response: the patient's central nervous system (CNS) senses the beginning of a dream period (REM period), associates it with an oncoming unpleasant dream or nightmare, and produces an immediate arousal response.

Atypical Polysomnographic Features

Another example of a primary insomnia, atypical polysomnographic features, is a condition in which sleep is frequently interrupted and nonrestorative and in which the sleep stage structure is marked by abnormal physiological features. Most commonly, the patient describes the quality of sleep as poor, light, or unrestful.

PRIMARY HYPERSOMNIA

Primary hypersomnia is diagnosed when no other cause for excessive somnolence occurring for at least one month can be

Table 17.2–5. Diagnostic Criteria for Primary Hypersomnia

A. The predominant complaint is excessive sleepiness for at least 1 month (or less if recurrent) as evidenced by either prolonged sleep episodes or daytime sleep episodes that occur almost daily.

B. The excessive sleepiness causes clinically significant distress or impairment in social, occupational, or other important areas of functioning.

C. The excessive sleepiness is not better accounted for by insomnia and does not occur exclusively during the course of another sleep disorder (e.g., narcolepsy, breathing-related sleep disorder, circadian rhythm sleep disorder, or a parasomnia) and cannot be accounted for by an inadequate amount of sleep.

D. The disturbance does not occur exclusively during the course of another mental disorder.

E. The disturbance is not due to the direct physiological effects of a substance (e.g., a drug of abuse, a medication) or a general medical condition.

Table from DSM-IV, *Diagnostic and Statistical Manual of Mental Disorders*, ed 4. Copyright American Psychiatric Association, Washington, 1994. Used with permission.

Table 17.2–6. Diagnostic Criteria for Narcolepsy

A. Irresistible attacks of refreshing sleep that occur daily over at least 3 months.

B. The presence of one or both of the following:

(1) Cataplexy (i.e., brief episodes of sudden bilateral loss of muscle tone, most often in association with intense emotion).

(2) Recurrent intrusions of elements of rapid eye movement (REM) sleep into the transition between sleep and wakefulness, as manifested by either hypnopompic or hypnagogic hallucinations or sleep paralysis at the beginning or end of sleep episodes.

C. The disturbance is not due to the direct physiological effects of a substance (e.g., a drug of abuse, a medication) or another general medical condition.

Table from DSM-IV, *Diagnostic and Statistical Manual of Mental Disorders*, ed 4. Copyright American Psychiatric Association, Washington, 1994. Used with permission.

found. Some persons are long sleepers who, like short sleepers, show a normal variation. Their sleep, although long, is normal in architecture and physiology. Sleep efficiency and the sleep-wake schedule are normal. That pattern is without complaints about the quality of sleep, daytime sleepiness, or difficulties with the awake mood, motivation, and performance.

Long sleep may be a lifetime pattern, and it appears to have a familial incidence. Many persons are variable sleepers and may become long sleepers at certain times in their lives.

Some persons have subjective complaints of feeling sleepy without objective findings. They do not tend to fall asleep more often than normal or have any objective signs. One should try to rule out clear-cut causes of excessive somnolence. According to DSM-IV, the disorder should be coded as recurrent if the patient has periods of excessive sleepiness lasting at least three days and occurring several times a year for at least two years (Table 17.2–5).

The treatment of primary hypersomnia consists mainly of stimulant drugs, such as amphetamines, given in the morning or the evening. Nonsedating antidepressant drugs, such as serotonin-specific reuptake inhibitors, may be of value in some cases.

NARCOLEPSY

Narcolepsy consists of excessive daytime sleepiness and abnormal manifestations of REM sleep occurring daily for at least three months (Table 17.2–6). The REM sleep includes hypnagogic and hypnopompic hallucinations, cataplexy, and sleep paralysis. The appearance of REM sleep within 10 minutes of sleep onset (sleep-onset REM periods) is also considered evidence of narcolepsy.

Narcolepsy is not as rare as was once thought. It is estimated to occur in 0.02 to 0.16 percent of adults and shows some familial incidence. Narcolepsy is neither a type of epilepsy nor a psychogenic disturbance. It is an abnormality of the sleep mechanisms—specifically, REM-inhibiting mechanism—and it has been studied in dogs and humans.

The most common symptom is sleep attacks: the patient cannot avoid falling asleep. Often associated with the problem (close to 50 percent of long-standing cases) is cataplexy—a sudden loss of muscle tone, such as jaw drop, head drop, weakness of the knees, or paralysis of all skeletal muscles with collapse. The patient often remains awake during brief cataplectic episodes; the long episodes usually merge with sleep and show the electroencephalographic (EEG) signs of REM sleep.

Other symptoms include hypnagogic or hypnopompic hallucinations: vivid perceptual experiences, either auditory or visual, occurring at sleep onset or on awakening. The patient is often momentarily frightened but within a minute or two returns to an entirely normal frame of mind and becomes aware that nothing was actually there.

Another uncommon symptom is sleep paralysis, most often occurring on awakening in the morning; during the episode, the patient is apparently awake and conscious but unable to move a muscle. If the symptom persists for more than few seconds, as it often does in narcolepsy, it can become extremely uncomfortable. (Isolated brief episodes of sleep paralysis occur in many nonnarcoleptic persons.) Narcoleptic patients report falling asleep quickly at night but often experience broken sleep.

Narcolepsy can occur at any age, but it most frequently begins in adolescence or young adulthood, in most instances before the age of 30. The disorder either progresses slowly or reaches a plateau maintained throughout life. Narcolepsy can be dangerous because it can lead to automobile and industrial accidents.

When the diagnosis is not clear clinically, a nighttime polysomnographic reveals a characteristic sleep-onset REM period. A test of daytime multiple sleep latency (several recorded naps at two-hour intervals) shows rapid sleep onset and usually one or more sleep-onset REM periods. A type of human leukocyte antigen called HLA-DR2 is found in more than 90 to 100 percent of narcoleptic patients and only 10 to 35 percent of unaffected persons.

Occasionally, a regimen of forced naps at a regular time of day helps, and in some cases the regimen can almost cure the patient without medication. When medication is required, stimulants—for example, amphetamine and methylphenidate (Ritalin)—are most useful, sometimes combined with antidepressants—for example, protriptyline (Vivactil)—when cataplexy is prominent.

Modafinil, an experimental α_1 agonist, has been reported to reduce the number of sleep attacks and to improve psychomotor

Table 17.2-7.   Diagnostic Criteria for Breathing-Related Sleep Disorder

A. Sleep disruption, leading to excessive sleepiness or insomnia, that is judged to be due to a sleep-related condition (e.g., obstructive or central sleep apnea syndrome or central alveolar hypoventilation syndrome).

B. The disturbance is not better accounted for by another mental disorder and is not due to the direct physiological effects of a substance (e.g., a drug of abuse, a medication) or another general medical condition (other than a breathing-related disorder).

Table from DSM-IV, *Diagnostic and Statistical Manual of Mental Disorders*, ed 4. Copyright American Psychiatric Association, Washington, 1994. Used with permission.

performance in narcolepsy, suggesting the involvement of noradrenergic mechanisms in the disorder.

BREATHING-RELATED SLEEP DISORDER

Breathing-related sleep disorder is characterized by sleep disruption leading to excessive sleepiness or insomnia caused by a sleep-related breathing disturbance (Table 17.2–7). Breathing disturbances that may occur during sleep include apneas, hypopneas, and oxygen desaturations. Those disturbances invariably cause hypersomnia. Two disorders of the respiratory system that can produce hypersomnia are sleep apnea and central alveolar hypoventilation. Both disorders can also cause insomnia; however, hypersomnia is more common than insomnia.

Obstructive Sleep Apnea Syndrome

Many persons—elderly persons and obese persons, even those who do not have clinical symptoms—are likely to have apneic periods and, in general, more respiratory problems in sleep than when awake.

Sleep apnea refers to the cessation of air flow at the nose or the mouth. By convention an apneic period is one that lasts 10 seconds or more. Sleep apnea can be of several distinct types. In pure central sleep apnea, both air flow and respiratory effort (abdomen and chest) cease during the apneic episodes and begin again during arousals. In pure obstructive sleep apnea, air flow ceases, but respiratory effort increases during apneic periods, suggesting an obstruction in the airway and increasing efforts by the abdominal and thoracic muscles to force air past the obstruction. Again, the episode ceases with an arousal. The mixed types involve elements of both obstructive and central sleep apnea.

Usually, sleep apnea is considered pathological if the patient has at least five apneic episodes an hour or 30 apneic episodes during the night. In severe cases of obstructive sleep apnea, patients may have as many as 300 apneic episodes, each followed by an arousal. Almost no normal sleep occurs, although the patients have been in bed and often assume that they have been sleeping for the entire night.

Sleep apnea can be a dangerous condition. It is thought to account for some unexplained deaths and crib deaths of children and infants. It is probably also responsible for many pulmonary and cardiovascular deaths in adults and in the elderly. Episodes of sleep apnea can produce cardiovascular changes, including arrhythmias, and transient alterations in blood pressure for each apneic episode. Long-standing sleep apnea is associated with an increase in pulmonary blood pressure and eventually an increase in systemic blood pressure as well. Those cardiovascular changes in sleep apnea may account for a considerable number of cases in which the diagnosis is essential hypertension.

The prevalence of sleep apnea in the population has not been established, but an increasing number of cases are discovered as growing awareness of its existence develops. In a recent survey of patients with daytime sleepiness whose disorder was serious enough to warrant polygraphical evaluation at a sleep disorders center, 42 percent were found to be suffering from a variant of sleep apnea.

A tentative diagnosis of sleep apnea can be made even without polysomnographic recordings. The most characteristic picture is that of middle-aged or elderly men who report tiredness and inability to stay awake in the daytime, sometimes associated with depression, mood changes, and daytime sleep attacks. They may or may not complain of anything unusual during sleep. If a history is obtained from a spouse or bed partner, it includes reports of loud, intermittent snoring, at times accompanied by gasping. Sometimes, observers recall apneic periods when patients appeared to be trying to breathe but were unable to do so. Such patients almost certainly have obstructive sleep apnea. With central or mixed apnea, the complaints are of repeated awakenings during the night, with no difficulty of falling asleep, associated with morning headaches and mood changes. At onset, the patients may have no complaints at all, although bed partners or roommates report heavy snoring and restless sleep. Obese patients with the disorder are said to have Pickwickian syndrome.

Patients suspected of having sleep apnea should undergo laboratory recordings. The usual all-night sleep recordings—including electroencephalogram (EEG), electromyogram (EMG), electrocardiogram (ECG), and respiratory tracings of various kinds—are useful. Recording air flow and respiratory effort is usually necessary to make a diagnosis. The severity of apneic episodes is determined by using oximetry to measure oxygen saturation during the night. Twenty-four-hour ECG monitoring is sometimes useful to monitor cardiac changes.

Nasal continuous positive airway pressure (nCPAP) is the treatment of choice for obstructive sleep apnea. Other procedures include weight loss, nasal surgery, tracheostomy, and uvulopalatoplasty. No medications are consistently effective in normalizing sleep in apneic patients. When sleep apnea is established or suspected, the patient must avoid the use of sedative medication, including alcohol, because it can considerably exacerbate the condition, which may then become life-threatening.

Central Alveolar Hypoventilation

Central alveolar hypoventilation consists of several conditions marked by impaired ventilation in which the respiratory abnormality appears or greatly worsens only during sleep and in which significant apneic episodes are not present. The ventilatory dysfunction is characterized by inadequate tidal volume or respiratory rate during sleep. Death may occur during sleep (Ondine's curse). Central alveolar hypoventilation is treated with some form of mechanical ventilation (for example, nasal ventilation).

CIRCADIAN RHYTHM SLEEP DISORDER

Circadian rhythm sleep disorder includes a wide range of conditions involving a misalignment between desired and actual sleep periods. DSM-IV lists four types of circadian rhythm sleep disorder: (1) delayed sleep phase type, (2) jet lag type, (3) shift work type, and (4) unspecified (Table 17.2–8).

Table 17.2-8.   Diagnostic Criteria for Circadian Rhythm Sleep Disorder

A. A persistent or recurrent pattern of sleep disruption leading to excessive sleepiness or insomnia that is due to mismatch between the sleep-wake schedule required by a person's environment and his or her circadian sleep-wake pattern.

B. The sleep disturbance causes clinically significant distress or impairment in social, occupational, or other important areas of functioning.

C. The disturbance does not occur exclusively during the course of another sleep disorder or other mental disorder.

D. The disturbance is not due to the direct effects of a substance (e.g., a drug of abuse, a medication) or a general medical condition.

Table from DSM-IV, *Diagnostic and Statistical Manual of Mental Disorders*, ed 4. Copyright American Psychiatric Association, Washington, 1994. Used with permission.

Delayed Sleep Phase Type

Delayed sleep phase type of circadian rhythm sleep disorder is marked by sleep and wake times that are intractably later than desired, actual sleep times at virtually the same daily clock hour, no reported difficulty in maintaining sleep once begun, and an inability to advance the sleep phase by enforcing conventional sleep and wake times. The disorder often presents with the major complaint of difficulty in falling asleep at a desired conventional time and may be similar to a sleep-onset insomnia. Daytime sleepiness often occurs secondary to sleep loss.

Delayed sleep phase type can be treated by gradually delaying the hour of sleep over a period of several days until the desired sleep time is achieved. The strategy works when advancing the sleep time does not work. The process of sleep phase adjustment can be assisted by the brief use of short-half-life hypnotic agents, such as triazolam (Halcion), to enforce sleep.

Another approach to treating delayed sleep phase type is the use of light therapy. Evening light therapy tends to delay sleep; regular morning light exposure tends to advance sleep.

Jet Lag Type

Jet lag type usually disappears spontaneously in two to seven days, depending on the length of the east-to-west trip and individual sensitivity; no specific treatment is required. Some people find that they can prevent the symptoms by altering their mealtimes and sleep times in an appropriate direction before traveling. Others find that what appear to be symptoms of jet lag are actually associated with sleep deprivation and that simply obtaining enough sleep helps.

Shift Work Type

Shift work type of circadian rhythm sleep disorder occurs in persons who repeatedly and rapidly change their work schedules and occasionally in persons with self-imposed chaotic sleep schedules. The most frequent symptom found is a period of mixed insomnia and somnolence; however, many other symptoms and somatic problems, including peptic ulcer, may be associated with the pattern after some time. Some adolescents and young adults appear to withstand changes of that kind remarkably well with few symptoms, but older persons and persons with sensitivity to change are clearly affected.

The symptoms are generally worst the first few days after shifting to a new schedule, but in some persons the disrupted sleep-wake patterns persist for a long time. Enforcement of new sleep hours and light therapy may help workers adjust to their new schedules. Many persons never adapt completely to unusual shift schedules because they maintain the altered pattern only five days a week, returning to the prevailing pattern of the rest of the population on days off and on vacations.

Unspecified

Advanced sleep phase syndrome.   Advanced sleep phase syndrome is characterized by sleep onsets and wake times that are intractably earlier than desired, actual sleep times at virtually the same daily clock hour, no reported difficulty in maintaining sleep once begun, and an inability to delay the sleep phase by enforcing conventional sleep and wake times. Unlike delayed sleep phase type, the condition does not interfere with the work or school day. The major presenting complaint is the inability to stay awake in the evening and to sleep in the morning until desired conventional times.

Disorganized sleep-wake pattern.   Disorganized sleep-wake pattern is irregular and variable sleep and waking behavior that disrupts the regular sleep-wake pattern. The condition is associated with frequent daytime naps at irregular times and excessive bed rest. Sleep at night is not of adequate length, and the condition may present as insomnia, although the total amount of sleep in 24 hours is normal for the patient's age.

DYSSOMNIA NOT OTHERWISE SPECIFIED

According to DSM-IV, dyssomnia not otherwise specified includes insomnias, hypersomnias, and circadian rhythm disturbances that do not meet the criteria for any specific dyssomnia.

Nocturnal Myoclonus

Nocturnal myoclonus consists of highly stereotyped abrupt contractions of certain leg muscles during sleep. Patients lack any subjective awareness of the leg jerks. The condition may be present in about 40 percent of people over age 65.

The repetitive leg movements occur every 20 to 60 seconds, with extension of the large toe and flexion of the ankle, the knee, and the hips. Frequent awakenings, unrefreshing sleep, and daytime sleepiness are major symptoms. No treatment for nocturnal myoclonus is universally effective. Treatments that may be useful include benzodiazepines, levodopa (Larodopa), and, rarely, opioids.

Restless Legs Syndrome

In restless legs syndrome the person feels deep sensations of creeping inside the calves whenever sitting or lying down. The dysesthesias are rarely painful, but they are agonizingly relentless and cause an almost irresistible urge to move the legs, thus interfering with sleep. The syndrome is not limited to sleep but can interfere with falling asleep. It peaks in middle age and occurs in 5 percent of the population.

The syndrome has no established treatment. The symptoms are relieved by movement and leg message. When pharmacotherapy is required, the benzodiazepines, levodopa, opioids, propranolol (Inderal), and carbamazepine (Tegretol) are of some benefit.

Kleine-Levin Syndrome

Kleine-Levin syndrome is a relatively rare condition consisting of recurrent periods of prolonged sleep (from which the patient may be aroused) with intervening periods of normal sleep and alert waking. During the hypersomnic episodes, wakeful periods are usually marked by withdrawal from social contacts and return to bed at the first opportunity; however, the patient may also display apathy, irritability, confusion, voracious eating, loss of sexual inhibitions, delusions, hallucinations, frank disorientation, memory impairment, incoherent speech, excitation or depression, and truculence. Unexplained fevers have occurred in a few patients.

Kleine-Levin syndrome is uncommon. Almost 100 cases with features suggesting the diagnosis have been reported. In most cases, several periods of hypersomnia, each lasting for one or several weeks, are experienced by the patient in a year. With few exceptions the first attack occurs between the ages of 10 and 21 years. Rare instances of onset in the fourth and fifth decades of life have been reported. The syndrome is almost invariably self-limited, enduring remission occurring spontaneously before age 40 in early-onset cases.

Menstrual-Associated Syndrome

Some women experience intermittent marked hypersomnia, altered behavioral patterns, and voracious eating at or shortly before the onset of their menses. Nonspecific EEG abnormalities similar to the ones associated with Kleine-Levin syndrome have been documented in several instances. Endocrine factors are probably involved, but specific abnormalities in laboratory endocrine measures have not been reported. Increased cerebrospinal fluid (CSF) turnover of 5-hydroxytryptamine (5-HT) was identified in one case.

Insufficient Sleep

Insufficient sleep is an earnest complaint of daytime sleepiness and associated waking symptoms by a person who persistently fails to obtain sufficient daily sleep needed to support alert wakefulness. The person is voluntarily, but often unwittingly, chronically sleep-deprived.

The diagnosis can usually be made based on the history, including a sleep log. Some persons, especially students and shift workers, want to maintain an active daytime life and perform their nighttime jobs. They may be seriously depriving themselves of sleep, producing somnolence during waking hours.

Sleep Drunkenness

Sleep drunkenness is an abnormal form of awakening in which the lack of a clear sensorium in the transition from sleep to full wakefulness is prolonged and exaggerated. A confusion state develops that often leads to individual or social inconvenience and sometimes to criminal acts. Essential to the diagnosis is the absence of sleep deprivation. It is a rare condition with a possible familial tendency. Before making the diagnosis, the clinician should examine the patient's sleep and rule out such conditions as apnea, nocturnal myoclonus, narcolepsy, and an excessive use of alcohol and other substances.

Parasomnias

NIGHTMARE DISORDER

A nightmare is characterized by a long, frightening dream from which one awakens frightened (Table 17.2–9). Like other dreams, nightmares almost always occur during REM sleep. They usually occur after a long REM period late in the night. Some persons have frequent nightmares as a lifelong condition; others experience them predominantly at times of stress and illness. About 50 percent of the adult population may report occasional nightmares.

Usually, no specific treatment is required for nightmare disorder. Agents that suppress REM sleep, such as tricyclic drugs, may reduce the frequency of nightmares. Benzodiazepines have also been used.

SLEEP TERROR DISORDER

A sleep terror is an arousal in the first third of the night during deep NREM (stages 3 and 4) sleep. It is almost invariably inaugurated by a piercing scream or cry and accompanied by behavioral manifestations of intense anxiety bordering on panic (Table 17.2–10).

Typically, patients sit up in bed with a frightened expression, scream loudly, and sometimes awaken immediately with a sense of intense terror. Sometimes patients remain awake in a disori-

Table 17.2–9. Diagjnostic Criteria for Nightmare Disorder

A. Repeated awakenings from the major sleep period or naps with detailed recall of extended and extremely frightening dreams, usually involving threats to survival, security, or self-esteem. The awakenings generally occur during the second half of the sleep period.

B. On awakening from the frightening dream, the person rapidly becomes oriented and alert (in contrast to the confusion and disorientation seen in sleep terror disorder and some forms of epilepsy).

C. The dream experience, or the sleep disturbance resulting from the awakening, causes clinically significant distress or impairment in social, occupational, or other important areas of functioning.

D. The nightmares do not occur exclusively during the course of another mental disorder (e.g., a delirium, posttraumatic stress disorder) and are not due to the direct physiological effects of a substance (e.g., a drug of abuse, a medication) or a general medical condition.

Table from DSM-IV, *Diagnostic and Statistical Manual of Mental Disorders*, ed 4. Copyright American Psychiatric Association, Washington, 1994. Used with permission.

Table 17.2–10. Diagnostic Criteria for Sleep Terror Disorder

A. Recurrent episodes of abrupt awakening from sleep, usually occurring during the first third of the major sleep episode and beginning with a panicky scream.

B. Intense fear and signs of autonomic arousal, such as tachycardia, rapid breathing, and sweating, during each episode.

C. Relative unresponsiveness to efforts of others to comfort the person during the episode.

D. No detailed dream is recalled and there is amnesia for the episode.

E. The episodes cause clinically significant distress or impairment in social, occupational, or other important areas of functioning.

F. The disturbance is not due to the direct physiological effects of a substance (e.g., a drug of abuse, a medication) or a general medical condition.

Table from DSM-IV, *Diagnostic and Statistical Manual of Mental Disorders*, ed 4. Copyright American Psychiatric Association, Washington, 1994. Used with permission.

ented state. More often, patients fall asleep, and, as with sleepwalking, they forget the episodes. Frequently, a night terror episode after the original scream develops into a sleepwalking episode. Polygraphic recordings of night terrors are somewhat like those of sleepwalking. In fact, the two conditions appear to be closely related. Night terrors, as isolated episodes, are especially frequent in children. About 1 to 6 percent of children have the disorder, which is more common in boys than in girls and tends to run in families.

Specific treatment for night terror disorder is seldom required. Investigation of stressful family situations may be important, and individual or family therapy is sometimes useful. In the rare cases in which medication is required, diazepam (Valium) in small doses at bedtime improves the condition and sometimes eliminates the attacks.

SLEEPWALKING DISORDER

Sleepwalking, also known as somnambulism, is a sequence of complex behaviors initiated in the first third of the night during deep NREM (stages 3 and 4) sleep and frequently, although not always, progress—without full consciousness or later memory of the episode—to leaving bed and walking about (Table 17.2–11).

The patient sits up and sometimes performs perseverative motor acts, such as walking, dressing, going to the bathroom, talking, screaming, and even driving. The behavior occasionally ends in an awakening with several minutes of confusion; more frequently, the person returns to sleep and has no recollection of the sleepwalking event. An artificially induced arousal from stage 4 sleep can sometimes produce the condition. For instance, in children, especially children with a history of sleepwalking, an attack can sometimes be provoked by standing them on their feet and thus producing a partial arousal during stage 4 sleep.

Sleepwalking usually begins between ages 4 and 8. Peak prevalence is at about age 12 years. The disorder is more common in boys than in girls, and about 15 percent of children have an occasional episode. It tends to run in families. A minor neurological abnormality probably underlies the condition; the episodes should not be considered purely psychogenic, although stressful periods are associated with an increase in sleepwalking

Table 17.2–11.   Diagnostic Criteria for Sleepwalking Disorder

A. Repeated episodes of rising from bed during sleep and walking about, usually occurring during the first third of the major sleep episode.

B. While sleepwalking, the person has a blank, staring face, is relatively unresponsive to the efforts of others to communicate with him or her, and can be awakened only with great difficulty.

C. On awakening (either from the sleepwalking episode or the next morning), the person has amnesia for the episode.

D. Within several minutes after awakening from the sleepwalking episode, there is no impairment of mental activity or behavior (although there may initially be a short period of confusion or disorientation).

E. The sleepwalking causes clinically significant distress or impairment in social, occupational, or other important areas of functioning.

F. The disturbance is not due to the direct physiological effects of a substance (e.g., a drug of abuse, a medication), or a general medical condition.

Table from DSM-IV, *Diagnostic and Statistical Manual of Mental Disorders*, ed 4. Copyright American Psychiatric Association, Washington, 1994. Used with permission.

Table 17.2–12.   Diagnostic Criteria for Parasomnia Not Otherwise Specified

The parasomnia not otherwise specified category is for disturbances that are characterized by abnormal behavioral or physiological events during sleep or sleep-wake transitions, but that do not meet criteria for a more specific parasomnia. Examples include

1. REM sleep behavior disorder: motor activity, often of a violent nature, that arises during rapid eye movement (REM) sleep. Unlike sleepwalking, these episodes tend to occur later in the night and are associated with vivid dream recall.
2. Sleep paralysis: an inability to perform voluntary movement during the transition between wakefulness and sleep. The episodes may occur at sleep onset (hypnagogic) or with awakening (hypnopompic). The episodes are usually associated with extreme anxiety and, in some cases, fear of impending death. Sleep paralysis occurs commonly as an ancillary symptom of narcolepsy and, in such cases, should not be coded separately.
3. Situations in which the clinician has concluded that a parasomnia is present but is unable to determine whether it is primary, due to a general medical condition, or substance induced.

Table from DSM-IV, *Diagnostic and Statistical Manual of Mental Disorders*, ed 4. Copyright American Psychiatric Association, Washington, 1994. Used with permission.

in affected persons. Extreme tiredness or prior sleep deprivation exacerbates attacks. The disorder is occasionally dangerous because of the possibility of accidental injury.

Treatment consists of measures to prevent injury and of drugs that suppress stages 3 and 4 sleep.

PARASOMNIA NOT OTHERWISE SPECIFIED

The diagnostic criteria for parasomnia not otherwise specified are given in Table 17.2–12.

Sleep-Related Bruxism

Bruxism, tooth grinding, occurs throughout the night, most prominently in stage 2 sleep. According to dentists, 5 to 10 percent of the population suffer from bruxism severe enough to produce noticeable damage to teeth. The condition often goes unnoticed by the sleeper, except for an occasional feeling of jaw ache in the morning; however,

bed partners and roommates are consistently awakened by the sound. Treatment consists of a dental bite plate and corrective orthodontic procedures.

REM Sleep Behavior Disorder

REM sleep behavior disorder is a chronic and progressive condition found mainly in men. It is characterized by the loss of atonia during REM sleep and subsequent emergence of violent and complex behaviors. In essence, patients with the disorder are acting out their dreams. Serious injury to the patient or the bed partner is a major risk. The development or the aggravation of the disorder has been reported in narcoleptic patients treated with psychostimulants and tricyclic drugs and in depressed and obsessive-compulsive disorder patients treated with fluoxetine (Prozac). REM sleep behavior disorder is treated with clonazepam (Klonopin), 0.5 to 2.0 mg a day. Carbamazepine, 100 mg three times a day, is also effective in controlling the disorder.

Sleeptalking (Somniloquy)

Sleeptalking is common in children and adults. It has been studied extensively in the sleep laboratory and is found to occur in all stages of sleep. The talking usually involves a few words that are difficult to distinguish. Long episodes of talking involve the sleeper's life and concerns, but sleeptalkers do not relate their dreams during sleep, nor do they often reveal deep secrets. Episodes of sleeptalking sometimes accompany night terrors and sleepwalking. Sleeptalking alone requires no treatment.

Sleep-Related Head Banging (Jactatio Capitis Nocturna)

Sleep-related head banging is the term for a sleep behavior consisting chiefly of rhythmic to-and-fro head rocking, less commonly of total body rocking, occurring just before or during sleep. Usually, it is observed in the immediate presleep period and is sustained into light sleep. It uncommonly persists into or occurs in deep NREM sleep. Treatment consists of measures to prevent injury.

Sleep Paralysis

Familial sleep paralysis is characterized by a sudden inability to execute voluntary movements either just at the onset of sleep or on awakening during the night or in the morning.

SLEEP DISORDERS RELATED TO ANOTHER MENTAL DISORDER

Insomnia Related to an Axis I or Axis II Disorder

Insomnia that occurs for at least one month and that is clearly related to the psychological and behavioral symptoms of the clinically well-known mental disorders are classified here (Table 17.2–13). The category consists of a heterogeneous group of conditions. The sleep problem is usually but not always difficulty in falling asleep and is secondary to anxiety that is part of any of the various mental disorders listed. The insomnia is more common in females than in males. In clear-cut cases in which the anxiety has psychological roots, psychiatric treatment of the cause of the anxiety (for example, individual psychotherapy, group psychotherapy, or family therapy) often relieves the insomnia.

Hypersomnia Related to an Axis I or Axis II Disorder

Hypersomnia that occurs for at least one month and that is associated with a mental disorder is found in a variety of condi-

Table 17.2-13.   Diagnostic Criteria for Insomnia Related to an Axis I or Axis II Disorder

A. The predominant complaint is difficulty initiating or maintaining sleep, or nonrestorative sleep, for at least one month that is associated with daytime fatigue or impaired daytime functioning.

B. The sleep disturbance (or daytime sequelae) causes clinically significant distress or impairment in social, occupational, or other important areas of functioning.

C. The insomnia is judged to be related to another Axis I or Axis II disorder (e.g., major depressive disorder, generalized anxiety disorder, adjustment disorder with anxiety) but is sufficiently severe to warrant independent clinical attention.

D. The disturbance is not better accounted for by another sleep disorder (e.g., narcolepsy, breathing-related sleep disorder, a parasomnia).

E. The disturbance is not due to the direct physiological effects of a substance (e.g., a drug of abuse, a medication) or a general medical condition.

Table from DSM-IV, *Diagnostic and Statistical Manual of Mental Disorders,* ed 4. Copyright American Psychiatric Association, Washington, 1994. Used with permission.

Table 17.2-14.   Diagnostic Criteria for Hypersomnia Related to an Axis I or Axis II Disorder

A. The predominant complaint is excessive sleepiness for at least one month as evidenced by either prolonged sleep episodes or daytime sleep episodes that occur almost daily.

B. The excessive sleepiness causes clinically significant distress or impairment in social, occupational, or other important areas of functioning.

C. The hypersomnia is judged to be related to another Axis I or Axis II disorder (e.g., major depressive disorder, dysthymic disorder), but is sufficiently severe to warrant independent clinical attention.

D. The disturbance is not better accounted for by another sleep disorder (e.g., narcolepsy, breathing-related sleep disorder, a parasomnia) or by an inadequate amount of sleep.

E. The disturbance is not due to the direct physiological effects of a substance (e.g., a drug of abuse, a medication) or a general medical condition.

Table from DSM-IV, *Diagnostic and Statistical Manual of Mental Disorders,* ed 4. Copyright American Psychiatric Association, Washington, 1994. Used with permission.

Table 17.2-15.   Diagnostic Criteria for Sleep Disorder Due to a General Medical Condition

A. A prominent disturbance in sleep that is sufficiently severe to warrant independent clinical attention.

B. There is evidence from the history, physical examination, or laboratory findings that the sleep disturbance is the direct physiological consequence of a general medical condition.

C. The disturbance is not better accounted for by another mental disorder (e.g., an adjustment disorder in which the stressor is a serious medical illness).

D. The disturbance does not occur exclusively during the course of a delirium.

E. The disturbance does not meet criteria for a breathing-related sleep disorder or narcolepsy.

F. The sleep disturbance causes clinically significant distress or impairment in social, occupational, or other important areas of functioning.

Table from DSM-IV, *Diagnostic and Statistical Manual of Mental Disorders,* ed 4. Copyright American Psychiatric Association, Washington, 1994. Used with permission.

Some conditions are associated with insomnia even when pain and discomfort are not specifically present. Those conditions include neoplasms, vascular lesions, infections, and degenerative and traumatic conditions. Other conditions, especially endocrine and metabolic diseases, frequently involve some sleep disturbance.

Awareness of the possibility of such conditions and obtaining a good medical history usually lead to a correct diagnosis; the treatment, whenever possible, is treatment of the underlying medical condition.

Substance-Induced Sleep Disorder

Any type of sleep disturbance (for example, insomnia, hypersomnia, parasomnia, or a combination) can be caused by a substance (Table 17.2–16). According to DSM-IV, the clinician should also specify if the onset of the disorder occurred during intoxication or withdrawal.

Somnolence related to tolerance or withdrawal from a central nervous system (CNS) stimulant is common in persons withdrawing from amphetamines, cocaine, caffeine, and related substances. The somnolence may be associated with severe depression, which occasionally reaches suicidal proportions.

The sustained use of CNS depressants, such as alcohol, can cause somnolence. Heavy alcohol use in the evening produces sleepiness and difficulty in arising the next day. That reaction may present a diagnostic problem if the patient does not admit to alcohol abuse.

Insomnia is associated with tolerance to or withdrawal from sedative-hypnotic drugs, such as benzodiazepines, barbiturates, and chloral hydrate. With the sustained use of such agents, usually undertaken to treat insomnia arising from a different source, tolerance increases, and the drugs lose their sleep-inducing effects. Patients then often increase the dosage. On sudden discontinuation of the drug, severe sleeplessness supervenes, often accompanied by the general features of substance withdrawal. Typically the patient experiences a temporary increase in the severity of the insomnia.

Long-term use (more than 30 days) of a hypnotic agent is well tolerated by some patients, but other patients begin to complain of sleep disturbance, most often multiple brief awakenings

tions, including mood disorders. Excessive daytime sleepiness may be reported in the initial stages of many mild depressive disorders and characteristically in the depressed phase of bipolar I disorder. It is sometimes associated for a few weeks with uncomplicated grief. Other mental disorders—such as personality disorders, dissociative disorders, somatoform disorders, dissociative fugue, and amnestic disorders—can produce hypersomnia (Table 17.2–14). Treatment of the primary disorder should result in the resolution of the hypersomnia.

OTHER SLEEP DISORDERS

Sleep Disorder Due to a General Medical Condition

Any type of sleep disturbance (for example, insomnia, hypersomnia, parasomnia, or a combination) can be caused by a general medical condition (Table 17.2–15).

Almost any medical condition associated with pain and discomfort (for example, arthritis, angina) can produce insomnia.

Table 17.2–16. Diagnostic Criteria for Substance-Induced Sleep Disorder

A. A prominent disturbance in sleep which is sufficiently severe to warrant independent clinical attention.

B. There is evidence from the history, physical examination, or laboratory findings of either (1) or (2):

   (1) the symptoms in criterion A developing during, or within a month of, substance intoxication or withdrawal

   (2) medication use is etiologically related to the sleep disturbance

C. The disturbance is not better accounted for by a sleep disorder that is not substance induced. Evidence that the symptoms are better accounted for by a sleep disorder that is not substance induced might include the following: the symptoms precede the onset of the substance abuse (or medication use); the symptoms persist for a substantial period of time (e.g., about a month) after the cessation of acute withdrawal or severe intoxication, or are substantially in excess or what would be expected given the type or amount of the substance used or the duration of use; or there is other evidence that suggests the existence of an independent non-substance-induced sleep disorder (e.g., a history of recurrent non-substance-related episodes).

D. The disturbance does not occur exclusively during the course of a delirium.

E. The sleep disturbance causes clinically significant distress or impairment in social, occupational, or other important areas of functioning.

Table from DSM-IV, *Diagnostic and Statistical Manual of Mental Disorders*, ed 4. Copyright American Psychiatric Association, Washington, 1994. Used with permission.

during the night. Recordings show a disruption of sleep architecture, reduced stages 3 and 4 sleep, increases of stages 1 and 2 sleep, and a fragmentation of sleep throughout the night.

The clinician should be aware of CNS stimulants as a possible cause of insomnia and should remember that various medications for weight reduction, caffeinated beverages, and occasionally adrenergic drugs taken by asthmatic patients may all produce insomnia. Alcohol may help induce sleep but frequently results in nocturnal awakening. Alcohol use during the cocktail hour can produce difficulty in falling asleep later in the evening.

For reasons that are not always clear, a variety of drugs occasionally produce sleep problems as a side effect. Those drugs include antimetabolites and other cancer chemotherapeutic agents, thyroid preparations, anticonvulsant agents, antide-pressant drugs, adrenocorticotropic hormone (ACTH)-like drugs, oral contraceptives, α-methyldopa, and β-blocking drugs.

Another group of agents does not produce sleep disturbance while being used but may have that effect after withdrawal. Almost any drug with sedating or tranquilizing agents can have that effect, including at times the benzodiazepines, the phenothiazines, the sedating tricyclic drugs, and various street drugs, including marijuana, opiates, and opioids.

Alcohol is a CNS depressant and produces the serious problems of other CNS depressants, both during administration—perhaps related to the development of tolerance—and after withdrawal. The insomnia after long-term alcohol consumption is sometimes severe and lasts for weeks or longer. The clinician should not give a potentially addicting medication to a patient who has just recovered from an addiction; sleeping medications, if possible, should be avoided.

Among cigarette smokers, the combination of a relaxing ritual and the tendency of low doses of nicotine to cause sedation may actually help sleep. However, high doses of nicotine can interfere with sleep, particularly sleep onset. The typical cigarette smoker sleeps less than a nonsmoker. Nicotine withdrawal may cause drowsiness or arousal.

References

Boivin D B, Montplaisir J, Petit D, Lambert C, Lubin S: Effects of modafinil on symptomatology of human narcolepsy. Clin Neuropharmacol 16: 46, 1993.

Farney R J, Walker J M: Office management of common sleep-wake disorders. Med Clin North Am 79: 391, 1995.

Hartmann P M: Drug treatment of insomnia: Indications and newer agents. Am Fam Physician 51: 191, 1995.

Kryger M H, Roth T, Dement W C, editors: *Principles and Practice of Sleep Medicine*, ed 2. Saunders, Philadelphia, 1993.

Neylan T C: Treatment of sleep disturbances in depressed patients. J Clin Psychiatry 56: 56, 1995.

Papadimitriou G N, Christodoulou G N, Katsouyanni K, Stefanis C N: Therapy and prevention of affective illness by total sleep deprivation, J Affect Disord 27: 107, 1993.

Prinz P N: Sleep and sleep disorders in older adults. J Clin Neurophysiol 12: 139, 1995.

Regestein Q R, Monk T H: Delayed sleep phase syndrome: A review of its clinical aspects. Am J Psychiatry 152: 602, 1995.

Schramm E, Hohagen F, Grasshoff U, Riemann D, Hajak G, Weeb H-G, Berger M: Test-retest reliability and validity of the structured interview for sleep disorders according to DSM-III-R. Am J Psychiatry 150: 867, 1993.

Stradling J R: Recreational drugs and sleep. Br J Med 306: 573, 1993.

Williams, R L, Karacan I, Moore C A, Hirshkowitz M: Sleep disorders. In *Comprehensive Textbook of Psychiatry*, ed 6, H I Kaplan, B J Sadock, editors, p 1373. Williams & Wilkins, Baltimore, 1995.

18/ Impulse-Control Disorders Not Elsewhere Classified

Six categories of impulse-control disorders not elsewhere classified are listed in the fourth edition of *Diagnostic and Statistical Manual of Mental Disorders* (DSM-IV): intermittent explosive disorder, kleptomania, pyromania, pathological gambling, trichotillomania, and impulse-control disorder not otherwise specified.

Patients with disorders of impulse control share the following features: (1) They fail to resist an impulse, drive, or temptation to perform some action that is harmful to themselves or others. They may or may not consciously resist the impulse and may or may not plan the act. (2) Before committing the act, they feel an increasing sense of tension or arousal. (3) While committing the act, they feel pleasure, gratification, or release. The act is ego-syntonic in that it is consonant with patients' immediate conscious wishes. Immediately after the act, the patients may or may not feel genuine regret, self-reproach, or guilt.

ETIOLOGY

The causes of impulse disorders are unknown, but psychodynamic, biological, and psychosocial factors seem to interact to cause the disorders. The disorders may have common underlying neurobiological mechanisms.

Psychodynamic Factors

An *impulse* is a disposition to act to decrease the heightened tension caused by the buildup of instinctual drives or by diminished ego defenses against the drives. The impulse disorders have in common an attempt to bypass the experience of disabling symptoms or painful affects by attempting to act on the environment. In his work with delinquent adolescents, August Aichhorn understood impulsive behavior as related to a weak superego and weak ego structures associated with psychic trauma from childhood deprivation.

Otto Fenichel linked impulsive behavior to attempts to master anxiety, guilt, depression, and other painful affects by means of action. He thought that such actions defend against internal danger and that they produce a distorted aggressive or sexual gratification. To an outside observer, impulsive behaviors may seem greedy and acquisitive, but they may actually be closely related to relief from pain.

Heinz Kohut understood many forms of impulse-control problems—including gambling, kleptomania, and some paraphiliac behaviors—to be related to an incomplete sense of self. He observed that, when patients do not receive the validating and affirming responses that they seek from significant relationships in their lives, the self may fragment. As a way of dealing with that fragmentation and of regaining a sense of wholeness or cohesion in the self, those patients may engage in impulsive behaviors that appear to others to be self-destructive. Kohut's formulation has some similarities to Donald Winnicott's view that impulsive or deviant behavior is a way that a child hopes to recapture a primitive maternal relationship. Winnicott saw such behavior as hopeful in that the child is still searching for affirmation and love from the mother, rather than giving up on ever getting it. Several therapists have stressed the patients' fixation at the oral stage of development. The patients attempt to master anxiety, guilt, depression, and other painful affects by means of action, but such actions aimed at obtaining relief seldom succeed even temporarily.

BIOLOGICAL FACTORS

Many investigators have focused on a possible organic involvement in the impulse-control disorders, especially for those patients with overtly violent behavior. Experiments have shown that specific brain regions, such as the limbic system, are associated with impulsive and violent activity and that other brain regions are associated with the inhibition of such behaviors. Certain hormones, especially testosterone, have been associated with violent and aggressive behavior. Some reports have described a relation between temporal lobe epilepsy and certain impulsive violent behaviors, an association of aggressive behavior in patients with histories of head trauma, increased numbers of emergency room visits, and other potential organic antecedents. A high incidence of mixed cerebral dominance may be found in some violent populations.

Impulse-control disorder symptoms may continue into adulthood in persons who are classified as suffering from childhood attention-deficit/hyperactivity disorder. Lifelong or acquired mental deficiency, epilepsy, and even reversible brain syndromes have long been implicated in lapses of impulse control.

Considerable evidence indicates that the serotonin neurotransmitter system mediates symptoms evident in impulse-control disorders. A relation has been found between cerebrospinal fluid (CSF) levels of 5-hydroxyindoleacetic acid (5-HIAA) and impulsive aggression. Brainstem and CSF levels of 5-HIAA are decreased, and 5-hydroxytryptamine (5-HT) binding sites are increased in suicide victims. Involvement of the dopaminergic and noradrenergic systems has also been implicated in impulsivity.

In some disorders of impulse control, the ego defenses are overwhelmed without actual nervous system pathology. Fatigue, incessant stimulation, and psychic trauma can lower resistance and temporarily suspend the ego's control.

PSYCHOSOCIAL FACTORS

Some workers have stressed the importance of the disorder's psychosocial aspects, such as early life events. Improper models for identification and parental figures who themselves have difficulty in controlling impulses have also been implicated. In addition, such parental factors as violence in the home, alcohol abuse, promiscuity, and antisocial tendencies have been thought to be significant.

INTERMITTENT EXPLOSIVE DISORDER

Intermittent explosive disorder is found in persons who have discrete episodes of losing control of aggressive impulses, resulting in serious assault or the destruction of property. The aggressiveness expressed is grossly out of proportion to any stressors that may have helped elicit the episodes. The symptoms, which the patient may describe as spells or attacks, appear within minutes or hours and, regardless of the duration, remit spontaneously and quickly. Each episode is usually followed by genuine regret or self-reproach. Signs of generalized impulsivity or aggressiveness are absent between episodes. The diagnosis of intermittent explosive disorder should not be made if the loss of control can be accounted for by schizophrenia, antisocial or borderline personality disorder, attention-deficit/hyperactivity disorder, conduct disorder, or substance intoxication.

The term ''epileptoid personality'' has been used to convey the seizurelike quality of the characteristic outbursts, which are not typical of the patient, and to convey the suspicion of an organic disease process. Some associated features suggest the possibility of an epileptoid state: the patient may experience an aura; postictallike changes in the sensorium, including partial or spotty amnesia; or hypersensitivity to photic, aural, or auditory stimuli. Persons with the disorder have a high incidence of hyperactivity, soft neurological signs, nonspecific electroencephalogram (EEG) findings, and accident-proneness.

Epidemiology

Intermittent explosive disorder is underreported. It appears to be more common in men than in women. The men are likely to be found in a correctional institution and the women in a psychiatric facility. In one study about 2 percent of all admissions to a university hospital psychiatric service were given diagnoses of intermittent explosive disorder; 80 percent were men.

Evidence suggests that intermittent explosive disorder is more common in first-degree biological relatives of persons with the disorder than in the general population. A variety of factors, other than a simple genetic explanation, may be responsible.

Etiology

Some investigators suggest that disordered brain physiology, particularly in the limbic system, is involved in most cases of episodic violence. However, an unfavorable environment in childhood is generally believed to be the major determinant. Predisposing factors in childhood are thought to include perinatal trauma, infantile seizures, head trauma, encephalitis, minimal brain dysfunction, and hyperactivity. The patient's childhood environments are often filled with alcohol dependence, beatings, threats to life, and promiscuity.

Those workers who have concentrated on psychogenesis in the cause of episodic explosiveness have stressed identification with assaultive parental figures or the symbolism of the target of the violence. Early frustration, oppression, and hostility have been noted as predisposing factors. Situations that are directly or symbolically reminiscent of those early deprivations (for example, persons who directly or indirectly evoke the image of the frustrating parent) become targets for destructive hostility.

Typical patients have been described as physically large but dependent men whose sense of masculine identity is poor. A sense of being useless and impotent or of being unable to change the environment often precedes the episode of physical violence.

Compelling evidence indicates that serotonergic neurons

Table 18-1.   Diagnostic Criteria for Intermittent Explosive Disorder

A. Several discrete episodes of failure to resist aggressive impulses that result in serious assaultive acts or destruction of property.

B. The degree of aggressiveness expressed during the episodes is grossly out of proportion to any precipitating psychosocial stressors.

C. The aggressive episodes are not better accounted for by another mental disorder (e.g., antisocial personality disorder, borderline personality disorder, a psychotic disorder, a manic episode, conduct disorder, or attention-deficit/hyperactivity disorder) and are not due to the direct physiological effects of a substance (e.g., a drug of abuse, a medication) or a general medical condition (e.g., head trauma, Alzheimer's disease).

Table from DSM-IV, *Diagnostic and Statistical Manual of Mental Disorders*, ed 4. Copyright American Psychiatric Association, Washington, 1994. Used with permission.

mediate behavioral inhibition. Decreases in serotonergic transmission—as can be induced by inhibiting serotonin synthesis or antagonizing its effects—result in a decrease in punishment's effect as a deterrent to behavior. The restoration of serotonin activity—by administering serotonin precursors, such as tryptophan, or drugs that increase synaptic serotonin levels—restores the behavioral effect of punishment. Low levels of CSF 5-HIAA have been correlated with impulsive aggression.

Diagnosis and Clinical Features

The diagnosis of intermittent explosive disorder should be the result of history taking that reveals several episodes of loss of control associated with aggressive outbursts (Table 18–1). A single discrete episode does not justify the diagnosis. The history is typically of a childhood in the midst of alcohol dependence, violence, and emotional instability. The patients' work histories are poor. The patients report job losses, marital difficulties, and trouble with the law. Most have sought psychiatric help in the past but without success. A high level of anxiety, guilt, and depression is usually present after an episode. Neurological examination sometimes reveals soft neurological signs, such as left-right ambivalence and perceptual reversal. EEG findings are frequently normal or show nonspecific changes. Psychological tests for organicity frequently result in normal findings.

Differential Diagnosis

The diagnosis of intermittent explosive disorder can be made only after disorders associated with the occasional loss of control of aggressive impulses have been ruled out. Those other disorders include psychotic disorders, personality change due to a general medical condition, antisocial or borderline personality disorder, conduct disorder, and intoxication with a psychoactive substance.

One can differentiate intermittent explosive disorder from the antisocial and borderline personality disorders because, in the personality disorders, aggressiveness and impulsivity are part of the patient's character and are present between outbursts. In paranoid and catatonic schizophrenia, the patient may display violent behavior in response to delusions and hallucinations, and the patient has a gross impairment in reality testing. Hostile manic patients may be impulsively aggressive, but the underlying diagnosis is generally clear from their mental status examinations and clinical presentations. Epilepsy, brain tumors, degenerative diseases, and endocrine disorders must be considered and ruled out, as must acute intoxications with such substances as alcohol, barbiturates, hallucinogens, and amphetamines. Conduct disorder is ruled out by its repetitive and resistant pattern of behavior, as opposed to an episodic pattern.

Course and Prognosis

Intermittent explosive disorder may begin at any stage of life but usually begins in the second or third decade. In most cases the disorder decreases in severity with the onset of middle age. Heightened organic impairment, however, can lead to frequent and severe episodes.

Treatment

A combined pharmacological and psychotherapeutic approach has the best chance of success. Psychotherapy with the patients is difficult, dangerous, and often unrewarding, as the therapist may have difficulties with countertransference and limit setting. Group psychotherapy may be of some help, as may family therapy, particularly when the explosive patient is an adolescent or a young adult.

Anticonvulsants have long been used in treating explosive patients, with mixed results. Phenothiazines and antidepressants have been effective in some cases, but one must wonder whether schizophrenia or a mood disorder is the true diagnosis. When subcortical seizurelike activity is a likelihood, those medications can aggravate the situation. Benzodiazepines have been reported to produce a paradoxical reaction of dyscontrol in some cases. Lithium (Eskalith) has been reported to be useful in generally lessening aggressive behavior, and carbamazepine (Tegretol) and phenytoin (Dilantin) have also been reported to be helpful. Propranolol (Inderal), buspirone (BuSpar), and trazodone (Desyrel) have also been effective in some cases. Increasing reports indicate that fluoxetine (Prozac) and other serotonin-specific reuptake inhibitors (SSRIs) are useful in reducing impulsivity and aggression.

Some neurosurgeons have performed operative treatments for intractable violence and aggression. No evidence indicates that such treatment is effective.

KLEPTOMANIA

The essential feature of kleptomania is a recurrent failure to resist impulses to steal objects not needed for personal use or their monetary value. The objects taken are often given away, returned surreptitiously, or kept and hidden.

Persons with kleptomania usually have the money to pay for the objects they impulsively steal. Like other impulse-control disorders, kleptomania is characterized by mounting tension before the act, followed by gratification and less tension with or without guilt, remorse, or depression during the act. The stealing is not planned and does not involve others. Although the thefts do not occur when immediate arrest is probable, kleptomaniac persons do not always consider the chances of their apprehension, even though repeated arrests lead to pain and humiliation. Kleptomaniac persons may feel guilt and anxiety after the theft, but they do not feel anger or vengeance. Furthermore, when the object stolen is the goal, the diagnosis is not kleptomania, for in kleptomania the act of stealing is itself the goal.

Epidemiology

The prevalence of kleptomania is not known. The estimated rate of kleptomania ranges from 3.8 to 24 percent of those arrested for shoplifting. The sex ratio is unknown but kleptomania appears to be more common among females than among males. DSM-IV reports it occurring in fewer than 5 percent of identified shoplifters.

Etiology

PSYCHODYNAMIC FACTORS

Some psychoanalytic writers have stressed the expression of the aggressive impulses in kleptomania; others have discerned a libidinal aspect. Those who focus on symbolism see meaning in the act itself, the object stolen, and the victim of the theft.

Kleptomania is often associated with other disturbances, such as mood disorders, obsessive-compulsive disorder, and eating disorders. Kleptomania frequently occurs as part of bulimia nervosa. In some reports, nearly a quarter of the patients with bulimia nervosa meet the diagnostic criteria for kleptomania.

The symptoms of kleptomania tend to appear in times of significant stress—for example, losses, separations, and the ending of important relationships.

Analytic writers have focused on stealing by children and adolescents. Anna Freud pointed out that the first thefts from the mother's purse indicate the degree to which all stealing is rooted in the oneness between mother and child. Karl Abraham wrote of the central feeling of being neglected, injured, or unwanted. One theoretician established seven categories of stealing in chronically acting-out children: (1) as a means of restoring the lost mother-child relationship, (2) as an aggressive act, (3) as a defense against fears of being damaged (perhaps a search by females for a penis or a protection against castration anxiety in males), (4) as a means of seeking punishment, (5) as a means of restoring or adding to self-esteem, (6) in connection with and as a reaction to a family secret, and (7) as excitement and a substitute for a sexual act. One or more of those categories can also apply to adult kleptomania.

BIOLOGICAL FACTORS

Brain diseases and mental retardation have been associated with kleptomania, as they have with other disorders of impulse control. Focal neurological signs, cortical atrophy, and enlarged lateral ventricles have been found in some patients. Disturbances in monoamine metabolism, particularly of serotonin, have been postulated.

Diagnosis and Clinical Features

The essential feature of kleptomania consists of recurrent, intrusive, and irresistible urges or impulses to steal unneeded objects (Table 18–2). Kleptomaniac patients may also be distressed about the possibility or the actuality of their being apprehended and so manifest signs of depression and anxiety. Patients feel guilty, ashamed, and embarrassed about their behavior. They often have serious problems with interpersonal relation-

Table 18-2. Diagnostic Criteria for Kleptomania

A. Recurrent failure to resist impulses to steal objects that are not needed for personal use or for their monetary value.

B. Increasing sense of tension immediately before committing the theft.

C. Pleasure, gratification, or relief at the time of commiting the theft.

D. The stealing is not committed to express anger or vengeance and is not in response to a delusion or a hallucination.

E. The stealing is not better accounted for by conduct disorder, a manic episode, or antisocial personality disorder.

Table from DSM-IV, *Diagnostic and Statistical Manual of Mental Disorders*, ed 4. Copyright American Psychiatric Association, Washington, 1994. Used with permission.

ships and often, but not invariably, show signs of personality disturbance. In one study of kleptomaniac patients, the frequency of stealing ranged from less than one to 120 episodes a month.

Most kleptomaniac patients steal from retail stores, but they may steal from family members in their own households.

Differential Diagnosis

Because most kleptomaniac patients are referred for examination in connection with legal proceedings after apprehension, the clinical picture may be clouded by subsequent symptoms of depression and anxiety. The major differentiation is between kleptomania and other forms of stealing. For a diagnosis of kleptomania, the stealing must always follow a failure to resist the impulse and must be a solitary act, and the stolen articles must be without immediate usefulness or monetary gain. In ordinary stealing the act is usually planned, and the objects are stolen for their use or financial value. Malingerers may try to simulate kleptomania to avoid prosecution. Stealing that occurs in association with conduct disorder, antisocial personality disorder, and manic episodes is clearly related to the pervasive, underlying disorder. Persons with kleptomania do not typically display antisocial behavior other than stealing.

Schizophrenic patients may steal in response to hallucinations and delusions, and patients with cognitive disorders may be accused of stealing because of their forgetting to pay for objects.

Course and Prognosis

Kleptomania may begin in childhood, although most children and adolescents who steal do not become kleptomaniac adults. The course of the disorder waxes and wanes, but the disorder tends to be chronic. The spontaneous recovery rate is unknown. Serious impairment and complications are usually secondary to being caught, particularly when being arrested. Many individuals seem never to have consciously considered the possibility of having to face the consequences of their acts, a feature in line with some descriptions of kleptomaniac patients as people who feel wronged and, therefore, entitled to steal. Some persons have bouts of being unable to resist the impulse to steal, followed by free periods that last for weeks or months. The prognosis with treatment can be good, but few patients come for help of their own accord. Often, the disorder in no way impairs the person's social or work functioning. In quies-

cent cases, new bouts of the disorder may be precipitated by loss or disappointment.

Treatment

Because true kleptomania is rare, reports of treatment tend to be individual case descriptions or a short series of cases. Insight-oriented psychotherapy and psychoanalysis have been successful but depend on the patient's motivation. Persons who feel guilt and shame may be helped by insight-oriented psychotherapy, because of their increased motivation to change the behavior.

Behavior therapy—including systematic desensitization, aversive conditioning, and a combination of aversive conditioning and altered social contingencies—has been reported to be successful, even when motivation was lacking. The reports cite follow-up studies of up to two years.

Fluoxetine and other SSRIs appear to be effective in some kleptomaniac patients.

PYROMANIA

The essential features of pyromania are deliberate and purposeful fire setting on more than one occasion; tension or affective arousal before setting the fires; fascination with, interest in, curiosity about, or attraction to fire and the activities and equipment associated with fire fighting; and pleasure, gratification, or relief when setting fires or when witnessing or participating in their aftermath. The patient may make considerable advance preparations before starting the fire.

Epidemiology

No information is available on the prevalence of pyromania, but only a small percentage of those adults who set fires can be classified as having pyromania. The disorder is found far more often in males than in females, and people who set fires are more likely to be mildly retarded than are the general population. Some studies have noted an increased incidence of alcohol abuse in people who set fires. Fire setters also tend to have a history of antisocial traits, such as truancy, running away from home, and delinquency. Enuresis has been considered a common finding in the history of fire setters, although controlled studies have failed to confirm the findings. However, studies have found an association between cruelty to animals and fire setting.

Etiology

Sigmund Freud saw fire as a symbol of sexuality. The warmth that is radiated by fire evokes the same sensation that accompanies a state of sexual excitation, and a flame's shape and movements suggest a phallus in activity. Other therapists have associated pyromania with an abnormal craving for power and social prestige. Some pyromaniac patients are volunteer fire fighters who set fires to prove themselves brave, to force other fire fighters into action, or to demonstrate their power to extinguish a blaze. The incendiary act is a way to vent accumulated rage over the frustration caused by a sense of social, physical, or sexual inferiority. A number of studies have noted that the fathers of pyromanic patients were absent from the home. Thus, one explanation of fire setting is that it represents a wish for

Table 18–3.   Diagnostic Criteria for Pyromania

A. Deliberate and purposeful fire setting on more than one occasion.

B. Tension or affective arousal before the act.

C. Fascination with, interest in, curiosity about, or attraction to fire and its situational contexts (e.g., paraphernalia, uses, consequences).

D. Pleasure, gratification, or relief when setting fires, or when witnessing or participating in their aftermath.

E. The fire setting is not done for monetary gain, as an expression of sociopolitical ideology, to conceal criminal activity, to express anger or vengeance, to improve one's living circumstances, in response to a delusion or hallucination, or as a result of impaired judgment (e.g., in dementia, mental retardation, substance intoxication).

F. The fire setting is not better accounted for by conduct disorder, a manic episode, or antisocial personality disorder.

Table from DSM-IV, *Diagnostic and Statistical Manual of Mental Disorders*, ed 4. Copyright American Psychiatric Association, Washington, 1994. Used with permission.

the absent father to return home as a rescuer, to put out the fire, and to save the child from a difficult existence.

Female fire setters, in addition to being much fewer in number than male fire setters, do not start fires to put fire fighters into action, as men frequently do. Rather, promiscuity without pleasure and petty stealing, often approaching kleptomania, have been frequently noted to be delinquent trends in female fire setters.

Significantly low CSF levels of 5-HIAA and 3-methoxy-4-hydroxyphenylglycol (MHPG) were found in one group of male fire setters.

Diagnosis and Clinical Features

Persons with pyromania are often regular watchers at fires in their neighborhood, frequently set off false alarms, and show interest in fire-fighting paraphernalia (Table 18–3). Curiosity is very evident. The persons may be indifferent to the consequences of the fire for life or property, exhibiting a lack of remorse. Fire setters may gain satisfaction from the resulting destruction. Frequently, they leave obvious clues. Common associated features include alcohol intoxication, sexual dysfunctions, lower-than-average intelligence quotient (I.Q.), chronic personal frustrations, and resentment toward authority figures. In some cases, the fire setter becomes sexually aroused by the fire.

Differential Diagnosis

The clinician should have little trouble distinguishing between pyromania and the fascination of many young children with matches, lighters, and fire as part of the normal investigation of their environments. Pyromania must also be separated from incendiary acts of sabotage carried out by dissident political extremists or paid torches, who are called arsonists in the legal system.

When fire setting occurs in conduct disorder and antisocial personality disorder, it is a deliberate act, rather than the failure to resist an impulse. Fires may be set for profit, sabotage, or retaliation. Patients with schizophrenia or mania may set fires in response to delusions or hallucinations. And patients with brain dysfunction may set fires because of a failure to appreciate the consequences of the act.

A diagnosis of pyromania should not be made when fires are set to make money, to express a sociopolitical ideology, to conceal criminal activity, to express anger or vengeance, to improve one's living circumstances, or to respond to a delusion or a hallucination.

Course and Prognosis

Pyromania usually begins in childhood. When the onset is in adolescence or adulthood, the fire setting tends to be deliberately destructive. The prognosis for treated children is good, and complete remission is a realistic goal. The prognosis for adults is guarded, because of their frequent use of denial, their refusal to take responsibility, and their concurrent alcohol dependence and lack of insight.

Treatment

Little has been written about the treatment of pyromania. The treatment of fire setters has been difficult because of their lack of motivation. Incarceration may be the only method available to prevent a recurrence. Behavior therapy can then be administered in the institution.

Fire setting in children must be treated with the utmost seriousness. Intensive interventions should be undertaken when possible but as therapeutic and preventive measures, rather than as punishment. Because of the recurrent nature of pyromania, any treatment program should include supervision of the patient to prevent a repeated episode of fire setting.

PATHOLOGICAL GAMBLING

As defined by DSM-IV, the essential feature of pathological gambling is persistent and recurrent maladaptive gambling behavior. Features of the maladaptive behavior include a preoccupation with gambling; the need to gamble with increasing amounts of money to achieve the desired excitement; repeated unsuccessful efforts to control, cut back, or stop gambling; gambling as a way of escaping from problems; gambling to recoup losses; lying to conceal the extent of the involvement with gambling; the commission of illegal acts to finance gambling; the jeopardizing or loss of personal and vocational relationships because of gambling; and a reliance on others for money to pay off debts.

Epidemiology

Estimates place the number of pathological gamblers at 1 to 3 percent of the adult United States population. The disorder is more common in men than in women. Both the fathers of males and the mothers of females with the disorder are more likely to have the disorder than are the population at large. Women with the disorder are more likely than are those not so affected to be married to alcoholic men who are usually absent from the home. Alcohol dependence in general is more common among the parents of pathological gamblers than among the overall population.

Etiology

The following may be predisposing factors for the development of the disorder: loss of a parent by death, separation, divorce, or desertion before the child is 15 years of age; inappropriate parental discipline (absence, inconsistency, or harshness); exposure to and availability of gambling activities for the adolescent; a family emphasis on material and financial symbols; and a lack of family emphasis on saving, planning, and budgeting.

There is an association between pathological gambling and mood disorders, especially major depressive disorder. Other associated disorders include panic disorder, obsessive-compulsive disorder, and agoraphobia. Childhood attention-deficit/hyperactivity disorder may be a predisposing factor for pathological gambling. Disorders of catecholamine metabolism have been suggested, with the gambler seeking to experience the activating effect of norepinephrine that accompanies the tension associated with gambling.

DIAGNOSIS AND CLINICAL FEATURES

In addition to the features described above, pathological gamblers most often appear overconfident, somewhat abrasive, energetic, and free-spending when they have obvious signs of personal stress, anxiety, and depression (Table 18–4). They commonly have the attitude that money is both the cause of and the solution to all their problems. As their gambling increases, they are usually forced to lie to obtain money and to continue gambling while holding the extent of their gambling behavior a secret. They make no serious attempt to budget or save money. When their borrowing resources are strained, they are likely to engage in antisocial behavior to obtain money for gambling. Their criminal behavior is typically nonviolent, such as forgery, embezzlement, or fraud. The conscious intent is to return or repay the money.

Complications include alienation from family members and acquaintances, the loss of one's life accomplishments, suicide

attempts, and association with fringe and illegal groups. Arrest for nonviolent crimes may lead to imprisonment.

Differential Diagnosis

Social gambling is distinguished from pathological gambling in that the former is associated with gambling with friends, on special occasions, and with predetermined acceptable and tolerable losses.

Gambling that is symptomatic of a manic episode can usually be distinguished from pathological gambling by the history of a marked mood change and the loss of judgment preceding the gambling. Maniclike mood changes are common in pathological gambling but always follow winning and are usually followed by depressive episodes because of subsequent losses.

Persons with antisocial personality disorder may have problems with gambling. In cases in which both disorders are present, both should be diagnosed.

Course and Prognosis

Pathological gambling usually begins in adolescence for males and late in life for females. The disorder waxes and wanes and tends to be chronic. Three phases are seen in pathological gambling: (1) the winning phase, ending with a big win, equal to about a year's salary, which hooks the patient; (2) the progressive-loss phase, in which patients structure their lives around gambling and move from being excellent gamblers to stupid ones (taking considerable risks, cashing in securities, borrowing money, missing work, and losing jobs); and (3) the desperate phase, with the patients gambling in a frenzy with large amounts of money, not paying debts, becoming involved with loan sharks, writing bad checks, and possibly embezzling. The disorder may take up to 15 years to reach the third phase, but then, within a year or two, the patients are totally deteriorated.

Treatment

Gamblers seldom come forward voluntarily for treatment. Legal difficulties, family pressures, or other psychiatric complaints are what bring the gamblers into treatment. Gamblers Anonymous (GA) was founded in Los Angeles in 1957 and modeled on Alcoholics Anonymous (AA); it is accessible—at least in large cities—and is probably the most effective treatment for gambling. It is a method of inspirational group therapy, which involves public confession, peer pressure, and the presence of reformed gamblers available (as are sponsors in AA) to help members resist the impulse to gamble.

In some cases, hospitalizing the patients may help by removing them from their environments. Insight should not be expected until the patients have been away from gambling for three months. At that point, pathological gambling patients may become excellent candidates for insight-oriented psychotherapy.

If gambling is associated with depressive disorders, mania, anxiety, or other mental disorders, pharmacotherapy with antidepressants, lithium, or antianxiety agents is useful.

TRICHOTILLOMANIA

According to DSM-IV, the essential feature of trichotillomania is the recurrent pulling out of one's hair, resulting in

Table 18–4.   Diagnostic Criteria for Pathological Gambling

A. Persistent and recurrent maladaptive gambling behavior as indicated by five (or more) of the following:

   (1) is preoccupied with gambling (e.g., preoccupied with reliving past gambling experiences, handicapping or planning the next venture, or thinking of ways to get money with which to gamble)
   (2) needs to gamble with increasing amounts of money in order to achieve the desired excitement
   (3) has repeated unsuccessful efforts to control, cut back, or stop gambling
   (4) is restless or irritable when attempting to cut down or stop gambling
   (5) gambles as a way of escaping from problems or of relieving a dysphoric mood (e.g., feelings of helplessness, guilt, anxiety, depression)
   (6) after losing money gambling, often returns another day to get even (''chasing'' one's losses)
   (7) lies to family members, therapist, or others to conceal the extent of involvement with gambling
   (8) has committed illegal acts such as forgery, fraud, theft, or embezzlement to finance gambling
   (9) has jeopardized or lost a significant relationship, job, or educational or career opportunity because of gambling
   (10) relies on others to provide money to relieve a desperate financial situation caused by gambling

B. The gambling behavior is not better accounted for by a manic episode.

Table from DSM-IV, *Diagnostic and Statistical Manual of Mental Disorders*, ed 4. Copyright American Psychiatric Association, Washington, 1994. Used with permission.

noticeable hair loss. Other clinical symptoms include an increasing sense of tension before pulling the hair and a sense of pleasure, gratification, or relief when pulling out the hair. The diagnosis should not be made if the hair pulling is the result of another mental disorder (for example, those disorders manifesting delusions or hallucinations) or a general medical disorder (for example, a preexisting lesion of the skin).

Epidemiology

Trichotillomania is apparently more common in females than in males. No information is available on the familial pattern, but one study reported that 5 to 19 children had family histories of some form of alopecia. Prevalence data are unavailable, but trichotillomania may be more common than is now believed, especially if hair pulling without the sense of tension before the pulling and without the sense of relief afterward is considered trichotillomania. Some experts contend that the DSM-IV criteria are too restrictive. Associated disorders are obsessive-compulsive disorder, obsessive-compulsive personality disorder, borderline personality disorder, and depressive disorders.

Etiology

Although trichotillomania is regarded as multidetermined, its onset has been linked to stressful situations in more than a quarter of all cases. Disturbances in mother-child relationships, fear of being left alone, and recent object loss are often cited as critical factors contributing to the condition. Substance abuse may encourage the development of the disorder. Depressive dynamics are often cited as predisposing factors; however, no particular personality trait or disorder characterizes the patients. Some see self-stimulation as the primary goal of hair pulling.

Trichotillomania is increasingly being viewed as having a biologically determined substrate that may reflect inappropriately released motor activity or excessive grooming behaviors.

Diagnosis and Clinical Features

Before engaging in the behavior, trichotillomaniac patients experience an increasing sense of tension and achieve a sense of release or gratification from pulling out their hair (Table 18–5). All areas of the body may be affected. The most common site is the scalp. Other areas involved are the eyebrows, eye-

lashes, and the beard; less commonly, the trunk, armpits, and the pubic area are involved. Hair loss is often characterized by short, broken strands appearing together with long, normal hairs in the affected areas. No abnormalities of the skin or the scalp are present. Hair pulling is not reported to be painful, although pruritus and tingling in the involved area may be present.

Trichophagy, mouthing of the hair, may follow the hair plucking. Complications of trichophagy include trichobezoars, malnutrition, and intestinal obstruction.

Characteristic histopathological changes in the hair follicle, known as trichomalacia, are demonstrated by biopsy and help distinguish trichotillomania from other causes of alopecia. Patients usually deny the behavior and often try to hide the resultant alopecia. Head banging, nail biting, scratching, gnawing, excoriation, and other acts or self-mutilation may be present.

Differential Diagnosis

Hair pulling may be a wholly benign condition, or it may occur in the context of several mental disorders. The phenomenology of trichotillomania and obsessive-compulsive disorder overlap. Like obsessive-compulsive disorder, trichotillomania is often chronic and recognized by the patient as undesirable. Unlike obsessive-compulsive disorder, patients with trichotillomania do not experience obsessive thoughts, and the compulsive activity is limited to one act—hair pulling.

Patients with factitious disorder with predominantly physical signs and symptoms actively seek medical attention and the patient role and deliberately simulate illness toward those ends. Patients who malinger or have factitious disorder may mutilate themselves to get medical attention, but they do not acknowledge the self-inflicted nature of the lesions.

Patient with stereotypic movement disorder have stereotypical and rhythmic movements, and they usually do not seem distressed by their behavior.

Trichotillomania may be difficult to distinguish from alopecia areata.

Course and Prognosis

Trichotillomania generally begins in childhood or adolescence, but onsets have been reported much later in life. A late onset may be associated with an increased likelihood of chronicity. The course of the disorder is not well known. Both chronic and remitting forms occur. In some cases the disorder has persisted for more than two decades. About a third of the people presenting for treatment report a duration of one year or less.

Treatment

No consensus is available on the best treatment modality for trichotillomania. Treatment usually involves psychiatrists and dermatologists in a joint endeavor. Psychopharmacological methods that have been used to treat psychodermatological disorders include topical steroids and hydroxyzine hydrochloride, and anxiolytic with antihistamine properties; antidepressants; serotonergic agents; and antipsychotics. Whether depression is present or not, antidepressant agents may lead to dermatological improvement. Current evidence strongly points to the efficacy of drugs that alter central serotonin turnover. In patients who respond poorly to SSRIs, augmentation with pimozide (Orap), a dopamine blocker, may lead to improvement. A report of

---

Table 18–5.   Diagnostic Criteria for Trichotillomania

A. Recurrent pulling out of one's hair, resulting in noticeable hair loss.

B. An increasing sense of tension immediately before pulling out the hair or when attempting to resist the behavior.

C. Pleasure, gratification, or relief when pulling out the hair.

D. The disturbance is not better accounted for by another mental disorder and is not due to a general medical condition (e.g., a dermatological condition).

E. The disturbance causes clinically significant distress or impairment in social, occupational, or other important areas of functioning.

Table from DSM-IV, *Diagnostic and Statistical Manual of Mental Disorders*, ed 4. Copyright American Psychiatric Association, Washington, 1994. Used with permission.

successful lithium treatment for trichotillomania cited the possible effect of lithium on aggressivity, impulsivity, and mood instability as an explanation. Lithium also possesses serotonergic activity.

Successful behavioral treatments, such as biofeedback, have been reported; however, most of the reports have been about individual cases or small series of studies with relatively short follow-up periods. Further controlled study of the techniques is warranted. Trichotillomania has been treated successfully with insight-oriented psychotherapy.

Hypnotherapy and behavior therapy have been mentioned as potentially effective modalities in the treatment of dermatological disorders in which psychological factors may be involved. The skin has been shown to be susceptible to hypnotic suggestion. Most of the work has been research-oriented, with little effect yet on clinical management.

IMPULSE-CONTROL DISORDER NOT OTHERWISE SPECIFIED

The DSM-IV diagnostic category of impulse-control disorder not otherwise specified is a residual category for disorders of impulse control that do not meet the criteria for a specific impulse-control disorder. Included in the not otherwise specified (NOS) disorders are compulsive shopping, addiction to video games, compulsive sexual behavior, and repetitive self-mutilation.

References

Burt V K: Impulse-control disorders not elsewhere classified. In *Comprehensive Textbook of Psychiatry*, ed 6, H I Kaplan, B J Sadock, editors, p 1409. Williams & Wilkins, Baltimore, 1995.
Rugle L, Melamed L: Neuropsychological assessment of attention problems in pathological gamblers. J Nerv Ment Dis *181*: 107, 1993.
Stein D J, Hollander E, Liebowitz M R: Neurobiology of impulsivity and the impulse control disorders. J Neuropsychiatry *5*: 9, 1993.
Swedo S E: Trichotillomania. Psychiatr Ann *23*: 402, 1993.

19/ Adjustment Disorders

Emotional or behavioral symptoms may occur in response to stressful life events. A diagnosis of adjustment disorder should be made if those symptoms or behaviors appear within three months of the onset of the stressor and are clinically significant as is evidenced by (1) marked distress that exceeds what is expected from exposure to the stressor or (2) significant impairment in social, vocational, or academic functioning. According to the fourth edition of *Diagnostic and Statistical Manual of Mental Disorders* (DSM-IV), the stress-related disturbance should not meet the criteria for any specific Axis I disorder and should not be merely an exacerbation of a preexisting Axis I or Axis II disorder. Bereavement is not considered an adjustment disorder in DSM-IV.

Adjustment disorder is a short-term maladaptive reaction to what a layperson may call a personal misfortune or to what a psychiatrist calls a psychosocial stressor. Adjustment disorder is expected to remit soon after the stressor ceases or, if the stressor persists, a new level of adaptation is achieved. The response is maladaptive because of an impairment in social or occupational functioning or because of symptoms or behaviors that are beyond the normal, usual, or expected response to such a stressor.

EPIDEMIOLOGY

Adjustment disorder is one of the most common psychiatric diagnoses among patients hospitalized for medical and surgical problems. In one study 5 percent of hospital admissions over a three-year period were classified as having adjustment disorder. The disorder is most frequently diagnosed in adolescents but may occur at any age.

In one survey of psychiatric patients, 10 percent of the sample population were found to have adjustment disorder. The ratio of females to males was about 2 to 1. Single women are generally overly represented as being most at risk. Among adolescents of either sex, common types of precipitating stresses are school problems, parental rejection, parental divorce, and substance abuse. Among adults, common precipitating stresses are marital problems, divorce, moving to a new environment, and financial problems.

ETIOLOGY

Adjustment disorder is precipitated by one or more stressors. The severity of the stressor or stressors is not always predictive of the severity of adjustment disorder; the stressor severity is a complex function of degree, quantity, duration, reversibility, environment, and personal context. For example, the loss of a parent is different for a 10-year-old and a 40-year-old. Personality organization and cultural or group norms and values contribute to the disproportionate responses to stressors.

Stressors may be single, such as a divorce or the loss of a job, or multiple, such as the death of an important person occurring at the same time as one's own physical illness and loss of a job. Stressors may be recurrent, such as seasonal business difficulties, or continuous, such as chronic illness or living in poverty. A discordant intrafamilial relationship may produce adjustment disorder that affects the whole family system. Or the disorder may be limited to the patient, as when the patient is the victim of a crime or has a physical illness. Sometimes adjustment disorder occurs in a group or community setting, and the stressor affects several people, as in a natural disaster or in racial, social, or religious persecution. Specific developmental stages—such as beginning school, leaving home, getting married, becoming a parent, failing to achieve occupational goals, having one's last child leave home, and retiring—are often associated with adjustment disorder.

Psychoanalytic Factors

Several psychoanalytic researchers have discussed the capacity of the same stress to produce a range of responses in various normal human beings. Throughout his life Sigmund Freud remained interested in why the stresses of ordinary life produce illness in some and not in others, why an illness takes a particular form, and why some experiences and not others predispose a person to psychopathology. He gave considerable weight to constitutional factors and viewed them as interacting with a person's life experiences to produce fixation.

Psychoanalytic research has emphasized the role of the mother and the rearing environment in a person's later capacity to respond to stress. Particularly important was Donald W. Winnicott's concept of the good-enough mother, a person who adapts to the infant's needs and provides enough support to enable the growing child to tolerate the frustrations in life.

Psychodynamic Factors

A concurrent personality disorder or organic impairment may make a person vulnerable to adjustment disorder. Vulnerability is also associated with the loss of a parent during infancy. Actual or perceived support from key relationships may mediate behavioral and emotional responses to stressors.

Pivotal to the understanding of adjustment disorder is an understanding of three factors: (1) the nature of the stressor, (2) the conscious and unconscious meanings of the stressor, and (3) the patient's preexisting vulnerability. The clinician must undertake a detailed exploration of the patient's experience of the stressor. Certain patients commonly place all the blame on a particular event when a less obvious event may have been more significant in psychological meaning to the patient. Current events may reawaken past traumas or disappointments from childhood, so patients should be encouraged to think about how the current situation relates to similar past events.

Throughout early development, each child develops a unique set of defense mechanisms to deal with stressful events. Because of greater amounts of trauma or greater constitutional vulnerability, some children have less mature defensive constellations than do other children. That disadvantage may cause them as adults to react with substantial impairment in functioning when they are faced with a loss, a divorce, or a financial setback. However, those who have developed mature defense mechanisms are less vulnerable and bounce back more quickly from the stressor. Their resilience is also crucially determined by the nature of the children's early relationships with their parents. Studies of trauma repeatedly indicate that supportive, nurturant relationships prevent traumatic incidents from causing permanent psychological damage.

Psychodynamic clinicians must take into account the relation between a stressor and the human developmental life cycle. When adolescents leave home for college, for example, they are at high developmental risk for reacting with a temporary symptomatic picture. Similarly, if the child who leaves home is the youngest in the family, the parents may be particularly vulnerable to reacting with adjustment disorder. Moreover, middle-aged persons who are confronting their own mortality may be especially sensitive to the effects of loss or death.

DIAGNOSIS AND CLINICAL FEATURES

Although by definition adjustment disorder follows a stressor, the symptoms do not necessarily begin immediately. According to DSM-IV, up to three months may elapse between the stressor and the development of symptoms. Symptoms do not always subside when the stressor ceases. If the stressor continues, the disorder may be chronic. The disorder may occur at any age. Its symptoms vary considerably, with depressive, anxious, and mixed features the most common in adults.

Physical symptoms are most common in children and the elderly but may occur in any age group. Manifestations may also include assaultive behavior and reckless driving, excessive drinking, defaulting on legal responsibilities, and withdrawal.

The clinical presentations of adjustment disorder can vary widely. DSM-IV lists six types of adjustment disorder, including an unspecified category (Table 19–1).

Table 19-1.   Diagnostic Criteria for Adjustment Disorders

A. The development of emotional or behavioral symptoms in response to an identifiable stressor(s) occurring within 3 months of the onset of the stressor(s).

B. These symptoms or behaviors are clinically significant as evidenced by either of the following:

   (1) marked distress that is in excess of what would be expected from exposure to the stressor
   (2) significant impairment in social or occupational (academic) functioning

C. The stress-related disturbance does not meet the criteria for another specific Axis I disorder and is not merely an exacerbation of a preexisting Axis I or Axis II disorder.

D. The symptoms do not represent bereavement.

E. Once the stressor (or its consequences) has terminated, the symptoms do not persist for more than an additional 6 months.

Specify if:
   Acute: if the disturbance lasts less than 6 months
   Chronic: if the disturbance lasts for 6 months or longer
Adjustment disorders are coded based on the subtype, which is selected according to the predominant symptoms. The specific stressor(s) can be specified on Axis IV.
   With depressed mood
   With anxiety
   With mixed anxiety and depressed mood
   With disturbance of conduct
   With mixed disturbance of emotions and conduct
   Unspecified

Table from DSM-IV, *Diagnostic and Statistical Manual of Mental Disorders*, ed 4. Copyright American Psychiatric Association, Washington, 1994. Used with permission.

Adjustment Disorder with Anxiety

Symptoms of anxiety—such as palpitations, jitteriness, and agitation—are present in adjustment disorder with anxiety, which must be differentiated from anxiety disorders.

Adjustment Disorder with Depressed Mood

In adjustment disorder with depressed mood, the predominant manifestations are depressed mood, tearfulness, and hopelessness. This type must be distinguished from major depressive disorder and uncomplicated bereavement.

Adjustment Disorder with Disturbance of Conduct

In adjustment disorder with disturbance of conduct, the predominant manifestation involves conduct in which the rights of others are violated or age-appropriate societal norms and rules are disregarded. Examples of behavior in this category are truancy, vandalism, reckless driving, and fighting. The category must be differentiated from conduct disorder and antisocial personality disorder.

Adjustment Disorder with Mixed Disturbance of Emotions and Conduct

The combination of disturbances of emotions and conduct sometimes occurs. Clinicians are encouraged to try to make one or the other diagnosis in the interest of parsimony.

Adjustment Disorder with Mixed Anxiety and Depressed Mood

In adjustment disorder with mixed anxiety and depressed mood, patients exhibit features of both anxiety and depression that do not meet the criteria for an already established anxiety disorder or depressive disorder.

Adjustment Disorder Unspecified

Adjustment disorder unspecified is a residual category for atypical maladaptive reactions to stress. Examples include inappropriate responses to the diagnosis of physical illness, such as massive denial and severe noncompliance with treatment, and social withdrawal without significant depressed or anxious mood.

DIFFERENTIAL DIAGNOSIS

Adjustment disorder must be differentiated from other conditions that may be a focus of clinical attention. Patients with other conditions that may be a focus of clinical attention do not have impairment in social or occupational functioning or symptoms beyond the normal and expectable reaction to the stressor. Because no absolute criteria aid in distinguishing between adjustment disorder and a condition that may be a focus of clinical attention, clinical judgment is necessary.

Although uncomplicated bereavement often includes temporarily impaired social and occupational functioning, the person's dysfunction remains within the expectable bounds of a reaction to the loss of a loved one and, thus, is not considered adjustment disorder.

Other disorders from which adjustment disorder must be differentiated include major depressive disorder, brief psychotic disorder, generalized anxiety disorder, somatization disorder, various substance-related disorders, conduct disorder, academic problem, occupational problem, identity problem, and posttraumatic stress disorder. Those diagnoses should be given precedence in all cases that meet their criteria, even in the presence of a stressor or group of stressors that served as a precipitant. However, some patients meet the criteria for both adjustment disorder and a personality disorder.

Posttraumatic Stress Disorder

In posttraumatic stress disorder the symptoms develop after a psychologically traumatizing event or events outside the range of normal human experience. That is, the stressors producing such a syndrome are expected to do so in the average human being. The stressors may be experienced alone, as in rape or assault, or in groups, as in military combat. A variety of mass catastrophes—such as floods, airplane crashes, atomic bombings, and death camps—have also been identified as stressors. The stressor contains a psychological component and frequently a concomitant physical component that may directly damage the nervous system. Clinicians believe that the disorder is more severe and lasts longer when the stressor is of human origin, as in rape, than when it is not, as in floods. In adjustment disorder the precipitating stress need not be severe or unusual.

COURSE AND PROGNOSIS

The overall prognosis of adjustment disorder is generally favorable with appropriate treatment. Most patients return to their previous level of functioning within three months. Adolescents usually require a longer time to recover than do adults. Some persons (particularly adolescents) who receive a diagnosis of adjustment disorder later have mood disorders or substance-related disorders.

TREATMENT

Psychotherapy

Because a stressor can be clearly delineated in adjustment disorder, it is often believed that psychotherapy is not indicated and that the disorder will remit spontaneously. Yet such thinking fails to consider that many persons exposed to the same stressor do not experience similar symptoms and that the response is pathological. Psychotherapy can help the person adapt to the stressor if it is not reversible or time-limited and can serve as a preventive intervention if the stressor does remit.

Psychotherapy remains the treatment of choice for adjustment disorder. Group therapy can be particularly useful for patients who have undergone similar stresses—for example, a group of retired persons or renal dialysis patients. Individual psychotherapy offers the opportunity to explore the meaning of the stressor to the patient, so that earlier traumas can be worked through. After successful therapy, patients sometimes emerge from adjustment disorder stronger than in the premorbid period, although no pathology was evident during that period.

The psychiatrist treating adjustment disorder must be particularly mindful of problems of secondary gain. The illness role may be rewarding to some normal persons who have had little experience with its capacity to free one from responsibility. Thus, the therapist's attention, empathy, and understanding—which are necessary for success—can become rewarding in their own right, thereby reinforcing the symptoms. Such considerations must be weighed before intensive psychotherapy is begun. When a secondary gain has already been established, therapy is difficult.

Patients in whom adjustment disorder includes a conduct disturbance may have difficulties with the law, authorities, or school. Psychiatrists should not attempt to rescue such patients from the consequences of their actions. Too often, such kindness only reinforces socially unacceptable means of tension reduction and hinders the acquisition of insight and subsequent emotional growth. In those cases family therapy can help.

CRISIS INTERVENTION

Crisis intervention, a brief type of therapy, is aimed at helping the person with adjustment disorder resolve the situation quickly by supportive techniques, suggestion, reassurance, environmental modification, and even hospitalization, if necessary. The frequency and the length of visits for crisis support vary according to the patient's needs; daily sessions may be necessary, sometimes two or three times each day. Flexibility is essential in the approach.

Pharmacotherapy

The judicious use of medications can help patients with adjustment disorder, but they should be prescribed for brief periods. A patient may respond to an antianxiety agent or to an antidepressant, depending on the type of adjustment disorder. Patients with severe anxiety bordering on panic or decompensation can benefit from small dosages of antipsychotic medications. Patients in withdrawn or inhibited states may benefit from a short course of psychostimulant medication. Few, if any, cases of adjustment disorder can be adequately treated by medication alone. In most cases, psychotherapy should be added to the treatment regimen.

References

Newcorn J H, Strain J J: Adjustment disorders. In *Comprehensive Textbook of Psychiatry*, ed 6, H I Kaplan, B J Sadock, editors, p 1418. Williams & Wilkins, Baltimore, 1995.

Pollock D: Structured ambiguity and the definition of psychiatric illness: Adjustment among medical inpatients. Soc Sci Med *35*: 25, 1992.

Strain J W, Newcorn J, Wolf D, Fulop G, Davis W: Considering changes in adjustment disorder. Hosp Community Psychiatry *44*: 13, 1993.

20/ Personality Disorders

Personality can be defined as all emotional and behavioral traits that characterize the person in day-to-day living under ordinary conditions; it is relatively stable and predictable. A personality disorder is a variant of those character traits that goes beyond the range found in most people. Only when personality traits are inflexible and maladaptive and cause either significant functional impairment or subjective distress do they constitute a class of personality disorder. Patients with personality disorders show deeply ingrained, inflexible, and maladaptive patterns of relating to and perceiving both the environment and themselves.

Those persons are far more likely to refuse psychiatric help and to deny their problems than are persons with anxiety disorders, depressive disorders, or obsessive-compulsive disorder. Personality disorder symptoms are alloplastic (that is, capable of adapting and altering the external environment) and ego-syntonic (that is, acceptable to the ego); those with a personality disorder do not feel anxiety about their maladaptive behavior. Because such persons do not routinely acknowledge pain from what society perceives as their symptoms, they are often regarded as unmotivated for treatment and impervious to recovery.

CLASSIFICATION

The personality disorders are grouped into three clusters in the fourth edition of *Diagnostic and Statistical Manual of Mental Disorders* (DSM-IV). Cluster A comprises the paranoid, schizoid, and schizotypal personality disorders; persons with those disorders often seem odd and eccentric. Cluster B comprises the antisocial, borderline, histrionic, and narcissistic personality disorders; persons with those disorders often seem dramatic, emotional, and erratic. Cluster C comprises the avoidant, dependent, and obsessive-compulsive personality disorders and a category called personality disorder not otherwise specified (examples include passive-aggressive personality disorder and depressive personality disorder); persons with those disorders often seem anxious or fearful.

Many persons exhibit traits that are not limited to a single personality disorder. If a patient meets the criteria for more than one personality disorder, each should be diagnosed. Personality disorders are coded on Axis II of DSM-IV.

ETIOLOGY

Genetic Factors

The best evidence that genetic factors contribute to the genesis of personality disorders comes from the investigations of psychiatric disorders in 15,000 pairs of twins in the United States. Among monozygotic twins, the concordance for personality disorders was several times higher than that among dizygotic twins. Moreover, according to one study, on multiple measures of personality and temperament, occupational and leisure-time interests, and social attitudes, monozygotic twins reared apart are about as similar as are monozygotic twins reared together.

Cluster A personality disorders (paranoid, schizoid, and schizotypal) are more common in the biological relatives of schizophrenic patients than among control groups. Significantly more relatives with schizotypal personality disorder are found in the family histories of persons with schizophrenia than among control groups. Less correlation is found between paranoid or schizoid personality disorder and schizophrenia.

Cluster B personality disorders (antisocial, borderline, histrionic, and narcissistic) have a genetic base. Antisocial personality disorder is associated with alcohol use disorders. Depression is common in the family backgrounds of borderline personality disorder patients. Borderline personality disorder patients have more relatives with mood disorders than do control groups, and borderline personality disorder and mood disorder often coexist. A strong association is found between histrionic personality disorder and somatization disorder (Briquet's syndrome); patients with each disorder show an overlap of symptoms.

Cluster C personality disorders (avoidant, dependent, and obsessive-compulsive) may also have a genetic base. The avoidant personality disorder patient often has a high anxiety level. Obsessive-compulsive traits are more common in monozygotic twins than in dizygotic twins, and obsessive-compulsive personality disorder patients show some signs associated with depression—for example, shortened rapid eye movement (REM) latency period, abnormal dexamethasone-suppression test (DST) results.

Temperamental Factors

Temperamental factors identified in childhood may be associated with personality disorders in adulthood. For example, children who are temperamentally fearful may go on to have avoidant personality disorder.

Childhood central nervous system dysfunctions associated with soft neurological signs are most common in antisocial and borderline personality disorders. Children with minimal brain damage are at risk for personality disorders, particularly antisocial personality disorder.

Certain personality disorders may arise from poor parental fit—that is, a poor match between temperament and child-rearing practices. For example, an anxious child reared by an equally anxious mother is more vulnerable to a personality disorder than would be the same child raised by a tranquil mother. Stella Chess and Alexander Thomas referred to goodness of fit. Cultures that encourage aggression may unwittingly reinforce and thereby contribute to paranoid and antisocial personality disorders. The physical environment may also play a role. For example, an active young child may seem hyperactive if kept in a small closed apartment but might be normal in a large middle-class house with a fenced-in yard.

Biological Factors

HORMONES

Persons who show impulsive traits often also show increased levels of testosterone, 17-estradiol, and estrone. In nonhuman primates, androgens increase the likelihood of aggression and sexual behavior; however, the role of testosterone in human aggression is not clear. DST results are abnormal in some borderline personality disorder patients with depressive symptoms.

PLATELET MONOAMINE OXIDASE

Low platelet monoamine oxidase (MAO) levels have been associated with activity and sociability in monkeys. College students with low platelet MAO levels report spending more time in social activities than do students with high platelet MAO levels. Low platelet MAO levels have also been noted in some schizotypal patients.

SMOOTH PURSUIT EYE MOVEMENTS

Smooth pursuit eye movements are abnormal in persons with the traits of introversion, low self-esteem, and withdrawal and in patients with schizotypal personality disorder. Movements in those persons are saccadic (that is, jerky). Those findings have no clinical application, but they do indicate the role of inheritance.

NEUROTRANSMITTERS

Endorphins have effects similar to those of exogenous morphine, including analgesia and the suppression of arousal. High endogenous endorphin levels may be associated with a phlegmatic-passive person. Studies of personality traits and the dopaminergic and serotonergic systems indicate an arousal-activating function for those neurotransmitters. Levels of 5-hydroxyindoleacetic acid (5-HIAA), a metabolite of serotonin, are low in persons who attempt suicide and in patients who are impulsive and aggressive.

Raising serotonin levels with such serotonergic agents as fluoxetine (Prozac) may produce dramatic changes in some personality characteristics. Serotonin reduces depression, impulsivity, and rumination in many persons and can produce a sense of general well-being. Increased dopamine in the central nervous system, produced by certain psychostimulants (for example, amphetamines) can induce euphoria. The effects of neurotransmitters on personality traits have generated a great deal of interest and controversy about whether personality traits are inborn or acquired.

ELECTROPHYSIOLOGY

Changes in electrical conductance on the electroencephalogram (EEG) have been found in some patients with personality disorders, most commonly in the antisocial and borderline types, in which slow-wave activity is seen.

Psychoanalytic Factors

Sigmund Freud originally suggested that personality traits are related to a fixation at one of the psychosexual stages of development. For example, an oral character is passive and dependent because of being fixated at the oral stage, when the dependence on others for intake of food is prominent. Anal characters are stubborn, parsimonious, and highly conscientious because of struggles around toilet training during the anal period.

Subsequently, Wilhelm Reich coined the term ''character armor'' to describe characteristic defensive styles that persons use to protect themselves from internal impulses and from interpersonal anxiety in significant relationships. Reich's thinking has had a far-reaching influence on the contemporary conceptualization of personality and personality disorders. The unique stamp of personality on each human being is largely determined by that person's characteristic defense mechanisms. Each personality disorder in Axis II has a cluster of defenses that help a psychodynamic clinician recognize the type of character pathology present. For example, persons with paranoid personality disorder use projection; schizoid personality disorder is associated with withdrawal.

When defenses work effectively, patients with personality disorders can master feelings of anxiety, depression, anger, shame, and guilt, and other affects. Patients often view their behavior as *ego-syntonic*, meaning that it creates no distress for the patients themselves, although it may adversely affect others. The patients may also be reluctant to engage in a treatment process because their defenses are important in controlling unpleasant affects and they are not interested in giving up those defenses.

Another central feature of personality disorders is the patient's internal object relations. During development, particular patterns of the self in relation to others are internalized. Through introjection the child internalizes a parent or other significant person as an internal presence that continues to feel like an object, rather than the self. Through identification the patient internalizes parents and other persons so that the traits of the external object are incorporated into the self and the patient ''owns'' the traits. Those internal self-representations and object representations are crucial in personality development. Through externalization and projective identification, aspects of the self-representations and object representations are played out in interpersonal scenarios in which others are coerced into playing a role in the patient's internal life. Therefore, patients with personality disorders are also identified by particular patterns of interpersonal relatedness that stem from those internal object relations patterns.

DEFENSE MECHANISMS

To help patients with personality disorders, the psychiatrist needs to appreciate their underlying defenses. Defenses are unconscious mental processes that the ego uses to resolve conflicts among the four lodestars of the inner life—instinct (wish or need), reality, important people, and conscience. When defenses are most effective, especially in personality disorders, they can abolish anxiety and depression. Thus, a major reason that those with personality disorders are reluctant to alter their behavior is that to abandon a defense is to increase conscious anxiety and depression.

Although patients with personality disorders may be characterized by their most dominant or most rigid mechanism, each patient uses several defenses. Therefore, the management of the defense mechanisms used by patients with personality disorders is discussed here as a general topic, rather than under the specific disorders. Many formulations presented here in the language of psychoanalytic psychiatry can be translated into principles consistent with cognitive and behavioral approaches.

Fantasy

Many persons—especially eccentric, lonely, frightened persons who are often labeled schizoid—make extensive use of the defense of fantasy. They seek solace and satisfaction within themselves by creating imaginary lives, especially imaginary friends, within their minds. Often, such persons seem to be strikingly aloof. One needs to understand the unsociability of such persons as resting on a fear of intimacy, rather than to criticize them or feel rebuffed by their rejection. The therapist should maintain a quiet, reassuring, and considerate interest in them without insisting on reciprocal responses. Recognition of their fear of closeness and respect for their eccentric ways are useful.

Dissociation

Dissociation or denial consists of the replacement of unpleasant affects with pleasant ones. Frequent users of dissociation are often seen as dramatizing and as emotionally shallow; they may be labeled histrionic personalities. Their behavior is reminiscent of the stunts of anxious adolescents who, to erase anxiety, carelessly expose themselves to exciting dangers. Accepting such patients as exuberant and seductive is to miss their anxiety; however, confronting them with their vulnerabilities and defects is to make them still more defensive. Because they seek appreciation of their attractiveness and courage, the therapist should not be too reserved. While remaining calm and firm, the therapist should realize that those patients are often inadvertent liars. Patients who use dissociation benefit from having a chance to ventilate their own anxieties; in the process they may "remember" what they "forgot." Often, dissociation and denial are best dealt with by the therapist's using displacement. Thus, the clinician may talk with patients about the same affective issue but in a context of a less threatening circumstance. Empathy with such patients' denied affect without direct confrontation with the facts may allow the patients to raise the original topic themselves.

Isolation

Isolation is characteristic of the orderly, controlled person, often labeled an obsessive-compulsive personality, who, unlike the histrionic personality, remembers the truth in detail but without affect. In a crisis the patient may show an intensification of self-restraint, overformal social behavior, and obstinacy. The patient's quest for control may be annoying or boring to the clinician. Often, such patients respond well to precise, systematic, and rational explanations. They value efficiency, cleanliness, and punctuality as much as they do the clinician's effective responsiveness. Whenever possible, clinicians should allow such patients to control their own care, rather than engage in a battle of wills.

Projection

In projection the patients attribute their own unacknowledged feelings to others. Excessive faultfinding of the therapist and sensitivity to criticism are common. These patients are hypervigilant and collect what they perceive to be injustices. The therapist should not be defensive or engage in arguments. Instead, even minor mistakes by the examiner and the possibility of future difficulties should be frankly acknowledged. Strict honesty, concern for the patient's rights, and maintaining the same formal, concerned distance as with a patient using fantasy are helpful. Confrontation guarantees a lasting enemy and an early termination of the interview. The therapist need not agree with the patient's injustice collecting, though, but should ask if they can agree to disagree.

The technique of counterprojection is especially helpful. In that technique the clinician acknowledges and gives paranoid patients full credit for their feelings and for their perceptions. Further, the clinician neither disputes the patient's complaints nor reinforces them but acknowledges that the world the paranoid patient describes can be imagined. The interviewer can then talk about the real motives and feelings, although they are misattributed to someone else, and begin to cement an alliance with the patient.

Splitting

In splitting, the patient divides ambivalently regarded people, both past and present, into good people and bad people. For example, in an inpatient setting, some staff members are idealized, and others are uniformly disparaged. The effect of that defensive behavior on a hospital ward can be highly disruptive; it ultimately provokes the staff to turn against the patient. Splitting is best mastered if staff members anticipate the process, discuss it at staff meetings, and gently confront the patient with the fact that no one is all-good or all-bad.

Passive Aggression

In passive-aggressive defenses the anger is turned against the self: in psychoanalytic terminology it is most often termed masochism. It includes failure, procrastination, silly or provocative behavior, self-demeaning clowning, and frankly self-destructive behavior. The hostility in such behavior is never entirely concealed; indeed, the mechanism, as in wrist cutting, engenders such anger in others that they feel that they themselves have been assaulted and view the patient as a sadist, not a masochist. Passive aggression is best dealt with by trying to get the patients to ventilate their anger.

Acting Out

In acting out, direct expression through action of an unconscious wish or conflict avoids being conscious of either the idea or the affect that accompanies it. Tantrums, apparently motiveless assaults, child abuse, and pleasureless promiscuity are common examples. Because the behavior occurs outside reflective awareness, acting out often appears to the observer to be unaccompanied by guilt. Once acting out is not possible, the conflict behind the defense may be accessible. Faced with acting out, either aggressive or sexual, in an interview situation, the clinician must recognize (1) that the patient has lost control, (2) that anything the interviewer says will probably be misheard, and (3) that getting the patient's attention is of paramount importance. Depending on the circumstances, the clinician's response may be, "How can I help you if you keep screaming?" Or, if the patient's loss of control is escalating, "If you continue screaming, I'll leave." The interviewer who feels genuinely frightened of the patient can simply leave and ask for help, if necessary, from the police.

Projective Identification

The defense mechanism of projective identification is used mainly in borderline personality disorder. It consists of three steps: (1) an aspect of the self is projected onto someone else, (2) the projector tries to coerce the other person to identify with what has been projected, and (3) the recipient of the projection and the projector feel a sense of oneness or union.

PARANOID PERSONALITY DISORDER

Persons with paranoid personality disorder are characterized by longstanding suspiciousness and mistrust of people in general. They refuse responsibility for their own feelings and assign responsibility to others. They are often hostile, irritable, and angry. The bigot, the injustice collector, the pathologically jealous spouse, and the litigious crank often have paranoid personality disorder.

Epidemiology

The prevalence of paranoid personality disorder is 0.5 to 2.5 percent. Persons with the disorder rarely seek treatment themselves; when referred to treatment by a spouse or an employer, they can often pull themselves together and not appear to be distressed. Relatives of schizophrenic patients show a higher incidence of paranoid personality disorder than do controls. The disorder is more common in men than in women, and it does not appear to have a familial pattern. The incidence among homosexuals is no higher than usual, as was once thought, but it is believed to be higher among minority groups, immigrants, and the deaf than in the general population.

Table 20-1.   Diagnostic Criteria for Paranoid Personality Disorder

A. A pervasive distrust and suspiciousness of others such that their motives are interpreted as malevolent, beginning by early adulthood and present in a variety of contexts, as indicated by four (or more) of the following:

(1) suspects, without sufficient basis, that others are exploiting, harming, or deceiving him or her

(2) is preoccupied with unjustified doubts about the loyalty or trustworthiness of friends or associates

(3) is reluctant to confide in others because of unwarranted fear that the information will be used maliciously against him or her

(4) reads hidden demeaning or threatening meanings into benign remarks or events

(5) persistently bears grudges, i.e., is unforgiving of insults, injuries, or slights

(6) perceives attacks on his or her character or reputation that are not apparent to others and is quick to react angrily or to counterattack

(7) has recurrent suspicions, without justification, regarding fidelity of spouse or sexual partner

B. Does not occur exclusively during the course of schizophrenia, a mood disorder with psychotic features, or another psychotic disorder and is not due to the direct physiological effects of a general medical condition.

Table from DSM-IV, *Diagnostic and Statistical Manual of Mental Disorders*, ed 4. Copyright American Psychiatric Association, Washington, 1994. Used with permission.

Diagnosis

On psychiatric examination, patients with paranoid personality disorder may seem formal and baffled at having been required to seek psychiatric help. Muscular tension, an inability to relax, and a need to scan the environment for clues may be evident. The patient's affect is often humorless and serious. Although some premises of their arguments may be false, their speech is goal-directed and logical. Their thought content shows evidence of projection, prejudice, and occasional ideas of reference. The DSM-IV diagnostic criteria are listed in Table 20–1.

Clinical Features

The essential feature of paranoid personality disorder is a pervasive and unwarranted tendency—beginning by early adulthood and present in a variety of contexts—to interpret other people's actions as deliberately demeaning or threatening. Almost invariably, persons with the disorder expect to be exploited or harmed by others in some way. Frequently, they question, without justification, the loyalty or trustworthiness of friends or associates. Often, such persons are pathologically jealous, questioning without justification the fidelity of their spouses or sexual partners.

The patients externalize their own emotions and use the defense of projection—that is, they attribute to others the impulses and thoughts that they are unable to accept in themselves. Ideas of reference and logically defended illusions are common.

Patients with the disorder are affectively restricted and seem unemotional. They pride themselves on being rational and objective, but that is not the case. They lack warmth and are impressed with and pay close attention to power and rank, expressing disdain for those who are seen as weak, sickly, impaired, or defective in some way. In social situations, persons with paranoid personality disorder may appear businesslike and efficient, but they often generate fear or conflict in others.

Differential Diagnosis

Paranoid personality disorder can usually be differentiated from delusional disorder because fixed delusions are absent in paranoid personality disorder. It can be differentiated from paranoid schizophrenia because hallucinations and formal thought disorder are absent in the personality disorders. Paranoid personality disorder can be distinguished from borderline personality disorder because the paranoid patient is rarely as capable as the borderline patient is of overinvolved, tumultuous relationships with others. Paranoid patients lack the antisocial character's long history of antisocial behavior. Persons with schizoid personality disorder are withdrawn and aloof and do not have paranoid ideation.

Course and Prognosis

No adequate and systematic long-term studies of paranoid personality disorder have been conducted. In some persons the paranoid personality disorder is lifelong. In others it is a harbinger of schizophrenia. In still others, as they mature or as stress diminishes, paranoid traits give way to reaction formation, appropriate concern with morality, and altruistic concerns. In general, however, patients with paranoid personality disorder have lifelong problems working and living with others. Occupational and marital problems are common.

Treatment

Psychotherapy

Psychotherapy is the treatment of choice. Therapists should be straightforward in all their dealings with the patient. If a therapist is accused of some inconsistency or fault, such as lateness for an appointment, honesty and an apology are better than a defensive explanation. Therapists must remember that trust and toleration of intimacy are troubled areas for patients with the disorder. Individual psychotherapy thus requires a professional and not overly warm style from the therapist. Paranoid patients do not do well in group psychotherapy, nor are they likely to tolerate the intrusiveness of behavior therapy. The clinician's too zealous use of interpretation—especially interpretation concerning deep feelings of dependence, sexual concerns, and wishes for intimacy—significantly increases the patient's mistrust.

At times, the behavior of patients with paranoid personality disorder becomes so threatening that the therapist must control it or set limits on it. Delusional accusations must be dealt with realistically but gently and without humiliating the patient. Paranoid patients are profoundly frightened if they feel that those trying to help them are weak and helpless; therefore, therapists should never threaten to take over control unless they are both willing and able to do so.

Behavior therapy has been used to improve social skills and to diminish suspiciousness through role playing.

Pharmacotherapy

Pharmacotherapy is useful in dealing with agitation and anxiety. Frequently an antianxiety agent such as diazepam (Valium) is sufficient. It may be necessary to use an antipsychotic, such as thioridazine (Mellaril) or haloperidol (Haldol), in small dosages and for brief periods to manage severe agitation or quasidelusional thinking.

The antipsychotic drug pimozide (Orap) has been successfully used to reduce paranoid ideation in some patients.

SCHIZOID PERSONALITY DISORDER

Schizoid personality disorder is diagnosed in patients who display a lifelong pattern of social withdrawal. Their discomfort with human interaction, their introversion, and their bland, constricted affect are noteworthy. Persons with schizoid personality disorder are often seen by others as eccentric, isolated, or lonely.

Epidemiology

The prevalence of schizoid personality disorder is not clearly established. The disorder may affect 7.5 percent of the general population. The sex ratio of the disorder is unknown, although some studies report a 2 to 1 male-female ratio. Persons with the disorder tend to gravitate toward solitary jobs that involve almost no contact with others. Many prefer night work to day work, so that they do not have to deal with many people.

Diagnosis

On the initial psychiatric examination, patients with schizoid personality disorder may seem ill at ease. They rarely tolerate eye contact. The interviewer may surmise that such patients are eager for the interview to end. Their affect may be constricted, aloof, or inappropriately serious. Yet underneath the aloofness, the sensitive clinician may recognize fear. The patients find it difficult to act lightheartedly. Their efforts at humor may seem adolescent and off the mark. The patients' speech is goal-directed, but they are likely to give short answers to questions and avoid spontaneous conversation. Occasionally, they may use an unusual figure of speech, such as an odd metaphor. Their mental content may reveal an unwarranted sense of intimacy with people they do not know well or whom they have not seen for a long time. They may be fascinated with inanimate objects or metaphysical constructs. The patients' sensorium is intact, their memory functions well, and their proverb interpretations are abstract. The DSM-IV diagnostic criteria are listed in Table 20–2.

Table 20-2. Diagnostic Criteria for Schizoid Personality Disorder

A. A pervasive pattern of detachment from social relationships and a restricted range of expression of emotions in interpersonal settings, beginning by early adulthood and present in a variety of contexts, as indicated by four (or more) of the following:

(1) neither desires nor enjoys close relationships, including being part of a family
(2) almost always chooses solitary activities
(3) has little, if any, interest in having sexual experiences with another person
(4) takes pleasure in few, if any, activities
(5) lacks close friends or confidants other than first-degree relatives
(6) appears indifferent to the praise or criticism of others
(7) shows emotional coldness, detachment, or flattened affectivity

B. Does not occur exclusively during the course of schizophrenia, a mood disorder with psychotic features, another psychotic disorder, or a pervasive developmental disorder and is not due to the direct physiological effects of a general medical condition.

Clinical Features

Persons with schizoid personality disorder give an impression of being cold and aloof, and they display a remote reserve and a lack of involvement with everyday events and the concerns of others. They appear quiet, distant, seclusive, and unsociable. They may pursue their own lives with remarkably little need or longing for emotional ties with others. They are the last to catch on to changes in popular fashion.

The life histories of such persons reflect solitary interests and success at noncompetitive, lonely jobs that others find difficult to tolerate. Their sexual lives may exist exclusively in fantasy, and they may postpone mature sexuality indefinitely. Men may not marry because they are unable to achieve intimacy; women may passively agree to marry an aggressive man who wants the marriage. Usually, persons with schizoid personality disorder reveal a lifelong inability to express anger directly. They can invest enormous affective energy in nonhuman interests, such as mathematics and astronomy, and they may be very attached to animals. They are often engrossed in dietary and health fads, philosophical movements, and social improvement schemes, especially those that require no personal involvement.

Although persons with schizoid personality disorder appear to be self-absorbed and engaged in excessive daydreaming, they show no loss of capacity to recognize reality. Because aggressive acts are rarely included in their repertoire of usual responses, most threats, real or imagined, are dealt with by fantasied omnipotence or resignation. They are often seen as aloof; yet, at times, such persons can conceive, develop, and give to the world genuinely original, creative ideas.

Differential Diagnosis

In contrast to patients with schizophrenia and schizotypal personality disorder, patients with schizoid personality disorder do not have schizophrenic relatives, and they may have successful, if isolated, work histories. Schizophrenic patients also differ by exhibiting thought disorder or delusional thinking. Although they share many traits with schizoid personality disorder patients, those with paranoid personality disorder exhibit more social engagement, a history of aggressive verbal behavior, and a greater tendency to project their feelings onto others. If just as emotionally constricted, obsessive-compulsive and avoidant personality disorder patients experience loneliness as dysphoric, possess a richer history of past object relations, and do not engage as much in autistic reverie. Theoretically, the chief distinction between a schizotypal personality disorder patient and a schizoid personality disorder patient is that the schizotypal patient shows a greater similarity to the schizophrenic patient in oddities of perception, thought, behavior, and communication. Avoidant personality disorder patients are isolated but strongly wish to participate in activities, a characteristic absent in persons with schizoid personality disorder.

Course and Prognosis

The onset of schizoid personality disorder is usually in early childhood. Like all personality disorders, schizoid personality disorder is long-lasting but not necessarily lifelong. The proportion of patients who go on to schizophrenia is unknown.

Treatment

PSYCHOTHERAPY

The treatment of schizoid personality disorder patients is similar to that of those with paranoid personality disorder. However, schizoid patients' tendencies toward introspection are consistent with the psychotherapist's expectations, and schizoid patients may become devoted, if distant, patients. As trust develops, schizoid patients may, with great trepidation, reveal a plethora of fantasies, imaginary friends, and fears of unbearable dependence—even of merging with the therapist.

In group therapy settings, schizoid personality disorder patients may be silent for long periods; nonetheless, they do become involved. The patients should be protected against aggressive attack by group members regarding their proclivity for silence. With time the group members become important to schizoid patients and may provide the only social contact in their otherwise isolated existence.

PHARMACOTHERAPY

Pharmacotherapy with small dosages of antipsychotics, antidepressants, and psychostimulants has been effective in some patients.

SCHIZOTYPAL PERSONALITY DISORDER

Persons with schizotypal personality disorder are strikingly odd or strange, even to laypersons. Magical thinking, peculiar ideas, ideas of reference, illusions, and derealization are part of the schizotypal person's everyday world.

Epidemiology

This occurs in about 3 percent of the population. The sex ratio is unknown. There is a greater association of cases among the biological relatives of schizophrenic patients than among controls and a higher incidence among monozygotic twins than among dizygotic twins (33 percent versus 4 percent in one study).

Diagnosis

Schizotypal personality disorder is diagnosed based on the patients' peculiarities of thinking, behavior, and appearance. History taking may be difficult because of the patients' unusual way of communicating. The DSM-IV diagnostic criteria for schizotypal personality disorder are given in Table 20–3.

Clinical Features

In schizotypal personality disorder, thinking and communicating are disturbed. Like schizophrenic patients, persons with schizotypal personality disorder may not know their own feelings; yet they are exquisitely sensitive to detecting the feelings of others, especially negative affects like anger. They may be superstitious or claim clairvoyance. Their inner world may be filled with vivid imaginary relationships and childlike fears and fantasies. They may believe that they have special powers of thought and insight. Although frank thought disorder is absent, their speech may often require interpretation. They may admit that they have perceptual illusions or macropsia or that people appear to them as wooden and alike.

Table 20–3.   Diagnostic Criteria for Schizotypal Personality Disorder

A. A pervasive pattern of social and interpersonal deficits marked by acute discomfort with, and reduced capacity for, close relationships as well as by cognitive or perceptual distortions and eccentricities of behavior, beginning by early adulthood and present in a variety of contexts, as indicated by five (or more) of the following:

   (1) idea of reference (excluding delusions of reference)
   (2) odd beliefs or magical thinking that influences behavior and is inconsistent with subcultural norms (e.g., superstitiousness, belief in clairvoyance, telepathy, or ``sixth sense''; in children and adolescents, bizarre fantasies or preoccupations)
   (3) unusual perceptual experiences, including bodily illusions
   (4) odd thinking and speech (e.g., vague, circumstantial, metaphorical, overelaborate, or stereotyped)
   (5) suspiciousness or paranoid ideation
   (6) inappropriate or constricted affect
   (7) behavior or appearance that is odd, eccentric, or peculiar
   (8) lack of close friends or confidants other than first-degree relatives
   (9) excessive social anxiety that does not diminish with familiarity and tends to be associated with paranoid fears rather than negative judgments about self

B. Does not occur exclusively during the course of schizophrenia, a mood disorder with psychotic features, another psychotic disorder, or a pervasive developmental disorder.

Table from DSM-IV, *Diagnostic and Statistical Manual of Mental Disorders*, ed 4. Copyright American Psychiatric Association, Washington, 1994. Used with permission.

The speech of persons with schizotypal personality disorder may be odd or peculiar and have meaning only to them. They show poor interpersonal relationships and may act inappropriately. As a result, they are isolated and have few, if any, friends. The patients may show features of borderline personality disorder, and, indeed, both diagnoses can be made. Under stress, schizotypal personality disorder patients may decompensate and have psychotic symptoms, but the symptoms are usually of brief duration. In severe cases, anhedonia and severe depression may be present.

Differential Diagnosis

Theoretically, those with schizotypal personality disorder can be distinguished from schizotypal and avoidant personality disorder patients by the presence of oddities in their behavior, thinking, perception, and communication and perhaps by a clear family history of schizophrenia. Schizotypal personality disorder patients can be distinguished from schizophrenic patients by their absence of psychosis. If psychosis symptoms do appear, they are brief and fragmentary. Some patients meet the criteria for both schizotypal personality disorder and borderline personality disorder. The paranoid personality disorder patient is characterized by suspiciousness but lacks the odd behavior of the schizotypal personality disorder patient.

Course and Prognosis

A long-term study by Thomas McGlashan reported that 10 percent of persons with schizotypal personality disorder eventually committed suicide. Retrospective studies have shown that many patients thought to have been suffering from schizophrenia actually had schizotypal personality disorder, and the current clinical thinking is that the schizotype is the premorbid personality of the schizophrenic patient. Many patients, however, maintain a stable schizotypal personality throughout their lives and marry and work in spite of their oddities.

Treatment

PSYCHOTHERAPY

The principles of treatment of schizotypal personality disorder should be no different from those of schizoid personality disorder. However, the odd and peculiar thinking of schizotypal personality disorder patients must be handled carefully. Some patients are involved in cults, strange religious practices, and the occult. Therapists must not ridicule such activities or be judgmental about those beliefs or activities.

PHARMACOTHERAPY

Antipsychotic medication may be useful in dealing with ideas of reference, illusions, and other symptoms of the disorder and can be used in conjunction with psychotherapy. Positive results have been reported with haloperidol. Antidepressants are of use when a depressive component of the personality is present.

ANTISOCIAL PERSONALITY DISORDER

Antisocial personality disorder is characterized by continual antisocial or criminal acts, but it is not synonymous with criminality. Instead, it is an inability to conform to social norms that involves many aspects of the patient's adolescent and adult development. In the 10th revision of the International Classification of Diseases and Related Health Problems (ICD-10), the disorder is called dissocial personality disorder.

Epidemiology

The prevalence of antisocial personality disorder is 3 percent in men and 1 percent in women. It is most common in poor urban areas and among mobile residents of those areas. Boys with the disorder come from larger families than do girls with the disorders. The onset of the disorder is before the age of 15. Girls usually have symptoms before puberty, and boys even earlier. In prison populations the prevalence of antisocial personality disorder may be as high as 75 percent. A familial pattern is present in that it is five times more common among first-degree relatives of males with the disorder than among controls.

Diagnosis

The patients may appear composed and credible in the interview. However, beneath the veneer (or, to use Hervey Cleckley's term, the mask of sanity) there is tension, hostility, irritability, and rage. Stress interview, in which patients are vigorously confronted with inconsistencies in their histories, may be necessary to reveal the pathology. Even the most experienced clinicians have been fooled by such patients.

A diagnostic workup should include a thorough neurological examination. Because the patients often show abnormal EEG results and soft neurological signs suggesting minimal brain damage in childhood, those findings can be used to confirm the

Table 20-4. Diagnostic Criteria for Antisocial Personality Disorder

A. There is a pervasive pattern of disregard for and violation of the rights of others occurring since age 15 years, as indicated by three (or more) of the following:

    (1) failure to conform to social norms with respect to lawful behaviors as indicated by repeatedly performing acts that are grounds for arrest

    (2) deceitfulness, as indicated by repeated lying, use of aliases, or conning others for personal profit or pleasure

    (3) impulsivity or failure to plan ahead

    (4) irritability and aggressiveness, as indicated by repeated physical fights or assaults

    (5) reckless disregard for safety of self or others

    (6) consistent irresponsibility, as indicated by repeated failure to sustain consistent work behavior or honor financial obligations

    (7) lack of remorse, as indicated by being indifferent to or rationalizing having hurt, mistreated, or stolen from another

B. The individual is at least age 18 years.

C. There is evidence of conduct disorder with onset before age 15 years.

D. The occurrence of antisocial behavior is not exclusively during the course of schizophrenia or a manic episode.

Table from DSM-IV, *Diagnostic and Statistical Manual of Mental Disorders*, ed 4. Copyright American Psychiatric Association, Washington, 1994. Used with permission.

clinical impression. The DSM-IV diagnostic criteria are listed in Table 20–4.

Clinical Features

Patients with antisocial personality disorder often present a normal and even a charming and ingratiating exterior. Their histories, however, reveal many areas of disordered life functioning. Lying, truancy, running away from home, thefts, fights, substance abuse, and illegal activities are typical experiences that the patients report as beginning in childhood. Often, antisocial personality disorder patients impress opposite-sex clinicians with the colorful, seductive aspects of their personalities, but same-sex clinicians may regard them as manipulative and demanding. Antisocial personality disorder patients show a lack of anxiety or depression that may seem grossly incongruous with their situations, and their own explanations of their antisocial behavior seem mindless. Suicide threats and somatic preoccupations may be common. Nevertheless, the patient's mental content reveals the complete absence of delusions and other signs of irrational thinking. In fact, they frequently have a heightened sense of reality testing. They often impress observers as having good verbal intelligence.

Antisocial personality disorder patients are highly represented by so-called con men. They are highly manipulative and are frequently able to convince others to participate in schemes that involve easy ways to make money or achieve fame or notoriety, which may eventually lead the unwary to financial ruin, social embarrassment, or both. Antisocial personality disorder patients do not tell the truth and cannot be trusted to carry out any task or follow any conventional standard of morality. Promiscuity, spouse abuse, child abuse, and drunk driving are common events in the patients' lives. A notable finding is a lack of remorse for those actions; that is, the patients appear to lack a conscience.

Differential Diagnosis

Antisocial personality disorder can be distinguished from illegal behavior in that antisocial personality disorder involves many areas of the person's life. If antisocial behavior is the only manifestation, the patients are put in the DSM-IV category of additional conditions that may be a focus of clinical attention—specifically, adult antisocial behavior. Dorothy Lewis found that many of those persons have a neurological or mental disorder that has been either overlooked or not diagnosed. More difficult is the differentiation of antisocial personality disorder from substance abuse. When both substance abuse and antisocial behavior begin in childhood and continue into adult life, both disorders should be diagnosed. When, however, the antisocial behavior is clearly secondary to premorbid alcohol abuse or other substance abuse, the diagnosis of antisocial personality disorder is not warranted.

In diagnosing antisocial personality disorder, the clinician must adjust for the distorting effects of socioeconomic status, cultural background, and sex on its manifestations. Furthermore, the diagnosis of antisocial personality disorder is not warranted if mental retardation, schizophrenia, or mania can explain the symptoms.

Course and Prognosis

Once an antisocial personality disorder develops, it runs an unremitting course, with the height of antisocial behavior usually occurring in late adolescence. The prognosis is variable. Some reports indicate that symptoms decrease as patients grow older. Many patients have somatization disorder and multiple physical complaints. Depressive disorders, alcohol use disorders, and other substance abuse are common.

Treatment

PSYCHOTHERAPY

If antisocial personality disorder patients are immobilized (for example, placed in hospitals), they often become amenable to psychotherapy. When the patients feel that they are among peers, like lack of motivation for change disappears. Perhaps that is why self-help groups have been more useful than jails in alleviating the disorder.

Before treatment can begin, firm limits are essential. The therapist must find some way of dealing with the patient's self-destructive behavior. To overcome the antisocial personality disorder patient's fear of intimacy, the therapist must frustrate the patient's wish to run from honest human encounters. In doing so, the therapist faces the challenge of separating control from punishment and of separating help and confrontation from social isolation and retribution.

PHARMACOTHERAPY

Pharmacotherapy is used to deal with incapacitating symptoms—such as anxiety, rage, and depression—but, because the patients are often substance abusers, drugs must be used judiciously. If the patient shows evidence of attention-deficit/hyperactivity disorder, psychostimulants, such as methylphenidate (Ritalin), may be of use. Attempts have been made to alter catecholamine metabolism with drugs and to control impulsive behavior with antiepileptic drugs, especially if abnormal wave forms are noted on an EEG.

BORDERLINE PERSONALITY DISORDER

Borderline personality disorder patients stand on the border between neurosis and psychosis and are characterized by extraordinarily unstable affect, mood, behavior, object relations, and self-image. The disorder has also been called ambulatory schizophrenia, as-if personality (a term coined by Helene Deutsch), pseudoneurotic schizophrenia (described by Paul Hoch and Phillip Politan), and psychotic character (described by John Frosch). In ICD-10 it is called emotionally unstable personality disorder.

Epidemiology

No definitive prevalence studies are available, but borderline personality disorder is thought to be present in about 1 to 2 percent of the population and is twice as common in women as in men. An increased prevalence of major depressive disorder, alcohol use disorders, and substance abuse is found in first-degree relatives of persons with borderline personality disorder.

Diagnosis

According to DSM-IV, the diagnosis of borderline personality disorder can be made by early adulthood when the patient shows at least five of the criteria listed in Table 20–5.

Biological studies may aid in the diagnosis, as some borderline personality disorder patients show shortened rapid eye movement (REM) latency and sleep continuity disturbances, abnormal dexamethasone-suppression test results, and abnormal thyrotropin-releasing hormone test results. However, those changes are also seen in some cases of depressive disorders.

Clinical Features

Borderline personality disorder patients almost always appear to be in a state of crisis. Mood swings are common. The

Table 20–5.   Diagnostic Criteria for Borderline Personality Disorder

A pervasive pattern of instability of interpersonal relationships, self-image, and affects, and marked impulsivity beginning by early adulthood and present in a variety of contexts, as indicated by five (or more) of the following:

  (1) frantic efforts to avoid real or imagined abandonment. **Note:** Do not include suicidal or self-mutilating behavior covered in Criterion 5.
  (2) a pattern of unstable and intense interpersonal relationships characterized by alternating between extremes of idealization and devaluation
  (3) identity disturbance: markedly and persistently unstable self-image or sense of self
  (4) impulsivity in at least two areas that are potentially self-damaging (e.g., spending, sex, substance abuse, reckless driving, binge eating). **Note:** Do not include suicidal or self-mutilating behavior covered in criterion 5.
  (5) recurrent suicidal behavior, gestures, or threats, or self-mutilating behavior
  (6) affective instability due to a marked reactivity of mood (e.g., intense episodic dysphoria, irritability, or anxiety usually lasting a few hours and only rarely more than a few days)
  (7) chronic feelings of emptiness
  (8) inappropriate, intense anger or difficulty controlling anger (e.g., frequent displays of temper, constant anger, recurrent physical fights)
  (9) transient, stress-related paranoid ideation or severe dissociative symptoms

Table from DSM-IV, *Diagnostic and Statistical Manual of Mental Disorders*, ed 4. Copyright American Psychiatric Association, Washington, 1994. Used with permission.

patients can be argumentative at one moment and depressed at the next and then complain of having no feelings at another time.

The patients may have short-lived psychotic episodes (so-called micropsychotic episodes), rather than full-blown psychotic breaks, and the psychotic symptoms of borderline personality disorder patients are almost always circumscribed, fleeting, or in doubt. The behavior of borderline personality disorder patients is highly unpredictable; consequently, they rarely achieve up to the level of their abilities. The painful nature of their lives is reflected in repetitive self-destructive acts. Such patients may slash their wrists and perform other self-mutilations to elicit help from others, to express anger, or to numb themselves to overwhelming affect.

Because they feel both dependent and hostile, borderline personality disorder patients have tumultuous interpersonal relationships. They can be dependent on those to whom they are close, and they can express enormous anger at their intimate friends when frustrated. However, borderline personality disorder patients cannot tolerate being alone, and they prefer a frantic search for companionship, no matter how unsatisfactory, to sitting by themselves. To assuage loneliness, if only for brief periods, they accept a stranger as a friend or are promiscuous. They often complain about chronic feelings of emptiness and boredom and the lack of a consistent sense of identify *(identity diffusion)*; when pressed, they often complain about how depressed they feel most of the time is spite of the flurry of other affects.

Otto Kernberg described the defense mechanism of projective identification used in borderline personality disorder patients. In that primitive defense mechanism, intolerable aspects of the self are projected onto another person. The other person is induced to play the role of what is projected, and the two persons act in unison. Therapists must be aware of the process so that they can act neutrally toward such patients.

Most therapists agree that borderline personality disorder patients show ordinary reasoning abilities on structured tests, such as the Wechsler Adult Intelligence Scale, and show deviant processes only on unstructured projective tests, such as the Rorschach test.

Functionally, borderline personality disorder patients distort their present relationships by putting every person into either an all-good or an all-bad category. They see people as either nurturant and attachment figures or hateful and sadistic persons who deprive them of security needs and threaten them with abandonment whenever they feel dependent. Because of that splitting, the good person is idealized, and the bad person is devalued. Shifts of allegiance from one person or group to another are frequent.

Some clinicians use the concepts of panphobia, pananxiety, panambivalence, and chaotic sexuality to delineate the borderline personality disorder patient's characteristics.

Differential Diagnosis

The differentiation from schizophrenia is made based on the borderline patient's having no prolonged psychotic episodes, thought disorder, or other classic schizophrenic signs. Schizotypal personality disorder patients show marked peculiarities of thinking, strange ideation, and recurrent ideas of reference. Paranoid personality disorder patients are marked by extreme suspiciousness. Histrionic and antisocial personality disorder patients are difficult to distinguish from borderline personality disorder patients. In general, the borderline personality disorder patient shows chronic feelings of emptiness, impulsivity, self-mutilation, short-lived psychotic episodes, manipulative suicide attempts, and unusually demanding involvement in close relationships.

Course and Prognosis

The disorder is fairly stable in that patients change little over time. Longitudinal studies do not show a progression toward schizophrenia, but the patients have a high incidence of major depressive disorder episodes. The diagnosis is usually made before the age of 40, when the patients are attempting to make occupational, marital, and other choices and are unable to deal with the normal stages in the life cycle.

Treatment

PSYCHOTHERAPY

Psychotherapy for borderline personality disorder patients is an area of intensive investigation and has been the treatment of choice. Recently, pharmacotherapy has been added to the treatment regimen.

Psychotherapy is difficult for patient and therapist alike. Regression occurs easily in borderline personality disorder patients, who act out their impulses and show labile or fixed negative or positive transferences, which are difficult to analyze. Projective identification may also cause countertransference problems if the therapist is unaware that the patient is unconsciously trying to coerce the therapist to act out a particular type of behavior. Splitting as a defense mechanism causes the patient to alternately love and hate the therapist and others in the environment. A reality-oriented approach is more effective than in-depth interpretations of the unconscious.

Behavior therapy has been used with borderline personality disorder patients to control impulses and angry outbursts and to reduce sensitivity to criticism and rejection. Social skills training, especially with videotape playback, is helpful to enable patients to see how their actions affect others and thereby to improve their interpersonal behavior.

Borderline personality disorder patients often do well in a hospital setting in which they receive intensive psychotherapy on both an individual basis and a group basis. They also interact with trained staff members from a variety of disciplines and are provided with occupational, recreational, and vocational therapy. Such programs are especially helpful if the home environment is detrimental to the patient's rehabilitation because of intrafamilial conflicts or other stresses, such as parental abuse. The borderline personality disorder patient who is excessively impulsive, self-destructive, or self-mutilating can be provided with limits and observation within the protected environment of the hospital. Under ideal circumstances, patients remain in the hospital until they show marked improvement, which may take up to one year in some cases. Patients can then be discharged to special support systems, such as day hospitals, night hospitals, and halfway houses.

PHARMACOTHERAPY

Pharmacotherapy for borderline personality disorder is useful to deal with specific personality features that interfere with the patients' overall functioning. Antipsychotics have been used to control anger, hostility, and brief psychotic episodes. Antidepressants improve the depressed mood that is common in the patients. The MAO inhibitors (MAOIs) have been effective in modulating impulsive behavior in some patients. Benzodiazepines, particularly alprazolam (Xanax), help anxiety and depression, but some patients show a disinhibition with that class of drugs. Anticonvulsants, such as carbamazepine (Tegretol), may improve global functioning in some patients. Serotonergic agents, such as fluoxetine, have been helpful in some cases.

HISTRIONIC PERSONALITY DISORDER

Histrionic personality disorder is characterized by colorful, dramatic, extroverted behavior in excitable, emotional persons. Accompanying their flamboyant presentations, however, is often an inability to maintain deep, long-lasting attachments.

Epidemiology

According to DSM-IV, limited data from general population studies suggest a prevalence of histrionic personality disorder of about 2 to 3 percent. Rates of about 10 to 15 percent have been reported in inpatient and outpatient mental health settings when structured assessment is used. It is diagnosed more frequently in women than in men. Some studies have found an association with somatization disorder and alcohol use disorders.

Diagnosis

In the interview, histrionic personality disorder patients are generally cooperative and eager to give a detailed history. Gestures and dramatic punctuation in their conversations are common. They may make frequent slips of the tongue, and their language is colorful. Affective display is common, but, when pressed to acknowledge certain feelings (such as anger, sadness, and sexual wishes), they may respond with surprise, indignation, or denial. The results of the cognitive examination are usually normal, although a lack of perseverance may be shown on arithmetic or concentration tasks, and the patients' forgetfulness of affect-laden material may be astonishing. The DSM-IV diagnostic criteria are listed in Table 20–6.

Table 20–6. Diagnostic Criteria for Histrionic Personality Disorder

A pervasive pattern of excessive emotionality and attention seeking, beginning by early adulthood and present in a variety of contexts, as indicated by five (or more) of the following:

(1) is uncomfortable in situations in which he or she is not the center of attention
(2) interaction with others is often characterized by inappropriate sexually seductive or provocative behavior
(3) displays rapidly shifting and shallow expression of emotions
(4) consistently uses physical appearance to draw attention to self
(5) has a style of speech that is excessively impressionistic and lacking in detail
(6) shows self-dramatization, theatricality, and exaggerated expression of emotion
(7) is suggestible, i.e., easily influenced by others or circumstances
(8) considers relationships to be more intimate than they actually are

Table from DSM-IV, *Diagnostic and Statistical Manual of Mental Disorders*, ed 4. Copyright American Psychiatric Association, Washington, 1994. Used with permission.

Clinical Features

Patients with histrionic personality disorder show a high degree of attention-seeking behavior. They tend to exaggerate their thoughts and feelings, making everything sound more important than it really is. They display temper tantrums, tears, and accusations if they are not center of attention or are not receiving praise or approval.

Seductive behavior is common in both sexes. Sexual fantasies about persons with whom the patients are involved are common, but the patients are inconsistent about verbalizing those fantasies and may be coy or flirtatious, rather than sexually aggressive. In fact, histrionic patients may have a psychosexual dysfunction: the women may be anorgasmic, and the men may be impotent. They may act on their sexual impulses to reassure themselves that they are attractive to the other sex. Their need for reassurance is endless. Their relationships tend to be superficial, however, and the patients can be vain, self-absorbed, and fickle. Their strong dependence needs make them overly trusting and gullible.

The major defenses of histrionic personality disorder patients are repression and dissociation. Accordingly, such patients are unaware of their true feeling and are unable to explain their motivations. Under stress, reality testing easily becomes impaired.

Differential Diagnosis

The distinction between histrionic personality disorder and borderline personality disorder is difficult. In borderline personality disorder, suicide attempts, identity diffusion, and brief psychotic episodes are more likely. Although both conditions may be diagnosed in the same patient, the clinician should separate the two. Somatization disorder (Briquet's syndrome) may occur with histrionic personality disorder. Patients with brief psychotic disorder and dissociative disorders may warrant a coexisting diagnosis of histrionic personality disorder.

Course and Prognosis

With age, patients with histrionic personality disorder tend to show fewer symptoms, but because they lack the same energy they had when younger, that difference may be more apparent than real. The patients are sensation seekers and may get into trouble with the law, abuse substances, and act promiscuously.

Treatment

PSYCHOTHERAPY

Patients with histrionic personality disorder are often unaware of their own real feelings; therefore, clarification of those feelings is an important therapeutic process. Psychoanalytically oriented psychotherapy, whether group or individual, is probably the treatment of choice for histrionic personality disorder.

PHARMACOTHERAPY

Pharmacotherapy can be adjunctive when symptoms are targeted—for example, use of antidepressants for depression and somatic complaints, antianxiety agents for anxiety, and antipsychotics for derealization and illusions.

NARCISSISTIC PERSONALITY DISORDER

Persons with narcissistic personality disorder are characterized by a heightened sense of self-importance and grandiose feelings that they are unique in some way.

Epidemiology

According to DSM-IV, estimates of prevalence of narcissistic personality disorder range from 2 to 16 percent in the clinical population and are less than 1 percent in the general population. There may be a higher than usual risk in the offspring of parents with the disorder who impart to their children an unrealistic sense of omnipotence, grandiosity, beauty, and talent. The number of cases reported is increasing steadily.

Diagnosis

Table 20–7 gives the DSM-IV diagnostic criteria for narcissistic personality disorder.

Clinical Features

Persons with narcissistic personality disorder have a grandiose sense of self-importance. They consider themselves special people and expect special treatment. They handle criticism poorly and may become enraged that anyone would dare to criticize them, or they may appear to be completely indifferent to criticism. They want their own way and are frequently ambitious, desiring fame and fortune. Their sense of entitlement is striking. Their relationships are fragile, and they can make others furious because they refuse to obey the conventional rules of behavior. They are unable to show empathy, and they feign sympathy only to achieve their selfish ends. Interpersonal exploitiveness is commonplace. The patients have fragile self-esteem and are prone to depression. Interpersonal difficulties, rejection, loss, and occupational problems are among the

Table 20-7.   Diagnostic Criteria for Narcissistic Personality Disorder

A pervasive pattern of grandiosity (in fantasy or behavior), need for admiration, and lack of empathy, beginning by early adulthood and present in a variety of contexts, as indicated by five (or more) of the following:

(1) has a grandiose sense of self-importance (e.g., exaggerates achievements and talents, expects to be recognized as superior without commensurate achievements)
(2) is preoccupied with fantasies of unlimited success, power, brilliance, beauty, or ideal love
(3) believes that he or she is ''special'' and unique and can only be understood by, or should associate with, other special or high-status people (or institutions)
(4) requires excessive admiration
(5) has a sense of entitlement, i.e., unreasonable expectations of especially favorable treatment or automatic compliance with his or her expectations
(6) is interpersonally exploitative, i.e., takes advantage of others to achieve his or her own ends
(7) lacks empathy: is unwilling to recognize or identify with the feelings and needs of others
(8) is often envious of others or believes that others are envious of him or her
(9) shows arrogant, haughty behaviors or attitudes

stresses that narcissists commonly produce by their behavior—stresses they are least able to handle.

Differential Diagnosis

Borderline, histrionic, and antisocial personality disorders are often present with narcissistic personality disorder, which means that a differential diagnosis is difficult. Patients with narcissistic personality disorder have less anxiety than do patients with borderline personality disorder, and their lives tend to be less chaotic. Suicidal attempts are also more likely to be associated with borderline personality disorder patients than with narcissistic personality disorder patients. Antisocial personality disorder patients give a history of impulsive behavior, often associated with alcohol or other substance abuse, that frequently gets them into trouble with the law. Histrionic personality disorder patients show features of exhibitionism and interpersonal manipulativeness that are similar to those of narcissistic personality disorder patients.

Course and Prognosis

Narcissistic personality disorder is chronic and difficult to treat. Patients with the disorder must constantly deal with blows to their narcissism resulting from their own behavior or from life experience. Aging is handled poorly, as the patient values beauty, strength, and youthful attributes, to which they cling inappropriately. They may be more vulnerable, therefore, to midlife crises than are other groups.

Treatment

PSYCHOTHERAPY

The treatment of narcissistic personality disorder is difficult, as the patients must renounce their narcissism if progress is to be made. Psychiatrists such as Otto Kernberg and Heinz Kohut advocate using psychoanalytic approaches to effect change; however, much research is required to validate the diagnosis and to determine the best treatment.

PHARMACOTHERAPY

Lithium (Eskalith) has been used with patients who have mood swings as part of the clinical picture. Because narcissistic personality disorder patients tolerate rejection poorly and are prone to depression, antidepressants may also be of use.

AVOIDANT PERSONALITY DISORDER

Persons with avoidant personality disorder show an extreme sensitivity to rejection, which may lead to a socially withdrawn life. They are not asocial and show a great desire for companionship but are shy; they need unusually strong guarantees of uncritical acceptance. Such persons are commonly referred to as having an inferiority complex. In ICD-10 the patients are classified as having anxious personality disorder.

Epidemiology

The prevalence of avoidant personality disorder is 1 to 10 percent; as defined, it is common. No information is available on sex ratio or familial pattern. Infants classified as having a

Table 20-8.   Diagnostic Criteria for Avoidant Personality Disorder

A pervasive pattern of social inhibition, feelings of inadequacy, and hypersensitivity to negative evaluation, beginning by early adulthood and present in a variety of contexts, as indicated by four (or more) of the following:

(1) avoids occupational activities that involve significant interpersonal contact, because of fears of criticism, disapproval, or rejection
(2) is unwilling to get involved with people unless certain of being liked
(3) shows restraint within intimate relationships because of the fear of being shamed or ridiculed
(4) is preoccupied with being criticized or rejected in social situations
(5) is inhibited in new interpersonal situations because of feelings of inadequacy
(6) views self as socially inept, personally unappealing, or inferior to others
(7) is unusually reluctant to take personal risks or to engage in any new activities because they may prove embarrassing

Table from DSM-IV, *Diagnostic and Statistical Manual of Mental Disorders*, ed 4. Copyright American Psychiatric Association, Washington, 1994. Used with permission.

timid temperament may be more prone to the disorder than are those high on activity-approach scales.

Diagnosis

In clinical interviews the most striking aspect is the patients' anxiety about talking with the interviewer. The patients' nervous and tense manner appears to wax and wane with their perception of whether the interviewer likes them. They seem vulnerable to the interviewer's comments and suggestions and may regard a clarification or an interpretation as a criticism. The DSM-IV diagnostic criteria for avoidant personality disorder are listed in Table 20-8.

Clinical Features

Hypersensitivity to rejection by others is the central clinical feature of avoidant personality disorder. Persons with the disorder desire the warmth and security of human companionship but justify their avoidance of forming relationships by their alleged fear of rejection. When talking with someone, they express uncertainty and a lack of self-confidence and may speak in a self-effacing manner. They are afraid to speak up in public or to make requests of others, because they are hypervigilant about rejection. They are apt to misinterpret another person's comments as derogatory or ridiculing. The refusal of any request leads them to withdraw from others and to feel hurt.

In the vocational sphere, avoidant personality disorder patients often take jobs on the sidelines. They rarely attain much personal advancement or exercise much authority. Instead, at work they may seem simply shy and eager to please.

Persons with the disorder are generally unwilling to enter relationships unless they are given an unusually strong guarantee of uncritical acceptance. Consequently, they often have no close friends or confidants. In general, their main personality trait is timidity.

Differential Diagnosis

Avoidant personality disorder patients desire social interaction, compared with schizoid personality disorder patients, who

want to be alone. Avoidant personality disorder patients are not as demanding, irritable, or unpredictable as are borderline and histrionic personality disorder patients. Avoidant personality disorder and dependent personality disorder are similar. The dependent personality disorder patient is presumed to have a greater fear of being abandoned or not loved than does the avoidant personality disorder patient; however, the clinical picture may be indistinguishable.

Course and Prognosis

Many avoidant personality disorder patients can function, provided they are in a protected environment. Some marry, have children, and live their lives surrounded only by family members. Should their support system fail, however, they are subject to depression, anxiety, and anger. Phobic avoidance is common, and avoidant personality disorder patients may give histories of social phobia or go on to social phobia during their illness.

Treatment

PSYCHOTHERAPY

Psychotherapeutic treatment depends on solidifying an alliance with the patient. As trust develops, the therapist conveys an accepting attitude toward the patient's fears, especially the fear of rejection. The therapist eventually encourages the patient to move out into the world to take what are perceived as great risks of humiliation, rejection, and failure. Nevertheless, the therapist should be cautious when giving assignments to exercise new social skills outside therapy, because failure may reinforce the patient's already poor self-esteem. Group therapy may help patients understand the effect that their sensitivity to rejection has on themselves and others. Assertiveness training is a form of behavior therapy that may teach patients to express their needs openly and to improve their self-esteem.

PHARMACOTHERAPY

Pharmacotherapy has been used to manage anxiety and depression when present as associated features. Some patients are helped by β-blockers, such as atenolol (Tenormin), to manage autonomic nervous system hyperactivity, which tends to be high in patients with avoidant personality disorder, especially when they approach feared situations.

DEPENDENT PERSONALITY DISORDER

Persons with dependent personality disorder subordinate their own needs to those of others, get others to assume responsibility for major areas in their lives, lack self-confidence, and may experience intense discomfort when alone for more than a brief period. In the first edition of *Diagnostic and Statistical Manual of Mental Disorders* (DSM-I), the condition was called passive-dependent personality. Freud described an oral-dependent dimension to personality characterized by dependence, pessimism, fear of sexuality, self-doubt, passivity, suggestibility, and lack of perseverance, which is similar to the DSM-IV categorization of dependent personality disorder.

Epidemiology

Dependent personality disorder is more common in women than in men. One study diagnosed 2.5 percent of all personality

Table 20–9.   Diagnostic Criteria for Dependent Personality Disorder

A pervasive and excessive need to be taken care of that leads to submissive and clinging behavior and fears of separation, beginning by early adulthood and present in a variety of contexts, as indicated by five (or more) of the following:

(1) has difficulty making everyday decisions without an excessive amount of advice and reassurance from others
(2) needs others to assume responsibility for most major areas of his or her life
(3) has difficulty expressing disagreement with others because of fear of loss of support or approval. **Note:** Do not include realistic fears of retribution.
(4) has difficulty initiating projects or doing things on his or her own (because of a lack of self-confidence in judgment or abilities rather than a lack of motivation or energy)
(5) goes to excessive lengths to obtain nurturance and support from others, to the point of volunteering to do things that are unpleasant
(6) feels uncomfortable or helpless when alone because of exaggerated fears of being unable to care for himself or herself
(7) urgently seeks another relationship as a source of care and support when a close relationship ends
(8) is unrealistically preoccupied with fears of being left to take care of himself or herself

Table from DSM-IV, *Diagnostic and Statistical Manual of Mental Disorders*, ed 4. Copyright American Psychiatric Association, Washington, 1994. Used with permission.

disorders as falling into that category. It is more common in young children than in older children. Persons with chronic physical illness in childhood may be most prone to the disorder.

Diagnosis

In the interview the patients appear to be compliant. They try to cooperate, welcome specific questions, and look for guidance. The DSM-IV diagnostic criteria for dependent personality disorder are listed in Table 20–9.

Clinical Features

Dependent personality disorder is characterized by a pervasive pattern of dependent and submissive behavior. Persons with the disorder are unable to make decisions without an excessive amount of advice and reassurance from others.

Dependent personality disorder patients avoid positions of responsibility and become anxious if asked to assume a leadership role. They prefer to be submissive. When on their own, they find it difficult to persevere at tasks but may find it easy to perform those tasks for someone else.

Persons with the disorder do not like to be alone. They seek out others on whom they can depend, and their relationships are thus distorted by their need to be attached to that other person. In *folie à deux* (shared psychotic disorder), one member of the pair is usually suffering from dependent personality disorder. The submissive person takes on the delusional system of the more aggressive, assertive person on whom he or she is dependent.

Pessimism, self-doubt, passivity, and fears of expressing sexual and aggressive feelings characterize the behavior of the dependent personality disorder patient. An abusive, unfaithful, or alcoholic spouse may be tolerated for long periods in order not to disturb the sense of attachment.

Differential Diagnosis

The traits of dependence are found in many psychiatric disorders, which makes the differential diagnosis difficult. Dependence is a prominent factor in histrionic and borderline personality disorder patients; however, dependent personality disorder patients usually have a longstanding relationship with one person on whom they are dependent, rather than on a series of persons, and they do not tend to be overtly manipulative.

Dependent behavior may occur in patients with agoraphobia, but agoraphobic patients tend to have a high level of overt anxiety or even panic.

Course and Prognosis

Little is known about the course of dependent personality disorder. There tends to be impaired occupational functioning, as the patients have an inability to act independently and without close supervision. Social relationships are limited to those on whom the persons can depend, and many suffer physical or mental abuse because they cannot assert themselves. They risk major depressive disorder if they sustain the loss of the person on whom they are dependent. However, the prognosis with treatment is favorable.

Treatment

PSYCHOTHERAPY

The treatment of dependent personality disorder can often be successful. Insight-oriented therapies enable patients to understand the antecedents of their behavior, and, with the support of a therapist, patients can become more independent, assertive, and self-reliant than they were before therapy.

A pitfall in the treatment may appear when the therapist encourages the patient to change the dynamics of a pathological relationship (for example, encourages a physically abused wife to seek help from the police). At that point the patient may become anxious, be unable to cooperate in therapy, and feel torn between complying with the therapist and losing a pathological external relationship. The therapist must show great respect for a dependent personality disorder patient's feelings of attachment, no matter how pathological those feelings may seem.

Behavior therapy, assertiveness training, family therapy, and group therapy have all been used, with successful outcomes in many cases.

PHARMACOTHERAPY

Pharmacotherapy has been used to deal with such specific symptoms as anxiety and depression, which are common associated features of dependent personality disorder. Those patients who experience panic attacks or who have high levels of separation anxiety may be helped by imipramine (Tofranil). Benzodiazepines and serotonergic agents have also been useful. If the patient's depression or withdrawal symptoms respond to psychostimulants, they may be used.

OBSESSIVE-COMPULSIVE PERSONALITY DISORDER

Obsessive-compulsive personality disorder is characterized by emotional constriction, orderliness, perseverance, stubbornness, and indecisiveness. The essential feature of the disorder is a pervasive pattern of perfectionism and inflexibility. In ICD-10 the disorder is called anankastic personality disorder.

Epidemiology

The prevalence of obsessive-compulsive personality disorder is unknown. It is more common in men than in women and is diagnosed most often in oldest children. The disorder also occurs more frequently in first-degree biological relatives of persons with the disorder than in the general population. Patients often have backgrounds characterized by harsh discipline. Freud hypothesized that the disorder is associated with difficulties in the anal stage of psychosexual development, generally around the age of 2. However, in various studies that theory has not been validated.

Diagnosis

In the interview, obsessive-compulsive personality disorder patients may have a stiff, formal, and rigid demeanor. Their affect is not blunted or flat but can be described as constricted. They lack spontaneity. Their mood is usually serious. Such patients may be anxious about not being in control of the interview. Their answers to questions are unusually detailed. The defense mechanisms they use are rationalization, isolation, intellectualization, reaction formation, and undoing. The DSM-IV diagnostic criteria for obsessive-compulsive personality disorder are listed in Table 20–10.

Clinical Features

Persons with obsessive-compulsive personality disorder are preoccupied with rules, regulations, orderliness, neatness, details, and the achievement of perfection. Those traits account for a general constriction of the entire personality. Such persons

Table 20-10. Diagnostic Criteria for Obsessive-Compulsive Personality Disorder

A pervasive pattern of preoccupation with orderliness, perfectionism, and mental and interpersonal control, at the expense of flexibility, openness, and efficiency, beginning by early adulthood and present in a variety of contexts, as indicated by four (or more) of the following:

   (1) is preoccupied with details, rules, lists, order, organization, or schedules to the extent that the major point of the activity is lost
   (2) shows perfectionism that interferes with task completion (e.g., is unable to complete a project because his or her own overly strict standards are not met)
   (3) is excessively devoted to work and productivity to the exclusion of leisure activities and friendships (not accounted for by obvious economic necessity)
   (4) is overconscientious, scrupulous, and inflexible about matters of morality, ethics, or values (not accounted for by cultural or religious identification)
   (5) is unable to discard worn-out or worthless objects even when they have no sentimental value
   (6) is reluctant to delegate tasks or to work with others unless they submit to exactly his or her way of doing things
   (7) adopts a miserly spending style toward both self and others; money is viewed as something to be hoarded for future catastrophes
   (8) shows rigidity and stubbornness

Table from DSM-IV, *Diagnostic and Statistical Manual of Mental Disorders*, ed 4. Copyright American Psychiatric Association, Washington, 1994. Used with permission.

are formal and serious and often lack a sense of humor. They insist that rules be followed rigidly and are unable to tolerate what they perceive to be infractions. Accordingly, they lack flexibility and are intolerant. They are capable of prolonged work, provided it is routinized and does not require changes to which they cannot adapt.

Obsessive-compulsive personality disorder patients' interpersonal skills are limited. They alienate people, are unable to compromise, and insist that others submit to their needs. They are, however, eager to please those whom they see as more powerful than themselves and carry out their wishes in an authoritarian manner. Because of their fear of making mistakes, they are indecisive and ruminate about making decisions. Although a stable marriage and occupational adequacy are common, obsessive-compulsive personality disorder patients have few friends.

Anything that threatens the patients' routines or their perceived stability can precipitate a great deal of anxiety that is otherwise bound up in the rituals they impose on their lives and try to impose on others.

Differential Diagnosis

When recurrent obsessions or compulsions are present, obsessive-compulsive disorder should be noted on Axis I. Perhaps the most difficult distinction is between the outpatient with some obsessive-compulsive traits and one with obsessive-compulsive personality disorder. The diagnosis of personality disorder is reserved for those patients with significant impairments in their occupational or social effectiveness. Sometimes, delusional disorder coexists with personality disorders and should be noted.

Course and Prognosis

The course of obsessive-compulsive personality disorder is variable and not predictable. From time to time, obsessions or compulsions may develop in the course of the personality disorder. Some adolescents with obsessive-compulsive personality disorder evolve into warm, open, and loving adults; however, in others the disorder can be either the harbinger of schizophrenia or—decades later and exacerbated by the aging process—major depressive disorder.

Persons with obsessive-compulsive personality disorder may do well in positions demanding methodical, deductive, or detailed work, but they are vulnerable to unexpected changes, and their personal lives may remain barren. Depressive disorders, especially those of late onset, are common.

Treatment

PSYCHOTHERAPY

Unlike patients with the other personality disorders, obsessive-compulsive personality disorder patients often know that they are suffering, and they seek treatment on their own. Free association and no-directive therapy are highly valued by the overtrained, oversocialized obsessive-compulsive personality disorder patient. However, the treatment is often long and complex, and countertransference problems are common.

Group therapy and behavior therapy occasionally offer certain advantages. In both contexts interrupting the patients in the midst of their maladaptive interactions or explanations is easy. Having the completion of their habitual behavior prevented raises patients' anxiety and leaves them susceptible to learning new coping strategies. Patients can also receive direct rewards for change in group therapy, something less often possible in individual psychotherapies.

PHARMACOTHERAPY

Clonazepam (Klonopin) is a benzodiazepine with anticonvulsant use that has reduced symptoms in patients with severe obsessive-compulsive disorder. Whether it is of use in the personality disorder is not known. Clomipramine (Anafranil) and such serotonergic agents as fluoxetine may be of use if obsessive-compulsive signs and symptoms break through.

PERSONALITY DISORDER NOT OTHERWISE SPECIFIED

This category in DSM-IV is reserved for disorders that do not fit into any of the previously described personality disorders. Passive-aggressive personality disorder and depressive personality disorder are now listed as examples of personality disorder not otherwise specified (NOS). A narrow spectrum of behavior or a particular trait—such as oppositionalism, sadism, or masochism—can also be classified here. A patient who has features of more than one personality disorder but does not meet the full criteria for any one personality disorder can be classified here.

The DSM-IV diagnostic criteria for personality disorder not otherwise specified are presented in Table 20–11.

Passive-Aggressive Personality Disorder

The person with passive-aggressive personality disorder is characterized by covert obstructionism, procrastination, stubbornness, and inefficiency. Such behavior is a manifestation of underlying aggression, which is expressed passively. In DSM-IV the disorder is also called negativistic personality disorder.

EPIDEMIOLOGY

No data are available about the epidemiology of the disorder. Sex ratio, familial patterns, and prevalence have not been adequately studied.

DIAGNOSIS

The diagnostic criteria for passive-aggressive disorder are presented in Table 20–12.

Table 20-11.   Diagnostic Criteria for Personality Disorder Not Otherwise Specified

This category is for disorders of personality functioning that do not meet criteria for any specific personality disorder. An example is the presence of features of more than one specific personality disorder that do not meet the full criteria for any one personality disorder (''mixed personality''), but that together cause clinically significant distress or impairment in one or more important areas of functioning (e.g., social or occupational). This category can also be used when the clinician judges that a specific personality disorder that is not included in the classification is appropriate. Examples include depressive personality disorder and passive-aggressive personality disorder.

Table from DSM-IV, *Diagnostic and Statistical Manual of Mental Disorders,* ed 4. Copyright American Psychiatric Association, Washington, 1994. Used with permission.

Table 20-12.   Research Criteria for Passive-Aggressive Personality Disorder

A. A pervasive pattern of negativistic attitudes and passive resistance to demands for adequate performance, beginning by early adulthood and present in a variety of contexts, as indicated by four (or more) of the following:

   (1) passively resists fulfilling routine social and occupational tasks
   (2) complains of being misunderstood and unappreciated by others
   (3) is sullen and argumentative
   (4) unreasonably criticizes and scorns authority
   (5) expresses envy and resentment toward those apparently more fortunate
   (6) voices exaggerated and persistent complaints of personal misfortune
   (7) alternates between hostile defiance and contrition

B. Does not occur exclusively during major depressive episodes and is not better accounted for by dysthymic disorder.

Table from DSM-IV, *Diagnostic and Statistical Manual of Mental Disorders,* ed 4. Copyright American Psychiatric Association, Washington, 1994. Used with permission.

CLINICAL FEATURES

Passive-aggressive personality disorder patients characteristically procrastinate, resist demands for adequate performance, find excuses for delays, and find fault with those on whom they depend; yet they refuse to extricate themselves from the dependent relationships. They usually lack assertiveness and are not direct about their own needs and wishes. They fail to ask needed questions about what is expected of them and may become anxious when forced to succeed or when their usual defense of turning anger against themselves is removed.

In interpersonal relationships, passive-aggressive personality disorder patients attempt to manipulate themselves into a position of dependence, but their passive, self-detrimental behavior is often experienced by others as punitive and manipulative. Others must do their errands and carry out their routine responsibilities. Friends and clinicians may become enmeshed in trying to assuage the patients' many claims of unjust treatment. The close relationships of passive-aggressive personality disorder patients are rarely tranquil or happy. Because the patients are bounded to their resentment more closely than to their satisfaction, they may never even know what enjoyment they want for themselves. People with the disorder lack self-confidence and are typically pessimistic about the future.

DIFFERENTIAL DIAGNOSIS

Passive-aggressive personality disorder needs to be differentiated from histrionic and borderline personality disorders. The passive-aggressive personality disorder patient is less flamboyant, dramatic, affective, and openly aggressive than are the histrionic and borderline personality disorder patients.

COURSE AND PROGNOSIS

In a follow-up study averaging 11 years of 100 passive-aggressive inpatients, Ivor Small found that passive-aggressive personality disorder was the primary diagnosis in 54 of them, 18 were also alcohol abusers, and 30 could be clinically labeled as depressed. Of the 73 former patients found, 58 (79 percent) had persistent psychiatric difficulties, and 9 (12 percent) were considered symptom-free. Most seemed irritable, anxious, and depressed; somatic complaints were many. Only 32 (44 percent) were employed full-time as workers or homemakers. Although neglect of responsibility and suicide attempts were common, only 1 patient had committed suicide in the interim.

Although 28 (38 percent) were readmitted to a hospital, only 3 patients were called schizophrenic.

TREATMENT

Psychotherapy

Passive-aggressive personality disorder patients who receive supportive psychotherapy have good outcomes. However, psychotherapy for patients with passive-aggressive personality disorder has many pitfalls: to fulfill their demands is often to support their pathology, but to refuse their demands is to reject them. The therapy session can thus become a battleground in which the patient expresses feelings of resentment against a therapist on whom the patient wishes to become dependent. With passive-aggressive personality disorder patients, the clinician must treat suicide gestures as one would any covert expression of anger and not as one would treat object loss in major depressive disorder. The therapist must point out the probable consequences of passive-aggressive behaviors as they occur. Such confrontations may be more helpful in changing the patient's behavior than is a correct interpretation.

Pharmacotherapy

Antidepressants should be prescribed only when clinical indications of depression and the possibility of suicide exist. Some patients have responded to benzodiazepines and psychostimulants, depending on the clinical features.

Depressive Personality Disorder

Persons with depressive personality disorder are characterized by lifelong traits that fall along the depressive spectrum. They are pessimistic, anhedonic, duty-bound, self-doubting, and chronically unhappy. The disorder is newly classified in DSM-IV, but melancholic personality was described by early 20th-century European psychiatrists, such as Ernst Kretschmer.

EPIDEMIOLOGY

Because depressive personality disorder is a new category, no epidemiological figures are available. However, based on the prevalence of depressive disorders in the overall population, depressive personality disorder seems common, to occur equally in men and women, and to occur in families in which depressive disorders are found.

ETIOLOGY

The cause of depressive personality disorder is unknown, but the factors involved in dysthymic disorder and major depressive disorder may be at work. Psychological theories involve early loss, poor parenting, punitive superegos, and extreme feelings of guilt. Biological theories involve the hypothalamic-pituitary-adrenal-thyroid axis, including the noradrenergic and serotonergic amine systems. Genetic predisposition, as indicated by Stella Chess's studies of temperament, may also play a role.

DIAGNOSIS AND CLINICAL FEATURES

A classic description of the depressive personality was provided in 1963 by Arthur Noyes and Laurence Kolb:

They feel but little of the normal joy of living and are inclined to be lonely and solemn, to be gloomy, submissive, pessimistic, and self-depreciatory. They are prone to express regrets and feelings of inadequacy and hopelessness. They are often meticulous, perfectionistic, overconscientious, preoccupied with work, feel responsibility keenly, and are easily discouraged under new conditions. They fear disapproval, tend to suffer in silence and perhaps to cry easily, although usually not in the presence of others. A tendency to hesitation, indecision, and caution betrays an inherent feeling of insecurity.

More recently, Hagop Akiskal described 7 groups of depressive traits: (1) quiet, introverted, passive, and nonassertive; (2) gloomy, pessimistic, serious, and incapable of fun; (3) self-critical, self-reproaching, and self-derogatory; (4) skeptical, critical of others, and hard to please; (5) conscientious, responsible, and self-disciplined; (6) brooding and given to worry; (7) preoccupied with negative events, feelings of inadequacy, and personal shortcomings.

Patients with depressive personality disorder complain of chronic feelings of unhappiness. They admit to feelings of low self-esteem and find it difficult to find anything in their lives about which they are joyful, hopeful, or optimistic. They are likely to denigrate their work, themselves, and their relationships with others; and they are self-critical and derogatory. Their physiognomy often reflects their mood—poor posture, depressed facies, hoarse voice, and psychomotor retardation.

DIFFERENTIAL DIAGNOSIS

Dysthymic disorder is a mood disorder characterized by greater fluctuation in mood than that found in depressive personality disorder. The personality disorder is chronic and lifelong, whereas dysthymic disorder is episodic, can occur anytime, and usually has a precipitating stressor. The depressive personality can be conceptualized as part of a spectrum of affective conditions in which dysthymic disorder and major depressive disorder are more severe variants.

Avoidant personality disorder patients are introverted and dependent but tend to be more anxious than depressed, compared with persons with depressive personality disorder.

COURSE AND PROGNOSIS

Persons with depressive personality disorder may be at great risk for dysthymic disorder and major depressive disorder. In a recent study by Donald Klein and Gregory Mills subjects with depressive personality exhibited significantly higher rates of current mood disorder, lifetime mood disorder, major depression, and dysthymia than subjects without depressive personality.

TREATMENT

Psychotherapy is the treatment of choice for depressive personality disorder. Patients respond to insight-oriented psychotherapy, and, because their reality testing is good, they can gain insight into the psychodynamics of their illness and to appreciate its effects on their interpersonal relationships. Treatment is likely to be long-term. Cognitive therapy helps the patients understand the cognitive manifestations of their low self-esteem and pessimism. Other types of psychotherapy that are useful include group psychotherapy and interpersonal therapy. Some persons respond to self-help measures.

Psychopharmalogical approaches include the use of antidepressant medications, especially such serotonergic agents as sertraline (Zoloft), 50 mg a day. Some patients respond to small dosages of psychostimulants, such as amphetamine, 5 to 15 mg a day. Psychopharmacological agents should always be combined with psychotherapy to achieve maximum effects.

Sadomasochistic Personality Disorder

Some personality types are characterized by elements of sadism or masochism or a combination of both. Sadomasochistic personality disorder is listed here because it is of major clinical and historical interests in psychiatry. It is not an official diagnostic category in DSM-IV or its appendix, but it can be diagnosed as personality disorder not otherwise classified.

Sadism is named after the Marquis de Sade, who wrote in the 18th century about persons who experienced sexual pleasure while inflicting pain on others; it is the desire to cause others pain by being either sexually abusive or physically or psychologically abusive in general. Freud believed that sadists ward off castration anxiety and can achieve sexual pleasure only when they can do to others what they fear will be done to them.

Masochism is named after Leopold von Sacher-Masoch, a 19th-century Austrian novelist; it is the achievement of sexual gratification by inflicting pain on the self. Generally, the so-called moral masochist seeks humiliation and failure, rather than physical pain. Freud believed that masochists' ability to achieve orgasm is disturbed by anxiety and guilt feelings about sex that are alleviated by their own suffering and punishment.

Clinical observations indicate that elements of both sadistic and masochistic behavior are usually present in the same person. Treatment with insight-oriented psychotherapy, including psychoanalysis, has been effective in some cases. Because of therapy, the patients become aware of the need for self-punishment secondary to excessive unconscious guilt and come to recognize their repressed aggressive impulses, which originate in early childhood.

Sadistic Personality Disorder

Sadistic personality disorder was a controversial addition to an appendix in DSM-III-R, and it is not included in DSM-IV. However, it still appears in the literature and may be of descriptive use. Persons with sadistic personality disorder show a pervasive pattern of cruel, demeaning, and aggressive behavior, beginning in early adulthood, that is directed toward others. Physical cruelty or violence is used to inflict pain on others and not to achieve some other goal, such as mugging someone as part of a theft. Persons with the disorder like to humiliate or demean people in front of others; they have usually treated or disciplined someone unusually harshly, especially children. In general, persons with sadistic personality disorder are fascinated by violence, weapons, injury, or torture. To be included in the category, such persons are not motivated solely by the desire to derive sexual arousal from their behavior; if they are so motivated, the paraphilia of sexual sadism should be diagnosed.

Personality Change Due to a General Medical Condition

Personality change due to a general medical condition deserves some discussion here. ICD-10 lists the diagnosis of personality and behavioral disorders due to brain disease, damage, and dysfunction, which includes organic personality disorder (Table 20–13), postencephalic syndrome, and postconcussional syndrome.

Personality change due to a general medical condition is characterized by a marked change in personality style and traits from a previous level of functioning. The patient must show evidence of a causative organic factor antedating the onset of the personality change.

ETIOLOGY

Structural damage to the brain is usually the cause of the personality change. Head trauma is probably the most common cause. Cerebral neoplasms and vascular accidents, particularly of the temporal and frontal lobes, are also common causes. The conditions most often associated with personality change are listed in Table 20–14.

DIAGNOSIS AND CLINICAL FEATURES

A change in personality from previous patterns of behavior or an exacerbation of previous personality characteristics is no-

Table 20–13.   ICD-10 Criteria for Organic Personality Disorder

This disorder is characterized by a significant alteration of the habitual patterns of premorbid behaviour. The expression of emotions, needs, and impulses is particularly affected. Cognitive functions may be defective mainly or even exclusively in the areas of planning and anticipating the likely personal and social consequences, as in the so-called frontal lobe syndrome. However, it is now known that this syndrome occurs not only with frontal lobe lesions but also with lesions to other circumscribed areas of the brain.

Diagnostic guidelines
In addition to an established history or other evidence of brain disease, damage, or dysfunction, a definitive diagnosis requires the presence of two or more of the following features:

(a) consistently reduced ability to persevere with goal-directed activities, especially those involving longer periods of time and postponed gratification;
(b) altered emotional behaviour, characterized by emotional lability, shallow and unwarranted cheerfulness (euphoria, inappropriate jocularity), and easy change to irritability or short-lived outbursts of anger and aggression; in some instances apathy may be a more prominent feature;
(c) expression of needs and impulses without consideration of consequences or social convention (the patient may engage in dissocial acts, such as stealing, inappropriate sexual advances, or voracious eating, or may exhibit disregard for personal hygiene);
(d) cognitive disturbances, in the form of suspiciousness or paranoid ideation, and/or excessive preoccupation with a single, usually abstract, theme (e.g. religion, ''right'' and ''wrong'');
(e) marked alteration of the rate and flow of language production, with features such as circumstantiality, overinclusiveness, viscosity, and hypergraphia;
(f) altered sexual behaviour (hyposexuality or change of sexual preference).

Table from World Health Organization: *The ICD-10 Classification of Mental and Behavioural Disorders: Clinical Descriptions and Diagnostic Guidelines.* World Health Organization, Geneva, 1992. Used with permission.

table. Impaired control of the expression of emotions and impulses is a cardinal feature. Emotions are characteristically labile and shallow, although euphoria or apathy may be prominent. The euphoria may mimic hypomania, but true elation is absent, and the patient may admit to not really feeling happy. There is a hollow and silly ring to the patient's excitement and facile jocularity, particularly if the frontal lobes are involved. Also associated with damage to the frontal lobes, the so-called frontal lobe syndrome, are prominent indifference and apathy, characterized by a lack of concern for events in the immediate environment. Temper outbursts with little or no provocation may occur, especially after alcohol ingestion, and may result in violent behavior. The expression of impulses may be manifested by inap-

Table 20–14.   Medical Conditions Associated with Personality Change

Head trauma
Cerebrovascular diseases
Cerebral tumors
Epilepsy (particularly complex partial epilepsy)
Huntington's disease
Multiple sclerosis
Endocrine disorders
Heavy metal poisoning (manganese, mercury)
Neurosyphilis
Acquired immune deficiency syndrome (AIDS)

propriate jokes, a coarse manner, improper sexual advances, and antisocial conduct resulting in conflicts with the law, such as assaults on others, sexual misdemeanors, and shoplifting. Foresight and the ability to anticipate the social or legal consequences of one's actions are typically diminished. People with temporal lobe epilepsy characteristically show humorlessness, hypergraphia, hyperreligiosity, and marked aggressiveness during seizures.

Patients with personality change due to a general medical condition have a clear sensorium. Mild disorders of cognitive function often coexist but do not amount to intellectual deterioration. Patients tend to be inattentive, which may account for disorders of recent memory. With some prodding, however, patients are likely to recall what they claim to have forgotten. The diagnosis should be suspected in patients who show marked behavioral or personality changes involving emotional lability and impaired impulse control, who have no history of mental disorder, and whose personality changes occur abruptly or over a relatively brief period (see Table 4.5–3).

Anabolic Steroids

An increasing number of high school and college athletes and other persons involved with weight lifting are using anabolic steroids as a shortcut to maximize their physical development. Anabolic steroids include such drugs as oxymetholone (Anadrol), somatropin (Humatrope), stanozolol (Winstrol), and testosterone cypionate (DEPO-Testosterone).

DSM-IV does not include a diagnostic category for substance-induced personality disorder, so it is unclear whether a personality change due to a steroid abuse is better diagnosed as personality change due to a general medical condition or as one of the other (or unknown) substance use disorders. It is discussed here because anabolic steroids can cause persistent alterations of personality and behavior.

DIFFERENTIAL DIAGNOSIS

Dementia involves global deterioration in intellectual and behavioral capacities, of which personality change is just one category. A personality change may herald a cognitive disorder that will eventually evolve into dementia. In those cases, as the deterioration begins to encompass significant memory and cognitive deficits, the diagnosis is changed from personality change due to a general medical condition to a dementia. In differentiating the specific syndrome from other disorders in which personality change may occur—such as schizophrenia, delusional disorder, mood disorders, and impulse-control disorders—the physician must consider the most important factor, the presence in the personality change disorder of a specific organic causative factor.

COURSE AND PROGNOSIS

Both the course and the prognosis of personality change due to a general medical condition depend on its cause. If the disorder is the result of structural damage to the brain, the disorder tends to persist. The disorder may follow a period of coma and delirium in cases of head trauma or vascular accident and may be permanent. The personality change may evolve into dementia in cases of brain tumor, multiple sclerosis, and Huntington's disease. Personality changes produced by chronic intoxication, medical illness, or drug therapy (such as levodopa [Larodopa] for parkinsonism) may be reversed if the underlying cause is treated. Some patients require custodial care or, at least, close supervision to meet their basic needs, avoid repeated conflicts with the law, and protect them and their families from the hostil-

ity of others and from destitution resulting from impulsive and ill-considered actions.

TREATMENT

Management of the personality change disorder involves treatment of the underlying organic condition if the condition is treatable. Psychopharmacological treatment of specific symptoms may be indicated in some cases, such as imipramine or fluoxetine for depression.

Patients with severe cognitive impairment or weakened behavioral controls may need counseling to help avoid difficulties at work or to prevent social embarrassment. As a rule, the patient's family needs emotional support and concrete advice on how to help minimize the patient's undesirable conduct. Alcohol should be avoided. Social engagements should be curtailed if the patient tends to act in a grossly offensive manner.

Enduring Personality Changes after Catastrophic Experience and after Psychiatric Illness

ICD-10 has two categories for personality changes that occur after either a catastrophic experience or a psychiatric illness in persons who had no previous personality disorder. According to ICD-10:

These diagnoses should be made only when there is evidence of a definite and enduring change in a person's pattern of perceiving, relating to, or thinking about the environment and the self. The personality change should be significant and associated with inflexible and maladaptive behaviour which was not present before the pathogenic experience. The change should not be a manifestation of another mental disorder, or a residual symptom of any antecedent mental disorder. Such enduring personality change is most often seen following devastating traumatic experience but may also develop in the aftermath of a severe, recurrent, or prolonged mental disorder. It may be difficult to differentiate between an acquired personality change and the unmasking or exacerbation of an existing personality disorder following stress, strain, or psychotic experience. Enduring personality change should be diagnosed only when the change represents a permanent and different way of being, which can be etiologically traced back to a profound, existentially extreme experience. The diagnosis should not be made if the personality disorder is secondary to brain damage or disease.

ENDURING PERSONALITY CHANGE AFTER CATASTROPHIC EXPERIENCE

According to ICD-10:

Enduring personality change may follow the experience of catastrophic stress. The stress must be so extreme that it is unnecessary to consider personal vulnerability in order to explain its profound effect on the personality. Examples include concentration camp experiences, torture, disasters, prolonged exposure to life-threatening circumstances (e.g. hostage situations—prolonged captivity with a imminent possibility of being killed). Post-traumatic stress disorder . . . may precede this type of personality change, which may then be seen as a chronic, irreversible sequel of stress disorder. In other instances, however, enduring personality change meeting the description given below may develop without an interim phase of a manifest post-traumatic stress disorder. However, long-term change in personality following short-term exposure to a life-threatening experience such as a car accident should *not* be included in this category, since recent research indicates that such a development depends on a pre-existing psychological vulnerability. . . .

The personality change should be enduring and manifest as inflexible and maladaptive features leading to an impairment in interpersonal, social, and occupational functioning. Usually the personality change has to be confirmed by a key informant. In order to make the diagnosis, it is essential to establish the presence of features not previously seen, such as: (a) a hostile or mistrustful attitude towards the world; (b) social withdrawal; (c) feelings of emptiness or hopelessness; (d) a chronic feeling of being "on edge," as if constantly threatened; (e) estrangement.

This personality change must have been present for at least 2 years, and should not be attribute to a pre-existing personality disorder or to a mental disorder other than post-traumatic stress disorder. . . . The presence of brain damage or disease which may cause similar clinical features should be ruled out.

Enduring Personality Change After Psychiatric Illness

Personality changes after psychiatric illness is described in ICD-10 as follows:

The personality change should be enduring and manifest as an inflexible and maladaptive pattern of experiencing and functioning, leading to long-standing problems in interpersonal, social, or occupational functioning and subjective distress. There should be no evidence of a pre-existing personality disorder that can explain the personality change, and the diagnosis should not be based on any residual symptoms of the antecedent mental disorder. The change in personality develops following clinical recovery from a mental disorder that must have been experienced as emotionally extremely stressful and shattering to the patient's self-image. Other people's attitudes or reactions to the patient following the illness are important in determining and reinforcing his or her perceived level of stress. This type of personality change cannot be fully understood without taking into consideration the subjective emotional experience and the previous personality, its adjustment, and its specific vulnerabilities.

Diagnostic evidence for this type of personality change should include such clinical features as the following: (a) excessive dependence on and a demanding attitude towards others; (b) conviction of being changed or stigmatized by the preceding illness, leading to an inability to form and maintain close and confiding personal relationships and to social isolation; (c) passivity, reduced interests, and diminished involvement in leisure activities; (d) persistent complaints of being ill, which may be associated with hypochondriacal claims and illness behaviour; (e) dysphoric or labile mood, not due to the presence of a current mental disorder or antecedent mental disorder with residual affective symptoms; (f) significant impairment in social and occupational functioning compared with the premorbid situation.

The above manifestations must have been present over a period of 2 or more years. The change is not attributable to gross brain damage or disease. A previous diagnosis of schizophrenia does not preclude the diagnosis.

References

Fabrega H, Ulrich R, Pilkonis P, Mezzich J: Personality disorders diagnosed at intake at a public psychiatric facility. Hosp Community Psychiatry 44: 159, 1993.

Gunderson J G, Phillips K A: Personality disorders. In *Comprehensive Textbook of Psychiatry*, ed 6, H I Kaplan, B J Sadock, editors, p 1425. Williams & Wilkins, Baltimore, 1995.

Gunderson J G, Sabo A N: The phenomenological and conceptual interface between borderline personality disorder and PTSD. Am J Psychiatry 150: 19, 1993.

Hubbard J R, Saathoff G B, Bernardo M J, Barnett B L Jr: Recognizing borderline personality disorder in the family practice setting. Am Fam Physician 52: 908, 1995.

Miller D: Diagnostic assessment and therapeutic approaches to borderline disorders in adolescents. Adolesc Psychiatry 20: 237, 1995.

Perkins D O, Davidson E J, Leserman J, Liao D: Personality disorder in patients infected with HIV: A controlled study with implications for clinical care. Am J Psychiatry 150: 309, 1993.

Sansone R A, Sansone L A: Borderline personality disorder. Interpersonal and behavioral problems that sabotage treatment success. Postgrad Med 97: 169, 1995.

Silverman J M, Siever L J, Horvath T B, Coccaro E F: Schizophrenia-related and affective personality disorder traits in relatives of probands with schizophrenia and personality disorders. Am J Psychiatry 150: 435, 1993.

Sternlicht H C: Obsessive-compulsive disorder, fluoxetine, and buspirone. Am J Psychiatry 150: 526, 1993.

Vollema M G, van den Bosch R J: The multidimensionality of schizotypy. Schizophr Bull 21: 19, 1995.

21/ Psychological Factors Affecting Medical Condition (Psychosomatic Disorders)

Psychosomatic medicine emphasizes the unity of mind and body and the interaction between them. In general, the conviction is that psychological factors are important in the development of all diseases. Whether that role is in the initiation, the progression, the aggravation, or the exacerbation of a disease or in the predisposition or the reaction to a disease is open to debate and varies from disorder to disorder. The term "psychosomatic" has become part of the concept of behavioral medicine, which was defined in 1978 by the National Academy of Science as "the interdisciplinary field concerned with the development and integration of behavioral and biomedical science knowledge and techniques relevant to health and illness and the application of this knowledge and these techniques to prevention, diagnosis, and rehabilitation." Behavioral medicine, thus, is an inclusive term for the field of psychosomatic medicine.

CLASSIFICATION

In the fourth edition of *Diagnostic and Statistical Manual of Mental Disorders* (DSM-IV), the diagnostic criteria for psychological factors affecting medical condition (that is, psychosomatic disorders) specify that psychological factors adversely affect the patient's medical condition in one of a variety of ways.

The diagnostic criteria are presented in Table 21.1–1. Excluded are (1) classic mental disorders that present with physical symptoms as part of the disorder (for example, conversion disorder, in which a physical symptom is produced by psychological conflict); (2) somatization disorder, in which the physical symptoms are not based on organic pathology; (3) hypochondriasis, in which patients have an exaggerated concern with their health; (4) physical complaints that are frequently associated with mental disorders (for example, dysthymic disorder, which usually has such somatic accompaniments as muscle weakness, asthenia, fatigue, and exhaustion); and (5) physical complaints associated with substance-related disorders (for example, coughing associated with nicotine dependence).

ETIOLOGY

Investigators have questioned the validity of the concept of psychophysiological medicine. Some have suggested that it is too vague a term; others say that it is too narrow. But most agree that chronic, severe, and perceived stress plays some causative role in the development of many somatic diseases. The character of the stress, the general underlying psychophysiological factors, the patient's genetic and organ vulnerability, the nature of the patient's emotional conflicts (whether they are specific or nonspecific), and the way they interact to produce diseases—all are still controversial.

General Stress

A stressful life event or situation—internal or external, acute or chronic—generates challenges to which the organism cannot adequately respond. Thomas Holmes and Richard Rahe, in their social readjustment rating scale, listed 43 life events associated with varying amounts of disruption and stress in the average person's life—for example, the death of a spouse, 100 life-change units; divorce, 73 units; marital separation, 65 units; and the death of a close family member, 63 units (Table 21.1–2). The scale was constructed after querying hundreds of persons with varying backgrounds to rank the relative degree of adjustment necessitated by changing life events. An accumulation of 200 or more life-change units in a single year increases the incidence of psychosomatic disorders.

Recent studies have found that persons who face general stresses optimistically, rather than pessimistically, are not apt to experience a psychosomatic disorder; if they do, they are apt to recover from the disorder easily.

Specific versus Nonspecific Stress

In addition to general stresses, such as a divorce and the death of a spouse, some investigators have suggested that specific personalities and conflicts are associated with specific psychosomatic diseases. Other investigators believe that nonspecific generalized anxiety from any type of conflict may lead to a number of diseases.

Specific psychic stress may be defined as a specific personality or unconscious conflict that causes a homeostatic disequilibrium that contributes to the development of a psychosomatic disorder. Specific personality types were first identified in regard to the coronary personality (a hard-driving, aggressive person who tends to experience myocardial occlusion). For example, the so-called type A personality (similar to the coronary personality) was singled out as one that predisposes a person to coronary disease. Type A and type B personalities were first defined by Meyer Friedman and Ray Rosenman.

That specific unconscious conflicts are associated with specific psychosomatic disorders (for example, unconscious dependence conflict predisposes one to peptic ulcer) was hypothesized by Franz Alexander. Alexander's multifactorial theories were later confirmed by Arthur Mirsky and Herbert Weiner. Both the specific personality type and the unconscious conflicts fall under the rubric of specific causative theories of psychosomatic diseases. Table 21.1–3 gives some psychological correlates of psychophysiological disorders.

Alternatively, chronic nonspecific stress, usually with the intervening variable of anxiety, has been suggested as having physiological correlates that, combined with genetic organ vulnerability or debility, predisposes certain persons to a psychosomatic disorder. Alexithymic persons are unable to read their own emotions; they have impoverished fantasy lives and are not conscious of their emotional conflicts; psychosomatic disorders may serve as an outlet for their accumulated tensions. Nonspecific casual theories are supported by experimental evidence that, under chronic stress, animals have psychosomatic disorders (such as peptic ulcer); clearly, animals do not have the specific personality or unconscious psychological conflicts that people do.

Table 21.1-1. Diagnostic Criteria for Psychological Factors Affecting Medical Condition

A. A general medical condition (coded on Axis III) is present.

B. Psychological factors adversely affect the general medical condition in one of the following ways:

  (1) the factors have influenced the course of the general medical condition as shown by a close temporal association between the psychological factors and the development or exacerbation of, or delayed recovery from, the general medical condition.

  (2) the factors interfere with the treatment of the general medical condition.

  (3) the factors constitute additional health risks for the individual.

  (4) stress-related physiological responses precipitate or exacerbate symptoms of a general medical condition

Table from DSM-IV, *Diagnostic and Statistical Manual of Mental Disorders*, ed 4. Copyright American Psychiatric Association, Washington, 1994. Used with permission.

Physiological Variables

The mediator between cognitively based stress and disease may be hormonal, as in the general-adaption syndrome of Hans Selye, in which hydrocortisone is the mediator; or the mediator may be changes in the functioning of the anterior pituitary-hypothalamic-adrenal axis, with autonomic effects, adrenal enlargement, and lymphoid shrinkage. In the hormonal linkage, hormones are released from the hypothalamus and travel to the anterior pituitary, where the trophic hormones interact directly or release hormones from other endocrine glands. Alexander pointed to the autonomic nervous system—for example, the parasympathetic nervous system in peptic ulcer and the sympathetic nervous system in hypertension—as the mechanism linking chronic stress and psychosomatic disorders.

Another intervening variable may be the action of the immune system's monocytes. The monocytes interact with brain neuropeptides, which serve as messengers between brain cells.

Table 21.1-2. Life-Change Scaling Results Across Time

Life Events	1967		1978		1994	
	Rank	LCU	Rank	LCU	Rank	LCU
Death of spouse	1	100	1	105	1	123
Divorce	2	73	4	62	2	100
Marital separation	3	65	8	52	4	82
Jail term	4	63	6	57	7	74
Death of close family member	5	63	2	73	3	94
Serious personal injury or illness	6	53	16	42	5	80
Marriage	7	50	10	50	19	50
Fired from work	8	47	3	64	6	79
Marital reconciliation	9	45	17	42	12	59
Retirement	10	45	11	49	16	55
Change in health or behavior of family member	11	44	9	52	14	58
Pregnancy	12	40	5	60	9	66
Sexual difficulties	13	39	12	49	21	45
Gain of new family member	14	39	14	47	13	58
Business readjustment	15	38	21	38	10	64
Change in financial state	16	38	13	48	15	57
Death of a close friend	17	37	15	46	8	71
Change to different line of work	18	36	22	38	17	52
Change in number of arguments with spouse	19	35	24	34	18	51
Major purchase (>$10,000)	20	31	18	39	23	44
Foreclosure on a mortgage or loan	21	30	7	57	11	63
Change in responsibilities at work	22	29	32	30	24	43
Son or daughter leaving home	23	29	36	29	22	45
Trouble with in-laws	24	29	34	29	28	38
Outstanding personal achievement	25	28	25	33	27	39
Spouse begins or ends work	26	26	23	37	20	48
Begin or end school	27	26	28	32	29	38
Change in living conditions	28	25	19	39	25	42
Revision of personal habits	29	24	30	31	36	27
Trouble with boss	30	23	20	39	32	30
Change in work hours or conditions	31	20	27	33	31	36
Change in residence	32	20	26	33	26	40
Change in schools	33	20	39	28	30	36
Change in recreation	34	19	30	30	34	28
Change in church activities/religious beliefs	35	19	35	29	42	22
Change in social activities	36	18	40	28	38	27
Moderate purchase (<$10,000)	37	17	42	26	35	28
Change in sleeping habits	38	16	31	31	40	26
Change in number of family get-togethers	39	15	41	26	39	27
Change in eating habits	40	15	38	29	37	27
Vacation	41	13	37	29	41	25
Christmas	42	12	*	*	33	30
Minor violations of the law	43	11	29	32	43	22
MEAN LCU VALUE for all events		**34**		**42**		**50**

Values for the original list of life changes published by Thomas Holmes and Richard Rahe in 1967 have been rescaled twice over the past 27 years—in 1978 and by Mark Miller and Richard Rahe in 1994. The table gives the life change unit (LCU) values for those events across these years. A gradual rise in these values is indicated by the mean LCU values calculated for all events in a testing, shown at the bottom of the table. It appears that life became progressively more difficult, in terms of life change and readjustment required for those events, across the past three decades.
* Christmas was not scaled in 1978.

Table 21.1-3. Some Hypothesized Psychological Correlates of Psychophysiological Disorders

Disorder	Psychogenic Causes, Personality Characteristics, and Coping Aims
Peptic ulcer	Feels deprived of dependence needs; is resentful; represses anger; cannot vent hostility or actively seek dependence security; characterizes self-sufficient and responsible go-getter types who are compensating for dependence desires; has strong regressive wish to be nurtured and fed; revengeful feelings are repressed and kept unconscious
Colitis	Was intimidated in childhood into dependence and conformity; feels conflict over resentment and desire to please; anger restrained for fear of retaliation; is fretful, brooding, and depressive or passive, sweet and bland; seeks to camouflage hostility by symbolic gesture of giving
Essential hypertension	Was forced in childhood to restrain resentments; inhibited rage; is threatened by and guilt-ridden over hostile impulses that may erupt; is a controlled, conforming, and ''mature'' personality; is hard-driving and conscientious; is guarded and tense; needs to control and direct anger into acceptable channels; wishes to gain approval from authority
Migraine	Is unable to fulfill excessive self-demands; feels intense resentment and envy toward intellectually or financially more successful competitors; has meticulous, scrupulous, perfectionistic, and ambitious personality; failure to attain perfectionist ambitions results in self-punishment
Bronchial asthma	Feels separation anxiety; was given inconsistent maternal affection; has fear and guilt that hostile impulses will be expressed toward loved persons; is demanding, sickly, and cranky or clinging and dependent; symptom expresses suppressed cry for help and protection
Neurodermatitis	Has overprotective but ungiving parents; has craving for affection; has conflict regarding hostility and dependence; shows guilt and self-punishment for inadequacies; is a superficially friendly and oversensitive personality with depressive features and low self-image; symptoms are atonement for inadequacy and guilt by self-excoriation; displays oblique expression of hostility and exhibitionism in need for attention and soothing

Table from T Millon, R. Millon: Psychophysiologic disorders. In *Medical Behavioral Science*, T Millon, editor, p 211. Saunders, Philadelphia, 1975. Used with permission.

Thus, immunity may influence psychic state and mood. Herbert Benson, in explaining the effects of relaxation therapy on certain psychosomatic disorders, postulated that relaxation decreases the activity of cerebral adrenergic catecholamines and that those substances affect the limbic system—the Papez circuit—which is important in the cause of psychosomatic and mental disorders.

TREATMENT

Both psychosomatic medicine and behavioral medicine are concerned with the interaction of the psyche and the soma. Traditionally, psychoanalysis and psychotherapy have been used to treat psychosomatic disorders. Since the 1970s, a great deal of interest has developed in the use of behavior modification (learning theory) techniques to treat those disorders. Among the therapeutic techniques emphasized in behavior modification are muscle relaxation therapy, biofeedback, hypnosis, controlled breathing, yoga, and massage. The goal of both the behavioral techniques and the usual psychotherapeutic modalities is to improve the psychosomatic equation.

References

Angell M: Disease as a reflection of the psyche. N Engl J Med *312*: 1570, 1985.
Feifel H, Strack S, Nagy V T: Degree of life-threat and differential use of coping modes., J Psychol Res *31*: 91, 1987.
Schneider W, Heuft G, Freyberger H J, Janssen P L: Diagnostic concepts, multimodal and multiaxial approaches in psychotherapy and psychosomatics. Psychother Psychosom *63*: 63, 1993.
Stoudemire A, McDaniel J S: History, Classification, and current trends in psychosomatic medicine. In *Comprehensive Textbook of Psychiatry*, ed 6, H I Kaplan, B J Sadock, editors, p 1463. Williams & Wilkins, Baltimore, 1995.

21.2 SPECIFIC DISORDERS

CARDIOVASCULAR SYSTEM

Coronary Artery Disease

Coronary artery disease causes a decrease in blood flow to the heart and is characterized by episodic chest and heart pain,

discomfort, or pressure. It is usually produced by exertion or stress and is relieved by rest or sublingual nitroglycerin.

PERSONALITY TYPE

Flanders Dunbar first described coronary disease patients as aggressive-compulsive personalities with a tendency to work long hours and to seize authority. Later, Meyer Friedman and Ray Rosenman defined type A and type B personalities. Type A personalities are strongly associated with the development of coronary heart disease. They are action-oriented persons who struggle to achieve poorly defined goals by means of competitive hostility. They are aggressive, impatient, upwardly mobile, and striving and angry when frustrated. Type B personalities are the opposite: they are relaxed and less aggressive and tend to strive less vigorously to achieve their goals. Type A personalities have increased amounts of low-density lipoprotein, serum cholesterol, triglycerides, and 17-hydroxycorticosteroids, and they tend to have coronary heart disease. Sudden loss may cause death by coronary occlusion.

TREATMENT

When coronary occlusion occurs, various medications for the patient's cardiac status are used. To alleviate the psychic distress associated with the disease, clinicians use psychotropics—for example, diazepam (Valium). Pain is treated with analgesics (for example, morphine). Medical treatment should be supportive and reassuring, with some psychological emphasis on the alleviation of psychic stress, compulsivity, and tension.

Essential Hypertension

Hypertension is a disease characterized by a blood pressure of 160/95 mm Hg or higher. Twenty percent of the adult population in the United States are hypertensive.

PERSONALITY TYPE

Hypertensive persons appear to be outwardly congenial, compliant, and compulsive; although their anger is not expressed openly, they have much inhibited rage, which they handle poorly. There appears to be a familial genetic predisposition to hypertension; that is, when chronic stress occurs in a genetically predisposed compulsive personality who has repressed and suppressed rage, hypertension may result. It also tends to occur in type A personalities.

TREATMENT

Supportive psychotherapy and behavioral techniques (for example, biofeedback, meditation, and relaxation therapy) have been reported to be useful in treating hypertension. Medically, the patient must comply with the antihypertensive medication regimen.

Congestive Heart Failure

Congestive heart failure is a disorder in which the heart fails to move the blood forward normally, causing congestion in the lungs and the systemic circulation and decreased tissue blood flow with diminished cardiac output. Psychological factors, such as nonspecific emotional stress and conflict, are frequently significant in the initiation or the exacerbation of the disorder. Thus, supportive psychotherapy is important in its treatment.

Vasomotor (Vasodepressor) Syncope

Vasomotor (vasodepressor) syncope is characterized by a sudden loss of consciousness (fainting) caused by a vasovagal attack. Sympathetic autonomic activity is inhibited, and parasympathetic vagal nerve activity is augmented, resulting in decreased cardiac output, decreased vascular peripheral resistance, vasodilation, and bradycardia. According to Franz Alexander, acute fear or fright inhibits the impulse to fight or flee, thereby pooling the blood in the lower extremities, from the vasodilation of the blood vessels in the extremities. That reaction results in decreased ventricular filling, a drop in the blood supply to the brain, and consequent brain hypoxia and loss of consciousness.

TREATMENT

Because patients with vasomotor syncope normally put themselves or fall into a prone position, the decreased cardiac output is corrected. Raising their legs also helps correct the physiological imbalance. Psychotherapy should be used to determine the cause of the fright or the trauma associated with syncope. When syncope is related to orthostatic hypotension, the patient should be advised to shift slowly from a sitting to a standing position.

Cardiac Arrhythmias

Potentially life-threatening arrhythmias—such as palpitations, ventricular tachycardia, and ventricular fibrillation—sometimes occur in conjunction with an emotional upset. Also associated with emotional trauma are sinus tachycardia, ST wave and T wave changes, ventricular ectopy, increased plasma catecholamines, and free fatty acid concentrations. Emotional stress is nonspecific, as is the personality description associated with the disorders.

TREATMENT

Psychotherapy and (β-adrenergic receptor antagonists, such as propranolol (Inderal), help protect against emotionally induced arrhythmias.

Raynaud's Phenomenon

Idiopathic paroxysmal bilateral cyanosis of the digits due to arteriolar contraction is frequently caused by external stress.

TREATMENT

Raynaud's phenomenon may be treated with supportive psychotherapy, progressive relaxation, or bio-feedback and by protecting the body from cold and using a mild sedative. Smoking must cease, because nicotine is a vasoconstrictor. β-adrenergic receptor antagonists, clonidine (Catapres), and ergot preparations also cause vasoconstriction and are contraindicated.

Psychogenic Cardiac Nondisease

Some patients are free of heart disease yet complain of symptoms suggestive of cardiac disease. They often exhibit a morbid concern about their hearts and exaggerated fears of heart disease. Their fear may range from an anxious concern, manifested by a severe phobia or hypochondriasis, to a delusional conviction that they have cardiac disease. Many of the patients suffer from an ill-defined syndrome often referred to as neurocirculatory asthenia.

Neurocirculatory asthenia was first described in 1871 by Jacob M. DaCosta, who named it irritable heart. It has some 20 names, including effort syndrome, DaCosta's syndrome, cardiac neurosis, vasoregulatory asthenia, hyperkinetic heart syndrome, and hyperdynamic-adrenergic circulatory state. Psychiatrists tend to view it as a clinical variant of anxiety disorders, although it does not appear in the fourth edition of *Diagnostic and Statistical Manual of Mental Disorders* (DSM-IV).

DIAGNOSIS

The diagnostic criteria for neurocirculatory asthenia are (1) respiratory complaints, such as sighing respiration, inability to take a deep breath, smothering and choking, and dyspnea; (2) palpitations, chest pain, or discomfort; (3) nervousness, dizziness, faintness, or discomfort in crowds; (4) undue fatigue or limitation of activities; and (5) excessive sweating, insomnia, and irritability. The symptoms usually start in adolescence or the early 20s but may begin in middle age. Such symptoms are twice as common in women as in men and tend to be chronic, with recurrent acute exacerbations.

TREATMENT

The management of neurocirculatory asthenia may be difficult, and the prognosis is guarded if the condition is chronic. Phobic elements are prominent, and patients often derive primary or secondary gains from the disability. Psychotherapy aimed at uncovering psychodynamic factors—often relating to hostility, unacceptable sexual impulses, dependence, guilt, and death anxiety—may be effective in some cases, but most patients with the condition tend to shun psychiatric help. Other behavioral techniques may be useful. Physical training programs aimed at correcting faulty breathing habits and gradually increasing the patient's effort tolerance may be helpful, especially if the programs are combined with group psychotherapy. Psychopharmacological treatment focuses on the predominant symptoms. The use of propranolol may interrupt the vicious circle of cardiac symptoms and have a positive reinforcement feedback effect on anxiety, which aggravates the symptoms.

Antianxiety agents (for example, diazepam) can be used for major anxiety symptoms. If fatigue, lassitude, and weakness are the major complaints, the judicious use of amphetamines or methylphenidate (Ritalin) may be helpful.

RESPIRATORY SYSTEM

Bronchial Asthma

Bronchial asthma is a chronic recurrent obstructive disease of the bronchial airways, which tend to respond to various stimuli by bronchial constriction, edema, and excessive secretion. Genetic factors, allergic factors, infections, and acute and chronic stress all combine to produce the disease. Whereas the rate and the depth of a healthy person's breathing can be changed voluntarily to correlate with various emotional states, such changes are aggravated and prolonged in a person with asthma.

PSYCHOLOGICAL FACTORS

Although asthmatic patients are characterized as having excessive dependence needs, no specific personality type has been identified. Alexander pointed to psychodynamic conflictual factors, as he found in many asthmatic patients a strong unconscious wish for protection and for envelopment by the mother or surrogate mother. The mother figures tend to be overprotective and oversolicitous, perfectionistic, dominating, and helpful. When protection is sought but is not received, an asthmatic attack occurs.

TREATMENT

Some asthmatic children improve by being separated from the mother (so-called parentectomy). All standard psychotherapies are used: individual, group, behavioral (systematic desensitization), and hypnotic. Asthmatic patients should be treated jointly by internists, allergists, and psychiatrists.

Hay Fever

Strong psychological factors combine with allergic elements to produce hay fever. One factor may dominate over the others, and they may alternate in importance.

TREATMENT

Psychiatric, medical, and allergic factors must be considered in treating hay fever.

Hyperventilation Syndrome

Normal persons can voluntarily change the rate, depth, and regularity of their breathing, which can also be correlated with various emotional states. Hyperventilative patients breathe rapidly and deeply for several minutes, feel light-headed, and then faint because of cerebral vasoconstriction and a respiratory alkalosis. Other symptoms, such as paresthesias and carpopedal spasm, may be present. Specific medical differentials for the syndrome are epilepsy, conversion disorder, vasovagal or hypoglycemic attacks, myocardial attacks, bronchial asthma, acute porphyria, Ménière's disease, and pheochromocytoma. Psychiatric differentials include anxiety attacks, panic attacks, schizophrenia, borderline or histrionic personality disorder, and phobic or obsessive complaints.

TREATMENT

Instruction or retraining regarding particular symptoms and how they are evoked by hyperventilation should be provided, so that patients can consciously avoid precipitating symptoms. Breathing into a paper bag can abort the attack. Reassurance and supportive psychotherapy are also indicated.

Tuberculosis

The onset and the aggravation of tuberculosis are often associated with acute and chronic stress. Psychological factors affect the immune system and may influence the patient's resistance to the disease.

TREATMENT

Treatment in the past was effective with antituberculosis drugs and antibiotics. The 1990s have seen a significant resurgence in the incidence of tuberculosis and the development of antibiotic-resistant tubercle bacilli. That resurgence has been partially attributed to the increase in the incidence of acquired immune deficiency syndrome (AIDS). Immune-compromised systems readily become hosts to tuberculosis, so many patients with AIDS and human immunodeficiency virus (HIV) also have tuberculosis, particularly the miliary type. The role of stress on the incidence of tuberculosis has not been thoroughly studied, but most AIDS patients have psychiatric and neurological complications and are liable to stress. Supportive psychotherapy is valuable because of the role of stress and the complicated psychosocial situation.

GASTROINTESTINAL SYSTEM

Peptic Ulcer

Peptic ulcer is a circumscribed ulceration of the mucous membrane of the stomach or the duodenum, penetrating to the muscularis mucosae and occurring in areas exposed to gastric acid and pepsin.

ETIOLOGY

Specific Theory

Alexander hypothesized that chronic frustration of intense dependence needs results in a characteristic unconscious conflict. That unconscious conflict pertains to intense dependent oral-receptive longings to be cared for and loved, which causes a chronic regressive unconscious hunger and anger. That reaction is manifested physiologically by persistent vagal hyperactivity leading to gastric acid hypersecretion, which is particularly ominous in a genetically predisposed hypersecretor of acid. With the aforementioned equation, ulcer formation may result. Genetic factors and preexisting organ damage or disease (for example, gastritis) are causally important. Such gastritis may result from excessive caffeine, nicotine, or alcohol.

Nonspecific Theories

Stress and anxiety caused by various nonspecific conflicts may produce gastric hyperacidity and hypersecretion of pepsin, resulting in an ulcer. Because various traumatic occurrences in animals (for example, electric shock in dogs) may produce ulcers, such experimental data support a nonspecific approach. Peptic ulcers have been diagnosed in all personality types.

Recent studies have implicated *Helico pylori,* a bacterium, as an infectious agent that may contribute to the cause of ulcer.

TREATMENT

Psychotherapy is directed toward the patient's dependence conflicts. Biofeedback and relaxation therapy may be useful. Medical treatment with cimetidine (Tagamet), ranitidine (Zantac), sucralfate (Carafate), or famotidine (Pepcid); antacid medications; and dietary control (for example, no alcohol) are indicated in ulcer management. The treatment of ulcer caused by *H. pylori* may include antimicrobial drugs.

Ulcerative Colitis

Ulcerative colitis is a chronic inflammatory ulcerative disease of the colon and is usually associated with bloody diarrhea. Familial incidence and genetic factors are significant. Related diseases include regional ileitis and irritable bowel syndrome.

PERSONALITY TYPE

Most studies show a predominance of compulsive personality traits. Patients with ulcerative colitis are neat, orderly, clean, punctual, hyperintellectual, timid, and inhibited in expressing their anger.

ETIOLOGY

Specific Theory

Alexander described a typical specific conflictual constellation in ulcerative colitis. The key issue is an inability to fulfill an obligation (usually of accomplishment) to a key dependency figure. Essentially, frustrated dependence stimulates oral-aggressive feelings, producing guilt and anxiety and resulting in restitution through the ''gifting'' of diarrhea. In regard to colitis, George Engel described a pathological mother-child relationship, resulting in feelings of hopelessness-helplessness and a giving up-given up complex.

Nonspecific Theory

Nonspecific stress of many types may aggravate ulcerative colitis.

TREATMENT

Nonconfrontive, supportive psychotherapy is indicated during acute ulcerative colitis, with interpretative psychotherapy during the quiescent periods. Medical treatment consists of nonspecific supportive medical measures, such as anticholinergics and antidiarrheal agents. Prednisone therapy is useful in severe cases. Bismuth-containing medications (for example, Pepto-Bismol) are useful in managing diarrhea.

Obesity

Obesity is a condition characterized by the excessive accumulation of fat (when the body weight exceeds by 20 percent the standard weight listed in the usual height-weight tables).

PSYCHOSOMATIC CONSIDERATIONS

There is a familial genetic predisposition to obesity, and early developmental factors are seen in childhood obesity. Those factors indicate that obese children increase the number of their fat cells (hyperplastic obesity), which predisposes them to adult obesity. When obesity occurs first in adult life, it is usually hypertrophic obesity (an increase in the size of fat cells), rather than an increase in the number of fat cells. Obesity also tends to limit physical activity, which aggravates the condition. Psychological factors are important in hyperphagic obesity (overeating), especially binge eating. Among psychodynamic fac-

tors suggested are oral fixation, oral regression, and the overvaluation of food. Bulimia—usually associated with binge eating—may be present. In addition, the patient often has a history of body-image disparagement and poor early conditioning to food intake.

TREATMENT

Obesity must be controlled through dietary limitation and the reduction of calorie intake. Emotional support and behavior modification are helpful for the anxiety and the depression associated with overeating and dieting. Gastric reduction surgery and similar techniques are of limited value.

Anorexia Nervosa

Anorexia nervosa is characterized by behavior directed toward losing weight, peculiar patterns of handling food, weight loss, intense fear of gaining weight, disturbance of body image, and, in women, amenorrhea. It is one of the few psychiatric illnesses that may have a course unremitting until death. Anorexia nervosa is discussed further in Section 16.1.

MUSCULOSKELETAL SYSTEM

Rheumatoid Arthritis

Rheumatoid arthritis is a disease characterized by chronic musculoskeletal pain caused by inflammatory disease of the joints. The disorder has significant hereditary, allergic, immunological, and psychological causative factors. Psychological stress may predispose patients to rheumatoid arthritis and other autoimmune diseases by immune suppression. The arthritic person feels restrained, tied down, and confined. Because many arthritic persons have a history of physical activity (for example, dancers), they often have repressed rage about the inhibition of their muscle function, which aggravates their stiffness and immobility.

TREATMENT

Treatment should include psychotherapy, which is usually supportive during chronic (sharp) attacks and interpretive between acute attacks. Rest and exercise should be structured, and patients should be encouraged not to become bed-bound and to return to their former activities. The rest and exercise program should be coordinated with the medical treatment of the pain and the inflammation of the joints.

Low Back Pain

Low back pain is felt in the lower lumbar, lumbosacral, and sacroiliac regions. It is often accompanied by sciatica, with pain radiating down one or both buttocks or following the distribution of the sciatic nerve. Although low back pain may be caused by a ruptured intervertebral disk, a fracture of the back, congenital defects of the lower spine, or a ligamentous muscle strain, many cases are psychosomatic in origin. Some reports indicate that 95 percent of cases are psychological in origin.

The examining physician should be particularly alert to a patient who gives a history of minor back trauma followed by severe disabling pain. Often, the patient with low back pain reports that the pain was initiated at a time of psychological trauma or stress. In addition, the patient's reaction to the pain is disproportionately emotional, with excessive anxiety and depression. Furthermore, the distribution of the pain rarely follows a normal neuroanatomical distribution (for example, of sciatica).

TREATMENT

Treatment should be conservative. Aspirin—up to a total of 4 grams daily—is a useful analgesic. Diazepam, 5 to 10 mg every four to six hours, acts as both a muscle relaxant and an anxiolytic. A careful exercise and physical therapy regimen, supportive psychotherapy regarding the precipitating emotional trauma, relaxation therapy, and biofeedback are helpful. Patients should be encouraged to return to their usual activities as soon as possible. Surgical intervention is rarely indicated.

HEADACHES

Headaches are the most common neurological symptom and one of the most common medical complaints. Every year about 80 percent of the population are estimated to suffer from at least one headache, and 10 to 20 percent of the population go to physicians with headache as their primary complaint. Headaches are also a major cause of absenteeism from work and avoidance of social and personal activities.

The majority of headaches are not associated with significant organic disease. Many persons are susceptible to headaches at times of emotional stress. Moreover, many psychiatric disorders, including anxiety and depressive disorders, frequently have headaches as a prominent symptom. Patients with headaches are often referred to psychiatrists by primary care physicians and neurologists after extensive biomedical workups, which often include a computed tomography (CT) scan of the head. The overwhelming majority of such workups for common headache complaints have negative findings, and such results may be frustrating for both the patient and the physician. The psychologically unsophisticated physician may attempt to reassure such patients by telling them that there is no disease. But that reassurance may have the opposite effect, increasing the patients' anxiety and even escalating into a disagreement about whether the pain is real or imagined.

Psychological stresses usually exacerbate headaches, whether their primary underlying cause is physical or psychological. Psychosomatic headaches are sometimes differentiated from psychogenic (for example, anxiety, depression, hypochondriacal, delusional) headaches. Headaches may be a conversion symptom of inpatients. In those patients the headache symbolizes unconscious psychological conflicts, and the symptoms are mediated through the voluntary sensorimotor nervous system. In contrast, psychosomatic or unconscious conflicts are not symbolic in nature. That distinction is important for psychiatrists to make so as to reach the proper diagnosis, which then allows the most specific treatment to be recommended.

Migraine (Vascular) Headaches

Migraine (vascular) headaches are a paroxysmal disorder characterized by recurrent headaches, with or without related visual and gastrointestinal disturbances. They are probably caused by a functional disturbance in the cranial circulation.

PERSONALITY TYPE

Two thirds of all patients with migraine headaches have family histories of similar disorders. Obsessional personalities

who are overly controlled and perfectionistic, who suppress anger, and who are genetically predisposed to migraines may have such headaches under severe nonspecific emotional conflict or stress.

TREATMENT

Migraines are best treated during the prodromal period with ergotamine tartrate (Cafergot) and analgesics. The prophylactic administration of propranolol or phenytoin (Dilantin) is useful if the headaches are frequent. Psychotherapy to diminish the effects of conflict and stress and certain behavioral techniques (for example, biofeedback) have been reported to be useful.

Tension (Muscle Contraction) Headaches

Emotional stress is often associated with the prolonged contraction of head and neck muscles, which over several hours may constrict the blood vessels and result in ischemia. A dull, aching pain often begins suboccipitally and may spread over the head, sometimes feeling like a tightening band. The scalp may be tender to the touch, and, in contrast to a migraine, the headache is usually bilateral and not associated with prodromata, nausea, and vomiting. The onset is often toward the end of the workday or in the early evening, possibly after the person has been removed from stressful job pressures, has tried to relax, and has focused on somatic sensations. But if family or personal pressures are equal to or greater than those at work, the headaches may be worse later in the evening, on weekends, or during vacations.

Tension headaches may occur to some degree in about 80 percent of the population during periods of emotional stress. Anxiety and depression are frequently associated with the headaches. Tense, high-strung, competitive, type A personalities are especially prone to the disorder. They may be treated in the initial stage with antianxiety agents, muscle relaxants, and massage or heat application to the head and the neck. If an underlying depression is present, antidepressants may be prescribed. However, psychotherapy is usually the treatment of choice for patients chronically afflicted by tension headaches. Learning to avoid or better cope with tension is the most effective long-term management approach. Electromyogram (EMG) feedback from the frontal or temporal muscles may help some tension-headache patients. Relaxation associated with practice periods, meditation, or other changes in a pressured life-style may provide symptomatic relief for some patients.

ENDOCRINE SYSTEM

Hyperthyroidism

Hyperthyroidism (thyrotoxicosis) is a syndrome characterized by biochemical and psychological changes that occur as a result of a chronic endogenous or exogenous excess of thyroid hormone.

PSYCHOSOMATIC CONSIDERATIONS

In a genetically predisposed person, stress is often associated with the onset of hyperthyroidism. According to psychoanalytic theory, during childhood, hyperthyroid patients have an unusual attachment to and dependence on a parent, usually the mother, and so they find intolerable any threat to their mother's approval. As children, such patients often have inadequate support because of economic stress, divorce, death, or multiple siblings.

That persistent threat to security in early life leads to premature and unsuccessful attempts to identify with an adult object. It also causes early stress and overuse of the endocrine system and further frustration of childhood dependence cravings. The patients continuously strive toward premature self-sufficiency and tend to dominate others with smothering attention and affection. They need to build defenses against a repetition of the unbearable feelings of rejection and isolation that occurred in childhood. Should those mechanisms break down, requiring a premature stimulation of the body's psychophysiological defense in a genetically predisposed patient, thyrotoxicosis may result.

TREATMENT

Antithyroid medication, tranquilizers, and supportive psychotherapy are useful. Crisis intervention may be helpful at the onset of the disease.

Diabetes Mellitus

Diabetes mellitus is a disorder of metabolism and the vascular system manifested by a disturbance of the body's handling of glucose, lipid, and protein.

ETIOLOGY

Heredity and family history are important in the onset of diabetes. A sudden onset is often associated with emotional stress, which disturbs the homeostatic balance in a predisposed patient. Psychological factors that seem significant are those provoking feelings of frustration, loneliness, and dejection. Diabetic patients must usually maintain some sort of dietary control of their diabetes. When they are depressed and dejected, they often overeat or overdrink self-destructively, causing their diabetes to get out of control. That reaction is especially common in juvenile diabetic patients. In addition, terms such as oral, dependent, seeking maternal attention, and excessive passivity have been applied to diabetic patients.

TREATMENT

Supportive psychotherapy is necessary to achieve cooperation in the medical management of the complex disease. Therapy should encourage diabetic patients to lead as normal a life as possible, with the recognition that they have a chronic but manageable disease.

Female Endocrine Disorders

PREMENSTRUAL DYSPHORIC DISORDER

Premenstrual dysphoric disorder, also known as premenstrual syndrome (PMS), is characterized by cyclical subjective changes in mood and the general sense of physical and psychological well-being correlated with the menstrual cycle. The symptoms usually begin soon after ovulation, increase gradually, and reach a maximum of intensity about five days before the menstrual period begins. Psychological, social, and biological factors have been implicated in the disorder's pathogenesis. In particular, changes in estrogen, progesterone, androgen, and prolactin levels have been hypothesized to be important to the cause. Excessive exposure to and subsequent abrupt withdrawal from endogenous opiate peptides, which fluctuate under the influence of gonadal steroids, may contribute to premenstrual dysphoric disorder. An increase in prostaglandins secreted by

the uterine musculature has been implicated in the pain associated with the disorder. Premenstrual dysphoric disorder also occurs in women past menopause and after hysterectomy, provided the ovaries remain intact. Seventy to 90 percent of all women of childbearing age report at least some symptoms.

MENOPAUSAL DISTRESS

Menopause is a natural physiological event. It is usually dated as having occurred after an absence of menstrual periods for one year. Usually, the menses tamper off during a two- to five-year span, most often between the ages of 48 and 55; the median age is 51.4 years. Menopause also occurs immediately after the surgical removal of the ovaries. The term "involutional period" refers to advancing age, and "climacteric" refers to involution of the ovaries.

Clinical Features

Many psychological symptoms have been attributed to the menopause, including anxiety, fatigue, tension, emotional lability, irritability, depression, dizziness, and insomnia. There is no general agreement on the relative contribution of those complaints or of the physiological changes to the psychological and social meanings of menopause and that development era in a woman's life.

Physical signs and symptoms include night sweats, flushes, and hot flashes. A hot flash is a sudden perception of heat within or on the body that may be accompanied by sweating and color change. The cause of the hot flash is unknown; it may be linked to pulsatile luteinizing hormone (LH) secretion. Estrogen-dependent functions are sequentially lost, and the woman may have atrophic changes in mucosal surfaces, accompanied by vaginitis, pruritus, dyspareunia, and stenosis. The woman may also have changes in calcium and lipid metabolism, probably as secondary effects of the lowered levels of estrogen, and those changes may be associated with a number of medical problems occurring in the postmenopausal era, such as osteoporosis and coronary arthrosclerosis. The physical changes may begin as much as four to eight years before the last menstrual period. During that time, women may have irregular menstrual periods with variations in the menstrual intervals and the quantity of the menstrual flow.

Hormonal Changes

Blood levels of ovarian hormones decline gradually during the climacteric period, usually over a period of several years. For many years, decreasing estrogen levels were thought to be primarily important to the clinical manifestations of menopause. Both estrogen and progesterone bind directly to brain tissue and were thought to act directly on brain function. Recently, however, it has been thought that other hormones, such as androgens and LH, are also involved. The effects of estrogen on mood may be indirectly moderated through its influence on androgen production. In any case the significance of hormonal changes is evidenced by the severe physical and psychological symptoms that follow abrupt (surgical) depletion of ovarian hormones. One difficulty in those studies that have attempted to assess the relations of changing hormonal levels in normal women is that the date of the last menstrual period is often difficult to establish, as is the menopause, for they merely mark a point on a curve of changing hormonal function. That is, the presence or the absence of menstrual bleeding is not an exact measure of hormonal status.

The severity of the symptoms at the menopause seems to be related to the rate of hormone withdrawal; the amount of hormone depletion; the woman's constitutional ability to withstand the overall aging process, including her overall health and level of activity; and the psychological meaning of aging for her.

Psychological and Psychosocial Factors

Clinically significant psychiatric difficulties may develop during the life cycle's involutional phase. Women who have previously experienced psychological difficulties, such as low self-esteem and low life satisfaction, are likely to be vulnerable to difficulties during menopause. A woman's response to menopause has been noted to parallel her response to other crucial development events in her life, such as puberty and pregnancy. Attempts to link the severity of menopausal distress with the premenstrual tension syndrome have been inconclusive.

Women who have invested heavily in childbearing and child-rearing activities are most likely to suffer distress during the postmenopausal years. Concerns about aging, loss of childbearing capacity, and changes in appearance all may be focused on the social and symbolic significance attached to the physical changes of the menopause.

Although in the past it was assumed that the incidence of mental disorders and depression would increase during the menopause, epidemiological evidence casts some doubt on that assumption as an all-inclusive and complete explanation. Epidemiological studies of mental disorders showed no increase in symptoms of mental disorders or in depression during the menopausal years, and studies of psychological complaints found no greater frequency in menopausal women than in younger women.

Treatment

Treatment programs must be individualized. Postclimacteric women may be asymptomatic for estrogen deprivation or may manifest estrogen excess (dysfunctional uterine bleeding).

The use of estrogen replacement treatment is still controversial. For women with signs of estrogen depletion, recent studies have been encouraging in regard to the use of long-term combined estrogen and progesterone replacement therapy, both in estrogen depletion syndrome and to prevent osteoporosis. Topical estrogen cream used to treat mucosal atrophy is readily absorbed systemically. The increased risk of cancer, particularly endometrial cancer, has been implicated in the use of exogenous estrogen, but the addition of a progestational agent to the replacement estrogen regimen is thought to reduce that increased risk.

Exercise, diet, and symptomatic treatment are all helpful in reducing physical discomfort. Psychological distress should be evaluated and treated primarily by appropriate psychotherapeutic and sociotherapeutic measures. Psychotherapy should include an exploration of the life stages and the meaning of aging and reproduction to the patient. The patient should be encouraged to accept the menopause as a natural life event and to develop new activities, interests, and gratifications. Psychotherapy should also attend to family dynamics and should enlist family and other social support systems when necessary.

Idiopathic Amenorrhea

The cessation of normal menstrual cycles in nonpregnant, premenopausal women with no demonstrable structural abnormalities in the brain, the pituitary, or the ovaries is called idiopathic amenorrhea.

The diagnosis is made first by exclusion and then, if possible, by identifying the primary psychogenic cause. Amenorrhea may occur as one feature of complex clinical psychiatric syndromes, such as anorexia nervosa and pseudocyesis. Other conditions associated with amenorrhea include massive obesity, diseases of the pituitary and the hypothalamus, and, in some cases, excessive amounts of running or jogging. Drugs such as reserpine (Serpasil) and chlorpromazine (Thorazine) can block ovulation and so delay the menses. Drug-induced amenorrhea is almost always accompanied by galactorrhea and elevated levels of prolactin.

The patterns of hormone defect that result in psychogenic amenorrhea are not well understood. Disturbed menstrual function with delayed or precipitate menses is a well-known response by healthy women to stress. The stress can be as minor as going away to college or as catastrophic as being put into a concentration camp.

In most women the menstrual cycling returns without medical intervention, sometimes even in continuing stressful conditions. Psychotherapy should be undertaken for psychological reasons, not just in response to the symptom of amenorrhea and to determine its cause. However, if the amenorrhea has been protracted and refractory, psychotherapy may be helpful in restoring regular menses.

CHRONIC PAIN

Persistent pain is the most frequent complaint of patients, yet it is one of the most difficult symptoms to treat because of differing causes and individual responses to pain.

Pain is affected by a myriad of subjective, unmeasurable factors, including level of attention, emotional state, personality, and past experiences. Pain may simultaneously serve as a symptom of psychological stress and as a defense against it. Psychological factors may cause a person to become somatically preoccupied and to magnify even normal sensations to chronic pain. Patients may be excessively responsive to pain for personal, social, or financial secondary gain. Chronic pain may be a way of justifying failure in establishing relationships with others. Cultural, ethnic, or religious affiliations may influence the degree and the manner in which persons express pain and the way in which their families react to the symptoms. Therefore, in evaluating and treating persistent pain, the physician should realize that pain is not a simple stimulus-response phenomenon. Rather, the perception of a reaction to pain is multifactorial, combining many biopsychosocial variables.

Pain Threshold and Perception

Peripheral sensations are transmitted through the pain pathways (for example, lateral spinothalamic tract, posterior thalamus of the diencephalon) to cortical somatosensory regions of the central nervous system (CNS) for conscious perception. The parietal cortex both localizes pain and perceives intensity. However, psychogenic pain may be entirely of CNS origin. Complex reactions to pain involve areas of the cortex responsible for memory and conscious and unconscious elements of a person's personality.

The threshold for the perception of pain is the same for most people but may be increased by about 40 percent by biofeedback, a positive emotional state, relaxation exercises, physical therapy or other physical activity, medication, guided imagery, suggestion, hypnosis, placebos, and analgesics. The beneficial response to placebos is sometimes falsely thought to differentiate organic from functional causes. In fact, about one third of normal persons, those with organic causes of pain, have at least a transient positive response to a placebo.

Variations in the effectiveness and the responsiveness of person's endorphin or other neurotransmitter systems may modulate pain perception and tolerance. A proposed gate-control theory suggests that large peripheral afferent nerve fibers modulate sensory input by inhibiting hypothetical sensory transmitting neurons (gateway cells) in the substantia gelatinosa of the spinal cord. Relief of pain by transcutaneous or dorsal column electrical stimulators may result from that system's activation.

Classification

DSM-IV classifies pain disorder under somatoform disorders. If patients have multiple recurrent pains of at least several year's duration that began before age 30, they are considered to have a somatization disorder. If the patients' pain suggests a physical illness but may be attributed to psychological factors alone, the diagnosis is conversion disorder or pain disorder (if pain is the only symptom). Patients with somatization disorder, major depressive disorder, or schizophrenia complain of various aches and pains, but pain is not the major complaint. In conversion disorder the distribution and the referral of pain are inconsistent.

Treatment

Patients with pain disorder are often undermedicated with analgesics because of a lack of knowledge of the pharmacology of analgesics, an unrealistic fear of causing addiction (even in terminal patients), and the ethical judgment that only bad physicians prescribe large dosages of narcotics. The clinician must separate patients with chronic benign pain (who tend to do much better with psychotherapy and psychotropic drugs) from those with chronic pain caused by cancer or other chronic medical disorders. The former often respond to the combination of an antidepressant and a phenothiazine. The latter usually respond better to analgesics or nerve blocks. Many cancer patients may be kept relatively active, alert, and comfortable with the judicious use of morphine, avoiding costly and incompletely effective surgical procedures, such as peripheral nerve section, cordotomy, and stereotaxic thalamic ablations.

A behavior modification, deconditioning program may also be useful. Analgesics should be prescribed at regular intervals, rather than only as needed. Otherwise, patients must suffer before receiving relief, which only increases their anxiety and sensitivity to pain. Standing orders dissociate experiencing pain from receiving medication. The deconditioning of needed care from experiencing increased pain should also extend to patients' interpersonal relationships. Patients should receive as much or more attention for displaying active and healthy behavior as they receive for passive, dependent, pain-related behaviors. Their spouses, bosses, friends, physicians, and health care or social agencies should not reinforce chronic pain and penalize patients (including threatening to discontinue disability payments) if the patients begin to relinquish the sick role. Patients should be assured of regular and supportive appointments that are not contingent on pain. Hospitalization should be avoided, if possible, to prevent further regression.

Pain clinics with a multispecialty staff evaluate and treat patients with complex pain disorders. The clinics involve psychiatrists early on, rather than only after the organic causes of pain have been ruled out and the patient and the physicians are frustrated. The patients are managed without addictive drugs, although many patients commence treatment already addicted. Exploratory or neurodestructive surgery is not encouraged, especially if the patient has a hysterical personality or a history of multiple surgical procedures. Pain clinics also recognize that most chronic pain patients experience a vicious circle of biological and psychosocial factors, so that the most effective treatment involves a systems approach that addresses each biopsychosocial component relevant to the patient.

IMMUNE DISORDERS

Considerable evidence points to a relation among psychosocial factors, immune function, and health and illness. Psychosocial processes—including a range of the person's life experiences, stresses, and trait characteristics—seem to influence the CNS, thereby encouraging the suppression of immune activity.

Infectious Diseases

Clinical studies have indicated that psychological variables influence the rate of recovery from infectious mononucleosis and influenza and the susceptibility to rhinovirus-induced common cold symptoms and tularemia. Recurrent herpes simplex and genital herpes lesions occur most frequently in patients who have a clinical depression or who experience unusual stress. Stressful life events and a poor psychological state decrease resistance to tuberculosis and influence the course of the illness. Social supports play a role in recovery from tuberculosis. Life experiences that induce anger alter the intestine's bacterial composition. College students who respond to upsetting events with maladaptive aggression or affective changes have a high incidence of subsequent upper respiratory infections. Studies indicate that the primary immune response was cell-mediated. In AIDS, transmitted by the HIV, psychiatric symptoms are common, and many think that the progress of the disease is influenced by the person's psychological state.

Allergic Disorders

Considerable clinical evidence indicates that psychological factors are related to the precipitation of many allergic disorders. Bronchial asthma is a prime example of a pathological process involving immediate hypersensitivity that is associated with psychosocial processes. Emotional reactions to life experience, personality patterns, and conditioning have been reported to contribute to the onset and the course of asthma.

Organ Transplantation

Psychosocial factors seem to play a role in organ transplantation. A number of clinical studies have found that stressful life events, anxiety, and depression precede some cases of graft rejection. Psychosocial effects on the immune system may contribute to the mechanisms involved in such rejections.

Autoimmune Diseases

A prime function of the immune system is to distinguish between self and nonself and to reject foreign antigens (nonself). Occasionally, for reasons that are unclear at the present time, a cell-mediated or humoral immune response develops against a person's own cells. That reaction results in a variety of pathological effects that are known clinically as autoimmune diseases. Disorders in which an autoimmune component has been implicated include Graves' disease, Hashimoto's disease, rheumatoid arthritis, ulcerative colitis, regional ileitis, systemic lupus erythematosus, psoriasis, myasthenia gravis, and pernicious anemia.

Mental Disorders

Although a number of investigators have found evidence suggesting altered immunity and autoimmunity in patients with schizophrenia, the specific findings have been difficult to replicate. Whether the immune abnormalities are involved in the pathogenesis of some or all types of schizophrenia or whether such abnormalities are related to a wide range of factors, including long-term institutionalization and antipsychotic agents, remains to be determined.

Immune phenomena in mental disorders other than schizophrenia have been less extensively studied. Work indicates that psychiatric patients manifest increased immunoglobulin M (IgM) and immunoglobulin A (IgA) levels. Those findings indicate the need for further study. The notion that patients with depressive disorders have an increased incidence of autoimmune antibodies has sparked some controversy. Marvin Stein concluded that the effect of depression on the modulation of immunity is complex and may involve a range of neurobiological mechanisms.

PSYCHOSOCIAL AND PSYCHOTHERAPEUTIC IMPLICATIONS

Various research groups have reported positive effects on immunological functioning from biofeedback, relaxation therapy, aerobic exercise training, and group therapy support.

CANCER

Because improved treatment has changed cancer from an incurable to a frequently chronic and often curable disease, the psychiatric aspects of cancer—the reaction to both the diagnosis and the treatment—are of increasing importance. At least half of the 1 million patients who contracted cancer in the United States in 1987 were alive five years later. Currently, an estimated 3 million cancer survivors have no evidence of the disease.

Patient Problems

When patients learn that they have cancer, their psychological reactions include fear of death, disfigurement, and disability; fear of abandonment and loss of independence; fear of disruption in relationships, role functioning, and financial standing; and denial, anxiety, anger, and guilt.

About half of all cancer patients have mental disorders. The largest group have adjustment disorder (68 percent), with major depressive disorder (13 percent) and delirium (8 percent) being the next most common diagnoses. Most of those disorders are thought to be reactive to the knowledge of having cancer.

Treatment-Related Problems

The most common medical treatments used with cancer are radiation and drugs (chemotherapy). Drugs are toxic when given in tumoricidal dosages. Patients undergoing long courses of treatment may become much sicker symptomatically from the treatment than from their disease.

RADIATION THERAPY

The side effects of radiation therapy include encephalopathy associated with increased intracranial pressure (nausea, vomiting, dizziness), headache, somnolence, personality changes, cognitive disturbances, and reactive psychic symptoms of fear and depression.

CHEMOTHERAPY

The most common adverse effects of chemotherapy are nausea and vomiting.

PAIN

Pain in cancer patients should not be underestimated or undermedicated. Because cancer patients with pain have a signifi-

cantly higher incidence of depression and anxiety than those without pain, proper and adequate treatment is essential for their psychological well-being. Cancer patients with acute pain respond well to treatment with antipain medications, such as opiates and opioids, but their tolerance levels rise, and they require more medication if the pain lasts more than a few days. That need is often inappropriately viewed as addiction, for studies have shown that cancer patients easily and voluntarily wean themselves when pain eases. Cancer patients with acute pain require sympathetic and supportive treatment from medical personnel, as do those with chronic pain, whose addictive problems are common and who nevertheless may require additional medication. As tolerance levels rise, as they always do, patients require increased dosages of narcotics, and there appears to be no ceiling to the dosage required. In cancer patients, however, tolerance to opiates and opioids does not imply addiction. Adjuvants to opiate and opioid medications, which potentiate their effects, are antidepressants, anticonvulsants, phenothiazines, and butyrophenones. One should be cautious about drug-drug interactions, such as that between meperidine (Demerol) and monoamine oxidase inhibitors (MAOIs), which can be fatal.

PALLIATIVE CARE

For the medical staff, palliation should be an active and involved process, with no hint of withdrawal or abandonment. Psychotherapy is useful in pain management.

ETHICAL ISSUES

Included among the ethical issues are questions on informed consent for both traditional and experimental treatments and third-party consent (for example, insurance companies, which may not pay for such treatments in certain cases).

Family Problems

Because cancer strikes not only the patient but also the family, caretakers in the family must provide care for the patient and respond to the increased demands of other family members. Anxiety and depression in family members require active intervention. The family problems requiring treatment are preexisting intrafamily conflicts, family abandonment, and family exhaustion.

Cancer in Children

Fewer children than adults have cancer. Of about 7,000 new cases of cancer in children in the United States in 1986, more than 60 percent had leukemia, lymphoma, and CNS tumors, and they received a combination of chemotherapy and radiation therapy. Five-year survival rates for children with fibrosarcomas, retinoblastomas, Hodgkin's disease, and gonadal and germ cell tumors have passed the 80 percent mark, and the survival rate for most other childhood cancers is between 40 and 60 percent.

SKIN DISORDERS

Psychosomatic skin disorders include a great variety of abnormal skin sensations. Emotional factors are important in every aspect of skin disorders: manifestations, aggravations, responses, causes, and prognoses.

Generalized Pruritus

Itch, tickle, and pain are all conveyed by the same afferent fibers and are differentiated only by the frequency of the electrical impulse.

The itching disorders include scabies, pediculosis, bites of insects, urticaria, atopic dermatitis, contact dermatitis, lichen ruber planus, and miliaria. Internal disorders that frequently cause itching are diabetes mellitus, nephritis, diseases of the liver, gout, diseases of the thyroid gland, food allergies, Hodgkin's disease, leukemia, and cancer. Itching can also occur during pregnancy and senility.

The term ''generalized psychogenic pruritus'' denotes that no organic cause for the itching exists or, at least, no longer exists and that, on psychiatric examination, emotional conflicts are seen to account for its occurrence.

The emotions that most frequently lead to generalized psychogenic pruritus are repressed anger and repressed anxiety. Whenever persons consciously or unconsciously experience anger or anxiety, they scratch themselves, often violently. An inordinate need for affection is a common characteristics of the patients. Frustrations of that need elicit aggressiveness that is inhibited. The rubbing of the skin provides a substitute gratification of the frustrated need, and the scratching represents aggression turned against the self.

Localized Pruritus

Pruritus Ani

The investigation of pruritus ani commonly yields a history of local irritation (for example, thread worms, irritant discharge, fungal infection) or general systemic factors (for example, nutritional deficiencies, drug intoxication). However, after running a conventional course, pruritus ani often fails to respond to the therapeutic and acquires a life of its own, apparently perpetuated by scratching and superimposed inflammation. It is a distressing complaint that often interferes with work and social activity. Investigation of large numbers of patients with the disorder has revealed that personality deviations often precede the condition and that emotional disturbances often precipitate and maintain it.

Pruritus Vulvae

As in pruritus ani, specific physical causes, either localized or generalized, may be demonstrable in pruritus vulvae, and the presence of glaring psychopathology in no way lessens the need for adequate medical investigation. In some patients, pleasure derived from rubbing and scratching is conscious—they realize that it is a symbolic form of masturbation—but more often than not the pleasure element is repressed. Most of the patients studied gave a long history of sexual frustration, which was frequently intensified at the time of the onset of the pruritus.

Hyperhidrosis

States of fear, rage, and tension can induce increased sweat secretion. Perspiration in humans has two distinct forms: thermal and emotional. Emotional sweating appears primarily on the palms, the soles, and the axillae; thermal sweating is most evident on the forehead, the neck, the trunk, and the dorsum of the hands and the forearms. The sensitivity of the emotional sweating response serves as the basis for the measurement of sweat by the galvanic skin response (an important tool of psychosomatic research), biofeedback, and the polygraph lie detector test).

Under conditions of prolonged emotional stress, excessive sweating (hyperhidrosis) may lead to secondary skin changes, rashes, blisters, and infections; therefore, hyperhidrosis may underlie a number of other dermatological conditions that are not primarily related to emotions. Basically, hyperhidrosis may be viewed as an anxiety phenomenon mediated by the autonomic nervous system; it must be differentiated from drug-induced states of hyperhidrosis.

References

Berman W H, Berman E R, Heymsfield S, Fauci M, et al: The incidence and comorbidity of psychiatric disorders in obesity. J Pers Disord 6: 168, 1992.

Goldstein M G, Niaura R: Psychological factors affecting physical condition: Cardiovascular disease literature review. Psychosomatics 33: 134, 1992.

Kaplan H I, Sadock B J, editors: Psychological factors affecting medical condition (psychosomatic disorders). In Comprehensive Textbook of Psychiatry, ed 6, H I Kaplan, B J Sadock, editors, p 1463. Williams & Wilkins, Baltimore, 1995.

Massie M J, Holland J C: The cancer patient with pain: Psychiatric complications and their management. J Pain Symp Manag 7: 99, 1992.

Niaura R, Goldstein M G: Psychological factors affecting physical condition: Cardiovascular disease literature review: II. Coronary artery disease and sudden death and hypertension. Psychosomatics 33: 146, 1992.

Stein M, Miller A H, Restman T: Depression and the immune system, and health and illness. Arch Gen Psychiatry 8: 171, 1991.

Whitehead W E: Behavioral medicine approaches to gastrointestinal disorders. J Consult Clin Psychol 60: 605, 1992.

21.3 Consultation-Liaison Psychiatry

In consultation-liaison (C-L) psychiatry, a rapidly growing area of expertise and an expanding field of concentration, the psychiatrist serves as a consultant to a medical colleague (either another psychiatrist or, more commonly, a nonpsychiatric physician) or another mental health professional (psychologist, social worker, or psychiatric nurse). In addition, the C-L psychiatrist consults in regard to patients in medical or surgical settings and provides follow-up psychiatric treatment as needed. In general, C-L psychiatry is associated with all the diagnostic, therapeutic, research, and teaching services that the psychiatrist performs in the general hospital and serves as a bridge between psychiatry and other specialties.

The C-L psychiatrist must play many roles in the medical wards of the hospital: a skillful and brief interviewer, a good psychiatrist and psychotherapist, a teacher, and a knowledgeable physician who understands the medical aspects of the case. The C-L psychiatrist must be viewed as part of the medical team who makes a unique contribution to the patient's total medical treatment.

DIAGNOSIS

Knowledge of psychiatric diagnosis is essential to the C-L psychiatrist. Both dementia and delirium frequently complicate organic medical illness, especially among hospital patients. Psychoses and other mental disorders often complicate the treatment of medical illness. Furthermore, deviant illness behavior, such as suicide, is a common problem in organically ill patients. The C-L psychiatrist must be aware of the many medical illnesses that can present with psychiatric symptoms. (A list of such medical problems is presented in Table 21.3–1.) The

Table 21.3-1.   Medical Conditions That Present with Psychiatric Symptoms

Disease	Common Medical Symptoms	Psychiatric Symptoms and Complaints	Impaired Performance and Behavior	Laboratory Tests and Findings	Diagnostic Problems
Hyperthyroidism (thyrotoxicosis)	Heat intolerance Excessive sweating Diarrhea Weight loss Tachycardia Palpitations Vomiting	Nervousness Excitability Irritability Pressured speech Insomnia May express fear of impending death Psychosis	Fine tremor Impaired cognition Decreased concentration Hyperactivity Intrusiveness	Free T_4 increased T_3 increased TSH decreased T_3 uptake decreased ECG: Tachycardia Atrial fibrillation P and T wave changes	Full range of symptoms may not be present Hyperthyroidism and anxiety states may coexist Rule out occult malignancy, cardiovascular disease, amphetamine intoxication, cocaine intoxication, anxiety states, mania
Hypothyroidism (myxedema)	Cold intolerance Dry skin Constipation Weight gain Brittle hair Goiter	Lethargy Depressed affect Personality change Maniclike psychosis Paranoia Hallucinations	Muscle weakness Decreased concentration Psychomotor slowing Apathy Unusual sensitivity to barbiturates	TSH increased TSH low if pituitary disease Free T_4 ECG: Bradycardia	More common in women Associated with lithium carbonate therapy Rule out pituitary disease, hypothalamic disease, major depressive disorder, bipolar I disorder
Hypoglycemia	Sweating Drowsiness Stupor Coma Tachycardia	Anxiety Confusion Agitation	Tremor Restlessness Seizures	Hypoglycemia Tachycardia	Excess insulin often complicated by exercise, alcohol, decreased food intake Rule out insulinoma, postictal states, agitated depression, paranoid psychosis
Hyperglycemia	Polyuria Anorexia Nausea Vomiting Dehydration Abdominal complaints	Anxiety Agitation Delirium	Acetone breath Seizures	Hyperglycemia Serum ketones Urine ketones Anion gap acidosis	Almost always associated with brittle diabetes in young juvenile diabetics and elderly non-insulin-dependent diabetics Rule out depressive disorders, anxiety disorders
Brain neoplasms	Headache Vomiting Papilledema Focal findings on neurology examination	Personality changes		Lumbar puncture: increased CSF pressure, skull X-ray, CT scan, EEG	40–50% gliomas most common in 40–50 year age group Cerebellar tumors most common in children Rule our intracranial abscess, aneurysm, subdural hematoma, seizure disorder, cerebrovascular disease, reactive depression, mania, schizophreniform disorder, dementia
Frontal lobe tumor		Mood changes Irritability Facetiousness Impaired judgment Impaired memory Delirium	Seizures Loss of speech Loss of smell	Angiogram: space-occupying lesion	
Parietal lobe tumor	Hyperreflexia Babinski's sign Astereognosis		Sensory and motor abnormalities Contralateral hemiparesis Focal seizures		
Occipital lobe tumor	Headache Papilledema Homonymous hemianopsia	Aura Visual hallucinations	Visual problems Seizures		
Temporal lobe tumor	Contralateral homonymous field cut		Psychomotor seizures Aphasia		
Cerebellar tumor	Early evidence of increased intracranial pressure Papilledema		Disturbed equilibrium Disturbed coordination		

(continued)

Table 21.3-1. *(continued)*

Disease	Common Medical Symptoms	Psychiatric Symptoms and Complaints	Impaired Performance and Behavior	Laboratory Tests and Findings	Diagnostic Problems
Head trauma	History or evidence of head trauma Headache Dizziness Bleeding from ear Altered level of consciousness Loss of consciousness Focal neurological findings	Confusion Personality changes Memory impairment	Seizures Paralysis	Lumbar puncture, skull X-rays, CT scan show evidence of bleeding or increased intracranial pressure Cerebral angiogram EEG	History of blow to head or bleeding confirms cause of ALS Rule out cerebrovascular disease, seizure disorder, alcohol dependence, diabetes mellitus, hepatic encephalopathy, depression, dementia
AIDS	Fever Weight loss Ataxia Incontinence Focal findings on neurological examination	Progressive dementia Personality changes Depression Loss of libido Psychosis Mutism	Impaired memory Decreased concentration Seizures	HIV testing CT, MRI, lumbar puncture, CSF, and blood cultures	>60% of patients have neuropsychiatric symptoms; always consider in high-risk populations and young patients with signs of dementia Rule out other infections, brain neoplasmas, dementia, depression, schizophreniform disorder
Injuries requiring ambulatory surgical evaluation and treatment (for example, wrist slashing)	Alcohol abuse and other substance abuse Recent surgery Chronic pain Chronic illness Terminal illness	>90% have major psychiatric disease History of prior suicide attempts Depressed mood Postpartum psychosis in women	Frequent accidents Repeated emergency room visits Eager to leave emergency room before full evaluation		Suicidal behavior is a symptom of underlying psychiatric illness Knowledge of risk factors is helpful but not a substitute for good clinical judgment Prediction is best done through assessment of current risk projected into the immediate future
Hyponatremia	Excessive thirst Polydipsia Stupor Coma	Confusion Lethargy Personality changes	Seizures Speech abnormalities	Decreased serum Na$^+$ Serum Na$^+$ and osmolalities to document syndrome of inappropriate secretion of antidiuretic hormone (SIADH)	Caused by excessive free water for level of total body Na$^+$ Often abnormal SIADH May be psychogenic Rule out nephrotic syndrome, liver disease, congestive heart failure, schizophreniform disorder, schizotypal personality disorder
Pancreatic carcinoma	Weight loss Abdominal pain	Depression Lethargy Anhedonia	Apathy Decreased energy	Elevated amylase	Always consider in depressed middle-aged patients Rule our other GI illnesses, major depressive disorder
Cushing's syndrome	Central obesity Purple striae Easy bruising Osteoporosis Proximal muscle weakness Hirsutism	Depression Insomnia Emotional lability Suicidality Euphoria Mania Psychosis Delirium	Disturbed sleep Decreased energy Agitation Difficulty in concentrating	Elevated blood pressure Poor glucose tolerance Dexamethasone-suppression test (may be falsely positive)	Must distinguish other causes—for example cancer from exogenous steroid excess Suicide rate in untreated cases is about 10% Rule out major depressive disorder, bipolar I disorder
Adrenocortical insufficiency (Addison's disease)	Nausea Vomiting Anorexia Stupor Coma Hyperpigmentation	Lethargy Depression Psychosis Delirium	Fatigue	Decreased blood pressure Decreased Na$^+$ Increased K$^+$ Eosinophilia	May be primary (Addison's disease) or secondary Rule out eating disorders, mood disorders

(continued)

Table 21.3-1. *(continued)*

Disease	Common Medical Symptoms	Psychiatric Symptoms and Complaints	Impaired Performance and Behavior	Laboratory Tests and Findings	Diagnostic Problems
Seizure disorder	Sensory distortions Aura	Confusion Psychosis Dissociative states Catatoniclike state	Violence Motor automatisms Belligerence Bizarre behavior	EEG, including NP leads	Consider complex partial seizures in all dissociative states Rule out postictal states, catatonic schizophrenia
Hyperparathyroidism	Constipation Polydipsia Nausea	Depression Paranoia Confusion		Increased Ca++ PTH variable ECG: shortened QT interval	Causes hypercalcemia Rule out major depressive disorder, schizoaffective disorder
Hypoparathyroidism	Headache Paresthesias Tetany Carpopedal spasm Laryngeal spasm Abdominal pain	Anxiety Agitation Depression Confusion	Impaired memory	Low Ca++, normal albumin Low blood pressure ECG: QT prolongation, ventricular arrhythmias	Causes hypocalcemia Rule out anxiety disorders, mood disorders
Systemic lupus erythematosus	Fever Photosensitivity Butterfly rash Joint pains Headache	Depression Mood disturbances Psychosis Delusions Hallucinations	Fatigue	Positive ANA Positive lupus erythematosus test Anemia Thrombocytopenia Chest X-ray: pleural effusion, pericarditis	Multisystemic autoimmune disease most frequent in women Psychiatric symptoms are present in 50% of cases Steroid treatment can cause psychiatric symptoms Rule out depressive disorders, paranoid psychosis, psychotic mood disorder
Multiple sclerosis	Sudden transient motor and sensory disturbances Impaired vision Diffuse neurological signs with remissions and exacerbations	Anxiety Euphoria Mania	Slurred speech Incontinence	CSF may show increased gamma globulin CT: degenerative patches in brain and spinal cord	Onset usually in young adults Rule out tertiary syphillis, other degenerative diseases, hysteria, mania (late)
Acute intermittent porphyria	Abdominal pain Fever Nausea Vomiting Constipation Peripheral neuropathy Paralysis	Acute depression Agitation Paranoia Visual hallucinations	Restlessness Diaphoresis Weakness	Leukocytosis Elevated δ aminolevulinic acid Elevated porphobilinogen Tachycardia	Autosomal dominant More common in women in the 20–40 age group May be precipitated by a variety of drugs Rule out acute abdominal disease, acute psychiatric episode, schizophreniform disorder, major depressive disorder
Hepatic encephalopathy	Asterixis Hyperreflexia Spider angiomata Palmar erythema Ecchymoses Liver enlargement and atrophy	Euphoria Disinhibition Psychosis Depression	Restlessness Decreased activities of daily living (ADL) Impaired cognition Impaired concentration Ataxia Dysarthria	Abnormal liver function test results Abnormal albumin EEG: diffuse slowing	May be acute or chronic depending on cause Rule out substance intoxication, mania, depressive disorder, dementia
Injuries requiring inpatient surgical evaluation and treatment (for example, suicide attempts, self-mutilation)	Alcohol abuse and other substance abuse Serious injury Major blood loss Damage to genitals, eyes, face, etc.	99% have severe psychiatric disease associated with psychosis, psychotic depression Impaired mental status secondary to substance intoxication Bizarre, inappropriate affect	Remain at great risk for suicide		Must assess and treat the underlying psychiatric condition on a priority basis Maintain a high index of suspicion for suicide risk

(continued)

Table 21.3-1. *(continued)*

Disease	Common Medical Symptoms	Psychiatric Symptoms and Complaints	Impaired Performance and Behavior	Laboratory Tests and Findings	Diagnostic Problems
Pheochromocytoma	Paroxysmal hypertension Headache	Anxiety Apprehension Feeling of impending doom	Panic Diaphoresis Tremor	Hypertension Elevated VMA in 24-hr. urine Tachycardia	Adrenal medulla secreting catecholamines Rule out anxiety disorders
Wilson's disease	Kayser-Fleischer corneal ring Hepatitislike picture	Mood disturbances Delusions Hallucinations	Choreoathetoid movements Gait disturbance Clumsiness Rigidity	Decreased serum ceruloplasmin Increased copper in urine	Hepatolenticular degeneration Autosomal recessive disorder of copper metabolism Often presents in adolescence, early adulthood Rule out extrapyramidal reactions, schizophreniform disorder, mood disorders
Huntington's disease	Family history	Depression Euphoria	Rigidity Choreoathetoid movements		Autosomal dominant Rule out mood disorders, mania, schizophrenia
Vitamin deficiencies Thiamine	Neuropathy Cardiomyopathy Wernike-Korsakoff syndrome Nystagmus Headache Amnesia	Confusion Confabulation	General malaise Inablity to sustain a conversation Poor concentration	Low thiamine level	Most common in alcoholic persons Rule out hypomania, depressive disorder, dementia
Nicotinamide	Diarrhea Stocking-glove dematitis	Confusion Irritability Insomnia Depression Psychosis Dementia	Memory disturbances		Rule out mood disorder, mania, schizophreniform disorder, dementia
Pyridoxine		Apathy Irritability	Memory disturbance Muscle weakness Seizures		Often caused by medication; isoniazid Rule out mood disorders, dementia
Vitamin B$_{12}$	Pallor Dizziness Peripheral neuropathy Dorsal column signs	Irritability Inattentiveness Psychosis Dementia	Fatigue Ataxia	Low B$_{12}$ level Schilling test Megaloblastic anemia	Often due to pernicious anemia Rule out dementia, mania, mood disorders
Tertiary syphilis	Skin lesions Leukoplakia Periostitis Arthritis Respiratory distress Progressive cardiovascular distress	Personality changes Irritability Confusion Psychosis	Irresponsible behavior Decreased attention to activities of daily living (ADL)	VDRL, Treponema antibody test CSF abnormal	General paresis Rule out neoplasias, meningitis, dementia, psychotic mood disorder, schizophrenia

C-L psychiatrist's tools for diagnosis are the interview and serial clinical observations. The purposes of the diagnosis are to identify mental disorders and psychological responses to the physical illness, to identify the patient's personality features, and to identify the patient's characteristic coping techniques in order to recommend the therapeutic intervention that is most appropriate to the patient's needs.

TREATMENT

The C-L psychiatrist's principal contribution to medical treatment is a comprehensive analysis of the patient's response to illness, psychological and social resources, coping style, and psychiatric illness, if any.

That assessment is the basis of the plan for patient treatment.

In discussing the plan, the C-L psychiatrist makes known his or her assessment of the patient to nonpsychiatric health professionals. The psychiatrist's recommendations should be clear, concrete guidelines for action. The C-L psychiatrist may recommend a specific therapy, suggest areas for further medical inquiry, inform doctors and nurses of their roles in the patient's psychosocial care, recommend a transfer to a psychiatric facility for long-term psychiatric treatment, or suggest or undertake with the patient brief psychotherapy on the medical ward.

The range of problems with which the C-L psychiatrist must deal is broad. Studies show that up to 65 percent of medical inpatients have psychiatric disorders, the most common symptoms being anxiety, depression, and disorientation. Treatment problems account for 50 percent of the consultation request

Table 21.3–2.   Common Consultation-Liaison Problems

Reason for Consultation	Comments
Suicide attempt or threat	High-risk factors are men over 45, no social support, alcohol dependence, previous attempt, incapacitating medical illness with pain, and suicidal ideation. If risk is present, transfer to psychiatric unit or start 24-hour nursing care.
Depression	Suicidal risks must be assessed in every depressed patient (see above); presence of cognitive defects in depression may cause diagnostic dilemma with dementia; check for history of substance abuse or depressant drugs (e.g., reserpine, propranolol); use antidepressants cautiously in cardiac patients because of conduction side effects, orthostatic hypotension.
Agitation	Often related to cognitive disorder, withdrawal from drugs, (e.g., opiods, alcohol, sedative-hypnotics); haloperidol most useful drug for excessive agitation; use physical restraints with great caution; examine for command hallucinations or paranoid ideation to which patient is responding in agitated manner; rule out toxic reaction to medication.
Hallucinations	Most common cause in hospital is delirium tremens; onset three to four days after hospitalization. In intensive care units, check for sensory isolation; rule out brief psychotic disorder, schizophrenia, cognitive disorder. Treat with antipsychotic medication.
Sleep disorder	Common cause is pain; early morning awakening associated with depression; difficulty in falling asleep associated with anxiety. Use antianxiety or antidepressant agent, depending on cause. Those drugs have no analgesic effect, so prescribe adequate painkillers. Rule out early substance withdrawal.
No organic basis for symptoms	Rule our conversion disorder, somatization disorder, factitious disorder, and malingering; glove and stocking anesthesia with autonomic nervous system symptoms seen in conversion disorder; multiple body complaints seen in somatization disorder; wish to be hospitalized seen in factitious disorder; obvious secondary gain in malingering (e.g., compensation case).
Disorientation	Delirium versus dementia; review metabolic status, neurological findings, substance history. Prescribe small dose of antipsychotics for major agitation; benzodiazepines may worsen condition and cause sundowner syndrome (ataxia, confusion); modify environment so patient does not experience sensory deprivation.
Noncompliance or refusal to consent to procedure	Explore relationship of patient and treating doctor; negative transference is most common cause of noncompliance; fears of medication or of procedure require education and reassurance. Refusal to give consent is issue of judgment; if impaired, patient can be declared incompetent but only by a judge; cognitive disorder is main cause of impaired judgment in hospitalized patients.

made of psychiatrist. (Table 21.3–2 covers the most common C-L problems with which the psychiatrist must deal.)

SPECIAL SETTINGS

Intensive Care Units

The central psychological aspect of patients in intensive care units (ICUs) is that they are suffering life-threatening illnesses with psychological responses that are predictable and that, if untreated, may threaten life or recovery. Coronary and medical ICU staff members see patients' reactions to acute unexpected illnesses. At first, the patient shows fear and anxiety, followed by the psychological behaviors associated with denial, such as acting out, signing out, hostility, and excessive dependence. Staff members working in burn units encounter patients going through the problems of acute unexpected illness and, later, depression, grief, and dissociation related to pain and disfigurement. Staff members in surgical ICUs see patients recovering from major surgery with the expected disorientation of delirium, depression, and adjustment reactions to surgery.

Treatment of the psychological problems in the ICU requires close attention to diagnostic possibilities and details of the environment, as well as careful team communication. Clinicians are clearly helped by familiarity with the patient's premorbid character, because the reactions to disease and illness are influenced by prior conditioning. The most common initial reactions to medical disasters include shock, fear, and anxiety. In many patients those reactions respond to treatment by the care team, especially succinct, authoritative, and consistent reassurance. When those measures are insufficient, benzodiazepines—preferably the short-acting forms—should be considered and used cautiously. When fear leads to panic or psychotic loss of control,

fast-acting antipsychotics—for example, haloperidol (Haldol)—should be used.

Denial and associated behaviors of acting out, hostility, dependence, and demanding behavior must be dealt with individually on the basis of knowledge of the patient and the reasons for those reactions. Several general points are pertinent. Direct communication with the patient, which allows but does not force a discussion of feelings, often eliminates disruptive behaviors without dealing with them directly. Allowing patients as much mastery as they want and can handle is the most reassuring approach. Permitting patients to make small choices restores some sense of control over the self and the future and calms them far beyond the meaning of the specific choices. They feel a symbolic sense of progress. For example, allowing patients to control pain medications, the lighting level, or where they sit reassures and relaxes them. Whether the disruptive behavior is hostility, dependence, or panic, patients are reassured when they are allowed to show some behavior while limits are set on behavioral extremes. Thus, the independent patient can be allowed to move around but not too far; the dependent patient can be allowed a limited number of interactions, such as use of the call button; and the hostile patient can be permitted some disagreement and ventilation but be limited in disruptive acts.

All ICUs deal mainly with anxiety, depression, and delirium. ICUs also impose extraordinarily high stress, both on the staff and on the patients, related to the intensity of the problems. Patients and staff members alike frequently observe cardiac arrests, deaths, and medical disasters, which leave all autonomically aroused and psychologically defensive. ICU nurses and their patients experience particularly high levels of anxiety, depression, turnover, and burnout.

Attention is often given, especially in the nursing literature, to the problem of stress in the ICU staff. Much less attention is given to the house staff, especially on the surgical services. All persons in ICUs need to be able to deal directly with their feelings about the extraordinary experiences they are having and the difficult emotional and physical circumstances they are experiencing. Regular support groups in which those persons are able to discuss how they are feeling are important to the ICU staff and the house staff. Such support groups are needed to protect the staff members from the otherwise predictable psychiatric morbidity that some persons experience and to protect their patients from the loss of concentration, the decreased energy, and the psychomotor-retarded communications that some staff members otherwise exhibit.

Hemodialysis Units

Hemodialysis units present a paradigm of complex modern medical treatment settings. Patients are coping with lifelong, debilitating, and limiting disease; they are totally dependent on a multiplex group of caretakers for access to a machine controlling their well-being. Dialysis is scheduled three times a week and takes four to six hours, thereby disrupting the patients' previous living routines.

In that context, such patients' major struggle is with the disease. Invariably, however, they also have to come to terms with a level of dependence on others, a dependence they probably have not experienced since childhood. Predictably, patients entering dialysis struggle for their independence; regress to childhood states; show denial by acting out against doctor's orders, by breaking their diet, or by missing sessions; show anger directed against staff members; bargain and plead or become infantilized and obsequious; but most often are accepting and courageous. The determinants of the patient's responses to entering dialysis include personality styles and their prior experiences with that or another chronic illness. Patients who have had time to react and adapt to their chronic renal failure face less new psychological work of adaptation than do those to whom renal failure and machine dependence are new.

Although little has been written about social factors, the effect of cultural factors in reaction to dialysis and the management of the dialysis unit are known to be important. Units that are run with a firm hand, that are consistent in dealing with patients, that have clear contingencies for behavioral failures, and that have adequate psychological support for staff members tend to do the best.

Complications of dialysis treatment can include psychiatric problems, such as depression, and suicide is not rare. Sexual problems can be neurogenic, psychogenic, or related to gonadal dysfunction and testicular atrophy.

Dialysis dementia is a rare condition that consists of loss of memory, disorientation, dystonias, and seizures. It occurs in patients who have been receiving dialysis treatment for many years. The cause is unknown.

The psychological treatment of dialysis patients falls into two areas. First, careful preparation before dialysis, including the work of adaptation to chronic illness, is important, especially in dealing with denial and unrealistic expectations. All predialysis patients should have a psychosocial evaluation. Second, once in a dialysis program, the patient needs periodic specific inquiries about adaptation, which does not encourage dependence or the sick role. The staff members should be sensitive to the likelihood of depression and sexual problems. Group sessions function well for support, and patient self-help groups restore a useful social network, self-esteem, and self-mastery. When needed, tricyclic drugs or phenothiazines can be used for dialysis patients. Psychiatric care is best if brief and problem-oriented.

The use of home dialysis units has been of great help. The home-treated patients, compared with hospital-treated patients, are better able to integrate the treatment into their daily lives and feel more autonomous and less dependent on others for their care.

Surgical Units

Some surgeons believe that patients who expect to die during surgery will do so. That belief now seems less superstitious than it did earlier. Chase Patterson Kimball and others have studied the premorbid psychological adjustment of patients headed for surgery and have shown that those who show evident depression or anxiety and deny it have a higher risk for morbidity and mortality than do those who, given similar depression or anxiety, are able to express it. Even better is to have a positive attitude toward impending surgery. The factors that contribute to an improved outcome for surgery are informed consent and the education of patients so that they know what to expect concerning what they will feel, where they will be (for example, it is useful to show patients the recovery room), what loss of function to expect, what tubes and gadgets will be in place, and how to cope with the anticipated pain. In cases in which the patients will not be able to talk or see, it is helpful to explain before the surgery what they can do to compensate for those losses. If postoperative states such as confusion, delirium, and pain can be predicted, they should be discussed with the patients in advance to avoid their experiencing them as unwarranted or as signs of danger. The presence of constructive family support members is helpful both before and after the surgery. Table 21.3–3 lists various surgical conditions with which the C-L psychiatrist must deal.

ALTERNATIVE MEDICINE

The use of alternative or unconventional medical therapy is increasing (Table 21.3–4). *The New England Journal of Medicine* found that one in three people uses such therapies at some point for such common ailments as depression, anxiety, chronic pain, and low back pain. Practitioners of holistic medicine use a total approach to the patient, evaluating psychosocial, environmental, and life-style parameters that have been subsumed under the psychosomatic approach in previous years. The establishment of a National Institutes of Health office, the Office of Alternative Medicine, now shows the increasing importance of the area.

Of all the alternative therapies, only hypnosis and biofeedback have entered the mainstream of psychiatry. Each treatment method requires exhaustive evaluation, but most methods appear to work through the power of suggestion. Whether other factors operate in a particular type of therapy remains to be evaluated. Patients should inform their medical doctors that they are using alternative medicine, something that most patients do not do (7 to 10 patients do not tell their physicians of such encounters).

Table 21.3-3. Transplantation and Surgical Problems

Organ	Biological Factors	Psychological Factors
Kidney	50 to 90 percent success rate; may not be done if patient is over age 55; increasing use of cadaver kidneys, rather than those from living donors	Living donors must be emotionally stable; parents are best donors, siblings may be ambivalent; donors are subject to depression. Patients who panic before surgery may have poor prognoses; altered body image with fear of organ rejection is common. Group therapy for patients is helpful.
Bone marrow	Used in aplastic anemias and immune system disease	Patients are usually very ill and must deal with death and dying; compliance is important. The procedure is commonly done in children who present problems of prolonged dependence; siblings are often donors and may be angry or ambivalent about procedure.
Heart	End-stage coronary artery disease and cardiomyopathy	Donor is legally dead; relatives of the deceased may refuse permission or be ambivalent. No fall-back position is available if the organ is rejected; kidney rejection patient can go on hemodialysis. Some patients seek transplantation hoping to die. Postcardiotomy delirium is seen in 25 percent of patients.
Breast	Radical mastectomy versus lumpectomy	Reconstruction of breast at time of surgery leads to postoperative adaptation; veteran patients are used to counsel new patients; lumpectomy patients are more open about surgery and sex than are mastectomy patients; group support is helpful.
Uterus	Hysterectomy performed on 10 percent of women over 20	Fear of loss of sexual attractiveness with sexual dysfunction may occur in a small percentage of women; loss of childbearing capacity is upsetting.
Brain	Anatomical location of lesion determines behavioral change	Environmental dependence syndrome in frontal lobe tumors is characterized by inability to show initiative, memory disturbances are involved in periventricular surgery; hallucinations are involved in parieto-occipital area.
Prostate	Cancer surgery has more negative psychobiological effects and is more technically difficult than is surgery for benign hypertrophy	Sexual dysfunction is common except in transurethral prostatectomy. Perineal prostatectomy produces the absence of emission, ejaculation, and erection; penile implant may be of use.
Colon and rectum	Colostomy and ostomy are common outcomes, especially for cancer	One third of patients with colostomies feel worse about themselves than before bowel surgery; shame and self-consciousness about the stoma can be alleviated by self-help groups that deal with those issues.
Limbs	Amputation performed for massive injury, diabetes, or cancer	Phantom-limb phenomenon occurs in 98 percent of cases; the experience may last for years; sometimes the sensation is painful, and neuroma at the stump should be ruled out; the condition has no known cause or treatment; it may stop spontaneously.

Table 21.3-4. Alternative Therapies

Some alternative approaches that may be studied by the NIH Office of Alternative Medicine under Joseph J. Jacobs. Some approaches have achieved medical recognition; others have only anecdotal support.

Manipulation
Acupuncture: Use of needles to stimulate areas that are supposed to have neural connections with specific organs and body functions.
Acupressure, reflexology: Similar to acupuncture in concept except that finger pressure is used; reflexology involves only the hands and the feet.
Chiropractic: Manipulation or subluxation of the spinal vertebrae to relieve back problems and other ailments.

Altered mental states
Relaxation response, visualization, guided imagery: Use of relaxed state—through meditation, for example—to alter body responses.

Medication
Antineoplastic therapy: Use of compounds from human urine, now synthesized, that seem to halt the division of some cancer cells.
Bee pollen: Use as a possible treatment for asthma, multiple sclerosis, and allergies.
Herbalism: Use of natural plant substances to treat illnesses, based on folk medicine and modern research.
Homeopathy: Medication based on the premise that with diluted minidoses of various substances, the immune system can fight diseases.
Ozone therapy: Introduction of ozone gas into the bloodstream as a possible way to fight diseases.
Shark cartilage: Use as a possible cancer treatment because of sharks' natural resistance to cancer.

Table from *Medical World News 34:* 54, April 1993. Used with permission.

References

Houpt J L: Introduction: Psychosomatic medicine, consultation-liaison psychiatry, and behavioral medicine. In *Psychiatry*, R Michael, A M Cooper, S B Guze, L L Judd, G L. Klerman, A J Solnit, A J Stunkard, P J Wilner, editors. Lippincott, Philadelphia, 1991.

Levenson J L, Mishra A, Hammer R, Hastillo A: Denial and medical outcome in unstable angina. Psychosom Med *51*: 27, 1989.

Lipowski Z J: Consultation-Liaison psychiatry at century's end. Psychosomatics *33*: 128, 1992.

Olfson M: Depressed patients who do and do not receive psychiatric consultation in general hospitals. Gen Hosp Psychiatry *13*: 39, 1991.

Popkin M K: Consultation-liaison psychiatry. In *Comprehensive Textbook of Psychiatry*, ed 6, H I Kaplan, B J Sadock, editors, p 1592. Williams & Wilkins, Baltimore, 1995.

Strain J, Hammer J S, Huertas D, Lam H C, et al: The problem of coping as a reason for psychiatric consultation. Gen Hosp Psychiatry *15*: 1, 1993.

21.4 TREATMENT

The concept of combined psychotherapeutic and medical treatment—that is, the approach that emphasizes the interrelation of mind and body in the genesis of symptom and disorder—calls for a greatly expanded sharing of responsibility among various professions. If one views disease from a multicausal point of view, every disease can be considered psychosomatic, since every disease is affected in some fashion by emotional factors. All those factors are best evaluated by the primary care physician, who may need the participation of the psychiatrist to explain the psychological factors fully.

Hostility, depression, and anxiety in varying proportions are at the root of most psychosomatic disorders. Psychosomatic medicine is principally concerned with those illnesses that present primarily somatic manifestations. The presenting complaint is usually physical; patients rarely complain of their anxiety or depression or tension but, rather, compliant of their vomiting or diarrhea or anorexia.

TYPES OF PATIENTS

A special evaluation of the psychological and somatic factors of three major groups of medical patients is required.

Psychosomatic Illness Group

Patients in the psychosomatic illness group suffer from such classic psychosomatic disorders as peptic ulcer and ulcerative colitis. In those disease processes one cannot posit a strictly psychogenic explanation, since the particular set of emotional factors found, for example, in the typical ulcer case may also appear in the patient with no history of ulcer.

Psychiatric Group

Patients in the psychiatric group suffer from physical disturbances caused by psychological illness, rather than physical illness. Their somatic disabilities may be real (objective) or unreal. When real, the disability involves the voluntary nervous system and is called conversion disorder. Among the unreal disabilities are hypochondriasis and delusional preoccupation with physical functioning, which is often seen in schizophrenic patients. Patients in this group suffer primarily from a psychological disturbance that requires psychiatric treatment, but auxiliary medical therapy may be necessary.

Reactive Group

Patients in the reactive group have actual organic disorders, but they also suffer from an associated psychological disturbance. For example, a patient with heart disease or rental disease requiring dialysis may have a reactive anxiety and depression regarding the life-threatening condition. That anxiety, in turn, may produce physical manifestations that complicate the somatic situation.

COMBINED TREATMENT

The combined treatment approach, in which the psychiatrist handles the psychiatric aspects of the case and the internist or other specialist treats the somatic aspects, requires the closest collaboration between the two physicians. The purpose of the medical therapy is to build up the patient's physical state so that the patient can successfully participate in psychotherapy for total cure.

Disorders such as bronchial asthma, in which psychosocial processes play a distinct role in the development and the course, may respond well to the combined treatment approach. Although the asthmatic attacks themselves may be treated successfully by the internist, psychiatric treatment can be useful in the short run by helping to alleviate the anxiety associated with the attacks and in the long run by helping to uncover the causes of the interdependence involved in the disorder.

In an acute somatic illness, such as an acute attack of ulcerative colitis, medical therapy is the primary form of treatment; psychotherapy, with its long-range goals, consists at that stage of reassurance and support. As the pendulum of disease activity

shifts and the illness becomes chronic, psychotherapy assumes the primary role, and medical therapy takes the less active position.

Sometimes reassurance is all that is needed in the treatment of psychosomatic syndromes.

Patients must participate in the process of improving their life situations. The symptoms themselves must be treated by the internist, but the psychiatric can help patients focus on their feelings about the symptoms and gain understanding of the unconscious processes involved.

If patients are handled insensitively or if their illness is regarded unsympathetically, the results can be grave.

Indications for Combined Treatment

If during an initial attack of a psychosomatic disorder the patient responds to active medical therapy in association with the superficial support, ventilation, reassurance, and environmental manipulation provided by the internist, additional psychotherapy by a psychiatrist may not be required. Psychosomatic illness that does not respond to medical treatment or that is chronic should receive psychosomatic evaluation by a psychiatrist and combined therapy as indicated.

Goal of Combined Treatment

It is useful to set up a tentative, flexible spectrum of therapeutic goals in the treatment of psychosomatic disorders. The end desired is cure, which means resolution of the structural impairment and reorganization of the personality, so that needs and tensions no longer produce pathophysiological results. Treatment should aim at a mature general life adjustment, increased capacity for physical and occupational activity, amelioration of the progression of the disease, reversal of the pathology, avoidance of complications of the basic disease process, decreased use of secondary gain associated with the illness, and increased capacity to adjust to the presence of the disease.

PSYCHIATRIC ASPECTS

Treatment of psychosomatic disorders from the psychiatric viewpoint is difficult. The purpose of therapy should be to understand the motivations and the mechanisms of disturbed functioning and to help patients understand the nature of their illness and the implications of the costly adaptive patterns. That insight should result in changed and healthier patterns of behavior.

Psychotherapy based on analytic principles is effective in treating psychosomatic disorders mainly in terms of the patients' experiences in the treatment, particularly regarding their relationships with the therapist. Psychosomatic patients are usually even more reluctant to deal with their emotional problems than are patients with other psychiatric problems. Psychosomatic patients try to avoid responsibility for their illness by isolating the diseased organ and presenting it to the doctor for diagnosis and cure. The patients may be satisfying an infantile need to be cared for passively, at the same time denying that they are adults, with all the attendant stresses and conflicts.

Resistance of Entering Psychotherapy

When psychosomatic patients first become ill, they are usually convinced that the illness is purely organic in origin. They reject psychotherapy as treatment for their sickness, and, in fact, the very idea of emotional illness may be repugnant because of personal prejudices concerning psychiatry.

In the initial phase, physical treatment and psychotherapeutic procedures must be combined subtly. A good arrangement in the early stage is treatment by a psychologically oriented physician, one who is sensitive to unconscious and transference phenomena and who is perhaps working with a psychotherapist.

Development of Relationship and Transference

Psychotherapy with the psychosomatic patient must often proceed more slowly and cautiously than with other psychiatric patients. Positive transference should be developed gradually. The psychiatrist must be supportive and reassuring during the acute illness. As the disorder becomes chronic, the psychiatrist may make exploratory interpretations, but a strong patient-physician relationship is essential for any such exploration. The psychosomatic patient is dependent, and that characteristic may be used supportively and interpretatively at crucial periods in the treatment. During therapy, a great deal of hostility appears—first in the form of overt ventilation and then in the framework of the transference. Free and appropriate expression of the patient's hostility is to be encouraged.

Interpretation

The therapist must pay particular attention to current problems in the patient's immediate life situation and must deal with the patient's reaction to the therapist and to treatment. There should be increased emphasis on evaluation of the patient's characterological difficulties and habitual reactions, particularly reactions to himself or herself (self-esteem, guilt) and reactions to his or her environment (dependence, submission, need for affection). The psychiatrist should also analyze the patient's anxieties and coping mechanisms for stress situations, such as asking for complete care, always having to be right, refraining from self-assertion, and suppressing all forbidden impulses.

Some psychoanalytic investigators have reported dramatic results when unconscious material was interpreted as a drastic measure during an acute illness. Although most Freudian psychoanalysts seem to think that genetic material must eventually be interpreted for a complete cure, new approaches have shown that adequate results can be obtained when psychotherapy is limited to the analysis of characterological and ego defenses associated with disturbed interpersonal relationships.

Psychosomatic patients are often involved in a repetitious pattern involving stress in their interpersonal relationships. Because such patients are usually unaware of the pattern, it is helpful to show them that the pattern is not accidental but is determined by factors of which they are unaware, and it is essential to show them how they may change the disturbing pattern and act in a new and healthier manner.

Psychosomatic patients tend to drive toward psychologically regressed mental and physical behavior. Usually, their regression is to a traumatic or highly conflictual period. By reenacting certain specific attitudes of childhood or infancy, they are attempting to master the anxiety and illness first manifested during those earlier stages.

In the treatment of psychosomatic disorders, the key concept is flexibility in technique. Because of the patient's poor motivation and poor physical condition, it may be necessary to make frequent changes in the psychotherapeutic approach.

Resistance during Therapy

Since psychosomatic patients frequently have a great deal of resistance to entering psychotherapy, the resistance often continues unabated during therapy. In many patients the motivation for entering treatment is so poor that they frequently drop out of therapy for minor reasons.

Interruption of Psychotherapy for a Medical Emergency

During a course of psychotherapy, a patient with a psychosomatic disorder may require medical or surgical treatment for the organic disorder. The psychiatrist should cooperate closely with the surgeon or medical personnel and should maintain contact with the patient—in person or by telephone—during the emergency. Such interest offers valuable emotional support in a time of crisis.

If a patient is hospitalized, the psychiatrist should help other hospital personnel recognize and learn to tolerate the frequently difficult and provocative behavior of certain psychosomatic patients. The preparation can be of use to such patients as well; if they see their demands being met considerately, they may be less inclined to view their world as hostile and formidable.

Danger of Psychosis

There are no simple relations between psychosomatic disorders and psychoses. Some people in whom physiological and psychological processes are poorly integrated manifest both psychosomatic disorders and psychoses. In other people, the ego integration is such that stress produces a breakdown of bodily function, rather than a psychotic maladjustment. Some nonpsychotic psychosomatic patients can become psychotic or exhibit psychotic symptoms as a result of too active an interpretation and the removal of defensive elements in the personality structure.

MEDICAL ASPECTS

The internist's treatment of psychosomatic disorders should follow the established rules for their medical management. Generally, the internist should spend as much time as possible with the patient and listen sympathetically to the many complaints. The internist must be reassuring and supportive. Before performing a physically manipulative procedure—particularly if it is painful, such as a colonoscopy—the internist should explain to the patient just what will happen. The explanation allays the patient's anxiety, makes the patient more cooperative, and actually facilitates the examination.

The patient's attitude toward taking drugs may also affect the outcome of the psychosomatic treatment. For example, patients suffering from diabetes who do not accept their illness and who have self-destructive impulses of which they are unaware may purposely not control their diet and, as a result, end up in a hyperglycemic coma. In the case of cardiac patients, some refuse to curtail their physical activity after a myocardial infarction because of a reluctance to admit weakness or because of a fear that they will somehow be considered unsuccessful. Others use their illness as a welcome punishment for guilt or as a way of avoiding responsibility. Therapy in such cases must strive to help patients minimize their fears and focus on self-care and the reestablishment of a healthy body image.

ACCEPTANCE OF PSYCHOMEDICAL TREATMENT

The advantages of the collaborative approach are that the patient receives the benefit of the efforts of specialists trained in various medical disciplines, each working in the area in which he or she is best equipped to function. However, some physicians have resisted the psychiatric approach because of inadequate training in psychiatry in medical school, unfamiliarity with the specialized language of psychiatry, and a general prejudice based on the cost of psychotherapy and the alleged unscientific and subjective aspects of psychiatry.

OTHER TYPES OF THERAPY

Other types of treatment have been introduced for psychosomatic disorders, some of which are described below. The first category includes psychotherapies based on psychological insight and change, such as group and family psychotherapy; the second category is composed of behavior therapy techniques based on Pavlovian principles of learning new behavior, such as biofeedback and relaxation therapy.

Group Psychotherapy and Family Therapy

Because of the psychopathological significance of the mother-child relationship in the development of psychosomatic disorders, modification of that relationship has been suggested as a likely focus of emphasis in the psychotherapy of psychosomatic disorders. Toksoz Byram Karasu wrote that the group

approach should also offer greater interpersonal contact, providing increased ego support for the weak egos of psychosomatic patients who fear the threat of isolation and parental separation. Family therapy offers hope of a change in the relationship between the family and the child. Both therapies have had excellent initial clinical results.

However, the long-term evaluation of the results of the various psychotherapies, individual and group, for psychosomatic disorders remains to be carried out.

Behavior Therapy

BIOFEEDBACK

The application of biofeedback techniques to patients with hypertension, cardiac arrhythmias, epilepsy, and tension headaches has led to encouraging but inconclusive therapeutic results.

RELAXATION TECHNIQUES

The treatment of hypertension may include the use of the relaxation techniques. Positive results have been published about the treatment of alcohol and other substance abuse by using transcendental meditation. Workers have also used meditation in the treatment of headaches.

References

Book H E: Empathy: Misconceptions and misuses in psychotherapy. Am J Psychiatry *145*: 4, 1988.
Dolinar L J: Obstacles to the care of patients with medical-psychiatric illness on general hospital psychiatry units. Gen Hosp Psychiatry *15*: 14, 1993.
Fink P: Surgery and medical treatment in persistent somatizing patients. J Psychosom Res *36*: 439, 1992.
Lipowski Z J: Psychosomatic medicine: Past and present. Can J Psychiatry *31*: 2, 1986.
Stoudemire A, McDaniel J S: History, classification, and current trends in psychosomatic medicine. In *Comprehensive Textbook of Psychiatry*, ed 6, H I Kaplan, B J Sadock, editors, p 1463. Williams & Wilkins, Baltimore, 1995.
Vitaliano P P, Maivro R D, Russo J, Mitchell E S, Carr J E, Van Citters R L: A biopsychosocial model of medical student distress. J Behav Med *11*: 311, 1988.

22/ Relational Problems

Relationships form the matrix within which most people live their lives. Relationships are the sources of comfort, connection, and happiness for people; they are also the sources of obligation, responsibility, and friction. Psychological problems affect the way people function in a variety of relationships. External events (illness, war, natural disaster, economic crises, and social change) can also stress relationships. The lack of relationships or the loss of relationships can lead to feelings of isolation and depression.

The fourth edition of *Diagnostic and Statistical Manual of Mental Disorders* (DSM-IV) considers relational problems in a variety of relationships in which the focus of attention is a pattern of interaction that results in clinically significant impairment in one or more persons involved in those relationships.

RELATIONAL PROBLEM RELATED TO A MENTAL DISORDER OR GENERAL MEDICAL CONDITION

According to DSM-IV, this category should be used when the focus of clinical attention is a pattern of impaired interaction associated with a mental disorder or a general medical condition in a family member.

Adults often assume the responsibility of caring for aging parents while they are still caring for their children. That dual obligation often creates stress. Also, caring for elderly parents involves the adaptation of both parties to a reversal of their former roles, facing the potential loss of the parent, and coping with evidence of one's own mortality.

A problem that is now receiving attention is the abuse of the elderly by some caretaking children. The problem is most likely to occur when the abusing offspring have substance abuse problems, are under economic stress, and have no relief from their caretaking duties and when the elderly parent is bedridden or has a chronic illness that requires constant nursing attention. More elderly women are abused than are elderly men, and most abuse occurs in the elderly over age 75.

The development of a chronic illness in a family member stresses the family system. It requires adaptation on the part of the sick person and other family members. The sick person frequently deals with some loss of autonomy, an increased sense of vulnerability, and sometimes a taxing medical regimen. Other family members also experience the loss of the person as he or she was before the illness and usually have substantial caretaking responsibility—for example, in debilitating neurological diseases, including dementia of the Alzheimer's type, and with such diseases as acquired immune deficiency syndrome (AIDS) and cancer. In those cases the whole family has to deal with the stress of both prospective death and the current illness. Some families use the anger engendered by such situations to create support organizations, increase public awareness of the disease, and rally the family around the sick member. However, chronic illness frequently causes depression in family members and may cause them to withdraw from one another or to attack one another. The burden of caring for ill family members falls disproportionately on the women in a family—mothers, daughters, and daughters-in-law.

Chronic emotional illness also requires major adaptations by families. For instance, family members may react with chaos or fear to the psychotic productions of a schizophrenic family member. Family systems are stressed by the schizophrenic member's regression, exaggerated emotions, frequent hospitalizations, and economic and social dependence. Family members may react with hostile feelings (referred to as expressed emotion) that are associated with poor prognoses in the sick patients. Similarly, families are stressed when a family member has bipolar I disorder, particularly during manic episodes.

Illness devastates a family when it suddenly strikes a previously healthy family member, when it occurs earlier than expected in the life cycle (some impairment of physical capacities is expected in old age, although many elderly people are healthy), when the economic stability of the family is affected by the illness, and when little can be done to improve or ease the condition of the sick family member.

PARENT-CHILD RELATIONAL PROBLEM

Parent-child problems apply to the parent or to the child or to both and are often conflicts that fall within the range of the normal developmental stages or crises of each. According to DSM-IV, this category should be used when the focus of clinical attention is a pattern of interaction between parent and child (for example, impaired communication, overprotection, inadequate discipline) associated with clinically significant impairment in individual or family functioning or clinically significant symptoms.

Difficulties arise in a variety of situations that stress the usual parent-child interaction. For instance, in a family in which the parents are divorced, parent-child problems may arise in the relationship with either the custodial or the noncustodial parent. The remarriage of a divorced or widowed parent can also lead to a parent-child problem. The resentment of a stepparent and the favoring of a natural child are usual in the initial phases of adjustment of a new family. The birth of a second child is an occasion for both familial stress and happiness. The birth of a child can also be troublesome if the parents had adopted a child in the belief that they were infertile.

Other situations that may cause a parent-child problem are the development, in either a parent or a child, of a fatal, crippling, or chronic illness—such as leukemia, epilepsy, sickle-cell anemia, or a spinal cord injury—or the birth of a child with congenital defects (for example, cerebral palsy, blindness, and deafness). Although those situations are not rare, they challenge the emotional resources of the people involved. The parents and the child have to face present and potential loss and must adjust their day-to-day lives physically, economically, and emotionally. Those situations can try the healthiest families and produce parent-child problems, not just with the sick child but also with the unaffected siblings. Those siblings may be resented, preferred, or neglected because the ill child requires so much time and attention.

PARTNER RELATIONAL PROBLEM

According to DSM-IV, this category should be used when the focus of clinical attention is a pattern of interaction between the spouses or the partners characterized by negative communication (for example, criticisms), distorted communication (for example, unrealistic expectations), or noncommunication (for example, withdrawal) associated with clinically significant impairment in individual or family functioning or symptoms in one or both partners.

When a person presents with a partner relational problem, the psychiatrist must assess whether the patient's distress arises from the relationship or whether it is part of a mental disorder. Mental disorders are more common among single people—the never married, widowed, separated, and divorced—than among married people. The developmental, sexual, and occupational histories and the relationship history of the patients are necessary for purposes of diagnosis.

Couples therapy is discussed in Section 26.4.

Demands of Marriage

Marriage demands a sustained level of adaptation from both partners. Areas to be explored in a troubled marriage include the extent of communication between the partners, their ways of solving disputes, their attitudes toward childbearing and child rearing, their relationships with their in-laws, their attitudes toward social life, their handling of finances, and the couple's sexual interaction. Stressful periods in the relationship may be precipitated by the birth of a child, abortion or miscarriage, economic stresses, moves to new areas, episodes of illness, major career changes, and any situations that involve a significant change in marital roles. Illness in a child exerts the greatest strain on a marriage, and marriages in which a child has died through illness or an accident end in divorce more often than not. Complaints of primary anorgasmia or impotence by marital partners are usually indicative of intrapsychic problems, although sexual dissatisfaction is involved in many cases of marital maladjustment.

Adjustment to marital roles can be a problem if the partners are of different backgrounds and have been raised with different value systems. For example, members of low socioeconomic status groups perceive the wife as making most of the decisions regarding the family and accept physical punishment as a way to discipline children. Middle-class persons perceive the decision-making process as shared, the husband often being the final arbiter, and they prefer to discipline children by verbal chastisement.

Problems involving conflicts in values, adjustment to new roles, and poor communication are most effectively handled when the relationship between the partners is examined, as in marital therapy.

Sibling Relational Problem

According to DSM-IV, this category should be used when the focus of clinical attention is a pattern of interaction between siblings associated with clinically significant impairment in individual or family functioning or symptoms in one or more of the siblings.

Problems arising from sibling rivalry can occur with the birth of a child and can recur as the children grow up. Competition among children for the attention, affection, and esteem of their parents is a fact of family life. That rivalry can extend to others who are not siblings and remains a factor in normal and abnormal competitiveness throughout life. In some families, children receive labels early in life, such as "the good child" or "the black sheep," and may turn those labels into self-fulfilling prophesies. In good sibling relationships the pleasures of companionship and the bonds created by kinship and shared experiences outweigh feelings of rivalry.

RELATIONAL PROBLEM NOT OTHERWISE SPECIFIED

According to DSM-IV, this category should be used when the focus of clinical attention is on relational problems not classifiable by any of the specific problems listed above—for example, difficulties with coworkers.

Problems causing sufficient strain to bring a person into contact with the mental health care system may arise in relationships with romantic partners, coworkers, neighbors, teachers, students, friends, and social groups.

Racial and religious prejudices cause problems in interpersonal relationships. Some social scientists believe that racism and religious bigotry do not have a strong psychological base, and they emphasize social and class factors as causative. Other investigators view prejudice as a learned attitude and consider it a cultural variant. A number of psychiatrists believe that people are motivated to change their prejudices only if they see them as part of a mental disorder. Prejudice may be a maladaptive defense erected to protect the prejudiced person from profound feelings of inadequacy. It involves the projection of unwanted and devalued attributes onto the scapegoated group.

References

Cook W L: Interdependence and the interpersonal sense of control: An analysis of family relationships. J Pers Soc Psychol 64: 587, 1993.

Hetherington E M, Clingempeel W G: Coping with marital transitions: A family systems perspective. Monogr Soc Res Child Dev 57: 1, 1992.

Hibbs E D, Hamburger S D, Kruesi M J, Lenane M: Factors affecting expressed emotion in parents of ill and normal children. Am J Orthopsychiatry 63: 103, 1993.

Krauss M W: Child-related and parenting stress: Similarities and differences between mothers and fathers of children with disabilities. Am J Ment Retard 97: 393, 1993.

O'Connor B P: Family and friend relationships among older and younger adults: Interaction motivation, mood, and quality. Int J Aging Hum Dev 40: 9, 1995.

Pruchno R, Kleban M H: Caring for an institutionalized parent: The role of coping strategies. Psychol Aging 8: 18, 1993.

Sadock V: Relational problems. In Comprehensive Textbook of Psychiatry, ed 6, H I Kaplan, B J Sadock, editors, p 1607. Williams & Wilkins, Baltimore, 1995.

Scheer S D, Unger D G: Parents' perceptions of their adolescence: Implications for parent-youth conflict and family satisfaction. Psychol Rep 76: 131, 1995.

Takigiku S K, Brubaker T H, Hennon C B: A contextual model of stress among parent caregivers of gay sons with AIDS. AIDS Educ Prev 5: 25, 1993.

23/ Problems Related to Abuse or Neglect

The fourth edition of *Diagnostic and Statistical Manual of Mental Disorders* (DSM-IV) specifies five problems related to abuse or neglect: (1) physical abuse of child, (2) sexual abuse of child, (3) neglect of child, (4) physical abuse of adult, and (5) sexual abuse of adult (Table 23–1).

CHILD ABUSE AND NEGLECT

Children who have been physically or sexually abused present with a multitude of psychiatric disturbances, including anxiety, aggressive behavior, paranoid ideation, posttraumatic stress disorder, depressive disorders, and an increased risk of suicidal behavior. Abuse appears to increase the risk of psychiatric disturbances in already vulnerable children. Abused children of parents with psychopathology are more likely to experience a mental disorder than are nonabused children of psychiatrically disturbed parents. Children who have been sexually abused reportedly have an increased frequency of poor self-esteem, depression, dissociative disorders, and substance abuse. Chronic maltreatment appears to promote aggressive and violent behavior in vulnerable children.

Epidemiology

According to the National Committee for the Prevention of Child Abuse, in 1992 about 3 million cases of child abuse and neglect were reported to public and social service agencies; of that number, about 1 million cases were substantiated. Each year in the United States, 2,000 to 4,000 deaths are caused by child abuse and neglect. Each year 150,000 to 200,000 new cases of sexual abuse are reported. An estimated one of every three to four girls will be sexually assaulted by the age of 18 years, and an estimated one of every seven to eight boys will be sexually assaulted by the age of 18 years. The actual occurrence rates are likely to be higher than those estimates, because many maltreated children go unrecognized, and many are reluctant to report the abuse. Of those children physically abused, 32 percent are under 5 years of age, 27 percent are between 5 and 9 years, 27 percent are between 10 and 14 years, and 14 percent are between 15 and 18 years. More than 50 percent of all abused and neglected children were born prematurely or had low birth weights.

Recently, sexual attacks on children by groups of other children have increased. Of 1,600 young sex abusers whose cases were analyzed by a university abuse-prevention center, more than 25 percent started abusing other children before the age of 12 years. The group leaders have often been abused themselves, but the followers seem to succumb to peer pressure and to a society that glamorizes violence and links violence with sex.

Etiology

Many factors contribute to the development of child abuse and neglect. Many abusive parents have themselves been victims of physical and sexual abuse and of long-term exposure to violent home lives. A powerful promoter of aggression is long-term exposure to pain and physical torment. Thus, parents who were brought up with harsh corporal punishment and cruel treatment by their own families may continue the abuse tradition with their children. In some cases, the adults believe that their methods are acceptable ways of teaching discipline. In other cases, parents are ambivalent about their methods of abusive parenting but find themselves without coping mechanisms, so they fall into behaviors similar to their own parents' behaviors.

Certain childhood characteristics may increase a child's vulnerability to neglect and physical and sexual abuse. Children who are premature, mentally retarded, or physically handicapped and those who cry excessively or are unusually demanding may be at high risk for being abused or neglected.

The perpetrator of the battered child syndrome (that is, physical abuse) is more often the mother than the father. One parent is usually the active batterer, and the other passively accepts the battering. Of the perpetrators studied, 80 percent were regularly living in the homes of the children they abused. More than 80 percent of the children studied were living with married parents, and about 20 percent were living with a single parent. The average age of the mother who abused her children is reported to be around 26 years; the average age of the father is 30 years. Many abused children come from poor homes, and the families tend to be socially isolated.

Sexual abuse is usually committed by men, although women acting in concert with men or alone have also been involved, especially in child pornography. Sexual abuse is usually perpetrated by someone known to the child. Males are the perpetrators in about 95 percent of the cases of sexual abuse of girls and about 80 percent of the cases of sexual abuse of boys. In many cases the perpetrator of sexual abuse has been a victim of physical or sexual abuse. In some circumstances, pedophilia is a factor; the adult perpetrator is more aroused by children than by adult partners. In other cases the sexual abuse may be mixed with physical abuse. In many instances the perpetrator shows no specific preference for child sexual partners.

Diagnosis and Clinical Features

PHYSICAL ABUSE OF CHILD

Physical abuse must always be considered when a child presents with bruises or injuries that cannot be adequately explained or that are not compatible with the history given by the parent. Suspicious physical indicators include bruises and marks that form symmetrical patterns, such as injuries to both sides of the face, and regular patterns on the back, the buttocks, and the thighs. Accidental injuries are not likely to result in symmetrical patterns. Bruises may have the shape of the instrument used to make them, such as a belt buckle or a cord. Burns by cigarettes may result in symmetrical round scars, and immersions in boiling water result in burns that look like socks or gloves or that are doughnut-shaped. Multiple and spiral fractures, especially in a young baby, may be the result of physical aggression; retinal hemorrhages in an infant may be due to shaking.

Children who are repeatedly brought to hospitals for treat-

Table 23-1. Problems Related to Abuse or Neglect

Physical abuse of child
This category should be used when the focus of clinical attention is physical abuse of a child.
Sexual abuse of child
This category should be used when the focus of clinical attention is sexual abuse of a child.
Neglect of child
This category should be used when the focus of clinical attention is child neglect.
Physical abuse of adult
This category should be used when the focus of clinical attention is physical abuse of an adult (e.g., spouse beating, abuse of elderly parent).
Sexual abuse of adult
This category should be used when the focus of clinical attention is sexual abuse of an adult (e.g., sexual coercion, rape).

Table from DSM-IV, *Diagnostic and Statistical Manual of Mental Disorders*, ed 4. Copyright American Psychiatric Association, Washington, 1994. Used with permission.

ment of peculiar or puzzling problems by parents who at first appear to be overly cooperative may be victims of Munchausen syndrome by proxy. In that abuse scenario a parent repeatedly inflicts illness or injury on a child—by injecting toxins or inducing the child to ingest drugs or toxins so as to cause diarrhea, dehydration, or other symptoms—and then eagerly seeks medical attention. Since the pathological parents are sneaky and on the surface compliant, the diagnosis is difficult to make.

Behaviorally, abused children may appear withdrawn and frightened or may present with aggressive behavior and labile mood. They often exhibit depression, poor self-esteem, and anxiety. They may try to physically cover up injuries and are usually reticent to disclose the abuse for fear of retaliation. They may show some delay in developmental milestones, often have difficulties with peer relationships, and may engage in self-destructive or suicidal behaviors.

SEXUAL ABUSE OF CHILD

No specific behavioral manifestations prove the sexual abuse has taken place, but children may exhibit many behaviors that raise suspicion. Young children who present a detailed knowledge of sexual acts have usually witnessed or participated in sexual behavior. Young sexually abused children often exhibit their sexual knowledge through play and may initiate sexual behaviors with their peers. Aggressive behavior is common among abused children. Children who are extremely fearful of adults, particularly men, may have been subjected to sexual abuse.

The diagnosis of sexual abuse in children is full of pitfalls. An estimated 2 to 8 percent of the allegations of sexual abuse are false. A much higher percentage of reports cannot be substantiated. Many investigation are done hastily or by inexperienced evaluators. In custody cases an allegation of sexual abuse can be used as a maneuver to limit a parent's visitation rights. Alleged sexual abuse of a preschool-age child is particularly difficult to evaluate because of the child's immature cognitive and language development. The use of anatomically correct dolls has grown in popularity, but the use of such dolls is controversial. Patient and careful evaluations by experienced objective professionals are necessary; leading questions must be avoided. Children under the age of 3 years are unlikely to produce a verbal memory of past trauma or abuses; however, their experience may be reflected in their play or fantasies. Some abused

children meet the DSM-IV diagnostic criteria for posttraumatic stress disorder. The psychological and physical effects of sexual abuse can be devastating and long-lasting. Children who are sexually stimulated by an adult feel anxiety and overexcitement, lose confidence in themselves, and become mistrustful of adults. Seduction, incest, and rape are important predisposing factors to later symptom formations, such as phobias, anxiety, and depression. The abused children tend to be hyperalert to external aggression, as shown by an inability to deal with their own aggressive impulses toward others or with others' hostility directed toward them.

Depressive symptoms are commonly reported among children who have been sexually abused. The depressive feelings are usually combined with shame, guilt, and a sense that the victim has been permanently damaged. Poor impulse control and self-destructive and suicidal behaviors are reported to be high among adolescents who have been sexually abused. Posttraumatic stress disorder and dissociative disorders are seen in some patients who have been sexually abused. Sexual abuse is a common preexisting factor in the development of dissociative identity disorder (also known as multiple personality disorder). Signs of dissociation are described as periods in which the children are amnestic, do not feel the pain, or feel that they are somewhere else. Borderline personality disorder has been reported in some patients with histories of sexual abuse. Substance abuse has also been reported with high frequency among adolescents and adults who were sexually abused as children.

Incest

Incest is defined as the occurrence of sexual relations between close blood relatives. A broader definition describes incest as intercourse between participants who are related to one another by some formal or informal bond of kinship that is culturally regarded as a bar to sexual relations. For example, sexual relations between stepparents and stepchildren or among stepsiblings are usually considered incestuous, even though no blood relationship exist.

The strongest and most universal taboo exists against mother-son incest. It occurs much less frequently than any other form of incest. Such behavior is usually indicative of more severe psychopathology in the participants than are father-daughter and sibling incest.

Accurate figures on the incidence of incest are difficult to obtain because of the general shame and embarrassment of the entire family. Girls are victims more often than are boys. About 15 million women in the United States have been the objects of incestuous attention, and one third of all sexually abused persons have been molested before the age of 9.

Incestuous behavior is reported much more frequently among families of low socioeconomic status than among other families. The difference may be due to greater contact with reporting officials—such as welfare workers, public health personnel, and law enforcement agents—and is not a true reflection of a higher incidence in families of low socioeconomic status. Incest is more easily hidden by economically stable families than by the poor.

Social, cultural, physiological, and psychological factors—all contribute to the breakdown of the incest taboo. Incestuous behavior has been associated with alcohol abuse, overcrowding, increased physical proximity, and rural isolation that prevents adequate extrafamilial contacts. Some communities may be more tolerant of incestuous behavior than is society in general. Major mental disorders and intellectual deficiencies have been described in some cases of clinical incest. Some family therapists view incest as a defense designed to maintain a dysfunctional family unit. The older and stronger participant in incestuous behavior is usually male. Thus, incest may be viewed as a form of child abuse, as a pedophilia, or as a variant of rape.

About 75 percent of reported cases involve father-daughter incest. However, many case of sibling incest are denied by parents or involve nearly normal interaction if the activity is prepubertal sexual play and exploration.

The daughter in father-daughter incest has frequently had a close relationship with her father throughout her childhood and may be pleased at first when he approaches her sexually. The incestuous behavior usually begins when the daughter is 10 years old. As the behavior continues, however, the abused daughter becomes bewildered, confused, and frightened. As she nears adolescence, she undergoes physiological changes that add to her confusion. She never knows whether her father will be parental or sexual. Her mother may be alternately caring and competitive; the mother often refuses to believe her daughter's reports or refuses to confront her husband with her suspicion. The daughter's relationships with her siblings are also affected as they sense her special position with her father and treat her as an outsider. The father, fearful that his daughter may expose their relationship and often jealously possessive of her, interferes with her development of normal peer relationships.

The physician must be aware of the possibility of intrafamilial sexual abuse as the cause of a wide variety of emotional and physical symptoms, including abdominal pain, genital irritations, separation anxiety disorder, phobias, nightmares, and school problems. When incest is suspected, the clinician must interview the child apart from the rest of the family.

Father-son incest. The family in which the father-son incest occurs is usually highly disturbed, with a violent, alcohol-dependent, or psychopathic father; a dependent or disabled mother who is unable to protect her children; and an absence of the usual family roles and individual identities. Father-son and mother-daughter incest are rarely reported. The son in father-son incest is frequently the eldest child, and, if he has a sister, she is often sexually abused by the father as well. The father does not necessarily have any other history of homosexual behavior. The sons in the situation may experience homicidal or suicidal ideation and may first present to a psychiatrist with self-destructive behavior.

Statutory Rape

Intercourse is unlawful between a male more than 16 years of age and a female under the age of consent, which varies from 14 to 21 years, depending on the jurisdiction. Thus, a man of 18 and a girl of 15 may have consensual intercourse, yet the man may be held for statutory rape. Statutory rape may vary dramatically from other types of rape in being nonassaultive, not a violent act. Nor is it a deviant act, unless the age discrepancy is sufficient for the man to be defined as a pedophile—that is, when the girl is less than 13 years old. Charges of statutory rape are rarely pressed by the consenting girl; they are brought by her parents.

NEGLECT OF CHILD

A maltreated child often presents no obvious signs of being battered but has multiple minor physical evidences of emotional and, at times, nutritional deprivation, neglect, and abuse. The maltreated child is often taken to a hospital or a private physician and has a history of failure to thrive, malnutrition, poor skin hygiene, irritability, withdrawal, and other signs of psychological and physical neglect.

Children who have been neglected may show overt failure to thrive at less than 1 year of age; their physical and emotional development is drastically impaired. The children may be physically small and not able to show appropriate social interaction. Hunger, chronic infections, poor hygiene, and inappropriate dress may be present. Malnutrition may eventually be evident. Behaviorally, children who are chronically neglected may be indiscriminately affectionate, even with strangers, or they may

be socially unresponsive, even in familiar social situations. Neglected children may present as runaways or with conduct disorder.

An extreme form of failure to thrive in children of 5 years or older is psychosocial dwarfism, in which a chronically deprived child does not grow and develop, even when adequate amounts of food are present. Such children have normal proportions but are exceedingly small for their age. They often have reversible endocrinological changes resulting in decreased growth hormone, and they cease to grow for a time. Behaviorally, children with the disorder exhibit bizarre eating behaviors and disturbed social relationships. Binge eating, the ingestion of garbage or nonedible substances, the drinking of toilet water, and induced vomiting have been reported.

Parents who neglect their children are often overwhelmed, depressed, isolated, and impoverished. Unemployment, the lack of a two-parent family, and substance abuse may exacerbate the situation. Several prototypes of neglectful mothers have been suggested. Some mothers are young, inexperienced, socially isolated, and ignorant, leading to a temporary period of inability to care for their children. Other neglectful mothers are chronically passive and withdrawn women who may have been raised in chaotic, abusive, and neglectful homes. In those cases, once the situation comes to the attention of a child protective agency, the mother often accepts help. Mothers with major mental disorders who view their children as evil or as purposely driving them crazy are difficult to help.

PATHOLOGY AND LABORATORY EXAMINATION

Although no definitive laboratory tests are available to help the clinician make a diagnosis of child physical or sexual abuse or neglect, a physical examination is indicated when abuse is suspected to identify physical stigmata. In cases of failure to thrive, endocrinological screening is indicated. An external genital examination is indicated in cases of suspected child sexual abuse to identify scars, tears, and genital infections.

Differential Diagnosis

Factors that complicate the identification and the substantiation of abuse and neglect situations include parental feuding and custody disputes. When the marital discord is severe or the separated parents are in conflict, children are often caught in the line of fire. For example, a mother who is overwhelmingly hostile toward a separated father may be convinced and may convince a child that the father is abusive. In some cases, parents have gone so far as to fabricate entire abuse scenarios and to coach children to repeat them. In other cases a parent may refuse to accept the possibility that a spouse or a close relative is the perpetrator of abuse, may repeatedly insist that a child stop telling lies, and may coerce a child into retracting the disclosures. In either scenario the child suffers profoundly, and the alleged abuse situation is never disentangled. Factors that support the veracity of abuse allegations are the use of phrases by the child that are consistent with the child's language development and that do not sound like rehearsed adult phrasing. Distress, the display of precocious sexual behavior, and a knowledge of or a preoccupation with sexual material also support the possibility of sexual abuse. A child who is not being abused but who is being coached to report sexual or physical abuse is also being placed under unbearable duress. Therefore, the clinician must recognize that severe chronic discord between the parents in which a child is caught in the crossfire can be as abusive as physical and sexual abuse. Controversies are arising in the courts because children are accusing caregivers and teachers of sexual abuse and the children's veracity is being challenged.

Course and Prognosis

The outcome of cases of child physical and sexual abuse and neglect is multifactorial. The outcome of a case depends on the severity, the duration, and the nature of the abuse and on the child's vulnerabilities. Children who already suffer from mental retardation, pervasive developmental disorders, physical handicaps, and disruptive behavior and attention-deficit disorders are likely to have a poorer outcome than are children unhampered by mental or physical disorders. Children who are abused for long periods of time, starting when they are babies or toddlers and going on into adolescence, are likely to be more profoundly damaged than are those who have experienced only brief episodes of abuse. The development of mental disorders—such as major depressive disorder, suicidal behavior, posttraumatic stress disorder, dissociative identity disorder, and substance abuse—further complicates the long-term prognosis. The nature of the relationship between the victim and the abuser and the adult support figures available to the child after the disclosure also affect the prognosis. The best outcomes are expected when the children are intact cognitively, the abuse is recognized and interrupted in an early phase, and the entire family is capable of participating in treatment.

Treatment

CHILD

The first part of the treatment of child abuse and neglect is to ensure the child's safety and well-being. The child may need to be removed from an abusive or neglectful family to ensure protection, yet, on an emotional level, the child may feel additionally vulnerable in an unfamiliar setting. Because of the high risk for psychiatric symptoms in abused and neglected children, a comprehensive psychiatric evaluation is in order. Next, along with providing specific treatments for any mental disorders present, the therapist may have to deal with the immediate situation and the long-term implications of the abuse or neglect. Psychotherapeutic issues to be addressed with an abused child include dealing with the child's fears, anxieties, and self-esteem; building a trusting relationship with an adult (the therapist) in which the child will not be exploited or betrayed; and gaining a beneficial perspective over time of the factors that contributed to the child's victimization at home.

Ideally, each abused and neglected child should be given the benefit of an intervention plan based on the assessment of (1) the factors responsible for the parent's psychopathology, (2) the overall prognosis for the parent's achieving adequate parenting skills, (3) the time estimated to achieve meaningful change in the parent's ability to parent, (4) an estimate of whether the parent's dysfunction is confined to this child or involves other children, (5) the extent to which the parent's overall malfunctioning, if that is the case, is short-term or long-term (reflecting a lifelong pattern), (6) the extent to which the mother's malfunctioning is confined to infants, as opposed to

older children (that is, the incidence of abuse is inversely related to the child's age), (7) the parent's willingness to participate in the intervention plan, (8) the availability of personnel and physical resources to implement the various intervention strategies, and (9) the risk of the child's sustaining additional physical or sexual abuse by remaining in the home.

PARENTS

On the basis of the information obtained, several options can be selected to improve the parent's functioning: (1) eliminate or diminish the social or environmental stresses, (2) lessen the adverse psychological effects of the social factors on the parents, (3) reduce the demands on the mother to a level that is within her capacity through day-care placement of the child or the provision of a housekeeper or baby-sitter, (4) provide emotional support, encouragement, sympathy, stimulation, instruction in maternal care, and aid in learning to plan for, assess, and meet the needs of the infant (supportive casework), and (5) resolve or diminish the parents' inner psychic conflicts (psychotherapy).

Incestuous Behavior

The first step in the treatment of incestuous behavior is its disclosure. Once a breakthrough of the denial and the collusion or fear by the family members has been achieved, incest is not likely to recur. When the participants suffer from severe psychopathology, treatment must be directed toward the underlying illness. Family therapy is useful to reestablish the group as a functioning unit and to develop healthier role definitions for each member. While the participants are learning to develop internal restraints and appropriate ways to gratify their needs, the external control provided by therapy helps prevent further incestuous behavior. At times, legal agencies are involved to help enforce external controls.

REPORTING

In cases of suspected child abuse and neglect, the physician should diagnose the suspected maltreatment; secure the child's safety by admitting the child to a hospital or by arranging out-of-home placement; report the case to the appropriate social service department, child protection unit, or central registry; make an assessment with the help of a history, a physical examination, a skeletal survey, and photographs; request a social worker's report and appropriate surgical and medical consultations; confer with members of a child abuse committee within 72 hours; arrange a program of care for the child and the parents; and arrange for social service follow-up.

Mandated child-abuse reporters include physicians, psychologists, school officials, police officers, hospital personnel engaged in the treatment of patients, district attorneys, and providers of child day care and foster care.

PREVENTION

To prevent child abuse and neglect, the clinician must identify those families who are at high risk and intervene before a child becomes a victim. Once high-risk families have been identified, a comprehensive program should include psychiatric monitoring of the families, including the identified high-risk child. Families can be educated to recognize when they are being neglectful or abusive, and alternative coping strategies can be suggested.

In general, child abuse and neglect prevention and treatment programs should try to (1) prevent the separation of parents and children if possible, (2) prevent the placement of children in institutions, (3) encourage the parents' attainment of self-care status, and (4) encourage the family's attainment of self-sufficiency. As a last resort and to prevent further abuse and neglect, children may have to be removed from families who are unwilling or unable to profit from the treatment program. In cases of sexual abuse, the licensing of day-care centers and the psychological screening of those persons who work in them should be mandatory to prevent further abuses. Education of the medical profession, members of allied health fields, and all who come in contact with children will aid in early detection. Furthermore, providing support services to stressed families will aid in preventing the problem in the first place.

PHYSICAL ABUSE OF ADULT

Spouse Abuse

Spouse abuse is estimated to occur in 2 million to 12 million families in the United States. That aspect of domestic violence has been recognized as a severe problem, largely as a result of recent cultural emphasis on civil rights and the work of feminist groups. However, the problem itself is one of long standing.

The major problem in spouse abuse is wife abuse. One study estimated that there are 1.8 million battered wives in the United States, excluding divorced women and girls battered on dates. Wife beating occurs in families of every racial and religious background and in all socioeconomic strata. It is most frequent in families with problems of substance abuse, particularly alcohol abuse and crack abuse.

Behavioral, cultural, intrapsychic, and interpersonal factors—all contribute to the development of the problem. Abusive men are likely to have come from violent homes where they witnessed wife beating or were abused themselves as children. The act itself is reinforcing; once a man has beaten his wife, he is likely to do so again. Abusive husbands tend to be immature, dependent, and nonassertive and to suffer from strong feelings of inadequacy.

The husbands' aggression is bullying behavior, designed to humiliate their wives to build up their own low self-esteem. The abuse is most likely to occur when the man feels threatened or frustrated at home, at work, or with his peers. The United States Surgeon General's office has identified pregnancy as a high-risk period for battering; 15 to 25 percent of pregnant women are physically abused while pregnant, and the abuse often results in birth defects.

Impatient and impulsive, abusive husbands physically displace aggression provoked by others onto their wives. The dynamics include identification with an aggressor (father, boss), testing behavior (Will she stay with me, no matter how I treat her?), distorted desires to express manhood, and dehumanization of the woman. As in rape, aggression is deemed permissible when the woman is perceived as property. About 50 percent of battered wives grew up in violent homes. The trait most commonly found in abused wives is dependence.

Recently, hot lines, emergency shelters for women, and other organizations (such as the National Coalition Against Domestic Violence) have been developed to aid battered wives and to educate the public. A presidential commission was established to investigate spouse abuse. A major problem for abused women has been finding a place to go when they leave home, frequently

in fear of their lives. Battering is often severe, involving broken limbs, broken ribs, internal bleeding, and brain damage. When an abused wife tries to leave her husband, he often becomes doubly intimidating and threatens, ''I'll get you.'' If the woman has small children to care for, her problem is compounded. The abusive husband wages a conscious campaign to isolate his wife and to make her feel worthless.

The woman faces a risk in leaving an abusive husband; women who leave their batterers are at a 75 percent greater risk for being killed by their batterers than are women who stay. In 1990 California passed the first antistalking law, making stalking a crime. In 1992 a total of 28 states passed similar laws.

Some men feel remorse and guilt after an episode of violent behavior and become particularly loving. That behavior gives the wife hope, and she remains until the next cycle of violence, which is inevitable.

Change is initiated when the man is convinced that the woman will not tolerate the situation and when she begins to exert control over his behavior. She can do so by leaving for a prolonged period—if she is physically and economically able to do so—with therapy for the man as a condition of return. Family therapy is effective in treating the problem, usually in conjunction with social and legal agencies. With relatively less impulsive men, external controls, such as calling the neighbors or the police, may be sufficient to stop the behavior.

Some beatings of husbands are also reported. In those cases the husbands complain of fear of ridicule if they expose the problem, fear of charges of counterassault, and inability to leave the situation because of financial difficulties. Husband abuse has also been reported when a frail elderly man is married to a much younger woman.

Elder Abuse

Elder abuse is discussed in Chapter 44.

SEXUAL ABUSE OF ADULT

Rape

The problem of rape is most appropriately discussed under the heading of aggression. Rape is an act of violence and humiliation that happens to be expressed through sexual means. Rape is used to express power or anger. Rapes in which sex is the dominant issue are rare; sexuality is usually used in the service of nonsexual needs.

Rape is the perpetration of an act of sexual intercourse with a female, against her will and consent, whether her will is overcome by force, by fear resulting from the threat of force, or by drugs or intoxicants; when because of mental deficiency she is incapable of exercising rational judgment; or she is below an arbitrary age of consent. Rape can occur between married persons and persons of the same sex.

The crime of rape requires only slight penile penetration of the victim's outer vulva. Full erection and ejaculation are not necessary. Forced acts of fellatio and anal penetration, although they frequently accompany rape, are legally considered sodomy.

RAPE OF WOMEN

Recent research has categorized male rapists into separate groups: sexual sadists, who are aroused by the pain of their victims; exploitive predators, who impulsively use their victims as objects for their gratification; inadequate men, who believe that no woman would voluntarily sleep with them and who are obsessed with fantasies about sex; and men for whom rape is a displaced expression of anger and rage. Some workers believe that the anger was originally directed toward a wife or mother. Feminist theory, however, proposes that the woman serves as an object for the displacement of aggression that the rapist cannot express directly toward other men. The woman is considered men's property or a vulnerable possession and is the rapist's instrument for revenge against other men.

Rape often occurs as an accompaniment to another crime. The rapist always threatens his victim with fists, a gun, or a knife and frequently harms her in nonsexual ways, as well as in sexual ways. The victim may be beaten, wounded, and sometimes killed.

Statistics show that most men who commit rapes are between 25 and 44 years of age; 51 percent are white and tend to rape white victims, 47 percent are black and tend to rape black victims, and the remaining 2 percent come from all other races. Alcohol is involved in 34 percent of all forcible rapes. A composite characterization of the archetypical rapist drawn from police statistics portrays a single 19-year-old man from the low socioeconomic groups who has a police record of acquisitive offenses.

According to the Federal Bureau of Investigation (FBI) Uniform Crime Reports, 106,590 rapes were reported in the United States in 1991. However, rape is a highly underreported crime. An estimated 1 of 4 to 1 of 10 rapes is reported. The underreporting is attributed to feelings of shame on the part of the victim and to the belief that she has no recourse through the legal system.

Victims of rape can be of any age. Cases have been reported in which the victims were as young as 15 months and as old as 82 years. The greatest danger exists for women aged 16 to 24. Rape most commonly occurs in a woman's own neighborhood, frequently inside or near her own home. Most rapes are premeditated. About half are committed by strangers and half by men known, to varying degrees, by the victims; 7 percent of all rapes are perpetrated by close relatives of the victim; 10 percent of rapes involve more than one attacker.

The woman being raped is frequently in a life-threatening situation. During the rape she experiences shock and fright approaching panic. Her prime motivation is to stay alive. In most cases, rapists choose victims slightly smaller than themselves. The rapist may urinate or defecate on his victim, ejaculate into her face and hair, force anal intercourse, and insert foreign objects into her vagina and rectum.

After the rape the woman may experience shame, humiliation, confusion, fear, and rage. The type and the duration of the reaction are variable, but women report that the effects last for a year or longer. Many women experience the symptoms of posttraumatic stress disorder. Some women are able to resume sexual relations with men, particularly if they have always felt sexually adequate. Other women become phobic about sexual interaction or have such symptoms as vaginismus. Few women emerge from the assault completely unscathed. The manifestations and the degree of damage depend on the violence of the attack itself, the vulnerability of the woman, and the support system available to her immediately after the attack.

The victim fares best when she receives immediate support and is able to ventilate her fear and rage to loving family members and to sympathetic physicians and law enforcement officials. She is helped when she knows that she has socially acceptable means of recourse, such as the arrest and conviction of the rapist.

Therapy is usually supportive unless the woman has a severe underlying disorder. Therapy focuses on restoring the victim's sense of adequacy and control over her life and relieving the feelings of helplessness, dependence, and obsession with the assault that frequently follow rape. Group therapy with homogeneous groups composed of rape victims is particularly effective.

The rape victim experiences a physical and psychological trauma when she is assaulted. Until recently, she also frequently faced skepticism from those to whom she reported the crime (if she had sufficient strength to do so) or accusations of having provoked or desired the assault. In reality, the National Commission on the Causes and Prevention of Violence found discernible victim participation of rape in only 4.4 percent of all cases. That statistic is lower than in any other crime of violence. The education of police officers and the assignment of policewomen to deal with rape victims have helped increase the reporting of the crime. Rape crisis centers and telephone hot lines are available for immediate aid and information for victims. Volunteer groups work in emergency rooms in hospitals and with physician education programs to assist in the treatment of victims.

Legally, women no longer have to prove in court that they actively struggled against the rapist. Testimony regarding the victim's prior sexual history has recently been declared inadmissible as evidence in a number of states. Also, penalties for first-time rapists have been reduced, making juries likely to consider a conviction. In some states, wives can now prosecute husbands for rape.

Date Rape

Date or acquaintance rape is a term applied to rapes in which the rapist is known to the victim. The assault can occur on a first date or after the man and the woman have known each other for many months. Considerable data on date rape have been gathered from college populations. In one study, 38 percent of male students said that they would commit rape if they thought they could get away with it, and 11 percent stated that they had committed rape; 16 percent of the female students said that they had been raped by men they knew or were dating.

In addition to suffering the symptoms of all rape survivors, victims of date rape berate themselves for exercising poor judgment in their choice of male friends and are more likely to blame themselves for provoking the rapist than are other victims. Many schools have set up programs for rape prevention and for counseling those who have been assaulted.

RAPE OF MEN

In some states the definition of rape is being changed to substitute the word ''person'' for ''female.'' In most states, male rape is legally defined as sodomy. Same-sex rape is much more frequent among men than among women, and it occurs frequently in closed institutions, such as prisons and maximum-security hospitals.

The dynamics are identical to those of heterosexual rape. The crime enables the rapist to discharge aggression and to aggrandize himself. The victim is usually smaller than the rapist, is always perceived as passive and unmanly (weaker), and is used as an object. The rapist selecting a male victim may be heterosexual, bisexual, or homosexual. The most common act is anal penetration of the victim; the second most common act is fellatio.

Male rape victims often feel, as do raped women, that they have been ruined. In addition, some fear that they will become homosexual because of the attack.

Sexual Coercion

Sexual coercion is a term used in DSM-IV for incidents in which one person dominates another by force or compels the other person to perform a sexual act.

References

Botsis A J, Plutchik R, Kotler M, van Praag H M: Parental loss and family violence as correlates of suicide and violence risk. Suicide Life Threat Behav *25*: 253, 1995.

Fitzpatrick K M, Boldizar J P: The prevalence and consequences of exposure to violence among African-American youth. J Am Acad Child Adolesc Psychiatry *32*: 424, 1993.

Lovett B B: Child sexual abuse: the female victim's relationship with her nonoffending mother. Child Abuse Negl *19*: 729, 1995.

McCall G J: Risk factors and sexual assault prevention. J Interpers Violence *8*: 277, 1993.

McCloskey L A, Figueredo A J, Koss M P: The effects of systemic family violence on children's mental health. Child Dev *66*: 1239, 1995.

O'Brien J D: The effects of incest on female adolescent development. J Am Acad Psychoanal *15*: 83, 1987.

Ogletree R J: Sexual coercion experience and help-seeking behavior of college women. J Am Coll Health *41*: 149, 1993.

Resick P A: The psychological impact of rape. J Interpers Violence *8*: 223, 1993.

Salzinger S, Feldman, R S, Hammer M, Rosario M: The effects of physical abuse on children's social relationships. Child Dev *64*: 169, 1993.

Sternberg K J, Lamb M E, Greenbaum C, Cicchetti D, et al: Effects of domestic violence on children's behavior problems and depression. Dev Psychol *29*: 44, 1993.

Strait R T, Siegel R M, Shapiro R A: Humeral fractures without obvious etiologies in children less than 3 years of age: When is it abuse? Pediatrics *96*: 667, 1995.

Vizard E, Monck E, Misch P: Child and adolescent sex abuse perpetrators: A review of the research literature. J Child Psychol Psychiatry *36*: 731, 1995.

Wardinsky T D: Genetic and congenital defect conditions that mimic child abuse. J Fam Pract *41*: 377, 1995.

24/ Additional Conditions That May Be a Focus of Clinical Attention

The fourth edition of *Diagnostic and Statistical Manual of Mental Disorders* (DSM-IV) lists 13 conditions that make up the category of additional conditions that may be a focus of clinical attention. They include the following: bereavement, occupational problem, adult antisocial behavior, malingering, phase of life problem, noncompliance with treatment for a mental disorder, religious or spiritual problem, acculturation problem, and age-associated memory decline, each of which is discussed in this chapter. Borderline intellectual functioning, academic problem, childhood or adolescent antisocial behavior, and identity problem are discussed in Chapter 42.

The additional conditions that may be a focus of clinical attention are not true mental disorders and are not considered as such by DSM-IV. Rather, they are conditions that have led to contact with the mental health care system. Once in the system, a person with an additional condition that may be a focus of clinical attention should have a thorough neuropsychiatric evaluation, which may or may not uncover a mental disorder. The categories listed above are of clinical interest to psychiatrists because they may accompany mental illness or, in some cases, be early harbingers of underlying mental disorders. For recording purposes in DSM-IV, the disorders are coded on Axis I.

According to DSM-IV, even if a person has a mental disorder, the focus of attention or treatment may be on a condition that is not due to the mental disorder. For example, the treatment of a person with social phobia who has an occupational problem not directly related to the phobia may focus on the occupational problem. At times, however, the distinction is not clear-cut, and it behooves the clinician to do as thorough a workup as possible so as not to overlook a diagnosable mental disorder.

BEREAVEMENT

Immediately after or within a few months of the loss of a loved one, a normal period of bereavement begins. Feelings of sadness, preoccupation with thoughts about the deceased, tearfulness, irritability, insomnia, and difficulties in concentrating and carrying out one's daily activities are some of the signs and symptoms. The bereavement is limited to a varying period of time, based on one's cultural group (usually no longer than six months). Normal bereavement, however, may lead to a full depressive disorder, which requires treatment.

OCCUPATIONAL PROBLEM

Occupational or industrial psychiatry is that area of psychiatry specifically concerned with the psychiatric aspects of problems at work and with vocational maladjustment. The practical symptoms of job dissatisfaction are mistakes at work, accident-proneness, absenteeism, and sabotage. The psychiatric symptoms include insecurity, reduced self-esteem, anger, and resentment at having to work.

People are particularly vulnerable to occupational problems at several points in their working lives—on entry into the working world, at times of promotion or transfer, during periods of unemployment, and at retirement. Specific situations—such as having too much or too little to do, being subjected to conflicting demands, feeling distracted by family problems, having responsibility without authority, and working for demanding and unhelpful managers—also create occupational distress.

Career Choices and Changes

The choice of a career is a major life decision. A significant number of young people follow in their parents' footsteps, but many are unsure of what to do and try several jobs before settling on an occupation. Disadvantaged youngsters frequently have little choice about a career. When young adults have a poor education and lack training and skills, even overwhelming ambition rarely leads them out of poverty or into occupational satisfaction. When the disadvantaged are women or members of minority groups, they have even less chance of occupational success. In discussing career choices with a patient, a psychiatrist should explore special talents and interests, childhood goals, the patient's models, family influences, future expectations, work and academic histories, and motivation to work.

Distress about work is readily understood when an employee has been fired, demoted, or passed over for promotion. Minorities and those in low socioeconomic groups are particularly vulnerable to losing their jobs. In one five-year period, 11.5 million persons in the United States age 20 or over lost their jobs as a result of industrial plant closings and cutbacks. Some left the labor force altogether. Others moved to lower-paying, low-skill jobs with fewer benefits than their former jobs. Some worked intermittently.

Women are specifically at risk for stress when they leave outside employment for homemaking, a transition that researchers have found to be extremely stressful.

Psychological Problems and the Workplace

Maladaptation at work may arise from psychodynamic conflicts. Those conflicts can be reflected in the person's inability to accept the authority of competent superiors or, conversely, in overdependence on authority figures to fulfill infantile needs. People with unresolved conflicts about their competitive and aggressive impulses may experience great difficulties in the work area. They may suffer from a pathological envy of the success of others or fear success for themselves because of their inability to tolerate envy from others. Those conflicts are also manifest in other areas of the patient's life, and the maladaptation is not limited to the patient's occupation.

Career Problems of Women

A number of changes have occurred in the business world in the United States since the 1960s. A significant number of women have entered the work force; many corporations are now willing to employ a husband and wife in the same firm; and teenagers have entered the work force, on a part-time basis, on a large scale.

Ninety percent of all females alive today in the United States will have to work to support themselves and probably one or two people. Economic necessity now prompts the homemaker to enter the labor force. Rejection by employers on the basis of age, lack of recent experience, or insufficient training can cause dysphoria and depression. That is particularly true for the recently divorced woman in her 40s or 50s who has spent most of her adult life in the occupations of wife and mother.

The young woman has different stresses, primarily related to the conflicting demands of work and family responsibilities. More than 50 percent of all mothers in the work force have children 1 year old or younger. However, women's organizations and other critics charge that few corporations are removing barriers to women's advancement or are concerned about reducing the tension that arises when job and family demands conflict. Specific issues that need to be addressed are provisions for child care or for the care of elderly parents, the option of flexible work hours, and the availability and use of unpaid parental leaves. Studies reveal that, when those leaves are made available to both parents, fathers rarely take them; that managers are more sensitive to crises in men's lives than to crises in the lives of female employees; and that managers respond to such major events as divorce and the death of a family member but ignore the stress placed on a worker by the illness of a child or a school closing because of a snow day. A few socially conscious corporations are holding workshops to address the changes arising from the influx of women into the work force and such issues as family responsibilities, sexual harassment in the workplace, personal safety during business travel, and rape prevention.

Dual-career families (in which both the husband and the wife have jobs) now constitute more than 40 percent of all families. A problem arises if the employer wants one partner to make a geographic move to a new post. Even if the transfer is a promotion, it can result in lower total income for the family because of the spouse's loss of job or disruption of career. Some corporations offer new jobs to both spouses when one is asked to relocate; however, such approaches are rare. A more common advance is the acceptance of couples, married or unmarried, as employees of the same corporation. Formerly, the employment of a husband and a wife by the same firm was considered taboo by many businesses. Couples employed by the same firm seem to suffer only if they compete with each other. The couples who fare best treat their spouses differently at the office than at home. Resentment from coworkers occurs if one spouse reports directly to the other. Otherwise, no adverse responses from other employees have been noted.

ADULT ANTISOCIAL BEHAVIOR

Antisocial behavior is a pattern that usually begins in childhood and often persists throughout life. It is characterized by activities that are illegal, immoral, or both and that violate the society's legal system.

Epidemiology

Estimates of the prevalence of adult antisocial behavior range from 5 to 15 percent of the population, depending on the criteria and the sampling. Within the prison population, investigators report prevalence figures of between 20 and 80 percent. Men account for more adult antisocial behavior than do women.

Etiology

Antisocial behaviors in adulthood are characteristic of a variety of persons, ranging from those with no demonstrable psychopathology to those who are severely impaired, suffering from psychotic disorders, cognitive disorders, and retardation, among other conditions. A comprehensive neuropsychiatric assessment of antisocial adults usually reveals a myriad of potentially treatable psychiatric and neurological impairments that can easily be overshadowed by offensive behaviors and thus be overlooked. However, only in the absence of mental disorders should patients be categorized as displaying adult antisocial behavior.

GENETIC FACTORS

Data supporting the genetic transmission of antisocial behavior are based on studies that find a 60 percent concordance rate in monozygotic twins and about a 30 percent concordance rate in dizygotic twins. Adoption studies show a high rate of antisocial behavior in the biological relatives of adoptees identified with antisocial behavior and a high incidence of antisocial behavior in the adopted-away offspring of those with antisocial behavior. A high incidence of abnormalities are seen during the prenatal and perinatal periods of those who subsequently display antisocial behavior.

SOCIAL FACTORS

Studies note that in neighborhoods in which low socioeconomic status (SES) families predominate, the sons of unskilled workers are more likely to commit more numerous and more serious criminal offenses than are the sons of middle-class and skilled workers, at least during adolescence and early adulthood. Those data are not as clear for women, but the findings are generally similar in studies from many countries. Areas of family training that have been particularly cited as differing by SES group are the use in middle-SES parents of love-oriented techniques in discipline, the withdrawal of affection versus physical punishment, negative parental attitudes toward aggressive behavior, attempts to curb aggressive behavior, and the ability to verbally communicate the various reasons for the parents' values and proscriptions of such behavior.

Adult antisocial behavior is associated with the use and abuse of alcohol and other substances. Violent antisocial acts are also associated with the easy availability of handguns.

Diagnosis and Clinical Features

The diagnosis of adult antisocial behavior is one of exclusion. Substance dependence in such behavior often makes it difficult to separate the antisocial behavior related primarily to substance dependence from disordered behaviors that occurred either before substance use or during episodes unrelated to substance dependence.

During the manic phases of bipolar I disorder, certain aspects of behavior can be similar to adult antisocial behavior, such as wanderlust, sexual promiscuity, and financial difficulties. Schizophrenic patients may have episodes of adult antisocial behavior, but the symptom picture is usually clear, especially with regard to thought disorder, delusions, and hallucinations on the mental status examination.

Neurological conditions may be associated with adult antisocial behavior, and so electroencephalograms (EEGs), computed tomography (CT) scans, magnetic resonance imaging (MRI), and a complete neurological examination should be done. Temporal lobe epilepsy is often considered in the differential diagnosis. When a diagnosis of temporal lobe epilepsy or encephalitis is clear-cut, the condition may contribute to the adult antisocial behavior. Abnormal EEG findings are prevalent among violent offenders. An estimated 50 percent of aggressive criminals have abnormal EEG findings.

Persons with adult antisocial behavior have difficulties in work, marriage, and money matters and conflicts with various authorities.

Antisocial personality disorder is discussed in Chapter 20.

Treatment

In general, adult antisocial behavior provokes therapeutic pessimism. That is, therapists have little hope of changing a pattern of behavior that has been present almost continuously throughout the patient's life. Psychotherapy has not been effective, and there have been no major breakthroughs with biological treatments, including the use of medications.

Enthusiasm is greater for the use of therapeutic communities and other forms of group treatment, even though the data are not encouraging. Many adult criminals who are incarcerated and in institutional settings have shown some response to group therapy approaches. The history of violence, criminality, and antisocial behavior has shown that such behaviors seem to decrease after age 40. Recidivism in criminals, which can reach 90 percent in some studies, also decreases in middle age.

MALINGERING

Malingering is characterized by the voluntary production and presentation of false or grossly exaggerated physical or psychological symptoms. The patient always has an external motivation, which falls into one of three categories: (1) to avoid difficult or dangerous situations, responsibilities, or punishment, (2) to receive compensation, free hospital room and board, a source of drugs, or haven from the police, and (3) to retaliate when the patient feels guilt or suffers a financial loss, legal penalty, or job loss. The presence of a clearly definable goal is the main factor that differentiates malingering from factitious disorders.

Epidemiology

The incidence of malingering is unknown, but it is common. It occurs most frequently in settings with a preponderance of men—the military, prisons, factories, and other industrial settings—although the condition also occurs in women.

Diagnosis and Clinical Features

In DSM-IV the following statement about malingering appears:

The essential feature of Malingering is the intentional production of false or grossly exaggerated physical or psychological symptoms, motivated by external incentives such as avoiding military duty, avoiding work, obtaining financial compensation, evading criminal prosecu-

tion, or obtaining drugs. Under some circumstances Malingering may represent adaptive behavior, for example, feigning illness while a captive of the enemy during wartime.

Malingering should be strongly suspected if any combination of the following is noted:

(1) medicolegal context of presentation (e.g., the person is referred by an attorney to the clinician for examination)
(2) marked discrepancy between the person's claimed stress or disability and the objective findings
(3) lack of cooperation during the diagnostic evaluation and in complying with the prescribed treatment regimen
(4) the presence of Antisocial Personality Disorder

Many malingerers express mostly subjective, vague, ill-defined symptoms—for example, headache; pains in the patient's neck, lower back, chest, or abdomen; dizziness; vertigo; amnesia; anxiety; and depression—and the symptoms often have a family history, in all likelihood not organically based but incredibly difficult to refute. Malingerers may complain bitterly, describing how much the symptoms impair their normal function and how much they dislike the symptoms. The patients may use the best doctors who are the most trusted (and perhaps most easily fooled) and promptly and willingly pay all their bills, even if excessive, to impress the doctors with their integrity. To seem credible, malingerers must report the symptoms but tell their physicians as little as possible. But often they complain of misery without objective signs or other symptoms congruent with recognized diseases and syndromes; if they do describe all the symptoms of a disease, the symptoms are said to come and go. Malingerers are often preoccupied with cash, rather than cure, and have a knowledge of the law and precedents relative to their claims.

Differential Diagnosis

As DSM-IV notes:

Malingering differs from Factitious Disorder in that the motivation for the symptom production in Malingering is an external incentive, whereas in Factitious Disorder external incentives are absent. Evidence of an intrapsychic need to maintain the sick role suggests Factitious Disorder.

Malingering is differentiated from Conversion and other Somatoform Disorders by the intentional production of symptoms and by the obvious, external incentives associated with it. In Malingering (in contrast to Conversion Disorder), symptom relief is not often obtained by suggestion or hypnosis.

Treatment

A patient suspected of malingering should be thoroughly and objectively evaluated, and the physician should refrain from showing any suspicion. If the clinician becomes angry (a common response to malingerers), a confrontation may occur, with two consequences: (1) The doctor-patient relationship is disrupted, and no further positive intervention is possible. (2) The patient will be even more on guard, and proof of deception may become virtually impossible. If the patient is accepted and not discredited, subsequent observation, while the patient is hospitalized or an outpatient, may reveal the versatility of the symptoms, which are consistently present only when patients know that they are being observed. Preserving the doctor-patient relationship is often essential to the diagnosis and long-term treatment of the patient. Careful evaluation usually reveals the relevant issue without the need for a confrontation. It is usually best to use an intensive treatment approach, as though the symptoms were real. The symptoms can then be given up in response to treatment, without the patient's losing face.

PHASE OF LIFE PROBLEM

In DSM-IV the following statement about phase of life problem appears:

This category can be used when the focus of clinical attention is a problem associated with a particular developmental phase or some other life circumstance that is not due to a mental disorder, or if it is due to a mental disorder, is sufficiently severe to warrant independent clinical attention. Examples include problems associated with entering school, leaving parental control, starting a new career, and changes involved in marriage, divorce, and retirement.

External events are most likely to overwhelm a person's adaptive capacities if they are unexpected, if they are numerous—that is, a number of stresses occurring within a short time—if the strain is chronic and unremitting, or if one loss heralds a myriad of concomitant adjustments that strain a person's recuperative powers.

The strains most likely to produce anxiety and depression relate to major life-cycle changes: marriage, occupation, and parenthood changes. Those events affect both men and women, but women, the poor, and minority groups seem particularly vulnerable to adverse reactions. Again, the change creates significant strain when it is unexpected and when it involves not only adjustment to a loss (a spouse or a job) but also the need to adjust to a new status that entails further hardships and problems.

In general, people are able to adjust to life changes if they have mature defense mechanisms, such as altruism, humor, and capacity for sublimation. Flexibility, reliability, strong family ties, regular employment, adequate income, job satisfaction, a pattern of regular recreation and social participation, realistic goals, and a history of adequate performance—in short, a full and satisfying life—create resilience to deal with life changes.

NONCOMPLIANCE WITH TREATMENT

In DSM-IV the following statement appears:

This category can be used when the focus of clinical attention is noncompliance with an important aspect of the treatment for a mental disorder or a general medical condition. The reasons for noncompliance may include discomfort resulting from treatment (e.g., medication side effects), expense of treatment, decisions based on personal value judgments of religious or cultural beliefs about the advantages and disadvantages of the proposed treatment, maladaptive personality traits or coping styles (e.g., denial or illness), or the presence of a mental disorder (e.g., Schizophrenia, Avoidant Personality Disorder). This category should be used only when the problem is sufficiently severe to warrant independent clinical attention.

RELIGIOUS AND SPIRITUAL PROBLEM

In DSM-IV the following statement appears:

This category can be used when the focus of clinical attention is a religious or spiritual problem. Examples include distressing experiences that involve loss or questioning of faith, problems associated with conversion to a new faith, or questioning of other spiritual values which may not necessarily be related to an organized church or religious institution.

Cults

Cults are charismatic groups that can affect participants in adverse ways, which may eventually bring them into contact with the mental health care system. Cults are characterized by an intensely held belief system and ideology that are imposed on their members, by a high level of group cohesion that tries to prevent members' freedom of choice to leave the group, and by a profound influence on the members' behavior that may include frank psychiatric symptoms, including psychotic disorders.

Most potential cult members are in their adolescence or otherwise struggling with establishing their own identities. They are drawn to the cult, which holds out the false promise of emotional well-being and purports to offer the sense of direction for which the persons are searching. Cult members are encouraged to proselytize and to draw new members into the group. They are often encouraged to break with family members and friends and to socialize only with other group members. Cults are invariably led by charismatic personalities, who are often ruthless in their quest for financial, sexual, and power gains and in their insistence on conformity to the cult's ideological belief system, which may have strong religious or quasireligious overtones. Exit therapy has been developed to guide cult members out of the group, provided their lingering emotional ties to persons outside the cult can be mobilized.

ACCULTURATION PROBLEM

Periods of cultural transition, with changing mores and fluidity of role definition, may increase a person's vulnerability to life strain. Extreme cultural transition can create a condition of severe distress. The problem, also called culture shock, occurs when a person is suddenly thrust into an alien culture or has divided loyalties to two different cultures. In a less extreme form, culture shock occurs when young men and women enter the army, when people change jobs, when families move or undergo a significant change in income, when children have their first day in school, and when black ghetto children are bused to white middle-class schools.

Brainwashing

First practiced by the Chinese Communists on American prisoners in the Korean war, brainwashing is the deliberate creation of cultural shock. A condition of isolation, alienation, and intimidation is developed for the express purpose of assaulting ego strengths and leaving the person to be brainwashed vulnerable to the imposition of alien ideas and behavior that would usually be rejected. Brainwashing relies on both mental and physical coercion. All people are vulnerable to brainwashing if they are exposed to it for a sufficient length of time, if they are alone and without support, and if they are without hope of escape from the situation. Help from the mental health care system is usually necessary to help brainwashed persons readjust to their usual environments after the brainwashing experience, a process known as deprogramming. Supportive therapy is offered, with emphasis on reeducation, restitution of ego strengths that existed before the trauma, and alleviation of the guilt and depression that are remnants of the frightening experience and the lost confidence and confusion in identity that results from it.

AGE-RELATED COGNITIVE DECLINE

In DSM-IV the following statement appears:

This category can be used when the focus of clinical attention is an objectively identified decline in cognitive functioning consequent to the aging process that is within normal limits given the person's age. Persons with this condition may report problems remembering names or appointments or may experience difficulty in solving complex problems. This category should be considered only after it has been determined that the cognitive impairment is not attributable to a specific mental disorder or neurological condition.

References

Bebbington P E: The content and context of compliance. Int Clin Psychopharmacol 9: 41, 1995.

Bernard L C, Houston W, Natoli L: Malingering on neuropsychological memory tests: Potential objective indicators. J Clin Psychol 49: 45, 1993.

Blackwell B: Noncompliance with treatment. In Comprehensive Textbook of Psychiatry, ed 6, H I Kaplan, B J Sadock, editors, p 1611. Williams & Wilkins, Baltimore, 1995.

Caine E D: Should aging-associated cognitive decline be included in DSM-IV? J Neuropsychiatry Clin Neurosci 5: 1, 1993.

Faust D: The detection of deception. Neurol Clin 13: 255, 1995.

Lehman D R, Davis C G, DeLongis A, Wortman C B: Positive and negative life changes following bereavement and their relations to adjustment. J Soc Clin Psychol 12: 90, 1993.

Mills M J, Lipian M S: Malingering. In Comprehensive Textbook of Psychiatry, ed 6, H I Kaplan, B J Sadock, editors, p 1614. Williams & Wilkins, Baltimore, 1995.

Morley R E: Physiological aspects. In Comprehensive Textbook of Psychiatry, ed 6, H I Kaplan, B J Sadock, editors, p 2534. Williams & Wilkins, Baltimore, 1995.

Repetti R L: Short-term effects of occupational stressors on daily mood and health complaints. Health Psychol 12: 125, 1993.

Sadock V: Other additional conditions that may be a focus of clinical attention. In Comprehensive Textbook of Psychiatry, ed 6, H I Kaplan, B J Sadock, editors, p 1633. Williams & Wilkins, Baltimore, 1995.

Tardiff K: Adult antisocial behavior and criminality. In Comprehensive Textbook of Psychiatry, ed 6, H I Kaplan, B J Sadock, editors, p 1622. Williams & Wilkins, Baltimore, 1995.

25/ Psychiatric Emergencies

25.1 SUICIDE

Suicide is intentional self-inflicted death. Edwin Schneidman defined suicide as "the conscious act of self-induced annihilation, best understood as a multidimensional malaise in a needful individual who defines an issue for which the act is perceived as the best solution." Suicide is not a random or pointless act. On the contrary, it is a way out of a problem or a crisis that is invariably causing intense suffering. Suicide is associated with thwarted or unfulfilled needs, feelings of hopelessness and helplessness, ambivalent conflicts between survival and unbreakable stress, a narrowing of perceived options, and a need for escape; the suicidal persons sends out signals of distress.

Suicide in children and adolescents is discussed in Chapter 40.

EPIDEMIOLOGY

Incidence and Prevalence

Each year about 30,000 deaths are attributed to suicide in the United States (30,232 deaths in 1989). That figure is for successful suicides; the number of attempted suicides is estimated to be 8 to 10 times that number. Lost in the reporting are intentional misclassifications of the cause of death, accidents of undetermined cause, and the so-called chronic suicides—for example, deaths through alcohol and other substance abuse and consciously poor adherence to medical regimens for diabetes, obesity, and hypertension.

Between 1970 and 1980 more than 230,000 people committed suicide in the United States—about one every 20 minutes, 75 suicides a day. The total suicide rate has remained fairly constant over the years. The current rate is 12.5 suicide deaths per 100,000. In 1977 suicide was at a peak of 13.3 per 100,000. Since then, there has been a slight decline. Currently, suicide is ranked as the eighth overall cause of death in this country, after heart disease, cancer, cerebrovascular disease, accidents, pneumonia, diabetes mellitus, and cirrhosis.

Suicide rates in the United States are at the midpoint of the national rates reported to the United Nations by the industrialized countries. Internationally, suicide rates range from highs of more than 25 per 100,000 people in Scandinavia, Switzerland, Germany, Austria, the eastern European countries (the suicide belt), and Japan to fewer than 10 per 100,000 in Spain, Italy, Ireland, Egypt, and the Netherlands.

A state-by-state analysis of suicides from 1979 to 1981 among those aged 15 to 44 revealed that New Jersey had the nation's lowest suicide rates for both sexes. Nevada and New Mexico had the highest rates for men, and Nevada and Wyoming had the highest rates for women. Women in Nevada killed themselves at a higher frequency than did men in New Jersey. The number-one suicide site in the world is the Golden Gate Bridge in San Francisco, with more than 800 suicides since it opened in 1937.

Associated Factors

SEX

Men commit suicide more than three times as often as do women, a rate that is stable over all ages. Women, however, are four times as likely to attempt suicide as are men.

METHODS

The higher rate of successful suicide for men is related to the methods they use. Men use firearms, hanging, or jumping from high places. Women are more likely to take an overdose of psychoactive substances or a poison, but they are beginning to use firearms more often than in the past. The use of guns has decreased as a method of suicide in those states with gun control laws.

AGE

Suicide rates increase with age. The significance of the midlife crisis is underscored by suicide rates. Among men, suicides peak after age 45; among women, the greatest number of completed suicides occur after age 55. Rates of 40 per 100,000 population are found in men aged 65 and older. The elderly attempt suicide less often than do younger people but are successful more often. The elderly account for 25 percent of suicides, although they make up only 10 percent of the total population. The rate for those 75 or older is more than three times the rate among the young.

The suicide rate is rising most rapidly in young people. For males 15 to 24 years old, the rate increased 40 percent between 1970 and 1980, and the rate is still rising. The suicide rate for females in the same age group showed only a slight increase. Among men 25 to 34 years old, the suicide rate increased almost 30 percent. Suicide is the third leading cause of death in the 15 to 24-year-old age group after accidents and homicides. Attempted suicides in that age group number between 1 million and 2 million annually. The majority of suicides now occur among those 15 to 44.

RACE

The rate of suicide among whites is nearly twice that among nonwhites, but the figures are being questioned, as the suicide rate among blacks is increasing. In 1989 the suicide rate for white males (19.6 per 100,000 persons) was 1.6 times that for black males (12.5), 4 times that for white females (4.8), and 8.2 times that for black females (2.4). Among ghetto youth and certain Native American and Alaskan Indian groups, suicide rates have greatly exceeded the national rate. Suicide among immigrants is higher than in the native-born population. Two out of every three suicides are white males.

RELIGION

Historically, suicide rates among Catholic populations have been lower than the rates among Protestants and Jews. It may be that a religion's degree of orthodoxy and integration is a more accurate measure of risk in this category than is simple institutional religious affiliation.

MARITAL STATUS

Marriage reinforced by children seems to significantly lessen the risk of suicide. Among married persons the rate is 11 per 100,000. The overall rate for never-married persons is nearly double the rate for married persons. However, previously married persons show sharply higher rates than do never-married persons: 24 per 100,000 among the widowed; 40 per 100,000 among divorced persons, with divorced men registering 69 suicides per 100,000, as compared with 18 per 100,000 for divorced women. Suicide is more common in persons who have a history of suicide (attempted or real) in the family and who are socially isolated than in the general population. So-called anniversary suicides are suicides by persons who take their lives on the same day as did a member of their families.

OCCUPATION

The higher a person's social status is, the greater is the suicide risk, but a fall in social status also increases the risk. Work, in general, protects against suicide.

Among occupational rankings, professionals, particularly physicians, have traditionally been considered to be at the greatest risk for suicide. However, the best recent studies have found no increased suicide risk for male physicians in the United States. Their annual suicide rate is about 36 per 100,000, which is the same as that for white men over 25. Recent British and Scandinavian data, by contrast, show that the suicide rate for male physicians is two to three times the rate found in the general male population of the same age.

Studies agree that female physicians have a higher risk of suicide than do other women. In the United States the annual suicide rate for female physicians is about 41 per 100,000, compared with the rate of 12 per 100,000 among all white women over 25 years of age. Similarly, in England and Wales the suicide rate for unmarried female physicians is 2.5 times greater than the rate among unmarried women in the general population, although it is comparable to that found among other groups of professional women.

Studies show that the physician who commits suicide has a mental disorder. The most common mental disorders found among physicians and among physician suicide victims are depressive disorders and substance dependence. Often, the physician who commits suicide has experienced recent professional, personal, or family difficulties. Both male and female physicians commit suicide significantly more often by substance overdoses and less often by firearms than do persons in the general population; drug availability and knowledge about toxicity are important factors in physician suicides. Some evidence indicates that female physicians have an unusually high lifetime risk for mood disorders, which may be the major determinant of the elevated suicide risk.

Among physicians, psychiatrists are considered to be at greatest risk, followed by ophthalmologists and anesthesiologists, but the trend is toward an equalization among all specialties. Special at-risk populations are musicians, dentists, law enforcement officers, lawyers, and insurance agents. Suicide is higher among unemployed persons than among employed persons. During economic recessions and depressions and times of high unemployment, the suicide rate increases. During times of high employment and during war, the rate decreases.

CLIMATE

No seasonal correlation with suicide has been found. The spring and the fall see a slight increase in suicides, but, contrary to popular belief, suicides do not increase during December and holiday periods.

PHYSICAL HEALTH

The relation of physical health and illness to suicide is significant. Prior medical care appears to be a positively correlated risk indicator of suicide: 32 percent of all people who commit suicide have had medical attention within six months of death. Postmortem studies show that a physical illness is present in some 25 to 75 percent of all suicide victims; a physical illness is estimated to be an important contributing factor in 11 to 51 percent of all suicides. In each instance the percentage increases with age.

Some endocrine conditions are associated with increased suicide risk: Cushing's disease, Klinefelter's syndrome, and porphyria. Mood disorders also attend those disorders. The two gastrointestinal disorders with an increased suicide risk are peptic ulcer and cirrhosis, both physical disorders found among alcohol-dependent persons. The two urogenital problems with an increased suicide risk are prostatic hypertrophy and renal disease treated with hemodialysis, both problems in which changes in mood occur.

Factors associated with illness and contributing to both suicides and suicide attempts are loss of mobility among persons to whom physical activity is occupationally or recreationally important; disfigurement, particularly among women; and chronic, intractable pain. In addition to the direct effects of illness, the secondary effects of illness—for example, disruption of relationships and loss of occupational status—are prognostic factors.

Certain drugs can produce depression, which may lead to suicide in some cases. Among those drugs are reserpine (Serpasil), corticosteroids, antihypertensives (for example, propranolol [Inderal]), and some anticancer agents.

MENTAL HEALTH

Highly significant psychiatric factors in suicide include substance abuse, depressive disorders, schizophrenia, and other mental disorders. Almost 95 percent of all patients who commit or attempt suicide have a diagnosed mental disorder. Depressive disorders account for 80 percent of that figure, schizophrenia accounts for 10 percent, and dementia or delirium accounts for 5 percent. Among all mentally disordered persons, 25 percent are also alcohol-dependent and have dual diagnoses. Patients who suffer from delusional depression are at the highest risk for suicide. The risk of suicide in patients with depressive disorders is about 15 percent. Twenty-five percent of all patients with a history of impulsive behavior or violent acts are also at high risk for suicide. Previous psychiatric hospitalization for any reason increases the risk for suicide.

Among adult suicide victims, differences between the young and the old are significant for both psychiatric diagnoses and antecedent stressors. A study in San Diego showed that diagnoses of substance abuse and antisocial personality disorder were found most often among suicide victims under 30 years of age, and diagnoses of mood disorders and cognitive disorders were found most often among suicides aged 30 and over. Stressors associated with suicide in those under 30 were separation, rejection, unemployment, and legal troubles; illness stressors were found most often among suicide victims over 30.

PSYCHIATRIC PATIENTS

Psychiatric patients' risk for suicide is 3 to 12 times greater than that of nonpatients. The degree of risk varies according to age, sex, diagnosis, and inpatient or outpatient status. After adjustment for age, male and female psychiatric patients who have at some time been inpatients have 5 and 10 times higher suicide risks, respectively, than do their counterparts in the general population. For male and female outpatients who have never been admitted to a hospital for psychiatric treatment, the suicide risks are three and four times greater, respectively, than are those of their counterparts in the general population. The higher suicide risk for psychiatric patients who have been inpatients reflects the fact that patients with severe mental disorders tend to be hospitalized—for example, depressive disorder patients requiring electroconvulsive therapy (ECT). The psychiatric diagnosis that carries that greatest risk for suicide in both sexes is a mood disorder.

Persons in the general population who commit suicide tend to be middle-aged or elderly; however, increasingly, studies report that psychiatric patients who commit suicide tend to be relatively young. In one study the mean age of male suicide victims was 29.5 years and that of women 38.4 years. The relative youthfulness of those suicide victims was due partly to the fact that two early-onset, chronic mental disorders—schizophrenia and recurrent major depressive disorder—accounted for just over half of all those suicides, reflecting an age and diagnostic pattern found in most studies of psychiatric patient suicides.

A small but significant percentage of psychiatric patients who commit suicide do so while they are inpatients. The majority of inpatients who commit suicide do not kill themselves in the psychiatric ward itself but do so on the hospital grounds, while on a pass or weekend leave, or when absent without leave.

The suicide risk is highest for both sexes in the first week of the psychiatric admission; after three to five weeks, the risk for inpatients is no greater than the risk in the general population. Also, the inpatient rates of suicide do not rise uniformly with age, as they do in the general population. In fact, the rates for female psychiatric patients fall with advancing age. That difference is due mainly to the fact that suicidal elderly persons do not present themselves to medical services. Times of staff rotation, particularly of the psychiatric residents, are periods associated with inpatient suicides. Epidemics of inpatient suicides tend to be associated with periods of ideological change on the ward, staff disorganization, and staff demoralization.

Among psychiatric outpatients the period after discharge is a period of increased suicide risk. A follow-up study of 5,000 patients discharged from an Iowa psychiatric hospital showed that, in the first three months after discharge, the rate of suicide for female patients was 275 times higher than that of all Iowa females; the rate of suicide for male patients was 70 times higher than that of all Iowa males.

Patients attending emergency services, especially those with panic disorder, also have an increased suicide risk. One study reported that the suicide rate for such patients is more than seven times the age-adjusted and sex-adjusted rate for the general population (but the rate is similar to that of other clinical psychiatric populations). There are two main risk groups: patients with depressive disorders, schizophrenia, and substance abuse and patients who repeatedly visit the emergency room. Thus, mental health professionals working in the emergency services must be well-trained in the taking of the patient's psychiatric history, the examination of the patient's mental state, the assessment of the patient's suicidal risk, and the making of appropriate dispositions and must be aware of the need to contact patients at risk who fail to keep follow-up appointments.

Depressive Disorders

Mood disorders are the diagnoses most commonly associated with suicide. As the suicide risk in depressive disorders is raised mainly when the patient is depressed, the psychopharmacological advances of the past 25 years may have reduced the suicide risk among depressive disorder patients. Nevertheless, the age-adjusted suicide rates for patients suffering from mood disorders has been estimated to be 400 per 100,000 for male patients and 180 per 100,000 for female patients.

Schizophrenia

The suicide risk is high among schizophrenic patients: up to 10 percent die by committing suicide. In the United States an estimated 4,000 schizophrenic patients commit suicide each year. The age of onset of schizophrenia is typically in adolescence or early adulthood, and most schizophrenic patients who commit suicide do so during the first few years of their illness; therefore, schizophrenic patients who commit suicide tend to be relatively young.

Alcohol Dependence

Up to 15 percent of all alcohol-dependent persons commit suicide. The suicide rate for alcoholics is estimated to be about 270 per 100,000 a year; in the United States, between 7,000 and 13,000 alcohol-dependent persons are suicide victims each year.

About 80 percent of all alcohol-dependent suicide victims are male, largely reflecting the sex ratio for alcohol dependence. Alcohol-dependent suicide victims tend to be white, middle-aged, unmarried, friendless, socially isolated, and currently drinking. Up to 40 percent have made a previous suicide attempt. Up to 40 percent of all suicides by alcohol-dependent patients occur within a year of the patient's last hospitalization; elderly alcohol-dependent patients are at particular risk during the postdischarge period.

Other Substance Dependence

Studies in various countries have found an increased suicide risk among substance abusers. The suicide rate for heroin-dependent persons is about 20 times greater than the rate for the general population. Adolescent girls who use intravenous substances also have a high suicide rate. The availability of a lethal amount of substances, intravenous use, associated antisocial personality disorder, a chaotic life-style, and impulsivity are some of the factors that predispose substance-dependent persons to suicidal behavior, particularly when they are dysphoric, depressed, or intoxicated.

Personality Disorders

A high proportion of suicide victims have various associated personality difficulties or disorders. Having a personality disorder may be a determinant of suicidal behavior in several ways: by predisposing to major mental disorders like depressive disorders or alcohol dependence, by leading to difficulties in relationships and social adjustment, by precipitating undesirable life events, by impairing the ability to cope with a mental or physical disorder, and by drawing persons into conflicts with those around them, including family members, physicians, and hospital staff members.

PREVIOUS SUICIDAL BEHAVIOR

A past suicide attempt is perhaps the best indicator that a patient in at increased risk for suicide. Studies show that about

40 percent of depressed patients who commit suicide have made a previous attempt. The risk of a patient's making a second suicide attempt is highest within three months of the first attempt.

ETIOLOGY

Sociological Factors

DURKHEIM'S THEORY

The first major contribution to the study of the social and cultural influences on suicide was made at the end of the last century by the French sociologist Emile Durkheim. In an attempt to explain statistical patterns, Durkheim divided suicides into three social categories: egoistic, altruistic, and anomic. Egoistic suicide applies to those who are not strongly integrated into any social group. The lack of family integration can be used to explain why the unmarried are more vulnerable to suicide than are the married and why couples with children are the best-protected group of all. Rural communities have more social integration than do urban areas and, thus, less suicide. Protestantism is a less-cohesive religion than Catholicism is, and so Protestants have a higher suicide rate than do Catholics.

Altruistic suicide applies to those whose proneness to suicide stems from their excessive integration into a group, with suicide being the outgrowth of that integration—for example, the Japanese soldier who sacrifices his life in battle.

Anomic suicide applies to those persons whose integration into society is disturbed, thereby depriving them of the customary norms of behavior. Anomie can explain why those whose economic situation has changed drastically are more vulnerable than they were before their change in fortune. Anomie also refers to social instability, with a breakdown of society's standards and values.

Psychological Factors

FREUD'S THEORY

The first important psychological insight into suicide came from Sigmund Freud. He described only one patient who made a suicide attempt, but he saw many depressed patients.

In his paper, ''Mourning and Melancholia'' Freud stated his belief that suicide represents aggression turned inward against an introjected, ambivalently cathected love object. Freud doubted that there would be a suicide without the earlier repressed desire to kill someone else.

MENNINGER'S THEORY

Building on Freud's concepts, Karl Menninger in *Man Against Himself* conceived of suicide as a retroflexed murder, inverted homicide as a result of the patient's anger toward another person, which is either turned inward or used as an excuse for punishment. He also described a self-directed death instinct (Freud's concept of Thanatos). He described three components of hostility in suicide: the wish to kill, the wish to be killed, and the wish to die.

RECENT THEORIES

Contemporary suicidologists are not persuaded that a specific psychodynamic or personality structure is associated with suicide. However, they have written that much can be learned about the psychodynamics of suicidal patients from their fantasies as to what would happen and what the consequences would be if they were to commit suicide. Such fantasies often include wishes for revenge, power, control, or punishment; for atonement, sacrifice, or restitution; for escape or sleep; or for rescue, rebirth, reunion with the dead, or a new life. The suicidal patients who are most likely to act out suicidal fantasies may be those who have suffered the loss of a love object or had a narcissistic injury, who experience overwhelming affects like rage and guilt, or who identify with a suicide victim. Group dynamics underlie mass suicides like those at Masada and Jonestown.

Depressed persons may attempt suicide just as they appear to be recovering from their depression. And a suicide attempt can cause a long-standing depression to disappear, especially if it fulfills the patient's need for punishment. Of equal relevance, many suicide patients use a preoccupation with suicide as a way of fighting off intolerable depression and a sense of hopelessness. In fact, hopelessness was found, in a study by Aaron Beck, to be one of the most accurate indicators of long-term suicidal risks.

Physiological Factors

GENETICS

A genetic factor in suicide has been suggested. Studies show that suicide tends to run in families. For example, at all stages of the life cycle, a family history of suicide is present significantly more often among persons who have attempted suicide than among those who have not. One major study found that the suicide risk for first-degree relatives of psychiatric patients was almost eight times greater than that for the relatives of controls. Furthermore, the suicide risk among the first-degree relatives of the psychiatric patients who had committed suicide was four times greater than that found among the relatives of patients who had not committed suicide. In some situations, particularly among adolescents, the family member who has committed suicide may serve as a role model with whom to identify when the option of committing suicide becomes one possible solution to intolerable psychological pain.

NEUROCHEMISTRY

A serotonin deficiency, measured as a decrease in the metabolism of 5-hydroxyindoleacetic acid (5-HIAA), was found in a group of depressed patients who attempted suicide. Those patients who attempted suicide by violent means (for example, guns or jumping) had a lower 5-HIAA level in the cerebrospinal fluid (CSF) than did those depressed patients who were not suicidal or who attempted suicide in a less violent manner (for example, a substance overdose).

Some animal and human studies have indicated an association between a deficiency in the central serotonin system and poor impulse control. Some workers have viewed suicide as one type of impulsive behavior. Furthermore, a significant negative correlation between CSF 5-HIAA levels and lifetime aggression scores has been reported among personality disorder patients. Other patient groups thought to have problems with impulse control include violent offenders, arsonists, and those with alcohol dependence, groups who have also been noted to have lower CSF 5-HIAA levels than do controls.

Possible peripheral markers of suicidal behavior have also

been examined. High outputs of urinary free cortisol, non-suppression of plasma cortisol after the administration of dexamethasone, an exaggerated plasma cortisol response to the infusion of 5-hydroxytryptophan, a blunted plasma thyroid-stimulating hormone (TSH) response to the infusion of thyrotropin-releasing hormone (TRH), skin conductance abnormalities, altered urinary catechol ratios, and decreases in platelet serotonin uptake or titrated imipramine (Tofranil) binding number have all been associated with suicidal behavior among depressed patients.

A few studies have found ventricular enlargement and abnormal electroencephalograms (EEGs) in some suicidal patients.

Blood samples analyzed for platelet monoamine oxidase (MAO) from a group of normal volunteers revealed that those persons with the lowest level of the enzyme in their platelets had eight times the prevalence of suicide in their families, compared with persons with high levels of the enzyme. There is strong evidence for an alteration of platelet MAO activity in depressive disorders.

SELF-INJURY

Studies show that about 4 percent of all patients in psychiatric hospitals have cut themselves; the female-to-male ratio is almost 3 to 1. The incidence of self-injury in psychiatric patients is estimated to be more than 50 times greater than in the general population. Cutters presenting to psychiatrists tend to have cut themselves chronically over several years. Self-injury is found in about 30 percent of all abusers of oral substances and 10 percent of all intravenous users admitted to substance-treatment units.

The patients are usually in their 20s and may be single or married. Most cut delicately, not coarsely. Cutting is usually done in private with a razor blade, a knife, broken glass, or a mirror. The wrists, arms, thighs, and legs are the most common sites cut; the face, breasts, and abdomen are cut infrequently. Most cutters claim to experience no pain. The reasons given include anger at themselves or others, relief of tension, and the wish to die. The great majority of cutters are classified as those with personality disorders and are significantly more introverted, neurotic, and hostile than are controls. Alcohol abuse and other substance abuse are common, and the majority of cutters have attempted suicide.

Self-mutilitation has been viewed as localized self-destruction, with mishandling of aggressive impulses caused by an unconscious wish to punish either oneself or an introjected object. Some have referred to cutters as pseudosuicidal.

PREDICTION

The clinician must assess an individual patient's risk for suicide on the basis of the clinical examination. The most predictive items associated with suicide risk are listed in Table 25.1–1. Among the high-risk characteristics are age over 45, male sex, alcohol dependence (the suicide rate is 50 times higher in alcohol dependent persons than in those who are not alcohol-dependent), violent behavior, prior suicidal behavior, and previous psychiatric hospitalization.

The clinician should always ask about suicide ideation as part of every mental status examination, especially if the patient is depressed. The patient should be asked directly: "Are you

Table 25.1–1. Factors Associated with Suicide Risk

Rank Order	Factor
1	Age (45 and older)
2	Alcohol dependence
3	Irritation, rage, violence
4	Prior suicidal behavior
5	Male
6	Unwilling to accept help
7	Longer than usual duration of current episode of depression
8	Prior inpatient psychiatric treatment
9	Recent loss or separation
10	Depression
11	Loss of physical health
12	Unemployed or retired
13	Single, widowed, or divorced

Table modified from R E Litman, N L Faberow, C I Wold, T R Brown: Prediction models of suicidal behaviors. In *The Prediction of Suicide.* H Beck, L P Resnik, D J Lettieri, editors, p 141. Charles Press, Bowie, MD. 1974. Used with permission.

or have you ever been suicidal? Do you want to die?" Eight out of 10 persons who eventually kill themselves give warnings of their intent. Fifty percent say openly that they want to die. If the patient admits to a plan of action, that is a particularly dangerous sign. Also, if a patient who has been threatening suicide becomes quiet and less agitated than in the past, that may be an ominous sign.

TREATMENT

The great majority of suicides among psychiatric patients are preventable. Some patients experience suffering so great and intense or so chronic and unresponsive to treatment that their eventual suicides may be perceived as inevitable; fortunately, such patients are relatively uncommon. Some other patients have severe personality disorders, are highly impulsive, and apparently commit suicide impulsively, often when dysphoric or intoxicated or both. The evidence that inadequate assessment or treatment is associated with suicide indicates that the great majority of suicides of psychiatric patients are probably preventable.

Inpatient versus Outpatient Treatment

Whether to hospitalize patients with suicidal ideation is the most important clinical decision to be made. Not all such patients require hospitalization; some may be treated as outpatients. But the absence of a strong social support system, a history of impulsive behavior, and a suicidal plan of action are indications for hospitalization. To determine whether outpatient treatment is feasible, the clinician should use a straightforward clinical approach—asking patients considered suicidal to agree to call when reaching a point beyond which they are uncertain of their ability to control their suicidal impulses. Patients who can make such an agreement reaffirm the belief that they have sufficient strength to control such impulses and to seek help.

In return for the patient's commitment, the clinician should be available to the patient 24 hours a day. If a patient who is considered seriously suicidal cannot make the commitment, immediate emergency hospitalization is indicated, and both the patient and the patient's family should be so advised. If, however, the patient is to be treated as an outpatient, the therapist should note the patient's home and work telephone numbers for emergency reference; occasionally, a patient hangs up unexpectedly during a late night call or gives only a name to the answering service. If the patient refuses hospitalization, the family must take the responsibility to be with the patient 24 hours a day.

In the hospital the patient can receive antidepressant or antipsychotic medications as indicated; individual therapy, group therapy, and family therapy are available; and the patient receives the hospital's social support and sense of security. Other therapeutic measures depend on the patient's underlying diagnosis. For example, if alcohol dependence is an associated problem, treatment must be directed toward alleviating that condition.

Although patients classified as acutely suicidal may have favorable prognoses, chronically suicidal patients are difficult to treat, and they exhaust the caretakers. Constant observation by special nurses, seclusion, and restraints cannot prevent suicide if the patient is resolute. Electroconvulsive therapy (ECT) may be necessary for some severely depressed patients, who may require several treatment courses.

Useful measures for the treatment of the depressed suicidal inpatient include searching the patient's belongings and person on arrival in the ward for objects that may be used for suicide and repeating the search at times of exacerbation of the suicidal ideation. Ideally, the suicidal depressed inpatient should be treated on a locked ward where the windows are shatterproof, and the patient's room should be located near the nursing station to maximize observation by the nursing staff. The treating team has to assess how much to restrict the patient and whether to make regular checks or continued direct observation. Vigorous treatment with antidepressant medication should be initiated.

Supportive psychotherapy by the psychiatrist shows concern and may alleviate some of the patient's intense suffering. Some patients may be able to accept the idea that they are suffering from a recognized illness and that they will probably make a complete recovery. Patients should be dissuaded from making major life decisions while they are suicidally depressed, because such decisions are often morbidly determined and may be irrevocable. The consequences of such bad decisions can cause further anguish and misery when the patient has recovered.

Patients recovering from a suicidal depression are at particular risk. As the depression lifts, patients become energized and are thus able to put their suicidal plans into action. Sometimes depressed patients, with or without treatment, suddenly appear to be at peace with themselves, because they have reached a secret decision to commit suicide. The clinician should be especially suspicious of such a dramatic clinical change, which may portend a suicidal attempt.

A patient may commit suicide even when in the hospital. According to one survey, about 1 percent of all suicides were committed by patients who were being treated in general medical-surgical or psychiatric hospitals; however, the annual suicide rate in psychiatric hospitals is only 0.003 percent.

LEGAL AND ETHICAL CONSIDERATIONS

Liability issues stemming from suicides in psychiatric hospitals frequently involve questions about the patient's rate of deterioration, the presence during hospitalization of clinical signs indicating risk, and the psychiatrist's and the staff members' awareness of and response to those clinical signs.

About half of cases of suicide while the patient is on a psychiatric unit result in a lawsuit. What the courts require is not that suicide never occur but that the patient be periodically evaluated for suicidal risk, that a treatment plan with a high level of security be formulated, and that the staff members follow that treatment plan.

At present, suicide and attempted suicide are variously viewed as a felony and a misdemeanor, respectively; in some states the acts are considered not crimes but unlawful under common law and statutes. The role of an aider and abettor in suicide adds another dimension to the legal morass; some court decisions have held that, although neither suicide nor attempted suicide is punishable, anyone who assists in the act may be punished.

Community Organizations

Community organizations seem to have fewer problems than do individual therapists with the ethics and the legalities of helping suicidal people. Prevention centers, crisis listening posts, and suicide hot lines are clear attempts to intervene and diminish the isolation, withdrawal, and loneliness of the suicidal patient. Outreach programs enable highly motivated laypersons to respond to cries for help in a variety of ways. But such responses do no more than just diminish an acute crisis; highly suicidal people place fewer than 10 percent of such calls. Two studies in the United States have failed to find that suicide prevention centers had an effect on suicide rates. Nevertheless, suicide prevention centers are important mental health resources for persons in distress.

References

Asnis G M, Friedman T A, Sanderson W C, Kaplan M L: Suicidal behaviors in adult psychiatric outpatients: I. Description and prevalence. Am J Psychiatry 150: 108, 1993.
Conwell Y: Suicide among elderly people. Psychiatr Serv 46: 563, 1995.
Duberstein P R, Conwell Y, Caine E D: Interpersonal stressors, substance abuse, and suicide. J Nerv Ment Dis 181: 80, 1993.
Hillard J R: Predicting suicide. Psychiatr Serv 46: 223, 1995.
Kaplan M, Asnis G M, Lipschitz D S, Chorney P: Suicidal behavior and abuse in psychiatric outpatients. Compr Psychiatry 36: 229, 1995.
Malone K M, Haas G L, Sweeney J A, Mann J J: Major depression and the risk of attempted suicide. J Affect Disord 34: 17, 1995.
Murphy G E, Wetzel R D, Robins E, McEvoy L: Multiple risk factors predict suicide in alcoholism. Arch Gen Psychiatry 49: 459, 1992.
Rich C L, Runeson B S: Mental illness and youth suicide. Am J Psychiatry 152: 1239, 1995.
Roy A: Are there genetic factors in suicide? Int Rev Psychiatry 4: 169, 1992.
Roy A: Suicide. In Comprehensive Textbook of Psychiatry, ed 6, H I Kaplan, B J Sadock, editors, p 1739. Williams & Wilkins, Baltimore, 1995.
Tsuang M T, Simpson J C, Fleming J A: Epidemiology of suicide. Int Rev Psychiatry 4: 117, 1992.

25.2 OTHER PSYCHIATRIC EMERGENCIES

A psychiatric emergency is any disturbance in thoughts, feelings, or actions for which immediate therapeutic intervention is necessary. For a variety of reasons—such as the growing incidence of violence, the increased appreciation of the role of organic disease in altered mental status, and the epidemic of alcohol dependence and other substance-related disorders—the number of emergency patients is on the rise. Physicians, including psychiatrists, are performing an expanded role as the primary clinician or consultant as part of integrated emergency medicine services. The widening scope of emergency psychiatry goes beyond general psychiatric practice to include such specialized problems as the abuse of substances, children, and spouses; violence in the form of suicide, homicide, and rape; and such social issues as homelessness, aging, competence, and acquired immune deficiency syndrome (AIDS). The emergency psychiatrist must be up-to-date on medicolegal issues and managed care.

EPIDEMIOLOGY

Psychiatric emergency rooms are used equally by men and women and more by single persons than by married persons. About 20 percent of patients are suicidal, and about 10 percent are violent. The most common diagnoses are mood disorders (including depressive disorders and manic episodes), schizophrenia, and alcohol dependence. About 40 percent of all patients seen in psychiatric emergency rooms require hospitalization. Most visits occur during the night hours, but there is no utilization difference based on the day of the week or the month of the year. Contrary to popular belief, studies have not found that psychiatric emergency rooms are used more often during a full moon or during the Christmas season.

EMERGENCY PSYCHIATRIC INTERVIEW

The emergency interview is similar to the standard psychiatric interview except for the time limitation imposed by the other patients waiting to be seen and by the potential sense of urgency in assessing the risk to the patient or others. In general, the physician focuses on the presenting complaint and the reasons that the patient has come to the emergency room at that time. The time constraint requires that the clinician structure the interview, particularly with patients who may respond with long, rambling accounts of their illnesses. If friends, relatives, or the police accompany the patient, a supplemental history should be obtained from them, especially if the patient is mute, negativistic, uncooperative, or otherwise unable to give a coherent history.

Patients may be highly motivated to reveal themselves to gain relief from suffering, but they may also be both consciously and unconsciously motivated to conceal innermost feelings that they perceive to be shameful or threatening. If the patient has been brought to the hospital involuntarily, willingness or ability to cooperate may be impaired for that reason. The psychiatrist's relationship with the patient strongly influences what the patient does and does not say, even within the context of a first interview in an emergency room; therefore, a large portion of the psychiatric emergency interview involves the specific and sophisticated techniques of listening, observation, and interpretation that provide the foundation of psychiatric training in general. Being straightforward, honest, calm, and nonthreatening is of utmost importance, as is the ability to convey to patients the idea that the clinician is in control and will act decisively to protect them from hurting themselves or others.

Sometimes the contact with the emergency room is by telephone. In such cases the psychiatrist should obtain the number from which the call is made and the exact address. Those items are important in case the call is interrupted; they allow the psychiatrist to direct help to the patient. If the patient is alone and the psychiatrist ascertains that the patient is in danger, the police should be alerted. If possible, an assistant should call the police on another line while the psychiatrist keeps the patient engaged

until help arrives. The patient should not be told to drive alone to the hospital. Rather, an emergency medical team should be dispatched to bring the patient to the hospital.

The greatest potential error in emergency room psychiatry is overlooking a physical illness as the cause of the emotional illness. Head traumas, medical illnesses, substance abuse (including alcohol), cerebrovascular diseases, metabolic abnormalities, and medications may all cause abnormal behavior, and the psychiatrist should take a concise medical history that concentrates on those areas.

Violence and Assaultive Behavior

The first task in evaluating violent behavior is to ascertain its cause. Cause directs treatment. Patients with thought disorders characterized by hallucinations commanding them to kill someone require psychiatric hospitalization and antipsychotic medication. If they are unwilling to accept treatment, certification is necessary to protect the intended victim and the patient. Those who take an extreme civil libertarian perspective fail to recognize that medical certification has evolved legally not only to protect society from the violent patient but also to protect patients from the consequences of their uncontrollable behavior. Patients who, while psychotic, destroy families' and friends' property or threaten to commit or do commit violent assaults destroy social supports that they need to help them function after the aberrant mood or delusional ideation is corrected.

Violence and assaultive behavior are difficult to predict. However, the fear with which some people regard all psychiatric patients is completely out of proportion to the small group who are an authentic danger to others. The best predictors of potential violent behavior are (1) excessive alcohol intake, (2) a history of violent acts with arrests or criminal activity, and (3) a history of childhood abuse. Although violent patients can arouse a realistic fear in the psychiatrist, they can also touch off irrational fears that impair clinical judgment and that may lead to the premature and excessive use of sedation or physical restraint. Violent patients are usually frightened by their own hostile impulses and desperately seek help to prevent loss of control. Nevertheless, restraints should be applied if there is a reasonable risk of violence.

DIFFERENTIAL DIAGNOSIS

The emergency psychiatrist must consider a wide range of conditions that may account for the presenting signs and symptoms. The most common complaints fall within the categories of anxiety, depression, mania, and thought disorder. Those conditions may overlap and have multiple causes.

Anxiety is different from depression, mania, and thought disorder in that a number of the illnesses that can cause anxiety are life-threatening. Incipient myocardial infarctions, pulmonary emboli, cardiac arrhythmias, and internal hemorrhages cause acute anxiety to the degree of panic. Untreated congestive heart failure secondary to a silent myocardial infarction or malignant cardiac arrhythmia may be fatal. Elderly people and those who have just suffered a loss may be perceived as having depressive or nihilistic ideation when, in fact, age or stress has propelled them into a life-threatening illness manifested by anxiety and a sense of impending doom. Persons who experience depression as a side effect of antihypertensive medication—for example, propranolol (Inderal)—may perceive spouse, children, friends, or work in a negative light that changes on cessation of the medication.

The differential diagnosis of violent behavior includes substance-induced persisting dementia, antisocial personality-disorder, catatonic schizophrenia, cerebral infection, cerebral neoplasm, obsessive-compulsive personality disorder, dissociative disorders, impulse control disorders, sexual disorders, idiosyncratic alcohol intoxication, delusional disorder, paranoid personality disorder, schizophrenia, social maladjustment without mental disorder, temporal lobe epilepsy, bipolar I disorder, and uncontrollable violence secondary to interpersonal stress.

TREATMENT

Patients in the grip of a violent episode pay no attention to the rational intercessions of others and probably do not even hear them. When armed, they are particularly dangerous and capable of murder. Such patients should be disarmed by trained law enforcement personnel without their harming the patients if at all possible. If unarmed, such patients should be approached with sufficient help and with overwhelming strength, so that there is, in effect, no contest. In the emergency room, armed police should always remove bullets from their weapons. In numerous instances, disturbed patients have grabbed a loaded gun and randomly killed others.

Patients must be placed in a safe setting. Some need to be transferred to a forensic unit because of the magnitude of their violent potential. Medication specific to a disorder is administered when indicated, unless a nonspecific measure is required to modify behavior until the cause is ascertained and specific therapy can be initiated.

The use of medication is contraindicated in acutely agitated patients who have suffered a head injury, because medication can confuse the clinical picture. In general, intramuscular (IM) haloperidol is one of the most useful emergency treatments for violent psychotic patients.

Electroconvulsive therapy (ECT) has also been used in emergencies to control psychotic violence. One or several ECT sessions within several hours usually ends an episode of psychotic violence.

Psychotherapy

In an emergency psychiatric intervention, all attempts are made to help patients' self-esteem. Empathy is critical to healing in a psychiatric emergency. The acquired knowledge of how biogenetic, situational, developmental, and existential forces converge at one point in history to create a psychiatric emergency is tantamount to the maturation of skill in emergency psychiatry.

Adjustment disorder in all age groups may result in tantrumlike outbursts of rage. Those outburst are seen particularly in marital quarrels. Police are often summoned by neighbors distressed by the sounds of a violent altercation. Such family quarrels should be approached with caution, because they may be completed by the use of alcohol and the presence of dangerous weapons. The warring couple frequently turn their combined fury on the unwary outsider. Wounded self-esteem is a big issue. Therefore, patronizing or contemptuous attitudes must be avoided, and an effort must be made to communicate an attitude of respect and an authentic peacemaking concern.

In family violence the psychiatrist should note the special vulnerability of selected close relatives. A wife or a husband may have a curious masochistic attachment to the spouse and provoke violence by taunting and otherwise undermining the partner's self-esteem. Such relationships often end in the murder of the provoking partner and sometimes in the suicide of the other partner, the dynamics behind most so-called suicide pacts.

As in the case of many suicidal patients, many violent patients require hospitalization and usually accept the offer of inpatient care with a sense of relief.

More than one psychotherapist or psychotherapy is frequently used in emergency therapy. For example, a 28-year-old man, depressed and suicidal after a colostomy for intractable colitis, whose wife was threatening to leave him because of his irritability and their constant altercations, may be referred to a psychiatrist for supportive psychotherapy and antidepressant, to a marital therapist with his wife to improve their marital functioning, and to a colostomy support group to learn ways of coping with a colostomy. Emergency psychiatric clinicians are pragmatic. They use every necessary mode of therapeutic intervention available to resolve the crisis and to facilitate value exploration and growth. There is less concern than usual about the dilution of a therapeutic relationship. Emphasis is on how various psychiatric modalities act synergistically to enhance recovery.

No one word is appropriate for all people in similar situations. What does one say to a patient and family experiencing a psychiatric emergency, such as a suicide attempt or a schizophrenic break? For some a genetic rationale helps. The information that an illness has a strong biological components relieves some people. For others it underlines lack of control and increases depression and anxiety; they feel helpless because neither the family nor the patient can alter the behavior to minimize the likelihood of recurrence. Others may benefit from an explanation of family or individual dynamics. Still others only want someone to listen; in time, they will reach their own understanding.

In the emergency situation, as in any other psychiatric situation, when a clinician does not know what to say, the best approach is to listen. People in crisis reveal how much they need support, denial, ventilation, and words to conceptualize the meaning of their crisis and to discover paths to resolution.

Pharmacotherapy

The major indications for the use of psychotropic medication in the emergency room include violent or assaultive behavior, massive anxiety or panic, and extrapyramidal reactions, such as dystonia and akathisia as side effects of psychiatric drugs. A rare form of dystonia is laryngospasm, and the psychiatrist should be prepared to maintain an open airway with intubation if necessary.

Persons who are paranoid or in a state of catatonic excitement require tranquilization. Episodic outbursts of violence respond to lithium (Eskalith), β-adrenergic receptor antagonists, and carbamazepine (Tegretol). If the history suggests a seizure disorder, clinical studies are performed to confirm the diagnosis, and an evaluation is performed to ascertain the cause. If the findings are positive, anticonvulsants are commenced, or appropriate surgery is provided (for example, in the instance of a cerebral mass). For intoxication from recreational substances,

Table 25.2–1   Common Psychiatric Emergencies

Syndrome	Emergency Manifestations	Treatment Issues
Adolescent crises	Suicidal attempts and ideation; substance abuse, truancy, trouble with law, pregnancy, running away; eating disorders; psychosis	Evaluation of suicidal potential, extent of substance abuse, family dynamics; crisis-oriented family and individual therapy; hospitalization if necessary; consultation with appropriate extrafamilial authorities
Agoraphobia	Panic; depression	Alprazolam (Xanax), 0.25 mg to 2 mg; propranolol (Inderal); antidepressant medication
Agranulocytosis (Clozapine (Clozaril)-induced)	High fever, pharyngitis, oral and perianal ulcerations	Discontinue medication immediately; administer granulocyte-colony stimulating factor
Akathisia	Agitation, restlessness, muscle discomfort; dysphoria	Reduce antipsychotic dosage; propranolol (30 to 120 mg a day); benzodiazepines; diphenhydramine (Benadryl) orally or IV; benztropine (Cogentin) IM
Alcohol-related emergencies		
Alcohol delirium	Confusion, disorientation, fluctuating consciousness and perception, autonomic hyperactivity; may be fatal	Chlordiazepoxide; haloperidol (Haldol) for psychotic symptoms may be added if necessary
Alcohol intoxication	Disinhibited behavior, sedation at high doses	With time and protective environment, symptoms abate
Alcohol persisting amnestic disorder	Confusion, loss of memory even for all personal identification data	Hospitalization; hypnosis; amobarbital (Amytal) interview; rule out organic cause
Alcohol persisting dementia	Confusion, agitation, impulsivity	Rule out other causes for dementia; no effective treatment; hospitalization if necessary
Alcohol psychotic disorder with hallucinations	Vivid auditory (at times visual) hallucinations with affect appropriate to content (often fearful); clear sensorium	Haloperidol for psychotic symptoms
Alcohol seizures	Grand mal seizures; rarely status epilepticus	Diazepam (Valium), phenytoin (Dilantin); prevent by using chlordiazepoxide (Librium) during detoxification
Alcohol withdrawal	Irritability, nausea, vomiting, insomnia, malaise, autonomic hyperactivity, shakiness	Fluid and electrolytes maintained; sedation with benzodiazepines; restraints; monitoring of vital signs; 100 mg thiamine IM
Idiosyncratic alcohol intoxication	Marked aggressive or assaultive behavior	Generally no treatment required other than protective environment
Korsakoff's syndrome	Alcohol stigmata, amnesia, confabulation	No effective treatment; institutionalization often needed.
Wernicke's encephalopathy	Oculomotor disturbances, cerebellar ataxia; mental confusion	Thiamine, 100 mg IV or IM, with $MgSO_4$ given before glucose loading
Amphetamine intoxication	Delusions, paranoia; violence; depression (from withdrawal); anxiety, delirium	Antipsychotics; restraints; hospitalization if necessary; no need for gradual withdrawal; antidepressants may be necessary
Anorexia nervosa	Loss of 25 percent of body weight of the norm for age and sex	Hospitalization; electrocardiogram (ECG), fluid and electrolytes; neuroendocrine evaluation
Anticholinergic intoxication	Psychotic symptoms, dry skin and mouth, hyperpyrexia, midriasis, tachycardia, restlessness, visual hallucinations	Discontinue drug, IV physostigmine (Antilirium), 0.5 to 2 mg, for severe agitation or fever, benzodiazepines; antipsychotics contraindicated
Anticonvulsant intoxication	Psychosis; delirium	Dosage of anticonvulsant is reduced
Benzodiazepine intoxication	Sedation, somnolence, and ataxia	Supportive measures; midazolam (Versed), 7.5 to 45 mg a day, titrated as needed, should be used only by skilled personnel with resuscitative equipment available
Bereavement	Guilt feelings; irritability; insomnia; somatic complaints	Must be differentiated from major depressive disorder; antidepressants not indicated; benzodiazepines for sleep; encouragement of ventilation
Brief psychotic disorder	Emotional turmoil, extreme lability; acutely impaired reality testing after obvious psychosocial stress	Hospitalization often necessary; low dosage of antipsychotics may be necessary but often resolves spontaneously
Caffeine intoxication	Severe anxiety, resembling panic disorder; mania; delirium; agitated depression; sleep disturbance	Cessation of caffeine-containing substances; benzodiazepines
Cannabis intoxication	Delusions; panic; dysphoria; cognitive impairment	Benzodiazepines and antipsychotics as needed; evaluation of suicidal or homicidal risk; symptoms usually abate with time and reassurance
Catatonic schizophrenia	Marked psychomotor disturbance (either excitement or stupor); exhaustion, can be fatal	Rapid tranquilization with antipsychotics; monitor vital signs; amobarbital may release patient from catatonic mutism or stupor but can precipitate violent behavior
Clonidine withdrawal	Irritability; psychosis; violence; seizures	Symptoms abate with time, but antipsychotics may be necessary; gradual lowering of dosage
Cocaine intoxication and withdrawal	Paranoia and violence; severe anxiety; manic state; delirium; schizophreniform psychosis; tachycardia, hypertension, myocardial infarction, cerebrovascular disease; depression and suicidal ideation	Antipsychotics and benzodiazepines; antidepressants or ECT for withdrawal depression if persistent; hospitalization

(continued)

Table 25.2-1   *(continued)*

Syndrome	Emergency Manifestations	Treatment Issues
Delirium	Fluctuating sensorium; suicidal and homicidal risk; cognitive clouding; visual, tactile, and auditory hallucinations; paranoia	Evaluate all potential contributing factors and treat each accordingly; reassurance, structure, clues to orientation; benzodiazepines and low-dosage, high-potency antipsychotics must be used with extreme care because of their potential to act paradoxically and increase agitation
Delusional disorder	Most often brought in to emergency room involuntarily; threats directed toward others	Antipsychotics if patient will comply (IM if necessary); intensive family intervention; hospitalization if necessary
Dementia	Unable to care for self; violent outbursts; psychosis; depression and suicidal ideation; confusion	Small dosages of high-potency antipsychotics; clues to orientation; organic evaluation, including medication use; family intervention
Depressive disorders	Suicidal ideation and attempts; self-neglect; substance abuse	Assessment of danger to self; hospitalization if necessary; nonpsychiatric causes of depression must be evaluated
L-Dopa intoxication	Mania; depression; schizophreniform disorder; may induce rapid cycling in patients with bipolar I disorder	Lower dosage or discontinue drug
Dystonia, acute	Intense involuntary spasm of muscles of neck, tongue, face, jaw, eyes, or trunk	Decrease dosage of antipsychotic; benztropine or diphenhydramine IM
Hallucinogen psychotic disorder with hallucinations	Symptom picture is result of interaction of type of substance, dose taken, duration of action, user's premorbid personality, setting; panic; agitation; atropine psychosis	Serum and urine screens; rule out underlying medical or mental disorder; benzodiazepines (2 to 20 mg) orally; reassurance and orientation; rapid tranquilization; often responds spontaneously
Homicidal and assaultive behavior	Marked agitation with verbal threats	Seclusion, restraints, medication
Hypertensive crisis	Life-threatening hypertensive reaction secondary to ingestion of tyramine-containing foods in combination with MAOIs; headache, stiff neck, sweating, nausea, vomiting	α-Adrenergic blockers (e.g., phentolamine (Regitine)); nifedipine (Procardia) 10 mg orally; chlorpromazine (Thorazine); make sure symptoms are not secondary to hypotension (side effect of monoamine oxidase inhibitors (MAOIs) alone)
Hyperthermia	Extreme excitement or catatonic stupor or both; extremely elevated temperature; violent hyperagitation	Hydrate and cool; may be drug reaction, so discontinue any drug; rule out infection
Hyperventilation	Anxiety, terror, clouded consciousness; giddiness, faintness; blurring vision	Shift alkalosis by having patient breathe into paper bag; patient education; antianxiety agents
Hypothermia	Confusion; lethargy; combativeness; low body temperature and shivering; paradoxical feeling of warmth	IV fluids and rewarming; cardiac status must be carefully monitored; avoidance of alcohol
Incest and sexual abuse of a child	Suicidal behavior; adolescent crises; substance abuse	Corroboration of charge; protection of victim; contact social services; medical and psychiatric evaluation; crisis intervention
Insomnia	Depression and irritability; early morning agitation; frightening dreams; fatigue	Hypnotics only in short term; e.g., triazolam (Halcion), 0.25 to 0.5 mg, at bedtime; treat any underlying mental disorder; rules of sleep hygiene (see Table 17.2–4)
Intermittent explosive disorder	Brief outbursts of violence; periodic episodes of suicide attempts	Benzodiazepines or antipsychotics for short term; long-term evaluation with computed tomography (CT) scan, sleep-deprived electroencephalogram (EEG), glucose tolerance curve
Lithium toxicity	Vomiting; abdominal pain; profuse diarrhea; severe tremor, ataxia; coma; seizures; confusion; dysarthria; focal neurological signs	Lavage with wide-bore tube; osmotic diuresis; medical consultation; may require ICU treatment
Major depressive episode with psychotic features	Major depressive episode symptoms with delusions; agitation, severe guilt; ideas of reference; suicide and homicide risk	Antipsychotics plus antidepressants; evaluation of suicide and homicide risk; hospitalization and ECT if necessary
Manic episode	Violent, impulsive behavior; indiscriminate sexual or spending behavior; psychosis; substance abuse	Hospitalization; restraints if necessary; rapid tranquilization with antipsychotics; restoration of lithium levels
Migraine	Throbbing, unilateral headache	Sumatriptan (Imitrex) 6 mg IM
Neuroleptic malignant syndrome	Hyperthermia; muscle rigidity; autonomic instability; parkinsonian symptoms; catatonic stupor; neurological signs; 10 to 30 percent fatality; elevated creatine phosphokinase	Discontinue antipsychotic; IV dantrolene (Dantrium); bromocriptine (Parlodel) orally; hydration and cooling; monitor CPK levels
Opioid intoxication and withdrawal	Intoxication can lead to coma and death; withdrawal is not life-threatening	IV naloxone, narcotic antagonist; urine and serum screens; psychiatric and medical illnesses (e.g., AIDS) may complicate picture

(continued)

Table 25.2-1   *(continued)*

Syndrome	Emergency Manifestations	Treatment Issues
Panic disorder	Panic, terror; acute onset	Must differentiate from other anxiety-producing disorders, both medical and psychiatric; ECG to rule out mitral valve prolapse; propranolol (10 to 30 mg); alprazolam (0.25 to 2.0 mg); long-term management may include an antidepressant
Paranoid schizophrenia	Command hallucinations; threat to others or themselves	Rapid tranquilization; hospitalization; long-acting depot medication; threatened persons must be notified and protected
Parkinsonism	Stiffness, tremor, bradykinesia, flattened affect, shuffling gait, salivation, secondary to antipsychotic medication	Oral antiparkinsonian drug for four weeks to three months; decrease dosage of the antipsychotic
Perioral (rabbit) tremor	Perioral tremor (rabbitlike facial grimacing) usually appearing after long-term therapy with antipsychotics	Decrease dosage or change to a medication in another class
Phencyclidine intoxication	Paranoid psychosis; can lead to death; acute danger to self and others	Serum and urine assay; benzodiazepines may interfere with excretion; antipsychotics may worsen symptoms because of anticholinergic side effects; medical monitoring and hospitalization for severe intoxication
Phenylpropanolamine toxicity	Psychosis, paranoia; insomnia; restlessness; nervousness; headache	Symptoms abate with dosage reduction or discontinuation (found in over-the-counter diet aids and oral and nasal decongestants)
Phobias	Panic, anxiety, fear	Treatment same as for panic disorder
Photosensitivity	Easy sunburning secondary to use of antipsychotic medication	Patient should avoid strong sunlight and use high-level sunscreens
Postpartum psychosis	Childbirth can precipitate schizophrenia, depression, reactive psychoses, mania, and depression; affective symptoms are most common; suicide risk is reduced during pregnancy but increased in the postpartum period	Danger to self and others (including infant) must be evaluated and proper precautions taken; medical illness presenting with behavioral aberrations is included in the differential diagnosis and must be sought and treated; care must be paid to the effects on father, infant, grandparents, and other children
Posttraumatic stress disorder	Panic, terror; suicidal ideation; flashbacks	Reassurance; encouragement of return to responsibilities; avoid hospitalization if possible to prevent chronic invalidism; monitor suicidal ideation
Priapism (trazodone (Desyrel)-induced)	Persistent penile erection accompanied by severe pain	Intracorporeal epinephrine; mechanical or surgical drainage
Rape	Not all sexual violations are reported; silent rape reaction is characterized by loss of appetite, sleep disturbance, anxiety, and, sometimes, agoraphobia; long periods of silence, mounting anxiety, stuttering, blocking, and physical symptoms during the interview when the sexual history is taken; fear of violence and death and of contracting a sexually transmitted disease or being pregnant	Rape is a major psychiatric emergency; victim may have enduring patterns of sexual dysfunction; crisis-oriented therapy, social support, ventilation, reinforcement of healthy traits, and encouragement to return to the previous level of functioning as rapidly as possible; legal counsel; thorough medical examination and tests to identify the assailant (e.g., obtaining samples of pubic hairs with a pubic hair comb, vaginal smear to identify blood antigens in semen); if a woman, methoxyprogesterone or diethylstilbestrol orally for five days to prevent pregnancy; if menstruation does not commence within one week of cessation of the estrogen, all alternatives to pregnancy, including abortion, should be offered; if the victim has contracted a venereal disease, appropriate antibiotics; witnessed written permission is required for the physician to examine, photograph, collect specimens, and release information to the authorities; obtain consent, record the history in the patient's own words, obtain required tests, record the results of the examination, save all clothing, defer diagnosis, and provide protection against disease, psychic trauma, and pregnancy; men's and women's responses to rape affectively are reported similarly, although men are more hesitant to talk about the assault, particularly if it was homosexual, for fear they will be assumed to have consented
Schizophrenia in exacerbation	Withdrawn; agitation; suicidal and homicidal risk	Suicide and homicide evaluation; screen for medical illness; restraints and rapid tranquilization if necessary; hospitalization if necessary; reevaluation of medication regimen
Sedative, hypnotic, or anxiolytic intoxication and withdrawal	Alterations in mood, behavior, thought—delirium; derealization and depersonalization; untreated, can be fatal; seizures	Naloxone (Narcan) to differentiate from opioid intoxication; slow withdrawal with phenobarbital (Luminal) or sodium thiopental or benzodiazepine; hospitalization
Seizure disorder	Confusion; anxiety; derealization and depersonalization; feelings of impending doom; gustatory or olfactory hallucinations; fugue-like state	Immediate EEG; admission and sleep-deprived and 24-hour EEG; rule out pseudoseizures; anticonvulsants

(continued)

Table 25.2–1   *(continued)*

Syndrome	Emergency Manifestations	Treatment Issues
Substance withdrawal	Abdominal pain; insomnia, drowsiness; delirium; seizures; symptoms of tardive dyskinesia may emerge; eruption of manic or schizophrenic symptoms	Symptoms of psychotropic drug withdrawal disappear with time and disappear with reinstitution of the substance; symptoms of antidepressant withdrawal can be successfully treated with anticholinergic agents, such as atropine; gradual withdrawal of psychotropic substances over two to four weeks generally obviates development of symptoms
Suicide	Suicidal ideation; hopelessness	Hospitalization, antidepressants
Tardive dyskinesia	Dyskinesia of mouth, tongue, face, neck, and trunk; choreoathetoid movements of extremities; usually but not always appearing after long-term treatment with antipsychotics, especially after a reduction in dosage; incidence highest in the elderly and brain-damaged; symptoms are intensified by antiparkinsonian drugs and masked but not cured by increased dosages of antipsychotic	No effective treatment reported; may be prevented by prescribing the least amount of drug possible for as little time as is clinically feasible and using drug-free holidays for patients who need to continue taking the drug; decrease or discontinue drug at first sign of dyskinetic movements
Thyrotoxicosis	Tachycardia; gastrointestinal dysfunction; hyperthermia; panic, anxiety, agitation; mania; dementia; psychosis	Thyroid function test (T_3, T_4, thyroid-stimulating hormone (TSH)); medical consultation

conservative measures may be adequate. In some instances, drugs such as thiothixene (Navane) and haloperidol (Haldol), 5 to 10 mg every half hour to an hour, are needed until a patient is stabilized. Benzodiazepines are used instead of or in addition to antipsychotics (to reduce the antipsychotic dosage). If a recreational drug has strong anticholinergic properties, benzodiazepines are more appropriate than antipsychotics. Persons with allergic or aberrant responses to antipsychotics and benzodiazepines are treated with sodium amobarbital (Amytal) (for example, 130 mg orally or IM, paraldehyde (Paral), or diphenhydramine (Benadryl), 50 to 100 mg orally or IM).

Violent, struggling patients are most effectively subdued with an appropriate sedative or antipsychotic. Diazepam (Valium), 5 to 10 mg, or lorazepam (Ativan), 2 to 4 mg, may be given slowly intravenously (IV) over two minutes. The clinician must give the IV medication with great care to prevent respiratory arrest. Patients who require IM medication can be sedated with haloperidol, 5 to 10 mg IM, or with chlorpromazine (Thorazine), 25 mg IM. If the furor is due to alcohol or is part of a postseizure psychomotor disturbance, the sleep produced by a relatively small amount of an IV medication may go on for hours. On awakening, the patients are often entirely alert and rational and typically have a complete amnesia for the violent episode.

If the furor is part of an ongoing psychotic process and returns as soon as the IV medication wears off, continuous medication may be given. It is sometimes better to use small IM or oral doses at half-hour to one-hour intervals—for example, haloperidol, 2 to 5 mg, or diazepam, 20 mg—until the patient is controlled than to use large dosages initially and end up with an overmedicated patient. As the patient's disturbed behavior is brought under control, successively smaller and less frequent doses should be used. During the preliminary treatment, the patient's blood pressure and other vital signs should be monitored.

RAPID TRANQUILIZATION

Antipsychotic medication can be given rapidly at 30- to 60-minute intervals to achieve a therapeutic result as quickly as possible. The procedure is useful in agitated patients and those in excited states. The drugs of choice for rapid tranquilization are haloperidol and other high-potency antipsychotics. In adults 5 to 10 mg of haloperidol can be given orally or IM and repeated every 20 to 30 minutes until the patient becomes calm. Some patients may experience mild extrapyramidal symptoms within the first 24 hours after rapid tranquilization; although the side effects are rare, the psychiatrist should not overlook them. In general, most patients respond before a total dose of 50 mg is given. The goal is not to produce sedation or somnolescence; rather, the patient should be able to cooperate in the assessment to process and, ideally, be able to provide some explanation of the agitated behavior. Agitated or panic-stricken patients can be treated with small doses of lorazepam, 2 to 4 mg IV or IM, which can be repeated if necessary in 20 to 30 minutes until the patient has quieted down.

The extrapyramidal emergencies respond to benztropine (Cogentin), 2 mg orally or IM, or diphenhydramine, 50 mg IM or IV. Some patients respond to diazepam, 50 to 10 mg orally or IV.

Restraints

Restraints are used when patients are so dangerous to themselves or others that they pose a severe threat that cannot be controlled in any other way. Patients may be restrained temporarily to receive medication or for long periods if medication cannot be used. Most often, patients in restraints quiet down after some time has elapsed. On a psychodynamic level, such patients may even welcome the control of their impulses that restraints provide.

SPECIFIC PSYCHIATRIC EMERGENCIES

Table 25.2–1 outlines in alphabetical order common psychiatric emergencies.

References

Boyer W F, Bakalar N H, Lake C R: Anticholinergic prophylaxis of acute haloperidol-induced acute dystonic reactions. J Clin Psychopharmacol 7: 264, 1987.

Fauman B J: Other psychiatric emergencies. In *Comprehensive Textbook of Psychiatry*, ed 6, H I Kaplan, B J Sadock, editors, p 1752. Williams & Wilkins, Baltimore, 1995.

Hillard J R, editor: *Manual of Clinical Emergency Psychiatry*. American Psychiatric Press, Washington, 1990.

Monahan J, Shah S A: Dangerousness and commitment of the mentally disordered in the United States. Schizophr Bull 15: 541, 1989.

Rosenberg R C, Kesselman M: The therapeutic alliance and the psychiatric emergency room. Hosp Community Psychiatry 44: 78, 1993.

Sanguineti V R, Brooks M O: Factors related to emergency commitment of chronically mentally ill patients who are substance abusers. Hosp Community Psychiatry 43: 237, 1992.

Schorr S J, Richardson D: Psychiatric emergencies. Obstet Gynecol Clin North Am 22: 369, 1995.

Tueth M J: Emergencies caused by side effects of psychiatric medications. Am J Emerg Med 12: 212, 1994.

Tueth M J: Management of behavioral emergencies. Am J Emerg Med 13: 344, 1995.

26/ Psychotherapies

26.1 PSYCHOANALYSIS AND PSYCHOANALYTIC PSYCHOTHERAPY

The problems that take people to psychiatrists for treatment are of two kinds: those that seem to have their origins largely in the remote past of patients' lives and those that seem to arise largely from current stresses and pressures that seem beyond the patients' conscious control. However, current external stresses may occur in combination with older problems, and some patients who have old but still active and unsolved problems may arrange their lives in such a way that they appear to be the victims of current life situations.

When a patient's problem stems mainly from the past with relatively little contribution from the present, psychoanalysis may well be the treatment of choice. During classic psychoanalysis, regressive patters often appear in the patient's feelings and fantasies toward the psychoanalyst. Those patterns provide the necessary ingress into the past.

Psychoanalytic therapy uses the theoretical framework provided by psychoanalysis, but its therapeutic goals are less extensive than the goals of psychoanalysis, and it uses some techniques that are not part of the analytic model. Current interpersonal and intrapsychic dynamics are likely to receive the greatest emphasis in psychoanalytic therapy, and there is less concern with detailed reconstructions of the patient's past life. The contrast, however, between the historical and the current loses its sharp outline in the treatment of the individual patient.

Psychoanalysis and the analytic psychotherapies, uniquely among the available therapies, provide a theoretical and clinical framework for investigating the richly complex and multidetermined psychological forces (psychodynamics) that shape human development—from motivation, impulse, and conflict to attachment, intimacy, and the nature of self-esteem.

PSYCHOANALYSIS

Psychoanalysis began with the treatment of patients by hypnosis. In 1881 Anna O, a neurotic young woman who suffered from multiple visual and motor disturbances and alterations of consciousness, was treated by the Viennese internist Josef Breuer. He observed that the patient's symptoms disappeared when she expressed them verbally while hypnotized. Sigmund Freud used the technique with Breuer, and they reported their findings in 1895 in *Studies on Hysteria*. They explained hysteria (now called conversion disorder) as the result of a traumatic experience, which was usually sexual in nature and associated with a large quantity of affect, that was barred from consciousness and that expressed itself in a disguised form through various symptoms. Freud eventually gave up placing his patients in a hypnotic trance; instead, he urged them to recline on a couch and concentrate with their eyes closed on past memories related to their symptoms. That concentration method eventually became the technique of free association. Freud instructed his patients to say whatever came into their minds, without censoring any of their thoughts. That method is still used today

and is one of the hallmarks of psychoanalysis, through which thoughts and feelings that are kept in the unconscious are brought into consciousness.

In *The Interpretation of Dreams* Freud described the topographical model of the mind as consisting of a conscious, preconscious, and unconscious. The conscious mind was conceptualized as awareness; the preconscious, as thoughts and feelings that are easily available to consciousness; and the unconscious, as thoughts and feelings that cannot be made conscious without overcoming strong resistances. The unconscious contains nonverbal forms of thought function and gives rise to dreams, parapraxes (slips of the tongue), and psychological symptoms. Psychoanalysis emphasizes the conflict between unconscious drives and moral judgments that patients may make about their impulses. That conflict accounts for the phenomenon of repression, which is regarded as pathological. Free association allows repressed memories to be recovered and thereby contributes to cure.

In 1923 Freud described his structural theory of the mind in *The Ego and the Id*. He saw the ego as a group of functions accessible to consciousness that mediate among the demands of the id, the superego, and the environment. He viewed anxiety as the ego's reaction to the threatened breakthrough of forbidden impulses.

Modern advances in psychoanalysis have focused on the increased understanding of the ego's functions (ego psychology), the role of early relationships (object relations), and the relationship between the analyst and the patient (transference and countertransference).

Goal

The chief requirement of psychoanalysis is the gradual integration of the previously repressed material into the total structure of the personality. It is a slow process, requiring the analyst to maintain a balance between the interpretation of unconscious material and the patient's ability to deal with increased awareness. If the work proceeds too rapidly, the patient may experience the analysis as a new trauma. The work of analysis initially is preparing the patient to deal with the anxiety-producing material that has been uncovered. The patient is taught to be aware of innermost thoughts and feelings and to recognize the natural resistances to the mind's willingness or ability to deal directly with noxious psychic material. The patient and the analyst seldom follow a straight path to insight. Instead, the process of analysis is more like putting together pieces of an immense and complicated jigsaw puzzle.

Analytic Setting

The usual analytic setting is for the patient to lie on a couch or sofa, behind which the analyst sits, partially or totally outside the patient's field of vision. The couch helps the analyst produce the controlled regression that favors the emergence of repressed material. The patient's reclining position in the presence of an attentive analyst almost re-creates symbolically the early parent-child situation, which varies from patient to patient. The position also helps the patient focus on inner thoughts, feelings, and fantasies, which can then become the focus of free associations. Moreover, the use of the couch introduces an element of sensory deprivation because the patient's visual stimuli are limited and the analyst's verbalizations are relatively few. That state promotes regression. There has been some disagreement, however, about the use of the couch as always characteristic of psychoanalysis. Otto Fenichel stated that whether the patient lies down or sits and whether certain rituals of procedure are used do not matter. The best condition is the one most appropriate to the analytic task.

Role of the Analyst

For the most part, the analyst's activity is limited to timely interpretation of the patient's associations. Ideally, analysts—who have undergone a personal psychoanalysis as part of their training—are able to maintain an attitude of benevolent objectivity or neutrality toward the patient, trying not to impose their own personalities or systems of values. Nevertheless, it is not possible or desirable for the analyst to be a so-called blank screen, *tabula rasa*, or analyst incognito. A real relationship underlies the analytic setting, and the handling of the real relationship may make the difference between success and failure in treatment.

Duration of Treatment

The patient and the psychoanalyst must be prepared to persevere in the process for an indefinite period. Psychoanalysis takes time—between three and six years, sometimes even longer. Sessions are usually held four or more times a week for 45 to 50 minutes each. Some analyses are conducted with less frequency and with the sessions varying from 20 to 30 minutes. The French psychoanalyst Jacques Lacan introduced sessions of variable length (3 to 45 minutes), which he believed to be equally effective.

Treatment Methods

FUNDAMENTAL RULE OF PSYCHOANALYSIS

The fundamental or basic rule is that the patient agrees to be completely honest with the analyst and to tell everything without selection. Freud referred to the technique that allowed for such honesty as free association.

FREE ASSOCIATION

In free association, patients say everything that comes to mind without any censoring, regardless of whether they believe the thought to be unacceptable, unimportant, or embarrassing. Associations are directed by three kinds of unconscious forces: The pathogenic conflicts of the neurosis, the wish to get well, and the wish to please the analyst. The interplay among those factors becomes complex. For example, a thought or an impulse that is unacceptable to patients and that is a part of their neuroses may conflict with their wishes to please the analyst, who, they assume, also finds the impulse unacceptable. But if patients follow the fundamental rule, they overcome the resistance.

FREE-FLOATING ATTENTION

The analysts' counterpart to the patients' free association is a special way of listening called free-floating attention. Analysts

allow the patients' associations to stimulate their own associations and are thereby able to discern a theme in the patients' free associations that may be reflected back to the patients then or at some later time. Analysts' careful attention to their own subjective experiences is an indispensable part of analysis.

RULE OF ABSTINENCE

By following the rule of abstinence, the patient is able to delay gratifying any instinctual wishes so as to talk about them in treatment. The tension thus engendered produces relevant associations that the analyst uses to increase the patient's awareness. The rule does not refer to sexual abstinence but, rather, to not allowing the treatment setting to gratify the patient's infantile longing for love and affection.

Analytic Process

TRANSFERENCE

A major criterion by which psychoanalysis can be differentiated in principle from other forms of psychotherapy is the management of the transference. Indeed, psychoanalysis has been defined as the analysis of transference.

Transference was first described by Freud and concerns the patient's feelings and behavior toward the analyst that are based on infantile wishes the patient has toward parents or parental figures. Those feelings are unconscious but are revealed in the transference neurosis, in which patients struggle to gratify their unconscious infantile wishes through the analyst. The transference may be positive, in which the analyst needs to be seen as a person of exceptional worth, ability, and character; or it may be negative, in which the analyst becomes the embodiment of what the patient experienced or feared from parental figures in the past. Negative transferences can be expressed and experienced in highly labile and volatile ways, especially in patients whose personalities are described as borderline or narcissistic. Both situations reflect the patient's need to repeat unresolved childhood conflicts.

The analyst's role is to help the patient gain true insight into the distortions of transference and, through insight, to increase the patient's capacity for gratifying relationships based on mature and realistic expectations, rather than on irrational, childhood-derived fantasies.

INTERPRETATION

In psychoanalysis the analyst provides the patient with interpretations about psychological events that were neither previously understood by nor meaningful to the patient. The transference constitutes a major frame of reference for interpretation. A complete psychoanalytic interpretation includes meaningful statements of current conflicts and the historical factors that influenced them. However, such complete interpretations constitute a relatively small part of the analysis. Most interpretations are limited in scope and deal with matters of immediate concern.

Interpretations must be well-timed. The analyst may have a formulation in mind, but the patient may not be prepared to deal with it directly because of a variety of factors, such as anxiety level, negative transference, and external life stress. The analyst may decide to wait until the patient can fully understand the interpretation. The proper timing of interpretations requires great clinical skill.

Dream Interpretation

In his classic work *The Interpretation of Dreams*, Freud referred to the dream as the "royal road to the unconscious." The *manifest content* of a dream is what the dreamer reports. The *latent content* is the unconscious meaning of the dream after the condensations, substitutions, and symbols are analyzed. The dream arises from what Freud referred to as the *day's residue* (that is, the events of the preceding day that stimulated the patient's unconscious mind). Dreams may serve as a wish-fulfillment mechanism and as a way of mastering anxiety about a life event.

Freud outlined several technical procedures to use in dream interpretation: (1) have the patient associate to elements of the dream in the order in which they occurred, (2) have the patient associate to a particular dream element that the patient or the therapist chooses, (3) disregard the content of the dream, and ask the patient what events of the previous day could be associated with the dream (the day's residue), and (4) avoid giving any instructions, and leave it to the dreamer to begin. The analyst uses the patient's associations to find a clue to the workings of the unconscious mind.

COUNTERTRANSFERENCE

Just as the term "transference" is used to encompass the patient's total range of feelings for and against the analyst, "countertransference" encompasses a broad spectrum of the analyst's reactions to the patient. Countertransference has unconscious components based on conflicts of which the analyst is not aware. Ideally, the analyst ought to be aware of countertransference issues, which may interfere with the analyst's ability to remain detached and objective. The analyst should remove such impediments by either further analysis or self-analysis. However, with some patients or groups of patients, a particular analyst does not work well, and the experienced clinician, recognizing that fact, refers such patients to a colleague.

THERAPEUTIC ALLIANCE

In addition to transferential and countertransferential issues, a real relationship between the analyst and the patient involves two adults entering into a joint venture, referred to as the therapeutic or working alliance. Both commit themselves to exploring the patient's problems, to establishing mutual trust, and to cooperating with each other to achieve a realistic goal of cure or the amelioration of symptoms.

RESISTANCE

Freud believed that unconscious ideas or impulses are repressed and prevented from reaching awareness because they are unacceptable to consciousness for some reason. He referred to that phenomenon as resistance, which has to be overcome if the analysis is to proceed. Resistance may sometimes be a conscious process manifested by withholding relevant information. Other examples of resistance are remaining silent for a long time, being late or missing appointments, and paying bills late or not at all. The signs of resistance are legion, and almost any feature of the analytic situation can be used in resistance. Freud once said that any treatment can be considered psychoanalysis that works by undoing resistance and interpreting transferences.

Indications for Treatment

The primary indications for psychoanalysis are long-standing psychological conflicts that have produced a symptom or

disorder. The connection between the conflict and the symptom may be direct or indirect. Psychoanalysis is considered effective in treating certain anxiety disorders, such as phobias and obsessive-compulsive disorder, mild depressive disorders (dysthymic disorder), some personality disorders, and some impulse-control and sexual disorders. More important than diagnosis, however, is the patient's ability to form an analytic pact and to maintain a commitment to a progressively deepening analytic process that brings about internal change through increasing self-awareness. Freud believed that the patient also has to be able to form a strong transference attachment to the analyst (termed *transference neurosis*), without which analysis is not possible. That excluded most psychotic patients because of the difficulty they have in forming the affective and realistic bonds that are essential to the development and the resolution of the transference neurosis. The ego of a patient in analysis must be able to tolerate frustration without responding with some serious form of acting out or shifting from one pathological pattern to another. That excludes most substance-dependent patients, who are regarded as unsuitable because their egos are unable to tolerate the frustration and the emotional demands of psychoanalysis.

Contraindications for Treatment

The various contraindications to psychoanalysis are relative, but each must be considered before embarking on a course of treatment.

AGE

Traditionally, many analysts believed that most adults over age 40 lack sufficient flexibility for major personality changes. However, most analysts now believe that more important than age is the patient's individual capacity for thoughtful introspection and desire for change. The ideal candidates are generally young adults. Children are unable to follow the rule of free association, but, with modifications of technique (for example, play therapy), they have been successfully analyzed.

INTELLIGENCE

Patients must be intelligent enough to be able to understand the procedure and to cooperate in the process.

LIFE CIRCUMSTANCES

If the patient's life situation cannot be modified, analysis may only make it worse. For example, it can be hazardous to create goals for patients who are unable to fulfill them because of external limitations.

ANTISOCIAL PERSONALITY DISORDER

Clinicians and researchers seem to agree that the absence of relatedness to others is the single most negative predictor of psychotherapy response. The true antisocial personality is a person who may benefit from certain types of therapy, such as group therapy with other antisocial personalities, but who is not suited for analytically oriented psychotherapy. J. R. Meloy defined five clinical features that contraindicate any attempt at psychotherapy. Table 26.1–1 summarizes those features.

Meloy believed that sadistic cruelty to others, total absence of remorse, and lack of emotional attachment are the key distinguished features that lead to an inability to engage in therapy. Also, countertransference fears often paralyze therapists, mak-

Table 26.1-1. Clinical Features That Contraindicate Psychotherapy of Any Kind

1. A history of sadistic, violent behavior towqrd others that resulted in serious injury or death

2. A total absence of remorse or rationalization for such behavior

3. Intelligence that is in either the very superior or the mildly mentally retarded range

4. A historical incapacity to develop emotional attachments to others

5. An intense countertransference fear of predation on the part of experienced clinicians even without clear precipitating behavior on the part of the patient

Table based on J R Meloy: *The Psychopathic Mind: Origins, Dynamics and Treatment.* Aronson, Northvale, N J, 1988.
Table from G O Gabbard: *Psychodynamic Psychiatry in Clinical Practice.* p 417. American Psychiatric Press, Washington, 1990. Used with permission.

ing therapy impossible. An extremely intelligent person with antisocial personality disorder can be expert at sabotaging therapy; and a mildly retarded antisocial personality may not have the cognitive ability to engage in the psychoanalysis.

TIME CONSTRAINTS

Unless the patient has time to participate and to wait for change, another type of therapy should be considered. The constraint applies especially to emergency symptoms and to those that the patient can no longer tolerate, including those that are dangerous (for example, strong suicidal impulses).

NATURE OF THE RELATIONSHIP

The analysis of friends, relatives, and acquaintances is contraindicated because it distorts the transference and the analyst's objectivity.

OTHER CONTRAINDICATIONS

Some patients work better with some analysts than with others. Sometimes that determination can be made after a single consultation, but often a trial analysis of several sessions is necessary. That time also allows patients to see whether they wish to continue. Experience has shown that it does not matter whether the analyst is a man or a woman, although some patients may initially prefer to see one or the other, a preference that is eventually understood as the analysis proceeds.

Dynamics of Therapeutic Results

The process of cure improvement involves the release of repression safely and effectively. The structural apparatus of the mind—id, ego, and superego—are modified. The ego is able to deal with repressed impulses and is finally in a position to accept or renounce them.

Analysis helps reduce the intensity of the conflicts and helps find acceptable ways of handling impulses that cannot be reduced. Instead of an acceptable method of channeling unmodified infantile strivings, the drives' primary-process quality itself is lessened, and they become adapted to reality. The ultimate goal is the elimination of symptoms, thereby increasing the patient's capacity for work, enjoyment, and self-understanding.

Few long-term outcome studies of psychoanalysis have been conducted because of the complex patient-therapist variables. Nevertheless, psychoanalysis is thought to be effective under some circumstances for many disorders.

PSYCHOANALYTIC PSYCHOTHERAPY

Psychoanalytic psychotherapy is therapy based on psychoanalytic formulations that have been modified conceptually and technically. Unlike psychoanalysis, which has as its ultimate concern the uncovering and the subsequent working through of infantile conflicts as they arise in the transference neurosis, psychoanalytic psychotherapy takes as its focus the patient's current conflicts and current dynamic patterns—that is, the analysis of the patient's problems with other persons and with themselves. Also unlike psychoanalysis, which has as its technique the use of free association and the analysis of the transference neurosis, psychoanalytic psychotherapy is characterized by interviewing and discussion techniques that infrequently use free association. And again unlike psychoanalysis, psychoanalytic psychotherapy usually limits its work on transference to a discussion of the patient's reactions to the psychiatrist and others. The reaction to the psychiatrist is not interpreted as much as it is in psychoanalysis. Nevertheless, transference attitudes and responses to the therapist may arise from time to time and can be used productively. For example, spontaneous transferences in the therapeutic situation may give valuable clues to patients' behavior in extratherapeutic situations and, at times, to their childhood. Those transferences may tell the therapist the probable focus for the patient at any given time, inside or outside the treatment relationship.

Treatment Techniques

One way in which psychoanalytic psychotherapy differs from classic psychoanalysis is that the former does not usually use a couch. The stimulation of temporary regressive patterns of feeling and thinking, which is valuable to psychoanalysis, is much less necessary in psychoanalytic psychotherapy, with its focus on current dynamic patterns. In psychoanalytic psychotherapy the patient and the therapist are usually in full view of each other, which may make the therapist seem real and not a composite of projected fantasies. That type of therapy is much more flexible than psychoanalysis, and it may be used in conjunction with psychotropic medication more often than is psychoanalysis.

Psychoanalytic psychotherapy can range from a single supportive interview, centering on a current but pressing problem, to many years of treatment, with one to three interviews a week of varying length. In contrast to psychoanalysis, psychoanalytic psychotherapy treats most of the disorders in the field of psychopathology.

Types

Many clinicians and researchers have conceptualized the types of psychotherapies as occurring along a spectrum, with expressive (insight-oriented) therapies, such as psychoanalysis and analytically oriented therapies, at one end of the spectrum and supportive therapies at the other end. The Menninger Clinic Treatment Intervention Project has indicated that therapist intervention can be placed in seven categories along an expressive (insight-oriented)-supportive continuum.

INSIGHT-ORIENTED PSYCHOTHERAPY

Insight is patients' understanding of their psychological functioning and personalities. The clinician should specify the area or the level of understanding or experience into which the patient is to achieve insight. In insight-oriented therapy (also called expressive therapy and intensive psychoanalytic psychotherapy), the psychiatrist emphasizes the value of new insights into the current dynamics of patients' feelings, responses, behavior, and, especially, current relationships with other persons. To a smaller extent the emphasis is on the value of developing some insight into patients' responses to the therapist and responses in childhood.

Insight-oriented therapy is the treatment of choice for a patient who has adequate ego strength but who, for one reason or another, should not or cannot undergo psychoanalysis.

The therapy's effectiveness does not depend solely on the insights developed or used. The patient's therapeutic response is also based on such factors as the ventilation of feelings in a nonjudgmental but limit-setting atmosphere, identification with the therapist, and other relationship factors. A therapeutic relationship does not require an indiscriminate acceptance of all that a patient says and does. At times, the therapist must intervene on the side of a relatively weak ego by giving unmistakable evidence that the patient could try to achieve a better adjustment or by setting realistic limits to the patients' maladaptive behavior. In so doing, therapists try to be guided by their dynamic assessments of the situation and not by their countertransference responses.

Inevitably, the therapist's attitudes and responses to the patient are different from those of important figures in the patient's childhood. At times, the therapist discusses those differences. Patients may come to see that they have generalized their parents' attitudes as being universal and have generalized their own responses; thus their responses to all parental or significant figures have become automatic.

Insight-oriented psychotherapy is frequently complicated by spontaneous strong transferences to the therapist that at times threaten to disrupt the treatment. The insight-oriented therapist must decide, on the basis of an understanding of each individual patient, how to respond to those transference reactions. If the patient is highly introspective and psychologically minded, the therapist may choose to make relatively deep transference interpretations (for example, relating the reactions to significant childhood fantasies). If the patient is fragile and not capable of tolerating an interpretation that is perceived as emotionally threatening, the therapist may choose to remain relatively superficial in approach (for example, relating the reactions to current, reality-based feelings).

SUPPORTIVE PSYCHOTHERAPY

Supportive psychotherapy (also called relationship-oriented psychotherapy) offers the patient support by an authority figure during a period of illness, turmoil, or temporary decompensation. It also has the goal of restoring and strengthening the patient's defenses and integrating capacities that have been impaired. It provides a period of acceptance and dependence for a patient who needs help in dealing with guilt, shame, and anxiety and in meeting the frustrations or the external pressures that may be too great to handle.

Supportive therapy uses a number of methods, either singly or in combination, including (1) warm, friendly, strong leadership, (2) gratification of dependence needs, (3) support in the ultimate development of legitimate independence, (4) help in the development of pleasurable sublimations (for example, hob-

bies), (5) adequate rest and diversion, (6) removal of excessive external strain if possible, (7) hospitalization when indicated, (8) medication to alleviate symptoms, and (9) guidance and advice in dealing with current issues. It uses the techniques that help the patient feel secure, accepted, protected, encouraged, and safe and not anxious.

One of the greatest dangers lies in the possibility of fostering too great a regression and too strong a dependence. From the beginning, the psychiatrist must plan to work persistently to enable the patient to assume independence. But some patients require supportive therapy indefinitely, often with just the goal of maintaining a marginal adjustment that enables them to function in society.

The expression of emotion is an important part of supportive psychotherapy. The verbalization of unexpressed strong emotions may bring considerable relief. The goal of such talking out is not primarily to gain insight into the unconscious dynamic patterns than may be intensifying current responses. Rather, the reduction of inner tension and anxiety may result from the expression of emotion, and its subsequent discussion may lead to insight into a current problem and objectivity in evaluating it.

Corrective Emotional Experience

The relationship between the therapist and the patient gives the therapist an opportunity to display behavior different from the destructive or unproductive behavior of the patient's parents. At times, such experiences seem to neutralize or reverse some of the effects of the parents' mistakes. If the patient had overly authoritarian parents, the therapist's friendly, flexible, nonjudgmental, nonauthoritarian—but at times firm and limit-setting—attitude means that the patient has an opportunity to adjust to, be led by, and identify with a new type of parent figure. Franz Alexander called that process a corrective emotional experience.

Supportive psychotherapy is suitable for a variety of psychogenic illnesses. For example, it may be useful when a patient resists an expressive psychotherapy or is considered too emotionally disturbed for such a procedure. Supportive therapy may be chosen when the diagnostic assessment indicates that a gradual maturing process, based on the elaboration of new foci for identification, is the most promising path toward improvement. Table 26.1–2 outlines a comparison and description of the types of therapies discussed in this section.

REFERRAL BY A NONPSYCHIATRIC PHYSICIAN

Nonpsychiatric physicians often treat psychiatric patients in their practices. Those patients may require referral to a psychiatrist for more in-depth evaluation and treatment than can be provided in the nonpsychiatric setting. Or nonpsychiatric physicians may think that some of their patients would benefit from psychotherapy. Those patients may or may not carry an Axis I or Axis II diagnosis.

CURRENT PROBLEMS

With the advent of managed care, increasing pressure is put on psychiatrists to provide psychotherapy that is short-term and thus, theoretically, low in cost. Short-term therapies—enthusiastically promoted by private insurance companies, health maintenance organizations, and a number of psychiatric residency programs—have parameters that are explicitly delineated with regard to such issues as the number of sessions, concrete goals, and outcome evaluation criteria. They are largely designed so that the techniques involved can be learned quickly and per-

Table 26.1–2.   Scope of Psychoanalytic Practice: A Clinical Continuum*

Feature	Psychoanalysis	Psychoanalytic Psychotherapy	
		Expressive Mode	Supportive Mode
Frequency	Regular four to five times a week: 50-minute hour	Regular one to three times a week: half to full hour	Flexible one time a week or less; or as needed, half to full hour
Duration	Long-term: usually three to five + years	Short-term or long-term: several sessions to months or years	Short-term or intermittent long-term; single session to lifetime
Setting	Patient primarily on couch with analyst out of view	Patient and therapist face-to-face; occasional use of couch	Patient and therapist face-to-face; couch contraindicated
Modus operandi	Systematic analysis of all (positive and negative) transference and resistance; primary focus on analyst and intrasession events; transference neurosis facilitated; regression encouraged	Partial analysis of dynamics and defenses; focus on current interpersonal events and transference to others outside sessions; analysis of negative transference; positive transference left unexplored unless it impedes progress; limited regression encouraged	Formation of therapeutic alliance and real object relationship; analysis of transference contraindicated with rare exceptions; focus on conscious external events; regression discouraged
Analyst-therapist role	Absolute neutrality; frustration of patient; reflector-mirror role	Modified neutrality; implicit gratification of patient and great activity	Neutrality suspended; limited explicit gratification, direction, and disclosure
Mutative change agents	Insight predominates within relatively deprived environment	Insight within empathic environment; identification with benevolent object	Auxiliary or surrogate ego as temporary substitute; holding environment; insight to degree possible
Patient population	Neuroses; mild character psychopathology	Neuroses; mild to moderate character psychopathology, especially narcissistic and borderline personality disorders	Severe character disorders; latent or manifest psychoses; acute crises; physical illness
Patient requisites	High motivation; psychological-mindedness; good previous object relationships; ability to maintain transference neurosis; good frustration tolerance	High to moderate motivation and psychological-mindedness; ability to form therapeutic alliance; some frustration tolerance	Some degree of motivation and ability to form therapeutic alliance
Basic goals	Structural reorganization of personality; resolution of unconscious conflicts; insight into intrapsychic events; symptom relief an indirect result	Partial reorganization of personality and defenses; resolution of preconscious and conscious derivatives of conflicts; insight into current interpersonal events; improved object relations; symptom relief a goal or prelude to further exploration	Reintegration of self and ability to cope; stabilization or restoration of preexisting equilibrium; strengthening defenses; better adjustment or acceptance of pathological symptom relief and environmental restructuring as primary goals
Major techniques	Free association method predominates; fully dynamic interpretation (including confrontation, clarification, and working through), with emphasis on genetic reconstruction	Limited free association; confrontation, clarification, and partial interpretation predominate, with emphasis on here-and-now interpretation and limited genetic interpretation	Free association method contraindicated; suggestions (advice) predominates; abreaction useful; confrontation, clarification, and interpretation in the here and now secondary; genetic interpretation contraindicated
Adjunct treatment	Primarily avoided; if applied, all negative and positive meanings and implications thoroughly analyzed	May be necessary (e.g., psychotropic drugs as temporary measure); if applied, negative implications explored and diffused	Often necessary (e.g., psychotropic drugs, family therapy, rehabilitative therapy, or hospitalization) if applied, positive implications are emphasized

* This division is not categorical; all practice resides on a clinical continuum.
Table by Toksoz Byram Karasu, MD.

formed with the aid of instructional manuals by a variety of practitioners other than psychiatrists.

Although the pressure to develop less expensive, less training-intensive, and less time-involving therapies than psychoanalysis stems from some legitimate concerns about the accessibility of the traditional insight-oriented approaches typical of psychoanalysis and analytically oriented psychotherapy, the rush to relegate such powerfully effective treatment to the periphery of the mainstream seems short-sighted and ultimately impoverishing to the field.

References

Altman A, Selzer M A: Delusions in the transference. Psychotherapy with the paranoid patient. Psychiatr Clin North Am *18*: 407, 1995.

Blechner J: Psychoanalysis and HIV disease. Contemp Psychoanal *29*: 61, 1993.
Bowden C L: Implications of psychopharmacological studies for the practice of psychoanalysis. J Am Acad Psychoanal *20*: 477, 1992.
Hirsch I: An interpersonal perspective: The analyst's unwitting participation in the patient's change. Psychoanal Psychol *9*: 299, 1992.
Karasu T B: Psychoanalysis and psychoanalytic psychotherapy. In *Comprehensive Textbook of Psychiatry*, ed 6, H I Kaplan, B J Sadock, editors, p 1767. Williams & Wilkins, Baltimore, 1995.
Kernberg O F: The current status of psychoanalysis. J Am Psychoanal Assoc *41*: 45, 1993.
Langs R: Psychoanalysis and the science of evolution. Am J Psychother *49*: 47, 1995.
Solms M: New findings on the neurological organization of dreaming: implications for psychoanalysis. Psychoanal Q *64*: 43, 1995.
Vaughan S C, Roose S P: The analytic process: clinical and research definitions. Int J Psychoanal *76*: 343, 1995.
Yorke V: Boundaries, psychic structure, and time. J Anal Psychol *38*: 57, 1993.

Brief dynamic psychotherapies are short-term therapies based on psychoanalytic concepts. Most of those therapies have specific patient selection criteria and treatment techniques that are designed for specific problems. The therapies have become increasingly popular since the mid-1980s, as numerous clinical reports have indicated their effectiveness with select groups of patients. With the renewed emphasis on primary care and cost containment in the health care delivery system, a good deal of worldwide interest has been aroused by the treatment modalities. Although time limitation is an essential and obvious feature of all short-term therapies, their adherents share no clear consensus about exactly what is meant by the concept. Thus, a number of therapies are subsumed under the category of "brief psychotherapies."

Crisis intervention, by definition, is a therapy limited by the parameters of whatever crisis has led the patient to be seen. Crisis intervention is based on crisis theory, which emphasizes not only immediate responses to an immediate situation but also long-term development of psychological adaption aimed at preventing future problems.

BRIEF PSYCHOTHERAPY

History

Most of the basic characteristics of brief psychotherapy were identified by Franz Alexander and Thomas French in 1946. They described a therapeutic experience that puts the patient at ease, manipulates the transference, and flexibly uses trial interpretations. The emphasis was on developing a corrective emotional experience capable of repairing traumatic events of the past and convincing the patient that new ways of thinking, feeling, and behaving are possible.

At about the same time Eric Lindemann established a consultation service at the Massachusetts General Hospital for persons experiencing a crisis. New treatment methods were developed to deal with those situations and were eventually applied to persons who were not in crisis but who were experiencing emotional distress from a variety of sources.

Selection Criteria

The most valuable predictor of a successful outcome is the patient's motivation for treatment. In addition, patients must be able to deal with psychological concepts, to respond to interpretation, and to concentrate on and resolve the conflict around the central issue or focus that underlies their basic problems. Patients must also be able to develop a therapeutic alliance and work with the therapist toward achieving emotional health.

Types

BRIEF FOCAL PSYCHOTHERAPY (TAVISTOCK-MALAN)

Brief focal psychotherapy was originally developed by the Michael Balint team at the Tavistock Clinic in London in the 1950s. Daniel Malan, a member of that team, reported the results of the therapy. Malan's selection criteria for treatment are elimi-

nating absolute contraindications; rejecting patients for whom certain dangers seem inevitable; clearly assessing the patient's psychopathology; and determining the patient's capacity to consider problems in emotional terms, face disturbing material, respond to interpretations, and endure the stress of the treatment. Malan found that high motivation invariably correlated with successful outcome.

Contraindications to treatment are serious suicide attempts, substance dependence, chronic alcohol abuse, incapacitating chronic obsessional symptoms, incapacitating chronic phobic symptoms, and gross destructive or self-destructive acting out.

REQUIREMENTS AND TECHNIQUES

Malan emphasized using the following routine: Identify the transference early and interpret it. Interpret also the negative transference. Link transferences to patients' relationships to their parents. Both patient and therapist must be willing to become deeply involved and to bear the ensuing tension. A circumscribed focus is formulated, and a termination date is set in advance. Grief and anger about termination are worked through.

About 20 sessions is suggested as an average length for the therapy for an experienced therapist and about 30 sessions for a trainee. However, Malan did not go beyond 40 interviews.

TIME-LIMITED PSYCHOTHERAPY (BOSTON UNIVERSITY-MANN)

A psychotherapeutic model of exactly 12 interviews focusing on a specified central issue was developed at Boston University by James Mann and his colleagues in the early 1970s. In contrast with Malan's emphasis on clear-cut selection and rejection criteria, Mann has not been as explicit as to who is a good candidate for time-limited psychotherapy.

The main points that Mann considers important are the determination of a reasonably correct central conflict in the patient and, in young people, maturational crises with many psychological and somatic complaints.

Mann also mentioned a few exceptions, which are similar to Mann's rejection criteria. Those exceptions are major depressive disorder that interferes with the treatment agreement, an acute psychotic state, and a desperate patient who needs but is incapable of tolerating object relations.

Requirements and Techniques

The following are Mann's technical requirements: strict limitation to 12 sessions; positive transference predominating early; specification and strict adherence to a central issue involving transference; positive identification; making separation a maturational event for the patient; absolute prospect of termination, avoiding development of dependence; clarification of present and past experiences and resistances; an active therapist who supports and encourages the patient; and education of the patient through direct information, reeducation, and manipulation.

The conflicts likely to be encountered include independence versus dependence, activity versus passivity, unresolved or delayed grief, and adequate versus inadequate self-esteem.

SHORT-TERM DYNAMIC PSYCHOTHERAPY (McGILL UNIVERSITY-DAVANLOO)

As conducted by Habib Davanloo at McGill University, short-term dynamic psychotherapy encompasses all the varieties of brief psychotherapy and crisis intervention. Patients treated in Davanloo's series are classified as those whose psychological conflicts are predominantly oedipal, those whose conflicts are not oedipal, and those whose conflicts have more than one focus.

In addition, Davanloo devised a specific psychotherapeutic technique for patients suffering from severe, long-standing neurotic problems, specifically those suffering from incapacitating obsessive-compulsive disorders and phobias.

Davanloo's selection criteria emphasize the evaluation of those ego functions that are of primary importance to the psychotherapeutic work: the establishment of a psychotherapeutic focus; the psychodynamic formulation of the patient's psychological problem; the ability to emotionally interact with the evaluator; the history of a give-and-take relationship with a significant person in the patient's life; the patient's ability to experience and tolerate anxiety, guilt, and depression; the patient's motivation for change; the patient's psychological-mindedness; and the patient's ability to respond to interpretation and to link the evaluator with people in the present and in the past.

Both Malan and Davanloo emphasize the patient's response to interpretation and consider it both an important selection criterion and a prognostic criterion.

Requirements and Techniques

The highlights of Davanloo's psychotherapeutic approach are flexibility (the therapist should adapt the technique to the patient's needs); control of the patient's regressive tendencies; active intervention, so as not to allow the development of overdependence on the therapist; and intellectual insight and emotional experiences by the patient in the transference. Those emotional experiences become corrective as a result of the interpretation.

SHORT-TERM ANXIETY-PROVOKING PSYCHOTHERAPY (HARVARD UNIVERSITY-SIFNEOS)

Short-term anxiety-provoking psychotherapy was first developed at the Massachusetts General Hospital by Peter Sifneos during the 1950s. The following criteria for selection are used: circumscribed chief complaint (implying an ability to select one of a variety of problems to which the patient assigns top priority and that the patient wants to resolve in treatment); one meaningful or give-and-take relationship during early childhood; the ability to interact flexibly with the evaluator and to express feelings appropriately; above-average psychological sophistication (implying not only on above-average intelligence but also an ability to respond to interpretations); a specific psychodynamic formulation (usually a set of psychological conflicts underlying the patient's difficulties and centering on an oedipal focus); a contract between the therapist and the patient to work on the specified focus and the formulation of minimal expectations of outcome; and good-to-excellent motivation for change and not just for symptom relief.

Requirements and Techniques

The treatment can be divided into four major phases; patient-therapist encounter, early therapy, height of the treatment, and evidence of change and termination. The therapist uses the following techniques during the four phases:

Patient-therapist encounter.   The therapist establishes a working alliance by using the quick rapport and the positive feelings for the therapist that appear in this phase. Judicious use of open-ended and forced-choice questions enables the therapist to outline and concentrate on a therapeutic focus. The therapist specifies the minimum expectations of outcome to be achieved by the therapy.

Early therapy.   In transference, feelings for the therapist are clarified as soon as they appear, leading to the establishment of a true therapeutic alliance.

Height of the treatment.   This phase emphasizes active concentration on the oedipal conflicts that have been chosen as the therapeutic focus for the therapy; repeated use of anxiety-provoking questions and confrontations; avoidance of pregenital characterological issues, which the patient uses defensively to avoid dealing with the therapist's anxiety-provoking techniques; avoidance at all costs of a transference neurosis; repetitive demonstration of the patient's neurotic ways or maladaptive patterns of behavior; concentration on the anxiety-laden material, even before the defense mechanisms have been clarified; repeated demonstrations of parent-transference links by the use of properly timed interpretations based on material given by the patient; establishment of a corrective emotional experience; encouragement and support of the patient, who becomes anxious while struggling to understand the conflicts; new learning and problem-solving patterns; and repeated presentations and recapitulations of the patient's psychodynamics until the defense mechanisms used in dealing with oedipal conflicts are understood.

Evidence of change and termination of psychotherapy.   This phase emphasizes the tangible demonstration of change in the patient's behavior outside the therapy, evidence that adaptive patterns of behavior are being used, and initiation of talk about terminating the treatment.

INTERPERSONAL PSYCHOTHERAPY

A specific type of short-term psychotherapy called interpersonal psychotherapy (IPT), described by Myrna Weissman and Gerald Klerman, is used to treat depressive disorders. Therapy consists of 45- to 50-minute sessions held weekly over a three- to four-month period. Interpersonal behavior is emphasized as a cause of depressive disorders and as a method of cure. Patients are taught to evaluate realistically their interactions with others and to become aware of how they isolate themselves, which contributes to or aggravates the depression about which they complain. The therapist offers direct advice, aids the patient in making decisions, and helps clarify areas of conflict. Little or no attention is given to the transference. The therapist attempts to be consistently supportive, empathic, and flexible. Studies of interpersonal psychotherapy have shown that, in selected cases of depressive disorders, it compares favorably with drug therapy with antidepressant agents.

Outcome

The shared techniques of all those kinds of brief psychotherapy (except interpersonal psychotherapy) far out-distance their differences. They include the therapeutic alliance or dynamic interaction between the therapist and the patient, the use of transference, the active interpretation of a therapeutic focus or central issue, the repetitive links between parental and transference issues, and the early termination of the therapy.

More than in any other form of psychotherapy, the outcomes of those brief treatments have been investigated extensively. Contrary to prevailing ideas that the therapeutic factors in psychotherapy are nonspecific, controlled studies and other assessment methods (for example, interviews with unbiased evaluators, patients' self-evaluations) point to the importance of the specific techniques used. Malan summarized the results in five major generalizations: (1) The capacity for genuine recovery in certain patients is far greater than was thought. (2) A certain type of patient receiving brief psychotherapy can benefit greatly from a practical working through of his or her nuclear conflict in the transference. (3) Such patients can be recognized in advance through a process of dynamic interaction, because they are responsive and motivated and able to face disturbing feelings, and a circumscribed focus can be formulated for them. (4) The more radical the technique is in terms of transference, depth of interpretation, and the link to childhood, the more radical the therapeutic effects will be. (5) For some disturbed patients a carefully chosen partial focus can be therapeutically effective.

CRISIS INTERVENTION

Theory

A crisis is a response to hazardous events and is experienced as a painful state. Consequently, it tends to mobilize powerful reactions to help the person alleviate the discomfort and return to the state of emotional equilibrium that existed before its onset. If that takes place, the crisis can be overcome, but, in addition, the person learns how to use adaptive reactions. Furthermore, by resolving the crisis, the patient may be in a better state of mind, superior to that before the onset of psychological difficulties. If, however, the patient uses maladaptive reactions, the painful state will intensify, the crisis will deepen, and a regressive deterioration will take place, producing psychiatric symptoms. Those symptoms, in turn, may crystallize into a neurotic pattern of behavior that restricts the patient's ability to function freely. At times, however, the situation cannot be stabilized; new maladaptive reactions are introduced; and the consequences can be of catastrophic proportions, leading at times to death by suicide. In that sense, psychological crises are painful and may be viewed as turning points for better or for worse.

A crisis is self-limited and can last anywhere from a few hours to weeks. The crisis as such is characterized by an initial phase, in which anxiety and tension rise. That phase is followed by a phase in which problem-solving mechanisms are set in motion. Those mechanisms may be successful, depending on whether they are adaptive or maladaptive.

During a period of turmoil patients are receptive to minimal help and obtain meaningful results. All sorts of services, therefore, have been devised for such purposes. Some are open-ended; others limit the time available or the number of sessions.

Crisis theory helps one understand healthy normal people in crisis and develop therapeutic tools aimed at preventing future psychological difficulties.

Crisis intervention is offered to persons who are incapacitated or severely disturbed by a crisis.

Criteria for Selection

The criteria used to select patients are a history of a specific hazardous situation of recent origin that produced the anxiety, a precipitating event that intensified the anxiety, clear-cut evidence that the patient is in a state of psychological crisis as previously defined, high motivation to overcome the crisis, a potential for making a psychological adjustment equal or superior to the one that existed before the development of the crisis, and a certain degree of psychological sophistication—an ability to recognize psychological reasons for the present predicament.

Requirements and Techniques

Crisis intervention deals with persons in the midst of a crisis in which rapidity is of the essence. Therapy requires a joint

understanding of the psychodynamics involved and an awareness of how they are responsible for the crisis. The participants work together, aiming at resolving the crisis. In addition, the patient, as well as the therapist, actively participates in the treatment.

Techniques include reassurance, suggestion, environmental manipulation, and psychotropic medications. Brief hospitalization may be added as part of the treatment plan. All those therapeutic maneuvers are aimed at decreasing the patient's anxiety. The length of crisis intervention varies from one or two sessions to several interviews over a period of one or two months. The technical requirements for crisis intervention involve rapidly establishing a rapport with the patient that is aimed at creating a therapeutic alliance; reviewing the steps that have led to the crisis; understanding the maladaptive reactions that the patient is using to deal with the crisis; focusing only on the crisis; learning to use adaptive ways to deal with crises; avoiding the development of symptoms; using the predominating positive transference feelings for the therapist, so as to transform the work into a learning experience; teaching the patient how to avoid hazardous situations that are likely to produce future crises; and ending the intervention as soon as evidence indicates that the crisis has been resolved and that the patient clearly understands all the steps that led to its development and its resolution.

Outcome

The most striking result of crisis therapy pertains to the patient's ability to become better equipped to avoid or, if necessary, to deal with future hazards. In addition, on the basis of some patients' objective observations, the therapeutic experience has enabled them to attain a level of emotional functioning that is superior to that before the onset of the crisis. In that sense, therefore, crisis intervention is not only therapeutic but also preventive.

References

Brom D, Kleber R J, Defares P B: Brief psychotherapy for posttraumatic stress disorders. J Consult Clin Psychol *57*: 607, 1989.

Flesenheimer W V, Pollack J: The time limit in brief psychotherapy. Bull Menninger Clin *53*: 44, 1989.

Klar H, Coleman W L: Brief solution-focused strategies for behavioral pediatrics. Ped Clin North Am *42*: 131, 1995.

Maxim R E, Hunt D D: Appraisal and coping in the process of patient change during short-term psychotherapy. J Nerv Ment Dis *178*: 235, 1990.

Mohl P C: Brief psychotherapy. In *Comprehensive Textbook of Psychiatry*, ed 6, H I Kaplan, B J Sadock, editors, p 1873. Williams & Wilkins, Baltimore, 1995.

Rosenberg S A, Zimet C N: Brief group treatment and managed mental health care. Int J Group Psychother *45*: 367, 1995.

Sifneos P E, Greenberg W E: Patient management. In *The New Harvard Guide to Psychiatry*, p 589. Harvard University Press, Cambridge, 1988.

Swinson R P, Soulios C, Cox B J, Kuch K: Brief treatment of emergency room patients with panic attacks. Am J Psychiatry *149*: 944, 1992.

Werner M J: Principles of brief intervention for adolescent alcohol, tobacco, and other drug use. Ped Clin North Am *42*: 335, 1995.

26.3 GROUP PSYCHOTHERAPY, COMBINED INDIVIDUAL AND GROUP PSYCHOTHERAPY, AND PSYCHODRAMA

GROUP PSYCHOTHERAPY

Group psychotherapy is a treatment in which carefully selected emotionally ill persons are placed into a group guided by a trained therapist to help one another effect personality change. By using a variety of technical maneuvers and theoretical constructs, the leader uses the group members' interactions to make that change.

Group psychotherapy encompasses the theoretical spectrum of therapies in psychiatry: supportive, structured, limit-setting (for example, groups with chronically psychotic people), cognitive-behavior, interpersonal, family, and analytically oriented groups. Two of the main strengths of group therapy, when compared with individual therapies, are (1) the opportunity for immediate feedback from the patient's peers and (2) the opportunity for both the patient and the therapist to observe the patient's psychological, emotional, and behavioral responses to a variety of persons, eliciting a variety of transferences.

Classification

Many approaches are used in the group method of treatment. Many clinicians work within a psychoanalytic frame of reference. Other therapy techniques include transactional group therapy, which was devised by Eric Berne and which emphasizes the here-and-now interactions among group members; behavioral group therapy, which relies on conditioning techniques based

on learning theory; Gestalt group therapy, which was created from the theories of Frederick Perls and enables patients to abreact and express themselves fully; and client-centered group psychotherapy, which was developed by Carl Rogers and is based on the nonjudgmental expression of feelings among group members. Table 26.3–1 outlines the major group psychotherapy approaches.

Patient Selection

To determine a patient's suitability for group psychotherapy, the therapist needs a great deal of information, which is gathered in a screening interview. The psychiatrist should take a psychiatric history and perform a mental status examination to obtain certain dynamic, behavioral, and diagnostic information.

AUTHORITY ANXIETY

Those patients whose primary problem is their relationship to authority and who are extremely anxious in the presence of authority figures may or may not do well in group therapy. However, they often do better in a group setting than in a dyadic (one-to-one) setting, because they are more comfortable in a group. Patients with a great deal of authority anxiety may be

Table 26.3–1. Comparison of Types of Group Psychotherapy

Parameters	Supportive Group Therapy	Analytically Oriented Group Therapy	Psychoanalysis of Groups	Transactional Group Therapy	Behavioral Group Therapy
Frequency	Once a week	1 to 3 times a week	1 to 5 times a week	1 to 3 times a week	1 to 3 times a week
Duration	Up to 6 months	1 to 3+ years	1 to 3+ years	1 to 3 years	Up to 6 months
Primary indications	Psychotic and anxiety disorders	Anxiety disorders, borderline states, personality disorders	Anxiety disorders, personality disorders	Anxiety and psychotic disorders	Phobias, passivity, sexual problems
Individual screening interview	Usually	Always	Always	Usually	Usually
Communication content	Primarily environmental factors	Present and past life situations, intragroup and extragroup relationships	Primarily past life experiences, intragroup relationships	Primarily intragroup relationships; rarely, history; here and now stressed	Specific symptoms without focus on causality
Transference	Positive transference encouraged to promote improved functioning	Positive and negative transference evoked and analyzed	Transference neurosis evoked and analyzed	Positive relationships fostered, negative feelings analyzed	Positive relationships fostered, no examination of transference
Dreams	Not analyzed	Analyzed frequently	Always analyzed and encouraged	Analyzed rarely	Not used
Dependence	Intragroup dependence encouraged, members rely on leader to great extent	Intragroup dependence encouraged, dependence on leader variable	Intragroup dependence not encouraged, dependence on leader variable	Intragroup dependence encouraged, dependence on leader not encouraged	Intragroup dependence not encouraged; reliance on leader is high
Therapist activity	Strengthen existing defenses, active, give advice	Challenge defenses, active, give advice or personal response	Challenge defenses, passive, give no advice or personal response	Challenge defenses, active, give personal response, rather than advice	Create new defenses, active and directive
Interpretation	No interpretation of unconscious conflict	Interpretation of unconscious conflict	Interpretation of unconscious conflict extensive	Interpretation of current behavioral patterns in the here and now	Not used
Major group processes	Universalization, reality testing	Cohesion, transference, reality testing	Transference, ventilation, catharsis, reality testing	Abreaction, reality testing	Cohesion, reinforcement, conditioning
Socialization outside of group	Encouraged	Generally discouraged	Discouraged	Variable	Discouraged
Goals	Improved adaptation to environment	Moderate reconstruction of personality dynamics	Extensive reconstruction of personality dynamics	Alteration of behavior through mechanism of conscious control	Relief of specific psychiatric symptoms

blocked, anxious, resistant, and unwilling to verbalize thought, and feelings in an individual setting, generally for fear of censure or disapproval from the therapist. Thus, they may welcome the suggestion of group psychotherapy so as to avoid the scrutiny of the dyadic situation. Conversely, if the patient reacts negatively to the suggestion of group psychotherapy or is openly resistant to the idea, the therapist should consider the possibility of a high degree of peer anxiety.

PEER ANXIETY

Patients, such as those with borderline and schizoid personality disorders, who have destructive relationships with their peer groups or who have been extremely isolated from peer group contact generally react negatively or anxiously when placed in a group setting. If such patients can work through their anxiety, however, group therapy can be beneficial.

DIAGNOSIS

The diagnosis of patients' disorders is important in determining the best therapeutic approach and in evaluating patients' motivations for treatment, capacities for change, and personality structure strengths and weaknesses.

There are few contraindications to group therapy. Antisocial patients generally do poorly in a heterogeneous group setting because they cannot adhere to group standards. However, if the group is composed of other antisocial patients they may respond better to peers than to perceived authority figures. Depressed patients do well after they have established a trusting relationship with the therapist. Actively suicidal or severely depressed patients should not be treated solely in a group setting. Manic patients are disruptive, but, once under pharmacological control, they do well in the group setting. Patients who are delusional and who may incorporate the group into their delusional system should be excluded, as should patients who pose a physical threat to other members because of uncontrollable aggressive outbursts.

Preparation

Patients who are prepared by the therapist for a group experience tend to continue in treatment longer and report less initial anxiety than do those who are not so prepared. The preparation consists of the therapist's explaining, before the first session, the procedure in as much detail as possible and answering any questions the patient may have.

Structural Organization

SIZE

Group therapy has been successful with as few as 3 members and as many as 15, but most therapists consider 8 to 10 members the optimal size. With fewer members there may not be enough interaction unless the members are especially verbal. But with more than 10 members the interaction may be too great for the members or the therapist to follow.

FREQUENCY OF SESSIONS

Most group psychotherapists conduct group sessions once a week. Maintaining continuity in sessions is important. When alternate sessions are used, the group meets twice a week, once with the therapist and once without the therapist.

LENGTH OF SESSIONS

In general, group sessions last anywhere from one to two hours, but the time limit set should be constant.

Time-extended therapy (marathon group therapy) is a method in which the group meets continuously for 12 to 72 hours. Enforced interactional proximity and, during the longest time-extended sessions, sleep deprivation break down certain ego defenses, release affective processes, and theoretically promote open communication. However, time-extended sessions may be dangerous for patients with weak ego structures, such as schizophrenic and borderline personality disorder patients. Marathon groups were most popular in the 1970s but are much less often used today.

HOMOGENEOUS VERSUS HETEROGENEOUS GROUPS

In general, most therapists believe that the group should be as heterogeneous as possible to ensure maximum interaction. Thus, the group should be composed of members from different diagnostic categories and with varied behavioral patterns; from all races, social levels, and educational backgrounds; and of varying ages and both sexes.

In general, patients between ages 20 and 65 can be effectively included in the same group. Age differences aid in the development of parent-child and brother-sister models. Moreover, patients have the opportunity to relive and rectify interpersonal difficulties that may have appeared insurmountable.

Both children and adolescents are best treated in groups composed mostly of patients of their own age group. Some adolescent patients are capable of assimilating the material of an adult group, regardless of content, but they should not be deprived of a constructive peer experience that they may otherwise not have.

OPEN VERSUS CLOSED GROUPS

Some groups have a set number and composition of patients. If members leave, no new members are taken on; that is termed a closed group. An open group is one in which there is more fluidity of membership; new members are taken on whenever old members leave.

Mechanisms

GROUP FORMATION

Each patient approaches the group differently, and in that sense the group is a microcosm. Patients use typical adaptive abilities, defense mechanisms, and ways of relating, which are ultimately reflected back to them by the group, thus allowing them to become introspective about their personality functioning. But a process inherent in group formation requires that the patients suspend their previous ways of coping. In entering the group, they allow their executive ego functions—reality testing, adaptation to and mastery of the environment, and perception—to be assumed to some degree by the collective assessment provided by the total membership, including the leader.

THERAPEUTIC FACTORS

Table 26.3–2 outlines 20 significant therapeutic factors that account for change in group psychotherapy.

Role of the Therapist

Although opinions differ regarding how active or passive the therapist should be, the consensus is that the therapist's

Table 26.3–2. Twenty Therapeutic Factors in Group Psychotherapy

Factor	Definition
Abreaction	A process by which repressed material, particularly a painful experience or conflict, is brought back to consciousness. In the process, the person not only recalls but relives the material, which is accompanied by the appropriate emotional response; insight usually results from the experience.
Acceptance	The feeling of being accepted by other members of the group; differences of opinion are tolerated, and there is an absence of censure.
Altruism	The act of one member's being of help to another; putting another person's need before one's own and learning that there is value in giving to others. The term was originated by Auguste Comte (1798–1857), and Sigmund Freud believed it was a major factor in establishing group cohesion and community feeling.
Catharsis	The expression of ideas, thoughts, and suppressed material that is accompanied by an emotional response that produces a state of relief in the patient.
Cohesion	The sense that the group is working together toward a common goal; also referred to as a sense of ''we-ness''; believed to be the most important factor related to positive therapeutic effects.
Consensual validation	Confirmation of reality by comparing one's own conceptualizations with those of other group members; interpersonal distortions are thereby corrected. The term was introduced by Harry Stack Sullivan; Trigant Burrow had used the phrase ''consensual observation'' to refer to the same phenomenon.
Contagion	The process in which the expression of emotion by one member stimulates the awareness of a similar emotion in another member.
Corrective familial experience	The group re-creates the family of origin for some members who can work through original conflicts psychologically through group interaction (e.g., sibling rivalry, anger toward parents).
Empathy	The capacity of a group member to put himself or herself into the psychological frame of reference of another group member and thereby understand his or her thinking, feeling, or behavior.
Identification	An unconscious defense mechanism in which the person incorporates the characteristics and the qualities of another person or object into his or her ego system.
Imitation	The conscious emulation or modeling of one's behavior after that of another (also called role modeling); also known as spectator therapy, as one patient learns from another.
Insight	Conscious awareness and understanding of one's own psychodynamics and symptoms of maladaptive behavior. Most therapists distinguish two types: (1) intellectual insight—knowledge and awareness without any changes in maladaptive behavior; and (2) emotional insight—awareness and understanding leading to positive changes in personality and behavior.
Inspiration	The process of imparting a sense of optimism to group members; the ability to recognize that one has the capacity to overcome problems; also known as instillation of hope.
Interaction	The free and open exchange of ideas and feelings among group members; effective interaction is emotionally charged.
Interpretation	The process during which the group leader formulates the meaning or significance of a patient's resistance, defenses, and symbols; the result is that the patient has a cognitive framework within which to understand his or her behavior.
Learning	Patients acquire knowledge about new areas, such as social skills and sexual behavior; they receive advice, obtain guidance, and attempt to influence and are influenced by other group members.
Reality testing	Ability of the person to evaluate objectively the world outside the self; includes the capacity to perceive oneself and other group members accurately. *See also* Consensual validation.
Transference	Projection of feelings, thoughts, and wishes onto the therapist, who has come to represent an object from the patient's past. Such reactions, while perhaps appropriate for the condition prevailing in the patient's earlier life, are inappropriate and anachronistic when applied to the therapist in the present. Patients in the group may also direct such feelings toward one another, a process called multiple transferences.
Universalization	The awareness of the patient that he or she is not alone in having problems; others share similar complaints or difficulties in learning; the patient is not unique.
Ventilation	The expression of suppressed feelings, ideas, or events to other group members; the sharing of personal secrets that ameliorate a sense of sin or guilt (also referred to as self-disclosure).

Table by Benjamin J. Sadock, MD.

role is primarily a facilitative one. Ideally, the group members themselves are the primary source of cure and change.

The climate produced by the therapist's personality is a potent agent of change. The therapist is more than an expert applying techniques; the therapist exerts a personal influence that taps such variables as empathy, warmth, and respect.

Inpatient Group Psychotherapy

Group therapy is an important part of the hospitalized patient's therapeutic experiences. Groups may be organized on a ward in a variety of ways: in a community meeting, an entire inpatient unit meets with all the staff members (for example, psychiatrists, psychologists, and nurses); in a team meeting, 15 to 20 patients and staff members meet; and a regular or small group composed of 8 to 10 patients may meet with one or two therapists, as in traditional group therapy. Although the goals of each type of group vary, they all have common purposes:

(1) to increase the patient's awareness of themselves through their interactions with the other group members, who provide feedback about their behavior, (2) to provide patients with improved interpersonal and social skills, (3) to help the members adapt to the inpatient setting, and (4) to improve communication between the patients and the staff. In addition, one type of group meeting is composed of only the inpatient hospital staff; it is used to improve communication among the staff members and to provide mutual support and encouragement in their day-to-day work with the patients. The community meeting and the team meeting are more helpful in dealing with patient treatment problems than they are for providing insight-oriented therapy, which is the province of the small-group therapy meeting.

GROUP COMPOSITION

Two key factors of the inpatient group, common to all short-term therapies, are the heterogeneity of its members and the rapid turnover of patients. Outside the hospital, the therapist has a large caseload from which to select patients for group therapy. On the ward, the therapist has a limited number of patients from which to draw and is restricted further to those patients who are both willing to participate in and suitable for a small-group experience. In certain settings, group participation may be mandatory (for example, in substance abuse and alcohol dependence units). But that is not usually true for a general psychiatry unit; in fact, most group experiences are better when the patients themselves choose to enter them.

More sessions are preferable to fewer sessions. During a patient's hospital stay, groups may meet daily, allowing for interactional continuity and the carryover of themes from one session to the next. A new member of the group can quickly be brought up-to-date, either by the therapist in an orientation meeting or by one of the members. A newly admitted patient has often learned many details about the small-group program from another patient before actually attending the first session. The less frequently the group sessions are held, the more the therapist needs to structure the group and be active.

INPATIENT VERSUS OUTPATIENT GROUPS

Although the therapeutic factors that account for change in the small inpatient group are similar to those in the outpatient setting, there are qualitative differences. For example, the relatively high turnover of patients in the inpatient group complicates the process of cohesion. But the fact that all the members of the group are together in the hospital aids the cohesion, as do efforts by the therapist to foster the process, emphasizing other similarities. Sharing of information, universalization, and catharsis are the main therapeutic factors at work in inpatient groups. Although insight is more likely in outpatient groups because of their long-term nature, some patients can obtain a new understanding of their psychological makeup within the confines of a single group session. A unique quality of the inpatient group is the patients' extragroup contact, which is extensive, as they live together on the same ward. Verbalizing their thoughts and feelings about such contacts in the therapy sessions encourages interpersonal learning. In addition, conflicts between patients or between patients and staff members can be anticipated and resolved.

Self-Help Groups

Self-help groups are composed of persons who want to cope with a specific problem or life crisis. Usually organized with a particular task in mind, such groups do not attempt to explore individual psychodynamics in great depth or to change personality functioning significantly. But self-help groups have improved the emotional health and well-being of many people.

A distinguishing characteristic of the self-help group is its homogeneity. The members suffer from the same disorders, and they share their experiences—good and bad, successful and unsuccessful—with one another. By so doing, they educate one another, provide mutual support, and alleviate the sense of alienation that is usually felt by the person drawn to that type of group.

Self-help groups emphasize cohesion, which is exceptionally strong in those groups. Because of the group members' similar problems and symptoms, a strong emotional bond and the group's own characteristics develop, to which the members may

attribute magical qualities of healing. Examples of self-help groups are Alcoholics Anonymous (AA), Gamblers Anonymous (GA), and Overeaters Anonymous (OA).

The self-help group movement is in its ascendancy. The groups meet their members' needs by providing acceptance, mutual support, and help in overcoming maladaptive patterns of behavior or states of feeling with which traditional mental health and medical professionals have not been generally successful. Self-help groups and therapy groups have begun to converge: the self-help groups have enabled their members to give up a pattern of unwanted behavior; the therapy groups help their members understand why and how they got to be the way they were or are.

COMBINED INDIVIDUAL AND GROUP PSYCHOTHERAPY

In combined individual and group psychotherapy, patients are seen individually by the therapist and also take part in group sessions. The therapist for the group and for the individual sessions is usually the same person.

Groups can vary in size from 3 to 15 members, but the best size is 8 to 10. Patients must attend all group sessions. Attendance at individual sessions is also important, and the failure to attend either group or individual sessions should be examined as part of the therapeutic process.

Combined therapy is a particular treatment modality. It is not a system by which individual therapy is augmented by an occasional group session, nor does it mean that a participant in group therapy meets alone with the therapist from time to time. Rather, it is an ongoing plan in which the group experience interacts meaningfully with the individual sessions and in which reciprocal feedback helps form an integrated therapeutic experience. Although the one-to-one doctor-patient relationship makes possible a deep examination of the transference reaction for some patients, it may not provide the corrective emotional experiences necessary for therapeutic change for other patients. The group gives patients a variety of persons with whom they can have transferential reactions. In the microcosm of the group, patients can relieve and work through familial and other important influences.

Techniques

Various techniques based on varying theoretical frameworks have been used in the combined therapy format. Some clinicians increase the frequency of the individual sessions to encourage the emergence of the transference neurosis. In the behavioral model, individual sessions are regularly scheduled but tend to be less frequent than in other approaches. Depending on the therapist's orientation, during the individual sessions the patient may use a couch or a chair. Techniques such as alternate meetings may be used in the group setting. Harold Kaplan and Benjamin Sadock developed a combined therapy approach called structured interactional group psychotherapy, in which a different member is the focus at each weekly group session and is discussed in some depth by the other members.

Results

Most workers in the field believe that combined therapy has the advantages of both the dyadic setting and the group setting, without sacrificing the qualities of either. Generally, the dropout rate in combined therapy is lower than that in group therapy alone. In many cases, combined therapy appears to bring problems to the surface and to resolve them more quickly than may be possible with either method alone.

PSYCHODRAMA

Psychodrama is a method of group psychotherapy originated by the Viennese-born psychiatrist Jacob Moreno in which personality makeup, interpersonal relationships, conflicts, and emotional problems are explored by means of special dramatic methods. The therapeutic dramatization of emotional problems includes (1) the protagonist or patient, the person who acts out problems with the help of (2) auxiliary egos, persons who enact varying aspects of the patient, and (3) the director, psychodramatist, or therapist, the person who guides those in the drama toward the acquisition of insight.

Roles

DIRECTOR

The director is the leader or therapist and so must be active and participating. He or she encourages the members of the group to be spontaneous and so has a catalytic function. The director must also be available to meet the group's needs and not superimpose his or her values on it. Of all the group psychotherapies, psychodrama requires of the therapist the most participation and ability to lead.

PROTAGONIST

The protagonist is the patient in conflict. The patient chooses the situation to portray in the dramatic scene, or the therapist may choose it if the patient so desires.

AUXILIARY EGO

An auxiliary ego is another group member who represents something or someone in the protagonist's experience. The auxiliary egos help account for the great range of therapeutic effects available in psychodrama.

GROUP

The members of the psychodrama and the audience make up the group. Some are participants, and others are observers, but all benefit from the experience to the extent that they can identify with the ongoing events. The concept of spontaneity in psychodrama refers to the ability of each member of the group, especially the protagonist, to experience the thoughts and feelings of the moment and to communicate emotion as authentically as possible.

Techniques

The psychodrama may focus on any special area of functioning (a dream, a family, or a community situation), a symbolic role, an unconscious attitude, or an imagined future situation. Such symptoms as delusions and hallucinations can also be acted out in the group. Techniques to advance the therapeutic process, productivity, and creativity include the soliloquy (a recital of overt and hidden thoughts and feelings), role reversal (the exchange of the patient's role with the role of a significant person), the double (an auxiliary ego acting as the patient), the

multiple double (several egos acting as the patient did on varying occasions), and the mirror technique (an ego imitating the patient and speaking for him or her). Other techniques include the use of hypnosis and psychoactive drugs to modify the acting behavior in various ways.

References

Dies R R: The future of group therapy. Psychotherapy 29: 58, 1992.
Fawzy F I, Fawzy N W, Arndt L A, Pasnau R O: Critical review of psychosocial interventions in cancer care. Arch Gen Psychiatry 52: 100, 1995.
Kaplan H I, Sadock B J, editors: Comprehensive Group Psychotherapy, ed 3. Williams & Wilkins, Baltimore, 1993.
Karterud S W: Reflections on group-analytic research. Group Analysis 25: 353, 1992.
Kleinberg J L: Group treatment of adults in midlife. Int J Group Psychother 45: 207, 1995.
Marshall J R: Integrated treatment of social phobia. Bull Menninger Clin 59 (2 Suppl A): A27, 1995.
Ormont L R: Subjective countertransference in the group setting: The modern analytic experience. Mod Psychoanal 17: 3, 1992.
Sigrell B: The long-term effects of group psychotherapy: A thirteen-year follow-up study. Group Anal 25: 333, 1992.
Wong N: Group psychotherapy, combined individual and group psychotherapy, and psychodrama. In Comprehensive Textbook of Psychiatry, ed 6, H I Kaplan, B J Sadock, editors, p 1821. Williams & Wilkins, Baltimore, 1995.

26.4 FAMILY THERAPY AND MARITAL THERAPY

Family systems theory states that a family behaves as if it were a unit with a particular homeostasis of relating that is maintained regardless of how maladaptive it is. The goals of family therapy are to recognize and acknowledge the often covert pattern of maintaining balance within a family and to help the family understand the pattern's meaning and purpose.

Family therapists generally believe that one member of the family has been labeled the identified patient. That person is identified by the family as ''the one who is the problem, is to blame, needs help.'' The family therapist's goal is to help the family understand that the identified patient's symptoms are, in fact, serving a crucial function in maintaining the family's homeostasis. The process of family therapy helps reveal a family's repetitious and ultimately predictable communication patterns that are sustaining and reflecting the identified patient's behavior.

Inherent in family systems theory is the belief, to one degree or another, that the marital relationship strongly influences the nature of a family's system and homeostasis. One influential family therapist has described that concept as the marital dyad's being the ''architects of the family.''

FAMILY THERAPY

Initial Consultation

Family therapy is well-enough known that families with a high level of conflict may request it specifically. When the initial complaint is about an individual family member, however, pretreatment work may be necessary. Typical fears underlying resistance to a family approach are fears (1) by parents that they will be blamed for their child's difficulties, (2) that the entire family will be pronounced sick, (3) that a spouse will object, and (4) that open discussion of one child's misbehavior will have a negative influence on younger siblings. Refusal by an adolescent or young adult patient to participate in family therapy is frequently a disguised collusion with the fears of one or both parents.

Interview Technique

The special quality of the family interview proceeds from two important facts: (1) The family comes to treatment with its history and dynamics firmly in place. To the family therapist, it is the established nature of the group, more than the symptoms, that constitutes the clinical problem. (2) Family members usually live together and, at some level, depend on one another for their physical and emotional well-being. Whatever transpires in the therapy session is known to all. Central principles of technique derive from those facts. For example, the catharsis of anger by one family member toward another must be carefully channeled by the therapist. The person who is the object of the anger is present and will react to the attack, running the danger of escalation toward violence, fractured relationships, and withdrawal from therapy. Free association is likewise not appropriate, because it would encourage one person to dominate the session. For those reasons the therapist must always control and direct the family interview.

Frequency and Length of Treatment

Unless an emergency arises, sessions are usually held no more than once a week. Each session, however, may require as much as two hours. Long sessions can include an intermission to give the therapist time to organize the material and plan a response. A flexible schedule is necessary when geography or personal circumstances make it physically difficult for the family to get together. The length of treatment depends not only on the nature of the problem but also on the therapeutic model. Therapists who use problem-solving models exclusively may accomplish their goals in a few sessions; therapists using growth-oriented models may work with a family for years, with sessions at long intervals.

Models of Intervention

Psychodynamic-Experiential Models

Psychodynamic-experiential models emphasize individual maturation in the context of the family system, free from unconscious patterns of anxiety and projection rooted in the past. Therapists seek to establish an intimate bond with each family member, alternating between the therapists' exchanges with the members and the members' exchanges with one another. Clarity of communication and honestly admitted feelings are given high priority; toward that end, family members may be encouraged to change their seats, to touch one another, and to make direct eye contact. Their use of metaphor, body language, and parapraxes helps reveal the unconscious pattern of family relationships. The therapist may also use *family sculpting*, in which family members physically arrange one another in tableaus depicting their personal view of relationships, past or present. The therapist both interprets the sculpture and modifies it in a way to suggest new relationships. In addition, the therapist's subjective responses to the family are given great importance. At appropriate moments the responses are expressed to the family to form yet another feedback loop of self-observation and change.

Bowen Model

Murray Bowen called his model simply "family systems," but in the field it has rightfully been given the name of its originator. Its hallmark is personal differentiation from the family of origin, the ability to be one's true self in the face of the familial or other pressures that threaten the loss of love or social position. The problem family is assessed on two levels: (1) the degree of their enmeshment versus the degree of their ability to differentiate and (2) the analysis of emotional triangles in the presenting problem. An *emotional triangle* is defined as a three-party system (of which there can be many within a family) arranged so that the closeness of two members tends to exclude a third. The closeness may be expressed as either love or repetitive conflict. In either case, emotional cross-currents are activated when the excluded third party attempts to join with one or the other or when one of the involved parties shifts in the direction of the excluded one. The role of the therapist is, first, to stabilize or shift the hot triangle—the one that relates to the presenting symptoms—and, second, to work with the most psychologically available family members, individually if necessary, on achieving enough personal differentiation so that the hot triangle does not recur. To stay neutral in their triangles, the therapist minimizes emotional contact with family members. Bowen originated the *genogram*, which is a historical survey of the family going back several generations.

Structural Model

In a structural model the family is viewed as a single interrelated system assessed along the following lines: (1) significant alliances and splits among family members, (2) hierarchy of power (that is, the parents in charge of the children), (3) the clarity and firmness of boundaries between the generations, and (4) the family's tolerance of one another. The structural model uses concurrent individual and family therapy.

General Systems Model

Based on general systems theory, a general systems model holds that the family is a system and that every action in the family produces a reaction in one or more of its members. Every member is presumed to play a role (for example, spokesperson, persecutor, victim, rescuer, symptom bearer, nurturer), which is relatively stable: however, the member who fills each role may change. Some families try to scapegoat one member by blaming him or her for the family's problems (the identified patient). If the identified patient improves, another family member may become the scapegoat. The family is defined as having external boundaries and internal rules. The general systems model overlaps with some of the other models presented, particularly the Bowen and structural models.

Techniques

Family Group Therapy

Family group therapy combines several families into a single group. Mutual problems are shared, and families compare their interactions with those of the other families in the group. Multiple family groups have been used effectively in the treatment of schizophrenia. Parents of disturbed children may also be gathered together to share their situations.

SOCIAL NETWORK THERAPY

Social network therapy gathers together the social community or network of a disturbed patient, all of whom meet in group sessions with the patient. The network includes those persons with whom the patient comes into contact in daily life, not only the immediate family but also relatives, friends, tradespersons, teachers, and coworkers.

PARADOXICAL THERAPY

This approach, which evolved from the work of Gregory Bateson, consists of suggesting that the patient intentionally engage in the unwanted behavior (called the paradoxical injunction), such as avoiding the phobic object or performing the compulsive ritual. Although paradoxical therapy and the use of paradoxical injunctions are relatively new, the therapy may create new insights for some patients. The danger of the approach is that it may be used in an arbitrary or routinized fashion.

POSITIVE CONNOTATION

Positive connotation or reframing is a relabeling of all negatively expressed feelings or behavior as positive. The therapist attempts to get family members to view behavior from a new frame of reference—for example, ''This child is impossible'' becomes ''This child is desperately trying to distract and protect you from what he or she perceives as an unhappy marriage.''

Goals

The goals of treatment are (1) to resolve or reduce pathogenic conflict and anxiety within the matrix of interpersonal relationships,(2) to enhance the perception and fulfillment by family members of one another's emotional needs, (3) to promote appropriate role relationships between the sexes and between the generations, (4) to strengthen the capacity of individual members and the family as a whole to cope with destructive forces inside and outside the surrounding environment, and (5) to influence family identity and values so that members are oriented toward health and growth.

A final goal is to integrate the family into the large systems in the society, which include not only the extended family but also society—as represented by such systems as schools, medical facilities, and social, recreational, and welfare agencies—so that the family is not isolated.

MARITAL THERAPY

Marital therapy is a form of psychotherapy designed to psychologically modify the interaction of two people who are in conflict with each other over one parameter or a variety of parameters—social, emotional, sexual, economic. In marital therapy a trained person establishes a therapeutic contract with the patient-couple and, through definite types of communication, attempts to alleviate the disturbance, to reverse or change maladaptive patterns of behavior, and to encourage personality growth and development.

Marriage counseling may be considered more limited in scope than marital therapy in that only a particular familial conflict is discussed. Marriage counseling may also be primarily task-oriented, geared to solving a specific problem, such as child rearing. Marriage therapy emphasizes restructuring the interaction between the couple, sometimes exploring the psychody-namics of each partner. Both therapy and counseling stress helping the marital partners cope effectively with their problems. Most important is the definition of appropriate and realistic goals, which may involve extensive reconstruction of the union or problem-solving approaches or a combination of both.

Types of Therapy

INDIVIDUAL THERAPY

In individual therapy the marital partners may be seen by different therapists, who may not necessarily communicate with each other. Indeed, they may not even know each other. The goal of the treatment is to strengthen each partner's adaptive capacities. At times, only one of the partners is in treatment; in such cases, a visit by the spouse who is not in treatment with the therapist may be helpful. The visiting partner may give the therapist data about the patient that may otherwise be overlooked; overt or covert anxiety in the visiting partner as a result of change in the patient can be identified and dealt with, irrational beliefs about treatment events can be corrected, and conscious or unconscious attempts by the partner to sabotage the patient's treatment can be examined.

INDIVIDUAL MARITAL THERAPY

In individual marital therapy each of the marriage partners is in therapy. When the same therapist conducts the treatment, it is called concurrent therapy; when the partners are seen by different therapists, it is called collaborative therapy.

CONJOINT THERAPY

Conjoint therapy is the treatment of partners in joint sessions conducted by either one or two therapists; it is the treatment method most frequently used in marital therapy. Cotherapy with therapists of both sexes prevents a particular patient from feeling ganged up on when confronted by two members of the opposite sex.

FOUR-WAY SESSION

In a four-way session each partner is seen by a different therapist, with regular joint sessions in which all four persons participate. A variation of the four-way session is the roundtable interview, developed by William Masters and Virginia Johnson for the rapid treatment of sexually dysfunctional couples. Two patients and two opposite-sex therapists meet regularly.

GROUP PSYCHOTHERAPY

Therapy for married couples placed in a group allows a variety of group dynamics to affect the couples. The group usually consists of three to four couples and one or two therapists. The couples identify with one another and recognize that others have similar problems; each gains support and empathy from fellow group members of the same or opposite sex; they explore sexual attitudes and have an opportunity to gain new information from their peer groups, and each receives specific feedback about his or her behavior, either negative or positive, that may have more meaning and be better assimilated coming from a neutral nonspouse member than from the spouse or the therapist.

When only one partner is in a therapy group, the spouse may occasionally visit the group, so as to allow the members to test reality. At times, a group may be so organized that only one married couple is part of the large group.

COMBINED THERAPY

Combined therapy refers to all or any of the preceding techniques used concurrently or in combination. Thus, a particular patient-couple may begin treatment with one or both partners in individual psychotherapy, continue to conjoint therapy with the partner, and terminate therapy after a course of treatment in a married couples group. The rationale for combined therapy is that no single approach to marital problems has been shown to be superior to another. A familiarity with a variety of approaches thus allows the therapist a degree of flexibility that provides maximum benefit for the couple in distress.

Indications

Regardless of the specific therapeutic technique used, certain indications for initiating marital therapy have been agreed on: (1) when individual therapy has failed to resolve the marital difficulties, (2) when the onset of distress in one or both partners is clearly related to marital events, and (3) when marital therapy is requested by a couple in conflict. Problems in communication between partners are a prime indication for marital therapy. In such instances one spouse may be intimidated by the other, may become anxious when attempting to tell the other about thoughts or feelings, or may project unconscious expectations onto the other. The therapy is geared toward enabling each of the partners to see the other realistically.

Conflicts in one or several areas, such as the partners' sexual life, are also indications for treatment. Similarly, difficulty in establishing satisfactory social, economic, parental, or emotional roles is an indication for help. The clinician should evaluate all aspects of the marital relationship before attempting to treat only one problem, as it may be a symptom of a pervasive marital disorder.

Contraindications

Contraindications for marital therapy include patients with severe forms of psychosis, particularly patients with paranoid elements and those in whom the marriage's homeostatic mechanism is a protection against psychosis; when one or both of the partners really wants to divorce; or when one spouse refuses to participate because of anxiety or fear.

Goals

According to Nathan Ackerman, the goals of therapy for marital disorders are to alleviate emotional distress and disability and to promote the levels of well-being of both partners together and individually. In a general way, the therapist moves toward those goals by strengthening the shared resources for problem solving, by encouraging the substitution of adequate controls and defenses for pathogenic ones, by enhancing both the immunity against the disintegrative effects of emotional upset and the complementarity of the relationship, and by promoting the growth of the relationship and each partner.

Part of the therapeutic task is to persuade each partner in the marriage to take responsibility in understanding the psychodynamic makeup of his or her personality. Accountability for the effects of behavior on one's own life, the life of the spouse, and the lives of others in the environment is emphasized, which often results in a deep understanding of the problems that created the marital discord.

Marital therapy does not ensure the maintenance of any marriage. Indeed, in certain instances it may show the partners that they are in a nonviable union that should be dissolved. In those cases the couple may continue to meet with the therapist to work through the difficult process of separating and obtaining a divorce. That has been called divorce therapy.

References

Babcock J C, Waltz J, Jacobson N S, Gottman J M: Power and violence: The relation between communication patterns, power discrepancies, and domestic violence. J Consult Clin Psychol 61: 40, 1993.

Boddington S J A, Lavender A: Treatment models for couples therapy: A review of the outcome literature and the Dodo's verdict. Sex Marital Ther 10: 69, 1995.

Dunn R L, Schwebel A I: Meta-analytic review of marital therapy outcome research. J Fam Psychology 9: 58, 1995.

Houlihan M M, Jackson J, Rogers T R: Decision making of satisfied and dissatisfied married couples. J Soc Psychol 130: 89, 1990.

Kadis L B, McClendon R A: Couples and marital therapy. In Comprehensive Textbook of Psychiatry, ed 6, H I Kaplan, B J Sadock, editors, p 1857. Williams & Wilkins, Baltimore, 1995.

Lebow J L, Gurman A S: Research assessing couple and family therapy. Annu Rev Psychol 46: 27, 1995.

Markman H J, Hahlweg K: The prediction and prevention of marital distress: An international perspective. Clin Psychol Rev 13: 29, 1993.

O'Leary K D, Beach S R: Marital therapy: A viable treatment for depression and marital discord. Am J Psychiatry 147: 183, 1990.

Pinsof W M: A conceptual framework and methodological criteria for family therapy process research. J Consult Clin Psychol 57: 53, 1989.

Steinglass P: Family therapy. In Comprehensive Textbook of Psychiatry, ed 6, H I Kaplan, B J Sadock, editors, p 1838. Williams & Wilkins, Baltimore, 1995.

Tatum, D W, DelCampo R L: Selective mutism in children: A structural family therapy approach to treatment. Comtemp Fam Ther 17: 177, 1995.

26.5 BIOFEEDBACK

Biofeedback provides information to a person regarding one or more physiological processes in an effort to enable the person to gain some element of voluntary control over bodily functions that normally operate outside consciousness. Biofeedback is based on the concept that autonomic responses can be controlled through the process of operant or instrumental conditioning. Physiological manifestations of anxiety or tension (for example, headaches, tachycardia, and pain) can be reduced by teaching the patient to be aware of the physiological differences between tension and relaxation. The teaching involves immediate feedback to the patient through concrete, visible or audible recordings of the patient's biological functioning during anxiety versus relaxation states; the procedure reinforces the patient's awareness of which state is present and helps the patient control it.

THEORY

Neal Miller demonstrated the medical potential of biofeedback by showing that the normally involuntary autonomic nervous system can be operantly conditioned, using appropriate feedback. By means of instruments, the patient is given information about the status of certain involuntary biological functions, such as skin temperature and electrical conductivity, muscle tension, blood pressure, heart rate, and brain wave activity. The patient is then taught to regulate one or more of those biological states, which affect symptoms. For example, the ability to raise the temperature of one's hands may be used to reduce the frequency of migraines, palpitations, or angina pectoris. A presumptive mechanism is a lowering of sympathetic activation and a voluntary self-regulation of arterial smooth muscle vasoconstrictive tendencies in predisposed persons. Section 21.3 discusses biofeedback further.

Table 26.5-1.   Biofeedback Applications

Condition	Effects
Asthma	Both frontal EMG and airway resistance biofeedback have been reported as producing relaxation from the panic associated with asthma, as well as improving air flow rate.
Cardiac arrhythmias	Specific biofeedback of the electrocardiogram has permitted patients to lower the frequency of premature ventricular contractions.
Fecal incontinence and enuresis	The timing sequence of internal and external and sphincters has been measured, using triple lumen rectal catheters providing feedback to incontinent patients in order for them to reestablish normal bowel habits in a relatively small number of biofeedback sessions. An actual precursor of biofeedback dating to 1938 was the sounding of a buzzer for sleeping enuretic children at the first sign of moisture (the pad and bell).
Grand mal epilepsy	A number of EEG biofeedback procedures have been used experimentally to suppress seizure activity prophylactically in patients not responsive to anticonvulsant medication. The procedures permit patients to enhance the sensorimotor brain wave rhythm or to normalize brain activity as computed in real-time power spectrum displays.
Hyperactivity	EEG biofeedback procedures have been used on children with attention-deficit/hyperactivity disorder to train them to reduce their motor restlessness.
Idiopathic hypertension and orthostatic hypotension	A variety of specific (direct) and nonspecific biofeedback procedures—including blood pressure feedback, galvanic skin response, and foot-hand thermal feedback combined with relaxation procedures—have been used to teach patients to increase or decrease their blood pressure. Some follow-up data indicate that the changes may persist for years and often permit the reduction or elimination of antihypertensive medications.
Migraine	The most common biofeedback strategy with classic or common vascular headaches has been thermal biofeedback from a digit accompanied by autogenic self-suggestive phrases encouraging hand warming and head cooling. The mechanism is thought to help prevent excessive cerebral artery vasoconstriction, often accompanied by an ischemic prodromal symptom, such as scintillating scotomata, followed by rebound engorgement of arteries and stretching of vessel wall pain receptors.
Myofacial and temporomandibular joint (TMJ) pain	High levels of EMG activity over the powerful muscles associated with bilateral temporomandibular joints have been decreased, using biofeedback in patients who are jaw clenchers or have bruxism.
Neuromuscular rehabilitation	Mechanical devices or an EMG measurement of muscle activity displayed to a patient increases the effectiveness of traditional therapies, as documented by relatively long clinical histories in peripheral nerve-muscle damage, spasmodic torticollis, selected cases of tardive dyskinesia, cerebral palsy, and upper motor neuron hemiplegias.
Reynaud's syndrome	Cold hands and cold feet are frequent concomitants of anxiety and also occur in Raynaud's syndrome, caused by vasospasm of arterial smooth muscle. A number of studies report that thermal feedback from the hand, an inexpensive and benign procedure compared with surgical sympathectomy, is effective in about 70 percent of cases of Raynaud's syndrome.
Tension headaches	Muscle contraction headaches are most frequently treated with two large active electrodes spaced on the forehead to provide visual or auditory information about the levels of muscle tension. The frontal electrode placement is sensitive to EMG activity regarding the frontalis and occipital muscles, which the patient learns to relax.

METHODS

The type of feedback instrument used depends on the patient and the specific problem. The most effective instruments are the electromyogram (EMG), which measures the electrical potentials of muscle fibers; the electroencephalogram (EEG), which measures alpha waves that occur in relaxed states; the galvanic skin response (GSR) gauge, which shows decreased skin conductivity during a relaxed state; and the thermistor, which measures skin temperature, which drops during tension because of peripheral vasoconstriction. The patient is attached to one of the measuring instruments, which measures a physiological function and translates the impulse into an audible or visual signal that the patient uses to gauge his or her responses. For example, in the treatment of bruxism, an EMG is attached to the masseter muscle. The EMG emits a high tone when the muscle is contracted and a low tone when at rest. The patient can learn to alter the tone to indicate relaxation. The patient receives feedback about the masseter muscle, the tone reinforces the learning, and the condition ameliorates—all those events interacting synergistically.

Table 26.5-1 outlines some of the important clinical applications of biofeedback. As can be seen in the table, a wide variety of biofeedback modalities have been used to treat numerous conditions. Many less specific clinical applications—such as treating insomnia, dysmenorrhea, and speech problems; improving athletic performance; treating volitional disorders; achieving altered states of consciousness; managing stress; and using biofeedback as an adjunct to psychotherapy for anxiety associated with somatoform disorders—use a model in which frontalis muscle EMG biofeedback is combined with thermal biofeedback and verbal instructions in progressive relaxation.

References

Arnold L E: Some nontraditional (unconventional and/or innovative) psychosocial treatments for children and adolescents: critique and proposed screening principles. J Abnorm Child Psychol 23: 125, 1995.

Burgio K L, Engel B T: Biofeedback-assisted behavioral training for elderly men and women. J Am Geriatr Soc *38*: 338, 1990.

Burish T G, Jenkins R A: Effectiveness of biofeedback and relaxation training in reducing the side effects of cancer chemotherapy. Health Psychol *11*: 17, 1992.

Elton D: Combined use of hypnosis and EMG biofeedback in the treatment of stress-induced conditions. Stress Med *9*: 25, 1993.

McGrady A, Conran P, Dickey D, Garman D, et al: The effects of biofeedback-assisted relaxation on cell-mediated immunity, cortisol, and white blood cell count in healthy and adult subjects. J Behav Med *15*: 343, 1992.

Mulholland T: Human EEG, behavioral stillness and biofeedback. Int J Psychophysiol *19*: 263, 1995.

Whitehead W E: Biofeedback treatment of gastrointestinal disorders. Biofeedback Self Regul *17*: 59, 1992.

26.6 BEHAVIOR THERAPY

Behavior therapists focus on overt behavior, emphasizing the removal of overt symptoms, without regard for the patient's private experiences of inner conflicts. The behaviorist's therapeutic goal is straightforward and concrete: the extinction of maladaptive habits or attitudes and the substitution of new, appropriate, nonanxiety-provoking patterns of behavior. The methods inherent to behavior therapies are based on the fundamental belief that persistent maladaptive behaviors and anxieties have been conditioned (or learned); therefore, successful treatment consists of various forms of deconditioning (or unlearning)—that is, whatever bad behavior has been learned can be unlearned.

Behavior therapy is based on the principles of learning theory—in particular, operant and classical conditioning. Behavior therapy is most often used when it is directed at specific, delineated habits of reacting with anxiety to objectively nondangerous stimuli (for example, phobias, compulsions, psychophysiological reactions, and sexual dysfunctions).

HISTORY

As early as the 1920s, scattered reports began to appear on the application of learning principles to the treatment of behavioral disorders. Those reports, however, had little effect on the mainstream of psychiatry and clinical psychology. Not until the 1960s did behavior therapy emerge as a systematic and comprehensive approach to psychiatric (behavioral) disorders. Those developments arose independently of one another on three continents. Joseph Wolpe and his colleagues in Johannesburg, South Africa, used largely Pavlovian techniques to produce and eliminate experimental neuroses in cats. From that research Wolpe developed systematic desensitization, the prototype of many current behavioral procedures for the treatment of maladaptive anxiety that is produced by identifiable stimuli in the environment. At about the same time a group at the Institute of Psychiatry of the University of London, particularly Hans Jurgen Eysenck and M. B. Shapiro, stressed the importance of an empirical, experimental approach to the understanding and treatment of the individual patient, using own-control, single-case experimental paradigms and modern learning theory. The third origin of behavior therapy was work inspired by the research of Harvard psychologist B. F. Skinner. Skinner's students began to apply his operant-conditioning technology, which was developed in animal-conditioning laboratories, to human beings in clinical settings.

SYSTEMATIC DESENSITIZATION

Systematic desensitization was developed by Joseph Wolpe and is based on the behavioral principle of counterconditioning, which states that a person can overcome maladaptive anxiety elicited by a situation or object by approaching the feared situation gradually and in a psychophysiological state that inhibits anxiety.

In systematic desensitization the patient attains a state of complete relaxation and is then exposed to the stimulus that elicits the anxiety response. The negative reaction of anxiety is then inhibited by the relaxed state, a process called *reciprocal inhibition*.

Rather than use actual situations or objects that elicit fear, the patient and the therapist prepare a graded list or hierarchy of anxiety-provoking scenes associated with the patient's fears. The learned relaxation state and the anxiety-provoking scenes are systematically paired in the treatment. Thus, systematic desensitization consists of three steps: relaxation training, hierarchy construction, and the desensitization of the stimulus.

Relaxation Training

Relaxation produces physiological effects that are opposite to those of anxiety—that is, slow heart rate, increased peripheral blood flow, and neuromuscular stability. A variety of relaxation methods have been developed, although some, such as yoga and Zen, have been known for centuries.

Most methods of achieving relaxation are based on a method called progressive relaxation. The patient relaxes major muscle groups in a fixed order, beginning with the small muscle groups of the feet and working cephalad or vice versa. Some clinicians use hypnosis to facilitate relaxation or use tape-recorded procedures to allow patients to practice relaxation on their own.

Mental imagery is a relaxation method in which patients are instructed to imagine themselves in a place associated with pleasant relaxed memories. Such images allow the patients to enter a relaxed state or experience or, as H. Benson termed it, the relaxation response.

Hierarchy Construction

When constructing the hierarchy, the clinician determines all the conditions that elicit anxiety and then has the patient create a list of hierarchy of 10 to 12 scenes in order of increasing anxiety. For example, the acrophobic hierarchy may begin with the patient's imagining standing near a window on the second floor and end with being on the roof of a 20-story building, leaning on a guard rail and looking straight down.

Desensitization of the Stimulus

Desensitization is done systematically by having the patient proceed through the list from the least anxiety-provoking scene to the most anxiety-provoking one while in a deeply relaxed state. The rate at which patients progress through the list is determined by their responses to the stimuli. When patients can vividly imagine the most anxiety-provoking scene of the hierarchy with equanimity, they experience little anxiety in the corresponding real-life situation.

Adjunctive Use of Drugs

Various drugs have been used to hasten desensitization, but they should be used with caution and only by clinicians trained and experienced in potential adverse effects. The widest experience is with the ultrarapidly acting barbiturate methohexital (Brevital), which is given intravenously in subanesthetic doses. Usually, up to 60 mg of the drug is given in divided doses in a session. Intravenous diazepam (Valium) may also be used cautiously. If the procedural details are carefully followed, almost all patients find the procedure pleasant, with few unpleasant side effects. The advantages of pharmacological desensitization are that preliminary training in relaxation can be shortened, almost all patients are able to become adequately relaxed, and the treatment itself seems to proceed more rapidly than without the drugs.

Indications

Systematic desensitization works best when there is a clearly identifiable anxiety-provoking stimulus. Phobias, obsessions, compulsions, and certain sexual disorders have been successfully treated with the technique.

GRADED EXPOSURE

Graded exposure is similar to systematic desensitization except that relaxation training is not involved and treatment is usually carried out in a real-life context.

FLOODING

Flooding is based on the premise that escaping from an anxiety-provoking experience reinforces the anxiety through conditioning. Thus, by not allowing the person to escape, the clinician can extinguish the anxiety and prevent the conditioned avoidance behavior.

The technique is to encourage the patient to confront the feared situation directly, without a gradual build-up as in systematic desensitization or graded exposure. No relaxation exercises are used, as in systematic desensitization. The patient experiences fear, which gradually subsides after a time. The success of the procedure depends on patients' remaining in the fear-generating situation until they are calm and feeling a sense of mastery. Prematurely withdrawing from the situation or prematurely terminating the fantasized scene is equivalent to an escape, which reinforces both the conditioned anxiety and the avoidance behavior, the opposite of what was intended. A variant of flooding is called *implosion*, in which the feared object or situation is confronted only in the imagination, rather than in real life. Many patients refuse flooding because of the psychological discomfort involved. It is also contraindicated in patients for whom intense anxiety would be hazardous (for example, patients with heart disease or fragile psychological adaptation). The technique works best with specific phobias.

PARTICIPANT MODELING

In participant modeling the patient learns by imitation. The patient learns a new behavior primarily by observation, without having to perform the behavior until the patient feels ready. Just as irrational fears may be acquired by learning, they can be unlearned by observing a fearless model confront the feared object. The technique has been useful with phobic children who are placed with other children of their own age and sex who approach the feared object or situation. With adults a therapist may describe the feared activity in a calm manner with which the patient can identify, or the therapist may act out with the patient the process of mastering the feared activity. Sometimes a hierarchy of activities is established, with the least anxiety-provoking activity being dealt with first. The participant-modeling technique has been used successfully with agoraphobia by having a therapist accompany the patient into the feared situation. A variant of the procedure is called *behavior rehearsal*, in which real-life problems are acted out under the therapist's observation or direction. The technique is useful for complex behavioral patterns, such as job interviews and shyness.

ASSERTIVENESS AND SOCIAL SKILLS TRAINING

To be assertive requires that persons have confidence in their judgment and sufficient self-esteem to express their opinions. Assertiveness and social skills training teaches people how to respond appropriately in social situations, to express their opinions in acceptable ways, and to achieve their goals. A variety of techniques—including role modeling, desensitization, and positive reinforcement (reward of desired behavior)—are used to increase assertiveness. Social skills training deals with assertiveness but also attends to a variety of real-life tasks, such as food shopping, looking for work, interacting with other people, and overcoming shyness.

AVERSION THERAPY

When a noxious stimulus (punishment) is presented immediately after a specific behavioral response, theoretically the response is eventually inhibited and extinguished. Many types of noxious stimuli are used: electric shocks, substances that induce vomiting, corporal punishment, and social disapproval. The negative stimulus is paired with the behavior, which is thereby suppressed. The unwanted behavior usually disappears after a series of such sequences. Aversion therapy has been used for alcohol abuse, paraphilias, and other behaviors with impulsive or compulsive qualities. Aversion therapy is controversial for many reasons. For example, punishment does not always lead to the expected decrease in response and can sometimes be positively reinforcing.

POSITIVE REINFORCEMENT

If a behavioral response is followed by a generally rewarding event—for example, food, avoidance of pain, or praise—it tends to be strengthened and to occur more frequently than before the reward. That principle has been applied in a variety of situations. On inpatient hospital wards, mental disorder patients have been rewarded for performing a desired behavior with tokens that they may use to purchase luxury items or certain privileges. The process has been successful in altering behavior and is known as a *token economy*. Some workers have suggested that psychotherapy is effective, in part, because patients want to please the therapist and so change their behavior to receive the therapist's praise. Sigmund Freud stated that, in treating phobias, the doctor needs to encourage the patient to face the phobia at some point determined by the positive relationship between the doctor and the patient.

RESULTS

Behavior therapy has been successful in a variety of disorders (Table 26.6–1) and can be easily taught. It requires less time than other therapies and is less expensive to administer. A limitation of the method is that it is useful for circumscribed

Table 26.6–1. Some Common Clinical Applications of Behavior Therapy

Disorder	Comments
Agoraphobia	Graded exposure and flooding can reduce the fear of being in crowded places. About 60 percent of patients so treated are improved. In some cases the spouse can serve as the model while accompanying the patient into the fear situation, however, the patient cannot get a secondary gain by keeping the spouse nearby and displaying symptoms.
Alcohol dependence	Aversion therapy in which the alcohol-dependent patient is made to vomit (by adding an emetic to the alcohol) every time a drink is ingested is effective in treating alcohol dependence. Disulfiram (Antabuse) can be given to alcohol-dependent patients when they are alcohol-free. Such patients are warned of the severe physiological consequences of drinking (e.g., nausea, vomiting, hypotension, collapse) with disulfiram in the system.
Anorexia nervosa	Observe eating behavior; contingency management; record weight.
Bulimia nervosa	Record bulimic episodes; log moods.
Hyperventilation	Hyperventilation test; controlled breathing; direct observation.
Other phobias	Systematic desensitization has been effective in treating phobias, such as fears of heights, animals, and flying. Social skills training has also been used for shyness and fear of other people.
Paraphilias	Electric shocks or other noxious stimuli can be applied at the time of a paraphilic impulse, and eventually the impulse subsides. Shocks can be administered by either the therapist or the patient. The results are satisfactory but must be reinforced at regular intervals.
Schizophrenia	The token economy procedure, in which tokens are awarded for desirable behavior and can be used to buy ward privileges, has been useful in treating inpatient schizophrenic patients. Social skills training teaches schizophrenic patients how to interact with others in a socially acceptable way so that negative feedback is eliminatedl. In addition, the aggressive behavior of some schizophrenic patients can be diminished through those methods.
Sexual dysfunctions	Dual-sex therapy, developed by William Masters and Virginia Johnson, is a behavior therapy technique used for various sexual dysfunctions, especially male erectile disorder, orgasm disorders, and premature ejaculation. It uses relaxation, desensitization, and graded exposure as the primary techniques.
Shy bladder	Inability to void in a public bathroom; relaxation exercises.
Type A behavior	Physiological assessment; muscle relaxation, biofeedback (on EMG)

behavioral symptoms, rather than for global areas of dysfunction (for example, neurotic conflicts, personality disorders). Analytically oriented theorists have criticized behavior therapy by saying that simple symptom removal may lead to symptom substitution. In other words, if symptoms are not viewed as consequences of inner conflicts and if the core cause of the symptoms is not addressed or altered, the result is the production of new symptoms. One interpretation of behavior theory is epitomized by Eysenck's controversial statement: ''Learning theory regards neurotic symptoms as simply learned habits; there is no neurosis underlying the symptoms, but merely the symptom itself. Get rid of the symptom and you have eliminated the neurosis.'' Some therapists believe that behavior therapy is an oversimplified approach to psychopathology and the complex interaction between therapist and patient. Symptom substitution may not be inevitable, but its possibility is an important consideration in the evaluation of behavior therapy's efficacy.

As with other forms of treatment, the patient's problems, motivation, and psychological strengths should be evaluated before instituting any behavior therapy approach.

References

Achenbach T M: Implications of multiaxial empirically based assessment for behavior therapy with children. Behav Ther 24: 91, 1993.
Agras W S: Behavior therapy. In Comprehensive Textbook of Psychiatry, ed 6, H I Kaplan, B J Sadock, editors, p 1788. Williams & Wilkins, Baltimore, 1995.
Collins F L, Thompson J K: The integration of empirically derived personality assessment data into behavioral conceptualization and treatment plan: Rationale, guidelines, and caveats. Behav Modif 17: 58, 1993.
Forehand R, Wierson M: The role of developmental factors in planning behavioral interventions for children: Disruptive behavior as an example. Behav Ther 24: 117, 1993.
Kellner R, Neidhardt J, Krakow B, Pathak D: Changes in chronic nightmares after one session of desensitization or rehearsal instructions. Am J Psychiatry 149: 659, 1992.
Kohlenberg R J, Tsai M, Kohlenberg B S: Functional analysis in behavior therapy. Prog Behav Modif 30: 1, 1996.
Wadden T A, Foster G D, Letizia K A: Response of obese binge eaters to treatment by behavior therapy combined with very low calorie diet. J Consult Clin Psychol 60: 808, 1992.
Woods D W, Miltenberger R G: Habit reversal: a review of applications and variations. J Behav Therapy Exp Psychiatry 26: 123, 1995.

26.7 HYPNOSIS

A pioneer in the field of clinical hypnotic induction, Milton Erickson, described the process of a clinical trance as ''a free period in which individuality can flourish.'' Martin Orne defined hypnosis as that state or condition in which a person is able to respond to appropriate suggestions by experiencing alterations of perceptions, memory, or mood. The essential feature of hypnosis is the subjective experiential change.

Hypnotherapists generally believe that clinical hypnosis and therapeutic trance are extensions of common processes inherent in everyday life. The experiences of daydreaming and inner preoccupation during which one goes through the motions of one's daily routine, seemingly automatically, are typical examples. During those periods, attention is spontaneously focused inward, just as in the clinical use of a trance state a patient is induced to be receptive to inner experiences. The primary view that hypnotherapists share with other psychotherapists is an appreciation and understanding of the dynamics of unconscious processes in behavior.

Hypnosis is a complex mental phenomenon that has been defined as a state of heightened focal concentration and receptivity to the suggestions of another person. It has also been called an altered state of consciousness, a dissociated state, and a stage of repression. However, there is no known psychophysiological basis for hypnosis, as there is for sleep, in which characteristic electroencephalogram (EEG) changes appear.

HISTORY

Modern hypnosis originated with the Austrian physician Friedrich Anton Mesmer (1734–1815), who believed the phenomenon, known as mesmerism, to be the result of animal magnetism or an invisible fluid that passes between the subject and the hypnotist. The term ''hypnosis'' originated in the 1840s with a Scottish physician, James Braid (1795–1860), who believed the subject to be in a particular state of sleep (*hypnos* is the Greek word for sleep). In the late 19th century the French neurologist Jean-Martin Charcot (1825–1893) thought hypnotism to be a special physiological state, and his contemporary Hippolyte-Marie Bernheim (1840–1919) believed it to be a psychological state of heightened suggestibility.

Sigmund Freud, who studied with Charcot, used hypnosis early in his career to help patients recover repressed memories. He noted that patients would relive traumatic events while under hypnosis, a process known as abreaction. Freud later replaced hypnosis with the technique of free association.

Today, hypnosis is a method that is used as a form of therapy (hypnotherapy), a method of investigation to recover lost memories, and a research tool.

HYPNOTIC CAPACITY AND INDUCTION

The therapist can use a number of specific procedures to help the patient be hypnotized and respond to suggestion. Those procedures involve capitalizing on some naturally occurring hypnosislike phenomena that have probably occurred in the life experiences of most patients. However, those experiences are rarely talked about; consequently, patients find them fascinating. For example, when discussing what hypnosis is like with a patient, the therapist may say: ''Have you ever had the experience of driving home while thinking about an issue that preoccupies you and suddenly realize that, although you have arrived safe and sound, you can't recall having driven past familiar landmarks? It's as if you had been asleep, and yet you stopped at all the red lights, and you avoided collisions. You were somehow traveling on automatic pilot.'' Most people resonate to that experience and are usually happy to describe similar personal experiences.

A discussion about experiences of that kind gives patients examples of hypnosislike episodes that they have probably had; thus, the patients realize that they have the capacity to use the hypnotic mode, as it is merely an extension of that kind of episode. Although the episodes were not necessarily hypnotic states, the extent to which a person experiences them is correlated with hypnotizability.

TRANCE STATE

Persons under hypnosis are said to be in a trance state, which may be light, medium, or heavy (deep). In a light trance there are changes in motor activity such that the person's muscles can feel relaxed, the hands can levitate, and paresthesia can be induced. A medium trance is characterized by diminished pain

sensation and partial or complete amnesia. A deep trance is associated with induced visual or auditory experiences and deep anesthesia. Time distortion occurs at all trance levels but is most profound in the deep trance.

Posthypnotic suggestion is characterized by the person's being instructed to perform a simple act or to experience a particular sensation after awakening from the trance state. It may be used to give a bad taste to cigarettes or a particular food, thus aiding in the treatment of nicotine dependence or obesity. Posthypnotic suggestions are associated with deep trance states.

HYPNOTHERAPY

The patient in a hypnotic trance can recall memories that are not available to consciousness in the nonhypnotic state. Such memories can be used in therapy to corroborate psychoanalytic hypotheses regarding the patient's dynamics or to enable the patient to use such memories as a catalyst for new associations. Some patients can experience age regression, during which they reexperience events that occurred at an earlier time in life. Whether the patient experiences the events as they actually occurred is controversial; however, the material elicited can be used to further the therapy. Patients in a trance state may describe an event with an intensity similar to that when it occurred (abreaction) and experience a sense of relief as a result. The trance state plays a role in the treatment of amnestic disorders and dissociative fugue, although the clinician should be aware that it may be hazardous to bring the repressed memory into consciousness quickly, as the patient may be overwhelmed by anxiety.

Indications and Uses

Hypnosis has been used, with varying degrees of success, to control obesity and substance-related disorders, such as alcohol abuse and nicotine dependence. It has been used to induce anesthesia, and major surgery has been performed with no anesthetic except hypnosis. It has also been used to manage chronic pain disorder, asthma, warts, pruritus, aphonia, and conversion disorder.

Relaxation can be achieved easily with hypnosis, so that patients may deal with phobias by controlling their anxiety. It has also been used to induce relaxation in systematic desensitization.

Contraindication

Hypnotized patients are in a state of atypical dependence on the therapist, and so a strong transference may develop, characterized by a positive attachment that must be respected and interpreted. In other instances a negative transference may erupt in patients who are fragile or who have difficulty in testing reality. Patients who have difficulty with basic trust, such as paranoid patients, or who have problems giving up control, such as obsessive-compulsive patients, are not good candidates for hypnosis. A secure ethical value system is important to all therapy and particularly to hypnotherapy, in which patients (especially those in a deep trance) are extremely suggestible and malleable. There is controversy about whether patients will perform acts during a trance state that they otherwise find repugnant or that run contrary to their moral code.

References

Barnier A J, McConkey K M: Reports of real and false memories: The relevance of hypnosis, hypnotizability, and context of memory test. J Abnorm Psychol *101*: 521, 1992.

Brown D: Pseudomemories: the standard of science and the standard of care in trauma treatment. Am J Clin Hypn *37*: 1, 1995.

Dywan J: The illusion of familiarity: an alternative to the report-criterion account of hypnotic recal. Int J Clin Exp Hypn *43*: 194, 1995.

Ganaway G K: Hypnosis, childhood trauma, and dissociative identity disorder: toward an integrative theory. Int J Clin Exp Hypn *43*: 127, 1995.

Kingsbury S J: Brief hypnotic treatment of repetitive nightmares. Am J Clin Hypn *35*: 161, 1993.

Miller M E, Bowers K S: Hypnotic analgesia: Dissociated experience or dissociated control? J Abnorm Psychol *102*: 29, 1993.

Orne M R, Dinges D P, Bloom P B: Hypnosis. In *Comprehensive Textbook of Psychiatry*, ed 6, H I Kaplan, B J Sadock, editors, p 1807. Williams & Wilkins, Baltimore, 1995.

Patterson D R, Everett J J, Burns G L, Marvin J A: Hypnosis for the treatment of burn pain. J Consult Clin Psychol *60*: 713, 1992.

Silva C E, Kirsch I: Interpretive sets, expectancy, fantasy proneness, and dissociation as predictors of hypnotic response. J Pers Soc Psychol *63*: 847, 1992.

26.8 COGNITIVE THERAPY

Cognitive therapy—according to its originator, Aaron Beck—is "based on an underlying theoretical rationale that an individual's affect and behavior are largely determined by the way in which he structures the world." A person's structuring of the world is based on cognitions (verbal or pictorial ideas available to consciousness), which are based on assumptions (schemas developed from previous experiences). According to Beck, if a person interprets all his experiences in terms of whether he is competent and adequate, his thinking may be dominated by the schema, "Unless I do everything perfectly, I'm a failure." Consequently, he reacts to situations in terms of adequacy even when they are unrelated to whether or not he is personally competent.

GENERAL CONSIDERATIONS

Cognitive therapy is a short-term structure therapy that uses active collaboration between the patient and the therapist to achieve the therapeutic goals. It is oriented toward current problems and their resolution. Therapy is usually conducted on an individual basis, although group methods are also used. Therapy may also be used in conjunction with drugs.

Cognitive therapy has been applied mainly to depressive disorders (with or without suicidal ideation); however, it is also used with other conditions, such as panic disorder, obsessive-compulsive disorder, paranoid personality disorder, and somatoform disorders. The treatment of depression can serve as a paradigm of the cognitive approach.

COGNITIVE THEORY OF DEPRESSION

The cognitive theory of depression holds that cognitive dysfunctions are the core of depression and that affective and physical changes and other associated features of depression are consequences of the cognitive dysfunctions. For example, apathy and low energy are results of a person's expectation of failure in all areas. Similarly, paralysis of will stems from a person's pessimism and feelings of hopelessness.

The cognitive triad of depression consists of (1) a negative self-percept that sees oneself as defective, inadequate, deprived, worthless, and undesirable, (2) a tendency to experience the world as a negative, demanding, and self-defeating place and to expect failure and punishment, and (3) the expectation of continued hardship, suffering, deprivation, and failure.

The goal of therapy is to alleviate depression and to prevent its recurrence by helping the patient (1) to identify and test negative cognitions, (2) to develop alternative and more flexible schemas, and (3) to rehearse both new cognitive responses and new behavioral responses. The goal is to change the way a person thinks and, subsequently, to alleviate the depressive disorder.

STRATEGIES AND TECHNIQUES

Overall, therapy is relatively short, lasting up to about 25 weeks. If the patient does not improve in that time, the diagnosis should be reevaluated. Maintenance therapy can be carried out over a period of years.

As with other psychotherapies, the therapists' attributes are important to successful therapy. The therapists must be able to exude warmth, understand the life experience of each patient, and be truly genuine and honest with themselves and with their patients. Therapists must be able to relate skillfully and interactively with their patients.

The cognitive therapist sets the agenda at the beginning of each session, assigns homework to be performed between sessions, and teaches new skills. The therapist and the patient actively collaborate. Cognitive therapy has three components: didactic aspects, cognitive techniques, and behavioral techniques.

Didactic Aspects

The didactic aspects include explaining to the patient the cognitive triad, schemas, and faulty logic. The therapist must tell the patient that they will formulate hypotheses together and test them over the course of the treatment. Cognitive therapy requires a full explanation of the relationship between depression and thinking, affect, and behavior, as well as the rationale for all aspects of the treatment. The explanation contrasts with the psychoanalytically oriented therapies, which require little explanation.

Cognitive Techniques

The cognitive approach includes four processes: (1) eliciting automatic thoughts, (2) testing automatic thoughts, (3) identifying maladaptive underlying assumptions, and (4) testing the validity of maladaptive assumptions.

ELICITING AUTOMATIC THOUGHTS

Automatic thoughts are cognitions that intervene between external events and the person's emotional reaction to the event. An example of an automatic thought is the belief that "everyone is going to laugh at me when they see how badly I bowl"—a thought that occurs to someone who has been asked to go bowling and responds negatively. Another example is a person's thought that "she doesn't like me" if someone passes the person in the hall without saying hello.

Automatic thoughts are also termed cognitive distortions. Every psychopathological disorder has its own specific cognitive profile of distorted thought, which, if known, provides a framework for specific cognitive interventions.

TESTING AUTOMATIC THOUGHTS

Acting as a teacher, the therapist helps the patient test the validity of automatic thoughts. The goal is to encourage patients to reject inaccurate or exaggerated automatic thoughts after careful examination.

Patients often blame themselves for things that go wrong that may well have been outside their control. The therapist reviews with the patient the entire situation and helps reattribute the blame or the cause of the unpleasant events. Generating alternative explanations for events is another way of undermining inaccurate and distorted automatic thoughts.

IDENTIFYING MALADAPTIVE ASSUMPTIONS

As the patient and the therapist continue to identify automatic thoughts, patterns usually become apparent. The patterns represent rules or maladaptive general assumptions that guide the patient's life. Samples of such rules are ''In order to be happy, I must be perfect'' and ''If anyone doesn't like me, I'm not lovable.'' Such rules inevitably lead to disappointments and failure and then to depression.

TESTING THE VALIDITY OF MALADAPTIVE ASSUMPTIONS

Similar to the testing of the validity of automatic thoughts is the testing of the accuracy of maladaptive assumptions. One particularly effective test is for the therapist to ask the patient to defend the validity of an assumption. For example, if a patient stated that he should always work up to his potential, the therapist might ask, ''Why is that so important to you?''

Behavioral Techniques

Behavioral techniques go hand in hand with cognitive techniques: Behavioral techniques are used to test and change maladaptive and inaccurate cognitions. The overall purposes of such techniques are to help the patients understand the inaccuracy of their cognitive assumptions and to learn new strategies and ways of dealing with issues.

Among the behavioral techniques used in therapy are scheduling activities, mastery and pleasure, graded task assignments, cognitive rehearsal, self-reliance training, role playing, and diversion techniques.

Among the first things done in therapy is to *schedule activities* on an hourly basis. A record of the activities is kept and reviewed with the therapist.

In addition to scheduling activities, patients are asked to rate the amount of *mastery and pleasure* their activities bring them. Patients are often surprised at how much more mastery and pleasure they get out of activities than they had otherwise believed.

To simplify the situation and to allow for miniaccomplishments, therapists often break tasks down into subtasks, as in *graded task assignments*, to demonstrate to patients that they can succeed.

Cognitive rehearsal has the patient imagine the various steps in meeting and mastering a challenge and rehearse the various aspects of it.

Patients, especially inpatients, are encouraged to become self-reliant by doing such simple things as making their own beds, doing their own shopping, and preparing their own meals, rather than relying on other people. That is known as *self-reliance training*.

Role playing is a particularly powerful and useful technique to elicit automatic thoughts and to learn new behaviors.

Diversion techniques are useful in helping patients get through particularly difficult times and include physical activity, social contact, work, play, and visual imagery.

Imagery is a phenomenon that affects behavior, as first discussed by Paul Schilder in his book *The Image and Appearance of the Human Body*, in which he described images as having physiological components. According to Schilder, *visualizing* oneself running activates subliminally the same muscles used in running, which can be measured with electromyography. That phenomenon is used in sports training, in which athletes visualize every conceivable event in a performance and develop a muscle memory for the activity. It can also be used to master anxiety or to deal with feared situations by combining behavioral and cognitive theories.

Impulsive or obsessive behavior has been treated with *thought stoppage*. For instance, patients imagine a stop sign with a police officer nearby or another image that evokes inhibition at the same time that they recognize an impulse or obsession that is alien to the ego. Similarly, obesity can be treated by having patients visualize themselves as thin, athletic, trim, and well-muscled and then training them to evoke that image whenever they have an urge to eat. Such imagery can be enhanced with hypnosis or autogenic training. In a technique called *guided imagery*, patients are encouraged to have fantasies that can be interpreted as wish fulfillments or attempts to master disturbing affects or impulses.

EFFICACY

Cognitive therapy can be used alone in the treatment of mild to moderate depressive disorders or in conjunction with antidepressant medication for major depressive disorder. Studies have clearly shown that cognitive therapy is effective and in some cases is superior or equal to medication alone. It is one of the most useful psychotherapeutic interventions currently available for depressive disorders and shows promise in the treatment of other disorders.

Cognitive therapy has also been studied in relation to increasing compliance with lithium (Eskalith) in bipolar I disorder patients and as an adjunct in treating withdrawal from heroin.

References

Barlow D H: Cognitive-behavioral approaches to panic disorder and social phobia. Bull Menninger Clin *56* (2, Suppl A): *14*, 1992.

Beck A T, Rush A J: Cognitive therapy. In *Comprehensive Textbook of Psychiatry*, ed 6, H I Kaplan, B J Sadock, editors, p 1847. Williams & Wilkins, Baltimore, 1995.

Elliott C H, Adams R L, Hodge G K: Cognitive therapy: Possible strategies for optimizing outcome. Psychiatr Ann *34:* 459, 1992.

Epstein N, Baucom D H, Rankin L A: Treatment of marital conflict: A cognitive-behavioral approach. Clin Psychol Rev *13*: 45, 1993.

Garner D M, Rockert W, Davis R, Garner M V, et al: Comparison of cognitive-behavioral and supportive-expressive therapy for bulimia nervosa. Am J Psychiatry *150*: 37, 1993.

Hoffart A: Cognitive treatments of agoraphobia: A critical evaluation of theoretical basis and outcome evidence. J Anx Disord *7*: 75, 1993.

Kendall P C, Panichelli-Mindel S M: Cognitive-behavioral treatments. J Abnorm Child Psychol *23*: 107, 1995.

March J S: Cognitive-behavioral psychotherapy for children and adolescents with OCD: a review and recommendations for treatment. J Am Acad Child Adolesc Psychiatry *34*: 7, 1995.

Teasdale J D, Segal Z, Williams J M: How does cognitive therapy prevent depressive relapse and why should attentional control (mindfulness) training help? Behav Res Ther *33*: 25, 1995.

27/ Biological Therapies

27.1 GENERAL PRINCIPLES OF PSYCHOPHARMACOLOGY

Because the pharmacotherapy for mental disorders is one of the most rapidly evolving areas of clinical medicine, any practitioner who prescribes such drugs must remain current with the research literature. The key areas for regular update are the emergence of new agents—for example, risperidone (Risperdal), tacrine (Cognex), venlafaxine (Effexor)—new indications for existing agents—for example, valproate (Depakene)—the clinical usefulness of plasma concentrations, and the identification and treatment of drug-related adverse effects.

Because of incomplete knowledge regarding the brain and the disorders that affect it, the drug treatment of mental disorders is empirical. Nevertheless, many organic therapies have proved to be highly effective and constitute the treatment of choice for certain psychopathological conditions. Organic therapies form a key part of the armamentarium for the treatment of mental disorders.

The practice of pharmacotherapy in psychiatry should not be oversimplified—for example, a one diagnosis-one pill approach. Many variables impinge on the practice of psychopharmacology, including drug selection, prescription, administration, psychodynamic meaning to the patient, and family and environmental influences. Some patients may view a drug as a panacea, and other patients may view a drug as an assault. The nursing staff and relatives, as well as the patient, must be instructed regarding the reasons, the expected benefits, and the potential risks of pharmacotherapy. In addition, the clinician often finds it useful to explain the theoretical basis for pharmacotherapy to the patient, the patient's caretakers, and psychiatric staff members. Moreover, the theoretical biases of the treating psychiatrist are critical to the success of drug treatment, since psychiatrists prescribe pharmacotherapeutic drugs as a function of their theoretical beliefs about such treatments.

Drugs must be used in effective dosages for sufficient time periods, as determined by previous clinical investigations and personal experience. Subtherapeutic dosages and incomplete trials should not be given to a patient because the psychiatrist is excessively concerned about the development of adverse effects. Drugs for mental disorders must be prescribed by a qualified practitioner and require continuous clinical observation. Treatment response and the emergence of adverse effects must be monitored closely. The dosage of the drug should be adjusted accordingly, and appropriate treatments for emergent adverse effects must be instituted as quickly as possible.

PHARMACOLOGICAL ACTIONS

Pharmacokinetic interactions concern how the body handles a drug; pharmacodynamic interactions concern the effects of the drug on the body. In a parallel fashion, pharmacokinetic drug interactions concern the effects of drugs on the plasma concentrations of each other, and pharmacodynamic drug interactions concern the effects of drugs on the receptor activities of each other.

Pharmacokinetics

ABSORPTION

A psychotherapeutic drug must first reach the blood on its way to the brain, unless it is directly administered into the cerebrospinal fluid or the brain. Orally administered drugs must dissolve in the fluid of the gastrointestinal (GI) tract before the body can absorb them. Drug tablets can be designed to disintegrate quickly or slowly, the absorption depending on the drug's concentration and lipid solubility and the GI tract's local pH, motility, and surface area. Depending on the drug's pK_a and the GI tract's pH, the drug may be present in an ionized form that limits its lipid solubility. If the pharmacokinetic absorption factors are favorable, the drug may reach therapeutic blood concentrations quickly if it is administered intramuscularly. If a drug is coupled with an appropriate carrier molecule, intramuscular administration can sustain the drug's release over a long period of time. Some antipsychotic drugs are available in depot forms that allow the drug to be administered only once every one to four weeks. Even though intravenous administration is the quickest route to achieve therapeutic blood levels, it also carries the highest risk of sudden and life-threatening adverse effects.

DISTRIBUTION

Drugs can be freely dissolved in the blood plasma, bound to dissolved plasma proteins (primarily albumin), or dissolved within the blood cells. If a drug is bound too tightly to plasma proteins, it may have to be metabolized before it can leave the bloodstream, thus greatly reducing the amount of active drug reaching the brain. The lithium ion is an example of a water-soluble drug that is not bound to plasma proteins. The distribution of a drug to the brain is determined by the blood-brain barrier, the brain's regional blood flow, and the drug's affinity with its receptors in the brain. Both high blood flow and high affinity favor the distribution of the drug to the brain. Drugs may also reach the brain after passively diffusing into the cerebrospinal fluid from the bloodstream. The volume of distribution is a measure of the apparent space in the body available to contain the drug. The volume distribution can also vary with the patient's age, sex, and disease state.

METABOLISM AND EXCRETION

Metabolism is synonymous with the term ''biotransformation.'' The four major metabolic routes for drugs are oxidation, reduction, hydrolysis, and conjugation. Although the usual result of metabolism is to produce inactive metabolites that are more readily excreted than are the parent compounds, many examples of active metabolites are produced from psychoactive drugs. The liver is the principal site of metabolism, and bile, feces, and urine are the major routes of excretion. Psychoactive drugs are also excreted in sweat, saliva, tears, and breast milk; therefore, mothers who are taking psychotherapeutic drugs should not breastfeed their children. Disease states and coadministered drugs can both raise and lower the blood concentrations of a psychoactive drug.

Four concepts regarding metabolism and excretion are time

of peak plasma level, half-life, first-pass effect, and clearance. The time between the administration of a drug and the appearance of peak concentrations of the drug in the plasma varies primarily according to the route of administration and absorption. A drug's half-life is defined as the amount of time it takes for half of the drug's peak plasma level to be metabolized and excreted from the body. A general guideline is that, if a drug is administered repeatedly in doses separated by time intervals shorter than its half-life, the drug will reach 97 percent of its steady-state plasma concentrations in a time equal to five times its half-life. The first-pass effects concern the extensive initial metabolism of some drugs within the portal circulation of the liver, thereby reducing the amount of unmetabolized drug that reaches the systemic circulation. Clearance is a measure of the amount of the drug excreted in each unit of time. If some disease process or other drug interferes with the clearance of a psychoactive drug, the drug accumulates in the patient and may reach toxic plasma concentrations.

An increasingly important area of consideration is the specific isoform of the hepatic cytochrome P_{450} (CYP) enzyme that is involved in the metabolism of any drug. In particular, there is a genetic heterogeneity in CYP2D6 that puts some individuals at risk for developing high drug levels of drugs that are metabolized by the enzyme, especially when two drugs metabolized in CYP2D6 are taken concurrently by a person with genetically low CYP2D6 activity.

Pharmacodynamics

The major pharmacodynamic considerations include receptor mechanisms; the dose-response curve; the therapeutic index; and the development of tolerance, dependence, and withdrawal phenomena. The receptor for a drug can be defined generally as the cellular component that binds to the drug and initiates the drug's pharmacodynamic effects. A drug can be an agonist for its receptor, thereby stimulating a physiological effect; conversely, a drug can be an antagonist for the receptor, most often by blocking the receptor so that an endogenous agonist cannot affect the receptor. The receptor site for most psychotherapeutic drugs is also a receptor site for an endogenous neurotransmitter. For example, the primary receptor site for chlorpromazine (Thorazine) is the dopamine type 2 (D_2) receptor. However, for other psychotherapeutic drugs, that may not be the case. The receptor for lithium may be the enzyme inositol-1-phosphatase, and the receptor for verapamil (Calan) is a calcium channel.

The dose-response curve plots the drug concentration against the effects of the drug. The potency of a drug is the relative dose required to achieve a certain effect. Haloperidol (Haldol), for example, is more potent than is chlorpromazine because about 5 mg of haloperidol is required to achieve the same therapeutic effect as 100 mg of chlorpromazine. However, haloperidol and chlorpromazine are equal in their clinical efficacy—that is, the maximum clinical response achievable by the administration of a drug.

The side effects of most drugs are often direct results of their primary pharmacodynamic effects and are conceptualized as adverse effects. The therapeutic index is a relative measure of a drug's toxicity or safety. It is defined as the ratio of the median toxic dose (TD_{50}) to the median effective dose (ED_{50}). The TD_{50} is the dose at which 50 percent of patients experience toxic effects, and the ED_{50} is the dose at which 50 percent of

patients experience therapeutic effects. Haloperidol, for example, has a high therapeutic index, as evidenced by the wide range of dosages in which it is prescribed. Conversely, lithium has a low therapeutic index, thereby requiring the monitoring of serum lithium levels. A specific drug can produce both interindividual and intraindividual variation in response. An individual patient may be hyporeactive, normally reactive, or hyperreactive to a particular drug. For example, some patients require 150 mg a day of imipramine, whereas other patients require 300 mg a day. Idiosyncratic drug responses occur when a patient experiences a particularly unusual effect from a drug. For example, some patients become agitated when given benzodiazepines, such as diazepam (Valium).

A patient may become less responsive to a particular drug as it is administered over time, which is referred to as tolerance. The development of tolerance can be associated with the appearance of physical dependence, which may be defined as the necessity to continue administering the drug to prevent the appearance of withdrawal symptoms.

CLINICAL GUIDELINES

The practice of clinical psychopharmacology requires skill as both a diagnostician and a psychotherapist, knowledge of the available drugs, and the ability to plan a pharmacotherapeutic regimen. The selection and the initiation of drug treatment should be based on the patient's history, the patient's current clinical state, and the treatment plan. The psychiatrist should know the purpose or the goal of a drug trial, the length of time that the drug needs to be administered to assess its efficacy, the approach to be taken to reduce any adverse effects that may occur, alternative drug strategies should the current one fail, and whether long-term maintenance of the patient on the drug is indicated. In almost all cases the psychiatrist should explain the treatment plan to the patient and often to the family and other caretakers. The patient's reaction to and ideas about a proposed drug trial should be considered. However, if the psychiatrist believes that accommodating the patient's wishes would hinder treatment, that should also be explained to the patient.

Choice of Drug

The first two steps in selecting drug treatment, the diagnosis and the identification of the target symptoms, should ideally be carried out when the patient has been in a drug-free state for one to two weeks. The drug-free state should include the absence of medications for sleep, such as hypnotics, as the quality of sleep can be both an important diagnostic guide and a target symptom. However, if a patient is hospitalized, insurance guidelines may make a drug-free period difficult or even impossible to obtain. Psychiatrists often evaluate symptomatic patients who are already receiving one or more psychoactive medications, and so it is usually necessary to wean the patient from the current medication and then to make an assessment. An exception to that practice occurs when a patient is taking a suboptimal dosage of an otherwise appropriate drug. In such cases the psychiatrist may decide to continue the drug at a higher dosage to complete a full therapeutic trial.

From among the drugs appropriate to a particular diagnosis, the specific drug should be selected according to the patient's history of drug response (compliance, therapeutic response, and adverse effects), the patient's family history of drug response, the profile of adverse effects for that drug with regard to a particular patient, and the psychiatrist's usual practice. If a drug has previously been effective in treating a patient or a family member, the same drug should be used again unless there is some specific reason not to use the drug. A history of severe adverse effects from a specific drug is a strong indicator that the patient would not comply with that drug regimen. Patients and their families are often ignorant about what drugs have been used before, in what dosages, and for how long. That ignorance may reflect the tendency of psychiatrists not to explain drug trials to their patients. Psychiatrists should consider giving their patients written records of drug trials for their personal medical records. A caveat to obtaining a history of drug response from patients is that, because of their mental disorders, they may inaccurately report the effects of a previous drug trial. If possible, therefore, the patients' medical records should be obtained to confirm their reports. Most psychotherapeutic drugs of a single class are equally efficacious; however, the drugs do differ in their adverse effects on individual patients. A drug should be selected that minimally exacerbates any preexisting medical problems with a particular patient.

NONAPPROVED DOSAGES AND USES

Under the federal Food, Drug, and Cosmetic (FDC) Act, the Food and Drug Administration (FDA) has authority to control the initial availability of a drug by approving only those new drugs that demonstrate both safety and effectiveness and then to ensure that the drug's proposed labeling is truthful and contains all pertinent information for the safe and effective use of that drug. An additional level of government regulation is directed by the Drug Enforcement Agency (DEA), which has classified drugs according to their abuse potential. Clinicians are advised to exercise increased caution when prescribing controlled substances.

According to Medical Liability Mutual Insurance Company, once a drug is approved for commercial use, the physician may, as part of the practice of medicine, lawfully prescribe a different dosage for a patient or otherwise vary the conditions of use from what is approved in the package labeling without notifying the FDA or obtaining its approval. Specifically, the FDC Act does not limit the manner in which a physician may use an approved drug. However, although physicians may treat patients with an approved drug for unapproved purposes—that is, indications not included on the drug's official labeling—without violating the FDC Act, the patient's right to redress for possible medical malpractice remains. That is a significant concern, because the failure to follow the FDA-approved label may lead to an inference that the physician was varying from the prevailing standard of care. Although the failure to follow the contents of the drug label does not impose liability per se and should not preclude a physician from using good clinical judgment in the interest of the patient, the physician should be aware that the drug label presents important information regarding the safe and effective use of the drug.

When using a drug for an unapproved indication or in a dosage outside the usual range, the physician should document the reason for those treatment decisions in the patient's chart. If clinicians are in doubt about a treatment plan, they should consult a colleague or suggest that the patient obtain a second opinion.

THERAPEUTIC TRIALS

A drug's therapeutic trial should last for a previously determined length of time. Because behavioral symptoms are more difficult to assess than are other physiological symptoms, such as hypertension, it is particularly important for specific target symptoms to be identified at the initiation of a drug trial. The psychiatrist and the patient can then assess the target symptom over the course of the drug trial to help determine whether the drug has been effective. A number of objective rating scales, such as the Brief Psychiatric Rating Scale (BPRS) and the Hamilton Rating Scale for Depression (HAM-D), are available to help assess a patient's progress over the course of a drug trial. If a drug has not been effective in reducing target symptoms within the specified length of time and if other reasons for the lack of response can be eliminated, the drug should be tapered and stopped. The brain is not a group of on-off neurochemical switches; rather, it is an interactive network of neurons in a complex homeostasis. Thus, the abrupt discontinuation of virtually any psychoactive drug is likely to disrupt the brain's functioning. Another common clinical mistake is the routine addition of medications without the discontinuation of a prior drug. Although that practice is indicated in specific circumstances, such as lithium potentiation of an unsuccessful trial of antidepressants, it often results in increased noncompliance and adverse effects and the clinician's not knowing whether it was the second drug alone or the combination of drugs that resulted in a therapeutic success or adverse effect.

THERAPEUTIC FAILURES

The failure of a specific drug trial should prompt the clinician to reconsider a number of possibilities. First, was the original diagnosis correct? That reconsideration should include the possibility of an undiagnosed cognitive disorder, including illicit drug abuse. Second, are the observed remaining symptoms the drug's adverse effects and not related to the original disease? Antipsychotic drugs, for example, can produce akinesia, which resembles psychotic withdrawal; akathisia and neuroleptic malignant syndrome resemble increased psychotic agitation. Third, was the drug administered in sufficient dosage for an appropriate period of time? Patients can have varying drug absorption and metabolic rates for the same drug, and plasma drug levels should be obtained to assess that variable. Fourth, did a pharmacokinetic or pharmacodynamic interaction with another drug the patient was taking reduce the efficacy of the psychotherapeutic drug? Fifth, did the patient take the drug as directed? Drug noncompliance is a common clinical problem. The reasons for drug noncompliance include complicated drug regimens (more than one drug in more than one daily dose), adverse side effects (especially if unnoticed by the clinician), and poor patient education about the drug treatment plan.

Combined Psychotherapy and Pharmacotherapy

Using drugs that effect the brain in combination with psychotherapy is one of the fastest growing practices in contemporary psychiatry. In that therapeutic approach, individual or group therapy is combined with pharmacological therapy. It should not be a system in which the therapist meets with the patient occasionally or irregularly to monitor the effects of medication or to make notations on a rating scale to assess progress and adverse effects; rather, it should be a system in which both therapies are integrated and synergistic. In many cases the results of combined therapy are superior to either type of therapy used alone. The term ''pharmacotherapy-oriented psychotherapy'' is used by some practitioners for the combined approach. The methods of psychotherapy used can vary, and all can be combined with pharmacotherapy.

Countertransference

As in all types of psychotherapy, psychiatrists must be aware of their conscious and unconscious feelings toward their patients, known as countertransference. Similarly, psychiatrists must be aware of their own psychological attitudes toward drugs. Medications cannot replace the therapeutic alliance. They are not a shortcut to cure and are no substitute for the intense concentration and involvement on the part of the psychiatrist who is conducting psychotherapy. Therapists who are pessimistic about the value of psychotherapy or who misjudge the patient's motivation may prescribe medications out of their own nihilistic beliefs. Others may withhold medication if they overvalue psychotherapy or devalue pharmacological agents. Withholding medication is most likely to occur with borderline personality disorder patients, suicidal patients, and patients with a history of substance abuse. Each case must be evaluated individually, and the risk-benefit ratio must be carefully assessed so that the patient is not punished, deprived, or mistreated.

SPECIAL TREATMENT CONSIDERATIONS

Children

Special care must be given when administering psychotherapeutic drugs to children. Although the small volume of distribution suggests the use of lower dosages than in adults, children's higher rate of metabolism indicates that higher ratios of milligrams of drug to kilograms of body weight should be used. In practice, it is best to begin with a small dose and to increase the dosage until clinical effects are observed (see Table 43.4–1). The clinician, however, should not hesitate to use adult dosages in children if the dosages are effective and the side effects are acceptable.

Geriatric Patients

The two major concerns when treating geriatric patients with psychotherapeutic drugs are that elderly persons may be especially susceptible to adverse effects (particularly cardiac effects) and may metabolize drugs slowly, thus requiring low dosages of medication. Another concern is that geriatric patients are often taking other medications, thereby requiring the psychiatrist to consider the possible drug interactions. In practice, psychiatrists should begin treating geriatric patients with a small dose, usually about one half the usual dose. The dosage should be raised in small amounts more slowly than in middle-aged adults until either a clinical benefit is achieved or unacceptable adverse effects appear. Although many geriatric patients require a small dosage of medication, many others require the usual adult dosage.

Pregnant and Nursing Women

The basic rule is to avoid administering any drug to a woman who is pregnant (particularly during the first trimester) or who is breast-feeding a child. That rule, however, occasionally needs to be broken when the mother's mental disorder is severe. If psychotherapeutic medications need to be administered during a pregnancy, the possibility of therapeutic abortion should be discussed. The two most teratogenic drugs in the psychopharmacopeia are lithium (Eskalith) and anticonvulsants. Lithium administration during pregnancy is associated with a high incidence of birth abnormalities, including Ebstein's anomaly, a serious abnormality in cardiac development. Other psychoactive drugs (antidepressants, antipsychotics, and anxiolytics), although less clearly associated with birth defects, should also be avoided during pregnancy if at all possible. The most common clinical situation is a pregnant woman who becomes psychotic. If a decision is made not to terminate the pregnancy, antipsychotics or electroconvulsive therapy (ECT) is preferable to lithium.

The administration of psychotherapeutic drugs at or near delivery may cause the baby to be overly sedated at delivery, requiring a respirator, or to be physically dependent on the drug, requiring detoxification and the treatment of a withdrawal syndrome. Virtually all psychotropic drugs are secreted in the milk of a nursing mother; therefore, mothers taking those agents should not breast-feed their infants.

Medically Ill Patients

Considerations in administering psychotropic drugs to medically ill patients include a potentially increased sensitivity to the drug's adverse effects, either increased or decreased metabolism and excretion of the drug, and interactions with other medications. As with children and geriatric patients, the most reasonable clinical practice is to begin with a small dose, increase it slowly, and watch for both clinical and adverse effects. The testing of plasma drug levels may be particularly helpful in those patients.

ADVERSE EFFECTS

Most psychotherapeutic drugs do not affect a single neurotransmitter system, nor are their effects localized to the brain. Psychotherapeutic drugs result in a wide range of adverse effects on neurotransmitter systems. For example, some of the most common adverse effects of psychotherapeutic drugs are caused by the blockade of muscarinic acetylcholine receptors. Several other commonly observed adverse effects involve neurotransmitters that have not been specifically identified.

Patients generally have less trouble with adverse effects if they have been told to expect them. The psychiatrist can explain the appearance of adverse effects as evidence that the drug is working. But clinicians should distinguish between probable or expected adverse effects and rare or unexpected adverse effects.

Treatment of Common Adverse Effects

Many adverse effects are seen with psychotherapeutic drugs. The management of the adverse effects is similar, regardless of which psychotherapeutic drug the patient is taking.

DRY MOUTH

Dry mouth is caused by the blockade of muscarinic acetylcholine receptors. When patients attempt to relieve the dry mouth by constantly sucking on sugar-containing hard candies, they increase their risk for dental caries. They can avoid the problem by chewing sugarless gum or sucking on sugarless hard candies. Some clinicians recommend the use of a 1 percent solution of pilocarpine (Salagen), a cholinergic agonist, as a mouth wash three times daily. Other clinicians suggest bethanechol (Urecholine, Myotonachol) tablets, another cholinergic agonist, 10 to 30 mg, once or twice daily. It is best to start with 10 mg once a day and to increase the dosage slowly. Adverse effects of cholinomimetic drugs, such as bethanechol, include tremor, diarrhea, abdominal cramps, and excessive eye watering.

BLURRED VISION

The blockage of muscarinic acetylcholine receptors causes mydriasis (pupillary dilation) and cycloplegia (ciliary muscle paresis), resulting in presbyopia (blurred near vision). The symptom can be relieved by cholinomimetic eyedrops. A 1 percent solution of pilocarpine can be prescribed as one drop four times daily. As an alternative, bethanechol can be used as it is used for dry mouth.

URINARY RETENTION

The anticholinergic activity of many psychotropic drugs can lead to urinary hesitation, dribbling, urinary retention, and increased urinary tract infections. Elderly persons with enlarged prostates are at increased risk for those adverse effects. Ten to 30 mg of bethanechol three to four times daily is usually effective in the treatment of the adverse effects.

CONSTIPATION

The anticholinergic activity of psychotropic drugs can result in the particularly disturbing adverse effect of constipation. The first line of treatment involves the prescribing of bulk laxatives, such as Metamucil and Fiberall. If that treatment fails, cathartic laxatives, such as milk of magnesia, can be tried. Prolonged use of cathartic laxatives can result in a loss of their effectiveness. Bethanechol, 10 to 30 mg three to four times daily, can also be used.

ORTHOSTATIC HYPOTENSION

Orthostatic hypotension is caused by the blockade of α_1-adrenergic receptors. The psychiatrist should warn patients of that possible adverse effect, particularly if the patient is elderly. The risk of hip fractures from falls is significantly elevated in patients who are taking psychotropic drugs. With patients at high risk for orthostatic hypotension, the clinician should choose a drug with low α_1-adrenergic activity. Most simply, the patient can be instructed to get up slowly and to sit down immediately if dizziness is experienced. The patient can also try support hose to help reduce venous pooling. Specific adjuvant medications have been recommended for specific pharmacotherapeutic drugs.

SEXUAL DYSFUNCTION

Psychotropic drug use can be associated with sexual dysfunctions—decreased libido, impaired ejaculation and erection, and inhibition of female orgasm. Warning a patient about those adverse effects may increase the patient's concern. Alternatively, patients are not likely to report adverse sexual effects spontaneously to the physician. Also, some sexual dysfunctions may be related to the primary mental disorder. Nevertheless, if sexual dysfunctions emerge after pharmacotherapy has begun, it may be worthwhile to treat them. Neostigmine (Prostigmin), 7.5 to 15 mg orally 30 minutes before sexual intercourse, may help alleviate impaired ejaculation. Impaired erectile function may be helped with bethanechol given regularly or possibly yohimbine (Yocon). Cyproheptadine (Periactin), 4 mg every morning, can be used for the treatment of inhibited female orgasm; 4 to 8 mg orally can be taken one to two hours before anticipated sexual activity for the treatment of inhibited male orgasm secondary to serotonergic agents.

WEIGHT GAIN

Weight gain accompanies the use of many psychotropic drugs. The weight gain can be the result of retained fluid, increased caloric intake, or decreased exercise. Edema can be treated by elevating the affected body parts or by administering a thiazide diuretic. If the patient is taking lithium or cardiac medications, the clinician must monitor blood levels, blood chemistries, and vital signs. The patient should also be instructed to minimize the intake of fats and carbohydrates and to exercise regularly. However, if the patient has not been exercising, the clinician should recommend that the patient start an exercise program at a modest level of exertion.

Overdoses

An extreme adverse effect of drug treatment is an attempt by a patient to commit suicide by overdosing on a psychotherapeutic drug. One psychodynamic theory of such behavior is that the patients are angry at their therapists for not having been able to help them. Whatever the motivation, psychiatrists should be aware of the risk and attempt to prescribe the safest possible drugs. It is good clinical practice to write nonrefillable prescriptions for small quantities of drugs when suicide is a consideration. In extreme cases, an attempt should be made to verify that patients are taking the medication and not hoarding the pills for a later overdose attempt. Patients may attempt suicide just as they are beginning to get better. Clinicians, therefore, should continue to be careful about prescribing large quantities of medication until the patient is almost completely recovered. Another consideration for psychiatrists is the possibility of an accidental overdose, particularly by children in the household. Patients should be advised to keep psychotherapeutic medications in a safe place.

References

Baldessarini R J: Enhancing treatment with psychotropic medicines. Bull Menninger Clin 58: 224, 1994.

Grebb J A: General principles of psychopharmacology. In Comprehensive Textbook of Psychiatry, ed 6, H I Kaplan, B J Sadock, editors, p 1895. Williams & Wilkins, Baltimore, 1995.

Rush A J, Prien R F: From scientific knowledge to the clinical practice of psychopharmacology: can the gap be bridged? Psychopharmacol Bull 31: 7, 1995.

Schmidt L G: Neurobiology of psychotropic drugs: Modes of action and therapeutic efficacy. Pharmacopsychiatry 27 (Suppl, 1): 2, 1994.

Spina E, Caputi A P: Pharmacogenetic aspects in the metabolism of psychotropic drugs: Pharmacokinetic and clinical implications. Pharmacological Res 29: 121, 1994.

Stevens N G: Guidelines for the diagnosis and treatment of major depression. J Am Board Fam Pract 7: 49, 1994.

27.2 MEDICATION-INDUCED MOVEMENT DISORDERS

The fourth edition of *Diagnostic and Statistical Manual of Mental Disorders* (DSM-IV) introduces a new diagnostic category, "medication-induced movement disorders." In reality, however, the category includes not only medication-induced movement disorders but also any medication-induced adverse effect that becomes a focus of clinical attention. When one of the diagnoses is made and included as a focus of treatment, the movement disorder or adverse effect diagnosis should be listed on Axis I of the DSM-IV multiaxial diagnostic formulation.

The advent of the diagnostic category recognizes the fact that many, if not most, of the pharmacological therapies available to treat mental disorders can cause adverse effects that themselves may require the formulation of a specific treatment plan. The most common of the adverse effects are the movement disorders related to the dopamine receptor antagonists, which are also referred to as neuroleptics and antipsychotics. However, the term "antipsychotics" also includes drugs that are seldom associated with the production of movement disorders—for example, clozapine (Clozaril).

In addition to providing a systematized and standardized diagnosis for the drug-induced movement disorders and adverse effects, the formalization of the diagnoses encourages the clinician to consider the differential diagnoses for those symptoms. For example, anxiety needs to be distinguished from akathisia, catatonia from neuroleptic malignant syndrome, parkinsonism from depression, and tardive dyskinesia from other basal ganglia-related movement disorders.

The extrapyramidal system is that part of the central nervous system (CNS) motor control system that is outside the pyramidal system, which includes the cortical motor areas and the spinal pyramidal tracts. The major component of the extrapyramidal system is the group of nuclei collectively known as the basal ganglia. The key symptoms of medication-induced movement disorders are those of parkinsonism (tremor, rigidity, and bradykinesia), dystonia, akathisia, and tardive dyskinesia. The pathophysiology of neuroleptic malignant syndrome is not completely understood, but it may involve the basal ganglia, although its symptoms also involve nonmotor symptoms (for example, autonomic instability). The common mechanism of many of the disorders includes some involvement with the dopamine type 2 (D_2) receptor antagonism by that class of antipsychotic drugs. The association between D_2 blockade and the extrapyramidal system is not straightforward, as indicated by the lack of an immediate and direct temporal association between the administration of the drugs and the appearance of the various symptom patterns, which occur at different times after the administration of dopamine receptor antagonists.

NEUROLEPTIC-INDUCED MOVEMENT DISORDERS

The most common neuroleptic-related movement disorders are parkinsonism, acute dystonia, and acute akathisia. Neuroleptic malignant syndrome is a life-threatening and often misdiagnosed condition. Neuroleptic-induced tardive dyskinesia is a late-appearing adverse effect of neuroleptic drugs and can be irreversible; however, recent data indicate that the syndrome, although still serious and potentially disabling, is less pernicious than was previously thought.

Neuroleptic-Induced Parkinsonism

Neuroleptic-induced parkinsonism is characterized principally by the triad of a tremor that is most pronounced at rest, rigidity, and bradykinesia (Table 27.2–1). Rigidity is a disorder of muscle tone—that is, the degree of tension in the muscles. Disorders of tone can result in either hypertonia (that is, rigidity) or hypotonia. The hypertonia associated with neuroleptic-induced parkinsonism is of either the lead-pipe type or the cogwheel type, two terms that are descriptive of the subjective impression of the affected limbs or joints. The syndrome of bradykinesia can include the masklike facial appearance of the patient, the decreased accessory arm movements while the patient is walking, and a characteristic difficulty in initiating movement. The so-called rabbit syndrome is a tremor affecting the lips and the perioral muscles; it is most commonly thought to be part of the syndrome of neuroleptic-induced parkinsonism, although it often appears later in treatment than do other symptoms. The pathophysiology of neuroleptic-induced parkinsonism involves the blockade of D_2 receptors in the caudate at the termination of the nigrostriatal dopamine neurons, the same neurons that degenerate in idiopathic Parkinson's disease. Patients who are elderly and female are at the highest risk for neuroleptic-induced parkinsonism.

Table 27.2–1. Diagnostic and Research Criteria for Neuroleptic-Induced Parkinsonism

Parkinsonian tremor, muscular rigidity or akinesia developing within a few weeks of starting or raising the dose of a neuroleptic medication (or after reducing a medication used to treat extrapyramidal symptoms).

A. One (or more) of the following signs or symptoms has developed in association with the use of neuroleptic medication:

    (1) parkinsonian tremor (i.e., a coarse, rhythmic, resting tremor with a frequency between 3 and 6 cycles per second, affecting the limbs, head, mouth, or tongue)

    (2) parkinsonian muscular rigidity (i.e., cogwheel rigidity or continuous "lead-pipe" rigidity)

    (3) akinesia (i.e., a decrease in spontaneous facial expressions, gestures, speech, or body movements)

B. The symptoms in criterion A developed within a few weeks of starting or raising the dose of a neuroleptic medication, or of reducing medication used to treat (or prevent) acute extrapyramidal symptoms (e.g., anticholinergic agents).

C. The symptoms in criterion A are not better accounted for by a mental disorder (e.g., catatonic or negative symptoms in schizophrenia, psychomotor retardation in a major depressive episode). Evidence that the symptoms are better accounted for by a mental disorder might include the following: the symptoms precede the exposure to neuroleptic medication or are not compatible with the pattern of pharmacologic intervention (e.g., no improvement after lowering the neuroleptic dose or administering anticholinergic medication).

D. The symptoms in criterion A are not due to a nonneuroleptic substance or to a neurological or other general medical condition (e.g., Parkinson's disease, Wilson's disease). Evidence that the symptoms are due to a general medical condition might include the following: the symptoms precede exposure to neuroleptic medication, unexplained focal neurological signs are present, or the symptoms progress despite a stable medication regimen.

Table from DSM-IV, *Diagnostic and Statistical Manual of Mental Disorders*, ed 4. Copyright American Psychiatric Association, Washington, 1994. Used with permission.

TREATMENT

The benefits and the risks of prophylactic treatment with anti-extrapyramidal system medications—for example, anticholinergics and amantadine (Symmetral, Symadine) or antihistamines—continue to be debated. However, once parkinsonian symptoms do appear, the three steps in treatment are to reduce the dosage of the neuroleptic, institute antiextrapyramidal system medications, and possibly change the neuroleptic. A poorly understood phenomenon is the common development of tolerance to the parkinsonian adverse effects of those drugs. Once treatment is initiated, therefore, the clinician should attempt to reduce or stop the antiextrapyramidal system medications after 14 to 21 days of treatment to assess whether the medications continue to be necessary.

Neuroleptic Malignant Syndrome

Neuroleptic malignant syndrome is a life-threatening complication of antipsychotic treatment and can occur anytime during the course of treatment (Table 27.2–2). The symptoms include muscular rigidity and dystonia (hence the classification of the disorder as a movement disorder), akinesia, mutism, obtundation, and agitation. The autonomic symptoms include high fever, sweating, and increased blood pressure and heart rate. In addition to supportive medical treatment, the most commonly used medications for the condition are dantrolene (Dantrium) and bromocriptine (Parlodel), although amantadine is sometimes used.

Neuroleptic-Induced Acute Dystonia

Dystonias are brief or prolonged contractions of muscles, usually resulting in obviously abnormal movements or postures,

Table 27.2–2. Diagnostic and Research Criteria for Neuroleptic Malignant Syndrome

Severe muscle rigidity, elevated temperature, and other related findings (e.g., diaphoresis, dysphagia, incontinence, changes in level of consciousness ranging from confusion to coma, mutism, elevated or labile blood pressure, elevated creatine phosphokinase (CPK)) developing in association with the use of neuroleptic medication.

A. The development of severe muscle rigidity and elevated temperature associated with the use of neuroleptic medication.

B. Two (or more) of the following:

   (1) diaphoresis
   (2) dysphagia
   (3) tremor
   (4) incontinence
   (5) changes in level of consciousness ranging from confusion to coma
   (6) mutism
   (7) tachycardia
   (8) elevated or labile blood pressure
   (9) leucocytosis
   (10) laboratory evidence of muscle injury (e.g., elevated CPK)

C. The symptoms in criteria A and B are not due to another substance (e.g., phencyclidine) or a neurological or other general medical condition (e.g., viral encephalitis).

D. The symptoms in criteria A and B are not better accounted for by a mental disorder (e.g., mood disorder with catatonic features).

Table from DSM-IV, *Diagnostic and Statistical Manual of Mental Disorders*, ed 4. Copyright American Psychiatric Association, Washington, 1994. Used with permission.

Table 27.2–3. Diagnostic and Research Criteria for Neuroleptic-Induced Acute Dystonia

Abnormal positioning or spasm of the muscles of the head, neck, limbs, or trunk developing within a few days of starting or raising the dose of a neuroleptic medication (or after reducing a medication used to treat extrapyramidal symptoms).

A. One (or more) of the following signs or symptoms has developed in association with the use of neuroleptic medication:

   (1) abnormal positioning of the head and neck in relation to the body (e.g., retrocollis, torticollis)
   (2) spasms of the jaw muscles (trismus, gaping, grimacing)
   (3) impaired swallowing (dysphagia), speaking, or breathing (laryngeal-pharyngeal spasm, dysphonia)
   (4) thickened or slurred speech due to hypertonic or enlarged tongue (dysarthria, macroglossia)
   (5) tongue protrusion or tongue dysfunction
   (6) eyes deviated up, down, or sideward (oculogyric crisis)
   (7) abnormal positioning of the distal limbs or trunk

B. The signs or symptoms in criterion A developed within seven days of starting or rapidly raising the dose of neuroleptic medication, or of reducing a medication used to treat (or prevent) acute extrapyramidal symptoms (e.g., anticholinergic agents).

C. The symptoms in criterion A are not better accounted for by a mental disorder (e.g., catatonic symptoms in schizophrenia). Evidence that the symptoms are better accounted for by a mental disorder might include the following: the symptoms precede the exposure to neuroleptic medication or are not compatible with the pattern of pharmacologic intervention (e.g., no improvement after neuroleptic lowering or anticholinergic administration).

D. The symptoms in criterion A are not due to a nonneuroleptic substance or to a neurological or other general medical condition. Evidence that the symptoms are due to general medical condition might include the following: the symptoms precede the exposure to the neuroleptic medication, unexplained focal neurological signs are present, or the symptoms progress in the absence of change in medication.

Table from DSM-IV, *Diagnostic and Statistical Manual of Mental Disorders*, ed 4. Copyright American Psychiatric Association, Washington, 1994. Used with permission.

including oculogyric crises, tongue protrusion, trismus, torticollis, laryngeal-pharyngeal dystonias, and dystonic postures of the limbs and the trunk (Table 27.2–3). The development of dystonic symptoms is characterized by their early onset during the course of treatment with neuroleptics and their high incidence in men, in patients under age 30, and in patients given high dosages of high-potency medications. The pathophysiological mechanism for dystonias is not clearly understood, although changes in neuroleptic concentrations and the resulting changes in homeostatic mechanisms within the basal ganglia may be the major causes of dystonias.

TREATMENT

Treatment of dystonias should be immediate, most commonly with anticholinergic or antihistaminergic drugs. If a patient fails to respond to three doses of those drugs within two hours, the clinician should consider a cause of the dystonic movements other than neuroleptic medications.

Neuroleptic-Induced Acute Akathisia

Akathisia is characterized by the subjective feelings of restlessness or the objective signs of restlessness or both. Examples include a sense of anxiety, an inability to relax, jitteriness, pacing, rocking motions while sitting, and the rapid alternation

Table 27.2–4.   Diagnostic and Research Criteria for Neuroleptic-Induced Acute Akathisia

Subjective complaints of restlessness accompanied by observed movements (e.g., fidgety movements of the legs, rocking from foot to foot, pacing, or inability to sit or stand still) developing within a few weeks of starting or raising the dose of a neuroleptic medication (or reducing medication used to treat extrapyramidal symptoms).

A. The development of subjective complaints of restlessness after exposure to a neuroleptic medication.

B. At least one of the following observed:

   (1) fidgety movements or swinging of the legs
   (2) rocking from foot to foot while standing
   (3) pacing to relieve restlessness
   (4) inability to sit or stand for at least several minutes

C. The onset of the symptoms in criteria A and B occur within four weeks of initiating or increasing the dose of the neuroleptic, or of reducing medication used to treat (or prevent) acute extrapyramidal symptoms (e.g., anticholinergic agents).

D. The symptoms in criterion A are not better accounted for by a mental disorder (e.g., schizophrenia, substance withdrawal, agitation from a major depressive or manic episode, hyperactivity in attention-deficit/hyperactivity disorder). Evidence that symptoms may be better accounted for by a mental disorder might include the following: the onset of symptoms preceding the exposure to the neuroleptics, the absence of increasing restlessness with increasing neuroleptic doses, and the absence of relief with pharmacological interventions (e.g., no improvement after decreasing the neuroleptic dose or treatment with medication intended to treat the akathisia).

E. The symptoms in criterion A are not due to a nonneuroleptic substance or to a neurological or other general medical condition. Evidence that symptoms are due to a general medical condition might include the onset of the symptoms preceding the exposure to neuroleptics or the progression of symptoms in the absence of a change in medication.

Table from DSM-IV, *Diagnostic and Statistical Manual of Mental Disorders*, ed 4. Copyright American Psychiatric Association, Washington, 1994. Used with permission.

Table 27.2–5.   Diagnostic and Research Criteria for Neuroleptic-Induced Tardive Dyskinesia

Involuntary choreiform, athetoid, or rhythmic movements (lasting at least a few weeks) of the tongue, jaw, or extremities developing in association with the use of neuroleptic medication for at least a few months (may be for a shorter period of time in elderly persons).

A. Involuntary movements of the tongue, jaw, trunk, or extremities have developed in association with the use of neuroleptic medication.

B. The involuntary movements are present over a period of at least four weeks, and occur in any of the following patterns:

   (1) chloreiform movements (i.e., rapid, jerky, nonrepetitive)
   (2) athetoid movements (i.e., slow, sinuous, continual)
   (3) rhythmic movements (i.e., stereotypies)

C. The signs or symptoms in criteria A and B develop during exposure to a neuroleptic medication or within 4 weeks of withdrawal from an oral (or within 8 weeks of withdrawal from a depot) neuroleptic medication.

D. There has been exposure to neuroleptic medication for at least three months (one month if age 60 or older).

E. The symptoms are not due to a neurological or general medical condition (e.g., Huntington's disease, Sydenham's chorea, spontaneous dyskinesia, hyperthyroidism, Wilson's disease); ill-fitting dentures; or exposure to other medications that cause acute reversible dyskinesia (e.g., L-dopa, bromocriptine). Evidence that the symptoms are due to one of these etiologies might include the following: the symptoms precede the exposure to the neuroleptic medication or unexplained focal neurological signs are present.

F. The symptoms are not better accounted for by a neuroleptic-induced acute movement disorder (e.g., neuroleptic-induced acute dystonia, neuroleptic-induced acute akathisia).

Table from DSM-IV, *Diagnostic and Statistical Manual of Mental Disorders*, ed 4. Copyright American Psychiatric Association, Washington, 1994. Used with permission.

of sitting and standing (Table 27.2–4). Akathisia can often be misdiagnosed as anxiety or as increased psychotic agitation. Middle-aged women are at increased risk of akathisia, and the time course of akathisia is similar to that for neuroleptic-induced parkinsonism.

TREATMENT

The three basic steps in the treatment of akathisia are to reduce the neuroleptic medication dosage, to attempt treatment with appropriate drugs, and to consider changing the neuroleptic. The most efficacious drugs in the treatment of akathisia are the β-adrenergic receptor antagonists, although the anticholinergic drugs and the benzodiazepines may also be useful in some cases. Patients may be less likely to experience akathisia on low-potency neuroleptics—for example, thioridazine (Mellaril)—than on high-potency neuroleptics—for example, haloperidol (Haldol); some of the new antipsychotics (for example, risperidone [Risperdal]) may be associated with a low incidence of akathisia.

Neuroleptic-Induced Tardive Dyskinesia

Neuroleptic-induced tardive dyskinesia is a late-appearing disorder of involuntary, choreoathetoid movements (Table

27.2–5). The most common movements involve the orofacial region and choreoathetoid movements of the fingers and the toes. Athetoid movements of the head, the neck, and the hips are also present in seriously affected patients. In the most serious cases the patients may have irregularities in breathing and swallowing, resulting in aerophagia, belching, and grunting. The risk factors for tardive dyskinesia include long-term treatment with neuroleptics, increasing age, female sex, the presence of a mood disorder, and the presence of a cognitive disorder. Although various treatments for tardive dyskinesia have not been successful, the course of tardive dyskinesia is considered less relentless than was previously thought. A recent alternative for such patients is to be treated with one of the new antipsychotics that may be little associated with the development of tardive dyskinesia (for example, clozapine and risperidone).

MEDICATION-INDUCED POSTURAL TREMOR

Tremor is defined as a rhythmical alteration in movement that is usually faster than one beat a second (Table 27.2–6). Typically, tremors decrease during periods of relaxation and sleep and increase during periods of anger and increased tension. Those characteristics sometimes mistakenly lead inexperienced clinicians to assume that the patient is faking the tremor. Whereas all the above DSM-IV diagnoses specifically include an association with neuroleptics, DSM-IV acknowledges that a range of psychiatric medications can produce tremor—most notably lithium (Eskalith), antidepressants, and valproate (De-

Table 27.2–6. Diagnostic and Research Criteria for Medication-Induced Postural Tremor

Fine tremor occurring during attempts to maintain a posture and developing in association with the use of medication (e.g., lithium, antidepressants, valproate).

A. A fine postural tremor that has developed in association with the use of a medication (e.g., lithium, antidepressants, valproic acid).

B. The tremor (i.e., a regular, rhythmic oscillation of the limbs, head, mouth, or tongue) has a frequency between 8 and 12 cycles per second.

C. The symptoms are not due to a pre-existing nonpharmacologically-induced tremor. Evidence that the symptoms are due to a pre-existing tremor might include the following: the tremor was present prior to the introduction of the medication, the tremor does not correlate with serum levels of the medication, and the tremor persists after discontinuation of the medication.

D. The symptoms are not better accounted for by neuroleptic-induced parkinsonism.

Table from DSM-IV, *Diagnostic and Statistical Manual of Mental Disorders*, ed 4. Copyright American Psychiatric Association, Washington, 1994. Used with permission.

Table 27.2–7. Drug-Induced Movement Disorders

Syndrome	Drugs Responsible	
Postural tremor	Sympathomimetics	+ +
	Levodopa	+ +
	Amphetamines	+ +
	Bronchodilators	+ +
	Tricyclic drugs	+ +
	Lithium carbonate	+ +
	Caffeine	+ +
	Thyroid hormone	+ +
	Valproate	+ +
	APDs	+ +
	Hypoglycemic agents	+ +
	Adrenocorticosteroids	+ +
	Alcohol withdrawal	+ +
	Amiodarone	+
	Cyclosporin A	+
	MAOIs	+ +
Acute dystonic reactions	APDs	+ +
	Metoclopramide	+ +
	Antimalarial agents	+
	Tetrabenazine	+ / −
	Diphenhydramine	+ / −
	Mefenamic acid	+ / −
	Oxatomide	+ / −
	Tricyclic drugs	+ / −
	Flunarizone and cinnarizine	+ / −

Tonda M E, Guthrie S K: Treatment of acute neuroleptic-induced movement disorders. Pharmacotherapy *14*: 543, 1994.
Whitworth A B, Fleischhacker W W: Adverse effects of antipsychotic drugs. Int Clin Psychopharmacol 9: 21, 1995.

pakene)–although still other psychiatric medications are associated with the induction of tremor.

The treatment of tremor involves four general steps. First, the lowest possible dosage of the psychiatric drug should be used. Second, patients should minimize their caffeine consumption. Third, the psychiatric drug should be taken at bedtime to minimize the amount of daytime tremor. Fourth, β-adrenergic receptor antagonists can be given in the treatment of drug-induced tremors.

MEDICATION-INDUCED MOVEMENT DISORDER NOT OTHERWISE SPECIFIED

Although neuroleptics are the psychiatric drugs most commonly associated with movement disorders, almost all the most commonly used psychiatric drugs can produce movement disorders in some patients. Furthermore, many nonpsychiatric drugs can also produce movement disorders, and patients who are treated with both psychiatric and nonpsychiatric drugs may experience the additive effects of those medications with movement disorders. DSM-IV also defines the diagnostic category as including movement disorders other than those specified above. Such movement disorders include tardive dystonia and tardive parkinsonism. Table 27.2±7 lists a number of movement disorders and the drugs that induce them.

ADVERSE EFFECTS OF MEDICATION NOT OTHERWISE SPECIFIED

This category allows clinicians to record the adverse effects of medications, other than movement symptoms, that become a focus of treatment. Examples of such adverse effects include priapism, severe hypotension, and cardiac abnormalities.

References

Blaisdell G D: Akathisia: A comprehensive review and treatment summary. Pharmacopsychiatry *27*: 139, 1994.
Comella C L, Goetz C G: Akathisia in Parkinson's disease. Mov Disord *9*: 545, 1994.
Grebb J A: Medication-induced movement disorders. In *Comprehensive Textbook of Psychiatry*, ed 6, H I Kaplan, B J Sadock, editors, p 1909. Williams & Wilkins, Baltimore, 1995.
Sachdev P, Kruk J: Clinical characteristics and predisposing factors in acute drug-induced akathisia. Arch Gen Psychiatry *51*: 963, 1994.

27.3 PSYCHOTHERAPEUTIC DRUGS

27.3.1 β-ADRENERGIC RECEPTOR ANTAGONISTS

The β-adrenergic receptor antagonists, which are variously referred to as β-blockers and β-antagonists, are commonly used in medical practice for the treatment of hypertension, angina, and certain cardiac arrhythmias, but the drugs are also used for the treatment of glaucoma, migraine, and the symptoms of hyperthyroidism. Although the drugs are not officially approved for use in psychiatric indications, their effectiveness has been well demonstrated for social phobia (for example, performance anxiety), lithium-induced postural tremor, and neuroleptic-induced acute akathisia. Preliminary research regarding their use in other psychiatric conditions has also been reported and is described below (Table 27.3.1±1).

THERAPEUTIC INDICATIONS

Although the β-adrenergic receptor antagonists have been studied for use in many mental disorders and medication-induced movement disorders, the use of the β-adrenergic receptor antagonists is best supported for social phobia, lithium-induced postural tremor, and neuroleptic-induced acute akathisia. The data on the use of those drugs as adjuncts to benzodiazepines for alcohol withdrawal and for the control of impulsive aggression or violence are also promising.

Social Phobia

Propranolol has been well-studied for the treatment of social phobia, primarily of the performance type (for example, disa-

Table 27.3.1-1.   β-Adrenergic Drugs Used in Psychiatry

Generic Name	Trade Name	Lipophilic	Metabolism	Receptor Selectivity	Half-Life (hrs)	Usual Starting Dose (mg)	Usual Maximal Dose (mg)
Atenolol	Tenormin	No	Renal	β_1	6–9	50 once a day	50–100 once a day
Metoprolol	Lopressor	Yes	Hepatic	β_1	3–4	50 twice a day	75–150 twice a day
Nadolol	Corgard	No	Renal	β_1–β_2	14–24	40 once a day	80–240 once a day
Pindolol	Visken	Yes	Hepatic anel renal	β_1–β_2	3–4	5 twice a day	20 three times a day
Propranolol	Inderal	Yes	Hepatic	β_1–β_2	3–6	10–20 two or three times a day	80–140 three times a day

bling anxiety before a musical performance). Although the beneficial effects probably result primarily from the reduction of the sympathetic peripheral manifestations of anxiety (for example, tremor, sweating, and tachycardia), the blocking of central nervous system β-adrenergic receptors may be of some additional benefit. However, studies of the least lipophilic β-adrenergic receptor antagonists have also shown them to be of benefit for that indication. A common treatment approach is to have the patient take 10 to 40 mg of propranolol (Inderal) 20 to 30 minutes before the anxiety-provoking situation. Patients may try a test run of the β-adrenergic antagonist before using it before an anxiety-provoking situation to be sure that they do not experience any adverse effects from the drug or the dosage.

Lithium-Induced Postural Tremor

Lithium-induced postural tremor is perhaps the most common of the medication-induced postural tremors. Although most of the studies of the β-adrenergic receptor antagonists for medication-induced postural tremor have been conducted for lithium-induced postural tremor, a β-adrenergic receptor antagonist would probably also be beneficial in other medication-induced postural tremors—for example, induced by tricyclic drugs and valproate (Depakene). Propranolol in the range of 20 to 160 mg a day, given two or three times daily, is generally effective for the treatment of lithium-induced postural tremor. Some studies have found that the least lipophilic β-adrenergic receptor antagonists are also effective, although other studies have reported that those drugs are not as effective as propranolol.

Neuroleptic-Induced Acute Akathisia

Neuroleptic-induced acute akathisia is recognized in the fourth edition of *Diagnostic and Statistical Manual of Mental Disorders* (DSM-IV) as one of the medication-induced movement disorders. Many studies have shown that β-adrenergic receptor antagonists can be effective in the treatment of neuroleptic-induced acute akathisia. The majority of clinicians and researchers believe that β-adrenergic receptor antagonists are more effective for that indication than are anticholinergics and benzodiazepines, although the relative efficacy of those agents may vary among patients. However, the clinician must realize that the β-adrenergic receptor antagonists are not effective in the treatment of such neuroleptic-induced movement disorders as acute dystonia and parkinsonism. Propranolol is the drug that has been most studied for neuroleptic-induced acute akathisia, and at least one study has reported that a less lipophilic compound was not effective in the treatment of the disorder.

Aggression and Violent Behavior

A number of studies have shown that β-adrenergic receptor antagonists may be effective in reducing the number of aggres-

sive and violent outbursts in patients with impulse disorders, schizophrenia, and aggression associated with brain injuries, such as trauma, tumors, anoxic injury, encephalitis, alcohol dependence, and degenerative disorders (for example, Huntington's disease). Many of those studies have added a β-adrenergic receptor antagonist to the ongoing therapy (for example, antipsychotics, anticonvulsants, lithium); therefore, it is difficult to distinguish additive effects from independent effects. Nevertheless, about 50 percent of all patients studied in various trials showed a clinically significant reduction in their aggressive and violent symptoms after the addition of a β-adrenergic receptor antagonist. Many controlled and anecdotal reports indicate that high doses of β-adrenergic receptor antagonists, sometimes up to a gram of propranolol, were used.

Alcohol Withdrawal

Propranolol has been reported to be useful as an adjuvant to benzodiazepines but not as a sole agent in the treatment of alcohol withdrawal. One study used the following dose schedule: no propranolol for a pulse less than 50; 50 mg propranolol for a pulse between 50 and 79; and 100 mg propranolol for a pulse equal to or greater than 80. The patients who received propranolol and benzodiazepines had less severe withdrawal symptoms, more stable vital signs, and a shorter hospital stay than did the patients who received only benzodiazepines.

Other Disorders

A number of case reports and controlled studies have reported data indicating that β-adrenergic receptor antagonists may benefit patients with generalized anxiety disorder, schizophrenia, and manic symptoms. The efficacy of β-adrenergic receptor antagonists in generalized anxiety disorder may be due to their reducing the autonomic symptoms that are associated with the disorder. The clinician must be cognizant of the possibility that the β-adrenergic receptor antagonists induce depression in some patients. The data regarding the effectiveness of β-adrenergic receptor antagonists in schizophrenia and mania are not robust, although a trial of the medications may be warranted under extreme or research situations.

PRECAUTIONS AND ADVERSE REACTIONS

The β-adrenergic receptor antagonists are contraindicated for use in patients with asthma, insulin-dependent diabetes, congestive heart failure, significant vascular disease, persistent angina, and hyperthyroidism. The contraindication in diabetic patients is due to the drugs' antagonizing the normal physiological response to hypoglycemia. The β-adrenergic receptor antagonists can worsen atrioventricular (A-V) conduction defects and lead to complete A-V heart block and death. If the clinician decides that the risk-benefit ratio warrants a trial of a β-adrenergic receptor antagonist in a patient with one of those coexisting medical conditions, a β_1-selective agent should probably be the first choice.

The most common adverse effects of β-adrenergic receptor antagonists are hypotension and bradycardia. In patients at risk for those adverse effects, a test dosage of 20 mg a day of propranolol can be given to assess the patient's reaction to the drug. Depression has been associated with lipophilic β-adrenergic receptor antagonists, such as propranolol, but it is probably rare. Nausea, vomiting, diarrhea, and constipation may also be caused by treatment with those agents. Serious central nervous system (CNS) adverse effects (for example, agitation, confusion, and hallucinations) are rare.

DRUG INTERACTIONS

A number of studies have found that concomitant administration of propranolol has resulted in increases in plasma concentrations of antipsychotics, theophylline (Primatene), and thyroxine (T_4). The plasma concentrations of antiepileptics would probably be affected similarly. Other β-adrenergic receptor antagonists possibly have similar effects. The β-adrenergic receptor antagonists that are eliminated by the kidneys may have similar effects on drugs that are also eliminated by the renal route. When there is a possibility of a drug-drug interaction, the plasma concentrations of the involved drugs should be monitored whenever possible. Barbiturates increase the elimination of β-adrenergic receptor antagonists that are metabolized by the liver. Several reports have associated hypertensive crises and bradycardia with the coadministration of β-adrenergic receptor antagonists and monoamine oxidase inhibitors. Patients on those two types of drugs should be treated with low dosages of both drugs and should have their blood pressure and pulse rates monitored regularly.

DOSAGE AND ADMINISTRATION

Since some β-adrenergic receptor antagonists act peripherally and others act both peripherally and centrally, peripherally acting drugs may be safer than the drugs that act both centrally and peripherally, especially with regard to such CNS side effects as depression, lassitude, and changes in sleep patterns. The problem with the data is that for most indications it remains unclear whether the peripherally acting drugs (that is, those that are least lipophilic) are as effective as the most lipophilic drugs.

For the treatment of chronic disorders, propranolol is usually initiated at 10 mg by mouth three times a day or 20 mg by mouth twice daily. The dosage can be raised by 20 to 30 mg a day until a therapeutic effect begins to emerge. The dosage should be leveled off at the appropriate range for the disorder under treatment. The treatment of aggressive behavior sometimes requires dosages up to 800 mg a day, and therapeutic effects may not be seen until the patient has been receiving the maximal dosage for four to eight weeks.

The patient's pulse and blood pressure readings should be taken regularly, and the drug should be withheld if the patient's pulse is less than 50 or the patient's systolic blood pressure is less than 90. The drug should be temporarily withheld if the patient has severe dizziness, ataxia, or wheezing. Treatment

with β-adrenergic receptor antagonists should never be discontinued abruptly. Propranolol should be tapered by 60 mg a day until a dosage of 60 mg a day is reached, after which the drug should be tapered by 10 to 20 mg a day every three or four days.

References

Arana G W, Santos A B: β-Adrenergic receptor antagonists. In *Comprehensive Textbook of Psychiatry*, ed 6, H I Kaplan, B J Sadock, editors, p 1915. Williams & Wilkins, Baltimore, 1995.
Eisele G, Gilmore L L, Blanchard E B: Close clinical observation minimized the complications of beta-blocker withdrawal. Ann Pharmacother 28: 849, 1994.
Gottlieb L D, Horwitz R I, Kraus M L, Segal S R, et al: Randomized controlled trial in alcohol relapse prevention: Role of atenolol, alcohol craving, and treatment adherence. J Subst Abuse Treat 11: 253, 1994.
Lang C, Remington D: Treatment with propranolol of severe self-injurious behavior in a blind, deaf, retarded adolescent. J Am Acad Child Adolesc Psychiatry 33: 265, 1994.
Mazzola-Pomietto P, Azorin J M, Tramoni V, Jeanningros R: Relation between lymphocyte beta-adrenergic responsivity and the severity of depressive disorders. Biol Psychiatry 35: 920, 1994.
Schlager D S: Early-morning administration of short-acting beta blockers for treatment of winter depression. Am J Psychiatry 151: 1385, 1994.

27.3.2 ANTICHOLINERGICS AND AMANTADINE

In the clinical practice of psychiatry, the anticholinergic drugs and amantadine (Symmetrel, Symadine), like the antihistamines, are primarily used as treatments for medication-induced movement disorders, particularly neuroleptic-induced parkinsonism, neuroleptic-induced acute dystonia, and medication-induced postural tremor. The anticholinergic drugs and amantadine may also be of limited use in the treatment of neuroleptic-induced acute akathisia. Before the introduction of levodopa (Larodopa), the anticholinergic drugs were commonly used in the treatment of idiopathic Parkinson's disease. The antiparkinsonian effects of amantadine, which was initially developed as an antiviral compound, were initially discovered when its use improved the parkinsonian symptoms of a patient who was being treated with amantadine for influenza A2.

The common use of the term "anticholinergic drugs" is misleading. There are two general types of acetylcholine receptors, the muscarinic receptors and the nicotinic receptors. The muscarinic receptors are G protein-linked receptors, and the nicotinic receptors are ligand-gated ion channels. The anticholinergic drugs discussed in this subsection are specific for the muscarinic receptors and, therefore, are also referred to as antimuscarinic drugs. Another name used for the general class of drugs (that is, the antimuscarinic drugs, amantadine, and the antihistamines) used to treat the symptoms of medication-induced movement disorders is antiparkinsonian drugs.

THERAPEUTIC INDICATIONS

Neuroleptic-Induced Parkinsonism

The primary indication for the use of anticholinergics or amantadine in psychiatric practice is for the treatment of neuroleptic-induced parkinsonism, which, in the full clinical syndrome, is characterized by tremor, rigidity, cogwheeling, bradykinesia, sialorrhea, stooped posture, and festination. Akinesia and the so-called rabbit syndrome may be related to the characteristic parkinsonian symptoms. Neuroleptic-induced akinesia can sometimes be confused clinically with catatonic symptoms. Rabbit syndrome is characterized by a rhythmic, involuntary, approximately 5 Hz perioral tremor that resembles the masticatory movements of a rabbit. Neuroleptic-induced parkinsonism is most common in the elderly is most frequently seen with high-potency antipsychotics—for example, haloperidol (Haldol). Symptoms usually begin after two or three weeks of treatment.

All the available anticholinergics and amantadine are equally effective in the treatment of parkinsonian symptoms, although the efficacy of amantadine may diminish in some patients within the first month of treatment. Amantadine may be more effective than the anticholinergics in the treatment of rigidity and tremor. Amantadine may also be the drug of choice if a clinician does not want to add additional anticholinergic drugs to a patient's treatment regimen, particularly if a patient is taking an antipsychotic or an antidepressant with high anticholinergic activity—for example, chlorpromazine (Thorazine) or amitriptyline (Elavil)—or is elderly and, therefore, at risk for anticholinergic adverse effects.

Neuroleptic-Induced Acute Dystonia

Neuroleptic-induced acute dystonia is most common in young men. The syndrome often occurs early in the course of treatment and is commonly associated with high-potency antipsychotics (for example, haloperidol). The dystonia most commonly affects the muscles of the neck, the tongue, the face, and the back. Opisthotonos (involving the entire body) and oculogyric crises (involving the muscles of the eyes) are examples of specific dystonias. Dystonias are uncomfortable, sometimes painful, and often frightening to the patient. Although the onset is often sudden, onset in three to six hours may occur, often resulting in patients' complaining about having a thick tongue or difficulty in swallowing. Dystonic contractions can be powerful enough to dislocate joints, and laryngeal dystonias can result in suffocation if the patient is not treated immediately.

Anticholinergic drugs are effective both in the short-term treatment of dystonias and in prophylaxis against neuroleptic-induced acute dystonias. Prophylactic treatment may, in fact, be indicated in the treatment of young patients, particularly men. If anticholinergics are not effective or if a patient cannot tolerate anticholinergics, treatment with antihistamines (for example, diphenhydramine) or benzodiazepines (for example, lorazepam [Ativan]) may be effective. Amantadine is not generally considered as effective as the anticholinergics for the treatment of acute dystonias.

Neuroleptic-Induced Acute Akathisia

Akathisia is characterized by a subjective and objective sense of restlessness, anxiety, and agitation. Although a trial of anticholinergics or amantadine for the treatment of neuroleptic-induced acute akathisia is reasonable, those drugs are not generally considered the first drugs of choice for the syndrome. The β-adrenergic receptor antagonists and perhaps the benzodiazepines and clonidine (Catapres) are preferable as the drugs to try initially.

PRECAUTIONS AND ADVERSE REACTIONS

The adverse effects of the anticholinergic drugs are those resulting from the blockade of muscarinic acetylcholine recep-

tors. Anticholinergic drugs should be given cautiously, if at all, to patients with prostatic hypertrophy, urinary retention, and narrow-angle glaucoma because the antimuscarinic activity exacerbates those problems. The anticholinergics are occasionally used as drugs of abuse on the street and by patients. Their abuse potential is related to their mild mood-elevating properties.

Amantadine is generally well tolerated, especially in dosages below 200 mg a day; dosages above 400 mg a day should be avoided. Amantadine is generally better tolerated than the anticholinergics, and preliminary data indicate that amantadine is associated with less memory impairment than are the anticholinergics. The most common CNS effects of amantadine are mild dizziness, insomnia, and impaired concentration, which occur in 5 to 10 percent of all patients. Irritability, depression, anxiety, and ataxia occur in 1 to 5 percent of all patients. Severe CNS adverse effects, including seizures, have been reported. Nausea is the most common peripheral adverse effect of amantadine. Livedo reticularis, usually affecting the lower extremities, is seen in a few patients who are treated with amantadine for a long time. Amantadine is relatively contraindicated in patients with renal disease and seizure disorders. Some evidence indicates that amantadine is teratogenic and, therefore, should not be given to pregnant women. Because amantadine is excreted in breast milk, women who are breast-feeding should not be given the drug. Suicide attempts with amantadine overdoses are life-threatening. The symptoms can include toxic psychoses (confusion, hallucinations, and aggressiveness) and cardiopulmonary arrest. Emergency treatment beginning with gastric lavage or the induction of emesis is indicated.

Anticholinergic Intoxication

The most serious adverse effect associated with anticholinergic toxicity is anticholinergic intoxication, which can be characterized by delirium, coma, seizures, agitation, hallucinations, severe hypotension, supraventricular tachycardia, and the usual peripheral manifestations—flushing, mydriasis, dry skin, hyperthermia, and decreased bowel sounds. Treatment should begin with the immediate discontinuation of all anticholinergic drugs. The syndrome of anticholinergic intoxication can be diagnosed and treated with physostigmine (Antilirium), an inhibitor of anticholinesterase, 1 to 2 mg intravenously (IV) (1 mg every two minutes) or intramuscularly (IM) every 30 to 60 minutes, although the absorption of IM physostigmine can be erratic. The first dose should be repeated in 15 to 20 minutes if no improvement is seen. Benzodiazepines can be used to treat agitation. Treatment with physostigmine should be used only when emergency cardiac monitoring and life-support services are available, because physostigmine can lead to severe hypotension and bronchial constriction. Those effects of physostigmine can be reversed with rapid IV administration of atropine, 0.5 mg per each milligram of physostigmine administered. Physostigmine is also contraindicated in patients with unstable vital signs, asthma, or a history of cardiac abnormalities. In general, physostigmine should be used only to confirm a diagnosis of anticholinergic activity or to treat the most serious symptoms of anticholinergic intoxication—seizures, severe hypotension, and delirium.

DRUG INTERACTIONS

The most common drug-drug interactions with the anticholinergics occur when they are coadministered with psychotropics that also have high anticholinergic activity, such as most antipsychotics, tricyclic and tetracyclic drugs, and monoamine oxidase inhibitors (MAOIs). Elderly patients may be taking other medications that may also contribute significant anticholinergic activity. Many over-the-counter cold preparations also induce significant anticholinergic activity. The coadministration of those drugs can result in a life-threatening anticholinergic intoxication syndrome. Anticholinergic drugs can also delay gastric emptying, thereby decreasing the absorption of drugs that are broken down in the stomach and usually absorbed in the duodenum (for example, levodopa and antipsychotics). Coadministration of amantadine with anticholinergics may result in an increased incidence of cognitive impairment, confusion, nightmares, and psychotic symptoms (for example, hallucinations). That combination of drugs, therefore, should be used cautiously, especially in elderly patients.

In one case report, amantadine coadministered with phenelzine (Nardil) resulted in a significant increase in resting blood pressure. Because of the dopaminergic activity of amantadine, the drug may augment the stimulatory effects of CNS stimulant substances, such as cocaine and other sympathomimetics (for example, amphetamines).

DOSAGE AND ADMINISTRATION

Although the anticholinergic drugs and amantadine are the most commonly used drugs for the treatment of neuroleptic-induced parkinsonism and neuroleptic-induced acute dystonia, antihistamines and benzodiazepines are also effective. Amantadine and the six anticholinergic drugs discussed in this subsection are available in a range of preparations (Table 27.3.2–1).

Neuroleptic-Induced Parkinsonism

In addition to the use of antiparkinsonian drugs, the treatment of neuroleptic-induced parkinsonism can involve the reduction of the antipsychotic dosage or switching to a less potent antipsychotic. Both anticholinergics and amantadine are effective, as are antihistaminergic drugs. For the treatment of neuroleptic-induced parkinsonism, the equivalent of 1 to 4 mg benztropine (Cogentin) should be given one to four times daily. Patients usually respond to that dosage of benztropine in one or two days. When amantadine is used for the treatment of neuroleptic-induced parkinsonism, the starting dosage is usually 100 mg orally twice a day, although that dosage can be cautiously increased up to 200 mg orally twice a day if indicated. The anticholinergic drug or amantadine should be administered for four to eight weeks; then it should be discontinued to assess whether the patient still requires the drug. Anticholinergic drugs and amantadine should be tapered over a period of one to two weeks.

Treatment with anticholinergics or amantadine as prophylaxis against the development of neuroleptic-induced parkinsonism is usually not indicated, since the symptoms of neuroleptic-induced parkinsonism are usually mild enough and gradual enough in onset to allow the clinician to initiate treatment only after it is clearly indicated. However, in young men, prophylaxis may be indicated, especially if a high-potency antipsychotic is being used. The clinician should attempt to discontinue the antiparkinsonian agent in four to six weeks to assess whether its continued use is necessary.

Neuroleptic-Induced Acute Dystonia

Although anticholinergics are indicated for the short-term treatment and prophylaxis of neuroleptic-induced acute dystonia, amantadine is not considered effective. For the treatment of neuroleptic-induced acute dystonia, 1 to 2 mg benztropine or its equivalent in another drug should be given IM. If that dose is not effective in 20 to 30 minutes, the drug should be administered again. If the patient still does not improve in another 20 to 30 minutes, a benzodiazepine (for example, 1 mg IM or IV lorazepam) should be given. Laryngeal dystonia is a medical emergency and should be treated with benztropine, up to 4 mg in a 10-minute period, followed by 1 to 2 mg of lorazepam, administered slowly by the IV route.

Prophylaxis against dystonias is indicated in patients who have had one episode or in patients at high risk (young men taking high-potency antipsychotics). The clinician should continue prophylactic treatment for four to eight weeks and then gradually taper the drug over a period of one to two weeks to assess whether the prophylactic treatment should be continued. Whether prophylaxis with anticholinergics is indicated when first giving a patient an antipsychotic continues to be debated. Clinicians in favor of prophylaxis argue that patient compliance is hindered if uncomfortable neurological adverse effects occur. Clinicians opposed to prophylactic treatment cite the increased risk of anticholinergic toxicity. Studies have shown that prophylactic treatment with anticholinergic drugs does reduce the incidence of acute dystonias.

References

Arana G W, Santos A B: Anticholinergics and amantadine. In *Comprehensive Textbook of Psychiatry*, ed 6, H I Kaplan, B J Sadock, editors, p 1919. Williams & Wilkins, Baltimore, 1995.

Freudenreich O, McEvoy J P: Added amantadine may diminish tardive dyskinesia in patients requiring continued neuroleptics. J Clin Psychiatry 56: 173, 1995.

King G R, Joyner C M, Ellinwood E H: Continuous or intermittent cocaine administration: Effects of amantadine treatment during withdrawal. Pharmacol Biochem Behav 47: 451, 1994.

Kosten T R, Morgan C M, Falcione J, Schottenfeld R S: Pharmacotherapy for cocaine-abusing methadone-maintained patients using amantadine or desipramine. Arch Gen Psychiatry 40: 894, 1992.

Spine E Sturiale V, Valvo S, Ancione M, DiRosa A E, Meduri M, Caputi A P: Prevalence of acute dystonic reactions associated with neuroleptic treatment with and without anticholinergic prophylaxis. Int Clin Psychopharmacol 8: 21, 1993.

Tune L, Carr S, Hoag E, Cooper T: Anticholinergic effects of drugs commonly prescribed for the elderly: Potential means for assessing risk of delirium. Am J Psychiatry 149: 1393, 1992.

Table 27.3.2–1. Anticholinergic Drugs

Name	Tablet Size	Injectable
Benztropine mesylate	0.5, 1.2 mg	1 mg per mL
Biperiden hydrochloride (tab) luctate (inj)	2 mg	5 mg per mL
Ethopropazine hydrochloride	10, 50 mg	—
Procyclidine hydrochloride	5 mg	
Trihexyphenidyl hydrochloride	2, 5 mg elixir 2 mg per 5 mL	—
Orphenadrine citrate	100 mg	30 mg per mL

27.3.3 ANTIHISTAMINES

A group of drugs that block the histamine type 1 (H_1) receptor are used in clinical psychiatry for the treatment of neuroleptic-induced parkinsonism and neuroleptic-induced acute dystonia and as hypnotics and anxiolytics. Although the drugs are generally referred to as antihistamines, another class of antihistamines that block the histamine type 2 (H_2) receptor—for example, cimetidine (Tagamet)—are used for the treatment of gastric ulcer. Diphenhydramine (Benadryl) is used for the treatment of neuroleptic-induced parkinsonism and neuroleptic-induced acute dystonia and sometimes as a hypnotic. Hydroxyzine hydrochloride (Atarax) and hydroxyzine pamoate (Vistaril) are used as anxiolytics. Cyproheptadine (Periactin) has been used for the treatment of inhibited male and female orgasm caused by serotonergic agents, such as fluoxetine (Prozac).

THERAPEUTIC INDICATIONS

The most justified indication for the use of the antihistamines is as a treatment for neuroleptic-induced parkinsonism and neuroleptic-induced acute dystonia. The use of cyproheptadine for impaired orgasms is also reasonable. The availability of carefully investigated drugs (for example, benzodiazepines) for use as hypnotics and anxiolytics makes the routine use of antihistamines for those indications a questionable practice.

Neuroleptic-Induced Parkinsonism and Neuroleptic-Induced Acute Dystonia

The use of diphenhydramine is a reasonable alternative to anticholinergics and amantadine for neuroleptic-induced parkinsonism and neuroleptic-induced acute dystonia, especially in patients who are particularly sensitive to the adverse effects of the other drugs.

Hypnotic and Anxiolytic Applications

The antihistamines are relatively safe hypnotics, but they are not superior to the benzodiazepines, which are a much-better-studied class of drugs in terms of efficacy and safety. The antihistamines have not been proved to be effective as long-term anxiolytic therapy; therefore, either the benzodiazepines or buspirone (BuSpar) is preferable for such treatment.

Other Indications

A number of case reports have asserted that cyproheptadine (4 to 8 mg before coitus) is efficacious in the treatment of abnormal orgasm, especially abnormal orgasm resulting from treatment with serotonergic drugs (for example, fluoxetine). A number of case reports and small studies have also reported that cyproheptadine may be of some use in the treatment of eating disorders, such as anorexia nervosa.

PRECAUTIONS AND ADVERSE REACTIONS

Antihistamines are commonly associated with sedation, dizziness, and hypotension, all of which can be severe in elderly patients, who are also likely to suffer from the anticholinergic effects of those drugs. Paradoxical excitement and agitation is an adverse effect that is seen in a small proportion of patients. Poor motor coordination can result in accidents; therefore, patients should be warned about driving and operating dangerous machinery. Other common adverse effects include epigastric distress, nausea, vomiting, diarrhea, and constipation. Because of the drugs' mild anticholinergic activity, some patients experience dry mouth, urinary retention, blurred vision, and constipation. The use of cyproheptadine in some patients has been associated with weight gain, which may contribute to its reported efficacy in some patients with anorexia nervosa.

In addition to the above adverse effects, antihistamines have some potential for abuse by susceptible patients. The coadministration of antihistamines and opioids can increase the rush experienced by persons abusing those drugs. Also, overdoses of antihistamines can be fatal. Antihistamines are excreted in breast milk, so their use should be avoided by nursing mothers. Because of some potential for teratogenicity, the use of antihistamines should also be avoided by pregnant women.

DRUG INTERACTIONS

The sedative property of antihistamines can be additive with other central nervous system (CNS) depressants, such as alcohol, other sedative-hypnotic drugs, and many psychotropic drugs, including tricyclic drugs and monoamine oxidase (MAO) inhibitors. The anticholinergic activity can also be additive with other drugs producing anticholinergic effects, sometimes resulting in severe anticholinergic symptoms or intoxication.

LABORATORY INTERFERENCES

Hydroxyzine has been reported to falsely elevate the values of urinary 17-hydroxycorticosteroids when assayed with either the Poster-Silber chromogens test or the Glenn-Nelson test.

DOSAGE AND ADMINISTRATION

The antihistamines are available in a variety of preparations (Table 27.3.3–1). Diphenhydramine is used in the short-term and the long-term treatment of neuroleptic-induced parkinsonism and neuroleptic-induced acute dystonia. When the drug is used for intramuscular (IM) injections, it should be given deep, since superficial administration can cause local irritation. Short-term intravenous (IV) administration of 25 to 50 mg is an effective treatment for neuroleptic-induced acute dystonia. Treatment with 25 mg three times a day—up to 50 mg four times a day if necessary—can be used to treat neuroleptic-induced parkinsonism, akinesia, and rabbit syndrome. When diphenhydramine is used as a hypnotic, doses of 50 mg are recommended, since doses of 100 mg have not been shown to be superior to 50 mg.

Hydroxyzine is most commonly used as a short-term anxiolytic, although the data supporting that indication are limited. Dosages of 50 to 100 mg orally four times a day for long-term treatment or 50 to 100 mg every four to six hours for short-term treatment are usually recommended. However, recent studies have indicated that 150 mg a day is ineffective as an anxiolytic, although 400 mg a day may be as effective as chlordiazepoxide (Librium). Other studies have indicated that hydroxyzine is not useful as an anxiolytic in children and that it should be used for that indication with some caution.

Table 27.3.3-1. Antihistamine Preparations

Name	Tablets (mg)	Capsules (mg)	Elixir[1] (mg/5 mL)	Solution[2] (mg/5 mL)	Parenteral (mg/mL)	Suspension[3] (mg/5 mL)
Diphenhydramine	25, 50	25, 50	12.5	8.3, 12.5	10, 50	—
Hydroxyzine	10, 25, 50, 100	25, 50, 100	—	10	25, 50	25
Cyproheptadine	4	—	—	2	—	—

[1] A sweetened hydroalcoholic liquid intended for oral use.
[2] A drug incorporated into an aqueous or alcoholic solution.
[3] Undissolved drug dispersed in a liquid for oral or parenteral use.

References

Etzel J V: Diphenhydramine-induced acute dystonia. Pharmacotherapy *14*: 492, 1994.

Kutcher S P, Reiter S Gardner D M, Klwin R G: The pharmacotherapy of anxiety disorders in children and adolescents. Psychiatr Clin North Am *15*: 41, 1992.

Moss W, Ojukwu C, Chiriboga C A: Phenytoin-induced movement disorder. Unilateral presentation in a child and response to diphenhydramine. Clin Pediatr *33*: 634, 1994.

Tejera C A, Saravay S M, Goldman E, Gluck L: Diphenhydramine-induced delirium in elderly hospitalized patients with mild dementia. Psychosomatics *35*: 399, 1994.

Tharion W J, McMenemy D J, Rauch T M: Antihistamine effects on the central nervous system, cognitive performance and subjective states. Neuropsychobiology *29*: 97, 1994.

Uhde T W, Tancer M E: Antihistamines. In *Comprehensive Textbook of Psychiatry*, ed 6, H I Kaplan, B J Sadock, editors, p 1923. Williams & Wilkins, Baltimore, 1995.

27.3.4 BARBITURATES AND SIMILARLY ACTING DRUGS

BARBITURATES

The barbiturates were first introduced into clinical psychiatry in 1903 and were the sedative-hypnotic drugs of first choice until chlordiazepoxide (Librium) and other benzodiazepines were introduced in the early 1960s. The introduction of the benzodiazepines and other anxiolytics—for example, buspirone (BuSpar)—and hypnotics—for example, zolpidem (Ambien)—has practically eliminated the use of the barbiturates and other prebenzodiazepine-era compounds—for example, meprobamate (Miltown)—because of the lower abuse potential, higher therapeutic index, and lack of hepatic enzyme induction by the new compounds.

Therapeutic Indications

All the barbiturates were approved by the Food and Drug Administration (FDA) before the current rigorous guidelines for drug approval were instituted. Therefore, the FDA-approved indications for those drugs should be viewed with some caution. Nevertheless, the FDA has approved the use of amobarbital (Amytal), aprobarbital (Alurate), butabarbital (Butisol), mephobarbital (Mebaral), pentobarbital (Nembutal), phenobarbital (Luminal), and secobarbital (Seconal) for the treatment of anxiety and apprehension. However, there have been no carefully conducted clinical trials of those agents for diagnoses of anxiety specified by the revised third edition of *Diagnostic and Statistical Manual of Mental Disorders)* (DSM-III-R) or the fourth edition of DSM (DSM-IV). The FDA has approved the use of amobarbital, aprobarbital, butabarbital, pentobarbital, phenobarbital, and secobarbital for the treatment of insomnia. Methohexital (Brevital) is approved for use as an anesthetic agent for

Table 27.3.4-1. Pentobarbital Challenge Test

1. Give pentobarbital 200 mg orally.
2. Observe for intoxication after one hour (e.g., sleepiness, slurred speech, or nystagmus).
3. If patient is not intoxicated, give another 100 mg of pentobarbital every two hours (maximum 500 mg over six hours).
4. Total dose given to produce mild intoxication is equivalent to daily abuse level of barbiturates.
5. Substitute phenobarbital 30 mg (longer half-life) for each 100 mg of pentobarbital.
6. Decrease by about 10 percent a day.
7. Adjust rate if signs of intoxication or withdrawal are present.

electroconvulsive therapy (ECT), and amobarbital is approved for use in narcoanalysis, which includes the concept of drug-assisted interviewing.

Although the FDA guidelines approve of the wide application of the barbiturates, the availability of newer, safer, better-studied drugs reduced the number of reasonable applications of the barbiturates to nine circumstances: (1) Amobarbital (50 to 250 mg intramuscular [IM]) may be used in emergency settings to control agitation. However, the use of IM lorazepam (Ativan) or intravenous (IV) diazepam (Valium) is replacing that use because of the risk of laryngospasm and respiratory depression associated with the barbiturates. (2) Amobarbital interviews are sometimes used for diagnostic purposes. However, several studies have reported that other sedative drugs, particularly the benzodiazepines, are as effective as the barbiturates. (3) Several reports indicate that barbiturates can activate some catatonic patients, although benzodiazepines may also have that effect. (4) Barbiturate use may be indicated for patients in whom serious adverse effects are associated with the use of benzodiazepines or buspirone. (5) Some patients who do not respond adequately to benzodiazepines or buspirone may respond to barbiturates. (6) Some patients, particularly elderly patients, may have received barbiturates in the past and may insist on taking barbiturates currently, rather than switching to a benzodiazepine or buspirone. (7) Methohexital is a safe and effective anesthetic agent to use during ECT. (8) The pentobarbital challenge test (Table 27.3.4–1) is a safe and effective way to assess the degree of CNS tolerance for barbiturates once a patient's period of initial barbiturate intoxication has resolved. That test is particularly useful when the patient's history regarding the previously used daily dosage of barbiturates is unreliable. (9) Phenobarbital is the barbiturate of choice to be used when detoxifying a patient from barbiturate dependence.

Precautions and Adverse Reactions

Some of the adverse effects of the barbiturates are similar to those of the benzodiazepines, including paradoxical dysphoria, hyperactivity, and cognitive disorganization. Rare adverse effects associated with barbiturate use include the development of Stevens-Johnson syndrome (exfoliative dermatitis), megaloblastic anemia, and osteopenia.

A major difference between the barbiturates and the benzodiazepines is the low therapeutic index of the barbiturates, an overdose of which can easily prove fatal. In addition to narrow therapeutic indexes, the barbiturates are associated with a significant risk of abuse potential and the development of tolerance and dependence. That increased risk is reflected by the fact that the Drug Enforcement Agency (DEA) has classified most of the barbiturates as control level (schedule) II drugs; the benzodiazepines are classified as control level IV drugs. Barbiturate intoxication is manifested by confusion, drowsiness, irritability, hyporeflexia or areflexia, ataxia, and nystagmus. The symptoms of barbiturate withdrawal are similar to those of benzodiazepine withdrawal but are more marked.

Because of some evidence of teratogenicity, barbiturates should not be used by pregnant women or nursing women. Barbiturates should be used with caution in patients with a history of substance abuse, depression, diabetes, hepatic impairment, renal disease, severe anemia, pain, hyperthyroidism, or hypoadrenalism. Barbiturates are also contraindicated in patients with acute intermittent porphyria, impaired respiratory drive, or limited respiratory reserve.

Drug Interactions

The primary area for concern regarding drug interactions is the potentially additive effects of respiratory depression. Barbiturates should be used with great caution with other prescribed central nervous system (CNS) drugs (including antipsychotic and antidepressant drugs) and nonprescribed CNS agents (for example, alcohol). Caution must also be exercised when prescribing barbiturates to patients who are taking other drugs that are metabolized in the liver, especially cardiac drugs and anticonvulsants. Because individual patients have a wide range of sensitivities to barbiturate-induced enzyme induction, it is not possible to predict the degree to which the metabolism of concurrently administered medications will be affected. Drugs whose metabolism may be enhanced by barbiturate administration include narcotic analgesics, antiarrhythmic agents, antibiotics, anticoagulants, anticonvulsants, antidepressants, β-adrenergic receptor antagonists, contraceptives, and immunosuppressants.

Dosage and Administration

The dosages of barbiturates vary, and treatment should begin with low dosages that are increased to achieve a clinical effect.

Children and the elderly are more sensitive than are young adults to the effects of the barbiturates. The most commonly used barbiturates are available in a variety of dose forms (Table 27.3.4–2). Barbiturates with half-lives in the 15 to 40-hour range are preferable, because long-acting drugs tend to accumulate in the body. The clinician should clearly instruct the patient about the adverse effects and the potential for dependence associated with barbiturates.

Although plasma levels of barbiturates are rarely necessary in psychiatry, plasma monitoring of phenobarbital levels is standard practice when the drug is used as an anticonvulsant. The therapeutic blood concentrations for phenobarbital in that indication range from 15 to 40 mg/L, although some patients may experience significant adverse effects within that range.

OTHER SEDATIVE-HYPNOTICS

Chloral hydrate (Noctec) and four other classes of drugs—carbamates, piperidinediones, cyclic ethers, and tertiary carbinols—are still available for use as sedatives and hypnotics. Those drugs are even more rarely used than are barbiturates, because of their high abuse potential and additional toxic effects.

Chloral Hydrate

Chloral hydrate is one of the oldest sedative-hypnotic drugs still in use, having been used since 1869. It is now used only as a short-term (two- or three-day) hypnotic. Long-term treatment with chloral hydrate is associated with an increased incidence and severity of adverse effects (nausea, vomiting, diarrhea, residual daytime sedation, and impaired motor coordination). Tolerance develops to the hypnotic effects of chloral hydrate after two weeks of treatment. The major indication for chloral hydrate is insomnia.

Chloral hydrate is available in 250 and 500 mg capsules, 250 and 500 mg per 5 mL solutions, and 325, 500, and 650 mg rectal suppositories. The standard dose of chloral hydrate is 500 to 2,000 mg at bedtime. Because the drug is a GI irritant, it should be administered with excess water, milk, other liquids, or antacids to decrease the gastric irritation.

In addition to the development of tolerance, dependence on chloral hydrate can occur, with symptoms similar to those of alcohol dependence. The lethal dose of chloral hydrate is between 5,000 and 10,000 mg, thus making chloral hydrate a particularly poor choice for potentially suicidal patients. The lethality of chloral hydrate is potentiated by other CNS depressants, including alcohol. Chloral hydrate is not expected to cause particular difficulties in children or the elderly; however, no specific information is available.

Table 27.3.4–2. Barbiturate Preparations

Name	Tablets	Capsules	Elixir	Parenteral	Rectal Suppositories
Amobarbital	30 mg	200 mg	—	250, 500 mg	—
Butabarbital	15, 30, 50, 100 mg	—	30 mg/5 L, 33.3 mg/5 mL	—	—
Mephobarbital	32, 50, 100 mg	—	—	—	—
Pentobarbital	—	50, 100 mg	18.2 mg/5 mL	50 mg/mL	30, 60, 120, 200 mg
Phenobarbital	15, 16, 30, 32, 60, 65, 100 mg	16 mg	15 mg/5 mL, 20 mg/5 mL	30 mg/mL, 60 mg/mL, 65 mg/mL, 130 mg/mL	—
Secobarbital	—	50, 100 mg	—	50 mg/mL	—

Carbamates

Meprobamate (Miltown, Equanil), ethinamate (Valmid), and carisoprodol (Soma) are carbamates that are effective as anxiolytics, sedatives, hypnotics, and muscle relaxants. Those drugs have a lower therapeutic index and a higher abuse potential than do the benzodiazepines, and their use is indicated only if the previously described drugs are not options. The carbamates have even more abuse potential and may be more dependence-inducing than the barbiturates.

The usual dosage of meprobamate is 400 mg, three or four times daily. Drowsiness is a common adverse effect, and patients should be warned about the additive effects of sedative drugs. Sudden withdrawal may cause anxiety, restlessness, weakness, delirium, and seizures. Adverse effects can include urticarial or erythematous rashes, anaphylactoid and other allergic reactions, angioneurotic edema, dermatitis, blood dyscrasias, gastrointestinal distress, and extraocular muscular paralysis. Fatal overdoses can occur with meprobamate in doses as low as 12 grams (thirty 400 mg tablets) without the ingestion of other sedatives. Meprobamate is available in 200, 400, and 600 mg tablets and 200 and 400 mg extended-release capsules. Carisoprodol is available in 350 mg tablets. Ethinamate is no longer manufactured in the United States.

Piperidinediones

Glutethimide and methyprylon (Noludar) are piperidinediones that are effective as hypnotics, sedatives, and anxiolytics but are even more subject to abuse and more lethal in overdose than are the barbiturates and carbamates. Glutethimide has a slow and unpredictable absorption after oral administration. Seizures, shock, and anticholinergic toxicity are more common in glutethimide overdoses than in barbiturate overdoses. Treatment with piperidinediones is rarely indicated. The usual dose of glutethimide is 250 to 500 mg at bedtime. Glutethimide is available in 500 mg tablets. Methyprylon is no longer manufactured in the United States.

Cyclic Ethers

Paraldehyde (Paral) was introduced in 1882 as a hypnotic. When 5 mL is given IM or 5 to 10 mL is administered orally, it is an effective, albeit old-fashioned, treatment for alcohol withdrawal symptoms, anxiety, and insomnia. Paraldehyde is almost completely metabolized, but its excretion in unmetabolized form by the lungs limits its usefulness because of its offensive taste and ubiquitous odor.

Tertiary Carbinols

Ethchlorvynol (Placidyl) is a tertiary carbinol, another nonbarbiturate sedative-hypnotic. It was marketed for use as a short-term treatment for insomnia. The drug is rapidly absorbed and has a fast onset of action and a relatively short duration of action. The liver is the major site for the drug's metabolism. Ethchlorvynol has sedative-hypnotic, muscle relaxant, and anticonvulsant properties. The usual hypnotic dose is 500 mg at bedtime. It is available in 200, 500, and 750 mg capsules.

The drug has significant potential for abuse, physical dependence, and tolerance. It is particularly dangerous in overdose. The lethal dose range is 10 to 25 grams, although death has been reported with as little as 3 grams. There is little to recommend the drug, especially in view of the much safer alternatives that are available. It is cross-tolerant with other sedative-hypnotics, and detoxification can be achieved with barbiturates by using the pentobarbital challenge tests (Table 27.3.4–1) to establish an appropriate dose of barbiturates.

References

Anthenelli R M, Klein J L, Smith T L, Schuckit M A: Comparison of the subjective and amnestic effects of diazepam and amobarbital in healthy young men. Am J Addict 2: 131, 1993.
Durbin C G Jr: Sedation in the critically ill patient. New Horizons 2: 64, 1994.
Piper A: ''Truth serum'' and ''recovered memories'' of sexual abuse: A review of the evidence. J Psychiatry Law 21:447, 1993.
Sylvester C E, Marchlewski A, Manaligod J M: Primidone or phenobarbital use complicating disruptive behavior disorders. Clin Pediatr 33: 252, 1994.
Uhde T W, Tancer M E: Barbiturates. In Comprehensive Textbook of Psychiatry, ed 6, H I Kaplan, B J Sadock, editors, p 1926. Williams & Wilkins, Baltimore, 1995.
Wolff K, Hay A A, Raistrick D, Feely M: Use of ''very low-dose phenobarbital'' to investigate compliance in patients on reducing doses of methadone (detoxification). J Subst Abuse Treat 10: 453, 1993.

27.3.5 Benzodiazepine Receptor Agonists and Antagonists

The benzodiazepine receptor agonists and antagonists have a common site of action on the γ-aminobutyric acid type A (GABA$_A$) receptor complex, which consists of a binding site for the neurotransmitter GABA, a binding site for benzodiazepines, and a chloride ion channel. This subsection discusses the benzodiazepines, a group of compounds that enhance the activity of the GABA$_A$ receptor by binding to the benzodiazepine receptor site; zolpidem (Ambien), a nonbenzodiazepine agonist at the benzodiazepine site; and flumazenil (Romazicon), a benzodiazepine receptor antagonist. The primary indications of benzodiazepines, zolpidem, and other benzodiazepine receptor agonists that are under development are anxiety and insomnia; the primary indication of flumazenil is the treatment of benzodiazepine overdose.

Basic neuroscience research has found evidence for two subtypes of central nervous system (CNS) benzodiazepine receptors (also called omega [ω] receptors)—BZ$_1$ (also called ω_1) and BZ$_2$ (also called ω_2). BZ$_1$ receptors are believed to be involved in the mediation of sleep. BZ$_2$ receptors are believed to be involved in cognition, memory, and motor control. Theoretically, a benzodiazepine hypnotic that affects only BZ$_1$ receptors may have fewer adverse cognitive effects. Both quazepam (Doral) and halazepam (Paxipam) are more specific for the BZ$_1$ receptors than the BZ$_2$ receptor and, therefore, may be associated with less amnesia and other cognitive impairments than are other currently available benzodiazepines.

BENZODIAZEPINES

The benzodiazepine-type benzodiazepine receptor agonists are commonly referred to simply as the benzodiazepines. Benzodiazepines are also variously referred to as antianxiety agents, anxiolytics, and minor tranquilizers. All those terms are misleading, since the benzodiazepines have multiple nonanxiety-related indications. Furthermore, the use of the term ''minor tranquilizer'' may cause confusion between this class of drugs and the major tranquilizers, another faulty but commonly used term for the antipsychotic drugs.

Benzodiazepines are sometimes classified as sedative-hypnotics, although other drugs can also be classified in that group (for example, barbiturates). A *sedative drug* reduces daytime anxiety, tempers excessive excitement, and generally quiets or calms the patient. Although sedatives and anxiolytics are sometimes distinguished because sedatives treat less pathological conditions than do anxiolytics, that is a poorly defined distinction that should be avoided. A *hypnotic drug* is one that produces drowsiness and facilitates the onset and the maintenance of sleep. In general, benzodiazepines act as hypnotics in high doses and as anxiolytics or sedatives in low doses.

In addition to their use as sedatives and hypnotics, some benzodiazepines are useful in other psychiatric indications, including panic disorder, phobias, and agitation associated with bipolar I disorder. In addition, the benzodiazepines are used as anesthetics, anticonvulsants, and muscle relaxants.

The benzodiazepines have become the sedative-hypnotic drugs of first choice because they have a higher therapeutic index and significantly less abuse potential than do many of the other sedative hypnotics (for example, barbiturates). One exception is buspirone (BuSpar), which is also a safe and effective drug.

Therapeutic Indications

ANXIETY

Generalized anxiety disorder, adjustment disorder with anxiety, and not necessarily pathological anxiety associated with life events (for example, after an accident) are the major clinical applications for benzodiazepines in psychiatry and general medical practice. Most patients should be treated for a predetermined, specific, and relatively brief period. Some patients with generalized anxiety disorder may warrant maintenance treatment with benzodiazepines.

INSOMNIA

Flurazepam (Dalmane), temazepam (Restoril), quazepam, estazolam (ProSom), and triazolam (Halcion) are the benzodiazepines approved for use as hypnotics. The benzodiazepine hypnotics differ principally in their half-lives; flurazepam has the longest half-life, and triazolam has the shortest half-life. Flurazepam may be associated with minor cognitive impairment on the day after its administration, and triazolam may be associated with mild rebound anxiety. Temazepam or estazolam may be a reasonable compromise for the usual adult patient. Because of its high specificity for the BZ_1 receptor, quazepam may be associated with few adverse cognitive effects; however, quazepam shares the final metabolite with flurazepam—desalkylflurazepam (half-life of about 100 hours)—and, therefore, may be associated with daytime impairment when used for a long time. Estazolam produces a rapid onset of sleep and a hypnotic effect for six to eight hours. All the benzodiazepines produce a moderate decrease in rapid eye movement (REM) sleep, although their use is not associated with REM rebound. The benzodiazepines are also associated with a decrease in stage 3 and stage 4 sleep, although the significance is not known.

DEPRESSION

Unique among the benzodiazepines, alprazolam (Xanax) has antidepressant effects equal to those of the tricyclic drugs, but alprazolam is not effective in seriously depressed inpatients.

The efficacy of alprazolam in depressive disorders may be a reflection of its potency; the antidepressant effects of other benzodiazepines may be evident only at doses that also induce sedation or sleep. The starting dosage of alprazolam for the treatment of depression should be 1 to 1.5 mg a day and should be raised in 0.5 mg a day intervals every three or four days. The maximal dosage is usually 4 to 5 mg a day, although some investigators and clinicians have used dosages as high as 10 mg a day. The use of high dosage is controversial because of the possibility of withdrawal symptoms. The clinician must taper alprazolam, rather than abruptly stop, usually at the rate of 0.5 mg a day every three to four days.

PANIC DISORDER AND SOCIAL PHOBIA

For two anxiety disorders, panic disorder with or without agoraphobia and social phobia, the two high-potency benzodiazepines, alprazolam and clonazepam (Klonopin), are effective. The Food and Drug Administration (FDA) has approved the use of alprazolam for the treatment of panic disorder. The dosage guidelines for the use of alprazolam in panic disorder are similar to those for depression.

BIPOLAR I DISORDER

Clonazepam is effective in the management of manic episodes and as an adjunct to lithium (Eskalith) therapy in lieu of antipsychotics. As an adjunct to lithium, clonazepam may result in an increased time between cycles and fewer than usual depressive episodes. The other high-potency benzodiazepine, alprazolam, may be as effective as clonazepam for that indication, which is not recognized by the FDA, and alprazolam should be considered a second-line treatment.

AKATHISIA

Standard anticholinergic drugs—for example, benztropine (Cogentin)—are often ineffective in treating neuroleptic-induced acute akathisia. The first-line drug for akathisia is most commonly a β-adrenergic receptor antagonist—for example, propranolol (Inderal). However, several studies have found that benzodiazepines are also effective in treating some cases of akathisia.

OTHER PSYCHIATRIC INDICATIONS

Chlordiazepoxide (Librium) is used to manage the symptoms of alcohol withdrawal. The benzodiazepines (especially intramuscular [IM] lorazepam) are used to manage both substance-induced (except amphetamine) and psychotic agitation in the emergency room. A few studies report the use of high dosages of benzodiazepines in patients with schizophrenia who had not responded to antipsychotics or who were unable to take the traditional drugs because of adverse effects. The use of IM lorazepam for the treatment of catatonia has been reported. Furthermore, benzodiazepines have been used instead of amobarbital (Amytal) for drug-assisted interviewing.

Precautions and Adverse Reactions

The most common adverse effect of benzodiazepines is drowsiness, which occurs in about 10 percent of all patients. Because of that adverse effect, patients should be advised to be careful while driving or using dangerous machinery when taking the drugs. Drowsiness can be present during the day after the use of a benzodiazepine for insomnia the previous night, so-called residual daytime sedation. Some patients also experience dizziness (less than 1 percent) and ataxia (less than 2 percent). Those symptoms can result in falls and hip fractures, especially in elderly patients. The most serious adverse effects of benzodiazepines occur when other sedative substances, such as alcohol, are taken concurrently. The combinations can result in marked drowsiness, disinhibition, or even respiratory depression. Other relatively rare adverse effects have been mild cognitive deficits that may impair job performance in patients who are taking benzodiazepines. Anterograde amnesia has also been associated with benzodiazepines, particularly high-potency benzodiazepines. A rare, paradoxical increase in aggression has been reported in patients given benzodiazepines, although that effect may be most common in patients with brain damage. Allergic reactions to the drugs are also rare, but a few studies report maculopapular rashes and generalized itching. The symptoms of benzodiazepine intoxication include confusion, slurred speech, ataxia, drowsiness, dyspnea, and hyporeflexia.

Triazolam has received significant attention in the media because of an alleged association with serious aggressive behavioral manifestations. Although little evidence supports the association, the Upjohn Company, which manufacturers triazolam, has issued a statement emphasizing that the drug is best used as a short-term (fewer than 10 days) treatment of insomnia and that physicians should carefully evaluate the emergence of any abnormal thinking or behavioral changes in patients treated with triazolam, giving appropriate consideration to all potential causes.

Patients with hepatic disease and elderly patients are particularly likely to have adverse effects and toxicity from the benzodiazepines, especially when the drugs are administered in repeated or high doses, because of the patient's impairment in the metabolism of the compounds. Benzodiazepines can produce clinically significant impairment of respiration in patients with chronic obstructive pulmonary disease and sleep apnea. Benzodiazepines should be used with caution in patients with a history of substance abuse, cognitive disorders, renal disease, hepatic disease, porphyria, central nervous system (CNS) depression, and myasthenia gravis.

Some data indicate that benzodiazepines are teratogenic; therefore, their use during pregnancy is not advised. Moreover, the use of benzodiazepines in the third trimester can precipitate a withdrawal syndrome in the newborn. The drugs are secreted in the breast milk in sufficient concentrations to affect the newborn. Benzodiazepines may cause dyspnea, bradycardia, and drowsiness in nursing babies.

TOLERANCE, DEPENDENCE, AND WITHDRAWAL

When benzodiazepines are used for short periods of time (one to two weeks) in moderate dosages, they usually cause no significant tolerance, dependence, or withdrawal effects. The short-acting benzodiazepines (for example, triazolam) may be an exception to that rule, as some patients have reported increased anxiety the day after taking a single dose of the drug. Some patients also report a tolerance for the anxiolytic effects of benzodiazepines and require increased dosages to maintain the clinical remission of symptoms. There is also a cross-tolerance among most of the classes of antianxiety drugs, with the notable exception of buspirone.

The appearance of a withdrawal syndrome, also called a discontinuation syndrome, depends on the length of time the patient has taken a benzodiazepine, the dosage the patient has been taking, the rate at which the drug is tapered, and the half-life of the compound. Abrupt discontinuation of benzodiazepines, particularly those with short half-lives, is associated with severe withdrawal symptoms. Serious symptoms may include depression, paranoia, delirium, and seizures. The incidence of the syndrome is controversial; however, some features of the syndrome may occur in as many as 50 percent of the patients treated with the drugs. A severe withdrawal syndrome develops only in patients who have taken high dosages for long periods. The appearance of the syndrome may be delayed for one or two weeks in patients who had been taking 2-keto benzodiazepines with long half-lives (Table 27.3.5–1). Alprazolam seems to be particularly associated with an immediate and severe withdrawal syndrome and should be tapered gradually.

OVERDOSES

Overdoses with benzodiazepines alone have a predictably favorable outcome. When the overdose involves drugs in addition to the benzodiazepines, however, respiratory depression, coma, seizures, and death are likely. Drugs that are commonly taken with benzodiazepines in fatal overdoses include alcohol, antipsychotics, and antidepressants. The availability of flumazenil has facilitated the medical management of benzodiazepine overdoses.

Drug Interactions

Because benzodiazepines are widely used, clinicians must be aware of the possible interactions of benzodiazepines and other drugs. Cimetidine (Tagamet), disulfiram (Antabuse), isoniazid (Nydrazid), and estrogens increase the plasma levels of 2-keto benzodiazepines. Antacids and food may decrease the plasma levels of benzodiazepines, and smoking may increase the metabolism of benzodiazepines. The benzodiazepines may increase the plasma levels of phenytoin (Dilantin) and digoxin (Lanoxin). All benzodiazepines have additive CNS effects with other sedative drugs. Ataxia and dysarthria may be likely to occur when lithium, antipsychotics, and clonazepam are combined.

Table 27.3.5–1. Classification of Benzodiazepines

2-Keto	3-Hydroxy	Triazolo	Imidazo	Nitro	2-Thione
Chlordiazepoxide	Oxazepam	Alprazolam	Midazolam	Clonazepam	Quazepam
Diazepam	Lorazepam	Triazolam			
Prazepam	Temazepam	Estazolam			
Clorazepate					
Halazepam					
Flurazepam					

Dosage and Administration

The clinical decision to treat an anxious patient with a benzodiazepine should be carefully considered. Medical causes of anxiety (for example, thyroid dysfunction, caffeinism, and medications) should be ruled out. The benzodiazepine should be started at a low dosage, and the patient should be instructed regarding the drug's sedative properties and abuse potential. An estimated length of therapy should be decided at the beginning of therapy, and the need for continued therapy should be reevaluated at least monthly because of the problems associated with long-term use.

DURATION OF TREATMENT

Benzodiazepines can be used to treat illnesses other than anxiety disorders. In such cases the duration of treatment should generally be similar to that for the standard drugs used to treat those disorders. The use of benzodiazepines over a long period for the chronically anxious patient is often valuable, although controversial. In his 1980 textbook on drug treatment in psychiatry, Donald Klein stated, "There are many reports of patients maintained on benzodiazepines for years with apparent benefit and without the development of tolerance. Nonetheless, it is dubious practice to prescribe such medications indefinitely without accompanying psychotherapy."

DISCONTINUATION OF THERAPY

Benzodiazepine withdrawal syndrome occurs when patients discontinue benzodiazepines abruptly; 90 percent of patients after long-term use experience some symptoms of withdrawal on discontinuation, even if the drug is tapered slowly. Benzodiazepine withdrawal syndrome consists of anxiety, nervousness, diaphoresis, restlessness, irritability, fatigue, light-headedness, tremor, insomnia, and weakness. The higher the dose and the shorter the half-life, the more severe the withdrawal symptoms can be.

When the medication is to be discontinued, the drug must be tapered slowly (25 percent a week); otherwise, recurrence or rebound of symptoms is likely. Monitoring of any withdrawal symptoms (possibly with a standardized rating scale) and psychological support of the patient are helpful in the successful discontinuation of benzodiazepine. Concurrent use of carbamazepine (Tegretol) during benzodiazepine discontinuation has been reported to permit a more rapid and better-tolerated withdrawal than does a gradual taper alone. The dosage range of carbamazepine used to facilitate withdrawal is 400 to 500 mg a day. Some clinicians report particular difficulty in tapering and discontinuing alprazolam, particularly in patients who have been receiving high dosages for long periods. There have been reports of successful discontinuation of alprazolam by switching to clonazepam, which is then gradually withdrawn.

CHOICE OF DRUG AND POTENCY

The wide range of benzodiazepines are available in an equally wide range of formulations (Table 27.3.5–2). The drugs differ primarily in their half-lives. Another difference is in the rate of onset of their potency and anxiolytic effects. Potency is a general term used to express the pharmacological activity of a drug. Some benzodiazepines are more potent than others in that one compound requires a relatively smaller dose than another compound to achieve the same effect. For example, clonazepam requires 0.25 mg to achieve the same effect as 5 mg

of diazepam; thus, clonazepam is considered a high-potency benzodiazepine. Conversely, oxazepam (Serax) has an approximate dose equivalence of 15 mg and is a low-potency drug. The four high-potency benzodiazepines—alprazolam, triazolam, estazolam, and clonazepam—are the drugs most likely to be effective for the new applications, such as depression, bipolar I disorder, panic disorder, and the phobias.

The advantages of the long-half-life drugs over the short-half-life drugs include less frequent dosing, less variation in plasma concentration, and less severe withdrawal phenomena. The disadvantages include drug accumulation, increased risk of daytime psychomotor impairment, and increased daytime sedation. The advantages of the short-half-life drugs over the long-half-life drugs include no drug accumulation and less daytime sedation. The disadvantages include more frequent dosing and earlier and more severe withdrawal syndromes. Rebound insomnia and anterograde amnesia are thought to be more of a problem with the short-half-life drugs than with the long-half-life drugs.

DRUG COMBINATIONS

The most common drug combinations with benzodiazepines involve the antipsychotics and the antidepressants, in addition to the benzodiazepines' obvious use as adjuvant hypnotics. The combination of a benzodiazepine and an antidepressant may be indicated in the treatment of markedly anxious depressed patients and patients with panic disorder. Several reports indicate that the combined use of alprazolam and an antipsychotic may further reduce psychotic symptoms in patients who did not respond adequately to the antipsychotic alone. The combined use of benzodiazepines and tricyclic drugs may improve compliance by reducing the subjective side effects and producing an immediate reduction in anxiety and insomnia. However, the combination may also cause excessive sedation, cognitive impairment, and even exacerbations of the depression, and it significantly adds to the lethality of an overdose.

ZOLPIDEM

Zolpidem is a new hypnotic that acts at the GABA-benzodiazepine complex as the benzodiazepines do, but it is not itself a benzodiazepine. The only indication for zolpidem at this time is as a hypnotic. The drug lacks the muscle-relaxant effects that are common to the benzodiazepines.

Therapeutic Indications

The sole indication at this time for zolpidem is as a hypnotic. Several studies have found an absence of rebound REM after the use of the compound for the induction of sleep. The comparatively few data available indicate that zolpidem may not be associated with rebound insomnia after the discontinuation of its use for short periods.

Precautions and Adverse Reactions

Because of the short half-life of zolpidem, the clinician may reasonably evaluate the patient for the possibility of anterograde amnesia and anxiety the day after its administration, although neither of those adverse effects has been reported. Emesis and dysphoric reactions have been reported as adverse effects. Although tolerance and dependence have not been demonstrated or reported, that may be due to the still limited experience with the drug. Patients taking zolpidem should be advised to exercise

Table 27.3.5-2. Benzodiazepines

Drug	Approximate Dose Equivalents[1]	Dose Forms	Benzodiazepines Rate of Absorption	Major Active Metabolites	Average Half-Life of Metabolites (hrs)	Short-Acting/ Long-Acting[3]	Usual Adult Dosage Range (mg per day)
Alprazolam (Xanax)	0.25	0.25, 0.5, 1, 2 mg tablets	Medium	α-Hydroxyalprazolam, 4-hydroxyalprazolam	12	Short	0.5–6
Chlordiazepoxide (Librium)	10	5, 10 25 mg tablets; 5, 10, 25 mg capsules; 100 mg parenteral	Medium	Desmethylchlordiazepoxide, demoxopam, desmethyldiazepam, oxazepam	100	Long	15–100
Clonazepam (Klonopin)	0.5	0.5, 1, 2 mg tablets	Rapid	None	34	Long	0.5–10
Clorazepate (Tranxene)	7.5	3.75, 7.5, 11.25, 15, 22.5 mg tablets; 3.75, 7.5, 15 mg capsules	Rapid	Desmethyldiazepam, oxazepam	100	Long	7.5–60
Diazepam (Valium)	5	2, 5, 10 mg tablets; 15 mg capsules (extended release); 5 mg/mL parenteral; 5 mg/5 mL, 5 mg/mL solution	Rapid	Desmethyldiazepam, oxazepam	100	Long	2–60
Estazolam (ProSom)	0.33	1, 2 mg tablets	Rapid	4-Hydroxy estazolam, 1-oxo estazolam	17	Short	1–2
Flurazepam (Dalmane)	5	15, 30 mg tablets	Rapid	Desalkylflurazepam, N-hydroxyethylflurazepam	100	Long	15–30
Halazepam (Paxipam)	20	20, 40 mg tablets	Medium	Desmethyldiazepam, oxazepam	100	Long	60–160
Lorazepam (Ativan)	1	0.5, 1, 2 mg tablets; 2 mg/mL, 4 mg/mL parenteral	Medium	None	15	Short	2–6
Midazolam (Versed)[2]	1.25–1.7	1 mg/mL, 5 mg/mL parenteral	N/A	1-Hydroxymethylmidazolam	2.5	Short	Parenteral form only; 7.5–45
Oxazepam (Serax)	15	15 mg tablets; 10, 15, 30 mg capsules	Slow	None	8	Short	30–120
Prazepam (Centrax)	10	10 mg tablets; 5, 10, 20 mg capsules	Slow	Desmethyldiazepam, oxazepam	100	Long	20–60
Quazepam (Doral)	5	7.5, 15 mg tablets	Rapid	2 oxoquazepam, N-desalkyl-2-oxoquazepam, and 3-hydroxy-2-oxoquazepam glucoronide	100	Long	7.5–30
Temazepam (Restoril)	5	15, 30 mg tablets	Medium	None	11	Short	15–30
Triazolam (Halcion)	0.1	0.125, 0.25 mg tablets	Rapid	None	2	Short	0.125–0.25

[1] High-potency drugs have an approximate dose equivalent of under 1.0; 1.0–10, medium potency; over 10, low potency.
[2] Used only by anesthesiologists.
[3] Short-acting benzodiazepines have a half-life of under 25 hrs.

additional caution when driving or operating dangerous machinery. Zolpidem is secreted in breast milk and is, therefore, contraindicated for use by nursing mothers. The dosage of zolpidem should be reduced in patients with renal and hepatic impairment. Preliminary data indicate that zolpidem has a longer than usual half-life in the elderly and a shorter than usual half-life in children.

Drug Interactions and Laboratory Interferences

Information on drug interactions and laboratory interferences is limited. Therefore, the clinician should consider the possibility of such an interaction or interference in a patient who is being treated with zolpidem.

Dosage and Administration

Zolpidem is available in 5, 10, 15, and 20 mg tablets, and a single 10 mg dose is the usual dose for the treatment of insomnia. For patients under age 65, the initial dose of 10 mg can be increased to 15 or 20 mg if necessary. For patients over age 65, an initial dose of 5 mg may be advised. Prolonged use of zolpidem or any hypnotic is not recommended.

FLUMAZENIL

Flumazenil is a benzodiazepine receptor antagonist. It reverses the psychophysiological effects of the benzodiazepine agonists (for example, diazepam). The use of flumazenil is limited to emergency rooms and other emergency settings.

Therapeutic Indications

Flumazenil is used to reverse the effects of benzodiazepine receptor agonists that have been used for clinical indications (for example, sedation and anesthesia) or in overdose.

Precautions and Adverse Reactions

The most common adverse effects of flumazenil are nausea, vomiting, dizziness, agitation, emotional lability, cutaneous vasodilation, injection-site pain, fatigue, impaired vision, and headache.

Drug Interactions

No deleterious drug interactions have been noted when flumazenil is administered after narcotics, inhalation anesthetics, muscle relaxants, and muscle-relaxant antagonists administered in conjunction with sedation or anesthesia. In mixed-drug overdose the toxic effects (for example, seizures and cardiac arrhythmias) of other drugs (for example, tricyclic drugs) may emerge with the reversal of the benzodiazepine effects of flumazenil. For example, seizures caused by an overdose of tricyclic drugs may have been partially treated in a patient who had also taken an overdose of benzodiazepines. With flumazenil treatment, the tricyclic-induced seizures or cardiac arrhythmias may present themselves and may result in a fatal outcome.

Dosage and Administration

For the initial management of a known or suspected benzodiazepine overdose, the recommended initial dose of flumazenil is 0.2 mg (2 mL) administered intravenously over 30 seconds. If the desired level of consciousness is not obtained after waiting 30 seconds, a further dose of 0.3 mg (3 mL) can be administered over 30 seconds. Further doses of 0.5 mg (5 mL) can be administered over 30 seconds at one-minute intervals up to a cumulative dose of 3.0 mg. The clinician should not rush the administration of flumazenil. A secure airway and intravenous access should be established before the administration of the drug. Patients should be awakened gradually.

Most patients with a benzodiazepine overdose respond to a cumulative dose of 1 to 3 mg of flumazenil; doses beyond 3 mg of flumazenil do not reliably produce additional effects. If a patient has not responded five minutes after receiving a cumulative dose of 5 mg flumazenil, the major cause of sedation is probably not due to benzodiazepine receptor agonists, and additional flumazenil is likely to have no effect.

RETURN OF SEDATION

Sedation can return in 1 to 3 percent of patients. It can be prevented or treated by giving repeated doses of flumazenil at 20-minute intervals. For repeat treatment, no more than 1 mg (given as 0.5 mg a minute) should be given at any one time, and no more than 3 mg should be given in any one hour.

References

Bailey L, Ward M, Musa M N: Clinical pharmacokinetics of benzodiazepines. J Clin Pharmacol 34: 804, 1994.

Hoey L L, Nahum A, Vance-Bryan K: A retrospective review and assessment of benzodiazepines in the treatment of alcohol withdrawal in hospitalized patients. Pharmacotherapy 14: 572, 1994.

Klein E, Colin V Stolk J, Lenox R H: Alprazolam withdrawal in patients with panic disorder and generalized anxiety disorder: Vulnerability and effect of carbamazepine. Am J Psychiatry 151: 1760, 1994.

Uhde T W, Tancer M E: Benzodiazepine receptor agonists and antagonists. In Comprehensive Textbook of Psychiatry, ed 6, H I Kaplan, B J Sadock, editors, p 1933. Williams & Wilkins, Baltimore, 1995.

Wardle J, Hayward P, Higgitt A, Stabl M, Blizard R, Gray J: Effects of concurrent diazepam treatment on the outcome of exposure therapy in agoraphobia. Behav Res Ther 32:203, 1994.

Woods J H, Winger G: Current benzodiazepine issues. Psychopharmacology 118: 107, 1995.

27.3.6 BROMOCRIPTINE

Bromocriptine (Parlodel) has been studied as a potential therapeutic agent in a number of psychiatric conditions. Those studies have been conducted because of interest in the mixed dopamine agonist-antagonist properties of bromocriptine, which is available in the United States as an approved treatment for Parkinson's disease. The most robust data are in support of the therapeutic benefit of bromocriptine in the treatment of antipsychotic-induced hyperprolactinemia and galactorrhea and in the treatment of neuroleptic malignant syndrome. Increasing data also support the use of bromocriptine for the treatment of cocaine withdrawal and depression, although the latter indication should be considered only after standard therapies have failed. Bromocriptine should only be used for a psychiatric indication after a review of the recent literature about those novel applications, which remain controversial.

THERAPEUTIC INDICATIONS

Antipsychotic-Induced Hyperprolactinemia

Because most antipsychotic drugs act as potent antagonists of dopamine type 2 (D_2) receptors, they cause an increase in prolactin release by blocking the inhibitory effects of endogenous dopamine in the pituitary. The increase in serum prolactin can result in amenorrhea and galactorrhea in women. Bromocriptine is an effective treatment because its dopamine agonist activity stimulates the D_2 receptors in the pituitary and inhibits prolactin release. In spite of the dopamine agonist activity of bromocriptine, its use does not appear to be associated with an exacerbation of psychotic symptoms. Bromocriptine is used in a dosage range of 5 to 15 mg a day for that indication.

Neuroleptic Malignant Syndrome

Neuroleptic malignant syndrome is a potentially fatal syndrome of autonomic instability associated with the use of antipsychotics—for example, haloperidol (Haldol). Because of the sporadic, unpredictable nature of neuroleptic malignant syndrome, most of the data regarding the effectiveness of bromocriptine in the condition come from case reports. Bromocriptine may be effective in neuroleptic malignant syndrome because its dopamine agonist activity reverses the effects of the dopamine antagonists on hypothalamic thermoregulatory function and peripheral muscle contraction.

The first and most crucial step in the treatment of neuroleptic malignant syndrome is the recognition of the syndrome in a patient. The first steps in the management of the syndrome are discontinuation of the antipsychotic drug and the initiation of supportive care. If bromocriptine or other drugs are used to treat neuroleptic malignant syndrome, the earlier they are begun, the more they are likely to benefit the patient. Amantadine (Symadine), another dopamine agonist, and dantrolene (Dantrium), a direct-acting skeletal muscle relaxant, are also of benefit in the treatment of neuroleptic malignant syndrome.

Treatment usually begins with 2.5 to 5.0 mg orally three times daily. The dosage can then be increased gradually up to 60 mg a day in divided doses to control fever, rigidity, and autonomic instability. In the available case reports published in the literature, the length of treatment has ranged from less than one week to two months.

Cocaine Withdrawal

The data in support of the use of bromocriptine in cocaine withdrawal come primarily from case reports and not well-controlled studies. Nevertheless, since there is no clearly superior treatment for cocaine withdrawal, a clinical trial of bromocriptine may be warranted in some patients. Bromocriptine has been used to treat both the withdrawal symptoms of cocaine and the long-term craving for cocaine. Dosages for the treatment of cocaine use disorders have ranged from 0.625 to 12.5 mg a day.

Depressive Disorders

The data in support of the use of bromocriptine in depressive disorders come primarily from case reports that have described its use in patients who have not responded to conventional antidepressant drugs. Although the neurotransmitters serotonin and norepinephrine have been emphasized in theories regarding depressive disorders, dopamine has also been hypothesized to be involved in the pathophysiology of mood disorders. Specifically, mania may be associated with dopaminergic hyperactivity, and depression may be associated with dopaminergic hypoactivity. In the studies of bromocriptine in depressive disorders, the daily dosages have ranged from 10 to 200 mg, with a mean dosage around 40 mg a day. Response to bromocriptine treatment has been reported to occur usually within two weeks, although it may take up to four weeks. Some investigators have suggested that bromocriptine is especially effective in the treatment of bipolar I disorder depressed patients and is particularly safe in elderly depressed patients because of its low sedative and anticholinergic activities. However, the use of bromocriptine in depressive disorders should be considered experimental and begun only after other treatments have failed.

Other Psychiatric Indications

Some reports support the use of bromocriptine in the treatment of antipsychotic-induced parkinsonism, antipsychotic-induced tardive dyskinesia, and alcohol withdrawal. Since bromocriptine is used to treat idiopathic Parkinson's disease, it may be effective in the treatment of antipsychotic-induced parkinsonism; however, the availability of other, probably safer, drugs—for example, benztropine (Cogentin)—should limit the use of bromocriptine for that indication. In several studies, bro-

mocriptine, in dosages ranging from 0.75 to 7.5 mg a day, has been reported to be effective in reducing tardive dyskinesia symptoms by about 50 percent in about 20 percent of the patients treated. Several case studies have reported that bromocriptine may be effective in the treatment of alcohol withdrawal.

On an experimental basis, bromocriptine has been reported to be effective in the treatment of anxiety disorders (including obsessive-compulsive disorder), mania, and schizophrenia. Bromocriptine should not be used for the treatment of those disorders unless many other drug trials have failed and the clinician has completely reviewed the available literature regarding the use of bromocriptine in the particular disorder.

PRECAUTIONS AND ADVERSE REACTIONS

The adverse effects of bromocriptine tend to be severe at the initiation of treatment and with dosages of more than 20 mg a day. The most common adverse effects are nausea, headache, and dizziness. Less common GI adverse effects include vomiting, abdominal cramps, and constipation. About 1 percent of patients have syncopal episodes 15 to 60 minutes after the first dose of the drug, although they can tolerate subsequent doses and dosage increases without syncope. Other patients, however, experience symptomatic orthostatic hypotension, for which they do not have tolerance with continued treatment. Other cardiovascular symptoms can include cardiac arrhythmias and an exacerbation of underlying angina. Rare psychiatric adverse effects can include hallucinations, delusions, confusion, and other behavioral changes, although those symptoms are most common after long-term use and in elderly patients. Bromocriptine should be used with caution in patients with hypertension, cardiovascular disease, and hepatic disease. Bromocriptine is not recommended for pregnant or breast-feeding patients.

DRUG INTERACTIONS

Although the concurrent use of bromocriptine and drugs that have dopamine antagonist activity (for example, phenothiazines) may theoretically decrease the activity of each of the drugs, the interaction has not proved to be of major clinical importance. The use of bromocriptine in conjunction with antihypertensive agents may produce additive hypotensive effects. Ergot alkaloids and bromocriptine should not be used concurrently, as they may cause hypertension and myocardial infarction. Progestins, estrogens, and oral contraceptives may interfere with the effects of bromocriptine.

DOSAGE AND ADMINISTRATION

Bromocriptine is available in 2.5 mg scored tablets and 5 mg capsules. The dosage of bromocriptine for mental disorders in uncertain, although it seems prudent to begin with low dosages (1.25 mg twice daily) and to increase the dosage gradually. Bromocriptine is usually taken with meals to help reduce the likelihood of nausea.

References

Boyd A: Bromocriptine and psychosis: A literature review. Psychiatr Q 66: 87, 1995.
Montastruc J L, Rascol O, Senard J M, Rascol A: A randomised controlled study comparing bromocriptine to which levodopa was later added, with levodopa alone in previously untreated patients with Parkinson's disease: A five year follow up. J Neurol Neurosurg Psychiatry 57: 1034, 1994.

Nunes E V, McGrath P J, Stewart J W, Quitkin F M: Bromocriptine treatment for cocaine addiction. Am J Addict 2: 169, 1993.
Perovich R M, Lieberman J A, Fleischhacker W W, Alvir J: The behavioral toxicity of bromocriptine in patients with psychiatric illness. J Clin Psychopharmacol 9: 417, 1989.
Kaplan H I, Sadock B J: Other pharmacological therapies. In *Comprehensive Textbook of Psychiatry*, ed 6, H I Kaplan, B J Sadock, editors, p 2122. Williams & Wilkins, Baltimore, 1995.
Sitland-Marken P A, Wells B G, Froemming J H, Chu C-C, Brown C S: Psychiatric applications of bromocriptine therapy. J Clin Psychiatry 51: 68, 1990.

27.3.7 BUPROPION

Bupropion (Wellbutrin) is a unique antidepressant in the available armamentarium of drugs, and it is unfortunate that its past inaccurate association with seizure liability has limited its use in the United States. Bupropion is a unicyclic antidepressant that is unrelated to any other antidepressant available in the United States. Bupropion has been shown to be as effective as any other antidepressant and has been proved to be safe and well-tolerated. The established safety and efficacy of bupropion should make it an option for the first-line treatment of depressive disorders.

THERAPEUTIC INDICATIONS

The therapeutic efficacy of bupropion in depression has been established in four well-controlled trials with depressed inpatients and outpatients. In comparison studies, bupropion has shown efficacy equal to fluoxetine (Prozac), nortriptyline (Aventyl), trazodone (Desyrel), doxepin (Adapin), amitriptyline (Elavil), and imipramine (Tofranil), although patients treated with bupropion may have less improvement in their sleep early in the course of treatment because of the lack of sedative effects.

Single reports have appeared about the use of bupropion in winter depression (that is, recurrent major depressive disorder with seasonal pattern) and in both childhood and adult attention-deficit/hyperactivity disorders. The use of bupropion in attention-deficit/hyperactivity disorder should be considered experimental at this time. Additional preliminary reports concern the use of bupropion in the treatment of cocaine abuse and chronic fatigue.

PRECAUTIONS AND ADVERSE REACTIONS

The side-effect profile of bupropion in placebo-controlled studies did not differ significantly from that for placebo-treated patients. No significant cardiovascular or clinical laboratory changes were reported in those placebo-controlled studies. A major advantage of bupropion over serotonin-specific reuptake inhibitors (SSRIs) is that bupropion is virtually devoid of any adverse effects on sexual functioning, whereas the SSRIs are associated with the occurrence of such effects in perhaps 25 to 50 percent of all patients.

The most common adverse effects are headache, insomnia, upper respiratory complaints, and nausea. Restlessness, agitation, and irritability may also occur. Most notable about bupropion is the absence of significant drug-induced orthostatic hypotension, weight gain, daytime drowsiness, and anticholinergic effects; however, some patients may experience dry mouth or constipation. In fact, weight loss may occur in about 25 percent of all patients. Bupropion may be a drug to consider early in the treatment of depressed patients with preexisting cardiovascular disease.

At dosages less than 450 mg a day, the incidence of seizures is about 0.4 percent, which is comparable to the incidence of seizures with tricyclic drugs. The risk of seizures increases to about 5 percent in dosages from 450 to 600 mg a day. Bupropion may be less likely than tricyclic drugs to cause a switch into mania or rapid cycling in bipolar I disorder patients; however, the drug can cause mania in some patients.

Overdoses with bupropion are associated with a generally favorable outcome, except in the cases of huge doses and mixed-drug overdoses. Seizures occur in about a third of all overdoses, and fatalities can involve uncontrollable seizures, bradycardia, and cardiac arrest. In general, however, bupropion is safer in overdose cases than are other antidepressants, except perhaps for the SSRIs.

The use of bupropion is contraindicated in patients with histories of head trauma, brain tumors, and other organic brain diseases because the drug may reduce the patient's seizure threshold. The presence of electroencephalographic abnormalities and the recent withdrawal of the patient from alcohol or a sedative-hypnotic may also increase the risk of having a bupropion-induced seizure. Because high dosages (more than 450 mg a day) of bupropion may be associated with a euphoric feeling, bupropion may be relatively contraindicated in patients with histories of substance abuse. The use of bupropion by pregnant women has not been studied and is not recommended. Because bupropion is secreted in breast milk, the use of bupropion in nursing women is not recommended.

DRUG INTERACTIONS

Bupropion should not be used concurrently with monoamine oxidase inhibitors (MAOIs) because of the possibility of inducing a hypertensive crisis, and at least 14 days should pass after the discontinuation of an MAOI before initiating treatment with bupropion. Delirium, psychotic symptoms, and dyskinetic movements may be associated with the coadministration of bupropion and dopamine agonists, such as amantadine (Symadine), levodopa (Larodopa), and bromocriptine (Parlodel). There have also been case reports of central nervous system (CNS) toxicity with the combination of lithium (Eskalith) and bupropion, although there have also been case reports that the combination is effective and well-tolerated in some patients with refractory depression. A few case reports indicate that delirium or seizures are associated with the combination of bupropion and fluoxetine. When bupropion is coadministered with drugs that are also metabolized in the liver, particular clinical attention should be given to the possibility of affecting the blood levels of the other drugs. Examples of other drugs metabolized in the liver are carbamazepine (Tegretol), cimetidine (Tagamet), barbiturates, and phenytoin (Dilantin).

DOSAGE AND ADMINISTRATION

Bupropion is available in 75 and 100 mg tablets. Initiation of treatment in the average adult patient should be at 100 mg orally twice a day. On the fourth day of treatment, the dosage can be raised to 100 mg orally three times a day. Because 300 mg is the recommended dosage, the patient should be maintained on that dosage for several weeks before further increasing the dosage. Because of the risk of seizures, increases in dosage should never exceed 100 mg in a three-day period; a single dose of bupropion should never exceed 150 mg; and the total daily dose should not exceed 450 mg.

One study of bupropion efficacy found that patients with trough blood levels of 10 to 29 ng per mL were more likely to respond to bupropion than were patients with trough blood levels of 30 ng per mL or more. That report was based on a small number of patients and needs to be replicated in a larger series before its accuracy can be assessed.

References

Brown E S, Dilsaver S C, Shoaib A M, Swann A C: Depressive mania: Response of residual depression to bupropion. Biol Psychiatry *35*: 493, 1994.

Goodnick P J: Blood levels and acute response to bupropion. Am J Psychiatry *149*: 399, 1992.

Labbate L A, Pollack M H: Treatment of fluoxetine-induced sexual dysfunction with bupropion: A case report. Ann Clin Psychiatry *6*: 13, 1994.

Sachs G S, Lafer B, Stoll A L, Banov M, Thibault A B, Tohen M, Tosenbaum J F: A double-blind trial of bupropion versus desipramine for bipolar depression. J Clin Psychiatry *55*: 391, 1994.

Sussman N: Bupropion. In *Comprehensive Textbook of Psychiatry*, ed 6, H I Kaplan, B J Sadock, editors, p 1951. Williams & Wilkins, Baltimore, 1995.

Weisler R H, Johnston J A, Lineberry C G, Samara B, Branconier R J, Billow A A: Comparison of bupropion and trazodone for the treatment of depression. J Clin Psychopharmacol *14*: 170, 1994.

27.3.8 BUSPIRONE

Buspirone (BuSpar) is the first clinically available azaperone drug in the United States. It is approved for the treatment of anxiety disorders. Buspirone is unrelated to the benzodiazepines or the barbiturates, and it does not directly affect the γ-aminobutyric acid (GABA) neurotransmitter system. Also unlike the benzodiazepines and the barbiturates, buspirone does not have sedative, hypnotic, muscle-relaxant, or anticonvulsant effects. In further contrast to those other drugs, buspirone carries a low potential for abuse and is not associated with withdrawal phenomena or cognitive impairment.

THERAPEUTIC INDICATIONS

The efficacy and the safety of buspirone in the treatment of generalized anxiety disorder have been demonstrated in at least 10 placebo-controlled trials. Most of those trials have found that the efficacy of buspirone did not differ from the efficacy of the benzodiazepines tested—diazepam (Valium), lorazepam (Ativan), clorazepate (Tranxene), and alprazolam (Xanax). However, all those studies used criteria in the third edition of *Diagnostic and Statistical Manual of Mental Disorders* (DSM-III) for generalized anxiety disorder, which differ from the criteria in the fourth edition of DSM (DSM-IV) by requiring only one month of symptoms, compared with the six months required in DSM-IV. Many clinicians are not convinced of the efficacy of buspirone, probably because of its delayed onset of action in comparison with the benzodiazepines and its lack of the mild euphoric effect or sense of well-being that can be associated with benzodiazepine use.

Both the benzodiazepines and buspirone have advantages and disadvantages. The beneficial effects of benzodiazepines are felt the same day the drug is started, and the full clinical response takes only days, whereas buspirone has no immediate effects, and the full clinical response may take two to four weeks. Sometimes the sedative effects of benzodiazepines, which are not found with buspirone, are desirable; however, those sedative effects are also associated with impaired motor performance and cognitive deficits. The major disadvantages

of benzodiazepine treatment are its addictive potential and the development of withdrawal phenomena on its discontinuation. Buspirone is not associated with any abuse potential, even in groups of patients who are at high risk for addictive behavior.

Buspirone has been studied in patient populations with symptoms in addition to anxiety. The studies produced mixed results regarding the efficacy of buspirone in depressive disorders and obsessive-compulsive disorder. The use of buspirone for those disorders should be considered experimental and should be undertaken only after traditional therapies have proved to be ineffective. The data indicate that buspirone is not effective in the treatment of panic disorder or social phobia of the performance type. Because buspirone does not act on the GABA-chloride ion channel complex, the drug is not recommended for the treatment of withdrawal from benzodiazepines, alcohol, or sedative-hypnotic drugs.

PRECAUTIONS AND ADVERSE REACTIONS

The most common adverse effects of buspirone are headache, nausea, dizziness, and, rarely, insomnia. No sedation is associated with buspirone. Some patients may report a minor feeling of restlessness, although that symptom may reflect an incompletely treated anxiety disorder. No deaths have been reported from overdoses of buspirone, and the median lethal dose (LD_{50}) is estimated to be 160 to 550 times the recommended daily dose. Buspirone should be used with caution in patients with hepatic and renal impairment, in pregnant women, and in nursing mothers. Buspirone can be used safely for the elderly; however, no specific information is available about its use for children.

DRUG INTERACTIONS

One study reported that the coadministration of buspirone and haloperidol (Haldol) resulted in increased blood concentrations of haloperidol. Buspirone should not be used with monoamine oxidase inhibitors, and a two-week washout period should pass between the discontinuation of an MAOI and the initiation of treatment with buspirone.

LABORATORY INTERFERENCES

Single doses of buspirone can cause transient elevations in growth hormone, prolactin, and cortisol concentrations, although the effects are not clinically significant.

DOSAGE AND ADMINISTRATION

Buspirone is available in 5 and 10 mg tablets, and treatment is usually initiated with 5 mg orally three times daily. The dosage can be raised 5 mg every two to three days to the usual dosage range of 15 to 30 mg a day. The maximum dosage is 60 mg a day.

Buspirone is as effective as the benzodiazepines in the treatment of anxiety in patients who have not received benzodiazepines in the past. However, buspirone does not cause the same response in patients who have received benzodiazepines in the past. The reason is probably buspirone's absence of the immediate mildly euphoric and sedative effects of the benzodiazepines. The most common clinical problem, therefore, is how to initiate buspirone therapy in a patient who is currently taking benzodiazepines. There are two alternatives: First, the clinician can start buspirone treatment gradually while the benzodiazepine is being withdrawn. Second, the clinician can start buspirone treatment and bring the patient up to a therapeutic dosage for two to three weeks while the patient is still receiving the regular dosage of the benzodiazepine; at that point the benzodiazepine can be slowly tapered. A few initial reports indicate that the coadministration of buspirone and benzodiazepines may be effective in the treatment of anxiety disorders that have not responded to treatment with either drug alone.

References

Buspirone: Seven-year update. J Clin Psychiatry 55: 222, 1994.

Duffy J D, Mallow P F: Efficacy of buspirone in the treatment of posttraumatic stress disorder: An open trial. Ann Clin Psychiatry 6: 33, 1994.

Kranzler H R, Burleson J A, Del Boca F K, Babor T F, Korner P, Brown J, Bohn M J: Buspirone treatment of anxious alcoholics. A placebo-controlled trial. Arch Gen Psychiatry 51: 720, 1994.

Norman T R, Apostolopoulos M, Burrows G D, Judd F K: Neuroendocrine responses to single doses of buspirone in obsessive-compulsive disorder. Int Clin Psychopharmacol 9: 89, 1994.

Uhde T W, Tancer M E: Buspirone. In Comprehensive Textbook of Psychiatry, ed 6, H I Kaplan, B J Sadock, editors, p 1957. Williams & Wilkins, Baltimore, 1995.

Zwier K J, Rao U: Buspirone use in an adolescent with social phobia and mixed personality disorder (cluster A type). J Am Acad Child Adolesc Psychiatry 33: 1007, 1994.

27.3.9 Calcium Channel Inhibitors

The calcium channel inhibitors are variously referred to as the calcium channel antagonists, calcium channel blockers, and organic calcium channel inhibitors. The calcium channel inhibitors were first developed as cardiac drugs for the treatment of hypertension, angina, and specific types of cardiac arrhythmias—indications that remain important in general medical practice. Although about a dozen calcium channel inhibitors are now available in the United States, most of the studies of calcium channel inhibitors in psychiatric disorders have been conducted with verapamil (Calan, Isoptin) and, recently, nimodipine (Nimotop), diltiazem (Cardizem) and nifedipine (Adalat, Procardia).

THERAPEUTIC INDICATIONS

Bipolar I Disorder

Case reports describing the efficacy of verapamil in bipolar I disorder first appeared in the early 1980s, and subsequent placebo-controlled and lithium-controlled studies have generally supported the initial finding of efficacy for that indication. Available data support the use of verapamil for both the short-term and maintenance treatment of bipolar I disorder, although verapamil should be considered a fourth-line drug, following trials of lithium (Eskalith), carbamazepine (Tegretol), and valproate (Depakene). Because of potential drug interactions, valproate should be coadministered with lithium or carbamazepine with caution. Some patients who are treated with lithium and calcium channel inhibitors concurrently may be at increased risk for the signs and symptoms of neurotoxicity.

Preliminary data indicate that nimodipine may be particularly effective in the treatment of rapid-cycling bipolar I disorder. Since nimodipine is currently an expensive drug and those data are preliminary, the use of nimodipine for bipolar I disorder is best limited to research settings at this time.

Hypertensive Crisis Associated with Monoamine Oxidase Inhibitors

One controversial use of a calcium channel inhibitor in psychiatry is the use of nifedipine to treat monoamine oxidase inhibitor (MAOI)-induced hypertensive crises. When patients begin to experience the symptoms of a hypertensive crisis, they are instructed to bite into a 20 mg capsule of nifedipine, to swallow the contents with water, to contact their physician, and to go to an emergency room. The concern is that patients may misidentify minor symptoms as hypertensive symptoms and take nifedipine unnecessarily, possibly resulting in a hypotensive episode or syncope.

Other Psychiatric Indications

Perhaps the most hopeful of the other indications studied with calcium channel inhibitors are the use of nimodipine for dementia and the use of a range of calcium channel inhibitors for tardive dyskinesia. Using nimodipine for dementia is strictly experimental at this time, but using a calcium channel inhibitor for tardive dyskinesia may be worth a therapeutic trial in severely affected patients. Case reports and small studies provide preliminary evidence of the efficacy of calcium channel inhibitors in Tourette's disorder, Huntington's disease, panic disorder, premenstrual dysphoric disorder, and intermittent explosive disorder. Well-controlled studies have found a lack of efficacy for calcium channel inhibitors in schizophrenia and depressive disorders.

PRECAUTIONS AND ADVERSE REACTIONS

The most common adverse effects associated with calcium channel inhibitors are hypotension, bradycardia, and antrioventricular (A-V) heart block, which sometimes necessitate discontinuing the drug. In all patients with cardiovascular disease, the drugs should be used with caution. Common gastrointestinal (GI) symptoms include constipation, nausea, and occasionally dry mouth, GI distress, and diarrhea. Adverse effects on the central nervous system include dizziness, headache, and fatigue. Adverse effects noted in case reports with diltiazem include hyperactivity, akathisia, and parkinsonism; with verapamil, delirium, hyperprolactinemia, and galactorrhea have been noted. The drugs have not been evaluated for safety in pregnant women and are best avoided. Because the drugs are secreted in breast milk, nursing mothers should also avoid the drugs. The elderly are more sensitive to the calcium channel inhibitors than are younger adults. No specific information is available regarding the use of the agents for children.

DRUG INTERACTIONS

Calcium channel inhibitors should not be prescribed for patients taking β-adrenergic receptor antagonists, hypotensives (for example, diuretics, vasodilators, and angiotensin-converting enzyme inhibitors), or antiarrhythmic drugs (for example, quinidine) without consultation with the patient's internist or cardiologist. Verapamil and diltiazem but not nifedipine have been reported to precipitate carbamazepine-induced neurotoxicity. Cimetidine (Tagamet) has been reported to increase plasma concentrations of nifedipine and diltiazem.

DOSAGE AND ADMINISTRATION

Verapamil is available in 40, 80, and 120 mg tablets; 180 and 240 mg extended-release tablets; and 120 and 240 mg capsules. The starting dosage is 40 mg orally three times a day and can be raised in increments every four to five days up to 80 to 120 mg three times a day. The patient's blood pressure, pulse, and electrocardiogram (ECG) (in patients more than 40 years old or with a history of cardiac illness) should be routinely monitored. Diltiazem is available in 30, 60, 90, and 120 mg tablets and 60, 90, and 120 mg capsules. It should be started at 30 mg orally four times a day and can be increased up to a maximum of 360 mg a day. Nifedipine is available in 10 and 20 mg capsules and 30, 60, and 90 mg tablets. It should be started at 10 mg orally three or four times a day and can be increased up to a maximum dosage of 180 mg a day.

References

Adlersberg S, Toren P, Mester R, Rehavi M, et al: Verapamil is not an antidepressant in patients resistant to tricyclic antidepressants. Clin Neuropharmacol *17*: 294, 1994.
Arana G W, Santos A B: Calcium channel inhibitors. In *Comprehensive Textbook of Psychiatry*, ed 6, H I Kaplan, B J Sadock, editors, p 1961. Williams & Wilkins, Baltimore, 1995.
Garza-Trevino E S, Overall J E, Hollister L E: Verapamil versus lithium in acute mania. Am J Psychiatry *149*: 108, 1992.
Hendrickson J L, Ellis C R, Singh N N, Singh Y N, et al: Effects of calcium channel blockers on tardive dyskinesia. J Dev Physical Disabilities *6*:125, 1994.
Pucilowski O: Psychopharmacological properties of calcium channel inhibitors. Psychopharmacology *109*: 12, 1992.
Schindler C W, Tella S R, Prada J, Goldberg S R: Calcium channel blockers antagonize some of cocaine's cardiovascular effects, but fail to alter cocaine's behavioral effects. J Pharmacol Exp Ther *272*: 791, 1995.

27.3.10 Carbamazepine

Carbamazepine (Tegretol) is an iminostilbene derivative structurally similar to imipramine (Tofranil) and approved for use in the United States for the treatment of temporal lobe epilepsy and trigeminal neuralgia. A large body of data supports the use of carbamazepine for the treatment of acute mania and for the prophylactic treatment of bipolar I disorder.

THERAPEUTIC INDICATIONS

Bipolar I Disorder

Almost two dozen well-controlled studies have shown that carbamazepine is effective in the treatment of acute mania, with efficacy comparable to lithium and antipsychotics. About 10 studies have also shown that carbamazepine is effective in the prophylaxis of both manic and depressive episodes in bipolar I disorder when it is used for prophylactic treatment. Carbamazepine is an effective antimanic agent in 50 to 70 percent of all patients. Additional evidence from those studies indicates that carbamazepine may be effective in some patients who are not responsive to lithium, such as patients with dysphoric mania, rapid cycling, or a negative family history of mood disorders. However, a few clinical and basic science data indicate that some patients may experience a tolerance for the antimanic effects of carbamazepine.

Schizophrenia and Schizoaffective Disorder

Several well-controlled studies have produced data indicating that carbamazepine is effective in the treatment of schizophrenia and schizoaffective disorder. Patients with positive symptoms (for example, hallucinations) and few negative symptoms (for example, anhedonia) may be likely to respond, as are patients who have impulsive aggressive outbursts as a symptom.

Depressive Disorders

The available data indicate that carbamazepine is an effective treatment for depression in some patients. About 25 to 33 percent of depressed patients respond to carbamazepine. That percentage is significantly smaller than the 60 to 70 percent response rate for standard antidepressants. Nevertheless, carbamazepine is an alternative drug for depressed patients who have not responded to conventional treatments, including electroconvulsive therapy (ECT), or who have a marked or rapid periodicity in their depressive episodes.

Impulse-Control Disorders

Several studies have reported that carbamazepine is effective in controlling impulsive, aggressive behavior in nonpsychotic patients. Other drugs for impulse-control disorders, particularly intermittent explosive disorder, include lithium (Eskalith), propranolol (Inderal), and antipsychotics. Because of the risk of serious adverse effects with carbamazepine, clinical trials with those other agents are warranted before initiating a trial with carbamazepine.

Carbamazepine is also effective in controlling nonacute agitation and aggressive behavior in schizophrenic patients. Diagnoses to be ruled out before treatment with carbamazepine is begun include akathisia and neuroleptic malignant syndrome. Lorazepam (Ativan) is more effective than carbamazepine for the control of acute agitation.

Alcohol Withdrawal

According to several studies, carbamazepine is as effective as the benzodiazepines in the control of symptoms associated with alcohol withdrawal. However, the lack of any advantage of carbamazepine over the benzodiazepines and the potential risk of adverse effects with carbamazepine limit the clinical usefulness of that application.

PRECAUTIONS AND ADVERSE REACTIONS

Although the drug's benign hematological effects are not dose-related, most of the adverse effects of carbamazepine are correlated with plasma concentrations above 9 μg per ml. The rarest but most serious adverse effects of carbamazepine are blood dyscrasias, hepatitis, and exfoliative dermatitis. Otherwise, carbamazepine is relatively well-tolerated by patients except for mild gastrointestinal (GI) and central nervous system (CNS) effects that can be significantly reduced if the dosage is increased slowly and minimal effective plasma concentrations are maintained.

Blood Dyscrasias

Severe blood dyscrasias (aplastic anemia, agranulocytosis) occur in about 1 in 20,000 patients treated with carbamazepine.

There appears to be no correlation between the degree of benign white blood cell suppression and the emergence of life-threatening blood dyscrasias. Patients should be warned that the emergence of such symptoms as fever, sore throat, rash, petechiae, bruising, and easy bleeding are potentially symptoms of a serious dyscrasia and should cause the patient to seek medical evaluation immediately. The benefit of routine hematological monitoring in carbamazepine-treated patients is uncertain.

Hepatitis

Within the first few weeks of therapy, carbamazepine can cause both a hypersensitivity hepatitis associated with increases in liver enzymes and a cholestasis associated with elevated bilirubin and alkaline phosphatase. Hepatitis will recur if the drug is reintroduced to the patient and can result in the death of the patient.

Exfoliative Dermatitis

A benign pruritic rash occurs in 10 to 15 percent of patients treated with carbamazepine, usually occurring within the first few weeks of treatment. Unfortunately, a small percentage of those patients may then experience life-threatening dermatological syndromes, including exfoliative dermatitis, erythema multiforme, Stevens-Johnson syndrome, and toxic epidermal necrolysis. The possible emergence of those serious dermatological problems causes most clinicians to discontinue carbamazepine use if any type of rash develops in a patient. If carbamazepine seems to be the only effective drug for a patient who has a benign rash with carbamazepine treatment, a retrial of the drug can be undertaken with pretreatment of the patient with prednisone (40 mg a day) in an attempt to treat the rash, although other symptoms of an allergic reaction (for example, fever and pneumonitis) may develop, even with steroid pretreatment.

Gastrointestinal Effects

The most common adverse effects of carbamazepine are nausea, vomiting, gastric distress, constipation, diarrhea, and anorexia. The severity of the adverse effects is reduced if the dosage of carbamazepine is increased slowly and kept at the minimal effective plasma concentration.

Central Nervous System Effects

Acute confusional states can occur with carbamazepine alone but occur most often in combination with lithium or antipsychotic drugs. The symptoms of CNS toxicity include drowsiness, confusion, ataxia, hyperreflexia, clonus, and tremor. Elderly patients and patients with cognitive disorders are at increased risk for CNS toxicity from carbamazepine. The common CNS effects of dizziness, ataxia, clumsiness, and sedation are often associated with carbamazepine treatment, although they are reduced by a slow upward titration of the dosage.

Other Adverse Effects

Carbamazepine decreases cardiac conduction (although less than the tricyclic drugs do) and can, thus, exacerbate preexisting cardiac disease. Carbamazepine should be used with caution in patients with glaucoma, prostatic hypertrophy, diabetes, or a history of alcohol abuse. Some evidence indicates that minor cranial facial abnormalities and spina bifida in infants may be associated with the maternal use of carbamazepine during pregnancy. Therefore, pregnant women should not use carbamazepine unless absolutely necessary. Carbamazepine is secreted in breast milk, so women taking carbamazepine should not nurse their babies.

Overdoses

Overdoses of carbamazepine, when taken alone, have a generally favorable outcome. Symptoms associated with an overdose include drowsiness, stupor, coma, sinus tachycardia, hypotension or hypertension, antrioventricular (A-V) conduction block, seizures, nystagmus, hypothermia, facial dyskinesias, and respiratory depression. Gastric lavage and the use of activated charcoal (50 to 100 grams, followed by 12.5 grams an hour until the patient has recovered) early in the course of emergency treatment are recommended. Some investigators have recommended the use of flumazenil (Romazicon) to block the effects of carbamazepine on central-type benzodiazepine receptors.

DRUG INTERACTIONS

The mechanisms for drug interactions with carbamazepine are many and result in many potentially relevant drug interactions. Coadministration with lithium (Eskalith), antipsychotic drugs, verapamil (Calan), or nifedipine (Procardia) can precipitate carbamazepine-induced CNS adverse effects. Carbamazepine can decrease the blood concentrations of oral contraceptives, resulting in breakthrough bleeding and uncertain prophylaxis against pregnancy. Carbamazepine should not be administered with monoamine oxidase inhibitors, which should be discontinued for at least two weeks before initiating treatment with carbamazepine.

LABORATORY INTERFERENCES

Carbamazepine treatment is associated with a decrease in thyroid hormones (thyroxine [T_4], free T_4, and triiodothyronine [T_3]) without an associated increase in thyroid-stimulating hormone (TSH). Carbamazepine is also associated with an increase in total serum cholesterol, primarily by increasing high-density lipoproteins. The thyroid and cholesterol effects are not clinically significant. Carbamazepine may also cause a false-positive result in a pregnancy test.

DOSAGE AND ADMINISTRATION

Carbamazepine can be used alone or with an antipsychotic drug for the treatment of manic episodes, although carbamazepine-induced CNS adverse effects (drowsiness, dizziness, ataxia) are likely with that combination of drugs. Patients who do not respond to lithium alone may respond when carbamazepine is added to the lithium treatment. If patients then respond, an attempt should be made to withdraw the lithium to assess whether the patient can be treated successfully with carbamazepine alone. When lithium and carbamazepine are used together, the clinician should minimize or discontinue any antipsychotics, sedatives, or anticholinergic drugs the patient may be taking to reduce the risks for adverse effects associated with taking multiple drugs. The lithium and the carbamazepine should both be used at standard therapeutic plasma concentrations before a trial of combined therapy is considered to have been a therapeutic failure. A three-week trial of carbamazepine at therapeutic plasma concentrations is usually sufficient to determine whether the drug will be effective in the treatment of acute mania; a longer trial is necessary to assess efficacy in the treatment of depression. Carbamazepine is also used in combination with valproate (Depakene), another anticonvulsant that is effective in bipolar I disorder. When carbamazepine and valproate are used in combination, the dosage of carbamazepine should be decreased, because valproate displaces carbamazepine binding on proteins, and the dosage of valproate may need to be increased.

Pretreatment Medical Evaluation

The patient's medical history should include information about preexisting hematological, hepatic, and cardiac diseases, because all three can be relative contraindications for carbamazepine treatment. Patients with hepatic disease require only one third to one half the usual dosage; the clinician should be cautious about raising the dosage in such patients and should do so only slowly and gradually. The laboratory examination should include a complete blood count with platelet count, liver function tests, serum electrolytes, and an electrocardiogram in patients more than 40 years of age or with a preexisting cardiac disease. An electroencephalogram (EEG) is not necessary before the initiation of treatment, but it may be helpful in some cases for the documentation of objective changes correlated with clinical improvement.

Initiation of Treatment

Carbamazepine is available in 100 and 200 mg tablets and as a 100 mg per 5 mL suspension. The usual starting dosage is 200 mg orally two times a day. Carbamazepine should be taken with meals, and the drug should be stored in a cool, dry place. Carbamazepine stored in a bathroom medicine cabinet can lose up to one third of its activity. In an inpatient setting with seriously ill patients, the dosage can be raised by not more than 200 mg a day until a dosage of 600 to 1,000 mg a day is reached. That relatively rapid titration, however, is often associated with adverse effects and may adversely affect compliance with the drug. In less ill patients and in outpatients, the dosage should be raised no more quickly than 200 mg every two to four days to minimize the occurrence of minor adverse effects, such as nausea, vomiting, drowsiness, and dizziness. When discontinuing treatment with carbamazepine, the clinician need not taper the dosage.

Blood Levels

The anticonvulsant blood level range for carbamazepine is 4 to 12 μg per mL, and that range should be reached before determining that carbamazepine is not effective in the treatment of a mood disorder. It is clinically prudent to come up to that range gradually, since the patient is likely to tolerate a gradual increase of carbamazepine better than a rapid increase. The clinician should titrate carbamazepine up to the highest well-tolerated dosage before deciding that the drug is ineffective. Plasma concentrations should be obtained when a patient has been re-

ceiving a steady dosage for at least five days. Blood for the determination of plasma levels is drawn in the morning before the first daily dose of carbamazepine is given. The total daily dosage necessary to achieve plasma concentrations in the usual therapeutic range varies from 400 to 1,600 mg a day, with a mean around 1,000 mg a day.

Routine Laboratory Monitoring

The most serious potential effects of carbamazepine are agranulocytosis and aplastic anemia. Although it has been suggested that complete laboratory blood assessments be performed every two weeks for the first two months of treatment and quarterly thereafter, that conservative approach may not be justified by a cost-benefit analysis and may not detect a serious blood dyscrasia before it occurs. The Food and Drug Administration (FDA) has revised the package insert for carbamazepine to suggest that blood monitoring be performed at the discretion of the physician. Patient education about the signs and the symptoms of a developing hematological problem is probably more effective than is frequent blood monitoring in protecting against that adverse event. It has also been suggested that liver and renal function tests be conducted quarterly, although the benefit of conducting those tests that frequently has been questioned. It seems reasonable, however, to assess hematological status, along with liver and renal functions, whenever the patient is routinely examined.

The following laboratory values should prompt the physician to discontinue carbamazepine treatment and to consult a hematologist: total white blood cell count less than 3,000 mm^3, erythrocytes less than 4.0×10^6 per mm^3, neutrophils less than 1,500 per mm^3, hematocrit less than 32 percent, hemoglobin less than 11 grams per 100 mL, platelet count less than 100,000 per mm^3, reticulocyte count less than 0.3 percent, and a serum iron level less than 150 mg per 100 mL.

References

Denicoff K D, Meglathery S B, Post R M, Tandeciarz S I: Efficacy of carbamazepine compared with other agents: A clinical practice survey. J Clin Psychiatry 55: 70, 1994.

Post R M: Carbamazepine. In *Comprehensive Textbook of Psychiatry*, ed 6, H I Kaplan, B J Sadock, editors, p 1919. Williams & Wilkins, Baltimore, 1995.

Pourcher E, Fliteau M, Bouchard R H, Barch P: Efficacy of the combination of buspirone and carbamazepine in early posttraumatic delirium. Am J Psychiatry 151: 150, 1994.

Schmidt S, Schmitz-Buhl M: Signs and symptoms of carbamazepine overdose. J Neurol 242: 169, 1995.

Stuppaeck C H, Barnas C, Schwitzer J, Flwischhacker W W: Carbamazepine in the prophylaxis of major depression: A 5-year follow-up. J Clin Psychiatry 55: 146, 1994.

Tohen M, Castillo J, Pope HG Jr, Herbstein J: Concomitant use of valproate and carbamazepine in bipolar and schizoaffective disorders. J Clin Psychopharmacol 14: 67, 1994.

27.3.11 CLONIDINE

Clonidine (Catapres) is an α_2-adrenergic receptor agonist used primarily as a hypotensive agent. Its major indications in psychiatry are the control of the withdrawal symptoms from opiates and opioids and the treatment of Tourette's disorder.

THERAPEUTIC INDICATIONS

Opioid Withdrawal

Clonidine is effective in reducing the autonomic symptoms of opiate and opioid withdrawal (for example, hypertension, tachycardia, dilated pupils, sweating, lacrimation, and rhinor-rhea) but not the associated subjective sensations. Clonidine can be used in withdrawing a patient from methadone. Usually, dosages of 0.15 mg twice a day are sufficient for that purpose. The efficacy of clonidine in treating opioid withdrawal may reflect its activity on the noradrenergic neurons of the locus ceruleus.

Tourette's Disorder

Some clinicians use clonidine as a first-line drug for the treatment of Tourette's disorder instead of the standard drugs, haloperidol (Haldol) and pimozide (Orap), because of the serious adverse effects associated with those antipsychotics. The starting child dosage is 0.05 mg a day; it can be raised to 0.3 mg a day in divided doses. Three months are needed before the beneficial effects of clonidine can be seen in Tourette's disorder.

Other Disorders

Other potential indications for clonidine include the anxiety disorders (panic disorder, phobias, obsessive-compulsive disorder, posttraumatic stress disorder, and generalized anxiety disorder) and mania, in which it may be synergistic with lithium (Eskalith) or carbamazepine (Tegretol). Anecdotal reports have noted the efficacy of clonidine in schizophrenia, tardive dyskinesia, and smoking cessation.

PRECAUTIONS AND ADVERSE REACTIONS

The most common adverse effects associated with clonidine are dry mouth and eyes, fatigue, sedation, dizziness, nausea, hypotension, and constipation, which result in the discontinuation from therapy of about 10 percent of all patients taking the drug. Some patients also experience sexual dysfunction. Uncommon central nervous system (CNS) adverse effects include insomnia, anxiety, and depression; rare CNS adverse effects include vivid dreams, nightmares, and hallucinations. Fluid retention associated with clonidine treatment can be treated with diuretics.

Patients who overdose on clonidine can present with coma and constricted pupils, symptoms similar to an opioid overdose. Other symptoms of overdose are decreased blood pressure, pulse, and respiratory rates. Clonidine should be used with caution in patients with heart disease, renal disease, Raynaud's syndrome, or a history of depression. Clonidine should be avoided during pregnancy and by nursing mothers. The elderly are more sensitive to the drug than are younger adults. Children are susceptible to the same side effects as are adults.

DRUG INTERACTIONS

The most relevant drug interaction is that the coadministration of clonidine and tricyclic drugs can inhibit the hypotensive effects of clonidine. Clonidine may also enhance the CNS depressive effects of barbiturates, alcohol, and other sedative-hypnotics. The concomitant use of β-adrenergic receptor antagonists can increase the severity of rebound phenomena when clonidine is discontinued.

DOSAGE AND ADMINISTRATION

Clonidine's is available in 0.1, 0.2, and 0.3 mg tablets. The usual starting dosage is 0.1 mg orally twice a day; the dosage can be raised by 0.1 mg a day to an appropriate level. Clonidine must always be tapered when it is discontinued to avoid rebound hypertension, which occurs about 20 hours after the last clonidine dose. Regardless of the indication for which clonidine is being used, the drug should be withheld if a patient becomes hypotensive (blood pressure less than 90/60).

References

Bierer L M, Aisen P S, Davidson M, Ryan T M Schmeidler J, Davis K L: A pilot study of clonidine plus physostigmine in Alzheimer's disease. Dementia 5: 243, 1994.
Gerra G, Marcato A, Caccavari R, Fontanesi B, Delsignore R, Fertonani G, Avanzini P, Rustichelli P, Passeri, M: Clonidine and opiate receptor antagonists in the treatment of heroin addiction. J Subst Abuse Treat 12: 35, 1995.
Muller N, Putz A, Klages U, Hofschuster E, Straube A, Ackenheil M: Blunted growth hormone response to clonidine in Gilles de la Tourette syndrome. Psychoneuroendocrinology 19: 335, 1994.
Rubinstein S, Silver L B, Licamele W L: Clonidine for stimulant-related sleep problems. J Am Acad Child Adolesc Psychiatry 33: 281, 1994.
Uhde T W, Tancer M E: Clonidine. In Comprehensive Textbook of Psychiatry, ed 6, H I Kaplan, B J Sadock, editors, p 1975. Williams & Wilkins, Baltimore, 1995.
Wilens T E, Biederman J, Spencer T: Clonidine for sleep disturbances associated with attention-deficit hyperactivity disorder. J Am Acad Child Adolesc Psychiatry 33: 424, 1994.

27.3.12 CLOZAPINE

Clozapine (Clozaril) is an effective antipsychotic drug that is associated with significantly fewer parkinsonianlike effects than are the conventional antipsychotics, which act primarily by their antagonist activity at dopamine type 2 (D_2) receptors. In addition, clozapine may be more effective in the treatment of the negative symptoms of schizophrenia than are the conventional antipsychotics and in the treatment of schizophrenic patients who have not responded to the traditional antipsychotic drugs. However, treatment with clozapine is associated with specific adverse events, the most serious of which is the occurrence of agranulocytosis in about 1 to 2 percent of all patients, an adverse event that necessitates the weekly hematological monitoring of patients who are being treated with clozapine.

THERAPEUTIC INDICATIONS

Treatment-Resistant Schizophrenia

The only FDA-approved indication for clozapine is as a therapy for treatment-resistant schizophrenia. Many studies suggested that indication; the most carefully conducted United States trial compared about 250 schizophrenic patients who had been defined as treatment-resistant because they had failed to improve during at least three adequate trials of various antipsychotic drugs. One group of patients were treated with clozapine, the others with both chlorpromazine (Thorazine) and benztropine (Cogentin). The treatment response of the clozapine group was clearly superior to the response of the chlorpromazine-benztropine group; only 4 percent of patients in the chlorpromazine-benztropine group showed significant improvement, compared with 30 percent in the clozapine group.

A challenge to today's clinician is to define the meaning of "treatment-resistant," since many patients have minimal responses to conventional antipsychotic drugs, resulting in minimally productive and rewarding lives. As clinicians become comfortable with the hematological monitoring necessary with clozapine treatment, clozapine may be used in a broad range of patients, since it may be a more effective treatment than the conventional antipsychotic drugs.

Other Indications

Many clinicians are using clozapine in patients who are seriously ill or who have severe tardive dyskinesia or a particular sensitivity to the extrapyramidal adverse effects of standard antipsychotic drugs. Clozapine treatment suppresses the abnormal movements of tardive dyskinesia, as does treatment with conventional antipsychotics; but, in contrast to conventional antipsychotics, clozapine may treat the movement disorder. Anecdotal reports and small, uncontrolled studies note the use of clozapine in schizoaffective disorder patients, severely ill bipolar I disorder patients, patients with borderline personality disorder, and patients with Parkinson's disease.

PRECAUTIONS AND ADVERSE REACTIONS

The feature of clozapine that distinguishes it from standard antipsychotics is its absence of extrapyramidal adverse effects. Clozapine does not cause acute dystonia, and it is associated with low incidences of parkinsonism (less than 5 percent), including perioral tremor (so-called rabbit syndrome), and akinesia, although there are reports that clozapine may be associated with akathisia. Clozapine may be associated with a much lower incidence of tardive dyskinesia than are other antipsychotics, although a few case reports do note that association. Because of its weak effects on D_2 receptors, clozapine does not affect prolactin secretion; thus, clozapine does not cause galactorrhea. The two most serious adverse effects associated with clozapine are agranulocytosis and seizures.

Agranulocytosis

Agranulocytosis is defined as a decrease in the number of white blood cells, with a specific decrease in the number of polymorphonuclear leukocytes. The erythrocyte and platelet concentrations are unaffected. Agranulocytosis occurs in 1 to 2 percent of all patients treated with clozapine; that percentage contrasts with an incidence of 0.04 to 0.5 percent of patients treated with standard antipsychotics. Early studies showed that a third of the patients who experienced agranulocytosis from clozapine died; however, careful clinical monitoring of the hematological status of clozapine-treated patients can virtually prevent fatalities by the early recognition of hematological problems and the cessation of clozapine use. Agranulocytosis can appear precipitously or gradually; it most often develops in the first six months of treatment, although it can appear much later than that. Increased age and female sex are additional risk factors for the development of clozapine-induced agranulocytosis. However, some undetermined genetic factor probably puts specific patients at risk for agranulocytosis.

Clozapine is also associated with the development of benign cases of leukocytosis (0.6 percent of patients), leukopenia (3 percent), eosinophilia (1 percent), and elevated erythrocyte sedimentation rates.

Seizures

About 5 percent of patients taking more than 600 mg a day of clozapine, 3 to 4 percent of patients taking 300 to 600 mg

a day, and 1 to 2 percent of patients taking less than 300 mg a day have clozapine-associated seizures. Those percentages are higher than those associated with the use of standard antipsychotic drugs. If seizures develop in a patient, clozapine should be temporarily stopped. Phenobarbital (Luminal) treatment can be initiated, and clozapine can be restarted at about 50 percent of the previous dosage, then gradually raised again. Carbamazepine (Tegretol) should not be used in combination with clozapine because of its association with agranulocytosis. The plasma concentrations of other antiepileptics must be monitored carefully because of the possibility of pharmacokinetic interactions with clozapine.

Cardiovascular Effects

Tachycardia, hypotension, and electrocardiographic (ECG) changes are associated with clozapine treatment. The tachycardia is due to vagal inhibition and can be treated with peripherally acting β-adrenergic antagonists, such as atenolol (Tenormin), although that treatment may aggravate the hypotensive effects of the clozapine. The hypotensive effects of clozapine may be severe enough to result in syncopal episodes, especially whenever the initial dosage exceed 75 mg a day. Syncopal episodes can usually be avoided if the starting dosage is low (25 mg a day) and the dosage is raised gradually, thus allowing tolerance for the hypotensive effects of the drug to develop. Additional treatment measures for hypotension include support stockings, increased sodium intake, and, possibly, fludrocortisone treatment. In addition to tachycardia, potential ECG changes with clozapine include nonspecific ST-T wave changes, T wave flattening, or T wave inversions, although those changes are usually not clinically significant.

Other Adverse Effects

The most common other adverse effects associated with clozapine treatment are sedation, fatigue, sialorrhea, weight gain, various GI symptoms (most commonly constipation), anticholinergic effects, and fever. Sedation and sialorrhea can often be the most troubling of those adverse effects to the patient. Sedation is most common early in the course of treatment, and the effects of daytime sedation can be reduced by giving most of the clozapine dosage at night. Sialorrhea can be a disturbing adverse effect, and it is often most severe at night, resulting in the complaint by patients that their pillows are wet when they awake in the morning. Because of the potentially additive effects of anticholinergic drugs and the anticholinergic activity of clozapine, treatment of sialorrhea with anticholinergic drugs is not advised; however, there have been reports of successful treatment with clonidine (Catapres) patches (0.1 mg weekly) and low doses of amitriptyline (Elavil) at bedtime. Although mild hypothermia is commonly associated with clozapine, fevers of 18 to 28F above normal may develop, usually during the first month of treatment, often causing concern regarding the development of an infection because of agranulocytosis. Clozapine should be withheld in those cases; if the white blood cell count (WBC) is normal, clozapine can be reinstituted slowly and at a low dosage. Because neuroleptic malignant syndrome has been reportedly associated with clozapine, the clinician must also consider that possibility in the differential diagnosis of fever in a clozapine-treated patient.

Precautions

Clozapine use by pregnant women has not been studied; because the drug can be excreted in breast milk, it should not be taken by nursing mothers. Clozapine should also not be used in patients with WBCs below 3,500, a history of a bone marrow disorder, or a history of clozapine-induced agranulocytosis. Because of the variety of cardiovascular changes associated with clozapine use, the drug should be used with caution by patients with preexisting cardiac disease. Patients with preexisting seizure disorders or histories of significant head trauma are at greater risk for seizures while taking clozapine.

DRUG INTERACTIONS

Clozapine should not be used with any other drug that is associated with the development of agranulocytosis or bone marrow suppression. Such drugs include carbamazepine (Tegretol), propylthiouracil, sulfonamides, and captopril (Capoten). Central nervous system depressants, alcohol, or tricyclic drugs coadministered with clozapine may increase the risk for seizures, sedation, and cardiac effects. The coadministration of benzodiazepines and clozapine may be associated with an increased incidence of orthostasis and syncope. There have been rare case reports of respiratory depression after the coadministration of benzodiazepines and clozapine at the initiation of clozapine treatment. Lithium (Eskalith) combined with clozapine may increase the risk of seizures, confusion, and movement disorders. A few case reports suggest that lithium not be used in combination with clozapine by patients who have experienced an episode of neuroleptic malignant syndrome.

DOSAGE AND ADMINISTRATION

Pretreatment Assessment

Once a physician has determined that a trial of clozapine is warranted for a particular patient, the risk and the benefits of clozapine treatment must be explained to the patient and the family. The informed consent procedure should be documented in the patient's chart. The patient's history should include information about blood disorders, epilepsy, cardiovascular disease, and hepatic and renal diseases. The presence of a hepatic or renal disease necessitates the use of low starting dosages of the drug. The laboratory examination should include an electrocardiogram (ECG), several complete blood counts (CBCs) with white blood cell counts (WBCs), which can then be averaged, and liver and renal function tests.

Titration and Dosage

Clozapine is available in 25 and 100 mg tablets; 1 mg of clozapine is equivalent to about $1\frac{1}{2}$ to 2 mg of chlorpromazine. The initial dosage is usually 25 mg one or two times daily, although a conservative initial dosage is 12.5 mg twice daily. The dosage can then be raised gradually (25 mg a day every two or three days) to 300 mg a day in divided doses, usually two or three times daily. The gradual increase in dosage is necessitated by the potential development of hypotension, syncope, and sedation, which are adverse effects for which the patient can usually develop tolerance if the dose titration is gradual enough. The usual effective treatment range is 400 to 500 mg a day, although dosages up to 600 mg a day can be used. If a patient stops taking clozapine for more than a 36-hour period, the clinician should restart the drug at 12.5 to 25 mg twice daily and then titrate the dosage upward to the previous dosage level. After the decision to terminate the drug, clozapine treatment should be tapered whenever possible to avoid cholinergic rebound symptoms, such as diaphoresis, flushing, diarrhea, and hyperactivity.

Plasma Concentrations

Data on the relation between plasma concentrations of clozapine and clinical efficacy are still limited, and many of the available data indicate a lack of any clear correlation. Nevertheless, for cases in which it seems indicated and possible to check plasma concentrations, the average range of plasma concentrations is 200 to 400 ng per mL, with concentrations below 100 ng per mL considered to be low and those above 500 ng per mL to be high, although one study indicated that concentrations above 500 ng per mL are associated with improved response.

Laboratory Monitoring

Weekly WBCs are indicated to monitor the patient for the development of agranulocytosis. Although monitoring is expensive, early indication of agranulocytosis can prevent a fatal outcome. If the WBC is less than 2,000 cells per mm^3 or the granulocyte count is less than 1,000 per mm^3, clozapine should be discontinued, a hematological consultation should be obtained, and a bone marrow sample should be considered. Patients with agranulocytosis should not be reexposed to the drug. Physicians can monitor the WBC through any laboratory. Proof of monitoring must be presented to the pharmacist to obtain the medication.

References

Fuchs D C: Clozapine treatment of bipolar disorder in a young adolescent. J Am Acad Child Adolesc Psychiatry 33: 1299, 1994.
Goldberg T E, Weinberger D R: The effects of clozapine on neurocognition: An overview. J Clin Psychiatry 55 (Suppl B): 88, 1994.
Gupta S, Baker P: Clozapine treatment of polydipsia. Ann Clin Psychiatry 6: 135, 1994.
Piscitelli S C, Frazier J A, McKenna K, Albus K E, Grothe D R, Gordon C T, Rapoport J L: Plasma clozapine and haloperidol concentrations in adolescents with childhood-onset schizophrenia: Association with response. J Clin Psychiatry 55 (Suppl B): 94, 1994.
Stern R G, Kahn R S, Davidson M, Nora R M Davis K L: Early response to clozapine in schizophrenia. Am J Psychiatry 151: 1817, 1994.
Van Kammen D P, Marder S R: Clozapine. In Comprehensive Textbook of Psychiatry, ed 6, H I Kaplan, B J Sadock, editors, p 1979. Williams & Wilkins, Baltimore, 1995.

27.3.13 DANTROLENE

Dantrolene (Dantrium) is a direct-acting skeletal muscles relaxant. The only indication for dantrolene in contemporary clinical psychiatry is as one of the potentially effective treatments for neuroleptic malignant syndrome.

THERAPEUTIC INDICATIONS

The primary psychiatric indication for intravenous (IV) dantrolene is spasticity in neuroleptic malignant syndrome. Dantrolene is almost always used in conjunction with appropriate supportive measures and a dopamine receptor agonist—for example, bromocriptine (Parlodel). If all available case reports and studies are summarized, about 80 percent of all patients with neuroleptic malignant syndrome who received dantrolene apparently benefited clinically from the drug. Muscle relaxation and a general and dramatic improvement in symptoms can appear within minutes of IV administration, although the beneficial effects usually take several hours to appear. Some evidence indicates that dantrolene treatment must be continued for some time, perhaps days to a week or more, to minimize the risk of the recurrence of symptoms, although the data for that clinical opinion are limited.

PRECAUTIONS AND ADVERSE REACTIONS

Muscle weakness, drowsiness, dizziness, light-headedness, nausea, diarrhea, malaise, and fatigue are the most common adverse effects of dantrolene. Those effects are generally transient. The central nervous system (CNS) effects of dantrolene can include speech disturbances (which may also reflect its effects on the muscles of speech), headache, visual disturbances, alteration of taste, depression, confusion, hallucinations, nervousness, and insomnia. Many of the serious adverse effects of dantrolene are associated with long-term treatment, rather than short-term use for the treatment of neuroleptic malignant syndrome. The potential serious adverse effects include hepatitis, seizures, and pleural effusion with pericarditis. Because of its potential for severe adverse effects, dantrolene should not be used by psychiatric patients for any long-term treatment. The effects are not associated with short-term IV use. Dantrolene should be used with caution by patients with hepatic, renal, and chronic lung diseases. Dantrolene can cross the placenta and is, thus, contraindicated for pregnant women and should not be used by nursing mothers except in emergency situations, such as neuroleptic malignant syndrome. Data are not available regarding the use of dantrolene by the elderly, and no unique problems have been associated with its use by children.

DRUG INTERACTIONS

The risk of liver toxicity may be increased in patients who are also taking estrogens. Dantrolene should be used with caution by patients who are using other drugs that produce drowsiness, most notably the benzodiazepines. In the case of neuroleptic malignant syndrome, however, the general guidelines regarding dantrolene must be weighed against the severity of the syndrome. Dantrolene should not be given IV in combination with calcium channel inhibitors.

DOSAGE AND ADMINISTRATION

In addition to the immediate discontinuation of antipsychotic drugs, medical support to cool the patient, and the monitoring of vital signs and renal output, dantrolene in dosages of 1 mg per kg can be given orally four times daily, or 1 to 5 mg per kg can be given IV to reduce muscle spasms in patients with neuroleptic malignant syndrome. Although some clinicians have recommended low dosages because of the side effects, other clinicians indicate that dosages of 10 mg per kg a day are most likely to be effective. Dantrolene is supplied as 25 mg, 50 mg, and 100 mg capsules and in a 20 mg parenteral preparation.

References

Becker B N, Ismail N: The neuroleptic malignant syndrome and acute renal failure. J Am Soc Nephrol 4: 1406, 1994.
Caroff S N, Mann S C: Neuroleptic malignant syndrome. Med Clin North Am 77: 185, 1993.
Kaplan H I, Sadock B J: Other pharmacological therapies. In Comprehensive Textbook of Psychiatry, ed 6, H I Kaplan, B J Sadock, editors, p 2122. Williams & Wilkins, Baltimore, 1995.
Khan A, Jaffe J H, Nelson W H, Morrison B: Resolution of neuroleptic malignant syndrome with dantrolene sodium: Case report. J Clin Psychiatry 46: 244, 1985.
Nisijima K, Ishiguro T: Does dantrolene influence central dopamine and serotonin metabolism in the neuroleptic malignant syndrome? A retrospective study. Biol Psychiatry 33: 45, 1993.
Wedel D J, Quinlan J G, Iaizzo P A: Clinical effects of intravenously administered dantrolene. Mayo Clin Proc 70: 241, 1995.

27.3.14 DISULFIRAM

Disulfiram (Antabuse) is used in the treatment of alcohol dependence. Its main effect is to produce an unpleasant reaction in a person who ingests even a small amount of alcohol while taking disulfiram. However, because of the risk of severe and even fatal disulfiram-alcohol reactions, disulfiram therapy is used less often today than previously.

THERAPEUTIC INDICATIONS

The primary indication for disulfiram use is an aversive conditioning treatment for alcohol dependence. Either the fear of having a disulfiram-alcohol reaction or the memory of having had one is meant to condition the patient not to use alcohol. Some clinicians induce a disulfiram-alcohol reaction in patients at the beginning of therapy to convince the patients of the severe unpleasantness of the symptoms. However, that practice is not recommended, since a disulfiram-alcohol reaction can lead to cardiovascular collapse. It is usually sufficient to describe the severity and the unpleasantness of the disulfiram-alcohol reaction graphically enough to discourage the patient from imbibing alcohol. Disulfiram treatment should be combined with such treatments as psychotherapy, group therapy, and support groups such as Alcoholic Anonymous (AA). The treatment of alcohol dependence requires careful monitoring; since a patient can simply decide not to take the disulfiram, compliance with the medication should be monitored if possible.

PRECAUTIONS AND ADVERSE REACTIONS

With Alcohol Consumption

The intensity of the disulfiram-alcohol reaction varies with each patient. In extreme cases it is marked by respiratory depression, cardiovascular collapse, myocardial infarction, convulsions, and death. Therefore, disulfiram is contraindicated for a patient with a significant pulmonary or cardiovascular disease. In addition, disulfiram should be used with caution, if at all, by a patient with nephritis, brain damage, hypothyroidism, diabetes, hepatic disease, seizures, polysubstance dependence, or an abnormal electroencephalogram (EEG). Most fatal reactions occur in patients who are taking more than 500 mg a day of disulfiram and who consume more than three ounces of alcohol. The treatment of a severe disulfiram-alcohol reaction is primarily supportive to prevent shock.

Without Alcohol Consumption

The adverse effects of disulfiram in the absence of alcohol consumption include fatigue, dermatitis, impotence, optic neuritis, a variety of mental changes, and hepatic damage. A metabolite of disulfiram inhibits dopamine hydroxylase, thus potentially exacerbating psychosis in patients with psychotic disorders.

DRUG INTERACTIONS

Disulfiram increases the blood concentration of diazepam (Valium), paraldehyde (Paral), phenytoin (Dilantin), caffeine, tetrahydrocannabinols (the active ingredient in marijuana), barbiturates, anticoagulants, isoniazid, and tricyclic drugs.

LABORATORY INTERFERENCES

In rare instances, disulfiram has been reported to decrease the uptake of iodine-131 (I^{131}) and protein-bound iodine test results. In research settings, disulfiram may reduce urinary concentrations of homovanillic acid, the major metabolite of dopamine, because of its inhibition of dopamine hydroxylase.

DOSAGE AND ADMINISTRATION

Disulfiram is supplied in tablets of 250 mg and 500 mg. The usual initial dosage is 500 mg a day taken by mouth for the first one or two weeks, followed by a maintenance dosage of 250 mg a day. The dosage should not exceed 500 mg a day. The maintenance dosage range is 125 to 500 mg a day.

The patient must be instructed that the ingestion of even the smallest amount of alcohol will bring on a disulfiram-alcohol reaction, with all its unpleasant effects. In addition, the patient should be warned against ingesting any alcohol-containing preparations, such as cough drops, tonics of any kind, and alcohol-containing foods and sauces. Some reactions have occurred in men who used alcohol-based after-shave lotions and inhaled the fumes; therefore, precautions must be explicit and should include any topically applied preparations containing alcohol, such as perfume.

Disulfiram should not be administered until the patient has abstained from alcohol for at least 12 hours. Patients should be warned that the disulfiram-alcohol reaction may occur as long as one or two weeks after the last dose of disulfiram. Patients should carry identification cards describing the disulfiram-alcohol reaction and listing the name and the telephone number of the physician to be called.

References

Barrera S E, Osinski W A, Davidoff E: The use of Antabuse (tetraethylthiuramdisulphide) in chronic alcoholics. 1950. Am J Psychiatry *151* (Suppl 6): 263, 1994.

Kaplan H I, Sadock B J: Other pharmacological therapies. In *Comprehensive Textbook of Psychiatry*, ed 6, H I Kaplan, B J Sadock, editors, p 2122. Williams & Wilkins, Baltimore, 1995.

Helander A, Lowenmo C, Johansson M: Distribution of acetaldehyde in human blood: Effects of ethanol and treatment with disulfiram. Alcohol Alcohol *28*: 461, 1993.

Myers W C, Donahue J E, Goldstein M R: Disulfiram for alcohol use disorders in adolescents. J Am Acad Child Adolesc Psychiatry *33*: 484, 1994.

Ryan T V, Sciara A D, Barth J T: Chronic neuropsychological impairment resulting from disulfiram overdose. J Stud Alcohol *54*: 389, 1993.

Wright C, Moore R D, Grodin D M, Spyker D A, Gill E V: Screening for disulfiram-induced liver test dysfunction in an inpatient alcoholism program. Alcohol Clin Exp Res *17*: 184, 1993.

27.3.15 L-DOPA

L-Dopa, also known as levodopa (Larodopa), is an indirectly acting dopamine agonist. L-Dopa, given in combination with a peripheral inhibitor of L-dopa decarboxylase (for example, carbidopa), is the most commonly used treatment for idiopathic Parkinson's disease. A commonly used commercially available combination of L-dopa and carbidopa is Sinemet. Within the field of clinical psychiatry, L-dopa is not a primary therapy for any single indication; rather, L-dopa is used as a second-line or third-line treatment for neuroleptic-induced parkinsonism.

THERAPEUTIC INDICATIONS

In psychiatry, L-dopa is used for the treatment of neuroleptic-induced parkinsonism, although anticholinergics, amantadine (Symadine), antihistamines, and bromocriptine (Parlodel) are more frequently used. L-Dopa is the least often used because the other drugs are equally effective and are associated with fewer adverse effects. Nonetheless, L-dopa can be used in patients to treat extrapyramidal symptoms, akinesia, and focal perioral tremors (sometimes called rabbit syndrome). Additional evidence, based on case reports and small studies, indicates that L-dopa may be effective in the treatment of restless legs syndrome and tardive dyskinesia. Preliminary data indicate that L-dopa may be effective in the treatment of the negative symptoms of schizophrenia, although that indication should be considered only in research settings.

PRECAUTIONS AND ADVERSE REACTIONS

Adverse effects are common with L-dopa therapy, thus limiting its usefulness in general psychiatric practice. Most adverse effects are dose-related or associated with withdrawal from the drug. Some adverse effects are seen early in treatment and include nausea, vomiting, orthostatic hypotension, and cardiac arrhythmias. After long-term use, patients may experience abnormal involuntary movements and psychiatric disturbances, including psychosis, depression, and mania. Anecdotal reports indicate that the abrupt discontinuation of L-dopa can precipitate a syndrome similar to neuroleptic malignant syndrome, especially if the patient is concomitantly receiving an antipsychotic. L-Dopa is contraindicated during pregnancy and is contraindicated for nursing mothers, especially since it inhibits lactation.

DRUG INTERACTIONS

Drugs that block dopamine type 2 (D_2) receptors—for example, haloperidol (Haldol)—are capable of reversing the effects of L-dopa. The concurrent use of tricyclic drugs and L-dopa has been reported to cause symptoms of neurotoxicity, such as rigidity, agitation, and tremor. L-Dopa is also capable of potentiating the hypotensive effects of diuretics and other antihypertensive medications. L-Dopa should not be used in conjunction with monoamine oxidase inhibitors (MAOIs), including selegiline (Eldepryl). MAOIs should be discontinued at least two weeks before the initiation of L-dopa therapy. Benzodiazepines, phenytoin (Dilantin), and pyridoxine may interfere with the therapeutic effects of L-dopa.

LABORATORY INTERFERENCES

L-Dopa administration has been associated with false reports of elevated serum and urinary uric acid concentrations, urinary glucose tests, urinary ketone tests, and urinary catecholamine concentrations. Whether L-dopa results in a false-positive result in those tests depends on the specific test method used, since some test methods are not affected by L-dopa.

DOSAGE AND ADMINISTRATION

Dosages of L-dopa for the treatment of antipsychotic-induced parkinsonism should be similar to the dosages used for idiopathic parkinsonism. Starting dosages of 100 mg three times a day may be increased until the patient is functionally improved. Hyperkinesias, in the form of choreiform and dystonic movements, are dose-related side effects. Particularly after prolonged therapy, periods of profound bradykinesia may alternate with periods during which the patient can move well or is hyperkinetic (on-off phenomenon). The addition of other antiparkinsonian medications, usually such dopamine agonists as bromocriptine, may ameliorate the problem, although the on-off phenomenon may eventually require the cessation of L-dopa therapy. L-Dopa is available in 100 mg, 250 mg, and 500 mg tablets and capsules.

References

Brannan T, Yahr M D: Comparative study of selegiline plus L-dopa-carbidopa versus L-dopa-carbidopa alone in the treatment of Parkinson's disease. Ann Neurol *37*: 95, 1995.

Kaplan B, Mason N A: Levodopa in restless legs syndrome. Ann Pharmacother *26*: 214, 1992.

Kaplan H I, Sadock B J: Other pharmacological therapies. In *Comprehensive Textbook of Psychiatry*, ed 6, H I Kaplan, B J Sadock, editors, p 2122. Williams & Wilkins, Baltimore, 1995.

McDermott M P, Jankovic J, Carter J, Fahn S, et al: Factors predictive of the need for levodopa therapy in early, untreated Parkinson's disease. Arch Neurol *52*: 565, 1995.

Tolosa E S, Valldeoriola F, Marti M J: New and emerging strategies for improving levodopa treatment. Neurology *44* (7 Suppl 6): S35, 1994.

27.3.16 DOPAMINE RECEPTOR ANTAGONISTS (ANTIPSYCHOTICS)

A diverse group of drugs that blockade the dopamine type 2 (D_2) receptor are commonly referred to as antipsychotic drugs. The major indication for the use of the drugs is the treatment of schizophrenia and other psychotic disorders. The antipsychotic drug class includes chlorpromazine (Thorazine), thioridazine (Mellaril), fluphenazine (Prolixin), and haloperidol (Haldol). One new antipsychotic drug, risperidone (Risperdal), has been introduced in the United States. Although risperidone is a potent antagonist of D_2 receptors, it has additional pharmacological features that may confer therapeutic advantages and improved side-effect profile, compared with previously available dopamine receptor antagonists.

"Antipsychotics" and "dopamine receptor antagonists" are not necessarily synonymous. Clozapine (Clozaril) is an effective antipsychotic but differs from all the drugs discussed here in that it has comparatively little activity at D_2 receptors. The drugs discussed here have also been referred to as neuroleptics and major tranquilizers. The term "neuroleptic" denotes the neurological or motor effects of most of the drugs. The development of new compounds, such as risperidone, that are associated with few neurological effects makes the continued use of the term "neuroleptic" inaccurate as an overall label for the compounds. The term "major tranquilizer" inaccurately implies that the primary effect of the drugs is to sedate patients and confounds the drugs with the so-called minor tranquilizers, such as the

benzodiazepines. An additional confusion in the nomenclature of the drugs is the common misuse of the term "phenothiazine" as a synonym for the term "antipsychotic." That use is inaccurate because the phenothiazines, such as chlorpromazine, are only one type of antipsychotic drug.

THERAPEUTIC INDICATIONS

Idiopathic Psychoses

The idiopathic psychoses include those in the fourth edition of *Diagnostic and Statistical Manual of Mental Disorders* (DSM-IV) that have no known cause. Those disorders include schizophrenia, schizophreniform disorder, schizoaffective disorder, delusional disorder, brief psychotic disorder, manic episodes, and major depressive disorder with psychotic features. Antipsychotic drugs are effective in both the short-term and the long-term management of those conditions; that is, antipsychotics both reduce acute symptoms and prevent future exacerbations.

SCHIZOPHRENIA

The short-term efficacy of antipsychotics in the treatment of schizophrenia has been demonstrated in hundreds of trials. The comparatively small number of trials that failed to demonstrate the superiority of the antipsychotics over a placebo almost always used dosages of an antipsychotic that were too low (less than 300 mg chlorpromazine equivalence) or were not rigorously designed studies in the first place. Similarly, dozens of well-controlled studies have demonstrated the efficacy of antipsychotic drugs in the maintenance treatment of psychotic patients. One survey of those studies found that about 75 percent of all schizophrenic patients relapse over the course of one year if treated with a placebo, in comparison with only 15 to 25 percent of patients who relapse after being treated with antipsychotic drugs. Furthermore, the severity of the symptoms during the relapses are less severe in the patients receiving maintenance treatment than in those patients not receiving antipsychotic treatment.

In general, the antipsychotics are thought to be more effective in the treatment of the positive symptoms (for example, hallucinations, delusions, and agitation) than in the treatment of the negative symptoms (for example, emotional withdrawal and ambivalence). A debate continues about that belief, since the antipsychotic drugs themselves may contribute to the negative symptoms. It is also generally believed that paranoid patients are more responsive than nonparanoid patients, that so-called reactive psychoses are more responsive than so-called process psychoses, and that female patients are more responsive than male patients. Some patients do not respond to any of the old antipsychotic drugs, and those patients are often referred to as treatment-resistant patients. Clozapine has been approved by the Food and Drug Administration (FDA) for the treatment of such patients. Although large-scale studies of the use of risperidone and remoxipride for that patient population have not yet been conducted, clinical trials of those drugs for treatment-resistant patients are warranted.

OTHER IDIOPATHIC PSYCHOSES

Antipsychotics are often used in combination with antimanic drugs to treat psychosis or manic excitement in bipolar I disorder. Although lithium (Eskalith), carbamazepine (Tegretol), and valproate (Depakene) are the drugs of choice for that condition, those drugs generally have a slower onset of action than do antipsychotics in the treatment of the acute symptoms. Thus, the general practice is to use combination therapy at the initiation of treatment and to gradually withdraw the antipsychotic after the antimanic agent has reached its onset of activity.

Combination treatment with an antipsychotic and an antidepressant is the treatment of choice for major depressive disorder with psychotic features, although electroconvulsive therapy (ECT) is also likely to be effective. Because of the potential adverse effects of long-term administration of the old antipsychotics (for example, tardive dyskinesia with long-term treatment), maintenance treatment with those drugs is indicated primarily for schizophrenia and not for the mood disorders. However, the introduction of such new antipsychotics as risperidone may make the long-term treatment of mood disorder patients with those drugs a clinically warranted treatment.

Schizoaffective disorder patients and delusional disorder patients often respond favorably to treatment with antipsychotic drugs. Some patients with borderline personality disorder who have marked psychotic symptoms as part of their disorder are also at least partially responsive to antipsychotic drugs, although those patients in particular also require psychotherapeutic treatment.

Secondary Psychoses

Secondary psychoses are psychotic syndromes that are associated with an identified organic cause, such as a brain tumor, a dementing disorder (for example, dementia of the Alzheimer's type), or substance abuse. The antipsychotic drugs are generally effective in the treatment of psychotic symptoms that are associated with those syndromes. The high-potency antipsychotics are usually safer than the low-potency antipsychotics in such patients because of the high-potency drugs' lower cardiotoxic, epileptogenic, and anticholinergic activities. However, antipsychotic drugs should not be used to treat withdrawal symptoms associated with ethanol or barbiturates because of the risk that such treatment will facilitate the development of withdrawal seizures. The drug of choice in such cases is usually a benzodiazepine. Agitation and psychosis associated with such neurological conditions as dementia of the Alzheimer's type are responsive to antipsychotic treatment; high-potency drugs and low dosages are generally preferable. Even with high-potency drugs, as many as 25 percent of elderly patients may experience episodes of hypotension. Risperidone may have a superior side-effect profile in those patients, although that has not been shown in well-controlled studies at this time. Low dosages of high-potency drugs, such as 0.5 to 5 mg a day of haloperidol, are usually sufficient for the treatment of those patients, although thioridazine, 10 to 50 mg a day, is also used because of its particularly potent sedative properties.

Severe Agitation and Violent Behavior

Antipsychotic drugs are commonly used for the treatment of patients who are severely agitated and violent, although other drugs, such as benzodiazepines and barbiturates, are also usually effective for the immediate control of such behavior. Symptoms such as extreme irritability, lack of impulse control, severe hos-

tility, gross hyperactivity, and agitation are responsive to short-term antipsychotic treatment. The long-term use of antipsychotic drugs for those indications must be weighed against the risk for neurological side effects (for example, tardive dyskinesia), although the advent of new antipsychotic drugs (for example, risperidone) may sometimes affect the risk-benefit consideration. Mentally handicapped children, especially those with profound mental retardation and autistic disorder, often have associated episodes of violence, aggression, and agitation, which are responsive to treatment with antipsychotic drugs. Again, the risk of the old antipsychotic drugs must be considered before instituting long-term treatment, and the potentially low risk of the new antipsychotic drugs will have to be evaluated in subsequent clinical trials. In general, the use of the high-potency antipsychotics, which cause little sedation, is preferred to the use of the more sedating low-potency drugs. Also, especially for long-term treatment, drugs such as lithium, the anticonvulsants (carbamazepine and valproate), the β-adrenergic receptor antagonists, and even serotonergic drugs should be considered before long-term treatment with antipsychotic drugs is undertaken.

Movement Disorders

Both the psychosis and the movement disorder of Huntington's disease are responsive to treatment with dopamine receptor antagonists, such as haloperidol. Clinical trials of risperidone, and clozapine in Huntington's disease patients have not yet been conducted, although such trials may show those drugs' superior efficacy, safety, or tolerability in the condition.

One of the antipsychotic drugs, pimozide (Orap), is specifically approved in the United States for the treatment of the motor and vocal tics of Tourette's disorder, although other dopamine receptor antagonists are likely to be equally effective. Pimozide is used for Tourette's disorder because of its alleged association with few extrapyramidal effects, although pimozide has its own side effects, such as marked prolongation of the QT interval of the electrocardiogram (ECG) in dosages over 10 mg a day and an increased risk for drug-induced seizures in dosages of 20 mg a day.

The rare neurological disorders ballismus and hemiballismus (which affects only one side of the body) are characterized by propulsive movements of the limbs away from the body. They are also responsive to treatment with dopamine receptor antagonists.

Other Psychiatric and Nonpsychiatric Indications

The use of thioridazine for the treatment of depression with marked anxiety or agitation has been approved in the United States, although that is an outdated indication for the drug because of the availability of drugs with superior efficacy and safety profiles. Nevertheless, some clinicians use small dosages of antipsychotic drugs (0.5 mg of haloperidol or 25 mg of chlorpromazine two or three times daily) to treat severe anxiety. The risk of inducing neurological side effects must be carefully weighed against the potential therapeutic benefits in such cases. The dopamine receptor antagonists are also sometimes used as adjuvants to treatment regimens for chronic pain, although the drugs should only be prescribed for that indication by specialists in the treatment of chronic pain. Miscellaneous indications for the use of dopamine receptor antagonists include the treatment of nausea, emesis, hiccups, and pruritus.

PRECAUTIONS AND ADVERSE REACTIONS

Nonneurological Adverse Effects

CARDIAC EFFECTS

Low-potency antipsychotics are more cardiotoxic than are high-potency antipsychotics. Chlorpromazine causes prolongation of the QT and PR intervals, blunting of the T waves, and depression of the ST segment. Thioridazine, in particular, has marked effects on the T wave and is associated with malignant arrhythmias, such as torsade de pointes, perhaps explaining why overdoses of piperidine phenothiazines may be the most lethal of this group of drugs. When QT intervals exceed 0.44 msec, there is some correlation with an increased risk for sudden death, possibly secondary to ventricular tachycardia or ventricular fibrillation. Although risperidone is associated with some increase in the QT interval, that is not clinically significant in the limited clinical data currently available. The early reports of remoxipride indicate that it may be a particularly safe antipsychotic from a cardiac standpoint.

SUDDEN DEATH

The cardiac effects of antipsychotics have been hypothesized to be related to sudden death in patients treated with the drugs. However, careful evaluation of the literature indicates that it is premature to attribute the sudden deaths to the antipsychotic drugs. Supporting that view is the observation that the introduction of antipsychotics had no effect on the incidence of sudden death in schizophrenic patients. In addition, both low-potency and high-potency drugs were involved in the reported cases. Furthermore, many reports were of patients with other medical problems who were also treated with several other drugs.

ORTHOSTATIC (POSTURAL) HYPOTENSION

Orthostatic (postural) hypotension is mediated by adrenergic blockade and is most common with low-potency antipsychotics, particularly chlorpromazine, thioridazine, and clozapine. It occurs most frequently during the first few days of treatment, and tolerance is rapidly developed for the adverse effects. The chief dangers of orthostatic hypotension are that the patients may faint, fall, and injure themselves, although such occurrences are not common.

When using intramuscular (IM) low-potency antipsychotics, the clinician should measure the patient's blood pressure (lying and standing) before and after the first dose and during the first few days of treatment. When appropriate, patients should be warned of the possibility of fainting and should be given the usual instructions to rise from bed gradually, sit at first with their legs dangling, wait for a minute, and sit or lie down if they feel faint. Support hose may help some patients.

If hypotension does occur in patients receiving the medications, the symptoms can usually be managed by having the patients lie down with the feet higher than the head. On rare occasions, volume expansion or vasopressor agents, such as norepinephrine (Levophed), may be indicated. Because hypotension is produced by α-adrenergic blockade, the drugs also block the α-adrenergic stimulating properties of epinephrine, leaving the β-adrenergic stimulating effects untouched. Therefore, the administration of epinephrine results in a paradoxical worsening of hypotension and is contraindicated in cases of antipsychotic-induced hypotension. Pure α-adrenergic pressor agents, such as metaraminol (Aramine) and norepinephrine, are the drugs of choice in the treatment of the disorder.

HEMATOLOGICAL EFFECTS

An often transient leukopenia with a white blood cell (WBC) count around 3,500 is a common but not serious problem. A life-threatening hematological problem is agranulocytosis, which occurs most often with chlorpromazine and thioridazine use but is seen with almost all antipsychotics. Agranulocytosis occurs most frequently during the first three months of treatment and with an incidence of around 5 in 10,000 patients treated with antipsychotics. Routine complete blood counts (CBCs) are not indicated; however, if a patient reports a sore throat and fever, a CBC should be done immediately to check for the possibility. If the blood indexes are low, the antipsychotic should be stopped, and the patient should be transferred to a medical facility. The mortality rate for the complication may be as high as 30 percent. Thrombocytopenic or nonthrombocytopenic purpura, hemolytic anemias, and pancytopenia may occur rarely in patients treated with antipsychotics. If remoxipride is approved for use in the United States, hematological monitoring may be required because of the possible association of the drug with aplastic anemia.

PERIPHERAL ANTICHOLINERGIC EFFECTS

Peripheral anticholinergic effects are common and consist of dry mouth and nose, blurred vision, constipation, urinary retention, and mydriasis. Some patients also have nausea and vomiting. Chlorpromazine, thioridazine, mesoridazine (Serentil), and trifluoperazine (Stelazine) are potent anticholinergics. Anticholinergic effects can be particularly severe if a low-potency antipsychotic is used with a tricyclic drug and an anticholinergic drug; such a practice is seldom warranted. In contrast to the dry nose of old antipsychotics, risperidone may be associated with nasal congestion or rhinitis, possibly a result of an α_1-adrenergic blockade.

Dry mouth can be a troubling symptom for some patients and can endanger continued compliance. The patients can be advised to rinse out their mouths frequently with water and not to chew gum or candy containing sugar, as that can result in fungal infections of the mouth or an increased incidence of dental caries. Constipation should be treated with the usual laxative preparations, but the condition can still progress to paralytic ileus in some patients. A decrease in the antipsychotic dosage or a change to another less anticholinergic drug is warranted in such a case. Pilocarpine may be used to treat paralytic ileus, although the relief is only transitory. Bethanechol (Urecholine) (20 to 40 mg a day) may be useful in some patients with urinary retention.

ENDOCRINE EFFECTS

Blockade of the dopamine receptors in the tuberoinfundibular tract results in the increased secretion of prolactin, which can result in breast enlargement, galactorrhea, impotence in men, and amenorrhea and inhibited orgasm in women.

SEXUAL EFFECTS

Psychiatrists may not find out about the disturbing sexual effects of an antipsychotic if they do not ask about the effects specifically. The incidence of those effects is believed to be significantly underestimated. As many as 50 percent of men taking antipsychotics may experience impotence. Several reports have stated that treatment of the condition with bromocriptine (Parlodel) or yohimbine (Yocon) is successful in some patients, although the risk of exacerbating the underlying psychosis must be considered with both drugs. Both men and women taking antipsychotics can experience anorgasmia and decreased libido. Thioridazine is particularly associated with decreased libido and retrograde ejaculation in men. Other antipsychotics have been associated with both delayed and retrograde ejaculation, although some therapeutic success has been reported after treatment with brompheniramine (Bromfed), ephedrine (Primatene), phenylpropanolamine (Comtrex), and imipramine (Tofranil) for the condition. Priapism and reports of painful orgasms have also been described, both possibly resulting from α_1-adrenergic antagonist activity.

WEIGHT GAIN

A common adverse effect of treatment with antipsychotics is weight gain, which can be significant in some cases. Molindone and, perhaps, loxapine are not associated with the symptom and may be indicated in patients for whom weight gain is a serious health hazard or a reason for noncompliance.

DERMATOLOGICAL EFFECTS

Allergic dermatitis and photosensitivity occur in a small percentage of patients, most commonly those taking low-potency drugs, particularly chlorpromazine. A variety of skin eruptions—urticarial, maculopapular, petechial, and edematous eruptions—have been reported. The eruptions occur early in treatment, generally in the first few weeks, and remit spontaneously. A photosensitivity reaction that resembles a severe sunburn also occurs in some patients taking chlorpromazine. Patients should be warned of that adverse effect, should spend no more that 30 to 60 minutes in the sun, and should use sun screens. Chlorpromazine is also associated with some cases of a blue-gray discoloration of the skin over areas exposed to sunlight. The skin changes often begin with a tan or golden brown color and progress to such colors as slate gray, metallic blue, and purple.

OPHTHALMOLOGICAL EFFECTS

Thioridazine is associated with irreversible pigmentation of the retina when given in dosages of more than 800 mg a day. An early symptom of the adverse effect can sometimes be nocturnal confusion related to difficulty with night vision. The pigmentation is similar to that seen in retinitis pigmentosa, and it can progress even after the thioridazine is stopped, finally resulting in blindness.

In contrast, chlorpromazine is associated with a relatively benign pigmentation of the eyes, characterized by whitish-brown granular deposits concentrated in the anterior lens and posterior cornea and visible only by slit-lens examination. The deposits can progress to opaque white and yellow-brown granules, often stellate. Occasionally, the conjunctiva is discolored by a brown pigment. Retinal damage is not seen in the patients, and their vision is almost never impaired. The majority of patients who show the deposits are those who have ingested 1 to 3 kg of chlorpromazine throughout their lives.

JAUNDICE

Obstructive or cholestatic jaundice is associated as a rare side effect with antipsychotic treatment. The adverse effect usually occurs in the first month of treatment and is heralded by symptoms of upper abdominal pain, nausea and vomiting, a flulike syndrome, fever, rash, eosinophilia, bilirubin in the urine, and increase in serum bilirubin, alkaline phosphatase, and hepatic transaminases. In the early days of chlorpromazine treatment, jaundice was not unusual, occurring in about 1 out of every 100 patients treated. For the past decade, the incidence has hovered around 1 in 1,000. The drop in the incidence is perhaps due to a reduction in impurities in the manufacturing of the compound, although the definitive reason for the drop in incidence is unknown.

If jaundice occurs, the clinician generally discontinues the medication, although the value of that practice has never been proved. Indeed, patients have continued to receive chlorpromazine throughout the illness without adverse effects, although that approach does not seem to be warranted, given the wide range of alternative treatments available. Jaundice has also been reported to occur with promazine (Sparine), thioridazine, and prochlorperazine (Compazine) and very rarely with fluphenazine and trifluoperazine. No convincing evidence indicates that haloperidol or many of the other nonphenothiazine antipsychotics can produce jaundice. The hepatotoxicity of risperidone is not known at this time; no particular evidence indicates that it is associated with jaundice, but risperidone does have nausea, vomiting, and abdominal pain as common side effects.

OVERDOSES OF ANTIPSYCHOTICS

The symptoms of antipsychotic overdose include extrapyramidal symptoms, mydriasis, decreased deep tendon reflexes, tachycardia, and hypotension. With the exception of overdoses of thioridazine and mesoridazine, the outcome of antipsychotic overdose is generally favorable unless the patient has also ingested other central nervous system (CNS) depressants, such as alcohol and benzodiazepines. The severe symptoms of overdose include delirium, coma, respiratory depression, and seizures. Haloperidol and possibly remoxipride may be among the safest antipsychotics in overdose. After an overdose, the electroencephalogram (EEG) shows diffuse slowing and low voltage. The piperazine phenothiazines (for example, thioridazine) can lead to heart block and ventricular fibrillation, resulting in death.

The treatment of antipsychotic overdose should include the use of activated charcoal, if possible, and gastric lavage. The use of emetics is not indicated, since the antiemetic actions of the antipsychotics inhibit their efficacy. Seizures can be treated with intravenous (IV) diazepam (Valium) or phenytoin (Dilantin). Hypotension can be treated with either norepinephrine or dopamine (Dopastat) but not epinephrine (Adrenalin).

Pregnancy and Lactation

If possible, antipsychotics should be avoided during pregnancy, particularly in the first trimester, unless the benefit outweighs the risk. In fact, however, very few data indicate a correlation between the presence of congenital malformations in the infant and the use of antipsychotics during pregnancy, except perhaps for chlorpromazine. Some data do indicate that the use of antipsychotics during pregnancy may result in decreased dopamine receptors in the neonate, increased cholesterol, and perhaps behavioral disturbances. Nevertheless, antipsychotic use in the second and third trimesters is probably relatively safe. High-potency antipsychotics are preferable to low-potency drugs, since the low-potency drugs are associated with hypotension. Although animal data indicate that risperidone is relatively safe for pregnant women, no clinical data support those basic science data.

Haloperidol and phenothiazines pass into breast milk. Whether loxapine (Loxitane), molindone (Moban), and pimozide pass into breast milk is not known, although they probably do. Women who are taking antipsychotics should not breastfeed their infants, since the available data do not prove that the practice is safe.

DRUG INTERACTIONS

Because of their many receptor effects and because of the metabolism of most of the dopamine receptor antagonists in the liver, many pharmacokinetic and pharmacodynamic drug interactions are associated with the drugs.

Antacids

Antacids and cimetidine (Tagamet), administered within two hours of antipsychotic administration, can reduce the absorption of antipsychotic drugs.

Anticholinergics

Anticholinergics may decrease the absorption of antipsychotics. The additive anticholinergic activity of antipsychotics, anticholinergics, and tricyclic drugs may result in anticholinergic toxicity.

Anticonvulsants

Phenothiazines, especially thioridazine, may decrease the metabolism of diphenylhydantoin, resulting in toxic levels of diphenylhydantoin. Barbiturates may increase the metabolism of antipsychotics, and the antipsychotics may lower the patient's seizure threshold.

Antidepressants

Tricyclic drugs and antipsychotics may decrease each other's metabolism, resulting in increased plasma concentrations of both drugs. The anticholinergic, sedative, and hypotensive effects of the drugs may also be additive.

Antihypertensives

Antipsychotics may inhibit the uptake of guanethidine (Esimil, Ismelin) in the synapse and may also inhibit the hypotensive effects of clonidine and α-methyldopa (Aldomet). Conversely, antipsychotics may have an additive effect on some hypotensive drugs. Antipsychotic drugs have a variable effect on the hypotensive effects of clonidine. Propranolol (Inderal) coadministration with antipsychotics increases the blood concentrations of both drugs.

CNS Depressants

Antipsychotics potentiate the CNS depressant effects of sedatives, opiates and opioids, antihistamines, and alcohol, particularly in patients with impaired respiratory status. When those agents are taken with alcohol, the risk for heat stroke may be increased.

Other Substances

Cigarette smoking may decrease the plasma levels of antipsychotic drugs. Epinephrine has a paradoxical hypotensive effect in patients taking antipsychotics. Antipsychotic drugs may decrease the blood concentration of warfarin (Coumadin), resulting in decreased bleeding time. Phenothiazines and pimozide should not be coadministered with other agents that prolong the QT interval.

LABORATORY INTERFERENCES

Antipsychotic drugs have been reported to interfere with some laboratory tests. Chlorpromazine and perphenazine have been reported to cause both false-positive results and false-negative results in immunological pregnancy tests and falsely elevated bilirubin (with reagent test strips) and urobilinogen (with Ehrlich's reagent test) values. Antipsychotic drugs have also been associated with an abnormal shift in the glucose tolerance test, although that shift may reflect the effects of the drugs on the glucose-regulating system. Phenothiazines have been reported to interfere with the measurement of 17-ketosteroids (with the Haltorff-Koch modification of the Zimmerman reaction) and 17-hydroxycorticosteroids (with the modified Glenn-Nelson reaction).

DOSAGE AND ADMINISTRATION

Antipsychotic drugs are remarkably safe in short-term use, and, if necessary, a clinician can administer the drugs without conducting a physical or laboratory examination of the patient. The major contraindications for antipsychotics are (1) a history of a serious allergic response, (2) the possibility that the patient has ingested a substance that will interact with the antipsychotic to induce CNS depression (for example, alcohol, opiates and opioids, barbiturates, and benzodiazepines) or anticholinergic delirium (for example, scopolamine [Donnatal] and possibly phencyclidine [PCP]), (3) the presence of a severe cardiac abnormality, (4) a high risk for seizures from organic and idiopathic causes, (5) the presence of narrow-angle glaucoma or prostatic hypertrophy if an antipsychotic with high anticholinergic activity is to be used, and (6) the presence or a history of tardive dyskinesia. Antipsychotics should be administered with caution in patients with hepatic disease, since impaired hepatic metabolism may result in high plasma concentrations of the antipsychotics. In the usual assessment, the clinician should obtain a CBC with white blood cell indexes, liver function tests, and an electrocardiogram, especially in women over 40 and men over 30. The elderly and children are more sensitive to adverse effects than are young adults; therefore, the dosage of the drug should be adjusted accordingly.

Choice of Drug

Although the potencies of the antipsychotics vary widely (Table 27.3.16–1), all available typical antipsychotics are

Table 27.3.16-1.   Dopamine Receptor Antagonists Drugs, Trade Names, Potencies, and Dosages

Generic Name	Trade Name	Potency* (mg of drug equivalent to 100 mg chlorpromazine)	Usual Adult Dosage Range (mg per day)	Usual Single IM Dose (mg)
Phenothiazines				
Aliphatic				
Chlorpromazine	Thorazine	100—low	300–800	25–50
Triflupromazine	Vespin	25–50—low	100–150	20–60
Promazine	Sparine	40—low	40–800	50–150
Piperazine				
Prochlorperazine	Compazine	15—medium	40–150	10–20
Perphenazine	Trilafon	10—medium	8–40	5–10
Trifluoperazine	Stelazine	3–5—high	6–20	1–2
Fluphenazine	Prolixin, Permitil	1.5–3—high	1–20	2–5
Acetophenazine	Tindal (no longer manufactured)	25—medium	60–120	—
Butaperazine	Repoise (not sold in U.S.)	10—medium	—	—
Carphenazine	Proketazine (not sold in U.S.)	25—medium	—	—
Piperidine				
Thioridazine	Mellaril	100—low	200–700[1]	—
Mesoridazine	Serentil	50—low	75–300	25
Piperacetazine	Quide (not sold in U.S.)	10—medium	—	—
Thioxanthenes				
Chlorprothixene	Taractan (no longer manufactured)	50—low	50–400	25–50
Thiothixene	Navane	2–5—high	6–30	2–4
Dibenzoxazepine				
Loxapine	Loxitane	10–15—medium	60–100	12.5–50
Dihydroindole				
Molindone	Moban, Lidone	6–10—medium	50–100	—
Butyrophenones				
Haloperidol	Haldol	2–5—high	60–20	2–5
Droperidol	Inapsine	10—medium	—	—
Diphenylbutylpiperidine				
Pimozide	Orap	1—high	1–10[2]	—
Benzamide				
Remoxipride[3]	Roxiam (not sold in U.S.)	50–75—low	200–400	—
Benzisoxasole				
Risperidone	Risperdal	2–3—low	4–8	—

* Recommended adult dosages are 200 to 400 mg a day of chlorpromazine or an equivalent amount of another drug.
[1] Maximum 800 mg.
[2] Second-line drug because of cardiotoxicity.
[3] Not currently available in the United States; association with hematological toxicity.

equally efficacious in the treatment of schizophrenia. The antipsychotics are available in a wide range of formulations and dose sizes (Table 27.3.16–2). Data support the conclusion that clozapine and risperidone may be more effective than other antipsychotic drugs for the treatment of the negative symptoms of schizophrenia. With the old antipsychotic drugs, no type of schizophrenia and no particular symptoms are most effectively treated by any single class of antipsychotics. However, risperidone may become the drug of first choice in the treatment of schizophrenia if its possibly superior efficacies with negative symptoms and its superior safety profiles are confirmed in wide clinical testing.

The general guidelines for choosing a particular psychotherapeutic drug should be followed when choosing an antipsychotic drug (Section 27.1). If no other rationale prevails, the choice should be based on adverse-effect profiles and the clinician's preference. Although high-potency antipsychotics are associated with increased neurological adverse effects, current clinical practice favors using them because of the high incidence of other adverse effects (for example, cardiac, hypotensive, epileptogenic, sexual, and allergic) with the low-potency drugs. A myth in psychiatry is that hyperexcitable patients respond best to chlorpromazine because it is highly sedating, whereas withdrawn patients respond best to high-potency antipsychotics, such as fluphenazine. That myth has never been proved; if sedation is a desired goal, either the antipsychotic can be given in

divided doses or a sedative drug, such as a benzodiazepine, can also be administered.

Some research supports the clinical observation that an unpleasant reaction by the patient to the first dose of an antipsychotic drug correlates highly with future poor response and noncompliance. Such experiences include a subjective negative feeling, oversedation, and acute dystonia. If a patient reports such a reaction, the clinician may be well-advised to switch the patient to a different antipsychotic. Similarly, if patients say that they did not feel well while taking a particular drug in the past, the clinician is well-advised not to initiate treatment with that drug again.

Dosage and Schedule

The therapeutic index for antipsychotics is favorable and has contributed to the unfortunate practice of routinely using high dosages of the drugs. Nevertheless, because of that common practice, physicians may be pressured by staff members to use very high dosages. Recent investigations of the dose-response curve for antipsychotics indicate that the equivalent of 10 to 20 mg of haloperidol is usually efficacious for either the short-term or the long-term treatment of schizophrenia. Some clinicians and researchers recommend that dosages equivalent to 5 to 10 mg of haloperidol be used before going to higher dosages. Antipsychotic drugs may have a bell-shaped dose-response

Table 27.3.16–2.   Dopamine Receptor Antagonist Preparations

	Tablets	Capsules	Solution	Parenteral	Rectal Suppositories
Chlorpromazine	10, 25, 50, 100, 200 mg	30, 75, 150, 200, 300 mg	10 mg/5 mL, 30 mg/mL, 100 mg/mL	25 mg/mL	25, 100 mg
Droperidol	—	—	—	2.5 mg/mL	—
Fluphenazine	1, 2.5, 5, 10 mg	—	2.5 mg/5 mL, 5 mg/mL	2.5 mg/mL (IM only)	—
Fluphenazine decanoate	—	—	—	25 mg/mL	—
Fluphenazine enanthate	—	—	—	25 mg/mL	—
Haloperidol	0.5, 1, 2, 3, 10, 20 mg	—	2 mg/mL	5 mg/mL (IM only)	—
Haloperidol decanoate	—	—	—	50 mg/mL, 100 mg/mL (IM only)	—
Loxapine	—	5, 10, 25, 50 mg	25 mg/mL	50 mg/mL	—
Mexonidazine	10, 25, 50, 100 mg	—	25 mg/mL	25 mg/mL	—
Molindone	5, 10, 75, 50, 100 mg	—	20 mg/mL	—	—
Perphenazine	2, 4, 8, 16 mg	—	16 mg/5 mL	5 mg/mL	—
Pimozide	2 mg	—	—	—	—
Prochlorperazine	5, 10, 25 mg	10, 15, 30 mg	5 mg/mL	5 mg/mL	2.5, 5, 25 mg
Promazine	25, 50, 100 mg	—	—	25 mg/mL, 50 mg/mL	—
Risperidone	1, 2, 3, 4 mg	—	—	—	—
Thioridazine	10, 15, 25, 50, 100, 150, 200 mg	—	25 mg/5 mL, 100 mg/5 mL, 30 mg/mL, 100 mg/mL	—	—
Thiothixene	—	1, 2, 5, 10, 20 mg	5 mg/mL	10 mg (IM only), 2 mg/mL (IM only)	—
Trifluoperazine	1, 2, 5, 10 mg	—	—	—	—
Triflupromazine	—	—	—	10 mg/mL, 20 mg/mL	—

curve. In general, the dosage of an antipsychotic drug should be evaluated over a six-week period before increasing the dosage or switching to another antipsychotic drug. Overly high dosages of antipsychotics may lead to neurological side effects, such as akinesia and akathisia, which are difficult to distinguish from exacerbations of psychosis.

Although patients can build up a tolerance for most of the adverse effects caused by antipsychotics, patients do not build up a tolerance for the antipsychotic effect. Nevertheless, the clinician should taper the dosage when a drug is being discontinued, as the patient may experience rebound effects from the other neurotransmitter systems that the drug may have blocked. Cholinergic rebound, for example, can produce a flulike syndrome in patients.

SHORT-TERM TREATMENT

The equivalent of 5 to 10 mg of haloperidol is a reasonable dose for an adult patient in an acute state. A geriatric patient may benefit from as little as 1 mg of haloperidol. The administration of more than 50 mg of chlorpromazine in one injection may result in serious hypotension. IM administration of the antipsychotic results in peak plasma levels in about 30 minutes versus 90 minutes with the oral route. Doses of antipsychotics for IM administration are about half the doses given by the oral route. In a short-term treatment setting, the patient should be observed for one hour after the first dose of antipsychotic medication. After that time, most clinicians administer a second dose of an antipsychotic or a sedative agent (for example, a benzodiazepine) to achieve effective behavioral control. Possible sedatives include lorazepam (Ativan) (2 mg IM) and amobarbital (50 to 250 mg IM).

Rapid Neuroleptization

Rapid neuroleptization (also called psychotolysis and digitalization) is the practice of administering hourly IM doses of antipsychotic medications until the patient is markedly sedated. However, several research studies have shown that merely waiting several more hours after one dose of an antipsychotic results in the same clinical improvement as that seen with repeated doses of antipsychotics. Nevertheless, clinicians must be careful to keep patients from becoming violent while they are psychotic. Clinicians can help prevent violent episodes by the use of adjuvant sedatives or by temporarily using physical restraints until the patients can control their behavior.

EARLY TREATMENT

Agitation and excitement are usually the first symptoms to improve with antipsychotic treatment. Psychotic symptoms improve significantly in about 75 percent of patients with a short history of illness. In patients with a long history of illness, a full six weeks may be necessary to evaluate the extent of the improvement in psychotic symptoms. Data indicate that psychotic symptoms, both positive and negative, continue to improve 3 to 12 months after the initiation of treatment.

The equivalent of 10 to 20 mg of haloperidol or 400 mg of chlorpromazine a day is adequate treatment for most patients with schizophrenia. Some research studies indicate that, in a significant proportion of patients, 5 mg of haloperidol or 200 mg of chlorpromazine may, in fact, be just as effective as higher doses. It is a reasonable practice to give antipsychotic drugs in divided doses when initiating treatment to minimize the peak plasma levels and reduce the incidence of adverse effects. The total daily dose can subsequently be consolidated into a single daily dose after the first week or two of treatment. The single daily dose is usually given at bedtime to help induce sleep and to reduce the incidence of adverse effects. However, in elderly patients that practice may increase the risk of their falling if they get out of bed during the night. The sedative effects of antipsychotics last only a few hours, in contrast to the antipsychotic effects, which last for one to three days.

Medications Given as Needed

It is common clinical practice to order medications to be given as needed (PRN). Although that practice may be reasonable during the first few days that a patient is hospitalized, the amount of time the patient takes antipsychotic drugs, rather than an increase in dosage, is what produces therapeutic improvement. Clinicians may feel pressured by their staff members to write PRN antipsychotic orders. Such orders for PRN medications should include specific symptoms, how often the drugs should be given, and how many doses can be given each day. Clinicians may choose to use small doses for the PRN doses (for example, 2 mg haloperidol) or use a benzodiazepine instead (for example, 2 mg lorazepam IM). If PRN doses of an antipsychotic are necessary after the first week of treatment, the clinician may want to consider increasing the standing daily dosage of the drug.

MAINTENANCE TREATMENT

The first three to six months after a psychotic episode is usually considered a period of stabilization for the patient. After that time, the dosage of the antipsychotic can be decreased about 20 percent every six months until the minimum effective dosage is found. A patient is usually maintained on antipsychotic medications for one to two years after the first psychotic episode. Antipsychotic treatment is often continued for five years after a second psychotic episode, and lifetime maintenance is considered after the third psychotic episode, although reduction of the daily dosage can be attempted every 6 to 12 months.

Antipsychotic drugs are effective in controlling psychotic symptoms, but patients may report that they prefer being off the drugs, because they feel better without them. That problem may be less common with the new antipsychotic drugs, such as risperidone and remoxipride. Normal persons who have taken antipsychotic drugs report a sense of dysphoria. The clinician must discuss maintenance medication with the patients and take into account the patients' wishes, the severity of their illnesses, and the quality of their support systems.

ALTERNATIVE MAINTENANCE REGIMENS

Alternative maintenance regimens have been designed to reduce both the risk of long-term adverse effects and any unpleasantness associated with taking antipsychotic medications. Intermittent medication is the use of antipsychotics only when patients require them. That arrangement requires that the patients or their caretakers be both willing and able to watch carefully for early signs of clinical exacerbations. At the earliest signs of such problems, antipsychotic medications should be reinstituted for a reasonable period, usually one to three months. Although that treatment approach is not indicated for the majority of patients, it is a safe and effective treatment approach for some patients.

Drug holidays are regular two- to seven-day periods during which the patient is not given antipsychotic medications. Currently, no evidence indicates that drug holidays reduce the risk of long-term adverse effects from antipsychotics, and drug holidays may increase the incidence of noncompliance.

LONG-ACTING DEPOT MEDICATIONS

Because some patients with schizophrenia do not comply with oral antipsychotic regimens, long-acting depot preparations may be needed. A clinician usually administers the IM preparations once every one to four weeks. Therefore, the clinician immediately knows if a patient has missed a dose of medication. Depot antipsychotics may be associated with increased adverse effects, including tardive dyskinesia, although the data for that increased association are controversial. Some researchers and clinicians limit their use of depot antipsychotics to those patients who are not compliant with oral medications; other researchers and clinicians, particularly in Europe, consider depot antipsychotics the formulation of choice for the treatment of schizophrenia.

Two depot preparations (a decanoate and an enanthate) of fluphenazine and a decanoate preparation of haloperidol are available in the United States. The preparations are injected IM into an area of large muscle tissue, from which they are absorbed slowly into the blood. Decanoate preparations can be given less frequently than are enanthate preparations because they are absorbed more slowly. Although stabilizing a patient on the oral preparation of the specific drugs is not necessary before initiating the depot form, it is good practice to give at least one oral dose of the drug to assess the possibility of an adverse effect, such as severe extrapyramidal symptoms or an allergic reaction.

The correct dosage and the time interval for depot preparations are difficult to predict. It is reasonable to begin with 12.5 mg (0.5 mL) of either fluphenazine preparation or 25 mg (0.5 mL) of haloperidol decanoate. If symptoms emerge in the next two to four weeks, the patient can be treated temporarily with additional oral medications or with additional small depot injections. After three to four weeks the depot injection can be increased to include the supplemental doses given during the initial period.

A good reason to initiate depot treatment with low doses is that the preparations may be absorbed faster than usual at the onset of treatment, resulting in frightening episodes of dystonia that eventually discourage compliance with the medication. Some clinicians keep patients drug-free for three to seven days before initiating depot treatment and give very small doses of the depot preparations (3.125 mg fluphenazine or 6.25 mg haloperidol) every few days to avoid those initial problems. Because the major indication for depot medication is poor compliance with oral forms, the clinician should go slowly with what is practically the last method of achieving compliance.

PLASMA CONCENTRATIONS

Interindividual variation in the metabolism of the antipsychotics is significant, resulting in part from genetic differences among patients and from pharmacokinetic interactions with other drugs. In patients who have not improved after four to six weeks of antipsychotic treatment, a plasma concentration of the drug should be obtained if such a test is available. Other possible indications for obtaining a plasma concentration are questions regarding compliance, concern regarding pharmacokinetic interactions, and the development of significant akathisia or akinesia.

The blood sample must be obtained after the patient has been taking a particular dosage for at least five times the half-life of the drug, so as to approach steady-state concentrations. It is also standard practice to obtain plasma samples at trough levels—that is, just before the daily dose is given, usually at least 12 hours after the previous dose and most commonly 20 to 24 hours after the previous dose. Unfortunately, the quality of the laboratories that perform the analyses varies significantly; therefore, the clinician must obtain the normal ranges for a particular laboratory and must test the laboratory with multiple plasma samples from well-controlled patients. Having taken all those precautions, the clinician is still left with the reality that most antipsychotics have no well-defined dose-response curve. The best-studied drug is haloperidol, which may have a therapeutic window ranging from 2 to 15 ng/mL. Other therapeutic ranges that have been reasonably well-documented are 30 to 100 ng/mL for chlorpromazine and 0.8 to 2.4 ng/mL for perphenazine (Tilafon).

TREATMENT-RESISTANT PATIENTS AND ADJUVANT MEDICATIONS

Various estimates have ranged from 10 to 35 percent for the proportion of schizophrenic patients who fail to obtain significant benefit from the old antipsychotic drugs (that is, all the drugs except clozapine, and risperidone). Patients are often defined as being treatment-resistant if they have failed at least two adequate trials of antipsychotics from two classes. Adequate trials are usually defined as lasting at least six weeks, and using daily dosages equivalent to 20 mg of haloperidol or 1,000 mg of chlorpromazine. It is useful to obtain plasma concentrations for such patients, since one possibility is that they are slow metabolizers and are grossly overmedicated with the antipsychotic drugs. More likely, however, they are simply nonresponsive to those typical antipsychotic drugs.

Adjuvant Treatments

Before the introduction of the new antipsychotics, the only approach to treatment-resistant schizophrenic patients was the use of adjuvant medications. Medications that have been reported to be useful as adjuvants to antipsychotics include lithium, carbamazepine, β-adrenergic receptor antagonists, antidepressants, and benzodiazepines. Of those medications, the most robust data support the use of lithium as an adjuvant to antipsychotic medications. When using the combination of lithium and antipsychotics, the clinician may want to use slightly lower dosages of each initially to avoid the development of delirium or neurotoxicity that has been reported in a few cases, with the combination. The use of carbamazepine has also been reported to be effective as an addition to antipsychotic drugs, although the coadministration of carbamazepine and an antipsychotic can lower the plasma concentrations of the antipsychotic as much as 50 percent because of the induction of hepatic enzymes. Although benzodiazepines have been reported to be effective as adjuvant treatments, their withdrawal can precipitate a significant worsening of symptoms. An increasing body of data supports the use of antidepressants in schizophrenic patients who have significant depressive symptoms.

New Antipsychotics

Clozapine has been shown to be effective in treating at least 30 percent of patients who are nonresponsive to typical antipsychotic drugs. Although other new antipsychotic drugs may also be effective in a proportion of treatment-resistant schizophrenic patients, that has yet to be demonstrated in large, well-controlled clinical trials.

References

Borison R L, Diamond B, Pathiraja A, Meibach R C: Pharmacokinetics of risperidone in chronic schizophrenic patients. Psychopharmacol Bull *30*: 193, 1994.

Grant S, Fitton A: Risperidone. A review of its pharmacology and therapeutic potential in the treatment of schizophrenia. Drugs *48*: 253, 1994.

He H, Richardson J S: A pharmacological, pharmacokinetic and clinical overview of risperidone, a new antipsychotic that blocks serotonin 5-HT$_2$ and dopamine D$_2$ receptors. Int Clin Psychopharmacol *10*: 19, 1995.

Pai B N, Janakiramaiah N, Gangadhar B N, Ravindranath V: Depletion of glutathione and enhanced lipid peroxidation in the CSF of acute psychotics following haloperidol administration. Biol Psychiatry *36*: 489, 1994.

Palao D J, Arauxo A, Brunet M, Bernardo M, Haor J M, Ferrer J, Gonzalez-

Monclus E: Haloperidol: Therapeutic window in schizophrenia. J Clin Psychopharmacol *14*: 303, 1994.

Van Kammen D P, Marder S R: Dopamine receptor antagonists. In *Comprehensive Textbook of Psychiatry*, ed 6, H I Kaplan, B J Sadock, editors, p 1987. Williams & Wilkins, Baltimore, 1995.

27.3.17 FENFLURAMINE

In psychiatry, fenfluramine (Pondimin) has been studied and used as a treatment for autistic disorder. Because of its anorectic effect, it has also been studied and used in the treatment of obesity.

THERAPEUTIC INDICATIONS

Fenfluramine has been studied primarily as a treatment for autistic disorder. Although several reports note that some patients have improved while taking the drug, fenfluramine is not an effective drug for that condition. Some data indicate that autistic disorder children with significant agitation and an intelligence quotient (I.Q.) above 40 are likely to benefit from treatment with the drug. The use of fenfluramine for weight reduction is controversial. Data indicate that tolerance develops for that effect. The advantage of fenfluramine over amphetamine as an anorectic agent is that fenfluramine does not produce euphoria.

PRECAUTIONS AND ADVERSE REACTIONS

Drowsiness, diarrhea, and dry mouth are the most common adverse effects of fenfluramine. Other adverse effects include dizziness, confusion, incoordination, headache, elevated mood, depressed mood, anxiety, nervousness, tension, insomnia, weakness, fatigue, agitation, dysarthria, and altered libido. Fenfluramine has not been studied in pregnant women and should be avoided during pregnancy. Whether fenfluramine passes into breast milk is not known.

DRUG INTERACTIONS

Patients should be advised to avoid alcoholic beverages during fenfluramine treatment. The drug may have additive effects when used with central nervous system (CNS) depressants. Fenfluramine may increase the efficacy of some antihypertensives. Coadministration of fenfluramine with serotonergic antidepressants—for example, fluoxetine (Prozac)—and monoamine oxidase inhibitors should be avoided.

DOSAGE AND ADMINISTRATION

In autistic disorder the dosage should be increased gradually to 1.0 to 1.5 mg per kg a day in divided doses. The reported therapeutic effects of fenfluramine include improved sleep, improved interpersonal skills, and a decrease in aggression, tantrums, irritability, self-mutilation, and hyperactivity. Fenfluramine is supplied in 20 mg tablets.

References

Coccaro E F, Klar H, Siever L J: Reduced prolactin response to fenfluramine challenge in personality disorder patients is not due to deficiency of pituitary lactotrophs. Biol Psychiatry *36*: 344, 1994.

Judd F K, Apostolopoulos M, Burrows G D, Norman T R: Serotonergic function in panic disorder: Endocrine responses to D-fenfluramine. Prog Neuropsychopharmacol Biol Psychiatry *18*: 329, 1994.

Kaplan H I, Sadock B J: Other pharmacological therapies. In *Comprehensive*

Textbook of Psychiatry, ed 6, H I Kaplan, B J Sadock, editors, p 2122. Williams & Wilkins, Baltimore, 1995.

Lichtenberg P, Shapira B, Blacker M, Gropp C, Calev A, Larer B: Effect of fenfluramine on mood: A double-blind placebo-controlled trial. Biol Psychiatry *31*: 351, 1992.

Varley C K, Holm V A: A two-year follow-up of autistic children treated with fenfluramine. J Am Acad Child Adolesc Psychiatry *29*: 137, 1990.

27.3.18 LITHIUM

Lithium (Eskalith, Lithonate, Lithotabs, Cibalith-S) is the most commonly used short-term and prophylactic treatment for bipolar I disorder.

THERAPEUTIC INDICATIONS

Bipolar I Disorder

Lithium has proved to be effective in both the short-term treatment and the prophylaxis of bipolar I disorder in about 70 to 80 percent of patients. Both manic and depressive episodes respond to lithium treatment alone. Lithium should also be considered as a potential treatment in patients with severe cyclothymic disorder.

MANIC EPISODES

About 80 percent of manic patients respond to lithium treatment, although the response to lithium alone can take one to three weeks of treatment at therapeutic concentrations. Because of the delay in response to lithium alone, benzodiazepines—for example, clonazepam (Klonopin) and lorazepam (Ativan)—or antipsychotics are used for the first one to three weeks to obtain immediate relief from the mania. Predictors of a poor response to lithium in the treatment of manic episodes include mixed and dysphoric manic episodes (which may occur in as many as 40 percent of patients), rapid cycling, and coexisting substance-related disorders.

DEPRESSIVE EPISODES

Although not approved by the Food and Drug Administration, lithium is effective in the treatment of bipolar I disorder depression. About 80 percent of bipolar I disorder depressive patients respond to lithium treatment alone, thereby eliminating the risk of an antidepressant-induced manic episode. When a depressive episode occurs in a patient already receiving maintenance lithium, the differential diagnosis should include lithium-induced hypothyroidism, substance abuse, and the lack of compliance with the lithium therapy. Possible treatment approaches include increasing the lithium concentration (up to 1.2 mEq per L), adding supplemental thyroid hormone (for example, 25 μg a day L-iodothyronine) even in the presence of normal findings on thyroid function tests, the judicious use of antidepressants, and electroconvulsive therapy (before which lithium should be discontinued to avoid complicating the cognitive assessment of the patient).

MAINTENANCE

Maintenance treatment with lithium markedly decreases the frequency, the severity, and the duration of manic and depressive episodes in bipolar I disorder patients. Only about 35 percent of lithium-treated patients relapse compared with placebo treatment, during which about 80 percent of bipolar I disorder patients relapse. Lithium maintenance is almost always indicated after the second episode of bipolar I disorder depression or mania. Lithium maintenance should be seriously considered after the first episode in patients who are adolescents, have a family history of bipolar I disorder, have poor support systems, had no precipitating factors for the first episode, had a serious first episode, have a high suicide risk, are 30 years old or older, had a sudden onset of their first episode, had a first episode of mania, or are male. Increased interest in initiating maintenance after the first episode is motivated by several observations: First, subsequent episodes may be increasingly likely after each additional episode. Second, some data indicate that relapses increase after lithium is discontinued. Third, case reports describe patients who were initially responsive to lithium but who lost their lithium-responsiveness with subsequent episodes. The treatment response of lithium is such that continued maintenance treatment may be associated with increasing efficacy. It is not necessarily representative of treatment failure, therefore, if an episode of depression or mania occurs after a relatively short time of lithium maintenance. If lithium treatment alone loses its effectiveness, the clinician should consider supplemental treatment with carbamazepine (Tegretol) or valproate (Depakene).

Schizoaffective Disorder

The use of lithium for schizoaffective disorder (bipolar type) is certainly indicated. If a patient has schizoaffective disorder (depressive type) with a particularly cyclic nature, a lithium trial may be warranted. In general, the more a schizoaffective disorder patient resembles a mood disorder patient, the more likely lithium is to be effective; the more a schizoaffective disorder patient resembles a schizophrenia patient, the less likely lithium is to be effective.

Major Depressive Disorder

The primary indication for lithium in major depressive disorder is as an adjuvant treatment to antidepressant in patients who have failed to respond to the antidepressants alone. Many studies have shown that about 50 percent of antidepressant nonresponders do respond when lithium, 300 mg given three times daily, is added to the antidepressant regimen. In some patients the response is dramatically rapid, occurring in days; in most patients, several weeks are required to assess the efficacy of the regimen. Lithium alone may be an effective treatment for depressed patients who are actually bipolar I disorder patients who have not yet had their first manic episode. Moreover, lithium has been reported to be effective in major depressive disorder patients whose disorder is particularly cyclic.

Schizophrenia

The symptoms of one fifth to one half of all schizophrenic patients are further reduced when lithium is coadministered with their antipsychotic drug. The therapeutic benefit of lithium does not seem to be correlated with the absence or the presence of affective symptoms in those patients. Some schizophrenic patients who cannot take antipsychotic drugs may benefit from lithium treatment alone. The intermittent aggressive outbursts of some schizophrenic patients may also be reduced by lithium treatment.

Aggression

Lithium has been used to treat aggressive outbursts in schizophrenic patients, prison inmates, and mentally retarded patients. Less success has been reported in the treatment of aggressiveness associated with head trauma and epilepsy. Other drugs for the treatment of aggression include anticonvulsants, β-adrenergic receptor antagonists, and antipsychotics. The treatment of aggressive patients requires a flexible approach to the use of those drugs and the use of psychosocial and behavioral treatment strategies.

Other Disorders

A few studies have reported that the episodic disorder characterizing premenstrual dysphoric disorder, the intermittent behaviors seen in borderline personality disorder, bulimia nervosa, and episodes of binge drinking respond to lithium treatment. Animal models of alcohol dependence have shown that lithium intake can reduce the intake of alcohol. In spite of those basic data, at least one large study has not shown any benefit of lithium treatment in alcohol dependence, although anecdotal case reports and small studies in the literature are hopeful.

PRECAUTIONS AND ADVERSE REACTIONS

The most common adverse effects of lithium treatment are gastric distress, weight gain, tremor, fatigue, and mild cognitive impairment. Gastrointestinal symptoms can include nausea, decreased appetite, vomiting, and diarrhea and can often be reduced by dividing the dosage, administering the lithium with food, or switching to another lithium preparation. Weight gain results from a poorly understood effect of lithium on carbohydrate metabolism. Weight gain can also result from lithium-induced edema. The only reasonable approach to weight gain is to encourage the patient to eat wisely and to engage in moderate exercise.

Tremor

The significance of drug-induced tremors is recognized in the fourth edition of *Diagnostic and Statistical Manual of Mental Disorders* (DSM-IV) by the inclusion of the diagnostic category medication-induced postural tremor. The tremor is usually an 8- to 10-Hz tremor and is most notable in outstretched hands, especially in the fingers. The tremor is sometimes worse during times of peak drug levels. The tremor can be reduced by dividing the daily dosage and reducing caffeine intake. Propranolol (Inderal) (30 to 160 mg a day in divided doses) is usually effective in reducing the tremor in most patients. When a lithium-treated patient has a severe tremor, the possibility of lithium toxicity should be suspected and evaluated.

Cognitive Effects

Lithium use has been associated with dysphoria, lack of spontaneity, slowed reaction times, and impaired memory. The differential diagnosis for such symptoms should include depressive disorders, hypothyroidism, other illnesses, and other drugs. Some patients have reported that fatigue and mild cognitive impairment decrease with time.

Renal Effects

The most common adverse renal effect of lithium is polyuria with secondary polydipsia. The symptom is particularly a problem in 25 to 35 percent of patients who may have a urine output of # 3 L a day (normal 1 to 2 L a day). The polyuria is a result of the lithium antagonism to the effects of antidiuretic hormone, thus decreasing the resorption of fluid from the distal tubules of the kidneys. Polyuria may be significant enough to result in problems at work and in social setting, with associated insomnia, weight gain, and dehydration. When polyuria is a significant problem, the patient's renal function should be evaluated and followed up with 24-hour urine collections for creatinine clearance and with consultation with a nephrologist. Treatment consists of fluid replacement, the use of the lowest effective dosage of lithium, and single daily dosing of lithium. Treatment can also involve the use of a thiazide or potassium-sparing diuretic—for example, amiloride (Midamor) or amiloride-hydrochlorothiazide (Moduretic). If treatment with a diuretic is initiated, the lithium dosage should be halved, and the diuretic should not be started for five days, because the diuretic is likely to increase the retention of lithium.

The most serious renal adverse effects, which are rarely associated with lithium administration, are minimal change glomerulonephritis, interstitial nephritis, and renal failure. The incidence of those severe renal complications is now thought to be lower than was originally thought: however, the clinician should consider such complications if the clinical picture warrants it.

Thyroid Effects

Lithium affects thyroid function, causing a generally benign and often transient diminution in the concentrations of circulating thyroid hormones. Reports have attributed goiter (5 percent of patients), benign reversible exophthalmos, and hypothyroidism (7 to 9 percent of patients) to lithium treatment. About 50 percent of patients receiving long-term lithium treatment have an abnormal thyrotropin-releasing hormone (TRH) response, and about 30 percent have elevated levels of thyroid-stimulating hormone (TSH). If symptoms of hypothyroidism are present, treatment with levothyroxine (Synthroid) is indicated. Even in the absence of hypothyroid symptoms, some clinicians treat patients with elevated TSH levels with levothyroxine. In lithium-treated patients, TSH levels should be measured every 6 to 12 months. Lithium-induced hypothyroidism should be considered when evaluating depressive episodes that emerge during lithium therapy.

Cardiac Effects

The cardiac effects of lithium, which resemble those of hypokalemia on the electrocardiogram (ECG), are caused by the displacement of intracellular potassium by the lithium ion. The most common changes on the ECG are T wave flattening or inversion. The changes are benign and disappear after the lithium is excreted from the body. Nevertheless, baseline ECGs are essential and should be repeated annually.

Because lithium also depresses the pacemaking activity of the sinus node, lithium treatment can result in sinus dysrhythmias and episodes of syncope. Lithium treatment, therefore, is contraindicated in patients with sick sinus syndrome. In rare cases, ventricular arrhythmias and congestive heart failure have been associated with lithium therapy.

Dermatological Effects

Several cutaneous adverse effects, which may be dose-dependent, have been associated with lithium treatment. The most prevalent effects include acneiform, follicular, and maculopapular eruptions; pretibial ulcerations; and worsening of psoriasis. Alopecia has also been reported. Many of those conditions respond favorably to changing to another lithium preparation and the usual dermatological measures. Lithium levels should be monitored if tetracycline is used for the treatment of acne because of several reports of its increasing the retention of lithium. Occasionally, aggravated psoriasis or acneiform eruptions may force the discontinuation of lithium treatment.

Lithium Toxicity and Overdose

The early signs and symptoms of lithium toxicity include coarse tremor, dysarthria, and ataxia; the later signs and symptoms include impaired consciousness, muscular fasciculations, myoclonus, seizures, and coma. The higher the lithium levels and the longer the lithium level have been high, the worse the symptoms of lithium toxicity are. Lithium toxicity is a medical emergency, since it can result in permanent neuronal damage and death. The treatment of lithium toxicity involves discontinuing the lithium and treating the dehydration. The value of forced diuresis has been disputed. In the most serious cases, hemodialysis is an effective means by which lithium can be removed from the body.

OVERDOSE

Overdose of lithium results in symptoms of severe lithium toxicity. Treatment should be similar to that for lithium toxicity in general but can also include gastric lavage with a wide-bore tube because of the tendency of the drug to form large clumps in the stomach.

Adolescents

The serum lithium levels for adolescents is similar to that used for adults. Although the side-effect profile is similar in adolescents and adults, the weight gain and the acne associated with lithium use can be particularly troublesome to an adolescent.

Geriatric Patient

Lithium is a safe and effective drug for the elderly. However, the treatment of elderly lithium-treated patients is complicated by the presence of other medical illnesses, decreased renal function, special diets that affect lithium clearance, and generally increased sensitivity to lithium-induced side effects. Because of that increased sensitivity, many elderly patients must be maintained on lower lithium concentrations than are younger adults. Elderly patients should be started on low dosage, their dosages should be switched less frequently than are dosages in younger patients, and a longer time must be allowed before assuming that their lithium concentrations are at steady-state levels because of possibly decreased renal function.

Pregnant Women

Early studies reported that about 10 percent of newborns who were exposed to lithium in the first trimester of pregnancy had major congenital malformations. The most common malformations involve the cardiovascular system, most commonly Ebstein's anomaly of the tricuspid valves. Recent epidemiological studies have found that the early studies may have significantly overestimated the risk. Although, ideally, a woman should not take any drug during pregnancy, the continuation of lithium therapy by a pregnant woman should not be considered out of the question. The possibility of fetal anomalies can be evaluated with fetal echocardiography. If a woman continues taking lithium during pregnancy, the lowest effective dosage should be used. Also, the maternal lithium level must be monitored closely during pregnancy and especially after pregnancy, because of the significant change in renal function that occurs over that time period. Lithium should be discontinued shortly before delivery, and the drug should be restarted after an assessment of the usually high risk of a postpartum mood disorder and the mother's desire to breast-feed her infant. Lithium should not be administered to a woman who is breast-feeding. Signs of lithium toxicity in infants include lethargy, cyanosis, abnormal reflexes, and sometimes hepatomegaly.

Miscellaneous Effects

Rare neurological adverse effects include symptoms of mild parkinsonism, ataxia, and dysarthria, although those last two symptoms are usually symptoms of lithium intoxication. Lithium should be used with caution in diabetic patients, who should monitor their blood glucose levels carefully. Leukocytosis is a common benign effect of lithium treatment. Dehydrated, debilitated, and mentally ill patients are susceptible to side effects and toxicity.

DRUG INTERACTIONS

Because of the possibility of lithium toxicity on the one hand and the need to maintain therapeutic lithium on the other hand, the clinician must be aware of the many drug interactions that can involve lithium. In lithium-treated patients who are about to undergo electroconvulsive therapy (ECT), the lithium should be discontinued two days before beginning ECT to reduce the risk of delirium resulting from the coadministration of the two treatments.

Most diuretics (for example, thiazide, potassium-sparing, and loop) can increase lithium levels; when treatment with such a diuretic is stopped, the clinician may need to increase the patient's daily lithium dosage. Osmotic diuretics, carbonic anhydrase inhibitors, and xanthines (including caffeine) may reduce lithium levels to below therapeutic levels. Increasing reports indicate that angiotensin-converting enzyme inhibitors cause an increase in lithium concentrations. A wide range of nonsteroidal anti-inflammatory drugs can decrease lithium clearance, thereby increasing lithium concentrations; those drugs include indomethacin (Indocin), phenylbutazone (Azolid), diclofenac (Voltaren), ketoprofen (Orudis), ibuprofen (Motrin), piroxicam (Feldene), and naproxen (Naprosyn). Aspirin and sulindac do not affect lithium concentrations.

When coadministered, antipsychotics and lithium may result in a synergistic increase in the symptoms of lithium-induced neurological adverse effects. That interaction is not, as was initially thought, specifically associated with the coadministration of lithium and haloperidol (Haldol). Although the validity of the clinical observation has been questioned, the clinician should probably avoid the coadministration of high dosages of antipsychotics in the presence of high serum concentrations of lithium.

The coadministration of lithium and anticonvulsants—including carbamazepine, valproate, and clonazepam—may increase lithium levels and aggravate lithium-induced neurological adverse effects. As with antipsychotic medications, the clinician should probably avoid the administration of high dosages of anticonvulsants in patients with high lithium concentrations. However, the coadministration of lithium and anticonvulsants can be therapeutically beneficial to some patients. Treatment with the combination should be initiated at slightly lower dosages than usual, and the dosages should be increased gradually. Lithium may have some protective effect against the granulocytopenia induced by carbamazepine, although no data indicate that the lithium reduces the risk of the serious carbamazepine-induced problems with agranulocytosis.

DOSAGE AND ADMINISTRATION

Lithium is a monovalent ion and is available as a carbonate (Li_2CO_3) for oral use in both rapidly acting and slow-release tablets and capsules. Lithium citrate (Cibalith-S) is available in a liquid form for oral administration. Regular-release capsules or tablets are usually used first, and the syrup or slow-release preparations are used if noncompliance, nausea, or other adverse effects occur and may improve with a different formulation.

Initial Medical Workup

Before the clinician administers lithium, a physician other than a psychiatrist should conduct a routine laboratory and physical examination. The laboratory examination should include a serum creatinine concentration level (or a 24-hour urine creatinine level if the clinician has any reason to be concerned about renal function), an electrolyte screen, thyroid function tests, a complete blood count (CBC), an ECG, and a pregnancy test if there is any possibility that the patient is pregnant.

Plasma Concentrations

Serum and plasma concentrations of lithium are the standard methods of assessing lithium concentrations, and they serve as the basis by which to titrate the dosages. Although reports have noted the measurement of lithium concentrations in saliva, tears, and red blood cells, those methods have no clinical superiority to the standard methods. The patient must be at steady state (usually after five days of constant dosing), and the blood sample must be drawn 12 hours (plus or minus 30 minutes) after the last dose in a twice- or thrice-daily dosing regimen. Because available data are based on those standards, the clinician should initiate lithium treatment with regular-release formulations of lithium given at least twice daily. Once the dosage has been adjusted, changing the formulation of the dosing schedule is reasonable. Lithium levels in patients treated with slow-release preparations are about 30 percent higher than the levels obtained with the normal-release preparations.

The most common guidelines are for 1.0 to 1.5 mEq per L for the treatment of acute mania and 0.6 to 1.2 mEq per L for maintenance treatment. It is almost never necessary to exceed 1.5 mEq per L, since patients with higher lithium levels are at much higher risk for lithium toxicity. If, in a very few patients, maximal therapeutic benefit has not been obtained and if adverse effects are absent, titration of the dose above 1.5 mEq per L may be warranted. One recent study found that patients with lithium concentrations in the range of 0.8 to 1.0 mEq per L are 2.6 times less likely to relapse than are patients with lithium concentrations in the range of 0.4 to 0.6 mEq per L. That study led some researchers and clinicians to consider 0.8 to 1.0 mEq per L as the most effective range for maintenance lithium concentrations.

LITHIUM DOSE PREDICTION

A number of researchers and clinicians have proposed various lithium dose prediction protocols. The protocols are generally based on the administration of a single dose of lithium, followed by the assessment of lithium concentrations at 12- or 24-hour time points. Those concentrations are then used to predict the final dose of lithium that a patient will require. Most clinicians and researchers have not adopted lithium dose prediction protocols for two reasons: First, the upward titration of lithium in patients is relatively straightforward and quick without the use of such a protocol. Second, the rapid dose increase associated with the use of a dose prediction protocol often results in adverse effects, especially gastrointestinal effects, that may adversely affect the patient's subsequent compliance with the medication regimen.

Dosage

If a patient has previously been treated with lithium and the previous dosage is known, the clinician should probably use that dosage for the current episode unless changes in the patient's pharmacokinetic parameters have affected lithium clearance. For most adult patients, the clinician should start lithium at 300 mg three times daily. The starting dosage in patients who are elderly or who have renal impairment should be 300 mg once or twice daily. The usual eventual dosage is between 900 and 1,800 mg a day, given in two or three divided doses.

The use of divided doses reduces gastric upset and avoids single high-peak lithium levels. A current debate concerns whether multiple small daily peaks are less likely than a single high daily peak to cause adverse effects. Single daily dosing is not considered standard practice at this time. Slow-release lithium preparations can be given two or three times daily; they result in low peak levels of lithium, but that procedure has not been proved to be of special value.

Patient Education

The clinician should advise the patient that changes in the body's water and salt content can affect the amount of lithium excreted, resulting in either increases or decreases in lithium levels. Excessive sodium intake (for example, a dramatic dietary change) lowers lithium levels. Conversely, too little sodium (for example, fad diets) can lead to potentially toxic levels of lithium. Decreases in body fluid (for example, excessive sweating) can lead to dehydration and lithium intoxication.

Failure of Drug Treatment

If the drug produces no clinical response after four weeks at therapeutic levels, slightly higher serum levels (up to 1.5 mEq per L) may be tried if there are no limiting adverse effects. If, after two weeks at a high serum concentration, the drug is still ineffective, the patient should be tapered off the drug over one to two weeks. Other drugs should be given therapeutic trials at that point.

RAPID CYCLING

Rapid cycling is defined as the presence of four or more episodes of illness during the year; some patients experience many more than four episodes. Rapid-cycling bipolar I disorder is present in as many as 20 percent of all patients and is associated with antidepressant treatment, thyroid abnormalities, and neurological disorders. If lithium treatment is ineffective in a rapid-cycling patient, thyroid hormones, carbamazepine, valproate, electroconvulsive therapy, calcium channel inhibitors, monoamine oxidase inhibitors, and clozapine are all potential treatment options for the clinician to consider.

References

Harvey N S, Merriman S: Review of clinically important drug interactions with lithium. Drug Safe *10*: 455, 1994.

Jefferson J W, Greist J H: Lithium. In *Comprehensive Textbook of Psychiatry*, ed 6, H I Kaplan, B J Sadock, editors, p 2022. Williams & Wilkins, Baltimore, 1995.

Lenox R H, Watson D G: Lithium and the brain: A psychopharmacological strategy to a molecular basis for manic depressive illness. Clin Chem *40*: 309, 1994.

Okusa M D, Crystal L J: Clinical manifestations and management of acute lithium intoxication. Am J Med *97*: 383, 1994.

Ozdemir M A, Sofuoglu S, Tanrikulu G, Aldanmaz F, Esel E, Dundar S: Lithium-induced hematologic changes in patients with bipolar affective disorder. Biol Psychiatry *35*: 210, 1994.

Schou M: Mortality-lowering effect of prophylactic lithium treatment: A look at the evidence. Pharmacopsychiatry *28*: 1, 1995.

27.3.19 METHADONE

Methadone hydrochloride (Dolophine) is used in psychiatry primarily for the detoxification and maintenance therapy for patients who are addicted to opiates and opioids.

THERAPEUTIC INDICATIONS

Methadone is used for the short-term detoxification (30 days), long-term detoxification (180 days), and maintenance of opiate and opioid addicts. Methadone is a schedule II drug; its administration is governed by specific federal laws and regulations. Those regulations are currently in a state of flux because of the increase in efforts to place intravenous drug abusers in methadone programs. The aim of such renewed efforts is to reduce the spread of acquired immune deficiency syndrome (AIDS), which can be contracted by the use of contaminated needles.

PRECAUTIONS AND ADVERSE REACTIONS

An overdose of methadone can cause respiratory and circulatory depression, leading to respiratory arrest, cardiac arrest, and death. Methadone is also capable of inducing tolerance, psychological dependence, and physical dependence. Other adverse effects on the central nervous system include dizziness, depres-

sion, sedation, euphoria, dysphoria, agitation, and seizures. Delirium and insomnia have also been reported in rare cases. Methadone should be used with caution in patients with respiratory disease, hepatic or renal dysfunction, and seizure disorders.

Pregnancy

Methadone should be administered to pregnant women only if the potential benefits outweigh the possible risks. Detoxification is not recommended for pregnant women; maintenance methadone may be appropriate in some circumstances. Whether methadone treatment is harmful to the fetus is not known. A significant number of infants born to mothers receiving methadone show withdrawal symptoms. Women should not breastfeed their babies if they are taking methadone.

DRUG INTERACTIONS

Methadone can potentiate the central nervous system (CNS) depressant effects of other opiate agonists, barbiturates, benzodiazepines, and alcohol. Antipsychotics, especially low-potency agents, tricyclic and tetracyclic drugs, and monoamine oxidase inhibitors (MAOIs), should be used cautiously with methadone. Two other opiate agonists, meperidine (Demerol) and fentanyl (Duragesic), have been associated with fatal drug-drug interactions with the MAOIs.

DOSAGE AND ADMINISTRATION

Methadone is supplied in tablets of 5, 10, and 40 mg; solutions of 5 mg per 5 mL, 10 mg per 5 mL, and 10 mg per mL; and a parenteral form of 10 mg per mL.

In maintenance programs, methadone is usually administered dissolved in water or fruit juice. For short-term detoxification, an initial dose of 15 to 20 mg usually suppresses withdrawal symptoms; additional doses can be given if the initial dose is insufficient. A dosage of 40 mg a day in single or divided doses is usually sufficient to control withdrawal symptoms in most patients. After stabilization, the methadone dosage is tapered at a rate that depends on the type of program, whether the patient is an inpatient or an outpatient, and the patient's level of tolerance for the withdrawal symptoms. If withdrawal takes more than 180 days, the treatment program is officially described as methadone maintenance. Maintenance should be at the lowest possible dosage of methadone, and, generally, the patient should eventually be withdrawn completely from methadone. The administration of methadone for both withdrawal and maintenance must follow strict federal guidelines, which generally require that patients receive the methadone in person to avoid its abuse by persons other than the patient.

References

Baker J G, Rounds J B, Carson C A: Monitoring in methadone maintenance treatment. Int J Addict *30*: 1177, 1995.

Hoffman J A, Moolchan E T: The phases-of-treatment model for methadone maintenance: Implementation and evaluation. J Psychoactive Drugs *26*: 181, 1994.

Jarvis M A, Schnoll S H: Methadone treatment during pregnancy. J Psychoactive Drugs *26*: 155, 1994.

Joe G W, Simpson D D, Sells S B: Treatment process and relapse to opioid use during methadone maintenance. Am J Drug Alcohol Abuse *20*: 173, 1994.

Milby J B, Hohmann A A, Gentile M, Huggins N, Sims M K, McLellan A T, Woody G, Haas N: Methadone maintenance outcome as a function of detoxification phobia. Am J Psychiatry *151*: 1031, 1994.

Schottenfeld R S, Kleber H D: Methadone. In *Comprehensive Textbook of Psy-*

chiatry, ed 6, H I Kaplan, B J Sadock, editors, p 2031. Williams & Wilkins, Baltimore, 1995.

27.3.20 MONOAMINE OXIDASE INHIBITORS

The monoamine oxidase inhibitors (MAOIs) are primarily used to treat depressive disorders and are generally accepted as being equal in efficacy to other antidepressant drugs (for example, tricyclic drugs and serotonin-specific reuptake inhibitors [SSRIs]). The MAOIs are currently used less frequently than other antidepressants because of the dietary precautions that must be followed to avoid tyramine-induced hypertensive crises. That clinical practice may change in the near future after the introduction of MAOIs that are less likely to cause tyramine-induced hypertensive crises.

Two advances in neurochemistry and pharmacology will probably affect the use of MAOIs in the future. First, two types of the monoamine oxidase (MAO) enzyme have been characterized, MAO_A and MAO_B. Inhibitors that are specific for MAO_B are not associated with tyramine-induced hypertensive crises, although those inhibitors are probably not effective in the treatment of depression. Second, a new class of MAOIs are the reversible inhibitors of monoamine oxidase (RIMAs). Currently available MAOIs irreversibly inactivate and destroy the MAO that is present in a patient, and a period of at least two weeks must follow the last dose of an MAOI before a patient can safely ingest tyramine-containing foods. Drugs of the RIMA class have a reversible binding to MAO and require that only an average of two to five days pass before tyramine-containing foodstuffs can be safely ingested.

THERAPEUTIC INDICATIONS

The indications for MAOIs are similar to those for tricyclic and tetracyclic drugs. MAOIs may be particularly effective in panic disorder with agoraphobia, posttraumatic stress disorder, eating disorders, social phobia, and pain disorder. Some investigators have reported that MAOIs may be preferable to tricyclic drugs in the treatment of atypical depression characterized by hypersomnia, hyperphagia, anxiety, and the absence of vegetative symptoms. Patients with that symptom pattern are often less severely depressed than are patients with classic symptoms of depression, which is often evidenced by less functional impairment. For those patients, many clinicians and researchers recommend a trial with an MAOI before a trial with a tricyclic drug, although the introduction of the SSRIs may change that practice. The failure of a patient to improve after treatment with a tricyclic or tetracyclic drug may be the most common reason why a patient is given a therapeutic trial of an MAOI.

PRECAUTIONS AND ADVERSE REACTIONS

The most frequent adverse effects of MAOIs are orthostatic hypotension, weight gain, edema, sexual dysfunction, and insomnia. If the orthostatic hypotension associated with phenelzine or isocarboxazid use is severe, it may respond to treatment with fludrocortisone (Florinef), a mineralocorticoid, 0.1 to 0.2 mg a day; support stockings; hydration; and increased salt intake. Orthostatic hypotension associated with tranylcypromine

use can usually be relieved by dividing the daily dose. A rare adverse effect of MAOIs, most commonly of tranylcypromine, is a spontaneous hypertensive crisis that occurs after the first exposure to the drug and that is not associated with tyramine ingestion. The mechanism for that rare event is not understood, but tolerance for the hypertensive response does not develop, and patients should not be rechallenged with the drug. Weight gain, edema, and sexual dysfunction are often not responsive to any treatment and may warrant switching from a hydrazine to a nonhydrazine MAOI or vice versa. When switching from one MAOI to another, the clinician should taper and stop the first drug for 10 to 14 days before beginning the second drug. Insomnia and behavioral activation can be treated by dividing the dose, not giving the medication after dinner, and using a benzodiazepine hypnotic if necessary.

Myoclonus, muscle pains, and parathesias are occasionally seen in patients treated with MAOIs. Parathesias may be secondary to MAOI-induced pyridoxine deficiency, which may respond to supplementation with pyridoxine, 50 to 150 mg orally each day. Occasionally, patients complain of feeling drunk or confused, perhaps indicating that the dosage should be reduced and then increased gradually. Reports that the hydrazine MAOIs are associated with hepatotoxic effects are relatively uncommon. MAOIs are less cardiotoxic and less epileptogenic than are the tricyclic and tetracyclic drugs that are used to treat depression.

MAOIs should be used with caution by patients with renal disease, seizure disorders, cardiovascular disease, or hyperthyroidism. MAOIs may alter the dosage of a hypoglycemic agent required by diabetic patients. MAOIs have been particularly associated with causing depressed bipolar I disorder patients to switch into manic episodes and causing psychotic decompensation in schizophrenic patients. MAOIs are contraindicated during pregnancy, although data on their teratogenic risk are minimal. MAOIs should not be taken by nursing women because the drugs can pass into the breast milk.

Tyramine-Induced Hypertensive Crisis

When patients who are taking nonselective MAOIs ingest foods rich in tyramine (Table 27.3.20–1), they are likely to have a hypertensive reaction that can be life-threatening (for example, a cerebrovascular disease). Patients should also be warned that bee stings may cause a hypertensive crisis. The mechanism involves MAO_A inhibition in the gastrointestinal tract, resulting in the increased absorption of tyramine, which then acts as a pressor in the general circulation.

Patients should be warned about the dangers of ingesting tyramine-rich foods while taking MAOIs, and they should be advised to continue the dietary restrictions for two weeks after they stop MAOI treatment to allow the body to resynthesize the enzyme. The risk of tyramine-induced hypertensive crises is decreased in patients who are taking RIMAs, such as moclobemide and brofaromine. The prodromal signs and symptoms of a hypertensive crisis may include headache, stiff neck, sweating, nausea, and vomiting. If those signs and symptoms occur, a patient should seek immediate medical treatment. An MAOI-induced hypertensive crisis can be treated with nifedipine (Procardia); however, some controversy exists regarding that practice because nifedipine produces a rapid drop in arterial pressure. That drop is a concern if a patient mistakes a headache

Table 27.3.20-1.   Tyramine-Rich Foods to Be Avoided while Taking MAOIs

Very high tyramine content:
Alcohol (particularly beer and wines, especially Chianti; a small amount of scotch, gin, vodka, or sherry is permissible)
Fava or broad beans
Aged cheese (e.g., Camembert, Liederkranz, Edam, and cheddar; cream cheese and cottage cheeses are permitted)
Beef or chicken liver
Orange pulp
Pickled or smoked fish, poultry, and meats
Soups (packaged)
Yeast vitamin supplements
Meat extracts (e.g., Marmite, Bovril)
Summer (dry) sausage
Moderately high tyramine content (no more than one or two servings a day):
Soy sauce
Sour cream
Bananas (green bananas can be included only if cooked in their skins; ordinary peeled bananas are fine)
Avocados
Eggplant
Plums
Raisins
Spinach
Tomatoes
Yogurt

Table 27.3.20-2.   Drugs to Be Avoided during MAOI Treatment

Never use:
Anesthetic—never spinal anesthetic or local anesthetic containing epinephrine (lidocaine and procaine are safe)
Antiasthmatic medications
Antihypertensives (α-methyldopa, guanethidine, reserpine, pargyline)
L-Dopa, L-tryptophan
Narcotics (especially meperidine (Demerol); morphine or codeine may be less dangerous)
Over-the-counter cold, hay fever, and sinus medications, especially those containing dextromethorphan (aspirin, acetaminophen, and menthol lozenges are safe)
Sympathomimetics (amphetamine, cocaine, methylphenidate, dopamine, metaraminol, epinephrine, norepinephrine, isoproterenol)
Serotonin-specific reuptake inhibitors, clomipramine
Use carefully:
Antihistamines
Hydralazine (Apresoline)
Propranolol (Inderal)
Terpin hydrate with codeine
Tricyclic and tetracyclic drugs

resulting from the rebound of MAOI-induced orthostatic hypotension for a hypertensive-related headache. When nifedipine is used, the patient should bite into a 10 mg nifedipine capsule and swallow its contents with water. Additional treatment can include the use of α-adrenergic antagonists—for example, phentolamine (Regitine) or chlorpromazine (Thorazine).

Overdose Attempts

In general, intoxication caused by MAOIs is characterized by agitation that progresses to coma with hyperthermia, hypertension, tachypnea, tachycardia, dilated pupils, and hyperactive deep tendon reflexes. Involuntary movements may be present, particularly in the face and the jaw. There is often an asymptomatic period of one to six hours after the ingestion of the drugs before the occurrence of the symptoms of toxicity. Acidification of the urine markedly hastens the excretion of MAOIs, and dialysis can be of some use. Nifedipine (Procardia), phentolamine, or chlorpromazine may be useful if hypertension is a problem.

DRUG INTERACTIONS

The inhibition of MAO can cause severe and even fatal interactions with various other drugs (Table 27.3.20–2). Patients should be instructed to tell any other physicians who are treating them that they are taking an MAOI. MAOIs may potentiate the action or be additive with central nervous system depressants, including alcohol and barbiturates. A serotonergic syndrome has been described when MAOIs are coadministered with serotonergic drugs, such as SSRIs and clomipramine (Anafranil), thus resulting in the recommendation that those combinations be avoided. The initial symptoms of a serotonin syndrome can include tremor, hypertonicity, myoclonus, and autonomic signs, which can then progress to hallucinosis, hyperthermia, and even death.

LABORATORY INTERFERENCES

The MAOIs are associated with the lowering of blood glucose levels, which are accurately reflected by laboratory analysis. However, MAOIs have been reported to be associated with a minimal false elevation in thyroid function tests.

DOSAGE AND ADMINISTRATION

There is no definitive rationale for choosing one MAOI over another, although some clinicians recommend tranylcypromine (Parnate) because of its activating qualities, possibly associated with a fast onset of action, and its low hepatotoxic potential. Phenelzine (Nardil) should be started with a test dose of 15 mg on the first day. On an outpatient basis, the dosage can be increased to 45 mg a day during the first week and increased by 15 mg a day each week thereafter until the dosage of 90 mg a day is reached by the end of the fourth week. Tranylcypromine should begin with a test dose of 10 mg and may be increased to 30 mg a day by the end of the first week. Many clinicians and researchers have recommended upper limits of 40 mg a day for tranylcypromine. If an MAOI trial is not successful after six weeks, lithium (Eskalith) or liothyronine (Cytomel) augmentation is warranted. The combined treatment of depressive disorders with MAOIs and tricyclic drugs is described in Section 27.3.27.

Liver functions tests should be monitored periodically because of the potential of hepatotoxicity, especially with phenelzine and isocarboxazid. The elderly may be more sensitive to MAOI adverse effects than are younger adults, although, because MAO activity increases with age, the usual dosages of MAOIs are required to treat elderly patients. The use of MAOIs for children has been minimally studied.

References

Berry M D, Juorio A V, Paterson I A: Possible mechanism of action of (-)deprenyl and other MAO-B inhibitors in some neurologic and psychiatric disorders. Prog Neurobiol *44*: 141, 1994.

Delumeau J C, Bentue-Ferrer D, Gandon J M, Amrein R, Belliart S, Allain H: Monoamine oxidase inhibitors, cognitive functions and neurodegenerative diseases. J Neural Transm Suppl *41*: 259, 1994.

Heinonen E H, Anttila M I, Lammintausta R A: Pharmacokinetic aspects of l-deprenyl (selegiline) and its metabolites. Clin Pharmacol Ther *56*: 742, 1994.

Himmelhoch J M: Monoamine oxidase inhibitors. In *Comprehensive Textbook of Psychiatry*, ed 6, H I Kaplan, B J Sadock, editors, p 2038. Williams & Wilkins, Baltimore, 1995.

Hublin C, Partinen M, Heinonen E H, Puukka P, Salmi T: Selegiline in the treatment of narcolepsy. Neurology *44*: 2095, 1994.

Tipton K F: Monoamine oxidase inhibition. Biochem Soc Trans *22*: 764, 1994.

27.3.21 NALTREXONE

Naltrexone (ReVia) is a synthetic opioid antagonist with no opioid agonist properties.

THERAPEUTIC INDICATIONS

Naltrexone is indicated for the treatment of alcoholism and narcotic dependence. It is available in 50 mg scored tablets.

Alcoholism

Naltrexone decreases alcohol craving, probably by blocking the release of endogenous opioids. A dosage of 50 mg once daily is recommended for most patients. That aids in achieving the goal of abstinence by preventing relapse and decreasing alcohol consumption. Naltrexone is only one of many factors in the treatment of alcoholism. Factors associated with a good outcome include the type, intensity, and duration of treatment; appropriate management of comorbid conditions; use of community-based support groups (for example, Alcoholics Anonymous), and good medication compliance. To achieve the best possible treatment outcome, appropriate compliance-enhancing techniques should be implemented for all components of the treatment program, especially medication compliance.

Narcotic Dependence

Naltrexone blocks the euphoric effect of opiates and opioids and aids in the goal of abstinence by preventing the high associated with the use of narcotics. Naltrexone is not effective against nonnarcotic drugs (for example, cocaine). Treatment should be initiated with an initial dose of 25 mg of naltrexone and is increased to 50 mg a day thereafter.

Treatment should not be attempted unless the patient has remained opioid-free for at least 7 to 10 days. Self-reporting of abstinence from opioids in narcotic addicts should be verified by analysis of the patient's urine for absence of opioids. If there is any question of occult opioid dependence, a naloxone (Narcan) challenge test should be performed (Table 27.3.21–1). If signs of opioid withdrawal are still observed following naloxone challenge, treatment with naltrexone should not be attempted.

A flexible approach to a dosing regimen may be used to enhance compliance. Thus, patients may receive 50 mg of naltrexone every weekday with a 100 mg dose on Saturday, patients may receive 100 mg every other day, or patients may receive 150 mg every third day. Those dosing schedules may enable many naltrexone patients to successfully maintain their opioid-free state.

PRECAUTIONS AND ADVERSE REACTIONS

Alcohol Dependence

Five to 15 percent of patients taking naltrexone for alcohol dependence will complain of nonspecific side effects, chiefly

Table 27.3.21–1. Naloxone (Narcan) Challenge Test

The naloxone challenge test should not be performed in a patient showing clinical signs or symptoms of opioid withdrawal, or in a patient whose urine contains opioids. The naloxone challenge test may be administered by either the intravenous or subcutaneous routes.

Intravenous challenge: Following appropriate screening of the patient, 0.8 mg of naloxone should be drawn into a sterile syringe. If the intravenous route of administration is selected, 0.2 mg of naloxone should be injected, and, while the needle is still in the patient's vein, the patient should be observed for 30 seconds for evidence of withdrawal signs or symptoms. If there is not evidence of withdrawal, the remaining 0.6 mg of naloxone should be injected, and the patient observed for an additional period of 20 minutes for signs and symptoms of withdrawal.

Subcutaneous challenge: If the subcutaneous route is selected, 0.8 mg should be administered subcutaneously, and the patient observed for signs and symptoms of withdrawal for 20 minutes.

Conditions and technique for observation of patient: During the appropriate period of observation, the patient's vital signs should be monitored, and the patient should be monitored for signs of withdrawal. It is also important to question the patient carefully. The signs and symptoms of opioid withdrawal includes, but are not limited to, the following:

Withdrawal signs: stuffiness or running nose, tearing, yawning, sweating, tremor, vomiting, or piloerection.

Withdrawal symptoms: feeling of temperature change, joint or bone and muscle pain, abdominal cramps, and formication (feeling of bugs crawling under skin).

Interpretation of the challenge: Warning—the elicitation of the enumerated signs or symptoms indicates a potential risk for the subject, and naltrexone should not be administered. If no signs or symptoms of withdrawal are observed, elicited, or reported, naltrexone may be administered. If there is any doubt in the observer's mind that the patient is not in an opioid-free state, or is in continuing withdrawal, naltrexone should be withheld for 24 hours and the challenge repeated.

gastrointestinal upset. To avoid adverse effects one may use an initial 25 mg dose, split the daily dose, or adjust the time of dosing; however, no dose or pattern of dosing is more effective than any other in reducing side effects for all patients.

Narcotic Dependence

Severe opioid withdrawal syndromes can be precipitated by the administration of naltrexone in opioid-dependent persons. Symptoms of withdrawal usually appear within five minutes of ingestion of naltrexone and may last for up to 48 hours. Mental status changes include confusion, somnolence, and visual hallucinations. Significant fluid losses from vomiting and diarrhea may require intravenous fluid administration. Therefore, the clinician should be certain that the patient is opioid-free before beginning treatment with naltrexone.

The effect of naltrexone administration on pregnant or nursing women is unknown and should therefore be avoided. The safe use of naltrexone in children has not been established.

DRUG INTERACTIONS

Studies to evaluate possible interactions between naltrexone and drugs other than opioids have not been performed. Consequently, caution is advised if the concomitant administration of naltrexone with other drugs is required.

Patients taking naltrexone may not benefit from opioid-containing medicines, such as cough and cold preparations, antidiarrheal preparations, and opioid analgesics. In an emergency situation when opioid analgesia must be administered to a patient receiving naltrexone, the amount of opioid required may be greater than usual, and the resulting respiratory depression may be deeper and more prolonged; caution should be exercised.

References

Jaffe J H: Cocaine-related disorders. In *Comprehensive Textbook of Psychiatry*, ed 6, H I Kaplan, B J Sadock, editors, p 817. Williams & Wilkins, Baltimore, 1995.
Jaffe J H: Opioid-related disorders. In *Comprehensive Textbook of Psychiatry*, ed 6, H I Kaplan, B J Sadock, editors, p 842. Williams & Wilkins, Baltimore, 1995.
O'Mara N B, Wesley L C: Naltrexone in the treatment of alcohol dependence. Ann Pharmacother 28: 210, 1994.
Sax D S, Kornetsky C, Kim A: Lack of hepatotoxicity with naltrexone treatment. J Clin Pharmacol *34*: 898, 1994.
Shufman E N, Porat S, Witztum E, Gandacu D, Bar-Hamburger R, Ginath Y: The efficacy of naltrexone in preventing reabuse of heroin after detoxification. Biol Psychiatry *35*: 935, 1994.
Volpicelli J R, Watson N T, King A C, Sherman C E, et al: Effect of naltrexone on alcohol "high" in alcoholics. Am J Psychiatry *152*: 613, 1995.

27.3.22 SEROTONIN-SPECIFIC REUPTAKE INHIBITORS

The group of drugs discussed here are widely known as antidepressants. The drugs, along with the tricyclic and tetracyclic drugs and the monoamine oxidase inhibitors (MAOIs), are often considered the major antidepressant drugs. Although depressive disorders were the initial indications for the drugs, they are effective in a wide range of disorders, including eating disorders, panic disorder, obsessive-compulsive disorder, and borderline personality disorder. Therefore, it is misleading to call the drugs antidepressants. In this textbook they are referred to as the serotonin-specific reuptake inhibitors (SSRIs) because they share the pharmacodynamic property in that they are specific inhibitors of serotonin reuptake by presynaptic neurons.

Fluoxetine (Prozac), the SSRI first introduced for clinical use in the United States in 1988, was discovered in the early 1970s. Since its introduction, fluoxetine has become the most widely prescribed (27 million people) antidepressant in the United States. Currently, three SSRIs are available in the United States and approved by the Food and Drug Administration (FDA) for the treatment of depression: fluoxetine, paroxetine (Paxil), and sertraline (Zoloft). Fluoxetine and a fourth SSRI, fluvoxamine (Luvox), are approved by the FDA for the treatment of obsessive-compulsive disorder. A fifth SSRI, citalopram, is in widespread clinical use in Europe. Clomipramine (Anafranil) is another drug that is specific in its actions as an inhibitor of serotonin reuptake, but, because it is structurally similar to the tricyclic drugs used to treat depression, it is classified along with the tricyclic and tetracyclic drugs. The SSRIs have dramatically changed the treatment approach to depression because they are as effective as the old antidepressants yet are associated with a generally more favorable side-effect profile.

THERAPEUTIC INDICATIONS

Depression

The major indication for SSRI use is short-term treatment of major depressive disorder; studies with fluoxetine have also shown that it is effective for the treatment of depressive episodes in bipolar I disorder. The majority of studies and data support the conclusions that the SSRIs are equal in efficacy to tricyclic drugs in the treatment of depression and that the SSRIs have a significantly superior side-effect profile, compared with those other antidepressant drugs.

Preliminary reports indicate that fluoxetine is useful in the treatment of dysthymic disorder and mild depressive episodes.

Other Indications

SSRIs are widely used with other disorders including impulse-control disorders, posttraumatic stress disorder, borderline personality disorder, and eating disorders. Because fluoxetine has been available clinically the longest, most studies regarding other indications have been done with fluoxetine, although it is likely that the other SSRIs are similar to fluoxetine in their efficacies for those additional indications. In particular, fluoxetine and fluvoxamine are approved for the treatment of obsessive-compulsive disorder. The most data on other indications involve anorexia bulimia nervosa and obesity. In several well-controlled studies, fluoxetine has been effective in reducing the vomiting and binge-eating symptoms of bulimia nervosa, in promoting weight loss in overweight persons, and in reducing the symptoms of obsessive-compulsive disorder. However, whereas the most commonly effective dosage of fluoxetine in the treatment of depression is 20 mg a day, the effective dosage of fluoxetine for those other indications appears to be 60 mg a day.

Other indications for which there is preliminary evidence of efficacy for the SSRIs are borderline personality disorder, panic disorder, and pain disorder. In contrast to the higher dosages of fluoxetine for some disorders, panic disorder patients are best started on lower dosages of fluoxetine, around 5 mg a day. That variation in dosages for fluoxetine among the indications suggests that it may not be wise to use nonfluoxetine SSRIs for nondepression indications without knowing the approximate dosage range in which a patient is likely to respond.

PRECAUTIONS AND ADVERSE REACTIONS

Studies have shown that some degree of nervousness or agitation, sleep disturbances, gastrointestinal (GI) symptoms, and sexual side effects are more common in SSRI-treated patients than in tricyclic drug-treated patients.

Fluoxetine

Because fluoxetine has been available the longest time and has been used in the most patients, the available data on its adverse effects are the most complete of the SSRIs. The side-effect profile of fluoxetine shows that it is a well-tolerated drug. The most common adverse effects of fluoxetine involve the central nervous system (CNS) and the GI system. The most common CNS effects include headache, nervousness, insomnia, drowsiness, and anxiety. Seizures have been reported in 0.2 percent of all patients treated with the drug, an incidence that is comparable to the incidence reported with other antidepressants. The most common GI complaints are nausea, diarrhea, anorexia, and dyspepsia. Data indicate that the nausea is dose-related and is an adverse effect for which patients apparently develop tolerance.

Other adverse effects involve sexual functioning and the

skin. Anorgasmia, delayed ejaculation, and impotence apparently affect at least 5 percent of all patients treated. Those sexual side effects may respond to yohimbine (Yocon) or to cyproheptadine (Periactin). Various types of rashes may appear in about 4 percent of all patients; in a small subset of those patients, the allergic reaction may generalize and involve the pulmonary system, resulting rarely in fibrotic damage and dyspnea. Fluoxetine treatment may have to be discontinued in patients with drug-related rashes. Fluoxetine is associated with a decrease in glucose concentrations; therefore, diabetic patients should be carefully monitored regarding the possibility of decreasing the dosage of their hypoglycemic drug. Rare cases of fluoxetine-associated hyponatremia have occurred in patients treated with diuretics who are also water-deprived.

Fluoxetine, compared with non-SSRI antidepressants, is a safe drug when taken in overdoses. Only one report has noted a lethal overdose of fluoxetine taken by itself and only a small number of lethal overdoses when fluoxetine was taken with other drugs. The symptoms of overdose include agitation, restlessness, insomnia, tremor, nausea, vomiting, tachycardia, and seizures. The clinician should ascertain whether other drugs were taken with the fluoxetine. The first steps in the treatment of overdose are gastric lavage and emesis. In the late 1980s a widely publicized report suggested an association between fluoxetine administration and violent acts, including suicide, but many subsequent reviews have clearly proved no increased likelihood of such an association with fluoxetine. However, a few patients become especially anxious and agitated, almost in an akathisialike fashion, when given fluoxetine, and the appearance of those symptoms in an already-suicidal patient may aggravate the seriousness of the suicidal ideation.

Because of the large number of patients who have taken fluoxetine, it is possible to state that the number of birth defects and birth complications when the mothers took fluoxetine during pregnancy is not significantly different from those seen when mothers did not take fluoxetine during pregnancy. Nevertheless, the general rule of avoiding all drugs during pregnancy should be adhered to unless there is a compelling reason to treat a pregnant woman with an antidepressant drug. Fluoxetine is excreted in breast milk; therefore, nursing mothers should not take fluoxetine. Fluoxetine should also be used with caution by patients with hepatic disease.

Other SSRIs

The adverse effects associated with other SSRIs are similar to those seen with fluoxetine, including nausea and vomiting, weight loss, headache, dry mouth, sedation and sexual side effects, although the fact that the other drugs have been given to fewer patients increases the possibility that some rare adverse effects are not fully recognized. The data on paroxetine, sertraline, and fluvoxamine are too limited at this point to differentiate them from fluoxetine, although their use in medically ill patients should be carried out with the appreciation that clinical exposure of the new compounds has been relatively limited.

DRUG INTERACTIONS

The clinician must be informed about a number of potential drug interactions with the SSRIs. No SSRI should be administered with L-tryptophan or a monoamine oxidase inhibitor

(MAOI) because of the possibility of inducing a potentially fatal serotonin syndrome. Fluoxetine can be administered with tricyclic drugs, but the clinician should use low dosages of the tricyclic drug. Possibly significant drug interactions have been described for fluoxetine with benzodiazepines, antipsychotics, and lithium (Eskalith). Fluoxetine has no interactions with warfarin (Coumadin), tolbutamide (Orinase), or chlorothiazide (Diuril). The drug interaction data on sertraline support a generally similar profile, although sertraline does not interact with the hepatic $P_{450}IID6$ enzyme. Paroxetine has a higher risk for drug interactions than does either fluoxetine or sertraline because of its metabolic pathway through the $P_{450}IID6$ hepatic enzyme. Cimetidine (Tagamet) can increase the concentration of paroxetine, and phenobarbital (Luminal) and phenytoin (Dilantin) can decrease the concentrations of paroxetine. The coadministration of paroxetine with other antidepressants and antiarrhythmic drugs should be undertaken with caution.

DOSAGE AND ADMINISTRATION

Fluoxetine

Fluoxetine is available in 10 mg and 20 Pulvules (that is, capsules) and as a liquid (20 mg per 5 mL). Fluoxetine may be available in 60 mg preparations in the near future. For depression, the initial dosage is usually 20 mg orally each day, usually given in the morning, because insomnia is a potential adverse effect of the drug. Fluoxetine should be taken with food to minimize the possible nausea. The long half-lives of the drug and its metabolite contribute to a four-week period to reach steady-state concentrations. As with all available antidepressants, the antidepressant effects of fluoxetine may be seen in the first one to three weeks, but the clinician should wait until the patient has been taking the drug for four to six weeks before evaluating its antidepressant activity. Several studies indicate that 20 mg is as effective as higher doses. The maximum daily dosage recommended by the manufacturer is 80 mg a day. A reasonable strategy is to maintain a patient with 20 mg a day for three weeks. If the patient shows no signs of clinical improvement at that time, an increase to 20 mg twice a day may be warranted, although at least one study has found that keeping a patient on the 20 mg a day dosage longer is as effective as increasing the dosage.

To minimize the early adverse effects of anxiety and restlessness, some clinicians initiate fluoxetine at 5 to 10 mg a day either by instructing the patient to dissolve the contents of a capsule in water or juice or by using the liquid preparation. If a patient mixes the contents of a capsule with a liquid, the mixture should be kept refrigerated. Alternatively, because of the long half-life of fluoxetine, the drug can be initiated with an every-other-day administration schedule.

With depressed patients who do not respond to fluoxetine treatment, the clinician can augment fluoxetine with other drugs, including tricyclic drugs (for example, desipramine [Norpramin]), sympathomimetics (for example, pemoline [Cylert]), buspirone (BuSpar), and lithium. Adding those drugs when a patient has been nonresponsive to fluoxetine alone has resulted in a significant proportion of patients' converting to treatment-responders. At least two weeks should elapse between the discontinuation of MAOIs and the initiation of fluoxetine. Fluoxetine must be discontinued for at least five weeks before the initiation of MAOI treatment.

The dosage of fluoxetine that is effective in other indications may differ from the 20 mg a day that is generally used for depression. A dosage of 60 mg a day has been reported to be the most efficacious dosage for obsessive-compulsive disorder, obesity, and bulimia nervosa. In contrast, a starting dosage of 5 mg a day with minimal increases has been reported to be effective in the treatment of panic disorder.

Fluvoxamine

Fluvoxamine is available in 50 and 100 mg tablets. The effective daily dosage range is from 50 mg a day to 300 mg a day. A usual starting dosage is 100 mg a day for the first week, after which the dosage can be adjusted according to the adverse effects and the patient's response. A tapered reduction of the dosage may be necessary if nausea develops over the first two weeks of therapy. Fluvoxamine can be administered as a single evening dose to minimize its adverse effects. Tablets should be swallowed with water and, preferably, food without chewing the tablet.

Paroxetine

Paroxetine is available in scored 20 mg and 30 mg unscored tablets. Paroxetine is usually initiated for the treatment of depression at a dosage of 20 mg a day. An increase in the dosage should be considered when patients do not show an adequate response in one to three weeks. At that point, the clinician can initiate upward dose titration in 10 mg increments at weekly intervals to a maximum of 50 mg a day. Patients who experience GI upsets may benefit by taking the drug with food. Paroxetine should be taken as a single daily dose in the morning. Patients with melancholic features may require dosages greater than 20 mg a day. The suggested therapeutic dosage range for elderly patients is 20 to 40 mg a day, as mean plasma concentrations are higher in the elderly than in younger adults.

Sertraline

For the initial treatment of depression, sertraline should be initiated with a dosage of 50 mg once daily. Patients who do not respond after one to three weeks may benefit from dosage increases of 50 mg every week up to a maximum of 200 mg given once daily. Sertraline can be administered in the morning or the evening without regard for meals.

References

Freeman C P, Trimble M R, Deakin J F, Stokes T M, Ashford J J: Fluvoxamine versus clomipramine in the treatment of obsessive compulsive disorder: A multicenter, randomized, double-blind, parallel group comparison. J Clin Psychiatry 55: 301, 1994.
Gram L F: Fluoxetine. N Engl J Med 331: 1354, 1994.
Harris M G, Benfield P: Fluoxetine. A review of its pharmacodynamic and pharmacokinetic properties, and therapeutic use in older patients with depressive illness. Drugs Aging 6: 64, 1995.
Mitchell P B: Selective serotonin reuptake inhibitors: Adverse effects, toxicity and interactions. Adverse Drug React Toxicol Rev 13: 121, 1994.
Serotonin-specific reuptake inhibitors. In Comprehensive Textbook of Psychiatry, ed 6, H I Kaplan, B J Sadock, editors, p 2054. Williams & Wilkins, Baltimore, 1995.
Stein D J, Hollander E, Josephson S C: Serotonin reuptake blockers for the treatment of obsessional jealousy. J Clin Psychiatry 55: 30, 1994.

27.3.23 Sympathomimetics

The sympathomimetics are a class of drugs that act primarily by stimulating the release of dopamine from presynaptic termi- nals. The drugs are also referred to as stimulants, psychostimu- lants, and analeptics. The first sympathomimetic, amphetamine (Benzedrine), was synthesized in 1935 and was recognized as efficacious in the treatment of narcolepsy, depressive disorders, and hyperactive children shortly thereafter. The use of ampheta- mine was soon replaced by the use of dextroamphetamine (Dexedrine), which was then joined by two other currently available sympathomimetics, methylphenidate (Ritalin) and pemoline (Cylert). The Food and Drug Administration (FDA)- approved indications for dextroamphetamine and methylpheni- date are narcolepsy and attention-deficit/hyperactivity disorder, and the approved indication for pemoline is attention-deficit/ hyperactivity disorder. The drugs are also effective in the treat- ment of depressive disorders in special populations (for exam- ple, the medically ill).

THERAPEUTIC INDICATIONS

Attention-Deficit/Hyperactivity Disorder

The major indication for the sympathomimetics is attention- deficit/hyperactivity disorder in children. The sympathomi- metics are effective in about 75 percent of those patients. Many well-controlled studies have shown that the drugs increase the attention span, increase the ability to concentrate, and decrease oppositional behaviors. Although those effects were once thought of as paradoxical effects for psychostimulants, subse- quent studies found that normal children also display decreased activity and increased cognitive performance when given the drugs. Although methylphenidate is the most commonly used drug for the indication, dextroamphetamine is equally effective. The data on the efficacy of pemoline are less robust, and the onset of action for pemoline is slower (three to four weeks) than the onset for the other drugs. Some clinicians, nevertheless, prefer pemoline because of its low abuse potential.

A syndrome of affective lability, inability to complete tasks, explosive temper, impulsivity, and stress intolerance has been described in adults, who often have a history of childhood atten- tion-deficit/hyperactivity disorder. Data indicate that the sympa- thomimetics are effective in the treatment of those adults. Am- phetamines (5 to 60 mg a day) or methylphenidate (5 to 60 mg a day) may be efficacious, and psychopharmacological therapy may need to be continued indefinitely.

Narcolepsy

Narcolepsy is the second approved use of sympathomimetics in the United States. The symptoms of narcolepsy include exces- sive daytime sleepiness and transient, irresistible attacks of day- time sleep. Unfortunately, patients with narcolepsy, unlike pa- tients with attention-deficit/hyperactivity disorder, develop tolerance for the therapeutic effects of the sympathomimetics.

Depressive Disorders

Sympathomimetics may be used to treat depressive disor- ders. Possible indications for their use include treatment-resis- tant depressive disorders; depression in the elderly, who are at increased risk for adverse effects from tricyclic and tetracyclic drugs and monoamine oxidase inhibitors (MAOIs); depression in medically ill patients—especially acquired immune defi- ciency (AIDS) patients—and clinical situations in which a rapid response is important but for which electroconvulsive therapy (ECT) is contraindicated.

Dextroamphetamine may be useful in differentiating pseudodementia of depression from dementia. A depressed patient generally responds to a 5 mg dose with increased alertness and improved cognition. Sympathomimetics are thought to provide only short-term benefit (two to four weeks) for depression, because tolerance for the antidepressant effects of the drugs develops rapidly in most patients. However, some research data and some clinicians report that long-term treatment of patients with sympathomimetics can be of benefit in some cases. Certainly, long-term treatment must be monitored to assess the continuing benefit of the drugs and to assess the patient's abuse of the drugs.

PRECAUTIONS AND ADVERSE REACTIONS

The most common adverse effects associated with sympathomimetics are anxiety, irritability, insomnia, and dysphoria. Sympathomimetics cause a decreased appetite, although tolerance develops for that effect. The treatment of common adverse effects in children with attention-deficit/hyperactivity disorder is usually straightforward. The drugs can also cause increases in the heart rate and the blood pressure and may cause palpitations. Less common adverse effects include the induction of movement disorders, such as tics and dyskinesia. In children, sympathomimetics may cause a transient suppression of growth. The most limiting adverse effect of sympathomimetics is their association with psychological and physical dependence. Sympathomimetics may exacerbate glaucoma, hypertension, cardiovascular disorders, hyperthyroidism, anxiety disorders, psychotic disorders, and seizure disorders.

High dosages of sympathomimetics can cause dry mouth, pupillary dilation, bruxism, formication, and emotional lability. Long-term use of high dosages can cause a delusional disorder that is indistinguishable from paranoid schizophrenia. Overdosages of sympathomimetics present with hypertension, tachycardia, hyperthermia, toxic psychosis, delirium, and occasionally seizures. Overdosages of sympathomimetics can also result in death, often due to cardiac arrhythmias. Seizures can be treated with benzodiazepines, cardiac effects with β-adrenergic receptor antagonists, fever with cooling blankets, and delirium with dopamine receptor antagonists.

There is virtually no justifiable indication for the use of sympathomimetics during pregnancy. Dextroamphetamine and methylphenidate pass into the breast milk, and it is not known whether pemoline does.

DRUG INTERACTIONS

The coadministration of sympathomimetics and tricyclic or tetracyclic drugs used for the treatment of depressive disorders, warfarin (Coumadin), primidone (Mysoline), phenobarbital (Luminal), phenytoin (Dilantin), or phenylbutazone (Butazolidin) decreases the metabolism of those compounds, resulting in increased plasma levels. Sympathomimetics decrease the therapeutic efficacy of many hypertensives, especially guanethidine (Esimil, Ismelin). The sympathomimetics should be used with extreme caution with MAOIs.

LABORATORY INTERFERENCES

Dextroamphetamine may elevate plasma corticosteroid levels and interfere falsely with some assay methods or urinary corticosteroids.

DOSAGE AND ADMINISTRATION

The dosage ranges and the available preparations for sympathomimetics are presented in Table 27.3.23–1. Sympathomimetics are schedule II drugs and in some states require triplicate prescriptions. Many clinicians initiate treatment with pemoline, because it is associated with less abuse potential than either dextroamphetamine or methylphenidate. Pretreatment evaluation should include an evaluation of the patient's cardiac function, with particular attention to the presence of hypertension or tachyarrhythmias. The clinician should also examine the patient for the presence of movement disorders, such as tics and dyskinesia, because those conditions can be exacerbated by the administration of sympathomimetics. Liver function and renal function should be assessed, and dosages of sympathomimetics should be reduced if the patient's metabolism is impaired.

When treating children for attention-deficit/hyperactivity disorder, the clinician can give dextroamphetamine or methylphenidate at 8 AM and 12 noon. Pemoline is given at 8 AM. The dosage of dextroamphetamine is 2.5 to 40 mg a day up to 0.5 mg per kg a day. Pemoline is given in dosages of 18.75 to 112.5 mg a day. Liver function tests should be monitored when using pemoline. Children are generally more sensitive to adverse effects than are adults.

Many psychiatrists believe that amphetamine use has been overly regulated by governmental authorities. Amphetamines and narcotics are listed as schedule II drugs by the U.S. Drug Enforcement Agency (DEA). In addition, in New York State, for example, physicians must use triplicate prescriptions for such drugs; one copy is filed with a state government agency.

Table 27.3.23—1. Sympathomimetics

Generic Name	Trade Name	Preparations	Adult Starting Dose (mg a day)	Adult Average Daily Dose (mg)	Adult Maximum Daily Dose (mg)
Dextroamphetamine	Dexedrine	5, 10 mg tablets 5 mg per 5 mL elixir 5, 10, 15 mg sustained-release capsules	2.5–10	10–20	60
Methylphenidate	Ritalin	5, 10, 20 mg tablets 20 mg sustained-release tablets	5–10	20–30	60–80
Pemoline	Cylert	18.75, 37.5, 75 mg tablets	18.75–37.5	56.25–75	112.5

Such mandates worry both patients and physicians about breaches in confidentiality, and physicians are concerned that their prescribing practices may be misinterpreted by official agencies. Consequently, some physicians may withhold sympathomimetics, even from patients who may benefit from the medications.

The controversial use of triplicate prescriptions is discussed further in Section 6.12.

References

Burns M M, Eisendrath S J: Dextroamphetamine treatment for depression in terminally ill patients. Psychosomatics 35: 80, 1994.

Ernst M, Zamtkin A J, Matochik J A, Liebenauer L, Fitzgerald G A, Cohen R M: Effects of intravenous dextroamphetamine on brain metabolism in adults with attention-deficit hyperactivity disorder (ADHS). Preliminary findings. Psychopharmacol Bull 30: 219, 1994.

Joffe G M, Kasnic T: Medical prescription of dextroamphetamine during pregnancy. J Perinatol 14: 301, 1994.

Klein R G: The role of methylphenidate in psychiatry. Arch Gen Psychiatry 52: 429, 1995.

Nelson J C: Sympathomimetics. In Comprehensive Textbook of Psychiatry, ed 6, H I Kaplan, B J Sadock, editors, p 2073. Williams & Wilkins, Baltimore, 1995.

Pawluk L K, Hurwitz T D, Schluter J L, Ullevig C, Mahowald M W: Psychiatric morbidity in narcoleptics on chronic high dose methylphenidate therapy. J Nerv Ment Dis 183: 45, 1995.

27.3.24 Tacrine

Tacrine (Cognex) is the first drug approved in the United States for the treatment of cognitive impairment in Alzheimer's disease. Tacrine has inhibition of acetylcholinesterase, the enzyme that catabolizes acetylcholine, as its primary mechanism of action. For at least two decades, a deficit in acetylcholine function may be involved in the pathophysiology of dementia of the Alzheimer's type. Several pharmacological approaches to address the deficit have been studied. In addition to the inhibition of acetylcholinesterase, the approaches include the administration of acetylcholine precursors (that is, lecithin and choline) and the direct stimulation of acetylcholine receptors (both muscarinic and nicotinic). Preliminary studies suggest the efficacy of physostigmine, an old acetylcholinesterase inhibitor; however, tacrine has a longer half-life and a wider therapeutic window than the old drug possesses.

THERAPEUTIC INDICATIONS

The only indication for tacrine at this time is the treatment of mildly to moderately cognitively impaired patients with dementia of the Alzheimer's type. The efficacy of tacrine in mildly demented patients and in patients with other forms of dementia has not been studied at this time. Tacrine was approved for clinical use primarily on the basis of two large multicenter placebo-controlled studies, although a number of other studies with various designs have also demonstrated the clinical efficacy of tacrine. The two studies demonstrated tacrine's beneficial effect as measured both by a specific cognitive rating scale and by a clinically based global impression scale.

PRECAUTIONS AND ADVERSE REACTIONS

The data presented here are based on studies of about 10,000 patients given tacrine. The safety data base for tacrine will expand quickly now that it has been introduced into clinical practice. On the basis of the available studies, researchers believe that about 70 percent of all patients started on tacrine will be able to tolerate long-term treatment with the drug. The most troublesome and common side effects are potentially significant elevations in hepatic transaminase levels in 25 to 30 percent of the patients, nausea and vomiting in about 20 percent of the patients, and diarrhea and other cholinergic symptoms in about 11 percent of the patients. Aside from elevations in transaminase levels, the most common specific adverse effects associated with tacrine treatment are nausea, vomiting, myalgia, anorexia, and rash, but only nausea, vomiting, and anorexia have been found to be clearly related to dosage. Decreases in weight, eructation, and increased sweating may also be caused by tacrine treatment, but those effects occur in less than 2 percent of tacrine-treated patients. Transaminase elevations characteristically develop during the first 6 to 12 weeks of treatment, and cholinergically mediated events are dosage-related. No significant effects of tacrine treatment have been seen in vital signs, cardiac function as indicated by electrocardiograms (ECGs), or laboratory measures of anything other than transaminases. Although a low incidence of white blood cell dyscrasias (for example, neutropenia, leukopenia, and agranulocytosis) has been associated with a metabolite of tacrine (1-hydroxytacrine, velnacrine), there is no evidence at this time that such blood dyscrasias are associated with tacrine treatment.

DRUG INTERACTIONS

Data on drug interactions with tacrine are not available at this time, but tacrine should be used cautiously with drugs that also possess cholinomimetic activity. The coadministration of tacrine and drugs that have cholinergic antagonist activity (for example, tricyclic drugs) is probably counterproductive.

DOSAGE AND ADMINISTRATION

Before the initiation of tacrine treatment, a complete physical and laboratory examination should be conducted, with special attention to liver function tests and baseline hematological indexes. Treatment should be initiated at 40 mg a day and then raised by 40 mg a day increments every six weeks up to 160 mg a day; the patient's tolerance of each dosage is indicated by the absence of unacceptable side effects and elevated ALT concentrations. Some small studies and case reports have used dosages up to 200 mg a day, but those higher dosages should probably be avoided at this time. Tacrine should be given three or four times daily—ideally one hour before meals, since the absorption of tacrine is reduced by about 25 percent when it is taken with meals or within two hours after meals.

Management of ALT Concentration Elevations

Although experience regarding the management of ALT concentration elevations is based only on the research populations, specific guidelines have been proposed. For routine monitoring of hepatic enzymes, asparate aminotransferase (AST) and alanine aminotransferase (ALT) concentrations should be measured weekly for the first 18 weeks, every month for the second four months, and every three months thereafter. AST and ALT concentrations should be assessed weekly for at least six weeks after any increase in dosage. For patients with elevated ALT concentrations between $3 \times$ ULN and $5 \times$ ULN, their ALT concentrations should be monitored weekly, and the tacrine dosage should not be increased until the ALT concentration drops to below 3 × ULN. For patients with ALT concentrations # 5 × ULN, the clinician should stop tacrine immediately, monitor ALT concentrations weekly, and not rechallenge the patients with tacrine until the ALT concentrations return to the normal range. When tacrine treatment is reinitiated, the same upward titration schedule can be followed, but ALT concentrations should be assessed weekly. For patients with ALT concentrations greater than 10 × ULN, the clinician should stop tacrine and monitor the patients until their ALT concentrations return to normal; the decision to rechallenge the patients should be based on a careful assessment of the risk-benefit ratio for each patient. For any patient with elevated ALT concentrations and jaundice, tacrine treatment should be stopped, and the patients should not be given the drug again.

References

Crismon M L: Tacrine: First drug approved for Alzheimer's disease. Ann Pharmacother 28: 744, 1994.
Grebb J A: Tacrine. In Comprehensive Textbook of Psychiatry, ed 6, H I Kaplan, B J Sadock, editors, p 2079. Williams & Wilkins, Baltimore, 1995.
Knapp M J, Knopman D S, Solomon P R, Pendlebury W W, Davis C S, Gracon S I: A 30-week randomized controlled trial of high-dose tacrine in patients with Alzheimer's disease. The Tacrine Study Group. JAMA 271: 985, 1994.
Lahiri D K, Lewis S, Farlow M R: Tacrine alters the secretion of the beta-amyloid precursor protein in cell lines. J Neurosci Res 37: 777, 1994.
Madden S, Spaldin V, Park B K: Clinical pharmacokinetics of tacrine. Clin Pharmacokinet 28: 449, 1995.
Wagstaff A J, McTavish D: Tacrine. A review of its pharmacodynamic and pharmacokinetic properties, and therapeutic efficacy in Alzheimer's disease. Drugs Aging 4: 510, 1994.

27.3.25 Thyroid Hormones

Thyroid hormones are used in psychiatry as adjuvants to antidepressants, often in an attempt to convert an antidepressant-nonresponsive patient into an antidepressant-responsive patient. Thyroid hormones have also been used in the treatment rapid-cycling bipolar I disorder patients. The most commonly used thyroid hormone is L-triiodothyronine (sometimes called liothyronine) (Cytomel), which is the levorotatory isomer of triiodothyronine (T_3); L-thyroxine (also known as levothyroxine) (Levoxine, Levothroid, Synthroid), the levorotatory isomer of thyroxine (T_4), is sometimes used for the same purpose. Endogenous thyroxine and exogenous thyroxine are converted into triiodothyronine in the body.

THERAPEUTIC INDICATIONS

The major indication for thyroid hormones in psychiatry is as adjuvants to antidepressants. There is no correlation between the laboratory measures of thyroid function and the response to thyroid hormone supplementation of antidepressants. If a patient has been nonresponsive to a six-week course of an antidepressant at an appropriate dosage, adjuvant therapy with either lithium (Eskalith) or a thyroid hormone is an alternative. Most clinicians use adjuvant lithium before trying a thyroid hormone. The available clinical data indicate that L-triiodothyronine is more effective than thyroxine. Although several controlled trials have indicated that the use of L-triiodothyronine converts 33 to 75 percent of antidepressant nonresponders to responders, several other studies have failed to support that finding.

PRECAUTIONS AND ADVERSE REACTIONS

The most common adverse effects associated with thyroid hormones are weight loss, palpitations, nervousness, diarrhea, abdominal cramps, sweating, tachycardia, increased blood pressure, tremors, headache, and insomnia. Osteoporosis may also occur with long-term treatment. Overdoses of thyroid hormones can lead to cardiac failure and death.

Thyroid hormones should not be administered to patients with cardiac disease, angina, or hypertension. The hormones are contraindicated in thyrotoxicosis and uncorrected adrenal insufficiency and in patients with acute myocardial infarctions. Thyroid hormones can be administered safely to pregnant women, because the thyroid hormones do not cross the placenta. Thyroid hormones are minimally excreted in the breast milk and have not been shown to cause problems in nursing babies.

DRUG INTERACTIONS

Thyroid hormones can potentiate the effects of warfarin (Coumadin) and other anticoagulants by increasing the catabolism of clotting factors. Thyroid hormones may increase the insulin requirement for diabetic patients. Sympathomimetics and thyroid hormones should not be coadministered because of the risk of cardiac decompensation.

LABORATORY INTERFERENCES

Thyroxine has not been reported to interfere with any laboratory test. L-Triiodothyronine, however, causes a suppression in the release of endogenous T_4, thereby lowering the value of any thyroid function test dependent on the measure of T_4. The value for thyroid-stimulating hormone (TSH) is not affected by either thyroxine or L-triiodothyronine administration.

DOSAGE AND ADMINISTRATION

L-Triiodothyronine is available in 5, 25, and 50 μg tablets. Thyroxine is available in 12.5, 25, 50, 75, 88, 100, 112, 125, 150, 175, 200, and 300 μg tablets; it is also available in a 200 and 500 μg parenteral form. The dosage of L-triiodothyronine is 25 or 50 μg a day added to the patient's antidepressant regimen. L-Triiodothyronine has been used as an adjuvant for all the available antidepressant drugs. An adequate trial of L-triiodothyronine supplementation should last 7 to 14 days. If L-triiodothyronine supplementation is successful, it should be continued for two months and then tapered at the rate of 12.5 μg a day every three to seven days.

References

Baumgartner A, Bauer M, Hellweg R: Treatment of intractable non-rapid cycline bipolar affective disorder with high-dose thyroxine: An open clinical trial. Neuropsychopharmacology 10: 183, 1994.
Joffe R T, Sokolov S T, Singer W: Thyroid hormone treatment of depression. Thyroid 5: 235, 1995.
Kathmann, N, Kuisle U, Bommer M, Naber D, et al: Effects of elevated triiodothyronine on cognitive performance and mood in healthy subjects. Neuropsychobiology 29: 136, 1994.
Mason J, Southwick S, Yehuda R, Wang S, et al: Elevation of serum free triiodothyronine, total triiodothyronine, thyroxine-binding globulin, and total thyroxine levels in combat-related posttraumatic stress disorder. Arch Gen Psychiatry 51: 629, 1994.
Prange A J, Stern R A: Thyroid hormones. In Comprehensive Textbook of Psychiatry, ed 6, H I Kaplan, B J Sadock, editors, p 2083. Williams & Wilkins, Baltimore, 1995.
Ryan W G, Roddam R F, Grizzle W E: Thyroid function screening in newly admitted psychiatric inpatients. Ann Clin Psychiatry 6: 7, 1994.

27.3.26 TRAZODONE AND NEFAZODONE

Trazodone (Desyrel) and nefazodone (Serzone) are effective in the treatment of depressive disorders. Trazodone and nefazodone are structurally unrelated to the tricyclic and tetracyclic drugs used to treat depressive disorders, the monoamine oxidase inhibitors (MAOIs), serotonin-specific reuptake inhibitors (SSRIs), and other currently available antidepressant drugs.

Trazodone differs from tricyclic and tetracyclic drugs and from monoamine oxidase inhibitors in having almost no anticholinergic adverse effects. Trazodone is also distinctive in having more marked sedative effects than those found with other antidepressants.

Nefazodone is distinct from trazodone in its pharmacological effects and its adverse-effect profile, especially its lack of sedation.

TRAZODONE

Therapeutic Indications

DEPRESSIVE DISORDERS

The primary indication for the use of trazodone is major depressive disorder. Trazodone is as effective as the standard antidepressants in the short-term and long-term treatment of major depressive disorder. The drug is particularly effective at improving sleep quality—increasing total sleep time, decreasing the number and the duration of nighttime awakenings, and decreasing the amount of rapid eye movement (REM) sleep. Unlike tricyclic drugs, trazodone does not decrease stage 4 sleep.

INSOMNIA

The marked sedative qualities of trazodone and its favorable effects on sleep architecture have suggested to many clinicians that it would be effective as a hypnotic, and a number of clinicians have used trazodone effectively as a hypnotic. It has also been used effectively as a hypnotic in combination with less sedating psychotropic drugs. Trazodone has been reported to be useful in treating fluoxetine (Prozac)-induced insomnia. The usual dosage is 50 to 100 mg at bedtime.

OTHER INDICATIONS

Some data indicate that trazodone may be useful in low dosages for controlling severe agitation in elderly patients. A few case reports and uncontrolled trials of trazodone have indicated its usefulness for the treatment of depression with marked anxiety symptoms and for panic disorder with agoraphobia. The final evaluation of the use of trazodone for those disorders requires further research.

Precautions and Adverse Reactions

The most common adverse effects associated with trazodone are sedation, orthostatic hypotension, dizziness, headache, and nausea. As a result of α_1-adrenergic blockade, some patients experience dry mouth. Trazodone may also cause gastric irritation in some patients. The drug is not associated with the usual anticholinergic adverse effects, such as urinary retention and constipation. A few case reports have noted an association between trazodone and arrhythmias in patients with preexisting premature ventricular contractions or mitral valve prolapse.

Trazodone is relatively safe in overdose attempts. No fatalities from trazodone overdoses have been reported when the drug was taken alone; however, there have been fatalities when trazodone was taken with other drugs. The symptoms of an overdose include the loss of muscle coordination, nausea and vomiting, and drowsiness. Trazodone does not have the quinidinelike antiarrhythmic effects of imipramine (Tofranil).

Trazodone is associated with the rare occurrence of priapism, prolonged erection in the absence of sexual stimuli. Patients should be advised to tell their clinicians if erections are gradually becoming frequent or prolonged. In such cases, physicians should consider switching the patients to another antidepressant medication. Untreated priapism can lead to impotence. A patient who experiences priapism while taking trazodone should stop taking the drug and consult a physician immediately. One effective treatment for priapism involves the intracavernosal injection of a 1 μg per mL solution of epinephrine (an α_1-adrenergic agonist). Other forms of sexual dysfunction may also occur with trazodone treatment.

The use of trazodone is contraindicated in pregnant and nursing women. Trazodone should be used with caution in patients with hepatic and renal diseases.

Drug Interactions

Trazodone potentiates the central nervous system depressant effects of other centrally acting drugs and alcohol. The combination of MAOIs and trazodone should be avoided. Concurrent use of trazodone and antihypertensives may cause hypotension. Electroconvulsive therapy (ECT) concurrent with trazodone administration should also be avoided. Trazodone increases plasma concentrations of fluoxetine.

Dosage and Administration

Trazodone is available in 50, 100, 150, and 300 mg tablets. The usual starting dose is 50 mg orally the first day. The dosage can be increased to 50 mg orally twice daily on the second day and possibly 50 mg orally three times daily on the third and fourth days if sedation or orthostatic hypotension does not become a problem. The therapeutic range for trazodone is 200 to 600 mg a day in divided doses. Some reports indicate that dosages of 400 to 600 mg a day are required for maximal therapeutic effects; other reports indicate that 300 to 400 mg a day is sufficient. The dosage may be titrated up to 300 mg a day; then the patient can be evaluated for the need for further dosage increases if there are no signs of clinical improvement.

NEFAZODONE

Therapeutic Indications

Nefazodone is approved as a safe and effective treatment for depressive disorders (for example, major depressive disorder with melancholia) on the basis of the positive results of several well-controlled efficacy studies. Preliminary clinical reports indicate that nefazodone may also be an effective treatment for premenstrual dysphoric disorder, and preliminary preclinical reports indicate that nefazodone may be effective in the management of chronic pain.

Precautions and Adverse Reactions

The adverse-effect profile for nefazodone has not yet been reported in the literature, but its relatively specific effects on the serotonin system indicate that the side-effect profile will be fairly benign. Nefazodone will probably not produce the sedation, orthostatic hypotension, and priapism that have been associated with trazodone use.

Drug Interactions and Laboratory Interferences

Although the effects of combined use of nefazodone and MAOIs have not been evaluated in humans or animals, because nefazodone is an inhibitor of both serotonin and norepinephrine reuptake, it is recommended that nefazodone not be used in combination with an MAOI, or within 14 days of discontinuing treatment with an MAOI. At least one week should be allowed after stopping nefazodone before starting an MAOI.

Interaction studies of nefazodone with triazolam (Halcion) and alprazolam (Xanax) have revealed substantial and clinically important increases in plasma concentration of these compounds when administered concomitantly with nefazodone. Astemizole (Hismanal) and terfenadine (Seldane) should not be used with nefazodone.

Dosage and Administration

On the basis of the clinical studies to date, the recommended dosage of nefazodone will probably be in the range of 300 to 500 mg a day; some data indicate that dosages of less than 300 mg a day and dosages of more than 500 mg a day are less effective, thus suggesting the presence of a therapeutic window for nefazodone. Nefazodone will be available in 100, 150, and 200 mg tablets.

References

Anton S F, Robinson D S, Roberts D L, Kensler T T, English P A, Archibald D G: Long-term treatment of depression with nefazodone. Psychopharmacol Bull *30*: 165, 1994.
Armitage R, Rush A J, Trivedi M, Cain J, Roffwarg H P: The effects of nefazodone on sleep architecture in depression. Neuropsychopharmacology *10*: 123, 1994.
Barry J J, Schatzberg A F: Trazodone and nefazodone. In *Comprehensive Textbook of Psychiatry*, ed 6, H I Kaplan, B J Sadock, editors, p 2089. Williams & Wilkins, Baltimore, 1995.
Haria M, Fitton A, McTavish D: Trazodone. A review of its pharmacology, therapeutic use in depression and therapeutic potential in other disorders. Drugs Aging *4*: 331, 1994.
Neirenberg A A, Adler L A, Peselow E, Zornberg G, Rosenthal M: Trazodone for antidepressant-associated insomnia. Am J Psychiatry *151*: 1069, 1994.
Taylor D P, Carter R B, Eison A S, Mullins U L, Smith H L, Torrente J R, Wright R N, Yocca F D: Pharmacology and neurochemistry of nefazodone, a novel antidepressant drug. J Clin Psychiatry *56* (suppl 6): 3, 1995.

27.3.27 TRICYCLIC AND TETRACYCLIC DRUGS (ANTIDEPRESSANTS)

The group of drugs discussed here are widely known as the tricyclic antidepressants and the tetracyclic antidepressants (both commonly abbreviated as the TCAs). The drugs, along with the monoamine oxidase inhibitors (MAOIs), are often considered the classic antidepressant drugs. Although depressive disorders were the initial indications for the drugs, they are effective in a wide range of disorders, including panic disorder, generalized anxiety disorder, posttraumatic stress disorder, obsessive-compulsive disorder, eating disorders, and pain disor-

der. Therefore, it seems at least misleading, if not incorrect, to call the drugs antidepressants. For that reason, in this textbook they are referred to as the tricyclic and tetracyclic drugs.

The tricyclic drugs share many pharmacokinetic and pharmacodynamic properties and possess similar adverse reaction profiles. Three tetracyclic drugs were initially introduced as being significantly different from the tricyclics; however, further study and clinical use have shown that the tetracyclic drugs and the tricyclic drugs can best be conceptualized as constituting one large family of drugs. They are sometimes referred to as the heterocyclic drugs, which potentially include monocyclic, dicyclic, tricyclic, and tetracyclic drugs. That term is not used in this textbook because it is an overinclusive classification of a diverse group of drugs with no single side-effect or therapeutic profile.

THERAPEUTIC INDICATIONS
Major Depressive Disorder

The treatment of a major depressive episode and the prophylactic treatment of major depressive disorder are the principal indications for using tricyclic and tetracyclic drugs. The drugs are also effective in the treatment of depression in bipolar I disorder patients. Melancholic features, prior major depressive episodes, and a family history of depressive disorders increase the likelihood of a therapeutic response. The treatment of a major depressive episode with psychotic features almost always requires the coadministration of an antipsychotic drug and an antidepressant.

Mood Disorder Due to a General Medical Condition with Depressive Features

Depression associated with a general medical condition (secondary depression) may respond to tricyclic and tetracyclic drug treatment. The depression may occur after cerebrovascular diseases and central nervous system (CNS) trauma. Depression can also be associated with dementias and movement disorders, such as Parkinson's disease. Depression associated with acquired immune deficiency syndrome (AIDS) may also respond to the drugs.

Panic Disorder with Agoraphobia

Imipramine is the tricyclic most studied for panic disorder with agoraphobia, but other tricyclic and tetracyclics are also effective. Early reports indicated that small dosages of imipramine (50 mg a day) were often effective; however, recent studies indicate that the usual antidepressant dosages are usually required.

Generalized Anxiety Disorder

The use of doxepin (Adapin, Sinequan) for the treatment of anxiety disorders is approved by the Food and Drug Administration (FDA). Some research data show that imipramine may also be useful, and some clinicians use a drug containing a combination of chlordiazepoxide and amitriptyline (marketed as Limbitrol) for mixed anxiety and depressive disorders.

Obsessive-Compulsive Disorder

In the fourth edition of *Diagnostic and Statistical Manual of Mental Disorders* (DSM-IV), obsessive-compulsive disorder is classified under the anxiety disorders. The disorder appears to respond specifically to clomipramine and the serotonin-specific reuptake inhibitors (SSRIs). None of the other tricyclic and tetracyclic drugs appears to be nearly as effective as clomipramine (Anafranil) for the disorder.

Eating Disorders

Both anorexia nervosa and bulimia nervosa have been successfully treated with imipramine and desipramine, although other tricyclics and tetracyclics may also be effective.

Pain Disorder

Chronic pain disorder, including headache (such as migraine), is often treated with tricyclics and tetracyclics.

Other Disorders

Childhood enuresis is often treated with imipramine (Tofranil). Peptic ulcer disease can be treated with doxepin, which has marked antihistaminergic effects. Other indications for tricyclics and tetracyclics are narcolepsy, nightmare disorder, and posttraumatic stress disorder. The drugs are sometimes used for children and adolescents with attention-deficit/hyperactivity disorder, sleepwalking disorder, separation anxiety disorder, and sleep terror disorder.

PRECAUTIONS AND ADVERSE REACTIONS

Psychiatric Effects

A major adverse effect of all tricyclic and tetracyclic drugs and other antidepressants is the possibility of inducing a manic episode in both bipolar I disorder patients and in patients without a history of bipolar I disorder. Clinicians should watch for that effect in bipolar I disorder patients, especially if substance-induced mania has been a problem in the past. It is prudent to use low dosages of tricyclic and tetracyclic drugs in such patients or to use an agent such as fluoxetine (Prozac) or bupropion (Wellbutrin), which may be less likely to induce a manic episode. Tricyclic and tetracyclic drugs have also been reported to exacerbate psychotic disorders in susceptible patients.

Anticholinergic Effects

Clinicians should warn patients that anticholinergic effects are common but that the patient may develop a tolerance for them with continued treatment. Amitriptyline (Endep, Elavil), imipramine, trimipramine (Surmontil), and doxepin are the most anticholinergic drugs; amoxapine (Asendin), nortriptyline (Pamelor), and maprotiline (Ludiomil) are less anticholinergic; and desipramine may be the least anticholinergic. Anticholinergic effects include dry mouth, constipation, blurred vision, and urinary retention. Sugarless gum, candy, or fluoride lozenges can alleviate the dry mouth. Bethanechol (Urecholine), 25 to 50 mg three or four times a day, may reduce urinary hesitancy and may be helpful in cases of impotence when the drug is taken 30 minutes before sexual intercourse. Narrow-angle glaucoma can also be aggravated by anticholinergic drugs, and the precipitation of glaucoma requires emergency treatment with a miotic agent. Tricyclic and tetracyclic drugs can be used in patients with glaucoma, provided pilocarpine eye drops are administered

concurrently. Severe anticholinergic effects can lead to a CNS anticholinergic syndrome with confusion and delirium, especially if tricyclic and tetracyclic drugs are administered with antipsychotics or anticholinergic drugs. Some clinicians have used IM or intravenous (IV) physostigmine (Antilirium) as a diagnostic tool to confirm the presence of anticholinergic delirium.

Sedation

Sedation is a common effect of tricyclic and tetracyclic drugs and may be welcomed if sleeplessness has been a problem. The sedative effect of tricyclic and tetracyclic drugs is a result of serotonergic, cholinergic, and histaminergic (H_1) activities. Amitriptyline, trimipramine, and doxepin are the most sedating agents; imipramine, amoxapine, nortriptyline, and maprotiline have some sedating effects; and desipramine (Norpramin, Pertofrane) and protriptyline (Vivactil) are the least sedating agents.

Autonomic Effects

The most common autonomic effect, partly because of α_1-adrenergic blockade, is orthostatic hypotension, which can result in falls and injuries in affected patients. Nortriptyline may be the drug least likely to cause the problem, and some patients respond to fludrocortisone (Florinef), 0.02 to 0.05 mg twice a day. Other possible autonomic effects are profuse sweating, palpitations, and increased blood pressure.

Cardiac Effects

When administered in their usual therapeutic dosages, the tricyclic and tetracyclic drugs may cause tachycardia, flattened T waves, prolonged QT intervals, and depressed ST segments in the electrocardiographic (ECG) recording. Imipramine has a quinidinelike effect at therapeutic plasma levels and may reduce the number of premature ventricular contractions. Because the drugs prolong conduction time, their use in patients with preexisting conduction defects is contraindicated. In patients with cardiac histories, tricyclic and tetracyclic drugs should be initiated at low dosages, with gradual increases in dosage and monitoring of cardiac functions. At high plasma levels, as seen in overdoses, the drugs become arrhythmogenic. The agents should be discontinued several days before elective surgery because of the occurrence of hypertensive episodes during surgery in patients receiving tricyclic and tetracyclic drugs.

Neurological Effects

In addition to the sedation induced by tricyclics and tetracyclics and the possibility of anticholinergic-induced delirium, two tricyclics—desipramine and protriptyline—are associated with psychomotor stimulation. Myoclonic twitches and tremors of the tongue and the upper extremities are common. Rare effects include speech blockage, paresthesia, peroneal palsies, and ataxia.

Amoxapine is unique in causing parkinsonian symptoms, akathisia, and even dyskinesia because of the dopaminergic blocking activity of one of its metabolites. Amoxapine may also cause neuroleptic malignant syndrome in rare cases. Maprotiline may cause seizures when the dosage is increased too quickly or is kept at high levels for too long. Clomipramine and amoxapine may lower the seizure threshold more than do other drugs in the class. As a class, however, the tricyclic and tetracyclic drugs have a relatively low risk for inducing seizures, except in patients who are at risk for seizures (for example, epileptic patients and patients with brain lesions). Although tricyclics and tetracyclics can still be used in such patients, the initial dosages should be lower than usual, and subsequent dosage increases should be gradual.

Allergic and Hematological Effects

Exanthematous skin rashes are seen in 4 to 5 percent of all patients treated with maprotiline. Jaundice is rare. Agranulocytosis, leukocytosis, leukopenia, and eosinophilia are rare complications of tetracyclic drug treatment. However, a patient who has a sore throat or a fever during the first few months of tricyclic and tetracyclic drug treatment should have a complete blood count (CBC) done immediately.

Other Adverse Effects

Weight gain, primarily an effect of the blockade of histamine type 2 (H_2) receptors, is common. If it is a major problem, changing to a different class of antidepressants may help. Impotence, an occasional problem, is perhaps most often associated with amoxapine because of the drug's blockade of dopamine receptors in the tuberoinfundibular tract. Amoxapine can also cause hyperprolactinemia, galactorrhea, anorgasmia, and ejaculatory disturbances. Other tricyclic and tetracyclic drugs have also been associated with gynecomastia and amenorrhea. Inappropriate secretion of antidiuretic hormone has also been reported with tricyclic and tetracyclic drugs. Other effects include nausea, vomiting, and hepatitis.

Precautions

The tricyclic and tetracyclic drugs should be avoided during pregnancy. The drugs pass into breast milk and have the potential to cause serious adverse reactions in nursing infants. The drugs should be used with caution in patients with hepatic and renal diseases.

Tricyclics and tetracyclics should not be administered during a course of electroconvulsive therapy (ECT), primarily because of the risk of serious adverse cardiac effects.

Overdoses

Overdoses with tricyclic and tetracyclic drugs are serious and can often be fatal. Prescriptions for the drugs should be nonrefillable and for no longer than a week at a time for patients who are at risk for suicide attempts. Amoxapine may be more likely than are other tricyclic and tetracyclic drugs to result in death when taken in an overdose, but all drugs in the class can be lethal in an overdose.

Symptoms of an overdose include agitation, delirium, convulsions, hyperactive deep tendon reflexes, bowel and bladder paralysis, dysregulation of the blood pressure and the temperature, and mydriasis. The patient then progresses to coma and perhaps respiratory depression. Cardiac arrhythmias may not respond to treatment. Because of the long half-lives of tricyclic and tetracyclic drugs, patients are at risk for cardiac arrhythmias

for three to four days after the overdose, so they should be monitored in an intensive care medical setting.

DRUG INTERACTIONS

Antihypertensives

Tricyclic and tetracyclic drugs block the neuronal reuptake of guanethidine (Esimil, Ismelin), which is required for antihypertensive activity. The antihypertensive effects of β-adrenergic receptor antagonists—for example, propranolol (Inderal)—and clonidine (Catapres) may also be blocked by tricyclic and tetracyclic drugs. The coadministration of a tricyclic or tetracyclic drug and α-methyldopa (Aldomet) may cause behavioral agitation.

Antipsychotics

The plasma levels of tricyclic and tetracyclic drugs and antipsychotics are increased by their coadministration. Antipsychotics also add to the anticholinergic and sedative effects of the tricyclic and tetracyclic drugs.

CNS Depressants

Opiates, opioids, alcohol, anxiolytics, hypnotics, and over-the-counter cold medications have additive effects by causing CNS depression when coadministered with tricyclic or tetracyclic drugs.

Sympathomimetics

Tricyclic drug use with sympathomimetic drugs may cause serious cardiovascular effects.

Oral Contraceptives

Birth control pills may decrease tricyclic and tetracyclic drug plasma levels through the induction of hepatic enzymes.

Other Interactions

Tricyclic and tetracyclic drug plasma levels may also be increased by acetazolamide (Diamox), acetylsalicylic acid, cimetidine (Tagamet), thiazide diuretics, fluoxetine, and sodium bicarbonate. Decreased plasma levels may be caused by ascorbic acid, ammonium chloride, barbiturates, cigarette smoking, chloral hydrate (Nortec), lithium (Eskalith), and primidone (Mysoline). Tricyclic drugs that are metabolized by CYP2D6 may interfere with the metabolism of other drugs metabolized by the hepatic enzyme.

DOSAGE AND ADMINISTRATION

Choice of Drug

The choice of which tricyclic or tetracyclic to use should be based on the general guidelines outlined in Subsection 27.1. All available tricyclic and tetracyclic drugs are equally effective in the treatment of depressive disorders. In the case of an individual patient, however, one tricyclic or tetracyclic may be effective, whereas another one may be ineffective. The adverse effects among the tricyclic and tetracyclic drugs differ. The tertiary amine tricyclics tend to produce more adverse effects—including sedation, orthostatic hypotension, and such anticholinergic effects as dry mouth—than do the secondary amines. Among the secondary amine tricyclics, nortriptyline is associated with the least orthostatic hypotension, and desipramine is associated with the least anticholinergic activity. Among the tetracyclic drugs, amoxapine is sometimes recommended for the treatment of a major depressive episode with psychotic features because of the drug's antidopaminergic activity.

Researchers have found differences among the tricyclics and the tetracyclics in their relative abilities to block either serotonin reuptake or norepinephrine reuptake. No study has found that the serotonin-to-norepinephrine ratio for each of the drugs can be used to help choose a specific drug to treat a particular patient. Switching from a strongly serotonergic drug to a strongly noradrenergic drug or vice versa may be reasonable if the first drug is ineffective in relieving the patient's symptoms.

Initiation of Treatment

A routine physical and laboratory examination of a patient to be administered a tricyclic or a tetracyclic should be conducted. The routine laboratory tests should include a CBC, a white blood cell (WBC) count with differential, and serum electrolytes (sequential multichannel autoanalyzer [SMA]-6) with liver function tests (SMA-12). An electrocardiogram (ECG) should probably be obtained for all patients, especially women over 40 and men over 30. The initial dose should be small and should be raised gradually. The clinician can raise the dosage for inpatients more quickly than for outpatients because of the inpatients' close clinical supervision.

The clinician should explain to patients that, although sleep and appetite may improve in one to two weeks, tricyclics and tetracyclics usually take three to four weeks to have significant

antidepressant effects, and a complete trial should last six weeks. The clinician may also explain to patients exactly what the drug treatment plan is if no clinical response is seen after six weeks.

The elderly and children are more sensitive to adverse effects of antidepressants than are young adults. In children, ECG monitoring is needed. A baseline electroencephalogram (EEG) is recommended, as children are sensitive to the epileptogenic effects of antidepressants and are prone to medication-induced constipation.

Dosage

The available preparations of tricyclic and tetracyclic drugs are presented in Table 27.3.27–1.

DEPRESSIVE DISORDERS

The dosage schedule for the tricyclics and tetracyclics varies among the drugs (Table 27.3.27–2). Imipramine, amitriptyline, doxepin, desipramine, clomipramine, and trimipramine can be started at 75 mg a day. Divided doses at first reduce the severity of the side effects, although most of the dosage should be given at night to help induce sleep if a sedating drug, such as amitriptyline, is used. Eventually, the entire daily dose can be given at bedtime. Protriptyline and less-sedating drugs should be given at least two to three hours before a patient goes to sleep. For outpatients the dosage can be raised to 150 mg a day the second week, 225 mg a day the third week, and 300 mg a day the fourth week. A common clinical mistake is to stop increasing the dosage when the patient is taking less than 250 mg a day and does not show clinical improvement. Doing so can result in a further delay in obtaining a therapeutic response, disenchantment with the treatment, and premature discontinuation of

Table 27.3.27–1.　Tricyclic and Tetracyclic Drug Preparations

Drug	Tablets	Capsules	Parenteral	Solution
Imipramine	10, 25, 50 mg	75, 100, 125, 150 mg	12.5 mg/mL	—
Desipramine	10, 25, 50, 75, 100, 150 mg	25, 50 mg	—	—
Trimipramine	—	25, 50, 100 mg	—	—
Amitriptyline	10, 25, 50, 75, 100, 150 mg	—	10 mg/mL	—
Nortriptyline	—	10, 25, 50, 75 mg	—	10 mg/5 mL
Protriptyline	5, 10 mg	—	—	—
Amoxapine	25, 50, 100, 150 mg	—	—	—
Doxepin	—	10, 25, 50, 75, 100, 150 mg	—	10 mg/mL
Maprotiline	25, 50, 75 mg	—	—	—
Clomipramine	—	25, 50, 75 mg	—	—

Table 27.3.27–2.　Clinical Information for the Tricyclic and Tetracyclic Drugs

Generic Name	Trade Name	Usual Adult Dosage Range (mg a day)	Therapeutic Plasma Levels* (ng per mL)
Imipramine	Tofranil	150–300†	150–300
Desipramine	Norpramin, Pertofrane	150–300†	150–300
Trimipramine	Surmontil	150–300†	?
Amitriptyine	Elavil, Endep	150–300†	100–250†
Nortriptyline	Pamelor, Aventyl	50–150	50–150 (maximum)
Protriptyline	Vivactil	15–60	75–250
Amoxapine	Asendin	150–400	?
Doxepin	Adapin, Sinequan	150–300†	100–250
Maprotiline	Ludiomil	150–225	150–300
Clomipramine	Anafranil	150–250	?

* Exact range may vary among laboratories.
† Includes parent compound and desmethyl metabolite.

the drug. The clinician should routinely assess the patient's pulse and orthostatic changes in blood pressure while the dosage is being increased.

Nortriptyline should be started at 50 mg a day and raised to 150 mg a day over three or four weeks unless a response occurs at a lower dosage, such as 100 mg a day. Amoxapine should be started at 150 mg a day and raised to 400 mg a day. Protriptyline should be started at 15 mg a day and raised to 60 mg a day. Maprotiline has been associated with an increased incidence of seizures if the dosage is raised too quickly or is maintained at too high a level. Maprotiline should be started at 75 mg a day and maintained at that level for two weeks. The dosage can be increased over four weeks to 225 mg a day but should be kept at that level for only six weeks and then reduced to 175 to 200 mg a day.

PAIN

Pain disorder patients or patients with chronic pain may be particularly sensitive to adverse effects when tricyclics or tetracyclics are started. Therefore, it may be prudent to begin with low dosages that are raised in small increments. Some clinicians coadminister benzodiazepines until the patients are stabilized on an antidepressant.

CHILDREN

In children, imipramine can be initiated at 1.5 mg per kg a day. The dosage can be titrated to no more than 5 mg per kg a day. In enuresis the dosage is usually 50 to 100 mg a day taken at bedtime. Clomipramine can be initiated at 50 mg a day and increased to no more than 3 mg per kg a day or 200 mg a day.

Failure of Drug Trial and Treatment-Resistant Depression

If a tricyclic or a tetracyclic has been used for four weeks at maximal dosages without a therapeutic effect, the clinician should obtain a plasma level and adjust the dosage accordingly. If plasma levels are adequate, supplementation with lithium or L-triiodothyronine (Cytomel) should be considered.

LITHIUM

Lithium (900 to 1,200 mg a day, serum level between 0.6 and 0.8 mEq per L) can be added to the tricyclic or tetracyclic dosage for 7 to 14 days. That approach converts a significant number of nonresponders into responders. The mechanism of action is not known, but the lithium may potentiate the serotonergic neuronal system.

L-TRIIODOTHYRONINE

The addition of 25 to 50 μg a day of L-triiodothyronine to the regimen for 7 to 14 days may convert a tricyclic or tetracyclic nonresponder into a responder. The mechanism of action for L-triiodothyronine augmentation is not known. Empirical data indicate that L-triiodothyronine is more effective than L-thyroxine (Levoxyl) as an adjunct to tricyclic and tetracyclic drugs. If L-triiodothyronine augmentation is successful, the L-triiodothyronine should be continued for two months and then tapered at the rate of 12.5 μg a day every three to seven days.

MAOIs

MAOIs should be discontinued for two weeks before initiating treatment with a tricyclic or a tetracyclic. A minimum of a one-week washout is needed when switching from a tricyclic or tetracyclic to an MAOI. The two classes of drugs are sometimes used in combination for resistant depressions. Certain precautions must be taken to avoid hypertensive crises. Desipramine, imipramine, clomipramine, and tranylcypromine (Parnate) should be avoided in combination with MAOIs. A low dosage of a tricyclic should be initiated after at least a one-week washout of the tricyclics. The MAOI is then added, also in a low dosage. Every few days, each of the medications is alternately increased in dosage while the patient is monitored.

Termination of Short-Term Treatment

Tricyclics and tetracyclics effectively resolve the acute symptoms of depression. If treatment is stopped prematurely, symptom reemergence is likely. To minimize the risk for recurrence or relapse, the clinician should continue the tricyclic or the tetracyclic at the same treatment dosage throughout the course of treatment. When treatment is discontinued, the clinician may reasonably reduce the dosage to three fourths the maximal dosage for another month. At that time, if no symptoms are present, the drug can be tapered by 25 mg (5 mg for protriptyline) every two to three days. The slow tapering process is indicated for most psychotherapeutic drugs; in the case of most tricyclics and tetracyclics, slow tapering avoids a cholinergic rebound syndrome, consisting of nausea, upset stomach, sweating, headache, neck pain, and vomiting. That syndrome can be treated by reinstituting a small dosage of the drug and tapering more slowly than before. Several case reports note the appearance of rebound mania or hypomania after the abrupt discontinuation of tricyclic and tetracyclic drugs. If a patient has been treated with lithium augmentation, the clinician should probably taper and stop the lithium first and then the tricyclic or tetracyclic drug. However, clinical studies supporting that approach are lacking, and the guidelines may change as more physicians report their experience with the drug combination.

Maintenance

Tricyclics and tetracyclics are effective in preventing the recurrence of major depressive episodes. The decision to institute prophylactic treatment is based on the severity and the nature of the disorder in a particular patient. However, increasing data argue for prophylactic treatment in patients with major depressive disorder. Conversely, some data indicate that the long-term use of antidepressants may induce a rapid-cycling bipolar I disorder. Lithium prophylaxis, therefore, has been suggested as an alternative treatment in selected patients who have frequent, episodic, and serious depressive episodes.

Several investigators have noted that neuroendocrine tests may be a guide for deciding when to maintain the use of tricyclics, tetracyclics, and other antidepressant drugs. Specifically, the investigators note that the normalization of a previously abnormal result in a dexamethasone-suppression test or a thyrotropin-releasing hormone (TRH) stimulation test may indicate that a patient can safely discontinue drug treatment. That use of neuroendocrine testing and monitoring is still in the research phases of development.

Plasma Levels

Research has defined the dose-response curves for a number of the tricyclic and tetracyclic drugs when given to treat depressive disorders. Clinical determinations of plasma levels should be conducted 8 to 12 hours after the last dose and after five to seven days on the same dosage of medication. Because of variations in absorption and metabolism, there is a 30- to 50-fold difference in the plasma concentrations in humans given the same dosage of a tricyclic or tetracyclic drug. The therapeutic ranges for plasma levels have been determined (Table 27.3.27–2). Nortriptyline is unique in its association with a therapeutic window; that is, plasma concentrations of more than 150 ng per mL may reduce its efficacy. Clinicians must follow the directions for collection from the testing laboratory and have confidence in the assay procedure used at a particular laboratory.

The use of plasma levels in clinical practice is still an evolving skill. Plasma levels may be useful in confirming compliance, assessing reasons for drug failures, and documenting effective plasma levels for future treatment. Clinicians should always treat the patient and never the plasma level. Some patients have adequate clinical responses with seemingly subtherapeutic plasma levels, and other patients have responses only at supratherapeutic plasma levels without experiencing adverse effects. The latter situation, however, should alert the clinician to monitor the patient's condition with, for example, serial ECG recordings.

References

Casper R C, Katz M M, Bowden C L, Davis J M, et al: The pattern of physical symptom changes in major depressive disorder following treatment with amitriptyline or imipramine. J Affect Dis *31*: 151, 1994.

Friedman R A, Parides M, Baff R, Moran M, Kocsis J H: Predictors of response to desipramine in dysthymia. J Clin Psychopharmacol *15*: 280, 1995.

Kessel J B, Simpson G M: Tricyclic and tetracyclic drugs. In *Comprehensive Textbook of Psychiatry*, ed 6, H I Kaplan, B J Sadock, editors, p 2096. Williams & Wilkins, Baltimore, 1995.

Leitenberg H, Rosen J C, Wolf J, Vara L S, et al: Comparison of cognitive-behavior therapy and desipramine in the treatment of bulimia nervosa. Behav Res Ther *32*: 37, 1994.

Pollack M G, Otto M W, Sachs G S, Leon A, Shear M K, Deltito J A, Keller M B, Rosenbaum J F: Anxiety psychopathology predictive of outcome in patients with panic disorder and depression treated with imipramine, alprazolam and placebo. J Affect Disord *30*: 273, 1994.

Wilens T E, Biederman J, Mick E Spencer T J: A systematic assessment of tricyclic antidepressants in the treatment of adult attention-deficit hyperactivity disorder. J Nerv Ment Dis *183*: 48, 1995.

27.3.28 L-TRYPTOPHAN

L-Tryptophan is the amino acid precursor of the neurotransmitter serotonin. L-Tryptophan administration to humans results in increased concentrations of serotonin in the central nervous system. That pharmacological effect led to the use of orally administered L-tryptophan as a hypnotic and as an adjuvant to antidepressant treatment.

In 1989 L-tryptophan and L-tryptophan-containing products were recalled in the United States because of an outbreak of eosinophilia-myalgia syndrome associated with those products. However, those drugs will probably be reintroduced in the United States.

THERAPEUTIC INDICATIONS

Primary Insomnia

The most common indication for L-tryptophan is insomnia, although that indication does not have the approval of the Food and Drug Administration (FDA). Whether the hypnotic effects

of L-tryptophan persist with long-term treatment is not certain. L-Tryptophan is not associated with visuospatial, cognitive, or memory deficits the day after drug ingestion, as are many of the standard hypnotic agents. Low doses of L-tryptophan are not associated with any change in the sleep electroencephalogram (EEG) other than earlier than usual sleep onset; high doses of L-tryptophan are associated with increases in slowwave sleep.

Antidepressant Adjuvant Treatment

L-Tryptophan has been used as an adjuvant to tricyclic and tetracyclic drug administration for depressed patients who have not responded to the tricyclic or tetracyclic drug alone. The use of either lithium (Eskalith) or L-triiodothyronine (Cytomel) adjuvant therapy with antidepressant nonresponders was more common than was L-tryptophan supplementation when L-tryptophan was still available. L-tryptophan has also been used as an adjuvant to lithium treatment for bipolar I disorder patients who had incomplete symptom remission with lithium treatment alone.

PRECAUTIONS AND ADVERSE REACTIONS

Except for experiencing eosinophilia-myalgia syndrome, most patients tolerate moderate doses of L-tryptophan. The only significant adverse effect reported is nausea, which is sometimes compared to the nausea associated with pregnancy. L-Tryptophan has also been associated with hepatotoxicity in rare cases.

Eosinophilia-Myalgia Syndrome

The symptoms of eosinophilia-myalgia syndrome include fatigue, myalgia, shortness of breath, rashes, and swelling of the extremities. Congestive heart failure and death can occur. The syndrome was related to a contaminant in a single manufacturing plant. Remaining concerns about protecting against the contaminant have slowed the reintroduction of L-tryptophan in the United States market.

DRUG INTERACTIONS

L-Tryptophan should not be coadministered with serotonin-specific reuptake inhibitors (SSRIs)—for example, fluoxetine (Prozac) and clomipramine (Anafranil)—or monoamine oxidase inhibitors. Those combinations can result in a syndrome related to serotonin excess and characterized by diarrhea, insomnia, nausea, headaches, chills, agitation, and poor concentration.

DOSAGE AND ADMINISTRATION

L-Tryptophan is currently not available in the United States. When it was used as a hypnotic, the dosage ranged from 1 to 15 grams taken at bedtime. The use of L-tryptophan as an adjuvant to antidepressant treatment was often in the range of 5 to 10 mg a day in divided doses.

References

D'Arcy P F: L-tryptophan: eosinophilia-myalgia syndrome. Adverse Drug React Toxicol Rev *14*: 37, 1995.

Delgado P L, Price L H, Miller H L, Salomon R M, Aghajanian G K, Heninger G R, Charney D S: Serotonin and the neurobiology of depression. Effects of tryptophan depletion in drug-free depressed patients. Arch Gen Psychiatry *51*: 865, 1994.

Kaplan H I, Sadock B J: Other pharmacological therapies. In *Comprehensive*

Textbook of Psychiatry, ed 6, H I Kaplan, B J Sadock, editors, p 2122. Williams & Wilkins, Baltimore, 1995.

Karege F, Widmer J, Bovier P, Gaillard J M: Platelet serotonin and plasma tryptophan in depressed patients: Effect of drug treatment and clinical outcome. Neuropsychopharmacology *10*: 207, 1994.

Menkes D B, Coates D C, Fawcett J P: Acute tryptophan depletion aggravates premenstrual syndrome. J Affect Dis *32*: 37, 1994.

Taracha E, Szukalski B: Serum tryptophan levels in patients with endogenous depression: I. Differences between unipolar and bipolar forms of affective disorder. New Trends Exp Clin Psychiatry *10*: 9, 1994.

27.3.29 VALPROATE

Valproate (Depakene), also called valproic acid (because it is rapidly converted to the acid form in the stomach), was first recognized as an effective antiepileptic drug in 1963 in France. Valproic acid (Depakene) was approved for use in certain types of epilepsy in the United States in 1978. Since that time, valproate has been shown to be effective in a range of epileptic conditions. In addition, valproate and two other anticonvulsant drugs, carbamazepine (Tegretol) and clonazepam (Klonopin), have been shown to be effective in the treatment of bipolar I disorder. Divalproex (Depakote)—a compound comprised of sodium valproate and valproic acid—was approved by the Food and Drug Administration (FDA) as a safe and effective treatment for bipolar I disorder. Many clinicians consider valproate at least equal in efficacy and better tolerated than lithium (Eskalith) in the treatment of bipolar I disorder; many clinicians consider valproate at least equal in efficacy and safety to carbamazepine as a second-line drug.

THERAPEUTIC INDICATIONS

Bipolar I Disorder

About a half-dozen well-controlled but small studies have shown that valproate is effective in the treatment of manic episodes. Data from uncontrolled studies support the hypothesis that valproate is effective in the prophylactic treatment of bipolar I disorder. Specifically, the patients who were treated with valproate had fewer, less severe, and shorter manic episodes while taking valproate than when they were not taking the drug prophylactically. Some of the available data from both uncontrolled and controlled studies have reported that valproate may be particularly effective in patients with rapid-cycling bipolar I disorder, dysphoric or mixed mania, and mania due to a general medical condition and in patients who have not had complete favorable responses to lithium treatment. Additional data from case reports indicate that valproate can be used effectively in combination with lithium or carbamazepine in patients who do not respond sufficiently to a treatment regimen with a single drug. The data are less supportive of the use of valproate alone for the short-term treatment of depressive episodes in bipolar I disorder, although the data from open-label studies support the conclusion that valproate is effective in the prophylactic treatment of depressive episodes in bipolar I disorder patients.

Schizoaffective Disorder

Although no controlled studies of valproate in schizoaffective disorder have been conducted, data from uncontrolled studies and case reports support the conclusion that valproate is effective in treating the short-term phase of the bipolar type of schizoaffective disorder. However, some data indicate that valproate is less effective in schizoaffective disorder than in bipolar I disorder.

Other Mental Disorders

Preliminary reports note the therapeutic efficacy of valproate in other mental disorders, including major depressive disorder; panic disorder; posttraumatic stress disorder; bulimia nervosa; alcohol and sedative, hypnotic, or anxiolytic withdrawal; and intermittent explosive disorder. Although the data for those indications are limited, the use of valproate for patients who have not responded to other treatments may be indicated, although it should be used only after a thorough review of the most recent literature. The available data have led many researchers to conclude that valproate is not effective in the treatment of schizophrenia.

PRECAUTIONS AND ADVERSE REACTIONS

Valproate treatment is generally well-tolerated and safe, although a range of common mild adverse effects and serious and rare adverse effects have been associated with valproate treatment. The common adverse effects associated with valproate are those affecting the gastrointestinal system, such as nausea (25 percent of all patients treated), vomiting (5 percent of patients), and diarrhea. The gastrointestinal effects are generally most common in the first month of treatment but are also common when the treatment is with valproic acid or sodium valproate, rather than enteric-coated divalproex sodium, especially the sprinkle formulation. Some clinicians have also treated gastrointestinal symptoms with histamine type 2 (H_2) receptor antagonists, such as cimetidine (Tagamet). Other common adverse effects involve the nervous system, such as sedation, ataxia, dysarthria, and tremor. Valproate-induced tremor has been reported to respond well to treatment with β-adrenergic receptor antagonists. Treatment of the other neurological adverse effects usually requires lowering of the valproate dosage. Weight gain is a common adverse effect, especially in long-term treatment, and can best be treated by recommending a combination of a reasonable diet and moderate exercise. Hair loss has been reported to occur in 5 to 10 percent of all patients treated; rare cases of complete loss of body hair have been reported. Some clinicians have recommended treatment of valproate-associated hair loss with vitamin supplements that contain zinc and selenium. Another adverse effect that may occur in 5 to 40 percent of patients is a persistent elevation in liver transaminases, which is usually asymptomatic and resolves after discontinuation of the drug. Other rare adverse events include effects on the hematopoietic system, including thrombocytopenia and platelet dysfunction, occurring most commonly at high dosages and resulting in the prolongation of bleeding times. Overdoses of valproate can lead to coma and death. There are reports that valproate-induced coma can be successfully treated with naloxone (Narcan) and reports that hemodialysis and hemoperfusion can be useful in the treatment of valproate overdoses.

The two most serious adverse effects of valproate treatment involve the pancreas and the liver. Rare cases of pancreatitis have been reported; they occur most often in the first six months of treatment, and the condition occasionally results in death. The most attention has been paid to an association between

Tale 27.3.29–1.   Valproate Preparations Available in the United States

Generic Name	Trade Name, Form (doses)	Time to Peak Serum Concentration
Valproic acid	Depakene capsules (250 mg)	1–2 hrs
Sodium valproate	Depakene syrup (250 mg/5 mL)	1–2 hrs
Divalproex sodium	Depakote tablets (125, 250, 500 mg)	4–8 hrs
Divalproex sodium coated particles in capsules	Depakote sprinkle capsules (125 mg)	Compared with divalproex tablets, divalproex sprinkle has earlier onset and slower rate of absorption, with slightly lower peak plasma concentrations

valproate and fatal hepatotoxicity. A result of that focus has been the identification of risk factors, including young age (less than 2 years), the use of multiple anticonvulsants, and the presence of neurological disorders in addition to epilepsy. The rate of fatal hepatotoxicity in patients who have been treated with only valproate is 0.85 per 100,000 patients; no patients over the age of 10 years are reported to have died from fatal hepatotoxicity. Therefore, the risk of that adverse reaction in adult psychiatric patients seems to be extremely low. Nevertheless, if symptoms of malaise, anorexia, nausea and vomiting, edema, and abdominal pain occur in a patient treated with valproate, the clinician must consider the possibility of severe hepatotoxicity. However, a modest increase in liver function test results does not correlate with the development of serious hepatotoxicity.

Valproate should not be used by pregnant or nursing women. The drug has been associated with neural tube defects (for example, spinal bifida) in about 1 to 2 percent of all women who took valproate during the first trimester of the pregnancy. Valproate is contraindicated in nursing mothers because it is excreted in breast milk. Clinicians should not administer the drug to patients with hepatic diseases.

DRUG INTERACTIONS

Valproate is commonly coadministered with lithium and the antipsychotics. The only consistent drug interaction with lithium is the exacerbation of drug-induced tremors, which can be usually treated with β-adrenergic receptor antagonists. The combination of valproate and antipsychotics may result in increased sedation, as can be seen when valproate is added to any CNS depressant (for example, alcohol), and increased severity of extrapyramidal symptoms, which usually respond to treatment with the usual antiparkinsonian drugs. The plasma concentrations of diazepam (Valium) and phenobarbital (Luminal) may be increased when those drugs are coadministered with valproate, and the plasma concentrations of phenytoin (Dilantin) may be decreased when phenytoin is combined with valproate. The plasma concentrations of valproate may be decreased when the drug is coadministered with carbamazepine and may be increased when coadministered with amitriptyline (Elavil) or fluoxetine (Prozac). Patients who are treated with anticoagulants—for example, aspirin and warfarin (Coumadin)—should also be monitored when valproate is initiated to assess the development of any undesired augmentation of the anticoagulation effects.

LABORATORY INTERFERENCES

Valproate has been reported to cause an overestimation of serum free fatty acids in almost half of the patients tested. Val-

proate has also been reported to elevate urinary ketone estimations falsely and to result in falsely abnormal thyroid function test results.

DOSAGE AND ADMINISTRATION

Valproate is available in a number of formulations and dosages (Table 27.3.29–1). It is best to initiate drug treatment gradually, so as to minimize the common adverse effects of nausea, vomiting, and sedation. The dose on the first day should be 250 mg administered with a meal. The dosage can be raised up to 250 mg orally three times daily over the course of three to six days. Plasma levels can be assessed in the morning before the first daily dose of the drug is administered. Therapeutic plasma levels for the control of seizures range between 50 to 100 mg per mL, although some physicians use 125 or even 150 mg per mL if the drug is well-tolerated. It is reasonable to use the same range for the treatment of mental disorders; most of the controlled studies have used 50 to 100 mg per mL. Most patients attain therapeutic plasma levels on a dosage between 1,200 and 1,500 mg a day in divided doses.

References

Bowden C L, McElroy S L: History of the development of valproate for treatment of bipolar disorder. J Clin Psychiatry. 56 (suppl 3): 3, 1995.
Pope G H Jr, McElroy S L: Valproate. In Comprehensive Textbook of Psychiatry, ed 6, H I Kaplan, B J Sadock, editors, p 2112. Williams & Wilkins, Baltimore, 1995.
Sival R C, Haffmans P M J, van Gent P P, van Neiuwkerk J F, et al: The effects of sodium valproate on disturbed behavior in dementia. J Am Geriatr Soc 42: 906, 1994.
Wilcox J: Divalproex sodium in the treatment of aggressive behavior. Ann Clin Psychiatry 6: 17, 1994.
Woodman C L, Noyes R: Panic disorder: Treatment with valproate. J Clin Psychiatry 55: 134, 1994.
Yassa R, Cvejic J: Valproate in the treatment of posttraumatic bipolar disorder in a psychogeriatric patient. J Geriatr Psychiatry Neurol 7: 55, 1994.

27.3.30 VENLAFAXINE

Venlafaxine (Effexor) is an effective antidepressant drug that is chemically distinct from other antidepressants, possesses a slightly different mechanism of action, and may have unique efficacy properties. Those efficacy properties may include a faster than usual onset of action and demonstrated efficacy in seriously depressed patients (for example, patients with melancholic features), although the data in support of those properties are limited at this time.

THERAPEUTIC INDICATIONS

The available data support the use of venlafaxine in the treatment of depressive disorders (for example, major depressive disorder). A number of well-controlled studies with a sufficient number of patients have shown the efficacy of venlafaxine for that indication. Some of the data from those studies have indicated that venlafaxine may be associated with a faster onset of action of antidepressant effects than are currently available antidepressants. However, the methods for demonstrating a faster onset of effect have not been carefully worked out, and subsequent studies may not support the initial findings. Another study with venlafaxine included 93 depressed inpatients with melancholic features. Those patients also responded to venlafaxine in a relatively short time period, indicating that venlafaxine may become a preferred drug for seriously ill patients. Again, the data require replication before they can be considered to be well-proved.

PRECAUTIONS AND ADVERSE REACTIONS

In the published clinical reports, venlafaxine has generally been reported to be well-tolerated. However, caution is warranted with the use of all newly introduced drugs until enough patients have been treated with the drug under usual clinical conditions. The following were the most common adverse reactions reported in the placebo-controlled studies: nausea (37 percent of all patients treated), somnolence (23 percent), dry mouth (22 percent), dizziness (19 percent), nervousness (13 percent), constipation (15 percent), asthenia (12 percent), anxiety (6 percent), anorexia (11 percent), blurred vision (6 percent), abnormal ejaculation or orgasm (12 percent), and impotence (6 percent). Nausea, somnolence, and insomnia were the three most common adverse reactions associated with patient discontinuation of venlafaxine.

The most potentially worrisome adverse effect associated with venlafaxine is an increase in blood pressure in some patients, particularly in patients who are treated with more than 300 mg a day. In clinical trials a mean increase of 1.2 mm Hg was observed in diastolic blood pressure in patients who were receiving venlafaxine, in contrast to a mean increase of 1.3 mm Hg in patients who were receiving imipramine (Tofranil) and a mean decrease of 1.6 mm Hg in patients who were receiving a placebo. In one study, sustained elevations of blood pressure higher than 140/90 were experienced by 1 percent of the patients who received a placebo, by no patients who received 75 mg a day of venlafaxine, by 1 percent of the patients who received 225 mg a day of venlafaxine, and by 3 percent of the patients who received 375 mg a day of venlafaxine. That adverse effect may lead the Food and Drug Administration to suggest that the drug be used cautiously in patients with preexisting hypertension. The clinical significance of the side effect may be less worrisome if low dosages of venlafaxine are found to be as efficacious as high dosages.

Information concerning use of venlafaxine by pregnant and nursing women is not available at this time. However, clinicians should avoid the use of all newly introduced drugs by pregnant and nursing women until more clinical experience has been gained.

DRUG INTERACTIONS

Venlafaxine should not be used in combination with a monoamine oxidase inhibitor (MAOI) or within 2 weeks of discontinuing treatment with an MAOI. Based on the half-life of venlafaxine, at least seven days should be allowed after stopping venlafaxine before starting an MAOI.

DOSAGE AND ADMINISTRATION

Venlafaxine is available in 37.5, 50, 75, and 100 mg tablets. The usual starting dose in depressed outpatients is 75 mg a day, given in two to three divided doses. In that patient population the dose can be raised to 150 mg a day, given in two or three divided doses after an appropriate period of clinical assessment at the lower dose (usually two to three weeks). The dose can be raised in 75 mg a day increments. Doses of venlafaxine that are over 300 mg a day should be given in three divided doses. The maximum dose of venlafaxine is 375 mg a day. The dose of venlafaxine should be halved in patients with significantly diminished renal function. In those patients the drug can be administered in one daily dosing. The clinician should be guided by the reports yet to be published and by the manufacturer's product insert.

References

Entsuah A R, Bradley M M, Littman G S: Cumulative mean change procedure: Application to a comparative trail of venlafaxine, imipramine, and placebo in the treatment of major depression. Prog Neuropsychopharmacol Biol Psychiatry 18: 695, 1994.
Feighner J P: The role of venlafaxine in rational antidepressant therapy. J Clin Psychiatry 55 (Suppl A): 62, 1994.
Grebb J A: Venlafaxine. In Comprehensive Textbook of Psychiatry, ed 6, H I Kaplan, B J Sadock, editors, p 2120. Williams & Wilkins, Baltimore, 1995.
Mendels, J, Johnston R, Mattes J A, Riesenberg R: Efficacy and safety of b.i.d. doses of venlafaxine in a dose-response study. Psychopharmacol Bull 29: 169, 1993.
Schweizer E, Feighner J, Mandos L A, Rickels K: Comparison of venlafaxine and imipramine in the acute treatment of major depression in outpatients. J Clin Psychiatry 55: 104, 1994.
Shrivastava R K, Cohn C, Crowder J, Davidson J, et al: Long-term safety and clinical acceptability of venlafaxine and imipramine in outpatients with major depression. J Clin Psychopharmacol 14: 322, 1994.

27.3.31 YOHIMBINE

Yohimbine (Yocon) is a β_2-adrenergic receptor antagonist that has been used as a treatment for both idiopathic and substance-induced sexual dysfunction in men. The efficacy of the drug for that indication remains controversial.

THERAPEUTIC INDICATIONS

In psychiatry, yohimbine has been used experimentally as a possible treatment for organic, psychogenic, and substance-induced erectile disorder and other male sexual dysfunctions. Its effects on male sexual performance are possibly related to its peripheral autonomic nervous system effects, although it is not possible to rule out central nervous system effects completely. Urologists have also used yohimbine for the diagnostic classification of certain types of male impotence.

PRECAUTIONS AND ADVERSE REACTIONS

The adverse effects of yohimbine include elevated blood pressure and heart rate, increased psychomotor activity, irritability, tremor, headache, skin flushing, dizziness, urinary frequency, nausea, vomiting, and sweating. Patients with panic disorder show heightened sensitivity to yohimbine, experiencing increased anxiety, a rise in blood pressure, and increased plasma 3-methoxy-4-hydroxy-phenylglycol (MHPG), the major metabolite of norepinephrine. Yohimbine should not be used by female patients or by patients with renal disease, cardiac disease, glaucoma, or a history of gastric or duodenal ulcers.

DRUG INTERACTIONS

Yohimbine should not be used with clonidine (Catapres), an α_2-adrenergic receptor agonist, because the two drugs have mutually canceling pharmacodynamic effects.

DOSAGE AND ADMINISTRATION

The dosage of yohimbine in the treatment of impotence is about 18 mg a day. The dosage range is 4 to 7.5 mg three times a day. In the event of significant adverse effects, the dosage should first be reduced and then gradually increased. Yohimbine is available in 5.4 mg tablets.

References

Clark J, Smieth E R, Davidson J M: Enhancement of sexual motivation in male rats with yohimbine. Science 225: 847, 1984.

Hollander E, McCarley A: Yohimbine treatment of sexual side effects induced by serotonin reuptake blockers. J Clin Psychiatry 53: 207, 1992.

Kaplan H I, Sadock B J: Other pharmacological therapies. In *Comprehensive Textbook of Psychiatry*, ed 6, H I Kaplan, B J Sadock, editors, p 2122. Williams & Wilkins, Baltimore, 1995.

Kenney W L, Zappe D H, Tankersley C G, Derr J A: Effect of systemic yohimbine on the control of skin blood flow during local heating and dynamic exercise. Am J Physiol 266: H371, 1994.

Montorsi F, Strambi L F, Guazzoni G, Galli L, Barbieri L, Rigatti P, Pizzine G, Miani A: Effect of yohimbine-trazodone on psychogenic impotence: A randomized, double-blind, placebo-controlled study. Urology 44: 732, 1994.

Price J, Grunhaus L J: Treatment of clomipramine-induced anorgasmia with yohimbine: A case report. J Clin Psychiatry 51: 32, 1990.

Reid K, Morales A, Harris C: Double-blind trial of yohimbine in treatment of psychogenic impotence. Lancet 2: 421, 1987.

27.4 ELECTROCONVULSIVE THERAPY

Electroconvulsive therapy (ECT) is a safe and effective treatment of patients with major depressive disorder, manic episodes, and other serious mental disorders. Many clinicians and researchers believe that ECT is grossly underused as a treatment. The major reason for the underuse is hypothesized to be misconceptions and biases about ECT, at least partly fueled by widespread misinformation and inflammatory articles in the lay press. Because ECT requires the use of electricity and the production of a seizure, many laypersons, patients, and patient's families are understandably frightened by ECT. Many inaccurate reports have appeared in both professional and lay literature about alleged permanent brain damage resulting from ECT. Although those reports have been largely disproved, the specter of ECT-induced brain damage remains.

The decision to suggest ECT to a patient, like all treatment recommendations, should be based on both the treatment options available to the patient and the risk-benefit considerations. The major alternatives to ECT are usually pharmacotherapy and psychotherapy; both have their own risks and benefits. ECT has been shown to be a safe and effective treatment; clinicians should not allow their biases to deprive patients of this effective treatment.

INDICATIONS

Patients with bipolar I disorder account for about 70 percent of the patients who receive ECT; patients with schizophrenia

account for about 17 percent. The three clearest indications for ECT are major depressive disorder, manic episodes, and, in some instances, schizophrenia.

Major Depressive Disorder

The primary indication for ECT is major depressive disorder. ECT should be considered as a treatment for patients who have failed medication trials, have not tolerated medications, have severe or psychotic symptoms, are acutely suicidal or homicidal, or have marked symptoms of agitation or stupor. Most clinicians believe that ECT results in at least the same degree of clinical improvement as does standard treatment with antidepressant drugs. Recently, the old studies that reported those comparisons have been questioned because of their use of low dosages of antidepressant drugs. In spite of that controversy, few clinicians doubt that ECT and pharmacotherapy are at least equal in their efficacy and response times.

ECT is effective for depression in both major depressive disorder and bipolar I disorder. Delusional or psychotic depression has long been thought to be particularly responsive to ECT; however, recent studies have indicated that major depressive episodes with psychotic features are no more responsive to ECT than are nonpsychotic depressive disorders. Nevertheless, since major depressive episodes with psychotic features are poorly responsive to antidepressant pharmacotherapy alone, ECT should be considered much more often as the first-line treatment for patients with the disorder. Major depressive disorder with melancholic features (such as markedly severe symptoms, psychomotor retardation, early morning awakening, diurnal variation, decreased appetite and weight, and agitation) is thought to be likely to respond to ECT. Elderly patients tend to respond to ECT more slowly than do young patients. However, ECT is a treatment for major depressive episode and does not provide prophylaxis unless it is administered on a long-term maintenance basis.

Manic Episodes

ECT is at least equal to and perhaps superior to lithium (Eskalith) in the treatment of manic episodes. Some data indicate that bilateral placement of electrodes during ECT is more effective than unilateral placement in the treatment of manic episodes. However, the pharmacological treatment of manic episodes is so effective in the short-term and for prophylaxis that the use of ECT for the treatment of manic episodes is generally limited to when all available pharmacological approaches are specifically contraindicated.

Schizophrenia

ECT is an effective treatment for the symptoms of distinct episodes of schizophrenia and not for chronic schizophrenia. Schizophrenic patients with marked positive symptoms, catatonia, or affective symptoms are thought to be most likely to respond to ECT. The efficacy of ECT in such patients is about equal to that of antipsychotics.

Other Indications

Small studies have found ECT to be effective in the treatment of catatonia, a symptom associated with mood disorders, schizophrenia, and medical and neurological disorders. ECT has also been reported to be useful in the treatment of episodic psychoses, atypical psychoses, obsessive-compulsive disorder, and delirium and such medical conditions as neuroleptic malignant syndrome, hypopituitarism, intractable seizure disorders, and the on-off phenomenon of Parkinson's disease. ECT may also be the treatment of choice for depressed pregnant women who require treatment and cannot take medication, geriatric and medically ill patients who cannot take antidepressant drugs safely, and perhaps even depressed children and adolescents who may be less likely to respond to antidepressant drugs than are adults.

CLINICAL GUIDELINES

Patients and their families are often apprehensive about ECT; therefore, the clinician must explain its beneficial and adverse effects and alternative treatment approaches to them. That informed-consent process should be documented in the patient's medical record and should include a discussion of the disorder, its natural course, and the option of receiving no treatment. Printed literature and videotapes about ECT may be useful in attempting to obtain a truly informed consent. The use of involuntary ECT is rare today and should be reserved for patients for whom the treatment is urgent and for whom a legally appointed guardian has agreed to its use. The clinician must know the local, state, and federal laws about the use of ECT.

Pretreatment Evaluation

The pretreatment evaluation should include standard physical, neurological, and preanesthesia examinations and a complete medical history. Laboratory evaluations should include blood and urine chemistries, a chest X-ray, and an electrocardiogram (ECG). A dental examination to assess the state of the patient's dentition is advisable in elderly patients and patients who have had inadequate dental care. An X-ray of the spine is needed if there is other evidence of a spinal disorder. Computed tomography (CT) or magnetic resonance imaging (MRI) should be performed if the clinician suspects the presence of a seizure disorder or a space-occupying lesion.

CONCOMITANT MEDICATIONS

The patient's ongoing medications should be assessed for possible interactions with the induction of a seizure and for drug interactions with the medications used during ECT. The presence of tricyclic and tetracyclic drugs, monoamine oxidase inhibitors, and antipsychotics are generally thought to be acceptable. Benzodiazepines should be withdrawn, because of their anticonvulsant activity; lithium should be withdrawn, because it can result in increased postictal delirium and prolonged seizure activity; and clozapine (Clozaril) should be withdrawn, because it is associated with the development of late-appearing seizures. Lidocaine (Xylocaine) should not be administered during ECT, because it markedly increases the seizure threshold, and theophylline (Theo-Dur) is also contraindicated, because it increases the duration of the seizures. Reserpine (Serpasil) is also contraindicated, because it is associated with further compromise of the respiratory and cardiovascular systems during ETC.

Premedications, Anesthetics, and Muscle Relaxants

Patients should not be given anything orally for six hours before treatment. Just before the procedure, the patient's mouth should be checked for dentures and other foreign objects, and an intravenous (IV) line should be established. A bite block is inserted in the mouth just before the treatment is administered to protect the patient's teeth and tongue during the seizure. Except for the brief interval of electrical stimulation, 100 percent oxygen is administered at a rate of 5 L a minute during the procedure until spontaneous respiration returns. Emergency equipment for the establishment of an airway should be immediately available in case it is needed.

MUSCARINIC ANTICHOLINERGIC DRUGS

Muscarinic anticholinergic drugs are administered before ECT to minimize oral and respiratory secretions and to block bradycardias and asystoles. Some ECT centers have stopped the routine use of anticholinergics as premedications, although their use is still indicated for patients talking β-adrenergic receptor antagonists and for patients with ventricular ectopic beats. The most commonly used drug is atropine, which can be administered 0.3 to 0.6 mg intramuscularly (IM) or subcutaneously 30 to 60 minutes before the anesthetic or 0.4 to 1.0 mg IV two or three minutes before the anesthetic. An option is to use glycopyrrolate (Robinul) (0.2 to 0.4 mg IM, IV, or subcutaneously), which is less likely to cross the blood-brain barrier and less likely to cause cognitive dysfunction and nausea, although it is thought to have less cardiovascular protective activity than does atropine.

GENERAL ANESTHETICS

The administration of ECT requires general anesthesia and oxygenation. The depth of anesthesia should be as light as possible, not only to minimize the adverse effects but also to avoid elevating the seizure threshold associated with many anesthetics. Methohexital (Brevital) (0.75 to 1.0 mg per kg IV bolus) is the most commonly used anesthetic because of its short duration of action and lower association with postictal arrhythmias than is seen with thiopental (Pentothal) (usual dose 2 to 3 mg per kg IV), although that difference in cardiac effects is not universally accepted. Three other anesthetic alternatives are etomidate, ketamine (Ketalar), and alfentanil (Alfenta). Etomidate (0.15 to 0.3 mg per kg IV) is sometimes used because it does not increase the seizure threshold, which can be particularly useful in elderly patients, because the seizure threshold increase with age. Ketamine (6 to 10 mg per kg IM) is sometimes used because it does not increase the seizure threshold, although its use is limited by the frequent association of psychotic symptoms with emergence from anesthesia. Alfentanil (2 to 9 mg per kg IV) is sometimes coadministered with barbiturates to allow the use of low doses of the barbiturate anesthetics and thus to reduce the seizure threshold less than usual, although its use may be associated with an increased incidence of nausea.

MUSCLE RELAXANTS

After the onset of the anesthetic effect, usually within a minute, a muscle relaxant is administered to minimize the risk of bone fractures and other injuries resulting from motor activity during the seizure. The goal is to produce a profound relaxation of the muscles, not necessarily to paralyze the muscles, unless the patient has a history of osteoporosis or spinal injury or has a pacemaker and is, therefore, at risk for injury related to the motor activity during the seizure. Succinylcholine (Anectine), an ultrafast-acting depolarizing blocking agent, has gained virtually universal acceptance for the purpose. Succinylcholine is usually administered in a dose of 0.5 to 1.0 mg per kg as an IV bolus or IV drip. Because succinylcholine is a depolarizing agent, its action is marked by the presence of muscle fasciculations, which move in a rostrocaudal progression. The disappearance of those movements in the feet or the absence of muscle contractions after peripheral nerve stimulation indicates that maximal muscle relaxation has been achieved. In some patients, tubocurarine (3 mg IV) is administered to prevent myoclonus and increases in potassium and muscle enzymes, which may be a problem in patients with musculoskeletal disease or cardiac disease.

If the patient has a known history of pseudocholinesterase deficiency, atracurium (Tracrium) (0.5 to 1.0 mg per kg IV) or curare can be used instead of succinylcholine. In such a patient, the metabolism of succinylcholine is disrupted, and a prolonged apnea may occur, thus necessitating emergency airway management. In general, however, because of the short half-life of succinylcholine, the duration of apnea after its administration is generally shorter than the delay in regaining consciousness caused by the anesthetic and the postictal state.

Stimulus Electrode Placement

ECT can be conducted with either bilaterally or unilaterally placed electrodes. In general, bilateral placement results in a more rapid therapeutic response, and unilateral placement results in less marked cognitive adverse effects in the first week or weeks after treatment, although that difference between placements is absent two months after treatment. In bilateral placement, which was introduced first, one stimulating electrode is placed over each hemisphere of the brain. In unilateral ECT, both electrodes are placed over the nondominant hemisphere, almost always the right hemisphere. Some attempts have been made to vary the location of the electrodes in unilateral ECT; however, those attempts have not been successful in obtaining the rapidity of response seen with bilateral ECT or in further reducing the cognitive adverse effects. The most common approach is to initiate treatment with unilateral ECT because of its more favorable side-effect profile. However, if the patient does not improve after four to six unilateral treatments, the technique is switched to the bilateral placement. Initial bilateral placement of the electrodes may be indicated in the following situations: severe depressive symptoms, marked agitation, immediate suicide risk, manic symptoms, catatonic stupor, and treatment-resistant schizophrenia. Some patients are particularly at risk for anesthetic-related adverse effects, and those patients may also be treated with bilateral placement from the beginning to minimize the number of treatments and exposures to anesthetics.

Traditional bilateral ECT places electrodes bifrontotemporally; each electrode has its center about one inch above the midpoint of an imaginary line drawn from the tragus to the external canthus. With unilateral ECT, one stimulus electrode is typically placed over the nondominant frontotemporal area. Although several locations for the second stimulus electrode have been proposed, placement on the nondominant centroparietal scalp, just lateral to the midline vertex, appears to be most effective.

Which cerebral hemisphere is dominant can generally be determined by a simple series of performance tasks (for example, for handedness and footedness) and stated preference. Right body responses correlate highly with left brain dominance. If the responses are mixed or if they clearly indicate left body dominance, clinicians should alternate the polarity of unilateral stimulation during successive treatments. Clinicians should also monitor the time that it takes for patients to recover consciousness and to answer simple orientation and naming questions. The side of stimulation associated with less rapid recovery and return of function is considered dominant. The left hemisphere is dominant in the vast majority of persons; therefore, unilateral electrode placement is almost always over the right hemisphere.

Electrical Stimulus

The electrical stimulus must be sufficiently strong to reach the seizure threshold (the level of intensity needed to produce a seizure). The electrical stimulus is given in cycles, each cycle containing a positive wave and a negative wave. Old machines used a sine wave; however, that type of machine is now considered obsolete because of the inefficiency of that wave shape. When a sine wave is delivered, the electrical stimulus in the sine wave before the seizure threshold is reached and after the seizure is activated is unnecessary and excessive. Modern ECT machines use a brief pulse wave form, which administers the electrical stimulus usually in a 1 to 2 msec time period. Machines that use an ultrabrief pulse (0.5 msec) are not as effective as brief pulse machines.

The establishment of a patient's seizure threshold is not straightforward. A 40-fold variability in seizure thresholds is seen among patients. In addition, during the course of ECT treatment, a patient's seizure threshold may increase 25 to 200 percent. Also, the seizure threshold is higher in men than in women, and higher in elderly patients than in younger adults. A common technique is to initiate treatment at an electrical stimulus that is thought to be lower than the seizure threshold for a particular patient and then to increase that intensity by 100 percent for unilateral placement and by 50 percent for bilateral placement until the seizure threshold is reached. A debate in the literature concerns the question of whether a minimally superthreshold dose, a moderately superthreshold dose ($1\frac{1}{2}$ times the threshold), or a high superthreshold dose (three times the threshold) is preferable. The debate about stimulus intensity is like the debate regarding electrode placement. Essentially, the data support the conclusion that doses of three times the threshold are the most rapidly effective and that minimal superthreshold doses are associated with the fewest and least severe cognitive adverse effects.

Induced Seizures

A brief muscular contraction, usually strongest in the patient's jaw and facial muscles, is seen concurrently with the flow of stimulus current, regardless of whether a seizure occurs. The first behavioral sign of the seizure is often a plantar extension, which lasts 10 to 20 seconds and marks the tonic phase. That phase is followed by rhythmic (that is, clonic) contractions that decrease in frequency and finally disappear. The tonic phase is marked by high-frequency, sharp EEG activity on which an even higher-frequency muscle artifact may be superimposed. During the clonic phase, bursts of polyspike activity occur simultaneously with the muscular contractions but usually persist for at least a few seconds after the clonic movements stop.

MONITORING SEIZURES

The physician must have an objective measure that a bilateral generalized seizure has occurred after the stimulation. The physician should be able to observe either some evidence of tonic-clonic movements or electrophysiological evidence of seizure activity from the EEG or electromyogram (EMG). Seizures with unilateral ECT are asymmetrical, with higher ictal EEG amplitudes over the stimulated hemisphere than over the nonstimulated hemisphere. Occasionally, unilateral seizures are induced; for that reason, at least a single pair of EEG electrodes should be placed over the contralateral hemisphere when using unilateral ECT. For a seizure to be effective in the course of ECT, the seizure should last at least 25 seconds.

Number and Spacing of ECT Treatments

ECT treatments are usually administered two to three times a week; twice-weekly treatments are associated with less memory impairment than are thrice-weekly treatments. In general, the course of treatment of major depressive disorder can take 6 to 12 treatments (although up to 20 sessions is possible), the treatment of manic episodes can take 8 to 20 treatments, the treatment of schizophrenia can take more than 15 treatments, and the treatment of catatonia and delirium can take as few as one to four treatments. Treatment should continue until the patient achieves what is thought to be the maximum therapeutic response. Treatment past that point does not result in any therapeutic benefit but increases the severity and the duration of the side effects. The point of maximal improvement is usually thought to be that point at which a patient fails to continue to improve after two consecutive treatments. If a patient is not improving after 6 to 10 sessions, bilateral placement and high-density treatment (three times the seizure threshold) should be attempted before ECT is abandoned.

MULTIPLE MONITORED ECT

Multiple monitored ECT (MMECT) involves giving multiple ECT stimuli during a single session, most commonly two bilateral stimuli within two minutes. That approach may be warranted in severely ill patients and in patients who are at especially high risk from the anesthetic procedures. MMECT is associated with the most frequent occurrences of serious cognitive adverse effects.

Maintenance Treatment

A short-term course of ECT induces a remission in symptoms but does not, in itself, prevent a relapse. Post-ECT maintenance treatment should always be considered. Generally, the maintenance therapy is pharmacological, but maintenance ECT treatments (weekly, biweekly, or monthly) have been reported to be effective relapse prevention treatments, although data from large studies are lacking. Indications for maintenance ECT treatments may include a rapid relapse after initial ECT, severe symptoms, psychotic symptoms, and the inability to tolerate medications.

ADVERSE EFFECTS

Contraindications

ECT has no absolute contraindications, only situations in which the patient is at increase risk and has an increased need for close monitoring. Pregnancy is not a contraindication for ECT, and fetal monitoring is generally thought to be unnecessary unless the pregnancy is high-risk or complicated. Patients with space-occupying central nervous system (CNS) lesions are at increased risk for edema and brain herniation after ECT. However, if the lesion is small, the patient is pretreated with dexamethasone, and hypertension is controlled during the seizure, the risk of serious complications can be minimized in those patients. Patients who have increased intracerebral pressure or are at risk for cerebral bleeding (for example, with cerebrovascular diseases and aneurysms) are at risk during ECT because of the increased cerebral blood flow during the seizure. That risk can be lessened, although not eliminated, by control of the patient's blood pressure during the treatment. Patients with recent myocardial infarctions are another high-risk group, although the risk is greatly diminished two weeks after the myocardial infarction and is even further reduced three months after the myocardial infarction. Patients with hypertension should be stabilized on their antihypertensive medications before ECT is administered. Propranolol (Inderal), sublingual nifedipine (Procardia), and sublingual nitroglycerin can also be used to protect such patients during treatment.

Mortality

The mortality rate with ECT is about 0.002 percent per treatment and 0.01 percent for each patient. Those numbers compare favorably with the risks associated with general anesthesia and childbirth. ECT death is usually from cardiovascular complications and is most likely in patients whose cardiac status is already compromised.

Central Nervous System Effects

Common adverse effects associated with ECT are confusion and delirium shortly after the seizure while the patient is coming out of anesthesia. Marked confusion may occur in up to 10 percent of patients within 30 minutes of the seizure and can be treated with barbiturates and benzodiazepines. Delirium is usually most pronounced after the first few treatments and in patients who receive bilateral ECT or who have coexisting neurological disorders. The delirium characteristically clears within days or a few weeks at the longest.

MEMORY

The greatest concern regarding ECT is the association between ECT and memory loss. About 75 percent of all patients given ECT say that the memory impairment is the worst side effect of the treatment. Although memory impairment during a course of treatment is almost the rule, follow-up data indicate that almost all patients are back to their cognitive baselines after six months. However, some patients do complain of persistent memory difficulties. For example, a patient may not remember the events leading up to the hospitalization and ECT, and such autobiographical memories may never be recalled. The degree of cognitive impairment during treatment and the time it takes to return to baseline are related in part to the amount of electrical stimulation used during treatment. Memory impairment is most reported by patients who have experienced little improvement with ECT. In spite of the memory impairment, which usually resolves, there is no evidence of brain damage caused by ECT.

The subject has been the focus of a number of brain imaging studies, using a variety of modalities; virtually all concluded that permanent brain damage is not an effect of ECT.

Systemic Effects

Occasionally, mild transient cardiac arrhythmias occur during ECT, particularly in patients with existing cardiac disease. The arrhythmias are usually a by-product of the brief postictal bradycardia and, therefore, can often be prevented by increasing the dosage of anticholinergic premedication. Other arrhythmias are secondary to a tachycardia during the seizure and may occur as the patient returns to consciousness. The prophylactic administration of a β-adrenergic receptor antagonist can be useful in such cases. As mentioned above, an apneic state may be prolonged if the metabolism of succinylcholine is impaired. Toxic and allergic reactions to the pharmacological agents used in ECT have rarely been reported. Sore muscles resulting from the seizure motor activity can be generally alleviated by pretreatment with curare or atracurium or by increasing the succinylcholine dose by 10 to 25 percent.

References

Abrams R, Swartz C M, Vedak C: Antidepressant effects of high-dose right unilateral electroconvulsive therapy. Arch Gen Psychiatry *48*: 746, 1991.

O'Connor M K, Rummans T A (editors): Updating ECT. Psychiatr Ann *23*: 2, 1993.

Potter W Z, Rudorfer M V: Electroconvulsive therapy: A modern medical procedure. N Engl J Med *328*: 882, 1993.

Prudic J. Sackheim H A, Devanand D P, Kiersky J E: The efficacy of ECT in double depression. Depression *1*: 38, 1993.

Zielinski R J, Roose S P, Devanand D P, Woodring S, Sackeim H A: Cardiovascular complications of ECT in depressed patients with cardiac disease. Am J Psychiatry *150*: 904, 1993.

27.5 OTHER BIOLOGICAL THERAPIES

LIGHT THERAPY

The major indication for light therapy is major depressive disorder with seasonal pattern, a disorder characterized by symptoms that appear on a seasonal basis, usually in the fall and the winter. In light therapy, also called phototherapy, the patient is exposed to a bright artificial light source on a daily basis during the treatment.

Mechanism of Action

PHASE-RESPONSE CURVES

Human circadian rhythms result from the entrainment of endogenous pacemakers by exogenous zeitgebers. The suprachiasmatic nucleus of the hypothalamus is thought to be the major endogenous pacemaker; the light-dark cycle is thought to be the major exogenous zeitgeber. The rhythms of the body exhibit a biological feature called a phase-response curve, which is based on a 24-hour unit. Perturbations, such as exposure to light, have a differential effect on bodily rhythms (for example, sleep and hormone secretion), depending on the time of day—hence, the location on the phase-response curve. Exposure to light in the morning results in a phase advance—that is, rhythms are shifted to an earlier time; exposure to light in the evening results in a phase delay—that is, rhythms are shifted to a later time. Therefore, the entrainment of the endogenous

pacemakers by light is the result of a phase advance at dawn and a phase delay at dusk. Melatonin is secreted by the pineal gland during the night. Secretion is stopped by exposure to light during the night but is not stimulated by exposure to darkness during the day.

EFFECTS OF LIGHT EXPOSURE

More than 50 controlled studies have shown that light therapy is effective, although its mechanism of action is still uncertain. The most accepted theory is that exposure to bright artificial light in the morning causes a phase advance of biological rhythms that effectively treats the delayed circadian rhythms associated with major depressive disorder with seasonal pattern. That hypothesis is supported by the observations of several investigators that other types of depressive disorders do not respond to phototherapy. The initial theory that light exposure works by affecting melatonin secretion has not been supported by subsequent experiments. A high intensity of light was thought to be required for therapeutic effects, but that hypothesis has been disputed by recent studies. Most studies support the idea that two hours of exposure is more effective than 30 minutes of exposure. Whether light should be administered in the morning or the evening or at both times to obtain maximal benefit is undetermined, but the majority of studies support the administration of light in the morning. Full-spectrum light is effective, and some studies have found that narrow-spectrum light is ineffective. Whether an intermediate spectrum of light would be effective is not known.

Indications

The major indication for light therapy is major depressive disorder with seasonal pattern, seen predominantly (80 percent) in women. The mean age of presentation is 40, although the mean age may decrease with better recognition of the disorder. The symptoms usually appear during the winter and remit spontaneously in the spring, but sometimes the symptoms appear in the summer. The most common symptoms include depression, fatigue, hypersomnia, hyperphagia, carbohydrate craving, irritability, and interpersonal difficulties. One third to one half of all patients with the disorder have not previously sought psychiatric help. The remainder have most often been previously classified as having a mood disorder. More than 50 percent of the patients with the disorder have a first-degree relative with a mood disorder. Some recent evidence indicates that persons with mild, subsyndromal symptoms of a seasonal pattern mood disorder may also experience some relief with phototherapy.

Clinical Guidelines

The treatment requires exposure to bright light (2,500 lux) that is about 200 times brighter than the usual indoor lighting. The initial experiments exposed patients to the light for two to three hours before dawn and sometimes an additional two to three hours after dusk every day. The patients were instructed not to look directly into the light but to glance at it only occasionally. Patients usually responded after two to four days of treatment and relapsed two to four days after the treatment was stopped. Recent studies have indicated that only morning exposure may be necessary and that one hour of daily exposure may be sufficient. A debate remains about the required intensity of the light.

The most commonly reported adverse effects are headache, eyestrain, and feeling wired or irritable. Those adverse effects can usually be managed by reducing the length of time that the patient is exposed to the light.

SLEEP DEPRIVATION AND ALTERATIONS OF SLEEP SCHEDULES

Sleep deprivation has been suggested as a short-term treatment of depressive disorder, as an adjuvant to antidepressant drugs to facilitate improvement, and as a treatment for premenstrual dysphoric disorder. One night's sleep deprivation results in a dramatic reduction of depressive symptoms in about 60 percent of all patients with depressive disorders. Unfortunately, the beneficial effects last only one day. The depressive disorder symptoms are often brought back quickly if the patient takes even a short nap after the night of sleep deprivation. That finding caused some researchers to hypothesize that some sleep-related depressogenic process may be temporarily aborted by the sleep deprivation. Some studies have reported that preventing only rapid eye movement (REM) sleep has the same effects as preventing all sleep, causing some researchers to hypothesize that a REM-related process may be related to maintaining or even causing depressive disorders.

Phase-advancing the sleep cycle—that is, going to bed early and waking up early—may have antidepressant effects in some depressed patients, especially when used as an adjuvant to pharmacotherapy. In contrast to the single-day improvement associated with sleep deprivation, the beneficial effects of sleep phase advance sometimes last for a week.

DRUG-ASSISTED INTERVIEWING

To facilitate gathering information during a psychiatric interview, some psychiatrists advocate drug-assisted interviewing. The common use of an intravenous injection of amobarbital (Amytal) led to the popular name of ''Amytal interview'' for the technique. Narcotherapy or narcoanalysis consists of a series of drug-assisted psychotherapy sessions. Both sedatives (for example, barbiturates and benzodiazepines) and stimulants—for example, methylphenidate (Ritalin)—have been used. Narcotherapy was thought to benefit patients by allowing them to experience the catharsis of having a repressed memory or thought brought to conscious awareness. Although narcotherapy is rarely used in modern psychiatry, there has been some renewed interest in it. Some noted psychiatrists have proposed that 3,4-methylenedioxymethamphetamine (MDMA, ecstasy) may be beneficial when used as an agent for drug-assisted psychotherapy. That suggestion has been extremely controversial.

Indications

Although much has been written about drug-assisted interviewing, the literature consists mainly of uncontrolled studies and anecdotal reports, thus making it difficult to determine a definite statement about its indications. Furthermore, several controlled trials have shown that the use of drugs does not guarantee that patients will tell the truth, in spite of the popular misconception that amobarbital is a truth serum. A few studies have shown, in fact, that drug-assisted interviews are no better at eliciting information than an empathic interviewer, hypnosis, or the administration of a placebo.

The most common reasons for drug-assisted interviews in modern practice are the presentation of uninformative or mute patients, catatonia, and supposed conversion disorder. Although drug-assisted interviews often elicit information sooner than interviews without the drug, no evidence indicates that the technique has a positive effect on the therapeutic outcome. Patients may be silent because of excessive anxiety about recounting a traumatic event (for example, a rape or an accident), and drug-assisted interviews have been used successfully in such cases. But hypnosis, daytime sedation, empathic and supportive approaches, and time also help elicit information and do not have the risks of drug-assisted interviewing.

Mute patients with a mental disorder may have catatonic schizophrenia or conversion disorder or may be malingering. Barbiturates or benzodiazepines help in temporarily activating catatonic patients; therefore, catatonic schizophrenia may be a reasonable indication for using drug-assisted interviewing. Patients with conversion disorder or malingering may or may not improve during a drug-assisted interview. The commonly held but controversial belief is that a functional or psychological disorder improves during a drug-assisted interview, whereas an organic or medical disorder does not improve or even worsens. If patients do improve, there is no indication that the drug-assisted interview facilitated their improvement; if they do not improve or if they worsen, the information gained from the interview is of little help in guiding the patient's treatment.

Another indication for drug-assisted interviewing is the differential diagnosis of confusion; the assumption is that functional confusion will clear during the procedure and that organic confusion will not. False-positive results occur when a confused patient is withdrawing from alcohol or barbiturates and when a patient has an epileptic disorder. False-negative results occur when the interviewer uses too much drug and sometimes when the patient has conversion disorder or is a malingerer. Another proposed indication for drug-assisted interviewing is to differentiate between schizophrenia and a depressive disorder. When given amobarbital, schizophrenic patients, it was once thought, would recall bizarre material, and depressed patients would recall depressive material. That hypothesis has not been confirmed in controlled studies. Amobarbital has also been suggested as an adjuvant in supportive therapy; the drug is used to reinforce a therapeutic suggestion (for example, to stop smoking). Furthermore, muscle relaxation is more powerful than sodium amobarbital as an adjuvant in behavior therapy.

Clinical Guidelines

A 10 percent solution of amobarbital is administered at a rate of about 0.5 to 1.0 mL a minute. The rate and the total dose should be adjusted for each patient. The total dose may vary between 0.25 and 0.5 grams, although some patients need up to 1 gram. The end point is a state of mild sedation but not sleep. The benzodiazepines—for example, diazepam (Valium)—are just as effective as the barbiturates and less dangerous.

Barbiturates should not be given to patients with liver, renal, or cardiopulmonary diseases or to patients with porphyria or a history of sedative abuse. Patients may have allergic reactions or respiratory suppression during barbiturate interviews, and the clinician must be prepared for both those possibilities. Furthermore, the use of what patients may perceive as a truth serum may increase their paranoia and interfere with the development of a psychotherapeutic transference.

PSYCHOSURGERY

Psychosurgery involves surgical modification of the brain with the goal of reducing the symptoms of the most severely ill psychiatric patients who have not responded adequately to less radical treatments. Psychosurgical procedures lesion specific brain regions (for example, in lobotomies and cingulotomies) or their connecting tract (for example, in tractotomies and leukotomies). Psychosurgical techniques are also used in the treatment of neurological disorders, such as epilepsy and chronic pain disorder.

The interest in psychosurgical approaches to mental disorders has only recently been rekindled. The renewed interest is based on a number of factors, including much-improved techniques that allow the neurosurgeon to make exact stereotactically placed lesions, improved preoperative diagnoses, comprehensive preoperative and postoperative psychological assessments, complete follow-up data, and a growing understanding regarding the neuroanatomical basis of some mental disorders.

Modern Psychosurgical Techniques

Stereotactic neurosurgical equipment now allows the neurosurgeon to place discrete lesions in the brain. Radioactive implants, cryoprobes, electrical coagulation, proton beams, and ultrasonic waves are used to make the actual lesions.

Indications

The major indication for psychosurgery is the presence of a debilitating, chronic mental disorder that has not responded to any other treatment. A reasonable guideline is that the disorder should have been present for five years, during which a wide variety of alternative treatment approaches were attempted. Chronic intractable major depressive disorder and obsessive-compulsive disorder are the two disorders reportedly most responsive to psychosurgery. The presence of vegetative symptoms and marked anxiety further increases the likelihood of a successful therapeutic outcome. Whether psychosurgery is a reasonable treatment for intractable and extreme aggression is still controversial. Psychosurgery is not indicated for the treatment of schizophrenia, and data regarding manic episodes are controversial.

Therapeutic and Adverse Effects

When patients are carefully selected, between 50 and 70 percent have significant therapeutic improvement with psychosurgery. Fewer than 3 percent become worse. Continued improvement is often noted from one to two years after surgery, and patients are often more responsive than they were before psychosurgery to traditional pharmacological and behavioral treatment approaches. Postoperative seizures are present in fewer than 1 percent of patients, and those seizures are usually controlled with phenytoin (Dilantin). As measured by intelligence quotient (I.Q.) scores, cognitive abilities improve after surgery, probably because of the patient's increased ability to attend to cognitive tasks. Undesired changes in personality have not been noted with the modern limited procedures.

PLACEBOS

Placebos are substances that have no known pharmacological activity. Although it is usually thought that placebos act through suggestion, rather than biological action, that idea is based on the artificial distinction between the mind and the body. Virtually every treatment modality is accompanied by poorly understood factors affecting its outcome (for example, the taste of a medicine and the patient's emotional response to a physician). Indeed, those poorly understood factors and the effects of placebos are better called nonspecific therapeutic factors. For example, at least one study has shown that naloxone (Narcan), an opiate antagonist, can block the analgesic effects of a placebo, thus indicating that a release of an endogenous opiate may explain some placebo effects.

Long-term treatment with placebos should never be undertaken when patients have clearly stated an objection to such a treatment. Furthermore, deceptive treatment with placebos seriously undermines patients' confidence in their physicians. And placebos should never be used when an effective therapy is available, as placebos can lead to both a dependence on pills and various adverse effects.

ACUPUNCTURE AND ACUPRESSURE

An ancient Chinese treatment, acupuncture is the stimulation of specific points of the body with electrical stimulation or the twisting of a needle. Acupressure is the stimulation of those same points with pressure; however, acupressure was not a part of traditional Chinese medicine. The stimulation of specific points is associated with the relief of certain symptoms and is identified with particular organs. Many Chinese doctors have reported therapeutic success with those treatments in combination with herbal treatment (given orally, topically, or intradermally) for a variety of disorders, including mental disorders. Several American investigators have reported that acupuncture is an effective treatment for some patients with depressive disorders and substance (for example, nicotine, caffeine, cocaine, and opioid) dependence. Although it is difficult to approach Eastern treatments with a Western mind, it is also true that history has shown that many ancient remedies have a firm biological basis.

ORTHOMOLECULAR THERAPY

Megavitamin therapy is treatment with large dosages of niacin, ascorbic acid, pyridoxine, folic acid, vitamin B_{12}, and various minerals. Special diets and hormone treatments are often part of those treatment protocols. Uncontrolled reports of the successful treatment of schizophrenia with niacin have not been replicated in controlled collaborative studies. Despite claims to the contrary, megavitamin and diet therapies currently have no proved clinical use in psychiatry. However, a balanced diet reasonably supplemented with vitamins is a good prescription for all patients and physicians.

HISTORICAL TREATMENTS

A variety of treatments were used before the introduction of effective pharmacological agents. Although most of the treatments never underwent controlled therapeutic trials, many clinicians report that the treatments were, in fact, effective. But because most of them were associated with unpleasant or dangerous adverse effects, they have been virtually supplanted by pharmacotherapy.

Subcoma Insulin Therapy

Psychiatrists used to inject small doses of insulin to induce mild hypoglycemia and the resultant sedative effects. Because of the possible complications of the treatment and the introduction of sedating drugs, the treatment has been abandoned.

Coma Therapy

Insulin coma therapy was introduced in 1933 by Manfred Sakel after his observation that schizophrenic patients who went into coma appeared to have decreased psychiatric symptoms after the coma. Insulin was used to induce a comatose state lasting 15 to 60 minutes. The risk of death or cognitive impairment and the introduction of antipsychotic drugs led to the abandonment of the treatment in the United States.

Atropine sulfate was first used in 1950 to induce coma in psychiatric patients. The atropine-induced comas lasted six to eight hours, and the patients took warm and cold showers after awakening. Atropine coma is no longer used in the United States.

Carbon Dioxide Therapy

Carbon dioxide therapy, first used in 1929, involved having the patients inhale carbon dioxide, resulting in an abreaction with severe motor excitement after removing the breathing mask. The treatment was used principally for neurotic patients, and there was doubt, even when it was in use, that the treatment

was effective. Carbon dioxide therapy is no longer used in the United States.

Electrosleep Therapy

Electrosleep therapy involves applying a low level of current through electrodes applied to the patient's head. The patient usually feels a tingling sensation at the sites of the electrodes, but sleep is not necessarily induced. The treatment is applied to a wide variety of disorders, with mixed reports of efficacy, but it is not used in the United States.

Continuous Sleep Treatment

Continuous sleep treatment is a symptomatic method of treatment in which the patient is sedated with any of a variety of drugs to induce 20 hours of sleep a day, sometimes for as long as three weeks in severely agitated patients. Klaesi introduced the name in 1922 and used barbiturates to obtain deep narcosis. The treatment is not used in the United States.

References

Hay P, Sachdev P, Cumming S, Smith J S, Lee T, Kitchener P, Matheson J: Treatment of obsessive-compulsive disorder by psychosurgery. Acta Psychiatr Scand 87: 197, 1993.
Leibenluft E, Wehr T A: Is sleep deprivation useful in the treatment of depression? Am J Psychiatry 149: 159, 1992.
Levitt A J, Joffe R T, Moul D E, Lam R W, Teicher M H, Lebegue B, Murray M G, Oren D A, Schwartz P, Buchanan A, Glod C A, Brown J: Side effects of light therapy in seasonal affective disorder. Am J Psychiatry 150: 650, 1993.
Quitkin F M, McGrath P J, Rabkin J G, Stewart J W, Harrison W, Ross D C, Tricamo E, Fleiss J, Markowitz J, Klein D F: Different types of placebo response in patients receiving antidepressants. Am J Psychiatry 148: 197, 1991.
Rosenthal N E, Moul D E, Hellekson C J, Oren D A, Frank A, Brainard G C, Murray M G, Wehr T A: A multicenter study of the light visor for seasonal affective disorder: No difference in efficacy found between two different intensities. Neuropsychopharmacology 8: 151, 1993.
Sadock B J, Kaplan H I: Other biological therapies. In Comprehensive Textbook of Psychiatry, ed 6, H I Kaplan, B J Sadock, editors, p . Williams & Wilkins, Baltimore, 1995.

28/ Child Psychiatry: Assessment, Examination, and Psychological Testing

A comprehensive evaluation of a child includes clinical interviews with the parents, the child, and the family; information regarding the child's current school functioning; and a standardized assessment of the child's intellectual level and academic achievement. In some cases, developmental tests and neuropsychological assessments are useful. Since psychiatric evaluations of children are rarely initiated by the child, the clinician must obtain information from the family, the school, and any involved community agencies to understand the reasons for the referral. Although children can be excellent informants about symptoms related to mood and inner experiences—such as psychotic phenomena, sadness, fears, and anxiety—they often have difficulty with the chronology of symptoms and are sometimes reticent to report behaviors that have gotten them into trouble. Very young children often cannot articulate their experiences verbally and are better at showing their feelings and preoccupations in a play situation.

Sources often disagree about a variety of symptoms and behaviors during a comprehensive assessment of a child. When faced with contradictory information, the clinician must realize that those differences may reflect an accurate picture of the child's presentation in different settings. Once a full history is obtained from the parents, the child is examined, the child's current functioning at home and at school is assessed, and psychological testing is completed, the clinician can make a best-estimate diagnosis by using all the available information and can make recommendations.

CLINICAL INTERVIEWS

To conduct a useful interview with a child of any age, the clinician must be familiar with normal development, so that the child's responses can be put in the proper perspective. For example, a young child's discomfort on separation from a parent and the lack of clarity regarding the purpose of the interview in a school-age child are perfectly normal and should not be misconstrued as psychiatric symptoms. Furthermore, behavior that is normal in a child of one age, such as temper tantrums in a 2-year-old, takes on a different meaning if present, for example, in a 17-year-old.

The first task of the interviewer is to engage the child and develop a rapport, so that the child is comfortable. The interviewer should find out the child's concept of the purpose of the interview and should ask what a parent has told the child. The interviewer can then briefly describe the reason the interview is taking place in a way that the child understands and that is supportive of the child. During the interview, the clinician should learn about the child's relationships with family members and peers, how well the child is functioning academically and behaviorally in school, and what the child enjoys doing. A general sense of the child's cognitive functioning is a part of the mental status examination.

The level of confidentiality in a child assessment is correlated with the age of the child—that is, just about all specific information is shared with the parents of a very young child,

and more privacy is reasonable with an adolescent. School-age and older children may be told that, if the clinician becomes concerned that the children are dangers to themselves or to others, that information must be shared with other adults. However, the clinician must determine whether the children are safe in their environments and make clinical judgments about whether the children are victims of abuse or neglect.

Toward the end of the interview, children may be asked in an open-ended manner whether they would like to bring up anything else. Every child should be complimented for his or her cooperation and thanked for participating in the interview, and the interview should end on a positive note.

Infants and Young Children

Assessments of infants usually begin with their parents present, since very young children may be frightened by the interview situation; also, the interview with the parents present provides the best way for the clinician to assess the parent-infant interaction. Infants may be referred for a variety of reasons, including high levels of irritability, difficulty in being consoled, disturbances of eating, poor weight gain, sleep disturbances, withdrawn behavior, lack of engagement in play, and developmental delay. Areas of functioning to be assessed include motor development, activity level, verbal communication, ability to engage in play, problem-solving skills, adaptation to daily routines, relationships, and social responsivity. The parent's ability to provide a nurturing, safe, and stimulating environment for the child is assessed through observation and discussions with the parents. The child's developmental level of functioning is determined by combining observations made during the interview with standardized developmental measures. Observations of play reveal a child's developmental level and reflect the child's emotional state and preoccupations. The examiner can playfully interact with an infant of 18 months or less by using such games as peekaboo. Children between the ages of 18 months and 3 years can be observed in a playroom. Children over 2 years old may exhibit symbolic play with toys and may reveal more in that mode than through conversation. The use of puppets and dolls with children under 6 years is often an effective way to elicit information, especially if questions are directed to the dolls, rather than to the child.

School-Age Children

Some school-age children are comfortable while conversing with an adult; others are hampered by fear, anxiety, poor verbal skills, or oppositionalism. School-age children can usually tolerate a 45-minute session. The room should be spacious enough for the child to be able to move around but not so large as to reduce intimate contact between the examiner and the child. Part of the interview can be reserved for unstructured play, and a variety of toys can be made available to capture the child's interest and to elicit themes and feelings.

The initial part of the interview should explore the child's understanding of the reasons for the meeting and should confirm the fact that the interview was not set up because the child did something wrong. Techniques that can facilitate the disclosure of feelings include asking the child to draw a person, family members, and a house and then questioning the child about the drawings. Children may be asked to reveal three wishes, to describe the best and worst events of their lives, and who would be a favorite person to be stranded with on a desert island. Games such as Donald Winnicott's squiggle, in which the examiner draws a curved line and then the examiner and the child take turns continuing the drawing, may open lines of communication.

Questions that are partially open-ended with some multiple choices may elicit the most comprehensive answers in school-age children. Simple, closed (yes-no) questions may not elicit enough information, and completely open-ended questions can overwhelm a school-age child who is not able to construct a chronological narrative, resulting in a shrugging of the child's shoulders. The use of indirect commentary—such as "I once knew a child who felt very sad when he moved away from all his friends"—is helpful, although the clinician must be careful not to lead the child into confirming what the child thinks the clinician wants to hear. School-age children respond well to a clinician who helps them compare moods or feelings by asking them to rate feelings on a scale of 1 to 10.

Adolescents

Adolescents can usually give a chronological account of the events leading to the evaluation, although some may disagree with the need for the evaluation. The clinician should communicate the value of hearing the story from the adolescent's point of view and must be careful to reserve judgment and not assign blame. Adolescents may be concerned about confidentiality. The clinician can assure them that permission will be requested from them before any specific information is shared with parents, except for situations involving danger to the adolescents or others, in which case confidentiality must be sacrificed. Adolescents can be approached in an open-ended manner, but, when silences occur during the interview, the clinician should break the ice and attempt to reengage them. The clinician can explore what the adolescents believe the outcomes of the evaluation will be (change of school, hospitalization, removal from home, removal of privileges).

Some adolescents approach the interview with apprehension or outright hostility but open up when the clinician is neither punitive not judgmental. Clinicians must be aware of their own responses to an adolescent's behavior (countertransference), so as to remain therapeutic, even in the face of a defiant, angry, or difficult adolescent. Clinicians should set appropriate limits: they should postpone or end the interview if they feel threatened or if patients become destructive to property or to themselves. The interview should always include an exploration of suicidal thoughts, assaultive behavior, psychotic phenomena, substance use, and sexual relationships. Once rapport has been established, many adolescents appreciate the opportunity to tell their side of the story and may reveal things that have not been disclosed to anyone else.

Family Interview

An interview with the parents and the patient together may be done first or as a later part of the evaluation. Sometimes an interview with the entire family, including the parents' other children, can be enlightening. The purpose is to observe the attitudes of the parents toward the patient and the affective responses of the children to their parents. The clinician's job is to maintain a nonthreatening atmosphere in which each member of the family can speak freely without feeling that the clinician is taking sides with any particular member. Although child psychiatrists generally function as advocates for the child, the clinician must validate each family member's feelings in the setting, because lack of communication within the family often contributes to their problems.

Parents

The interview with the patient's parents or caretakers is necessary to get a chronological picture of the child's growth and development. A thorough developmental history and details of any stressors or important events that have influenced the child's development must be elicited. The parents' view of the family dynamics, their marital history, and their own emotional adjustment are also elicited. The family's psychiatric history and the parenting styles of the grandparents are pertinent. Parents can be the best informants about the child's previous psychiatric and medical illnesses, evaluations, and treatments and about the time frame and severity of any preexisting problems. The clinician should question the parents about their understanding of the causes and the nature of their child's problems and about their expectations regarding the assessment and potential treatments.

STRUCTURED AND SEMISTRUCTURED INTERVIEWS

The advantage of a structured interview is that information that might otherwise be overlooked or minimized is collected comprehensively. Structured interviews, however, cannot replace clinical interviews, since structured interviews do not adequately address the chronology of symptoms, the interplay between environmental stressors and emotional responses, and developmental issues. Nevertheless, the clinician may find it helpful to combine the data from a structured interview with other materials in a comprehensive evaluation.

Kiddie Schedule for Affective Disorders and Schizophrenia (K-SADS)

This semistructured interview presents multiple items with some space for further clarification of symptoms keyed to many diagnoses in the third edition of *Diagnostic and Statistical Manual of Mental Disorders* (DSM-III). It comes in a form for parents about their child and a version to be used with the child directly. It takes about 1 to $1\frac{1}{2}$ hours to administer and is applicable for children between the ages of 6 and 17 years. The interviewer should have some training in the field of child psychiatry but need not be a psychiatrist.

Diagnostic Interview Schedule for Children-Revised (DISC-R)

This structured interview was designed to be administered by trained laypersons. It is available in parallel child and parent forms and is applicable for a multitude of diagnoses keyed to the revised third edition of DSM (DSM-III-R); a computer scoring algorithm is available. Since it is fully structured interview, the instructions serve as a complete guide for the questions, and the examiner need not have any knowledge of child psychiatry to conduct the interview correctly. It is applicable to children between the ages of 8 and 17 years of age. The interview assesses symptoms over the previous six months and, thus, may be useful adjunctively in the evaluation process.

RATING SCALES

Child Behavior Checklist

The parent and teacher versions of this checklist were developed to cover a broad range of symptoms and several positive attributes related to academic and social competence. It presents items related to mood, frustration tolerance, hyperactivity, oppositional behavior, anxiety, and variety of other behaviors. The parent version consists of 118 items rated on a scale of 0 (not true), 1 (sometimes true), and 2 (very true). The teacher version is similar but without the items that apply only to home life. Profiles were developed that are based on normal children of three different age groups (4 to 5, 6 to 11, and 12 to 16).

Such a checklist identifies specific problem areas that would otherwise be overlooked. Although the checklist is not used specifically to make diagnoses, it may point out areas in which the child's behavior is deviant compared with normal children of the same age group.

Revised Behavior Problem Checklist

This scale consists of 150 items that cover a variety of childhood behavioral and emotional symptoms. It discriminates between clinic-referred and nonreferred children. Separate subscales have been found to correlate in the appropriate direction with other measures of intelligence, academic achievement, clinical observations, and peer popularity. As with the other broad rating scales, such an instrument can be helpful in gaining a comprehensive view of many behavioral areas, but it is not designed to make psychiatric diagnoses.

CHILD PSYCHIATRIC EVALUATION

The child psychiatric evaluation should include a description of the reason for the referral, the child's past and present functioning, and any test results.

Identifying Data

To understand the clinical problems to be evaluated, the clinician must first identify the patient and keep in mind the family constellation surrounding the child. The clinician must also pay attention to the source of the referral—that is, whether it is the child's family, school, or some other agency, since that influences the family's attitude toward the evaluation. Finally, many informants contribute to the child's evaluation, so identifying each of them is important is gaining insight into the functioning of the child in different settings.

History

A comprehensive history comprises information about the child's current and past functioning, based on the reports of the parents from clinical and structured interviews and on the re-

ports of teachers and previous medical and psychiatric physicians and therapists. The chief complaint, the history of the present illness, and the child's developmental history are usually obtained from the parents. Psychiatric and medical histories, current physical examination findings, and immunization histories are usually obtained from the psychiatrists and pediatricians who treated the child in the past. The child is helpful in reporting the current situation regarding peer relationships, adjustment to school, and family functioning. The family's psychiatric and social histories are best obtained from the parents.

Mental Status Examination

A detailed description of the child's current mental functioning can be obtained through observation and specific questioning.

PHYSICAL APPEARANCE

The examiner should note and document the child's size, grooming, nutritional state, bruising, head circumference, physical signs of anxiety, facial expressions, and mannerisms.

PARENT-CHILD INTERACTION

The examiner can observe the interactions between the parents and the child in the waiting area before the interview and in the family session. The manner in which the parents and the child converse and the emotional overtones are pertinent.

SEPARATION AND REUNION

The examiner should note both the manner in which the child responds to the separation from a parent for an individual interview and the reunion behavior. Either lack of affect at separation and reunion or severe distress on separation or reunion can indicate the presence of problems in the parent-child relationship or other psychiatric disturbances.

ORIENTATION TO TIME, PLACE, AND PERSONS

Impairments in orientation can reflect organic damage, low intelligence, or a thought disorder; however, the age of the child must be kept in mind, since very young children are not expected to know the date, other chronological information, or the name of the interview site.

SPEECH AND LANGUAGE

The examiner should note whether the level of speech and language acquisition is appropriate for the child's age. An observable disparity between expressive and receptive language is notable. The examiner should note the child's rate of speech, rhythm, latency to answer, spontaneity of speech, intonation, articulation of words, and prosody. Echolalia, repetitive stereotypical phrases, and unusual syntax are important psychiatric findings. Children who do not use words by 18 months or who do not use phrases by $2\frac{1}{2}$ to 3 years but who have a history of normal babbling and appropriate response to nonverbal cues are probably developing normally. The examiner should consider the possibility that a hearing loss is contributing to a speech and language deficit.

MOOD

A child's sad expression, lack of appropriate smiling, tearfulness, anxiety, euphoria, and anger are valid indicators of mood, as are verbal admissions of feelings. Persistent themes in play and fantasy also reflect the child's mood.

AFFECT

The examiner should note the child's range of emotional expressivity, appropriateness of affect to the content of thought, ability to move smoothly from one affect to another, and sudden labile emotional shifts.

THOUGHT PROCESS AND CONTENT

In evaluating a thought disorder in a child, the clinician must always consider what is developmentally expected for the child's age and what is deviant for any age group. The evaluation of the form of thought considers loosening of associations, excessive magical thinking, perseveration, echolalia, the child's ability to distinguish fantasy from reality, coherence of sentences, and the ability to reason logically. The evaluation of the content of thought considers delusions, obsessions, themes, fears, wishes, preoccupations, and interests.

Suicidal ideation is always a part of the mental status examination in children who are verbal enough to understand the questions and old enough to understand the concept. Children of average intelligence over 4 years of age usually have some understanding of what is real and what is make believe. They may be asked about suicidal ideation, although a firm concept of the permanence of death may take several more years.

Aggressive thoughts and homicidal ideation are assessed here. Perceptual disturbances, such as hallucinations, are also assessed. Very young children are expected to have short attention spans and may change the topic and conversation abruptly without exhibiting a symptomatic flight of ideas. Transient visual and auditory hallucinations in very young children do not necessarily represent major psychotic illnesses, but they do deserve further investigation.

SOCIAL RELATEDNESS

The examiner assesses the child's appropriateness of response to the interviewer, general level of social skills, eye contact, and degree of familiarity in or withdrawal from the interview process. Overly friendly or familiar behavior may be as troublesome as extremely retiring and withdrawn presentations. The examiner assesses the child's self-esteem, general and specific areas of confidence, and success with family and peer relationships.

MOTOR BEHAVIOR

This part of the mental status examination includes observations regarding the child's activity level, ability to pay attention and carry out developmentally appropriate tasks, coordination, involuntary movements, tremors, motor overflow, and any unusual focal asymmetries of muscle movement.

COGNITION

The examiner assesses the child's intellectual functioning, problem-solving abilities, and memory. An approximate level of intelligence can be estimated by the child's general information, vocabulary, and comprehension. For a specific assessment of the child's cognitive abilities, the examiner can use a standardized test.

MEMORY

School-age children should be able to remember three objects after five minutes and to repeat five digits forward and three digits backward. Anxiety may interfere with the child's performance, but an obvious inability to repeat digits or to add simple numbers may reflect brain damage, mental retardation, or learning disabilities.

JUDGMENT AND INSIGHT

The child's view of problems, the reactions to them, and the potential solutions suggested by the child may give the clinician a good idea of the child's judgment and insight. In addition, the child's understanding of what is realistic for the child to do to help and what the clinician can do adds to the assessment of the child's judgment.

Neuropsychiatric Assessment

A neuropsychiatric assessment is appropriate for children who are suspected of having a neurological disorder, a psychiatric impairment that coexists with neurological signs, or psychiatric symptoms that may be due to neuropathology. The neuropsychiatric evaluation combines information from a neurological examination, a physical examination, and the mental status examination. The neurological examination can identify asymmetrical abnormal signs (hard signs) that may indicate lesions in the brain. A physical examination can evaluate the presence of physical stigmata of particular syndromes in which neuropsychiatric symptoms or developmental aberrations play a role (for example, fetal alcohol syndrome, Down's syndrome).

Part of the neuropsychiatric examination is the assessment of neurological soft signs and minor physical anomalies. The term "neurological soft signs" was first used by Loretta Bender in the 1940s in reference to nondiagnostic abnormalities in the neurological examinations of schizophrenic children. Soft signs are not indicative of focal neurological disorders, but they are associated with a variety of developmental disabilities and are seen frequently in children with low intelligence, learning disabilities, and behavioral disturbances. Soft signs may refer to both behavioral symptoms (which are sometimes associated with brain damage, such as severe impulsivity and hyperactivity), physical findings (including contralateral overflow movements), and a variety of nonfocal signs (such as mild choreiform movements, poor balance, mild incoordination, asymmetry of gait, nystagmus, and the persistence of infantile reflexes). Soft signs can be divided into (1) those that are normal in a young child but become abnormal when they persist in an older child and (2) those that are abnormal at any age. The Physical and Neurological Examination for Soft Signs (PANESS) is an instrument used with children up to age 15 years. It consists of 15 questions regarding general physical status and medical history and 43 physical tasks (for example, touch your finger to your nose, hop on one foot to the end of the line, tap this fast with your finger). Neurological soft signs are important to note but are not specific in making a psychiatric diagnosis.

Minor physical anomalies or dysmorphic features occur with a higher than usual frequency in children with developmental disabilities, learning disabilities, speech and language disorders, and hyperactivity. As with soft signs, the documentation of minor physical anomalies is part of the neuropsychiatric assessment, but they are rarely helpful in the diagnostic process, nor do they imply a good or bad prognosis. Minor physical anomalies include a high-arched palate, epicanthus folds, hypertelorism, low-set ears, transverse palmar creases, multiple hair whorls, a large head, a furrowed tongue, and partial syndactyly of several toes.

When a seizure disorder is being considered in the differential diagnosis or a structural abnormality in the brain is suspected, an electroencephalogram (EEG), computed tomography (CT), or magnetic resonance imaging (MRI) may be indicated.

Developmental, Psychological, and Educational Testing

Psychological tests are not always required to assess psychiatric symptoms, but they are valuable in determining a child's developmental level, intellectual functioning, and academic difficulties. A measure of adaptive functioning (including the child's competence in communication, daily living skills, socialization, and motor skills) is a prerequisite when a diagnosis of mental retardation is being considered.

DEVELOPMENT TESTS FOR INFANTS AND PRESCHOOLERS

The Gesell Infant Scale, the Cattell Infant Scale, the Bayley Infant Scale of Development, and the Denver Developmental Screening Test include developmental assessments of infants as young as 2 months of age. When used with very young infants, the tests focus on sensorimotor and social responses to a variety of objects and interactions. When those instruments are used with older infants and preschoolers, language acquisition is emphasized. The Gesell Infant Scale measures development in four areas: motor, adaptive functioning, language, and social. The Cattell Infant Scale was developed as a downward extension of the Stanford-Binet Intelligence Scale and is administered as a test.

An infant's score on one of the above developmental assessments is not a reliable way to predict a child's future intelligence quotient (I.Q.) in most cases. Infant assessments are valuable, however, in detecting developmental deviation and mental retardation and in raising suspicions of a developmental disorder. Whereas infant assessments rely heavily on sensorimotor functions, intelligence testing in older children and adolescents comprises later-developing functions, including verbal, social, and abstract cognitive abilities.

INTELLIGENCE TESTS FOR SCHOOL-AGE CHILDREN AND ADOLESCENTS

The most widely used test of intelligence for school-age children and adolescents is the Wechsler Intelligence Scale for Children-III (WISC-III). It can be given to children from 6 to 17 years old, yields a verbal I.Q., a performance I.Q., and a combined full-scale I.Q. The verbal subtests consist of vocabulary, information, arithmetic, similarities, comprehension, and digit span (supplemental) categories. The performance subtests include block design, picture completion, picture arrangement, object assembly, coding, mazes (supplemental), and symbol search (supplemental). The scores of the supplemental subtests are not included in the computation of the intelligence quotient.

Each subcategory is scored from 1 to 19, with 10 being the average score. An average full-scale I.Q. is 100, with 70 to 80 representing borderline intellectual function, 80 to 90 being in the low average range, 90 to 109 being average, 110 to 119 being high average, and above 120 being in the superior or very superior range. The multiple breakdowns of the performance and verbal subscales allow a great deal of flexibility in identify-

ing specific areas of deficit and scatter in intellectual abilities. Since a larger part of intelligence testing measures abilities used in academic settings, the breakdown of the WISC-III can also be helpful in pointing out skills in which a child is weak and may benefit from remedial education.

The Stanford-Binet Intelligence Scale covers an age range that extends from 2 to 24 years. It relies on pictures, drawings, and objects for very young children and on verbal performance in older children and adolescents. The Stanford-Binet Intelligence Scale, the earliest version of an intelligence test of its kind, leads to a mental age score and an intelligence quotient.

The McCarthy Scales of Children's Abilities and the Kaufman Assessment Battery for Children are two other tests of intelligence that are available for preschool and school-age children. They do not cover the adolescent age group.

Long-Term Stability of Intelligence

Although a child's intelligence is relatively stable throughout the school-age years and adolescence, some factors can influence intelligence and a child's score on an intelligence test. The intellectual functions of children with severe mental illnesses and of those from socioeconomically deprived environments may decrease over time, whereas the intelligence quotients of children whose environments have been enriched may increase over time. Factors that influence a child's score on a given test of intellectual functioning and thus affect the accuracy of the test are motivation, emotional state, anxiety, and cultural milieu.

PERCEPTUAL AND PERCEPTUAL MOTOR TESTS

The Bender Visual-Motor Gestalt test can be given to children between the ages of 4 and 12 years. It consists of a set of spatially related figures that the child is asked to copy. The scores are based on the child's number of errors. Although not a diagnostic test, it is useful in identifying developmentally age-inappropriate perceptual performances.

PERSONALITY TESTS

Personality tests are not of much use in making diagnoses, and they are less satisfactory than intelligence tests in regard to norms, reliability, and validity. However, they can be helpful in eliciting themes and fantasies.

Rorschach test is a projective technique in which ambiguous stimuli—a set of bilaterally symmetrical inkblots—are shown to a child, who is then asked to describe what he or she sees in each one. The hypothesis is that the child's interpretation of the vague and ambiguous stimuli reflects basic characteristics of the child's personality. The examiner notes the themes and patterns. Two sets of norms have been established for the Rorschach test, one for children between 2 and 10 years and one for adolescents between 10 and 17 years.

A more structured projective test is the Children's Apperception Test (CAT), which is an adaption of the Thematic Apperception Test (TAT). The CAT consists of cards with pictures of animals in situations that are somewhat ambiguous but that show scenes related to parent-child and sibling issues, caretaking, and other relationships. The child is asked to describe what is happening and to tell a story about what happens. Animals are used because it was hypothesized that children may respond more readily to the animal images than to human figures.

Drawings, toys, and play are also applications of projective techniques that can be used during the evaluation of a child. Doll houses, dolls, and puppets have been especially helpful in allowing the child a nonconversational mode in which to express a variety of attitudes and feelings. Play materials that reflect household situations are likely to elicit the child's fears, hopes, and conflicts about the family.

Projective techniques have not fared well as standardized instruments. Rather than being considered tests, projective techniques are best considered as additional clinical modalities.

EDUCATIONAL TESTS

Achievement tests measure the attainment of knowledge and skills based on a particular academic curriculum. The Wide-Range Achievement Test-Revised (WRAT-R) consists of tests of knowledge and skills and timed performances of reading, spelling, and mathematics. It is used with children ranging from 5 years to adulthood. The test yields a score that is compared with the average expected score for the child's chronological age and grade level.

The Peabody Individual Achievement Test (PIAT) includes word identification, spelling, mathematics, and reading comprehension.

The Kaufman Test of Educational Achievement, the Gray Oral Reading Test-Revised (GORT-R), and the Sequential Tests of Educational Progress (STEP) are achievement tests that determine whether the child has achieved the level expected for the child's grade level. Children with an average I.Q. whose achievement is significantly lower than expected for their grade level in one or more subjects are considered learning-disabled. Thus, achievement testing, combined with a measure of intellectual function, can identify specific learning disabilities for which remediation is recommended. Children who do not reach their grade level according to their chronological age but who function intellectually in the borderline range or lower are not necessarily learning-disabled unless there is a disparity between their I.Q.s and their levels of achievement.

Formulation and Summary

Once all the information is available, the clinician must put all the pieces together in a formulation that includes the psychodynamic summary, family environmental stressors, the psychiatric symptoms and any disorders that they constitute, and the specific physical, neuromotor, or developmental abnormalities that are causing the impairment. The clinician should also use the information from standardized psychological and developmental assessments in the summary. Since children are pervasively influenced by their environments, the psychiatric formulation includes not only the child's impairments but also the manner in which the family functions and affects the child's impairments. The clinician should also comment on the appro-priateness of the child's educational setting and the issue of the child's general well-being with respect to abuse and neglect.

Diagnosis

At the close of the evaluation process, the clinician should make a diagnosis. A child whose daily function is significantly impaired either in a school setting or at home is likely to meet the criteria for one or more psychiatric disorders. The fourth edition of DSM (DSM-IV) provides a guideline for psychiatric diagnosis that reflects a consensus of current expertise in the field; other clinical situations may not fall within DSM-IV's categories, but they require psychiatric attention and treatment. When dealing with children who are an integral part of a family and are vulnerable to environmental stressors, the clinician must consider interventions that go beyond the DSM-IV diagnoses.

Recommendations and Treatment Plan

Along with recommending appropriate courses of treatment for psychiatric disorders, the clinician must consider the family's level of functioning and the need for family and environmental interventions that are likely to ameliorate the child's condition. The clinician's decisions in those areas may range from determining that a child's entire family needs psychotherapy, to recommending that a child's school setting be changed, to recommending that the child live outside the family setting. The clinician must communicate the recommendations and proposed treatment plan to the parents and the child; without the parent's cooperation, treatment may not be obtained.

In many cases the child was referred by an outside agency, such as a school, a therapist, or a protective service agency. Therefore, with the family's permission, the clinician needs to communicate the recommendations to the referring source.

References

Chandler M C, Gualtieri C T, Barnhill L J: The neuropsychiatric examination of the child. In *Handbook of Studies on Child Psychiatry*, B J Tonge, G D Burrows, J C Werry, editors, p 91. Elsevier, Amsterdam, 1990.

Kaminer Y, Feinstein C, Seifer R: Is there a need for observationally based assessment of affective symptomatology in child and adolescent psychiatry? Adolescence *30*: 483, 1995.

Ollendick T H, Hersen M, editors: *Handbook of Child and Adolescent Assessment.* Allyn & Bacon, Boston, 1993.

Parrott R., Burgoon M, Ross C: Parents and pediatricians talk: Compliance-gaining strategies's use during well-child exams. Health Commun *4*: 57, 1992.

Wilens T E, Spencer T, Biederman J, Wozniak J, Connor D: Combined pharmacotherapy: an emerging trend in pediatric psychopharmacology. J Am Acad Child Adolesc Psychiatry *34*: 110, 1995.

Young J G, O'Brien J B, Gutterman E M, Cohen P: Research on the clinical interview. J Am Acad Child Adolesc Psychiatry *26*: 613, 1987.

Young J G, Kaplan D, Pascualvaca D M, Brasic J R: Psychiatric examination of the infant, child, and adolescent. In *Comprehensive Textbook of Psychiatry*, ed 6, H I Kaplan, B J Sadock, editors, p. 2169. Williams & Wilkins, Baltimore, 1995.

29/ Mental Retardation

Mental retardation is a heterogeneous disorder consisting of below-average intellectual functioning and impairment in adaptive skills that is present before the person is 18 years of age. The impairments are influenced by genetic, environmental, and psychosocial factors. Since the 1980s, increased recognition has been given to subtle biological factors, including small chromosomal abnormalities, genetic syndromes, subclinical lead intoxication, and various prenatal toxic exposures in persons with mild mental retardation (up to 85 percent of the mentally retarded population). The development of mild mental retardation had traditionally been attributed mainly to psychosocial deprivation.

The American Association of Mental Deficiency (EMETE) and the fourth edition of *Diagnostic and Statistical Manual of Mental Disorder* (DSM-IV) define mental retardation as significantly subaverage general intellectual functioning resulting in or associated with concurrent impairments in adaptive behavior and manifested during the developmental period—that is, before the age of 18. The diagnosis is made regardless of whether the patient has a coexisting physical disorder or other mental disorder. Table 29–1 presents an overview of development levels in communication, academic functioning, and vocational skills expected of persons with various degrees of mental retardation.

General intellectual functioning is determined by using standardized tests of intelligence, and the term "significantly subaverage" is defined as an intelligence quotient (I.Q.) of approximately 70 or below or two standard deviations below the mean for the particular test. Adaptive functioning can be measured with a standardized scale, such as the Vineland Adaptive Behavior Scale.

CLASSIFICATION

The degrees or levels of mental retardation are expressed in various terms. DSM-IV presents four types of mental retardation, reflecting the degree of intellectual impairment: mild mental retardation, moderate mental retardation, severe mental retardation, and profound mental retardation. Table 29–2 shows the degrees of mental retardation by I.Q. range. The category of borderline mental retardation (between one and two standard deviations below the test mean) was eliminated in 1973. Borderline intellectual functioning, according to DSM-IV, is not within the category of mental retardation but refers to an I.Q. in the 71 to 84 range and may be a focus of psychiatric attention.

In addition, DSM-IV lists mental retardation, severity unspecified, as a type reserved for those persons who are strongly suspected of having mental retardation but cannot be tested by standard intelligence tests or are too impaired or uncooperative to be tested. That type may be applicable to infants whose significantly subaverage intellectual functioning is clinically judged but for whom the available tests (for example, Bayley Infant Scale of Development and Cattell Infant Scale) do not yield numerical I.Q. values. That type should not be used when the intellectual level is presumed to be above 70.

EPIDEMIOLOGY

The prevalence of mental retardation at any one time is estimated to be about 1 percent of the population. The incidence of mental retardation is difficult to calculate because of the difficulty of identifying its onset. In many cases, retardation may be latent for a long time before the person's limitations are recognized or, because of good adaptation, the formal diagnosis cannot be made at a particular point in the person's life. The highest incidence is in school-age children, with the peak at ages 10 to 14. Mental retardation is about $1\frac{1}{2}$ times more common among men than among women. In the elderly, prevalence is less, as those with severe or profound mental retardation have high mortality rates resulting from the complications of associated physical disorders.

ETIOLOGY

Causative factors in mental retardation include genetic (chromosomal and inherited) conditions, prenatal exposure to infections and toxins, perinatal trauma (such as prematurity), acquired conditions, and sociocultural factors. The severity of the resulting mental retardation is related to the timing and the duration of the trauma or exposure to the central nervous system. The more severe the mental retardation, the more likely it is that the cause is evident. In about three fourths of the persons with severe mental retardation, the cause is known, whereas the cause is apparent in only half of persons with mild mental retardation. No cause is known for three fourths of persons with borderline intellectual functioning. Overall, in up to two thirds of all mentally retarded persons, the probable cause can be identified.

Low socioeconomic groups may be overrepresented in cases of mild mental retardation, the significance of which is not clear. Current knowledge suggests that genetic factors, environmental biological factors, and psychosocial factors work additively in mental retardation.

Chromosomal Abnormalities

DOWN'S SYNDROME

Down's syndrome was first described by the English physician Langdon Down in 1866 and was based on the physical characteristics associated with subnormal mental functioning. Since then, Down's syndrome has remained the most investigated and the most discussed syndrome in mental retardation. Children with the syndrome were originally called "mongoloid" because of their physical characteristics of slanted eyes, epicanthal folds, and flat nose.

Despite a plethora of theories and hypotheses advanced in the past 100 years, the cause of Down's syndrome is still unknown. There is agreement on a few predisposing factors in chromosomal disorders—among them, the increased age of the mother, possibly the increased age of the father, and X-ray radiation. The problem of cause is complicated even further by the recent recognition of three types of chromosomal aberrations in Down's syndrome:

1. The overwhelming majority of patients have trisomy 21 (three of chromosome 21, instead of the usual two); they have 47 chromosomes, with an extra chromosome 21. The

Table 29-1.   Developmental Characteristics of Mentally Retarded Persons

Degree of Mental Retardation	Preschool Age (0–5) Maturation and Development	School Age (6–20) Training and Education	Adult (21 and Over) Social and Vocational Adequacy
Profound	Gross retardation; minimal capacity for functioning in sensorimotor areas; needs nursing care; constant aid and supervision required	Some motor development present; may respond to minimal or limited training in self-help	Some motor and speech development; may achieve very limited self-care; needs nursing care
Severe	Poor motor development; speech minimal; generally unable to profit from training in self-help; little or no communication skills	Can talk or learn to communicate; can be trained in elemental health habits; profits from systematic habit training; unable to profit from vocational training	May contribute partially to self-maintenance under complete supervision; can develop self-protection skills to a minimal useful level in controlled environment
Moderate	Can talk or learn to communicate; poor social awareness; fair motor development; profits from training in self-help; can be managed with moderate supervision	Can profit from training in social and occupational skills; unlikely to progress beyond second-grade level in academic subjects; may learn to travel alone in familiar places	May achieve self-maintenance in unskilled or semiskilled work under sheltered conditions; needs supervision and guidance when under mild social or economic stress
Mild	Can develop social and communication skills; minimal retardation in sensorimotor areas; often not distinguished from normal until later age	Can learn academic skills up to approximately sixth-grade level by late teens; can be guided toward social conformity	Can usually achieve social and vocational skills adequate to minimum self-support but may need guidance and assistance when under unusual social or economic stress

Table adapted from *Mental Retardation Activities of the US Department of Health, Education and Welfare*, p 2. US Government Printing Office, Washington, 1983. Used with permission. DSM-IV criteria are adapted essentially from this chart.

Table 29-2.   Diagnostic Criteria for Mental Retardation

A. Significantly subaverage intellectual functioning: an I.Q. of approximately 70 or below on an individually administered I.Q. test (for infants, a clinical judgment of significantly subaverage intellectual functioning).

B. Concurrent deficits or impairments in present adaptive functioning (i.e., the person's effectiveness in meeting the standards expected for his or her age by his or her cultural group) in at least two of the following areas: communication, self-care, home living, social/interpersonal skills, use of community resources, self-direction, functional academic skills, work, leisure, health and safety.

C. The onset is before age 18 years.

Code based on degree of severity reflecting level of intellectual impairment:

Mild mental retardation: IQ level 50–55 to approximately 70
Moderate retardation: IQ level 35–40 to 50–55
Severe mental retardation: IQ level 20–25 to 35–40
Profound mental retardation: IQ level below 20 or 25
Mental retardation, severity unspecified: when there is a strong presumption of mental retardation but the person's intelligence is untestable by standard tests

Table from DSM-IV, *Diagnostic and Statistical Manual of Mental Disorders*, ed 4. Copyright American Psychiatric Association, Washington, 1994. Used with permission.

mothers' karyotypes are normal. A nondisjunction during meiosis, occurring for unknown reasons, is held responsible for the disorder.

2. Nondisjunction occurring after fertilization in any cell division results in mosaicism, a condition in which both normal and trisomic cells are found in various tissues.

3. Translocation involves a fusion of two chromosomes, mostly 21 and 15, resulting in a total of 46 chromosomes, despite the presence of an extra chromosome 21. The disorder, unlike trisomy 21, is usually inherited, and the translocated chromosome may be found in unaffected parents and siblings. Those asymptomatic carriers have only 45 chromosomes.

The incidence of Down's syndrome in the United States is about 1 in every 700 births. In his original description, Down mentioned the frequency of 10 percent among all mentally retarded patients. Today, around 10 percent of patients with Down's syndrome are in institutions for the mentally retarded. For a middle-aged mother (more than 32 years old), the risk of having a Down's syndrome child with trisomy 21 is about 1 in 100 births, but, when translocation is present, the risk is about one in three. Those facts assume special importance in genetic counseling.

Mental retardation is the overriding feature of Down's syndrome. The majority of patients belong to the moderately and severely retarded groups, with only a minority having an I.Q. above 50. Mental development seems to progress normally from birth to 6 months of age. I.Q. scores gradually decrease from near normal at 1 year of age to about 30 at older ages. The decline in intelligence may be real or apparent. It could be that infantile tests do not reveal the full extent of the defect, which may become manifest when sophisticated tests are used in early childhood. According to many sources, patients with Down's syndrome are placid, cheerful, and cooperative, which facilitates their adjustment at home. The picture seems to change in adolescents, who may experience various emotional difficulties, behavior disorders, and (rarely) psychotic disorders.

The diagnosis of Down's syndrome is made with relative ease in an older child but is often difficult in newborn infants. The most important signs in a newborn include general hypotonia, oblique palpebral fissures, abundant neck skin, a small flattened skull, high cheekbones, and a protruding tongue. The hands are broad and thick, with a single palmar transversal crease, and the little fingers are short and curved inward. Moro reflex is weak or absent. More than 100 signs or stigmata are described in Down's syndrome, but rarely are all found in one person.

Life expectancy used to be about 12 years. With the advent of antibiotics, few young patients succumb to infections, but many of them do not live beyond the age of 40.

Persons with Down's syndrome tend to show a marked deterioration in language, memory, self-care skills, and problem solving in their 30s. Postmortem studies of those with Down's syndrome over 40 have shown a high incidence of senile plaques and neurofibrillary tangles, as seen in Alzheimer's disease. Neurofibrillary tangles are known to occur in a variety of degenerative diseases, whereas senile plaques seem to be found most often in Alzheimer's disease and in Down's syndrome, suggesting that the two disorders share some degree of pathophysiology.

FRAGILE X SYNDROME

Fragile X syndrome is the second most common single cause of mental retardation. The syndrome results from a mutation on the X chromosome at what is known as the fragile site (Xq27.3). The fragile site is expressed in only some cells, and it may be absent in asymptomatic males and female carriers. Both genetic and phenotypic expressions vary widely. Fragile X syndrome is believed to occur in about 1 in every 1,000 males and 1 in every 2,000 females. The typical phenotype includes a large long head and ears, short stature, hyperextensible joints, and postpubertal macro-orchidism. The degree of mental retardation ranges from mild to severe. The behavioral profile of persons with the syndrome includes a high rate of attention-deficit/hyperactivity disorder, learning disorders, and pervasive developmental disorders, such as autistic disorder. Deficits in language function include rapid perseverative speech with abnormalities in combining words into phrases and sentences. Persons with fragile X syndrome seem to have relatively strong skills in communications and socialization, and their intellectual functions seem to decline in the pubertal period. Female carriers are often less impaired than are males with fragile X syndrome, but females can manifest the typical physical characteristics and can be mildly retarded.

PRADER-WILLI SYNDROME

Prader-Willi syndrome is postulated to be the result of a small deletion involving chromosome 15, usually occurring sporadically. Its prevalence is less than 1 in 10,000. Persons with the syndrome exhibit compulsive eating behavior and often also exhibit obesity, mental retardation, hypogonadism, small stature, hypotonia, and small hands and feet. Children with the syndrome often have oppositional and defiant behavior.

CAT-CRY (CRI-DU-CHAT) SYNDROME

Children with cat-cry syndrome are missing part of chromosome 5. They are severely retarded and show many stigmata often associated with chromosomal aberrations, such as microcephaly, low-set ears, oblique palpebral fissures, hypertelorism, and micrognathia. Laryngeal abnormalities cause the characteristic catlike cry that gave the syndrome its name. The cry gradually changes and disappears with increasing age.

OTHER CHROMOSOMAL ABNORMALITIES

Other syndromes of autosomal aberrations associated with mental retardation are much less prevalent than Down's syndrome. Various types of autosomal and sex chromosome aberration syndromes are described in Table 29–3.

Other Genetic Factors

PHENYLKETONURIA

Phenylketonuria (PKU) was first described by Ivar Asbjörn Fölling in 1934 as the paradigmatic inborn error of metabolism.

Table 29–3.   Thirty-Five Important Syndromes with Multiple Handicaps

Syndrome	Diagnostic Manifestations			Mental Retardation	Short Stature	Genetic Transmission
	Craniofacial	Skeletal	Other			
Aarskog-Scott syndrome	Hypertelorism; broad nasal bridge, anteverted nostrils, long philtrum	Small hands and feet; mild interdigital webbing; short stature	Scrotal shawl above penis		+	X-linked semidominant
Apert's syndrome (acrocephalosyndactyly)	Craniosynostosis; irregular midfacial hypoplasia; hypertelorism	Syndactyly; broad distal thumb and toe		±		Autosomal dominant
Cerebral gigantism (Sotos syndrome)	Large head; prominent forehead, narrow anterior mandible	Large hands and feet	Large size in early life; poor coordination	±		?
Cockayne's syndrome	Pinched facies; sunken eyes; thin nose; prognathism; retinal degeneration	Long limbs, with large hands and feet; flexion deformities	Hypotrichosis; photosensitivity; thin skin; diminished subcutaneous fat; impaired hearing	+	+	Autosomal recessive
Cohen syndrome	Maxillary hypoplasia with prominent central incisors	Narrow hands and feet	Hypotonia; obesity	+	±	?Autosomal recessive
Cornelia de Lange syndrome	Synophrys (continuous eyebrows); thin down-turning upper lip; long philtrum; anteverted nostrils; microcephaly	Small or malformed hands and feet; proximal thumb	Hirsutism	+	+	?
Cri-du-chat syndrome	Epicanthic folds, slanting palpebral fissures; round facial contour; hypertelorism; microcephaly	Short metacarpals or metatarsals; four-finger line in palm	Catlike cry in infancy	+	+	?
Crouzon's syndrome (craniofacial dysostosis)	Proptosis with shallow orbits; maxillary hypoplasia; craniosynostosis					Autosomal dominant
Down's syndrome	Upward slant to palpebral fissures; midface depression; epicanthic folds; Brushfield spots; brachycephaly	Short hands; clinodactyly of fifth finger; four-finger line in palm	Hypotonia; loose skin on back of neck	+	+	Trisomy 21

(continued)

Table 29-3. *(continued)*

Syndrome	Diagnostic Manifestations			Mental Retardation	Short Stature	Genetic Transmission
	Craniofacial	Skeletal	Other			
Dubowitz syndrome	Small facies; lateral displacement of inner canthi; ptosis; broad nasal bridge; sparse hair; microcephaly		Infantile eczema; high-pitched hoarse voice	±	+ +	?Autosomal recessive
Fetal alcohol syndrome	Short palpebral fissures; mid-facial hypoplasia; microcephaly		±Cardiac defect; fine motor dysfunction	+	+	
Fetal hydantoin syndrome (phenytoin)	Hypertelorism; short nose; occasional cleft lip	Hypoplastic nails, especially fifth	Cardiac defect	±	±	
Goldenhar's syndrome	Malar hypoplasia; macrostomia; micrognathia; epibulbar dermoid, lipodermoid; malformed ear with preauricular tags	±Vertebral anomalies				?
Incontinentia pigmenti	±Dental defect; deformitis of ears; ±patchy alopecia		Irregular skin pigmentation in fleck, whorl, or spidery form	±		?Dominant, X-linked ?Lethal in males
Laurence-Moon-Bardet-Biedl syndrome	Retinal pigmentation	Polydactyly; syndactyly	Obesity; seizures; hypogenitalism	+	±	Automated recessive
Linear nevus sebaceus syndrome	Nevus sebaceus, face or neck		+/−Seizures	+	±	?
Lowe's syndrome (oculocerebrorenal syndrome)	Cataract	Renal tubular dysfunction	Hypotonia	+	+	X-linked recessive
Möbius' syndrome (congenital facial diplegia)	Expressionless facies; ocular palsy	±Clubfoot; syndactyly		±	±	?
Neurofibromatosis	±Optic gliomas; acoustic neuromas	±Bone lesions; pseudarthroses	Neurofibromas; café-au-lait spots; seizures	±		Autosomal dominant
Noonan's syndrome	Webbing of posterior neck; malformed ears; hypertelorism	Pectus excavatum; cubitus valgus	Cryptorchidism; pulmonic stenosis	±	+	?
Prader-Willi syndrome	±Upward slant to palpebral fissures	Small hands and feet	Hypotonia, especially in early infancy; then polyphagia and obesity; hypogenitalism	+	+	?
Robin's syndrome	Micrognathia; glossoptosis; cleft palate, U-shaped		±Cardiac anomalies			?
Rubella	Cataract; retinal pigmentation; ocular malformations		Sensorineural deafness; patent ductus arteriosus	±	±	
Rubinstein-Taybi syndrome	Slanting palpebral fissures; maxillary hypoplasia; microcephaly	Broad thumbs and toes	Abnormal gait	+	+	?
Seckel syndrome	Facial hypoplasia; prominent nose; microcephaly	Multiple minor joint and skeletal abnormalities		+	+	Autosomal recessive
Sjögren-Larsson syndrome		Spasticity, especially of legs	Ichthyosis	+	+	Autosomal recessive
Smith-Lemli-Opitz syndrome	Anteverted nostrils, ptosis of eyelid	Syndactyly of second and third toes	Hypospadias; cryptorchidism	+	+	Autosomal recessive
Sturge-Weber syndrome	Flat hemangioma of face, most commonly trigeminal in distribution		Hemangiomas of meninges with seizures	±		?
Treacher Collins' syndrome (mandibulofacial dysostosis)	Malar and mandibular hypoplasia; downslanting palpebral fissures; defect of lower eyelid; malformed ears					Autosomal dominant
Trisomy 18	Microstomia; short palpebral fissures; malformed ears; elongated skull	Clenched hand, second finger over third; low arches on fingertips; short sternum	Cryptorchidism; congenital heart disease	+	+	Trisomy 18
Trisomy 13	Defects of eyes, nose, lips, ears, and forebrain of holoprosencephaly type	Polydactyly; narrow hyperconvex fingernails	Skin defects, posterior scalp	+	+	Trisomy 13
Tuberous sclerosis	Hamartomatous pink to brownish facial skin nodules	±Bone lesions	Seizures; intracranial calcification	±		Autosomal dominant
Waardenburg syndrome	Lateral displacement of inner canthi and puncta		Partial albinism; white forelock; heterochromia of iris; vitiligo; +/− deafness			Autosomal dominant
Williams syndrome	Full lips; small nose with anteverted nostrils; iris dysplasia	Mild hypoplasia of nails	±Hypercalcemia in infancy; supravalvular aortic stenosis	+	+	?
Zellweger syndrome (cerebrohepato-renal syndrome)	High forehead; flat facies		Hypotonia; hepatomegaly; death in early infancy			

Table from L Syzmanski, A Crocker and adapted from D W Smith: Patterns of malformation. In *Nelson Textbook of Pediatrics*, ed 11, V C Vaughan III, R J McKay, R E Behrman, editors, p 2035. Saunders, Philadelphia, 1979. Used with permission.

PKU is transmitted as a simple recessive autosomal Mendelian trait and occurs in about 1 in every 10,000 to 15,000 live births. For parents who have already had a child with PKU, the chance of having another child with PKU is one in every four to five successive pregnancies. Although the disease is reported predominantly in people of north European origin, a few cases have been described in blacks, Yemenite Jews, and Asians. The frequency among institutionalized retarded patients is about 1 percent.

The basic metabolic defect in PKU is an inability to convert phenylalanine, an essential amino acid, to paratyrosine because of the absence or the inactivity of the liver enzyme phenylalanine hydroxylase, which catalyzes the conversion. Two other types of hyperphenylalaninemia have recently been described. One is due to a deficiency of an enzyme, dihydropteridine reductase, and the other to a deficiency of a cofactor, biopterin. The first defect can be detected in fibroblasts, and biopterin can be measured in body fluids. Both of those rare disorders carry a high risk of fatality.

The majority of patients with PKU are severely retarded, but some are reported to have borderline or normal intelligence. Eczema, vomiting, and convulsions are present in about a third of all cases. Although the clinical picture varies, typical PKU children are hyperactive and exhibit erratic, unpredictable behavior, which makes them difficult to manage. They frequently have temper tantrums and often display bizarre movements of their bodies and upper extremities and twisting hand mannerisms; their behavior sometimes resembles that of autistic or schizophrenic children. Verbal and nonverbal communication is usually severely impaired or nonexistent. The children's coordination is poor, and they have many perceptual difficulties.

The disease was previously diagnosed based on a urine test: phenylpyruvic acid in the urine reacts with ferric chloride solution to yield a vivid green color. However, that test has its limitations, as it may not detect the presence of phenylpyruvic acid in urine before the baby is 5 or 6 weeks old; it may give positive responses with other aminoacidurias. Currently, a more reliable screening test that is widely used is the Guthrie inhibition assay, which uses a bacteriological procedure to detect blood phenylalanine.

Early diagnosis is important, as a low-phenylalanine diet, in use since 1955, significantly improves both behavior and developmental progress. The best results seem to be obtained with early diagnosis and the start of dietary treatment before the child is 6 months of age.

Dietary treatment, however, is not without risk. Phenylalanine is an essential amino acid, and its omission from the diet may lead to such severe complications as anemia, hypoglycemia, edema, and even death. Dietary treatment of PKU should be continued indefinitely. Children who receive a diagnosis before the age of 3 months and are placed on an optimal dietary regimen may have normal intelligence. For untreated older children and adolescents with PKU, a low-phenylalanine diet does not influence the level of mental retardation. However, the diet does decrease their irritability and abnormal electroencephalogram (EEG) changes and does increase their social responsiveness and attention span.

The parents of PKU children and some of the children's normal siblings are heterozygous carriers. The disease can be detected by a phenylalanine tolerance test, which may be important in genetic counseling.

RETT'S DISORDER

Rett's disorder is hypothesized to be an X-linked dominant mental retardation syndrome that is degenerative and affects only females. Andreas Rett reported on 22 girls with serious progressive neurological disability in 1966. Deterioration in communications skills, motor behavior, and social functioning starts at $1\frac{1}{2}$ years of age. Autisticlike symptoms are common, as are ataxia, facial grimacing, teeth grinding, and loss of speech. Intermittent hyperventilation and a disorganized breathing pattern are characteristic while the child is awake. Stereotypical hand movements, including handwringing, are typical. Progressive gait disturbance, scoliosis, and seizures occur. Severe spasticity is usually present by middle childhood. Cerebral atrophy occurs with decreased pigmentation of the substantia nigra, suggesting abnormalities of the dopaminergic nigrostriatal system. Chapter 33 discusses the disorder further.

NEUROFIBROMATOSIS

Also called von Recklinghausen's disease, neurofibromatosis is the most common of the neurocutaneous syndromes caused by a single dominant gene. It may be inherited, or it may be a new mutation. It occurs in about 1 in 5,000 births. The disorder is characterized by café-au-lait spots on the skin and neurofibromas, including optic gliomas and acoustic neuromas, caused by abnormal cell migration. Mild mental retardation is present in up to one third of persons with the disease.

TUBEROUS SCLEROSIS

Tuberous sclerosis is the second most common of the neurocutaneous syndromes; a progressive mental retardation is present in up to two thirds of all affected persons. It occurs in about 1 in 15,000 persons and is caused by autosomal dominant transmission. Seizures are present in all the patients who are mentally retarded and in two thirds of those who are not mentally retarded. Infantile spasms may occur as early as 6 months. The phenotypic presentation includes adenoma sebaceum and ash-leaf spots that can be identified with a slit lamp. The rate of autism is higher than the intellectual impairment would lead one to expect.

LESCH-NYHAN SYNDROME

Lesch-Nyhan syndrome is a rare disorder caused by a deficiency of an enzyme involved in purine metabolism. It is associated with severe compulsive self-mutilation by biting of the mouth and the fingers. It is an X-linked disorder and presents with mental retardation, microcephaly, seizures, choreoathetosis, and spasticity. The disorder is another example of a genetically determined syndrome in which a specific behavioral pattern is predictable.

ADRENOLEUKODYSTROPHY

The most common of several disorders of sudanophilic cerebral sclerosis, adrenoleukodystrophy is characterized by diffuse demyelination of the cerebral white matter resulting in visual and intellectual impairment, seizures, spasticity, and progression to death. Adrenocortical insufficiency accompanies the cerebral degeneration in adrenoleukodystrophy. The disorder is transmitted by a sex-linked gene on the distal end of the long arm of the X chromosome. The clinical onset is generally between 5 and 8 years, with early seizures, disturbances in gait, and mild intellectual impairment. Abnormal pigmentation reflecting adrenal insufficiency sometimes precedes the neurological symptoms, and attacks of crying are common. Spastic contractures, ataxia, and disturbances of swallowing are common. Although the course is often rapidly progressive, some patients may have a relapsing and remitting course.

MAPLE SYRUP URINE DISEASE

The clinical symptoms of maple syrup urine disease appear during the first week of life. The infant deteriorates rapidly and has decerebrate rigidity, seizures, respiratory irregularity, and hypoglycemia. If untreated, most patients die in the first months of life, and the survivors are severely retarded. Some variants have been reported with transient ataxia and only mild retardation.

Treatment follows the general principles established for PKU and consists of a diet very low in the three involved amino acids—leucine, isoleucine, and valine.

OTHER ENZYME DEFICIENCY DISORDERS

Several enzyme deficiency disorders associated with mental retardation have been identified, and still more diseases are being added as new discoveries are made. Some of them include Hartnup disease, galactosemia, and glycogen-storage disease. Thirty important disorders with inborn errors of metabolism, hereditary transmission patterns, defective enzymes, clinical signs, and relation to mental retardation are listed in Table 29–4.

Prenatal Factors

Important prerequisites for the overall development of the fetus include the mother's physical, psychological, and nutritional health during pregnancy. Maternal chronic illnesses and conditions affecting the normal development of the fetus's central nervous system include uncontrolled diabetes, anemia, emphysema, hypertension, and long-term use of alcohol and narcotic substances. Maternal infections during pregnancy, especially viral infections, have been known to cause fetal damage and mental retardation. The degree of fetal damage depends on such variables as the type of viral infection, the gestational age of the fetus, and the severity of the illness. Although many infectious diseases have been reported to affect the fetus's central nervous system, the following medical disorders have been definitely identified as high-risk conditions for mental retardation.

RUBELLA (GERMAN MEASLES)

Rubella has replaced syphilis as the major cause of congenital malformations and mental retardation caused by maternal infection. The children of affected mothers may present a number of abnormalities, including congenital heart disease, mental retardation, cataracts, deafness, microcephaly, and microphthalmia. Timing is crucial, as the extent and the frequency of the complications are inversely related to the duration of the pregnancy at the time of the maternal infection. When mothers are infected in the first trimester of pregnancy, 10 to 15 percent of the children are affected, but the incidence rises to almost 50 percent when the infection occurs in the first month of pregnancy. The situation is often complicated by subclinical forms of maternal infection, which often go undetected. Immunization can prevent maternal rubella.

CYTOMEGALIC INCLUSION DISEASE

Often, cytomegalic inclusion disease remains dormant in the mother. Some children are stillborn, and others have jaundice, microcephaly, hepatosplenomegaly, and radiographic findings of intracerebral calcification. Children with mental retardation from the disease frequently have cerebral calcification, microcephaly, or hydrocephalus. Positive findings on throat and urine cultures of the virus and the recovery of inclusion-bearing cells in the urine confirm the diagnosis.

SYPHILIS

Syphilis in pregnant women used to be the main cause of various neuropathological changes in their offspring, including mental retardation. Today, the incidence of syphilitic complications of pregnancy fluctuates with the incidence of syphilis in the general population. Some recent alarming statistics from several major cities in the United States indicate that there is still no room for complacency.

TOXOPLASMOSIS

Toxoplasmosis can be transmitted by the mother to the fetus. It causes mild or severe mental retardation and, in severe cases, hydrocephalus, seizures, microcephaly, and chorioretinitis.

HERPES SIMPLEX

The herpes simplex virus can be transmitted transplacentally, although the most common mode of infection is during birth. Microcephaly, mental retardation, intracranial calcification, and ocular abnormalities may result.

ACQUIRED IMMUNE DEFICIENCY SYNDROME (AIDS)

Many fetuses of mothers with AIDS never come to term because of stillbirth or spontaneous abortion. In those who are born infected with the human immunodeficiency virus (HIV), up to half have progressive encephalopathy, mental retardation, and seizures within the first year of life. Children born infected with HIV often live only a few years.

FETAL ALCOHOL SYNDROME

Fetal alcohol syndrome consists of mental retardation and a typical phenotypic picture of facial dysmorphism that includes hypertelorism, microcephaly, short palpebral fissures, inner epicanthal folds, and a short turned-up nose. Often, the affected children have learning disorders and attention-deficit/hyperactivity disorder. Cardiac defects are also frequent. The entire syndrome occurs in up to 15 percent of babies born to women who regularly ingest large amounts of alcohol. Babies born to women who consume alcohol regularly during pregnancy have a high incidence of attention-deficit/hyperactivity disorder, learning disorders, and mental retardation without the facial dysmorphism.

PRENATAL SUBSTANCE EXPOSURE

Prenatal exposure to opiates, such as heroin, often results in an infant who is small for its gestational age, with a head circumference below the 10th percentile and withdrawal symptoms manifested within the first two days of life. The withdrawal symptoms in the infant include irritability, hypertonia, tremor, vomiting, a high-pitched cry, and an abnormal sleep pattern. Seizures are unusual, but the withdrawal syndrome can be life-threatening to the infant if it is untreated. Diazepam (Valium),

Table 29-4.   Thirty Important Disorders with Inborn Errors of Metabolism

Disorder	Hereditary Transmission*	Enzyme Defect	Prenatal Diagnosis	Mental Retardation	Clinical Signs
I. LIPID METABOLISM					
Niemann-Pick disease					
Group A, infantile					
Group B, adult	A.R.	Sphingomyelinase	+	±	Hepatosplenomegaly
Groups C and D, intermediate		Unknown	−	+	Pulmonary infiltration
Infantile Gaucher's disease	A.R.	β-Glucosidase	+	±	Hepatosplenomegaly, pseudobulbar palsy
Tay-Sachs disease	A.R.	Hexosaminidase A	+	+	Macular changes, seizures, spasticity
Generalized gangliosidosis	A.R.	β-Galactosidase	+	+	Hepatosplenomegaly, bone changes
Krabbe's disease	A.R.	Galactocerebroside β-Galactosidase	+	+	Stiffness, seizures
Metachromatic leukodystrophy	A.R.	Cerebroside sulfatase	+	+	Stiffness, developmental failure
Wolman's disease	A.R.	Acid lipase	+	−	Hepatosplenomegaly, adrenal calcification, vomiting, diarrhea
Farber's lipogranulomatosis	A.R.	Acid ceramidase	+	+	Hoarseness, arthropathy, subcutaneous nodules
Fabry's disease	X.R.	α-Galactosidase	+	−	Angiokeratomas, renal failure
II. MUCOPOLYSACCHARIDE METABOLISM					
Hurler's syndrome MPS I	A.R.	Iduronidase	+	+	
Hunter's disease II	X.R.	Iduronate sulfatase	+	+	
Sanfilippo's syndrome III	A.R.	Various sulfatases (types A–D)	+	+	Varying degrees of bone changes, hepatosplenomegaly, joint restriction, etc.
Morquio's disease IV	A.R.	N-Acetylgalactosamine-6-sulfate sulfatase	+	−	
Maroteaux-Lamy syndrome VI	A.R.	Arylsulfatase B	+	±	
III. OLIGOSACCHARIDE AND GLYCOPROTEIN METABOLISM					
I-cell disease	A.R.	Glycoprotein N-acetylglucosaminyl-phosphotransferase	+	+	Hepatomegaly, bone changes, swollen gingivae
Mannosidosis	A.R.	Mannosidase	+	+	Hepatomegaly, bone changes, facial coarsening
Fucosidosis	A.R.	Fucosidase	+	+	Same as above
IV. AMINO ACID METABOLISM					
Phenylketonuria	A.R.	Phenylalanine hydroxylase	−	+	Eczema, blonde hair, musty odor
Homocystinuria	A.R.	Cystathionine β-synthetase	+	+	Ectopia lentis, Marfanlike phenotype, cardiovascular anomalies
Tyrosinosis	A.R.	Tyrosine amine transaminase	−	+	Hyperkeratotic skin lesions, conjunctivitis
Maple syrup urine disease	A.R.	Branched chain ketoacid decarboxylase	+	+	Recurrent ketoacidosis
Methylmalonic acidemia	A.R.	Methylmalonyl-CoA mutase	+	+	Recurrent ketoacidosis, hepatomegaly, growth retardation
Propionicacidemia	A.R.	Propionyl-CoA carboxylase	+	+	Same as above
Nonketotic hyperglycinemia	A.R.	Glycine cleavage enzyme	+	+	Seizures
Urea cycle disorders	Mostly A.R.	Urea cycle enzymes	+	+	Recurrent acute encephalopathy, vomiting
Hartnup disease	A.R.	Renal transport disorder	−	−	None consistent
V. OTHERS					
Galactosemia	A.R.	Galactose-1-phosphate uridyltransferase	+	+	Hepatomegaly, cataracts, ovarian failure
Wilson's hepatolenticular degeneration	A.R.	Unknown factor in copper metabolism	−	±	Liver disease, Kayser-Fleischer ring, neurological problems
Menkes's kinky-hair disease	X.R.	Same as above	+	−	Abnormal hair, cerebral degeneration
Lesch-Nyhan syndrome	A.R.	Hypoxanthine guanine phosphoribosyltransferase	+	+	Behavioral abnormalities

* A.R. = autosomal recessive transmission. X.R. = X-linked recessive transmission.
Table by L Syzmanski, A Crocker and adapted from J G Leroy: Heredity, development, and behavior. In *Developmental-Behavioral Pediatrics*, M D Levine, W B Carey, A C Crocker, editors, p 315. Saunders, Philadelphia, 1983. Used with permission.

phenobarbital (Luminal), chlorpromazine (Thorazine), and paregoric have been used to treat neonatal opiate and opioid withdrawal. The long-term sequelae of prenatal opiate exposure are not fully known; the children's developmental milestones and intellectual functions may be within the normal range, but they have an increased risk for impulsivity and behavioral problems.

Infants exposed to cocaine prenatally are at high risk for low birth weight and premature delivery. In the early neonatal period, they may have transient neurological and behavioral abnormalities, including abnormal results on electroencephalograms (EEGs), tachycardia, poor feeding patterns, irritability, and excessive drowsiness. The physiological and behavioral abnormalities are a response to the cocaine, rather than a withdrawal reaction, since the children may excrete the cocaine for up to a week postnatally.

COMPLICATIONS OF PREGNANCY

Toxemia of pregnancy and uncontrolled maternal diabetes present hazards to the fetus and sometimes result in mental retardation. Maternal malnutrition during pregnancy often results in prematurity and other obstetrical complications. Vaginal hemorrhage, placenta previa, premature separation of the placenta, and prolapse of the cord may damage the fetal brain by causing anoxia.

The potential teratogenic effect of pharmacological agents administered during pregnancy was widely publicized after the thalidomide tragedy (the drug produced a high percentage of deformed babies when given to pregnant women). So far, except for metabolites used in cancer chemotherapy, no usual dosages are known to damage the fetus's central nervous system, but caution and restraint in prescribing drugs to pregnant women are certainly indicated. The use of lithium (Eskalith) during pregnancy was recently implicated in some congenital malformations, especially of the cardiovascular system (for example, Ebstein's anomaly).

Perinatal Factors

Some evidence indicates that premature infants and infants with low birth weight are at high risk for neurological and intellectual impairments manifested during their school years. Infants who sustain intracranial hemorrhages or evidence of cerebral ischemia are especially vulnerable to cognitive abnormalities. The degree of neurodevelopmental impairment generally correlates with the severity of the intracranial hemorrhage. Socioeconomic deprivation can also affect the adaptive function of those vulnerable infants. Early intervention may improve their cognitive, language, and perceptual abilities.

Acquired Childhood Disorders

Occasionally, a child's developmental status changes dramatically as a result of a specific disease or physical trauma. In retrospect, it is sometimes difficult to ascertain the full picture of the child's developmental progress before the insult, but the adverse effects on the child's development or skills are apparent after the insult.

INFECTION

The most serious infections affecting cerebral integrity are encephalitis and meningitis. Measles encephalitis has been vir-

tually eliminated by the universal use of measles vaccine, and the incidences of other bacterial infections of the central nervous system have been markedly reduced with antibacterial agents. Viral organisms cause most episodes of encephalitis. Sometimes a clinician must retrospectively consider a probable encephalitic component in a past obscure illness with high fever and lasting encephalopathy. Meningitis that was diagnosed late, even when followed by antibiotic treatment, can seriously affect a child's cognitive development. Thrombotic and purulent intracranial phenomena secondary to septicemia are rarely seen today except in small infants.

HEAD TRAUMA

The best-known causes of head injury in children that produce developmental handicaps, including seizures, are motor vehicle accidents. However, more head injuries are caused by household accidents, such as falls from tables, from open windows, and on stairways. Child abuse is also a cause of head injury.

OTHER ISSUES

Brain damage from cardiac arrest during anesthesia is rare. One cause of complete or partial brain damage is asphyxia associated with near drowning. Long-term exposure to lead is a well-established cause of compromised intelligence and learning skills. Intracranial tumors of various types and origins, surgery, and chemotherapy can also adversely affect brain function.

Environmental and Sociocultural Factors

Mild retardation is significantly prevalent among persons of culturally deprived, low socioeconomic groups, and many of their relatives are affected with similar degrees of mental retardation. No biological causes have been identified in those cases.

Children in poor, socioculturally deprived families are subjected to potentially pathogenic and developmentally adverse conditions. Poor medical care and poor maternal nutrition compromise the prenatal environment. Teenage pregnancies are frequent and are associated with obstetrical complications, prematurity, and low birth weight. Poor postnatal medical care, malnutrition, exposure to such toxic substances as lead, and physical traumata are frequent. Family instability, frequent moves, and multiple but inadequate caretakers are common. Furthermore, the mothers in such families are often poorly educated and ill-equipped to give the child appropriate stimulation.

Another unresolved issue is the influence of severe parental mental disorders. Such disorders may adversely affect the child's care and stimulation and other aspects of the environment, thus putting the child at a developmental risk. Children of parents with mood disorders and schizophrenia are known to be at risk for those and related disorders. Recent studies indicate a high prevalence of motor skills disorder and other developmental disorders among the children but not necessarily mental retardation.

DIAGNOSIS

The diagnosis of mental retardation can be made after the history, a standardized intellectual assessment, and a measure of adaptive function indicate that the child's current behavior is significantly below the expected level. The diagnosis itself does not specify either the cause or the prognosis. A history and a psychiatric interview are useful in obtaining a longitudinal picture of the child's development and functioning, and examination of physical stigmata, neurological abnormalities, and laboratory tests can be used to ascertain the cause and the prognosis.

History

The history is most often taken from the parents or the caretaker, with particular attention to the mother's pregnancy, labor, and delivery; the presence of a family history of mental retardation; consanguinity of the parents; and hereditary disorders. As part of the history, the clinician assesses the parents' sociocultural background, the home's emotional climate, and the parents' intellectual functioning.

Psychiatric Interview

Two factors are of paramount importance when interviewing the patient: the interviewer's attitude and the manner of communication with the patient. The interviewer should not be guided by the patient's mental age, as it cannot fully characterize the person. A mildly retarded adult with a mental age of 10 is not a 10-year-old child. When addressed as if they were children, some retarded persons become justifiably insulted, angry, and uncooperative. Passive and dependent persons, alternatively, may assume the child's role that they think is expected of them. In both cases, no valid diagnostic data can be obtained.

The patient's verbal abilities, including receptive and expressive language, should be assessed as soon as possible by observing the verbal and nonverbal communication between the caretakers and the patient and from the history. The clinician often finds it helpful to see the patient and the caretakers together. If the patient uses sign language, the caretaker may have to stay during the interview as an interpreter.

Retarded persons have the lifelong experience of failing in many areas, and they may be anxious before seeing an interviewer. The interviewer and the caretaker should attempt to give such patients a clear, supportive, and concrete explanation of the diagnostic process, particularly those patients with sufficient receptive language. Giving patients the impression that their bad behavior is the cause of the referral should be avoided. Support and praise should be offered in language appropriate to the patient's age and understanding. Leading questions should be avoided, as retarded persons may be suggestible and wish to please others. Subtle directiveness, structure, and reinforcements may be necessary to keep them on the task or topic.

The patient's control over motility patterns should be ascertained, and clinical evidence of distractibility and distortions in perception and memory may be evaluated. The use of speech, reality testing, and the ability to generalize from experiences are important to note.

The nature and the maturity of the patient's defenses—particularly exaggerated or self-defeating uses of avoidance, repression, denial, introjection, and isolation—should be observed. Sublimation potential, frustration tolerance, and impulse control—especially over motor, aggressive, and sexual drives—should be assessed. Also important are self-image and its role in the development of self-confidence, as well as the assessment of tenacity, persistence, curiosity, and the willingness to explore the unknown.

In general, the psychiatric examination of the retarded patient should reveal how the patient has coped with the stages of development. As for failure or regression, the clinician can develop a personality profile that allows the logical planning of management and remedial approaches.

Physical Examination

Various parts of the body may have certain characteristics that are commonly found in mentally retarded persons and have prenatal causes. For example, the configuration and the size of the head offer clues to a variety of conditions, such as microcephaly, hydrocephalus, and Down's syndrome. The patient's face may have some of the stigmata of mental retardation, which greatly facilitate the diagnosis. Such facial signs are hypertelorism, a flat nasal bridge, prominent eyebrows, epicanthal folds, corneal opacities, retinal changes, low-set and small or misshapen ears, a protruding tongue, and a disturbance in dentition. Facial expression, such as a dull appearance, may be misleading and should not be relied on without other supporting evidence. The color and the texture of the skin and the hair, a high-arched palate, the size of the thyroid gland, and the size of the child and his or her trunk and extremities are further areas to be explored. The circumference of the head should be measured as part of the clinical investigation. The clinician should bear in mind during the examination that mentally retarded children, particularly those with associated behavioral problems, are at increased risk for child abuse.

Dermatoglyphics may offer another diagnostic tool, as uncommon ridge patterns and flexion creases are often found in retarded persons. Abnormal dermatoglyphics may be found in chromosomal disorders and in patients who were infected prenatally with rubella. Table 29–3 lists the multiple handicaps associated with the syndromes discussed.

Neurological Examination

Sensory impairments occur frequently among mentally retarded persons; for example, up to 10 percent of mentally retarded persons are hearing-impaired at a rate that is four times that of the general population. A variety of other neurological impairments are also high in mentally retarded persons; seizure disorders occur in about 10 percent of all mentally retarded persons and in one third of persons with severe mental retardation.

When neurological abnormalities are present, their incidence and severity generally rise in direct proportion to the degree of retardation. However, many severely retarded children have no neurological abnormalities; conversely, about 25 percent of all children with cerebral palsy have normal intelligence.

Disturbances in motor areas are manifested in abnormalities of muscle tone (spasticity or hypotonia), reflexes (hyperreflexia), and involuntary movements (choreoathetosis). A smaller degree of disability is revealed in clumsiness and poor coordination.

Sensory disturbances may include hearing difficulties, ranging from cortical deafness to mild hearing deficits. Visual disturbances may range from blindness to disturbances of spatial concepts, design recognition, and concept of body image.

The infants with the poorest prognoses are those who manifest a combination of inactivity, general hypotonia, and exaggerated response to stimuli. In older children, hyperactivity, short attention span, distractibility, and a low frustration tolerance are often signs of brain damage.

In general, the younger the child is at the time of investigation, the more caution is indicated in predicting future ability, as the recovery potential of the infantile brain is very good. Observing the child's development at regular intervals is probably the most reliable approach.

Skull X-rays are usually taken routinely but are illuminating only in a relatively few conditions, such as craniosynostosis, hydrocephalus, and others that result in intracranial calcifications (for example, toxoplasmosis, tuberous sclerosis, cerebral angiomatosis, and hypoparathyroidism). Computed tomography (CT) scans and magnetic resonance imaging (MRI) have become important tools for uncovering central nervous system pathology associated with mental retardation. The occasional findings of internal hydrocephalus, cortical atrophy, or porencephaly in a severely retarded, brain-damaged child are not considered important to the general picture.

An EEG is best interpreted with caution in cases of mental retardation. The exceptions are patients with hypsarhythmia and grand mal seizures, in whom the EEG may help establish the diagnosis and suggest treatment. In most other conditions a diffuse cerebral disorder produces nonspecific EEG changes, characterized by slow frequencies with bursts of spikes and sharp or blunt wave complexes. The confusion over the significance of the EEG in the diagnosis of mental retardation is best illustrated by the reports of frequent EEG abnormalities in Down's syndrome, which range from 25 percent to the majority of patients examined.

Laboratory Tests

Laboratory tests used in cases of mental retardation include examination of the urine and the blood for metabolic disorders. Enzymatic abnormalities in chromosomal disorders, particularly Down's syndrome, promise to become useful diagnostic tools. The determination of the karyotype in a suitable genetic laboratory is indicated whenever a chromosomal disorder is suspected.

Amniocentesis, in which a small amount of amniotic fluid is removed from the amniotic cavity transabdominally between the 14th and the 16th weeks of gestation, has been useful in diagnosing various infant chromosomal abnormalities, especially Down's syndrome. Amniotic fluid cells, mostly fetal in origin, are cultured for cytogenetic and biochemical studies. Many serious hereditary disorders can be predicted with amniocentesis, and therapeutic abortion is the only method of prevention. Amniocentesis is recommended for all pregnant women over the age of 29. Fortunately, most chromosomal anomalies occur only once in a family.

Chronic villi sampling (CVS) is a new screening technique to determine fetal abnormalities. It is done at 8 to 10 weeks of gestation, which is six weeks earlier than amniocentesis, is done. The results are available in a short time (hours or days), and, if the result is abnormal, the decision to terminate the pregnancy can be made within the first trimester. The procedure has a miscarriage risk of between 2 and 5 percent.

Hearing and Speech Evaluations

Hearing and speech evaluations should be done routinely. The development of speech may be the most reliable criterion in investigating mental retardation. Various hearing impairments are often present in mentally retarded persons: however, the impairments sometimes simulate mental retardation. Unfortunately, the commonly used methods of hearing and speech evaluation require the patient's cooperation and, thus, are often unreliable in severely retarded persons.

Psychological Assessment

Examining clinicians may use several screening instruments for infants and toddlers. As in many areas of mental retardation, the controversy over the predictive value of infant psychological tests is heated. Some report the correlation of abnormalities during infancy with later abnormal functioning as very low, and others report it as very high. However, the correlation rises in direct proportion to the age of the child at the time of the developmental examination.

Copying geometric figures, the Goodenough Draw-a-Person Test, the Kohs Block Test, and geometric puzzles—all may be used as quick screening tests of visual-motor coordination.

Psychological testing, performed by an experienced psychologist, is a standard part of a evaluation for mental retardation. The Gesell, Bayley, and Cattell tests are most commonly used with infants. For children the Stanford-Binet and the Wechsler Intelligence Scale for Children-Revised (WISC-R, WISC-3) are the most widely used in this country. Both tests have been criticized for penalizing the culturally deprived child, for being culturally biased, for testing mainly the potential for academic achievement and not for adequate social functioning, and for their unreliability in children with I.Q.s of less than 50. Some people have tried to overcome the language barrier of mentally retarded patients by devising picture vocabulary tests, of which the Peabody Vocabulary Test is the most widely used.

The tests often found useful in detecting brain damage are the Bender Gestalt and the Benton Visual Retention tests. Those tests are also useful for mildly retarded children. In addition, a psychological evaluation should assess perceptual, motor, linguistic, and cognitive abilities. Information about motivational, emotional, and interpersonal factors is also important.

CLINICAL FEATURES

Mild Mental Retardation

Mild mental retardation may not be diagnosed until the affected children enter school, since their social skills and communication may be adequate in the preschool years. As they get older, however, such cognitive deficits as poor ability to abstract and egocentric thinking may distinguish them from others of their age. Although mildly retarded persons can function academically at the high elementary level and their vocational skills are sufficient to support themselves in some cases, social assimilation may be difficult. Communication deficits, poor self-esteem, and dependence may contribute to their relative lack of social spontaneity. Some mildly retarded persons may fall into relationships with peers who exploit their shortcomings. Usually, persons with mild mental retardation can achieve some degree of social and vocational success in a supportive environment.

Moderate Mental Retardation

Moderate mental retardation is likely to be diagnosed at a younger age than is mild mental retardation because communication skills develop more slowly in moderately retarded persons, and their social isolation may begin in the elementary school years. Although academic achievement is usually limited to the mid-elementary level, moderately retarded children benefit from individual attention focused on the development of self-help skills. Children with moderate mental retardation are aware of their deficits and often feel alienated from their peers and frustrated by their limitations. They continue to require a relatively high level of supervision but can become competent at occupational tasks set in supportive conditions.

Severe Mental Retardation

Severe mental retardation is generally obvious in the preschool years, since the affected children's speech is minimal, and their motor development is poor. Some language development may occur in the school-age years; by adolescence, if language is poor, nonverbal forms of communication have evolved. The inability to fully articulate needs may reinforce the physical means of communicating. Behavioral approaches can help promote some degree of self-care, although persons with severe mental retardation generally need extensive supervision.

Profound Mental Retardation

Children with profound mental retardation require constant supervision and are severely limited in communication and motor skills. By adulthood, some speech development may be present, and simple self-help skills may be acquired. Even in adulthood, nursing care is needed.

Other Features

Surveys have identified a number of clinical features that occur with greater frequency in mentally retarded persons than in the general population. The features, which may occur in isolation or as part of a mental disorder, include hyperactivity, low frustration tolerance, aggression, affective instability, repetitive stereotypic motor behaviors, and self-injurious behaviors of various kinds. Self-injurious behaviors may be more frequent and more intense with increasingly severe mental retardation. It is often difficult to decide whether those clinical features are comorbid mental disorders or direct sequelae of the developmental limitations imposed by mental retardation.

COMORBID PSYCHOPATHOLOGY

Prevalence

Since the 1980s, several epidemiological surveys have indicated that the rates of other mental disorders in children and adults with mental retardation range between one third and two thirds, rates that are several times higher than those in nonmentally retarded community samples. The prevalence of psychopathology seems to be correlated with the degree of mental retardation; the more severe the mental retardation, the higher the risk for other mental disorders.

The types of mental disorders appear to run the gamut of those seen in nonmentally retarded persons, including mood disorders, schizophrenia, attention-deficit/hyperactivity disorder, and conduct disorder. Persons with severe mental retardation have a particularly high rate of autistic disorder and pervasive developmental disorders. About 2 to 3 percent of mentally retarded persons meet the criteria for schizophrenia; that is several times higher than the rate for the general population. Up to 50 percent of mentally retarded children and adults had a mood disorder when such instruments as the Kiddie Schedule for Affective Disorders and Schizophrenia, the Beck Depression Inventory, and the Children's Depression Inventory were used in pilot studies. Since those instruments have not been standardized within the mentally retarded population, those findings must be considered preliminary.

Highly prevalent psychiatric symptoms that can occur in mentally retarded persons outside the context of a mental disorder include hyperactivity and short attention span, self-injurious behaviors (for example, head banging and self-biting), and repetitive stereotypical behaviors (hand flapping and toe walking).

Personality styles and traits in mentally retarded persons are not unique to them. However, negative self-image, low self-esteem, poor frustration tolerance, interpersonal dependence, and a rigid problem-solving style are overrepresented in mentally retarded persons. Specific causal syndromes seen in mental retardation may also predispose the affected persons to various types of psychopathology.

Risk Factors

NEUROLOGICAL IMPAIRMENT

Reports indicate that the risk for psychopathology increases in a variety of neurological conditions, such as seizure disorders. Rates of psychopathology increase with the severity of mental retardation, indicating an increase in neurological impairment as intellectual impairment increases.

GENETIC SYNDROMES

Some evidence indicates that genetically based syndromes—such as fragile X syndrome, Prader-Willi syndrome, and Down's syndrome—are associated with specific behavioral manifestations.

Persons with fragile X syndrome are known to have extremely high rates (up to three fourths of those studied) of attention-deficit/hyperactivity disorders. High rates of aberrant interpersonal behavior and language function often meet the criteria for autistic disorder and avoidant personality disorder.

Prader-Willi syndrome is almost always associated with compulsive eating disturbances, hyperphagia, and obesity. Children with the syndrome have been described as oppositional and defiant. Socialization is an area of weakness, especially in coping skills. Externalizing behavior problems—such as temper tantrums, irritability, and arguing—seem to be heightened in adolescence.

In Down's syndrome, language function is a relative weakness, whereas sociability and social skills, such as interpersonal cooperation and conformity with social conventions, are relative strengths. Most studies have noted muted affect in children with Down's syndrome relative to nonretarded children of the same mental age. Persons with Down's syndrome also manifest deficiencies in scanning the environment and are likely to focus on a single stimulus, making it difficult for them to notice environmental changes and to communicate. A variety of mental disorders occur in persons with Down's syndrome, but the rates appear to be lower than those in other mental retardation syndromes, especially of autistic disorder.

PSYCHOSOCIAL FACTORS

A negative self-image and poor self-esteem are common features of mildly and moderately mentally retarded persons, who are well aware of being different from others. They experience repeated failure and disappointment in not meeting their parents' and society's expectations and of progressively falling behind their peers and even their younger siblings. Communication difficulties further increase their vulnerability to feelings of ineptness and frustration. Inappropriate behaviors, such as withdrawal, are common. The perpetual sense of isolation and inadequacy has been linked to feelings of anxiety, anger, dysphoria, and depression.

DIFFERENTIAL DIAGNOSIS

By definition, mental retardation must begin before the age of 18. A mentally retarded child has to cope with so many difficult social and academic situations that maladaptive patterns often form, complicating the diagnostic process. However, vulnerable children who are exposed to perpetual environmental stressors may not develop at the expected rate.

Children who come from deprived homes that provide inadequate stimulation may manifest motor and mental retardation that can be reversed if an enriched, stimulating environment is provided in early childhood. A number of sensory handicaps, especially deafness and blindness, may be mistaken for mental retardation if, during testing, no compensation for the handicap is allowed. Speech deficits and cerebral palsy often make a child seem retarded, even in the presence of borderline or normal intelligence.

Chronic, debilitating diseases of any kind may depress the child's functioning in all areas. Convulsive disorders may give an impression of mental retardation, especially in the presence of uncontrolled seizures.

Chronic brain syndromes may result in isolated handicaps—failure to read (alexia), failure to write (agraphia), failure to communicate (aphasia), and several other handicaps—that may exist in a person of normal and even superior intelligence.

Children with learning disorders, which can coexist with mental retardation, experience a delay or a failure of development in a specific area, such as reading or mathematics, but the children develop normally in other areas. In contrast, children with mental retardation show general delays in most areas of development.

Mental retardation and pervasive developmental disorders often coexist; 70 to 75 percent of those with pervasive developmental disorders have an I.Q. of less than 70. A pervasive developmental disorder results in the distortion of the timing, the rate, and the sequence of many basic psychological functions necessary for social development. Because of their general level of functioning, children with pervasive developmental disorders have more problems with social relatedness and have more deviant language than do those with mental retardation. In mental retardation, generalized delays in development are present, and mentally retarded children behave in some ways as though they were passing through an earlier normal developmental stage, rather than with completely aberrant behavior.

A most difficult differential diagnostic problem concerns children with severe mental retardation, brain damage, autistic disorder, schizophrenia with childhood onset, or, according to some, Heller's disease. The confusion stems from the fact that details of the child's early history are often unavailable or unreliable. In addition, when the children are evaluated, many with the conditions display similar bizarre and stereotyped behavior—mutism, echolalia, or functioning on a retarded level. By the time the children are usually seen, it does not matter from a practical point of view whether the child's retardation is secondary to a primary early infantile autistic disorder or schizophrenia or whether the personality and behavioral distortions are secondary to brain damage or mental retardation. When ego functions are delayed in development or are atrophic because of other reasons, the physician must first concentrate on overcoming the child's unrelatedness. A relationship with the child must be established before remedial education measures can be successful.

Children under the age of 18 years who meet the diagnostic criteria for dementia and who manifest an I.Q. of less than 70 are given the diagnostics of dementia and mental retardation. Persons whose I.Q.s drop to less than 70 after the age of 18 years and who have new onsets of cognitive disorders are not given the diagnosis of mental retardation but receive only the diagnosis of dementia.

COURSE AND PROGNOSIS

In most cases of mental retardation, the underlying intellectual impairment does not improve, yet the affected person's level of adaptation can be positively influenced by an enriched and supportive environment. As in persons who are not mentally retarded, the more comorbid mental disorders occur, the more guarded is the overall prognosis. When clear-cut mental disorders are superimposed on mental retardation, standard treatments for the comorbid mental disorders are often beneficial. However, there is still a lack of clarity about the classification of such aberrant behaviors as hyperactivity, emotional lability, and social dysfunction; are they additional psychiatric symptoms or direct sequelae of the mental retardation? In general, persons with mild and moderate mental retardation have the most flexibility in adapting to various environmental conditions.

TREATMENT

Mental retardation is associated with several heterogeneous groups of disorders and many psychosocial factors. The best treatment of mental retardation is primary, secondary, and tertiary prevention.

Primary Prevention

Primary prevention concerns actions taken to eliminate or reduce the conditions that lead to the development of the disorders associated with mental retardation. Such measures include (1) education to increase the general public's knowledge and awareness of mental retardation, (2) continuing efforts of health professionals to ensure and upgrade public health policies, (3) legislation to provide optimal maternal and child health care, and (4) the eradication of the known disorders associated with central nervous system damage. Family and genetic counseling helps reduce the incidence of mental retardation in a family with a history of a genetic disorder associated with mental retardation. For the children and the mothers of low socioeconomic status, proper prenatal and postnatal medical care and various supplementary enrichment programs and social service assistance may help minimize the medical and psychosocial complications.

Secondary and Tertiary Prevention

Once a disorder associated with mental retardation has been identified, the disorder should be treated to shorten the course of the illness (secondary prevention) and to minimize the sequelae or consequent handicaps (tertiary prevention).

Hereditary metabolic and endocrine disorders, such as PKU and hypothyroidism, can be effectively treated in an early stage by dietary control or hormone replacement therapy.

Mentally retarded children frequently have emotional and behavioral difficulties requiring psychiatric treatment. Those children's limited cognitive and social capabilities require modified psychiatric treatment modalities based on the children's level of intelligence.

EDUCATION FOR THE CHILD

Educational settings for mentally retarded children should include a comprehensive program that addresses adaptive skills training, social skills training, and vocational training. Particular attention should be focused on communication and efforts to improve the quality of life. Group therapy has often been a successful format in which mentally retarded children can learn and practice hypothetical real-life situations and receive supportive feedback.

BEHAVIOR, COGNITIVE, AND PSYCHODYNAMIC THERAPIES

The difficulties in adaptation among mentally retarded persons are widespread and so varied that a number of interventions alone or in combinations may be beneficial.

Behavior therapy has been used for many years to shape and enhance social behaviors and to control and minimize the patient's aggressive and destructive behaviors. Positive reinforcement for desired behaviors and benign punishment (such as loss of privileges) for objectionable behaviors have been helpful.

Cognitive therapy, such as dispelling false beliefs and relaxation exercises with self-instruction, has also been recommended for those mentally retarded patients who can follow the instructions.

Psychodynamic therapy has been used with mentally retarded patients and their families to decrease conflicts regarding expectations that result in persistent anxiety, rage, and depression.

FAMILY EDUCATION

One of the most important areas that a clinician can address is that of educating the family of a mentally retarded patient regarding ways to enhance competence and self-esteem while

maintaining realistic expectations for the patient. The family often finds it difficult to balance fostering independence and providing a nurturing and supportive environment for the mentally retarded child, who is likely to experience some degree of rejection and failure outside the family context.

The parents may benefit from continuous counseling or family therapy. The parents should be allowed opportunities to express their feelings of guilt, despair, anguish, recurring denial, and anger regarding the child's disorder and future. The psychiatrist should be prepared to give the parents all the basic and current medical information regarding causes, treatment, and other pertinent areas (such as special training and the correction of sensory defects).

PHARMACOLOGICAL INTERVENTION

Pharmacological approaches to the treatment of comorbid mental disorders in mentally retarded patients are much the same as for patients who are not mentally retarded. Increasing data support the use of a variety of medications for patients with mental disorders who are not mentally retarded. Some studies have focused on the use of medications for the following behavioral syndromes that are frequent among the mentally retarded.

Aggression and Self-Injurious Behavior

Some evidence from controlled and uncontrolled studies indicates that lithium has been useful in decreasing aggression and self-injurious behavior. Narcotic antagonists such as naltrexone (ReVia) have been reported to decrease self-injurious behaviors in mentally retarded patients who also meet the diagnostic criteria for infantile autistic disorder. One hypothesis proposed as the mechanism of naltrexone treatment is that it interferes with the release of endogenous opioids presumed to be associated with self-injury. Carbamazepine (Tegretol) and valproate (Depakene) are medications that have also been beneficial in some cases of self-injurious behavior.

Stereotypical Motor Movements

Antipsychotic medications, such as haloperidol (Haldol) and chlorpromazine, decrease repetitive self-stimulatory behaviors in mentally retarded patients, but those medications have not increased adaptive behavior. Some mentally retarded children and adults (up to one third) face a high risk for tardive dyskinesia with the continued use of antipsychotic medications.

Explosive Rage Behavior

β-adrenergic receptor antagonists, such as propranolol (Inderal) and buspirone (BuSpar), have been reported to result in a decrease in explosive rages among patients with mental retardation and autistic disorder. Systematic study is necessary before efficacy of those drugs can be confirmed.

Attention-Deficit/Hyperactivity Disorder

Studies of methylphenidate treatment in mildly retarded patients with attention-deficit/hyperactivity disorder have shown a significant improvement in the ability to maintain attention and to stay on tasks. Methylphenidate treatment studies have not shown evidence of long-term improvement in social skills or learning.

References

Bodensteiner J B, Schaefer G B: Evaluation of the patient with idiopathic mental retardation. J Neuropsychiatry Clin Neurosci 7: 261, 1995.
Bregman J D: Current developments in the understanding of mental retardation: Part II, Psychopathology. J Am Acad Child Adolesc Psychiatry 30: 861, 1991.
Bregman J D, Harris J C: Mental retardation. In Comprehensive Textbook of

Psychiatry, ed 6, H I Kaplan, B J Sadock, editors, p 2207. Williams & Wilkins, Baltimore, 1995.

Bregman J D, Hodapp R M: Current developments in the understanding of mental retardation: Part I. Biological and phenomenological perspectives. J Am Acad Child Adolesc Psychiatry *30*: 707, 1991.

Dykens E M, Hodapp R M, Walsh K, Nash L J: Adaptive and maladaptive behavior in Prader-Willi syndrome. J Am Acad Child Adolesc Psychiatry *31*: 1131, 1992.

Rosebush P I, MacQueen G M, Clarke J T, Callahan J W, Strasberg P M, Mazurek M F: Late-onset Tay-Sachs disease presenting as catatonic schizophrenia: diagnostic and treatment issues. J Clin Psychiatry *56*: 347, 1995.

Sturmey P: Diagnostic-based pharmacological treatment of behavior disorders in persons with developmental disabilities: a review and a decision-making typology. Res Dev Disabil *16*: 235, 1995.

Sturmey P: The use of DSM and ICD diagnostic criteria in people with mental retardation: A review of empirical studies. J Nerv Ment Dis *181*: 38, 1993.

30/ Learning Disorders

30.1 READING DISORDER

Reading disorder is characterized by an impaired ability to recognize words, slow and inaccurate reading, and poor comprehension in the absence of low intelligence or significant sensory deficits. The relatively common school-age childhood disorder seems to run in families and is often associated with disorder of written expression, mathematics disorder, or one of the communication disorders. In addition, children with attention-deficit/hyperactivity disorder have a high risk for reading disorder. Over the years, a variety of labels have been used to describe reading disabilities, including ''dyslexia,'' ''reading backwards,'' ''learning disability,'' ''alexia,'' and ''developmental word blindness.'' The term ''dyslexia'' was used extensively for many years to describe a reading disability syndrome that often included speech and language deficits and right-left confusion. When it became evident that reading disorder is frequently accompanied by disabilities in other academic skills, the use of the term ''dyslexia'' diminished, and general terms, such as ''learning disorder,'' began to be used.

In the fourth edition of *Diagnostic and Statistical Manual of Mental Disorders* (DSM-IV), reading disorder is defined as reading achievement that is below the expected level for the child's age, education, and intelligence, and the impairment significantly interferes with academic success or the daily activities that involve reading. According to DSM-IV, if a neurological condition or sensory disturbance is present, the reading disability exhibited exceeds that usually associated with it.

The DSM-IV definition of reading disorder differs from that in the 10th revision of the International Classification of Diseases and Related Health Problems (ICD-10). According to ICD-10, children with specific reading disorder frequently have a history of impaired speech, language, and spelling.

EPIDEMIOLOGY

An estimated 4 percent of school-age children in the United States have reading disorder; prevalence studies find rates ranging between 2 and 8 percent. Three to four times as many boys as girls are reported to have reading disability in school and clinically referred samples. The rate for boys may be inflated, since boys with reading disorder are apt to be picked up because of their increased behavioral difficulties. Adults with reading backwardness or reading retardation reportedly show no sex difference in the frequency of the disorder.

ETIOLOGY

No unitary cause is known for reading disorder. Given the many associated learning disorders and language difficulties, reading disorder is probably multifactorial. One recent study found an association between dyslexia and birth in the months of May, June, and July, suggesting that prenatal exposure to a maternal infectious illness, such as influenza, in the winter months may contribute to reading disorder.

Reading disorder tends to be more prevalent among family members of persons affected by the disorder than in the general population, leading to the speculation that the disorder may have a genetic origin. However, family and twin studies have not supplied definitive evidence to support that theory.

Studies in the 1930s attempted to explain reading disorder with the cerebral hemispheric function model, which suggested positive correlations of reading disorder with left-handedness, left-eyedness, or mixed laterality. However, subsequent epidemiological studies did not find any consistent association between reading disorder and laterality of handedness or eyedness. However, right-left confusion has been associated with reading difficulties. The reversal of cerebral asymmetry may result in the transference of language lateralization to a cerebral hemisphere that is less differentiated to accommodate language function, thereby leading to reading disorder. A few recent studies (computed tomography [CT] scan, magnetic resonance imaging [MRI], and on autopsy) have shown abnormal symmetries in the temporal or parietal lobes of persons with reading disorder.

Many attribute reading disorder to subtle deficits that are either visual or verbal (that is, auditory). More evidence exists for verbal deficits than for visual deficits; thus, reading disorder is considered part of an oral language disorder.

Reading requires a brain that is mature enough and sufficiently intact to integrate information arriving through various processing systems and to relegate disturbing stimuli to the background. In addition, reading requires sufficient freedom from conflict to permit the investment of energy in the task and a sociocultural value system that views reading as basic to survival.

A high incidence of reading disorder tends to be found among children with cerebral palsy who are of normal intelligence. A slightly increased incidence of reading disorder is seen among epileptic children. Complications during pregnancy, prenatal and perinatal difficulties (including prematurity), and low birth weight are common in the histories of children with reading disorder.

Secondary reading disorder may be seen in children with postnatal brain lesions in the left occipital lobe resulting in right visual field blindness. The disorder may also be seen in children with lesions in the splenium of the corpus callosum that block the transmission of visual information from the intact right hemisphere to the language areas of the left hemisphere.

Reading disorder may be one manifestation of developmental delay or maturational lag. Temperamental attributes have been reported to be closely associated with reading disorder. Compared with nonreading-disordered children, children with reading disorder often have more difficulty in concentrating and a shorter attention span.

Some studies suggest an association between malnutrition and cognitive function. Children who were malnourished for a long time during early childhood show subaverage performances in various cognitive tests. Their cognitive performances are lower than those of their siblings who grew up in the same family environment but who were not subjected to the same degree of malnutrition.

Severe reading disorder is often associated with psychiatric problems. Reading disorder may be the result of a preexisting psychiatric disorder or the cause of emotional and behavior

Table 30.1-1.   Diagnostic Criteria for Reading Disorder

A. Reading achievement, as measured by individually administered standardized tests of reading accuracy or comprehension, is substantially below that expected given the person's chronological age, measured intelligence, and age-appropriate education.

B. The disturbance in criterion A significantly interferes with academic achievement or activities of daily living that require reading skills.

C. If a sensory deficit is present, the reading difficulties are in excess of those usually associated with it.

Table from DSM-IV, *Diagnostic and Statistical Manual of Mental Disorders*, ed 4. Copyright American Psychiatric Association, Washington, 1994. Used with permission.

disorders; however, ascertaining the causal relation between reading disorder and a coexisting psychiatric disorder is not always easy.

DIAGNOSIS

The main diagnostic feature of reading disorder is reading achievement markedly below the person's intellectual capacity (Table 30.1–1). Other characteristic features include difficulties with the recall, evocation, and sequencing of printed letters and words; with the processing of sophisticated grammatical constructions; and with the making of inferences. Clinically, the observer is impressed by the interaction between emotional and specific features. The experience of school failure seems to confirm preexisting doubts that some children have about themselves. The energy of some children is so bound to their psychological conflicts that they are unable to use their assets. The psychiatric evaluation should assess the need for psychiatric intervention and select the appropriate treatment.

The diagnosis of reading disorder cannot be established without confirmation by a standardized reading achievement test; pervasive developmental disorders and mental retardation must be ruled out.

Psychoeducational Tests

Besides standardized intelligence tests, psychoeducational diagnostic tests should be administered. The diagnostic battery may include a standardized spelling test, the writing of a composition, the processing and the use of oral language, and design copying (a judgment of the adequacy of pencil use). A screening projective battery may include human-figure drawings, picture-story tests, and sentence completion. The evaluation should also include a systematic observation of behavior variables.

CLINICAL FEATURES

Reading disorder is usually apparent by age 7 (second grade). In severe cases, evidence of reading difficulty may be apparent as early as age 6 (first grade). Sometimes reading disorder is compensated for in the early elementary grades, particularly when it is associated with high scores on intelligence tests. In those cases the disorder may not be apparent until age 9 (fourth grade) or later.

Reading-disordered children make many errors in their oral reading. The faulty reading is characterized by omissions, additions, and distortions of words. Such children have difficulty in distinguishing between printed letter characters and sizes, especially those that differ only in spatial orientation and length of line. The problems in managing printed or written language may pertain to individual letters, sentences, and even a whole page. The children's reading speed is slow, often with minimal comprehension. Most children with reading disorder have an age-appropriate ability to copy from a written or printed text, but nearly all are poor spellers.

Associated problems include language difficulties, which show often as impaired sound discrimination and difficulties in properly sequencing words. The reading-disordered child may start a word in the middle or at the end of a printed or written sentence. At times, such children transpose letters that are to be read because of a poorly established left-to-right tracking sequence. Failures in both memory recall and sustained elicitation result in the poor recall of letter names and sounds.

Most children with reading disorder dislike and avoid reading and writing. Their anxiety is heightened when they are confronted with demands that involve printed language.

Most reading-disordered children who do not receive remedial education have a sense of shame and humiliation because of their continuing failure and subsequent frustration. Those feelings become more intense as time progresses. Older children tend to be angry and depressed, and they exhibit poor self-esteem.

DIFFERENTIAL DIAGNOSIS

Deficits in expressive language and speech discrimination are usually present in reading disorder and may be severe enough to warrant the additional diagnosis of expressive language disorder or mixed receptive-expressive language disorder. Disorder of written expression is often present. Sometimes there is a discrepancy between verbal and performance intelligence scores. Visual perceptual deficits are seen in only about 10 percent of cases.

Reading difficulties may be caused primarily by the generalized impairment in intellectual functioning seen in mental retardation, which can be checked by administering a standardized intelligence test.

Inadequate schooling resulting in poor reading skills can be determined by finding out whether other children in the same school have similarly poor reading performances on standardized reading tests.

Hearing and visual impairments should be ruled out with screening tests.

Reading disorder often accompanies other emotional and behavioral disorders, especially attention-deficit/hyperactivity disorder, conduct disorder, and depressive disorders, particularly in older children and adolescents.

COURSE AND PROGNOSIS

Even without any remedial assistance, many reading-disordered children acquire a little information about printed language during their first two years in grade school. By the end of the first grade, some have learned how to read a few words. However, if no remedial educational intervention is given by the third grade, the children remain reading-impaired. Under the best circumstances, a child is classified as being at risk for a reading disorder during the kindergarten year or early in the first grade.

When remediation is instituted early, it can sometimes be discontinued by the end of the first or second grade. In severe cases and depending on the pattern of deficits and strengths, remediation may be continued into the middle and high school years. Children who have either compensated satisfactorily or recovered from early reading disorder are overrepresented in families with socioeconomically advantaged backgrounds.

TREATMENT

The treatment of choice for reading disorder is a remedial educational approach; however, the relative efficacy of various remedial teaching strategies is controversial.

One frequently used method, developed by Samuel Orton, urges therapeutic attention to the mastery of simple phonetic units, followed by the blending of those units into words and sentences. An approach that systematically engages several senses is recommended. The rationale for that and similar methods is that children's difficulties in managing letters and syllables are basic to their failures to learn to read; therefore, if they are taught to cope with graphemes, they will learn to read.

As in psychotherapy, the therapist-patient relationship is important to a successful treatment outcome in remedial educational therapy.

Reading-disordered children should be placed in a grade as close as possible to their social functional level and given special remedial work in reading. Coexisting emotional and behavioral problems should be treated by appropriate psychotherapeutic means. Parental counseling may also be helpful.

References

Cantwell D P, Baker L: Reading disorder. In *Comprehensive Textbook of Psychiatry*, ed 6, H I Kaplan, B J Sadock, editors, p 2246. Williams & Wilkins, Baltimore, 1995.

Hyrid G W, Semrod-Clikeman E: Dyslexia and neurodevelopmental pathology: Relationships to cognition, intelligence, and reading skill acquisition. J Learn Disabil 22: 204, 1989.

Lerner J W: Educational interventions in learning disabilities. J Am Acad Child Adolesc Psychiatry 28: 326, 1989.

Maughan B: Long-term outcomes of developmental reading problems. J Child Psychol Psychiatry 36: 357, 1995.

Semrod-Clikeman E, Biederman J, Sprich-Buckminster S, Lehman B K, Faraone S V, Norman D: Comorbidity between ADDH and learning disability: A review and report in a clinically referred sample. J Am Acad Child Adolesc Psychiatry 31: 439, 1992.

Shankweiler D, Crain S, Katz L, Fowler A E: Cognitive profiles of reading-disabled children: Comparison of language skills in phonology, morphology, and syntax. Psychol Sci 6: 149, 1995.

Smith S D, Pennington B F, Kimberling W J, Ing P S: Familial dyslexia: Use of genetic linkage data to define subtypes. J Am Acad Child Adolesc Psychiatry 29: 204, 1990.

30.2 MATHEMATICS DISORDER

Mathematics disorder is essentially a disability in performing arithmetic skills expected for a person's intellectual capacity and educational level. Standardized, individually administered tests measure arithmetic skills. The lack of expected mathematics ability interferes with school performance or daily life activities, and the difficulties are in excess of impairments associated with any existing neurological or sensory deficits.

According to the fourth edition of *Diagnostic and Statistical Manual for Mental Disorders* (DSM-IV), mathematics disorder is a learning disorder. Impairments in four groups of skills have been identified in mathematics disorder: linguistic skills (those related to understanding mathematical terms and converting written problems into mathematical symbols), perceptual skills (the ability to recognize and understand symbols and to order clusters of numbers), mathematical skills (basic addition, subtraction, multiplication, and division and following sequencing of basic operations), and attentional skills (copying figures correctly and observing operational symbols correctly).

Other disorders often accompany mathematics disorder, including reading disorder, developmental coordination disorder, and mixed receptive-expressive language disorder. Unlike DSM-IV, the equivalent disorder in the 10th revision of the International Classification of Diseases and Related Health Problems (ICD-10) excludes reading and spelling disabilities.

EPIDEMIOLOGY

The prevalence of mathematics disorder has not been well studied and can be only roughly estimated to be 6 percent of school-age children who are not mentally retarded. The extent to which educational limitations influence that number is not clear. Data do suggest that children with mathematics disorder are likely to exhibit another learning disorder or language disability. The sex ratio of mathematics disorder is still under investigation. The disorder may be more common in girls than in boys.

ETIOLOGY

The cause of mathematics disorder is not known. An early theory proposed a neurological deficit in the right cerebral hemisphere, particularly in the occipital lobe areas. Those regions are responsible for processing visual-spatial stimuli that, in turn, are responsible for mathematical skills. However, the validity of that theory has received little support in subsequent neuropsychiatric studies.

The current view is that the cause is multifactorial. Maturational, cognitive, emotional, educational, and socioeconomic factors account in varying degrees and combinations for mathematics disorder. Compared with reading, arithmetic abilities may be more dependent on the amount or the quality of instruction.

DIAGNOSIS

In a typical case of mathematics disorder, a careful inquiry into the child's school performance history reveals early difficulties with arithmetic subjects. The definitive diagnosis can be made only after the child takes an individually administered standardized arithmetic test and scores markedly below the expected level, considering the child's schooling and intellectual capacity measured by a standardized intelligence test. A pervasive developmental disorder and mental retardation should also be ruled out before confirming the diagnosis of mathematics disorder. The diagnosis criteria for mathematics disorder are given in Table 30.2–1.

CLINICAL FEATURES

Most children with mathematics disorder can be classified during the second and third grades in elementary school. The affected child's performance in handling basic number concepts, such as counting and adding even one-digit numbers, is

Table 30.2–1.   Diagnostic Criteria for Mathematics Disorder

A. Mathematical ability, as measured by individually administered standardized tests, is substantially below that expected given the person's chronological age, measured intelligence, and age-appropriate education.

B. The disturbance in criterion A significantly interferes with academic achievement or activities of daily living that require mathematical ability.

C. If a sensory deficit is present, the difficulties in mathematical ability are in excess of those usually associated with it.

Table from DSM-IV, *Diagnostic and Statistical Manual of Mental Disorders*, ed 4. Copyright American Psychiatric Association, Washington, 1994. Used with permission.

significantly below the age-expected norms, but the child shows normal intellectual skills in other areas.

During the first two or three years of elementary school, a child with mathematics disorder may appear to make some progress in mathematics by relying on rote memory. However, soon, as arithmetic progresses into complex levels requiring discrimination and manipulation of spatial and numerical relations, the presence of the disorder becomes conspicuous.

Some investigators have classified mathematics disorder into several categories: (1) difficulty in learning to count meaningfully, (2) difficulty in mastering cardinal and ordinal systems, (3) difficulty in performing arithmetic operations, and (4) difficulty in envisioning clusters of objects as groups. In addition, affected children may have difficulties in associating auditory and visual symbols, understanding the conservation of quantity, remembering sequences of arithmetic steps, and choosing principles for problem-solving activities. Children with those problems are presumed to have good auditory and verbal abilities.

Mathematics disorder often coexists with other disorders affecting the following skills: reading, expressive writing, coordination, and expressive and receptive language. Spelling problems, deficits in memory or attention, and emotional or behavioral problems may be present. Young grade-school children often present first with other learning disorders and should be checked for mathematics disorder. Children with cerebral palsy may have mathematics disorder with normal overall intelligence.

The relation between mathematics disorder and other communication and learning disorders is not yet clear. Although mathematics disorder does not affect children with mixed receptive-expressive language disorder and expressive language disorder, the conditions often coexist, as they are associated with impairments in both decoding and encoding processes.

DIFFERENTIAL DIAGNOSIS

Arithmetic difficulties seen in mental retardation are accompanied by a generalized impairment in overall intellectual functioning. In unusual cases of mild mental retardation, arithmetic skills may be significantly below the expected level, given the person's schooling and level of mental retardation. In such cases the additional diagnosis of mathematics disorder should be made, as treatment of the arithmetic difficulties can be particularly helpful to the child's chances for employment in adulthood.

Inadequate schooling can often affect the child's poor arithmetic performance on a standardized arithmetic test. If so, most

of the other children in the same class probably have similarly poor arithmetic performances.

Conduct disorder and attention-deficit/hyperactivity disorder may be present with mathematics disorder, and in those cases both diagnoses should be made.

COURSE AND PROGNOSIS

Mathematics disorder is usually apparent by the time the child is 8 years old (third grade). In some children the disorder is apparent as early as 6 years (first grade), and in others it may not occur until age 10 (fifth grade) or later. Thus far, few longitudinal study data are available to predict clear patterns of developmental and academic progress of children classified as having mathematics disorder in early school grades. However, untreated children with a moderate mathematics disorder and those children whose arithmetic difficulties cannot be resolved by intensive remedial interventions may have complications, including continuing academic difficulties, poor self-concept, depression, and frustration. Those complications may then lead to a reluctance to attend school, truancy, or conduct disturbance.

TREATMENT

The currently most effective treatment of mathematics disorder is remedial education. Controversy continues as to the comparative effectiveness of various remedial educational treatments. However, the current consensus is that the treatment methods and materials are useful only when they fit the particular child, the disorder, and the severity and feasibility of the teaching plans. Project MATH, a multimedia self-instructional or group-instructional in-service training program, has been successful for some children with mathematics disorder. Computer programs can be helpful and can increase compliance with remediation efforts. Poor coordination may accompany the disorder, so physical therapy and sensory integration activities may be helpful.

References

Baker L, Cantwell D P: Mathematics disorder. In *Comprehensive Textbook of Psychiatry*, ed 6, H I Kaplan, B J Sadock, editors, p 2251. Williams & Wilkins, Baltimore, 1995.
Jordan N C, Levine S C, Huttenlocher J: Calculation abilities in young children with different patterns of cognitive functioning. J Learn Disabil 28: 53, 1995.
Lerner J W: Educational intervention in learning disabilities. J Am Acad Child Adolesc Psychiatry 28: 326, 1989.
Naglieri J A, Gottling S H: A study of planning and mathematics instruction for students with learning disabilities. Psychol Rep 76: 1343, 1995.
Nussbaum N L, Grant M L, Roman M J, Poole J H, Bigler E D: Attention-deficit disorder and the mediating effect of age on academic and behavioral variables. J Dev Pediatr 1: 22, 1990.
Share D L, Moffitt T E, Silva P A: Factors associated with arithmetic and reading disability and specific arithmetic disability. J Learn Disabil 21: 313, 1988.

30.3 DISORDER OF WRITTEN EXPRESSION AND LEARNING DISORDER NOS

DISORDER OF WRITTEN EXPRESSION

Disorder of written expression is characterized by writing skills that are significantly below the expected level for a person's age, intellectual capacity, and education as measured by a standardized test. The impairment interferes with the person's school performance and with the demands for writing in everyday life, and the disorder is not due to a neurological or sensory deficit. The components of writing disability include poor spelling, errors in grammar and punctuation, and poor handwriting.

Writing disabilities are often associated with other learning disorders but may be diagnosed later than others, since expressive writing is acquired later than language and reading.

The 10th revision of the International Classification of Diseases and Related Health Problems (ICD-10), in addition to a disorder of written expression similar to the one in the fourth edition of *Diagnostic and Statistical Manual of Mental Disorders* (DSM-IV), also includes a separate specific spelling disorder.

Epidemiology

The prevalence of disorder of written expression is not known but has been estimated at 3 to 10 percent of school-age children. The male-to-female ratio is also unknown. Some evidence indicates that affected children are frequently from families with a history of the disorder.

Etiology

One hypothesis holds that disorder of written expression results from the combined effects of one or more of the following disorders: expressive language disorder, mixed receptive-expressive language disorder, and reading disorder. That view suggests the possible existence of neurological and cognitive defects or malfunctions somewhere in the central information-processing areas of the brain.

Empirical findings that most children with disorder of written expression have relatives with the disorder have suggested hereditary predisposition to the disorder.

Temperamental characteristics may play some role in disorder of written expression, especially such characteristics as short attention span and easy distractibility.

Diagnosis

The diagnosis of disorder of written expression is made based on the person's consistently poor performance on the composition of written text. Performance is markedly below the person's intellectual capacity, as confirmed by an individually administered standardized expressive writing test (Table 30.3–1). The presence of a major disorder, such as a pervasive developmental disorder or mental retardation, may obviate the

Table 30.3–1. Diagnostic Criteria for Disorder of Written Expression

A. Writing skills, as measured by individually administered standardized tests (or functional assessments of writing skills), are substantially below those expected given the person's chronological age, measured intelligence, and age-appropriate education.

B. The disturbance in criterion A significantly interferes with academic achievement or activities of daily living that require the composition of written texts (e.g., writing grammatically correct sentences and organized paragraphs).

C. If a sensory deficit is present, the difficulties in writing skills are in excess of those usually associated with it.

Table from DSM-IV, *Diagnostic and Statistical Manual of Mental Disorders*, ed 4. Copyright American Psychiatric Association, Washington, 1994. Used with permission.

diagnosis of disorder of written expression. Other disorders to be differentiated from disorder of written expression are communication disorders, reading disorder, and impaired vision and hearing.

Dyslexia is characterized by an inability to read and dysgraphia by an inability to write. Any person suspected of having disorder of written expression should first be given a standardized intelligence test, such as the third version of Wechsler Intelligence Scale for Children (WISC-3) or the Weschsler Adult Intelligence Scale-Revised (WAIS-R), to determine the person's intellectual capacity before administering a standardized expressive writing test.

Clinical Features

Children with disorder of written expression present difficulties early in grade school in spelling words and expressing their thoughts according to age-appropriate grammatical norms. Their spoken and written sentences contain an unusually large number of grammatical errors and poor paragraph organization. During and after the second grade, the children commonly make simple grammatical errors in writing a short sentence. For example, they frequently fail, despite constant reminders, to start the first letter of the first word in a sentence with a capital letter and to end a sentence with a period.

As they grow older and progress into higher grades in school, such children's spoken and written sentences become more conspicuously primitive, odd, and inferior to what is expected of students at their grade level. Their word choices are erroneous and inappropriate; their paragraphs are disorganized and not in proper sequence; and spelling correctly becomes more difficult as their vocabulary becomes more abstract and larger in number and characters.

Associated features of disorder of written expression include refusal or reluctance to go to school and to do assigned written homework, poor academic performance in other areas (such as mathematics), general disinterest in school work, truancy, attention-deficit, and conduct disturbance.

Most children with disorder of written expression become frustrated and angry because of their feelings of inadequacy and failure in their academic performance. They may have a chronic depressive disorder because of their growing sense of isolation, estrangement, and despair.

Adults with disorder of written expression who do not receive remedial intervention continue to have difficulties in social adaptation involving writing skills and a continuing sense of incompetence, inferiority, isolation, and estrangement. Some of them even try to avoid or procrastinate writing a response letter or a simple greeting card for fear that their writing incompetence will be exposed. When their coping mechanisms fail, the severity of their psychopathology is likely to be increased. Most adults with the disorder choose occupations that require minimal writing skills, such as in trade, custodianship, and other menial work; seldom do they achieve or hold a socially desirable occupational position requiring a high level of expressive writing. Common associated disorders are reading disorder, mixed receptive-expressive language disorder, expressive language disorder, mathematics disorder, developmental coordination disorder, and attention-deficit and disruptive behavior disorders.

Course and Prognosis

Because writing, language, and reading disorders often coexist and because a child normally speaks well before learning to read and learns to read well before writing well, a child with all three disorders has expressive language disorder diagnosed first and disorder of written expression diagnosed last. In severe cases a disorder of written expression is apparent by age 7 (second grade); in less severe cases the disorder may not be apparent until age 10 (fifth grade) or later. Most persons with mild and moderate disorder of written expression fare well if they receive timely remedial education early in grade school. Severe disorder of written expression requires continual extensive remedial treatment through the late part of high school and even into college.

The prognosis depends on the severity of the disorder, the age or grade when the remedial intervention is started, the length and the continuity of treatment, and the presence or the absence of associated or secondary emotional or behavioral problems.

Those persons who later become well compensated or who recover from disorder of written expression are often from families with high socioeconomic backgrounds.

Treatment

Disorder of written expression responds to treatment. The best treatment to date is remedial education. Although controversy continues as to the effectiveness of various remedial expressive writing modalities, an intensive and continuous administration of individually tailored one-to-one expressive and creative writing therapy appears to show the most favorable treatment outcomes. Teachers in some special schools devote as much as two hours a day to such writing instruction.

The treatment of the disorder requires an optimal patient-therapist relationship, as in psychotherapy. Success or failure in sustaining the patient's motivation greatly affects the treatment's long-term efficacy.

Associated and secondary emotional and behavioral problems should be given prompt attention, with appropriate psychiatric treatment and parental counseling.

LEARNING DISORDER NOS

Learning disorder not otherwise specified (NOS) is a new category in DSM-IV for disorders that do not meet the criteria for any specific learning disorder but that cause impairment and reflect learning abilities below those expected for a person's intelligence, education, and age. An example of a disability that could be placed in the category is a spelling skills deficit.

References

Baker L, Cantwell D P: Disorder of written expression. In *Comprehensive Textbook of Psychiatry*, ed 6, H I Kaplan, B J Sadock, editors, p 2253. Williams & Wilkins, Baltimore, 1995.

Devel R K: Developmental dysgraphia and motor skills disorders. J Child Neurol *10* (Suppl 1): 56, 1995.

Friedland J: Development and breakdown of written language. J Commun Disord *23*: 171, 1990.

Houck C K, Billingsley B S: Written expression of students with and without learning disabilities: Differences across the grades. J Learn Disabil *22*: 561, 1989.

Oliver C E: A sensorimotor program for improving writing readiness skills in elementary-age children. Am J Occup Ther *44*: 111, 1990.

Outhred L: Work processing: Its impact on children's writing. J Learn Disabil *22*: 262, 1989.

Weiss C E, Lillywhite H S: *Communicative Disorders: Prevention and Early Intervention*, Mosby, St. Louis, 1981.

31/ Motor Skills Disorder: Developmental Coordination Disorder

Developmental coordination disorder is currently the only disorder in the category of motor skills disorder, according to the fourth edition of *Diagnostic and Statistical Manual of Mental Disorders* (DSM-IV).

The disorder is characterized by markedly lower than expected performance in activities requiring motor coordination. The child may have delays in achieving motor milestones, such as sitting up, crawling, and walking. The patient is usually clumsy in gross and fine motor skills but is not globally impaired. Developmental coordination disorder may also include deficits in handwriting and in the frequency of dropping things. Children with the disorder may motorically resemble children of a younger age. Motor skills are significantly poor for the child's chronological and mental age, and they interfere with daily functioning or school performance. Motor impairment in the disorder cannot be explained on the basis of a medical condition, such as cerebral palsy, muscular dystrophy, or any other neuromuscular disorder.

Clumsiness in children has been associated with learning disorders, communication disorders, and disruptive behavior and attention-deficit disorders, such as attention-deficit/hyperactivity disorder. Children who are clumsy are often poor in sports and may be socially ostracized.

EPIDEMIOLOGY

The prevalence of developmental coordination disorder is not known but has been estimated at about 6 percent of school-age children. The male-to-female ratio is also not known, but more boys than girls have developmental coordination disorder. Reports in the literature of the male-to-female ratio have ranged from 2 to 1 to as much as 4 to 1.

ETIOLOGY

The causes of developmental coordination disorder are unknown, but hypotheses include both organic and developmental causes. Risk factors postulated in the disorder include prematurity, hypoxia, perinatal malnutrition, and low birth weight. Neurochemical abnormalities and parietal lobe lesions have also been suggested as contributors to coordination deficits.

Developmental coordination disorder and communication disorders have strong associations, although the specific causative agents are unknown for both. Coordination problems are also more than usually frequent in children with impulsive behavior and a variety of learning disorders. Developmental coordination disorder probably has a multifactorial cause.

DIAGNOSIS

The diagnosis of developmental coordination disorder requires a history of the child's early motor behavior, including the direct observation of motor activities. Informal screening for developmental coordination disorder can be done by asking the child to perform tasks involving gross motor coordination (for example, hopping, jumping, and standing on one foot), fine

motor coordination (for example, finger tapping and shoelace tying), and hand-eye coordination (for example, catching a ball and copying letters). The diagnosis is supported by below-normal scores on the performance subtests of standardized intelligence tests and by normal or above-normal scores on the verbal subtests. Specialized tests of motor coordination can be useful, such as the Bender Gestalt Visual Motor test, the Frostig Movement Skills Test Battery, and the Bruininks-Oseretsky Test of Motor Development. The child's chronological age and intellectual capacity must be considered, and the disorder cannot be caused by a neurological or neuromuscular condition. However, slight reflex abnormalities and other soft neurological signs may occasionally be found on examination. The DSM-IV diagnostic criteria are given in Table 31–1.

CLINICAL FEATURES

The clinical signs suggesting the existence of developmental coordination disorder are evident as early as infancy, when the affected child begins to attempt tasks requiring motor coordination. The essential clinical feature is the child's markedly impaired performance in motor coordination. The difficulties in motor coordination may vary with the child's age and developmental stage.

In infancy and early childhood the disorder may manifest delays in normal developmental milestones, such as turning over, crawling, sitting, standing, walking, buttoning shirts, and zipping up pants. Between the ages of 2 and 4 years clumsiness appears in almost all activities requiring motor coordination. The affected children cannot hold objects, and they drop them easily; their gait is unsteady; they often trip over their own feet; and they may bump into other children while attempting to go around them.

In older children the impaired motor coordination may be shown in table games, such as putting together puzzles or building blocks, and in any type of ball game. Although no specific features are pathognomonic of developmental coordination disorder, developmental milestones are frequently delayed. Many children with the disorder also have a speech disorder. Older children may also have secondary problems of school difficulties, including behavioral and emotional problems, that require appropriate therapeutic interventions.

DIFFERENTIAL DIAGNOSIS

The differential diagnosis includes medical disorders that produce coordination difficulties (such as cerebral palsy and muscular dystrophy), pervasive developmental disorders, and mental retardation. In mental retardation and in the pervasive developmental disorders, coordination usually does not stand out as a deficit compared with other skills. Children with neuromuscular disorders may exhibit more global muscle impairment than clumsiness and delayed motor milestones. In those cases, neurological workups usually reveal more extensive deficits

Table 31-1.   Diagnostic Criteria for Developmental Coordination Disorder

A. Performance in daily activities that require motor coordination is substantially below that expected given the person's chronological age and measured intelligence. This may be manifested by marked delays in achieving motor milestones (e.g., walking, crawling, sitting), dropping things, ''clumsiness,'' poor performance in sports, or poor handwriting.

B. The disturbance in criterion A significantly interferes with academic achievement or activities of daily living.

C. The disturbance is not due to a general medical condition (e.g., cerebral palsy, hemiplegia, or muscular dystrophy) and does not meet criteria for a pervasive developmental disorder.

D. If mental retardation is present, the motor difficulties are in excess of those usually associated with it.

Table from DSM-IV, *Diagnostic and Statistical Manual of Mental Disorders*, ed 4. Copyright American Psychiatric Association, Washington, 1994. Used with permission.

than are present in developmental coordination disorder. Extremely hyperactive and impulsive children may be physically careless because of their high levels of motor activity. Clumsy motor behavior and attention-deficit/hyperactivity disorder seem to be associated.

COURSE AND PROGNOSIS

No reliable data are available on the prospective longitudinal outcomes of both treated and untreated children with developmental coordination disorder. Some studies suggest a favorable outcome for those children who have an average or above-average intellectual capacity, because they can learn to compensate for their coordination deficits. In general, the clumsiness persists into adolescence and adult life.

In severe cases that remain untreated, the patient may have some secondary complications, such as repeated failures in both nonacademic and academic school tasks, repeated problems in attempting to integrate with a peer group, and inability to play games and sports. Those problems may lead to low self-esteem, unhappiness, withdrawal, and, in some cases, increasingly severe behavioral problems as a reaction to the frustration engendered by the disorder. All levels of adaptive functioning can be expected in the children. Commonly associated features include delays in nonmotor milestones, expressive language disorder, and mixed receptive/expressive language disorder.

TREATMENT

The treatments of developmental coordination disorder include perceptual motor training, neurophysiological techniques of exercise for motor dysfunction, and modified physical education. The Montessori technique (developed by Maria Montessori) may be useful with many preschool children, as it emphasizes the development of motor skills. No single exercise or training method appears more advantageous or effective than another. Secondary behavioral or emotional problems and coexisting communication disorders must be managed by appropriate treatment methods.

No large-scale controlled studies have reported on the effects of treatment, although small studies have suggested that exercises in rhythmic coordination, practicing motor movements, and learning to use typewriters are all helpful.

Parental counseling helps reduce the parents' anxiety and guilt over the child's impairment and increases their awareness, giving them confidence to cope with the child.

References

Baker L, Cantwell D P: Developmental coordination disorders. In *Comprehensive Textbook of Psychiatry*, ed 6, H I Kaplan, B J Sadock, editors, p 2257. Williams & Wilkins, Baltimore, 1995.

Henderson L, Rose P, Henderson S: Reaction time and movement time in children with a Developmental Coordination Disorder. J Child Psychol Psychiatry *33*: 895, 1992.

Losse A, Henderson S E, Elliman D, Hall D, Knight E, Jongmans M: Clumsiness in children: Do they grow out of it? A ten-year follow-up study. Dev Med Child Neurol *33*: 55, 1991.

Smyth T R: Abnormal clumsiness in children: A defect of motor programming? Child Care Health Dev *17*: 283, 1991.

Thelen E: Motor development. A new synthesis. Am Psychol *50*: 79, 1995.

32/ Communication Disorders

32.1 EXPRESSIVE LANGUAGE DISORDER

With expressive language disorder the child is below expected ability in vocabulary, the use of correct tenses, the production of complex sentences, and the recall of words. Language disability can be acquired at any time during childhood (for example, secondary to a trauma or a neurological disorder), or it can be developmental and is usually congenital without an obvious cause. Most childhood language disorders fall within the developmental category. In either case, deficits in receptive skills (comprehension of language) or in expressive skills (ability to express language) can occur. Expressive language disturbance often occurs in the absence of comprehension difficulties, whereas receptive dysfunction generally also affects the expression of language.

Children with only expressive language disorder have courses, prognoses, and comorbid diagnoses that are different from those of children with mixed receptive-expressive language disorder. In the revised fourth edition of *Diagnostic and Statistical Manual of Mental Disorders* (DSM-IV), the diagnosis of expressive language disorder still exists but not receptive language disorder. In DSM-IV, mixed receptive-expressive language disorder is diagnosed when both receptive and expressive language syndromes are present and mixed receptive-expressive language disorder is an exclusionary criterion for expressive language disorder. Thus, according to DSM-IV, receptive language disorder can be diagnosed only if the full syndrome of expressive disorder is also present.

In DSM-IV, expressive language disorder and mixed receptive-expressive language disorder are not limited to developmental language disabilities; the acquired forms of language disturbances are included.

To meet the criteria for expressive language disorder, the patient must have scores from standardized measures of expressive language that are markedly below those of standardized nonverbal I.Q. subtests and standardized tests of receptive language.

EPIDEMIOLOGY

The prevalence of expressive language disorder ranges from 3 to 10 percent of all school-age children, with most estimates between 3 and 5 percent. The disorder is two to three times more common in boys than in girls. The disorder is also most prevalent among children whose relatives have a family history of phonological disorder or other communication disorders.

ETIOLOGY

The cause of expressive language disorder is not known. Subtle cerebral damage and maturational lags in cerebral development have been postulated as the underlying causes, but no evidence supports those theories. Left-handedness or ambilaterality appears to increase the risk.

Unknown genetic factors have been suspected to have a role, because the relatives of children with learning disorders have a relatively high incidence of expressive language disorder.

DIAGNOSIS

The presence of markedly below age-level verbal or sign language, accompanied by a low score on standardized expressive verbal tests, is diagnostic of expressive language disorder (Table 32.1–1). The disorder is not caused by a pervasive developmental disorder, as the child shows a desire to communicate. If the child uses any language, it is severely retarded, vocabulary is limited, grammar is simple, and articulation is variable. Inner language or the appropriate use of toys and household objects is present.

To confirm the diagnosis, the clinician should have the child tested with standardized expressive language and nonverbal intellectual tests. Observations of the child's verbal and sign language patterns should be made in various settings (for example, in the schoolyard, the classroom, the home, and the playroom) and during interactions with other children. That will help ascertain the severity and the specific areas of the child's impairment and aid in the early detection of behavioral and emotional complications.

The family history should include the presence or the absence of expressive language disorder among relatives.

An audiogram is indicated for very young children and for those children whose hearing acuity appears impaired.

CLINICAL FEATURES

Severe forms of the disorders are evident before the age of 3 years. Less severe forms may not occur until early adolescence, when language ordinarily becomes complex. The essential feature of the child with expressive language disorder is a marked impairment in the development of age-appropriate expressive language, which results in the use of verbal or sign language that is markedly below the expected level, considering the child's nonverbal intellectual capacity. The child's language understanding (decoding) skills remain relatively intact.

The disorder becomes conspicuous by about the age of 18 months, when the child fails to speak spontaneously or even to echo single words or sounds. Even simple words, such as "mama" and "dada," are absent from the child's active vocabulary, and the child points or uses gestures to indicate desires. The child seems to want to communicate, maintains eye contact, relates well to the mother, and enjoys games such as pat-a-cake and peekaboo.

The child's repertoire of vocabulary is severely limited. At 18 months the child can, at most, comprehend simple commands and can point to common objects when they are named. When the child finally begins to speak, the language deficit becomes apparent. Articulation is usually immature. Many articulation errors are present but are inconsistent, particularly with such sounds as /th/, /r/, /s/, /z/, /y/, and /l/, which are either omitted or are substituted for other sounds.

By the age of 4, most children with expressive language disorder can speak in short phrases, but they appear to forget old words as they learn new ones. After beginning to speak, they acquire language more slowly than do normal children. Their use of various grammatical structures is also markedly lower than the age-expected level. Their developmental mile-

Table 32.1–1.   Diagnostic Criteria for Expressive Language Disorder

A. The scores obtained from standardized individually administered measures of expressive language development are substantially below those obtained from standardized measures of both nonverbal intellectual capacity and receptive language development. The disturbance may be manifest clinically by symptoms that include having a markedly limited vocabulary, making errors in tense, or having difficulty recalling words or producing sentences with developmentally appropriate length or complexity.

B. The difficulties with expressive language interfere with academic or occupational achievement or with social communication.

C. Criteria are not met for mixed receptive-expressive language disorder or a pervasive developmental disorder.

D. If mental retardation, a speech-motor or sensory deficit, or environmental deprivation is present, the language difficulties are in excess of those usually associated with these problems.

Table from DSM-IV, *Diagnostic and Statistical Manual of Mental Disorders*, ed 4. Copyright American Psychiatric Association, Washington, 1994. Used with permission.

stones may also be slightly delayed. Phonological disorder is often present. Developmental coordination disorder and enuresis are common associated disorders.

Complications

Emotional problems involving poor self-image, frustration, and depression may develop in school-age children. Children with expressive language disorder may also have a learning disorder, manifested by reading retardation, that may result in serious difficulties in various academic subjects. The major learning difficulties are in perceptual skills and skills of recognizing and processing symbols in the proper sequence.

Other behavioral symptoms and problems that may appear in children with expressive language disorder include hyperactivity, short attention span, withdrawing behavior, thumb sucking, temper tantrums, bed-wetting, disobedience, accident-proneness, and conduct disorder. Neurological abnormalities have been reported in a number of children, including soft neurological signs, depressed vestibular responses, and electroencephalogram (EEG) abnormalities.

Many disorders—such as reading disorder, developmental coordination disorder, and other communication disorders—are associated with expressive language disorder. Children with expressive language disorder often have some degree of receptive impairment, although not always significant enough for the diagnosis of mixed receptive-expressive language disorder. Delayed motor milestones and a history of enuresis are common in children with expressive language disorder. Phonological disorder is commonly found in young children with the disorder.

DIFFERENTIAL DIAGNOSIS

In mental retardation, the patient has an overall impairment in intellectual functioning, as shown by below-normal intelligence test scores in all areas. The nonverbal intellectual capacity and functioning of children with expressive language disorder are within normal limits.

In mixed receptive-expressive language disorder, comprehension of language (decoding) is markedly below the expected

age-appropriate level, whereas, in expressive language disorder, language comprehension remains within normal limits.

In pervasive developmental disorders the affected children have, besides the cardinal cognitive characteristics, no inner language, no symbolic or imagery play, no appropriate use of gesture, nor any capacity to form warm and meaningful social relationships. Moreover, the children show little or no frustration with the inability to communicate verbally. In contrast, all those characteristics are present in children with expressive language disorder.

Children with acquired aphasia or dysphasia have a history of early normal language development, and the disordered language had its onset after a head trauma or another neurological disorder (for example, a seizure disorder).

Children with selective mutism have a history of normal language development, and their speech is limited to certain family members (for example, mother, father, and siblings). More girls than boys are affected by selective mutism, and the affected children are mostly shy and withdrawn outside the family.

COURSE AND PROGNOSIS

In general, the prognosis for expressive language disorder is favorable. The rapidity and the degree of recovery depend on the severity of the disorder, the child's motivation to participate in therapies, and the timely institution of speech and other therapeutic interventions. The presence or the absence of other factors—such as moderate to severe hearing loss, mild mental retardation, and severe emotional problems—also affects the prognosis for recovery. As many as 50 percent of children with mild expressive language disorder recover spontaneously without any sign of language impairment, but children with severe expressive language disorder may later display the features of mild to moderate language impairment.

TREATMENT

Language therapy should start immediately after the diagnosis of expressive language disorder. Therapy consists of behaviorally reinforced exercises and practice with phonemes (sound units), vocabulary, and sentence construction. The goal is to increase the number of phrases by using block-building methods and conventional speech therapies.

Psychotherapy is not usually indicated unless the language-disordered child shows signs of concurrent or secondary behavioral or emotional difficulties.

Supportive parental counseling may be indicated in some cases. The parents may need help to reduce intrafamilial tensions arising from difficulties in rearing the language-disordered child and to increase their awareness and understanding of the child's disorder.

References

Campbell T F, Dollaghan C A: Expressive language recovery in severely brain-injured children and adolescents. J Speech Hear Disord *55*: 567, 1990.

Cantwell D P, Baker L: Expressive language disorder. In *Comprehensive Textbook of Psychiatry*, ed 6, H I Kaplan, B J Sadock, editors, p 2260. Williams & Wilkins, Baltimore, 1995.

Cantwell D P, Baker L: *Psychiatric and Developmental Disorders in Children with Communication Disorders*, American Psychiatric Association Press, Washington, 1991.

Coplan J: Normal speech and language development: An overview. Pediatr Rev *16*: 91, 1995.

Strand E: Treatment of motor speech disorders in children. Semin Speech Language *16*: 126, 1995.

32.2 MIXED RECEPTIVE-EXPRESSIVE LANGUAGE DISORDER

In mixed receptive-expressive language disorder the child is impaired in both the understanding and the expression of language. The fourth edition of *Diagnostic and Statistical Manual of Mental Disorders* (DSM-IV) is the first diagnostic manual to combine receptive language disorder with expressive language disorder. The implication is that clinically significant receptive language impairment is always accompanied by expressive language dysfunction. With DSM-IV, it is not possible to code receptive language disorder in the absence of expressive language disorder. DSM-IV allows for receptive and expressive disorders that are acquired, as well as those that are congenital or developmental.

The essential features of mixed receptive-expressive language disorder require that scores from standardized tests of both receptive (comprehension) and expressive language development fall substantially below those obtained from standardized measures of nonverbal intellectual capacity. The language difficulties must be severe enough to impair academic achievement or daily social communication. The patient may not meet the criteria for a pervasive developmental disorder, and the language dysfunctions must be in excess of those usually associated with mental retardation and other neurological and sensory-deficit syndromes.

EPIDEMIOLOGY

Prevalence estimates range from 1 to 13 percent for either receptive or expressive language disorder. Expressive language disorder alone is thought to be much more common than receptive language disorder alone. Both disorders are believed to be more common in boys than in girls.

No studies have examined the prevalence of the DSM-IV category of mixed receptive-expressive language disorder, but prevalence estimates of children who possess both receptive and expressive language disorders are in the 3 to 5 percent range.

ETIOLOGY

The cause of mixed receptive-expressive language disorder is not known. Early theories listed perceptual dysfunction, subtle cerebral damage, maturational lag, and genetic factors as probable causative factors, but no definitive evidence supports those theories. Several studies suggest the presence of underlying impairment of auditory discrimination, as most children with the disorder are more responsive to environmental sounds than to speech sounds. As with expressive language disorder, left-handedness and ambilaterality seem to increase the risk.

DIAGNOSIS

The presence of a markedly below age-appropriate level of comprehension of verbal sign language with intact age-appropriate nonverbal intellectual capacity, the confirmation of the

Table 32.2–1. Diagnostic Criteria for Mixed Receptive-Expressive Language Disorder

A. The scores obtained from a battery of standardized individually administered measures of both receptive and expressive language development are substantially below those obtained from standardized measures of nonverbal intellectual capacity. Symptoms include those for expressive language disorder as well as difficulty understanding words, sentences, or specific types of words, such as spatial terms.

B. The difficulties with receptive and expressive language significantly interfere with academic or occupational achievement or with social communication.

C. Criteria are not met for a pervasive developmental disorder.

D. If mental retardation, a speech-motor or sensory deficit, or environmental deprivation is present, the language difficulties are in excess of those usually associated with these problems.

Table from DSM-IV, *Diagnostic and Statistical Manual of Mental Disorders*, ed 4. Copyright American Psychiatric Association, Washington, 1994. Used with permission.

language difficulties by standardized receptive language tests, and the absence of pervasive developmental disorders confirm the diagnosis of mixed receptive-expressive language disorder (Table 32.2–1). In mixed receptive-expressive language disorder, receptive dysfunction coexists with expressive dysfunction. Therefore, standardized tests for both receptive and expressive language abilities must be given to anyone suspected of having mixed receptive-expressive language disorder.

An audiogram is indicated in all suspected mixed receptive-expressive language-disordered children to rule out or to confirm the presence of deafness and to determine the types of auditory deficits.

A history of the child and the family and observation of the child in various settings help clarify the diagnosis.

CLINICAL FEATURES

The essential clinical feature of the disorder is significant impairment in both language comprehension and language expression. In the mixed disorder, the expressive impairments are similar to those seen in expressive language disorder but can be more severe.

The clinical features of the receptive component of the disorder typically appear before the age of 4 years. Severe forms are apparent by age 2; mild forms may not become evident until age 7 (second grade) or older, when language becomes complex. Children with mixed receptive-expressive language disorder show markedly delayed and below-normal ability to comprehend (decode) verbal or sign language, although they do have age-appropriate nonverbal intellectual capacity. In most cases of receptive dysfunction, verbal or sign expression (encoding) of language is also impaired. The clinical features of mixed receptive-expressive language disorder in children between the ages of 18 and 24 months are the results of the child's failure to make spontaneous utterances of a single phoneme (sound unit) or to mimic another person's words.

Many children with mixed receptive-expressive language disorder have auditory sensory difficulties or are unable to process visual symbols, such as the meaning of a picture. They have deficits in integrating both auditory and visual symbols—for example, recognizing the basic common attributes of a toy truck and a toy passenger car. Whereas a child with expressive language disorder only at 18 months can comprehend simple commands and can point to familiar household objects when told to do so, the child of the same age with mixed receptive-expressive language disorder can neither point to common objects nor obey simple commands. A child with mixed receptive-expressive language disorder usually seems deaf; however, the child does hear and responds normally to nonlanguage sounds from the environment but not to spoken language. If the child starts to speak later, the speech contains many articulation errors, such as omissions, distortions, and substitutions of phonemes. Language acquisition is much slower for children with mixed receptive-expressive language disorder than for normal children.

Children with mixed receptive-expressive language disorder also have difficulty in recalling early visual and auditory memories and recognizing and reproducing symbols in proper sequence. In some cases bilateral electroencephalogram (EEG) abnormalities are seen. Some children with mixed receptive-expressive language disorder have a partial hearing defect for true tones, an increased threshold of auditory arousal, and an inability to localize sound sources. Seizure disorders and reading disorder are more common among the relatives of children with mixed receptive-expressive language disorder than they are in the general population.

Associated comorbid disorders with mixed receptive-expressive language disorder include reading disorder, mathematics disorder, and disorder of written expression. In a large study of children with communication disorders, more than half of the children who met the criteria for mixed receptive-expressive language disorder also had a learning disorder. More than 70 percent in the same study had other mental disorders, especially attention-deficit/hyperactivity disorder, anxiety disorders, and depressive disorders.

DIFFERENTIAL DIAGNOSIS

In expressive language disorder alone, comprehension of spoken language (decoding) remains within age norms. Children with phonological disorder or stuttering have normal expressive and receptive language competence, despite their having speech impairments. Hearing impairment should be ruled out. Most children with mixed receptive-expressive language disorder have a history of variable and inconsistent responses to sounds; they respond more often to environmental sounds than to speech sounds.

Mental retardation, acquired aphasia, and pervasive developmental disorders should also be ruled out.

COURSE AND PROGNOSIS

The overall prognosis for mixed receptive-expressive language disorder is less favorable than for expressive language disorder alone. When the mixed disorder is identified in a young child, it is usually severe, and the short-term prognosis is poor, since early childhood is a time when language develops at a rapid rate. Young children with the disorder may appear to be falling behind. In view of the likelihood of comorbid learning disorders and other mental disorders, the prognosis is guarded. Young children with severe mixed receptive-expressive language disorder are likely to have learning disorders in the future. In children with mild versions of the mixed disorder, it may not be identified for several years, and the disruption in every-

day life may be less overwhelming than that seen in severe forms of the disorder. Over the long run, some children with mixed receptive-expressive language disorder achieve close to normal language functions.

The prognosis for children who acquire mixed receptive-expressive language disorder is widely variable and depends on the nature and the severity of the damage.

TREATMENT

A comprehensive speech and language evaluation, leading to speech and language therapy, is usually recommended for children with mixed receptive-expressive language disorder, despite the lack of controlled treatment studies for the disorder. Some language therapists favor a low-stimuli setting in which children are given individual linguistic instruction. Others recommend that speech and language instruction be integrated into a varied setting with a group of children who are taught several language structures simultaneously. Many symptoms are involved in the disorder, so a small specialized educational setting may be beneficial in maximizing the results.

Psychotherapy is often necessary because children with the mixed disorder frequently have emotional and behavioral problems. Particular attention should be paid to improving the child's self-image and social skills. Family counseling in which the parents are taught appropriate patterns of interaction with the child can also be helpful.

References

Benaisich A A, Curtiss S, Tallal P: Language, learning and behavioral disturbances in childhood: A longitudinal perspective. J Am Acad Child Adolesc Psychiatry 32: 585, 1993.
Cantwell D P, Baker L: Mixed receptive-expressive language disorder. In Comprehensive Textbook of Psychiatry, ed 6, H I Kaplan, B J Sadock, editors, p 2264. Williams & Wilkins, Baltimore, 1995.
Cantwell D P, Baker L: Psychiatric and Developmental Disorders in Children with Communication Disorders. American Psychiatric Association Press, Washington, 1991.
Mitchell P R, Mahoney G: Team management for young children with motor speech disorders. Semin Speech Language 16: 159, 1995.
Rapin I: Acquired aphasia in children. J Child Neurol 10: 267, 1995.
Robinson R J: Causes and associations of severe and persistent specific speech and language disorders in children. Dev Med Child Neurol 33: 943, 1991.
Tomblin J B, Hardy J C, Hein H A: Predicting poor communication status in preschool children using risk factors present at birth. J Speech Hear Res 34: 1096, 1991.

32.3 PHONOLOGICAL DISORDER

Phonological disorder includes many disorders in which developmentally expected speech sounds for the patient's age and intelligence are incorrect or delayed. The disorder can consist of errors in sound production, substitutions of one sound for another, and omissions of such sounds as final consonants. The difficulties interfere with academic achievement or social communication. According to the fourth edition of Diagnostic and Statistical Manual of Mental Disorders (DSM-IV), if mental retardation, a speech-motor or sensory deficit, or environmental deprivation is present, the language dysfunction is in excess of that associated with those problems.

Developmental articulation disorder is the most common phonological disorder in children and is the prototype of the disorders defined by the DSM-IV category of phonological disorder. Phonological disorder is characterized by frequent misarticulations, sound substitutions, and omissions of speech sounds, giving the impression of baby talk. It is not caused by any anatomical, structural, physiological, auditory, or neurological abnormalities. It varies from mild to severe and results in speech that ranges from completely intelligible to unintelligible.

EPIDEMIOLOGY

The prevalence of all phonological dysfunctions in children is unknown, and estimates vary widely with the diagnostic criteria used. The prevalence of phonological disorder is conservatively estimated to be 10 percent of children below 8 years of age and 5 percent of children 8 years of age and above. The disorder is two to three times more common in boys than in girls. It is also more common among the first-degree relatives of patients with the disorder than in the general population. DSM-IV reports 2 to 3 percent of 6 to 7 years olds have the disorder.

ETIOLOGY

The causes of phonological disturbance are variable and range from perinatal problems to hearing impairment to structural abnormalities related to speech. Phonological disorder in children has an unknown cause. A simple developmental lag or maturational delay in the neurological process underlying speech, rather than an organic dysfunction, is at fault.

A disproportionately high frequency of phonological disorder has been found among children from large families and from low socioeconomic status families, suggesting the possible causal effects of inadequate speech stimulation and reinforcement in those families.

Constitutional factors, rather than environmental factors, are of major importance in determining whether a child has phonological disorder. The high proportion of children with the disorder who have relatives with a similar disorder suggests that the disorder may have a genetic component.

Poor motor coordination, laterality, and handedness do not contribute to phonological disorder.

DIAGNOSIS

The essential feature of phonological disorder is an articulation defect characterized by the child's consistent failure to use developmentally expected speech sounds of certain consonants, including omissions, substitutions, and distortions of phonemes, which are generally late-learned phonemes. The disorder cannot be attributed to structural or neurological abnormalities and is accompanied by normal language development. The DSM-IV diagnostic criteria for phonological disorder are given in Table 32.3–1.

CLINICAL FEATURES

The essential clinical feature of phonological disorder is a variety of developmentally inappropriate speech sounds. The sounds are often substitutions—for example, the use of /t/ instead of /k/—and omissions, such as leaving off the final consonants of words.

Phonological disorder is recognized in early childhood. In severe cases the disorder is first recognized at about 3 years of age. In less severe cases the disorder may not be apparent until the age of 6 years. Articulation is judged to be defective when

Table 32.3–1. Diagnostic Criteria for Phonological Disorder

A. Failure to use developmentally expected speech sounds that are appropriate for age and dialect (e.g., errors in sound production, use, representation, or organization such as, but not limited to, substitutions of one sound for another (use of /t/ for target /k/ sound) or omissions of sounds such as final consonants).

B. The difficulties in speech sound production interfere with academic or occupational achievement or with social communication.

C. If mental retardation, a speech-motor or sensory deficit, or environmental deprivation is present, the speech difficulties are in excess of those usually associated with these problems.

Table from DSM-IV, *Diagnostic and Statistical Manual of Mental Disorders*, ed 4. Copyright American Psychiatric Association, Washington, 1994. Used with permission.

compared with the speech of children at the same age level, and the differences cannot be attributed to abnormalities in intelligence, hearing, or the physiology of the patient's speech mechanism. In very mild cases only one phoneme may be affected. Single phonemes are usually affected, most commonly those acquired late in the normal language acquisition process.

In phonological disorder the speech sounds that are most frequently misarticulated are those acquired late in the developmental sequence (/r/, /sh/, /th/, /f/, /z/, /l/, and /ch/). But in severe cases and in young children, sounds such as /b/, /m/, /t/, /d/, /n/, and /h/ may be mispronounced. One or many speech sounds may be affected, but vowel sounds are not among them.

The child with phonological disorder is not able to articulate certain phonemes correctly and may distort, substitute, or even omit the affected phonemes. With omissions, the phonemes are absent entirely—for example, "bu" for "blue," "ca" for "car," or "whaa?" for "what's that?" With substitutions, difficult phonemes are replaced with incorrect ones—for example, "wabbit" for "rabbit," "fum" for "thumb," or "whath dat?" for "what's that?" With distortions, the correct phoneme is approximated but is articulated incorrectly. Rarely do additions, usually of the vowel "schwa" or "uh," occur—for example, "puhretty" for "pretty," "what's uh that uh?" for "what's that?"

Omissions are thought to be the most serious type of misarticulation, with substitutions the next most serious type, and distortion the least serious type. Omissions are most frequently found in the speech of young children and usually occur at the end of words or in clusters of consonants ("ka" for "car," "scisso" for "scissors"). Distortions, which are found mainly in the speech of older children, result in a sound that is not part of the speaker's dialect. Distortions may be the last type of misarticulation remaining in the speech of children whose articulation problems have mostly remitted. The most common types of distortions are the *lateral lisp*—in which the child pronounces /s/ sounds with the air stream going across the tongue, producing a whistling effect—and the *palatal lisp*—in which the /s/ sound is formed with the tongue too close to the palate, producing a /sh/ sound. The misarticulations of children with phonological disorder are often inconsistent and random. A phoneme may be pronounced correctly in one situation and incorrectly another time. Misarticulations are most common at the ends of words, in long and syntactically complex sentences, and during rapid speech.

Omissions, distortions, and substitutions also occur normally in the speech of young children learning to talk. However, whereas young normal children soon replace those misarticulations, children with phonological disorder do not. Even as children with phonological disorder grow and finally acquire the correct phoneme, they may use it only in newly acquired words and may not correct earlier learned words that they have been mispronouncing for some time.

In most cases, recovery from phonological disorder is spontaneous, and often the child's beginning kindergarten or school hastens improvement. Speech therapy is clearly indicated for those children who have not shown a spontaneous improvement by the third or fourth grade. For those children whose articulation is significantly unintelligible and are clearly troubled by their inability to speak clearly, speech therapy should be initiated at an earlier age.

Other disorders are commonly present with phonological disorder, including expressive language disorder, mixed receptive-expressive language disorder, reading disorder, and developmental coordination disorder. Enuresis may also be present.

A delay in reaching speech milestones (such as first word and first sentence) has been reported in some children with phonological disorder, but most children with the disorder begin speaking at the appropriate age.

Children with phonological disorder may have various concomitant social, emotional, and behavioral problems. About a third of the children with the condition have psychiatric disorders, such as attention-deficit/hyperactivity disorder, separation anxiety disorder, adjustment disorders, and depressive disorders. Those children with a severe degree of articulation impairment or whose disorder is chronic and nonremitting are the ones most likely to suffer from psychiatric problems.

DIFFERENTIAL DIAGNOSIS

The differential diagnostic process for phonological disorder involves three steps. First, the clinician must determine that the misarticulations are severe enough to be considered abnormal and must rule out the normal misarticulations of young children. Second, the clinician must find that no physical abnormalities account for the articulation errors and must rule out dysarthria, hearing impairment, and mental retardation as the cause. And third, the clinician must establish that expressive language is within normal limits and must rule out expressive language disorder, mixed receptive-expressive language disorder, and pervasive developmental disorders.

A rough guideline for a clinical assessment of children's articulation is that normal 3-year-olds correctly articulate /m/, /n/, /ng/, /b/, /p/, /h/, /t/, /k/, /q/, and /d/; normal 4-year-olds correctly articulate /f/, /y/, /ch/, /sh/, and /z/; and normal 5-years-olds correctly articulate /th/, /s/, and /r/.

Children with dysarthria, a disorder caused by structural or neurological abnormalities, differ from children with phonological disorder in that dysarthria is difficult and sometimes impossible to remedy. Drooling, slow or uncoordinated motor behavior, abnormal chewing or swallowing, and awkward or slow protrusion and retraction of the tongue are indications of dysarthria. A slow rate of speech is another indication of dysarthria.

COURSE AND PROGNOSIS

Recovery is frequently spontaneous, particularly in children whose misarticulations involve only a few phonemes. Spontaneous recovery is rare after the age of 8 years.

TREATMENT

Speech therapy is considered the most successful treatment for most phonological errors: it is indicated when the child's articulation intelligibility is poor; when the affected child is over 8 years of age; when the speech problem is apparently causing problems with peers, learning, and self-image; when the disorder is so severe that many consonants are misarticulated; and when errors involve omissions and substitutions of phonemes, rather than distortions.

Monitoring of the child's peer relationships, school behavior, and parental counseling may be necessary for the timely implementation of psychiatric treatment when the need arises.

References

Baker L, Cantwell D P: Phonological disorder. In *Comprehensive Textbook of Psychiatry*, ed 6, H I Kaplan, B J Sadock, editors, p 2268. Williams & Wilkins, Baltimore, 1995.
Cantwell D P, Baker L: *Psychiatric and Developmental Disorders in Children with Communication Disorder*. American Psychiatric Association Press Washington, 1991.
Coplan J, Gleason J R: Unclear speech: Recognition and significance of unintelligible speech in preschool children. Pediatrics 82: 447, 1988.
Lewis B A: Familial phonological disorders: Four pedigrees. J Speech Hear Disord 55: 160, 1990.
Shriberg L D, Kwiatkowski J: A follow-up study of children with phonologic disorders of unknown origin. J Speech Hear Disord 53: 144, 1988.

32.4 STUTTERING AND COMMUNICATION DISORDER NOS

STUTTERING

In the fourth edition of *Diagnostic and Statistical Manual of Mental Disorders* (DSM-IV), stuttering is classified under communication disorders. It is defined by a disturbance in the normal fluency and time patterning of speech that is inappropriate for the patient's age and that consists of one or more of the following: sound repetitions, prolongations, interjections, pauses within words, observable word substitutions to avoid blocking, and audible or silent blocking. The disturbance in fluency is severe enough to interfere with academic or occupational achievement or social communication. Usually the disorder originates in childhood. The degree of stuttering may vary with situations and with particular words.

Epidemiology

Within the general population the prevalence of stuttering is about 1 percent, but the incidence is estimated at close to 3 percent a year. Stuttering tends to be most common in young children and to resolve in older children and in adults. Stuttering affects about three to four males for every female. The disorder is more common among family members of the affected child than in the general population.

Etiology

The precise cause of stuttering is unknown, but a variety of theories have been proposed. In the past it was hypothesized that stuttering occurs as a response to conflicts, fears, or neurosis. No evidence suggests that conflicts or anxiety causes stuttering or that persons who stutter have more psychiatric disturbances than do persons with other forms of speech and language disorders.

However, stuttering may be exacerbated by certain stressful situations.

Other theories about the cause of stuttering include organic models and learning models. The organic models include those that focus on incomplete lateralization or abnormal cerebral dominance. Several studies using electroencephalography (EEG) found that stuttering males had right-hemispheric alpha suppression across stimulus words and tasks; nonstutterers had left-hemispheric suppression. An overrepresentation of left-handedness and ambidexterity is found in stutterers. The theory of abnormal cerebral dominance essentially hypothesizes a conflict between the two halves of the cerebrum for control of language functions. The striking gender differences in stuttering and twin studies indicate that stuttering has some genetic basis.

The learning theories about the cause of stuttering include the semantogenic theory, in which stuttering is basically a learned response to normative early childhood dysfluencies. Another learning model focuses on classical conditioning, in which the stuttering becomes conditioned to environmental factors. In the cybernetic model, speech is viewed as a process that depends on appropriate feedback for regulation; stuttering is hypothesized to occur because of a breakdown in the feedback loop. The observations that stuttering is reduced by white noise and that delayed auditory feedback produces stuttering in normal speakers increase the potential validity of that theory.

Stuttering is probably caused by a set of interacting variables that include genetic and environmental factors.

Diagnosis

The diagnosis of stuttering is not difficult when the clinical features are apparent and well developed and each of the four phases, as described below, can be readily recognized. Diagnostic difficulties may arise when trying to determine the existence of stuttering in young children, as some preschool children experience transient dysfluency. It may not be clear whether the nonfluent pattern is part of normal speech and language development or whether it represents the initial stage in the development of stuttering. If incipient stuttering is suspected, referral to a speech pathologist is indicated. Table 32.4–1 presents the DSM-IV diagnostic criteria for stuttering.

Table 32.4-1.   Diagnostic Criteria for Stuttering

A. Disturbance in the normal fluency and time patterning of speech (inappropriate for the individual's age), characterized by frequent occurrences of one or more of the following:

(1) sound and syllable repetitions
(2) sound prolongations
(3) interjections
(4) broken words (e.g., pauses within a word)
(5) audible or silent blocking (filled or unfilled pauses in speech)
(6) circumlocutions (word substitutions to avoid problematic words)
(7) words produced with an excess of physical tension
(8) monosyllabic whole-word repetitions (e.g., ``I-I-I see him'')

B. The disturbance in fluency interferes with academic or occupational achievement or with social communication.

C. If a speech-motor or sensory deficit is present, the speech difficulties are in excess of those usually associated with these problems.

Table from DSM-IV, *Diagnostic and Statistical Manual of Mental Disorders*, ed 4. Copyright American Psychiatric Association, Washington, 1994. Used with permission.

Clinical Features

Stuttering usually appears before the age of 12 years, in most cases between 18 months and 9 years, with two sharp peaks of onset between the ages of 2 to $3\frac{1}{2}$ and 5 to 7 years. Some but not all stutterers have other speech and language problems, such as phonological disorder and expressive language disorder. Stuttering does not suddenly begin; it typically occurs over a period of weeks or months with a repetition of initial consonants, whole words that are usually the first words of a phrase, or long words. As the disorder progresses, the repetitions become more frequent, with consistent stuttering on the most important words or phrases. Even after it develops, stuttering may be absent during oral readings, singing, and talking to pets or inanimate objects.

Four gradually evolving phases in the development of stuttering have been identified.

Phase 1 occurs during the preschool period. Initially, the difficulty tends to be episodic, appearing for periods of weeks or months between long interludes of normal speech. There is a high percentage of recovery from those periods of stuttering. During phase 1, children stutter most often when excited or upset, when they seem to have a great deal to say, and under other conditions of communicative pressure.

Phase 2 usually occurs in the elementary school years. The disorder is chronic, with few if any intervals of normal speech. Affected children become aware of their speech difficulties and regard themselves as stutterers. In phase 2 the stuttering occurs mainly on the major parts of speech—nouns, verbs, adjectives, and adverbs.

Phase 3 is usually seen after age 8 and up to adulthood. It occurs most often in late childhood and early adolescence. During phase 3 the stuttering comes and goes largely in response to specific situations, such as reciting in class, speaking to strangers, making purchases in stores, and using the telephone. Some words and sounds are regarded as more difficult than others.

Phase 4 is typically seen in late adolescence and adulthood. Stutterers show a vivid, fearful anticipation of stuttering. They fear words, sounds, and situations. Words substitutions and circumlocutions are common. Stutterers avoid situations requiring speech and show other evidence of fear and embarrassment.

Stutterers may have associated clinical features: vivid, fearful anticipation of stuttering, with avoidance of particular words, sounds, or situations in which stuttering is anticipated; eye blinks; tics; and tremors of the lips or the jaw. Frustration, anxiety, and depression are common among those with chronic stuttering. Other disorders that coexist with stuttering include phonological disorder, expressive language disorder, mixed receptive-expressive language disorder, and attention-deficit/hyperactivity disorder.

Differential Diagnosis

Normal speech dysfluency in the preschool years is difficult to differentiate from incipient stuttering. In stuttering there are more part-word repetitions, sound prolongations, and disruptions in voice airflow through the vocal track.

Spastic dysphonia is a stutteringlike speech disorder and is distinguished from stuttering by the presence of an abnormal pattern of breathing.

Cluttering is a speech disorder characterized by erratic and dysrhythmic speech patterns of rapid and jerky spurts of words and phrases. In cluttering, the affected persons are usually unaware of the disturbance, whereas, after the initial phase of the disorder, stutterers are aware of their speech difficulties.

Course and Prognosis

The course of stuttering is usually long-term, with some periods of partial remission lasting for weeks or months and exacerbations occurring most frequently when the stutterer is under pressure to speak. Fifty to 80 percent of all children with stuttering, most with mild cases, recover spontaneously.

In chronic stuttering by school-age children, impairment in peer relationships may be a result of testing and social ostracism. The children may face academic difficulties if they avoid speaking in class. Later major complications include the affected person's limitations in occupational choice and advancement.

Treatment

Until the end of the 19th century, the most common treatments for stuttering were distraction, suggestion, and relaxation. Recent approaches using distraction include teaching stutterers to talk in time to rhythmic movements of the arm, the hand, or the fingers. Stutterers are also advised to speak slowly in a sing-song or monotone. Those approaches, however, remove the stuttering only temporarily. Suggestion techniques, such as hypnosis, also stop stuttering but, again, only temporarily. Relaxation techniques are based on the premise that it is almost impossible to be relaxed and at the same time to stutter in the usual manner. Because of their lack of long-term benefits, distraction, suggestion, and relaxation approaches as such are not currently used.

Classic psychoanalysis, insight-oriented psychotherapy, group therapy, and other psychotherapeutic modalities have not been successful in treating stuttering. However, if stutterers have a poor self-image, are anxious or depressed, or show evidence of an established emotional disorder, individual psychotherapy is indicated and effective for the associated condition. In one study the reaction of nonstuttering listeners to stutterers who acknowledged their stuttering was much more positive than to stutterers who did not acknowledge their stuttering.

Family therapy should also be considered if there is evidence of family dysfunction, family contribution to the stutterer's symptoms, or family stress caused by trying to cope with or to help the stutterer.

Most of the modern treatments of stuttering are based on the view that stuttering is essentially a learned form of behavior that is not necessarily associated with a basic mental disorder or neurological abnormality. The approaches work directly with the speech difficulty to minimize the issues that maintain and strengthen the stuttering, to modify or decrease the severity of the stuttering by eliminating the secondary symptoms, and to encourage the stutterer to speak, even if stuttering, in a relatively easy and effortless fashion, thereby avoiding fears and blocks.

One example of that approach is the self-therapy proposed by the Speech Foundation of America. Self-therapy is based on the premise that stuttering is not a symptom but a behavior that can be modified. Stutterers are told that they can learn to control their difficulty partly by modifying their feelings about stuttering and attitudes toward it and partly by modifying the deviant behaviors associated with their stuttering blocks. The approach includes desensitization, reducing the emotional reaction to and fears of stuttering, and substituting positive action to control the moment of stuttering. The basic principle is that stuttering is something one is doing and that stutterers can learn to change what they are doing.

Recently developed therapies focus on the restructuring of fluency. The entire pattern of speech production is reshaped, with emphasis on a variety of target behaviors, including rate reduction, easy or gentle onset of voicing, and smooth transitions between sounds, syllables, and words. With adults, the approaches have met with substantial success in establishing perceptually fluent speech. However, the maintenance of fluency over long periods and relapses remain problems for all involved in adult stuttering treatment.

Whichever therapeutic approach is used, individual and family assessments and supportive interventions may be helpful. A team assessment of the child or the adolescent and his or her family should be made before any approaches to treatment are begun.

COMMUNICATION DISORDER NOT OTHERWISE SPECIFIED

This category is used for disorders that do not meet the diagnostic criteria for any specific communication disorder. An example is voice disorder, in which the patient has an abnormality in pitch, loudness, quality, tone, or resonance. To be coded as a disorder, the voice abnormality must be severe enough to cause an impairment in academic achievement or social communication.

References

Baker L, Cantwell D P: Stuttering. In *Comprehensive Textbook of Psychiatry*, ed 6, H I Kaplan, B J Sadock, editors, p 2272. Williams & Wilkins, Baltimore, 1995.

Conture E G: *Stuttering*, ed 2. Prentice-Hall, Englewood Cliffs, NJ, 1990.

Cordes A K, Ingham R J: Stuttering includes both within-word and between-word disfluencies. J Speech Hear Res 38: 382, 1995.

Louko L J: Phonological characteristics of young children who stutter. Top Language Disord 15: 48, 1995.

Nippold M A: Concomitant speech and language disorders in stuttering children: A critique of the literature. J Speech Hear Disord 55: 51, 1990.

Pool K D, Devous M D, Freeman F J, Watson B, Flinitzo T: Regional cerebral blood flow in developmental stutterers. Arch Neurol 48: 509, 1991.

Rosenfield D B, Derman H S: Physician referral patterns for stutterers. J Otolaryngol 19: 19, 1990.

Zebrowski P M: The topography of beginning stuttering. J Commun Disord 28: 75, 1995.

33/ Pervasive Developmental Disorders

The pervasive developmental disorders are a group of psychiatric conditions in which expected social skills, language development, and behavioral repertoire either do not develop appropriately or are lost in early childhood. In general, the disorders affect multiple areas of development, manifest early in life, and cause persistent dysfunction. Autistic disorder (also known as infantile autism), best-known of the disorders, is characterized by sustained impairments in reciprocal social interactions, communication deviance, and restricted, stereotypical behavioral patterns. According to the fourth edition of *Diagnostic and Statistical Manual of Mental Disorders* (DSM-IV), abnormal functioning in the above areas must be present by age 3. More than two thirds of the persons with autistic disorder have mental retardation, but that is not required for the diagnosis.

DSM-IV includes several other disorders in the category of pervasive developmental disorders: Rett's disorder, childhood disintegrative disorder, and Asperger's disorder. Rett's disorder appears to occur exclusively in girls; it is characterized by normal development for at least six months, followed by a degenerating developmental course. Typically, the child begins to show stereotyped hand movements, a loss of purposeful motions, diminishing social engagement, poor coordination, and decreasing language use. In childhood disintegrative disorder, development progresses normally for the first two years, after which the child shows a loss of previously acquired skills in two or more of the following areas: language use, social responsiveness, play, motor skills, and bladder or bowel control. Asperger's disorder is a condition in which the child shows a marked impairment in social relatedness and repetitive and stereotyped patterns of behavior without a delay in language development. The child's cognitive abilities and adaptive skills are normal.

AUTISTIC DISORDER

Epidemiology

PREVALENCE

Autistic disorder occurs at a rate of 2 to 5 cases per 10,000 children (0.02 to 0.05 percent) under age 12. If severe mental retardation with some autistic features is included, the rate can rise as high as 20 per 10,000. Usually autism begins before 36 months but may not be evident to parents, depending on their awareness and the severity of the disorder.

SEX DISTRIBUTION

Autistic disorder is found more frequently in boys than in girls. Three to five times more boys than girls have autistic disorder. However, autistic girls tend to be more seriously affected and more likely to have family histories of cognitive impairment than are boys.

SOCIOECONOMIC STATUS

Early studies suggested that a high socioeconomic status was common in families with autistic children; however, those findings were probably based on referral biases. Over the past 25 years, an increasing proportion of cases has been found in the low socioeconomic groups. That finding may well be due to an increased awareness of the disorder and the increased availability of child mental health workers for poor children.

Etiology and Pathogenesis

Autistic disorder is a developmental behavioral disorder. Although autistic disorder was first considered psychosocial or psychodynamic in origin, much evidence has accumulated to support a biological substrate.

PSYCHODYNAMIC AND FAMILY FACTORS

In his initial report Leo Kanner noted that few parents of autistic children were really warmhearted and that, for the most part, the parents and other family members were preoccupied with intellectual abstractions and tended to express little genuine interest in their children. That finding, however, has not been replicated over the past 50 years. Other theories, such as parental rage and rejection and parental reinforcement of autistic symptoms, have also not been substantiated. Recent studies comparing parents of autistic children with parents of normal children have not shown significant differences in child-rearing skills. No satisfactory evidence indicates that any particular kind of deviant family functioning or psychodynamic constellation of factors leads to the development of autistic disorder. Nevertheless, some autistic children respond to psychosocial stressors, such as the birth of a sibling or the move to a new home, with an exacerbation of symptoms.

ORGANIC-NEUROLOGICAL-BIOLOGICAL ABNORMALITIES

Autistic disorder and autistic symptoms are associated with conditions that have neurological lesions, notably congenital rubella, phenylketonuria (PKU), tuberous sclerosis, and Rett's disorder. Autistic children show more evidence of perinatal complications than do comparison groups of normal children and those with other disorders.

The finding that autistic children have significantly more minor congenital physical anomalies than do their siblings and normal controls suggests that complications of pregnancy in the first trimester are significant. Four to 32 percent of autistic persons have grand mal seizures at some point in life, and about 20 to 25 percent of autistic persons show ventricular enlargement on computed tomography scans. Various electroencephalogram (EEG) abnormalities are found in 10 to 83 percent of autistic children, and, although no EEG finding is specific to autistic disorder, there is some indication of failed cerebral lateralization. Recently, one magnetic resonance imaging (MRI) study revealed hypoplasia of cerebellar vermal lobules VI and VII, and another MRI study revealed cortical abnormalities, particularly polymicrogyria, in some autistic patients. Those abnormalities may reflect abnormal cell migrations in the first six months of gestation. An autopsy study revealed decreased Purkinje's cell counts, and in another study was increased diffuse cortical metabolism during positron emission tomography (PET) scanning.

GENETIC FACTORS

In several surveys, between 2 and 4 percent of siblings of autistic persons have been found to be afflicted with autistic disorder, a rate 50 times greater than in the general population. The concordance rate of autistic disorder in the two largest twin studies was 36 percent in monozygotic pairs versus 0 percent in dizygotic pairs in one study and about 96 percent in monozygotic pairs versus about 27 percent in dizygotic pairs in the second study. In the second study, however, zygosity was confirmed in only about half of the sample. Clinical reports and studies suggest that the nonautistic members of the families share various language or other cognitive problems with the autistic person but have them in a less severe form. Fragile X syndrome appears to be associated with autistic disorder, but the number of persons with both autistic disorder and fragile X syndrome is unclear.

IMMUNOLOGICAL FACTORS

Some evidence suggests that immunological incompatibility between the mother and the embryo or fetus may contribute to autistic disorder. The lymphocytes of some autistic children react with maternal antibodies, raising the possibility that embryonic neural or extraembryonic tissues may be damaged during gestation.

PERINATAL FACTORS

A high incidence of various perinatal complications seems to occur in children with autistic disorder, although no complication has been directly implicated as causative. During gestation, maternal bleeding after the first trimester and meconium in the amniotic fluid have been reported in autistic children more often than in the general population. In the neonatal period, autistic children have a high incidence of respiratory distress syndrome and neonatal anemia. Some evidence suggests a high incidence of medication usage during pregnancy in the mothers of autistic children.

NEUROANATOMICAL FINDINGS

The temporal lobe has been suggested as a critical part of the brain that may be abnormal in autistic disorder. That suggestion is based on reports of autisticlike syndromes in some persons who have temporal lobe damage. When the temporal region of animals is damaged, expected social behavior is lost, and restlessness, repetitive motor behavior, and a limited behavioral repertoire are seen. Other findings in autistic disorder include decreased Purkinje's cells in the cerebellum, potentially resulting in abnormalities of attention, arousal, and sensory processes.

BIOCHEMICAL FINDINGS

At least one third of autistic disorder patients have elevated plasma serotonin. That finding is not specific to autistic disorder, since persons with mental retardation without autistic disorder also have that trait. Autistic disorder patients without mental retardation also have a high incidence of hyperserotonemia.

In some autistic children, increased cerebrospinal fluid (CSF) homovanillic acid (the major dopamine metabolite) is associated with increased withdrawal and stereotypies. Some evidence indicates that symptom severity decreases as the ratio of CSF 5-hydroxyindoleacetic acid (5-HIAA, metabolite of serotonin) to CSF homovanillic acid increases. CSF 5-HIAA may be inversely proportional to blood serotonin levels; those levels are increased in one third of autistic disorder patients, a nonspecific finding that is also found in mentally retarded persons.

Table 33-1.   Diagnostic Criteria for Autistic Disorder

A. A total of six (or more) items from (1), (2), and (3), with at least two from (1), and one each from (2) and (3):

  (1) qualitative impairment in social interaction, as manifested by at least two of the following:
   (a) marked impairment in the use of multiple nonverbal behaviors such as eye-to-eye gaze, facial expression, body postures, and gestures to regulate social interaction
   (b) failure to develop peer relationships appropriate to developmental level
   (c) a lack of spontaneous seeking to share enjoyment, interests, or achievements with other people (e.g., by a lack of showing, bringing, or pointing out objects of interest)
   (d) lack of social or emotional reciprocity

  (2) qualitative impairments in communication as manifested by at least one of the following:
   (a) delay in, or total lack of, the development of spoken language (not accompanied by an attempt to compensate through alternative modes of communication such as gesture or mime)
   (b) in individuals with adequate speech, marked impairment in the ability to initiate or sustain a conversation with others
   (c) stereotyped and repetitive use of language or idiosyncratic language
   (d) lack of varied, spontaneous make-believe play or social imitative play appropriate to developmental level

  (3) restricted repetitive and stereotyped patterns of behavior, interests, and activities, as manifested by at least one of the following:
   (a) encompassing preoccupation with one or more stereotyped and restricted patterns of interest that is abnormal either in intensity or focus
   (b) apparently inflexible adherence to specific, nonfunctional routines or rituals
   (c) stereotyped and repetitive motor mannerisms (e.g., hand or finger flapping or twisting, or complex whole-body movements)
   (d) persistent preoccupation with parts of objects

B. Delays or abnormal functioning in at least one of the following areas, with onset prior to age 3 years: (1) social interaction, (2) language as used in social communication, or (3) symbolic or imaginative play.

C. The disturbance is not better accounted for by Rett's disorder or childhood disintegrative disorder.

Table from DSM-IV, *Diagnostic and Statistical Manual of Mental Disorders*, ed 4. Copyright American Psychiatric Association, Washington, 1994. Used with permission.

Diagnosis and Clinical Features

The DSM-IV diagnostic criteria for autistic disorder are given in Table 33–1.

PHYSICAL CHARACTERISTICS

Appearance

Kanner was struck by autistic children's intelligent and attractive appearance. Between the ages of 2 and 7, they also tend to be shorter than the normal population.

Handedness

Many autistic children have a failure of lateralization. That is, they remain ambidextrous at an age when cerebral dominance is established in normal children. Autistic children also have a higher incidence of abnormal dermatoglyphics (for example, fingerprints) than do the general population, which may suggest a disturbance in neuroectodermal development.

Intercurrent Physical Illness

Young autistic disorder children have a higher incidence of upper respiratory infections, excessive burping, febrile seizures, constipation, and loose bowel movements than do controls. Many autistic children react differently to illness than do normal children, which may reflect an immature or abnormal autonomic nervous system. Autistic children may not have elevated temperatures with infectious illnesses, may not complain of pain either verbally or by gesture, and may not show the malaise of ill children. Their behavior and relatedness may improve to a noticeable degree when they are ill, and in some cases that is a clue to physical illness.

BEHAVIORAL CHARACTERISTICS

Qualitative Impairments in Social Interaction

All autistic children fail to show the usual relatedness to their parents and other people. As infants, many lack a social smile and anticipatory posture for being picked up as an adult approaches. Abnormal eye contact is a common finding. The social development of autistic children is characterized by a lack (but not always a total absence) of attachment behavior and a relatively early failure of person-specific bonding. Autistic children often do not seem to recognize or differentiate the most important people in their lives—parents, siblings, and teachers. And they may show virtually no separation anxiety on being left in an unfamiliar environment with strangers.

When autistic children have reached school age, their withdrawal may have diminished or not be as obvious, particularly in better-functioning children. Instead, their failure to play with peers and to make friends, their social awkwardness and inappropriateness, and, particularly, their failure to develop empathy are observed.

In late adolescence, those autistic persons who make the most progress often have a desire for friendships. However, their ineptness of approach and their inability to respond to another's interests, emotions, and feelings are major obstacles in developing friendships. Autistic adolescents and adults have sexual feelings, but their lack of social competence and skills prevents most of them from developing a sexual relationship. It is extremely rare for autistic persons to marry.

Disturbances of Communication and Language

Gross deficits and deviances in language development are among the principal criteria for diagnosing autistic disorder. Autistic children are not simply reluctant to speak, and their speech abnormalities are not due to lack of motivation. Language deviance, as much as language delay, is characteristic of autistic disorder. In contrast to normal and mentally retarded children, autistic children make little use of meaning in their memory and thought processes. When autistic persons do learn to converse fluently, they lack social competence, and their conversations are not characterized by reciprocal responsive interchanges.

In the first year of life, the autistic child's amount and pattern of babbling may be reduced or abnormal. Some children emit noises—clicks, sounds, screeches, and nonsense syllables—in a stereotyped fashion with no seeming intent of communication.

Unlike normal young children, who always have better receptive language skills and understand much before they can speak, verbal autistic children may say more than they understand. Words and even entire sentences may drop in and out of a child's vocabulary. Autistic children may use a word once and then not use it again for a week, a month, or years. Their speech contains echolalia, both immediate and delayed, or stereotyped phrases out of context. Those abnormalities are often associated with pronominal reversal; that is, a girl asks, "Do you want the toy?" when she means she wants it. Difficulties in articulation are also noted. The use of peculiar voice quality and rhythm is observed clinically in many cases. About 50 percent of all autistic children never have useful speech. Some of the brightest children show a particular fascination with letters and numbers. A few literally teach themselves to read at a preschool age (hyperlexia), often astonishingly well. In nearly all cases, however, the children read without any comprehension at all.

Stereotyped Behavior

In the first years of an autistic child's life, much of the normal child's exploratory play is absent or minimal. Toys and objects are often manipulated in a way that was not intended, with little variety, creativity, and imagination and few symbolic features. Autistic children cannot imitate or use abstract pantomime. The activities and play, if any, of the autistic child are rigid, repetitive, and monotonous. Ritualistic and compulsive phenomena are common in early and middle childhood. Autistic children often spin, bang, and line up objects and become attached to inanimate objects. In addition, many autistic children, particularly those who are the most intellectually impaired, exhibit various abnormalities of movements. Stereotypies, mannerisms, and grimacing are most frequent when the child is left alone and may decrease in a structured situation. Autistic children are resistant to transition and change. Moving to a new house, moving furniture in a room, and having breakfast before a bath when the reverse was the routine may result in panic or temper tantrums.

Instability of Mood and Affect

Some children with autistic disorder exhibit sudden mood changes, with bursts of laughing or crying for no apparent reason and without expressing thoughts congruent to the affect.

Response to Sensory Stimuli

Autistic children may be overresponsive or underresponsive to sensory stimuli (for example, to sound and pain). They may selectively ignore spoken language directed at them, and so they are often thought to be deaf. However, they may show unusual interest in the sound of a wristwatch. Many have a heightened pain threshold or an altered response to pain. Indeed, autistic children may injure themselves severely and not cry.

Many autistic children seem to enjoy music. They frequently hum a tune or sing a song or commercial jingle before saying words or using speech. Some particularly enjoy vestibular stimulation—spinning, swinging, and up-and-down movements.

Other Behavioral Symptoms

Hyperkinesis is a common behavior problem in young autistic children. Hypokinesis is less frequent; when present, it often alternates with hyperactivity. Aggressiveness and temper tantrums are observed, often for no apparent reason, or they are prompted by change or demands. Self-injurious behavior includes head banging, biting, scratching, and hair pulling. Short attention span, a complete inability to focus on a task, insomnia, feeding and eating problems, enuresis, and encopresis are also frequent.

INTELLECTUAL FUNCTIONING

About 40 percent of the children with infantile autism have intelligence quotient (I.Q.) scores below 50 to 55 (moderate, severe, or profound mental retardation); 30 percent have scores of 50 to approximately 70 (mild mental retardation); and 30 percent have scores of 70 or more. Epidemiological and clinical studies show that the risk for autistic disorder increases as the I.Q. decreases. About one fifth of all autistic children have a normal nonverbal intelligence. The I.Q. scores of autistic children tend to reflect problems with verbal sequencing and abstraction skills, rather than with visuospatial or rote memory skills, suggesting the importance of defects in language-related functions.

Unusual or precocious cognitive or visuomotor abilities are present in some autistic children. The abilities may exist even within the overall retarded functioning and are called splinter functions or islets of precocity. Perhaps the most striking examples are the idiot savants who have prodigious rote memories or calculating abilities. Their specific abilities usually remain beyond the capabilities of normal peers. Other precocious abilities in young autistic children include hyperlexia, an early ability to read well (although they are not able to understand what they read), memorizing and reciting, and musical abilities (singing tunes or recognizing musical pieces).

Differential Diagnosis

The major differential diagnoses are schizophrenia with childhood onset, mental retardation with behavioral symptoms, mixed receptive-expressive language disorder, congenital deafness or severe hearing disorder, psychosocial deprivation, and disintegrative (regressive) psychoses.

SCHIZOPHRENIA WITH CHILDHOOD ONSET

Whereas a wealth of literature on autistic disorder is available, there are few data on children under age 12 who meet the diagnostic criteria for schizophrenia. Schizophrenia is rare in children under the age of 5. It is accompanied by hallucinations or delusions, a lower incidence of seizures and mental retardation, and less discrepancy between the language and visuomotor facets of I.Q. than is present in autistic children.

MENTAL RETARDATION WITH BEHAVIORAL SYMPTOMS

About 40 percent of autistic children are moderately, severely, or profoundly retarded, and retarded children may have behavior symptoms that include autistic features. When both disorders are present, both should be diagnosed. The main differentiating features between autistic disorder and mental retardation are that (1) mentally retarded children usually relate to adults and other children according to their mental age; (2) they use the language they do have to communicate with others; and (3) they have a relatively even profile of impairments without splinter functions.

MIXED RECEPTIVE-EXPRESSIVE LANGUAGE DISORDER

Some children with mixed receptive-expressive language disorder have autisticlike features and may present a diagnostic problem.

ACQUIRED APHASIA WITH CONVULSION

Acquired aphasia with convulsion is a rare condition and is sometimes difficult to differentiate from autistic disorder and childhood disintegrative disorder. Children with the condition are normal for several years before losing both their receptive and their expressive language over a period of weeks or months. Most of them have a few seizures and generalized EEG abnormalities at the onset, but those signs usually do not persist. A profound disorder of language comprehension then follows, characterized by a deviant speech pattern and speech impairment. Some children recover but with considerable residual language impairment.

CONGENITAL DEAFNESS OR SEVERE HEARING IMPAIRMENT

Because autistic children are often mute or show a selective disinterest in spoken language, they are often thought to be deaf. The following may be differentiating features: Autistic infants may babble only infrequently, whereas deaf infants have a history of relatively normal babbling that then gradually tapers and may stop from 6 months to 1 year of age. Deaf children respond only to loud sounds, whereas autistic children may ignore loud or normal sounds and respond to soft or low sounds. Most important, audiogram or auditory evoked potentials indicate significant hearing loss in deaf children. Unlike autistic children, deaf children usually relate to their parents, seek their affection, and, as infants, enjoy being held.

PSYCHOSOCIAL DEPRIVATION

Severe disturbances in the physical and emotional environment (such as maternal deprivation, psychosocial dwarfism, hospitalism, and failure to thrive) can cause children to appear apathetic, withdrawn, and alienated. Language and motor skills can be delayed. Children with those signs almost always rapidly improve when placed in a favorable and enriched psychosocial environment, which is not so with autistic children.

Course and Prognosis

Autistic disorder has a long course and a guarded prognosis. Some autistic children suffer a loss of all or some of their preexisting speech. That occurs most often between 12 and 24 months of age. As a rule, the autistic children with I.Q.s above 70 and those who use communicative language by ages 5 to 7 have the best prognoses. Adult outcome studies suggest that about two thirds of autistic adults remain severely handicapped and live in complete dependence or semidependence, either with their relatives or in long-term institutions. Only 1 to 2 percent acquire a normal and independent status with gainful employment, and 5 to 20 percent achieve a borderline normal status. The prognosis is improved if the environment or the home is supportive and can meet the extensive needs of such a child.

Although a decrease of symptoms is noted in many cases, severe self-mutilation or aggressiveness and regression may develop in others. About 4 to 32 percent have grand mal seizures in late childhood or adolescence, and the seizures adversely affect the prognosis.

TREATMENT

The goals of treatment are to decrease the behavioral symptoms and to aid in the development of delayed, rudimentary, or nonexistent functions, such as language and self-care skills. In addition, the parents, often distraught, need support and counseling.

Insight-oriented individual psychotherapy has proved to be ineffective. Educational and behavioral methods are currently considered the treatments of choice.

Structured classroom training in combination with behavioral methods is the most effective treatment method for many autistic children and is superior to other types of behavioral approaches. Well-controlled studies indicate that gains in language and cognition and decreases in maladaptive behaviors are achieved by consistent behavioral programs. Careful training of parents in the concepts and the skills of behavior modification and the resolution of the parents' concerns may yield considerable gains in the child's language, cognitive, and social areas of behavior. However, the training programs are rigorous and require a great deal of the parents' time. The autistic child requires as much structure as possible, and a daily program for as many hours as feasible is desirable.

Although no drug has been found to be specific for autistic disorder, psychopharmacotherapy is a valuable adjunct in comprehensive treatment programs. The administration of haloperidol (Haldol) both reduces behavioral symptoms and accelerates learning. The drug decreases hyperactivity, stereotypies, withdrawal, fidgetiness, abnormal object relations, irritability, and labile affect. Supportive evidence indicates that, when used judiciously, haloperidol remains an effective long-term drug. Although tardive and withdrawal dyskinesias can occur with haloperidol treatment in autistic children, evidence suggests that those dyskinesias can resolve when haloperidol is discontinued. Fenfluramine (Pondimin), which reduces blood serotonin levels, is effective in a few autistic children. Improvement does not appear associated with a reduction in blood serotonin level. Naltrexone (ReVia), an opiate antagonist, is currently being investigated in the hope that blocking endogenous opioids will reduce autistic symptoms. Lithium (Eskalith) can be tried for aggressive or self-injurious behaviors when other medications fail.

RETT'S DISORDER

In 1965 Andreas Rett, an Australian physician, identified a syndrome in 22 girls who appeared to have had normal development for at least six months, followed by a devastating developmental deterioration. Although few surveys have been done, the ones available suggest a prevalence of 6 to 7 cases of Rett's disorder per 100,000 girls.

Etiology

The cause of Rett's disorder is unknown, although the progressive deteriorating course after an initial normal period is compatible with a metabolic disorder. In some patients with Rett's disorder, hyperammonemia has been found, leading to the postulation that an enzyme that metabolizes ammonia is deficient. However, hyperammonemia has not been found in most Rett's disorder patients. It is likely that Rett's disorder has a genetic basis, since it has been seen only in girls, and case reports so far indicate complete concordance in monozygotic twins.

Diagnosis and Clinical Features

During the first five months after birth, the infant has age-appropriate motor skills, a normal head circumference, and normal growth. Social interactions show the expected reciprocal quality. At 6 months to 2 years of age, the child has a progressive encephalopathy, with several characteristic features. The signs often include the loss of purposeful hand movements, which are replaced by stereotypic motions, such as hand wringing, the loss of previously acquired speech, psychomotor retardation, and ataxia. Other stereotypical movements of the hands may occur, such as licking or biting the fingers and tapping or slapping movements. The head-circumference growth decelerates, resulting in microcephaly. All language skills are lost, and both receptive and expressive communicative and social skills seem to plateau at developmental levels between 6 months and 1 year. Poor muscle coordination and an apraxic gait develop; the gait

Table 33-2. Diagnostic Criteria for Rett's Disorder

A. All of the following:

  (1) apparently normal prenatal and perinatal development
  (2) apparently normal psychomotor development through the first 5 months after birth
  (3) normal head circumference at birth

B. Onset of all of the following after the period of normal development:

  (1) deceleration of head growth between ages 5 and 48 months
  (2) loss of previously acquired purposeful hand skills between ages 5 and 30 months with the subsequent development of stereotyped hand movements (e.g., hand-wringing or hand washing)
  (3) loss of social engagement early in the course (although often social interaction develops later)
  (4) appearance of poorly coordinated gait or trunk movements
  (5) severely impaired expressive and receptive language development with severe psychomotor retardation

Table from DSM-IV, *Diagnostic and Statistical Manual of Mental Disorders*, ed 4. Copyright American Psychiatric Association, Washington, 1994. Used with permission.

has an unsteady and stiff quality. All the above clinical features are diagnostic criteria for the disorder (Table 33-2).

Associated features include seizures in up to 75 percent of affected children and disorganized EEGs with some epileptiform discharges in almost all young children with Rett's disorder, even in the absence of clinical seizures. An additional associated feature is irregular respiration, with episodes of hyperventilation, apnea, and breath holding. The disorganized breathing occurs in most patients while they are awake; during sleep the breathing usually normalizes. Many patients with Rett's disorder also have scoliosis. As the disorder progresses, muscle tone seems to increase from an initial hypotonic condition to spasticity to rigidity. Although children with Rett's disorder may live for well over a decade from the onset of the disorder, after 10 years of the disorder, many patients are wheelchair-bound, with muscle wasting, rigidity, and virtually no language ability. Long-term receptive and expressive communication and socialization abilities remain at a developmental level of less than 1 year.

Differential Diagnosis

Some children with Rett's disorder receive initial diagnoses of autistic disorder because of the marked disability in social interactions in both disorders. However, the two disorders have some predictable differences. In Rett's disorder, the child shows a deterioration of developmental milestones, head circumference, and total growth; in autistic disorder, aberrant development usually is present from early on. In Rett's disorder, specific and characteristic hand motions are always present; in autistic disorder, a variety of hand mannerisms may or may not occur. Poor coordination, ataxia, and apraxia are predictably part of Rett's disorder; many persons with autistic disorder have unremarkable gross motor function. In Rett's disorder, verbal abilities are usually lost completely; in autistic disorder, the patient uses characteristic aberrant language. Respiratory irregularity is characteristic of Rett's disorder, and seizures often appear early on; in autistic disorder, no respiratory disorganization is seen, and seizures do not develop in most patients; when seizures do develop, they are more likely in adolescence than in childhood.

Course and Prognosis

Rett's disorder is progressive. The prognosis is not fully known, but those patients who live into adulthood remain at a cognitive and social level equivalent to that in the first year of life.

Treatment

Treatment is aimed at symptomatic intervention. Physiotherapy has been beneficial for the muscular dysfunction, and anticonvulsant treatment is usually necessary to control the seizures. Behavior therapy is useful to control self-injurious behaviors, as it is in the treatment of autistic disorder, and may help regulate the breathing disorganization.

CHILDHOOD DISINTEGRATIVE DISORDER

Childhood disintegrative disorder, also known as Heller's syndrome and disintegrative psychosis, was described in 1908 as a deterioration over several months of intellectual, social, and language function occurring in 3- and 4-year-olds with previously normal functions. After the deterioration the children closely resembled children with autistic disorder.

Epidemiology

Epidemiological data have been complicated by the variable diagnostic criteria used, but childhood disintegrative disorder is estimated to be at least one tenth as common as autistic disorder, and the prevalence has been estimated to be about one case in 100,000 boys. The ratio of boys to girls seems to be between 4 and 8 boys to 1 girl.

Etiology

The cause is unknown, but the disorder has been associated with other neurological conditions, including seizure disorders, tuberous sclerosis, and various metabolic disorders.

Diagnosis and Clinical Features

The diagnosis is made on the basis of features that fit a characteristic age of onset, clinical picture, and course. Cases reported have ranged in onset from ages 1 to 9 years, but in the vast majority the onset is between 3 and 4 years; according to DSM-IV, the minimum age of onset is 2 years (Table 33–3). The onset may be insidious over several months, or it may be relatively abrupt, with diminishing abilities occurring in days or weeks. In some cases, the child displayed restlessness, increased activity level, and anxiety before the loss of function.

The core features of the disorder include a loss of communication skills, marked regression of reciprocal interactions, and the onset of stereotyped movements and compulsive behavior. Affective symptoms are common, particularly anxiety, as is the regression of self-help skills, such as bowel and bladder control. To receive the diagnosis, the child must exhibit a loss of skills in two of the following areas: language, social or adaptive behavior, bowel or bladder control, play, and motor skills. Abnormalities must be present in at least two of the following categor-

Table 33–3. Diagnostic Criteria for Childhood Disintegrative Disorder

A. Apparently normal development for at least the first 2 years after birth as manifested by the presence of age-appropriate verbal and nonverbal communication, social relationships, play, and adaptive behavior.

B. Clinically significant loss of previously acquired skills (before age 10 years) in at least two of the following areas:

   (1) expressive or receptive language
   (2) social skills or adaptive behavior
   (3) bowel or bladder control
   (4) play
   (5) motor skills

C. Abnormalities of functioning in at least two of the following areas:

   (1) qualitative impairment in social interaction (e.g., impairment in nonverbal behaviors, failure to develop peer relationships, lack of social or emotional reciprocity)
   (2) qualitative impairments in communication (e.g., delay or lack of spoken language, inability to initiate or sustain a conversation, stereotyped and repetitive use of language, lack of varied make-believe play)
   (3) restricted, repetitive, and stereotyped patterns of behavior, interests, and activities, including motor stereotypies and mannerisms

D. The disturbance is not better accounted for by another specific pervasive developmental disorder or by schizophrenia.

Table from DSM-IV, *Diagnostic and Statistical Manual of Mental Disorders*, ed 4. Copyright American Psychiatric Association, Washington, 1994. Used with permission.

ies: reciprocal social interaction, communication skills, and stereotyped or restricted behavior. The main neurological associated feature is seizure disorder.

Differential Diagnosis

The differential diagnosis of childhood disintegrative disorder includes autistic disorder and Rett's disorder. In many cases the clinical features overlap with autistic disorder, but childhood disintegrative disorder is distinguished from autistic disorder by the loss of previously acquired development. Before the onset of childhood disintegrative disorder (occurring at 2 years or older), language has usually progressed to sentence formation. That skill is strikingly different from the premorbid history of even high-functioning autistic disorder patients, in whom language generally does not exceed single words or phrases before the diagnosis of the disorder. Once the disorder occurs, however, those with childhood disintegrative disorder are more likely to have no language abilities than are high-functioning autistic disorder patients.

In Rett's disorder, the deterioration occurs much earlier than in childhood disintegrative disorder, and the characteristic hand stereotypies of Rett's disorder do not occur in childhood disintegrative disorder.

Course and Prognosis

The course of childhood disintegrative disorder is variable, with a plateau reached in most cases, a progressive deteriorating course in rare cases, and some improvement in occasional cases to the point of regaining the ability to speak in sentences. Most patients are left with at least moderate mental retardation.

Treatment

Because of the clinical similarity to autistic disorder, the treatment of childhood disintegrative disorder is the same as that for autistic disorder.

ASPERGER'S DISORDER

In 1994 Hans Asperger, an Austrian physician, described a syndrome that he named ''autistic psychopathy.'' His original description was of persons with normal intelligence who exhibit a qualitative impairment in reciprocal social interaction and behavioral oddities without delays in language development. Since then, persons with mental retardation but without language delay have received diagnoses of Asperger's disorder, and persons with language delay but without mental retardation have been given the diagnosis.

In the 10th revision of the International Classification of Diseases and Related Health Problems (ICD-10), Asperger's disorder is called Asperger's syndrome and is characterized by qualitative social impairment, a lack of significant language and cognitive delays, and the presence of restricted interests and behavior.

Assessing the prevalence of the disorder is difficult because of the lack of stability in the diagnostic criteria.

Etiology

The cause of Asperger's disorder is unknown, but family studies suggest a possible relation to autistic disorder. The similarity of Asperger's disorder to autistic disorder leads to genetic, metabolic, infectious, and perinatal hypotheses.

Diagnosis and Clinical Features

The clinical features include at least two of the following indications of qualitative social impairment: markedly abnormal nonverbal communicative gestures, the failure to develop peer relationships, the lack of social or emotional reciprocity, and an impaired ability to express pleasure in other people's happiness. Restricted interests and patterns of behavior are always present. According to DSM-IV, the patient shows no language delay, clinically significant cognitive delay, or adaptive impairment (Table 33–4).

Differential Diagnosis

The differential diagnosis includes autistic disorder, pervasive development disorder not otherwise specified, and, in patients approaching adulthood, schizoid personality disorder. According to DSM-IV, the most obvious distinctions between Asperger's disorder and autistic disorder are the criteria regarding language delay and dysfunction. The lack of language delay is a requirement for Asperger's disorder, but language impairment is a core feature in autistic disorder.

Course and Prognosis

Although little is known about the cohort described by the DSM-IV diagnostic criteria, past case reports have shown variable courses and prognoses for patients who have received diagnoses of Asperger's disorder. The factors associated with a good prognosis are a normal I.Q. and high-level social skills.

Table 33–4. Diagnostic Criteria for Asperger's Disorder

A. Qualitative impairment in social interaction, as manifested by at least two of the following:
  (1) marked impairment in the use of multiple nonverbal behaviors such as eye-to-eye gaze, facial expression, body postures, and gestures to regulate social interaction
  (2) failure to develop peer relationships appropriate to developmental level
  (3) a lack of spontaneous seeking to share enjoyment, interests, or achievements with other people (e.g., by a lack of showing, bringing, or pointing out objects of interest to other people)
  (4) lack of social or emotional reciprocity

B. Restricted repetitive and stereotyped patterns of behavior, interests, and activities, as manifested by at least one of the following:
  (1) encompassing preoccupation with one or more stereotyped and restricted patterns of interest that is abnormal either in intensity or focus
  (2) apparently inflexible adherence to specific, nonfunctional routines or rituals
  (3) stereotyped and repetitive motor mannerisms (e.g., hand or finger flapping or twisting, or complex whole-body movements)
  (4) persistent preoccupation with parts of objects

C. The disturbance causes clinically significant impairment in social, occupational, or other important areas of functioning.

D. There is no clinically significant general delay in language (e.g., single words used by age 2 years, communicative phrases used by age 3 years).

E. There is no clinically significant delay in cognitive development or in the development of age-appropriate self-help skills, adaptive behavior (other than in social interaction), and curiosity about the environment in childhood.

F. Criteria are not met for another specific pervasive developmental disorder or schizophrenia.

Table from DSM-IV, *Diagnostic and Statistical Manual of Mental Disorders*, ed 4. Copyright American Psychiatric Association, Washington, 1994. Used with permission.

Treatment

Treatment depends on the patient's level of adaptive function. For those patients with severe social impairment, some of the same techniques used for autistic disorder are likely to be beneficial in the treatment of Asperger's disorder.

PERVASIVE DEVELOPMENTAL DISORDER NOT OTHERWISE SPECIFIED

Pervasive development disorder not otherwise specified (NOS) should be diagnosed when a child manifests a qualitative impairment in the development of reciprocal social interaction and verbal nonverbal communication skills but does not meet the criteria for other pervasive developmental disorders, schizophrenia, or schizotypal or avoidant personality disorder.

Some children who receive the diagnosis exhibit a markedly restricted repertoire of activities and interest. The condition usually shows a better outcome than does autistic disorder.

TREATMENT

The treatment approach is basically the same as in autistic disorder. Mainstreaming in school may be possible. Compared with autistic children, those with pervasive developmental disorder not otherwise specified generally have better language skills and more self-awareness, so they are better candidates for psychotherapy.

References

Bauer S: Autism and the pervasive developmental disorders: Part 1. Pediatr Rev *16*: 130, 1995.

Bauer S: Autism and the pervasive developmental disorders: Part 2. Pediatr Rev *16*: 168, 1995.

Campbell M, Shay J: Pervasive developmental disorders. In *Comprehensive Text-book of Psychiatry*, ed 6, H I Kaplan, B J Sadock, editors, p 2277. Williams & Wilkins, Baltimore, 1995.

Ciaranello A L, Ciaranello R D: the neurobiology of infantile autism. Annu Rev Neurosci *18*: 101, 1995.

Gilman J T, Tuchman R F: Autism and associated behavioral disorders: Pharma-cotherapeutic intervention. Ann Pharmacother *29*: 47, 1995.

Kazdin A E: Replication and extension of behavioral treatment of autistic disorder. Am J Ment Retard *97*: 377, 1993.

Mundy P: Normal versus high-functioning status in children with autism. Am J Ment Retard *97*: 381, 1993.

Percy A K: Rett syndrome. Curr Opin Neurol *8*: 156, 1996.

Tsai L Y: Is Rett's syndrome a subtype of pervasive development disorders? J Autism Dev Disord *22*: 551, 1992.

Volkmar F R: Childhood disintegrative disorder: Issues for DSM-IV. J Autism Dev Disord *22*: 625, 1992.

34/ Attention-Deficit Disorders

ATTENTION-DEFICIT/HYPERACTIVITY DISORDER

Attention-deficit/hyperactivity disorder (ADHD) is characterized by a developmentally inappropriate poor attention span, age-inappropriate features of hyperactivity and impulsivity, or both. To meet the diagnostic criteria the disorder must be present for at least six months, cause impairment in academic or social functioning, and occur before the age of 7 years. According to the fourth edition of *Diagnostic and Statistical Manual of Mental Disorders* (DSM-IV), the diagnosis is made by confirming many symptoms in the inattention domain, the hyperactivity-impulsivity domain, or both. Thus, a child may qualify for the disorder with symptoms of inattention only or with symptoms of hyperactivity and impulsivity but not inattention. Some children exhibit multiple symptoms along both dimensions. Accordingly, DSM-IV lists three subtypes of attention-deficit/hyperactivity disorder: predominantly inattentive type, predominantly hyperactive-impulsive type, and combined type. An additional criterion is the presence of symptoms in two or more situations, such as at school, home, and work.

Epidemiology

Reports on the incidence of ADHD in the United States have varied from 2 to 20 percent of grade-school children. A conservative figure is about 3 to 5 percent of prepubertal elementary school children. In Great Britain the incidence is reported to be lower than in the United States, less than 1 percent. Boys have a greater incidence than do girls, with the ratio being from 3 to 1 to as much as 5 to 1. The disorder is most common in firstborn boys. The parents of children with ADHD show an increased incidence of hyperkinesis, sociopathy, alcohol use disorders, and conversion disorder. Although the onset is usually by the age of 3, the diagnosis is generally not made until the child is in elementary school and the formal learning situation requires structured behavioral patterns, including developmentally appropriate attention span and concentration.

Etiology

The causes of attention-deficit/hyperactivity disorders are not known. Most children with ADHD do not show evidence of gross structural damage in the central nervous system (CNS). Conversely, most children with known neurological disorders caused by brain injuries do not display attention deficits and hyperactivity. Despite the lack of a specific neurophysiological or neurochemical basis for the disorder, it is predictably associated with a variety of other disorders that affect brain function, such as learning disorders. The suggested contributing factors for ADHD include prenatal toxic exposures, prematurity, and prenatal mechanical insult to the fetal nervous system.

Food additives, colorings, preservatives, and sugar have also been suggested as possible causes of hyperactive behavior. No scientific evidence shows that those factors cause ADHD.

GENETIC FACTORS

Evidence for a genetic basis for ADHD includes the greater concordance in monozygotic twins than in dizygotic twins.

Also, siblings of hyperactive children have about twice the risk of having the disorder as does the general population. One sibling may have predominantly hyperactivity symptoms, and the others may have predominantly inattention.

Biological parents of children with the disorder have a higher risk for ADHD than do adoptive parents. When ADHD coexists with conduct disorder in the child, alcohol use disorders and antisocial personality disorder are more common in the parents than in the general population.

BRAIN DAMAGE

Researchers have long speculated that some children affected by ADHD received minimal and subtle brain damage to the CNS during their fetal and perinatal periods. Alternatively, infection, inflammation, and trauma during early infancy may have caused brain damage by adverse circulatory, toxic, metabolic, mechanical, and other effects. Minimal, subtle, and subclinical brain damage may be responsible for the genesis of learning disorders and ADHD. Nonfocal (soft) neurological signs are frequent.

Computed tomographic (CT) head scans in children with ADHD show no consistent findings. Studies using positron emission tomography (PET) have found decreased cerebral blood flow and metabolic rates in the frontal lobe areas of children with attention-deficit/hyperactivity disorder compared with controls. One theory is that the frontal lobes in children with ADHD are not adequately performing their inhibitory mechanism on lower structures, leading to disinhibition.

NEUROCHEMICAL FACTORS

Many neurotransmitters have been associated with attention-deficit and hyperactivity symptoms. In part, the findings have come out of the use of many medications that exert some positive effect on the disorder. The most widely studied drugs in the treatment of ADHD, the sympathomimetics, affect both dopamine and norepinephrine, leading to neurotransmitter hypotheses that include possible dysfunction in both the adrenergic and the dopaminergic systems. Sympathomimetics increase catecholamines by promoting their release and by blocking their uptake. Stimulants and some tricyclic drugs—for example, desipramine (Norpramin)—reduce urinary 3-methoxy-4-hydroxyphenylglycol (MHPG), which is a metabolite of norepinephrine. Clonidine (Catapres), a norepinephrine agonist, has been helpful in treating hyperactivity. Other drugs that have reduced hyperactivity include tricyclic drugs and monoamine oxidase inhibitors (MAOIs). Overall, no clear-cut evidence implicates a single neurotransmitter in the development of ADHD, but many neurotransmitters may be involved in the process.

NEUROPHYSIOLOGICAL FACTORS

The human brain normally undergoes major growth spurts at several ages: 3 to 10 months, 2 to 4 years, 6 to 8 years, 10 to 12 years, and 14 to 16 years. Some children have a maturational delay in the sequence and manifest symptoms of ADHD that seem temporary. A physiological correlate is the presence of a variety of nonspecific abnormal electroencephalogram

(EEG) patterns that are disorganized and characteristic of young children. In some cases the EEG findings normalize over time.

PSYCHOSOCIAL FACTORS

Children in institutions are frequently overactive and have poor attention spans. Those signs result from prolonged emotional deprivation, and they disappear when deprivational factors are removed, such as through adoption or placement in a foster home. Stressful psychic events, a disruption of the family equilibrium, and other anxiety-inducing factors contribute to the initiation or the perpetuation of ADHD. Predisposing factors may include the child's temperament, genetic-familial factors, and the demands of society to follow routinized ways of behaving and performing. Socioeconomic status does not seem to be a predisposing factor.

Diagnosis

The principal sign of hyperactivity should alert clinicians to the possibility of ADHD. A detailed prenatal history of the child's early developmental patterns and direct observation usually reveal excessive motor activity. Hyperactivity may be seen in some situations (for example, school) but not in others (for example, one-to-one interviews and watching television), and it may be less obvious in structured situations than in unstructured situations. However, the hyperactivity should not be an isolated, brief, and transient behavioral manifestation under stress but should have been present over a long time. According to DSM-IV, symptoms must be present in at least two settings (for example, school and home) to meet the diagnostic criteria for attention-deficit/hyperactivity disorder (Table 34–1).

Other distinguishing features of ADHD are short attention span and easy distractibility. In school, children with ADHD cannot follow instructions and often demand extra attention from their teachers. At home, they often do not follow through on their parents' requests. They act impulsively, show emotional lability, and are explosive and irritable.

Children who have hyperactivity as a predominant feature are more likely to be referred for treatment than are children with primarily symptoms of attention deficit. Children with the predominantly hyperactive-impulsive type of ADHD are more likely to have a stable diagnosis over time and are more likely to have concurrent conduct disorder than are children with the predominantly inattentive type without hyperactivity.

Disorders involving reading, arithmetic, language, and coordination may be found in association with ADHD. The child's history may give clues to prenatal (including genetic), natal, and postnatal factors that may have affected the CNS structure or function. Rates of development, deviations in development, and the parental reactions to significant or stressful behavioral transitions should be ascertained, as they may help the clinician determine the degree to which parents have contributed to or reacted to the child's inefficiencies and dysfunctions.

School history and teachers' reports are important in evaluating whether children's difficulties in learning and school behavior are primarily due to their attitudinal or maturational problems or to their poor self-image because of felt inadequacies. Those reports may also reveal how the children have handled those problems. How they have related to siblings, to peers, to adults, and to free and structured activities gives valuable diagnostic clues to the presence of ADHD and helps identify the complications of the disorder.

Table 34–1. Diagnostic Criteria for Attention-Deficit/Hyperactivity Disorder

A. Either (1) or (2):

(1) six (or more) of the following symptoms of **inattention** have persisted for at least 6 months to a degree that is maladaptive and inconsistent with developmental level:

Inattention
(a) often fails to give close attention to details or makes careless mistakes in schoolwork, work, or other activities
(b) often has difficulty sustaining attention in tasks or play activities
(c) often does not seem to listen when spoken to directly
(d) often does not follow through on instructions and fails to finish schoolwork, chores, or duties in the workplace (not due to oppositional behavior or failure to understand instructions)
(e) often has difficulty organizing tasks and activities
(f) often avoids, dislikes, or is reluctant to engage in tasks that require sustained mental effort (such as schoolwork or homework)
(g) often loses things necessary for tasks or activities (e.g., toys, school assignments, pencils, books, or tools)
(h) is often easily distracted by extraneous stimuli
(i) is often forgetful in daily activities

(2) six (or more) of the following symptoms of **hyperactivity-impulsivity** have persisted for at least 6 months to a degree that is maladaptive and inconsistent with developmental level:

Hyperactivity
(a) often fidgets with hands or feet or squirms in seat
(b) often leaves seat in classroom or in other situations in which remaining seated is expected
(c) often runs about or climbs excessively in situations in which it is inappropriate (in adolescents or adults, may be limited to subjective feelings of restlessness)
(d) often has difficulty playing or engaging in leisure activities quietly
(e) is often ''on the go'' or often acts as if ''driven by a motor''
(f) often talks excessively

Impulsivity
(g) often blurts out answers before questions have been completed
(h) often has difficulty awaiting turn
(i) often interrupts or intrudes on others (e.g., butts into conversations or games)

B. Some hyperactive-impulsive or inattentive symptoms that caused impairment were present before age 7 years.

C. Some impairment from the symptoms is present in two or more settings (e.g., at school (or work) and at home).

D. There must be clear evidence of clinically significant impairment in social, academic, or occupational functioning.

E. The symptoms do not occur exclusively during the course of a pervasive developmental disorder, schizophrenia, or other psychotic disorder and are not better accounted for by another mental disorder (e.g., mood disorder, anxiety disorder, dissociative disorder, or a personality disorder).

Code based on type:
Attention-deficit/hyperactivity disorder, combined type: if both criteria A1 and A2 are met for the past 6 months
Attention-deficit/hyperactivity disorder, predominantly inattentive type: if criterion A1 is met but Criterion A2 is not met for the past 6 months
Attention-deficit/hyperactivity disorder, predominantly hyperactive-impulsive type: if Criterion A2 is met but Criterion A1 is not met for the past 6 months

Coding note: For individuals (especially adolescents and adults) who currently have symptoms that no longer meet full criteria, ''in partial remission'' should be specified.

Table from DSM-IV, *Diagnostic and Statistical Manual of Mental Disorders*, ed 4. Copyright American Psychiatric Association, Washington, 1994. Used with permission.

The mental status examination may show a secondarily depressed mood but no thought disturbance, impaired reality testing, or inappropriate affect. The child may show great distractibility, perseveration, and a concrete and literal mode of thinking. Indications of visual-perceptual, auditory-perceptual, language, or cognition problems may be present. Occasionally, evidence appears of a basic, pervasive, organically based anxiety, often called body anxiety.

A neurological examination may reveal visual-motor-perceptual or auditory-discriminatory immaturity or impairments without overt signs of disorders of visual or auditory acuity. Children may show problems with motor coordination and difficulties in copying age-appropriate figures, rapid alternating movements, right-left discrimination, ambidexterity, reflex asymmetries, and a variety of subtle nonfocal neurological signs (soft signs). The clinician should obtain an EEG to recognize the child with frequent bilaterally synchronous discharges resulting in short absence spells. Such a child may react in school with hyperactivity out of sheer frustration. The child with an unrecognized temporal lobe seizure focus can present a secondary behavior disorder. In those instances, several features of ADHD are often present. Identification of the focus requires an EEG obtained during drowsiness and during sleep.

Clinical Features

ADHD may have its onset in infancy. Infants with ADHD are unduly sensitive to stimuli and are easily upset by noise, light, temperature, and other environmental changes. At times, the reverse occurs, and the children are placid and limp, sleep much of the time, and appear to develop slowly in the first months of life. It is more common, though, for infants with ADHD to be active in the crib, sleep little, and cry a great deal. ADHD children are far less likely than are normal children to reduce their locomotor activity when their environment is structured by social limits. In school, ADHD children may rapidly attack a test but answer only the first two questions. They may be unable to wait to be called on in school and may respond for everyone else. At home, they cannot be put off for even a minute.

Children with ADHD are often explosively irritable. The irritability may be set off by relatively minor stimuli, which may puzzle and dismay the children. They are frequently emotionally labile, easily set off to laughter or to tears, and their mood and performance are apt to be variable and unpredictable. Impulsiveness and an inability to delay gratification are characteristic. They are often accident-prone.

Concomitant emotional difficulties are frequent. The fact that other children grow out of that kind of behavior but ADHD children do not grow out of it at the same time and rate may lead to adults' dissatisfaction and pressure. The resulting negative self-concept and reactive hostility are worsened by the children's recognition that they have problems.

The characteristics of children with ADHD most often cited are, in order of frequency, (1) hyperactivity, (2) perceptual motor impairment, (3) emotional lability, (4) general coordination deficit, (5) disorders of attention (short attention span, distractibility, perseveration, failure to finish things, inattention, poor concentration), (6) impulsivity (action before thought, abrupt shifts in activity, lack of organization, jumping up in class), (7) disorders of memory and thinking, (8) specific learning disabilities, (9) disorders of speech and hearing, and (10) equivocal neurological signs and EEG irregularities.

About 75 percent of children with ADHD fairly consistently show behavioral symptoms of aggression and defiance. But, whereas defiance and aggression are generally associated with adverse intrafamily relationships, hyperactivity is more closely related to impaired performance on cognitive tests requiring concentration. Some studies claim that some relatives of hyperactive children show features of antisocial personality disorder.

School difficulties, both learning and behavioral, are common: they sometimes stem from concomitant communication or learning disorders or from the children's distractibility and fluctuating attention, which hamper their acquisition, retention, and display of knowledge. Those difficulties are noted especially on group tests. The adverse reactions of school personnel to the behavior characteristics of ADHD and the lowering of self-regard because of felt inadequacies may combine with the adverse comments of peers to make school a place of unhappy defeat, which may lead to acting-out antisocial behavior and self-defeating, self-punitive behaviors.

PATHOLOGY AND LABORATORY EXAMINATION

No specific laboratory measures are pathognomonic of ADHD. Several laboratory measures often yield nonspecific abnormal results in hyperactive children, such as a disorganized, immature result on an EEG, and PET may show decreased cerebral blood flow in the frontal regions.

Cognitive testing that is helpful in confirming the child's inattention and impulsivity includes the continuous performance task, in which the child is asked to press a button each time a particular sequence of letters or numbers is flashed on a screen. Children with poor attention make errors of omission—that is, they fail to press the button, even when the sequence has flashed. Impulsivity is manifested by errors of commission, in which they are unable to resist pushing the button, although the desired sequence has not yet appeared on the screen.

Differential Diagnosis

A temperamental constellation consisting of high activity level and short attention span should be first considered. Differentiating those temperamental characteristics from the cardinal symptoms of ADHD before age 3 is difficult, mainly because of the overlapping features of a normally immature nervous system and the emerging signs of visual-motor-perceptual impairments frequently seen in ADHD.

Anxiety in the child needs to be evaluated. Anxiety may accompany ADHD as a secondary feature, and anxiety by itself may be manifested by overactivity and easy distractibility.

Many children with ADHD have secondary depression in reaction to their continuing frustration over their failure to learn and their consequent low self-esteem. That condition must be distinguished from a primary depressive disorder, which is likely to be distinguished by hypoactivity and withdrawal.

Frequently, conduct disorder and ADHD coexist, and so both must be diagnosed.

Learning disorders of various kinds must also be distinguished from ADHD, since a child may be unable to read or do mathematics because of a learning disorder, rather than inattention. However, ADHD often coexists with one or more learning disorders, including reading disorder, mathematics disorder, and disorder of written expression.

Course and Prognosis

The course of ADHD is highly variable. Symptoms may persist into adolescence or adult life, they may remit at puberty, or the hyperactivity may disappear, but the decreased attention span and impulse-control problems may persist.

The overactivity is usually the first symptom to remit and distractibility the last. Remission is not likely before the age of 12. If remission does occur, it usually occurs between the ages of 12 and 20. Remission may be accompanied by a productive adolescence and adult life, satisfying interpersonal relationships, and few significant sequelae. The majority of patients with ADHD, however, undergo partial remission and are vulnerable to antisocial and other personality disorders and mood disorders. Learning problems often continue.

In about 15 to 20 percent of cases, the symptoms of ADHD persist into adulthood. Those with the disorder may show diminished hyperactivity but remain impulsive and accident-prone. Although their educational attainments are lower than those of persons without ADHD, their early employment histories are not different from those of persons with similar educations.

Children with ADHD whose symptoms persist into adolescence are at high risk for developing conduct disorder. Approximately 50 percent of children with conduct disorder will develop antisocial personality disorder in adulthood. Children with both ADHD and conduct disorder are also at risk for developing a substance-related disorder.

Overall, the outcome of ADHD in childhood appears related to the amount of persistent conduct disorder and chaotic family factors. Optimal outcomes may be promoted by ameliorating the children's aggression and by improving family functions as early as possible.

Treatment

PHARMACOTHERAPY

The pharmacological agents for ADHD are the CNS stimulants, primarily dextroamphetamine (Dexedrine), methylphenidate (Ritalin), and pemoline (Cylert). The Food and Drug Administration (FDA) approves of dextroamphetamine in children 3 years and older and methylphenidate in those 6 years and older; those two are the most commonly used drugs.

The precise mechanism of action of the stimulants remains unknown. The idea of paradoxical response by hyperactive children is no longer accepted. Methylphenidate has been shown to be highly effective in up to three quarters of all children with ADHD and to have relatively few side effects. Methylphenidate is a short-acting medication that is generally used during school hours, so that children with the disorder can attend to tasks and remain in the classroom. The drug's most common side effects include headaches, stomachaches, nausea, and insomnia. Some children experience a rebound effect, in which they become mildly irritable and appear slightly hyperactive for a brief period when the medication wears off. In children with a history of motor tics, some caution must be used, since, in some cases, methylphenidate may cause an exacerbation of the tic disorder. Another common concern about methylphenidate is whether it will cause some suppression of growth. During periods of use, methylphenidate is associated with growth suppression, but children tend to make up the growth when they are given drug holidays in the summer or on weekends. An important question

regarding the use of methylphenidate is how much it normalizes school performance. A recent study found that about 75 percent of a group of hyperactive children exhibited a significant improvement in their ability to pay attention in class and on measures of academic efficiency when treated with methylphenidate. The drug has been shown to improve hyperactive children's scores on tasks of vigilance, such as the continuous performance task and paired associations.

Antidepressants—including imipramine (Tofranil), desipramine, and nortriptyline (Pamelor)—have been used to treat ADHD with some success. In children with comorbid anxiety disorders or depressive disorders and in children in whom tic disorders preclude the use of stimulants, the antidepressants may be beneficial, although, for hyperactivity itself, the stimulants are more efficacious. The antidepressants require careful monitoring of cardiac function. Several studies have reported sudden death in children with ADHD who were being treated with desipramine. Why the deaths occurred is not clear, but the deaths reinforce the need for close follow-up of any child receiving a tricyclic drug.

A recent study of children with ADHD and depressive symptoms who were taking methylphenidate and desipramine simultaneously found that the combination enhanced the children's abilities to use visual search strategies on such cognitive tasks as comparing several pictures with subtle differences—for example, the matching familiar faces task.

Clonidine has also been used in the treatment of ADHD with some degree of success. It may be especially helpful in cases in which the patients also have tic disorders.

Generally, stimulants remain the first drug of choice in the pharmacological treatment of ADHD.

Evaluation of Therapeutic Progress

Monitoring starts with the initiation of the medication. Because school performance is most markedly affected, special attention and effort should be given to establishing and maintaining a close collaborative working relation with the child's school.

In most patients, stimulants reduce overactivity, distractibility, impulsiveness, explosiveness, and irritability. No evidence suggests that the medications directly improve any existing impairments in learning, although, when the attention deficits diminish, the children can learn more effectively than in the past. In addition, the medication can improve self-esteem when the ADHD children are no longer constantly reprimanded for their behavior.

PSYCHOTHERAPY

Medication alone rarely satisfies the comprehensive therapeutic needs of ADHD children and is usually but one facet of a multimodality regimen. Individual psychotherapy, behavior modification, parent counseling, and the treatment of any coexisting learning disorder may be necessary.

When taking medication, ADHD children should be given the opportunity to explore the meaning of the medication to them. Doing so helps dispel misconceptions about medication use (such as ''I'm crazy'') and makes it clear that the medication is only an adjuvant. The children have to understand that they need not always be perfect.

When ADHD children are helped to structure their environment, their anxiety diminishes. Therefore, their parents and teachers should set up a predictable structure of reward and punishment, using a behavior therapy model and applying it to the physical, temporal, and interpersonal environment. An almost universal requirement of therapy is to help the parents recognize that permissiveness is not helpful to their children. The parents should also be helped to recognize that, in spite of their children's deficiencies in some areas, they face the normal tasks of maturation, including the need to take responsibility for their actions. Therefore, children with ADHD do not benefit from being exempted from the requirements, expectations, and planning applicable to other children.

ATTENTION-DEFICIT/HYPERACTIVITY DISORDER NOT OTHERWISE SPECIFIED

DSM-IV includes attention-deficit/hyperactivity disorder not otherwise specified (NOS) as a residual category for disturbances with prominent symptoms of inattention or hyperactivity that do not meet the criteria for ADHD. The incidence of adult manifestations of ADHD is unknown; however, there are many more cases than were previously thought or diagnosed. This category of illness will be more frequently diagnosed and will require much greater attention and study.

In adults, residual signs of the disorder include impulsivity and attention deficit (for example, difficulty in organizing and completing work, inability to concentrate, increased distractibility, and sudden decision making without a thought of the consequences). Many patients with the disorder suffer from a secondary depressive disorder associated with low self-esteem related to their impaired performance and that affects both occupational and social functioning. The treatment of the disorder involves the use of amphetamines (5 to 60 mg a day) or methylphenidate (5 to 60 mg a day). Signs of a positive response are an increased attention span, decreased impulsiveness, and improved mood. Psychopharmacological therapy may need to be continued indefinitely. Because of the abuse potential of the drugs, clinicians should monitor drug response and patient compliance.

References

Arnold L E, Jensen P S: Attention-deficit disorders. In *Comprehensive Textbook of Psychiatry*, ed 6, H I Kaplan, B J Sadock, editors, p 2295. Williams & Wilkins, Baltimore, 1995.
Baxter P S: Attention-deficit hyperactivity disorder in children. Curr Opin Pediatr 7: 381, 1995.
Safer D J: Major treatment considerations for attention-deficit hyperactivity disorder. Curr Probl Pediatr 25: 137, 1995.
Searight H R, Nahlik J E, Campbell D C: Attention-deficit/hyperactivity disorder: assessment, diagnosis, and management. J Fam Pract 40: 270, 1995.
Steingard R, Biederman J, Spender T, Wilens T, Gonzales A: Comparison of clonidine response in the treatment of attention-deficit hyperactivity disorder with and without comorbid tic disorders. J Am Acad Child Adolesc Psychiatry 3: 350, 1993.
Wender E H: Attention-deficit hyperactivity disorders in adolescence. J Dev Behav Pediatr 16: 192, 1995.
Wilens T E, Biederman J, Geist D E, Steingard R, Spencer T: Nortriptyline in the treatment of ADHD: A chart review of 58 cases. J Am Acad Child Adolesc Psychiatry 32: 343, 1993.

35/ Disruptive Behavior Disorders

35.1 OPPOSITIONAL DEFIANT DISORDER

Oppositional defiant disorder is an enduring pattern of negativistic, hostile, and defiant behaviors in the absence of serious violations of social norms or the rights of others. In *Diagnostic and Statistical Manual of Mental Disorders* (DSM-IV), five symptoms are required for the diagnosis. The disorder cannot be diagnosed if the criteria for conduct disorder are met. Unlike conduct disorder, oppositional defiant disorder cannot be diagnosed if the symptoms emerge exclusively during a mood disorder or a psychotic disorder. The most common symptoms of oppositional defiant disorder include the following: often loses temper, often argues with adults, often actively defies or refuses to comply with adults' requests or rules, often deliberately does things that annoy other people, and often blames others for his or her mistakes or misbehavior.

EPIDEMIOLOGY

Oppositional, negativistic behavior may be developmentally normal in early childhood. Epidemiological studies of negativistic traits in nonclinical populations found them in between 16 and 22 percent of school-age children. Although oppositional defiant disorder can begin as early as 3 years of age, it typically begins by 8 years of age and usually not later than adolescence.

The disorder is more prevalent in boys than in girls before puberty, and the sex ratio is probably equal after puberty. One authority suggests that girls are classified as having oppositional disorder more frequently than boys, as boys are more often given the diagnosis of conduct disorder.

There are no distinct family patterns, but almost all parents of oppositional defiant disorder children are themselves overconcerned with issues of power, control, and autonomy. Some families contain several obstinate children, controlling and depressed mothers, and passive-aggressive fathers. In many cases, the patients were unwanted children.

ETIOLOGY

Asserting one's own will and opposing that of others is crucial to normal development. It is related to establishing one's autonomy, forming an identity, and setting inner standards and controls. The most dramatic example of normal oppositional behavior peaks between 18 and 24 months, the terrible twos, when the toddler behaves negativistically as an expression of growing autonomy. Pathology begins when that developmental phase persists abnormally, authority figures overreact, or oppositional behavior recurs considerably more frequently than in most children of the same mental age.

Children may have constitutional or temperamental predispositions to strong will, strong preferences, or great assertiveness. If power and control are issues for the parents or if they exercise authority for their own needs, a struggle can follow that sets the stage for the development of oppositional defiant disorder. What begins for the infant as an effort to establish self-determination becomes transformed into a defense against overdependence on the mother and a protective device against intrusion into the ego's autonomy. In late childhood, environmental traumata, illness, or chronic incapacity, such as mental retardation, may trigger oppositionalism as a defense against helplessness, anxiety, and loss of self-esteem. Another normative oppositional stage occurs in adolescence as an expression of the need to separate from the parents and to establish an autonomous identity.

Classic psychoanalytic theory implicates unresolved conflicts that developed during the anal period. Behaviorists have suggested that oppositionalism is a reinforced, learned behavior through which the child exerts control over authority figures—for example, by having a temper tantrum when some undesired act is requested, the child coerces the parents to withdraw their request. In addition, increased parental attention—for example, long discussions about the behavior—may reinforce the behavior.

DIAGNOSIS AND CLINICAL FEATURES

Children with oppositional defiant disorder often argue with adults, lose their temper, and are angry, resentful, and easily annoyed by others. They frequently actively defy adults' requests or rules and deliberately annoy other people. They tend to blame others for their own mistakes and misbehavior. Manifestations of the disorder are almost invariably present in the home but may not be present at school or with other adults or peers. In some cases, features of the disorder from the beginning of the disturbance are displayed outside the home; in other cases, they start in the home but are later displayed outside the home. Typically, symptoms of the disorder are most evident in interactions with adults or peers whom the child knows well. Thus, children with the disorder are likely to show little or no sign of the disorder when examined clinically. Usually, they do not regard themselves as oppositional or defiant but justify their behavior as a response to unreasonable circumstances. The disorder appears to cause more distress to those around the children than to the children themselves. The DSM-IV diagnostic criteria for oppositional defiant disorder are given in Table 35.1–1.

Chronic oppositional defiant disorder almost always interferes with interpersonal relationships and school performance. The children are often friendless and perceive human relationships as unsatisfactory. Despite adequate intelligence, they do poorly or fail in school, as they withhold participation, resist external demands, and insist on solving problems without others' help.

Secondary to those difficulties are low self-esteem, poor frustration tolerance, depressed mood, and temper outbursts. Adolescents may abuse alcohol and illegal substances. Often, the disturbance evolves into a conduct disorder or a mood disorder.

Pathology and Laboratory Examination

No specific laboratory tests or pathological findings help diagnose oppositional defiant disorder. Since some children with the disorder become physically aggressive and do violate the rights of others as they get older, they may share some of the same characteristics that are being investigated in violent

**Table 35.1–1.   Diagnostic Criteria for Oppositional
Defiant Disorder**

A. A pattern of negativistic, hostile, and defiant behavior lasting
   at least 6 months, during which four (or more) of the following
   are present:

   (1) often loses temper
   (2) often argues with adults
   (3) often actively defies or refuses to comply with adults'
       requests or rules
   (4) often deliberately annoys people
   (5) often blames others for his or her mistakes or misbehavior
   (6) is often touchy or easily annoyed by others
   (7) is often angry and resentful
   (8) is often spiteful or vindictive

B. The disturbance in behavior causes significant impairment in
   social, academic or occupational functioning.

C. The behaviors do not occur exclusively during the course of a
   psychotic or mood disorder.

D. Criteria are not met for conduct disorder and, if individual is
   age 18 years or older, criteria are not met for antisocial
   personality disorder.

Table from DSM-IV, *Diagnostic and Statistical Manual of Mental Disorders*, ed 4.
Copyright American Psychiatric Association, Washington, 1994. Used with permission.

persons, such as decreased serotonin in the central nervous system (CNS).

DIFFERENTIAL DIAGNOSIS

Because oppositional behavior is both normal and adaptive
at specific developmental stages, those periods of negativism
must be distinguished from oppositional defiant disorder. De-
velopmental-stage oppositional behavior is of shorter duration
than oppositional defiant disorder and is not considerably more
frequent or more intense than that seen in other children of the
same mental age.

Oppositional defiant behavior occurs temporarily in reaction
to a stress should be diagnosed as an adjustment disorder.

When features of oppositional defiant disorder appear during
the course of conduct disorder, schizophrenia, or a mood disorder, the diagnosis of oppositional defiant disorder should not
be made.

Oppositional and negativistic behaviors may also be present
in attention-deficit/hyperactivity disorder, cognitive disorders,
and mental retardation. Whether a concomitant diagnosis of
oppositional defiant disorder should be given depends on the
severity, pervasiveness, and duration of such behavior.

Some young children who receive a diagnosis of oppositional defiant disorder go on in several years to meet the criteria
for conduct disorder. Some investigators believe that the two
disorders may be developmental variants of each other, with
conduct disorder being the natural progression of oppositional
defiant disorder when the child matures. However, the majority
of children with oppositional defiant disorder do not later meet
the criteria for conduct disorder, and up to one quarter of children with oppositional defiant disorder may not meet the diagnosis or either several years later. Overall, the current consensus
suggests that, although certain symptoms of conduct disorder
(for example, fighting or bullying) seem to occur in children
with oppositional defiant disorder, the two disorders remain
distinct on the basis of the children's total impairment, with
oppositional defiant disorder producing less dysfunction than
does conduct disorder.

COURSE AND PROGNOSIS

The course and prognosis of children with oppositional defiant disorder depend on many variables, including the severity
of the disorder, its stability over time, the likelihood of comorbid
disorders (such as conduct disorders, learning disorders, mood
disorders, and substance use disorders), and the degree of the
family's intactness.

About one quarter of children who receive the diagnosis of
oppositional defiant disorder may no longer qualify for it within
the next several years. It is not clear in those cases whether the
criteria captured children whose behavior was not developmentally abnormal or whether the disorder spontaneously remitted. Such patients have the best prognosis.

Patients in whom the diagnosis persists may remain stable
or may go on to violate the rights of others, leading to conduct
disorder. Such patients should receive guarded prognoses. Parental psychopathology, such as antisocial personality disorder
and substance abuse, appears more common in families with
children with oppositional defiant disorder than in the general
population, creating additional risks for chaotic and troubled
home environments. The prognosis of a child with oppositional
defiant disorder depends somewhat on the degree of functioning
within the family and on the development of comorbid psychopathology.

TREATMENT

The primary treatment of oppositional defiant disorder is
individual psychotherapy for the child with counseling and direct training of the parents in child management skills.

Behavior therapists emphasize teaching parents how to alter
their behavior to discourage their child's oppositional behavior
and encourage appropriate behavior. Behavior therapy focuses
on selectively reinforcing and praising appropriate behavior and
ignoring or not reinforcing undesired behavior.

Clinicians who treat patients with individual psychotherapy
note that family patterns are rigid and difficult to alter unless
the children themselves have a new type of object relationship
with the therapist. Within the therapeutic relationship, the children can relive the autonomy-threatening experiences that produced their defenses. In the safety of a noncontrolling relationship, they can understand the self-destructive nature of their
behavior and risk expressing themselves directly. Their self-
esteem must be restored before their defenses against external
control can be relinquished. In that way, independence may
replace habitual defenses against intrusion and control. Once a
therapeutic relationship has been formed on the basis of respect
for the patient's separateness, the patient is ready to understand
the source of the defenses and to try new coping behavior.

References

Lahey B B, Loeber R, Quay H C, Frick P J, Grimm J: Oppositional defiant
    disorders: Issues to be resolved for DSM-IV. J Am Acad Child Adolesc Psy-
    chiatry *31*: 539, 1992.
Paternite C E, Loney J, Roberts M A: External validation of oppositional disorder
    and attention deficit disorder with hyperactivity. J Abnorm Child Psychol *23*:
    453, 1995.
Rey J M, Bashir M R, Schwartz M, Richards I N, Plapp J M, Stewart A W:
    Oppositional disorder: Fact or fiction. J Am Acad Child Adolesc Psychiatry
    27: 157, 1988.
Speltz M L, DeKlyen M, Greenberg M T, Dryden M: Clinic referral for opposi-
    tional defiant disorder: relative significance of attachment and behavioral vari-
    ables. J Abnorm Child Psychol *23*: 487, 1995.
Vitiello B, Jensen P S: Disruptive behavior disorders. In *Comprehensive Textbook
    of Psychiatry*, ed 6, H I Kaplan, B J Sadock, editors, p 2311. Williams &
    Wilkins, Baltimore, 1995.

35.2 CONDUCT DISORDER AND DISRUPTIVE BEHAVIOR DISORDER NOS

CONDUCT DISORDER

The essential feature of conduct disorder is a repetitive and persistent pattern of behavior in which either the basic rights of others or major age-appropriate societal norms or rules are violated. The behavior must be present for at least six months to qualify for the diagnosis. The criteria in the fourth edition of *Diagnostic and Statistical Manual of Mental Disorders* (DSM-IV) require three specific behaviors for the diagnosis. DSM-IV also specifies that truancy from school must begin before 13 years of age to be considered a symptom of conduct disorder. The disorder can be diagnosed in a person more than 18 years old only if the criteria for antisocial personality disorder are not met.

DSM-IV divides conduct disorder into two types with respect to age of onset: childhood-onset type and adolescent-onset type. In the childhood-onset type, at least one conduct problem must have its onset before the age of 10 years. In adolescent-onset type, no conduct problems were present before the age of 10 years. DSM-IV also labels severity, ranging from mild (few if any conduct problems in excess of those needed to make the diagnosis and conduct problems cause only minor harm to others), to moderate (intermediate between mild and severe), to severe (many conduct problems in excess of the minimal diagnostic criteria or conduct problems causing considerable harm to others).

Epidemiology

Conduct disorder is common during childhood and adolescence. An estimated 6 to 16 percent of boys and 2 to 9 percent of girls under the age of 18 years have the disorder. The disorder is more common among boys than among girls, and the ratio ranges from 4 to 1 to as much as 12 to 1. Conduct disorder is more common in the children of parents with antisocial personality disorder and alcohol dependence than it is in the general population. The prevalence of conduct disorder and antisocial behavior is significantly related to socioeconomic factors.

Etiology

No single factor can account for children's antisocial behavior and conduct disorder. Rather, a variety of biopsychosocial factors contribute to the development of the disorder.

PARENTAL FACTORS

Some parental attitudes and faulty child-rearing practices influence the development of children's maladaptive behaviors. Chaotic home conditions are associated with conduct disorder and delinquency. However, broken homes per se are not causatively significant; it is the strife between the parents that contributes to conduct disorder. Parental psychopathology, child abuse, and negligence often contribute to conduct disorder. Sociopathy, alcohol dependence, and substance abuse in the parents are associated with conduct disorder in their children. Parents may be so negligent that care of the child is shared by relatives or assumed by foster parents. Many such parents were

scarred by their own upbringing and tend to be abusive, negligent, or engrossed in getting their own needs met. In the 1980s, particularly in urban areas, cocaine abuse and acquired immune deficiency syndrome (AIDS) increased family dysfunction. Recent studies suggest that many parents of conduct disorder children suffer from serious psychopathology, including psychotic disorders. Psychodynamic hypotheses suggest that children with conduct disorder unconsciously act out their parent's antisocial wishes.

SOCIOCULTURAL FACTORS

Current theories suggest that socioeconomically deprived children, unable to achieve status and obtain material goods through legitimate routes, are forced to resort to socially unacceptable means to reach those goals and that such behavior is normal and acceptable under circumstances of socioeconomic deprivation, as the children are adhering to the values of their own subculture.

PSYCHOLOGICAL FACTORS

Children brought up in chaotic, negligent conditions generally become angry, disruptive, demanding, and unable to progressively develop the tolerance for frustration necessary for mature relationships. As their role models are poor and often frequently changing, the basis for developing both an ego-ideal and a conscience is lacking. The children are left with little motivation to follow societal norms and are relatively remorseless.

NEUROBIOLOGICAL FACTORS

Neurobiological factors in conduct disorder have been little studied. However, research in attention-deficit/hyperactivity disorder yields some important findings, and conduct disorder and attention-deficit/hyperactivity disorder often coexist. In some conduct-disordered children a low level of plasma dopamine β-hydroxylase, an enzyme that converts dopamine to norepinephrine, has been found. That finding supports a theory of decreased noradrenergic functioning in conduct disorder. Some conduct-disordered juvenile offenders have increased blood serotonin (5-hydroxytryptamine [5-HT]) levels. Some evidence indicates that blood 5-HT levels correlate negatively with levels of the 5-HT metabolite 5-hydroxyindoleacetic acid (5-HIAA) in the cerebrospinal fluid (CSF) and that low CSF 5-HIAA correlates with aggression and violence.

CHILD ABUSE AND MALTREATMENT

Children who are exposed to violence for long periods, especially those who endure physically abusive treatment, often behave in aggressive ways. Such children may have difficulty verbalizing their feelings, and that difficulty increases their tendency to express themselves physically. In addition, severely abused children and adolescents tend to be hypervigilant; in some cases they misperceive benign situations and respond with violence. Not all physical behavior is synonymous with conduct disorder, but children with a pattern of hypervigilance and violent responses are likely to violate the rights of others.

OTHER FACTORS

Attention-deficit/hyperactivity disorder, central nervous system (CNS) dysfunction or damage, and early extremes of temperament can predispose a child to conduct disorder. Propensity to violence correlates with CNS dysfunction and signs of severe psychopathology, such as delusional tendencies. Longitudinal temperament studies suggest that many behavioral deviations are initially a straightforward response to a poor fit between, on the one hand, a child's temperament and emotional needs and, on the other hand, parental attitudes and child-rearing practices.

Diagnosis and Clinical Features

Conduct disorder does not develop overnight; instead, a variety of symptoms evolve over time until a consistent pattern violates the rights of others. Very young children are unlikely to meet the criteria for the disorder, since they are not developmentally able to exhibit the symptoms typical of older children with conduct disorder. A 3-year-old does not break into someone's home, steal with confrontation, force someone into sexual activity, or deliberately use a weapon that can cause serious harm. However, school-age children may become bullies, initiate physical fights, destroy property, or set fires. The DSM-IV diagnostic criteria for conduct disorder are given in Table 35.2–1.

The average age of onset of conduct disorder is younger in boys than in girls. Boys most commonly meet the diagnostic criteria by 10 to 12 years of age, whereas girls often reach 14 to 16 years of age before the criteria are met.

Table 35.2-1.   Diagnostic Criteria for Conduct Disorder

A. A repetitive and persistent pattern of behavior in which either the basic rights of others or major age-appropriate societal norms or rules are violated, as manifested by the presence of three (or more) of the following criteria in the past 12 months, with at least one criterion present in the past 6 months:

Aggression to people and animals
(1) often bullies, threatens, or intimidates others
(2) often initiates physical fights
(3) has used a weapon that can cause serious physical harm to others (e.g., a bat, brick, broken bottle, knife, gun)
(4) has been physically cruel to people
(5) has been physically cruel to animals
(6) has stolen while confronting a victim (e.g., mugging, purse snatching, extortion, armed robbery)
(7) has forced someone into sexual activity
Destruction of property
(8) has deliberately engaged in fire setting with the intention of causing serious damage
(9) has deliberately destroyed others' property (other than by fire setting)
Deceitfulness or theft
(10) has broken into someone else's house, building, or car
(11) often lies to obtain goods or favors or to avoid obligations (i.e., ''cons'' others)
(12) has stolen items of nontrivial value without confronting a victim (e.g., shoplifting, but without breaking and entering; forgery)
Serious violations of rules
(13) often stays out at night despite parental prohibitions, beginning before 13 years
(14) has run away from home overnight at least twice while living in parental or parental surrogate home (or once without returning for a lengthy period)
(15) often truant from school, beginning before age 13 years

B. The disturbance in behavior causes clinically significant impairment in social, academic, or occupational functioning.

C. If the individual is age 18 years or older, criteria are not met for antisocial personality disorder.

Table from DSM-IV, *Diagnostic and Statistical Manual of Mental Disorders*, ed 4. Copyright American Psychiatric Association, Washington, 1994. Used with permission.

Children who meet the criteria for conduct disorder express their overt aggressive behavior in various forms. The aggressive antisocial behavior may take the form of bullying, physical aggression, and cruel behavior toward peers. The children may be hostile, verbally abusive, impudent, defiant, and negativistic toward adults. Persistent lying, frequent truancy, and vandalism are common. In severe cases there is often destructiveness, stealing, and physical violence. The children usually make little attempt to conceal their antisocial behavior. Sexual behavior and the regular use of tobacco, liquor, or nonprescribed psychoactive substances begin unusually early for such children and adolescents. Suicidal thoughts, gestures, and acts are frequent.

Many children with aggressive behaviors fail to develop social attachments, as manifested by their difficulty in peer relationships or their lack of sustained normal peer relationships. Such children are often socially withdrawn or isolated. Some of them may befriend a much older or younger person or have superficial relationships with other antisocial youngsters. Most of them have low self-esteem, although they may project an image of toughness. Characteristically, they do not put themselves out for others, even if doing so would have an obvious immediate advantage. Their egocentrism is shown by their readily manipulating others for favors without any effort to reciprocate. They lack concern for the feelings, wishes, and welfare of others. They seldom have feelings of guilt or remorse for their callous behavior and try to blame others.

Not only have the children frequently encountered unusual frustrations, particularly of their dependency needs, but they also have escaped any consistent pattern of discipline. Their deficient socialization is revealed in their excessive aggressiveness and in their lack of sexual inhibition. Their general behavior is unacceptable in almost any social setting. Unfortunately, severe punishment almost invariably increases their maladaptive expression of rage and frustration, rather than ameliorating the problem.

In evaluation interviews, aggressive conduct-disordered children are typically uncooperative, hostile, and provocative. Some have a superficial charm and compliance until they are urged to talk about their problem behaviors. Then they may angrily deny any problems. If the interviewer persists, children with conduct disorder may attempt to justify their misbehavior or become suspicious and angry about the source of the examiner's information and perhaps bolt from the room. Most often, they become angry at the examiner and express their resentment of the examination with open belligerence or sullen withdrawal. Their hostility is not limited to adult authority figures but is expressed with equal venom toward their age-mates and younger children. In fact, they often bully those who are smaller and weaker than they. By boasting, lying, and expressing little interest in the listener's responses, such children reveal their profoundly narcissistic orientation.

Evaluation of the family situation often reveals severe marital disharmony, which initially may center on disagreements concerning management of the child. Because of a tendency toward family instability, parent surrogates are often in the picture. Many children with conduct disorder are only children of unplanned or unwanted pregnancies. The parents, especially the father, often have antisocial personality disorder or alcohol dependence.

The aggressive child and the child's family show a stereotyped pattern of impulsive and unpredictable verbal and physical hostility. The child's aggressive behavior rarely seems directed toward any definable goal and offers little pleasure, success, or even sustained advantages with peers or authority figures.

In other cases, conduct disorder includes repeated truancy, vandalism, and serious physical aggression or assault against others by a gang, such as mugging, gang fighting, and beating.

Children who become part of a gang usually have age-appropriate friendships. They are likely to show concern for the welfare of their friends or their own gang members and are unlikely to blame them or inform on them.

In some cases, gang members have a history of adequate or even excessive conformity during early childhood that ended when the youngster became a member of the delinquent peer group, usually in preadolescence or during adolescence. Also present in the history is some evidence of early problems, such as marginal or poor school performance, mild behavior problems, anxiety, and depressive symptoms.

Some degree of family social or psychological pathology is usually evident. Patterns of paternal discipline are rarely ideal and may vary from harshness and excessive strictness to inconsistency or relative absence of supervision and control. The mother has often protected the child from the consequences of early mild misbehavior but does not seem to actively encourage delinquency. Delinquency, also called juvenile delinquency, is most often associated with conduct disorder but may also be the result of other psychological or neurological disorders.

PATHOLOGY AND LABORATORY EXAMINATION

No specific laboratory test or neurological pathology helps make the diagnosis of conduct disorder. Some evidence indicates that certain neurotransmitters, such as serotonin in the CNS, are low in some persons with a history of violent or aggressive behavior toward others or themselves. Whether that association is related to the cause or is the effect of violence or is unrelated to the violence is not clear.

Differential Diagnosis

Disturbances of conduct may be part of many childhood psychiatric conditions, ranging from mood disorders to psychotic disorders to learning disorders. Therefore, the clinician must obtain a history of the chronology of the symptoms to determine whether the conduct disturbance is a transient or reactive phenomenon. Isolated acts of antisocial behavior do not justify a diagnosis of conduct disorder; an enduring pattern must be present.

The relation of conduct disorder to oppositional defiant disorder is still under debate. Historically, oppositional defiant disorder has been understood as a mild precursor of conduct disorder that is likely to be diagnosed in young children at risk for conduct disorder. Children who progress from oppositional defiant disorder to conduct disorder do maintain their oppositional characteristics, but some evidence indicates that the two disorders are independent. Many children with oppositional defiant disorder never go on to have conduct disorder, and, when conduct disorder first appears in adolescence, it may be unrelated to oppositional defiant disorder. The main distinguishing clinical feature of the two disorders is that, in conduct disorder, the basic rights of others are violated, whereas, in oppositional defiant disorder, hostility and negativism fall short of seriously violating the rights of others.

Mood disorders are often present in children with some degree of irritability and aggressive behavior. Both major depressive disorder and bipolar disorders must be ruled out. However, the full syndrome of conduct disorder may occur and be diagnosed during the onset of a mood disorder. That is not true for oppositional defiant disorder, which cannot be diagnosed if it occurs exclusively during a mood disorder.

Attention-deficit/hyperactivity disorder and learning disorders are commonly associated with conduct disorder. Usually, the symptoms of those disorders predate the diagnosis of conduct disorder.

All those disorders should be noted when they co-occur. Children with attention-deficit/hyperactivity disorder often exhibit impulsive and aggressive behaviors that may not meet the full criteria for conduct disorder.

Course and Prognosis

In general, children who have conduct disorder symptoms at a young age, exhibit the greatest number of symptoms, and express them most frequently have the poorest prognoses. That is true partly because those with severe conduct disorder seem the most vulnerable to another disorder later in life, such as a mood disorder. Conduct disorder is also associated with substance-related disorders later in life. It stands to reason that, the more concurrent mental disorders a person suffers from, the more troublesome life will be. A recent report found that, although assaultive behavior in childhood and parental criminality predict a high risk for incarceration later in life, the diagnosis of conduct disorder per se was not correlated with imprisonment.

A good prognosis is predicted by mild conduct disorder, the absence of coexisting psychopathology, and normal intellectual functioning. Although assessing treatment strategies is difficult because of the many symptoms involved in conduct disorder, it seems more difficult to design effective treatment programs for the covert symptoms of conduct disorder than for overt aggression.

Treatment

Multimodality treatment programs that use all the available family and community resources are likely to effect the best control of conduct-disordered behavior. No treatment is considered curative for the entire spectrum of behaviors that contribute to conduct disorder. A variety of treatments may be helpful for certain components of the chronic disorder.

An environmental structure with consistent rules and expected consequences can help control a variety of problem behaviors. The structure can be applied to family life in some cases, so that the parents become aware of behavioral techniques and proficient at using them to foster appropriate behaviors. Families in which psychopathology or environmental stressors prevent the parent's grasping the techniques may require parental psychiatric evaluation and treatment before making such an endeavor. When the family is abusive or chaotic, the child may have to be removed from the home to benefit from a consistent and structured environment.

School settings can also use behavioral techniques to promote socially acceptable behavior toward peers and to discourage covert antisocial incidents.

Individual psychotherapy oriented toward improving problem-solving skills can be useful, since children with conduct disorder may have a long-standing pattern of maladaptive responses to daily situations. The age at which treatment begins is important, since, the longer the maladaptive behaviors continue, the more entrenched they become.

Medication can be a useful adjunctive treatment for a number of symptoms that often contribute to conduct disorder. Overt explosive aggression responds to several medications. Antipsychotics, most notably haloperidol (Haldol), decrease aggressive and assaultive behaviors that may be present in various disorders. Lithium (Eskalith) also has some benefit in the treatment of aggression within or outside the context of bipolar disorders. Some trials suggest that carbamazepine (Tegretol) may help control aggression. A recent pilot study found that clonidine (Catapres) may decrease aggression.

Since conduct disorder frequently coexists with attention-deficit/hyperactivity disorder, learning disorders, and, over time, mood disorders and substance-related disorders, the treatment of any concurrent disorders must also be addressed.

DISRUPTIVE BEHAVIOR DISORDER NOT OTHERWISE SPECIFIED

Disruptive behavior disorder not otherwise specified (NOS) can be used for disorders of conduct or oppositional defiant behaviors that do not meet the diagnostic criteria for either conduct disorder or oppositional defiant disorder but in which there is notable impairment.

References

Campbell M, Kafantaris V, Cueva J E: An update on the use of lithium carbonate in aggressive children and adolescents with conduct disorder. Psychopharmacol Bull *31*: 93, 1995.

Eyberg S M, Boggs S R, Algina J: Parent-child interaction therapy: a psychological model for the treatment of young children with conduct problem behavior and their families. Psychopharmacol Bull *31*: 83, 1995.

Kemph J P, DeVane C L, Levin G M, Jarecke R, Miller R L: Treatment of aggressive children with clonidine: Results of an open pilot study. J Am Acad Child Adolesc Psychiatry *32*: 577, 1993.

Lahey B B, Loeber R, Quay H C, Frick P J, Grimm J: Oppositional defiant disorder and conduct disorders: Issues to be resolved for DSM-IV. J Am Acad Child Adolesc Psychiatry *31*: 539, 1992.

Lewis D O: From abuse to violence: Psychophysiological consequences of maltreatment. J Am Acad Child Adolesc Psychiatry *31*: 383, 1992.

Moss H B, Kirisci L: Aggressivity in adolescent alcohol abusers: relationship with conduct disorder. Alcohol Clin Exp Res *19*: 642, 1995.

Vitiello B, Jensen P S: Disruptive behavior disorders. In *Comprehensive Textbook of Psychiatry*, ed 6, H I Kaplan, B J Sadock, editors, p 2311. Williams & Wilkins, Baltimore, 1995.

Zoccolillo M: Co-occurrence of conduct disorder and its adult outcomes with depressive and anxiety disorders: A review. J Am Acad Child Adolesc Psychiatry *31*: 547, 1992.

36/ Feeding and Eating Disorders of Infancy or Early Childhood

36.1 Pica

Pica is a pattern of eating nonnutritive substances for at least one month. According to the fourth edition of *Diagnostic and Statistical Manual of Mental Disorders* (DSM-IV), the ingestion of nonnutritive substances must be inappropriate to the child's developmental level. In addition, the eating behavior is not part of a culturally sanctioned practice. Pica is seen much more frequently in young children than in adults. It also occurs in mentally retarded persons. Among adults, certain forms of pica, including geophagia (clay eating) and amylophagia (starch eating), have been reported to occur in pregnant women. In certain regions of the world and among certain cultures, such as the Australian aborigines, rates of pica in pregnant women have been reported to be high. According to DSM-IV, however, if the practices are culturally determined, the diagnostic criteria for pica are not met.

EPIDEMIOLOGY

Pica is estimated to occur in 10 to 32 percent of children between 1 and 6 years of age. In children more than 10 years old, reports of pica have indicated a rate of about 10 percent. In older children and adolescents with normal intelligence, the frequency of pica diminishes. Pica has been reported to occur in up to one fourth of institutionalized mentally retarded children and adolescents. The presence of pica appears to affect both sexes equally.

ETIOLOGY

Several theories have been proposed to explain the phenomenon of pica, but none has been universally accepted. A higher than expected incidence of pica seems to occur in the relatives of persons with the symptoms.

Nutritional deficiencies have been postulated as causes of pica, since in particular circumstances cravings for nonedible substances have been produced by deficiencies. For example, cravings for dirt and ice are sometimes associated with iron and zinc deficiencies and are eliminated by their administration.

A high incidence of parental neglect and deprivation has been associated with cases of pica. Theories relating the child's psychological deprivation and subsequent ingestion of inedible substances have been suggested as compensatory mechanisms to satisfy oral needs.

DIAGNOSIS AND CLINICAL FEATURES

Eating nonedible substances after 18 months of age is usually considered abnormal. The onset of pica is usually between ages 12 and 24 months, and the incidence declines with age. The specific substances ingested vary with their accessibility, and they increase with the child's mastery of locomotion and the resultant increased independence and decreased parental supervision. Typically, young children ingest paint, plaster, string, hair, and cloth; older children have access to dirt, animal feces, stones, and paper.

The clinical implications may be benign or life-threatening, according to the objects ingested. Among the most serious complications are lead poisoning, usually from lead-based paint; intestinal parasites after the ingestion of soil or feces; anemia and zinc deficiency after the ingestion of clay; severe iron deficiency after the ingestion of large quantities of starch; and intestinal obstruction from the ingestion of hair balls, stones, or gravel.

Except in mentally retarded persons, pica usually remits by adolescence. Pica associated with pregnancy is usually limited to the pregnancy itself. The DSM-IV diagnostic criteria for pica are given in Table 36.1–1.

DIFFERENTIAL DIAGNOSIS

The differential diagnosis of pica includes iron and zinc deficiencies. Pica also may occur with failure to thrive and several other mental and medical disorders, including schizophrenia, autistic disorder, anorexia nervosa, and Kleine-Levin syndrome. In psychosocial dwarfism, a dramatic but reversible endocrinological and behavioral form of failure to thrive, children often present with bizarre behaviors, including the ingestion of toilet water, garbage, and other nonnutritive substances. A small minority of children with autistic disorder and schizophrenia may have pica. In children who exhibit pica along with another medical disorder, both disorders should be coded, according to DSM-IV.

COURSE AND PROGNOSIS

The prognosis for pica is variable. In children, pica usually resolves with increasing age; in pregnant women, pica is usually limited to the term of the pregnancy. However, in some adults, especially in the mentally retarded, pica may continue for years. Follow-up data on those populations are too limited to permit conclusions.

TREATMENT

There is no definitive treatment for pica. Treatments emphasize psychosocial, environmental, behavioral, and family guidance approaches.

An effort should be made to relieve any significant psychosocial stressors that are present. When lead is present in the surroundings, it must be eliminated or rendered inaccessible, or the child must be moved to new surroundings.

Several behavioral techniques have been used with some success. The most rapidly effective seems to be mild aversion therapy or negative reinforcement (for example, a mild electric shock, an unpleasant noise, or an emetic drug). Positive reinforcement, modeling, behavioral shaping, and overcorrection treatment have also been used. Increasing parental attention, stimulation, and emotional nurturance may have positive results.

Table 36.1-1.   Diagnostic Criteria for Pica

A. Persistent eating of nonnutritive substances for a period of at least 1 month.

B. The eating of nonnutritive substances is inappropriate to developmental level.

C. The eating behavior is not part of a culturally sanctioned practice.

D. If the eating behavior occurs exclusively during the course of another mental disorder (e.g., mental retardation, pervasive developmental disorder, schizophrenia), it is sufficiently severe to warrant independent clinical attention.

Table from DSM-IV, *Diagnostic and Statistical Manual of Mental Disorders*, ed 4. Copyright American Psychiatric Association, Washington, 1994. Used with permission.

In some patients, the correction of an iron or zinc deficiency has resulted in the elimination of pica. Medical complications (for example, lead poisoning) that develop secondarily to the pica must also be treated.

References

Blinder B J, Chaitin B, Goldstein R, editors: *The Eating Disorders*. Pergamon, New York, 1987.

Connors M E, Morse W: Sexual abuse and eating disorders: A review. Int J Eating Disord *13*: 1, 1993.

Cooper M: *Pica*. Charles C Thomas, Springfield, IL, 1957.

Garfinkel P E: Feeding and eating disorders of infancy or early childhood. In *Comprehensive Textbook of Psychiatry*, ed 6, H I Kaplan, B J Sadock, p 2321. Williams & Wilkins, Baltimore, 1995.

36.2 RUMINATION DISORDER AND FEEDING DISORDER OF INFANCY OR EARLY CHILDHOOD

RUMINATION DISORDER

Rumination disorder is the repeated regurgitation of food, usually in infants. Its onset generally occurs after 3 months of age. Once the regurgitation occurs, the food may be swallowed or spit out. The disorder is rare in older children, adolescents, and adults. It varies in its severity, and it is sometimes associated with medical conditions, such as hiatus hernia, that result in esophageal reflux. In its most severe form, the disorder can be fatal. According to the fourth edition of *Diagnostic and Statistical Manual of Mental Disorders* (DSM-IV), the disorder must be present for at least one month after a period of normal functioning, and it is not associated with gastrointestinal illness or other general medical conditions.

Epidemiology

Rumination disorder is rare. It seems most common among infants between 3 months and 1 year of age and among mentally retarded children and adults. Adults with rumination disorder usually maintain a normal weight. The disorder is apparently equally common in boys and girls. No reliable figures on predisposing factors or familial patterns are available. The disorder may be seen in up to 10 percent of persons with bulimia nervosa.

Etiology

Several causes of rumination have been proposed. In mentally retarded ruminators, the disorder may simply be self-stimulatory behavior. In nonretarded ruminators, psychodynamic theories hypothesize various disturbances in the mother-child relationship. The mothers of infants with the disorder are usually immature, involved in a marital conflict, and unable to give much attention to the baby. Those factors result in insufficient emotional gratification and stimulation for the infant, who seeks gratification from within. The rumination is interpreted as the infant's attempt to re-create the feeding process and provide gratification that the mother does not provide. Overstimulation and tension have also been suggested as causes of rumination.

A dysfunctional autonomic nervous system may be implicated. As sophisticated and accurate investigative techniques are refined, a substantial number of children classified as ruminators are shown to have gastroesophageal reflux or hiatal hernia.

Behaviorists attribute rumination to the positive reinforcement of the pleasurable self-stimulation and to the attention the baby receives from others because of the disorder.

Diagnosis and Clinical Features

The DSM-IV diagnostic criteria for rumination disorder are given in Table 36.2–1. DSM-IV notes that the essential feature of the disorder is repeated regurgitation and rechewing of food for at least one month after a period of normal functioning. Partially digested food is brought up into the mouth without nausea, retching, disgust, or associated gastrointestinal disorder. The food is then ejected from the mouth or reswallowed. A characteristic position of straining and arching of the back, with the head held back, is observed. The infant makes sucking movements with the tongue and gives the impression of gaining considerable satisfaction from the activity. An associated feature that is usually present is that the infant is generally irritable and hungry between episodes of rumination.

Although spontaneous remissions are common, severe secondary complications may develop, such as progressive malnutrition, dehydration, and lowered resistance to disease. Failure to thrive, with growth failure and developmental delays in all areas, may occur. Mortality as high as 25 percent has been reported in severe cases.

An additional complication is that the mother or caretaker is often discouraged by the failure to feed the infant successfully and may become alienated, if not already so. Further alienation often occurs as the noxious odor of the regurgitated material leads to avoidance of the infant.

Differential Diagnosis

To make the diagnosis of rumination disorder, the clinician must rule out gastrointestinal congenital anomalies, infections,

Table 36.2-1.   Diagnostic Criteria for Rumination Disorder

A. Repeated regurgitation and rechewing of food for a period of at least 1 month following a period of normal functioning.

B. The behavior is not due to an associated gastrointestinal or other general medical condition (e.g., esophageal reflux).

C. The behavior does not occur exclusively during the course of anorexia nervosa or bulimia nervosa. If the symptoms occur exclusively during the course of mental retardation or a pervasive developmental disorder, they are sufficiently severe to warrant independent clinical attention.

Table from DSM-IV, *Diagnostic and Statistical Manual of Mental Disorders*, ed 4. Copyright American Psychiatric Association, Washington, 1994. Used with permission.

and other medical illnesses. Pyloric stenosis is usually associated with projectile vomiting and is generally evident before 3 months of age, when rumination has its onset. Rumination has been associated with various mental retardation syndromes in which other stereotypic behaviors and eating disturbances, such as pica, have been present. Rumination disorder may occur in patients with other eating disorders, such as bulimia nervosa.

Course and Prognosis

Rumination disorder is believed to have a high rate of spontaneous remission. Indeed, many cases of rumination disorder may develop and remit without ever being diagnosed. Only limited data are available regarding the prognosis of rumination disorder in adults.

Treatment

The effectiveness of treatments is difficult to evaluate, as most reports are single-case studies and patients are not randomly assigned to controlled studies. Any concomitant medical complications must also be treated.

Treatments include improvement of the child's psychosocial environment, increased tender loving care from the mother or caretakers, and psychotherapy for the mother or both parents.

When anatomical abnormalities such as hiatal hernia are present, surgical repair may be necessary.

Behavioral techniques have been used effectively. Aversive conditioning involves administering a mild electric shock or squirting an unpleasant substance (such as lemon juice) in the child's mouth whenever rumination occurs. That practice appears to be the most rapidly effective treatment; rumination is eliminated in three to five days. In the aversive-conditioning reports on rumination disorder, the infants were doing well at 9- or 12-month follow-ups, with no recurrence of the rumination

Table 36.2-2.   Diagnostic Criteria for Feeding Disorder of Infancy or Early Childhood

A. Feeding disturbance as manifested by persistent failure to eat adequately with significant failure to gain weight or significant loss of weight over at least 1 month.

B. The disturbance is not due to an associated gastrointestinal or other general medical condition (e.g., esophageal reflux).

C. The disturbance is not better accounted for by another mental disorder (e.g., rumination disorder) or by lack of available food.

D. The onset is before age 6 years.

Table from DSM-IV, *Diagnostic and Statistical Manual of Mental Disorders*, ed 4. Copyright American Psychiatric Association, Washington, 1994. Used with permission.

and with weight gains, increased activity levels, and increased responsiveness to people.

FEEDING DISORDER OF INFANCY OR EARLY CHILDHOOD

According to DSM-IV, this diagnosis is used for feeding disturbances manifested by persistent failure to eat adequately, resulting in failure to gain expected weight or in significant weight loss over at least one month (Table 36.2–2). The disorder is not due to any gastrointestinal illness or other medical illness. It is not due to a lack of available food, and it cannot be better accounted for by another mental disorder. The disorder must have its onset before age 6 years.

References

Mayes S D, Humphrey F J, Handford H A, Mitchell J F: Rumination disorder: Differential diagnosis. J Am Acad Child Adolesc Psychiatry *27*: 300, 1988.

Nasser M: A prescription of vomiting; Historical footnotes. Int J Eating Disord *13*: 129, 1993.

Garfinkel P E: Feeding and eating disorders of infancy or early childhood. In *Comprehensive Textbook of Psychiatry*, ed 6, H I Kaplan, B J Sadock, p 2321. Williams & Wilkins, Baltimore, 1995.

37/ Tic Disorders

Tics are involuntary, sudden, rapid, recurrent, nonrhythmic, stereotyped motor movements or vocalizations. Motor and vocal tics are divided into those that are simple and those that are complex. Simple motor tics are those composed of repetitive, rapid contractions of functionally similar muscle groups—for example, eye blinking, neck jerking, shoulder shrugging, and facial grimacing. Common simple vocal tics include coughing, throat clearing, grunting, sniffing, snorting, and barking. Complex motor tics appear more purposeful and ritualistic than simple motor tics. Common complex motor tics include grooming behaviors, the smelling of objects, jumping, touching behaviors, echopraxia (the imitation of observed behavior), and copropraxia (the display of obscene gestures). Complex vocal tics include repeating words or phrases out of context, coprolalia (the use of obscene words or phrases), palilalia (the repetition of one's own words), and echolalia (the repetition of the last-heard words of others).

In all the tic disorders, stressful situations and anxiety may result in an exacerbation of tics. Some persons with tic disorders can suppress the tics for minutes or hours, but other persons, especially young children, either are not aware of their tics or experience them as irresistible. Tics may be attenuated by sleep, relaxation, or absorption in an activity. Tics often disappear during sleep, but tics do occur while some persons are asleep.

TOURETTE'S DISORDER

Georges Gilles de la Tourette first described a patient with what became known as Tourette's disorder in 1885, while he was studying with Jean-Martin Charcot in France. He noted a syndrome among several patients that included multiple motor tics, coprolalia, and echolalia.

Epidemiology

The lifetime prevalence of Tourette's disorder is estimated to be 4 to 5 per 10,000. The onset of the motor component of the disorder generally occurs by age 7 years; vocal tics emerge on average by age 11 years. Tourette's disorder occurs about three times more often in boys than in girls.

Etiology

GENETIC FACTORS

Increasing evidence suggests that genetic factors play a role in the development of Tourette's disorder. Twin studies have indicated that concordance for the disorder in monozygotic twins is significantly greater than in dizygotic twins. The fact that Tourette's disorder and chronic motor or vocal tic disorder are likely to occur in the same families lends support to the view that the disorders are part of a genetically determined spectrum. The sons of mothers with Tourette's disorder seem to be at the highest risk for the disorder. Evidence in some families indicates that Tourette's disorder is transmitted in an autosomal dominant fashion. There is a relation between Tourette's disorder and attention-deficit/hyperactivity disorder; up to half of all Tourette's disorder patients also have attention-defi-

cit/hyperactivity disorder. A relation has also been found between Tourette's disorder and obsessive-compulsive disorder; up to 40 percent of all Tourette's disorder patients also have obsessive-compulsive disorder. In addition, first-degree relatives of persons with Tourette's disorder are at high risk for the development of Tourette's disorder, chronic motor or vocal tic disorder, and obsessive-compulsive disorder. In view of the presence of symptoms of attention-deficit/hyperactivity disorder in more than half of the patients with Tourette's disorder, questions arise regarding a genetic relation between those two disorders.

NEUROCHEMICAL AND NEUROANATOMICAL FACTORS

Compelling evidence of dopamine system involvement in tic disorders includes the observations that pharmacological agents that antagonize dopamine—haloperidol (Haldol), pimozide (Orap), and fluphenazine (Prolixin)—suppress tics and that agents that increase central dopaminergic activity—methylphenidate (Ritalin), amphetamines, pemoline (Cylert), and cocaine—tend to exacerbate tics. However, the relation of tics to the dopamine system is not simple, since in some cases antipsychotic drugs, such as haloperidol, are not effective in the reduction of tics and the effect of stimulants on tic disorders has been reported as variable. In some cases, Tourette's disorder has emerged during treatment with antipsychotic medications, leading to a term "tardive Tourette's disorder" because of that disorder's similarity to tardive dyskinesia. Endogenous opiates may be involved in tic disorders and obsessive-compulsive disorder. Some evidence indicates that pharmacological agents that antagonize endogenous opiates—for example, naltrexone (ReVia)—reduce tics and attention deficits in Tourette's disorder patients.

Abnormalities in the noradrenergic system have been implicated by the reduction of tics in some cases by clonidine (Catapres), an α-adrenergic agonist that reduces the release of norepinephrine in the central nervous system, which may reduce activity in the dopaminergic system.

Abnormalities in the basal ganglia result in various movement disorders, such as in Huntington's disease, and are implicated as possible sites of disturbance in Tourette's disorder, obsessive-compulsive disorder, and attention-deficit/hyperactivity disorder.

Diagnosis and Clinical Features

To make a diagnosis of Tourette's disorder, the clinician must obtain a history of multiple motor tics and the emergence of at least one vocal tic at some point in the disorder. According to the fourth edition of *Diagnostic and Statistical Manual of Mental Disorders* (DSM-IV), the tics must occur many times a day nearly every day or intermittently for more than one year. The average age of onset of tics is 7 years, but the tics may occur as early as age 2 years. The onset must occur before age 18 years. According to DSM-IV, the tics may not be the direct result of a substance (such as stimulants) or a medical condition

Table 37-1.   Diagnostic Criteria for Tourette's Disorder

A. Both multiple motor and one or more vocal tics have been present at some time during the illness, although not necessarily concurrently. (A *tic* is a sudden, rapid, recurrent, nonrhythmic, stereotyped motor movement or vocalization.)

B. The tics occur many times a day (usually in bouts), nearly every day or intermittently throughout a period of more than 1 year, and during this period there was never a tic-free period of more than 3 consecutive months.

C. The disturbance causes marked distress or significant impairment in social, occupational, or other important areas of functioning.

D. The onset is before age 18 years.

E. The disturbance is not due to the direct physiological effects of a substance (e.g., stimulants) or a general medical condition (e.g., Huntington's disease or postviral encephalitis).

Table from DSM-IV, *Diagnostic and Statistical Manual of Mental Disorders*, ed 4. Copyright American Psychiatric Association, Washington, 1994. Used with permission.

(Table 37–1). In Tourette's disorder, the initial tics are in the face and the neck. Over time, the tics tend to occur in a downward progression.

The most commonly described tics are those affecting (1) the face and the head: grimacing; puckering of the forehead; raising of the eyebrows; blinking eyelids; winking; wrinkling of the nose; trembling nostrils; twitching mouth; displaying of the teeth; biting of the lips and other parts; extruding the tongue; protracting the lower jaw; nodding, jerking, or shaking the head; twisting the neck; looking sideways; and head rolling; (2) the arms and the hands: jerking of the hands, jerking of the arms, plucking fingers, writhing fingers, and clenching fists; (3) the body and the lower extremities: shrugging of the shoulders; shaking a foot, a knee, or a toe; peculiarities of gait; body writhing; and jumping; and (4) the respiratory and alimentary systems: hiccuping, sighing, yawning, snuffing, blowing through the nostrils, whistling inspiration, exaggerated breathing, belching, sucking or smacking sounds, and clearing the throat.

Typically, prodromal behavioral symptoms—such as irritability, attention difficulties, and poor frustration tolerance—are evident before or coincide with the onset of tics. More than 25 percent of the persons in some studies received stimulants for a diagnosis of attention-deficit/hyperactivity disorder before receiving a diagnosis of Tourette's disorder.

The most frequent initial symptom is an eye-blink tic, followed by a head tic or a facial grimace. Most of the complex motor and vocal symptoms emerge several years after the initial symptoms. Coprolalia usually begins in early adolescence and occurs in about one third of all cases. Mental coprolalia—in which the patient thinks a sudden, intrusive, socially unacceptable thought or obscene word—may also occur. In some severe cases, physical injuries, including retinal detachment and orthopedic problems, have resulted from severe tics.

Obsessions, compulsions, attention difficulties, impulsivity, and personality problems have been associated with Tourette's disorder. Attention difficulties often precede the onset of tics, whereas obsessive-compulsive symptoms often occur after the onset of tics. It is still being debated whether those problems usually develop secondarily to the patient's tics or are caused primarily by the same underlying pathobiological condition.

Many tics have an aggressive or sexual component, which may result in serious social consequences for the patient. Phe-

nomenologically, the tics resemble a failure of censorship, both conscious and unconscious, with increased impulsivity and a too-ready transformation of thought into action.

PATHOLOGY AND LABORATORY EXAMINATION

There is no specific laboratory diagnostic test for Tourette's disorder. However, many patients with Tourette's disorder have nonspecific abnormal electroencephalogram (EEG) findings. Computed tomography (CT) and magnetic resonance imaging (MRI) scans have not revealed specific structural lesions, although about 10 percent of all Tourette's disorder patients show some nonspecific abnormality on CT scans.

Differential Diagnosis

Tics must be differentiated from other disordered movements (for example, dystonic, choreiform, athetoid, myoclonic, and hemiballismic movements) and the neurological diseases of which they are characteristic (for example, Huntington's disease, parkinsonism, Sydenham's chorea, and Wilson's disease). Tremors, mannerisms, and stereotypic movement disorder (for example, head banging or body rocking) must also be distinguished from tic disorders. The voluntary nature of stereotypic movement disorder and the fact that such movements do not cause subjective distress differentiate it from tic disorders. Compulsions are also intentional behaviors.

Both autistic and mentally retarded children may exhibit symptoms similar to those seen in tic disorders, including Tourette's disorder. Tardive dyskinesia must also be considered in those patients who are receiving or have received medication that may cause that untoward effect. Before instituting antipsychotic medication, the clinician must make a baseline evaluation of preexisting abnormal movements, as such medication can mask abnormal movements. If the movements occur later, they can be mistaken for tardive dyskinesia.

Sympathomimetics (such as methylphenidate, amphetamines, and pemoline) have been reported to exacerbate preexisting tics in some cases. Those effects have been reported primarily in some children and adolescents being treated for attention-deficit/hyperactivity disorder. In most but not all cases, after the drug was discontinued, the tics remitted or returned to premedication levels. Most experts suggest that children and adolescents who experience tics while receiving stimulants are probably predisposed genetically and would have experienced tics regardless of their treatment with stimulants. Until the situation is clarified, clinicians should use great caution and should frequently monitor the children at risk for tics who are given stimulants.

Course and Prognosis

Untreated, Tourette's disorder is usually a chronic, lifelong disease with relative remissions and exacerbations. Initial symptoms may decrease, persist, or increase, and old symptoms may be replaced by new ones. Severely afflicted persons may have serious emotional problems, including major depressive disorder. Some of those difficulties appear to be associated with Tourette's disorder, whereas others result from severe social, academic, and vocational consequences, which are frequent sequelae of the disorder. In some cases, despair over the disruption of social and occupational functioning is so severe that the persons contemplate and attempt suicide. But some children with Tourette's disorder have satisfactory peer relationships, function well in school, and have adequate self-esteem; they may need no treatment and can be monitored by their pediatricians.

Treatment

Pharmacological treatments are most effective for Tourette's disorder, but patients with mild cases may not require medication. Psychotherapy is usually ineffective as a primary treatment modality, although it may help the patient cope with the symptoms of the disorder and any concomitant personality and behavioral difficulties that arise.

Several behavioral techniques—including massed (negative) practice, self-monitoring, incompatible response training, presentation and removal of positive reinforcement, and habit reversal treatment—were reviewed by Stanley A. Hobbs. He reported that tic frequency was reduced in many cases, particularly with habit reversal treatment, but relatively few studies have reported clinically significant changes. In general, behavioral treatments were most effective in treating transient and chronic motor or vocal tic disorders, but relatively few cases of Tourette's disorder responded favorably. Behavior therapy currently appears most useful in reducing stresses that may aggravate Tourette's disorder. Whether behavior therapy and pharmacotherapy together have a synergistic effect has not been sufficiently investigated.

PHARMACOTHERAPY

Haloperidol is the most frequently prescribed drug for Tourette's disorder. Up to 80 percent of the patients have a favorable response; their symptoms decrease by as much as 70 to 90 percent of baseline frequency. Follow-up studies, however, indicate that only 20 to 30 percent of those patients continue to take long-term maintenance therapy. Discontinuation is often based on the drug's adverse effects.

Haloperidol appears to be most effective at relatively low dosages. The initial daily dosage for adolescents and adults is usually between 0.25 and 0.5 mg of haloperidol. Haloperidol is not approved for use in children under 3 years of age. For children between 3 and 12, the recommended total daily dosage is between 0.05 and 0.075 mg per kg, administered in divided doses either two or three times a day. That dosage imposes a daily limit of 3 mg of haloperidol for a 40-kg child. The dosage for all patients should be increased slowly, to minimize the likelihood of an acute dystonic reaction. The maximum effective dosage in adolescents and adults is often in the range of 3 to 4 mg a day, but some patients require dosages of up to 10 to 15 mg a day.

Patients and their parents, when appropriate, must be made aware of the drug's possible immediate and long-term adverse effects. The clinician must forewarn them of the possibilities of acute dystonic reactions and parkinsonian symptoms. Although the prophylactic use of an anticholinergic agent is not recommended, it is appropriate to prescribe diphenhydramine (Benadryl) or benztropine (Cogentin) to the patient, so that it is available should an acute dystonic reaction or parkinsonian effects occur at home or on vacation. Other effects of special concern are cognitive dulling, which can impair school performance and learning, and the risk of tardive dyskinesia. School phobias in children and disabling social phobias in adults have

been reported during the early phase of treatment, but the phobias usually remit within a few weeks after discontinuing haloperidol.

Pimozide, an inhibitor of postsynaptic dopamine receptors, is also effective in treating Tourette's disorder. In a recent large study, haloperidol was more effective than pimozide. Pimozide, like haloperidol, should not be used to treat simple tics. Pimozide is an antipsychotic and has adverse effects similar to those of other antipsychotics. Furthermore, adverse cardiac effects are unusually frequent, and deaths have occurred at high dosages. Aside from that, pimozide appears to be safe at recommended dosages, with cardiotoxicity limited to prolonged QT wave intervals. Electrocardiograms must be performed at baseline and periodically during treatment. There is little experience in administering pimozide to children under age 12 years.

The initial dosage of pimozide is usually 1 to 2 mg daily in divided doses; the dosage may be increased every other day. Most patients are maintained at less than 0.2 mg per kg a day or 10 mg a day, whichever is less. A dosage of 0.3 mg per kg a day or 20 mg a day should never be exceeded.

Although not presently approved for use in Tourette's disorder, clonidine, a noradrenergic antagonist, has been reported in several studies to be efficacious; 40 to 70 percent of patients benefited from the medication. Some clinicians have used it after they have considered its risks and benefits and fully informed the patient and, when appropriate, the parents. Clonidine has a slower onset of action than does haloperidol, and improvement may continue for more than a year in some cases. Besides the improvement in tic symptoms, patients may experience less tension, a greater sense of well-being, and a longer attention span than before receiving clonidine.

Children suffering from tics and severe attention-deficit/hyperactivity disorder can be treated with desipramine (Norpramin) for their attention problems. The benzodiazepines may be useful in diminishing anxiety in some patients, but they do not appear to significantly reduce the frequency of tics.

Other tricyclic drugs, such as nortriptyline (Pamelor), have also been used to treat children with attention-deficit/hyperactivity disorder and Tourette's disorder with some degree of success. Although clinicians must weigh the risks versus the benefits of using stimulants in cases of severe hyperactivity and comorbid tics, a recent study reported that methylphenidate reduced the occurrence of vocal tics in some children with hyperactivity and tic disorders. Another recent case report indicated that bupropion (Wellbutrin), an antidepressant of the aminoketone class, resulted in increased tic behavior in several children being treated for Tourette's disorder and attention-deficit/hyperactivity disorder.

CHRONIC MOTOR OR VOCAL TIC DISORDER

In chronic motor or vocal tic disorder, motor or vocal tics but not both have been present intermittently or nearly every day for more than one year. According to DSM-IV criteria, the disorder must have its onset before the age of 18 years, and it is not diagnosed if the criteria for Tourette's disorder have ever been met.

Epidemiology

The rate of chronic motor or vocal tic disorder has been estimated to be from 100 to 1,000 times greater than that of

Tourette's disorder. School-age boys are at highest risk, but the incidence is not known. Although the disorder was once believed to be rare, current estimates of the prevalence of chronic motor of vocal tic disorder range from 1 to 2 percent.

Etiology

Both Tourette's disorder and chronic motor or vocal tic disorder aggregate within the same families. Twin studies have found a high concordance for either Tourette's disorder or chronic motor tics in monozygotic twins. That finding lends support to the importance of hereditary factors in the transmission of at least some tic disorders.

Diagnosis and Clinical Features

The onset of chronic motor or vocal tic disorder appears to be in early childhood. The types of tics and their locations are similar to those in transient tic disorder. Chronic vocal tics are considerably rarer than chronic motor tics. The chronic vocal tics are usually much less conspicuous than those in Tourette's disorder. The vocal tics are usually not loud or intense; they consist of grunts or other noises caused by thoracic, abdominal, or diaphragmatic contractions; the tics are not primarily from the vocal cords. The DSM-IV diagnostic criteria are given in Table 37–2.

Differential Diagnosis

Chronic motor tics must be differentiated from a variety of other motor movements, including choreiform movements, myoclonus, restless legs syndrome, akathisia, and dystonias. Involuntary vocal utterances can occur in certain neurological disorders, such as Huntington's disease and Parkinson's disease.

Course and Prognosis

Children whose tics start between the ages of 6 and 8 years seem to have the best outcomes. Symptoms usually last for four to six years and stop in early adolescence. Those children whose tics involve the limbs or the trunk tend to do less well than those with only facial tics.

Table 37–2.   Diagnostic Criteria for Chronic Motor or Vocal Tic Disorder

A. Single or multiple motor or vocal tics (i.e., sudden, rapid, recurrent, nonrhythmic, stereotyped motor movements or vocalizations), but not both, have been present at some time during the illness.

B. The tics occur many times a day nearly every day or intermittently throughout a period of more than 1 year, and during this period there was never a tic-free period of more than 3 consecutive months.

C. The disturbance causes marked distress or significant impairment in social, occupational, or other important areas of functioning.

D. The onset is before 18 years.

E. The disturbance is not due to the direct physiological effects of a substance (e.g., stimulants) or a general medical condition (e.g., Huntington's disease or postviral encephalitis)

F. Criteria have never been met for Tourette's disorder.

Table from DSM-IV, *Diagnostic and Statistical Manual of Mental Disorders*, ed 4. Copyright American Psychiatric Association, Washington, 1994. Used with permission.

Treatment

The treatment of chronic motor or vocal tic disorder depends on the severity and the frequency of the tics; the patient's subjective distress; the effects of the tics on school or work, job performance, and socialization; and the presence of any other concomitant mental disorder.

Psychotherapy may be indicated to minimize the secondary emotional problems caused by the tics. Several studies have found that behavioral techniques, particularly habit reversal treatments, have been effective in treating chronic motor or vocal tic disorder. Antianxiety agents have not been successful. Haloperidol has been helpful in some cases, but the risks must be weighed against the possible clinical benefits because of the drug's adverse effects, including the development of tardive dyskinesia.

TRANSIENT TIC DISORDER

Transient tic disorder consists of single or multiple motor or vocal tics that occur many times a day nearly every day for at least four weeks but for no longer than 12 consecutive months. According to DSM-IV, the disorder must have its onset before age 18 years; it is not diagnosed if either Tourette's disorder or chronic motor or vocal tic disorder has ever been diagnosed.

Epidemiology

Transient, ticlike habit movements and nervous muscular twitches are common in children. From 5 to 24 percent of all school-age children have a history of tics. The prevalence of tics as defined here is unknown.

Etiology

Transient tic disorder probably has either organic or psychogenic origins, with some tics combining elements of both. Organic tics are probably most likely to progress to Tourette's disorder and have an increased family history of tics, whereas psychogenic tics are most likely to remit spontaneously. Those tics that progress to chronic motor or vocal tic disorder are most likely to have components of both. Tics of all sorts are exacerbated by stress and anxiety, but no evidence is available that tics are caused by stress or anxiety.

Diagnosis and Clinical Features

The DSM-IV criteria for establishing the diagnosis of transient tic disorder are as follows: (1) The tics are single or multiple motor or vocal tics. (2) The tics occur many times a day nearly every day for at least four weeks but for no longer than 12 consecutive months. (3) The patient has no history of Tourette's disorder or chronic motor or vocal tic disorder. (4) The onset is before age 18. (5) The tics do not occur exclusively during substance intoxication or a general medical condition. The diagnosis should specify whether a single episode or recurrent episodes are present (Table 37–3).

Transient tic disorder can be distinguished from chronic motor or vocal tic disorder and Tourette's disorder only by observing the symptoms' progression over time.

Course and Prognosis

Most persons with transient tic disorder do not progress to a more serious tic disorder. Their tics either disappear perma-

Table 37-3. Diagnostic Criteria for Transient Tic Disorder

A. Single or multiple motor and/or vocal tics (i.e., sudden, rapid, recurrent, nonrhythmic, stereotyped motor movements or vocalizations).

B. The tics occur many times a day, nearly every day for at least four weeks but for no longer than 12 consecutive months.

C. The disturbance causes marked distress or significant impairment in social, occupational, or other important areas of functioning.

D. The onset is before age 18 years.

E. The disturbance is not due to the direct physiological effects of a substance (e.g., stimulants) or a general medical condition (e.g., Huntington's disease or postviral encephalitis).

F. Criteria have never been met for Tourette's disorder or chronic motor or vocal tic disorder.

Specify if:
 Single episode or **recurrent.**

Table from DSM-IV, *Diagnostic and Statistical Manual of Mental Disorders*, ed 4. Copyright American Psychiatric Association, Washington, 1994. Used with permission.

nently or recur during periods of special stress. Only a small percentage go on to chronic motor or vocal tic disorder or Tourette's disorder.

Treatment

Whether the tics will disappear spontaneously, progress, or become chronic is unclear initially. Focusing attention on tics may exacerbate them, so the clinician often recommends that, at first, the family disregard the tics as much as possible. But if the tics are so severe that they impair the patient's functioning or if they are accompanied by significant emotional disturbances, complete psychiatric and pediatric neurological examinations are recommended. Treatment depends on the results of the evaluations. Psychopharmacology is not recommended unless the symptoms are unusually severe and disabling. Several studies have found that behavioral techniques, particularly habit reversal treatment, have been effective in treating transient tics.

TIC DISORDER NOT OTHERWISE SPECIFIED

The DSM-IV category of tic disorder not otherwise specified (NOS) is used for tic disorders that do not meet the criteria for any of the above disorders.

References

Gadow K D, Nolan E E, Sverd J: Methylphenidate in hyperactive boys with comorbid tic disorder: II. Short-term behavioral effects in school settings. J Am Acad Child Adolesc Psychiatry *31*: 462, 1992.

Hanna G L: Tic disorders. In *Comprehensive Textbook of Psychiatry*, ed 6, H I Kaplan, B J Sadock, editors, p 2325. Williams & Wilkins, Baltimore, 1995.

Lombroso P J, Scahill L D, Chappell P B, Pauls D L, Cohen D J, Leckman J F: Tourette's syndrome: a multigenerational, neuropsychiatric disorder. Advances Neurol *65*: 305, 1995.

Rauch S L, Baer L, Cosgrove G R, Jenike M A: Neurosurgical treatment of Tourette's syndrome: a critical review. Compr Psychiatry *36*: 141, 1995.

Spencer T, Biederman J, Steingard R, Wilens T: Bupropion exacerbates tics in children with attention-deficit hyperactivity disorder and Tourette's syndrome. J Am Acad Child Adolesc Psychiatry *32*: 211, 1993.

Spencer T, Biederman J, Wilens T, Steingard R, Geist D: Nortriptyline treatment of children with attention-deficit hyperactivity disorder and tic disorder or Tourette's syndrome. J Am Acad Child Adolesc Psychiatry *32*: 205, 1993.

Woods D W, Miltenberger R G: Habit reversal: A review of applications and variations. J Behav Ther Exp Psychiatry *26*: 123, 1995.

38/ Elimination Disorders

Bowel and bladder control develop gradually over time. Many factors affect toilet training, such as the child's intellectual capacity and social maturity, cultural determinants, and the psychological interactions between the child and the parents. The fourth edition of *Diagnostic and Statistical Manual of Mental Disorders* (DSM-IV) includes two elimination disorders, encopresis and enuresis. DSM-IV defines encopresis as a pattern of passing feces into inappropriate places, whether the passage is involuntary or intentional. The pattern must be present for at least three months, and the child's chronological age must be at least 4 years, or the child must have the developmental level of a 4-year-old. The DSM-IV definition of enuresis is the repeated voiding of urine into clothes or bed, whether the voiding is involuntary or intentional. The behavior must occur twice weekly for at least three months or must cause clinically significant distress or impairment socially or academically. The child's chronological or developmental age must be at least 5 years.

The normal sequence of developing control over bowel and bladder functions is (1) the development of nocturnal fecal continence, (2) the development of diurnal fecal continence, (3) the development of diurnal bladder control, and (4) the development of nocturnal bladder control.

ENCOPRESIS

Epidemiology

In Western culture, bowel control is established in more than 95 percent of children by the fourth birthday and in 99 percent by the fifth birthday. After that, frequency decreases to virtual absence by the age 16. After age 4, encopresis at all ages is three to four times more common in boys than in girls. At ages 7 to 8, frequency is about 1.5 percent in boys and about 0.5 percent in girls. By ages 10 to 12, once-a-month soiling occurs in 1.3 percent of boys and in 0.3 percent of girls.

Etiology

The lack of appropriate toilet training or inadequate training may delay the child's attainment of continence. Evidence suggests that some encopretic children suffer from lifelong inefficient and ineffective sphincter control. Either of those factors alone but especially the two in combination offer an opportunity for a power struggle between the child and the parent over issues of autonomy and control; such battles often aggravate the disorder, frequently causing secondary behavioral difficulties. Many encopretic children, however, do not have behavioral problems. When behavioral problems do occur, they are the social consequences of soiling.

Encopretic children who are clearly able to control their bowel function adequately and who deposit feces of relatively normal consistency in abnormal places usually have a psychiatric difficulty.

Encopresis may be associated with other neurodevelopmental problems, including easy distractibility, short attention span, low frustration tolerance, hyperactivity, and poor coordination. Occasionally, the child has a special fear of using the toilet.

Life events may also precipitate encopresis, such as the birth of a sibling or a move to a new home.

Encopresis after a long period of fecal continence sometimes appears to be a regression after such stresses as a parental separation, a change in domicile, or the start of school.

PSYCHOGENIC MEGACOLON

Many encopretic children also retain feces and become constipated either voluntarily or secondarily to painful defecation. In those cases no clear evidence indicates that preexisting anorectal dysfunction contributes to the constipation. The resulting chronic rectal distention from large, hard fecal masses may cause loss of tone in the rectal wall and desensitization to pressure. Thus, many children become unaware of the need to defecate, and overflow encopresis occurs, usually with relatively small amounts of liquid or soft stool leaking out. Olfactory accommodation may diminish or eliminate sensory cues.

Diagnosis and Clinical Features

Encopresis is diagnosed when feces are passed into inappropriate places regularly (at least once a month) for three months. Encopresis may be present in children who have bowel control and intentionally deposit feces in their clothes or other places for a variety of emotional reasons. Some children engage in the inappropriate behavior when angry at parental figures or as part of a pattern of oppositional defiant disorder. The children often develop repetitive behaviors that seem to seek negative attention. In other children, sporadic episodes of encopresis may occur during times of stress—for example, proximal to the birth of a new sibling—but in such cases the behavior is usually transient and does not fulfill the diagnostic criteria for the disorder. Encopresis may also be present involuntarily in the absence of physiological abnormalities. In those cases the child may not exhibit adequate control over the sphincter muscles, either because the child is absorbed in another activity or because the child lacks an awareness of the process. The feces may be of normal, near-normal, or liquid consistency. Some involuntary soiling is due to the chronic retaining of stool, resulting in liquid overflow. In rare cases the involuntary overflow of stool results from psychological causes of diarrhea or anxiety disorder symptoms. DSM-IV breaks down the types of encopresis into (1) with constipation and overflow incontinence and (2) without constipation and overflow incontinence. To receive a diagnosis of encopresis, a child must have a developmental or chronological level of at least 4 years. If the fecal incontinence is directly related to a medical condition, encopresis is not diagnosed (Table 38–1).

Studies have indicated that children with encopresis who do not have gastrointestinal illnesses have high rates of abnormal anal sphincter contractions. That finding is particularly prevalent among children with encopresis with constipation and overflow incontinence. Those children have difficulty in relaxing their anal sphincter muscles when trying to defecate. Children with constipation who have difficulties with sphincter relaxation are not likely to be good responders to laxatives in the treatment of their encopresis. Encopretic children without abnormal sphincter tone are likely to improve over a short period.

Table 38-1. Diagnostic Criteria for Encopresis

A. Repeated passage of feces into inappropriate places (e.g., clothing or floor) whether involuntary or intentional.

B. At least one such event a month for at least 3 months.

C. Chronological age is at least 4 years (or equivalent developmental level).

D. The behavior is not due exclusively to the direct physiological effects of a substance (e.g., laxatives) or a general medical condition except through a mechanism involving constipation.

Code as follows:
With constipation and overflow incontinence
Without constipation and overflow incontinence

Table from DSM-IV, *Diagnostic and Statistical Manual of Mental Disorders*, ed 4. Copyright American Psychiatric Association, Washington, 1994. Used with permission.

Pathology and Laboratory Examination

Although no specific test indicates a diagnosis of encopresis, the clinician must rule out medical illnesses, such as Hirschsprung's disease, before making a diagnosis. If it is unclear whether fecal retention is responsible for encopresis with constipation and overflow incontinence, a physical examination of the abdomen is indicated, and an abdominal X-ray can be helpful in determining the degree of constipation present. Sophisticated tests to determine whether sphincter tone is abnormal are generally not conducted in simple cases of encopresis.

Differential Diagnosis

In encopresis with constipation and overflow incontinence, constipation can begin as early as the child's first year, peaking between the second and fourth years. Soiling usually begins at age 4. Frequent liquid stools and hard fecal masses are found in the colon and the rectum on abdominal palpation and rectal examination. Complications include impaction, megacolon, and anal fissures.

Encopresis with constipation and overflow incontinence can be caused by faulty nutrition; structural disease of the anus, the rectum, and the colon; medicinal side effects; or nongastrointestinal medical (endocrine or neurological) disorders. The chief differential problem is aganglionic megacolon or Hirschsprung's disease, in which the patient may have an empty rectum and no desire to defecate but may still have an overflow of feces. The disease occurs in 1 in 5,000 children; signs appear shortly after birth.

Course and Prognosis

The outcome of encopresis depends on the cause, the chronicity of the symptoms, and coexisting behavioral problems. In many cases, encopresis is self-limiting, and it rarely continues beyond middle adolescence.

Children who have contributing physiological factors, such as poor gastric motility and an inability to relax the anal sphincter muscles, are more difficult to treat than are those with constipation but normal sphincter tone.

Encopresis is a particularly repugnant disorder to most people, including family members; thus, family tension is often high. The child's peers are also sensitive to the developmentally inappropriate behavior and often ostracize the child. An encopretic child is often scapegoated by peers and shunned by adults.

Many encopretic children have abysmally low self-esteem and are aware of their constant rejection. Psychologically, the children may appear blunted regarding the symptoms, or they may be entrenched in a pattern of encopresis as a mode of expressing anger.

The outcome of cases of encopresis is affected by the family's willingness and ability to participate in treatment without being too punitive and by the child's awareness of when the passage of feces is about to occur.

Treatment

By the time a child is brought in for treatment, considerable family discord and distress are common. Family tensions regarding the symptom must be reduced, and a nonpunitive atmosphere must be created. Similar efforts should be made to reduce the child's embarrassment at school. Many changes of underwear with a minimum of fuss should be arranged.

Psychotherapy is useful in many ways: it can (1) ease family tensions, (2) treat the encopretic children's reactions to their symptoms (such as low self-esteem and social isolation), (3) address the psychodynamic causes present in those children who have bowel control but continue to deposit their feces in inappropriate locations, and (4) treat those cases of encopresis after a long period of fecal continence that are reactions to psychological stressors. A good outcome occurs when the child feels in control of life events. Coexisting behavior problems predict a poor outcome.

Behavioral techniques have been used with great success, including such behavior reinforcers as star charts, in which the child places a star on a chart for dry or continent nights.

A pediatrician should be consulted in cases of encopresis with constipation and overflow incontinence. First, the child's bowel must be cleared, and then stool movements must be maintained with stool softeners or laxatives. Proper bowel habits should be taught. Biofeedback techniques can be of help.

ENURESIS

Epidemiology

The prevalence of enuresis decreases with increasing age. Thus, 82 percent of 2-year-olds, 49 percent of 3-year-olds, 26 percent of 4-year-olds, and 7 percent of 5-year-olds have been reported to be enuretic on a regular basis. However, prevalence rates vary, depending on the population studied and the tolerance for the symptoms in various cultures and socioeconomic groups.

The Isle of Wight study reported that 15.2 percent of 7-year-old boys were enuretic occasionally and that 6.7 percent of boys were enuretic at least once a week. The study reported that 3.3 percent of girls at age 7 years were enuretic at least once a week. Studies have reported that the overall prevalence was 3 percent by age 10. The rate drastically drops for teenagers, in whom a prevalence of 1.5 percent has been reported for 14-year-olds. In adults, enuresis affects about 1 percent.

Mental disorders are present in only about 20 percent of enuretic children and are most common in enuretic girls, in children with symptoms during the day and the night, and in children who maintain the symptoms into older childhood.

Etiology

Normal bladder control is acquired gradually and is influenced by neuromuscular and cognitive development, socioemotional factors, toilet training, and, possibly, genetic factors. Difficulties in one or more of those areas may delay urinary continence. Although an organic cause precludes a diagnosis of enuresis, the correction of an anatomical defect or the cure of an infection does not always cure the enuresis, suggesting that the cause sometimes may be unrelated to organic abnormality.

In a longitudinal study of child development, those children who were enuretic were about twice as likely to have concomitant developmental delays as were dry children.

About 75 percent of enuretic children have a first-degree relative who is or was enuretic. The concordance rate is higher in monozygotic twins than in dizygotic twins. Although there may be a genetic component, much can be accounted for by tolerance for enuresis in those families and by other psychosocial factors.

Some studies report that enuretic children have a bladder with a normal anatomical capacity when anesthetized but a functionally small bladder, so that the child feels an urge to void with little urine in the bladder. Other studies report that bedwetting occurs because the bladder is full and there is an absence of the high levels of nighttime antidiuretic hormone. Those factors allow for a higher than usual urine output. Enuresis may not be related to a specific stage of sleep or time of night; instead, bed-wetting appears randomly. In most cases the quality of sleep is normal. Little evidence suggests that enuretic children sleep more soundly than do other children.

Psychosocial stressors appear to precipitate some cases of enuresis. In young children the disorder has been particularly associated with the birth of a sibling, hospitalization between the ages of 2 and 4, the start of school, the breakup of a family because of divorce or death, and a move to a new domicile.

Diagnosis and Clinical Features

Enuresis is the repeated voiding of urine into the patient's clothes or bed; the voiding may be involuntary or intentional. For the diagnosis to be made, the child must exhibit a developmental or chronological age of at least 5 years. According to DSM-IV, the behavior must occur twice weekly for at least three months or must cause distress and impairment in functioning to meet the diagnostic criteria. Enuresis is diagnosed only if the behavior is not due to a medical condition. DSM-IV breaks down the disorder into three types: (1) nocturnal only, (2) diurnal only, and (3) nocturnal and diurnal (Table 38–2).

PATHOLOGY AND LABORATORY EXAMINATION

No single laboratory finding is pathognomonic of enuresis. However, the clinician must rule out organic factors, such as the presence of urinary tract infections that may predispose a child to enuresis. Structural obstructive abnormalities may be present in up to 3 percent of children who present with apparent enuresis. Sophisticated radiographic studies are usually deferred in simple cases of enuresis with no signs of repeated infections or other medical problems.

Differential Diagnosis

Possible organic causes of bed-wetting must be ruled out. Organic features are found most often in children with both

Table 38–2. Diagnostic Criteria for Enuresis

A. Repeated voiding of urine into bed or clothes (whether involuntary or intentional).

B. The behavior is clinically significant as manifested by either a frequency of twice a week for at least 3 consecutive months or the presence of clinically significant distress or impairment in social, academic (occupational), or other important areas of functioning.

C. Chronological age is at least 5 years (or equivalent developmental level).

D. The behavior is not due exclusively to the direct physiological effect of a substance (e.g., a diuretic) or a general medical condition (e.g., diabetes, spina bifida, a seizure disorder).

Specify type:
Nocturnal only
Diurnal only
Nocturnal and diurnal

Table from DSM-IV, *Diagnostic and Statistical Manual of Mental Disorders,* ed 4. Copyright American Psychiatric Association, Washington, 1994. Used with permission.

nocturnal and diurnal enuresis combined with urinary frequency and urgency. The organic features include (1) genitourinary pathology—structural, neurological, and infectious—such as obstructive uropathy, spina bifida occulta, and cystitis; (2) other organic disorders that may cause polyuria and enuresis, such as diabetes mellitus and diabetes insipidus; (3) disturbances of consciousness and sleep, such as seizures, intoxication, and sleepwalking disorder, during which the patient urinates; and (4) side effects from treatment with antipsychotics—for example, thioridazine (Mellaril).

Course and Prognosis

Enuresis is usually self-limited. The child can eventually remain dry without psychiatric sequelae. Most enuretic children find their symptom ego-dystonic and have enhanced self-esteem and improved social confidence when they become continent.

About 80 percent of affected children never achieved a year-long period of dryness. Enuresis after at least one dry year usually begins between ages 5 and 8 years; if it occurs much later, especially during adulthood, organic causes must be investigated. Some evidence indicates that late onset of enuresis in children is more frequently associated with a concomitant psychiatric difficulty than is enuresis without at least one dry year. Relapses occur in enuretics who are becoming dry spontaneously and in those being treated.

The significant emotional and social difficulties of enuretic children usually include poor self-image, decreased self-esteem, social embarrassment and restriction, and intrafamilial conflict.

Treatment

Because there is usually no identifiable cause of enuresis and because the disorder tends to remit spontaneously, even if not treated, a few methods have achieved some success.

APPROPRIATE TOILET TRAINING

Appropriate toilet training with parental reinforcement should have been attempted, especially in enuresis in which a period of urinary continence did not precede the disturbance. If toilet training was not attempted, the parents and the patient should be guided in that undertaking. Record keeping is helpful in determining a baseline and following the child's progress and may itself be a reinforcer. A star chart may be particularly helpful. Other useful techniques include restricting fluids before bed and night lifting to toilet train the child.

BEHAVIORAL THERAPY

Classical conditioning with the bell (or buzzer) and pad apparatus is generally the most effective treatment for enuresis. Dryness results in more than 50 percent of all cases. The treatment is equally effective in children with and without concomitant mental disorders, and there is no evidence of symptom substitution. Difficulties may include child and family noncompliance, improper use of the apparatus, and relapse.

Bladder training—encouragement or reward for delaying micturition for increasing lengths of time during waking hours—has also been used. Although sometimes effective, the method is decidedly inferior to the bell and pad.

PHARMACOTHERAPY

Drugs should rarely be used to treat enuresis and then only finally in intractable cases causing serious socioemotional difficulties for the sufferer. Imipramine (Tofranil) is efficacious and has been approved for use in treating childhood enuresis, primarily on a short-term basis. Initially, up to 30 percent of enuretic patients stay dry, and up to 85 percent wet less frequently than before treatment. The success, however, does not often last. Tolerance often develops after six weeks of therapy. Once the drug is discontinued, relapse and enuresis at former frequencies usually occur within a few months. A serious problem is the drug's adverse effects, which include cardiotoxicity. Desmopressin (DDAVP), an antidiuretic compound that is available as an intranasal spray, has shown some initial success in reducing enuresis.

PSYCHOTHERAPY

Although many psychological and psychoanalytic theories regarding enuresis have been advanced, controlled studies have found that psychotherapy alone is not an effective treatment of enuresis. Psychotherapy, however, may be useful in dealing with the coexisting psychiatric problems and the emotional and family difficulties that arise secondary to the disorder.

References

Mikkelsen E J. In *Child and Adolescent Psychiatry: A Comprehensive Textbook*, ed 2, M Lewis, editor, p 593. Williams & Wilkins, Baltimore, 1996.

Mikkelsen E J: Elimination disorders. In *Comprehensive Textbook of Psychiatry*, ed 6, H I Kaplan, B J Sadock, editors, p 2337. Williams & Wilkins, Baltimore, 1995.

Monda J M, Husmann D A: Primary nocturnal enuresis: A comparison among observation, imipramine, desmopressin acetate and bed-wetting alarm systems. J Urol *154*: 745, 1995.

Rutter M: Isle of Wight revisited: Twenty-five years of child psychiatric epidemiology. J Am Acad Child Adolesc Psychiatry *28*: 633, 1989.

Thompson S, Rey J M: Functional enuresis: is desmopressin the answer? J Am Acad Child Adolesc Psychiatry *34*: 266, 1995.

Young M H, Brennen L C, Baker R D, Baker S S: Functional encopresis: Symptom reduction and behavioral improvement. J Dev Behav Pediatr *16*: 226, 1995.

39/ Other Disorders of Infancy, Childhood, or Adolescence

39.1 SEPARATION ANXIETY DISORDER

Some degree of separation anxiety is a universal phenomenon, and it is an expected part of a child's normal development. Infants exhibit separation anxiety as stranger anxiety at less than 1 year of age when the infant and the mother are separated. Some separation anxiety is also normal in young children who are entering school for the first time. Separation anxiety disorder, however, is present when developmentally inappropriate and excessive anxiety emerges concerning separation from the major attachment figure. School avoidance may occur. According to the fourth edition of *Diagnostic and Statistical Manual of Mental Disorders* (DSM-IV), separation anxiety disorder requires the presence of at least three symptoms related to excessive worry regarding separation from the major attachment figures. The worries may take the form of refusal to go to school, fears and distress on separation, repeated complaints of such physical symptoms as headaches and stomachaches when separation is anticipated, and nightmares related to separation issues. The DSM-IV diagnostic criteria include a duration of at least four weeks and an onset before the age of 18 years.

EPIDEMIOLOGY

Separation anxiety disorder is more common in young children than in adolescents and has been reported to occur equally in boys and girls. The onset may occur in preschool years but is most commonly seen in 7-to-8-year-olds. The prevalence of separation anxiety disorder has been estimated at 3 to 4 percent of all school-age children and 1 percent of all adolescents.

ETIOLOGY

Psychosocial Factors

Young children, immature and dependent on a mothering figure, are particularly prone to anxiety related to separation. Because children undergo a series of developmental fears—fear of losing the mother and the mother's love, fear of bodily damage, fear of their impulses, and fear of the punishing anxiety of the superego and of guilt—most have transient experiences of separation anxiety based on those fears. However, separation anxiety disorder occurs when the child has a disproportionate fear of mother-loss. A frequent dynamic is the child's disavowal and displacement of angry feelings toward the parents onto the environment, which then becomes too threatening. Fears of personal harm and of danger to one's parents are persistent preoccupations; the child can feel safe and secure only in the parents' presence. The syndrome is common in childhood, especially in mild forms that do not reach the physician's office. Only when the symptoms have become established and disturb the child's general adaptation to family life, peers, and school do they come to the attention of professionals.

The character structure pattern in many children with the disorder includes conscientiousness, eagerness to please, and a tendency toward conformity. Families tend to be close-knit and caring, and the children often seem spoiled or the objects of parental overconcern.

External life stresses often coincide with the development of the disorder. The death of a relative, illness in the child, a change in the child's environment, or a move to a new neighborhood or a new school is frequently noted in the histories of children with the disorder.

Learning Factors

Direct modeling may communicate phobic anxiety from parents to children. If a parent is fearful, the child will probably have a phobic adaptation to new situations, especially to the school environment. Some parents appear to teach their children to be anxious by overprotecting them from expected dangers or by exaggerating the dangers. For example, the parent who cringes in a room during a lightning storm teaches a child to do the same. The parent who is frightened of mice or insects conveys the affect of fright to the child. Conversely, the parent who becomes angry at a child during an incipient phobic concern about animals may inculcate a phobic concern in the child by the very intensity of the anger expressed.

GENETIC FACTORS

The intensity with which separation anxiety is experienced by individual children probably has a genetic basis. Family studies have shown that the biological offspring of adults with anxiety disorders are prone to suffer in childhood from separation anxiety disorder. Parents who have panic disorder with agoraphobia appear to have an increased risk of having a child with separation anxiety disorder. Separation anxiety disorder and depression overlap in children, and some clinicians view separation anxiety disorder as a variant of depressive disorders.

DIAGNOSIS AND CLINICAL FEATURES

Separation anxiety disorder is the most common anxiety disorder in childhood. To meet the diagnostic criteria, according to DSM-IV, the disorder must be characterized by three of the following symptoms for at least four weeks: (1) persistent and excessive worry about losing or possible harm befalling major attachment figures; (2) persistent and excessive worry that an untoward event will lead to separation from a major attachment figure; (3) persistent reluctance or refusal to go to school or elsewhere because of fear of separation; (4) persistent and excessive fear or reluctance to be alone or without major attachment figures at home or without significant adults in other settings; (5) persistent reluctance or refusal to go to sleep without being near a major attachment figure or to sleep away from home; (6) repeated nightmares involving the theme of separation; (7) repeated complaints of physical symptoms, including headaches and stomachaches, when separation from major attachment figures is anticipated; and (8) recurrent excessive distress when separation from home or major attachment figures is anticipated or involved. According to DSM-IV, the disturbance

Table 39.1–1. Diagnostic Criteria for Separation Anxiety Disorder

A. Developmentally inappropriate and excessive anxiety concerning separation from home or from those to whom the individual is attached, as evidence by three (or more) of the following:

  (1) recurrent excessive distress when separation from home or major attachment figures occurs or is anticipated

  (2) persistent and excessive worry about losing, or about possible harm befalling, major attachment figures

  (3) persistent and excessive worry that an untoward event will lead to separation from a major attachment figure (e.g., getting lost or being kidnapped)

  (4) persistent reluctance or refusal to go to school or elsewhere because of fear of separation

  (5) persistently and excessively fearful or reluctant to be alone or without major attachment figures at home or without significant adults in other settings

  (6) persistent reluctance or refusal to go to sleep without being near a major attachment figure or to sleep away from home

  (7) repeated nightmares involving the theme of separation

  (8) repeated complaints of physical symptoms (such as headaches, stomachaches, nausea, or vomiting) when separation from major attachment figures occurs or is anticipated

B. The duration of the disturbance is at least 4 weeks.

C. The onset is before age 18 years.

D. The disturbance causes clinically significant distress or impairment in social, academic (occupational), or other important areas of functioning.

F. The disturbance does not occur exclusively during the course of a pervasive developmental disorder, schizophrenia, or other psychotic disorder and, in adolescents and adults, is not better accounted for by panic disorder with agoraphobia.

Table from DSM-IV, *Diagnostic and Statistical Manual of Mental Disorders*, ed 4. Copyright American Psychiatric Association, Washington, 1994. Used with permission.

must also cause significant distress or impairment in functioning (Table 39.1–1).

The patient's history may reveal important episodes of separation in the child's life, particularly because of illness and hospitalization, illness of a parent, loss of a parent, or geographic relocation. The clinician should scrutinize the period of infancy for evidence of separation-individuation disorders or lack of an adequate mothering figure. The use of fantasies, dreams, and play materials and the observation of the child are of great help in making the diagnosis. The clinician should examine not only the content of thought but also the way in which thoughts are expressed. For example, children may express fears that their parents will die, even when their behavior does not show evidence of motor anxiety. Similarly, their difficulty in describing events or their bland denial of obviously anxiety-provoking events may suggest the presence of separation anxiety disorder. Difficulty with memory in expressing separation themes and patent distortions in the recital of such themes may give clues to the disorder's presence.

The essential feature of separation anxiety disorder is extreme anxiety precipitated by separation from parents, home, or other familiar surroundings. The child's anxiety may approach terror or panic. The distress is greater than that normally expected for the child's developmental level and cannot be explained by any other disorder. In many cases the disorder is a kind of phobia, although the phobic concern is a general one and not directed to a particular symbolic object. Because the disorder is associated with childhood, it is not included among the phobias of adulthood, which imply a much greater structuralization of the personality.

Morbid fears, preoccupations, and ruminations are characteristic of separation anxiety disorder. Children with the disorder become fearful that someone close to them will be hurt or that something terrible will happen to them when they are away from important caring figures. Many children worry that they or their parents will have an accident or become ill. Fears about getting lost and about being kidnapped and never again finding their parents are common.

Adolescents may not directly express any anxious concern about separation from a mothering figure; however, their behavior often reflects a separation anxiety. They may express discomfort about leaving home, engage in solitary activities, and continue to use the mothering figure as a helper in buying clothes and entering social and recreational activities.

Separation anxiety disorder in children is often manifested at the thought of travel or in the course of travel away from home. The children may refuse to go to camp, a new school, or even a friend's house. Frequently, a continuum exists between mild anticipatory anxiety before separation from an important figure and pervasive anxiety after the separation has occurred. Premonitory signs include irritability, difficulty in eating, whining, staying in a room alone, clinging to parents, and following a parent everywhere. Often, when a family moves, the child displays separation anxiety by intense clinging to the mother figure. Sometimes geographic relocation anxiety is expressed in feelings of acute homesickness or psychophysiological symptoms that break out when the child is away from home or is going to a new country. The child yearns to return home and becomes preoccupied with fantasies of how much better the old home was. Integration into the new life situation may become extremely difficult.

Sleep difficulties are frequent and may require that someone remain with the children until they fall asleep. Children often go to their parent's bed or even sleep at the parents' door when the bedroom is barred to them. Nightmares and morbid fears are other expressions of anxiety.

Associated features include fear of the dark and imaginary, bizarre worries. Children may see eyes staring at them and become preoccupied with mythical figures or monsters reaching out for them in their bedrooms.

Many children are demanding and intrusive in adult affairs and require constant attention to allay their anxieties. Symptoms emerge when separation from an important parent figure becomes necessary. If separation is threatened, many children with the disorder do not experience interpersonal difficulties. They may, however, look sad and may cry easily. They sometimes complain that they are not loved, express a wish to die, or complain that siblings are favored over them. They frequently experience gastrointestinal symptoms of nausea, vomiting, and stomachaches and have pains in various parts of the body, sore throats, and flulike symptoms. In older children, typical cardiovascular and respiratory symptoms of palpitations, dizziness, faintness, and strangulation are reported.

The most common anxiety disorder that coexists with separation anxiety disorder is specific phobia, which occurs in about one third of all referred separation anxiety disorder cases.

DIFFERENTIAL DIAGNOSIS

Some degree of separation anxiety is a normal phenomenon, and clinical judgment must be used in distinguishing that normal anxiety from separation anxiety disorder. In generalized anxiety disorder, the patient does not focus anxiety on separation. In pervasive developmental disorders and schizophrenia, anxiety about separation may occur but is viewed as caused by those conditions, rather than as a separate disorder. In depressive disorders occurring in children, the diagnosis of separation anxiety disorder should also be made when the criteria for both disorders are met; the two diagnoses often coexist. Panic disorder with agoraphobia is uncommon before age 18, and the fear is of being incapacitated by a panic attack, rather than of separation from parental figures; in some adult cases, however, many symptoms of separation anxiety disorder may be present. In conduct disorder, truancy is common, but the child stays away from home and does not have anxiety about separation. School refusal is a frequent symptom in separation anxiety disorder but is not pathognomonic of it. Children with other diagnoses, such as phobias, can present with school refusal; in those disorders, the age of onset may be later and the school refusal more severe than in separation anxiety disorder.

COURSE AND PROGNOSIS

The course and the prognosis of separation anxiety disorder are variable and are related to the age of onset, the duration of the symptoms, and the development of comorbid anxiety and depressive disorders. Young children who experience the disorder but can still attend school generally have a better prognosis than do adolescents with the disorder who refuse to attend school for long periods. Reports have indicated a significant overlap of separation anxiety disorder and depressive disorders. In those complicated cases, the prognosis is guarded.

Most follow-up studies have methodological problems and are of hospitalized, school-phobic children, not of children with separation anxiety disorder per se. Little is reported about the outcome of mild cases, whether the children are seen in outpatient treatment or receive no treatment. Despite the limitations of the studies, they indicate that some children with severe school phobia continue to resist attending school for many years.

During the 1970s the literature reported that many adult agoraphobic women suffered separation anxiety disorder in childhood. Although research suggests that many children with an anxiety disorder are at increased risk for an adult anxiety disorder, the specific link between separation anxiety disorder in childhood and agoraphobia in adulthood has not been clearly established. Studies do show that anxious parents are at increased risk to have children with anxiety disorders. In addition, in recent years some cases have been reported of children presenting with both panic disorder and separation anxiety disorder.

TREATMENT

A multimodal treatment approach—including individual psychotherapy, family education, and family therapy—is recommended for separation anxiety disorder. Family therapy helps the parents understand the need for consistent, supportive love and the importance of preparing for any important change in life, such as illness, surgery, or geographic relocation. Specific cognitive strategies and relaxation exercises may help the child control the anxiety. Pharmacotherapy is also useful when psychotherapy alone is not sufficient.

School refusal associated with separation anxiety disorder may be viewed as a psychiatric emergency. A comprehensive treatment plan involves the child, the parents, and the child's peers and school. The child should be encouraged to attend school, but, if a return to a full school day is overwhelming, a program should be arranged for the child to progressively increase his or her time spent at school. Graded contact with an object of anxiety is a form of behavior modification that can be applied to any type of separation anxiety. In some severe cases of school refusal, hospitalization is required.

Pharmacotherapy is useful for separation anxiety disorder. The tricyclic and tetracyclic drugs, such as imipramine (Tofranil), are usually begun in dosages of 25 mg daily, increased by additional 25 mg doses up to a total of 150 to 200 mg daily until a therapeutic effect is noted. If no effect is noted with 200 mg daily, the plasma levels of imipramine and its active metabolite, desmethylimipramine, should be studied to determine whether a therapeutic blood level has been attained. Apart from its antidepressant effect, imipramine has been postulated to yield results that reduce panic and fear related to separation. Diphenhydramine (Benadryl) can be used to break a dangerous cycle of sleep disturbances.

References

Bradley S J, Hood L: Psychiatrically referred adolescents with panic attacks: Presenting symptoms, stressors, and comorbidity. J Am Acad Child Adolesc Psychiatry *32*: 826, 1993.

Francis G, Last C G, Strauss C C: Avoidant disorder and social phobia in children and adolescents. J Am Acad Child Adolesc Psychiatry *31*: 1086, 1992.

Jellinek M S, Kearns M E: Separation anxiety. Pediatr Rev *16*: 57, 1995.

Mattison R E: Separation anxiety disorder and anxiety in children. In *Comprehensive Textbook of Psychiatry*, ed 6, H I Kaplan, B J Sadock, editors, p 2345. Williams & Wilkins, Baltimore, 1995.

39.2 SELECTIVE MUTISM

Selective mutism is an uncommon childhood condition in which a child who is fluent with language consistently fails to speak in specific social situations, such as school, in which language is expected. Most children with the disorder are silent in their mute situations, but some whisper or use single-syllable words. Despite the absence of speech, some children communicate with eye contact or nonverbal gestures. Those children speak fluently in other situations, such as at home and in certain familiar settings.

According to the fourth edition of *Diagnostic and Statistical Manual of Mental Disorders* (DSM-IV), the symptoms must be present for at least one month but are not limited to the first month of school; the disturbance must interfere with educational or occupational achievement or social communication. The disorder is diagnosed only if the condition is not better accounted for by a communication disorder, such as stuttering, or by a lack of knowledge of appropriate language skills.

EPIDEMIOLOGY

The prevalence of selective mutism estimated to range between 3 and 8 per 10,000. Young children are more vulnerable than older children to the disorder. Although still under investigation, selective mutism may be more common in girls than in boys.

ETIOLOGY

Selective mutism is a psychologically determined inhibition or refusal to speak. However, many children with selective mutism have histories of delayed onset of speech or speech abnormalities that may be contributory. Parental discord, maternal depression, and heightened dependence needs are noted in many of the families. Those factors result in maternal overprotection and an overly close but ambivalent relationship between the mother and her selectively mute child. Children with selective mutism usually speak freely at home; they have no significant biological disability. Some children seem predisposed to selective mutism after early emotional or physical trauma; therefore, some clinicians call the phenomenon traumatic mutism, rather than selective mutism.

DIAGNOSIS AND CLINICAL FEATURES

The diagnosis of selective mutism is not difficult to make once it is clear that the child has adequate language skills in some environments but not in others (Table 39.2–1). The mutism may develop gradually or suddenly after a disturbing experience. The onset can range from ages 4 to 8, and it is usually noticed in the school setting. Mute periods are most commonly manifested in school or outside the home; in rare cases a child is mute at home but not in school. Children who exhibit selective mutism may also have symptoms of separation anxiety disorder, school refusal, and delayed language acquisition. Since social anxiety is almost always present in children with selective mutism, some investigators have suggested that selective mutism is a symptom of social phobia. Behavioral disturbances, such as temper tantrums and oppositional behaviors, may also occur in the home.

DIFFERENTIAL DIAGNOSIS

Shy children may exhibit a transient muteness in new, anxiety-provoking situations. Those children often have histories of not speaking in the presence of strangers and of clinging to their mothers. Most of the children who are mute on entering school improve spontaneously and may be described as having transient adaptational shyness.

Selective mutism must also be distinguished from mental retardation, pervasive developmental disorders, and expressive language disorder. In those disorders, however, the symptoms are widespread, and there is not one situation in which the child communicates normally; the child may have an inability to speak, rather than a refusal to speak. In mutism secondary to conversion disorder, the mutism is pervasive.

Children introduced into an environment where a different language is spoken may be reticent to begin using the new language. Selective mutism should be diagnosed only when children also refuse to converse in their native language and when they have gained communicative competence in the new language.

COURSE AND PROGNOSIS

Although children with selective mutism are often abnormally shy in the preschool years, the onset of the disorder is usually at age 5 or 6. The most common pattern is that the children speak almost exclusively at home with the nuclear family but not elsewhere, especially not at school. Consequently, they may have significant academic difficulties and even failure. Children with selective mutism are generally shy, anxious, and depressed. They may not form social relationships, and teasing and scapegoating by peers may cause them to refuse to go to school. Frequently, the children display at home compulsive traits, negativism, temper tantrums, and oppositional and aggressive behavior.

Some children with selective mutism communicate with gestures, such as nodding and shaking the head and saying "um-hum" or "no." Most cases last only a few weeks or months, but some may persist for years. In one follow-up study, about half the children improved within 5 to 10 years. Children who do not improve by age 10 appear to have a long-term course and a worse prognosis than do children who do improve by age 10.

Some mute children appear to have negativistic and sadistic relationships with adults and use their defiant muteness to punish them. That behavior seems to improve concomitantly with increasing speech in the environments where the child had previously been mute.

TREATMENT

A multimodal approach using individual, behavioral, and family interventions is most likely to be successful. In the preschool years, counseling or psychotherapy for the parents may be indicated. The preschool child may also benefit from a therapeutic nursery. For the school-age child, individual psychotherapy or behavior therapy may be indicated. When a child's independence is being thwarted, marital counseling or psychotherapy for the parents is paramount.

Some reports suggest the use of pharmacological agents as adjunctive treatments for selective mutism. Those suggestions are based on the observation that children with the disorder often exhibit symptoms consistent with social phobia. Therefore, such medications as phenelzine (Nardil) may be helpful. No data confirm this treatment's efficacy, although case reports have been published. Further investigation is needed to determine the usefulness of pharmacological interventions for selective mutism.

Table 39.2–1. Diagnostic Criteria for Selective Mutism

A. Consistent failure to speak in specific social situations (in which there is an expectation for speaking, e.g., at school) despite speaking in other situations.

B. The disturbance interferes with educational or occupational achievement or with social communication.

C. The duration of the disturbance is at least 1 month (not limited to the first month of school).

D. The failure to speak is not due to a lack of knowledge of, or comfort with, the spoken language required in the social situation.

E. The disturbance is not better accounted for by a communication disorder (e.g., stuttering) and does not occur exclusively during the course of a pervasive developmental disorder, schizophrenia, or other psychotic disorder.

Table from DSM-IV, *Diagnostic and Statistical Manual of Mental Disorders*, ed 4. Copyright American Psychiatric Association, Washington, 1994. Used with permission.

References

Baker L, Cantwell D P: Selective mutism. In *Comprehensive Textbook of Psychiatry*, ed 6, H I Kaplan, B J Sadock, editors, p 2351. Williams & Wilkins, Baltimore, 1995.

Dow S P, Sonies B C, Scheib D, Moss S E, Leonard H L: Practical guidelines for the assessment and treatment of selective mutism. J Am Acad Child Adolesc Psychiatry *34*: 836, 1995.

Klin A, Volkmar F R: Elective mutism and mental retardation. J Am Acad Child Adolesc Psychiatry *32*: 860, 1993.

39.3 REACTIVE ATTACHMENT DISORDER OF INFANCY OR EARLY CHILDHOOD

Reactive attachment disorder of infancy or early childhood is a disturbance of social interaction and relatedness based on grossly inappropriate caretaking—that is, neglect of the child's basic physical or emotional needs or multiple changes in caretakers, preventing appropriate bonds. The fourth edition of *Diagnostic and Statistical Manual of Mental Disorders* (DSM-IV) specifies that before the age of 5 years, one of the following two patterns of inappropriate behavior is exhibited: (1) persistent failure to initiate or respond appropriately to most social interactions as manifested by excessively inhibited, hypervigilant, or ambivalent responses; (2) indiscriminate expressions of familiarity with relative strangers and diffuse attachments. Those developmentally inappropriate behaviors are presumed to be due largely to pathogenic caretaking, but less severe disturbances in parenting may also be associated with infants who exhibit the disorder. In DSM-IV, the disturbance cannot be accounted for solely based on developmental delay, such as in mental retardation, and is not a symptom of a pervasive developmental disorder. The disorder may result in a picture of failure to thrive, in which the infant shows physical signs of malnourishment and does not exhibit the expected developmental motor and verbal milestones. When that is the case, the failure to thrive is coded on Axis III.

EPIDEMIOLOGY

No specific data on the prevalence, sex ratio, or familial pattern are available at this time. Although patients with reactive attachment disorder of infancy or early childhood come from all socioeconomic (SES) groups, studies of some patients (such as infants with failure to thrive) indicate an increased vulnerability among the low SES groups. That finding is congruent with the likelihood of psychosocial deprivation, single-parent households, family disorganization, and economic difficulties in families in low SES groups.

A caregiver may be fully satisfactory for one child, but another child under the same care may have a reactive attachment disorder of infancy or early childhood.

ETIOLOGY

The cause of reactive attachment disorder of infancy or early childhood is included in the disorder's definition. Grossly pathogenic care of the infant or young child by the caretaker presumably causes the markedly disturbed social relatedness usually evident. The emphasis is on the unidirectional cause; that is, the caretaker does something inimical or neglects to do something essential for the infant or child. However, in evaluating a patient for whom such a diagnosis is appropriate, the clinician should consider the contributions of each member of the caretaker-child dyad and their interactions. The clinician should weigh such things as infant or child temperament, deficient or defective bonding, a developmentally disabled or sensorially impaired child, and a particular caretaker-child mismatch. The likelihood of neglect increases with parental mental retardation; lack of parenting skills because of personal upbringing, social isolation, or deprivation and lack of opportunities to learn about caretaking behavior; and premature parenthood (during early and middle adolescence), in which the parents are unable to respond to and care for the infant's needs and in which the parents' own needs take precedence over their infant's or child's needs.

Frequent changes of the primary caretaker—as may occur in institutionalization, repeated lengthy hospitalizations, and multiple foster home placements—may also cause a reactive attachment disorder of infancy or early childhood.

DIAGNOSIS AND CLINICAL FEATURES

Children with reactive attachment disorder of infancy or early childhood often first come to the attention of their pediatrician. The clinical picture varies greatly according to the child's chronological and mental ages. Perhaps the most typical clinical picture of the infant with the disorder is the nonorganic failure to thrive. In such infants, hypokinesis, dullness, listlessness, and apathy with a poverty of spontaneous activity are usually seen. The infants look sad, unhappy, joyless, and miserable. Some infants also appear frightened and watchful, with a radarlike gaze. In spite of that, the infants may exhibit delayed responsiveness to a stimulus that would elicit fright or withdrawal in a normal infant (Table 39.3–1). DSM-IV specifies two types: inhibited and disinhibited.

Most of the infants appear significantly malnourished, and many have protruding abdomens. Occasionally, foul-smelling, celiaclike stools are reported. In unusually severe cases a clinical picture of marasmus appears. The infant's weight is often below the third percentile and markedly below the appropriate weight for the infant's height. If serial weights are available, the weight percentiles may have progressively decreased because of an actual weight loss or a failure to gain weight as height increases. Head circumference is usually normal for the infant's age. Muscle tone may be poor. The skin may be colder and paler or more mottled than the normal child's skin. Laboratory findings are usually within normal limits except for those abnormal findings coincident with any malnutrition, dehydration, or concurrent illness. Bone age is usually retarded. Growth hormone levels are usually normal or elevated, suggesting that growth failure in the children is secondary to caloric deprivation and malnutrition. The children improve physically and gain weight rapidly after they are hospitalized.

Socially, the infants usually show little spontaneous activity and a marked diminution of both initiative toward others and reciprocity in response to the caretaking adult or examiner. Both the mother and the infant may be indifferent to their separation on hospitalization or the termination of subsequent hospital visits. The infants frequently show none of the normal upset, fretting, or protest about hospitalization. Older infants usually show little interest in their environment. They may have little interest in playing with toys, even if encouraged. However, they rapidly

Table 39.3-1.   Diagnostic Criteria for Reactive Attachment Disorder of Infancy or Early Childhood

A. Markedly disturbed and developmentally inappropriate social relatedness in most contexts, beginning before age 5 years, as evidenced by either (1) or (2):

   (1) persistent failure to initiate or respond in a developmentally appropriate fashion to most social interactions, as manifested by excessively inhibited, hypervigilant, or highly ambivalent and contradictory responses (e.g., the child may respond to caregivers with a mixture of approach, avoidance, and resistance to comforting, or may exhibit frozen watchfulness)

   (2) diffuse attachments as manifested by indiscriminate sociability with marked inability to exhibit appropriate selective attachments (e.g., excessive familiarity with relative strangers or lack of selectivity in choice of attachment figures)

B. The disturbance in criterion A is not accounted for solely by developmental delay (as in mental retardation) and does not meet criteria for a pervasive developmental disorder.

C. Pathogenic care as evidenced by at least one of the following:

   (1) persistent disregard of the child's basic emotional needs for comfort, stimulation, and affection

   (2) persistent disregard of the child's basic physical needs

   (3) repeated changes of primary caregiver that prevent formation of stable attachments (e.g., frequent changes in foster care)

D. There is a presumption that the care in criterion C is responsible for the disturbed behavior in A (e.g., the disturbances in criterion A began following the pathogenic care in criterion C).

Table from DSM-IV, *Diagnostic and Statistical Manual of Mental Disorders*, ed 4. Copyright American Psychiatric Association, Washington, 1994. Used with permission.

or gradually take an interest in and relate to their caretakers in the hospital.

Classic psychosocial dwarfism or psychosocially determined short stature is a syndrome that is usually first manifested in children 2 to 3 years of age. The children typically are unusually short and have frequent growth hormone abnormalities and severe behavioral disturbances. All those symptoms are the result of an inimical caretaker-child relationship, and the symptoms resolve without any medical or psychiatric treatment after the child is removed from the home and placed in a favorable domicile.

The affectionless character may appear with a failure or lack of opportunity to form attachments before age 2 to 3 years. The child is unable to form lasting relationships, and that inability is sometimes accompanied by a lack of guilt, an inability to obey rules, and a need for attention and affection. Some children are indiscriminately friendly. The disorder is usually not reversible.

Pathology and Laboratory Examination

Although no single specific laboratory test is used to make a diagnosis, many children with the disorder have disturbances of growth and development. Therefore, establishing a growth curve and examining the progression of developmental milestones may be helpful in determining whether associated phenomena, such as failure to thrive, are present.

DIFFERENTIAL DIAGNOSIS

Pervasive developmental disorders, mental retardation, various severe neurological abnormalities, and psychosocial dwarf-

ism are the primary considerations in the differential diagnosis. Autistic children are typically well-nourished and of age-appropriate size and weight; they are generally alert and active, despite their impairments in reciprocal social interactions. Moderate, severe, or profound mental retardation is present in about 50 percent of autistic children, whereas most children with reactive attachment disorder of infancy or early childhood are only mildly retarded or have normal intelligence. No evidence indicates that parental factors cause autistic disorder, and most parents of autistic children do not differ significantly from the parents of normal children. Unlike most children with reactive attachment disorder, autistic children do not improve rapidly if they are removed from their homes and placed in a hospital or other favorable environment.

Mentally retarded children may show delays in all social skills. Such children, unlike children with reactive attachment disorder, are usually adequately nourished, their social relatedness is appropriate to their mental age, and they show a sequence of development similar to that seen in normal children.

COURSE AND PROGNOSIS

The course and the prognosis of reactive attachment disorder depend on the duration and the severity of the neglectful and pathogenic parenting and on associated complications, such as failure to thrive. Constitutional and nutritional factors interact to result in children who may either respond resiliently to treatment or continue to fail to thrive. Outcomes range from the extremes of death to the developmentally healthy child. Usually, the longer a child remains in the adverse environment without adequate intervention, the more physical and emotional damage is done, and the worse the prognosis is. Once the pathological environmental situation is recognized, how much treatment and rehabilitation the family receives affects the child returning to that family. For children who have multiple problems stemming from the pathogenic caretaking, their physical recovery may be faster and more comprehensive than is their emotional well-being.

TREATMENT

Some general principles of treatment apply. Often, the first decision is whether to hospitalize the child or to attempt treatment while the child remains in the home. Usually, the severity of the child's physical and emotional state or the severity of the pathological caretaking determines the strategy. The overriding choice must be for the child's safety. The patient must be given appropriate psychological and, if necessary, pediatric treatment. Concomitantly, the treatment team must begin to alter the unsatisfactory relationship between the caretaker and the child. Doing so usually requires extensive and intensive long-term psychological therapy with the mother or, in intact households, both parents whenever possible.

Possible interventions include but are not limited to the following: (1) psychosocial support services, including hiring a homemaker, improving the physical condition of the apartment or obtaining more adequate housing, improving the family's financial status, and decreasing the family's isolation; (2) psychotherapeutic interventions, including individual psychotherapy, psychotropic medications, and family or marital therapy;

(3) educational counseling services, including mother-infant or mother-toddler groups, and counseling to increase awareness and understanding of the child's needs and to increase parenting skills; and (4) provisions for close monitoring of the progression of the patient's emotional and physical well-being. Should those interventions fail, foster care, adoption, or placement in a group home, in a residential treatment facility, or with relatives must be considered.

References

Ferholt J B: A psychodynamic study of psychosomatic dwarfism. J Am Acad Child Psychiatry *14*: 49, 1985.

Green W H, Campbell M, David R: Psychosocial dwarfism; A critical review of the evidence. J Am Acad Child Psychiatry, *23*: 39, 1984.

Rutter M: Clinical implications of attachment concepts: Retrospect and prospect. J Child Psychol Psychiatry *36*: 549, 1995.

Volkmar F R: Reactive attachment disorder of infancy or early childhood. In *Comprehensive Textbook of Psychiatry*, ed 6, H I Kaplan, B J Sadock, editors, p 2354. Williams & Wilkins, Baltimore, 1995.

Zeanah C H, Zeanah P D: Intergenerational transmission of maltreatment: Insights from attachment theory and research. Psychiatry *52*: 177, 1989.

39.4 STEREOTYPIC MOVEMENT DISORDER AND DISORDER OF INFANCY, CHILDHOOD, OR ADOLESCENCE NOS

STEREOTYPIC MOVEMENT DISORDER

The fourth edition of *Diagnostic and Statistical Manual of Mental Disorders* (DSM-IV) defines stereotypic movement disorder as repetitive, seemingly driven, and nonfunctional motor behavior—such as rocking, head banging, self-biting, picking, and waving—for at least four weeks. The behaviors markedly interfere with normal activities or would result in injury if preventive measures were not used. If the behaviors coexist with mental retardation or a pervasive developmental disorder, they must be sufficiently severe to be a focus of treatment. The disorder is diagnosed only if the symptoms are not better accounted for by a compulsion or a tic and are not restricted to hair pulling (as in trichotillomania).

According to DSM-IV, stereotypic movement disorder can be diagnosed with mental retardation or a pervasive developmental disorder when the stereotypic behaviors are severe enough to warrant treatment. Stereotypic behaviors are not specified as intentional in DSM-IV since it is not clear to what extent the patients maintain voluntary control over the behaviors. In DSM-IV, self-injurious behavior is specified if bodily damage requires medical treatment.

Epidemiology

The prevalence of stereotypic movement disorder is not known. Behaviors such as nail biting are common, affecting up to half of all school-age children; behaviors such as thumb sucking and rocking are normal in young children but are often maladaptive in older children and adolescents. In most cases, those behaviors do not constitute a stereotypic movement disorder, since most children who bite their nails function in daily activities without impairment or self-injury. In one pediatric clinic up to 20 percent of the children had a history of rocking, head banging, or swaying in one form or another. Deciding

which cases are severe enough to confirm a diagnosis of stereotypic movement disorder may be difficult.

The diagnosis is a compilation of many symptoms, and various behaviors have to be studied separately to obtain data concerning prevalence, sex ratio, and familial patterns. It is clear, however, that stereotypic movement disorder is more prevalent in boys than in girls. Stereotypic behaviors are common among the mentally retarded, affecting 10 to 20 percent. Self-injurious behaviors are seen in some genetic syndromes, such as Lesch-Nyhan syndrome, and are also present in some patients with Tourette's disorder. Self-injurious stereotypic behaviors are increasingly common in persons with severe mental retardation. Stereotypic behaviors are also common in children with sensory impairments, such as blindness and deafness.

Etiology

The causes of stereotypic movement disorder are essentially unknown, but several theories have been advanced. Many of the behaviors may be associated with normal development. For example up to 80 percent of all normal children show rhythmic activities that phase out by the age of 4 years. Those rhythmic patterns seem purposeful, to provide sensorimotor stimulation and tension release, and to be satisfying and pleasurable to the children. The movements may increase at times of frustration, boredom, and tension.

The progression from what are perhaps vicissitudes of normal development to stereotypic movement disorder is thought to reflect disordered development, as in mental retardation or a pervasive developmental disorder, or psychological conflict. Such behaviors as head banging may result from maternal neglect or abuse and the lack of psychosocial and physical stimulation.

Stereotypic movements may be associated with dopamine activity. Dopamine agonists induce or increase stereotypic behaviors, whereas dopamine antagonists decrease them. In one report four children with attention-deficit/hyperactivity disorder were treated with a stimulant medication and began to bite their nails and fingertips. The nail biting ceased when the medication was eliminated. Endogenous opiates have also been implicated in the production of self-injurious behaviors.

DIAGNOSIS AND CLINICAL FEATURES

Affected persons may suffer from one or more symptoms of stereotypic movement disorder; thus, the clinical picture varies considerably. Most commonly, one symptom predominates. The presence of several severe symptoms tends to occur among the most severely afflicted persons with mental retardation or a pervasive development disorder. Those persons frequently have other significant mental disorders, especially disruptive behavior disorders.

In extreme cases, severe mutilation and life-threatening injuries may result, and secondary infection and septicemia may follow self-inflicted trauma.

The DSM-IV diagnostic criteria for stereotypic movement disorder are given in Table 39.4–1.

Head Banging

Head banging is an example of a stereotypic movement disorder that can result in functional impairment. The reported

Table 39.4-1.   Diagnostic Criteria for Stereotypic Movement Disorder

A. Repetitive, seemingly driven, and nonfunctional motor behavior (e.g., hand shaking or waving, body rocking, head banging, mouthing of objects, self-biting, picking at skin or bodily orifices, hitting own body).

B. The behavior markedly interferes with normal activities or results in self-inflicted bodily injury that requires medical treatment (or would result in an injury if preventive measures were not used).

C. If mental retardation is present, the stereotypic or self-injurious behavior is of sufficient severity to become a focus of treatment.

D. The behavior is not better accounted for by a compulsion (as in obsessive-compulsive disorder) a tic (as in tic disorder), a stereotypy that is part of a pervasive developmental disorder, or hair pulling (as in trichotillomania).

E. The behavior is not due to the direct physiological effects of a substance or a general medical condition.

F. The behavior persists for 4 weeks or longer.

Table from DSM-IV, *Diagnostic and Statistical Manual of Mental Disorders*, ed 4. Copyright American Psychiatric Association, Washington, 1994. Used with permission.

incidence varies between 3.3 and 19 percent. Typically, head banging begins during infancy, between 6 and 12 months of age. Infants strike their heads with a definite rhythmic and monotonous continuity against the crib or other hard surface. Infants appear to be absorbed in the activity, which may persist until they become exhausted and fall asleep. The head banging is transitory in many children, but sometimes it persists into middle childhood.

Head banging that is a component of temper tantrums is different from stereotypic head banging and ceases once the tantrums and their secondary gains are controlled.

Nail Biting

Nail biting begins as early as 1 year of age and increase in incidence until age 12. Usually, the child bites all the nails. Most cases are not sufficiently severe to meet the DSM-IV diagnostic criteria. The other cases are those that cause physical damage to the fingers themselves, usually by associated biting of the cuticles and by secondary infections of the fingers and nail beds. Nail biting seems to occur or increase in intensity when the person is either anxious or bored. Some of the most severe nail biting occurs in the severely and profoundly mentally retarded and in some paranoid schizophrenia patients. Some nail-biters, however, have no obvious emotional disturbance.

Differential Diagnosis

The differential diagnosis of stereotypic movement disorder includes obsessive-compulsive disorder and tic disorders, both of which are exclusionary criteria in DSM-IV. Although stereotypic movements are not spasmodic and are voluntary, the clinician may find it difficult to differentiate those features from tics in all cases. Stereotypic movements are likely to be comforting, whereas tics are often associated with distress. In obsessive-compulsive disorder, the compulsions must be ego-dystonic, although that, too, is difficult to discern in young children.

Differentiating dyskinetic movements from stereotypic movements can be difficult. Because antipsychotic medications can suppress stereotypic movements, the clinician must note any stereotypic movements before initiating treatment with an antipsychotic.

Stereotypic movement disorder may be diagnosed concurrently with substance-related disorders (for example, amphetamine use disorders), severe sensory impairments, central nervous system and degenerative disorders (for example, Lesch-Nyhan syndrome), and severe schizophrenia.

COURSE AND PROGNOSIS

The duration and the course of stereotypic movement disorder are variable, and the symptoms may wax and wane. The disorder ranges from brief episodes occurring under stress or with transient mental conditions to an ongoing pattern in the context of a chronic disorder, such as mental retardation or a pervasive developmental disorder. Even in chronic conditions the emergence of stereotypic behaviors may come and go. Sometimes, stereotypic movements are prominent in early childhood and diminish as the child gets older.

The severity of the dysfunction caused by stereotypic movements also ranges with the associated frequency, quantity, and degree of self-injury. Persons who exhibit frequent, severe self-injurious stereotypic behaviors have the poorest prognosis. Repetitive episodes of head banging, biting oneself, and eye poking may be difficult to control without physical restraints.

Most nail biting is benign and often does not meet the diagnostic criteria for stereotypic movement disorder. In severe cases in which the nail beds are repetitively damaged, bacterial and fungal infections can occur.

Although chronic stereotypic movement disorders can severely impair daily functioning, a number of treatments help control the symptoms.

TREATMENT

Treatment should be related to the specific symptom or symptoms being treated, their causes, and the patient's mental age.

The psychosocial environment should be changed for those infants, young children, and mentally retarded persons for whom lack of adequate caretaking, little opportunity for physical expression, boring inactivity, and self-stimulation seem to be important causes. In those cases, increased nurturance and stimulation may be helpful. Such measures as padding hard surfaces may be important for head bangers.

Behavioral techniques, including reinforcement and behavioral shaping, are successful in some cases. A large, specialized literature addresses the problems in the seriously retarded.

Psychotherapy has been used primarily in older, mentally normal persons in whom intrapsychic conflict or interpersonal difficulties seem prominent.

For those cases in which severe physical damage occurs, especially in the severely retarded, psychopharmacology must be considered. Phenothiazines have been the most frequently used drugs; however, the psychiatrist must be particularly aware of adverse effects, including tardive dyskinesia and impairment of cognition. Opiate antagonists have reduced self-injurious behaviors in some patients without exposing them to tardive dyskinesia or impaired cognition.

Additional pharmacological agents tried in the treatment of stereotypic movement disorder include fenfluramine (Pondimin), clomipramine (Anafranil), and fluoxetine (Prozac). In some reports, fenfluramine diminished stereotypic behaviors in children with autistic disorder; in other studies, the results were less encouraging. Open trials indicate that both clomipramine and fluoxetine may decrease self-injurious behaviors and other stereotypic movements in some patients.

DISORDER OF INFANCY, CHILDHOOD, OR ADOLESCENCE NOT OTHERWISE SPECIFIED

This residual category is for disorders with an onset in infancy, childhood, or adolescence that do not meet the diagnostic criteria for any specific disorder in the DSM-IV classification.

References

Hanna G L: Stereotypic movement disorder and disorder of infancy, childhood, or adolescence NOS. In *Comprehensive Textbook of Psychiatry*, ed 6, H I Kaplan, B J Sadock, editors, p 2359. Williams & Wilkins, Baltimore, 1995.

Leonard H L, Lenane M C, Swedo S E, Rettew D C, Rapoport J L: A double-blind comparison of clomipramine and desipramine treatment of severe onychophagia (nail biting). Arch Gen Psychiatry 48: 821, 1992.

Oliver C: Annotation: Self-injurious behaviour in children with learning disabilities: Recent advances in assessment and intervention. J Child Psychol Psychiatry *36*: 909, 1995.

Ricketts R W, Goza A B, Ellis C R, Singh Y N, Singh N N, Cooke J C III: Fluoxetine treatment of severe self-injury in young adults with mental retardation. J Am Acad Child Adolesc Psychiatry *32*: 865, 1993.

Vivona J M, Ecker B, Halgin R P, Cates D, Garrison W T, Friedman M: Self- and other-directed aggression in child and adolescent psychiatric inpatients. J Am Acad Child Adolesc Psychiatry *34*: 434, 1995.

Wieseler N A, Hanson R H, Nord G: Investigation of mortality and morbidity associated with severe self-injurious behavior. Am J Ment Retard *100*: 1, 1995.

40/ Mood Disorders and Suicide in Children and Adolescents

MOOD DISORDERS

Mood disorders in children and adolescents have received increasing recognition and attention over the past few decades. For many generations, sadness and despair have been known to occur in children and adolescents, yet the concept of enduring disorders of mood has taken longer to be generally accepted. A criterion for mood disorders in childhood and adolescence is a disturbance of mood, such as depression or elation. In addition, irritability can be a sign of a mood disorder in children and adolescents.

Children's moods are especially vulnerable to the influences of severe social stressors, such as chronic family discord, abuse and neglect, and academic failure. The vast majority of young children with major depressive disorder have histories of abuse or neglect. Children with depressive disorders in the midst of toxic environments may have remission of some or much of their depressive symptoms when the stressors diminish or when the children are removed from the stressful environment. Bereavement often becomes a focus of psychiatric treatment when children have lost a loved one, even when a depressive disorder is not present.

Although the diagnostic criteria in the fourth edition of *Diagnostic and Statistical Manual of Mental Disorders* (DSM-IV) for mood disorders are almost identical across all age groups, the expression of disturbed mood varies in children according to their ages. Symptoms commonly seen in young depressed children and less often as their ages increase are mood-congruent auditory hallucinations, somatic complaints, withdrawn and sad appearance, and poor self-esteem. Other symptoms more common in depressed late adolescence than in young childhood are pervasive anhedonia, severe psychomotor retardation, delusions, and a sense of hopelessness. Symptoms that appear with the same frequency whatever the age and developmental status include suicidal ideation, depressed or irritable mood, insomnia, and diminished ability to concentrate. However, developmental issues do influence the expression of all the symptoms. For example, miserable young children who exhibit recurrent suicidal ideation are generally unable to come up with a realistic suicide plan or to put their ideas into action.

Epidemiology

Mood disorders increase with increasing age, and prevalence in any age group is drastically higher within psychiatrically referred groups than in the general population. Mood disorders in preschool-age children are extremely rare. The rate of major depressive disorder in preschoolers has been estimated to be about 0.3 percent in the community, compared with 0.9 percent in a clinic setting. Among school-age children in the community, about 2 percent have major depressive disorder. Depression is more common in boys than in girls in school-age children. Some bias may be present in the clinic reports, since boys outnumber girls in psychiatric clinics. Among adolescents, about 5 percent in the community have major depressive disor-

der. Among hospitalized children and adolescents, the rates of major depressive disorder are much higher than in the general community; up to 20 percent of children and 40 percent of adolescents are depressed.

Dysthymic disorder is estimated to be more common than major depressive disorder in school-age children, with rates up to 2.5 percent, compared with 2 percent for major depressive disorder. School-age children with dysthymic disorder have a high likelihood that major depressive disorder will develop at some point after one year of the dysthymic disorder. In adolescents, as in adults, dysthymic disorder is less common than major depressive disorder, with a rate of about 3.3 percent for dysthymic disorder, compared with about 5 percent to major depressive disorder.

The rate of bipolar I disorder is exceedingly low in prepubertal children and may take years to be diagnosed, since mania typically presents for the first time in adolescence. The lifetime rate of bipolar I disorder has been estimated to be 0.6 percent in a community study of adolescents. Adolescents with clinical variants of mania, such as bipolar II disorder, have rates of up to about 10 percent, according to some studies.

Etiology

Considerable evidence suggests that the mood disorders are the same fundamental disease or disease group, whatever the age of onset.

GENETIC FACTORS

Mood disorders in children, adolescents, and adult patients tend to cluster in the same families. An increased incidence of mood disorders is generally found in the children of mood-disordered parents and in the relatives of mood-disordered children. However, in one study, depression was equally increased in the parents of both depressed and nondepressed children and adolescent inpatients and outpatients. However, having one depressed parent probably doubles the risk for the offspring. Having both parents depressed probably quadruples the risk of a child's having a mood disorder before age 18 when compared with the risk for children with two unaffected parents.

Some evidence indicates that the number of recurrences of parental depression does increase the likelihood that their children will be affected, but that increase may be related, at least in part, to the affective loading of that parent's own family tree. Similarly, children with the most severe episodes of major depressive disorder have shown much evidence of dense and deep familial aggregation for major depressive disorder.

OTHER BIOLOGICAL FACTORS

Studies of prepubertal major depressive disorder and adolescent mood disorder have revealed biological abnormalities.

Prepubertal children in a depressive episode secrete significantly more growth hormone during sleep than do normal children and those with nondepressed mental disorders. They also secrete significantly less growth hormone in response to insulin-induced hypoglycemia than do nondepressed patients. Both abnormalities have been found to remain abnormal and basically unchanged after at least four months of full, sustained clinical response, the last month in a drug-free state.

In contrast, the data conflict about cortisol hypersecretion during major depressive disorder. Some workers report hypersecretion, and some report normal secretion. The dexamethasone-suppression test (DST) is used in childhood and adolescence but not as frequently or as reliably as in adults.

Sleep studies are inconclusive in depressed children and adolescents. Polysomnography shows either no change or changes characteristic of adults with major depressive disorder: reduced rapid eye movement (REM) latency and an increased number of REM periods.

Social Factors

The finding that identical twins do not have a 100 percent concordance rate suggests a role for nongenetic factors. So far, little evidence indicates that parental marital status, the number of siblings, the family's socioeconomic status, parental separation, divorce, marital functioning, or the familial constellation or structure plays much of a role in causing depressive disorders in children. However, some evidence suggests that boys whose fathers died before they were 13 years old are more likely than are controls to have depression.

The psychosocial deficits found in depressed children improve after sustained recovery from the depression. Those deficits appear to be secondary to the depression itself and compounded by the long duration of most dysthymic or depressive episodes, during which poorly accomplished or unaccomplished developmental tasks accumulated. Among preschoolers in whom depressive clinical presentations are described, the role of environmental influences will probably receive experimental support in the future.

Diagnosis and Clinical Features

Major Depressive Disorder

Major depressive disorder in children is most easily diagnosed when it is acute and occurs in a child without previous psychiatric symptoms. In many cases, however, the onset is insidious and presents in a child who had several years of difficulties with hyperactivity, separation anxiety disorder, or intermittent depressive symptoms.

According to the DSM-IV diagnostic criteria for major depressive disorder, at least five symptoms must be present for two weeks and must be a change from previous functioning (see Table 9.1–1). Among the necessary symptoms are either (1) a depressed or irritable mood or (2) a loss of interest or pleasure. Other symptoms from which the other four diagnostic criteria are drawn include the child's failure to make expected weight gains, daily insomnia or hypersomnia, psychomotor agitation or retardation, daily fatigue or loss of energy, feelings of worthlessness or inappropriate guilt, diminished ability to think or concentrate, and recurrent thoughts of death. Those symptoms must produce social or academic impairment. To meet the diagnostic criteria for major depressive disorder, the symptoms cannot be the direct effects of a substance (for example, alcohol) or a general medical condition. A diagnosis of major depressive disorder is not made within two months of the loss of a loved one except when marked functional impairment, morbid preoccupation with worthlessness, suicidal ideation, psychotic symptoms, or psychomotor retardation is present.

A major depressive episode in a prepubertal child is likely to be manifested by somatic complaints, psychomotor agitation, and mood-congruent hallucinations. Anhedonia is also frequent, but anhedonia, hopelessness, psychomotor retardation, and delusion are more common in adolescent and adult major depressive episodes than in young children. Adults have more problems with sleep and appetite than do depressed children and adolescents. In adolescence, negativistic or frankly antisocial behavior and the use of alcohol or illicit substances may be present and justify the additional diagnoses of oppositional defiant disorder, conduct disorder, and substance abuse or dependence. Feelings of restlessness, grouchiness, aggression, sulkiness, reluctance to cooperate in family ventures, withdrawal from social activities, and a desire to leave home are all common in adolescent depression. School difficulties are likely. The adolescent may be inattentive to personal appearance and show increased emotionality, with particular sensitivity to rejection in love relationships.

Children can be reliable reporters about their own behavior, emotions, relationships, and difficulties in psychosocial functions. They may, however, refer to their feelings by many names. Thus, the clinician must ask about feeling sad, empty, low, down, blue, very unhappy, or like crying or having a bad feeling inside that is there most of the time. Depressed children usually identify one or more of those terms as the persistent feeling they have had. The clinician should assess the duration and the periodicity of the depressive mood to differentiate relatively universal, short-lived, and sometimes frequent periods of sadness, usually after a frustrating event, from a true, persistent depressive mood. The younger the children, the more imprecise their time estimates are likely to be.

Mood disorders tend to be chronic if they begin early. Childhood onset may be the most severe form of a mood disorder and tends to appear in families with a high incidence of mood disorders and alcohol abuse. The children are likely to have such secondary complications as conduct disorder, alcohol and other substance abuse, and antisocial behavior.

Functional impairment associated with a depressive disorder in childhood extends to practically all areas of the child's psychosocial world; school performance and behavior, peer relationships, and family relationships—all suffer. Only highly intelligent and academically oriented children with no more than a moderate depression can compensate for their difficulties in learning by substantially increasing their time and effort. Otherwise, school performance is invariably affected by a combination of difficulty in concentrating, slowed-down thinking, lack of interest and motivation, fatigue, sleepiness, depressive ruminations, and preoccupations. Depression in a child may be misdiagnosed as a learning disorder. Learning problems secondary to depression, even when long-standing, correct themselves rapidly after the child's recovery from the depressive episode.

Children and adolescents with major depressive disorder may have hallucinations and delusions. Usually those psychotic symptoms are thematically consistent with the depressed mood, occur with the depressive episode (usually at its worst), and do not include certain types of hallucinations, such as conversing voices and a commenting voice, which are specific to schizophrenia. Depressive hallucinations usually consist of a single voice speaking to the person from outside his or her head, with derogatory or suicidal content. Depressive delusions center on themes of guilt, physical disease, death, nihilism, deserved punishment, personal inadequacy, and sometimes persecution. Those delusions are rare in prepuberty, probably because of cognitive immaturity, but are present in about half of all psychotically depressed adolescents.

A mood disorder with adolescent onset may be difficult to diagnose when first seen if the adolescent has attempted self-medication with alcohol or other illicit substances. In a recent study 17 percent of the youngsters with a mood disorder first presented to medical attention as substance abusers. Only after detoxification could the psychiatric symptoms be properly assessed and the correct mood disorder diagnosis be made.

Dysthymic Disorder

Dysthymic disorder in children and adolescents consists of a depressed or irritable mood for most of the day, for more days than not, over a period of at least one year. DSM-IV notes that, in children and adolescents, irritable mood can replace the depressed mood criterion for adults and that the duration criterion is not two years but one year for children and adolescents. According to the DSM-IV diagnostic criteria, at least three of the following symptoms must accompany the depressed or irritable mood: poor self-esteem, pessimism or hopelessness, loss of interest, social withdrawal, chronic fatigue, feelings of guilt or brooding about the past, irritability or excessive anger, decreased activity or productivity, and poor concentration or memory. During the year of the disturbance, the above symptoms have never resolved for more than two months at a time. In addition, no major depressive episode was present during the first year of the disturbance. To meet the DSM-IV diagnostic criteria for dysthymic disorder, the child must not have a history of a manic or hypomanic episode. Also, dysthymic disorder is not diagnosed if the symptoms occur exclusively during a chronic psychotic disorder or if they are the direct effects of a substance or a general medical condition. DSM-IV provides for the specification of early onset (before age 21 years) or late onset (after 21 years).

A child or an adolescent with dysthymic disorder may have had a previous major depressive episode before the onset of dysthymic disorder, but it is much more common for a child with dysthymic disorder for more than one year to have major depressive disorder. In that case, both depressive diagnoses are given (double depression).

Dysthymic disorder in children is known to have an average age of onset that is several years earlier than the age of onset of major depressive disorder. Clinicians disagree about whether dysthymic disorder is a chronic and insidious version of major depressive disorder or a separate disorder.

Occasionally, youngsters fulfill the criteria for dysthymic disorder except that their episodes last only two weeks to several months, with symptom-free intervals lasting for two to three months. Those minor mood presentations in children are likely to indicate severe mood disorder episodes in the future. Current knowledge suggests that the longer, the more recurrent, the more frequent, and perhaps the less related to social stress episodes are, the greater the likelihood of a severe mood disorder in the future.

However, when minor depressive episodes follow a significant stressful life event by less than three months, they do not indicate future mood disorder episodes, and so they should be diagnosed as adjustment disorder with depressed mood or bereavement.

Bipolar I Disorder

Bipolar I disorder is rarely diagnosed in prepubertal children, since manic episodes are uncommon in that age group, even when depressive symptoms have already appeared. Usually, a major depressive episode precedes a manic episode in an adolescent experiencing bipolar I disorder. However, when a classic manic episode appears in an adolescent, it is recognized as a definite change from a preexisting state and often presents with grandiose and paranoid delusions and hallucinatory phenomena. According to DSM-IV, the criteria for a manic episode remain the same for children and adolescents as for adults (see Table 9.1–2). The diagnostic criteria for a manic episode include a distinct period of an abnormally elevated, expansive, or irritable mood that lasts at least one week or for any duration if hospitalization is necessary. In addition, during periods of mood disturbance, at least three of the following significant and persistent symptoms must be present: inflated self-esteem or grandiosity, decreased need for sleep, pressure to talk, flight of ideas or racing thoughts, distractibility, an increase in goal-directed activity, and excessive involvement in pleasurable activities that may result in painful consequences. The mood disturbance is sufficient to cause marked impairment, and it is not due to the direct effect of a substance or a general medical condition. Thus, manic states precipitated by somatic medications (for example, antidepressants) cannot be counted as indicating a diagnosis of bipolar I disorder.

In contrast to the classic manic episode, childhood manic episodes may be variants but have a relation to bipolar I disorder. The atypical manic episodes are sometimes observed in children with family histories of classic bipolar I disorder; the atypical manic episodes consist of extreme mood variability, cyclic aggressive behavior, high levels of distractibility, and poor attention span. Those episodes are not likely to be clearly episodic, and they may be less treatment-responsive than are classic manic episodes. Children with atypical hypomanic episodes must be differentiated from children with severe attention-deficit/hyperactivity disorder, who share some features of mania but exhibit their behaviors on a long-term basis, rather than on an episodic basic. In attention-deficit/hyperactivity disorder, family histories of bipolar I disorder are uncommon.

When manic episodes appear in an adolescent, psychotic features often accompany them, and hospitalization is often necessary. Adolescents' delusions and hallucinations may involve grandiose notions about their power, worth, knowledge, family, or relationships. Persecutory delusions and flight of ideas are common. Overall, gross impairment of reality testing is common in adolescent manic episodes. In adolescents with major depressive disorder destined for bipolar I disorder, those at highest risk have family histories of bipolar I disorder and exhibit acute severe depressive episodes with psychosis, hypersomnia, and psychomotor retardation.

Cyclothymic Disorder

The only difference in the DSM-IV diagnostic criteria for child or adolescent cyclothymic disorder is that a period of one year of many mood swings is necessary, instead of the adult criterion of two years. Some cyclothymic adolescents eventually develop bipolar I disorder.

SCHIZOAFFECTIVE DISORDER

The criteria for schizoaffective disorder in children and adolescents are identical to those in adults. Although some adolescents and probably some children do fit the criteria for schizoaffective disorder, little is now known about the natural course of their illness, family history, psychobiology, and treatment. In DSM-IV schizoaffective disorder in children is classified as a psychotic disorder.

BEREAVEMENT

Bereavement is a state of grief related to the death of a loved one that may present with symptoms characteristic of a major depressive episode. Typical depressive symptoms associated with bereavement include feelings of sadness, insomnia, diminished appetite, and sometimes weight loss. Grieving children may become withdrawn and appear sad, and they are not easily drawn into even favorite activities. In DSM-IV bereavement is not a mental disorder but is in the category of additional conditions that may be a focus of clinical attention. Persons in the midst of a typical bereavement period may also meet the criteria for major depressive disorder when the symptoms persist longer than two months after the loss. In some instances, severe depressive symptoms within two months of the loss are considered beyond the scope of normal grieving, and a diagnosis of major depressive disorder is warranted. Symptoms indicative of major depressive disorder exceeding usual bereavement include guilt related to issues beyond those surrounding the death of the loved one, preoccupation with death other than thoughts of being dead to be with the deceased person, morbid preoccupation with worthlessness, marked psychomotor retardation, prolonged serious functional impairment, and hallucinations other than transient perceptions of the voice of the deceased person.

The duration of a normal period of bereavement varies; in children the duration may depend partly on the support system in place. For example, a child who must be removed from home because of the death of the only parent in the home may feel devastated and abandoned for a long time. Children who lose loved ones may feel that the death occurred because they were bad or did not perform as expected. The reaction to the loss of a loved one may be partly influenced by being prepared for the death in cases of chronic illness.

PATHOLOGY AND LABORATORY EXAMINATION

No single laboratory test is useful in making a diagnosis of a mood disorder. A screening test for thyroid function can rule out the possibility of an endocrinological contribution to a mood disorder. DSTs may be done serially in cases of major depressive disorder to document whether an initial nonsuppressor becomes a suppressor with treatment or with resolution of the symptoms.

Differential Diagnosis

Psychotic forms of depressive and manic episodes must be differentiated from schizophrenia. Substance-induced mood disorder can sometimes be differentiated from other mood disorders only after detoxification. Anxiety symptoms and conduct-disordered behavior can coexist with depressive disorders and can frequently pose problems in differentiating those disorders from nondepressed emotional and conduct disorders.

Of particular importance is the distinction between agitated depressive or manic episodes and attention-deficit/hyperactivity disorder, in which the persistent excessive activity and restlessness can cause confusion. Prepubertal children do not present with classic forms of agitated depression such as hand wringing and pacing. Instead, their inability to sit still and their frequent temper tantrums are the most common symptoms. Sometimes the correct answer becomes evident only after the depressive episode has remitted. If the child has no difficulty in concentrating and is not hyperactive while recovered from the depressive episode in a drug-free state, attention-deficit/hyperactivity disorder was probably not present.

Course and Prognosis

The course and the prognosis of mood disorders in children and adolescents depend on the age of onset, the severity of the episode, and the presence of comorbid disorders, with a young age of onset and multiple disorders predicting a bad prognosis.

Depressive disorders are likely to recur and, if not successfully treated, produce considerable short-term and long-term difficulties and complications: poor academic achievement, arrest or delay in psychological development patterns, suicide, substance abuse as self-medication, and conduct disorder. Follow-up studies to date suggest a continued risk for mood disorders.

Treatment

HOSPITALIZATION

The important immediate consideration is often whether hospitalization is indicated. When the patient is suicidal, hospitalization is indicated to provide maximum protection against the patient's own self-destructive impulses and behavior. Hospitalization may also be needed when the child or adolescent has coexisting substance abuse or dependence.

PSYCHOTHERAPY

Few data confirm the superiority of one kind of psychotherapeutic approach over another in the treatment of childhood and adolescent mood disorders. However, family therapy is needed to educate families about serious mood disorders that occur in children at times of overwhelming family stress. Psychotherapeutic approaches for depressed children include cognitive approaches and a more directed and structured approach than that usually used with adults. Since depressed children's psychosocial functions may remain impaired for long periods, even after the depressive episode has remitted, long-term social skills interventions are needed. In some treatment programs, modeling and role playing can help establish good problem-solving skills.

PHARMACOTHERAPY

No clear evidence from double-blind, placebo-controlled studies indicates that antidepressants are of benefit in child and adolescent depressive disorders. Moreover, antidepressants have yet to receive Food and Drug Administration (FDA) approval for use in depressed children. Nonetheless, if a trial of antidepressants is indicated, the following should be kept in mind: The use of antidepressants requires baseline studies, gradual titration of the drug, and monitoring of electrocardiogram (ECG) changes, blood pressure, adverse effects, and, whenever possible, serum concentrations. Because toxicity produces serious cardiac arrhythmias, seizures, coma, and death, monitoring is essential. The clinical response may be correlated with plasma level. In one uncontrolled study using imipramine (Tofranil) to treat prepubertal major depressive disorder, good responses were seen when blood levels were about 140 to 150 ng per mL. Because antidepressants have not yet been approved for use by depressed children and because of their potentially serious side effects and toxicity, clinicians should use antidepressants for children only after study or consultation with a clinician experienced in their use.

Fluoxetine (Prozac) has been used with some success in adolescents with major depressive disorder. Since some children and adolescents who have depressive episodes go on to experience bipolar II disorder, the clinician must note hypomanic symptoms that may occur during the use of fluoxetine and other antidepressants. In those cases the medication should be discontinued to determine if the hypomanic episode then resolves. However, hypomanic responses to antidepressants do not necessarily predict that bipolar II disorder has developed.

Bipolar I disorder and bipolar II disorder in childhood and adolescence are treated with lithium (Eskalith) with good results. However, children who have preexisting disruptive behavior disorders (for example, conduct disorder and attention-deficit/hyperactivity disorder) and then experience bipolar disorders early in adolescence are less likely to respond well to lithium than are those without the behavior disorders.

SUICIDE

Suicidal ideation, gestures, and attempts are frequently associated with depressive disorders, and those suicidal phenomena, particularly in adolescence, are a growing public mental health problem. Suicidal ideation occurs with greatest frequency when the depressive disorder is severe. More than 12,000 children and adolescents are hospitalized in the United States each year because of suicidal threats or behavior. However, completed suicide is rare under the age of 12 years. A young child is little able to design and carry out a realistic suicide plan. Cognitive immaturity seems to play a protective role in preventing even children who wish they were dead from committing suicide. Completed suicide occurs about five times more often in adolescent boys than in girls, although the rate of suicide attempts is at least three times higher among adolescent girls than among boys.

Suicidal ideation is not a static phenomenon; it may wax and wane with time. The decision to engage in suicidal behavior may be impulsive, without a great deal of forethought, or it may be the culmination of prolonged rumination. The method of the suicide attempt influences the morbidity and the completion rate independent of the severity of the intent to die at the time of the suicidal behavior. Thus, the most common method of completed suicide in children and adolescents is by using firearms, which account for about two thirds of all suicides in boys and almost half the suicides in girls. The second most common method of suicide in boys, occurring in about a fourth of all cases, is by hanging; in girls about a fourth commit suicide through the ingestion of toxic substances. Carbon monoxide poisoning is the next most common method for suicide in boys but occurs in less than 10 percent; suicide by hanging and carbon monoxide poisoning are equally frequent among girls, accounting for about 10 percent each.

Epidemiology

In recent years the suicide rate among adolescents in the United States has risen dramatically, although in some other countries it has not. There has been a steady increase in suicide rate for Americans 15 to 19 years of age. It is now 13.6 per 100,000 for boys and 3.6 per 100,000 for girls. More than 5,000 adolescents commit suicide each year in the United States, one every 90 minutes. The increased suicide rates are thought to reflect changes in the social environment, changing attitudes toward suicide, and the increasing availability of the means to commit suicide; for example, in the United States 66 percent of adolescent suicides in boys are committed by firearms, compared with 6 percent in the United Kingdom. Suicide is the third leading cause of death in the United States for persons aged 15 to 24 years and is second among white males in that age group.

The rates for suicide depend on age, and they increase significantly after puberty. Whereas less than 1 completed suicide per 100,000 occurs under 14 years of age, about 10 per 100,000 completed suicides occur in adolescents between 15 and 19 years of age. Under 14 years of age, suicide attempts are at least 50 times more common than are suicide completions. Between 15 and 19 years, however, the rate of suicide attempts is about 15 times greater than suicide completions. The number of adolescent suicides over the past several decades has increased three- or four-fold.

Etiology

Universal features in suicidal adolescents are their inability to synthesize solutions to problems and their lack of coping strategies to deal with immediate stressors. Thus, a narrow view of the options available to deal with recurrent family discord, rejection, or failure contributes to a decision to commit suicide.

GENETIC FACTORS

Evidence for a genetic contribution to suicidal behavior is based on family suicide risk studies and the higher concordance for suicide among monozygotic twins compared with dizygotic twins. Although the risk for suicide is high in persons with mental disorders—including schizophrenia, major depressive disorder, and bipolar I disorder—the risk for suicide is much higher in the relatives of those with mood disorders than in the relatives of persons with schizophrenia.

OTHER BIOLOGICAL FACTORS

Neurochemical findings show some overlap between persons with aggressive, impulsive behaviors and those who complete suicide. Low levels of serotonin and its major metabolite, 5-hydroxyindoleacetic acid (5-HIAA), have been found postmortem in the brains of suicide completers. Low levels of 5-HIAA have been found in the cerebrospinal fluid of depressed persons who attempted suicide by violent methods. Alcohol and other psychoactive substances may lower 5-HIAA, perhaps increasing the vulnerability to suicidal behavior in an already predisposed person. The mechanism linking decreased serotonergic function and aggressive or suicidal behavior is unknown, and low serotonin may turn out to be a marker, rather than a cause, of aggression and suicidal propensity.

The DST has produced less reliable findings in depressed children and adolescents than in adults. However, some studies of children and adolescents suggest an association of non-suppression on the DST and potentially lethal suicide attempts. In children and adolescents the association between suicidality and nonsuppression is not necessarily in the context of a major mood disorder.

SOCIAL FACTORS

Children and adolescents are vulnerable to overwhelmingly chaotic, abusive, and neglectful environments. A wide range of psychopathological symptoms may occur owing to exposure to violent and abusive homes. Aggressive, self-destructive, and suicidal behaviors seem to occur with greatest frequency in persons who have endured chronically stressful family lives.

Diagnosis and Clinical Features

Direct questioning of children and adolescents about suicidal thoughts is necessary, because studies have consistently shown that parents are frequently unaware of such ideas in their children. Suicidal thoughts (that is, children's talk about wanting to harm themselves) and suicidal threats (that is, children's statements that they want to jump in front of a car) are more common than is suicide completion.

The characteristics of adolescents who attempt suicide and those who complete suicide are similar, and about one third of those who complete suicide made prior attempts. Mental disorders present in some suicide attempters and completers include major depressive disorder, manic episodes, and psychotic disorders. Persons with mood disorders in combination with substance abuse and a history of aggressive behavior are particularly high-risk adolescents. Those without mood disorders who are violent, aggressive, and impulsive may be prone to suicide during family or peer conflicts. High levels of hopelessness, poor problem-solving skills, and a history of aggressive behavior are risk factors for suicide. Depression alone is a more serious risk factor for suicide in girls than in boys, but boys often have more severe psychopathology than do girls who commit suicide. The profile of an adolescent who commits suicide is occasionally one of high achievement and perfectionistic character traits; such an adolescent may have recently been humiliated by a perceived failure, such as diminished academic performance.

In psychiatrically disturbed and vulnerable adolescents, suicide attempts are often related to recent stressors. The precipitants of suicidal behavior include conflicts and arguments with family members and boyfriends or girlfriends. Alcohol and other substance use may further predispose an already vulnerable adolescent to suicidal behavior. In other cases, an adolescent attempts suicide in anticipation of punishment after being caught by the police or other authority figures for a forbidden behavior.

About 40 percent of youthful suicide completers had previous psychiatric treatment, and about 40 percent made a previous suicide attempt. A child who has lost a parent by any means before the age of 13 has a high risk for mood disorders and suicide. The precipitating factors include loss of face with peers, a broken romance, school difficulties, unemployment, bereavement, separation, and rejection.

Clusters of suicides among adolescents who know one another and go to the same school have been reported. Suicidal behavior may precipitate similar attempts within a peer group through identification—so-called copycat suicides. Some studies have found an increase in adolescent suicide after television programs were shown whose main theme was the suicide of a teenager. In general, however, many other factors are involved, including a necessary substrate of psychopathology. One recent study investigated two clusters of teenage suicide in Texas. The researchers found that indirect exposure to suicide through the media was not significantly associated with suicide. Factors that were associated included previous suicidal threats or attempts, self-injury, exposure to someone who had died violently, recent romantic breakups, and a high frequency of moves, schools attended, and parental figures lived with.

The tendency of disturbed young persons to imitate highly publicized suicides has been called the Werther syndrome, after the protagonist in Johann Wolfgang von Goethe's novel *The Sorrows of Young Werther*. The novel, in which the hero kills himself, was banned in some European countries after its publication more than 200 years ago because of a rash of suicides by young men who had read it; some, when they killed themselves, dressed like Werther or left the book open to the passage describing his death. In general, although imitation may play a role in the timing of suicide attempts by vulnerable adolescents, the overall suicide rate does not seem to increase when media exposure increases.

Treatment

Adolescent suicide attempters must be evaluated before the decision is made to hospitalize them or return them home. Those who fall into high-risk groups should be hospitalized until the suicidality is no longer present. High-risk persons include those who have made previous suicide attempts; boys more than 12 years old with histories of aggressive behavior or substance abuse; those who have made an attempt with a lethal method, such as a gun or a toxic ingested substance; those with major depressive disorder characterized by social withdrawal, hopelessness, and a lack of energy; girls who have run away from home, are pregnant, or have made an attempt with a method other than ingesting a toxic substance; and any person who exhibits persistent suicidal ideation. A child or an adolescent with suicidal ideation must be hospitalized if the clinician has any doubts about the family's ability to supervise the child or cooperate with treatment in an outpatient setting. In such a situation, child protective services must be involved before the child can be discharged.

When adolescents with suicidal ideation report that they are no longer suicidal, discharge can be considered only after a complete discharge plan is in place. The plan must include psychotherapy, pharmacotherapy, and family therapy as indicated. A written contract with the adolescent, outlining the adolescent's agreement not to engage in suicidal behavior and providing an alternative if suicidal ideation re-occurs, should be in place. In addition, a follow-up outpatient appointment should be made before the discharge, and a telephone number of a hot line should be provided to the adolescent and the family in case suicidal ideation reappears before treatment begins.

References

Berman A L, Jobes D A: Suicide prevention in adolescents (age 12–18). Suicide Life Threat Behav 25: 143, 1995.

Fennig S, Carlson G A: Advances in the study of mood disorders in childhood and adolescence. Curr Opin Pediatr 7: 401, 1995.

Garland A F, Zigler E: Adolescent suicide prevention: Current research and social policy implications. Am Psychol *48*: 169, 1993.

Kahn J P, Prowda K J, Trautman P D: Adolescent suicide: Diagnosis, psychopharmacology, and psychotherapeutic management. In *Treatment approaches with suicidal adolescents*, J K Zimmerman, G M Asnis, editors, p 219. John Wiley & Sons, New York, 1995.

Kazdin A E: Childhood depression. J Child Psychol Psychiatry *31*: 121, 1990.

Kovacs M, Goldston D, Gatsonis C: Suicidal behaviors and childhood-onset depressive disorders: A longitudinal investigation. J Am Acad Child Adolesc Psychiatry *32*: 8, 1993.

Lewinsohn P M, Rohde P, Seeley J R: Psychosocial characteristics of adolescents with a history of suicide attempt. J Am Acad Child Adolesc Psychiatry *32*: 60, 1993.

Pataki C S, Carlson G A: Bipolar disorder in children and adolescents. In *Clinical Guide to Depression in Children and Adolescents*, M Shafii, S Shafii, editors, p. 269. American Psychiatric Press, Washington, 1992.

Rotheram-Borus M J: Suicidal behavior and risk factors among runaway youths. Am J Psychiatry *150*: 103, 1993.

Ryland D H, Kruesi M J: Suicide among adolescents, Int Rev Psychiatry *4*: 185, 1992.

41/ Schizophrenia with Childhood Onset

Schizophrenia with childhood onset is conceptually the same as schizophrenia in adolescence and adulthood. Although rare, schizophrenia in prepubertal children includes the presence of at least two of the following: hallucinations, delusions, grossly disorganized speech or behavior, and severe withdrawal for at least one month. Social or academic dysfunction must be present, and continuous signs of the disturbance must persist for at least six months. The diagnostic criteria for schizophrenia in children are identical to the criteria for the adult form except that children may fail to achieve their expected levels of social and academic functioning, instead of having their functioning deteriorate.

EPIDEMIOLOGY

Schizophrenia in prepubertal children is exceedingly rare; it is estimated to occur less frequently than autistic disorder. In adolescents the prevalence of schizophrenia is estimated to be 50 times greater than in younger children, with probable rates of 1 to 2 per 1,000. Boys seem to have a slight preponderance among schizophrenic children, with an estimated ratio of about 1.67 boys to 1 girl. Boys often become symptomatic at a younger age than do girls. Schizophrenia is rarely diagnosed in children less than 5 years of age; it is commonly diagnosed in adolescents over 15 years. The symptoms usually emerge insidiously, and the diagnostic criteria are met gradually over time. Occasionally, the onset of schizophrenia is sudden and occurs in a previously well functioning child. Schizophrenia may also be diagnosed in a child who has had chronic difficulties and then experiences a significant exacerbation.

The prevalence of schizophrenia among the parents of schizophrenic children is about 8 percent, which is close to double the prevalence in the parents of adult-onset schizophrenic patients.

Schizotypal personality disorder is similar to schizophrenia in its inappropriate affects, excessive magical thinking, odd beliefs, social isolation, ideas of reference, and unusual perceptual experiences, such as illusions. However, schizotypal personality disorder does not have psychotic features; still, the disorder seems to aggregate in families with adult-onset schizophrenia, leading to an unclear relation between the two disorders.

ETIOLOGY

Although family and genetic studies provide substantial evidence of a biological contribution to the development of schizophrenia, no specific biological markers have been identified, and the precise mechanisms of transmission of schizophrenia are not understood.

Schizophrenia is significantly more prevalent among first-degree relatives of those with schizophrenia than in the general population. Adoption studies of adult-onset schizophrenic patients have shown that schizophrenia occurs in the biological relatives, not the adoptive relatives. Additional genetic evidence is supported by the higher concordance rates for schizophrenia in monozygotic twins than in dizygotic twins. The genetic transmission pattern of schizophrenia remains unknown; however,

more genetic loading is seen in the relatives of those with childhood-onset schizophrenia than in the relatives of those with adult-onset schizophrenia.

Currently, no reliable way is available to identify those persons who are at the highest risk for schizophrenia in a given family. However, higher than expected rates of neurological soft signs and impairments in sustaining attention and in strategies for information processing are seen among high-risk groups of children.

Increased rates of disturbed communication styles are found in families with a schizophrenic patient. High expressed emotion, characterized by overly reactive and critical responses in families, negatively affect the prognosis of schizophrenic patients.

A variety of abnormal, nonspecific results on computed tomography (CT) scans and electroencephalograms (EEGs) have been noted in schizophrenic patients.

Children and adolescents with schizophrenia are more apt to have a premorbid history of social rejection, poor peer relationships, clingy withdrawn behavior, and academic trouble than are those with adult-onset schizophrenia. Some children whose schizophrenia is first seen in middle childhood have early histories of delayed motor milestones and delayed language acquisition that are similar to some symptoms of autistic disorder.

The mechanism of biological vulnerability and environment influences resulting in the manifestations of schizophrenia remains under investigation.

DIAGNOSIS AND CLINICAL FEATURES

All the symptoms included in adult-onset schizophrenia may be manifested by children with the disorder. The onset is frequently insidious; after first exhibiting inappropriate affects of unusual behavior, a child may take months or years to meet all the diagnostic criteria for schizophrenia. Children who eventually meet the criteria are often socially rejected and clingy and have limited social skills. They may have histories of delayed motor and verbal milestones and do poorly in school in spite of normal intelligence. Although schizophrenic children and autistic children may be similar in their early histories, schizophrenic children have normal intelligence and do not meet the criteria for a pervasive developmental disorder. According to the fourth edition of *Diagnostic and Statistic Manual of Mental Disorders* (DSM-IV), a schizophrenic child may experience a deterioration of function, along with the emergence of psychotic symptoms, or the child may never achieve the expected level of functioning.

Auditory hallucinations are commonly manifested by children with schizophrenia. They may hear several voices making an ongoing critical commentary about them, or command hallucinations may tell the children to kill themselves or others. The voices may be of a bizarre nature, identified as a ''computer in my head'' or Martians or the voice of someone familiar, such as a relative.

Visual hallucinations are experienced by a significant number of children with schizophrenia and are often frightening;

the children may see the devil, skeletons, scary faces, or space creatures. Transient phobic visual hallucinations also occur in traumatized children who do not go on to have a major psychotic disorder.

Delusions are present in more than half of all schizophrenic children; the delusions take various forms, including persecutory, grandiose, and religious. Delusions increase in frequency with increased age.

Blunted or inappropriate affects are almost universally present in children with schizophrenia. Schizophrenic children may giggle inappropriately or cry without being able to explain why.

Formal thought disorders, including loosening of associations and thought blocking are common features among children with schizophrenia. Illogical thinking and poverty of thought are also often present. Schizophrenic children speak less than do other children of the same intelligence, and schizophrenic children are ambiguous in the way they refer to people, objects, and events.

The core phenomena for schizophrenia appear to be the same among various age groups, but the child's developmental level influences the presentation of the symptoms. Thus, delusions present in young children are less complex than are those in older children. Age-appropriate content, such as animal imagery and monsters, is a likely source of delusional fear in children.

Other features that seem to be present with a high frequency in schizophrenic children are poor motor functioning, visuospatial impairments, and attention deficits.

PATHOLOGY AND LABORATORY EXAMINATION

No specific laboratory tests are helpful in the diagnosis of schizophrenia with childhood onset. High incidences of complications in pregnancy and birth have been reported among schizophrenic children, but at the present time no specificity has been found in those risks for childhood schizophrenia. EEG studies have also not been helpful in distinguishing schizophrenic children from other children.

DIFFERENTIAL DIAGNOSIS

Children with schizotypal personality disorder and children with schizophrenia have many similarities. Blunted affect, social isolation, eccentric thoughts, ideas of reference, and bizarre behavior may be seen in both disorders; however, in schizophrenia, overt psychotic symptoms—such as hallucinations, delusions, and incoherence—must be present at some point. When they are present, they exclude a diagnosis of schizotypal personality disorder.

However, hallucinations alone are not evidence of schizophrenia, since the patient must show either a deterioration of function or an inability to meet the expected developmental level to warrant the diagnosis of schizophrenia. Auditory and visual hallucinations can appear as self-limited events in nonpsychotic young children who are faced with extreme psychosocial stressors, such as the breakup of their parents, and in children experiencing a major loss or significant change in lifestyle.

Psychotic phenomena are common among children with major depressive disorder, in which both hallucinations and, less commonly, delusions may occur. The congruence of mood with the psychotic features is most pronounced in depressed children, although schizophrenic children may also appear sad.

The hallucinations and the delusions of schizophrenia are more likely to have a bizarre quality than are those of children with depressive disorders. In children and adolescents with bipolar I disorder, it is often difficult to distinguish a first episode of mania with psychotic features from schizophrenia if the child has no history of prior depressions. Grandiose delusions and hallucinations are typical of manic episodes, but often the clinician must follow the natural history of the disorder to confirm the presence of a mood disorder.

Pervasive developmental disorders, including autistic disorder with normal intelligence, may share some features with schizophrenia. Most notably, difficulty with social relationships, an early history of delayed language acquisition, and ongoing communication deviance are manifested in both disorders; however, hallucinations, delusions, and formal thought disorder are core features of schizophrenia and are not expected features of pervasive developmental disorders. Pervasive developmental disorders are usually diagnosed by the age of 3 years, but schizophrenia with childhood onset is rarely diagnosable before the age of 5 years.

The abuse of alcohol and other substances can sometimes result in a deterioration of function, psychotic symptoms, and paranoid delusions. Amphetamines, lysergic acid diethylamide (LSD), and phencyclidine (PCP) may lead to a psychotic state. A sudden, flagrant onset of paranoid psychosis is more suspicious of drug-induced psychoses than is an insidious onset.

Medical conditions that may induce psychotic features include thyroid disease, systemic lupus erythematosus, and temporal lobe disease.

COURSE AND PROGNOSIS

Important predictors of the course and the outcome of childhood-onset schizophrenia include the child's level of functioning before the onset of schizophrenia, the age of onset, the child's degree of functioning regained after the first episode, and the degree of support available from the family.

Children who have developmental delays and premorbid behavioral disorders, such as attention-deficit/hyperactivity disorder and conduct disorder, and learning disorders seem to be poor responders to medication treatment of schizophrenia and are likely to have the most guarded prognoses. In a long-term outcome study of schizophrenic patients with onset before age 14 years, the worst prognoses occurred in children whose schizophrenia was diagnosed before they were 10 years of age and who had preexisting personality disorders.

An additional issue in outcome studies is the stability of the diagnosis of schizophrenia. Up to a third of all children who receive a diagnosis of schizophrenia may end up with a diagnosis of a mood disorder (instead of schizophrenia) in adolescence. Children and adolescents with bipolar I disorder may have a better long-term prognosis than do children and adolescents with schizophrenia.

In adult-onset schizophrenia, family interactions, such as high expressed emotion, may be associated with increased relapse rates. No clear-cut data are available in childhood schizophrenia, but the degree of supportiveness, as opposed to critical and overinvolved family responses, probably influences the prognosis.

In general, schizophrenia with childhood onset appears less medication-responsive than is adult-onset and adolescent-onset schizophrenia, and the prognosis may be poorer. The positive symptoms—that is, hallucinations and delusions—are likely to be more responsive to medication than are negative symptoms, such as withdrawal. In a recent report of 38 schizophrenic children who had been hospitalized, two thirds required placement in residential facilities, and only one third were improved enough to return home.

TREATMENT

The treatment of schizophrenia with childhood onset includes a multimodality approach. Antipsychotic medications are indicated and may be effective, although many patients show little or no response. In addition, family education and ongoing supportive family meetings are needed to maximize the level of support that the family can give the patient. The proper educational setting for the child is also important, since social skills deficits, attention deficits, and academic difficulties often accompany childhood schizophrenia.

Few studies document the efficacy of antipsychotic medications in children and adolescents with schizophrenia. The medications appear to be helpful, and high-potency medications, such as haloperidol (Haldol) and trifluoperazine (Stelazine), are favored because of their decreased sedative side effects. The dosages for haloperidol range from about 1 to 10 mg a day in divided doses. Acute dystonic reactions do occur in children, and 1 to 2 mg a day of benztropine (Cogentin) is usually enough to treat the extrapyramidal side effects. Children and adolescents who are treated with antipsychotic medications are at risk for withdrawal dyskinesias when the medication is withdrawn. The long-term side effects, including tardive dyskinesia, are perpetual risks for any patients treated with an antipsychotic medication.

Clozapine (Clozaril) has been used with some success in schizophrenic adults who are resistant to treatment with multiple conventional antipsychotics. Clozapine has the advantage that it generally does not induce extrapyramidal side effects and is not likely to cause tardive dyskinesia. However, because of its serious, potentially fatal side effect, agranulocytosis, the patient's white blood cell count must be monitored before treatment and frequently while the medication is being used. Agranulocytosis occurs in 1 to 2 percent of all patients. Other side effects associated with clozapine include somnolence, tachycardia, postural hypotension, hypersalivation, hyperthermia, and seizures. No available data evaluate its efficacy in treatment-resistant children and adolescents with schizophrenia. One published case study has reported on three successfully treated schizophrenic adolescents who were resistant to standard antipsychotic treatment. The adolescents treated with clozapine reported sedation and increased salivation but could tolerate the medication. However, because of the serious nature of agranulocytosis, patients and families should be counseled extensively, and clinicians should record that the families understand the risks and the need for close monitoring.

Psychotherapy with schizophrenic children must consider the child's developmental level, must continually support the child's good reality testing, and must include sensitivity to the child's sense of self.

References

Birmaher B, Baker R, Kapur S, Quinatana H, Ganguli R: Clozapine for the treatment of adolescents with schizophrenia. J Am Acad Child Adolesc Psychiatry 31: 160, 1992.
Green W H, Padron-Gayol M, Hardesty A S, Bassiri M: Schizophrenia with childhood onset: A phenomenological study of 38 cases. J Am Acad Child Adolesc Psychiatry 31: 968, 1992.
Quintana H, Keshavan M: Case study: Risperidone in children and adolescents with schizophrenia. J Am Acad child Adolesc Psychiatry 34: 1292, 1995.
Spencer E K, Campbell M: Children with schizophrenia: Diagnosis, phenomenology, and pharmacotherapy. Schizophr bull 20: 713, 1994.
Szatmari P: Schizophrenia with childhood onset. In Comprehensive Textbook of Psychiatry, ed 6, H I Kaplan, B J Sadock, editors, p 2393. Williams & Wilkins, Baltimore, 1995.
Towbin K E, Dykens E M, Pearson G S, Cohen D J: Conceptualizing ''borderline syndrome of childhood'' and ''childhood schizophrenia'' as a developmental disorder. J Am Acad Child Adolesc Psychiatry 32: 775, 1993.
Werry J S, McClellan J M: Predicting outcome in child and adolescent (early onset) schizophrenia and bipolar disorder. J Am Acad Child Adolesc Psychiatry 31: 147, 1992.
Werry J S. McClellan J M, Andrews L K, Ham M: Clinical features and outcome of child and adolescent schizophrenia. Schizophr Bull 20: 619, 1994.

42/ Child Psychiatry: Additional Conditions That May Be a Focus of Clinical Attention

BORDERLINE INTELLECTUAL FUNCTIONING

Borderline intellectual functioning is defined by the presence of an intelligence quotient (I.Q.) within the range of 71 to 84. According to the fourth edition of *Diagnostic and Statistical Manual of Mental Disorders* (DSM-IV), a diagnosis of borderline intellectual functioning is made when issues about that level of cognition become the focus of clinical attention.

The clinician must assess the patient's intellectual level and current and past levels of adaptive functioning to diagnose borderline intellectual functioning. In cases of major mental disorders in which the current level of adaptive functioning has deteriorated, the diagnosis of borderline intellectual functioning may not be evident. In such situations the clinician must evaluate the patient's chronological history to determine whether a compromised level of adaptive functioning was present even before the onset of the mental disorder.

Only about 6 to 7 percent of the population are found to have a borderline I.Q., as determined by the Stanford-Binet test or the Wechsler scales. The premise behind the inclusion of borderline intellectual functioning in DSM-IV is that persons at that level may experience difficulties in their adaptive capacities, which may ultimately become a focus of treatment. Thus, without specific intrapsychic conflicts, developmental traumas, biochemical abnormalities, and other factors linked to a mental disorder, such persons may experience severe emotional distress. Frustration and embarrassment over their difficulties may shape their life choices and lead to circumstances warranting psychiatric intervention.

Etiology

Heritable factors and environmental conditions can contribute to a variety of cognitive impairments. Twin and adoption studies support hypotheses that many genes contribute to the development of a particular intelligence quotient. Specific infectious processes (such as congenital rubella), prenatal exposures (such as fetal alcohol syndrome), and specific chromosomal abnormalities (such as fragile X syndrome) result in mental retardation, but such causal factors probably do not lead to borderline intellectual functioning.

Diagnosis

In DSM-IV the following statement about borderline intellectual functioning appears:

This category can be used when the focus of clinical attention is associated with borderline intellectual functioning, that is, an IQ in the 71–84 range. Differential diagnosis between Borderline Intellectual Functioning and Mental Retardation (an IQ of 70 or below) is especially difficult when the coexistence of certain mental disorders (e.g., Schizophrenia) is involved.

Treatment

Once the underlying problem is known to the therapist, psychiatric treatment can be useful. Many persons with borderline intellectual functioning can function at a superior level in some areas while being markedly deficient in other areas. By directing such persons to appropriate areas of endeavor, by pointing out socially acceptable behavior, and by teaching them living skills, the therapist can help improve their self-esteem.

ACADEMIC PROBLEM

In DSM-IV, academic problem is a condition that is not due to a mental disorder, such as a learning disorder or a communication disorder, or, if it is due to a mental disorder, it is severe enough to warrant independent clinical attention. Thus, a child or an adolescent who is of normal intelligence and is free of a learning disorder or a communication disorder but is failing in school or doing poorly falls into this category.

Etiology

An academic problem may result from a variety of contributing factors and may arise at any time during a child's school years. Adjustment and success in the school setting depend on the child's physical, cognitive, social, and emotional adjustment. Children's general coping mechanisms in a variety of developmental tasks are usually reflected in their academic and social success in school. Boys and girls must cope with the process of separation from parents, adjustments to new environments, adaptation to social contacts, competition, assertion, intimacy, and exposure to unfamiliar attitudes. A corresponding relation often exists between school performance and how well those tasks are mastered.

Other factors may play a major role in interfering with children's academic performances. Anxiety may hamper children's abilities to perform well on tests, to speak in public, and to ask questions when they do not understand something.

Depressed children may withdraw from academic pursuits; they require specific interventions to improve their academic performances and to treat their depression. Children consumed by family problems—such as financial troubles, marital discord in their parents, and mental illness in family members—may be distracted and unable to attend to academic tasks.

The loss of the parents as the primary and predominant teachers in the child's life may result in identity conflicts for some children. Some students lack a stable sense of self and are unable to identify goals for themselves, leading to a sense of boredom or futility as students.

Schools, teachers, and clinicians can share insights about how to foster productive and cooperative environments for all students in a classroom. The teacher's varying expectations can shape the differential development of students' skills and abilities. Negative conditioning can disturb academic performance.

Diagnosis

In DSM-IV the following statement about academic problem appears:

This category can be used when the focus of clinical attention is an academic problem that is not due to a mental disorder, or if due to a mental disorder, is sufficiently severe to warrant independent clinical attention. An example is a pattern of failing grades or of significant underachievement in a person with adequate intellectual capacity in the absence of a Learning or Communication Disorder or any other mental disorder that would account for the problem.

Treatment

Although not considered a mental disorder, academic problem can often be alleviated by psychological means. Psychotherapeutic techniques can be used successfully for scholastic difficulties related to poor motivation, poor self-concept, and underachievement.

Early efforts to relieve the problem are critical, as sustained problems in learning and school performance are frequently compounded and precipitate severe difficulties. Feelings of anger, frustration, shame, loss of self-respect, and helplessness—emotions that most often accompany school failures—emotionally and cognitively damage self-esteem, disabling future performance and clouding expectations for success.

Tutoring is an effective technique in dealing with academic problems and should be considered in most cases. Tutoring is of proven value in preparing for objective multiple-choice examinations, such as the Scholastic Aptitude Test (SAT), Medical College Aptitude Test (MCAT), and national boards. Taking such examinations repetitively and using relaxation skills are two behavioral techniques of great value to diminish anxiety.

CHILDHOOD OR ADOLESCENT ANTISOCIAL BEHAVIOR

Antisocial behavior in children and adolescents covers many acts that violate the rights of others, including overt acts of aggression and violence and such covert acts as lying, stealing, truancy, and running away from home. The DSM-IV definition of conduct disorder requires a repetitive pattern of at least three antisocial behaviors for at least six months, but childhood or adolescent antisocial behavior may consist of isolated events that do not constitute a mental disorder but do become the focus of clinical attention. The emergence of occasional antisocial symptoms is common among children who have a variety of mental disorders, including psychotic disorders, depressive disorders, impulse control disorders, and disruptive behavior and attention-deficit disorders, such as attention-deficit/hyperactivity disorder and oppositional defiant disorder.

The child's age and developmental level play roles in the manifestations of disturbed conduct and influence the child's likelihood to meet the diagnostic criteria for a conduct disorder, as opposed to childhood antisocial behavior. Thus, a child of 5 or 6 years is not likely to meet the criteria for three antisocial symptoms—for example, physical confrontations, the use of weapons, and forcing someone into sexual activity—but a single symptom, like initiating fights, is common in that age group.

The term "juvenile delinquent" is defined by the legal system as a youth who has violated the law in some way, but it does not mean that the youth meets the criteria for a mental disorder.

Epidemiology

Estimates of antisocial behavior range from 5 to 15 percent of the general population and somewhat less among children and adolescents. Reports have documented the increased frequency of antisocial behaviors in urban settings, compared with rural areas. In one report, the risk of coming into contact with the police for an antisocial behavior was estimated to be 20 percent for teenage boys and 4 percent for teenage girls.

Etiology

Antisocial behaviors may occur within the context of a mental disorder or in its absence. Antisocial behavior is multidetermined, occurring most frequently in children or adolescents with many risk factors. Among the most common risk factors are harsh and physically abusive parenting, parental criminality, and impulsive and hyperactive behavior in the child. Additional associated features of children and adolescents with antisocial behavior are low I.Q., academic failure, and low levels of adult supervision.

Chapter 24 discusses genetic and social factors as causes of adult antisocial behavior.

PSYCHOLOGICAL FACTORS

If the parenting experience is poor, children experience emotional deprivation, which leads to low self-esteem and unconscious anger. They are not given any limits, and their consequences are deficient because they have not internalized parental prohibitions that account for superego formation. Therefore, they have so-called superego lacunae, which allow them to commit antisocial acts without guilt. At times, such children's antisocial behavior is a vicarious source of pleasure and gratification for parents who act out through the children their own forbidden wishes and impulses. A consistent finding in persons with repeated acts of violent behavior is a history of physical abuse.

Diagnosis and Clinical Features

In DSM-IV the following statement about childhood or adolescent antisocial behavior appears:

This category can be used when the focus of clinical attention is antisocial behavior in a child or adolescent that is not due to a mental disorder (e.g., Conduct Disorder or an Impulse Control Disorder). Examples include isolated antisocial acts of children or adolescents (not a pattern of antisocial behavior).

The childhood behaviors most associated with antisocial behavior are theft, incorrigibility, arrests, school problems, impulsiveness, promiscuity, oppositional behavior, lying, suicide attempts, substance abuse, truancy, running away, associating with undesirable persons, and staying out late at night. The greater the number of symptoms present in childhood, the greater is the probability of adult antisocial behavior; however, the presence of many symptoms also indicates the development of other mental disorders in adult life.

Differential Diagnosis

Substance-related disorders (including alcohol, cannabis, and cocaine use disorders), bipolar I disorder, and schizophrenia in childhood often manifest themselves as antisocial behavior.

Treatment

The first step in determining the appropriate treatment for a child or an adolescent who is manifesting antisocial behavior is to evaluate the need to treat any coexisting mental disorder, such as bipolar I disorder, a psychotic disorder, or a depressive disorder that may be contributing to the antisocial behavior.

The treatment of antisocial behavior usually involves behavioral management, which is most effective when the patient is in a controlled environment or when the child's family members cooperate in maintaining the behavioral program. Schools can help modify antisocial behavior within classrooms. Rewards for prosocial behaviors and positive reinforcement for the control of unwanted behaviors have merit.

In cases of aggressive and violent behavior, medications have been used with some success. Lithium (Eskalith), haloperidol (Haldol), and methylphenidate (Ritalin) can decrease aggression in some cases.

It is more difficult to treat children and adolescents with long-term patterns of antisocial behavior—particularly covert behaviors, such as stealing and lying. Group therapy has been used to treat those behaviors, and cognitive problem-solving approaches are potentially helpful.

IDENTITY PROBLEM

Identity problem is related to severe distress about one's sense of self as it pertains to long-term goals, friendships, moral values, career aspirations, sexual orientation, and group loyalties. It is not a mental disorder in DSM-IV. Identity problem is sometimes manifested in the context of such mental disorders as mood disorders, psychotic disorders, and borderline personality disorder.

Epidemiology

No reliable information is available on predisposing factors, familial pattern, sex ratio, or prevalence. However, problems with identity formation appear to be a result of life in modern society. Today, children and adolescents experience greater instability of family life, increased problems with identity formation, increased conflicts between adolescent peer values and the values of parents and society, and increased exposure through the media and education to a variety of moral, behavioral, and lifestyle possibilities.

Etiology

The causes of identity problems are often multifactorial and include the pressures of a highly dysfunctional family and the influences of coexisting mental disorders. In general, adolescents who suffer from major depressive disorder, psychotic disorders, and other mental disorders report feeling alienated from family members and experience a degree of turmoil.

Children who have had difficulties in mastering expected developmental tasks all along are likely to have difficulties with the pressure to establish a well-defined identity during adolescence.

Erik Erikson used the term "identity versus role diffusion" to describe the developmental and psychosocial tasks challenging adolescents to incorporate past experiences and present goals into a coherent sense of self.

Diagnosis and Clinical Features

In DSM-IV the following statement about identity problem appears:

This category can be used when the focus of clinical attention is uncertainty about multiple issues relating to identity such as long-term goals, career choice, friendship patterns, sexual orientation and behavior, moral values, and group loyalties.

The essential features of identity problem seem to revolve around the question "Who am I?" Conflicts are experienced as irreconcilable aspects of the self that the adolescent is unable to integrate into a coherent identity. If the symptoms are not recognized and resolved, a full-blown identity crisis may develop. As Erikson described, youth manifests severe doubting and an inability to make decisions (abulia), a sense of isolation and inner emptiness, a growing inability to relate to others, disturbed sexual functioning, a distorted time perspective, a sense of urgency, and the assumption of a negative identity.

The associated features frequently include marked discrepancy between the adolescent's self-perception and the views that others have of the adolescent; moderate anxiety and depression that are usually related to inner preoccupation, rather than external realities; and self-doubt and uncertainty about the future, with either difficulty in making choices or impulsive experiments in an attempt to establish an independent identity. Some persons with identity problem join cultlike groups.

Differential Diagnosis

Identity problem must be differentiated from a mental disorder (such as borderline personality disorder, schizophreniform disorder, schizophrenia, or a mood disorder). At times, what initially appears to be identity problem may be the prodromal manifestations of one of those disorders.

Intense but normal conflicts associated with maturing, such as adolescent turmoil and mid-life crisis, may be confusing, but they are usually not associated with marked deterioration in school, vocational, or social functioning or with severe subjective distress. However, considerable evidence suggests that adolescent turmoil is often not a phase that is outgrown but indicates true psychopathology.

Course and Prognosis

The onset of identity problem is most frequently in late adolescence, as the teenager separates from the nuclear family and attempts to establish an independent identity and value system. The onset is usually manifested by a gradual increase in anxiety, depression, regressive phenomena (such as loss of interest in friends, school, and activities), irritability, sleep difficulties, and changes in eating habits.

The course is usually relatively brief, as developmental lags are responsive to support, acceptance, and the provision of a psychosocial moratorium. An extensive prolongation of adolescence with continued identity problem may lead to the chronic state of role diffusion that may indicate a disturbance of early developmental stages and the presence of borderline personality disorder, a mood disorder, or schizophrenia. Identity problem usually resolves by the mid-20s. If it persists, the person with identity problem may be unable to make career commitments or lasting attachments.

Treatment

Individual psychotherapy directed toward encouraging growth and development is usually considered the therapy of choice. Adolescents with identity problem often react as do borderline personality disorder patients to the psychotherapeutic technique in which the transference is allowed to develop in the context of a controlled regression without gratifying or infantilizing the patient. The patients' feelings and wishes are recognized, and the patients are encouraged to examine their longings and feelings of deprivation and to try to understand, with the empathic help of the therapist, what is happening to them.

References

Bleiberg E: Identity problem and borderline disorders. In *Comprehensive Textbook of Psychiatry*, ed 6, H I Kaplan, B J Sadock, editors, p 2483. Williams & Wilkins, Baltimore, 1995.

DuPaul G, Rapport M: Does methylphenidate normalize the classroom performance of children with attention deficit disorder. J Am Acad Child Adolesc Psychiatry *32*: 190, 1993.

Lundy M S, Pfohl B, Kuperman S: Adult criminality among formerly hospitalized child psychiatric patients. J Am Acad Child Adolesc Psychiatry *32*: 568, 1993.

Sadock V A: Other additional conditions that may be a focus of clinical attention. In *Comprehensive Textbook of Psychiatry*, ed 6, H I Kaplan, B J Sadock, editors, p 1633. Williams & Wilkins, Baltimore, 1995.

Verhulst I C, Eussen M L J M, Berden G F M G, Sanders-Woodstra J, van der Ende J: Pathways of problem behaviors from childhood to adolescence. J Am Acad Child Adolesc Psychiatry *32*: 388, 1993.

43/ Psychiatric Treatment of Children and Adolescents

THEORIES

Clinicians should have a working knowledge of several psychotherapeutic theories and their applications in children, since a combination of therapeutic interventions is often used in a child's treatment. Psychodynamic approaches are at times mixed with supportive components and behavioral management techniques to build a comprehensive treatment plan for a child. Individual psychotherapy with children is frequently done with family therapy, group therapy, and, when indicated, psychopharmacology.

Several theoretical systems underlie psychotherapeutic approaches with children, including (1) psychoanalytic theories, (2) behavioral theories, (3) family systems theories, and (4) developmental theories.

Psychoanalytic Theories

Classic psychoanalytic theory conceives of exploratory psychotherapy's working, with patients of all ages, by reversing the evolution of psychopathologic processes. A principal difference noted with advancing age is a sharpening distinction between psychogenetic and psychodynamic factors. The younger the child, the more the genetic and dynamic forces are intertwined.

The development of those pathological processes is generally thought to begin with experiences that have proven to be particularly significant to the patients and have affected them adversely. Although in one sense the experiences were real, in another sense they may have been misinterpreted or imagined. In any event, for the patients they were traumatic experiences that caused unconscious complexes. Being inaccessible to conscious awareness, the unconscious elements readily escape rational adaptive maneuvers and are subject to pathological misuse of adaptive and defensive mechanisms. The result is the development of conflicts leading to distressing symptoms, character attitudes, or patterns of behavior that constitute the emotional disturbance.

Increasingly, the psychoanalytic view of emotional disturbances in children has assumed a developmental orientation. Thus, the maladaptive defensive functioning is directed against conflicts between impulses that are characteristic of a specific developmental phase and environmental influences or the child's internalized representations of environment. In that framework the disorders are the result of environmental interferences with maturational timetables or conflicts with the environment engendered by developmental progress. The result is difficulty in achieving or resolving developmental tasks and achieving the capacities specific to later phases of development, which can be expressed in various ways, such as Anna Freud's lines of development and Erik Erikson's concept of sequential psychosocial capacities.

The goal of therapy is to help develop good conflict-resolution skills in the child, so that the child can function at the appropriate developmental level. Therapy may again be necessary as the child faces the challenges of subsequent developmental periods.

Psychoanalytic psychotherapy is a modified form of psychotherapy that is expressive and exploratory and that attempts to reverse the evolution of emotional disturbance through a reenactment and desensitization of the traumatic events by the free expression of thoughts and feelings in an interview-play situation. Ultimately, the therapist helps patients understand the warded-off feelings, fears, and wishes that have beset them.

Whereas the psychoanalytic psychotherapeutic approach seeks improvement by exposure and resolution of buried conflicts, suppressive-supportive-educative psychotherapy works in an opposite fashion. It aims to facilitate repression. The therapist, capitalizing on the patient's desire to please, encourages the patient to substitute new adaptive and defensive mechanisms. In that type of therapy, the therapist uses interpretations minimally; instead, the therapist emphasizes suggestion, persuasion, exhortation, operant reinforcement, counseling, education, direction, advice, abreaction, environmental manipulation, intellectual review, gratification of the patient's current dependent needs, and similar techniques.

Behavioral Theories

All behavior, no matter whether it is adaptive or maladaptive, is a consequence of the same basic principles of behavior acquisition and maintenance. Behavior is either learned or unlearned, and what renders behavior abnormal or disturbed is its social significance.

Although the theories and their derivative therapeutic intervention techniques have become increasingly complex over the years, all learning can be subsumed within two global basic mechanisms. One is classical respondent conditioning, akin to Ivan Pavlov's famous experiments, and the second is operant instrumental learning, which is associated with B. F. Skinner, although it is basic to both Edward Thorndike's law of effect regarding the influence of reinforcing consequences of behavior and to Sigmund Freud's pain-pleasure principle. Both of those basic mechanisms assign the highest priority to the immediate precipitants of behavior, deemphasizing those remote underlying causal determinants that are important in the psychoanalytic tradition. The theory asserts that there are but two types of abnormal behavior: behavioral deficits that result from a failure to learn and deviant maladaptive behaviors that are a consequence of learning inappropriate things.

Such concepts have always been an implicit part of the rationale underlying all child psychotherapy. Intervention strategies derive much of their success, particularly with children, from rewarding previously unnoticed good behavior, thereby highlighting it and making it more frequent than in the past.

Family Systems Theories

Although families have long been an interest of child psychotherapists, the understanding of transactional family processes has been greatly enhanced by conceptual contributions from cybernetics, systems theory, communications theory, object relations theory, social role theory, ethology, and ecology.

The bedrock premise entails the family's functioning as a self-regulating open system that possesses its own unique history and structure. Its structure is constantly evolving as a consequence of the dynamic interaction between the family's mutually interdependent systems and persons who share a complementarity of needs. From that conceptual foundation, a wealth of ideas has emerged under rubrics such as the family's development, life cycle, homeostasis, functions, identity, values, goals, congruence, symmetry, myths, rules, roles (spokesperson, symptoms bearer, scapegoat, affect barometer, pet, persecutor, victim, arbitrator, distractor, saboteur, rescuer, breadwinner, disciplinarian, nurturer), structure (boundaries, splits, pairings, alliances, coalitions, enmeshed, disengaged), double bind, scapegoating, pseudomutuality, and mystification. Increasingly, appreciation of the family system sometimes explains why a minute therapeutic input at a critical junction may result in far-reaching changes, whereas in other situations huge quantities of therapeutic effort appear to be absorbed with little evidence of change.

Developmental Theories

Underlying child psychotherapy is the assumption that, without unusual interferences, children mature in basically orderly, predictable ways that are codifiable in a variety of interrelated psychosociobiological sequential systematizations. The central and overriding role of a developmental frame of reference in child psychotherapy distinguishes it from adult psychotherapy. The therapist's orientation should entail something more than a knowledge of age-appropriate behavior derived from such studies as Arnold Gesell's description of the morphology of behavior. It should encompass more than psychosexual development with ego-psychological and sociocultural amendments, exemplified by Erikson's epigenetic schema. It extends beyond familiarity with Jean Piaget's sequence of intellectual evolution as a basis for acquaintance with the level of abstraction at which children of various ages may be expected to function or for assessing their capacities for a moral orientation.

TYPES OF PSYCHOTHERAPY

Among the common bases for the classification of child therapy is the identification of the element presumed to be helpful for the young patient. Isolating a single therapeutic element as the basis for classification tends to be artificial, because most, if not all, of the factors are present in varying degrees in every child psychotherapeutic undertaking. For example, in every psychotherapy the relationship between the therapist and the patient is a vital factor; nevertheless, child psychotherapists commonly talk of relationship therapy to describe a form of treatment in which a positive, friendly, helpful relationship is viewed as the primary, if not the sole, therapeutic ingredient. Probably one of the best examples of pure relationship therapy is found outside a clinical setting in the work of the Big Brother Organization.

Remedial, educational, and patterning psychotherapy attempts to teach new attitudes and patterns of behavior to children who persist in using immature and inefficient patterns, which are often presumed to be due to a maturational lag.

Supportive psychotherapy is particularly helpful in enabling a well-adjusted youngster to cope with the emotional turmoil engendered by a crisis. It is also used with disturbed youngsters whose less than adequate ego functioning may be seriously disrupted by an expressive-exploratory mode or by other forms of therapeutic intervention. At the beginning of most psychotherapy, whatever the patient's age and the nature of the therapeutic interventions, the principal therapeutic elements perceived by the patient tend to be the supportive ones, a consequence of therapists' universal efforts to be reliably and sensitively responsive. In fact, some therapy may never proceed beyond the supportive level, whereas others develop an expressive-exploratory or behavioral modification flavor on top of the supportive foundation.

Release therapy, described initially by David Levy, facilitates the abreaction of pent-up emotions. Although abreaction is an aspect of many therapeutic undertakings, in release therapy the treatment situation is structured to encourage only that factor. It is indicated primarily for preschool-age children who are suffering from a distorted emotional reaction to an isolated trauma.

Preschool-age children are sometimes treated through the parents, a process called filial therapy. The therapist using the strategy should be alert to the possibility that apparently successful filial treatment can obscure a significant diagnosis because the patient is not directly seen. The first case of filial therapy was that of Little Hans, reported by Sigmund Freud in 1905. Hans was a 5-year-old phobic child who was treated by Hans's father under Freud's supervision.

Psychotherapy with children is often psychoanalytically oriented, which means that it tries through the vehicle of self-understanding to enable the child's potential to develop further. That development is accomplished by liberating for constructive use the psychic energy presumed to be expended in defending against fantasied dangers. Children are generally unaware of those unreal dangers, their fear of them, and the psychological defenses they use to avoid both the danger and the fear. With the awareness that is facilitated, patients can evaluate the usefulness of their defensive maneuvers and can relinquish the unnecessary maneuvers that constitute the symptoms of their emotional disturbance.

Child psychoanalysis—an intensive, uncommon form of psychoanalytic psychotherapy—works on unconscious resistance and defenses during three to four sessions a week. Under those circumstances the therapist anticipates unconscious resistance and allows transference manifestations to mature to a full transference neurosis, through which neurotic conflicts are resolved.

Interpretations of dynamically relevant conflicts are emphasized in psychoanalytic descriptions. However, that does not imply the absence of elements that are predominant in other types of psychotherapies. Indeed, in all psychotherapy the child should derive support from the consistently understanding and accepting relationship with the therapist. Remedial educational guidance is provided when necessary.

Probably the most vivid examples of the integration of psychodynamic and behavioral approaches, though they are not always explicitly understood as such, are to be found in the milieu therapy of child and adolescent psychiatric inpatient, residential, and day treatment facilities. Behavioral change is initiated in those settings, and its repercussions are explored concurrently in individual psychotherapeutic sessions, so that the action in one arena and the information stemming from it augment and illuminate what transpires in the other arena.

Cognitive therapy has been used with children, adolescents, and adults. The approach attempts to correct cognitive distortions, particularly negative conceptions of oneself, and is used mainly in depressive disorders.

DIFFERENCES BETWEEN CHILDREN AND ADULTS

Reason suggests that psychotherapy with children, who are generally more flexible than adults and have simpler defenses and other mental mechanisms, should consume less time than comparable treatment of adults. Experience does not usually confirm that expectation, because of the relative absence in children of some elements that contribute to successful treatment.

A child, for example, typically does not seek help. Consequently, one of the first tasks for the therapist is to stimulate the child's motivation for treatment. Children commonly begin therapy involuntarily, often without the benefit of true parental support. Although the parents may want their child helped or changed, that desire is often generated by frustrated anger with the child. Typically, the anger is accompanied by relative insensitivity to what the therapist perceives as the child's need and the basis for a therapeutic alliance. Thus, whereas adult patients frequently perceive advantages in getting well, children may envision therapeutic change as nothing more than conforming to a disagreeable reality, which heightens the likelihood of perceiving the therapist as the parent's punitive agent. That is hardly the most fertile soil in which to nurture a therapeutic alliance.

Children tend to externalize internal conflicts in search of alloplastic adaptations, and they find it difficult to conceive of problem resolution except by altering an obstructing environment. The passive, masochistic boy who is the constant butt of his schoolmates' teasing finds it inconceivable that the situation can be rectified by altering his mode of handling his aggressive impulses, rather than by someone's controlling his tormentors, a view that may be reinforced by significant adults in his environment.

The tendency of children to reenact their feelings in new situations facilitates the early appearance of spontaneous and global transference reactions that may be troublesome. Concurrently, the eagerness that children have for new experiences, coupled with their natural developmental fluidity, tends to limit the intensity and the therapeutic usefulness of subsequent transference developments.

Children have a limited capacity for self-observation, with the notable exception of some obsessive children who resemble adults in that ability. Such obsessive children, however, usually isolate the vital emotional components. In the exploratory-interpretative psychotherapies, the development of a capacity for ego splitting—that is, simultaneous emotional involvement and self-observation—is most helpful. Only by means of identification with a trusted adult and in alliance with that adult are children able to approach such an ideal. The therapist's sex and the relatively superficial aspects of the therapist's demeanor may be important elements in the development of a trusting relationship with a child.

Regressive behavioral and communicative modes can be wearing on child therapists. Typically motor-minded, even

when they do not require external controls, children may demand a degree of physical stamina that is not of consequence in therapy with adults. The age appropriateness of such primitive mechanisms as denial, projection, and isolation hinders the process of working through, which relies on a patient's synthesizing and integrating capacities, both of which are immature in children. Also, environmental pressures on the therapist are generally greater in psychotherapeutic work with children than in work with adults.

Although children compare unfavorably with adults in many qualities that are generally considered desirable in therapy, children have the advantage of active maturational and developmental forces. The history of psychotherapy for children is punctuated by efforts to harness those assets and to overcome the liabilities. Recognition of the importance of play constituted a major forward stride in those efforts.

PLAYROOM

The playroom's structure, design, and furnishing are most important. Some therapists say that the toys should be few, simple, and carefully selected to facilitate the communication of fantasy. Other therapists suggest that a variety of playthings be available to increase the range of feelings the child may express. Those contrasting recommendations have been attributed to differences in therapeutic methods. Some therapists tend to avoid interpretation, even of conscious ideas, whereas others recommend the interpretation of unconscious content directly and quickly. Therapists tend to change their preferences in equipment as they accumulate experience and develop confidence in their abilities.

Although special equipment—such as genital dolls, amputation dolls, and see-through anatomically complete (except for genitalia) models—have been used in therapy, many therapists have observed that the unusual nature of such items risks making children wary and suspicious of the therapist's motives. Until the dolls available to the children in their own homes include genitalia, the psychic content that special dolls are designed to elicit may be more available at the appropriate time with conventional dolls.

Although the choices of play materials vary from therapist to therapist, the following equipment can constitute a well-balanced playroom or play area: multigenerational families of flexible but sturdy dolls of various races; additional dolls representing special roles and feelings, such as police officer, doctor, and soldier; dollhouse furnishings with or without a dollhouse; toy animals; puppets; paper, crayons, paint, and blunt-ended scissors; a spongelike ball; clay or something comparable; tools like rubber hammers, rubber knives, and guns; building blocks, cars, trucks, and airplanes; and eating utensils. The toys should enable children to communicate through play. The therapist should avoid toys and materials that are fragile or break easily, which can result in physical injury to the child or can increase the child's guilt.

A special drawer or box should be available to each child, space permitting, in which to store items the child brings to the therapy session or to store projects, such as drawings and stories, for future retrieval. Limits have to be set, so that the private storage area is not used to hoard communal play equipment, depriving the therapist's other patients. Some therapists assert than an absence of such arrangements evokes material about sibling rivalry; however, others think that assertion is a rationalization for not respecting the child's privacy, as such feelings can be expressed in other ways.

INITIAL APPROACH

A variety of approaches can be derived from the therapist's individual style and perception of the child's needs. The range extends from those in which the therapist attempts to direct the child's thought content and activity—as in release therapy, some behavior therapy, and certain educational patterning techniques—to those exploratory methods in which the therapist endeavors to follow the child's lead. Although the child determines the focus, the therapist structures the situation. Encouraging children to say whatever they wish and to play freely, as in exploratory psychotherapy, establishes a definite structure. The therapist creates an atmosphere in which to get to know all about the child—the good side, as well as the bad side, as children would put it. The therapist may communicate to the child that the child's response will elicit neither anger nor pleasure, only understanding from the therapist. Such an assertion does not imply that therapists do not have emotions, but it assures the young patient that the therapist's personal feelings and standards are subordinate to understanding the youngster.

THERAPEUTIC INTERVENTIONS

Therapeutic interventions with children encompass a range comparable to those used with adults in psychotherapy. If the amount of therapist activity is used as the basis for a classificatory continuum of interventions, at the least active end are the questions posed by the therapist requesting an elaboration of patient's statements or behavior. Next on the continuum of therapeutic activity are the exclamations and confrontations in which the therapist directs attention to some data of which the patients are cognizant. Then the therapist uses interpretations designed to expand patient's conscious awareness of themselves by making explicit those elements that have previously been implicitly expressed in their thoughts, feelings, and behavior. Beyond interpretation, the therapist may educatively offer information that is new because the patients have not been exposed to it previously. At the most active end of the continuum are advising, counseling, and directing, designed to help patients adopt a course of action or a conscious attitude.

Nurturing and maintaining a therapeutic alliance may require some education of children regarding the process of therapy. Another educational intervention may entail assigning labels to affects that have not been part of the youngster's past experience. Rarely does therapy have to compensate for a real absence of education regarding acceptable decorum and playing games. Usually, children are in therapy not because of the absence of educational efforts but because repeated educational efforts have failed. Therefore, therapy generally does not need to include additional teaching efforts, despite the frequent temptation to offer them.

Adult's natural educational fervor with children is often accompanied by a paradoxical tendency to protect them from learning about some of life's realities. In the past, that tendency contributed to the stork's role in childbirth, the dead having taken a long trip, and similar fairy-tale explanations for natural phenomena about which adults were uncomfortable in communicating with children. Although adults are more honest with children today, therapists can find themselves in a situation in which their overwhelming urge to protect the hurt child may be as disadvantageous to the child as was the stork myth. Alternatively, information given to the child must take into account individual problems and developmental levels.

The temptation to offer oneself as a model for identification may stem also from helpful educational attitudes toward children. Although that may sometimes be an appropriate therapeutic strategy, therapists should not lose sight of the pitfalls in that apparently innocuous strategy.

PARENTS

Psychotherapy with children is characterized by the need for parental involvement. The involvement does not necessarily reflect parental culpability for the youngster's emotional difficulties but is a reality of the child's dependent state. The fact cannot be stressed too much because of what can be considered an occupational hazard shared by many who work with children. The hazard is the urge to rescue children from the negative influences of their parents, sometimes related to an unconscious competitive desire to be a better parent than the child's or one's own parents.

Parents are involved to varying degrees in child psychotherapy. With preschool-age children the entire therapeutic effort may be directed toward the parents, without any direct treatment of the child. At the other extreme, children can be seen in psychotherapy without any parental involvement beyond the payment of fees and perhaps transporting the child to the therapy sessions. However, most practitioners prefer to maintain an informative alliance with the parents to obtain additional information about the child.

Probably the most frequent arrangements are those that were developed in a child guidance clinic—that is, parent guidance focused on the child or on the parent-child interaction and therapy for the parents' own individual needs concurrent with the child's therapy. The parents may be seen by the child's therapist or by someone else. In recent years increasing efforts have been made to shift the focus from the child as the primary patient to the child as the family's emissary to the clinic. In such family therapy, all or selected members of the family are treated simultaneously as a family group. Although the preferences of specific clinics and practitioners for either an individual or a family therapeutic approach may be unavoidable, the final decision about which therapeutic strategy or combination to use should be derived from the clinical assessment.

CONFIDENTIALITY

Consideration of parental involvement highlights the question of confidentiality in psychotherapy with children. There are advantages to creating an atmosphere in which the child can feel that all words and actions will be viewed by the therapist as simultaneously both serious and tentative. In other words, the child's communications do not bind the therapist to a commitment; nevertheless, they are too important to be communicated to a third party without the patient's permission. Although such an attitude may be conveyed implicitly, sometimes the therapist should explicitly discuss confidentiality with the child. Promising a child not to tell the parents what transpires in therapeutic sessions can be risky. Although the therapist has no intention of disclosing such data to the parents, the bulk of what children do and say in psychotherapy is common knowledge to the parents. Therefore, a child so motivated can easily manipulate the situation to produce circumstantial evidence that the therapist has betrayed a confidence. Accordingly, if confidentiality requires specific discussion during treatment, the therapist may not want to go beyond indicating that the therapist is not in the business of telling parents what goes on in therapy, as the therapist's role is to understand and help children.

The therapist should try to enlist the parents' cooperation in respecting the privacy of the child's therapeutic sessions. The respect is not always readily honored, as parents are naturally curious about what transpires and may be threatened by the therapist's apparently privileged position.

Routinely reporting to the child the essence of the communications with the third parties regarding the child underscores the therapist's reliability and respect for the child's autonomy. In certain types of treatment, the report may be combined with soliciting the child's guesses about those transactions. Also, the therapist may find it fruitful to invite children, particularly older children, to participate in discussions about them with third parties.

INDICATIONS AND CONTRAINDICATIONS

The present level of knowledge does not permit the compilation of a meaningful list of the multifaceted indications for child psychotherapy. Existing diagnostic classifications cannot serve as the basis for such a list because of invariable deficiencies in nosological specificity and comprehensiveness. In general, psychotherapy is indicated for children with emotional disorders that seem permanent enough to impede maturational and developmental forces. Psychotherapy may also be indicated when the child's development is not impeded but is inducing reactions in the environment considered pathogenic. Ordinarily, such disharmonies are dealt with by the child with parental assistance, but, when those efforts are persistently inadequate, psychotherapeutic interventions may be indicated.

Psychotherapy should be limited to those instances in which positive indicators point to its potential usefulness. For the child to benefit from psychotherapy, the home situation must provide a certain amount of nurturance, stability, and motivation for therapy. The child must have adequate cognitive resources to participate in the process and profit from it. If psychotherapy, despite contraindications, is invariably recommended after every child psychiatric evaluation by a particular therapist or clinic, that fact suggests not only unsatisfactory professional practice and a disservice to patients but also an indiscriminate use of psychotherapy.

Psychotherapy is contraindicated if the emotional disturbance is judged to be an intractable one that will not respond to treatment. That is a difficult judgment but one that is essential, considering the excess of the demand for psychotherapy over its supply. Because the potential for error in such prognostic assessments is great, therapists should bring to them both professional humility and a readiness to offer a trial of therapy. Sometimes the essential factor in intractability is the therapist. Certain patients may elicit a reaction from one therapist that is a contraindication for psychotherapy with that therapist but not necessarily with another.

Another contraindication is evidence that the therapeutic process will interfere with reparative forces. A difficult question is posed by suggestions that the forces mobilized as a consequence of psychotherapy may have dire social or somatic effects. For example, psychotherapy may upset a precarious family equilibrium, thereby causing more difficulty than the original problem posed.

References

Beardslee W R, Salt P, Porterfield K, Rothberg P C, van de Velde P, Swatling S, Hoke L, Moilanen D L, Wheelock I: Comparison of preventive interventions for families with parental affective disorder. J Am Acad Child Adolesc Psychiatry *32*: 254, 1993.

Cohen J A, Mannarino A P: A treatment model for sexually abused preschoolers. J Interpers Violence *8*: 115, 1993.

Forehand R, Wierson M: The role of developmental factors in planning behavioral interventions for children: Disruptive behavior as an example. Behav Ther *24*: 117, 1993.

Kernberg P F: Individual psychotherapy. In *Comprehensive Textbook of Psychiatry*, ed 6, H I Kaplan, B J Sadock, editors, p 2399. Williams & Wilkins, Baltimore, 1995.

Kernberg P F: A reevaluation of estimates of child therapy effectiveness: Discussion. J Am Acad Child Adolesc Psychiatry *31*: 710, 1992.

43.2 GROUP PSYCHOTHERAPY

Group psychotherapy can be modified to suit groups of children in various age groups and can focus on behavioral, educational, social skills, and psychodynamic issues. The mode in which the group functions depends on the children's developmental levels, intelligence, and problems to be addressed. In behaviorally oriented groups, the group leader is directive and an active participant, facilitating prosocial interactions and desired behaviors. In groups using psychodynamic approaches, the leader may monitor interpersonal interactions less actively than in behavior therapy groups.

Groups are highly effective in providing peer feedback and support to children who are either socially isolated or unaware of their effects on their peers.

Groups with very young children are generally highly structured by the leader and use imagination and play to foster socially acceptable peer relationships and positive behavior. The therapist must be keenly aware of the level of the children's attention span and the need for consistency and limit setting. Leaders of preschool-age groups can model supportive adult behavior in meaningful ways to children who have been deprived or neglected.

School-age children's groups may be single-sex groups or include both boys and girls. Children of school age are more sophisticated in verbalizing their feelings than are preschoolers, but they also benefit from structured therapeutic games. Children of school age need frequent reminders about rules, and they are quick to point out infractions of the rules to each other. Interpersonal skills can be addressed nicely in group settings with school-age children.

Among early adolescents, same-sex groups are often used. In early adolescence, physiological changes and the new demands of high school lead to stress that may be relieved when groups of same-age peers compare and share. In older adolescence, groups more often include both boys and girls. Even with older adolescents, the leader often uses structure and direct intervention to maximize the therapeutic value of the group. Adolescents who are feeling dejected or alienated may find a special sense of belonging in a therapy group.

PRESCHOOL-AGE AND EARLY SCHOOL-AGE GROUPS

Work with a preschool-age group is usually structured by the therapist through the use of a particular technique, such as puppets or artworks, or is couched in terms of a permissive play atmosphere. In therapy with puppets, the children project their fantasies onto the puppets in a way not unlike ordinary play. The main value lies in the cathexis afforded the children, especially if they show difficulty in expressing their feelings. Here the group aids the child less by interaction with other members than by action with the puppets.

In play group therapy the emphasis rests on the interactional qualities of the children with each other and with the therapist in the permissive playroom setting. The therapist should be a person who can allow the children to produce fantasies verbally and in play but who can also use active restraint when the children undergo excessive tension. The toys are the traditional ones used in individual play therapy. The children use the toys to act out aggressive impulses and to relive with the group members and with the therapist their home difficulties. The children catalyze each other and obtain libido-activating stimulation from the catalysis and from their play materials. The therapist interprets a child to the group in the context of the transference to the therapist and to other group members.

The children selected for group treatment show in common a social hunger, the need to be like their peers and to be accepted by them. Usually, the therapist excludes the children who have never realized a primary relationship, as with their mothers, since individual psychotherapy can better help those children. The children selected for group psychotherapy usually include those with phobias, effeminate boys, shy and withdrawn children, and children with disruptive behavior disorders.

Modifications of those criteria have been used in group psychotherapy for autistic children, parent group therapy, and art therapy.

A modification of group psychotherapy has been used for physically handicapped toddlers who show speech and language delays. The experience of twice-a-week group activities involves the mothers and their children in a mutual teaching-learning setting. The experience has proved effective for the mothers, who received supportive psychotherapy in the group experience; their formerly hidden fantasies about the children emerged, to be dealt with therapeutically.

LATENCY-AGE GROUPS

Activity group psychotherapy assumes that poor and divergent experiences have led to deficits in appropriate personality development in the behavior of children; therefore, corrective experiences in a therapeutically conditioned environment will modify them. Because some latency-age children present deep disturbances involving fears, high anxiety levels, and guilt, an activity-interview group psychotherapy modification has evolved. The format uses interview techniques, verbal explanations of fantasies, group play, work, and other communications.

In that type of group psychotherapy, the children verbalize in a problem-oriented manner, with the awareness that problems brought them together and that the group aims to change them. They report dreams, fantasies, daydreams, and traumatic and unpleasant experiences. Both the experiences and the group behavior undergo open discussion.

Therapists vary in their use of time, cotherapists, food, and materials. Most groups meet after school for at least one hour, although some group leaders prefer 90 minutes. Some therapists serve food in the last 10 minutes, and others prefer serving times when the children are more together for talking. Food, however, does not become a major feature, never becoming central to the group's activities.

PUBERTAL AND ADOLESCENT GROUPS

Group therapy methods similar to those used in latency-age groups can be used with pubertal children, who are often grouped monosexually, rather than mixed. Their problems resemble those of late latency-age children, but they are also beginning, especially the girls, to feel the effects and the pressures of early adolescence. In a way the groups offer help during a transitional period. The group appears to satisfy the social appetite of preadolescents, who compensate for feelings of inferiority and self-doubt by the formation of groups. That form of therapy puts to advantage the influence of the process of socialization during those years. Because pubertal children experience difficulties in conceptualizing, pubertal therapy groups tend to use play, drawing, psychodrama, and other nonverbal modes of expression. The therapist's role is active and directive.

Activity group psychotherapy has been the recommended type of group therapy for pubertal children who do not have significantly disturbed personality patterns. The children, usually of the same sex and in groups of not more than eight, freely engage in activities in a setting especially designed and planned for its physical and milieu characteristics.

Samuel Slavson, one of the pioneers in group psychotherapy, pictured the group as a substitute family in which the passive, neutral therapist becomes the surrogate for the parents. The therapist assumes various roles, mostly nonverbally, as each child interacts with the therapist and with other group members. Recent therapists, however, tend to see the group as a form of peer group, with its attendant socializing processes, rather than as a reenactment of the family.

Late adolescents, 16 years of age and up, may be included in groups of adults when indicated. Group therapy has been useful in the treatment of substance-related disorders. Combined therapy (the use of group and individual therapy) has also been used successfully with adolescents.

OTHER GROUP SITUATIONS

Some residential and day treatment units frequently use group psychotherapy techniques in their work. Group psychotherapy in schools for underachievers and for the underprivileged has relied on reinforcement and on modeling theory, besides traditional techniques, and has been supplemented by parent groups.

In controlled conditions, residential treatment units have been used for specific studies in group psychotherapy, such as behavioral contracting. Behavioral contracting with reward-punishment reinforcement provides positive reinforcements among preadolescent boys with severe concerns in basic trust, low self-esteem, and dependence conflicts. Somewhat akin to formal residential treatment units are social group work homes. The children undergo many psychological assaults before placement, so that supportive group psychotherapy offers ventilation and catharsis, but more often it succeeds in letting the children become aware of the enjoyment of sharing activities and developing skills.

Public schools—also a structured environment, although usually not considered the best site for group psychotherapy—have been used by many workers. Group psychotherapy as group counseling readily lends itself to school settings. One such group used gender- and problem-homogeneous selection for groups of six to eight students, who met once a week during school hours over two to three years.

INDICATIONS

There are many indications for group psychotherapy as a treatment modality. Some indications are situational; the therapist may work in a reformatory setting, where group psychotherapy seems to reach the adolescents better than does individual treatment. Another indication is time economics; more patients can be reached within a given time by using groups than by individual therapy. Using groups best helps the child at a given age and developmental stage and with a given type of problem. In the young age group the children's social hunger and their potential need for peer acceptance help to determine their suitability for group therapy. Criteria for unsuitability are controversial and have been progressively loosened.

PARENT GROUPS

In group psychotherapy, as in most treatment procedures for children, parental difficulties present obstacles. Sometimes uncooperative parents refuse to bring a child or to participate in their own therapy. The extreme of that situation reveals itself when severely disturbed parents use the child as their channel of communication in working out their own needs. In such circumstances the child is in an intolerable position of receiving positive group experiences that seem to create havoc at home.

Parent groups, therefore, can be a valuable aid to the group psychotherapy for their children. The parent of a child in therapy often has difficulty in understanding the nature of the child's ailment, in discerning the line of demarcation between normal and pathological behavior, in relating to the medical establishment, and in coping with feelings of guilt. A parent group assists them in those areas and helps the members formulate guidelines for action.

References

Garland J A: The establishment of individual and collective competency in children's groups as a prelude to entry into intimacy, disclosure, and bonding. Int J Group Psychother *42*: 395, 1992.

Licamele W L, Bernet W: Group psychotherapy. In *Comprehensive Textbook of Psychiatry*, ed 6, H I Kaplan, B J Sadock, editors, p 2412. Williams & Wilkins, Baltimore, 1995.

Schamess G: Reflections on a developing body of group-as-a-whole theory for children's therapy groups: An introduction. Int J Group Psychother *42*: 351, 1992.

43.3 RESIDENTIAL, DAY, AND HOSPITAL TREATMENT

Residential treatment centers and facilities are appropriate settings for children and adolescents with mental disorders who require a highly structured and supervised setting over a substantial period. Such settings have the advantage of being able to provide a stable and consistent environment with a high level of psychiatric monitoring but one that is less intensive than a hospital. Many treatments are offered in residential settings, including behavioral management, the therapeutic milieu itself, psychotherapy, medication, and special education. Children and adolescents who benefit from residential settings have a variety of psychiatric problems and commonly have difficulties with impulse control and structuring their own time. Many residents of such programs also have families with serious psychiatric, financial, and parenting difficulties.

Day treatment programs are excellent alternatives for children and adolescents who require more intensive support, monitoring, and supervision than is available in the community but can live successfully at home, given the right level of intervention. In most cases, children and adolescents who attend day hospital programs have serious mental disorders and may warrant psychiatric hospitalization without the support of the program. Family therapy, group and individual psychotherapy, psychopharmacology, behavioral management programs, and special education are integral parts of the programs.

Psychiatric hospitalization is needed when a child or an adolescent exhibits dangerous behavior, is contemplating suicide, or is experiencing an exacerbation of a psychotic disorder or another serious mental disorder. Safety, stabilization, and efficacious treatment are the goals of hospitalization. In recent years the length of stay of child and adolescent psychiatric patients has decreased because of financial pressures and the increased availability of day treatment programs. Psychiatric hospitalization may be the first opportunity for some children to experience a stable and safe environment. The hospital is often the most appropriate place to start new medications, and it provides a round-the-clock setting in which to observe a child's behavior. Children may show a remission of some symptoms by virtue of their removal from a stressful or abusive environment. Once the child has been observed for several weeks, the best treatment and disposition may become clear.

RESIDENTIAL TREATMENT

More than 20,000 emotionally disturbed children are in residential treatment centers in the United States, and that number is increasing. Deteriorating social conditions, particularly in cities, often make it impossible for a child with a serious mental disorder to live at home. In those cases, residential treatment centers serve a real need. They provide a structured living environment where children may form strong attachments to and receive commitments from the staff members. The purpose of the centers is to provide treatment and special education for the children and treatment of their families.

Staff and Setting

Staffing patterns include various combinations of child care workers, teachers, social workers, psychiatrists, pediatricians, nurses, and psychologists, making the cost of residential treatment very high.

The Joint Commission on the Mental Health of Children made the following structural and setting recommendations:

Besides space for therapy programs, there should be facilities for a first-rate school and a rich evening activity program, and there should be ample space for play, both indoors and out. Facilities should be small, seldom exceeding 60 in capacity, with 100 a maximum limit, and should make provision for children to live in small groups. The centers should be located near the families they serve and be readily accessible by public transportation. They should be located for ready access to special medical and educational services and to various community resources, including consultants. They should be open institutions whenever possible; locked buildings, wards, or rooms should only rarely be required. In designing residential programs, the guiding principle should be this: Children should be removed the least possible distance—in space, in time, and in the psychological texture of the experience—from their normal life setting.

Indications

Most children who are referred for residential treatment have already been seen by one or more professional persons, such as a school psychologist, a pediatrician, and members of a child guidance clinic, juvenile court, or state welfare agency. Attempts at outpatient treatment and foster home placement usually precede residential treatment. Sometimes the severity of the child's problems or the inability of the family to provide for the child's needs prohibits sending a child home. Many children sent to residential treatment centers have conduct disorder. The age range of the children varies from institution to institution, but most children are between 5 and 15 years of age. Boys are referred more frequently than are girls.

An initial review of the data enables the intake staff to determine whether a particular child is likely to benefit from their treatment program. Often, for every one child accepted for admission, three are rejected. The next step is usually interviews with the child and the parents by various staff members, such as a therapist, a group living worker, and a teacher. Psychological testing and neurological examinations are given when indicated if they have not already been done. The child and the parents should be prepared for those interviews.

Group Living

Most of the children's time in a residential treatment setting is spent in group living. The group living staff consists of child care workers who offer a structured environment that is a therapeutic milieu. The environment places boundaries and limitations on the children. Tasks are defined within the limits of the children's abilities; incentives, such as additional privileges, encourage them to progress, rather than regress. In milieu therapy the environment is structured, limits are set, and a therapeutic atmosphere is maintained.

The children often select one or more staff members with whom to form a relationship through which they express, consciously and unconsciously, many of their feelings about their parents. The child care staff should be trained to recognize such transference reactions and to respond to them in a way that is different from the children's expectations, based on their previous or even current relationships with their parents.

To maintain consistency and balance, the group living staff members must communicate freely and regularly with one another and with the other professional and administrative staff members of the residential setting, particularly the children's

teachers and therapists. The child care staff members must recognize any tendency toward becoming the good (or bad) parent in response to a child's splitting behavior. That tendency may be manifested as a pattern of blaming other staff members for a child's disruptive behavior. Similarly, the child care staff must recognize and avoid such individual and group countertransference reactions as sadomasochistic and punitive behavior toward a child.

The structured setting should offer a corrective emotional experience and opportunities for facilitating and improving the children's adaptive behavior, particularly when such deficiencies as speech and language deficits, intellectual retardation, inadequate peer relationships, bed-wetting, poor feeding habits, and attention deficits are present. Some of those deficits are the basis of the children's poor school academic performance and unsocialized behavior, including temper tantrums, fighting, and withdrawal.

Behavior modification principles have also been used, particularly in group work with children. Behavior therapy is part of the residential center's total therapeutic effort.

Education

Children in residential treatment frequently have severe learning disorders and disruptive behavior and attention-deficit disorders. Usually, the children cannot function in a regular community school and, consequently, need a special on-grounds school. A major goal of the on-grounds school is to motivate the children to learn.

Therapy

Traditional modes of psychotherapy have a place in residential treatment, including intensive, individual psychotherapy with the child; group therapy with selected children; individual therapy or group therapy or both for the parents; and, in some cases, family therapy. However, several modifications need to be kept in mind.

The child relates to the total staff of the setting and, therefore, needs to know that what transpires in the therapist's office is shared with all professional staff members. The therapist informs the child that what they discuss and do in individual therapy will not be revealed to other family members or to other children in the residential center but will be shared with the professional staff members within the setting itself.

Parents

Concomitant work with the parents is essential. The child usually has a strong tie to at least one parent, no matter how disturbed the parent is. Sometimes the child idealizes the parent, who repeatedly fails the child. Sometimes the parent has an ambivalent or unrealistic expectation that the child will return home. Sometimes the parent must be helped to enable the child to live in another setting when that is in the child's best interests. Most residential treatment centers offer individual or group therapy for the parents, couples or marital therapy, and in some cases conjoint family therapy.

DAY TREATMENT

The concept of daily comprehensive therapeutic experiences without removing the children from their homes or families derived in part from experiences with a therapeutic nursery school. The development of day hospital programs for children followed, and the number of programs continues to grow.

The main advantage of day treatment is that the children remain with their families, and so the families can be more involved in day treatment than in residential treatment or hospital treatment. Day treatment is also much less expensive than residential treatment. At the same time, the risks of day treatment are the child's social isolation and confinement to a narrow band of social contacts within the program's disturbed peer population.

Indications

The primary indication for day treatment is the need for a more structured, intensive, and specialized treatment program than can be provided on an outpatient basis. Simultaneously, the home in which the child is living should be able to provide an environment that is at least not destructive to the child's development. Children who are likely to benefit from day treatment may have a wide range of diagnoses, including autistic disorder, conduct disorder, attention-deficit/hyperactivity disorder, and mental retardation. Exclusion symptoms include behavior that is likely to be destructive to the children themselves or to others under the treatment conditions. Thus, some children who threaten to run away, set fires, attempt suicide, hurt others, or disrupt to a significant degree the lives of their families while they are at home may not be suitable for day treatment.

Programs

The same ingredients that lead to a successful residential treatment program apply to day treatment. Those ingredients include clear administrative leadership, team collaboration, open communication, and an understanding of the children's behavior. Indeed, having a single agency offer both residential and day treatment has advantages.

A major function of the child care staff in day treatment for psychiatrically disturbed children is to provide positive experiences and a structure that will enable the children and their families to internalize controls and to function better than in the past regarding themselves and the outside world. Again, the methods used are essentially similar to those found in the full residential treatment program.

Because the ages, needs, and range of diagnoses of children who may benefit from some form of day treatment vary, many day treatment programs have been developed. Some programs specialize in the special educational and structured environmental needs of mentally retarded children. Others offer the special therapeutic efforts required to treat autistic and schizophrenic children. Still other programs provide the total spectrum of treatment usually found in full residential treatment, of which they may be a part. The children may then move from one part of the program to another and may be in residential treatment or day treatment according to their needs. The school program is always a major component of day treatment, and the psychiatric treatment varies according to the children's needs and diagnoses.

Results

The results of day treatment have not yet been adequately evaluated. The assessment of the long-term effectiveness of day treatment is fraught with difficulties, whether one is making the assessment from the point of view of the child's maintenance of gains, the therapist's view of what has been accomplished, or society's concerns for such matters as cost-benefit ratios.

At the same time, the advantage of day treatment has encouraged further development of the programs. Moreover, the lessons learned from day treatment programs have moved the mental health disciplines toward having the services follow the children, rather than perpetuating discontinuities of care. The experiences of day treatment for the psychiatric conditions of children and adolescents have also encouraged pediatric hospitals and departments to adapt that model for the medical nursing care of children with physical disorders, particularly those with chronic physical illnesses.

HOSPITAL TREATMENT

Begun in the 1920s, inpatient psychiatric treatment of children includes two types of units: acute-care hospital units and long-term hospital units. Acute-care units generally accept children manifesting dangerous—that is, suicidal, assaultive, or psychotically disorganized—behavior. Diagnosis, stabilization, and the formulation and the initiation of a treatment plan are the goals of acute-care units. Disposition is usually to home, to residential treatment centers, or to long-term (usually state) hospitals for continued care. Acute-care hospitalization generally lasts from 6 to 12 weeks and is often extended because of the wait for beds in residential treatment centers and state hospitals. Long-term hospitalization generally lasts many months to years. The staffs on inpatient units are interdisciplinary, including psychiatrists, psychologists, social workers, nurses, activity therapists, and teachers.

References

Gold J, Shera D, Clarkson B: Private psychiatric hospitalization of children: Predictors of length of stay. J Am Acad Child Adolesc Psychiatry 32: 135, 1993.
Grizenko N, Papineau D, Sayegh L: Effectiveness of a multimodal day treatment program for children with disruptive behavior problems. J Am Acad Child Adolesc Psychiatry 32: 127, 1993.
Husain S A: Residential and inpatient treatment. In Comprehensive Textbook of Psychiatry, ed 6, H I Kaplan, B J Sadock, editors, p 2434. Williams & Wilkins, Baltimore, 1995.
Kiser L J, Heston J D, Pruitt D B: Partial hospitalization. In Comprehensive Textbook of Psychiatry, ed 6, H I Kaplan, B J Sadock, editors, p 2428. Williams & Wilkins, Baltimore, 1995.
Mikkelsen E J, Bereika G M, McKenzie J C: Short-term family-based residential treatment: An alternative to psychiatric hospitalization for children. Am J Orthopsychiatry 63: 28, 1993.
Perrin E C: Children in hospitals. J Dev Behav Pediatr 14: 50, 1993.

43.4 BIOLOGICAL THERAPIES

PHARMACOTHERAPY

In the 1990s, several interests and concerns about child and adolescent psychopharmacotherapy are particularly important, including the use of serotonin-specific reuptake inhibitors (SSRIs) in almost every childhood mental disorder. For example, will early-onset major depressive disorder respond better to SSRIs than to tricyclic drugs? Researchers are still trying to determine why tricyclic drugs seem ineffective in early-onset major depressive disorder. Another concern is the safety of medications, particularly tricyclic drugs, whose cardiotoxicity may have contributed to the mysterious deaths of four children who were taking desipramine (Norpramin). In addition, the management of disruptive behavior and attention-deficit disorders is a challenge. Multiple drugs are sometimes used in those cases, although few studies attest to the efficacy or the safety of the drug combinations used.

The goals of pediatric psychopharmacotherapy have not changed. One aim is to decrease maladaptive behaviors and promote adaptive behaviors in such areas as school performance. To accomplish that end, the clinician must try to avoid cognitive dulling. The medications used in pediatric psychopharmacotherapy are often associated with a specific disorder or target symptoms that appear in several disorders. For example, haloperidol (Haldol) is used to treat Tourette's disorder and also severe aggression, which may occur in many disorders.

Therapeutic Considerations

The evaluation for psychopharmacotherapy must first include an assessment of the child's psychopathology and physical condition to rule out any predisposition for adverse effects (Table 43.4–1). An assessment of the child's caretakers focuses on their ability to provide a safe and consistent environment in which the clinician can conduct a drug trial. The physician must consider the benefit-risk ratio and must explain it to the patient, if old enough, and to the child's caretakers and for others (for example, child welfare workers) who may be involved in the decision to medicate.

The clinician must obtain baseline ratings before medicating. Behavioral rating scales help objectify the child's response to medication. The physician generally starts at a low dosage and titrates upward on the basis of the child's response and the appearance of adverse effects. Optimal drug trials cannot be rushed (for example, by insurance-imposed inadequately short hospital stays or infrequent outpatient visits), nor can drug trials be prolonged by insufficient contact of the physician with the patient and the caretakers. The success of drug trials often hinges on the daily accessibility of the physician.

Childhood Pharmacokinetics

Children, compared with adults, have greater hepatic capacity, more glomerular filtration, and less fatty tissue. Therefore, stimulants, antipsychotics, and tricyclic drugs are eliminated more rapidly by children than by adults; lithium (Eskalith) may be eliminated more rapidly, and children may have less ability to store drugs in their fat. Because of children's quick elimination, the half-lives of many medications may be shorter in children than in adults.

Little evidence suggests that the clinician can predict a child's blood level from the dosage or predict a child's treatment

Table 43.4–1.   Common Psychoactive Drugs in Childhood and Adolescence

Drugs	Indications	Dosage	Adverse Reactions and Monitoring
Antipsychotics—also known as major tranquilizers, neuroleptics. Divided into (1) high-potency, low-dosage, e.g., haloperidol (Haldol), trifluoperazine (Stelazine), Thiothixene (Navane); (2) low-potency, high-dosage (more sedating), e.g., chlorpromazine (Thorazine), thioridazine (Mellaril); (3) clozapine (Clozaril); and (4) risperidone (Risperdal)	Psychoses; agitated, aggressive, self-injurious behaviors in mental retardation (MR), pervasive developmental disorders (PDD), and conduct disorder (CD) Studies support following indications: haloperidol—schizophrenia, PDD, CD with severe aggression, Tourette's disorder Clozapine—refractory schizophrenia in adolescence Risperidone—anecdotal reports of success in PDD	All can be given in two to four divided doses or combined into one dose after gradual buildup Haloperidol—child 0.5–6 mg a day, adolescent 0.5–16 mg a day Thiothixene—5–42 mg a day Chlorpromazine and thloridazine—child 10–200 mg a day, adolescent 50–600 mg a day, over 16 years of age 100–700 mg a day Clozapine—dosage not determined in children; <600 mg a day in adolescents Risperidone—1–3 mg a day in several children with PDD	Sedation, weight gain, hypotension, lowered seizure threshold, constipation, extrapyramidal symptoms, jaundice, agranulocytosis, dystonic reaction, tardive dyskinesia; with clozapine, no extrapyramidal adverse effects Monitor: blood pressure, complete blood count (CBC), liver function tests (LFTs), electroencephalogram, if indicated; with thioridazine pigmentary retinopathy is rare but dictates ceiling of 800 mg in adults and proportionately lower in children; with clozapine, weekly white blood counts (WBCs) for development of agranulocytosis and electroencephalogram (EEG) monitoring due to lowering of seizure threshold
Stimulants Dextroamphetamine (Dexedrine) FDA-approved for children 3 years and older Methylphenidate (Ritalin) and pemoline (Cylert) FDA-approved for children 6 years and older	In attention-deficit/hyperactivity disorder (ADHD) for hyperactivity, impulsivity, and inattentiveness	Dextroamphetamine and methylphenidate are generally given at 8 AM and noon (the usefulness of sustained-release preparations is not proved) Dextroamphetamine—2.5–40 mg a day up to 0.5 mg per kg a day Methylphenidate—10–60 mg a day or up to 1.0 mg per kg a day Pemoline—37.5–112.5 mg given at 8 AM	Insomnia, anorexia, weight loss (and possibly growth delay), headache, tachycardia, precipitation or exacerbation of tic disorders With pemoline, monitor LFTs, as hepatoxicity is possible

(continued)

Table 43.4–1. *(continued)*

Drugs	Indications	Dosage	Adverse Reactions and Monitoring
Lithium—considered an antipsychotic drug, also has antiaggression properties	Studies support use in MR and CD for aggressive and self-injurious behaviors; can be used for same in PDD; also indicated for early-onset bipolar I disorder	600–2, 100 mg in two or three divided doses; keep serum concentrations to 0.4–1.2 mEq per L	Nausea, vomiting, enuresis, headache, tremor, weight gain, hypothyroidism Experience with adults suggests renal function monitoring
Tricyclic drugs Imipramine (Tofranil) has been used in most child studies Nortriptyline (Pamelor) has been studied in children Clomipramine (Anafranil) is effective in child obsessive-compulsive disorder (OCD)	Major depressive disorder, separation anxiety disorder, bulimia nervosa, enuresis; sometimes used in ADHD, sleepwalking disorder, and sleep terror disorder Clomipramine is effective in child OCD and sometimes in PDD.	Imipramine—start with divided dosages totalling about 1.5 mg per kg a day; can build up to not more than 5 mg per kg a day and eventually combine in one dose; not FDA-approved for children except for enuresis; dosage is usually 50–100 mg before sleep Clomipramine—start at 50 mg a day; can raise to not more than 3 mg per kg a day or 200 mg a day	Dry mouth, constipation, tachycardia, drowsiness, postural hypotension, hypertension, mania Electrocardiogram (ECG) monitoring is needed because of risk for cardiac conduction slowing; consider lowering dosage if PR interval >0.20 seconds or QRS interval >0.12 seconds; baseline EEG is advised, as it can lower seizure threshold (especially with clomipramine); blood levels of drug are sometimes useful
Serotonin-specific reuptake inhibitors—fluoxetine (Prozac) sertraline (Zoloft), and fluvoxamine (Luvox)	OCD: may be useful in major depressive disorder anorexia, bulimia nervosa, repetetive behaviors in MR or PDD	Appears less than adult dosages	Nausea, headache, nervousness, insomnia, dry mouth, diarrhea, drowsiness
Carbamazepine (Tegretol)—an anticonvulsant	Aggression or dyscontrol in MR or CD, bipolar disorder	Start with 10 mg per kg a day; can build to 20–30 mg per kg a day; therapeutic serum concentration range appears to be 4–12 mg per L	Drowsiness, nausea, rash, vertigo, irritability Monitor: CBC and LFTs for possible blood dyscrasias and hepatotoxicity; blood levels are necessary
Benzodiazepines—have been insufficiently studied in childhood and adolescence	Sometimes effective in parasomnias: sleepwalking disorder or sleep terror disorder; can be tried in generalized anxiety disorder Clonazepam (Klonopin) can be tried in all anxiety disorders, especially panic disorder Alprazolam (Xanax) can be tried in separation anxiety disorder	Parasomnias: diazepam (Valium) 2–10 mg before bedtime	Can cause drowsiness, ataxia, tremor, dyscontrol; can be abused
Fenfluramine (Pondimin)—an amphetamine congener	Well-studied in autistic disorder; generally ineffective, but some patients show improvement	Gradually increase to 1.0–1.5 mg per kg a day in divided doses	Weight loss, drowsiness, irritability, loose bowel movements
Propranolol (Inderal)—a β-adrenergic receptor antagonist	Aggression in MR, PDD, and cognitive disorder; awaits controlled studies	Effective dosage in children and adolescents is not yet established; range is probably 40–320 mg a day	Bradycardia, hypotension, nausea, hypoglycemia, depression; avoid in asthma
Clonidine (Catapres)—a presynaptic α-adrenergic blocking agent	Some success in ADHD; clonidine in Tourette's disorder	Clonidine—0.1–0.3 mg a day; 3–5.5 µg per kg a day Guanfacine—up to 3 mg a day	Orthostatic hypotension, sedation, dry mouth
Cyproheptadine (Periactin)	Anorexia nervosa	Dosages up to 8 mg four times a day	Antihistaminic side effects, including sedation and dryness of the mouth
Naltrexone (ReVia)	Self-injurious behaviors in MR and PDD; currently being studied in PDD	0.5–2.0 mg per kg a day	Sleepiness, aggressivity Monitor LFTs, as hepatotoxicity has been reported in adults at high dosages
Desmopressin (DDAVP)	Nocturnal enuresis	20–40 µg intranasally	Headache; hyponatremic seizures (rare)

Table by Richard Perry, MD.

response from the plasma level. Relatively low serum levels of haloperidol appear adequate to treat Tourette's disorder in children. No correlation is seen between methylphenidate (Ritalin) serum level and the child's response. The data are incomplete and conflicting about major depressive disorder and serum levels of tricyclic drugs. A serum-level-to-response relation has been found for tricyclics in the treatment of enuresis.

With lithium therapy, a saliva-to-serum-lithium ratio can be established for a child by averaging three to four individual ratios. The average ratio can then be used to convert subsequent saliva levels to serum levels and thus avoid some venipunctures in children who are stressed by blood tests. As with serum levels, regular clinical monitoring for adverse side effects is necessary.

Table 43.4–1 lists representative drugs and their indications, dosages, adverse reactions, and monitoring requirements.

Indications

MENTAL RETARDATION

The psychopharmacotherapy for mental retardation most often addresses behavioral problems, especially aggression, and the coexistence of other mental disorders. Medications are overused to control the behavior of institutionalized retarded children because other therapies and services are not available. For severe aggression, antipsychotics are most commonly used, and cognitive dulling can best be avoided with high-potency drugs. β-Adrenergic receptor antagonists have reduced aggression in uncontrolled studies of adults and children with mental retardation. Lithium and anticonvulsants such as carbamazepine (Tegretol) may also be tried.

Antipsychotics have the advantage of a fast onset of action and little need for laboratory monitoring of their side effects. However, the use of other drugs eliminates the risk for tardive dyskinesia.

The endogenous opioid antagonists, such as naltrexone (ReVia), and the serotonin-specific reuptake inhibitors, such as fluoxetine (Prozac), reduce self-injurious behavior in some patients with mental retardation. When attention-deficit/hyperactivity disorder coexists with mental retardation, methylphenidate is often effective, and a small study showed behavioral improvements with fenfluramine (Pondimin).

Recent attempts have been made to treat the behavioral problems associated with fragile X syndrome with folic acid supplements. Some prepubescent children experienced less active or less aggressive behavior and concentrated better when they took folic acid than they did before treatment.

LEARNING DISORDERS

No pharmacological agent significantly improves any learning disorder. However, many children with other mental disorders also have learning disorders, and many who have learning disorders also have behavioral problems. Those associations and the importance of school and learning in children's lives raise questions about the cognitive effects of psychotropics.

In children with learning disorders but no other mental disorder, methylphenidate facilitates performance on several standard cognitive, psycholinguistic, memory, and vigilance tests but does not improve the child's academic achievement ratings or teacher ratings. Cognitive impairment from psychotropic drugs, especially antipsychotics, may be an even greater problem in mentally retarded persons than in those with learning disorders.

AUTISTIC DISORDER

The behavioral problems of children with autistic disorder can be extreme. In short-term and long-term studies, haloperidol, often in nonsedating dosages, has proved to be efficacious in reducing temper tantrums, aggression, stereotypies, self-injurious behavior, hyperactivity, and withdrawal. However, dyskinesia is a risk. In recent years the serotonin-specific reuptake inhibitors have been studied in autistic disorder as researchers posited an association between the compulsive behaviors in obsessive-compulsive disorder and the stereotypic behaviors common in autistic children. To date, clomipramine (Anafranil) and fluoxetine have shown promise in ending stereotypies and other behaviors in autistic children and adults.

The opioid antagonists naloxone (Narcan) and naltrexone are effective in reducing self-injurious behavior in some autistic children. However, to what degree other behaviors are benefited is not yet clear. Improvements appear to be modest.

The behavioral difficulties of autistic children can be difficult to manage. Much effort, firmness, and consistency are required from caretakers. The psychiatrist may need to try many medications. β-Blockers, lithium, or anticonvulsants may be helpful. Polypharmacy is not unusual but has not been formally studied. Stimulants can be tried to reduce hyperactivity and inattentiveness in relatively manageable autistic children.

ATTENTION-DEFICIT/HYPERACTIVITY DISORDER

Studies in recent years continue to support the use of stimulants in the treatment of attention-deficit/hyperactivity disorder. The most frequently researched and used stimulant is methylphenidate. Dextroamphetamine (Dexedrine) is of comparable efficacy and, unlike methylphenidate, is approved by the Food and Drug Administration (FDA) for children 3 years and older, whereas the starting age for methylphenidate is 6 years. Pemoline (Cylert) is a less effective but longer-acting stimulant that carries a small risk for hepatotoxicity. Stimulants reduce the hyperactivity, inattentiveness, and impulsivity in about 75 percent of children with attention-deficit/hyperactivity disorder. The effects are not paradoxical, as normal children respond similarly.

Attention-deficit/hyperactivity disorder often coexists with oppositional defiant disorder or conduct disorder. With those added disorders comes aggression; in some cases stimulants appear to reduce aggression. However, a common mistake is to prolong stimulant trials when the aggression is not subsiding and when a switch to or the addition of a more specifically antiaggression drug is indicated.

In those children with attention-deficit/hyperactivity disorder in which stimulants are ineffective and in children with preexisting tic disorders, antidepressants can be tried. Desipramine has proven to be effective in studies, but its use is limited because four children who took desipramine died suddenly. Other tricyclic drugs, including nortriptyline (Pamelor) and clomipramine, have been tried successfully. The response of children with attention-deficit/hyperactivity disorder to antidepressants can occur within days of the beginning of treatment.

Clonidine (Catapres) has also been tried with some success in attention-deficit/hyperactivity disorder in a few studies. Antipsychotics can be used to treat attention-deficit/hyperactivity disorder but only after other treatments have failed because of the risks for sedation and tardive dyskinesia.

Attention-deficit/hyperactivity disorder often precedes and then coexists with tic disorders. Chapter 37 discusses the pharmacotherapy for the child who has the two conditions.

The dietary management of hyperactivity has received a great amount of public attention, but controlled studies have not proved its benefit. Similarly, in most controlled studies, caffeine was not found superior to a placebo for attention-deficit/hyperactivity disorder.

CONDUCT DISORDER

The assaultiveness that is frequently associated with conduct disorder is targeted by pharmacotherapy. Antipsychotics such as haloperidol can quell aggression, but sedation and the risk of tardive dyskinesia are major drawbacks. Lithium has reduced aggression in conduct disorder, and propranolol (Inderal) and carbamazepine have been effective in open studies.

When conduct disorder is associated with attention-deficit/hyperactivity disorder and when the aggression is mild, a trial of a stimulant may be indicated, as stimulants are faster acting and easier to monitor than the drugs noted above. Clonidine may be effective and deserves further study.

The aggression associated with conduct disorder is often difficult to get under control, leading to the use of polypharmacy. No studies have demonstrated the benefits of that approach.

TIC DISORDERS

The strongly antidopaminergic antipsychotics haloperidol and pimozide (Orap) remain the most effective medications for Tourette's disorder. Pimozide prolongs the QT interval, requiring electrocardiographic monitoring. Clonidine, a presynaptic α-adrenergic blocking agent, is less effective than the two antipsychotics but avoids the risk for tardive dyskinesia; sedation is a frequent adverse effect of clonidine.

Tic disorders often coexist with attention-deficit/hyperactivity disorder in children and adolescents. Stimulants, which can precipitate tics, should be avoided in those cases, although recent studies indicate that the prohibition may not be totally warranted. Clonidine reduces tics in both attention-deficit/hyperactivity disorder and the comorbid cases. A small study supports the use of nortriptyline.

ENURESIS

Before initiating psychopharmacotherapy in the treatment of enuresis, the clinician has to consider the merits of waiting for a possible spontaneous remission and of using behavioral techniques; bell-and-pad conditioning (a bell awakens the child when the mattress becomes wet) is perhaps the most elaborate behavioral treatment and seems more successful than medications.

Tricyclic drugs are effective in reducing enuresis in about 60 percent of enuretic patients, and desmopressin (DDAVP) is effective in about 50 percent of enuretic patients. Improvement ranges from complete cessation of wetting to continued wetting but with less urine volume. Tricyclic drugs are given about one hour before bedtime. The starting dosage is usually 25 mg a day, a lower dosage than that used in trials for depression. One can increase the dosage to 75 mg a day for an adolescent, but the dosage should not exceed 2 mg per kg a day. The child usually responds within days. Desmopressin is taken intranasally in dosages of 10 to 40 mg a day. When used over months, nasal discomfort can occur. Water retention is potentially a problem. Those patients who respond with full dryness should continue to take the medication for several months to prevent relapses.

SEPARATION ANXIETY DISORDER

Few studies support the use of anxiolytics in pediatric psychopharmacology. A recent double-blind, placebo-controlled study did not replicate a similar study done by the same workers 20 years before, when imipramine (Tofranil) was shown to be effective for school refusal. Alprazolam (Xanax) may be helpful in separation anxiety disorder, but the data are conflicting.

SCHIZOPHRENIA

Antipsychotics are commonly used for schizophrenia in childhood and adolescence. However, only two double-blind studies showed a modest effectiveness of antipsychotics in adolescent schizophrenia and only one of those studies was placebo-controlled. In the only double-blind placebo-controlled study of childhood schizophrenia, haloperidol was significantly superior to the placebo. Schizophrenia with onset in late adolescence is treated like adult-onset schizophrenia.

MOOD DISORDERS

Tricyclic drugs have not been shown to be superior to a placebo in double-blind, placebo-controlled studies of children and adolescents with major depressive disorder. In children, developmental differences in neurotransmitters and neuroendocrine systems may be associated with responses to antidepressants. In any case, the 1990s will undoubtedly see a number of studies of serotonin-specific reuptake inhibitors in the treatment of early-onset major depressive disorder.

Most researchers still advocate a trial of antidepressant medication in severe, prolonged major depressive disorder. However, because of their potential cardiotoxic effects, tricyclic drugs require a knowledge of appropriate dosing, electrocardiographic monitoring, and circumspection about prescribing the drugs to those at risk for suicide.

Manic episodes in childhood and adolescence are treated as they are in adults. No double-blind, placebo-controlled studies have demonstrated the effectiveness of lithium in treating adolescent mania.

OBSESSIVE-COMPULSIVE DISORDER

In a growing number of studies, clomipramine has proved to be effective in diminishing obsessions and compulsions in children and adolescents. Fluoxetine has been studied less than clomipramine but also appears effective. Clomipramine is generally well tolerated. The side effects of fluoxetine appear more frequent, bothersome, and dramatic than the adverse effects of clomipramine. Other serotonin-specific reuptake inhibitors will probably be studied for their use in the treatment of early-onset obsessive-compulsive disorder.

EATING DISORDERS

Pharmacotherapy has little to offer in the treatment of anorexia nervosa. Cyproheptadine (Periactin) benefits some anorectic patients, and antidepressants may benefit those with comorbid depressive disorders. However, the compromised metabolism of many anorectic patients can put them at a high risk for cardiac arrhythmias if tricyclic drugs are administered.

Many antidepressants—imipramine, desipramine, trazodone (Desyrel), fluoxetine, and monoamine oxidase inhibitors (MAOIs)—reduce the binge eating and purging in bulimia nervosa. Bupropion (Wellbutrin) in one large study of bulimic nervosa patients was associated with a dramatic incidence of seizures.

SLEEP TERROR DISORDER AND SLEEPWALKING DISORDER

Sleep terror disorder and sleepwalking disorder occur in the transition from deep delta-wave sleep (stages 3 and 4) to light sleep. Benzodiazepines and tricyclic drugs are effective in those disorders. They work by reducing both delta-wave sleep and the arousals between sleep stages. The medications should be used temporarily and in only severe cases, because tolerance to the medications develops, cessation of the medications can lead to severe rebound worsening of the disorders, and reducing delta sleep in children may have deleterious effects. Therefore, behavioral approaches are preferred in both disorders.

ANXIETY DISORDERS

Buspirone (BuSpar) has been effective in an open trial of adolescents suffering from generalized anxiety disorder. Patients with early-onset panic disorder and panic attacks have benefited from clonazepam (Klonopin) in several open trials.

Adverse Effects and Complications

ANTIDEPRESSANTS

The adverse effects of antidepressants in children are usually similar to those in adults and result from the antidepressants' anticholinergic properties. The adverse effects include dry mouth, constipation, palpitations, tachycardia, loss of accommodation, and sweating. The most serious adverse effects are cardiovascular, although, in children, diastolic hypertension is more common, and postural hypotension occurs more rarely than in adults. Electrocardiographic (ECG) changes are most apt to be seen in children receiving high dosages. Slowed cardiac conduction (PR interval >0.20 seconds or QRS interval >0.12) may require lowering the dosage. FDA guidelines limit dosages to a maximum of 5 mg per kg a day. The drug can be toxic in an overdose, and, in small children, ingestions of 200 to 400 mg can be fatal. When the dosage is lowered too rapidly, withdrawal effects are manifested mainly by gastrointestinal symptoms: cramping, nausea, vomiting, and sometimes apathy and weakness. The treatment is a slower tapering of the dosage.

ANTIPSYCHOTICS

The best studied of the antipsychotics given to pediatric-age groups are chlorpromazine (Thorazine), thioridazine (Mellaril), and haloperidol. High-potency and low-potency antipsychotics are believed to differ in their side-effect profiles. The phenothiazine derivatives (chlorpromazine and thioridazine) have the most pronounced sedative and atropinic actions, whereas the high-potency antipsychotics are commonly thought to be associated with extrapyramidal reactions, such as parkinsonian symptoms, akathisia, and acute dystonias. Caution is warranted in assuming that those things are also true in children. In particular, when comparisons are made at low-dosage levels of equivalent potency, differences may not be detected.

Even if the frequency of adverse effects differs among the antipsychotics, the drugs always cause them. Evidence in children of impaired cognitive function and, most important, of tardive dyskinesia calls for great caution in the use of antipsychotic drugs. Tardive dyskinesia—which is characterized by persistent abnormal involuntary movements of the tongue, the face, the mouth, or the jaw and may also involve the extremities—is a known hazard when giving antipsychotics to patients of all age groups. No known treatment is effective. Tardive dyskinesia has not been reported in patients taking less than 375 to 400 grams of chlorpromazine equivalents. Because nonpersistent choreiform movements of the extremities and the trunk are common after an abrupt discontinuation of antipsychotics, the clinician must distinguish those symptoms from persistent dyskinesias.

Whenever clinically feasible, children receiving antipsychotics should be periodically withdrawn from the medication, so that the clinician can assess the patient's current clinical need and the possible development of tardive dyskinesia.

STIMULANTS

Problems with retarded growth associated with taking stimulants have been reported, although little evidence for the problems is available. The current thinking is that any growth suppression is temporary and that children taking stimulants will eventually reach their normal height.

OTHER BIOLOGICAL THERAPIES

Electroconvulsive therapy (ECT) is not indicated in childhood or adolescence. Psychosurgery for severe and intransigent obsessive-compulsive disorder should probably be delayed until adulthood, after all attempts at less drastic treatment have failed and when the patient can participate fully in the process of informed consent.

Little evidence indicates that food allergies or sensitivities play a role in childhood mental disorders. Diets that eliminate food additives, colorings, and sugar are difficult to maintain and usually have no effect. Megavitamin therapy is usually ineffective (unless the child has a frank vitamin deficiency) and can cause adverse effects.

References

Aman M G, Kern R A, McGhee O E, Arnold L E A: Fenfluramine and methylphenidate in children with mental retardation and ADHD: Clinical and side effects. J Am Acad Child Adolesc Psychiatry 32: 851, 1993.
Gordon C T, State R C, Nelson J E, Hamburger S D, Rapoport J L: A double-blind comparison of clomipramine, desipramine, and placebo in the treatment of autistic disorder. Arch Gen Psychiatry 50: 441, 1993.
Popper C W: Pharmacotherapy. In Comprehensive Textbook of Psychiatry, ed 6, H I Kaplan, B J Sadock, editors, p 2418. Williams & Wilkins, Baltimore, 1995.
Ratey J J, Gordon A: The psychopharmacology of aggression: Toward a new day. Psychopharmacol Bull 29: 65, 1993.
Riddle M A, Geller B, Rayn N: Another sudden death in a child treated with desipramine. J Am Acad Child Adolesc Psychiatry 32: 792, 1993.
Spencer T, Biederman J, Wilens T, Steingard R, Geist D: Nortriptyline treatment of children with attention-deficit hyperactivity disorder and tic disorder or Tourette's syndrome. J Am Acad Child Adolesc Psychiatry 32: 205, 1993.
Steingard R, Biederman J, Spencer T, Wilens T, Gonzalez A: Comparison of clonidine response in the treatment of attention-deficit hyperactivity disorder with and without comorbid tic disorders. J Am Acad Child Adolesc Psychiatry 32: 350, 1993.

43.5 PSYCHIATRIC TREATMENT OF ADOLESCENTS

Adolescence is a time when environmental demands increase and many serious mental disorders have their onset. Schizophrenia, bipolar I disorder, and the risk for completed suicide—all drastically increase during adolescence. Although some degree of stress is virtually universal during adolescence, most teenagers without mental disorders can cope well with the environmental demands. Those teenagers with preexisting mental disorders may have exacerbations during adolescence and become frustrated, alienated, and demoralized.

One must be sensitive to adolescents' perceptions of themselves, since a range of emotional maturity exists within a group of same-aged teenagers. Issues that are specific to adolescents are related to their new evolving identities, the development of sexual activities, and their plans to meet future life goals.

DIAGNOSIS

Adolescents can be assessed in both their specific stage-appropriate functions and their general progress in accomplishing the tasks of adolescence. For almost all adolescents in today's culture, at least until their late teens, school performance is the prime barometer of healthy functioning. Intellectually normal adolescents who are not functioning satisfactorily in some form of schooling have significant psychological problems whose nature and causes should be identified.

Questions to be asked regarding adolescents' stage-specific tasks are the following: What degree of separation from their parents have adolescents achieved? What sort of identities are evolving? How do they perceive their past? Do they perceive themselves as responsible for their own development or as only the passive recipients of their parents' influences? How do they perceive themselves regarding the future, and how do they anticipate future responsibilities for themselves and others? Can they think about the consequences of various ways of living? How do they express their sexual and affectionate interest? Those tasks occupy all adolescents and normally are performed at varying times.

Adolescents' object relations must be evaluated. Do they perceive and accept both the good and the bad qualities in their parents? Do they see their peers and boyfriends or girlfriends as separate persons with needs and identities of their own, or do they exist only for the patients' needs?

A respect for and, if possible, some actual understanding of the adolescent's subcultural and ethnic background are essential. For example, in some groups, depression is acceptable; in other groups, overt depression is a sign of weakness and is masked by antisocial acts, substance misuse, and self-destructive risks. However, a psychiatrist need not be of the same race or group identity as the adolescent to be effective. Respect and knowledgeable concern are human qualities, not group-restricted qualities.

INTERVIEWS

Whenever circumstances permit, both the adolescent patient and the parents should be interviewed. Other family members may also have to be included, depending on their degree of involvement in the youngster's life and difficulties. However, the clinician should see the adolescent first; that preferential treatment helps avoid the appearance of being the parents' agent.

In psychotherapy for an older adolescent, the therapist and the parents usually have little contact after the initial part of the therapy, because ongoing contact inhibits the adolescent's desire to open up.

Interview Techniques

All patients test and mistrust the therapist, but in adolescents those manifestations are likely to be crude, intense, provocative, and prolonged. Clinicians must establish themselves as trustworthy and helpful adults to promote a therapeutic alliance. They should have the adolescents tell their own stories, without interrupting to check out discrepancies, as that will sound like correcting and disbelief. Clinicians should obtain explanations and theories from the patients about what happened, why those behaviors or feelings occurred, when things changed, and what caused the identified problems to begin when they did.

Sessions with adolescents generally follow the adult model of the therapist's sitting across from the patient. However, in early adolescence board games (for example, checkers) may be helpful in stimulating conversation in an otherwise quiet, anxious patient.

Language is crucial. Even when a teenager and a clinician come from the same socioeconomic group, their languages are seldom the same. Psychiatrists should use their own language, explain any specialized terms or concepts, and ask for an explanation of unfamiliar in-group jargon or slang.

Many adolescents do not talk spontaneously about illicit substances and suicidal tendencies but do respond honestly to the therapist's questions. The therapist may need to ask specifically about each substance and the amount and the frequency of its use.

Adolescents' sexual histories and current sexual activities are increasingly important pieces of information for adequate evaluation. The nature of adolescents' sexual behaviors is often a vignette of their whole personality structures and ego development. However, a long time in therapy may pass before adolescents begin to talk about their sexual behavior.

TREATMENT

Usually, no single therapy modality is specific to a particular disorder. The best choice, then, is often what best fits the characteristics of the individual adolescent and the family or social milieu. Adolescents' real dependence needs may press clinicians to strive to maintain even the sickest youngster in a satisfactory home. But for the same reason, clinicians may be forced to remove adolescents from pathogenic homes, even when the severity of the illness alone does not dictate it, because the youngsters are not developmentally capable of handling the double burden of working to overcome their illness and being traumatized at home. Also, adolescents' striving for autonomy may so complicate problems of compliance with therapy that they force involuntary inpatient treatment of difficulties for which such treatment may not be necessary at a different stage of life. Thus, the following discussion is less a set of guidelines than a brief summary of what each treatment modality can or should offer.

Individual Psychotherapy

Few, if any, adolescent patients are trusting or open without considerable time and testing, and so it is helpful to anticipate the testing period by letting patients know that it is to be expected and is natural and healthy. Pointing out the likelihood of therapeutic problems—for instance, impatience and disappointment with the psychiatrist, with the therapy, with the time required, and with the often intangible results—may help keep the problems under control. Therapeutic goals should be stated in terms that adolescents understand and value. Although they may not see the point in exercising self-control, enduring dysphoric emotions, or foregoing impulsive gratification, they may value feeling more confident than in the past and gaining more control over their lives and the events that affect them.

Typical adolescent patients need a real relationship with a therapist whom they can perceive as a real person. The therapist becomes another parent, because adolescents still need appropriate parenting or reparenting. Thus, the professional who is impersonal and anonymous is a less useful model than is one who can accept and respond rationally to an angry challenge or confrontation without fear or false conciliation, can impose limits and controls when the adolescents cannot, can admit mistakes and ignorance, and can openly express the gamut of human emotions. The failure to take a stand regarding self-damaging and self-destructive behavior or a passive response to manipulative and dishonest behavior is perceived as indifference or collusion.

Countertransference reactions can be intense in psychotherapeutic work with an adolescent, and the therapist must be aware of them. The adolescent often expresses hostile feelings toward adults, such as parents and teachers. The therapist may react with an overidentification with the adolescent or with the parents. Such reactions are determined, at least in part, by the therapist's own experiences during adolescence or, when applicable, by the therapist's own experiences as a parent.

Individual outpatient therapy is appropriate for adolescents whose problems are manifested in conflicted emotions and non-dangerous behavior, who are not too disorganized to be maintained outside a structured setting, and whose families or other living environments are not so disturbed as to negate the influence of therapy. Such therapy characteristically focuses on intrapsychic conflicts and inhibitions; on the meanings of emotions, attitudes, and behavior; and on the influence of the past and the present.

Antianxiety agents can be considered in adolescents whose anxiety may be high at certain times during psychotherapy. However, the adolescent's potential for abusing those drugs must be carefully weighed.

Group Psychotherapy

In many ways group psychotherapy is a natural setting for adolescents. Most teenagers are more comfortable with peers than with adults. A group diminishes the sense of unequal power between the adult therapist and the adolescent patient. Participation varies, depending on the adolescent's readiness. Not all interpretations and confrontations need come from the parent-figure therapist; group members are often adept at picking up symptomatic behavior in one another, and adolescents may find it easier to hear and consider critical or challenging comments from their peers.

Group psychotherapy usually addresses interpersonal and present life issues. However, some adolescents are too fragile for group psychotherapy or have symptoms or social traits too likely to elicit peer group ridicule: they need individual therapy to attain enough ego strength to struggle with peer relationships. Conversely, other adolescents need to resolve interpersonal issues in a group before they can tackle intrapsychic issues in the intensity of one-to-one therapy.

Family Therapy

Family therapy is the primary modality when the adolescent's difficulties are mainly a reflection of a dysfunctional family (for example, teenagers with simple school phobia, runaways). The same may be true when developmental issues, such as adolescent sexuality and striving for autonomy, trigger family conflicts. Or the family pathology may be severe, as in cases of incest and child abuse. In those instances the adolescent usually needs individual therapy as well, but family therapy is mandatory if the adolescent is to remain in the home or return to it. Serious character pathology, such as that underlying antisocial and borderline personality disorders, often develops out of highly pathogenic early parenting. Family therapy is strongly indicated whenever possible in such disorders, but most authorities consider it adjunctive to intensive individual psychotherapy when individual psychopathology has become so internalized that it persists whatever the current family status.

Inpatient Treatment

Residential treatment schools are often preferable for long-term therapy, but hospitals are more suitable for emergencies, although some adolescent inpatient hospital units also provide educational, recreational, and occupational facilities for long-term patients. Adolescents whose families are too disturbed or incompetent, who are dangerous to themselves or others, who are out of control in ways that preclude further healthy development, or who are seriously disorganized require, at least temporarily, the external controls of structured environment.

Long-term inpatient therapy is the treatment of choice for those severe disorders considered wholly or largely psychogenic in origin, such as major ego deficits caused by early massive deprivation and that respond poorly or not at all to medication. Severe borderline personality disorder, for example, whatever the behavioral symptoms, requires a full-time corrective environment in which regression is possible and safe and in which ego development can take place. Psychotic disorders in adolescence often require hospitalization, but psychotic adolescents often respond to appropriate medication, so that therapy is usually feasible in an outpatient setting except during exacerbation. Schizophrenic adolescents who show a long-term deteriorating course may require hospitalization periodically.

Day Hospitals

In day hospitals, which have become increasingly popular, the adolescent spends the day in class, individual and group psychotherapy, and other programs but goes home in the evenings. Compared with full hospitalization, day hospitals are less expensive and are usually preferred by the patients.

CLINICAL PROBLEMS

Atypical Puberty

Pubertal changes that occur $2\frac{1}{2}$ years earlier or later than the average age are within the normal range. But body image is so important to adolescents that extremes of the norm may be distressing to some, either because markedly early maturation subjects them to social and sexual pressures for which they are unready or because late maturation makes them feel inferior and excludes them from some peer activities. Medical reassurance, even if based on examination and testing to rule out pathophysiology, may be insufficient. The adolescent's distress may show as sexual or delinquent acting out, withdrawal, or problems at school of such a degree as to warrant therapeutic intervention. Therapy may also be prompted by similar disturbances in some adolescents who fail to achieve the peer-valued stereotypes of physical development, despite normal pubertal physiology.

Substance-Related Disorders

Some experimentation with psychoactive substances is almost ubiquitous among adolescents, especially if one includes alcohol. But most adolescents do not become abusers, particularly of prescription drugs and illegal substances.

Regular substance abuse of any degree represents disturbance. Substance abuse is sometimes self-medication against depression or schizophrenic deterioration and is sometimes a sign of characterological disorder in teenagers whose ego deficits render them unequal to the stresses of puberty and the tasks of adolescence. However, many substances, especially cocaine, have a physiologically reinforcing action that acts independently of preexisting psychopathology. Regardless of why the abuse developed, it becomes a problem in itself. Ego development depends on confronting and learning to cope adaptively with reality. The substances become both a substitute for reality and an avoidance of it, thus impairing ego development and perpetuating substance abuse to conceal poor coping skills.

When substance abuse covers an underlying illness or is a maladaptive response to current stresses or disturbed family dynamics, treatment of the underlying cause may take care of the substance abuse. Outpatient psychotherapy, however, is generally useless with long-term abusers, who require a structured setting where the substances are not available.

Suicide

Suicide is now the second leading cause of death among adolescents. Many hospital admissions of adolescents result from suicidal ideation or behavior. Suicide is the final common pathway for a number of disorders, and its high incidence reflects grave psychopathology. Some authorities think that in adolescence, in contrast to adulthood, schizophrenia more often underlies suicide than do major mood disorders. Among adolescents who are not psychotic, the highest suicidal risks occur in those adolescents who have a history of parental suicide, who are unable to form stable attachments, who display impulsive behavior or episodic dyscontrol, and who abuse alcohol or other substances. Many adolescent suicides show a common pattern of long-standing family and social problems throughout childhood and an escalation of subjective distress under the pressure and stresses of puberty and adolescence. That is followed by a suicide attempt precipitated by the sudden real or perceived loss of some person or social support felt to be the one source of meaning or closeness.

Normal developmental losses—of childhood dependence, of the parents, of childhood—can also cause psychogenic depression in adolescents. The rapid and extreme mood swings in adolescence, coupled with the adolescent's difficulty in seeing beyond the intensity of the moment, contribute to catastrophic despair and impulsive suicide attempts over losses that adults could weather. Moreover, alcohol and other substances can decrease the resistance to suicidal impulses. Normally persistent magical thinking may impair the sense of permanence of one's own death, allowing adolescents to contemplate suicide more lightly than do adults.

During both evaluation and treatment, suicidal thoughts, plans, and past attempts must be discussed directly when the concern arises and information is not volunteered. Long-term or recurring thoughts should be taken seriously, and an agreement or contract should be negotiated with the adolescent not to attempt suicide without first calling and talking about it with the psychiatrist. Adolescents are usually honest about making and keeping, or refusing, such agreements; if they refuse, closed hospitalization is indicated. Hospitalization is a sign of serious, protective concern and may be as therapeutic as the opportunity to conduct or plan further treatment in a safe environment.

References

Bird H R: Psychiatric treatment of adolescents. In *Comprehensive Textbook of Psychiatry*, ed 6, H I Kaplan, B J Sadock, editors, p 2439. Williams & Wilkins, Baltimore, 1995.

O'Brien J D: Current prevention concepts in child and adolescent psychiatry. Am J Psychother *45*: 261, 1991.

44/ Geriatric Psychiatry

Geriatric psychiatry is the branch of medicine concerned with the prevention, diagnosis, and treatment of physical and psychological disorders in the elderly and with the promotion of longevity. Because Americans are living longer than in the past, the number and the relative percentage of elderly persons in the general population are markedly increased. According to the 1990 United States census, the oldest old—people at least 85 years old—are the fastest-growing segment of the elderly population. Although the oldest old constitute only 1.2 percent of the total population, they have increased 232 percent since 1960. People at least 85 years old now constitute 10 percent of those 65 and older. Since 1960 the elderly population has grown 89 percent; the total population has increased 39 percent. There are 39 men for every 100 women 85 years old or older.

Geriatric psychiatry is the fastest growing field in psychiatry. The diagnosis and the treatment of mental disorders in the elderly require special knowledge because of possible differences in clinical manifestations, pathogenesis, and pathophysiology of mental disorders between young adults and the elderly. Complicating factors in elderly patients also need to be considered; those factors include the frequent presence of coexisting chronic medical diseases and disabilities, the use of many medications, and the increased susceptibility to cognitive impairment.

PSYCHIATRIC ASSESSMENT

Psychiatric history taking and the mental status examination of an elderly patient should follow the same format that applies to young adults. Because of the high prevalence of cognitive disorders in elderly patients, the psychiatrist should determine whether the patient understands the nature and the purpose of the examination. If the patient is cognitively impaired, an independent history should be obtained from a family member or caregiver. The patient should still be seen alone—even if there is clear evidence of impairment—to preserve the privacy of the doctor-patient relationship and to elicit the patient's suicidal thoughts or paranoid ideation, which may not be voiced in the presence of a relative or a nurse.

Laboratory Studies

Laboratory and imaging studies can help the clinician establish a diagnosis and detect treatable conditions, especially disorders that might otherwise be regarded as part of normal aging. Computed tomography, magnetic resonance imaging (MRI), or single photon emission computed tomography scans are probably indicated whenever a notable change in mental status occurs.

Psychiatric History

A complete psychiatric history includes the preliminary identification (name, age, sex, marital status), chief complaint, history of the present illness, history of previous illnesses, personal history, and family history. A review of the medications (including over-the-counter medications) that the patient is currently using or has used in the recent past is also important.

Patients over age 65 often have subjective complaints of minor memory impairments, such as not remembering the names of persons and misplacing objects. Those age-associated memory impairments are of no significance. Minor cognitive problems may also occur because of anxiety in the interview situation. The term "benign senescent forgetfulness" has been used to describe those phenomena.

The patient's medical history should note all major illnesses, especially seizure disorders, loss of consciousness, headaches, visual problems, and hearing loss. A history of alcohol use should be ascertained. Although substance abuse is less of a problem in the aged than in young adults, a history of prolonged substance abuse may account for current deficits.

The patient's childhood and adolescent history can provide information about personality organization and give important clues about coping strategies and defense mechanisms that the aged person may use under stress. A history of learning disability or minimal cerebral dysfunction is significant.

The psychiatrist should ask about friends, sports, hobbies, social activity, and work. The occupational history should include the patient's feelings about work, relationships with peers, problems with authority, and attitudes toward retirement. The patient should also be questioned about plans for the future. What are the patient's hopes and fears?

The family history should include the patient's description of parent's attitudes and adaptation to their old age and, if applicable, information about the causes of their deaths. Alzheimer's disease is transmitted as an autosomal dominant trait in 10 to 30 percent of the offspring of parents with Alzheimer's disease; depression and alcohol dependence also run in families. The patient's current social situation should be evaluated: Who cares for the patient? Does the patient have children? What are the characteristics of the patient-child relationships? A financial history helps the psychiatrist evaluate the role of economic hardship in the patient's illness and make realistic treatment recommendations.

The marital history includes a description of the spouse and the characteristics of the relationship. If the patient is a widow or a widower, the psychiatrist should explore how grieving was handled. If the loss of the spouse occurred within the past year, the patient is at high risk for an adverse physical or psychological event.

The patient's sex history includes sexual activity, orientation, libido, masturbation, extramarital affairs, and sexual symptoms (such as impotence and anorgasmia). Young clinicians may have to overcome their own biases about taking a sex history in the aged; however, sex is an important area of concern for many geriatric patients, who welcome the chance to talk about their sexual feelings and attitudes.

Mental Status Examination

The mental status examination is a cross-sectional view of how the patient thinks, feels, and behaves during the examination. In the aged patient, the psychiatrist may not be able to rely on a single examination to answer all the diagnostic questions. Repeat mental status examinations may have to be performed because of fluctuating changes in the patient's mental status.

The longitudinal history from the patient or the patient's family is important.

General Description

A general description of the patient includes appearance, psychomotor activity, attitude toward the examiner, and speech activity.

Motor disturbances—such as shuffling gait, stooped posture, pill-rolling movements of the fingers, tremors, and body asymmetry—should be noted. Involuntary movements of the mouth or the tongue may be side effects of phenothiazine medication. Many depressed patients appear to be slow in speech and movement. A masklike facies occurs in Parkinson's disease.

The patient's speech may be pressured in agitated, manic, and anxious states. Tearfulness and overt crying are seen in depressive disorders and cognitive disorders, especially if the patient feels frustrated about being unable to answer one of the examiner's questions. The presence of a hearing aid or some other indication that the patient has a hearing problem, such as requesting the repetition of questions, should be noted.

The patient's attitude toward the examiner—cooperative, suspicious, guarded, ingratiating—can give clues about possible transference reactions. Elderly patients can react to younger physicians as if the physicians were parent figures, in spite of the age difference, because of transference distortions.

Functional Assessment

Elderly patients should be evaluated for their capacity to maintain independence and to perform the activities of daily life. Those activities include toileting, preparing meals, dressing, grooming, and eating. The degree of functional competence in their everyday behaviors is an important consideration in formulating a plan of treatment for elderly patients.

Mood, Feelings, and Affect

Suicide is a leading cause of death in the elderly, and an evaluation of the patient's suicidal ideation is essential. Feelings of loneliness, worthlessness, helplessness, and hopelessness are symptoms of depression. Loneliness is the most common reason cited by elderly persons who consider suicide. Depression carries a high risk for suicide. Nearly 75 percent of all suicide victims suffer from depression or alcohol abuse or both. The examiner should specifically ask the patient about any thoughts of suicide, whether the patient feels life is no longer worth living, whether one is better off dead or, when dead, is no longer a burden to others. Such thoughts—especially when associated with alcohol abuse, living alone, the recent death of the spouse, physical illness, and somatic pain—suggest a high suicidal risk.

Disturbances in mood states, most notably depression and anxiety, may interfere with memory functioning. An expansive or euphoric mood may indicate a manic episode or may be part of a dementing disorder. Frontal lobe dysfunction often produces *witzelsucht*, which is the tendency to make puns and jokes and then laugh aloud at them.

The patient's affect may be flat, blunted, constricted, shallow, or inappropriate, which can indicate a depressive disorder, schizophrenia, or brain dysfunction. Such an affect is an important abnormal finding, although it is not pathognomonic of a specific disorder. Dominant lobe dysfunction causes dysprosody, an inability to express emotions through speech intonation.

Perceptual Disturbances

Hallucinations and illusions in the elderly may be transitory phenomena resulting from decreased sensory acuity. The examiner should note whether the patient is confused about time or place during the hallucinatory episode; confusion points to an organic condition. Distorted perceptions of the body are particularly important to ask about in the elderly. Since hallucinations may be caused by brain tumors and other focal pathology, a diagnostic workup may be indicated. Brain diseases cause perceptive impairments.

Agnosia (the inability to recognize and interpret the significance of sensory impressions) is associated with organic brain diseases. The examiner should note the type of agnosia—the denial of illness (anosognosia), the denial of a body part (autopagnosia), or the inability to recognize objects (visual agnosia) or faces (prosopagnosia).

Language Output

This category of the geriatric mental status examination covers the aphasias, which are disorders of language output related to organic lesions of the brain. The best described are (1) nonfluent or Broca's aphasia, (2) fluent or Wernicke's aphasia, and (3) global aphasia, a combination of fluent and nonfluent aphasias.

Broca's aphasia is characterized by a terse nonfluent output, mostly intact comprehension, and poor repetition. Reading comprehension is largely preserved, and reading aloud has the same nonfluent characteristics as spoken language. Naming and writing are impaired.

Wernicke's aphasia has a fluent output with poor comprehension and impaired repetition. Naming is abnormal, reading comprehension is impaired, reading aloud is compromised, and writing contains errors similar to the fluent paraphasic output.

Visuospatial Functioning

Some decline in visuospatial capability is normal with aging. Asking a patient to copy figures or a drawing may be helpful in assessing the function. A neuropsychological assessment should be performed when visuospatial functioning is obviously impaired.

Thought

Disturbances in thinking include neologisms, word salad, circumstantiality, tangentiality, loosening of associations, flight of ideas, clang associations, and blocking. The loss of the ability to appreciate nuances of meaning (abstract thinking) may be an early sign of dementia. Thinking is then described as concrete or literal.

Thought content should be examined for phobias, obsessions, somatic preoccupations, and compulsions. Ideas about suicide or homicide should be discussed. The examiner should determine if delusions are present and how such delusions affect the patient's life. Delusions may be present in nursing home patients and may be a reason for admission. Patients who are hard of hearing may be mistakenly classified as paranoid or suspicious. Ideas of reference or of influence should be described.

Sensorium and Cognition

Sensorium concerns the functioning of the special senses; cognition concerns information processing and intellect. The survey of both areas is known as the neuropsychiatric examination and consists of the assessment done by the clinician and a comprehensive battery of psychological tests.

JUDGMENT

Judgment is the capacity to act appropriately in various situations: Does the patient show impaired judgment? What would the patient do if a stamped, sealed, addressed envelope was found in the street? What would the patient do if smoke was smelled in a theater? What is the difference between a dwarf and a boy? Why are persons required to get a marriage license?

Neuropsychological Assessment

A thorough neuropsychological examination includes a comprehensive battery of tests that can be replicated by various examiners and can be repeated over time to assess the course of a specific illness. The most widely used test of current cognitive functioning is the Mini-Mental State Examination (MMSE), which assesses orientation, attention, calculation, immediate and short-term recall, language, and the ability to follow simple commands (see Table 4.1–1). The MMSE is used to detect impairments, follow the course of an illness, and monitor the patient's treatment responses. It is not used to make a formal diagnosis.

The assessment of intellectual abilities is performed with the Wechsler Adult Intelligence Scale-Revised (WAIS-R), which gives verbal, performance, and full-scale intelligence quotient (I.Q.) scores. Some tests, such as vocabulary tests, hold up as aging progresses; others, such as tests of similarities and digit-symbol substitution, do not. The performance part of the WAIS-R is a more sensitive indicator of brain damage than is the verbal part.

Visuospatial functions are sensitive to the normal aging process. The Bender gestalt test is one of many instruments used to test visuospatial functions; another is the Halstead-Reitan battery, the most complex battery of tests covering the entire spectrum of information processing and cognition.

Depression, even in the absence of dementia, often impairs psychomotor performance, especially visuospatial functioning and timed motor performance. The Geriatric Depression Scale is a useful screening instrument that excludes somatic complaints from its list of items. The presence of somatic complaints on a rating scale tends to confound the diagnosis of a depressive disorder.

Current Medications Used

Elderly patients are susceptible to the adverse behavioral and cognitive effects of drugs. The most commonly used class of psychoactive drugs among the elderly, the benzodiazepines, can cause sedation, behavioral disinhibition, depression, and memory impairment as side effects. Benzodiazepine discontinuation can cause insomnia and anxiety. Many antidepressant drugs cause nervousness and insomnia. Medications used to treat cardiovascular, pulmonary, and endocrine disorders are known to cause psychiatric side effects. The clinician must obtain a complete list of all current medications used by the patient.

MENTAL DISORDERS OF OLD AGE

The National Institute of Mental Health's Epidemiologic Catchment Area (ECA) program has found that the most common mental disorders of old age are depressive disorders, cognitive disorders, phobias, and alcohol use disorders.

Dementing Disorders

Dementia, a generally progressive and irreversible impairment of the intellect, increases in prevalence with age. Of Americans over the age of 65, about 5 percent have severe dementia, and 15 percent have mild dementia. Of Americans over the age of 80, about 20 percent have severe dementia. Only arthritis is a more common cause of disability among the elderly than dementia. Known risk factors for dementia are age, family history, and female sex.

In contrast to mental retardation, the intellectual impairment in dementia develops over time—that is, previously achieved mental functions are gradually lost. The characteristic changes of dementia involve cognition, memory, language, and visuospatial functions, but behavioral disturbances are common. The behavioral disturbances include agitation, restlessness, wandering, rage, violence, shouting, social and sexual disinhibition, impulsiveness, sleep disturbances, and delusions. Delusions and hallucinations occur during the course of the dementias in nearly 75 percent of all patients.

Many conditions impair cognition. The conditions include brain injuries, cerebral tumors, acquired immune deficiency syndrome (AIDS), alcohol, medications, infections, chronic pulmonary diseases, and inflammatory diseases. Although dementias associated with advanced age are typically caused by primary degenerative central nervous system (CNS) disease and vascular disease, many factors contribute to cognitive impairment; in the elderly, mixed causes of dementia are common.

About 10 to 15 percent of all patients who exhibit symptoms of dementia have potentially treatable conditions. The treatable conditions include systemic disorders, such as heart disease, renal disease, and congestive heart failure; endocrine disorders, such as hypothyroidism; vitamin deficiency; medications; and primary mental disorders, most notably, depressive disorders.

Dementias have been classified as cortical and subcortical, depending on the site of the cerebral lesion. A subcortical dementia is seen in Huntington's disease, Parkinson's disease, normal pressure hydrocephalus, multi-infarct dementia, and Wilson's disease. The subcortical dementias are associated with movement disorders, gait apraxia, psychomotor retardation, apathy, and akinetic mutism that can be confused with catatonia. The cortical dementias are seen in dementias of the Alzheimer's type, Creutzfeldt-Jakob disease, and Pick's disease, which frequently manifest aphasia, agnosia, and apraxia. In clinical practice the two types of dementia overlap, and usually an accurate diagnosis can be made only by autopsy.

DEMENTIA OF THE ALZHEIMER'S TYPE

Of all patients with dementia, 50 to 60 percent have dementia of the Alzheimer's type, the most common type of dementia. About 5 percent of all persons who reach age 65 have dementia of the Alzheimer's type, compared with 15 to 25 percent of all persons age 85 or older. The prevalence of dementia of the Alzheimer's type is higher in women than in men. Patients with dementia of the Alzheimer's type occupy more than 50 percent of all the nursing home beds.

Dementia of the Alzheimer's type is characterized by the gradual onset and progressive decline of cognitive functions.

Memory is impaired, and at least one of the following is seen: aphasia, apraxia, agnosia, and disturbances in executive functioning. The general sequence of deficits is memory, language, and visuospatial functions. Initially, the patient may have an inability to learn and recall new information, then impaired naming, then an ability to copy figures. Early dementia of the Alzheimer's type may be difficult to diagnose, since the patient's I.Q. may be normal.

Personality changes—such as depression, obsessiveness, and suspiciousness—occur. Outbursts of anger are common, and violent acts are a risk. Disorientation leads to wandering, and the patient may be found far from home in a dazed condition. Loss of initiative is common. Neurological defects—such as gait disturbances, aphasia, apraxia, and agnosia—eventually appear.

The dementia has an insidious onset and is progressive. The mean survival for patients with dementia of the Alzheimer's type is about 8 years, with a range of 1 to 20 years. The diagnosis is made on the basis of the patient's history and a mental status examination. Brain-imaging techniques may also be useful.

Etiology

The cause of Alzheimer's disease is unknown, although postmortem neuropathological and biochemical studies have found a selective loss of cholinergic neurons. Structural and functional changes occur. Gross anatomical findings include reduced gyral volume in the frontal and temporal lobes, with relative sparing of the primary motor and sensory cortex. Typical microscopic alterations include senile plaques and neurofibrillary tangles. Those tangles are derived from tau proteins. Blocking the aberrant phosphorylation of tau proteins is being explored as a possible therapeutic intervention in dementia of the Alzheimer's type.

Treatment

Dementia of the Alzheimer's type has no known prevention or cure. Treatment is palliative, consisting of proper nutrition, exercise, and supervision of daily activity. Medication may be helpful in managing agitation and behavioral disturbances. Propranolol (Inderal), pindolol (Visken), buspirone (BuSpar), and valproate (Depakene) have all been reported to help reduce agitation and aggression. Haloperidol (Haldol) and other high-potency dopamine blocking agents may be used to control acute behavior disturbances. A subgroup of patients with dementia of the Alzheimer's type show improvement in cognitive and functional measures when treated with tacrine (Cognex), a potent centrally active, reversible acetylcholinesterase inhibitor.

VASCULAR DEMENTIA

Vascular dementia is the second most common type of dementia. It is characterized by the same cognitive deficits as dementia of the Alzheimer's type, but it has focal neurological signs and symptoms, such as an exaggeration of deep tendon reflexes, extensor plantar response, pseudobulbar palsy, gait abnormalities, and weakness of an extremity. Compared with dementia of the Alzheimer's type, vascular dementia has an abrupt onset and a stepwise deteriorating cause. Vascular dementia may be prevented through the reduction of known risk factors, such as hypertension, diabetes, cigarette smoking, and arrhythmias. Diagnosis can be confirmed with MRI and cerebral blood flow studies.

DEMENTIA DUE TO PICK'S DISEASE

Pick's disease causes a slowly progressing dementia. It is associated with focal cortical lesions, primarily in the frontal lobes, producing aphasia, apraxia, and agnosia. The disease lasts from 2 to 10 years, with an average duration of 5 years. Clinically, Pick's disease is difficult to distinguish from Alzheimer's disease. On autopsy, however, the brain reveals intraneuronal inclusions called Pick bodies, which are different from the neurofibrillary tangles of Alzheimer's dementia. Pick's disease is much rarer than Alzheimer's dementia, and no treatment is available.

DEMENTIA DUE TO CREUTZFELDT-JAKOB DISEASE

Creutzfeldt-Jakob disease is a diffuse degenerative disease that affects the pyramidal and extrapyramidal systems. Creutzfeldt-Jakob disease usually affects people in their 50s, and the usual course is about one year. Creutzfeldt-Jakob disease is not associated with aging. Its incidence actually decreases after age 60. The terminal stage is characterized by severe dementia, generalized hypertonicity, and profound speech disturbances. It is caused by a slow-growing infectious virus. Some cases have been traced to the transplantation of the cornea of an infected person to a previously noninfected person.

DEMENTIA DUE TO HUNTINGTON'S DISEASE

Huntington's disease is a hereditary disease associated with progressive degeneration of the basal ganglia and the cerebral cortex. Huntington's disease is transmitted as an autosomal dominant gene (traced to the G8 fragment of chromosome 4); each offspring of an affected parent has a 50 percent chance of getting the disease. Everyone with the gene eventually has the disease. A genetic screening test for the disorder is now available. Currently 25,000 Americans have Huntington's disease, and about 125,000 children are at risk. The onset of Huntington's disease occurs between 35 and 50 years of age, but the disease may begin later than that in rare cases. It is characterized by progressive dementia, muscular hypertonicity, and bizarre choreiform movements; death usually occurs 15 to 20 years after the onset of the disease. No treatment is available.

DEMENTIA DUE TO NORMAL PRESSURE HYDROCEPHALUS

In the elderly, normal pressure hydrocephalus causes gait disturbances (unstable or shuffling gait), urinary incontinence, and dementia. Enlargement of the ventricles with increased cerebrospinal fluid (CSF) pressure is found.

DEMENTIA DUE TO PARKINSON'S DISEASE

Parkinson's disease is characterized primarily by motor dysfunction, but cognitive disturbances, including dementia, may be part of the disorder. Frontal lobe symptoms and memory deficits are common. Nearly half of all affected patients are depressed, making depression the most common mental disturbance in Parkinson's disease. Patients are also at increased risk for anxiety.

Medications used to treat Parkinson's disease—particularly drugs that facilitate dopaminergic neurotransmission, such as levodopa (Laradopa), amantadine (Symmetrel), and bromocriptine (Parlodel)—may cause psychosis and delirium.

Depressive Disorders

Depressive symptoms are present in about 15 percent of all elderly community residents and nursing home patients. Age itself is not a risk factor for the development of depression, but being widowed and having a chronic medical illness are associated with vulnerability to depressive disorders. Late-onset depression is characterized by high rates of recurrence.

The common signs and symptoms of depressive disorders include reduced energy and concentration, sleep problems (especially early morning awakening and multiple awakenings), decreased appetite, weight loss, and somatic complaints. The presenting symptoms may be different in elderly depressed patients from those seen in younger adults because of an increased emphasis on somatic complaints in the elderly. The elderly are particularly vulnerable to major depressive episodes with melancholic features, characterized by depression, hypochondriasis, low self-esteem, feelings of worthlessness, and self-accusatory trends (especially about sex and sinfulness) with paranoid and suicidal ideation.

Cognitive impairment in depressed geriatric patients is called the dementia syndrome of depression (pseudodementia), which can easily be confused with true dementia. In true dementia, intellectual performance is usually global in nature, and impairment is consistently poor; in pseudodementia, deficits in attention and concentration are variable. Distinguishing between the two disorders is difficult. Compared with patients who have true dementia, patients with pseudodementia are less likely to have language impairment and to confabulate; when uncertain, they are more likely to say "I don't know"; memory difficulties are more limited to free recall, as compared with recognition on cued recall tests. Pseudodementia occurs in about 15 percent of depressed elderly patients, and 25 to 50 percent of patients with dementia are depressed. Table 44–1 compares dementia and pseudodementia.

Depression may be associated with physical illness and with the medications used for treating illness. The clinician needs to be aware of the many pharmacological agents that are common causes of depression.

Bipolar I Disorder

Bipolar I disorder usually begins in middle adulthood, although the lifetime prevalence of 1 percent remains steady throughout life. A vulnerability to recurrences remains, so the patient with a history of bipolar I disorder may present with a manic episode in late life. In most instances a first episode of manic behavior after age 65 should alert the clinician to search for an associated physiological or organic cause, such as the side effects of medication or an early dementia.

The signs and symptoms of mania in the elderly are similar to those in younger adults and include an elevated, expansive, or irritable mood; a decreased need to sleep; distractibility; impulsivity; and, often, excessive alcohol intake. Hostile or paranoid behavior is usually present. The presence of cognitive impairment, disorientation, or fluctuating levels of awareness should make the clinician suspicious of an organic cause.

Lithium (Eskalith) remains the treatments of choice for mania; however, its use by elderly patients must be carefully monitored, because their reduced renal clearance makes lithium toxicity a significant risk. Neurotoxic effects are also more common in the elderly than in younger adults.

Schizophrenia

Schizophrenia usually begins in late adolescence or young adulthood and persists throughout life. Although first episodes diagnosed after age 65 are rare, a late-onset type beginning after age 45 has been described. Women are more likely to have a

---

Table 44–1.   Major Clinical Features Differentiating Pseudodementia from Dementia

Pseudodementia	Dementia
Clinical course and history	
Family always aware of dysfunction and its severity	Family often unaware of dysfunction and its severity
Onset can be dated with some precision	Onset can be dated only within broad limits
Symptoms of short duration before medical help is sought	Symptoms usually of long duration before medical help is sought
Rapid progression of symptoms after onset	Slow progression of symptoms throughout course
History of previous psychiatric dysfunction common	History of previous psychiatric dysfunction unusual
Complaints and clinical behavior	
Patients usually complain much of cognitive loss	Patients usually complain little of cognitive loss
Patients' complaints of cognitive dysfunction usually detailed	Patients' complaints of cognitive dysfunction usually vague
Patients emphasize disability	Patients conceal disability
Patients highlight failures	Patients delight in accomplishments, however trivial
Patients make little effort to perform even simple tasks	Patients struggle to perform tasks
	Patients rely on notes, calendars, etc., to keep up
Patients usually communicate strong sense of distress	Patients often appear unconcerned
Affective change often pervasive	Affect labile and shallow
Loss of social skills often early and prominent	Social skills often retained
Behavior often incongruent with severity of cognitive dysfunctions	Behavior usually compatible with severity of cognitive dysfunction
Nocturnal accentuation of dysfunction uncommon	Nocturnal accentuation of dysfunction common
Clinical features related to memory, cognitive, and intellectual dysfunction	
Attention and concentration often well preserved	Attention and concentration usually faulty
"Don't know" answers typical	Near-miss answers frequent
On tests of orientation, patients often give "don't know" answers	On tests of orientation, patients often mistake unusual for usual
Memory loss for recent and remote events usually severe	Memory loss for recent events usually more severe than for remote events
Memory gaps for specific periods or events common	Memory gaps for specific periods unusual*
Marked variability in performance on tasks of similar difficulty	Consistently poor performance on tasks of similar difficulty

* Except when caused by delirium, trauma, seizures, etc.
Table from C E Wells: Pseudodementia. Am J Psychiatry *136*: 898, 1979. Used with permission.

late onset of schizophrenia than are men. Another difference between early-onset and late-onset schizophrenia is the greater prevalence of paranoid schizophrenia in the late-onset type.

About 20 percent of schizophrenic persons show no active symptoms by age 65; 80 percent show varying degrees of impairment. Psychopathology becomes less marked as the patient ages.

The residual type of schizophrenia occurs in about 30 percent of all schizophrenic persons. Its signs and symptoms include emotional blunting, social withdrawal, eccentric behavior, and illogical thinking. Delusions and hallucinations are not common. Since most residual schizophrenic persons are unable to care for themselves, long-term hospitalization is required.

Elderly persons with schizophrenic symptoms respond well to antipsychotic drugs. Medication must be judiciously administered. Lower than usual dosages are often effective in the elderly.

Delusional Disorder

The age of onset of delusional disorder is usually between 40 and 55; however, it can occur at any time in the geriatric period. Delusions can take many forms, the most common being persecutory in nature—patients believe that they are being spied on, followed, poisoned, or harassed in some way. Delusional disorder persons may become violent against their supposed persecutors. In some cases they lock themselves in their rooms and live reclusive lives. Somatic delusions, in which the persons believe they have a fatal illness, may also occur in the elderly. In one study of persons over 65, pervasive persecutory ideation was present in 4 percent of those sampled.

Delusional disorder occurs under physical or psychological stress in vulnerable persons and may be precipitated by the death of the spouse, loss of a job, retirement, social isolation, adverse financial circumstances, debilitating medical illness or surgery, visual impairment, and deafness. Delusions may also accompany another disorder—such as dementia of the Alzheimer's type, alcohol use disorders, schizophrenia, depressive disorders, and bipolar I disorder—which need to be ruled out. Delusional syndromes may also result from prescribed medications or from early signs of a brain tumor.

The prognosis is fair to good in most cases, with best results achieved through a combination of psychotherapy and pharmacotherapy.

A late-onset delusional disorder called paraphrenia is characterized by persecutory delusions. It develops over several years and is not associated with dementia. Some workers believe the disorder to be a variant of schizophrenia that first becomes manifest after age 60. Patients with a family history of schizophrenia show an increase in paraphrenia.

Anxiety Disorders

The anxiety disorders include panic disorder, phobias, obsessive-compulsive disorder, generalized anxiety disorder, acute stress disorder, and posttraumatic stress disorder. The ECA study has found that the one-month prevalence of anxiety disorders in persons aged 65 years and older is 5.5 percent. By far, the most common disorders are phobias (4 to 8 percent). The rate for panic disorder is 1 percent. Anxiety disorders begin in early or middle adulthood, but some appear for the first time

after age 60. An initial onset of panic disorder in the elderly is rare but can occur.

The signs and symptoms of phobias in the elderly are less severe than those that occur in younger persons, but the effects are equally, if not more, debilitating in aged patients.

Existential theories help explain anxiety when there is no specifically identifiable stimulus for a chronically anxious feeling. The aged person has to come to grips with death. The person may deal with the thought of death with a sense of despair and anxiety, rather than with equanimity and Erik Erikson's sense of integrity.

The fragility of the autonomic nervous system in the aged may account for the development of anxiety after a major stressor. Posttraumatic stress disorder is often more severe in the elderly than in younger persons because of concurrent physical disability in the aged.

Obsessions and compulsions may appear for the first time in the aged person, although one usually finds signs of obsessive-compulsive disorder in the personalities of patients who, when younger, were orderly, perfectionistic, punctual, and parsimonious. When symptomatic, the patients become excessive in their desire for orderliness, rituals, and sameness. They may also have compulsions to check things over and over, becoming generally inflexible and rigid. Obsessive-compulsive disorder, in contrast to obsessive-compulsive personality disorder, is characterized by ego-dystonic rituals and obsessions and may begin late in life.

Treatment of anxiety disorders must be individually tailored to the patient, considering the biopsychosocial interplay producing the disorder. Both pharmacotherapy and psychotherapy are required.

Somatoform Disorders

Somatoform disorders, characterized by physical symptoms resembling medical diseases, are relevant to geriatric psychiatry because somatic complaints are common among the aged. More than 80 percent of the aged have at least one chronic disease—usually arthritis or cardiovascular problems. After the age of 75 years, 20 percent have diabetes and an average of four diagnosable chronic illnesses that require medical attention.

Hypochondriasis is common in patients over 60, although the peak incidence is in the 40-to-45-year-old age group. The disorder is usually chronic, and the prognosis is guarded. Repeated physical examinations are useful in reassuring patients that they do not have a fatal illness; however, invasive and high-risk diagnostic procedures should be avoided unless medically indicated.

Telling patients that their symptoms are imaginary usually meets with resentment and is counterproductive. The clinician should acknowledge that the complaint is real, that the pain is really there and perceived as such by the patient, and that a psychological or pharmacological approach to the problem is indicated.

Substance-Related Disorders

Aged patients with alcohol dependence usually give a history of excessive drinking that began in young or middle adulthood. They are usually medically ill, primarily with liver disease, and are either divorced, widowed, or never married men. Many have arrest records and are numbered among the homeless poor. A large number have chronic dementing illness such as Wernicke's encephalopathy and Korsakoff's syndrome. Twenty percent of nursing home patients have alcohol dependence.

Overall, alcohol and other substance use disorders account for 10 percent of all emotional problems in the aged, and dependence on such substances as hypnotics, anxiolytics, and narcotics is more common in old age than is generally recognized. Substance-seeking behavior—characterized by crime, manipulativeness, and antisocial behavior—is relatively rare in the elderly, compared with younger adults. Elderly patients may abuse anxiolytics to allay chronic anxiety or to ensure sleep. The maintenance of the chronically ill cancer patient with narcotics prescribed by a physician produces dependence; however, the need to provide pain relief takes precedence over the possibility of narcotic dependence and is entirely justified.

The clinical presentation of elderly patients with alcohol and other substance use disorders is varied. It includes falls, confusion, poor personal hygiene, depression, malnutrition, and the effects of exposure. The sudden onset of delirium in elderly persons hospitalized for medical illness is most often caused by alcohol withdrawal. Alcohol abuse should be considered in elderly patients with chronic gastrointestinal problems.

Over-the-counter substances, including nicotine and caffeine, may also be misused by the elderly. Over-the-counter analgesics are the most common offenders (used by 35 percent), followed by laxatives (used by 30 percent). Unexplained gastrointestinal, psychological, and metabolic problems should alert the clinician to over-the-counter substance abuse.

Sleep Disorders

Advanced age is the single most important factor associated with the increased prevalence of sleep disorders. Sleep-related phenomena that are more frequently reported by the elderly than by younger adults are trouble sleeping, daytime sleepiness, daytime napping, and the use of hypnotic drugs. Clinically, the elderly experience higher rates of breathing-related sleep disorder and medication-induced movement disorders than do younger adults.

Besides altered regulatory and physiological systems, the causes of sleep disturbances in the elderly include primary sleep disorders, other mental disorders, general medical disorders, and social and environmental factors. Among the primary sleep disorders, dyssomnias are the most frequent, especially primary insomnia, nocturnal myoclonus, restless legs syndrome, and sleep apnea. Of the parasomnias, REM sleep behavior disorder occurs almost exclusively among elderly men. The conditions that commonly interfere with sleep in the elderly include pain, nocturia, dyspnea, and heartburn. The lack of a daily structure and of social or vocational responsibilities contributes to poor sleep.

Because of the decreased length of the daily sleep-wake cycle in the elderly, those without daily routines, especially patients in nursing homes, may experience an advanced sleep phase, in which they go to sleep early and awaken during the night.

Even modest amounts of alcohol can interfere with the quality of sleep, causing sleep fragmentation and early morning awakening. Alcohol may also precipitate or aggravate obstructive sleep apnea. Many elderly patients use alcohol, hypnotics, and other central nervous system depressants to help them fall asleep. However, data show that most elderly patients experience more early morning awakening than trouble in falling asleep. When prescribing sedative-hypnotic drugs for the elderly, clinicians must monitor the patients for unwanted cognitive, behavioral, and psychomotor effects, including memory impairment (anterograde amnesia), residual sedation, rebound insomnia, daytime withdrawal, and unsteady gait.

Dementia may be associated with sundowning, an increase in confusion and agitation after nightfall. Dementia is associated with an increased frequency of arousals, increased stage 1 sleep, and decreased stages 3 and 4 sleep. Many demented patients, however, have no sleep disturbance.

Changes in sleep structure among the elderly involve both rapid eye movement (REM) sleep and nonrapid eye movement (NREM) sleep. The REM changes include the redistribution of REM sleep throughout the night, an increased number of REM episodes, the decreased length of REM episodes, and reduced total REM sleep. The NREM changes include the decreased amplitude of delta waves, a decreased percentage of stages 3 and 4 sleep, and an increased percentage of stages 1 and 2 sleep. In addition, the elderly experience increased awakening after sleep onset.

Much of the observed deterioration in the quality of sleep in the elderly is due to the altered timing and consolidation of sleep. For example, with advanced age, people have a lower amplitude of circadian rhythms, a circasemidian (12-hour) sleep-propensity rhythm, and a decreased length of circadian cycles.

OTHER DISORDERS OF OLD AGE

Vertigo

Feelings of vertigo or dizziness, a common complaint in the elderly, cause many elderly persons to become inactive because they fear falling. The causes of vertigo are varied and include anemia, hypotension, cardiac arrhythmia, cerebrovascular disease, basilar artery insufficiency, middle ear disease, acoustic neuroma, and Ménière's disease. Most cases of vertigo have a strong psychological component, and the clinician should ascertain any secondary gain from the symptom. The overuse of anxiolytics can cause dizziness and daytime somnolence. Treatment with meclizine (Antivert), 25 to 100 mg daily, has been successful in many cases of vertigo.

Syncope

The sudden loss of consciousness associated with syncope results from a reduction of cerebral blood flow and brain hypoxia. A thorough medical workup is required to rule out the common causes, such as epilepsy, anemia, cardiac arrhythmia, cerebrovascular disease, and hypoglycemia.

ELDER ABUSE

An estimated 10 percent of those more than 65 years old are abused. Elder abuse is defined by the American Medical Association as "an act or omission which results in harm or threatened harm to the health or welfare of an elderly person." Mistreatment includes abuse and neglect—physically, psychologically, financially, and materially. Sexual abuse does occur.

Acts of omission include the withholding of food, medicine, clothing, and other necessities.

Family conflicts and other problems often underlie elder abuse. The victims tend to be very old and frail. They often live with their assailants, who are often financially dependent on the victims. Both the victim and the perpetrator tend to deny or minimize the presence of abuse. Interventions include providing legal services, housing, and medical, psychiatric, and social services.

PSYCHOPHARMACOLOGICAL TREATMENT OF GERIATRIC DISORDERS

In the elderly, certain guidelines should be followed regarding the use of all drugs. A pretreatment medical evaluation is essential, including an electrocardiogram (ECG). It is especially useful to have the elderly patient or the family bring in all currently used medications, because multiple drug use may be contributing to the symptoms.

Most psychotropic drugs should be given in equally divided doses three or four times over a 24-hour period. Elderly patients may not be able to tolerate a sudden rise in drug blood level resulting from one large daily dose. Any changes in blood pressure and pulse rate and other side effects should be watched. For patients with insomnia, however, giving the major portion of an antipsychotic or antidepressant at bedtime takes advantage of its sedating and soporific effects. Liquid preparations are useful for elderly patients who cannot or who refuse to swallow tablets. Clinicians should frequently reassess all patients to determine the need for maintenance medication, changes in dosage, and the development of side effects.

If the patient is taking psychotropic drugs at the time of the evaluation, the clinician should, if possible, discontinue those medications and, after a washout period, reevaluate the patient during a drug-free baseline state.

The elderly use the greatest number of medications of any age group, with 25 percent of all prescriptions written for those over age 65. Adverse drug reactions caused by medications result in the hospitalization of nearly 250,000 persons in the United States each year. Psychotropic drugs are among the most commonly prescribed, along with cardiovascular and diuretic medications; 40 percent of all hypnotics dispensed in the United States each year are to those over age 65, and 70 percent of elderly patients are over the-counter medications, compared with only 10 percent of young adults.

Principles

The major goals of the pharmacological treatment of the elderly are to improve the quality of life, maintain them in the community, and delay or avoid their placement in nursing homes. Individualization of dosage is the basic tenet of geriatric psychopharmacology.

Alterations of drug dosages are required because of the physiological changes that occur as the person ages. Renal disease is associated with decreased renal clearance of drugs; liver disease results in a decreased ability to metabolize drugs; cardiovascular disease and reduced cardiac output can effect both renal and hepatic drug clearance; and gastrointestinal disease and decreased gastric acid secretion influence drug absorption. As a person ages, the ratio of lean-to-fat body mass also changes.

With normal aging, lean body mass decreases, and body fat increases. Changes in the lean-to-fat body mass ratio that accompany aging affect the distribution of drugs. Many lipid-soluble psychotropic drugs are more widely distributed in fat tissue than in lean tissue, thus prolonging the drug action more than expected. Similarly, changes in end-organ or receptor-site sensitivity need to be taken into account. The increased risk of orthostatic hypotension in the elderly from psychotropic drugs is related to reduced functioning of blood-pressure regulating mechanisms.

As a rule, the lowest possible dosage should be used to achieve the desired therapeutic response. The clinician must know the pharmacodynamics, pharmacokinetics, and biotransformation of each drug prescribed and the effects of the interaction of the drug with other drugs that the patient is taking.

Antidepressants

All antidepressant drugs are equally effective in treating depression, making the dominant consideration in selecting a drug that of side effects. Elderly patients are often more susceptible to some antidepressant side effects than are younger adults. The consequences of adverse drug reactions in the elderly are also potentially more severe than in younger adults. Among the factors that contribute to side-effect prevalence and severity in the elderly are altered drug metabolism, compromised physiological functions, altered body composition, and drug interactions.

Tricyclic drugs are among the oldest psychopharmacological agents. When used by elderly patients, the secondary amine agents desipramine (Norpramin) and nortriptyline (Pamelor) are preferred because of their low propensity to cause anticholinergic, orthostatic, and sedative side effects. Nortriptyline is less likely than are other tricyclic agents to cause orthostatic hypotension in patients with congestive heart failure. Because of the quinidinelike effect of all tricyclics, a pretreatment electroencephalogram (EEG) is essential to determine if the patient has a preexisting cardiac conduction defect.

Monoamine oxidase inhibitors (MAOIs) are also useful in treating depression because monoamine oxidase (MAO) decreases in the aging brain and may account for diminished catecholamines and a resultant depression. MAOIs may be used with caution in elderly patients. Orthostatic hypotension is common and severe with MAOIs. Patients need to follow a tyramine-free diet to avoid hypertensive crises. The potential for serious drug interactions involving certain analgesics, such as meperidine (Demerol) and sympathomimetics, also requires that patients understand what food and drugs they may use. Tranylcypromine (Parnate) and phenelzine (Nardil) are representative drugs that should be used cautiously in patients prone to hypertension. Any kind of cognitive impairment precludes MAOI therapy.

Major adverse-effect considerations with some other antidepressants are as follows: for trazodone (Desyrel), sedation and orthostatic hypotension; for amoxapine (Asendin), extrapyramidal effects; and for maprotiline (Ludiomil), seizures. Except for the risk of seizures at high dosages, bupropion (Wellbutrin) is generally tolerated well. It is nonsedating and does not produce orthostasis; it should be given in three divided doses.

In general, the serotonin-specific reuptake inhibitors (SSRIs)—such as fluoxetine (Prozac) and paroxetine (Paxil)—are safe and well tolerated by elderly patients. As a group, those drugs may cause nausea and other gastrointestinal symptoms, nervousness, agitation, headache, and insomnia, most often to mild degrees. Fluoxetine is the drug most likely to cause nervousness, insomnia, and loss of appetite, particularly early in treatment. Sertraline (Zoloft) is the drug most likely to produce nausea and diarrhea. Paroxetine causes some anticholinergic effects. The SSRIs do not cause the characteristic side effects of the tricyclic agents. The absence of orthostatic hypotension is a clinically significant factor in the use of SSRIs by the elderly.

Psychostimulants

The psychostimulants, which are also called analeptics and sympathomimetics, include amphetamines (for example, dextroamphetamine [Dexedrine]), methylphenidate (Ritalin), and pemoline (Cylert). In selected cases they can improve the mood, apathy, and anhedonia of the depressed elderly patient, especially when those symptoms are caused by some associated chronic medical illness, such as rheumatoid arthritis or multiple sclerosis. Amphetamines may also augment analgesia in patients who require pain medication. The use of psychostimulants is controversial because of the risk of abuse; however, when prescribed judiciously in small dosages, they are of value.

Lithium

The use of lithium in aged patients is more hazardous than its use in young patients because of the common occurrence of age-related morbidity and physiological changes of the heart, the thyroid, and the kidneys. Lithium is excreted by the kidneys, and decreased renal clearance and renal disease can increase the risk of toxicity. Thiazide diuretics decrease the renal clearance of lithium; consequently, the concomitant use of those medications can require adjustments in lithium dosage. Other medications may also interfere with lithium clearance. Lithium may cause CNS effects to which the elderly may be especially sensitive. Because of those factors, frequent serum monitoring of lithium levels is recommended for the elderly. In addition, cardiac, kidney, and thyroid workups are essential before initiating therapy.

Antipsychotics

Besides treating overt signs of psychosis, such as hallucinations and delusions, antipsychotics have been used to deal effectively with violent, agitated, and abusive geriatric patients.

In general, psychosis in the elderly frequently responds to much lower dosages of medication than those used for younger patients. The elderly are also much more sensitive to many of the side effects of antipsychotic medications than are young patients, specifically to the extrapyramidal (parkinsonian) side effects. Elderly patients have been known to stop speaking, ambulating, and swallowing because of those side effects. The same dosages of medication are not likely to produce significant problems for younger patients.

Hip fracture resulting from falls, in part associated with medication use, is a major cause of morbidity in the elderly and can be a proximal or distal factor associated with death. Consequently, to minimize the potential deleterious and even life-threatening side effects, the clinician should monitor drug use.

Hip fractures are least often associated with short half-life anxiolytics and most often associated with antipsychotics.

Clinical experience suggests that the therapeutic effects of antipsychotic medications in the elderly may not become evident on a given dosage of medication for four weeks or longer. Because of the therapeutic factors and risks, the dictum in treating psychosis in the elderly is to start low and go slow. As in younger patients, side-effect profiles should help determine the choice of medication; however, no consensus exists regarding the choice or the dosages level of antipsychotics for the elderly. There is no need to administer prophylactic antiparkinsonian agents on a regular basis when prescribing antipsychotics. The anticholinergic aspects of those drugs can create unwanted side effects, especially memory impairment.

Anxiolytics

The geriatric patient with mild or moderate anxiety can benefit from anxiolytics. The benzodiazepines are the most widely used anxiolytics. Most patients are treated for brief periods, although some may have to be maintained on small dosages for long periods. The long-term use of benzodiazepines is controversial, because they are controlled substances with a potential for abuse. Benzodiazepines with short or intermediate half-lives are preferable for use as hypnotics. The benzodiazepines may cause short periods of memory impairment, such as anterograde amnesia, which may aggravate an elderly existing cognitive disorder in the elderly patient. Elderly patients accumulate the long-acting benzodiazepines (such as diazepam [Valium]) in adipose tissues, increasing such unwanted effects as ataxia, insomnia, and confusion (sundowner syndrome). That effect can be avoided if the smallest possible dosage is prescribed and if intake is monitored until a therapeutic response is achieved.

Barbiturates may be substituted for the benzodiazepines in the few patients who do not respond to benzodiazepines. The geriatric patient is particularly prone to paradoxical dysphoria and cognitive disorganization, which can result from barbiturates. The barbiturates have a higher abuse potential, compared with the benzodiazepines. Barbiturates are controlled substances (schedule II), and the Drug Enforcement Agency (DEA) imposes constraints on their use.

Buspirone is an anxiolytic drug without sedative properties. It has a longer onset of action—up to three weeks—than either the benzodiazepines or the barbiturates and does not cause cognitive impairment. Moreover, it does not have any potential for abuse.

Pharmacological Management of Agitation and Aggression in Dementia

A common issue in the treatment of elderly patients with dementia is the management of agitation and aggression. The use of antipsychotics is generally unsatisfactory because of their limited efficacy and their parkinsonian side effects. Benzodiazepines, although frequently used to treat behavior disturbances, may produce cognitive impairment, sedation, and paradoxical worsening of the patient's behavior. Some β-adrenergic antagonists, such as propranolol and pindolol, the partial 5-HT$_{1A}$ agonist buspirone, and the 5-HT$_2$ antagonist trazodone have been reported to reduce agitation, aggression, and impulsivity in patients with dementia and other cognitive disorders.

PSYCHOTHERAPY FOR THE AGED

The standard psychotherapeutic interventions—such as insight-oriented psychotherapy, supportive psychotherapy, cognitive therapy, group therapy, and family therapy—should be available to the geriatric patient. According to Sigmund Freud, persons more than 50 years of age are not suited for psychoanalysis because they lack elasticity of the mental processes. But in the view of many who followed Freud, psychoanalysis is possible after that age. Advanced age certainly limits the plasticity of the personality, but, as Otto Fenichel stated: ''It does so in varying degrees and at very different ages so that no general rule can be given.'' Insight-oriented psychotherapy may be tried for removing a specific symptom, even with old persons. It is of most benefit if the patient has possibilities for libidinal and narcissistic gratification, but it is contraindicated if it would bring only the insight that life has been a failure and that the patient has no opportunity to make up for it.

Common age-related issues in therapy involve the need to adapt to recurrent and diverse losses (such as the deaths of friends and loved ones), the need to assume new roles (such as the adjustment to retirement and the disengagement from previously defined roles), and the need to accept one's mortality.

Transference

In most cases the elderly patient parentifies the younger psychiatrist and transfers the infantile responses from the past relationship with the parent to the present relationship with the physician. A childlike dependence can then develop, or, conversely, a childlike defiance and disobedience may appear. The patient can be shown how the infantile behavior is at work now in relation to the psychiatrist and to others in the patient's life. Other transference reactions include the patient's reacting to the therapist as a brother, sister, uncle, or even grandparent.

Group Therapy

Group therapy with the aged provides an opportunity for mutual support and aids in helping patients deal with the stresses of adapting to declining resources. Group members provide new friendships at a time when there has been a loss of old friends by death. Patients have the opportunity to be of help to one another, thus increasing their self-esteem. Even patients with mild to moderate dementia can be helped to remain stimulated, active, and oriented through group interaction.

Family Therapy

Engaging the patient's family in treatment is frequently desirable and often necessary. Issues in family therapy are myriad. They include the distribution of family resources in providing care for the patient, the attitudes of the children toward their parent and their parent's need for therapy, the grandparenting role, and the examination of family conflicts.

Brief Therapy

Short-term therapy approaches, such as cognitive therapy, help the aged by correcting distortions in thinking, especially self-induced prejudices about the aging process. Persons who think they are too old for sports, sex, learning new things, ac-quiring new skills, helping others, and working at new jobs can have those cognitive distortions modified by direct therapeutic interventions. Patients can learn to use adaptive defense mechanism and can be persuaded to make an effort to fight phobic avoidances and other inhibitions.

INSTITUTIONAL CARE OF THE AGED

The placement of the aged person in an institution is often viewed as a failure in management. It is, however, often a carefully thought out and executed treatment option that improves the person's quality of life. Several types of institutions are available.

Old-age homes and board-and-care homes are voluntary nonprofit institutions in which old persons are expected to live together for the rest of their lives, with no attempt to rehabilitate them for discharge. Instead, they are helped to adjust to the protective setting and to have a better social life than they could have in their own homes.

Nursing homes and extended-care facilities are institutions for the long-term care of chronically ill or permanently impaired persons. Those institutions emphasize the admission of short-term convalescent patients and persons with the potential for rehabilitation to community life. However, only 50 percent stay less than three months, and 50 percent stay on as permanent residents. The government divides nursing homes into skilled nursing facilities and intermediate-care facilities. Seventy percent are proprietary, and 30 percent are nonproprietary or governmental. In 1988 the average cost to stay in a nursing home was $22,000 a year. The cost is now more than $30,000 a year. A total of $38 billion is spent annually on nursing home care; half of that is paid by the government (through Medicaid). An increasing number of private insurance companies now offer long-term care insurance to help cover nursing home costs.

Day-care centers and community centers for the aged are places for elderly persons to congregate, to enjoy socializing experiences, and to deal with feelings of depression, anxiety, boredom, and loneliness.

The state psychiatric hospitals used to have a large geriatric population with various cognitive disorders. Today those hospitals exclude aged persons with dementia unless the dementia is mild or reversible and the patient is not likely to become a permanent resident. As a result, both old-age homes and nursing homes have received patients who are similar to the disorganized, bizarre, and violent patients formerly in mental hospitals. The likelihood that these persons will ever be discharged from these long-term care facilities is slim, because even willing and effective families cannot cope with the many around-the-clock needs of those patients.

A new trend to help avoid institutionalization is the so-called retirement community composed of relatively healthy old persons who live and work together. The communities are usually run on a nonprofit basis and may have an associated medical facility for the treatment of medical problems. Increasingly, profit-making companies are establishing retirement communities.

Restraints

Restraints are belts and vests that keep patients from falling out of bed and wheelchairs or from wandering away. For some patients (such as patients who would pull out feeding or oxygen tubes) such restraints are necessary, but for most patients they are used excessively. Some federal surveys have found that about 40 percent of all nursing home residents are put in restraints each year. The alternatives include tilted recliners, safe wandering paths, and floor alarms. Patients without restraints have better muscle tone from the exercise of walking and, psychologically, have less rage and a greater sense of mastery than do patients in restraints.

Psychosocial Therapy

Institutions can provide a total-push approach to the patient that involves a variety of professional staff members, including psychologists; social workers; psychiatric aides; occupational, vocational, and activity therapists, nutritionists; and exercise therapists. Each has skills that, when brought to bear on the institutionalized resident either individually or in a group, can markedly improve the patient's quality of life.

Psychiatrists who work with the aged must be especially aware of their own attitudes toward the aging process and aged persons, particularly their own parents and grandparents. If the psychiatrists have unresolved resentments or unconscious anger toward the aged in their own lives, they are likely to have countertransference problems that interfere with their ability to do good psychotherapy. Similarly, if they have unresolved fears of death, dying, or chronic illness, they may have blind spots that interfere with therapy. Psychiatrists must have an optimistic view of the last stage of life cycle and a genuine belief that aged persons have a rightful place in society and a reservoir of wisdom from their accumulated years of experience that enables them to change.

References

Addonizio G, Alexopoulos G S: Affective disorders in the elderly. Int J Geriatr Psychiatry *8*: 41, 1993.

Coyne A C, Reichman W E, Berbig L J: The relationship between dementia and elder abuse. Am J Psychiatry *150*: 643, 1993.

Dal Forno G, Kawas C H: Cognitive problems in the elderly. Curr Opin Neurol *8*: 256, 1995.

Gomberg E S: Older women and alcohol. Use and abuse. Recent Dev Alcohol *12*: 61, 1995.

Kaplan H I, Sadock B J, Small G W, editors: Geriatric Psychiatry. In *Comprehensive Textbook of Psychiatry*, ed 6, H I Kaplan, B J Sadock, editors, p 2507. Williams & Wilkins, Baltimore, 1995.

Martin L M, Fleming K C, Evans J M: Recognition and management of anxiety and depression in elderly patients. Mayo Clin Proc *70*: 999, 1995.

Pollock B G, Mulsant B H: Antipsychotics in older patients. A safety perspective. Drugs Aging *6*: 312, 1995.

Rovner B W, Katz I R: Psychiatric disorders in the nursing home: A selective review of studies related to clinical care. Int J Geriatr Psychiatry *8*: 75, 1993.

Solomon K, Manepalli J, Ireland G A, Mahon G M: Alcoholism and prescription drug abuse in the elderly: St. Louis University grand rounds. J Am Geriatr Soc *41*: 57, 1993.

Weiss L J, Lazarus L W: Psychosocial treatment of the geropsychiatric patient. Int J Geriatr Psychiatry *8*: 95, 1993.

45/ Forensic Psychiatry

Forensic psychiatry is the branch of medicine that deals with disorders of the mind and their relation to legal principles. The word "forensic" means belonging to the courts of law. At various stages in their historical development, psychiatry and the law have converged. Today, the two disciplines often intersect when dealing with the social deviant who, by violating the rules of society secondary to some presumed or proposed mental disorder, adversely affects the functioning of the community. Traditionally, the psychiatrist's efforts are directed elucidation of the causes and, through prevention and treatment, reduction of self-destructive elements of harmful behavior. The lawyer, as the agent of society, is concerned with the fact that the social deviant is a potential threat to the safety and the security of other people. Both psychiatry and the law seek to implement their respective goals through the application of pragmatic techniques based on empirical observations.

The "legalization" of psychiatry has had a major serious side effect—the increasing practice of defensive medicine. Defensive practice converts patients into adversaries against whom clinicians must defend themselves. Patients readily sense the shift from the clinician's interest in the patient to the clinician's self-protection. The patient's feeling may trigger litigation. That feeling also negates the most important element the clinician has in avoiding lawsuits: the therapeutic alliance.

The interface between psychiatry and the law is complex and has the potential for gross misunderstandings.

During a routine outpatient psychotherapy appointment, a male middle-level manager began to complain to his therapist about his boss. Feeling the freedom of expression that the therapeutic situation is intended to foster, the man worked himself up to a higher pitch than usual, and, in the emotional intensity of the moment, he said that he would like to kill his boss. He then calmed down, somewhat relieved by having let off steam, went on to discuss other subjects, and departed at the end of the session.

The therapist did not believe that the patient was anywhere near the point of seriously acting on the feelings expressed. However, the therapist had heard of a case in which the therapist got into trouble for not warning third parties, so he decided to take action.

On a sheet with his letterhead, he typed a warning to the employer that his patient, John Jones, had expressed the desire to kill him. He sent the letter by first-class mail—not express or registered—and he addressed it not to the employer but to the personnel department of the company.

The resulting uproar, although perhaps predictable, surprised the therapist. During the subsequent liability suit for breach of confidentiality, he was heard to sputter, "But I was only doing what the law requires of me!"

PSYCHIATRISTS AND THE COURTS

Most psychiatric work with patients is based on the therapeutic alliance between the clinician and the patient, but the legal model works from an adversarial position. The complexity of medicolegal matters is inevitably divided (or, more often, polarized) into two sides, which pull against each other trying to place the truth in the hands of the fact finder (the judge or the jury). For the clinician exposed to merciless cross-examination scenes in all media, that fundamental element of the American legal system is apt to evoke fear, revulsion, and dismay. But those feelings may be tempered somewhat by insights into the process. From the clinician's viewpoint an important distinction must first be made regarding the clinician's role as witness. The earliest point to establish in sorting out the clinician's role is what kind of witness the psychiatrist will be.

WITNESS OF FACT

The first type of witness is witness of fact (also called an ordinary witness). As a witness of fact, the psychiatrist functions no differently from laypersons generally—for example, as observers of an accident on the street. The witness's input—the facts—are direct observations and material from direct scrutiny. A witness of fact may be a psychiatrist who reads portions of the medical record aloud to bring it into the legal record and thus make it available for testimony. In theory, any psychiatrist at any level of training can fulfill that role.

EXPERT WITNESS

In contrast, a psychiatrist under certain circumstances may be qualified as an expert. The qualifying process, however, consists not of popular recognition in one's clinical field but of being accepted by the court and both sides of the case as suitable to perform expert functions. Thus, the term "expert" has particular legal meaning and is independent of any actual or presumed expertise the clinician may have in a given area. The clinician's expertise is elucidated during direct examination and cross-examination of the clinician's education, publications, and certifications. In the context of the courtroom, an expert witness is one who may draw conclusions from data and thereby render an opinion—for example, that a patient meets the required criteria for commitment or for an insanity defense under the standards of a jurisdiction. Expert witnesses play a role in determining the standard of care and what constitutes the average practice of psychiatry.

The most common role of a psychiatrist in court proceedings is as an expert. When psychiatrists are asked to serve as experts, they are usually asked to do so for one side in the case; rarely are clinicians independent examiners reporting directly to the court. That can lead to a scenario known as the battle of the experts, in which each side hires an expert witness and the two experts give opposing opinions. The battle of the experts can leave the jury in a quandary and can result in their discounting the testimony of each expert and deciding the case on other evidence and testimony. Testimony is brought out by the hiring attorney in that part of the presentation known as the direct examination. The opposing attorney then draws out additional material through the cross-examination.

COURT-MANDATED EVALUATIONS

In several legal situations the judge asks clinicians to be consultants to the court, which raises the issue of for whom the clinicians work. Because clinical information may have to be revealed to the court, clinicians may not enjoy the same confidential relationship with their patients in those situations that they have in private practice. Clinicians who make such court-ordered evaluations are under an ethical obligation and, in some states, a legal obligation to so inform the patients at the outset of the examinations and to make sure that the patients understand that condition. Such court-mandated evaluations were supported by the Supreme Court of the United States in *Ake v. Oklahoma.* The Court held that, when a state allows a defense of sanity, it must provide funds for a psychiatric expert for an indigent defendant. Such an expert may be part of the defense if appropriate.

EVALUATION OF WITNESSES' CREDIBILITY

It is up to the trial judge to grant a psychiatric examination requested by one of the parties to the action. Before ordering an examination, the trial judge asks for evidence showing that it is necessary to determine the merits of the case and that the imposition on or inconvenience to the witness does not outweigh the examination's value. Many courts limit psychiatric examinations to complaining witnesses in rape and other sex-offense cases, in which corroborative proof is nearly always circumstantial. In incest cases, for example, the father and the daughter may jointly deny the incest that the mother persistently alleges; or the father may steadfastly deny the act, and the mother may support his denial; or, after accusing her father, the daughter may retract her accusation. Psychiatrists say that only a thorough psychiatric examination of the family can eliminate the confusion. Recognizing that false sex charges may stem from the psychodynamics of a victim who appears normal to a layperson, the courts permit psychiatrists to expose mental processes and defenses in complaining witnesses. The liberal attitude in that area is probably caused by the gravity of the charge or by the general lack of corroborating evidence.

PRIVILEGE AND CONFIDENTIALITY

Privilege

Privilege is the right to maintain secrecy or confidentiality in the face of a subpoena. Privileged communications are those statements made by certain persons within a relationship—such as husband-wife, priest-penitent, or doctor-patient—that the law protects from forced disclosure on the witness stand. Privilege is a right that belongs to the patient, not to the physician, and so the right can be waived by the patient. Psychiatrists, who are licensed to practice medicine, may claim medical privilege, but they have found that the privilege is so riddled with qualifications that it is practically meaningless. Purely federal cases have no psychotherapist-patient privilege. Moreover, the privilege does not exist at all in military courts, regardless of whether the physician is military or civilian and whether the privilege is recognized in the state where the court martial takes place. The privilege has many exceptions, which are often viewed as implied waivers. In the most common exception, patients are said to waive the privilege by injecting their condition into the litigation, thereby making their condition an element of their claim or defense. Another exception involves proceedings for hospitalization, in which the interests of both the patient and the public are said to call for a departure from confidentiality. In some contexts, clinicians may be ordered to give the court information that is ordinarily considered privileged. Yet another

exception is made in child-custody and child-protection proceedings regarding the best interest of the child. Furthermore, the privilege does not apply to actions between a therapist and a patient. Thus, in a fee dispute or a malpractice claim, the complainant's lawyer can obtain the necessary therapy records to resolve the dispute.

Psychiatrists and other physicians do not legally have the same privilege that exists between client and attorney, priest and churchgoer, and husband and wife. Most physicians are not aware of that fact.

Confidentiality

A long-held premise of medical ethics binds the physician to hold secret all information given by a patient. That professional obligation is what is meant by confidentiality. Understanding confidentiality requires an awareness that is applied to certain populations and not to others. That is, one can identify a group that is within the circle of confidentiality, meaning that sharing information with the members of that group does not require specific permission from the patient. Within that circle are other staff members treating the patient, clinical supervisors, and consultants. Parties outside the circle include the patient's family, attorney, and previous therapist; sharing information with such people requires the patient's permission. Nevertheless, often the psychiatrist may be asked to divulge information imparted by the patient. Although a court demand for information worries psychiatrists the most, the most frequent demand is by someone, such as the insurer, who cannot compel disclosure but who can withhold a benefit without it. Generally, the patient makes disclosures or authorizes the psychiatrist to make disclosures to receive a benefit, such as employment, welfare benefits, or insurance.

A psychiatrist can be forced to breach confidentiality by a subpoena. The law could not function adequately if courts did not have the right to compel witnesses to testify. A subpoena (meaning ''under penalty'') is an order to appear as a witness in court or at a deposition. Physicians are usually served with a *subpoena duces tecum,* which requires that they also produce their relevant records and documents. Although the power to issue subpoenas belongs to a judge, they are routinely issued at the request of an attorney representing a party to an action.

In bona fide emergencies, information may be released in as limited a way as feasible to carry out emergency interventions. Sound clinical practice holds that efforts should be made, time allowing, to obtain the patient's permission anyway. After the emergency the clinician should debrief the patient.

As a rule, clinical information may be shared with the patient's permission (preferably written permission), although oral permission suffices with proper documentation. Each permission is good for only one release of information, and permission should be reobtained for each subsequent release, even to the same party. Permission overcomes only the legal barrier, not the clinical one; the release is permission, not obligation. If the clinician believes that the information may be destructive, the matter should be discussed, and the release may be refused with some exceptions.

THIRD-PARTY PAYERS AND SUPERVISION

Increased insurance coverage for health care is precipitating a concern about confidentiality and the conceptual model of psychiatric practice. Today, insurance covers about 70 percent of all health care bills; to provide coverage, an insurance carrier must be able to obtain information with which it can assess the administration and the cost of various programs.

Quality control of care requires that confidentiality not be absolute; it also requires a review of individual patients and therapists. The therapist in training must breach a patient's confidence by discussing the case with a supervisor. Also, institutionalized patients who have been ordered by a court to get treatment must have their individualized treatment programs submitted to a mental health board.

DISCUSSIONS ABOUT PATIENTS

In general, psychiatrists have multiple loyalties: to patients, to society, and to the profession. Through their writings, teaching, and seminars, they can share their acquired knowledge and experience, providing information that may be valuable to other professionals and to the public. But it is not easy to write or talk about a psychiatric patient without breaching the confidentiality of the relationship. Unlike physical ailments, which can be discussed without anyone's recognizing the patient, a psychiatric history usually entails a discussion of distinguishing characteristics. Psychiatrists have an obligation not to disclose identifiable patient information (and, perhaps, any descriptive patient information) without appropriate informed consent. Failure to obtain informed consent may result in claims based on breach of privacy, defamation, or both.

CHILD ABUSE

In New York all physicians are legally required for medical licensure to take a course on child abuse. All states now legally require that psychiatrists, among others, who have reason to believe that a child has been the victim of physical or sexual abuse make an immediate report to an appropriate agency. In that situation, confidentiality is decisively limited by legal statute on the grounds that potential or actual harm to vulnerable children outweighs the value of confidentiality in a psychiatric setting. Although many complex psychodynamic nuances accompany the required reporting of suspected child abuse, such reports are generally considered ethically justified.

DISCLOSURE TO SAFEGUARD

In some situations the physician must report to the authorities, as specifically required by law. The classic example of mandatory reporting involves a patient with epilepsy who operates a motor vehicle. Another example of mandatory reporting—one in which penalties are imposed for failing to report—involves child abuse. Expanded definitions of what constitutes child abuse under the law have been amended in some jurisdictions to include both emotional and physical child abuse. Under the legislation, practitioners who learn that a patient is engaged in sexual activity with a child are obliged to report it. In the absence of a specific statute that mandates reporting, a report is optional. As a general principle, a person has no duty to come to the aid of another unless a special relationship mandates that duty. However, once a person does come to the aid of another, a relationship is established, and a duty may be imposed.

Tarasoff I

Does the establishment of a therapist-patient relationship obligate the therapist to care for the safety of not only the patient but also others?

The issue was raised in the case of *Tarasoff v. Regents of University of California* in 1976 (now known as *Tarasoff I*). In that case, Prosenjit Poddar, a student and a voluntary outpatient at the mental health clinic of the University of California, told his therapist that he intended to kill a student readily identified as Tatiana Tarasoff. Realizing the seriousness of the intention, the therapist, with the concurrence of a colleague, concluded that Poddar should be committed for observation under a 72-hour emergency psychiatric detention provision of the California commitment law. The therapist notified the campus police both orally and in writing that Poddar was dangerous and should be committed.

Concerned about the breach of confidentiality, the therapist's supervisor vetoed the recommendation and ordered all records relating to Poddar's treatment destroyed. At the same time, the campus police temporarily detained Poddar but released him on his assurance that he would "stay away from that girl." Poddar stopped going to the clinic when he learned from the police of his therapist's recommendation to commit him. Two months later, he carried out his previously announced threat to kill Tatiana. The young woman's parents then sued the university for negligence.

As a consequence, the California Supreme Court, which deliberated the case for the unprecedented period of some 14 months, ruled that a physician or a psychotherapist who has reason to believe that a patient may injure or kill someone must notify the potential victim, the victim's relatives or friends, or the authorities.

The discharge of the duty imposed on the therapist to warn intended victims against danger may take one or more various steps, depending on the case. Thus, said the court, it may call for the therapist to notify the intended victim or others likely to notify the victim of the danger, to notify the police, or to take whatever other steps are reasonably necessary under the circumstances.

The *Tarasoff I* decision has not drastically affected psychiatrists, as it has long been their practice to warn the appropriate persons or law enforcement authorities when a patient presents a distinct and immediate threat to someone. According to the American Psychiatric Association, confidentiality may, with careful judgment, be broken in the following ways: (1) A patient will probably commit murder, and the act can be stopped only by the psychiatrist's notification of the police. (2) A patient will probably commit suicide, and the act can be stopped only by the psychiatrist's notification of the police. (3) A patient, such as a bus driver or an airline pilot who has potentially life-threatening responsibilities, shows marked impairment of judgment.

The *Tarasoff I* ruling does not require a therapist to report fantasies; rather, it requires a therapist to report an intended homicide. It is the therapist's duty to exercise good judgment.

Tarasoff II

In 1982 the California Supreme Court issued a second ruling in the case of *Tarasoff v Regents of University of California* (now known as *Tarasoff II*), which broadened its earlier ruling, the duty to *warn,* to include the duty to *protect*.

The *Tarasoff II* ruling has stimulated intense debates in the medicolegal field. Lawyers, judges, and expert witnesses argue the definition of protection, the nature of the relationship between the therapist and the patient, and the balance between public safety and individual privacy.

Clinicians argue that the duty to protect hinders treatment because the patient may not trust the doctor if confidentiality is not maintained. Furthermore, because it is not easy to determine if a patient is dangerous enough to justify long-term incarceration, unnecessary involuntary hospitalization because of defensive practices may occur.

Because of such debates in the medicolegal field, since 1976 the state courts have not made a uniform interpretation of the *Tarasoff II* ruling (the duty to protect). Generally, one should note whether a specific identifiable victim appears to be in imminent and probable danger from the threat of an action contemplated by a mentally ill patient; the harm, in addition to being imminent, should be potentially serious or severe. Usually, the patient must be a danger to another person and not to property. And the therapist should take clinically reasonable actions.

Claims have already been advanced in few cases (none successful so far) that a *Tarasoff*-like duty applies to the infection of partners with human immunodeficiency virus (HIV) by patients under mental health treatment. The breach of confidentiality in *Tarasoff* cases is justified only by the threat of violence. Laws vary confusingly by jurisdiction. The ideal solution is to persuade the patient to make the disclosure and report the matter to the public health authorities.

HOSPITALIZATION

All states, as part of their police power, provide for some form of involuntary hospitalization. Such action is usually taken when psychiatric patients present a danger to themselves or to others in their environment to the degree that their urgent need for treatment in a closed institution is evident. Certain states allow for involuntary hospitalization if patients are unable to care for themselves adequately.

The doctrine of *parens patriae* allows the state to intervene and to act as a surrogate parent for those unable to care for themselves or who may harm themselves. *Parens patriae* (''father of his country'') in common law goes back to Edward I of England and derives from English common law. It was transformed into American common law to mean paternalism in which the state acts for its mentally ill and its minors.

The statutes governing hospitalization of the mentally ill have generally been designated commitment laws. However, psychiatrists have long considered the term an undesirable one, because commitment legally means a warrant for imprisonment. The American Bar Association and the American Psychiatric Association have recommended that the term ''commitment'' be replaced by the less offensive and more accurate term ''hospitalization,'' which has been adopted by most states. Although that change in terminology does not correct the attitudes of the past, the emphasis on hospitalization is in keeping with psychiatrists' views of treatment over punishment.

''False imprisonment'' is the name of the legal action that arises from the claim that a patient has been negligently hospitalized. It is an uncommon basis for malpractice litigation and is rarely successful when invoked; at present, society tends to emphasize social protection more than individual rights. The clinician's guidelines are to (1) obtain an emergency or involuntary hospitalization in good faith, for reasonable cause, with data obtained from personal examination or a reliable report of danger; (2) seclude the patient for proper indications according to local regulations; and (3) obtain consultation on ambiguous cases.

Procedures of Admission

Four procedures of admission to psychiatric facilities have been endorsed by the American Bar Association to safeguard civil liberties and to make sure that no person is railroaded into a mental hospital. Although each of the 50 states has the power to enact its own laws regarding psychiatric hospitalization, the procedures outlined here are gaining much acceptance.

INFORMAL ADMISSION

Informal admission operates on the general hospital model, in which the patient is admitted to a psychiatric unit of a general hospital in the same way that a medical or surgical patient is admitted. Under such circumstances the ordinary doctor-patient relationship applies, with the patient free to enter and to leave, even against medical advice.

VOLUNTARY ADMISSION

In cases of voluntary admission, patients apply in writing for admission to a psychiatric hospital. They may come to the hospital on the advice of their personal physician, or they may seek help on their own. In either case the patients are examined by a psychiatrist on the hospital staff and are admitted if that examination reveals the need for hospital treatment.

TEMPORARY ADMISSION

Temporary admission is used for patients who are so senile or so confused that they require hospitalization and are not able to make decisions of their own and for patients who are so acutely disturbed that they must be immediately admitted to a psychiatric hospital on an emergency basis. Under the procedure a person is admitted to the hospital on the written recommendation of one physician. Once the patient has been admitted, the need for hospitalization must be confirmed by a psychiatrist on the hospital staff. The procedure is temporary because patients cannot be hospitalized against their will for more than 15 days.

INVOLUNTARY ADMISSION

Involuntary admission involves the question of whether patients are a danger to themselves, such as suicidal patients, or a danger to others, such as homicidal patients. Because those persons do not recognize their need for hospital care, the application for admission to a hospital may be made by a relative or a friend. Once the application is made, the patients must be examined by two physicians, and, if both physicians confirm the need for hospitalization, the patients can then be admitted.

Involuntary hospitalization involves an established procedure for written notification of the next of kin. Furthermore, the patients have access at any time to legal counsel, who can bring the case before a judge. If the judge does not think that hospitalization is indicated, the patient's release can be ordered.

Involuntary admission allows the patient to be hospitalized for 60 days. After that time, if the patient is to remain hospitalized, the case must be reviewed periodically by a board consisting of psychiatrists, nonpsychiatric physicians, lawyers, and other citizens not connected with the institution. In New York State the board is called the Mental Health Information Service.

Persons who have been hospitalized involuntarily and who believe that they should be released have the right to file a petition for a writ of habeas corpus. Under law, a writ of habeas corpus may be proclaimed by those who believe that they have been illegally deprived of liberty. The legal procedure asks a court to decide whether a patient has been hospitalized without due process of law. The case must be heard by a court at once, whatever the manner or the form in which the motion is filed. Hospitals are obligated to submit the petitions to the court immediately.

Involuntary Discharge

Under a variety of circumstances, patients may have to be discharged from a hospital against their will—if they have intentionally broken a major hospital rule (for example, smuggled drugs or assaulted another patient), refused treatment, or been restored to health but still wish to remain hospitalized. Some people may wonder why many patients wish to remain in a psychiatric hospital. For some patients, such a protective environment is preferable to the streets, jail, or the family's home. Although the focus here is on discharge from an inpatient unit, similar issues are involved in unilateral termination with an outpatient.

ABANDONMENT AS CAUSE OF ACTION

For the clinician the potential pitfall of involuntary discharge or involuntary termination is the charge of abandonment. That claim can be a particularly fertile ground for malpractice litigation when inevitable bad feelings are combined with a bad result. The clinician's vulnerability in that context is augmented by the jury's tendency to project a prejudicial distaste for the mentally ill person onto the physician, viewing the physician as someone who probably wants to get rid of the patient and be free to play golf. That popular perception places an additional onus on the clinician to exercise special care in that charged situation.

ENDING THE RELATIONSHIP

An involuntary discharge entails all the pain of the usual therapy termination process with far less opportunity for perspective, healing, and growth. Most important, in that situation the clinician directly opposes the patient's proclaimed wishes, thereby severely straining the therapeutic alliance. Consultation and documentation of the rationale for the action are the two safeguards against liability.

Going the extra mile means smoothing the way for the patient to obtain care in the future. Termination does not mean abandonment when a good-faith transfer of services is made through an appropriate referral to another hospital or therapist. Furthermore, when possible, the patient should be told that the door is open for a negotiated return at some time after restitution has been made or the problem has otherwise been redressed.

The clinician is not obliged to accept any patient back into full treatment. Patients are owed only an evaluation to determine their needs. Referral to an appropriate source of care may then follow. Blanket refusal to see a patient is a dangerous course and, short of serious risk of bodily harm to the clinician, should be avoided.

EMERGENCIES

The one circumstance in which the clinician cannot terminate a patient is a state of emergency. A typical example is a patient who attacks a therapist. The therapist cannot terminate the patient's care, no matter how severe the assault, until the emergency has been resolved (for example, by hospitalizing the patient or by arranging for seclusion or restraint). Only then can the therapist terminate the relationship and transfer the patient.

RIGHT TO TREATMENT

Among the rights of patients, the right to a standard quality of care is fundamental. That right has been litigated in much-publicized cases in recent years under the slogan of "right to treatment."

In 1966, Judge David Bazelon, speaking for the District of Columbia Court of Appeals in *Rouse v. Cameron,* noted that the purpose of involuntary hospitalization is treatment and concluded that the absence of treatment draws into question the constitutionality of the confinement. Treatment in exchange for liberty is the logic of the ruling. In that case the patient was discharged on a writ of habeas corpus, the basic legal remedy to ensure liberty. Judge Bazelon further held that, if alternative treatments that infringe less on personal liberty are available, involuntary hospitalization cannot take place.

Alabama Federal District Court Judge Frank Johnson was more venturesome in the decree he rendered in 1971 in *Wyatt v. Stickney.* The *Wyatt* case was a class-action proceeding, brought under newly developed rules that sought not release but treatment. Judge Johnson ruled that persons civilly committed to a mental institution have a constitutional right to receive such individual treatment as will give them a reasonable opportunity to be cured or to have their mental condition improved. Judge Johnson set out minimum requirements for staffing, specified physical facilities and nutritional standards, and required individualized treatment plans.

The new codes, more detailed than the old ones, include the right to be free from excessive or unnecessary medication; the right to privacy and dignity; the right to the least restrictive environment; the unrestricted right to be visited by attorneys, clergy, and private physicians; and the right not to be subjected to lobotomies, electroconvulsive treatments, and other procedures without fully informed consent. Patients can be required to perform therapeutic tasks but not hospital chores unless they volunteer for them and are paid the federal minimum wage. That requirement is an attempt to eliminate the practice of peonage, in which psychiatric patients were forced to work at menial tasks, without payment, for the benefit of the state.

In a number of states today, medication or electroconvulsive therapy cannot be forcibly administered to a patient without first obtaining court approval, which may take as long as 10 days. The right to refuse treatment is a legal doctrine that holds that persons cannot be forced to have treatment against their will unless it is an emergency. An emergency is a condition in clinical practice that requires immediate intervention to prevent death or serious harm to the patient or others or deterioration of the patient's clinical state.

In the 1976 case of *O'Connor v. Donaldson,* the Supreme Court of the United States ruled that harmless mentally ill patients cannot be confined against their will without treatment if they can survive outside. According to the Court, a finding of mental illness alone cannot justify a state's confining persons in a hospital against their will. Instead, involuntarily confined patients must be considered dangerous to themselves or others or possibly so unable to care for themselves that they cannot survive outside. Because of the 1979 case of *Rennie v. Klein,* patients have the right to refuse treatment and to use an appeal process. Because of the 1981 case of *Roger v. Oken,* patients have an absolute right to refuse treatment but a guardian may authorize treatment.

Questions have been raised about psychiatrists' ability to accurately predict dangerousness and about the risk to psychiatrists, who may be sued for monetary damages if persons are thereby deprived of their civil rights.

The ethical controversy over applications of the law to psychiatric patients came to the fore through Thomas Szasz, a professor of psychiatry at the State University of New York. In his book *The Myth of Mental Illness,* Szasz argued that the various psychiatric diagnoses are totally without significance. He contended that psychiatrists have no place in the courts of law and that all forced confinements because of mental illness are unjust. Szasz's opposition to suicide prevention and the imposition of treatment, with or without confinement, is interesting but is viewed by the psychiatric community with strong misgivings.

SECLUSION AND RESTRAINT

Seclusion is the placement and retention of an inpatient in a bare room to contain a clinical situation that may result in an emergency. Restraint involves measures designed to confine a patient's bodily movements, such as the use of leather cuffs and anklets or straitjackets. The use of seclusion and restraint raises issues of safety. The American Psychiatric Association's *Task Force Report on Seclusion and Restraint* provides standards for the use of those interventions. Clinicians practicing in institutions that use such measures should be familiar with that report and with local statutes. In most areas the doctrine of the least restrictive alternatives is invoked. According to that concept, commitment should be used only when no less restrictive alternative is available. However, clinicians facing a genuine emergency should act conservatively. A patient can always be released from restraints or seclusion, whereas the harm caused by uncontained violence may be irreversible.

INFORMED CONSENT

Lawyers representing an injured claimant now invariably add to a claim of negligent performance of procedures (malpractice) an informed consent claim as another possible area of liability. Ironically, it is one claim under which the requirement of expert testimony may be avoided. The usual claim of medical malpractice requires the litigant to produce an expert to establish that the defendant physician departed from accepted medical practice. But in a case in which the physician did not obtain informed consent, the fact that the treatment was technically well performed, in accord with the generally accepted standard of care, and effected a complete cure is immaterial. However, as a practical matter, unless the treatment had adverse consequences, a complainant will not get far with a jury in an action based solely on an allegation that the treatment was performed without consent.

In classic tort theory (a *tort* is a civil wrongful act other than a breach of contract) an intentional touching to which one has not given consent is *battery*. Thus, the administration of electroconvulsive therapy or chemotherapy, though it may be therapeutic, is a battery when done without consent. Indeed, any unauthorized touching outside conventional social intercourse constitutes a battery. It is an offense to the dignity of the person, an invasion of the person's right of self-determination, for which punitive and actual damages may be imposed. Justice Benjamin Cardozo wrote: "Every human being of adult years and sound mind has a right to determine what shall be done with his own body; and a surgeon who performs an operation without his patient's consent commits [a battery] for which he is liable in damages." In addition to battery, a procedure done without informed consent may be malpractice, as informed consent has become a broadly recognized part of the standard of care.

According to Justice Cardozo, it is not the effectiveness or the timeliness of the treatment that allows taking care of another but the consent to it. Thus, a mentally competent adult may refuse treatment, although it is effective and involves little risk. But, for example, when gangrene sets in and the patient is psychotic, treatment—even of such momentous proportions as amputation—may be ordered to save the patient's life. The state is also said to have a compelling interest in preventing its citizens from committing suicide, thus allowing for treatment without consent in that situation as well.

In the case of minors, the parent or the guardian is the person legally empowered to consent to medical treatment. However, most states by statute list specific diseases and conditions that a minor can consent to have treated—including venereal disease, pregnancy, substance dependence, alcohol abuse, and contagious diseases. In an emergency a physician can treat a minor without parental consent. The trend is to adopt what is called the mature minor rule, allowing minors to consent to treatment under ordinary circumstances. Because of the Supreme Court's 1967 *Gault* decision, all juveniles must now be represented by counsel, must be able to confront witnesses, and must be given proper notice of any charges. Emancipated minors have the rights of an adult when it can be shown that they are living as adults with control over their own lives.

In the past, to obviate a claim of battery, physicians only needed to relate what they proposed to do and obtain the patient's consent thereto. However, simultaneously with the growth of product liability and consumer law, the courts began to require that physicians also relate sufficient information to allow the patient to decide whether such a procedure is acceptable in the light of the risks and the benefits and the available alternatives, including no treatment at all. In general, informed consent requires that there be (1) an understanding of the nature and the foreseeable risks and benefits of a procedure, (2) a knowledge of alternative procedures, (3) awareness of the consequences of withholding consent, and (4) the recognition that the consent is voluntary. The physician must convey to the patient a readiness to listen and to discuss anything the patient may fear as a risk, a side effect, or a concern about the proposed treatment.

Consent Form

The consent form is a written document outlining the patient's informed consent to a proposed procedure. The use of the consent form followed revelations of harm done to patients during clinical experimentation. Consent forms are usually designed by attorneys whose aim is to protect the institution from liability. Therefore, such forms are often exhaustive and require a level of reading comprehension that is beyond that of many patients. Paradoxically, if such a form truly covered all possible eventualities, it would probably be too long to be comprehensible, and, if it were short enough to be comprehensible, it might be incomplete. Some theorists have recommended that the form be replaced by a standardized discussion and a progress note. The basic elements of a consent form should include a fair explanation of the procedures to be followed and their purposes, including identification of any procedures that are experimental; a description of any attendant discomforts and risks reasonably to be expected; a description of any benefits reasonably to be expected; a disclosure of any appropriate alternative procedures that may be advantageous to the patient; an offer to answer any inquiries concerning the procedures; and an instruction that the patient is free to withdraw patient consent and to discontinue participation in the project or activity at any time without prejudice. The patient has the right to refuse treatment.

CHILD CUSTODY

The action of a court in a child-custody dispute is now predicted on the best interests of the child. The maxim reflects the idea that a natural parent does not have an inherent right to be named as the custodial parent, but the presumption, although a bit eroded, remains in favor of the mother in the case of young children. By a rule of thumb, the courts presume that the welfare of a child of tender years is generally best served by maternal custody when the mother is a good and fit parent. The best interest of the mother may be served by naming her as the custodial parent, as a mother may never resolve the effects of the loss of a child, but her best interest is not to be equated ipso facto with the best interest of the child. Care and protection proceedings are the court's interventions in the welfare of a child when the parents are unable to care for the child.

More and more fathers are asserting custodial claims. In about 5 percent of all cases, fathers are named custodians. The movement supporting women's rights is also enhancing the chances of paternal custody. With more and more women going outside the home to work, the traditional rationale for maternal custody has less force today than it did in the past.

Every state today has a statute allowing a court, usually a juvenile court, to assume jurisdiction over a neglected or abused child and to remove the child from parental custody. Most states provide several grounds for assuming jurisdiction, such as parental abuse and an injurious living environment. If the court removes the child from parental custody, it usually orders that the care and custody of the child be supervised by the welfare or probation department.

TESTAMENTARY AND CONTRACTUAL CAPACITY AND COMPETENCE

Psychiatrists may be asked to evaluate patients' testamentary capacity—that is, their competence to make a will. Three psychological abilities are necessary to prove that competence. Patients must know (1) the nature and the extent of their bounty (property), (2) that they are making a bequest, and (3) who their natural beneficiaries are—that is, the spouse, their children, and other relatives.

When a will is being probated, one of the heirs or some other person often challenges its validity. A judgment in such cases must be based on a reconstruction of what the testator's mental state was at the time the will was written, using data from documents and from expert psychiatric testimony.

When one is unable or does not exercise one's right to make a will, the law in all states provides for the distribution of one's property to the heirs; if there are no heirs, the estate goes to the public treasury.

Witnesses at the signing of the will, which may include a psychiatrist, may attest that the testator was rational at the time the will was executed. In unusual cases the lawyer may videotape the signing to safeguard the will from attack. Ideally, persons thinking of making a will who believe that questions may be raised about their testamentary competence hire a forensic psychiatrist to perform a dispassionate examination antemortem to validate and record that capacity.

An incompetence proceeding and the appointment of a guardian may be considered necessary when a member of the family is spending the family's assets. The guardianship process may be used when property is in danger of dissipation, as in the case of aged, retarded, alcohol-dependent, and psychotic persons. The issue is whether such persons can manage their own affairs. However, a guardian appointed to take control of the property of one deemed incompetent cannot make a will for the ward (the incompetent patient).

Competence is determined on the basis of a person's ability to make a sound judgment—that is, to weigh, to reason, and to make reasonable decisions. There is no such thing as general competence; competence is task-specific. The capacity of weighing decision-making factors (competence) is often best shown by the patient's asking pertinent and knowledgeable questions after the risks and the benefits have been explained. Although physicians (especially psychiatrists) often give opinions on competence, only a judge's ruling converts the opinion into a finding; a patient is not competent or incompetent until the court says so. The diagnosis of a mental disorder is not, in itself, sufficient to warrant a finding of incompetence. Rather, the mental disorder must cause an impairment in judgment regarding the specific issues involved. Once declared incompetent, persons are deprived of certain rights: they cannot make contracts, marry, start a divorce action, drive a vehicle, handle their own property, or practice their profession. Incompetence is decided at a formal courtroom proceeding, and the court usually appoints a guardian who will best serve the patient's interests. Another hearing is necessary to declare the patient competent. Admission to a mental hospital does not automatically mean the person is incompetent.

Competence is also essential in contracts, as a contract is an agreement between parties to do some specific act. The contract is declared invalid if, when it was signed, one of the parties was unable to comprehend the nature and the effect of his or her act. The marriage contract is subject to the same standard and, thus, can be voided if either party did not understand the nature, duties, obligations, and other characteristics entailed at the time they were married. In general, however, the courts are unwilling to declare a marriage void on the basis of incompetence.

Whether the competence is related to wills, contracts, or the making or breaking of marriages, the fundamental concern is the person's state of awareness and capacity to comprehend the significance of the particular commitment made.

Durable Power of Attorney

A modern development that permits persons to make provisions for their own anticipated loss of decision-making capacity is called a durable power of attorney. The document allows the advance selection of a substitute decision maker who can act without the necessity of court proceedings when the signatory becomes incompetent through illness, progressive dementia, or perhaps a relapse of bipolar I disorder.

Competence to Inform

Competence to inform is a relatively new concept involving the patient's interaction with the clinician; it is useful in ambiguous situations that may have a poor outcome. The clinician first explains to the patient the value of being honest with the clinician and then attempts to determine whether the patient is competent to weigh the risks and the benefits of withholding information about suicidal or homicidal intent. The process must be documented.

CRIMINAL LAW

Competence to Stand Trial

The Supreme Court of the United States stated that the prohibition against trying someone who is mentally incompetent is fundamental to the United States system of justice. Accordingly, the Court, in *Dusky v. United States,* approved a test of competence that seeks to ascertain whether a criminal defendant "has sufficient present ability to consult with his lawyer with a reasonable degree of rational understanding—and whether he has a rational as well as factual understanding of the proceedings against him."

One of the most useful clinical guides for determining a patient's competence to stand trial is the McGarry instrument, which identifies 13 areas of functioning:

1. Ability to appraise the legal defenses available
2. Level of unmanageable behavior
3. Quality of relating to the attorney
4. Ability to plan legal strategy
5. Ability to appraise the roles of various participants in the courtroom proceedings
6. Understanding of court procedure
7. Appreciation of the charges
8. Appreciation of the range and the nature of the possible penalties
9. Ability to appraise the likely outcome
10. Capacity to disclose to the attorney available pertinent facts surrounding the offense
11. Capacity to challenge prosecutive witnesses realistically
12. Capacity to testify relevantly
13. Manifestation of self-serving versus self-defeating motivation

An apparent strength of such a guide is that it helps the clinician picture the effects of the familiar forms of psychopathology on those parameters, even without courtroom experience.

Clinicians must remember that they merely offer opinions about competence. The judge is free to honor, modify, or disregard those opinions. A patient is not competent or incompetent until the judge says so. One would do well to refrain from protesting a competence judgment that contradicts one's clinical opinion—which is a matter for appeals courts, not clinical objections.

Competence to Be Executed

A new area of competence to emerge in the interface between psychiatry and the law is the question of the patient's competence to be executed. The requirement for competence is thought to rest on three general principles: First, the patient's awareness of what is happening is supposed to heighten the retributive element of the punishment. Punishment is held as meaningless unless the patient is aware of what it is and to what it is a response. The second element is a religious one; competent persons about to be executed are thought to be in the best position to make whatever peace is appropriate with their religious beliefs, including confession and absolution. Third, the competent person about to be executed preserves until the end the possibility (admittedly slight) of recalling some forgotten detail of the events or the crime that may prove exonerating.

The need to preserve competence was recently supported in the Supreme Court case of *Ford v. Wainwright.* But no matter how the courts struggle with the question, most medical bodies have gravitated toward the position that it is unethical for any clinician to participate, no matter how remotely, in state-mandated executions, as the physician's duty to preserve life transcends all other competing requirements. Thus, the average psychiatrist has ethical guidance on the point. However, ethical dilemmas are readily predictable. A psychiatrist who examines a patient slated for execution may find the person incompetent on the basis of a mental disorder but may incur a medical obligation to recommend a treatment plan, which, if implemented, would ensure that person's fitness to be executed. There is room for a difference of opinion about whether treatment under those circumstances is humane or inhumane.

Criminal Responsibility

According to criminal law, a socially harmful act is not the sole criterion of a crime. Rather, the objectionable act must have two components: voluntary conduct (*actus reus*) and evil intent (*mens rea*). There cannot be an evil intent if the offender's mental status is so deficient, so abnormal, or so diseased as to have deprived the offender of the capacity for rational intent. The law can be invoked only when an illegal intent is implemented. Neither behavior, however harmful, nor the intent to do harm is, in itself, a ground for criminal action.

Until recently, in most American jurisdictions, persons could be found not guilty by reason of insanity if they suffered from a mental illness, did not know the difference between right and wrong, and did not know the nature and the consequences of their acts.

The tenacity of the insanity defense appears to derive from two profound medicolegal forces. One is the moral imperative; the insanity defense is perhaps more nearly a moral issue than either a clinical issue or a legal issue. The moral dimension speaks to the reluctance to hold blameworthy or culpable those persons in society who do not appear to merit those labels because of their psychological or neurological condition—what the law calls mental disease or defect. Children and severely retarded persons have traditionally occupied that moral niche; the mentally ill have always been in an ambiguous position.

The second force is the perception of fairness. Society's sense of the fairness of its courts is undermined when, as one judge put it, "drooling idiots are treated as if they were responsible defendants." Ultimately, the legal system requires a class of nonculpable persons and a system and standards for defining that class—in short, the theory and practice of an insanity defense.

The main problem with the insanity defense, from a societal point of view, is that it generates two common misconceptions that make it unpopular. The first misconception is that many hardened criminals use the loophole in the law to escape conviction. In reality, the insanity defense is used in only a tiny fraction of cases, and it prevails in a tiny fraction of that fraction—precisely because of its unpopularity.

The second misconception is that the insanity defense allows psychiatrists to get criminals off by acting as apologists for their evil actions. That view fails because the adversarial system requires two psychiatric opinions and also because no psychiatrist ever decides a case.

M'NAGHTEN RULE

The precedent for determining legal responsibility was established in the British courts in 1843. The so-called M'Naghten rule, which has until recently determined responsibility in most of the United States, holds that people are not guilty by reason of insanity if they labored under a mental disease such that they were unaware of the nature, the quality, and the consequences of their acts or if they were incapable of realizing that their acts were wrong. Moreover, to absolve people from punishment, a delusion has to be one that, if true, would be an adequate defense. If the deluded idea does not justify the crime, such persons are presumably held responsible, guilty, and punishable. The M'Naghten rule is known commonly as the right-wrong test.

The M'Naghten rule derives from the famous M'Naghten case dating back to 1843. At that time Edward Drummond, the private secretary of Robert Peel, was murdered by Daniel M'Naghten. M'Naghten had been suffering from delusions of persecution for several years. He had complained to many people about his ''persecutors,'' and finally he decided to correct the situation by murdering Robert Peel. When Drummond came out of Peel's home, M'Naghten shot Drummond, mistaking him for Peel. The jury, as instructed under the prevailing law, found M'Naghten not guilty by reason of insanity. M'Naghten was later committed to a hospital for the insane. The case aroused great interest, causing the House of Lords to debate the problems of criminality and insanity. In response to questions about what guidelines could be used to determine whether a person could plead insanity as a defense against criminal responsibility, the English chief judge wrote:

1. To establish a defense on the ground of insanity it must be clearly proved that, at the time of committing the act, the party accused was laboring under such a defect of reason, from disease of the mind, as not to know the nature and quality of the act he was doing, or if he did know it, he did not know he was doing what was wrong.

2. Where a person labors under partial delusions only and is not in other respects insane and as a result commits an offense he must be considered in the same situation as to responsibility as if the facts with respect to which the delusion exists were real.

The M'Naghten rule does not ask whether the accused knows the difference in general between right and wrong; it asks whether the defendant understood the nature and the quality of the act and if the defendant knew the difference between right and wrong with respect to the act. It asks specifically whether the defendant knew the act was wrong or, perhaps, thought the act was correct—that is, was a delusion causing the defendant to act in legitimate self-defense.

IRRESISTIBLE IMPULSE

In 1922 a committee of jurists in England reexamined the M'Naghten rule. They suggested broadening the meaning of ''insanity'' in criminal cases to include the idea of the irresisti-

ble impulse, which holds that a person charged with a criminal offense is not responsible for an act if the act was committed under an impulse that the person was unable to resist because of mental disease. The courts have chosen to interpret the law so that it has been called the policeman-at-the-elbow law. In other words, the court grants the impulse to be irresistible only if it determines that the accused would have gone ahead with the act even if a policeman had been at the accused's elbow. To most psychiatrists the law is unsatisfactory because it covers only a small special group of those who are mentally ill.

DURHAM RULE

In the 1954 case of *Durham v. United States*, a decision was handed down by Judge David Bazelon in the District of Columbia Court of Appeals that resulted in the product rule of criminal responsibility: an accused is not criminally responsible if his or her unlawful act was the product of mental disease or mental defect.

In the *Durham* case, Judge Bazelon expressly stated that the purpose of the rule was to get good and complete psychiatric testimony. He sought to release the criminal law from the theoretical straitjacket of the M'Naghten rule. However, judges and juries in cases using the *Durham* rule became mired in confusion over the terms ''product,'' ''disease,'' and ''defect.'' In 1972, some 18 years after the rule's adoption, the Court of Appeals for the District of Columbia, in *United States v. Brawner,* discarded the rule. The court—all nine members, including Judge Bazelon—decided in a 143-page opinion to throw out its *Durham* rule and to adopt in its place the test recommended in 1962 by the American Law Institute in its model penal code, which is the law in the federal courts today.

MODEL PENAL CODE

In its model penal code the American Law Institute recommended the following test of criminal responsibility: (1) Persons are not responsible for criminal conduct if at the time of such conduct, as a result of mental disease or defect, they lacked substantial capacity either to appreciate the criminality (wrongfulness) of their conduct or to conform their conduct to the requirement of the law. (2) The term ''mental disease or defect'' does not include an abnormality manifested only by repeated criminal or otherwise antisocial conduct.

Subsection 1 of the American Law Institute rule contains five operative concepts: (1) mental disease or defect, (2) lack of substantial capacity, (3) appreciation, (4) wrongfulness, and (5) conformity of conduct to the requirements of law. The rule's second subsection, stating that repeated criminal or antisocial conduct is not of itself to be taken as mental disease or defect, aims to keep the sociopath or psychopath within the scope of criminal responsibility.

OTHER TESTS

The test of criminal responsibility and other tests of criminal liability refer to the time of the offense's commission, whereas the test of competence to stand trial refers to the time of the trial.

The 1982 verdict of a District of Columbia jury—finding John W. Hinckley, Jr., the would-be assassin of President Ronald Reagan, not guilty by reason of insanity—ignited moves to limit or abolish the special plea. Hinckley's trial by jury also turned out to be a trial of law and psychiatry. The psychiatrists and the law that allows their testimony were made the culprits for the unpopular verdict. ''The psychiatrists spun sticky webs of pseudoscientific jargon,'' wrote a prominent columnist, ''and in these webs the concept of justice, like a moth, fluttered feebly and was trapped.'' The American Bar Association and the American Psychiatric Association quickly issued statements calling for a change in the law. More than 40 bills were introduced in Congress to amend the law, but none was passed. However, the bills helped defuse the public criticism. At present, Hinckley is hospitalized indefinitely at the federal St. Elizabeth's Hospital in Washington, D.C.

Attempts at reform have included the plea of guilty but mentally ill, which is already used in some jurisdictions. That standard has the advantage of identifying guilt while allowing some adaptation to psychiatric conditions. For example, it allows for treatment in restricted settings while allowing the courts to maintain an active role. ''Guilty but insane'' is a contradiction in terms. Insanity has no legal meaning except the exculpation of guilt. The defense of diminished capacity is based on the claim that the defendant suffered some impairment (usually but not always because of mental illness) sufficient to interfere with the ability to formulate a specific element (such as forethought) of the particular crime charged. Therefore, the defense finds its most common use with so-called specific-intent crimes, such as first-degree murder.

Under that concept, Dan White, who had killed two city officials of San Francisco, had his crime reduced from murder to manslaughter. White's ''Twinkie defense'' involved psychiatrists who testified that he was depressed and that his compulsive eating of junk foods was a symptom of depression. His depression led to a manslaughter conviction, rather than a first-degree murder conviction. After he was released from prison, White committed suicide.

The American Medical Association has proposed yet another reform: limiting the insanity exculpation to cases in which the person is so ill as to lack the necessary criminal intent (*mens rea*). That approach would all but eliminate the insanity defense and place a burden on the prisons to accept many mentally ill persons.

The American Bar Association and the American Psychiatric Association in their 1982 statements recommended a defense of nonresponsibility, which focuses solely on whether defendants, because of mental disease or defect, are unable to appreciate the wrongfulness of their conduct. Those proposals would limit the evidence of mental illness to cognition and would exclude control, but apparently a defense would still be available under a not-guilty plea—such as extreme emotional disturbance, automatism, provocation, or self-defense—that would be established without psychiatric testimony about mental illness. The American Psychiatric Association also urged that ''mental illness'' be limited to severely abnormal mental conditions. Those proposals remain controversial, and the issue will probably rise again with each sensational case in which the insanity defense is used.

MALPRACTICE

''Malpractice'' is the term commonly used to refer to professional negligence. Legally, negligence is defined by what a reasonably prudent person would or would not do in the same or similar circumstances. An action based on negligence, whatever the specific situation, involves basic problems of the relationship among the parties, the risk, and the reason. A negligence action is often precipitated by a bad outcome and resultant bad feelings.

The usual claim of malpractice requires the litigant to produce an expert to establish the four D's of malpractice: that there was the Dereliction (negligent performance or omission) of a Duty that Directly led to Damages. In negligence (1) a standard of care requisite under the particular circumstances must exist; (2) a duty must have been owed by the defendant or by someone for whose conduct the defendant is answerable; (3) the duty must have been owed to the plaintiff; and (4) a breach of the duty must be the legal cause of the plaintiff's asserted damage or injury.

The requisite standard of care under the circumstances may be established in the federal or state constitution, statutes, administrative regulations, court decisions, or the custom of the community. However, the law, with few exceptions, does not specifically define the particular duties. And it is not possible to define the way in which a person ought to act under various circumstances and conditions. As a rule, professionals have the duty to exercise the degree of skill ordinarily used under similar circumstances by similar professionals.

Complainants in a malpractice action must prove their allegations by a preponderance of evidence. To sustain the burden of proof, the plaintiff must show (1) an act or omission on the part of the defendant or of someone for whose conduct the defendant is answerable, (2) a causal relation between the conduct and the damage or injury allegedly suffered by the plaintiff, and (3) the negligent quality of the conduct. Because most professional conduct is not within the common knowledge of the layperson, expert testimony must usually provide such information.

In relative frequency of malpractice suits, psychiatry ranks eighth among the medical specialties; in almost every suit for psychiatric malpractice in which liability was imposed, tangible physical injury was proved. The number of suits against psychiatrists is said to be small because of the patient's reluctance to expose a psychiatric history, the skill of the psychiatrist in dealing with the patient's negative feelings, and the difficulty in linking injury with treatment. Psychiatrists have been sued for malpractice for faulty diagnosis and screening, improper certification in hospitalization, suicide, harmful effects of electroconvulsive treatments and psychotropic drugs, improper divulgence of information, and sexual intimacy with patients.

Respondeat Superior

The Latin phrase *respondeat superior* expresses the axiom, ''Let the master answer for the deeds of the servant.'' That doctrine holds that a person occupying a high position in a chain or hierarchy of responsibility is liable for the actions of a person in a lower position. A typical example is the psychiatric attending physician who supervises a resident. By the same reasoning, when a state hospital, for example, is named in a lawsuit, the list of cited defendants may extend upward to include the commissioner of mental health and the governor of the state. After the traditional first response, the attorneys usually weed out the irrelevant defendants.

A few critical issues should be noted here. First, consultation from outside the line of clinical responsibility often does not fit the model. The consultant is an adviser, not a superior. Second, the question of the particular defendant's authority (whether that person can hire and fire, censure, or control subordinates in the system) is relevant to the assignment of blame. Third, as a rule, psychiatrists should remove themselves from situations in which they bear responsibility (liability) for the practice of other professionals but cannot control the activities of those persons or perform their own assessments of the patients. In addition, psychiatrists should clarify ambiguities of responsibility at the point of entry into a system.

Sexual Relations with Patients

Although sexual relations with patients is not a common form of malpractice, it is not rare enough. The most common form is heterosexual relations occurring in an outpatient context between a male therapist and a female patient, but all other permutations have come to light and to litigation.

Sexual relations with a patient is considered a breach of the fiduciary (trust-based) relationship of physician to patient and a negligent failure by the physician to work correctly with transference and countertransference issues in a manner consistent with the standard of care. The usual harms identified are the failure to provide treatment during the affair, the misuse of time that might be spent in treatment elsewhere, the creation of severe difficulties for future therapy, and the direct emotional harms of guilt, depression, anxiety, shame, humiliation, and suicidal intent.

As a ground for malpractice, engagement in sexual relations with patients poses many complex conundrums about the nature of consent, transference and transference love, countertransference, confidentiality, mutuality, and exploitation. Such situations may represent neurotic acting out by a therapist whose marriage is in difficulty, successful seduction by a patient, exploitative or psychopathic manipulation of a vulnerable patient by the therapist, the development of true love, or false (groundless) accusations by a vengeful borderline personality disorder patient expressing sadistic transference.

The consensus, drawn from the case law and the codes of practice espoused by national professional organizations, clearly dictates that sexual relations with a patient under any circumstances (usually including expatients) is unethical, a deviation from the standard of care, and, therefore, proscribed. Many social activities that are not overtly sexual are highly suspect (one famous case involved a therapist's taking tea with a patient). As a form of liability prevention, such activities should also be avoided.

Several questions are often raised on the subject. First, does some rule of limitations specify that, after a certain period has elapsed, an expatient can properly be dated? Although some states have defined time limits, the short answer is "probably not": once a patient, always a patient, as far as that issue is concerned. The judgment calls are more difficult with a colleague's patient or a patient seen for a one-time evaluation, but a conservative approach is recommended.

Second, what counts as sexual relations? Hugging? Hand holding? There is no way to tell what a court of law may consider sexual activity, but handshakes under appropriate circumstances should probably be the limit of physical contact between parties. Clinicians who perform physical examinations of their

patients should have them chaperoned, just as in medical practice.

Third, can a therapist refer and then date a patient, so that the patient's clinical needs are addressed and the therapist is not pretending to offer treatment while being paid and leaving the patient without psychiatric care? At that point in malpractice law, the answer must again be "no." The transference relationship with the original therapist is still thought to cloud the autonomy of the patient's consent. However, the therapist whose feelings of love (or hate, for that matter) toward the patient become unmanageable and who does not respond to the usual means of countertransference resolution should terminate and refer the patient elsewhere in the interests of sound, objective care.

The problem of sexual relations with patients is such a serious issue that some governmental authorities require that psychotherapists give a publication that explains patient rights to those patients who report having been involved in sexual relations with a previous therapist.

Suicide and Suicidal Attempts by Patients

Suicide and suicidal attempts are the most frequent causes for lawsuits against psychiatrists. An estimated one out of every two suicides leads to a malpractice action. Psychiatrists may be charged with negligence because they did not properly control a patient under treatment; such negligence causes injury, and the suicidal behavior must have been predictable. The psychiatrist may be judged with malpractice, in decreasing order of culpability, during the patient's hospitalization, while the patient is out of the hospital on a pass, and during outpatient treatment. Supervision is greatest during hospitalization, and supervision is least during outpatient treatment.

Misdiagnosis

For the clinician still grappling with the often counter-intuitive complexities of the various editions of the *Diagnostic and Statistical Manual of Mental Disorders*, the idea that misdiagnosis can result in litigation may precipitate needless anxiety. Cases on that point are not concerned with whether a patient unambiguously suffered from schizophrenia or bipolar I disorder. Rather, the imputation is that the clinician negligently missed some diagnostic point. Typical examples include failures to discover a patient's suicidal or homicidal intent, a concomitant or underlying medical condition, or a side effect of consequence. The diagnoses, by inference, are diagnoses that would be detected by the average practitioner.

Negligent Treatment

After diagnosis comes treatment, which may be claimed to be negligent in various ways, perhaps most succinctly summarized as "too much, too little, or wrong." Typical claims allege inadequate or insufficient treatment (undertreatment), excessive or overly aggressive treatment (overtreatment), and variations on the theme of improper treatment, such as using the wrong medication, failing to anticipate or respond to side effects appropriately, and creating iatrogenic harms or addictions.

Clinicians often worry about being sued for harm caused by a drug that is detected years after the drug was introduced, such as unsuspected, late-appearing side effects; but here the law is logical. The relevant standard is information available to the average practitioner at the time of the event. In court, for example, the latest edition of an appropriate textbook that was available at the time of the alleged negligence may be referred to in order to illuminate the issue.

Among the treatment modalities that are a source of professional liability are various antipsychotic medications associated with the development of tardive dyskinesia. Accordingly, psychiatrists should monitor their patients receiving such medications after warning the patients and their guardians of the risk. Documented evidence of informed consent should be in the patients' medical records. Other risks—such as retinopathy, teratogenicity, and kidney failure—should be noted when appropriate. Informed consent should be obtained before initiating electroconvulsive therapy. Recently, a hospital was judged liable for withholding medication in a case of depression when psychotherapy was the sole treatment used.

Preventing Liability

Although eliminating malpractice is impossible, some preventive approaches have proved valuable in clinical practice: (1) Clinicians should provide only those kinds of care that they are qualified to offer. They should not overload their practices or overstretch their abilities; they should take reasonable care of themselves; and they should treat their patients with respect. (2) The documentation of good care is a strong deterrent to liability. Such documentation should include the decision-making process, the clinician's rationale for treatment, and an evaluation of the costs and the benefits. (3) A conclusion affords protection against liability, because it allows the clinician to obtain information about the peer group's standard of practice. It also provides a second opinion, enabling the clinician to submit any judgment to the scrutiny of a peer. A clinician who takes the trouble to obtain a consultation in a difficult and complex case is unlikely to be viewed by a jury as careless or negligent. (4) The informed-consent process involves a discussion of the inherent uncertainty of psychiatric practice. Such a dialogue helps prevent a liability suit.

OTHER AREAS OF FORENSIC PSYCHIATRY
Emotional Damage and Distress

There has been a rapidly rising trend to sue for psychological and emotional damage in recent years: secondary to physical injury, as a consequence of witnessing a stressful act, or from the suffering endured under the stress of such circumstances as concentration camp experiences. The West German government heard many of those claims from persons detained in Nazi camps during World War II. In the United States the courts have moved from a conservative to a liberal position in awarding damages for such claims. Psychiatric examinations and testimony are sought in those cases, often by both the plaintiffs and the defendants.

Workmen's Compensation

The stresses of employment may cause or accentuate mental illness. Patients are entitled to be compensated for their job-related disabilities or to receive disability retirement benefits. A psychiatrist is often called on to evaluate such situations.

References

Colella U: HIV-related information and the tension between confidentiality and liberal discovery: The need for a uniform approach. J Leg Med *16*: 33, 1995.
Daniolos P T, Holmes V F: HIV public policy and psychiatry: An examination of ethical issues and professional guidelines. Psychosomatics *36*: 12, 1995.
Goldstein R L: Paranoids in the legal system: The litigious paranoid and the paranoid criminal. Psychiatr Clin North Am *18*: 303, 1995.
Gutheil T G: Legal issues in psychiatry. In *Comprehensive Textbook of Psychiatry*, ed 6, H I Kaplan, B J Sadock, editors, p 2747. Williams & Wilkins, Baltimore, 1995.
Hill J K: Countertransference in conflict: one client or two? Bull Am Acad Psychiatry Law *23*: 105, 1995.
Jobes D A, Berman A L: Suicide and malpractice liability: Assessing and revising policies, procedures, and practice in outpatient settings. Prof Psychol Res Pract *24*: 91, 1993.
Kant I: *Foundations of the Metaphysics of Morals*. Bobbs-Merrill, Indianapolis, 1959.
Miller R D: Need-for-treatment criteria for involuntary civil commitment: Impact in practice. Am J Psychiatry *149*: 1380, 1992.
Monahan J, Hoge S K, Lidz C, Roth L H, Bennett N, Gardner W, Mulvey E: Coercion and commitment: understanding involuntary mental hospital admission. Int J Law Psychiatry *18*: 249, 1995.
Perlin M L: Tarasoff and the dilemma of the dangerous patient: New directions for the 1990's. Law Psychol Rev *16*: 29, 1992.
Reid W H, Wise M, Sutton B: The use and reliability of psychiatric diagnosis in forensic settings. Psychiatr Clin North Am *15*: 529, 1992.
Rosenberg J E, Eth S: Ethics in psychiatry. In *Comprehensive Textbook of Psychiatry*, ed 6, H I Kaplan, B J Sadock, editors, p 2767. Williams & Wilkins, Baltimore, 1995.
Saks E: The criminal responsibility of people with multiple personality disorder. Psychiatr Q *66*: 119, 1995.
Werner P D, Meloy J R: Decision making about dangerousness in releasing patients from long-term psychiatric hospitalization. J Psychiatry Law *20*: 35, 1992.

Index

Page numbers in **boldface** type indicate major discussions; those followed by *t* or *f* indicate tables or figures, respectively.

beclouded, 49
catastrophic reaction in, 55
clinical course, 56–57
    psychosocial factors affecting, 56
clinical features, 50, 54–55
cortical, 591
in Creutzfeldt-Jakob disease, 52, 591, **592**
definition, 27
vs. delirium, 49, 56
vs. delusional disorder, 154
vs. depression, 56
depression and, 170
diagnosis, 53–54
    clinical, 54
differential diagnosis, 55–56
emergency manifestations and treatment, 370*t*
epidemiology, 50–51
etiology, 50–52
vs. factitious disorder, 56
family of patient with, interventions for, 57–58
head trauma-related, 52, 591
health care costs with, 51
HIV-related, 17, 52, 72, 591
    presenting as psychiatric disorder, 12
in Huntington's disease, 52, 591, **592**
inhalant-induced persisting, 104
language impairment in, 54–55
memory impairment in, 54
due to multiple etiologies, diagnosis, 54*t*
neurological findings in, 55
vs. normal aging, 56
with normal pressure hydrocephalus, 592
orientation in, 54
due to other general medical conditions, diagnosis, 53, 53*t*
in Parkinson's disease, 52, 591, **592**
personality changes in, 55
pharmacological treatment, 57
in Pick's disease, 52, 591, *592*
prognosis for, 56–57
vs. pseudodementia, 593, 593*t*
psychiatric impairment in, 55
psychodynamic factors in, 57–58
psychosis in, 55
vs. schizophrenia, 56
sedative-, hypnotic-, or anxiolytic-induced persisting, 117
stages, 54
subcortical, 52, 591
substance-induced persisting, diagnosis, 54, 54*t*
sundowner syndrome in, 55
treatment, 57–58
vascular, **52,** 592
    clinical course, 57
    vs. dementia of Alzheimer's type, 55
    diagnosis, 53, 53*t*
    epidemiology, 50, 52
    etiology, 52
    prognosis for, 57
    vs. transient ischemic attacks, 55–56
Dementia precox, 121
Dementia pugilistica, neuropathology, 51
Dementia syndrome of depression, definition, 27
Demerol. *See* Meperidine
Demyelinating disorders, mental disorders due to, 65–66
Denial, in delusional disorder, 151
Denver Developmental Screening Test, 479
Depakene. *See* Valproate
Depakote. *See* Divalproex
Dependence, on drug or substance. *See* Drug dependence; Substance dependence
Depersonalization, 9
    definition, 27, 240
Depersonalization disorder, **240–241**
    clinical course, 241
    clinical features, 241

diagnosis, 241
diagnostic criteria, 241, 241*t*
differential diagnosis, 241
epidemiology, 240
etiology, 240
prognosis for, 241
treatment, 241
Depression. *See also* Bipolar I disorder; Dysthymic disorder; Major depressive disorder; Minor depressive disorder; Mood disorder(s)
    with β-adrenergic blockers, 409
    alcohol dependence and, 168
    antihypertensive-related, 16
    anxiety and, 168
    benzodiazepines for, 416
    buspirone for, 422
    carbamazepine for, 425
    catecholamines and, 14
    in children and adolescents, 167
    cognitive therapy for, 397
    consultation-liaison psychiatry and, 339*t*
    definition, 23
    vs. delirium, 49
    vs. dementia, 56
    dementia syndrome of, definition, 27
    diagnosis, dexamethasone suppression test in, 13
    double, 166, 179
    drug-related, 170
    in elderly, 167, 592–593
        treatment, 452–453
    gastrointestinal manifestations, 17
    hormonal considerations, 13
    vs. hypochondriasis, 225
    vs. hypothyroidism, 13
    interview of patient with, 2
    life events and, 162–163
    with medical illness, 168
    in mental disorders, 170, 170*t*
    nefazodone for, 456
    objective rating scales for, 169
    primary, 166
    psychoanalytic theory, 163
    respiratory complaints in, 17
    secondary, 166
        tricyclic and tetracyclic drugs for, 457
    serotonin-specific reuptake inhibitors for, 450
    suicide and, 2, 167–169, 362–363
    sympathomimetics for, 452–453
    syndromes related to, 159
    trazodone for, 456
    treatment-resistant, 461
    unipolar, 159
    venlafaxine for, 464–465
Depression-related cognitive dysfunction, 56
Depressive disorder(s), **183–185**
    alcohol-related disorders and, 80
    emergency manifestations and treatment, 370*t*
    in HIV-infected (AIDS) patient, 72–73
    not otherwise specified, 183–185
Depressive episode(s), 166, **167**
    mental status examination in, 168–169
Depressive equivalent, 166
Derailment
    definition, 25
    in schizophrenia, 133
Derealization, 9
    definition, 27, 240
Dereism, definition, 24
Dermatoglyphics, 489
Desipramine (Norpramin, Pertofrane)
    adverse effects, 176*t*
    anticholinergic effects, 458
    dosage and administration, 460*t*
    neurological effects, 458

l disorder

onal disorder